THE PUNJAB "REBELLION" OF 1919 AND HOW IT WAS SUPPRESSED

THE PUNJAB "REBELLION" OF 1919

AND HOW IT WAS SUPPRESSED

AN ACCOUNT OF THE PUNJAB DISORDERS AND THE WORKING OF MARTIAL LAW

(In Two Volumes)

By
PANDIT PEARAY MOHAN

With a Foreword by
LALA LAJPAT RAI

Introduction to new edition by
BIPAN CHANDRA

Editor
RAVI M. BAKAYA

Volume I

GYAN PUBLISHING HOUSE
NEW DELHI-110002

First published in 1920
Original title
**AN IMAGINARY REBELLION:
AND HOW IT WAS SUPPRESSED**
AN ACCOUNT OF THE PUNJAB DISORDERS
AND THE WORKING OF MARTIAL LAW

ISBN : 81-212-0671-5 (Set)
ISBN : 81-212-0687-1 (Vol. I)

First Reprint 1999 by
Gyan Publishing House,
5, Ansari Road, Darya Ganj
New Delhi-110002

Laser Typesetting at A.S. Printers, Delhi

Printed at Chawla Offset Printers, Delhi

TO THE
Revered
and
Sacred memory
Of the Europeans
And Indians, who died
As the result of the disorders,
This book is most
Respectfully
Dedicated
by the
Author

Punjab, 1919

How shall our love console thee, or assuage
Thy hapless woe; how shall our grief requite
The hearts that scourge thee and the hands that smite
Thy beauty with their rods of bitter rage?
Lo ! let our sorrow be thy battle-gage
To wreck the terror of the tyrant's might
Who mocks with ribald wrath thy tragic plight,
And stains with shame thy radiant heritage !
O beautiful ! O broken and betrayed !
O mournful queen ! O martyred Draupadi !
Endure thou still, unconquered, undismayed !
The sacred rivers of thy stricken blood
Shall prove the five-fold stream of Freedom's flood,
To guard the watch-towers of our Liberty.

— *SAROJINI NAIDU*

AN IMAGINARY REBELLION: AND HOW IT WAS SUPPRESSED

AN ACCOUNT OF THE PUNJAB DISORDERS AND THE WORKING OF MARTIAL LAW

BY

PANDIT PEARAY MOHAN
B.A., L.L.B., VAKIL, HIGH COURT, LAHORE

With a Foreword by
LALA LAJPAT RAI

PRINTED AND PUBLISHED BY KHOSLA BROS. RAILWAY ROAD, LAHORE
1920

(The title page of the original edition)

CONTENTS

CHAPTER I

From Loyalty to Rebellion

CHAPTER II

The Rebellion

CHAPTER III
The Reign of Terror
1—Before Martial Law

2—Martial Law

APPENDIX I
Martial Law Ordinances and other Notifications, etc.

APPENDIX II

Judgments of Martial Law Commissions

APPENDIX III

Proceedings in Privy Council

APPENDIX IV

Martial Law and its Applicability

APPENDIX V

The Indemnity Act

VOL. II

FROM THE EDITOR

It is a matter of great satisfaction that this important book, first published in 1920 by Khosla Brothers, Railway Road, Lahore, under the original title *AN IMAGINARY REBELLION AND HOW IT WAS SUPPRESSED: An Account of the Punjab Disorders and the Working of Martial Law*, is at last being made available to readers in India and abroad. The book was promptly banned and all copies were confiscated by the then British rulers and it has since then remained a bibliographical rarity.

It is thanks mainly to the interest and persistence of the late author's elder son, Dr. Ram Mohan Dattatreya, an old friend of this writer, that the publication of this edition has become possible. Dr. Dattatreya is a distinguished surgeon who settled down in Holland several decades ago but has been regularly coming to India both on professional and personal visits. He found an old and lattered copy of his father's book, with nearly 200 pages missing, in Dehra Dun, in his brother Lt. Col. Hari Mohan Dattatreya's house. The missing matter was retrieved after long and sustained efforts of several people from a copy each in the possession of the National Library in Calcutta and the Nehru Memorial Library in Delhi. Those who saw the book felt strongly that considering its great historical value as the first detailed eyewitness account of events connected with the Jallianwala Bagh massacre and Martial Law in 1919 in the Punjab, the book should be made available to research workers and those interested in the history of our freedom movement. We are glad that Gyan Publishing House agreed to undertake the onerous task of recomposing the entire text and publishing a new edition, virtually the first that is now being made available to the readers.

The Editor wishes to thank all those without whose help this publication would not have been possible. Among them are veteran writer and journalist Mr. V.D. Chopra; Director in-charge (at the time) of the Nehru Memorial Museum and Library Dr. Hari Dev Sharma; Mr. Anand

Gupta, Dr. Neshat Quaiser, and also Mr. J.M. Kaul and Mr. Tapan Sarkar of Calcutta. Mr. B.K. Raina, a close relative of Dr. Dattatreya, contacted Mr. Hari Jaisingh, Editor-in-Chief of *The Tribune* at Chandigarh, who very kindly undertook to find the detailed obituary article published by the paper in Lahore on 25th December, 1936 (buried in old microfilms) and sent us a photocopy. Our thanks to both of them.

We are extremely grateful to Prof. Bipan Chandra, the eminent historian, who agreed at short notice to write a brief but insightful introduction to this edition.

The old edition of the book gave the reader little information about the author who, true to his character, said almost nothing about himself. He deserves to be known better to our readers. We have been able to get biographical details about him from Dr. R.M. Dattatreya and from the obituary article mentioned above.

Pearay Mohan Dattatreya was born in 1895, in a Kashmiri Pandit family. His father, Pt. Brij Mohan Dattatreya 'Kaifi', retired as Assistant Foreign Secretary to the then Maharaja of Jammu and Kashmir, and was a renowned Persian and Urdu scholar, writer and poet. Pearay Mohan graduated from the Government College in Lahore in 1915, winning first prizes in economics and philosophy. He was a good debater and a regular contributor to the prestigious college magazine *Ravi*. While still in college, he won the first prize for a philosophical eassy "Some Thoughts on Love" in a competition announced by a magazine published from Baghdad. He also collaborated with a prominent Urdu journalist of those days, L. Bishan Sahai Azad, in writing a large volume in Urdu called "A History of the Great War".

In 1917, he got his law degree and started practising in Lahore. He was soon afterwards called to the High Court Bar. But after the publication of his celebrated book he joined *The Tribune* in November, 1920 and by sheer dint of ability rose to become the second in command of its distinguished editor, Mr. Kali Nath Roy.

Pt. Pearay Mohan could never brook any insult to people of his profession. In days when "Public Interest Litigation" (PIL) was unknown, he was responsible for bringing several test cases against the Railway authorities to establish the illegal character of the once too common practice of reserving special accommodation for Anglo-Indians on railways, forcing them to give it up. He also successfully fought a case against the Secretary of State for India challenging his own wrongful detention by the Senior Superintendent of Police of Lahore, when he went as *The Tribune's* representative to report on the arrival of the Simon Commission.

At the time of his premature death at the age of 41, Pt. Pearay Mohan was Senior Vice-President of the Punjab Journalists' Association and prominent in many fields of public activity. He was connected with the Lahore Congress Committee and was contemplating to seek election to the Provincial Assembly on the Congress ticket.

We were fortunate to get a photograph of the author from the family album of Dr. Dattatreya. It is being published for the first time in this edition. Considering the large size of the book, it was decided to print this edition in two volumes.

In the end, the Editor wishes sincerely to thank Mr. B.P. Garg, head of the Gyan Publishing House, and his staff members for accomplishing the difficult task of recreating this book from the old edition.

1st September 1999

Ravi M. Bakaya

INTRODUCTION

For learning about our recent past we are well endowed with articles and newspaper sources. There are also a few autobiographical accounts which, however, suffer both from lapses of memory and influence of later events in the minds of the writers. But there is a surprising lack of contemporary, first-hand accounts based on personal observation, listening, conversation, etc. It is, therefore, a privilege to introduce Pearay Mohan's contemporary account of the historical anti-Rowlatt Acts agitation and its consequent brutal repression in Punjab, which had an abiding and immediate impact on the course of the Indian national movement.

Pearay Mohan's work tells us how a bright, young, politically and socially sensitive intellectual looked at events at the time. He brings out the political and intellectual atmosphere of the times, the elemental popular forces released by crude state repression and the extent to which British bureaucracy in Punjab went in preventing the popular political agitation from taking root.

As a young lawyer, Pearay Mohan interacted with the active participants, the local leaders and men of influence, who tried to prevent both the crowds and the authorities from exceeding the bounds of the then accepted decent behaviour, and later the victims of government repression. He studied newspaper reports, government documents, political discussions and arguments and court judgements, as they became available, and then pieced together a rivetting narrative of popular resistance and its ferocious repression by the Punjab authorities.

Pearay Mohan brings out the widespread nature of the anti-Rowlatt agitation in Punjab. Peaceful *hartals* and protest meetings on 6th April and later on 10th and 11th April, after Gandhiji's arrest, occurred not only in major towns and cities but also in small and rural towns and in large villages. The official effort to suppress these peaceful protests with force, and after the news of the Jallianwala massacre spread, hardened the popular mood and despite the efforts of the leaders, popular protest developed into riots in the five districts of Lahore, Amritsar, Gujranwala, Lyallpur and Gujrat, where it affected both the cities and towns, and rural areas.

Pearay Mohan details at length the form that the spontaneous popular fury took, fuelled by anger and news and rumours of the nature of official repression at Amritsar, Jallianwala Bagh, Lahore and other places. The main target of the crowds were symbols of government authority. They looted and burnt post offices, local and district courts, *tehsil* offices, dak bungalows and railway stations. They damaged railway lines, bridges and signals and cut telegraph wires. In some villages they attacked *patwaris'* offices and destroyed land records. Though missionaries were spared, a few churches and missionary offices were attacked.

Pearay Mohan stresses the spontaneous character of popular actions. There was no continuity. The fury was exhausted within a few days. As he puts it: "Everywhere the mobs voluntarily dispersed after their passions had cooled down; and there was no further disorder..... At every place where there was a disturbance, perfect quiet prevailed after a few hours' rioting; and the authorities were able to make arrests immediately after the riots without the slightest resistance". (p. 121)

Pearay Mohan raises several interesting and important questions regarding the events in Punjab during April and May 1919. Why was the response to Gandhi's call for protest so strong in Punjab, especially in the five central Punjab districts? Why was the protest so easily suppressed? What explains the utter brutality of the suppression under the Martial Law regime? And he gives detailed answers.

Punjab shared with the rest of India grievances regarding rise in prices, *khilafat* wrongs, disappointment with the promised reforms, and the impact of world events. In addition, specific to Punjab, he says, were the dubious and coercive methods used by the bureaucracy to raise soldiers and war loans. He discusses this question at length. Critical was also the presence after the war of the large number of disbanded soldiers who had served abroad and lost the awe in which they had earlier held the white man.

Not willing to tolerate any expression of political dissent in Punjab, the sword-arm of the Empire, the Punjab Government reacted to the popular protest in a spirit of vengeance which took the brutal from of the Jallianwala massacre, brutal flogging of men in public, crawling order in Amritsar, humiliating treatment meted out to students and teachers, arrest and torture of thousands, bombing and machine-gunning of unarmed citizens of Gujranwala, sentencing of nearly two thousand to varying terms in jail, with 265 sentenced to transportation for life and 108 to death. In fact, the entire population of the riot-affected areas was subjected to brutal retaliation and reprisal for having questioned the might of the British Empire and for having attacked the symbols of British domination.

The swiftness and brutality of official reaction in Punjab was influenced by the coincidence of several factors. One was the specific Punjab system of administration evolved since the 1850s, which lacked the checks and balances placed on the bureaucracy in the rest of India. The anti-Rowlatt agitation was seen as a direct challenge to this system. A second factor was the authoritarian personality of the then Punjab Governor, Sir Michael O'Dwyer, whose ego was hurt by his failure to prevent the *hartals* and demonstrations on 6th, 10th and 11th April. The Punjab bureaucracy was also alarmed to see the masses, especially the peasantry, and the intelligentsia, or as contemporaries put it, the 'educated classes', coming together. This was seen as a major threat in a province which had supplied in the war nearly 450,000 soldiers from a population of less than 20 million. Another significant factor was the widespread nature of racialism bred for over 70 years among the British army officers and soldiers and even ordinary Englishmen and women in India.

The entire narration brings out the spirit of the people of Punjab at that particular historical conjuncture and Pearay Mohan is percipient in predicting the dire consequences for the rulers if an attempt were made to whitewash those among the Punjab rulers who were responsible for the crimes he has detailed at length in his work, which also contains seven extremely valuable appendices and one supplement which are bound to be a real boon to the teachers and researchers in history.

Pearay Mohan's narration is written from a contemporary liberal-moderate point of view. This has its own historical value. But it also enables us to trace the transition of the Indian intelligentsia from the moderate to the Gandhian militant nationalist position. It explains two specific facets of this transition: the failure of the Moderates and Extremists to deal with British unwillingness to accept their demands for self-government by Indians; and their attraction both to Gandhian mass struggle and the emphasis on non-violence. On the one hand, Pearay Mohan is horrified by official brutality and spirit of vengeance and disappointed by the failure of the popular resistance to continue beyond a few days, and, on the other, he unhesitatingly condemns the attacks on Englishmen and women and deplores acts of crowd violence.

15 August, 1999

Bipan Chandra

PREFACE

The tragedy of errors enacted in the Punjab may be divided into five acts. The first act consisted of the events that led up to the disorders under the able and effective guidance of the principal actor Sir Michael O'Dwyer. The second act opened on 10th April at Amritsar with the murder of the bank managers and consisted of scenes of riot, arson, bloodshed and other disorderly acts at several places in the province. The third act was by far the most bloody performance and consisted of scenes of official bloodshed and vindictive lawlessness, both before and after the proclamation of martial law. The fourth act of the drama was an attempt to exaggerate the mob violence and magnify it into a rebellion in order to justify the official excesses, which interested persons were anxious to minimise. Some of the scenes of this act have already been played in the columns of the Anglo-Indian press and on the floor of the Imperial Legislative Council; and it is expected that the whitewashing process will be completed by Lord Hunter's Committee. Perhaps the most important part of the drama will be, as usual, the fifth act which will be fraught with grave issues for the future good government of India, on the proper settlement of which will depend in a large measure the contentment of the people of India and the honour and reputation of England, as well as the mutual goodwill of the European and the Indian communities. This act will depict the attempts of the people to bring the official offenders to justice, and the counter-attempts of the government to shield their *proteges* from the consequences of their misdeeds. The first scene of the act has already been enacted by the publication of the Congress Sub-Committee's Report; and before the curtain drops on this final act, we shall be in a position to say what is going to be the moral and the aftermath of this tragic drama.

This book was undertaken in December 1919, immediately after the curtain rose on the fourth act of the tragedy; and, therefore, the author has confined himself to the first three acts of this bloody drama. We are so near the actual enactment of the tragedy, that it is not possible for us to have the proper perspective which is necessary to obtain a detached view of the history of the disorders. But on the other hand, it may be pleaded that we are the men who have seen these events with our own eyes and have heard the harrowing tales of the afflicted Punjab with our own ears from the very lips of those who have suffered. Whatever view the reader may take, the author can assure him that he has tried his best to ascertain the truth and place it in its naked form before his readers, however unpleasant that task has been on many occasions.

These few lines have been written simply because a preface has come to be regarded as a necessary adjunct to every book; and the author has only to add his thanks to the publishers for undertaking the work at a time when few others were bold enough to do so.

LAHORE, PEARAY MOHAN

10th May, 1920

FOREWORD

The Punjab tragedy of 1919 is an event of historical importance. It is a chapter of the world's history—a bloody chapter *albeit*—dyed red by the high priests of Imperialism, which will retain its freshness whenever the future generations of men and women happen to read it. It has placed us in a position to visualise the barbaric possibilities of Imperialism run amuck. Modern Indians had been so well inoculated with the serum of "benevolent despotism", as to make them forget that it is easier for a leopard to change its spots than for Imperialism to alter its true nature. Benevolent Imperialism is like a caged lion. However, you may play with it so long as it is caged, or under the spell of a master-tamer, the moment it gets out of control, it is bound to behave in conformity with its real nature. The atrocities perpetrated at Amritsar have proved that Imperialism run mad is more dangerous, more destructive, more vindictive, more inhuman, than a frenzied uncontrollable mob. When a mob gets out of hand, it does things pretty bad and cruel; but its destructiveness is born of passion and is not deliberately planned and thought out. Imperialism, on the other hand, as represented by O'Dwyers, Dyers, O'Briens, Bosworth Smiths, Johnsons, Dovetons and others, takes revenge with a deliberate aim. It plans out with a fixed purpose, and carries out those plans in a spirit of military vindictiveness.

As to the causes of this tragedy, it should not be forgotten that the Punjab had been seething with discontent for more than twenty years. With its unique record of services in the cause of the Empire, having profusely shed its blood in the expansion and protection of British dominions all the world over, having given its best in developing British colonies and British possessions, the treatment it has received has been most cruel and bitter. In fact, that very circumstance has been the reason why the Imperial bureaucracy has considered it necessary to deny to this province the benefits of education and industrial development to the extent to which they have been fostered in other provinces. The Punjab peasantry has been deliberately kept in ignorance, because of its being the chief recruiting source of the Indian army and the military police. Its childlike faith in British justice and fairplay has kept it politically backward and, in a way, inarticulate. Whatever political life was in the province was crushed by various methods of repression and corruption. Numbers of educated youngmen were bought over to the Government side by rewards of lands, offices, titles and other inducements of a similar nature. Others, who proved above these temptations, were persecuted and maltreated. In this connection, I might mention in passing the unrest of 1907, the historic trial of Arya Samajists in 1909, the prosecutions for sedition of 1909-1910, the conspiracy cases of 1913-1914, and the political trials held during the war. This is neither the time nor the place to go into details; but it is obvious that these were indications of growing unrest and discontent which should have moved any wise administration to initiate measures of conciliation. Instead of that, the defiant attitude of Sir Michael O'Dwyer, his firm faith in militarism, his iron and blood policy of keeping down all agitation and stopping the free expression of public opinion, together with the contempt which he displayed towards the aspirations of the Indians for self-government, only added fuel to the fire. Thus, the Rowlatt Act was only the proverbial straw on the camel's back. The successful *hartals* of the 30th March and 6th April descended upon him and his henchmen like a bolt from the blue. The bureaucracy had all along been deluded and deceived by the false, though reassuring, reports of their agents, spies and admirers; but now they found themselves suddenly disillusioned and in a fit of anger decided to embark upon a policy of unbridled retaliation and reprisals against those who had participated in the agitation against the Rowlatt Act. This short-sighted policy of the late Lieutenant Governor and the arbitrary methods adopted to penalise those who had taken part in the agitation against the Rowlatt Act led to riots, which were followed by the declaration of martial law and all that followed in its wake.

We were brought up in an atmosphere of "benevolent despotism" and fed on the idea of British Imperialism being something quite different from other isms of the same character. Our disillusionment began some twenty years ago; but it required an O'Dwyer and a Dyer and a Jallianwala Bagh to complete the process. Coming so soon after the Great War, which was fought ostensibly to destroy Imperialism and Militarism, the Punjab tragedy has cleared the atmosphere which enveloped the war aims of the Allies and shown the brute in its naked form. The Indians are to-day cursing Sir Michael O'Dwyer, General Dyer and others; but, in my humble judgment, it is the system which needs cursing, if that can give any satisfaction to the persons aggrieved. The men are the mere tools of circumstances. They may overdo a thing; but so long as they are told that the maintenance of the system is the main thing and that it has to be done at any cost, their fault is only secondary. If the administration of Sir Michael O'Dwyer and the Punjab tragedy enacted by him awakens the Indians to a sense of their duty in the matter, the blood of hundreds (including children), who died at the Jallianwala Bagh, Gujranwala, Lahore and other places, would not have been spilled in vain. The blood of the innocents calls not for vengeance, but the putting forth of every iota of our energy to get rid of the bureaucratic system of Government, under which we have lived for the last 70 years or so. It is, therefore, extremely desirable that various accounts of what happened in the Punjab in the spring of 1919, with the necessary documents showing the causes and effects thereof; as also explaining the various incidents that happened under the martial law *regime,* should be available to people who wish to study the whole thing. for effective and constructive criticism. This book is an attempt to supply one such account. It has been written with a scrupulous regard for truth and with remarkable lucidity, precision and impartiality. It contains in supplements a unique collection of documents, needed to throw light on the various phases of the tragedy. As such, I recommend it for the perusal of such Indians and non-Indians, as are anxious to have a clear idea of what happened and how. I pass no judgment on the opinions expressed by the author, except that they are the opinions of a man who knows what he says and who says it on the strength of facts within his knowledge. A very valuable part of the book are the documents incorporated in the appendices, which enhance its value as a book of ready reference.

The reader might very well ask, what is going to be the upshot of the failure of the bureaucracy in the Punjab and the brutalities committed in the name of law and order by martial law administrators. A year ago, I had some kind of confidence in Mr. Montagu's statesmanship; and I was under the impression that when full facts are known to him, he would not fail to heal up the wounds inflicted on the Punjab by Sir Michael O'Dwyer and his lieutenants. I had no hope in the Government of India; I had no hope in the British Cabinet; but I had some little hope in Mr. Montagu, which has been completely shattered by the orders he has passed on the Hunter Committee's Report. The Government of India has failed us, as it was bound to, because it was practically a party to the whole series of oppressive measures which led to the disturbances and the subsequent introduction of martial law. The Government of India being one of the guilty parties, they could not be expected to pronounce an adverse judgment on themselves. The Secretary of State has also deserted us. Our only hope lies in ourselves. The duty is twofold: first, to leave nothing undone to bring the true facts to the knowledge of the civilised world as extensively as our resources would permit; and secondly, to think out and put into practice a plan of action which would impress upon the Government the fact that we are not prepared to tolerate similar outrages upon our honour and liberty. The Government must know that these methods of governing India are dead; and unless the ruling caste is ready to accept the change in the situation, the task of governing India would be extremely difficult and full of perils and pitfalls. Whether we shall inaugurate a campaign of non-cooperation or passive resistance or what, I cannot say yet, as the whole matter awaits decision by the Special Session of the Congress, which the All-India Congress Committee has resolved to hold as early as possible. But this much I might be permitted to say to my educated countrymen, that the question whether they will be treated in the future as men or as beasts of burden depends in a large measure on their own conduct and behaviour. It is for them to decide whether they are ready to sacrifice their individual preferments for the honour of the nation, or whether they will choose to be satisfied with the few crumbs that are thrown to them from the masters' table and go to sleep again. Let us never forget that "nations by themselves are made."

LAHORE, LAJPAT RAI
5th June, 1920

CHAPTER I

From Loyalty to Rebellion

India's Loyalty during the War.

The Government has admitted on several occasions during the War that India gave an unprecedented demonstration of her loyalty and attachment to the British Throne by her splendid response to the call of the Empire in its hour of need. In the hour of England's peril, India rushed to her help with unfailing faith and loyal enthusiasm. The voice of controversy was hushed; and the old grievances, which the people had against the Government, were laid aside. The whole country unhesitatingly placed her resources at the service of the Allied Cause; she did not stop to bargain for favour or even for bare justice to her demands. She supplied more men for the War than all the Colonies taken together; and while some of the latter took large loans of money from the mother country, she, in spite of her chronic poverty, made the generous gift of £100,000,000 to England for the expenses of the war. In a word, to quote Lord Hardinge, India allowed herself to be "bled white" in the larger interests of the Empire. This loyal response of all classes of the people to the call of the King-Emperor enabled the Government to withdraw without misgiving almost all the white troops from the country at a time when England was waging a gigantic war with varying success, and the elements of disorder might well have taken the opportunity to rise in insurrection against the Government had they desired to do so. But India was staunch in both faith and work in the darkest days of the conflict, when the fortunes of war were wavering. About one million men were sent overseas to fight the battles of the Empire and up to the 31st of March 1919, India had incurred an expenditure of £127,800,000 towards the War, in addition to the sum of £2,100,000 which was contributed by the princes and people of India to various war funds and charities. Considerable sums were also placed at the disposal of the Government for the purchase of horses, motors, aeroplanes, ambulance cars and comforts for the troops.

Punjab's share

Comparisons are odious; but it is a bare statement of fact that the Punjab did more in the War than any other province of India. Both in men and money the Punjab made sacrifices that could not reasonably have been expected from her in view of her population and economic condition. More than half the total number of recruits provided by the whole country came from the Punjab; and in the matter of the War Loans, the Punjab competed successfully with the richer provinces of the country.

These great sacrifices of the province in the cause of the Empire were recognised both by the Imperial and the Provincial Governments. In fact, Sir Michael O'Dwyer never lost an opportunity to proclaim to the rest of India the loyalty and magnificent sacrifices of the province, which had the advantage of his fostering care during the last six years. On some occasions, these praises took a most aggressive and offensive form; and the late Lieutenant-Governor came to grief over one of his panegyrics on Punjab's loyalty in the Imperial Legislative Council. In his last speech in the Punjab Legislative Council, which was delivered on the 7th of April 1919, Sir Michael O'Dwyer made the following observations with regard to the Punjab and its people :—

> "Gentlemen," I have often been criticised for dwelling on the achievements of the Punjab in season and out of season. But my pride in the province is based on no parochial spirit. I have spent 15 years away from it, during which I have seen many other parts of India.
>
> "I might say :—
>
> 'Much have I seen and known—cities of men,
> And manners, climates, councils, governments.'
>
> But nowwhere did I find the same qualities as the Punjab can show from the prince's palace down to the peasant's hut. I found I could meet the Punjabee, whatever, his class or condition, as man to man without suspicion or mistrust. I found him in the mass—and I refer primarily to the rural masses—loyal but not subservient, brave but not boastful, enterprising but not visionary, progressive but not pursuing false ideals or mistaking the shadow for the substance.....

> "I regard it as a great privilege to have lived and worked with such a people and to be closing my service amongst them....................."

These words were uttered by Sir Michael O'Dwyer a week before martial law was declared. In the same speech, the late Lieutenant-Governor admitted that the "province has continued to be free from political crime." Several passages may be cited from Sir Michael O'Dwyer's speeches showing that the places where disorder broke out were admitted to be loyal and credited with good work in connection with the War. For instance, at a durbar held by Sir Michael O'Dwyer at Gujranwala on the 29th of March, 1919, the day from which martial law took retrospective effect, he made the following remarks in the course of his speech :—

> "It is a very great pleasure to me to come among you to-day and to have this opportunity of meeting so many old friends whom I have not forgotten and who have not forgotten me, to hear such good accounts of the progress of the town and district and to be able to congratulate you on the *staunch and loyal support* which I and my officers have received from you during my six years term of office and particularly during the critical period of the war.....
>
> "As you know Gujranwala was slow in starting but under the stimulus given to your efforts by the vigorous personality of Colonel O'Brien, it made a notable advance in the last year of the war, and in the 11 months from December 1917 to October 1918 it raised 7,000 recruits for the Army.
>
> "When the war ceased you had about 13,000 men in the army and in proportion to your male population while far below Amritsar and Gurdaspur, you were equal to your neighbours in Sialkot and a good way better than Lahore. So Gujranwala though not in the first rank has removed the reproach that would have attached to it had you allowed other people to fight your battles. In the matter of War Charities the generosity of Gujranwala has been conspicuous and Lady O'Dwyer desires me to express her gratitude to the zealous workers who gave such liberal and unfailing support to the Red Cross and Comforts Fund.
>
> "And now, gentlemen, I take leave of you with a heart saddened by the thought that I shall not see you again. Many happy days I have spent here, but I find comfort in the recollection of the many and valued friends I have made here."

This was the district where a fortnight later machine guns and aeroplanes were employed to quell disorder. Amritsar was equally the object of Sir Michael O'Dwyer's benedictions for its great war-effort. Indeed, Sir Michael O'Dwyer had a warm corner in his heart for Amritsar on account of the large number of recruits supplied by that district; and his heart bled to see Amritsar occupy a secondary position in the favours of the Government. In his speech at a recruiting durbar held at Kasur, Sir Michael went so far as to solemnly declare that he would transfer the seat of Government from Lahore to Amritsar as a reward for the great war services of the latter and as a punishment to the former for its slackness in providing recruits. At a durbar held at Amritsar on the 9th June 1919, Sir Edward Maclagan expressed his surprise at the outbreak of rebellion in Amritsar in the following words:—

> "The city of Amritsar used to be one of the most peaceful cities in India and it was known in the Punjab for its religious associations, its commercial activity, its municipal development and its educational institutions. Then *suddenly* two months ago it became the scene of rebellious outrages."

When an apostle of law and order like Sir Michael O'Dwyer bestows such lavish praises on a province, we may take it that it was really loyal and law-abiding, otherwise it could not have extracted such praise from a man of his suspicious nature.

From loyalty to rebellion.

Is it not, therefore, a strange phenomenon that the people of a province are one day admired and congratulated by a ruler like Sir Michael O'Dwyer for their loyalty and splendid services to the Empire; and the very next day, they are declared to be in a state of "open rebellion"? It is, indeed, impossible to believe that a province, which had given its best men, not in their thousands but hundreds of thousands, to fight against the enemies of the Empire, should break out into open rebellion on the very morning of victory, when it should have expected to be rewarded for the great sacrifices of blood and money that it had made in the interests of the Empire as a whole. One of these two statements must be incorrect. Either Sir Michael O'Dwyer was wrong when he was recounting the splendid services of the Punjab to the Empire, and praising the people for their steadfast devotion to the British Crown; or, else, he had not rightly appreciated the situation in holding that this state of loyal homage to the King-Emperor was transformed by some invisible power into a state of open rebellion against the authority of Government in the course of a single night. Rebellions and revolutions are not the work of a moment and do not burst forth on a peaceful, contented people like a sleeping volcano without warning or premonition. The sentiments and emotions of men and their attitude towards their rulers are not transformed in a day. It is impossible to imagine that a loyal and contented province can become rebellious without grave and continued oppression; and in most cases rebellions must be preceded by longer or shorter periods of political crime, from which the Punjab was admittedly free.

The theory of Conspiracy.

Sir Michael O'Dwyer, therefore, realised the difficulty of reconciling the statement that there was open rebellion with his previous declarations about the loyal services of the province. He could not let go the theory of rebellion, which placed the hated agitator in his power; nor could he admit that the people were not satisfied and contented under his administration. His task became more difficult by the fact that the agitation against the Rowlatt Act, the *hartals* and the *Satyagraha* campaign, as well as the "false and malicious rumours" about the Rowlatt Act were unable to produce rebellion in other parts of the country. Strange explanations were, therefore, put forward to explain away a situation that was more or less the creation of Sir Michael O'Dwyer himself. The first theory which was propounded, and which still holds the field in an attenuated form, was that there was a huge conspiracy to subvert the British Government and seduce the Indian army from their allegiance, the ramifications of which had enveloped the whole country, the conspirators having been financed by Bolshevic money. The minor disorders in other parts of the country and the big rebellion in the Punjab were sought to be explained by reference to this common source, the magnitude of the rising in the Punjab being due to the fact that it was the home of warriors. This theory could not stand for any length of time as the evidence of the Bolshevic origin could not be made to assume even a plausible shape. The attempt to substitute an Afghan agency for the Bolshevists also failed for want of sufficient evidence. This conspiracy has, therefore, been given up, except by men like the Hon'ble Major Malik Sir Umar Hayat Khan Tiwana, who prefers to be consistent. Then the status of the conspiracy was whittled down to that of a mere indigenous organisation and the honour of being the "chief conspirator" was thrust upon Mr. Gandhi. The object of this conspiracy was said to be to overawe the Government by criminal means and thereby secure the repeal of the Rowlatt Act. This theory had the additional advantage of being capable of justifying the order of externment passed against Mr. Gandhi by the Punjab Government, under which he was arrested at Palwal and taken back to Bombay. But in this form also, the conspiracy could not be supported by facts and had to be abandoned in sheer despair. As a last resort, an attempt was made to build up several local conspiracies and ascribe the disorders to them. These conspiracies were not given even a provincial character, but were said to be autonomous independent bodies, in which irrepressible agitators like Lala Harkishen Lal, Lala Duni Chand, Dr. Kitchlew, Dr. Satyapal, Mr. Labh Singh, and Diwan Mangal Sen, were said to have participated. These conspiracies were invested with some sort of sanctity by the judgments of martial law commissions; but the theory broke down as the result of the cross-examination to which the supporters of this discovery were subjected by Lord Hunter's Enquiry Committee. One drawback was common to all these theories. To initiate and develop a conspiracy of a magnitude and character, which may be able to guide, organise and promote rebellion against an Empire upon which the sun never sets, is not the work of a day, nor can it be undertaken by an organisation which a few men can run or control. It is, therefore, strange that the ubiquitous police failed to find any trace of it before the disorders actually appeared. Now the theory of conspiracy seems to have been given up in disgust and is no longer put forward in any serious discussion.

Agitation against Rowlatt Act.

The most widely accepted official theory is that the agitation against the Rowlatt Act was directly responsible for the disturbances that occurred in various parts of the country. The Government of India Resolution on the disorders, which was published on April 14, 1919, puts the official view in the following words :—

> "When the Bill was under discussion its opponents publicly stated that if it passed into law a campaign of agitation against it on a scale hitherto unattained would be organised throughout India and a section of them indicated that they would support that campaign by resort to what is known as passive resistance. No one cognizant of the conditions of India could have been ignorant at the time of the dangers of initiating a widespread movement of this nature. They were clearly pointed out by many public men of moderate views and the representatives of government did not fail during the debates on the Bill to emphasise the serious consequences to the public peace which would follow from an agitation such as was then threatened. The warnings were unheeded, and to the agitation which has succeeded the passing of the Act must be directly attributed the open breaches of the public peace, the defiance of authority and the criminal attacks on life and property which have lately been witnessed in certain parts of India."

Obviously, the words quoted above refer to that part of the agitation against the Rowlatt Act, which was concerned with *Satyagraha* and passive resistance. But the *Satyagraha* movement was never followed in the Punjab; nor were any *Satyagraha Sabhas* formed anywhere except at Amritsar, where there was no disturbance on the 6th April, the *Satyagraha* day. It is true that in almost every important town and in several large villages, the 6th of April was observed as a day of humiliation and prayer; it is also true that on that day *hartals* took place throughout the province. The *hartals,* however, did not cause breach of the public peace in any part of the province; nor did they inaugurate the movement of passive resistance, as the following words from the Resolution quoted above imply:—

> "The agitation has followed a double line of action, namely, direct criticism of the Act by means of public speeches and publications and the initiation of the threatened movement of passive resistance. The latter movement was ushered in by a demonstration consisting of the

observance of a day of fasting and the closing of the shops and places of business. Such a demonstration was not in itself illegal; but there is ample evidence to prove that in more than one place those locally responsible for its organisation overstepped the limits of lawful persuasion and resorted to direct interference with the business of many who were not interested in the movement, and to forcible obstruction of the traffic in the public streets."

The allegations contained in these words are not true so far as the Punjab is concerned. The civil disobedience of laws or passive resistance was never practised in the Punjab nor did the *hartals* lead to breach of peace at any place in the Province. Assuming that the *hartals* were organised and not spontaneous, there is no truth in the statement that at any place in the Punjab the organisers of *hartals* had "overstepped the limits of lawful persuasion and resorted to direct interference with the business of many who were not interested in the movement." The traffic in the public streets was also not obstructed at any town in the Punjab. The Government, therefore, has no reason to complain of the manner in which the people of the Punjab behaved on the 6th of April.

False Rumours.

The Resolution quoted above goes on to say that in many quarters the campaign involved "the use of the most flagrant misrepresentations regarding the character of the Act." There is no doubt that false rumours about the provisions of the Rowlatt Act were in circulation at the time; but such rumours and misrepresentations were not circulated or made by those who took part in the agitation against the Act. The prevalence of such rumours was the natural outcome of the widespread agitation against the Act. Whenever large masses of ignorant persons think, or try to think, on questions which are beyond their understanding, they are bound to distort, cut up and re-arrange the facts presented to them in such a manner as to lead to grotesque, though honest, misrepresentation, however mischievous may be its effects. This was the case during the War. The ignorant masses of people failed to understand the true significance of the bits of war news that reached them in a fragmentary form; but they made up these scraps of information into a complete whole by filling the gaps in their own way. Exactly the same thing happened in connection with the Rowlatt Act. The agitation against it had assumed such proportions, that its echoes reached the countryside and led the simple villagers to make their own conjectures about its provisions. Perhaps a *jat* had gone to the neighbouring town in connection with a law suit and seeing that there was a *hartal* had inquired as to its meaning, and was told that the *sircar* had passed a new law increasing the powers of the police and taking away the right of appeal; or it may be that the village *patwari* who subscribed to a vernacular newspaper or a student who had come home for holidays had talked to him about the *Kala Qanun;* but the result in each case was that the *jat* imbibed wrong notions about the nature and scope of the Act, the correct provisions of which he was not able to understand. This naturally gave rise to false rumours, which might have grown in number and virulence, and become a real danger to public safety by creating discontent amongst large masses of the people who were easily excitable. But the man who takes part in political agitation is not to blame for such indirect consequences, nor can he be justly accused of having misrepresented the acts of Government. The Government having refused to respond to milder forms of agitation, the people were forced to take to strong, but constitutional, forms of protest by which the agitation was carried to the masses, in order to make the Government feel the pressure of public opinon. There is absolutely no evidence that the responsible public leaders of the Punjab or any other part of India ever misrepresented, *maliciously* or otherwise, the scope or intention of the Rowlatt Act. The Rowlatt Act was neither misrepresented in the press nor at the public meetings which were held all over the province. The provisions of the Act are so monstrous that no misrepresentation is required to make out a strong case against it. The leaders of the people, or the agitators as they are called in official parlance, have always been working in broad daylight; and these rumours should have been easily traceable to them, had they any responsibility in the matter. Besides, some of the rumours were so fanciful and stupid, that it is impossible to suppose that they could have been started by the educated classes.

Was the agitation honest?

The Indian members of the Imperial Legislative Council warned the Government in good time of the agitation that would result from the enactment of the Rowlatt Bill and foreshadowed the disastrous consequences that might follow it. These timely remonstrances of the members of the Council, many of whom intimately knew the feelings and sentiments of the people and faithfully voiced them in the Council, were unheeded; and the Government stubbornly persisted in passing this odious and unpopular measure. But when there was an agitation of unprecedented magnitude throughout the length and breadth of the country, and what the members had predicted actually came to pass, instead of being grateful to them for their sound advice and correct appraisement of the situation, the Viceroy called their motives into question, and accused them of having fomented disorder. These are His Excellency's words:—

> "Last session certain hon. members during the passage of the Rowlatt Bill gave me warnings of an almost minatory character that if that Bill passed into law there would be agitation of a serious nature. I think the hon. members will realise that no Government could deviate from a policy which it regarded as essential on account of any threat of agitation. However, there were those who thought that it was necessary to make good this threat, and as a consequence the deplorable events occurred which are to be the subject of an enquiry."

With the characteristic hauteur of a bureaucracy, the Government refuses to admit that there was anything in the Act itself which could have justified the agitation to which it gave rise, but accuses the leaders of manufacturing an artificial agitation and throwing the whole country into a state of unrest, simply in order to make good their threats of agitation. The question, therefore, is whether any decent man can be reasonably opposed to the Rowlatt Act or whether the agitation against it was merely engineered by certain unscrupulous leaders of the people in order to make good their threats.

Slur on India's loyalty.

The avowed object of the Rowlatt Act is to "cope with anarchical and revolutionary crime." A few months before the passing of this Act, the King-Emperor, in the course of a Message which His Majesty sent to the Princes and peoples of India on the signing of the armistice, was graciously pleased to acknowledge the loyal services rendered by India in the following words:—

> "The struggle now so happily ended has demanded unprecedented sacrifices from us all, and in responding to the call upon her for men and resources India has played a part worthy of her martial qualities and high traditions. She has fulfilled my faith in her single-minded devotion to my person and Empire, and she has vindicated my confidence in her loyalty"

The people of India were able to satisfy the King-Emperor with their loyalty and devotion to His Majesty and the Empire; but the Government of India was more difficult to please. Though anarchical and revolutionary crime had greatly decreased during the war, the Government came out with the Rowlatt Bills even before the peace treaty was signed. All self-respecting Indians, therefore, justly resented these measures as an unmerited slur on their loyalty and devotion to the British Crown.

Necessity of the Act.

The country objected to the Rowlatt Act not because it was in sympathy with the anarchists or revolutionaries, but because the Act was calculated to take away the legal safeguards which are vital to the protection of the life and liberties of law-abiding peaceful citizens. The Indians accepted without demur the provisions of the Defence of India Act and the rules made thereunder, because it was a temporary war measure and they did not want to embarrass the Government. More than a year before this Act was due to expire, the Government of India hurled the Rowlatt Bills at an unsuspecting people; and one of these Bills, which for all practical purposes re-enacted the extraordinary provisions of the Defence of India Act, was rushed through the Legislative Council, regardless of the fact that every non-official Indian member of the Council opposed it and the whole country emphatically disapproved of its provisions. In the absence of serious revolutionary crime, the only conclusion at which the public arrived was, that like every other bureaucracy, the Government of India was not willing to part with the powers that were once placed in its hands, no matter under what circumstances those powers were given. After the Government had for some years enjoyed the ample powers conferred on it for a temporary period by the Defence of India Act, it could not overcome the temptation to keep those powers for ever. The *speedy* trials, the freedom from the unnecessary inconvenience of appeals, the arbitrary orders of internment and externment without the embarrassing nuisance of a judicial trial, and the various other luxuries of despotism were too good to be relinquished. The Sedition Committee was, therefore, appointed to conduct a secret investigation into the anarchical and revolutionary movement in India. The old records of the Criminal Investigation Department were placed before this Committee, and a recommendation for the permanent enactment of the provisions of the Defence of India Act was obtained. Armed with these credentials, the Government rushed into the Council and pleaded in the most earnest tones that the safety of the country demanded the immediate enactment of the Rowlatt Bills, if the country was to be saved from the pestilence of anarchy and revolution. No definite proofs to substantiate these fears were placed before the Council; but the whole affair was given a romantic touch by reference to the mysterious anarchist who is everywhere and nowhere, who lurks in the background, does all his work in secret, and is not to be found. If the Press Act, the Seditious Meetings Act and the Defence of India Act have not been able to discover him, and if even the various formidable sections of the Penal Code that deal with offences against the State have not been able to unearth him, where is the guarantee that the Rowlatt Act will accomplish that extraordinary feat. This elusive being must be discovered, before the Rowlatt Act can be put into operation against him.

Opinion of Sir O'Moore Creagh

The Government has not been able to show that the formidable array of Acts and Regulations with which it is equipped for the purpose of suppressing sedition and anarchy, supplemented by the almost unlimited ordinance-making power of the Governor-General, were inadequate or had been worn out by constant use; and that the safety of the country would have been endangered had the Rowlatt Act not been placed on the statute-book. Even a man like Sir O'Moore Creagh, who was formerly the Commander-in-Chief of India and cannot be accused of making common cause with the Indian agitator, had to deny the necessity of passing the Rowlatt Act. In the course of an article in the *Sunday Express,* in which he strongly criticises the educated classes for their political agitation, he says :—

> "The present unrest about the Rowlatt Bill is typical of Indian maladministration. There would be no need for the Bill had certain old Bills of 1818 and earlier, now brought into action, been utilised. These having until now been declared obsolete or forgotten, new measures were considered unavoidable, but it is a matter of common knowledge that the Indian Government has a mania for new legislation ignoring the amazing array of equally suitable Acts that it possesses in its legal armoury.

Provisions of the Rowlatt Act

It has been insinuated that the Rowlatt Act is a harmless and beneficent measure, designed to protect the life and property of the people against outbursts of anarchy and revolution; and that the evilly disposed agitators made it a pretext for promoting a rising against the Government by a systematic campaign of falsehood and misrepresentation. This allegation was not confined to the Anglo-Indian Press but was publicly made by responsible officials. For instance, Sir Michael O'Dwyer in a speech delivered by him on April 10th, 1919, in reply to an address presented by representatives of the Martial Races of the Punjab, made the following remarks :—

"You have seen within the last few weeks how a law passed to safeguard the lives and property of the people against such outbursts of anarchy and revolution ..... has by the persistent falsehood and misrepresentation of a small but noisy class been made to appear as a deadly weapon aimed at the people whom it is intended to protect in situations of great emergency.....

"I would, therefore, ask you to.....expose the campaign of falsehood that is being carried on in certain quarters in order to mislead the ignorant and credulous masses and the scum of the bazaars of the towns and to incite them to crime and disorder....."

It may be that Sir Michael O'Dwyer had a lover's partiality for this masterpiece of the bureaucratic art of government, or that his words were actuated by a desire to fasten the responsibility for the dastardly crimes that had been committed at Amritsar on the agitators; but even a cursory glance at the provisions of the Act would show that the people were justified in agitating for its repeal. The Act is divided into five parts, the provisions of which may be briefly noted as follows :—

(*a*) *Part I* applies to a state of things when "the Governor-General in Council is satisfied that in the whole or any part of British India, anarchical or revolutionary movements are being promoted and that scheduled offences* in connection with such movements are prevalent to such an extent that it is expedient in the interests of public safety to provide for the *speedy* trial of such offences." In case the Government of India is of that opinion, it may make a declaration to that effect, which will render the provisions of this Part operative in the area to which the declaration relates. As soon as this declaration is made, the task of the Government of India is accomplished, and after that the Local Government concerned steps in and decides as to the persons who are to derive the benefit of a *speedy* trial. (*b*) Now, these trials are to be conducted not by the ordinary courts but by tribunals specially constituted for the purpose. The commitment proceedings, which gave

---

*The following is the list of offences given in the Schedule to the Act.

(i) Any offence under the following sections of the Indian Penal Code, namely :— sections 121, 121-A, 122, 123, 124, 131 and 132.

the accused a fair notice as to the charge against him and the evidence which the prosecution wanted to lead to substantiate that charge, are discarded and the accused is bound to be prejudiced in his defence. (*c*) In order to make the trial more *speedy*, the accused is also deprived of his right of appeal, on the assumption that the eminent judges who hold the trial are infallible. The only consideration shown is that "a sentence of death shall not be passed upon any accused person in respect of whose guilt there is a difference of opinion among the members of the Court". If justice is not to be cheated of its due, this concession in favour of the accused can only be justified on the ground that the difference of opininon amongst the judges raises a doubt as to the guilt of the accused. If that is true, there is no reason why the accused should not have a right of appeal to some other Court. (*d*) The provisions of the Criminal Procedure Code are superseded by the special rules of procedure laid down in the Act. (*e*) It is further provided that notwithstanding anything contained in the Evidence Act the statement of a witness may be admitted in evidence against the accused, even if the witness has not been cross-examined on his behalf, "if the person making the same is dead or cannot be found or is incapable of giving evidence, and it is established to the satisfaction of the court that such death, disappearance or incapacity has been caused in the interests of the accused." As the accused will be under custody of the police, it should be impossible for him to personally cause the disappearance of the witness

---

(2) Any of the following offences, if, in the opinion of Government, such offence is connected with any anarchical or revolutionary movement, namely :—

(a) any offence under sections 124-A, 148, 153-A, 302, 304, 326, 327, 329, 332, 333, 385, 386, 387, 392, 394, 395, 396, 397, 398, 399, 400, 401, 402, 431, 435, 436, 447, 438, 440, 454, 455, 457, 458, 459, 460 and 506 of the Indian Penal Code;

(b) any offence under the Explosive Substances Act, 1908;

(c) any offence under section 20 of the Indian Arms Act, 1878.

(3) Any attempt, or conspiracy to commit or any abetment of any of the above offences.

by kidnapping him, unless the accused himself first escapes from such custody. Nor is it likely that the accused, as long as he is under arrest, will be able to kill or incapacitate the witness, unless it be in the Court itself; and in that case the accused, besides losing all possible chance to be declared innocent of the charge on which he is being tried, will lay himself open to a certain conviction for another, and perhaps a graver, offence. If, however, the death, disappearance or incapacity of the witness has been brought about not by the accused himself but by some other persons alleged to be acting in his interests, the latter should suffer and not the accused, unless it be proved that this was done with his knowledge or consent. Until the persons, who may be alleged to have caused the incapacity, disappearance or death of the witness, are actually put on their trial and proved to have done so in the interests of the accused, no court should have a right to jeopardise the accused in his defence in the manner contemplated by the Act. (*f*) As if these provisions were not sufficient, it is further ordained that the trials may be held *in camera*, which is sure to remove the wholesome check which publicity always has on the acts of judges. It is clear that the secrecy of the trial is not considered to be an effective means of securing the protection of witnesses from the associates of the accused, as the possibility of their being incapacitated, kidnapped or put death is taken for granted in the Act itself. Besides, the counsel for the accused as well as his relatives, who may be attending the trial, are bound to disclose the evidence adduced in the case to the friends of the accused in order to prepare the defence. Therefore, the only effect of holding a trial *in camera* will be to keep the general public in ignorance as to the evidence on which the accused was convicted or acquitted, which will prevent its being able to form a correct judgment on the findings of the tribunal. As secret trials naturally make the people suspicious, secrecy in this matter is likely to make them sympathise with the accused, which must be prevented at all costs. (*g*) The Local Government is also authorised under

Section 4 Subsection (2) to give retrospective effect to the operation of the provisions contained in this Part of the Act. (*h*) *Part II* of the Act does not pretend to deal with actual offences or actual offenders; it is directed against potential criminals and is purely preventive in its character. "If the Governor-General in Council is satisfied that anarchical or revolutionary movements which are, in his opininon, *likely to lead* to the commission of scheduled offences are being promoted in the whole or any part of British India, he may ..... make a declaration to that effect, and thereupon the provisions of this Part shall come into force in the area specified." (*i*) When the provisions of this Part have been brought into operation in any area, and the Local Government believes that any person is or has been *actively concerned* (whatever these words may mean) in such area in any movement of the nature described above, "the Local Government may place all the materials in its possession relating to his case before a judicial officer qualified for appointment to a High Court and take his opinion thereon". (*j*) The person concerned is not entitled to claim that he should be heard by the judicial officer to whom his case is entrusted, nor is the Local Government bound to follow the opinion of that officer. (*k*) After considering such opinion, the Local Government may by order in writing direct (i) that the person concerned shall execute a bond with or without sureties undertaking, for a period not exceeding one year, that he will not commit, or attempt or conspire to commit or abet the commitment of any of the scheduled offences, or (ii) that he shall notify his residence and any change of residence to such authority as may be so specified, or (iii) that he shall reside in any area in British India specified by Government, or (iv) that he shall abstain from any act, specified in the order, which, in the opinion of the Local Government, is prejudicial to public safety, or (v) that he shall report himself to the officer in charge of the police station nearest to his residence at stated periods. (*l*) It is open to the Local Government to simultaneously issue any or all of these orders against any individual (Section 22). It must be remembered that these orders may be issued against a person who has not been given an opportunity to disprove the charges against him. (*m*) These orders are of an interim nature and shall remain in force for one month only, unless extended in the manner hereafter described. After making an order under section 22, the Local Government must forward the case of the person in question for opinion to an investigating authority which shall consist of three persons, of whom two shall not be inferior in rank to a District and Sessions Judge, and one shall be a person not in the service of the Crown in India. (*n*) This investigating authority shall hold an inquiry *in camera,* at which the unfortunate person whose actions are being inquired into shall not be entitled to be present. The investigating authority shall, however, *allow* the person in question to appear before it at *some* stage (not all the stages) of the proceedings. Presumably it is for the person in question to find out if an investigating authority is going through his case, and then to apply for permission to appear, because there is no provision in the Act which requires the Local Government or the investigating authority to inform him of that fact. (*o*) If the person in question appears before the investigating authority the nature of the charge will be explained to him and he shall be allowed to offer an explanation if he desires to do so; but the investigating authority shall not disclose to him any fact connected with the inquiry, the communication of which might endanger the public safety or the safety of an individual. The investigating authority shall also allow him to produce such evidence as it may think necessary; but "such authority shall not be bound to observe the rules of the law of evidence" nor shall the person in question have the right to be represented by Counsel. (*p*) On receipt of the report of the investigating authority, the Local Government may either confirm or cancel its previous order, no matter whether the finding of the investigating authority was in favour of or against the person in question. It will thus be seen that the Local Government is bound to refer the matter to such authority; but is not bound to follow its conclusions. (*q*) After the expiry of an order passed in this manner, the Local Government may, if it deems it necessary in the interests of public safety, again make an order authorised under section 22 against the same person, which shall not remain in force for more than another year. In other words, the acts and movements of a person may be restricted for two years without his having been brought to a proper trial. (*r*) *Part III* of the Act is more drastic, and differs from the foregoing parts in that it is made applicable when in the opinion of the Governor-General in Council the offences referred to above "are prevalent to such an extent as to endanger public safety." (*s*) Under the provisions contained in this Part, the Local Government may, in addition to an order under section 22, direct the arrest and confinement of the suspected person and may also order the search of any place specified in the order. The arrest may take place without a warrant; but the person imprisoned is not to be confined in that part of a prison where convicted criminals are kept. The confinement under such an order shall not exceed fifteen days. (*t*) Then the procedure laid down in Part II with respect to an inquiry by the investigating authority is to follow. (*u*) If a person evades or fails to comply with an order made under this part, he shall be punishable with imprisonment for a term which may extend to one year or with fine to the extent of one thousand rupees or with both. It would thus appear, that a person may be imprisoned for two years under a *lettre de cachet* of the Local Government, without being placed on his trial before a court of law. It is not difficult to imagine the widespread injustice and terror which may be caused by the operation of the provisions contained in this Part, when the Local Government is in a state of panic or excitement. (*v*) *Part IV* relates to persons who have been already dealt with under the Defence of India Act, the Bengal State Prisoners' Regulation, 1818, and the Ingress into India Ordinance; and brings such persons *ipso facto* under the provisions of the Act. This means that once a man finds himself in the clutches of the Government by some emergency legislation, he is not to be easily released. (*w*) *Part V* of the Act simply strengthens the grip of the executive. It provides that even when the orders applying the first three Parts to any area are cancelled, "such cancellation shall not affect any trial, investigation or order commenced or made under this Act, and such trial, investigation or order may be continued or enforced, and on the completion of any such investigation, any order which might otherwise have been made may be made and enforced, as if such notification had not been cancelled". (*x*) This Part also enacts an indemnifying clause which provides that, "no order under this Act shall be called in question in any court, and no suit or prosecution or other legal proceeding shall lie against any person for anything which is in good faith done or intended to be done under this Act." (*y*) The last section lays down that the powers given by this Act shall be exercisable in addition to the powers conferred on Government by any other enactment. One should have thought that the powers conferred by the previous laws were useless and antiquated; but even a bad coin may be useful in an emergency.

If these provisions are not hard on the accused and there is no likelihood of a miscarriage of justice, why is their operation confined to the scheduled offences, and that also only under certain stated circumstances. If the procedure followed at ordinary criminal trials is unnecessarily dilatory, the Rowlatt Act should be made applicable to all offences, whatever their nature may be, because the interests of public safety ought to demand a speedy trial not only of the anarchists but also of all murderers and dacoits. If the provision for appeal in the jurisprudence of all the civilised countries of the world is a hindrance and a danger to the course of justice, why not abolish this pernicious practice in all trials. If sections 32 and 33 of the Evidence Act give the accused an opportunity to escape punishment by keeping the witnesses away or otherwise doing injury to them, why should not these rules of evidence be discarded under similar circumstances in every trial. If a person accused of an anarchical or revolutionary crime is expected to derive great benefit by laying himself open to cross-examination, why should this privilege not be extended to persons accused of other offences. And lastly, if the *investigating authority* is a proper body to inquire into the conduct of persons suspected of such grave offences as are mentioned in the schedule to the Act, and if the presence of the suspected person is an unnecessary waste of his valuable time, and the rules of evidence a mere restriction on the liberty of the judge, why should not these advantages be made available to persons suspected of other offences. No sensible man desires to shield the anarchists. They are a danger to every civilised community; but even they should be treated like other criminals. The revolutionary is at war with the society; but he should have no ground to say that he was not given an open and fair trial, before he was sent to his doom.

This Act is no doubt an improvement on the Defence of India Act, inasmuch as some sort of an inquiry is to be held in every case; but its provisions do not exclude the chances of an innocent person being made to suffer by arbitrary action of the Executive. The critics of the Act are asked to rely on the good faith of the Executive, and in most cases that reliance may be justifiable; but there may be other cases in which in the absence of the wholesome checks provided in the constitution of every country, the arbitrary action of the Executive Government may lead to injustice and oppression.

Application of the Act.

The Government tried to make much of the fact that the Act was not in actual operation in any part of the country; and it was urged that the agitation against it, especially the passive resistance, was uncalled for, inasmuch as the Act was not in force. Obviously, this could not be a sufficient reason to hold the agitation in abeyance, because the Act was passed not merely to adorn the statute book but to be put to effective use. It was also argued that the Act could not be applied to any part of the country unless the Government was satisfied that the "interests of public safety" demanded its use to suppress revolutionary or anarchical crime. At the first blush, this sounds perfectly reasonable and reassuring; but the people know by their long and bitter experience, how easily and on what flimsy grounds such measures are brought into operation—the application of Regulation X of 1804 to various parts of the Punjab being the most recent of such experiences. The assurance that the Act is to be brought into operation only "in the interests of public safety" has been found to be more or less illusory, for the Government and the people hold very different ideas about "public safety." The Government has in recent years given a very wide interpretation to these words. Under the Defence of India Rules, the Government did numerous things in the interests of public safety, which the people think were highly detrimental to those interests. Mrs. Besant was interned, because her freedom would have endangered public safety. Mr. Bipin Chandra Pal and Lokamanya Tilak whre prohibited from setting their feet on the sacred land of the five rivers in the interests of public safety. Mrs. Besant's newspapers, the *New India* and the *Commonweal* were not allowed to be circulated in the Punjab on the same grounds. Thousands of persons, including men like Messrs. Mohamed Ali and Shaukat Ali, were interned in various parts of the country without trial or judicial proof in the interests of public safety. Thousands of persons were *speedily* tried by special tribunals, set up under the Defence of India Act, for offences wholly unconnected with the War on the plea that their being tried by ordinary courts, which would have secured to them a fair and open trial with a right of appeal, was prejudicial to the interests of public safety. Even the accused in cases like the Shahabad and Katarpur riot cases, which arose from purely religious disputes, were so tried. Mr. B.G. Horniman was deported from India, because his presence here would have jeopardised the public peace. Such being the notions of public safety which the Government entertains, the people naturally refused to attach any importance to this spurious safeguard embodied in the Rowlatt Act, especially when the Government's discretion in the matter of judging the requirements of public safety was not to be open to question in any court of law.

Object of the Act.

Ever since the Rowlatt Bill (No. 2) was introduced in the Council, the Government has been proclaiming from the house-tops, that it is intended to cope with anarchical and revolutionary crime, and that the law-abiding citizens have nothing to fear from it. A person who is not acquainted with the ways of the Indian bureaucracy may not have any objection to such a law; but unfortunately the Indian politicians have seen too much of the working of such laws to consider them to be as innocent as they appear to be. Recents events in India have shown that the Government has rather queer notions of sedition and anarchy. At one time or another constitutional workers like Lokamanya Tilak, Mr. Bipin Chandra Pal, Lala Lajpat Rai, Mr. Arabindo Ghose, Mrs. Annie Besant, Mr. B. G. Horniman, Messrs. Mohamed Ali and Shaukat Ali, Lala Harkishen Lal and Lala Duni Chand, have been held by the Government to be disloyal and seditious persons, whose remaining at large was a danger to society. If these persons, whom India literally adores, are counted among revolutionaries or the promoters of disloyal movements, then certainly the people of India are directly and vitally affected by the Rowlatt Act or any other repressive legislation, however much the Government may say to the contrary. The case of the opponents of the Act may be briefly put in the following words of the Hon'ble Mr. Srinivasa Sastri, which he used in the Imperial Legislative Council :—

> "A bad law once passed is not always used against the bad, ... When Government undertakes a repressive policy, the innocent are not safe. Men like me would not be considered innocent. Innocent then is he who forswears politics, who takes no part in the public movements of the times; who retires into his house, mumbles his prayers, pays his taxes and *salams* all the Government officials all round..... Now even in war, when all humanity throbs with excitement

and peril, and when nobody thinks of anything except how to conquer the enemy, even then, my Lord, there are the laws of war..... When there are criminals abroad in a country, there are certain ways in which they ought to be brought to book. You ought not to lay them by the heels and punish them in ways that will shock the sense of justice; in ways, that will make the innocent feel that there is no law in the land; in ways, that will make the virtuous and public-spirited work impossible. The price even for the extinction of wickedness that is demanded then is far too high."

The Government contends that the Act is limited in its application to anarchical and revolutionary crimes; but it refused to incorporate in the Act the definition of such a crime. The schedule of offences attached to the Act does not confine its operation only to such offences as may be considered to be anarchical and revolutionary, but includes even such crimes as sedition, rioting, promoting enmity between different classes of His Majesty's subjects, causing grievous hurt, extortion and criminal intimidation. The executive authority in India being subject to no constitutional check, the people are right in objecting to its arming itself with extraordinary powers, which may possibly jeopardise the life and liberties of His Majesty's Indian subjects; and the suspicion and distrust of the people regarding the use and effect of this legislation cannot be considered absolutely unreasonable and due to a desire to embarrass the Government.

Mistake of the Government.

The people thus had real objections to the passing of the Act, which have been correctly summarised in the following words used by Mr. M. A. Jinnah in a letter, which he addressed to the Viceroy resigning his seat in the Imperial Legislative Council :—

"Neither the unanimous opinion of the non-official Indian members, nor the entire public opinion and feeling outside has met with the least respect. The Government of India and Your Excellency, however, have thought it fit to place on the Statute Book a measure, admittedly obnoxious and decidedly coercive at a time of peace, thereby substituting the executive authority for the judicial.....

"The fundamental principles of justice have been uprooted and the constitutional rights of the people have been violated, at a time when there is no real danger to the State by an overfearful and incompetent bureaucracy, which is neither responsible to the people nor in touch with the real public opinion. And their whole plea is that powers when they are assumed will not be abused.....

"In my opinion the Government that passes or sanctions such a law in times of peace forfeits its claim to be called a civilized Government, and I still hope that the Secretary of State for India, Mr. Montagu, will advise His Majesty to signify his disallowance to this Black Act."

Such protests were bound to create a disquieting effect on the people; but that could not be avoided if the Government was to be informed of the real views and sentiments of the people. The constitutional issues involved were so grave that widespread agitation was bound to follow the passing of the Act; and the members of the Council were only echoing the views of the people when they warned the Government against the consequences of the agitation that must have resulted from the uncompromising attitude of the Government. But the Government did not heed these unequivocal indications of public opinion, and considered it a point of honour and the secret of power not to yield to popular criticism. The unanimous opposition of the non-official members of the Council was disregarded. The resignations of members like Pandit Madan Mohan Malaviya, Mr. Mazhar-ul-Haque, Mr. M.A. Jinnah and Mr. B.D. Shukul were received and accepted with a sense of relief. The numerous meetings of protest that were held all over the country when the Bill was still under consideration and the views of the Indian leaders and publicists were disregarded. The strong objections which were taken to the provisions of the Bill and which should have proved fatal to it were brushed aside as of no avail. The warnings of the Indian members of the Council were treated as vain threats. And the Government persisted in rushing the measure through the Council in the face of an almost universal opposition. After adopting this obstinate attitude, it did not lie in the mouth of the Viceroy to accuse the members of his Legislative Council of fomenting agitation and creating disorder in the country.

Burke repeated an obvious truth when he observed that "the natural rights of mankind are sacred things, and

Object of agitation.

if any public measure is proved to affect them, the objection ought to be fatal to that measure." Failing to make the Government of India agree to this axiom of democratic governance, the people hoped that the Secretary of State for India may, perchance, listen to them and persuade the Cabinet to disallow the Black Act. At the thousands of meetings that were held to protest against the measure, resolutions were adopted entreating the King-Emperor to disallow the Act. This was the object of the agitation that followed the Rowlatt legislation, and it is wrong to say that the members of the Indian Legislative Council promoted this agitation to make good their so-called threats. The chief object of the *hartals*, or suspension of business as a protest against the Act, in which people of all classes and creeds took part, was to falsify the position taken up by the Government that the opposition against the measure was confined to a few agitators, and to prove beyond all reasonable doubt to His Majesty's Government that even the masses disapproved of the repressive enactment. The people wanted that their voice should be heard, even though it were not heeded.

An example from Anglo-Indian history.

No people, with any sense of self-respect or a desire to uphold their rights, would have behaved differently under similar circumstances. The non-official European community in India went much further, in their opposition to the Ilbert Bill. Sir Henry Cotton in his book called the "Indian and Home Memories"* describes the doings of the European community in the following words:—

"The readers of Trevelyan's biography of Lord Macaulay will remember how the whole non-official world in India was banded together to resist what it conceived to be the monstrous injustice of Macaulay's 'Black Act,' which authorised Indian judges to exercise civil jurisdiction over British-born subjects. But this crisis was as nothing in comparison with that which occurred in Lord Ripon's time when Sir Ashley Eden, shortly before his retirement, proposed an amendment in the Criminal Law to give Indian Magistrates jurisdiction to try

*"Indian and Home Memories," by Sir Henry Cotton, K.C.S.I., pages 178-180.

European offenders. This is the measure known as the Ilbert Bill, because it was introduced into the Legislative Council by Sir Courtenay Ilbert, who was then Legal Member. A public meeting of protest by the European community was held at the Town Hall in Calcutta; members of the Bar abandoned the noble traditions of their profession, and speakers and audience, frenzied with excitement, were lost to all sense of moderation and propriety. The Viceroy was personally insulted at the gate of Government House. A gathering of tea planters assembled and hooted him at a railway station as he was returning from Darjeeling, when "Bill" Beresford, then an A.D.C., was with difficulty restrained from leaping from the railway carriage into their midst to avenge the insult to his Chief."

This was not all. The non-official Europeans to a man boycotted the entertainments at the Government House; and a conspiracy was hatched to overpower the sentries at Government House and kidnap the Viceroy in the event of the Government adhering to the proposed legislation. Sir Henry Cotton goes on to say :—

"It is with a feeling of shame that I am bound to add that the opposition to the Ilbert Bill was headed by members of my own Service..... Lord Ripon was thus harassed and hampered by the bigotry and race feeling of his own fellow-countrymen."

The community, which is now so loud in execrating the Indians for agitating to remove an unjust enactment from the statute book, which is fatal to their constitutional liberties, went to such lengths in order to protect a privilege which they had no right to retain.

Agitation against Rowlatt Act not responsible for disorders.

Always unwilling to admit that their own acts can ever lead to discontent among the people, many Government officials refused to believe that the general unrest in the province which burst forth into disorders could have been caused by the acts and policy of Government. They ascribed the excesses of the mobs to a deep-laid conspiracy spread throughout the country, possibly in alliance with the Bolshevists, which was using the Rowlatt Act as a convenient pretext for promoting a rising against the Government. *Hartals*, public meetings of protest and malicious misrepresentations of the provisions of the Act were considered to be the methods of inflaming the populace against the authorities. Even a cursory review of the facts will show that this is not a correct reading of the situation. The agitation against the Rowlatt Act was natural, proper and necessary, because its provisions are a menace to the elementary rights of citizenship and are an insult to India's loyalty. This agitation, however, was not confined to the Punjab. It was shared by her with the other provinces, with this difference that while it was accompanied by disturbances in certain other parts of the country, in the Punjab it did not result in a single act of violence. Both the 30th of March and the great *Satyagraha* day of the 6th of April, passed off quietly in the province, though a universal *hartal* was observed and mass meetings were held to protest against the Act in almost all the important towns and villages. The agitation against the Act reached its culminating point on the 6th of April, when at least a million men must have taken part in the demonstrations held all over the province, in the form of *hartals* or meetings or processions; but there was no violence or collision with the police at any place whatever. This is a clear proof of the fact that the disorders were not connected with the agitation against the Act. Even in other parts of the country, e.g., in Bombay, Calcutta, Ahmedabad, Viramgaum and Delhi, where there were disturbances, perfect quiet was restored almost immediately afterwards. If the discontent in the Punjab was due to the same causes, how is it that the disorders in the Punjab assumed the proportions of an "open rebellion"? It has been suggested that the martial races of the Punjab are excitable. Whenever the Government wants to treat this province in a differential manner, it seeks to justify its actions by referring to the fact that the Punjab is close to the frontier and is peopled by the martial races. The first consideration has no bearing on the question and cannot furnish any explanation of the disorders, unless it is proved that emissaries from beyond the frontier came over to the province to create unrest. Of this there is no evidence. The second fact—the Punjab being the province from which the Indian armies are largely recruited—should ensure the maintenance of peace and order rather than the propagation of rebellion, unless, of course, it be a fact that objectionable methods were adopted to secure recruits for the army. A province which contributes more than half the number of recruits for the Indian Army ought to be fully conscious of the vast resources of the Government and the futility of attempting to subvert British rule in India by means of sticks.

There is no doubt that the agitation against the Rowlatt Act had a disquieting effect on the masses, but the *hartals*. and other demonstrations would not have been so extensive and so successful had the people not been already smarting under numerous other grievances. The Punjab Government itself admits this fact when it says about the *hartal* at Amritsar that, "the rapidity with which a demonstration of this nature can be organised—*given the previous existence of a suitable atmosphere*—is proved by the fact that when the *hartal* was duly held next day, the 6th April, it was as complete as that of the 30th March."* The real cause, therefore, of the disorders in the Punjab is not to be found in passive resistance and *Satyagraha,* which were never practised in the Punjab, nor in the agitation against the Rowlatt Act, which was common to the whole country, nor in its proximity to the frontier or its being the home of soldiers; but the real causes of the disorders are the causes which brought about "the existence of a suitable atmosphere" and prepared the ground for an angry outburst of the pent-up feelings of the people at the slightest provocation.

Exxcessive Recruiting for the Army.

The allegation that oppressive methods were adopted to obtain recruits may be open to question; but there is no doubt that the heavy recruitment for the army, which went on in the Punjab, particularly during the year preceding the disturbances, had created a good deal of discontent among the masses. Speaking on the 7th of April

* Selections from the Punjab Government's report on the Disturbances, page 3.

in the Provincial Legislative Council Sir Michael O'Dwyer described the results of the recruiting operations in the Punjab in the following words :—

> ".....We started the war with 100,000 men in the Army.
>
> "In 1917, I was able to tell you that in the first two-and-a-half years of the war we had raised 124,000 combatants. In the next year we raised over 127,000 and a year ago the total was over a quarter of a million. We were then in the most critical stage of the war, and in response to His Majesty's August Message and the Premier's appeal I asked the Province to raise another 200,000 men including 180,000 fighting men within a year. Many people thought, that was *an extravagant demand*. Those people did not know the spirit of the Punjab. April and May 1918 were the harvest months and we advisedly did not push recruiting. But 21,000 men were enrolled.
>
> "From June to September the recruiting campaign was carried on everywhere with great enthusiasm, and in these four months 78,000 men or over 19,500 per month joined the colours. In October, owing to the influenza epidemic, the number dropped to 14,426; and in November when we were about to make a fresh effort, our enemies collapsed and hostilities came to an end, and the number fell to 6,313; but in six months, from June to November, we had raised 99,000 men or half the total promised, and in eight months, April to November, our total was 121,000 men, including 100,000 combatants. If the need had continued, we shall have completed our quota of 200,000. As it is, we can claim to have raised about 360,000 combatants during the four years of the war, or more than half the total raised in the Indian Empire, excluding, of course, the splendid contribution from our gallant neighbours and allies in Nepal."

In other words, the Punjab supplied about 460,000 men for the war. Now, according to the census of 1911, the population of the Punjab is a little less than 20 millions, while the total population of India is 315 millions. Was it, therefore, just or proper that the recruiting for the war should have been so unevenly distributed over the diffferent parts of the country, that a province possessing only one-fifteenth of the population should be made to supply more than half the number of recruits raised in the whole country? Even if such a heavy recruitment could have been carried on without resorting to the slightest pressure or compulsion, the campaign for obtaining recruits became so intensive in the chief recruiting areas of the province that it was bound to create discontent. In his speech of the 7th Apri1, 1919, Sir Michael O'Dwyer admitted that, "The active attempts to obtain recruits from an ignorant and home-loving population, who had not yet learnt the elementary duty of helping to defend their country, led to some serious riots and lawless outbreaks in the Multan Division and Shahpur." The Secretary of State for India in his last Budget Speech, while discussing the causes of unrest, had to admit that "recruiting for the army has gone on in parts particularly affected by these disturbances with such zeal and enthusiasm, that I think there is reason to believe many a family was left without its bread-winner or bread-winners". In the presence of such unequivocal admissions by officials of such eminence, it is not necessary to labour the argument that excessive recruiting for the Army, no matter how the recruits were obtained, was in itself a sufficient cause to create discontent amongst the people.

The methods adopted.

While discussing the methods adopted in various parts of the province to obtain recruits, we are on less firm ground, because no evidence of a convincing character is available either to state positively that in all places recruits were obtained without undue pressure from official or semi-official quarters, or to come to the conclusion that press-gang methods were adopted to secure recruits. There is, however, no doubt that Sir Michael O'Dwyer was a strong man, who did not do things by halves. He transformed the whole machinery of Government into a huge recruiting factory. He himself assumed the role of the chief recruiting-sergeant, tramping up and down the province, holding numerous recruiting durbars, distributing *sanads*, conferring titles, giving *inams*, eulogising the districts that had furnished a large number of recruits and threatening those that had not, and reciting the formula that there is no *izzat* without *khidmat*. Each district was assigned a quota of men, and it was understood that this number had to be produced within a stated period. The Commissioners, the Deputy Commissioners, the Magistrates, the Tahsildars, the Naib Tahsildars were all so many recruiters for the Army; and the very continuance in service and promotion of *Zaildars, Lambardars* and *Patwaris* depended on the number of recruits furnished by them. Even the services of the police-officers were requisitioned for this purpose. The number of recruits furnished by a man being the measure of favour that he got from the Government, the result was that unscrupulous officials began to practise oppression when they failed to obtain recruits by fair methods. The police got up false cases under the security sections of the Criminal Procedure Code against the inhabitants of villages that had not furnished their assigned quota of recruits; and the Magistrates threatened the accused with conviction unless they consented to be enlisted in the army. If the accused did not want to enlist in the army, he could earn his acquittal by purchasing a substitute for himself. A short time after the starting of this oppressive campaign, the recruit became an economic commodity and could be bought and sold in the open market. And the favour of Government being measured in terms of recruits, a large number of aspirants after honours and rewards made extensive transactions in this trade; and considering the squares of land that loomed in view and the coveted titles of Rai Sahibs and Khan Sahibs, this was indeed a profitable business for the wealthier persons. They sent their agents all over the province, who obtained recruits on payment for their masters, who in their turn passed them on to the Government in their own name. Thus by spending a sum of about eight or ten thousand rupees, these men got some squares or rectangles of land in the canal colonies or obtained titles, which are to some infinitely more valuable than the sordid gain of money. The natural result was that the price of a recruit rose up, and in some districts approached the four figures. Some Government officials also turned this new development in the art of recruitment to their own profit; and when they could get more recruits than they thought would appease the desire of their superiors, they passed on the surplus on payment to these *reises.* Some of the subordinate officials rendered themselves so obnoxious by the immoral, indecent and oppressive methods which they employed to obtain recruits, that the people were driven to deeds of violence; and in one case, a Tahsildar was murdered by the villagers who were infuriated at his conduct, which the Government admitted as almost amounting to conscription. As the result of this act, 46 men were put on their trial, of whom 4 were sentenced to be hanged and 12 to transportation for life. A large number of prisoners were also drafted into the army; and when they returned, their propensities for mischief had been whetted rather than diminished by a sojourn in foreign lands. In fact, the mania for recruits was carried to every department of the Government. The first question put to every applicant for employment in any Government office was whether any of his near relations were in the Army; and promotions of Government officials depended on the number of recruits furnished by them. Even the students who wanted to get admission in the Medical or other Government Colleges were given a precedence if any of their near relations were serving in the Army. Is it reasonable to expect that such a state of things would not lead to abuses among officials and consequent discontent amongst the people?

Who is responsible?

It must be admitted that most of the European officers and a large number of Indian officials did not adopt illegal or oppressive methods to obtain recruits. But it being impossible to obtain the required number of recruits by methods that would be above reproach, the promotions of these officers were in most cases stopped or were not so rapid as they should have been, on account of the poor results of recruiting that stood to their credit. Though there is ample evidence to show that over-zealous and unscrupulous subordinate officials of the Government used unfair and tyrannical methods to swell the number of recruits in order to obtain rewards from the Government, there is no evidence to justify the sweeping assertion that a systematic form of press-gang was in existence in the Punjab. Nor is there any evidence of a convincing kind that Sir Michael O'Dwyer was aware of these iniquitous methods of recruitment, by which unwilling men were shoved into the Army by force and fraud; but if he was not, he is to blame, for it was his duty to find out and put down these practices with a strong hand. These methods were adopted on such a large scale and became so scandalous in certain districts, *e.g.*, in Gujranwala and Shahpur, that Sir Michael O'Dwyer should not have been unaware of them. It is, therefore, suspected that he must have connived at the lapses of his over-zealous subordinates in the larger interests of his Empire, in the belief that he would be able to suppress any unrest that may result at home by his strong methods, an exhibition of which was recently given in several districts of the Punjab. Nor is there any doubt that the Government had fully anticipated the unrest that might result when these soldiers returned from the field of battle. The Rowlatt Committee stated that "there will, especially in the Punjab, be a large number of disbanded soldiers among whom it may be possible to stir up discontent." The Punjab Government also fully realised the situation and passed the Patrol Act to meet this danger. In the course of his speech on this Bill, the Hon'ble Mr. Craik said :—

> "At present the Punjab is peaceful and free from crime. Will any honourable member be bold enough to phrophesy that that state will last when after the war thousands and hundreds of thousands of the more adventrous spirits return to native land? It is quite possible that a year or two hence you may see a great recrudescence of armed dacoity or cattle theft or robbery."

If these men had entered the army out of their own free desire to serve the Empire, why should they become a source of danger on their return home after loyally and bravely fighting for the Empire and making all the sacrifices that it involves ?

The disbanded soldier.

As long as an Indian does not leave India, he has a dread for the European and looks upon him as a super-human being. But when he goes to European countries and sees not only the well-fed *sahib* of proud bearing, with a clean suit, shining boots, a roaring car and arrogant manners, but also meets the white man with baggy trousers and starved physique, talks to him on terms of equality and studies his morals and manners at close quarters, he loses the awe with which he used to regard the *sahib* in India and considers him to be an ordinary mortal of flesh and blood. So it was with the returned Punjabee soldiers. Many of them had gone to France and were acclaimed and received as saviours by the French, men and women alike; but when they came back to India, they had left behind in France the awe and fear which they previously had of the *sahib*. On their return to India, they found that the inducements and consolations held out to them, when they had been recruited—in whatever manner it might have been done—were not fulfilled. Only a few were able to get favours from the Government, and the rest grew jealous. As a matter of fact, the lion's share of the war rewards went to the wealthy *reis* who stayed at home and only managed to obtain recruits by methods which it was nobody's interest to inquire. In some cases, the disbanded soldier found that in his absence his wife had transferred her allegiance to some other youth of the village; and in other cases, his relations had invaded and occupied his land. The lands of several others were lying uncultivated. The convict-soldiers were again overpowered by their adventurous spirit. Such was the state of things in several rural areas when the disorders took place.

The War Loans.

What has been said about the methods adopted to obtain recruits applies *mutatis mutandis* to the raising of war loans. The Punjab is a poor province; but the war-loan campaigns were so strenuously carried on that it competed successfully with most of the richer provinces of India. The extent to which the Government wanted its officials to exercise their influence in this matter may be judged from the following instructions, which were contained in a confidential circular issued by the Punjab Government to all Deputy Commissioners :—

".....Deputy Commissioners might assist much in the campaign by estimating the contributions that might reasonably be expected from the various towns. In doing so they will derive much assistance from the local income-tax returns, especially where the assessments have recently been revised by the special establishment. Income-tax returns furnish, too, a fairly reliable index to the relative financial condition of individuals who are expected to help the loan. To judge of the adequacy of their investments in it, it would not be unreasonable to expect that on an average an assessee would be in a position to invest in the War loan from half to one-fourth of the income on which he is actually assessed.....

'The Deputy Commissioner should then, by special meetings, formation of local committee of *Sahukars* and such expedients endeavour to obtain the estimated sum as a minimum contribution. Local committee of traders and others presided over in large towns by Judicial Officers, Extra Assistant Commissioners or Tahsildars, will probably be able to effect a satisfactory distribution of the loan demand. Rivalry between towns and communities might be promoted by periodical publication and comparisons of the amounts subscribed. Help might be afforded by a promise to recognise liberal subscriptions by *sanads*, by the grant of chairs, and by the gift of Special Certificates. On the other hand, it should be made clear to wealthy citizens that failure to do their duty in this matter will be taken into account in nominations to Municipal and Notified Area Committees, in appointments of honorary magistrates and in other forms of Government recognition, on the ground that such honours are reserved for those who have shown in a practical form their desire to assist the administration."

It would be a pure euphemism to style the methods outlined in this circular as mere moral persuasion. But even if it be conceded that the Government officials did no more than exercise their official or social influence to secure contributions to the war loans and war charities, the pressing appeals of the officials are not unoften interpreted as orders. The Government was fully conscious of this weakness of the people and wanted to take full advantage of it, when it suggested that Judicial Officers, Extra Assistant Commissioners or Tahsildars should preside over the war loan committees. In several Government offices, the high officials persuaded their subordinates to subscribe to the war loans or buy the post-office cash certificates. It is true that these officers did not actually compel their subordinates to do so; but there is no doubt, that a request or a suggestion emanating from the superior officer to his subordinates is taken to be an order and obeyed in that belief. The result was that most of these poorly paid clerks, who were already suffering from the war prices, had to contribute their mite towards the war loan in order not to incur the displeasure of their superior officers. There is also no doubt that in some districts the revenue officers brought a good deal of pressure to bear upon the villagers to make them subscribe to the war loans. In some districts, the landowners had to pay a certain fixed percentage of the land revenue towards the war-funds. It is also stated that in parts of the Gujranwala district, pressure was brought to bear upon the villagers by certain subordinate officials to make them subscribe to the O'Dwyer Memorial Fund.

Illiteracy and War Loans.

The Punjab is not only a poor province; but the ignorance of its people is also appalling. According to the census of 1911, in the Punjab only one person in 28 is literate and only one in 270 has any knowledge of English. The masses were, therefore, unable to understand the expediency and propriety of the action of Government in floating public loans for the expenses of the war. Hence, the worst effect of carrying appeals for war loans to the villagers was that they suspected that the Government was on the verge of bankruptcy. The illiterate villager could understand the demand for recruits to fight the battles of the King-Emperor; but he failed to understand that the great and rich *sircar* can ever stoop to borrow money from him. He was familiar with the idea of recruitment for the Army; but the importunate demands of the Tahsildar for a loan to the Government made him suspicious, and set him athinking, which naturally resulted in wild conjectures and baseless rumours. And there is no doubt, that apart from the particular methods adopted to secure contributions, the fact that the Government was borrowing from the people was in itself a cause which added to the discontent of the masses.

Economic Causes.

Economic causes played not a small part in bringing about a state of discontent among the people. During the last seven years the prices of food grains like wheat, barley, *jowar, bajra,* gram and maize which are largely consumed by the poorer classes had risen enormously as is illustrated by the following table :—

Commodity	*Retail price during fortnight ending 15th Dec. 1912. (For a rupee)*	*Retail price during fortnight ending 15th June, 1919 (For a rupee)*
Wheat	12 seers 4 Chitacks.	6 Seers 9 Chitacks.
Barley...	15 " 13 "	8 " 3 "
Jowar	15 " 12 "	4 " 3 "
Bajra	12 " 3 "	4 " 2 "
Gram	15 " 1 "	7 " 7 "
Maize	16 " 3 "	6 " 6 "

And as compared with 1894, the prices of food-stuffs had risen five times. The wages of both rural and urban workmen had not increased so rapidly. The rise in wages during the last 6 years may be taken to be about 50 per cent. The result was that real wages fell down to the starving point. The case of those who had fixed incomes was even worse, and it is an open secret that the railway employees were about to go on a strike when the disorders broke out. Failure of monsoon, diminution of the area under cultivation owing to heavy recruitment and the terrible mortality due to influenza had much to do in bringing about this state of things, which was accentuated by the enormous purchases made by Government on public account. The prices of the other necessaries of life, for which India depended on foreign countries, had also increased immensely during the war. There was thus an enormous rise in the cost of living both in rural and urban areas, which was in itself a source of widespread discontent among all classes of the people, except that small class of big land-holders who produce grain for sale. This would have led to labour troubles in Europe, but in India it took a political form because of the *ma-bap* relationship between the Government and the people. The Government tried its best to alleviate suffering by prohibiting the export of grain, by selling salt at cheaper rates, by retailing of standard cloth and control of sale of kerosene. But these measures were utterly insufficient to meet the situation. This state of things had lasted for some years and the people, especially the poorer classes, were becoming desperate and were ready to join in any agitation against Government. This explains why the city riff-raff and the lower classes so readily took to violence when an occasion presented itself. This economic suffering was an important contributory cause of the disturbances. A hungry man is an angry man. Starved communities like starved individuals are easily provoked; and as Bacon says, "Rebellions of the belly are the worst."

The world forces.

The war had an unsettling effect on the minds of people all over the world. The principles of freedom and international justice and the doctrine of self-determination had caused a revolution in the ideas of men. The tremendous forces that were harnessed for the purposes of the war had stirred up the remotest corners of the world. And it was but natural that the convulsions of this mighty struggle should be felt for some time after the actual conflict was brought to a close. The fountains of the great deep had been broken up; and the people expected the birth of a new world on the ruins of the Belgium and France and Russia of old. The placid life of the Punjab did not remain unaffected by this great cataclysm. The sanguine utterances of the allied statesmen had led people to believe that victory would bring a millennium to the world; but no such millennium came. The mighty victory of the Allies did not bring any of the promised boons to the Punjabees, who had been literally bled white during the war. The country had been promised a liberal measure of constitutional reforms; but it was feared that the Punjab Government was trying its best to make the Punjab's share as small as possible. With regard to honours and rewards for military services, the soldiers got almost nothing except their pay. It were the *reises*, the wealthy magnates and Government officials, who got big *jagirs*, titles and rewards for securing recruits for the Army by methods which were well-known to the people. Instead of the application to India of the doctrine of self-determination which the Allies had adopted as a world programme, the people were stunned to see the Government rush through the Council a new law which surpassed all those enacted before in its severity and in its utter disregard of principles of justice. The people resented the action of the Government in flouting the unanimous vote of their representatives, and refused to allow the Government to impugn their loyalty without uttering a strong though ineffective protest. The peace had come; but the promised boons did not come with it. The poverty, the high prices, the starvation wages still continued; and the position of an Indian in India was the same as it was before the war. Naturally there was a deep discontent among the people.

Sir Michael O'Dwyer's regime.

When Sir Michael O'Dwyer was appointed the Lieutenant-Governor of the Punjab in the year 1913, the province was contented and peaceful and its people were prosperous and happy; but when six years later he relinquished the reins of his high office, the province was under martial law and its people were said to be in a state of open rebellion. By his fierce hatred of the educated classes, by his utter contempt of the wishes and sentiments of the public, by his unveiled dislike for the political aspirations of the people, by his belief in the infallibility of his administration, and by his overweening pride and brutal disregard of the principles on which the British Commonwealth is based, Sir Michael did more to shake the foundations of British rule in India, than all the anarchists and revolutionaries taken together can ever be able to do. He believed in strong methods, in throttling political agitation, in suppressing public criticism of the acts and policy of Government, and in keeping the people down with a strong hand. According to him, the only object of the Government is maintenance of law and order by striking terror in the minds of the people. Political agitation was regarded by him as a danger to the peace and safety of the province. He believed with the rulers of medievel times that the subjects have no right to think or act for themselves, nor to make any suggestions to the Government for the better administration of the country. He relied not on the contentment, love and willing allegiance of the people, but on sheer force to strengthen the foundations of British administration in India. Government actions he considered to be above criticism; and political agitation he regarded as a danger to good government. These being the principles upon which his administration was based, he did his utmost to weed out public life from the province. Like the engineer who stems the current at its source, he endeavoured to bring under his control the Press and the Platform, and isolate the province from the other parts of the country. The former he tried to accomplish by creating a special branch of the Criminal Investigation Department, called the Press Branch, whose business it was to keep newspaper criticism within *safe* limits. Public meetings were discouraged by browbeating and threatening the speakers and conveners. And the spread of infection to the Punjab from the other provinces, which were suffering from political diseases like the demands for home rule or constitutional reforms, was sought to be prevented by prohibiting the entry into the province of several leading men and prominent newspapers of other provinces. In one word, Sir Michael O'Dwyer governed the Punjab on the lines on which the Native States of India are governed, where he had had his training in the art of Government.

Sir Michael and the educated classes.

Sir Michael O'Dwyer displayed a marked antagonism towards the educated classes because of their desire for political advancement, which this high priest of the Indian bureaucracy regarded to be the greatest sin. He believed that the existing system of administration was the best for all concerned and any suggestion to alter it was doing a disservice to the best interests of the country. Sometimes he went further and plainly told the people that they should look to their duties and not to their alleged rights. For instance, only a few weeks after his appointment as the Lieutenant-Governor of the Province, he made the following remarks in his reply to an address of welcome which was presented to him :—

> "During the short time I have held charge of this province, I have received many excellent and well-meant suggestions, as to how I should carry on the administration, what I should do to meet the aspirations of the people, to further the movement towards self-government, towards the separation of executive and judicial function and in regard to other matters of State policy. *Abstract speculations* of this nature have their interest and value, though they would gain in value, if in addition to enforcing the duties of administration, some stress were laid on the elementary duties of the people as citizens and subjects. I should have welcomed and I shall welcome any practical suggestion, as to how Government can discharge more efficiently its primary obligation to secure life and property, and how the people can be aroused to a sense of their duty towards the community. All other questions of policy are, in my opinion, subsidiary to these two and should stand over till these obligations are adequately discharged."

Again, speaking in the Punjab Legislative Council on the 18th of April 1914, Sir Michael O'Dwyer referred to the proposal to create an Executive Council for the Punjab in the following words :—

> "..... The people of this Province have from the start been habituated to regard the Chief Commissioner or the Lieutenant-Governor as the sole head of, and in the last degree responsible for, the administration of the Province. The Province has progressed and prospered under that system in a manner which can stand comparison with any other Province or Presidency, whether with an Executive Council or not.....
>
> "If it could be shown that the present administration of the Province suffers from certain defects, and that the addition of an Executive Council would remove those defects, then the matter might come within practical politics. In the middle of the 18th century, when political controversies and religious discussions were almost as rife as they are in India to-day, a poet and philosopher summed up the situation in the following words :—
>
> 'For forms of government, let fools contest,
> Whate'er is best administered is best,
> For modes of faith, let graceless zealots fight,
> He can't be wrong whose life is in the right' "

Speaking in the Imperial Legislative Council on the 13th of September, 1917, Sir Michael referred to India's demand for self-government in the following derisive language :—

> "..... In these days when we are in danger of being deafened by political harangues and of being blinded by the shower of political manifestoes, it is well occasionally to return to mother earth to clear up our minds of shams and illusions, and to ask ourselves what will all this noise and talk do for the man on the soil, the man behind the plough, the man whose life is a long drawn question between a crop and a crop."

Sir Michael O'Dwyer did his utmost to discourage the demand for constitutional reforms; and when in spite of his efforts, the Punjab's demand for reforms grew in volume and intensity, he tried his utmost to whittle down the Punjab's share by all means in his power, by trying to create and promote dissension between the rural and urban classes and by attempting to prove that the masses in the Punjab had no desire for political reforms. This is what he says in his Reform Memorandum of January 10th, 1918:—

> "Do anything to weaken or shake the authority of the Government and you will be appalled to find how small is the margin of safety—how thin the partition that divides order from disorder."

Referring to the Home Rule propaganda, he tried to make out that it was allied to anarchy :—

> "The small section of advanced politicians in the Punjab, hitherto quiescent, were encouraged to assert themselves and come into line with other provinces," but "here is no repudiation on their part of the Home Rule propaganda as preached by Mrs. Besant and Mr. Tilak, because its methods and objects were then little known in the Punjab, which is however familiar enough with the revolutionary aspect of Home Rule as preached and practised by the now defunct *Ghadr* party."

Again, he deplored the release of Mrs. Besant from her unjust internment and the announcement of the British Cabinet that self-government was the goal of British rule in India :—

> "We now seem to be drifting into what is known as 'Birrclism' in Ireland, truckling to the Extremists, encouraging the idea that we are going to hand over the administration to them."

In the course of the same memorandum he belittled the demand for constitutional reforms in the following words :—

> "If it is clear that the demands emanate not from the mass of the people, whose interests are at stake, but from a small and not quite disinterested minority, naturally enough eager for power and place, we must, if we are faithful to our trust, place the interests of the

silent masses before the *clamour* of the politicians, however *troublesome* and insistent. Here I may quote Burke's warning, 'because half a dozen grasshoppers under a fern make the field ring with their importunate cries, while thousands of great cattle, who repose beneath the shadow of the British oak, chew their cud and are silent, pray do not imagine that those who make the noise are the only inhabitants of the field'."

How far Sir Michael O'Dwyer succeeded in gagging the 'grasshoppers' or lengthening the repose of the 'great cattle' is clear from recent happenings in the Punjab. When the war was going on, he demanded the suspension of all political agitation on the plea of national safety. At a meeting held on the 4th May, 1918, he said :— "It was said of a Roman Emperor that while he fiddled Rome was burning. Shall it be said of us that while we argued about reforms our very liberties were ascending to heaven in the fires of Louvain?" The people acted on this advice and did not take part in the strong agitation for constitutional reforms that was going on in other parts of the country, in the belief that they would not be made to suffer for their self-imposed silence. But Sir Michael O'Dwyer took advantage of this patriotic desire of the people not to embarrass Government at a critical time, and tried to do as much damage as he could to their interests by misrepresenting them.

The feeling in the Punjab before the Rowlatt Act agitation.

For six long years the Punjab had suffered in silent anguish the *zulum* of Sir Michael O'Dwyer. It had seen the Lieutenant-Governor carry on a ruthless and systematic campaign to crush public life in the province by gagging the newspapers and persecuting the public leaders, by isolating the Punjab from the other provinces, by discouraging independent criticism of the acts and policy of the Government, and by malicous misrepresentation and vilification of the educated classes and their leaders. The people had also borne the tortures of the iniquitous and barbarous methods of raising recruits and war loans. They had also felt the stir of the great social, intellectual and political revolution that the war had brought into the world; and saw with no small despair and resentment that while the principle of self-determination was being applied even to the enemy territories, the Punjab was to be treated as the Cinderella of the Indian Empire. High prices and influenza had made the life of the people miserable. The Mahommedans were greatly agitated over the Khilafat and the fate of Turkey. All these matters did not affect the minds of all the inhabitants of the Punjab. Some had been incensed at the oppression practised for obtaining recruits; some complained of the methods employed to secure contributions for the war loans; some were exasperated at the repressive policy of the Lieutenant-Governor in the matter of constitutional reforms, and at his deliberate and continued insults to their leaders; and almost all suffered from the economic conditions. But society is an organic whole, and it will not be correct to cut it up into different sections and argue that only certain parts of it were aggrieved. When such a multitude of causes were in operation, their cumulative effect was bound to render the whole population discontented. Such was the state of the public mind when the Rowlatt Act was passed; and all classes readily joined in the agitation against it. *Hartals* and mass meetings of protest were held all over the province. A large number of persons who had never before taken part in political movements addressed these meetings; and hundreds of thousands of persons who had till then evinced no interest in politics joined the agitation. The Hindus and Mahommedans merged their differences in common grievances; and the outburst of indignation was directly proportionate to the harshness of Sir Michael O'Dwyer's administration, as the people felt that, like every other repressive legislation, the Rowlatt Act would be applied with special rigour to the Punjab. But the agitation, which was undoubtedly of unprecedented vigour and magnitude, did not lead to a single unlawful act anywhere in the province. The Government had nothing to complain of, and a wise administrator should not have considered it necessary to meddle with it.

Sir Michael O'Dwyer, however, considered the agitation to be a direct challenge to his ideas of good government and was greatly enraged when his attempts to prevent the *hartals* and the demonstrations against the Rowlatt Act had failed. He was an astute administrator, who had learnt his lessons in government in the Native States of India. He, therefore, quietly waited to see if the agitation would lead to acts of violence and thus place its leaders in his power. But, in spite of the display of armed police and its interference to prevent demonstrations, the people refused to be provoked and the 6th of April did not witness a single deed of violence. At this Sir Michael O'Dwyer felt scandalised, as according to his code of government strong, though constitutional, agitation against a measure of government should have interfered with the maintenance of law and order; and failing to find any pretext to cavil at this peaceful expression of public opinion, be misrepresented its nature and threatened the public leaders in the following words :—

Sir Michael's threats to penalise the agitation.

> "As a result of the prompt measures taken in previous years to quell revolutionary and anarchical movements, the province has contined to be free from political crime..... I must make it clear that if conditions should recur threatening the public peace, Government will not delay to use all the means at its disposal to repress disorder. We have lately had public meetings at Lahore and Amritsar—I am not speaking of yesterday's meetings of which I have not yet had the details—where some of the speakers used wild and inflammatory language distorting the acts and misrepresenting the policy of the Government. We have had similar violent language in some organs of the Indian Press. In fact a section of agitators who kept very much in the background during the war, when loyal citizens were helping to fight the common enemy, are now coming forward to show their valour by attacking Government and its agents and endeavouring to intimidate and coerce quiet law-abiding people by their propaganda of so-called passive resistance. I have already said publicly that the Punjab repudiated what is or was known as 'passive loyalty.' It will repudiate even more emphatically that veiled disloyalty which while hiding itself under the cloak of passive resistance leads on its dupes (as we have seen at Delhi) into open defiance of authority and the penalties which such defiance entails.
>
> "The Government of this province is, and will remain, determined that public order which was maintained so successfully during the time of war shall not be disturbed in time of peace. Action has, therefore, been taken in the last few days under the Defence of India Act

against certain individuals in Lahore and Amritsar who, whatever their motive, were endeavouring to arouse public feeling against the Government. The British Government which has crushed foreign foes and quelled internal rebellion could afford to *despise* these agitators, but it has the duty of protecting the young and ignorant, whom they may incite to mischief and crime, while themselves standing aside. I, therefore, take this opportunity of warning all who are connected with political movements in the province, that they will be held responsible for the proper conduct of meetings which they organise, for the language used at, and the consequences that follow such meetings..... It may not be out of place to repeat Aesop's story of the enemy trumpeter who begged the soldier of the victorious army to spare him on the ground that he was a non-combatant. The soldier refused on the ground that without the trumpeter's summons the enemy's soldiers would not have advanced. That moral is clear..... The recent *puerile* demonstrations against the Rowlatt Act in both these cities (Lahore and Amritsar) would therefore be *ludicrous,* if they did not indicate how easily ignorant and credulous people–not one in thousand of whom knows anything of the measure–can be misled....."

These words were uttered by Sir Michael O'Dwyer at a meeting of the Legislative Council on the 7th of April 1919, after the demonstrations against the Rowlatt Act had taken place without causing any breach of the public peace. Failing to find any reasonable objection against the conduct of the people and their leaders during these huge demonstrations, and chagrined at their universal success, he vented his spleen by accusing the leaders of misrepresenting the provisions of the Act and inciting the masses to violence, of which no evidence was produced by Government either at the trials held by martial law commissions or before Lord Hunter's Enquiry Committee. Also, in order to enlist the sympathy and support of the Government of India in the repressive measures which he intended to take against the promoters of this peaceful agitation, be misrepresented these demonstrations by connecting them with passive resistance, which was never preached or practised in the Punjab. In order to make it clear to the people that the Government was impervious to popular demonstrations of public opinion, he mocked them by calling their actions 'puerile' and ludicrous, and threatened the leaders with dire consequences for having dared to effectively protest against a measure of the Government.

It is not difficult to understand the psychology of Sir Michael O'Dwyer's mind. At a time when the people of the whole of India were in a state of excitement and the rulers of other provinces were trying to pacify them by allowing the storm to blow over without causing unnecessary provocation by taking measures of uncalled-for severity, Sir Michael O'Dwyer was not an errant fool to have threatened and insulted the promoters or leaders of these demonstrations. He knew, as the whole country knew, that the object of these demonstrations was not to incite the masses to acts of violence nor to inflame them against the Government. But Sir Michael knew and feared what the administrators of other parts did not know and had no cause to fear. He was aware of the fact that the whole province was justly indignant at the oppressive methods of raising recruits and money for the war; he knew of thousands of old decrepit parents whose sons had been thrust into the army by force and fraud; he was conscious of the fact that hundreds of villages had been ruthlessly depleted of their manhood and were peopled mostly by women and children; he was also aware of thousands of other families which had been impoverished in their attempt to let the bread-winner escape from the clutches of the recruiting-agent by bribing him or buying other recruits for substitution; and above all he realised that by his persistent insults and continued antagonism towards their desires and aspirations, he had alienated the sympathies of the educated classes;—therefore it was that the late Lieutenant-Governor considered it dangerous for the masses to take part in any form of political agitation and wanted the people to quietly sleep out the after-effects of the splendid war effort of the Punjab Government. It is only on this reasoning that one can satisfactorily explain why Sir Michael O'Dwyer dreaded political agitation and was alarmed to see the masses unite with the educated classes in these peaceful demonstrations.

Psychology of Sir Michael O'Dwyer's mind.

A large number of meetings were held in various parts of the province to protest against the Rowlatt Bill, both

Penalising Agitation

before and after it was passed in the Legislative Council; and on the 30th of March *hartals* were held at some places as a protest against this legislation. The Indian Press of the Province, both English and vernacular, condemned the new law in scathing terms. Every day the agitation grew in volume and Sir Michael O'Dwyer thought that his reputation as a strong ruler would be irretrievably lost if he did not curb the agitation. As the agitation was more insistent at Lahore and Amritsar, he started with these two places. On the 29th March, 1919, an order was issued against Dr. Satyapal of Amritsar prohibiting him from speaking in the public or writing to the Press, and interning him at Amritsar, so that he might not go to other places and deliver public speeches. Three days later, security was demanded under the Press Act from the "New Herald" of Lahore; and an order of precensorship was passed against the "Vakil" of Amritsar. On the same day, Syed Habib Shah, the editor of "Syasat," a vernacular daily newspaper of Lahore, was interned in his village. On April 4th, four other "trumpeters" of Amritsar, *viz*., Dr. Saif-ud-Din Kitchlew, Pandit Kotu Mal, Lala Dina Nath and Swami Anubhawa Nand, who, to use Sir Michael O'Dwyer's words, had summoned the enemy's soldiers to collect in peaceful public meetings and protest against the Rowlatt Act, were served with orders not to speak in public. All this show of power, however, did not succeed in silencing the war of words which the people were waging against the Government; and on the 6th of April, voluntary *hartals* were observed and mass meetings were held throughout the Province. This was a cause of grave provocation to Sir Michael O'Dwyer; and he decided to take more drastic steps to punish the agitators.

Blazing Indiscretion.

As the town of Amritsar was the most prominent in its agitation against the Rowlatt Act, the vials of Sir Michael O'Dwyer's wrath were first poured forth on the leaders of this town. On the evening of the 9th of April, the fiat went forth that Dr. Saif-ud-Din Kitchlew and Dr. Satyapal, both of whom were greatly loved and esteemed by the people of Amritsar for their unselfish patriotism and great services for the cause of national uplift, be deported under the Defence of India Rules without any trial or judicial proof. As usual, the ostensible reason for these orders was that their presence at Amritsar was prejudicial to public safety. Even a cursory glance at the events that preceded these orders would show that the Government had not the slightest justification to indulge in this act of criminal folly. In all about six meetings had been held at Amritsar to protest against the Rowlatt Act, which were of an orderly and constitutional nature, some of these meetings being attended by as many as 35,000 men; there were also complete *hartals* on March 30th and April 6th. But, as is admitted by the Punjab Government in its Report on the Disturbances which it submitted to the Government of India on the 3rd of November, "there was no disorder or collision with the police," "the organisers avoiding anything to justify intervention." The only other public event of any importance that took place at Amritsar during the interval was the Ram Naumi festival, on the 9th of April. This festival was utilised by the Hindus and Musalmans of Amritsar to fraternise with each other, and both the communities joined the Ram Naumi procession. The people shouted out "*King-Emperor Ki Jai*," and as the various band-parties passed the Deputy Commissioner who was watching the procession they struck up "God save the King." The Punjab Government in its Report admits that at this procession "there was no hostility or even discourtesy exhibited to Europeans, who moved freely among the crowd, as they had in the *hartal* on the previous Sunday (April 6th)." Dr. Kitchlew and Dr. Satyapal were the principal organisers of this procession. Such was the state of Amritsar on the night preceding the day of riot and arson, and the Deputy Commissioner was watching these demonstrations of loyalty with the orders of deportation in his pocket, which within the brief space of a few hours were to convert the happy town into a scene of desolation and ruin and to plunge the whole Province into disorder and tumult.

The spark that lighted the fire.

The orders of deportation against Dr. Kitchlew and Dr. Satyapal were communicated to the Deputy Commissioner of Amritsar on the evening of the 9th and were executed on the morning of the 10th April. The Deputy Commissioner had not recommended to the Local Government that this extreme step should be taken against these two popular leaders; but had asked the Lieutenant-Governor to stay his hand and allow him time to persuade these gentlemen to refrain from acts which were not agreeable to the head of the Government. When these orders were conveyed to the Deputy Commissioner, knowing as he did the condition of the town and the peaceful nature of the agitation that had been going on, he did not anticipate any disturbance of the public peace. "His estimate of the situation was based on the fact that during the *hartal* of the 6th, and even during the excitement of the Ram Naumi on the 9th, there had been no tendency to violence and no demonstration of open hostility to authority."* But the Deputy Commissioner anticipated a possible demonstration in the Civil Lines; and in order to prevent it, he picketed the route to that part of the town by mounted troops and police. On the morning of the 10th, Dr. Kitchlew and Dr. Satyapal were sent for by the Deputy Commissioner on some pretext; and on their arrival at his bungalow, were shown the orders of deportation, arrested and removed from Amritsar in motor cars. The news of this high-handed act of the authorities spread in the town like wildfire and in a few minutes all business was suspended and there was a *hartal*. The people collected in their thousands in the public streets and decided to go in a body to the Deputy Commissioner to assure him that the deported leaders were as loyal as anyone of them and to entreat him to have the orders of deportation cancelled. At about noon, this crowd started for the residence of the Deputy Commissioner, not with the desire of doing mischief but with the idea of having a

* Vide the Punjab Government Report on the Disturbances.

personal interview with the head of the district and of praying for his intercession with the Local Government on their behalf. Many persons in the crowd were bare-headed and bare-footed and all were unarmed. The people were in a mourning rather than a fighting spirit; and it is admitted by the Punjab Government in its report that "the crowd passed several Europeans on the way but did not molest them." The progress of this peaceful body of citizens was barred by the picket that had been stationed at the railway overbridge for that purpose, and on their insisting to proceed were fired upon and repulsed, with the result that a number of them were killed and wounded. The sight of blood infuriated the excitable members of the crowd and they started on their mad career of destruction. The Government admits that the acts of arson and murder which the mob committed at Amritsar "followed and did not precede the repulse of the crowd at the Hall Gate Bridge."

Arrest of Mr. Gandhi

On April 4th, Sir Michael O'Dwyer had also issued an order against Mr. Gandhi under the Defence of India Rules, prohibiting him from entering the Punjab on the ground that his presence within the jurisdiction of Sir Michael O'Dwyer was prejudicial to public safety. This order was not served on Mr. Gandhi, but was treated as a state secret until he actually reached Palwal (a small railway station on the borders of the Punjab) on his way to Delhi. At this station, a police officer boarded the compartment in which Mr. Gandhi was travelling, and showed to him this order of the Punjab Government. Mr. Gandhi politely refused to obey it, and expressed his intention to continue the journey. He was thereupon placed under arrest and taken back to Bombay in police custody. This happened on the night of the 9th April and the news of Mr. Gandhi's arrest at Palwal reached Lahore on the afternoon of the 10th. The people were stunned at this astounding folly of the Punjab Government, and were overpowered with grief and consternation at the unjustifiable and humiliating treatment to which their adored leader was subjected, whom a large number of persons regarded as a *rishi* or a *wali* and whose "coming was compared to the coming of Christ, to the coming of Muhammad and to the coming of Krishna."* In about half-an-hour all business was suspended and there was a *hartal* throughout the town. People were in a state of excitement and began to collect in the public streets. In about an hour a sort of procession was formed, which proceeded towards the Mall with the object of demonstrating to the European population of the town the esteem and love which the people of all classes and creeds felt for Mr. Gandhi, and in order to entreat the Lieutenant-Governor to withdraw his order. The peaceful character of the demonstration is established by the fact that the demonstrators readily made way for European ladies and men whom they met on the Mall and did not show the slightest discourtesy to any of them; nor did they attempt the slightest mischief to the many churches, European shops, banks and public buildings which they passed on their way. That the demonstration was of a pacific character is further proved by the fact that the churches, the banks and the public buildings and the European business-houses were all unguarded, and the people could have burnt or damaged them without the slightest resistance, had they desired to do so. It is also significant that at about this time Sir Michael O'Dwyer was being feted at a garden party in the Montgomery Hall, where he was to receive a farewell address from the representatives of the martial races. The procession was stopped by the police when it was about a quarter of a mile from the Montgomery Hall. The authorities had in their mind the occurrences that had taken place only a few hours before at Amritsar; and did not want the people to interrupt the Lieutenant-Governor in his pleasant occupation. As usual, the processionists refused to disperse and were fired upon, which inflicted some casualties. The people were then driven down the Mall up the Anarkali Bazar to the Lohari

* See Mr. Hailey's speech in the Legislative Council, *Appendix VI page 762.*

Gate, an Indian quarter where no danger to European life or property could have been apprehended, and were again fired upon.

Justification of the Order.

No lengthy argument is needed to show that the order of the Punjab Government against Mr. Gandhi was without the slightest justification and should not have been issued when the people were already in a state of excitement. That Mr. Gandhi is eminently a man of peace does not require to be proved. If there is any man in the whole of India who is incapable of doing violence to man or beast it is Mr. Gandhi. Even during the recent disturbances, the weight of his authority and position was always thrown on the side of peace and order. Mr. Montagu in his last Budget Speech spoke of Mr. Gandhi as his friend and refused to associate violence with his name. Far from promoting disorder or violence in any form or shape, Mr. Gandhi is one of the strongest forces in the country on the side of peace and order. It has been admitted by the officials concerned in their evidence before Lord Hunter's Enquiry Committee, that the subsiding of the disturbances at Ahmedabad and Viramgaum was in a great measure due to the influence and effort of Mr. Gandhi. The Hon'ble Dr. Tej Bahadur Sapru, a recognised leader of the Moderates, who did not agree with Mr. Gandhi's *Satyagraha* propaganda, condemns the action of the Punjab Government in the following words :—

> "Indian opinion is convinced that the arrest of Mr. Gandhi was a blunder and has been, to a great extent, responsible for the excitement and bitterness that has followed. That Mr. Gandhi is a man who hates violence even his worst critics have not denied him. That he has spoken straight to the people at Ahmedabad and at the same time pacified them has also been acknowledged in quarters not altogether friendly to him. And I venture to think that if he had been allowed to proceed to Delhi, the story before us would have been different."

But Sir Michael O'Dwyer believed that Mr. Gandhi was the moving spirit of a huge conspiracy to subvert the British Government by means of public meetings and *hartals*; and he could not so far forget his duty of preserving law and order in the province committed to his charge, as to allow the "chief conspirator" to hold personal communion with the local members of the conspiracy.

The Jallianwala Massacre.

On the top of it all came the terrible massacre at the Jallianwala Bagh. People from all parts of the province were present at the unfortunate meeting, and they carried the tidings of General Dyer's brutal massacre to the furthest corners of the Punjab. The news of General Dyer's efficient firing spread far and wide, and if that was his object he should be the happiest man in the world. But the form which the news took in transmission did more credit to the General than he deserved. The rumour went forth that the General had not only shot down the 'rebels' but had also bombarded the Golden Temple at Amritsar. This rumour was so widespread and caused so much excitement all over the province, that the Government had to contradict it in an official communique. But the mischief had been done, and not a few acts of disorder that took place after the 13th of April are directly attributable to the Jallianwala massacre.

Firing at Lahore and Amritsar.

Apart from the question whether the firing upon unarmed crowds at Amritsar and Lahore and the Jallianwala massacre were justifiable or not, there is no doubt that they had a disquieting effect on the masses all over the province. The people had never before heard the Government shoot down persons at a time of peace. They could understand deportations and arrests; but they could not realise that the police and the military would use rifles unless there was an actual rebellion. The illiterate masses, therefore, gave credence to the wild rumours, that there was rebellion in Lahore and Amritsar, that certain regiments had mutinied and the forts at Lahore and Amritsar were in the hands of the insurgents. This inflamed the villagers, who were already discontented on account of the methods adopted to raise recruits and the war loans; and the more excitable amongst them uprooted railway lines, cut down telegraph wires, burnt railway stations and committed other acts of violence.

The immediate cause of the disorders was, therefore, Sir Michael O'Dwyer's attempt to punish the agitation against the Rowlatt Act, of which he was a great admirer. Sir Michael O'Dwyer endeavoured to cow down the people by deporting their leaders, by gagging their newspapers and by prohibiting the entry of Mr. Gandhi into the province. All these acts inflamed the people, who were already smarting under various other grievances, and the firing at Amritsar and Lahore upon unarmed and peaceful citizens, who had not done any acts of violence, further enraged them and gave birth to wild rumours which caused grave and widespread disorder. Referring to the manner in which popular discontentment develops into outbreaks of disorder, Bacon says :—

The efficient cause.

> "As for discontentments, they are in the politic body like to humours in the natural, which are apt to gather a preternatural heat and to inflame. And let no prince measure the danger of them by this, whether they be just or unjust; for that were to imagine people to be too reasonable; who do often spoon at their own good: nor yet by this, whether the griefs whereupon they rise be in fact great or small..... Neither let any prince or state be secure concerning discontentments, because they have been long, and yet no peril hath ensured: for as it is true that every vapour or fume doth not turn into a storm; so it is nevertheless true that storms, though they blow over divers times, yet may fall at last; and as the Spanish proverb noteth well, 'The cord breaketh at the last by the weakest pull'."

So it was in the Punjab. For six long years, the people of the Punjab allowed Sir Michael O'Dwyer to pursue his systematic campaign of ruthless repression. They patiently and silently allowed the decimation of their population by oppressive methods of recruitment. They kept quiet over the objectionable methods by which money was squeezed out of them for the war loans. They were willing to endure the sufferings that arose from the high prices and the epidemic of influenza. They tolerated the continued insults and abuse which Sir Michael O'Dwyer heaped on the educated classes and the persistent misrepresentation and vilification by which he sought to reduce to the inevitable minimum the Punjab's share in the new constitutional reforms. The result was that Sir Michael O'Dwyer became bolder and openly ridiculed the demonstrations against the Rowlatt Act. He went even further and punished the leaders of a peaceful and consititutional agitation, when he found that the masses were joining the educated classes against the Act. This was the last straw that broke the camel's back. The people could not allow Dr. Kitchlew and Dr. Satyapal to be deported without telling the authorities what they felt about it. So far there was no breach of the public peace. Even during the *Satyagraha* demonstrations, when there were disorders in various parts of the country, the Punjabees had kept within the bounds of law. But when they were fired upon at Amritsar without any reasonable excuse, they lost their self-control, and indulged in acts of murder, arson and pillage. The arrest of Mr. Gandhi and the firing at a peaceful crowd in Lahore further incensed the feelings of the people, which were accentuated by the brutal massacre at Amritsar and the rumours which originated in these rash acts of the authorities. These brought about fresh outbreaks of disorder and at last the nemesis overtook Sir Michael O'Dwyer. The policy of repression miserably failed; and the strong man, who prided himself over his resolute administration, in a fit of panic declared himself incapable of carrying on the government of the province. A state of "open rebellion" against Sir Michael O'Dwyer's government was declared in the capital of the Punjab and four other districts that surrounded it; and martial law was proclaimed to consummate the work which his repressive policy had failed to accomplish.

CHAPTER II

The Rebellion

I—URBAN AREAS

As a protest against the Rowlatt Act, Amritsar observed

Amritsar

a complete *hartal* on the 30th of March 1919; a mass meeting was also held the same evening, at which resolutions for the repeal of the Act were passed. But no untoward event happened on that day ; and there was no collision between the people and the police. As the previous *hartal* was due to a misreading of Mr. Gandhi's letter to the Press, on the 6th of April there was another *hartal* at Amritsar as in other parts of the country; but on this day no public meeting was held. As in the previous occasion, there was no breach of the public peace, because to quote the Punjab Government Report, "the organisers avoided anything to justify official intervention". After the 6th of April, there was no further agitation against the Rowlatt Act; and on the 7th, 8th and 9th of April normal conditions prevailed and there was not the slightest disorder. On the evening of the 9th, the annual Ram Naumi festival was observed as usual, with this difference that the Mohammedans cooperated with the Hindus in bringing out the usual procession to a grater extent than before. The processionists at intervals shouted out *King-Emperor ki jai* (Victory to King-Emperor) and the different band parties struck up the national anthem when they passed the Deputy Commissioner, who was watching the procession. The Punjab Government admits that "there was no hostility or even discourtesy exhibited to Europeans who moved freely among the crowd, as they had done in the *hartal* of the previous Sunday (April 6)." It would thus appear that till the night of the 9th of April the feelings of the people of Amritsar towards the Government and towards the Europeans were perfectly loyal and cordial. On the morning of the 10th April, Dr. Saif-ud-Din Kitchlew, a barrister of great repute, and Dr. Satyapal, who had for some time during the war held the King's Commission in the Indian Medical Service, were deported by orders of the Local Government without any trial of judcial inquiry. Both these gentlemen were held in high esteem by the people of Amritsar for their great services to the national cause; and their deportation plunged the whole town into grief and consternation. In less than an hour all shops were closed; and people began to collect in the public streets. After mutual consolation, they decided to approach the Deputy Commissioner and entreat him to have the orders of deportation cancelled by the Punjab Government. The people were absolutely unarmed, and most of them were bareheaded as a sign of mourning at the deportation of their beloved leaders. This crowd passed the National Bank, the Town Hall and Christian Mission Hall without doing any damage, and displayed not the slightest discourtesy or resentment against the Europeans whom it met on the way. It has been acknowledged in the Government Report that up to this point the crowd was well-behaved ; and there is no doubt that it was proceeding on a peaceful errand. Had it been allowed to proceed, it would have gone to the Deputy Commissioner's bungalow and pleaded with him for the release of Dr. Kitchlew and Dr. Satyapal. The Deputy Commissioner could have given the people a sympathetic hearing and sent them away by soft words of hope, which would certainly have appeased them ; he might have called the influential men of the town, and with their help could have induced the people to resume their work with the assurance that their request would be placed before the Government. As Ruskin has said,

> "You can talk a mob into anything; its feelings may be—usually are—on the whole, generous and right; but it has no foundation for them, no hold of them; you may tease or tickle it into anything, at your pleasure; it thinks by infection, for the most part, catching an opinion like a cold, and there is nothing so little that it will not roar itself wild about, when the fit is on; nothing so great but it will forget in an hour, when the fit is past."

The Deputy Commissioner, however, was imbued with the principles of Sir Michael O'Dwyer's government, and did not endeavour to humour the crowd or parley with it. The previous conduct of the crowd did not warrant the assumption that it was bent on mischief or violence; nor had it been formed in disobedience to any public orders of the authorities. The crowd was ordered to disperse. The people refused to obey and insisted on the right to go to the Deputy Commissioner and lay their *faryad* (prayer) before him. The picket, which had already been posted at the Hall Gate Bridge, refused to allow the people to proceed; and on their persisting to do so, fired upon them. A number of men were killed and wounded. After a short time, the crowd again attempted to cross over to the Civil Lines and was fired upon a second time. This time there were probably about 20 to 30 casualties (official estimate).* The people wanted the Deputy Commissioner to intercede with the Government on their behalf; but a shower of bullets greeted them. They wanted bread; but bullets were given to them. The sight of blood incensed the mob. A wild roar of anger issued from the mob, which had up to that time been perfectly peaceful and law-abiding. The unruly elements in the crowd suggested vengeance, which looked sweet to the maddened crowd. The mob armed itself with sticks and stones; and split itself up into different groups. Guard Robinson was caught and brutally murdered by a section of the mob at the railway goods-yard. Another section of the mob that had been repulsed by fire, led by some hooligans, "attacked the National Bank, murdered Mr. Stewart, Manager, and Mr. Scott, Assistant Manager, sacked and burnt the Bank, and looted the godown which contained cloth and other goods to the value of several lakhs of rupees."† These Europeans were murdered in the most brutal manner, and after beating them to death with sticks, their assailants poured some oil on the furniture, which, with the bodies, was then set alight. The Chartered Bank was also attacked and its doors and windows were set on

* In all 73 rounds were fired by troops on the 10th. This does not include firing by police.

† Martial Law Commission's Order (*Vide* Appendix II, pages 329-330)

fire. The mob then attacked the Alliance Bank and murdered its Manager, Mr. Thompson, who happened to possess a revolver and bravely defended himself to the last against such numerous odds. The Martial Law Commission thus describes the cruel deed:—

> "After the mob had sacked the National Bank, an attack was made on the Alliance Bank, and the Manager, Mr. Thompson, was cruelly murdered—his assailants even going back a second time, on a rumour that he was still breathing and brutally assaulting him again with clubs—and was flumg from an upper balcony into the street where the body was burnt under a pile of Bank furniture drenched in kerosene oil."

The Religious Book Society's Depot and Hall were also burnt down. The Town Hall and the Sub-Post Office attached to it were fired; and the Sub-Post Offices at the Golden Temple, Majith Mandi and Dhab Basti Ram were looted. In one case the post master himself, it is alleged, took advantage of the riots and made away with the cash. Not content with the destruction and butchery already committed by the mob, they also assaulted Miss Sherwood, Superintendent of the Mission School at Amritsar, who, as the Commission which tried her assailants noted, "had for many years been working in the city and was greatly respected." The Commission describes the assault that was committed on her in the following words :—

> "..... About 1 o'clock on the 10th of April, when she was bicycling from one of her schools to another, she encountered a mob which raised cries of 'kill her, she is English'. She wheeled round and tried to escape, but took a wrong turning and had to retrace her steps. She reached a lane where she was well-known, and thought she would be safe; but the mob overtook her and she was also attacked from the front. Being hit on the head with sticks, she fell down but got up and ran a little way where she was again felled, being struck with sticks even when she was on the ground. Again she got up and tried to enter a house, but the door was slammed in her face. Falling from exhaustion, she again struggled up, but everything seemed to get dark, and she thought she had become blind."*

The Commission further goes on to say that the mob left her for dead; and afterwards some Hindu shopkeepers picked her up and took her to a temporary refuge. In the

* For Order of the Commisssion in this case, see Appendix II, pages 328-329.

evening she was conveyed out of the city and her injuries were attended to by a doctor. The assault on Miss Sherwood was certainly the most brutal and cowardly act of the mob and General Dyer had a just cause of anger against her assailants. It is inconceivable that a lady of Miss Sherwood's nobility of character and generosity of nature, who even refused to accept the sum of Rs. 50,000 which the Government offered to her as a compensation for the cruel suffering to which she was put, could have given the slightest cause for offence to the mob. Earlier in the day the mob also entered the Municipal Zenana Hospital and made every effort to hunt out the lady-doctor, Mrs. Easdon, who, it is alleged, had laughed at the persons wounded in the day's firing, who were brought for treatment to a dispensary which is just opposite to her hospital. Mrs. Easdon is said to have mocked the wounded and told them that they deserved the fate they had met. If this allegation is correct, any words that Mrs. Easdon might have used were highly callous and inexpedient, but they did not furnish any justification to the mob for their behaviour towards her or the other acts of violence which they committed. Seeing the mob collect outside, Mrs. Easdon had the hospital locked and hid herself at the other end of the building. The Commission describes the incidents connected with the conduct of the mob at the Zenana Hospital in the following words:—

> "Shortly afterwards, Mrs Benjamin (Sub-Assistant Surgeon at the Hospital), whom she (Mrs. Easdon) had sent downstairs to get some milk, rushed back with the appalling news that, assisted by *Musammat* Mathri (the *dai*), the mob had succeeded in getting into the hospital and that her life was in imminent danger. Mrs. Easdon had just had time to hide herself a few steps down an adjoining staircase when the mob, which had failed to find her downstairs, rushed up into Mrs. Benjamin's room and demanded to know where she was. Mrs. Benjamin, terrified through she was, swore that Mrs. Easdon had left the hospital but the mob was not satisfied and in the endeavour to find Mrs. Easdon broke open and searched all the cupboards and boxes in Mrs. Benjamin's quarters. Mrs. Easdon who was within a few feet of them, could hear all that occurred.
>
> "When the mob got back to the entrance of the hospital, *Musammat* Mathri informed them that Mrs. Easdon was still inside. The search

for her began again; but by that time she had hidden herself in a latrine on the roof. Before the mob could find her, the news arrived of the burning of the National Bank and, in the hope of loot, the would-be murderers dispersed.

"Hussain Bakhsh *chaprasi,* who had behaved loyally and bravely throughout, then got out of the hospital and returned with a *burka* and a pair of Indian *paijamas*. Disguised in these, and having blackend her face with ink, Mrs. Easdon escaped by a back way ....."*

The whole story sounds like a romance which might have been turned into a serious tragedy but for the presence of mind of two ladies and a *chaprasi*. In the course of the afternoon, the mob also burnt the Indian Christian Church; and attempted to attack the Church Mission Society's Girls' School, but a European Police Inspector, who had a picket close by, hastened to the spot with half his picket and the mob thereupon fled. Finally the mob murdered Sergeant Rowlands of the Military Works near the Rigo Bridge.** The mob was able to accomplish all these deeds of murder, arson and pillage in about three hours. In this brief space of time, five Europeans had been most brutally done to death, one lady was assaulted in the most shameful manner and property worth lakhs of rupees had been destroyed and looted. No justification can be offered for these cruel and cowardly crimes.

Was it Rebellion ?

The passion of the mob was satiated with three hours' work of destruction, after which there was perfect quiet and the people waited in abject fear for the consequences of their terrible crimes. The people of Amritsar are peaceful and loyal and the acts of a small section of its population, however heinous they may be, cannot reflect any discredit on the whole town or the district. In the course of a speech delivered by him at a Durbar held at Amritsar on the 17th February, 1919, Sir Micheal O'Dwyer praised the loyalty of the people of Amritsar in the following words:—

"During the past 5 years, I have paid Amritsar many visits, some times when the internal situation was serious, to seek your counsel

* For full text of the Order, see Appendix II, pages 333-335.

** For Order of the Commission in this case, see Appendix II, pages 320-321.

> and support, sometimes to appeal to the loyal martial tradition for which Amritsar is famous when men were wanted to defend the Empire, or money to provide the sinews of war, sometimes to discuss with your representatives important schemes for the improvement of your great and prosperous city. Whatever was the occasion, I always found from Amritsar and its people a prompt and practical response, and I have always gone away heartened and stimulated by the spirit of loyal endeavour and practical co-operation which Amritsar has shown. It is to prove my appreciation and Government's recognition of these qualities, that I have come here to-day ....."

And it must be remembered that Sir Michael O'Dwyer was not easy to please in such matters. Partly because the fury of the mob had spent itself, and partly because the law-abiding and thoughtful element of the population—which was by far the largest—asserted itself, the riots ceased after about three hours. Order was restored not by the action of the police or the military, but by the return of the public mind to its normal condition. The authorities were never paralysed; and on the only three occasions when they asserted themselves, they were successful in their object. At the Hall Gate Bridge, the police and the military were successful on both occasions in preventing the mob from crossing over to the Civil Lines; and when the mob was attacking the Church Mission Society's Girls' School, the mere approach of Mr. Marshall, Inspector of Police, with half of his picket, made the rioters take to their heels, without even giving him time to fire upon them. There is no reason to believe that the authorities would not have been able to check the violence of the mob at other places, had they tried to do so. But the police and the military apparently thought that their duty was finished, as soon as they drove the mob away from the bridge that connected the City with the Civil Lines. While the Banks were being burnt and looted and their managers mercilessly beaten to death, no less than a hundred armed constables, with a Deputy Superintendent of Police, one Inspector and three Sub-Inspectors, were kept idle at the *Kotwali,* which was at a stone's throw from these scenes of arson and bloodshed. Even when the Town Hall was being gutted by the mob, these 100 police constables were not moved from the *Kotwali*, which is a part of the same building as the Town

Hall. It is, therefore, wrong to assert that the authorities had been overpowered by the mob or had at any stage of the riots lost control over the town. There is, however, no doubt that the authorities were guilty of a grave dereliction of duty. As has been stated above, after the fury of the mob had spent itself, order was automatically restored, without the intervention of the police or the military. After the evening of the 10th, no act of violence was committed at Amritsar; nor is there an evidence to show that the people defied the authority of Government in any manner after the riots of the 10th were over. On the other hand, there is ample evidence to prove that the civil authorities had full control of the town, only if they chose to exercise it; and there is certainly no doubt that they could enforce their orders with the assistance of the military without the slightest danger of a disturbance. For instance, the Deputy Commissioner issued certain orders on the morning of the 11th April with regard to the burial and cremation of the persons who had died as the result of the firing on the 10th. The Deputy Commissioner had ordered that not more than a certain number of persons should accompany the dead bodies, that they should go by the route stated by him, and return by the time fixed in his order, and so on. All these orders were strictly obeyed by the people; and there was no collision between them and the authorities, in spite of the fact that thousands of persons had collected and accompanied the dead bodies in a procession. Similarly, the police investigations into the previous day's riots were commenced on the 11th April and some persons were also arrested in that connection; but there was no resistance on the part of the people. Even during the riots of the 10th April, no Government official was injured by the mob; and the courts continued to work. Under these circumstances, it is simply ridiculous to say that Amritsar was in state of rebellion on the 10th April or ever afterwards. The happenings at Amritsar were no more than local riots of a serious nature, during the course of which the authorities allowed the mob a free hand to commit grave offences against life and property. The people committed these violent crimes under grave and sudden provocation, which may not justify their acts but explains how a peaceful, law-abiding and loyal population was in a fit of righteous anger driven to these regrettable acts. In about three hours the riots collapsed with the collapse of the fury of the mob; and peace and order was automatically restored without the intervention of the police or the military, there being no organisation or premeditated design behind the disturbances.

Lahore

Passive resistance or *Satyagraha* was never preached or followed in Lahore. There was, however, a *hartal* on the 6th April; and a mass meeting was also held the same evening to protest against the Rowlatt Act. There was no breach of the public peace; nor was any coercion practised by the promoters of the *hartal* or any one else to make the shopkeepers close their shops. Thousands of persons collected in the public streets and tried to proceed towards the Mall to give a visual representation of their feelings about the Rowlatt Act to the European population of the town. The authorities, however, succeeded in persuading the mob to disperse without resort to violent methods. The events of the day are thus described by the Punjab Government in its Report—"On the whole, however, the promoters obviously received an almost universal measure of support from the shopkeeping class. There were very large crowds in the streets. During the course of the morning processions were formed (usually preceded by a black flag with Mr. Gandhi's picture on it) which were with some difficulty controlled by the police, but the leaders were interested in preventing disorder, and on several occasions were instrumental in controlling the movements of the crowd. The processions were illegal, but steps were not taken to disperse the crowds as they did not appear to be bent on violence."* The *hartal*

* Dr. Gokal Chand Naurang, a leading barrister of Lahore, was mainly instrumental in dispersing the crowd. He was subsequently arrested and prosecuted for waging war against the King.

and meeting of the 6th constituted the first act of rebellion. Business was resumed on the morning of April 7th, and normal conditions prevailed till the afternoon of the 10th, when shops were again closed on receipt of the news of Mr. Gandhi's arrest at Palwal. A crowd was formed, and it proceeded towards the Mall where it was dispersed by fire under circumstances which have already been described in the previous chapter. This so-called riot was the second act of rebellion. The third act of rebellion consisted in the fact that the District Magistrate thought it advisable to order the police to fire a second time on the mob outside the Lohari Gate on the same evening. The crowd is said to have been sullen and defiant on both these occasions, but no violence was attempted or done by it. It is also significant of the attitude of the authorities towards the people, that Pandit Rambhaj Datta Chowdhry, one of the public leaders of Lahore, who was in close co-operation with the Deputy Commissioner in trying to disperse the crowd outside the Lohari Gate, was not given even two minutes to exhort the people to disperse before the order to fire was given. The firing on both these occasions caused several casualties; but the Government having the good sense not to have deported the leaders at this stage, the people were kept in check. Had there been no firing on the evening of the 10th, the shops would have reopened on the 11th; but as it was, the *hartal* continued on that day as well. The persons who were wounded or killed on the evening of the 10th were taken possession of by the police and were sent to the hospital or the jail. There was a general rumour at the time, that the wounded were not properly treated at the hospital, as some of the English nurses refused to touch the 'rebels.' The news of the events at Amritsar reached Lahore late on the night of the 10th or the morning of the 11th. The people were highly excited and demanded that the dead and the wounded should be returned to them, and said that they would not open their shops till they had performed the final rites of the persons who were killed as the result of official violence. On the morning of the 11th, the Deputy Commissioner summoned the popular leaders of the town, and after threatening and cajoling them, asked them to have the shops re-opened. The leaders assured the Deputy Commissioner that they had every desire to help the Government and would try to have the shops re-opened, but that their efforts were not likely to succeed until the excitement of the people subsided by return of the dead and the wounded to them or otherwise disposing of the dead bodies. The Deputy Commissioner could not himself decide this most difficult problem and wanted time to consult the Lieutenant-Governor about it. In this connection, it may be remembered that after the grave riots and bloodshed of the 10th, the Deputy Commissioner at Amritsar had allowed the people of that town to go in a huge procession with the dead bodies to the cremation and burial ground and that there was no breach of the public peace. At Lahore, on the other hand, where the mob had not committed any violence and where the number of the police and military forces available was much larger than at Amritsar, the people were not allowed to bury their dead, nor were the persons wounded restored to their relations. This difference was presumably due to the fact that Lahore was the seat of Sir Michael O'Dwyer's Government. The leaders were recalled by the Deputy Commissioner in the forenoon of the 11th and were requested to go to the Badshahi Mosque and try to calm the people who were collecting there. Those to whom this request was made readily accepted it; and Pandit Rambhaj Datta Chowdhry, Syed Moshin Shah, Dr. Khalifa Shuja-ud-Din, Lala Harkishen Lal, Mr. Duni Chand and others went to the Mosque, addressed the people assembled there, tried to pacify them and exhorted them to open their shops and to obey whatever orders might be given by the authorities. The people re-iterated their demand for the restoration of the dead and the wounded; and refused to open their shops till this was done. On their return, Pandit Rambhaj Datta Chowdhry and others reported to the Deputy Commissioner what had taken place at the Mosque.

Subsequently, this meeting was also considered to be an act of rebellion, the gravamen of the charge being that Hindu speakers had addressed the audience from the pulpit of the Mosque. The fifth act of rebellion consisted in another meeting held in the Badshahi Mosque on the following day, at which the leaders again urged upon the people the desirability of ending the *hartal* and behaving as the authorities wanted them to behave. Fearing that a continued *hartal* might cause hardship to the poor and possibly lead to a breach of the public peace by starving hooligans, and realising the difficulty of trying to persuade the people to re-open their shops in huge mass meetings, the leaders also formed at this meeting a committee of leading shopkeepers, chowdhris of mohallas, and others to deal with the question. This committee was later on termed a "Revolutionary Committee" by the Government, and formed one of the charges against the Lahore leaders. The sixth act of rebellion consisted in the fact that the thousands of persons, who left the Mosque for their homes after the meeting of the 12th, could not melt away into thin air at the bidding of the authorities and were consequently fired upon. More than 30 casualties were inflicted; but the people who were peacefully returing to their homes did not commit or attempt any violence. It is suspected that an incident which had happened at the Mosque earlier in the morning, before the arrival of the leaders, had not a small effect on the officials in inducing them to fire on the men who were coming from the Mosque. Chowdhry Ali Gauhar, an Inspector of Police in the Criminal Investigation Department, was present in the Mosque presumably to report its proceedings, or as the people thought to misrepresent them, to the authorities. He was recognised and thrashed with sticks. The Commission, which tried the case, describes the incident in the following words:— "His assailants had him at their mercy but did not kill him. Followed by the mob, he was chased to his house, where he shut himself in. There were shouts of 'burn the house' and the door was battered, but the mob did not proceed to extremes. Ali Gauhar's *pagri* was afterwards burnt in the Mosque."* The firing of the 12th and the proposed Durbar of Sir Michael O'Dwyer further prolonged the *hartal* and the demand for the return of the wounded became more insistent. But the people were not disposed to disorder as would appear from the fact that the dead body of Khushi Ram, who was killed by the firing on the 12th, was followed to the burning-ground by several thousands of persons and there was no riot or disorder. The fact that Chowdhri Ali Gauhar was not seriously injured, when the mob had him at their mercy, and his assailants contented themselves with chasing him to his house and quietly leaving him there, further shows the temper of the people. On the 12th and the 13th the "Revolutionary Committee" continued to devise means to end the *hartal;* and two meetings were held at the Town Hall and at the Hon'ble Mr. Mahomed Shafi's house for the same purpose, which were attended by the leaders of the "rebellion". At the former meeting the Dupty Commissioner was also present, and it was pointed out to him that all efforts to re-open the shops would be futile if the wounded were not returned to the people. At Mr. Shafi's meeting, at which the ultra-loyalist notables were also present, the following proposals were formulated by common consent and taken to the Chief Secretary of the Government by Raja Narindra Nath, Hon'ble Sir Zulfiqar Ali Khan, Hon'ble Mr. Muhammad Shafi, Hon'ble Rai Bahadur Ramsaran Das, Nawab Fateh Ali Khan and Rai Bahadur Amar Nath– (1) that the Government may return the bodies of those who had died; (2) that persons wounded may be made over to their relatives; (3) that the military may be withdrawn from the Indian quarter of the town; and (4) that the persons arrested be let out on adequate bail. The popular leaders said that they were prepared to co-operate with the Government and try to have the shops re-opened, even if these suggestions were not acceptable to the Government; but they urged that their efforts to end the *hartal* might

* For text of Order, see Appendix II, pages 289-290.

not be successful, if the Government did not accede to these recommendations. Sir Michael O'Dwyer spurned these proposals and considered it derogatory to the prestige of the Government to accept them. Seeing that it was impossible to expect any reasonable attitude from Sir Michael O'Dwyer's Government, the popular leaders finally decided on the evening of the 13th to approach the people and persuade them to unconditionally re-open their shops. In pursuance of this decision, Pandit Rambhaj Datta Chowdhry and others addressed the crowd outside Shahalmi Gate to end the *hartal,* to which the people did not seem agreeable. It was then considered desirable that instead of addressing large numbers of men at a time, the leaders should go from door to door in different parts of the town to impress on the people the necessity of immediately re-opening their shops by talking to them individually. At this juncture there was a shower of rain, and the popular leaders had to defer it till the next morning. In the meanwhile some of them went to the Deputy Commissioner and told him about their proposed house to house visit to remove the *hartal.* The Deputy Commissioner smiled a mysterious smile and asked them to see him again on the following morning, when, perchance, he might have some important decision of the Government to communicate to them. The next morning, Lala Harkishen Lal, Mr. Duni Chand and Pandit Rambhaj Datta Chowdhry were deported under the Defence of India Rules, in the interests of public safety.

The "rebellion" at Lahore was, therefore, no more than a closure of shops, which the people refused to open before the return of the dead and the wounded who were the innocent victims of official lawlessness. No violence was attempted or committed by the people, as, unlike Amritsar, the leaders were present on every occasion to keep the people in check. The "rebellion" was very much like the rebellion of a lover against his beloved, who gets angry and refuses to talk or take food until certain conditions are fulfilled. It is not necessary to point out that the civil authorities did not lose control over the town for a single moment, till martial law wrested it from their willing hands. The police made arrests almost every day between the 10th and the 15th; the Courts were open and working as usual; and on the day preceding the declaration of martial law, the civil authorities arrested and deported the three most popular leaders of the people without the slightest opposition or disturbance. The police and the military freely moved in and out of the town without molestation. No one, European or Indian, was assaulted or injured; nor was property worth a single pice damaged in this grave "rebellion," which it is said, could not be suppressed without resort to Martial Law. The Deputy Commissioner almost every day discussed the situation with the leaders of the "rebellion" without fear or hesitation; and the various Indian and European officers moved about in the town and performed their duties without any opposition from the people. Except Sir Malik Umar Hayat Khan Tiwana, who of course occupied a semi-official position, no officer or pro-official person was ever insulted by the mob, Mr. Tiwana's grievance being that the people were disloyal enough to address him as "*Sarkar-ka-Mama*" (Uncle of the Government). And if this one fact is not sufficient to make the people rebellious, a state of "open rebellion" cannot be said to have existed at Lahore.

Kasur

Kasur is a town of only 25,000 inhabitants; and is situated at a distance of about 40 miles from Lahore and 50 miles from Amritsar. This small town was not tainted with political activity of any description before the recent disturbances. The riots that took place at Kasur cannot, therefore, be ascribed to any political agitation or conspiracy. This fact has been admitted in the Report of the Punjab Government in the following words:–"It does not appear that the agitation in the town was of long duration, there is indeed no record of meetings or propaganda before April the 10th, and the town did not even observe the general *hartal* of April the 6th. It is safe, therefore, to exclude any suggestion that disorder was long pre-meditated or due to a definite organisation to that end." On the 11th April the news of the deportation of Dr. Satyapal and Dr. Kitchlew and of the arrest of Mr. Gandhi reached Kasur; exaggerated reports of the happenings at Lahore and Amritsar on the previous day were also in circulation during the course of the day. As a result of these disquieting news, there was a *hartal* during the latter part of that day, which was started by the traders themselves without any pressure from the other classes. In the evening, there was a public meeting, at which a number of pleaders and some members of the local Municipal Committee spoke. The Government admits in its Report, that the tone of the speeches delivered by the pleaders and the Municipal Commissioners was "moderate". The *hartal* continued on the 12th April; and the excitement increased. There is "a very unruly element of the menial, leather-worker and butcher class at Kasur" (Punjab Government Report); and in the morning, while the pleaders and other prominent men of the town were holding a meeting to discuss the situation and devise means to end the *hartal* and allay public excitement, a mob consisting of these and other unruly elements of the town collected in the bazar. This mob rapidly grew to thousands, and somebody suggested that they should have a funeral of liberty. Accordingly, a procession was formed which proceeded towards the railway station with a charpoy covered with black cloth, representing the coffin of liberty, at its head. The general feeling seems to have been that the people were ashamed to have kept away from the agitation, while their leaders like Mr. Gandhi, Dr. Kitchlew and Dr. Satyapal were being arrested and deported; and the idea of forming the procession and going to the railway station was due to a desire to show to the railway passengers that Kasur was not slow in expressing its grief at recent events. The idea of the procession appealed to the school-boys, and some of them also joined. The doings of the mob are described in the Report of the Punjab Government in the following words:–

> "It now resembled a Muharram procession; there were general cries of lamentation, and beating of breasts; it was deliberately working itself up into the state of frenzy which Muharram processions frequently exhibit. Upto this time apparently the intention had merely been to make a violent demonstration. Arrived at the station, the crowd did considerable damage by breaking doors and throwing stones at windows, but did not penetrate the station or interfere with the permanent way. It then commenced to turn away, but at the direct incitement of some of its leaders, surged back and commenced a more serious work of destruction. It burnt an oilshed, damaged the signal and telegraph wires, smashed a quantity of furniture and looted the ticket office."

By this time, the prominent citizens of the town reached the railway station, put out the fire and persuaded the mob to leave the station. But seeing a train, which was drawn up at the distant signal, the crowd rushed towards it. The train contained several Europeans, Mr. and Mrs. Sherbourne and their three children; Captain Limby and Lieutenant Munro of the XVII Royal Regiment; two warrant officers, Master Gunner Mallet and Conductor Selby; and Corporals Battson and Gringham of the Queen's Regiment. The crowd attacked these Europeans; but was prevented from going to extremes by the efforts of Mr. Ghulam Mohy-ud-Din, who saved the Sherbourne family from the violence of the mob. The official report acknowledges this fact in the following words:–

> "..... The Sherbournes would probably have fared badly but for the persistent efforts of Mr. Ghulam Mohy-ud-Din, Pleader.† He had been one of the promoters of the meeting of the previous day and was clearly recognised by the crowd as a leader; but he now showed undoubted courage in dissuading the mob from violence."

Ultimately, he succeeded in taking the Sherbournes off to the hamlet of Kot Halim Khan on the other side of the line, from where they were rescued by the police. Captain Limby, Lieutenant Munro and Corporal Battson and Gringham also escaped. The two warrant officers, however, relied on their revolvers and refused to leave the train. The mob followed the train to the platform; and began to stone the warrant officers from a distance, when they alighted from it. They fired off their revolvers at the mob,

† This gentleman was subsequently arrested; because the mob had obeyed him. He was kept in custody for some weeks and ultimately released without trial.

after which they were surrounded and most brutally beaten to death with sticks. After these murders, the crowd left the railway station and on its way looted and gutted the Wheat Mandi Post Office, burned the main Post Office, set fire to the Munsif's Court and attempted to burn the *Tahsil,* where the police dispersed them by fire. The constables and some *Tahsil* subordinates thereupon pursued the rioters and arrested eight of them. No attempt was made to rescue the prisoners; and no further trouble occurred. On the 13th, shops re-opened; and the town assumed its normal condition. As at Amritsar, the police succeeded in making arrests and dispersing the rioters, as soon as it tried to do so; and there is no reasonable ground to believe that the civil authorities were overpowered by the mob on any occasion, or ever lost control of the town. If the police succeeded in dispersing the rioters and making arrests after the mob had become bold by committing the heinous crimes detailed above, the police would undoubtedly have been able to do so at an earlier stage of the riot.

Gujranwala

Passive resistance or *Satyagraha* was never preached or practised at Gujranwala. On the evening of April 5th, a public meeting was held to protest against the Rowlatt Act. It was largely attended by all classes of the people; and the tone of the speeches was very moderate. Earlier in the day, the Deputy Commissioner and the Superintendent of Police had summoned some of the conveners of this meeting and endeavoured to coerce and intimidate them into abandoning their intention to protest against the Rowlatt Act. This attempt was apparently not successful. On the 6th of April, the shopkeepers did not open their shops, and there was a complete *hartal* throughout the town. The *hartal* was spontaneous and orderly; and the Punjab Government admits that it "passed off without incident or open excitement, the open exhibitions of lamentation and fasting manifested elsewhere being absent." This *hartal* and its peaceful character further incensed Colonel O'Brien, the Deputy Commissioner. During the week following the *hartal* the town was perfectly quiet. The news of the arrest and deportation of Dr. Kitchlew and Dr. Satyapal, of the firing at Amritsar and the riots that followed, of the shooting down of innocent persons at Lahore and of the arrest of Mr. Gandhi reached Gujranwala on the 11th; and as the accounts of these extraordinary events spread through the town, they assumed exaggerated forms. The people talked of observing another *hartal* to protest against Mr. Gandhi's arrest; but the local leaders, knowing as they did the views of Colonel O'Brien about *hartals,* were reluctant to provoke the local authorities by a popular demonstration, which might possibly lead to a repetition of the events at Amritsar and Lahore in their own town. For a time they were able to keep the people in check; and the *hartal* was averted. No *hartal,* much less a disturbance of the public peace was, therefore, apprehended; and on the 12th, Colonel O'Brien left the district on transfer, and a number of magistrates and local notables also left for Lahore to attend a Divisional Durbar. In the meantime, however, news of the *hartal* at other places reached Gujranwala, as also exaggerated reports of the third firing at Lahore. The news of the riots at Kasur was also received. Besides, *hartals* had been observed at two important villages in the district, *viz*., Chuharkana and Sangla; and people from these villages, who came to Gujranwala for the Baisakhi, twitted the inhabitants of the town for not having expressed their grief at Mr. Gandhi's arrest. All these causes, therefore, made it evident before the evening of the 13th that there would be a *hartal* on the next day. Failing in their desire to prevent the closing of shops, the local leaders decided to organise a mass meeting on the *hartal* day in order to keep the people busy. The 14th April opened with a complete *hartal.* This was the second day of the Baisakhi, when large number of persons from Gujranwala go to Wazirabad for the fair. The railway station was, therefore crowded with hundreds of persons. Early in the morning the Lahore train arrived, and the intending passengers, many of whom had come from the neighbouring villages, rushed towards it. The train was already packed and a large number of persons accommodated themselves on the foot-boards or clung to the bars of the carriages. Some of the passengers, who were coming from Amritsar, reproached the merry intruders for their light-heartedness and related to them harrowing details of the Jallianwala massacre of the previous evening. In a few moments the news was carried all over the railway station, and caused great excitement amongst the Baisakhi revellers, many of whom were already in a state of boisterous inebriation. The train at last moved away, but stopped near the distant-signal, probably because the guard did not want to allow a large number of persons to travel on the foot-board. Seeing the train stop, the crowd at the station rushed towards it. The cry of "all or none" was raised by those who were left behind; and most of the persons who had got into the train at the station also left it. So far there had been no disturbance, but now an incident took place, which inflamed the passions of the crowd. A slaughtered calf had been hung up by the neck to the Gurukul Bridge, which was only a few yards from the engine. The crowd was highly incensed at this sight and fired the bridge. It was openly stated by the mob that the killing of the calf and putting it at such a prominent place could only be the work of the police, who wanted to inflame the Hindus and wreck the mutual confidence and goodwill that prevailed between Hindus and Mohammedans, which was a special feature of these popular demonstrations. The local leaders in the meantime got information of this lamentable episode and with all possible speed repaired to the bridge and put out the fire.* About that time, information was received that a slaughtered pig was displayed at another culvert on the railway line towards the other side of the station, called the Kachi Bridge; and the infuriated mob proceeded in that direction, doing damage to the telegraph wires in the way. The popular leaders, as stated above, had arranged a public meeting to

* This act also formed an important count in the charge against some of the Gujranwala leaders.

keep the people busy; and diverted large crowds from the railway station to that meeting, where speeches on Hindu-Moslem unity, the coming municipal elections and other subjects were delivered. But in the meantime, the police had fired on the mob at the Kachi Bridge and two men who had been wounded in this encounter were taken to the meeting. This increased the excitement of the audience to such an extent that it became impossible to continue the meeting. The people left the meeting and proceeded towards the station to have vengeance. The leaders tried to restrain the mob but without success; and the mob set fire to the *Tahsil,* the Dak Bungalow, the District Court, the Church and the Railway Station. Sated with these acts of incendiarism, the rioters dispersed at about 1-30 P.M.; and no further damage was done to any public or Government property. It may be noted in this connection, that the buildings which wre burnt by the mob were all properly guarded by the police with loaded rifles; and there is no mention in the Government reports or elsewhere of the police forces in charge of these buildings having ever seriously tried to protect them from the rioters. It is not stated that the policemen were at any place overpowered by the mob. On the contrary, it is admitted in the Government Report that wherever the police offered any resistance to the crowds, it succeeded in dispersing them. For instance, the mob was successfully beaten off from the police lines and the jail without any difficulty. In fact, it has been alleged that the Superintendent of Police was extremely unpopular with his men, who, therefore, generally behaved as mere unconcerned spectators and in some instances incited the mobs to violence instead of checking them. However, it is an undeniable fact that no attempt was made by the police to extinguish the fires, which went on burning for a day after the riots. It is also significant that the police inspite of a so-called thorough investigation did not discover the person or persons who had initiated and fomented the trouble at Gujranwala by displaying the slaughtered calf and pork to public gaze at a time when the people were already excited. As stated above, the civil station was clear of the mob at about 1-30 p.m., after which there was no breach of the public peace. Even Colonel O'Brien admits in his evidence before Lord Hunter's Enquiry Committee that when he reached Gujranwala at about 2 p.m., the mob had finished their work of destruction and dispersed.

Wazirabad and Nizamabad.

Wazirabad is a small town in the Gujranwala District with a population of about 10,000. The people of this town did not participate in the agitation against the Rowlatt Act, what to say of *Satyagraha* and passive resistance. But the news of the arrest of Mr. Gandhi, the deportation of Dr. Kitchlew and Dr. Satyapal, firing on innocent persons at Amritsar and Lahore, the Amritsar and Kasur riots, the massacre at the Jallianwala Bagh and of the riots in the neighbouring town of Gujranwala caused a good deal of excitement among the people; and there was also a rumour that the Golden Temple at Amritsar had been bombarded with a machine-gun, which heightened the feeling of popular resentment. The thousands of persons who had assembled at Wazirabad from surrounding villages and towns for the Baisakhi twitted the local population for not holding a *hartal* as a protest against the Rowlatt Act and the high-handed acts of the authorities. There was, therefore, a general *hartal* on the 15th. During the previous night, the news that aeroplanes had bombarded Gujranwala with machine-guns and dropped bombs at persons not engaged in acts of violence had also reached Wazirabad. The news spread on the morning of the 15th and added considerably to the excitement and indignation of the people. An angry mob composed of the riff-raff of the town and the Baisakhi revellers collected in the streets; and the ring-leaders incited them to violent action. Telegraph wires were cut and the railway line was slightly damaged. A party of cavalry which had been posted at the railway station dispersed the mob by firing into the air. Part of the mob then moved on along the railway line, fired a small railway bridge, cut the telegraph wires and was ultimately dispersed by the police without firing. Another portion of the mob proceeded towards Nizamabad, a small village in the suburbs of the town, set fire to a gang hut and damaged the gates of a level crossing. Then the rioters sighted the house of Rev. Grahame Bailey, a Church of Scotland Missionary. What followed is described by the Commission, which tried this case, in the following words:–

> "The ring-leaders suggested that they should go and burn it. Some of the mob demurred saying that Mr. Bailey was an Irishman and therefore against the Government, but the more violent elements in the crowd prevailed and the whole body (with one or two exceptions) marched on the house..... A desperate scene of rioting and looting was witnessed, the house was thoroughly ransacked for treasure and then it was set ablaze..... Sated with their work, and probably anxious to dispose of their ill-gotten gains, the mob then dispersed. In the meanwhile the inhabitants of the neighbouring village of Wairoke had come to the spot, and the sight of so much abandoned loot proving too much for them, they picked up what the rioters had left and decamped with it to their houses."†

Mr. Bailey had resided in the town for many years and was very popular with the people; but as his house was located at an isolated spot, about two miles from Wazirabad and a mile from Nizamabad, it was not possible for them to save the building or the valuable collection of manuscripts that it contained. It appears that only a few hours after these acts of arson and pillage, the rioters felt sorry for what they had done, and some of them voluntarily returned the stolen property. In the words of the Commission, "they were moved by affection for Mr. Bailey." As stated in the findings of the Commission quoted above, the rioters dispersed of their own accord; and the police who were present at the scene of the riot, did not endeavour to prevent the incendiarism or disperse the mob, which was not a large one. The passions of the mob cooled down after they had committed the lawless acts described above, and there was no further disturbance of the public peace. Order was restored without any overt action of the authorities. In the words of the Official Report, "it is only necessary to add

† For full text of the Order, see Appendix II, pages 317-320.

here that on the following day additional troops reached Wazirabad and the arrival of the District Magistrate from Gujranwala *completed* the restoration of order." The manner in which the riots began and subsided negatives the idea that there was at Wazirabad a conspiracy to wage war against the King or that the people were in a state of open rebellion.

Gujrat has double the population of Wazirabad and is situated at a distance of about 70 miles from Lahore. To quote the Official Report, Gujrat has "no political history." The Report further admits that "the demand for a universal demonstration on April 6th met with absolutely no response in the district; there were no protest meetings held and no demonstration of any kind was reported." But during the following week, news of the arrest of Mr. Gandhi and the happenings at Lahore and Amritsar reached the town and caused some excitement. The people coming from Lahore and Amritsar also reproached the Gujratis for not having observed the Rowlatt Act *hartal.* Early on the morning of the 14th April, "a band of Baisakhi revellers," who returned from Wazirabad on their way from the railway station to the city formed a sort of a procession shouting *"Rowlatt Bill na Manzur"* and *"Mahatma Gandhi ki Jai;"* but these men peacefully dispersed to their houses. At about 9 A.M. there was a complete *hartal* in the town, which was not due to incitement from anybody. In fact, the Government admits that the pleaders and the prominent men of the town had no "previous knowledge" that the shops were going to be closed. A procession was formed, which marched through the town shouting the usual cries; but after parading through a part of the town, it quietly dispersed without any interference from the authorities. On the 14th, the news of the massacre at the Jallianwala Bagh was received; and as a result the *hartal* continued on the 15th. The incidents of the 15th are described in the Official Report in the following words:–

Gujrat.

"The shops remained closed, and during the morning a *somewhat* excitable crowd, mostly *youths,* marched about the city. About 10.30 A.M. they went to the Mission High School and compelled it to close, after breaking a number of windows and doors.

They visited other schools, but they had already closed. In the afternoon the crowd reassembled, and was observed to be moving towards the railway station, which was unguarded either by police or troops.... After smashing a number of lamps on the way, it reached the station, and swarming into it *began* destroying the telegraph and telephone instruments and furniture and setting fire to records. It had been followed by the force of police with a senior Indian Magistrate; in view of the damage which was being done to the station the latter ordered the police to open fire on the crowd. A few shots were fired—as far as is known without effect — and the crowd dispersed, some arrests being made. Additional troops were now sent for and arrived at midnight; but it was not found necessary to utilize them or the small force already in the city, in quelling disturbances. On the following morning (the 16th) notices were issued prohibiting meetings and processions without licence; practically all the shops were opened during the day and no further disturbances occurred."

The official account is substantially correct, except that most of the "youths" were mere boys; and that the Sub-Inspector of Police not only *followed,* but also incited the crowd to mischief. There were two factions at Gujrat, to one of which the Sub-Inspector belonged; and he wanted that the mob might create a disturbance and give him an opportunity of implicating the men of the other party. It may also be added that the so-called *crowd* was composed of only a few hundred persons; and that in the opinion of the Commission which tried the Gujrat case, the police fired not on the crowd but into the air.

Lyallpur

The population of Lyallpur is over 15,000; and it is situated at a distance of about 90 miles from Lahore. *Satyagraha* or passive resistance was never preached or practised at Lyallpur; but there was a *hartal* and a public meeting on the 6th April to protest against the Rowlatt Act. The *hartal* was spontaneous in its character; and the tone of the speeches delivered at the meeting was moderate. There was no breach of the public peace; and the authorities had nothing to complain of, except that the people had taken part in the general agitation against the Act in spite of the official and semi-official efforts to the contrary. It is admitted by the Government in the Official Report that "the behaviour of the crowds was orderly." The news of Mr. Gandhi's arrest was received on the 11th April, which caused general excitement. Later on the same day or on the 12th, information about the deportation of Dr. Kitchew and Dr. Satyapal, the firing at Amritsar and Lahore, and the Amritsar riots also reached Lyallpur; and added to the excitement of the people. There was again a general *hartal* on the 13th, in spite of the efforts of the local pleaders and other prominent citizens to prevent it. On the 14th, news of the Jallianwala Bagh massacre arrived, and it was stated that the Golden Temple at Amritsar had been bombarded. It was also rumoured that the police had taken the side of the mob at Amritsar, and that a number of Sikh girls belonging to the Kairon School had been outraged by British soldiers on the railway. The excitement of the people increased; and the *hartal* continued on the 14th and the 15th; but on the afternoon of the 15th, through the efforts of the local leaders, many of whom were pleaders, the *hartal* terminated and the shops were re-opened. After this there were no more demonstrations in the town and everything was quiet. But on the evening of the 17th, an incident took place of which the Government tried to take undue advantage. It appears that cinders from the chimneys of adjoining factories set fire to about 24,000 maunds of *bhusa* (hay) which belonged to the Government and was stacked near the railway station. The Government tried to connect this accident with the *hartal*; and sought to prove that the people of Lyallpur were in a state of open rebellion. The introduction of martial law and other repressive measures taken at Lyallpur mainly derive their justification from this alleged act of incendiarism. But the inquiries made into the circumstances under which the *bhusa* caught fire falsify the allegation of the Government and entirely free the people from any liability in the matter. It appears that on the 23rd May, 1919, the Government preferred a claim under section 15-A of the Police Act for compensation for the loss sustained by the Government on account of the destruction of this *bhusa*. The claim amounted to Rs. 48,037-6-2. Thereupon, Mr. F.P. DeMontMorency, the District Magistrate, investigated the whole matter and made the following order on the 5th of July:–

".....The facts of the case are as follows:–

"There were no riots or disturbances in Lyallpur that day (the 17th April); though shops were shut, no disorder or unlawful assemblies were noticed in the town itself.....

"The *bhusa* stacks consist of large pyramids of bales lying on some open ground between the goods sidings and the factories. They are separated from the town by the goods sidings and goods yard. The goods yard gate was closed that day. A considerable space, occupied by the Normal School and the District Board *sarai*, separates the goods yard from the town of Lyallpur. There was a picket of Indian Infantry on the road which leads past the Normal School and the *sarai* and separates them from the town. A patrol visits the goods yard and the Elevator.

"The *bhusa* appears to have gone on fire between 8.15 p.m. and 8.45 p.m. The fire was noticed by the picket at about 8.40. The night was dark; there was a strong wind blowing from the direction of the factories at the time. The wind later developed into a dust storm of great violence.

"The stack or rather pyramid of bales which was nearest to the factories had taken fire. The fire had begun on the side nearest to the factories. The *sirki* covering or roof over the bales had caught fire. The fire communicated itself to the bales at once. The *chowkidar* of the *bhusa* stacks was absent at the time. The store-keeper or the officer in charge of baling operations arrived shortly after the fire had begun. I reached the spot with cavalry very shortly after the fire had begun. A few people from the factories, a few members of the Municipal Staff and the store-keeper alluded to above were the only persons on the spot when I arrived. There was no information of any crowd having visited the stacks or of any single person having been seen near the stacks. The absence of the *chowkidar* seems to have been due to laziness and not to have been arranged or premeditated. Neither patrol nor picket saw anything suspicious in the vicinity of the goods yard. The subsequent dust storm and covering of the ground by footprints of the helpers who tried to prevent the fire spreading to other stacks prevented all possibility of track evidence.

"A very exhaustive police inquiry was made; no trace of anything bearing on the burning of the *bhusa* came out. There were some approvers in the Lyallpur cases who were associates and in the secrets of those who were convicted in the Lyallpur disorders. None of those, however, had any information to give in regard to the burning of *bhusa* which does not seem to have formed part of the plans of their associates.

"There was a strong suspicion at the time that this was the work of an incendiary, because,

1. Similar acts had occurred elsewhere is connection with the disorders.

2. A plot to burn *bhusa* had been alleged to have existed at Toba Tek Singh.

3. Of the fact that goods had been removed from the goods yard the day before.

"The police inquiry, however, has failed to connect the burning of this *bhusa* with the act of any incendiary or with any riot or rioters. Those convicted in jail in Lyallpur disorders have been questioned by me. They have now, after conviction, no object in concealing what they knew and have given information on a number of other points, but none of them have any information to give about the *bhusa*.

"I have examined the theory of whether it was the act of some villager or villagers but no clue has been obtained.

"Four factories were working on the day in question; one of them was in close proximity to the stacks. During the winter months no fires wre caused to the *bhusa* by factories working; but since April, there have been a number of fires in piles of open cotton in factory yards, due to cinders from chimneys, etc. It is possible, though not likely on account of the distance, that this may have been the cause of the *bhusa* fire.

"I have been unable to find anything, except suspicion, to point to this injury having arisen from riot and unlawful assembly within the area.

"I am unable, therefore, to make an assessment contemplated in section 15 A(a) (2) (c) of the Police Act."

After this inquiry and order, it should have been possible for the Government to have abandoned its suspicion of incendiarism; but the theory of rebellion had to be supported, and nothing else had happened at Lyallpur to furnish an excuse for the application of martial law. We, therefore, find the following statement in the Official Report which was submitted by the Local Government to the Government of India as late as the 3rd of November, *i.e.*, four months after the suspicion of mob-violence had been exposed by official inquiry:–

> "In the evening (of 17th) a serious act of suspected incendiarism occurred at Lyallpur, Government bhusa stacked near the railway station being burnt to the value of Rs. 50,000."

The Government is, of course, welcome to entertain any suspicions it pleases; but there should be some foundation for those suspicions, otherwise the suspicions are likely to degenerate into misrepresentation of facts. The Official Report proceeds to state that on the 18th, "in Lyallpur itself the arrival of the troops had checked further demonstrations and the *hartal* was abandoned. On the following day, the 19th, the moveable column arrived and all further apprehension of serious disorder at head-quarters was at an end."

2—RURAL AREAS

Amritsar District

The Official Report states that after the Amritsar riots, "many of the villagers in the neighbourhood gave way to disorder." A part of the Amritsar mob attacked the Bhagtanwala Railway Station which is only a mile from the Goldern Temple, looted the godown and set the station building on fire. Later at night a mob of villagers attacked the Chheharta Railway Station, which is 5 miles from Amritsar, broke the station lamps and looted a goods train which was standing in the yard. On the 12th, telegraph wires were cut between Chheharta and Amritsar, Khasa and Gurusar, and between Khasa and Chheharta. The same evening, the headman of Sanghana visited the neighbouring villages of Gumanpura and Basarke, where he described the riots at Amritsar and incited the villagers to cut the railway line and telegraph wires. Later in the evening a meeting of the villagers was held at Basarke at which the villagers recounted their grievances and decided to cut the railway line which runs close by. Accordingly, a body of men set out to accomplish this purpose. With the assistance of railway gang-men, two whole sections of the line were bodily removed with the result that a goods train, which was the first to pass, was derailed. On the 14th, telegraph wires were cut between Mananwala and Amritsar and between Patti and Karor; and there was a sympathetic *hartal* at Tarn Taran. On the 15th Telegraph wires were cut at Jandiala and Butari.

Neighbouring Villages.

Tarn Taran is about 16 miles from Amritsar and is a sacred town of the Sikhs. There was no disorder at this place; but the malignant ingenuity of the Inspector of Police ruined hundreds of persons. In order to prove his valour and loyalty to his superiors, he fabricated a false story that a body of two or three hundred villagers "armed with dangerous weapons" had collected outside the town to loot the *Tahsil*; but he with his dozen constables by a ruse attacked and dispersed

Tarn Taran

them before they had even entered the town. This brave exploit of the Inspector of Police and his devoted band of policemen is described by the court-martial, which tried the case; in the following words :-

> "Soon after dark an armoured train from Amritsar with a search light stopped at Tarn Taran, and appeared to have somewhat upset the confidence of the crowd, but the train moved on and information was brought that soldiers had stayed. The crowd then moved its position and sat down under some trees near the grave-yard close to the town, and began to get ready for the attack on the treasury. Meanwhile information of the collection of these intending looters had reached the Inspector of Police, who decided to go out to attack the mob, and took with him 13 of the police force, including the sub-inspector with Zaildar and a number of Lambardars and others; and remaining Police (out of 30) were left behind to guard the Tahsil and Thana. The leaders of the waiting band of looters appear to have seen the Inspector's force advancing towards them but to have taken them for more villagers coming to join them, and in consequence remained sitting and allowed the police to come close to them. On getting near, the Inspector called *"Pharlo"* and he, the Zaildar and the Sub-Inspector P. Ram Ditta Mall, fired their revolvers in the air. The crowd hearing the shots thought that soldiers had arrived after all, and scattered, fleeing in the dark in all directions. Some attempt to rally them is said to have been made by the leaders when they saw it was only a small police force, but this was unsuccessful."†

The story is on the face of it absurd. The Majha Jat cannot be scared away in this manner by a few policemen, if he is out for loot. It is significant that the soldiers were not detained to deal with the imaginary looters, who had admittedly assembled before the arrival of the armoured train; nor was the searchlight of the train able to detect this large assemblage of two or three hundred dacoits. It is also surprising that the Inspector did not choose to take the Tahsildar and Magistrate into his confidence, when he went out to attack this dangerous band of intending looters. It is extraordinary that the *Tahsil,* which contained about three lakhs of Government money, was left under the protection of a few constables who had not even a police officer with them. This was of course natural, as neither of the police officers would have liked to be said to have remained idle at the *Tahsil* when an imaginary band of

† *Vide* Order of Mr. G. D. Rudkin O. B. E., District Magistrate (exercising the powers of a Summary Court), dated the 15th May, 1919.

dacoits had to be attacked. It may be noted that all chance of the corroboration of the story is avoided by stating that the firing was "in the air" and, therefore, no one was injured. This cock and bull story was, however, believed; and no less than 102 men were arrested and tried for this supposed offence, out of whom 5 became approvers, 15 were acquitted and the remaining 82 were sentenced to various terms of imprisonment and fine. It may also be mentioned that the Inspector of Police (Chaudhri Aziz-ud-Din Ahmad) was not only responsible for this inconceivable deed of valour; but had also the supreme satisfaction of investigating the supposed occurrence and preparing the prosecution. This was indeed a piece of sheer good luck, as in other hands the investigation might have miscarried and the camouflage might have been seen through.

Lahore District

Minor Acts

On the 12th April about 20 men, mainly sweepers from Patti village, did a slight damage at the Khem Karan Railway Station ; but were driven off by some local *zamindars*. On the 13th, telegraph wires were cut at two places near Wagah and Patti. On the 15th, wires were cut near Chhanga Manga ; and two grass farm stacks were burnt at Banghali and Padri. On the 16th, wires were cut near Valtoha, Chhanga Manga and Premnagar. On the 17th, wires were cut near Chhanga Manga and Patti. On the 19th canal wire was cut and 300 feet wire was stolen between Valtoha and Manihala. On the 14th, 15th and 16th stones were thrown at passing trains by some rebel or rebels at Kot Radha Kishen.

Wagah.

Wagah is a village situated at a distance of about 13 miles from Lahore. On the 13th April, the Baisakhi fair was held at Maniala village, which is only a few miles from Wagah. Men from the neighbouring villages collected at the fair, at which an impromptu meeting was held and speeches were made attacking Government. That night, "Wagah Railway Station was sacked and burnt, telegraph wires were cut, a length of line was taken up and an armoured train was consequently derailed, but there was fortunately no loss of life." Forty-four men from different villages were tried by a Martial Law Commission† in connection with this offence; and the Commission found that the ring-leader of the rioters, as also the principal organiser of the meeting at Maniala, was a havildar in a Sikh regiment. It is admitted in the Official Report that the outrage was merely a local affair and was not organised from Lahore.

Gujranwala District

Sheikhupura

Sheikhupura is a small rural town with a population of about 2,500 persons. It is situated at a distance of 26 miles from Lahore. On the 6th April there was a *hartal* to protest against the Rowlatt Act. The *hartal* was complete and spontaneous. "This was followed by a mass meeting in the evening, but the language used was not inflammatory."* The local officials did their utmost to prevent the *hartal* as well as the meeting ; but their attempts failed. There was, however, no disturbance or breach of the public peace. During the next week nothing unusual happened. The news of the shooting down of innocent persons at Amritsar and Lahore, the exaggerated accounts of the Amritsar riots and the arrest of Mr. Gandhi caused great excitement among the people ; and there was another *hartal* on the 14th. During the day some men who went down to the railway station to learn the latest news about Lahore and Amritsar from the passengers, damaged the distant-signal on their way back. At night some unknown persons cut telegraph wires. Martial Law was proclaimed on the 19th April.

Hafizabad

Hafizabad is a fairly large rural town and has a population of about 5,000 persons. It is situated at a distance of about 38 miles from Wazirabad. A *hartal* was observed on the 6th April, which was not a complete success ; but no effort was made to

† For text of the Order, see Appendix II, pages 338-339.

* Punjab Government Report.

compel those who had not joined it to close their shops. In the evening a public meeting was held, at which speeches against the Rowlatt Act were delivered. The tone of the speeches was moderate.

The information about the occurrences at Lahore and Amritsar and the arrest of Mr. Gandhi caused widespread resentment and there was another *hartal* on the 14th, which was unanimous and spontaneous. A fairly large crowd collected but at the request of the *Tahsildar* dispersed. Another party composed of city riff-raff and boys had assembled near the railway station and seeing a train arrive, they rushed towards it. Lieutenant Tatam of the Military Farms Department with a small boy was travelling by the train. Seeing him, the mob went before his compartment and made a demonstration. Not satisfied with this, some mischievous persons in the mob who were probably drunk threw stones at the carriage and tried to assault the Lieutenant with sticks. A few windows of the carriage were broken; but further damage was prevented by the intervention of some Indian passengers of the train and the more sober members of the crowd. Ultimately Lieutenant Tatam was made to say that he was opposed to the Rowlatt Act; and the station master started the train to prevent further mischief. The *hartal* continued on the 15th. A small mob of about a hundred men collected and was led by a drunkard, called Top, towards the railway station, with the result that the distant-signals were damaged and telegraph wires were cut. Top and another person were arrested and taken to the Tahsil. The mob followed them and stoned the building but was dispersed on the police firing into the air. Without any action by the authorities, the shops reopened on the 16th. There was no further disturbance.

Akalgarh.

Akalgarh is situated at a distance of 23 miles from Wazirabad and 15 miles from Hafizabad. Its population is only 4,000. On the 6th April there was a *hartal* and a public meeting to protest against the Rowlatt Act. The Government admits that the speeches were not immoderate in tone. On the *hartal* day a small party of men collected and roamed about the town with cries of *"Mahatma Gandhi ki Jai"* and *"hai hai Rowlatt Bill"*. There was no breach of the public peace. On receipt of the news of the arrest of Mr. Gandhi and the events at Lahore and Amritsar, another *hartal* was observed on the 14th; but there was no disturbance. The shops reopened on the 15th. That night feeble attempts were made to set fire to a bridge, the glass of a signal was broken and an insulator smashed. Slight damage was also done to a telegraph wire at a distance of about a mile from the town. The Commission, which tried the Akalgarh Riot Case, did not regard the facts as indicating any serious disorder and in the course of its order made the following remarks:— "The mischief appears to have been done by boys......The fact is that the leaders...were able to obtain only lukewarm support and the people were not prepared to go to extremes. The mob, never a large one, was kept off the station premises without difficulty and its proceedings were a mere parody of rebellion."*

Ramnagar.

Ramnagar is about the same size as Akalgarh and is situated at a distance of 6 miles from it on the banks of the river Chenab. There was a *hartal* on the 6th April as a protest against the Rowlatt Act. But there was no breach of the public peace on this or any other day. The police had, therefore, nothing to investigate. This meant a double loss to the police—the loss of thousands of rupees; and the loss of a capital opportunity of winning rewards and favours from Government by displaying a feverish zeal to bring the "rebels" to book. The Revenue Officer, Malik Sahib Khan, was also in the same predicament. Till the 23rd of April they waited and ruminated; but there was no disturbance. It was hoping against hope; but the guardians of law and order refused to be disappointed. They then boldly adopted the only other course open to them, *viz.,* to invent an

---

* For text of Order, see Appendix II, pages 309-310.

imaginary offence and launch an arduous investigation to discover the supposed criminals. But as there was no damage to life or property, nor even an attempt at a disturbance of the public peace, the task of the local officials was not an easy one. At last by a happy inspiration, the official conspirators decided to make it appear that on the 15th April an effigy of the King-Emperor was taken in procession from the town to the river, where it was burnt with every species of insult after which the people threw the ashes into the river, took a ceremonial bath of purification and returned to the town. The originality and ingenuity of the authors of this story is indeed marvellous. On the 23rd of April, the occurrence of this supposed incident was reported. The interval of no less than seven days between the alleged offence and its mention in the police diaries was explained by a vague reference to the "absorption " of the police in other matters of public safety. The search for victims was a comparatively easy matter. A large number of persons were arrested Many were arrested, because they were expected to buy their release with large sums of money; others were arrested, because they were too poor to call the attention of the people or the Government to their unjust sufferings. Several others were taken into custody, because the police were paid by their enemies to perform that service. In addition to the persons actually arrested, there were many who were only threatened and made to pay bribes to the police to avoid arrests. This process of arrests and releases, which the Indian police has reduced to a fine art, went on for some weeks, till at last by a process of elimination, 28 persons were picked out for a trial; several others were forced to give evidence against the accused, one of whom was compelled to play the part of an approver. It is needless to mention that all the persons prosecuted were convicted and sentenced. These are, in brief, the real facts about the story that the King's effigy was burnt at Ramnagar. Had the incident been true, it would certainly have been the most shameful and disreputable episode in the whole history of the recent disorders in the Punjab; but, as it is, no blame attaches to the people of Ramnagar, who were merely the unfortunate victims of a few unscrupulous officials.

Aulakh. Aulakh is a big village, which is inhabited by *jats*. Exaggerated reports of the happenings at Amritsar, Lahore and Gujranwala and the rumour that the Golden Temple at Amritsar had been bombarded caused a deep excitement among the villagers. On the 16th April several landowners with the help of two *lambardars* attacked and burnt the *patwarkhana*, which contained the revenue records of six villages.

Sangla. Sangla is situated at a distance of 62 miles from Lahore and has a population of 4,000 persons. On the 12th April there was a *hartal* to protest against the Rowlatt Act and the arrest of Mr. Gandhi. The whole town observed the *hartal,* with the exception of the ginning factories and a drug shop. In the morning large numbers of persons went and bathed in the canal that passes close to the town; and returned in a procession with an effigy of the Rowlatt Act, over which cries of mourning were being raised. The crowd also went to the railway station; but did no more than hoot a missionary. There was no breach of the public peace. The shops reopened on the 13th; and there was no other *hartal*. On the 14th, a party of men threw stones at a passing train. During the night of the 15th a telegraph wire was cut between Sangla and Salarwala. It is possible that the offender or offenders belonged to Sangla; but of this there is no evidence. On the 16th, a Sikh who had run amok rescued a military prisoner from a detachment at Sangla Station. In the afternoon the same Sikh assaulted Mr. Wale, a Telegraph Inspector. Mr. Wale, however, managed to shoot down his assailant without much difficulty. Martial law was proclaimed on the 19th.

Chuharkana Chuharkana is a fairly big *Mandi* (market-place), which is an important centre of trade for the neighbouring villages. Chuharkana village is a little more than a mile away from the Mandi. The distance between Lahore and Chuharkana is about 35 miles. On the 11th April a public meeting was held in the mosque, attended by both Hindus and Musalmans, and it was resolved that a *hartal* should be held the next day as a mark of general protest against the Rowlatt Act. There was accordingly a *hartal* on the 12th which was followed by a meeting at which a considerable number of agriculturists were present. It is not alleged that the speakers who addressed the meeting incited the audience to violence or even spoke against the Government. The Government Report only says that "the language used was strongly condemnatory of the Act, and contained the usual misstatements as to the increased powers which it would give the police." There was no breach of the public peace; and on the 13th business was resumed. On the two following days, news of the happenings at Amritsar and Lahore reached Chuharkana, as also an account of the arrest of Mr. Gandhi. The rumour that the Golden Temple had been bombarded was also on everybody's lips. The people were naturally excited and there was general resentment against the supposed and actual acts of the Government. On the 15th, a large party of men, including several villagers, went to the station and in broad daylight damaged the permanent way, attacked and looted the brake-van of a passenger train, burnt and looted the station, damaged two canal bridges by fire and cut some telegraph wires. Sated with this work of destruction, the mob voluntarily dispersed. There was no further disorder at Chuharkana.

Dhaban Singh

Dhaban Singh is a small railway station on the Lahore-Lyallpore line. It is situated at a distance of 15 miles from Chuharkana and 50 miles from Lahore. The disorder at Dhaban Singh occurred on the night between the 15th and the 16th of April, and is described in the Punjab Government's Report in the following words:—

" Some Sikh Kambohs of Nawan Pind village summoned a meeting, announced that the Golden Temple at Amritsar had been bombarded, and urged their hearers to cut the railway communications. A mob of agriculturists marched down to the railway about a mile and a half from Dhaban Singh Station, tore up rails and cut the telegraph wires.

Subsequently collecting more men from Mahnianwala village, the leaders of the mob attacked, looted and burnt the railway station itself in the early hours of the morning."

The Commission which tried the rioters adds that the mob had also fired a railway bridge over the canal at a distance of a mile and a half from the station.

Moman.

Moman is another railway station on the same line, and is situated midway between Sangla and Dhaban Singh. As has already been stated, exaggerated reports of the happenings at Amritsar and Lahore and the rumour that the Golden Temple at Amritsar had been bombarded had produced a good deal of excitement in this area, with the result that the mischief-makers were out for mischief. The news of the massacre at the Jallianwala Bagh had also reached these parts on the 14th or the 15th April and had added to the indignation of the people. On the night of the 15th a mob of villagers, about 60 or 70 strong, attacked the railway station of Moman, warned the railway staff to leave the premises, and then proceeded to burn all the station buildings. The Official Report adds that the station was looted before it was set on fire; but in the findings of the Commission, which tried the persons accused of this outrage, there is no mention of looting. The ring-leader of the mob was Harnam Singh, who was the same man that rescued a military prisoner and assaulted Mr. Wale at Sangla on the next day.

Minor Acts.

On 15th April a telegraph wire was cut and some insulators were smashed between Mansurwali and Wazirabad. On the 16th April a wire was cut between Machhike and Muridke. On 19th April another wire was cut at Muridke. On the night between the 16th and 17th, some villagers from Barohoa cut the telegraph wires on the Shahdara-Lahore line near their village.

Lyallpur District

Gojra

Gojra is a big market of wheat and is situated at a distance of 31 miles from Lyallpur. There was no *hartal* at Gojra on the 6th April.

Exaggerated reports of the occurrences at Amritsar and Lahore, news of Mr. Gandhi's arrest and the rumour that the Golden Temple had been bombarded and thousands of persons massacred at Amritsar brought about a *hartal* on the 15th. A crowd collected in the public streets and proceeded to the railway station, where it mobbed a refreshment vendor and forced him to stop work. Some persons also climbed up into the engine of a train and endeavoured to presuade the driver to join in the *hartal* and not to take on the train. There was also a funeral procession of the Rowlatt Act in the Mandi. There was, however, no disorder or breach of the public peace. The *hartal* was resumed on the 16th, but the shops were re-opened towards the evening.

Toba Tek Singh.

Toba Tek Singh is the headquarters of a *tahsil* of that name and is situated at a distance of 48 miles from Lyallpur. On the 6th April there was a public meeting and a very brief *hartal* to protest against the Act; but it did not lead to the slightest disorder or breach of the peace. The reports of the Jallianwala Bagh massacre and rumours that the Golden Temple had been bombarded caused some excitement. On the night of the 18th, a gang of 18 Sikh youngmen of Chak No. 150, Gugera Branch, under the leadership of a deserter from the Army overturned some telegraph posts and cut wires between Toba Tek Singh and Janiwala. The damage done was slight. This was the only case from Lyallpur that was tried by a Commission. In their order, the judges stated that a relative of the leading men had actually received a bullet wound at Amritsar.

Minor Occurrences.

At Jaranwala, on the 6th of April, attempts were made to promote a *hartal* by lawful means, and subscriptions were collected for the families of the "Delhi Martyrs." There was also a *hartal* on the 14th. A brief *hartal* was observed at Tandlianwala on the 6th April. On the 15th, there was *hartal* at Dijkot; and the people hooted down the *Zaildar* when he started reading a pamphlet prepared by the Publicity Committee in support of the Rowlatt Act. At none of these places was there any breach of the public peace.

Gujrat District

Jalalpur Jattan. Jalalpur Jattan is a fairly big village some nine miles from Gujrat. The Commission, which tried the "Jalalpur Jattan riot case" describes the occurrences at this village in the following words:—

> "..... There was a *hartal* on the 15th but apparently little else. On the 16th, the Municipal Committee met in the morning to concert measures for dealing with *possible* disorder. They were too late. Hardly had they met when a mob invaded the room, snatched off the turbans of the members and impelled them from the building. Outside speeches were made against the Government and the Rowlatt Act, the mob moved off in two bodies, one to the Post Office and the other to the Mission School, where, however, no damage was done beyond the breaking of a few windows at the School by some boys, and the movement then subsided. The people ..... were obviously not prepared to go to extremes...."†

The Commission proceeded to say that the occurrence was not very serious and the occasion seemed to have been taken by the mob to emphasise its "antipathy to the Municipal Committee." The Commission further said, "We are unable to find that war was actually waged or that the actions of the mob ever amounted to insurrection." It is possible that even the events described in the passage quoted above might have been exaggerated, as the Commission itself admitted in its Order that the village was "a hotbed of partnership and petty faction" and much of the evidence produced in the case was "tainted" on that account. There were some English missionaries in the village; but the crowd did not touch them. The next morning shops reopened; and there was no further untoward incident.

Malakwal. Malakwal is a railway junction and contains a railway colony of some dimensions. It is a small town with a population of 3,000; and is situated at a distance of about ten miles from Gujrat. It has been admitted in the Government Report that for some

† For text of Order, see Appendix II, pages 302-303.

time past the railway staff of Malakwal had been showing signs of discontent. *Hartal* was not observed at Malakwal. On the morning of the 16th April, some railway employees went on strike. At night a small party of firemen and shunters from the railway station together with some others cut telegraph wires, removed the distant-signal lamps and uprooted a pair of rails. The party then dispersed. The damage to the lines was not noticed until the following morning, when a passenger train was derailed, as a result of which two persons died and several were injured. The general public of Malakwal admittedly had no hand in this outrage.

Minor Occurrences.

A mistri of Kunjah succeeded in bringing about an incomplete *hartal* in his village on the 15th April. He was later on tried and sentenced for this indiscretion by a summary Court under section 25 of the Defence of India Rules. On the 15th, some students of the Engineering College at Rasul "refused to attend their lectures, but did not resort to violence." The same day the canal officials at Rasul met in the mosque and offered prayers for the repeal of the Rowlatt Act.

3.—GENERAL CONCLUSIONS

The Cause

As would appear from the events described above, the agitation against the Rowlatt Act did not lead to disorder anywhere in the Punjab. All over the Punjab, the 6th of April, when the agitation reached its culminating point, passed off peacefully. The real cause of the disturbances is to be found in the action of the officials, not in the agitation against the Act. It is interesting to note that this view is taken not only by the promoters of the *Satyagraha* movement, but also by the moderates who have always condemned *Satyagraha* and passive resistance. The Hon'ble Mr. Surendranath Banerji, in the course of the statement which he issued on the 27th April 1919 as President of the Committee of the Moderates' Conference, states:—

> "While our countrymen all over India rendered all the service they could in furtherance of the British cause in the war, it is acknowledged by all that the brunt of suffering and sacrifice, particularly in the matter of supply of recruits, fell upon martial people of the Punjab. The Lieutenant-Governor of the Punjab bore repeated testimony to this. How has it come to pass that there is so much discontent in that Province, more than anywhere else.....? Has the character of the administrative measures and methods, partly in relation to war effort, anything to do with the temper of the people? There were disturbances in Ahmedabad, Veramgaum, Calcutta and Bombay, but they passed away and quiet has been prevailing from almost immediately after. In other parts of the country the Satyagraha demonstrations passed off without any incidents, although they consisted of crowds as large as the places where the peace was disturbed. The contrast is noteworthy, and cannot be explained wholly by a reference to the different characteristics of the people inhabiting the different provinces. The Committee think that there are grounds for the assumption that the character of the administration of the Punjab during the last few years has created discontent and alienated the people and that the Rowlatt Act and the Satyagraha demonstrations furnished the occasion for the ebullition of such feeling. The measures by which it has been answered are such as has not been resorted to elsewhere, and only strengthen the presumption against the Punjab administration. That Sir Michael O'Dwyer's methods have always been noted for strength rather than popularity is a well-known fact. The Committee apprehend that they are responsible to no small extent for the present crisis, and in this view they cannot but regret that his term of office has been extended even after the arrival of his successor at headquarters."

The very fact that the agitation was common to the whole country, and was in some provinces more acute and widespread than in the Punjab, falsifies the statement that it had anything to do with the disorder in the Punjab. To say that the people of Punjab are generally anti-government or disposed to crime or disorder is adding insult to the injury. Before the necessity of calling into question the law-abiding and loyal nature of the people of the Punjab arose, they had always been praised for their peaceful and law-abiding character. In his speech delivered in the Imperial Legislative Council on the 13th of September, 1917, Sir Michael O'Dwyer described the temper and mentality of the Punjabees in the following words:—

> "Eloquence is a common enough quality in India; Commonsense and sanity of judgement are unfortunately less common; both are essentially Punjab qualities. They are also pre-eminently British qualities and it is the common possession of these qualities..... that has led, ever since the destinies of the two were united, to mutual comprehension, to mutual confidence and mutual co-operation between the British Government and the people of the Punjab... But perhaps the most signal proof the province (the Punjab) has given of its practical loyalty is the manner in which it has combined to quell internal disorder and repressed incipient rebellion..... There was no hesitation, no sitting on the fence, no mawkish sympathy with red-handed crime, no insincere apologies for so-called misguided youths pursuing noble ideals, no subtle distinctions between evolutionary and revolutionary patriots. The Punjabi, like the British, is perhaps lacking in that mysterious quality known as spirituality. If you were to try and explain to him what it means, he would probably shake his head and say, 'no doubt it was an excellent thing, an admirable virtue, something like charity often used to cover a multitude of sins'. He might even go so far as to compare it in the latter respect with that equally vague term 'Home Rule', which many of our politicians propound as a legitimate and constitutional ideal, while many of our revolutionaries have put it forward as the goal they have in view, when attempting to subvert the King's Government by the sword, the pistol and the bomb..... But, Sir, if the Punjabi is lacking in comprehension of the mysteries of spirituality and Home Rule, he is lacking neither in moral or physical courage, nor in a sense of duty. ..... I claim that when the stability of the Empire is threatened, the Punjab, now as in the Mutiny, has set a noble example of loyalty and self-sacrifice to the rest of the Empire."

These words were uttered when Sir Michael O'Dwyer wanted to obtain recruits and money from the Punjab, and to discourage the idea of Home Rule in the province by offering mean adulation to the people. The same man less than two years later, in order to support his theory of rebellion and hence the declaration of martial law, maligned the same people by calling them inflammable rebels. The commonsense and sanity of judgement, which the people possessed in such an eniment degree in September 1917, evaporated during the 18 months' resolute rule of Sir Micheal O'Dwyer.

The real cause of the disorder in the Punjab was not the temper of the people but the temper of the man who unfortunately was at the head of its Government. It was Sir Michael O'Dwyer who was inflammable, not the people. He had alienated the sympathies of the educated classes, and had driven discontent into the masses by his ruthless campaign of pressing recruits and levying war loans. His antagonism to the proposed constitutional reforms had made his name hated all over the province. Economic starvation, no less than political grievances, brought together the classes and the masses in their agitation against the Rowlatt Act. Sir Michael O'Dwyer had already claimed for his administration that, "whatever its defects the Punjab Government has never been lacking in courage." Sir Michael, therefore, boldly started on his campaign of penalising the agitation against the Act, which had been conducted on strictly peaceful and constitutional lines. Newspapers were gagged, the public leaders were ordered to hold their tongue. The District Officers were instructed to prevent the *hartals* of the 6th April by veiled threats and open dispproval. All this proved insufficient, and the great demonstrations of the 6th of April were held all over the province and were joined by hundreds of thousands of persons. Sir Michael decided to administer another dose of repression. A Government which cannot face independent criticism is on the high-road which leads to tyranny, discontent and sedition. Dr. Kitchlew and Dr. Satyapal of Amritsar were deported without enquiry or trial. As the Punjab Government Report States, the object of these deportations was to "disorganise" the agitation against the Rowlatt Act. Mr. Gandhi was arrested and interned in Bombay, because his presence in the Punjab would have interfered with the successful working of the scheme which

Sir Michael had in view to "disorganise" the agitation. Innocent persons were shot down at Amritsar for no more fault than that they were going to the Deputy Commissioner to entreat him to have the orders of deportation cancelled. The Amritsar mob was infuriated and grave riots took place; the local officials simply looked on in wonderment at the crimes of the mob. All was quiet after about two hours. The officials regained their consciousness and openly talked of wreaking a terrible vengeance for the loss of European lives at Amritsar. It was proposed to bombard the whole town. The vengeance, however, took the form of the massacre at the Jallianwala Bagh. The exaggerated reports of these deeds spread throughout the length and breadth of the province, and the "splendid loyalty and virile manhood of the Punjab" burst forth in sporadic outbursts of indignation. Acts of lawlessness were perpetrated in places where the discontent already existing was the greatest. The attempt of Sir Michael O'Dwyer to torture the people and keep them silent, like the attempt of a mother who beats her child and when it weeps beats it the more to make it quiet, miserably failed.

Extent of Disorder

1. Urban Areas.

The disorder at Amritsar lasted for about two hours and was the direct result of the grave and sudden provocation given to the people by the deportation of Dr. Kitchlew and Dr. Satyapal and the shooting down of innocent persons in their attempt to see the District Magistrate and make their representation to him. These riots resulted in the brutal murder of five Europeans, the cowardly assault on Miss Sherwood, the burning and looting of the English banks and some other acts of incendiarism and destruction. The mob dispersed without any action of the authorities. The riots at Kasur were purely fortuitous acts of a mob excited by exaggerated reports from Lahore and Amritsar and the arrest of Mr. Gandhi; and resulted in the murder of two Europeans, the burning of the Post Office and the Munsif's Court and some damage at the Railway Station. After about two hours' rioting the mob was dispersed by the police. The immediate cause of the riots at Gujranwala was the provocation offered to the Baisakhi revellers, a large number of whom were drunken agriculturists, by the exhibition of a slaughtered calf to the public gaze. It is suspected that this was done by the police. The firing by the police had also the effect of infuriating the mob. The rioters set fire to the Dak Bungalow, the Tahsil, the District Court, the Church, the Telegraph Office, the Railway Station and the Post Office. No one was killed or wounded by the rioters, who dispersed of their own accord. The disturbance at Wazirabad was due to the bombing of Gujranwala, the arrest of Mr. Gandhi and the official excesses at Amritsar; and consisted in the cutting of wires, slightly damaging the railway line, burning a gang-hut, damaging the gates of a level-crossing and the burning and looting of the house of a missionary. The mob voluntarily dispersed. At Lahore there was no damage to life or property, except the casualties caused by police fire, which was neither necessary nor justifiable. The mob which confronted the police and the military on the 6th of April was a much bigger and a more truculent mob than the one that was fired on by the police on the evening of the 10th. But the great patience and forbearance shown by the police and the District Magistrate on the 6th was lacking on the 10th, because the excesses committed by the mob at Amritsar had frightened and enraged the officials, and they were not disposed to weigh the situation in a calm and reasonable manner. Two days later, another peaceful crowd of persons returning from the Badshahi Mosque was fired on. On neither of these occasions had the mob committed any violence; and there was no rioting or disorder at Lahore, as distinguished from peaceful demonstrations. It has been alleged that brickbats were thrown by the mob on the police or the military on each occasion before the order of firing was given; but no evidence has been forthcoming to show that any policeman or soldier was injured. At Gujrat and Lyallpur, there was no disorder worth mentioning.

As would appear from the facts narrated in this chapter, the disorder in the rural areas was more serious than in the urban. The railway stations of Wagah, Moman, Dhaban Singh and Chuharkana were set on fire, telegraph wires were cut and the railway lines were damaged at many villages. At Aulakh the *patwarkhana,* which contained the revenue records of six villages, was burnt. These acts of lawlessness were not the mere thoughtless acts of large mobs, which had been given an immediate cause for provocation or had been misled by a few mischievous persons in the heat of the moment; but were the deliberate and prearranged acts of small bands of men, who had set out with the definite intention of committing these crimes. The fact that the disorders in the rural areas did not result in much damage does not prove anything, because there were no Europeans to be killed nor any Government buildings to be burnt. There is no doubt that like the inhabitants of the towns, the vast majority of the rural population took no part in disorder, and that the acts of violence were more or less isolated; but the attempt of Sir Micheal O'Dwyer and other officials to minimise the outrages which happened on the countryside is highly significant. As the oppressive and illegal methods of recruitment were mainly practised in the villages and as the "agitators" and the educated classes, whom it was sought to humiliate and punish for promoting an imaginary rebellion, resided in the towns, Sir Micheal O'Dwyer and his confederates did their best to make it appear that the disorder was confined to the urban areas. Inasmuch as only a very small fraction of the population was concerned in the so-called disturbances, it is true that the villagers were on the whole loyal. But the same is true of the urban population of the province. Sir Michael, however, wanted to kill out political life, which was confined to the towns; and it was, therefore, doubly to his interest to minimise the disorder in rural tracts and exaggerate the occurrences that took place in the urban areas. By this simple device, Sir Michael O'Dwyer was no doubt able to

2. Rural Areas.

subject the urban population to the most shameful indignities and untold oppressions under martial law; but he could not annihilate historical facts. The connection between oppressive recruitment and disorder was so strong and clear that it could not be successfully concealed. During the last year of the war, the methods of recruitment of the army assumed the most tyrannical form in the district of Gujranwala, and it was in this district that rural disorders were the most widespread. It is admitted in the Punjab Government Report that, "The district, for many years a noticeably poor recruiting area, had been the scene of an intensive campaign from November 1917 to November 1918". When the war ceased, Gujranwala had 13,000 men in the army out of whom 7,000 had been raised in the 11 months from December 1917 to October, 1918. This "intensive campaign" is said to have been carried on with such zeal, that some of the officials with the help of the police actually raided villages in the dead hours of night and arrested sleeping villagers, who were forcibly marched to the headquarters where they were compelled to enlist in the army. It was also in a part of this district, in which the largest number of outrages were committed (the Shiekhupura Sub-division), that the villagers were forced to subscribe to the O'Dwyer Memorial Fund. And it is about this district that we read in the Official Report that, "The story here is one of damage and outrage done largely by agriculturists." No better example than that of the Gujranwala district can be given to show that the illegal and barbarous methods of recruitment for the army were to a large extent responsible for the general discontent which prevailed in the villages and burst forth into acts of disorder when the minds of the people were excited by exaggerated rumours of further acts of official lawlessness. The general mass of the rural population, however, like the general mass of the urban population, was unaffected by the unrest. In the Amritsar district, "the agricultural classes were not affected by unrest." About the district of Lahore, the Official Report states :— "Though there were some sporadic attacks on communications outside, the unrest in rural areas never reached serious proportions, nor did it lead to widespread outrage such as that which marked the rural areas of Gujranwala district." In the districts of Gujrat and Lyallpur there was no disturbance worth the name either in the rural or the urban areas.

The Educated Classes.

Once upon a time, a small boy of the Jewish persuasion who was playing at the end of the pier fell into the sea, and was only rescued after great difficulty by an intrepid swimmer, who dived off the end of the pier and succeeded in getting the boy into a rowing boat. Half an hour afterwards, much exhausted by his effort, the rescuer was walking off the pier when a man came up and tapped him on the shoulder. "Are you the man who saved my son Ikey's life ?" he asked. "Yes," answered the much exhausted hero. "Then" said the Hebrew in indignant tones, "where's his cap?" So it was with the educated classes and the pleaders during the disturbances. The pleaders specially and the educated community generally, did their utmost to prevent disorder where it did not exist and to restore order where there had been excesses; but the Government ignored their great services in the cause of law and order, and subjected them to grave persecution and hardship for their supposed faults. At Amritsar, though the only two popular leaders who could control the people were unavoidably absent, the pleaders and barristers readily offered their services to the authorities and did all they could to help them both on the 10th April and on the following days. At Lahore, the local leaders were in constant attendance on the District Magistrate and gave willing help to the officials on every occasion ; and it was mainly due to the strenuous efforts of the leaders, that in spite of the grave and uncalled for provocation which the authorities caused on several occasions, there was no breach of the public peace. At Kasur, the leaders gave every help to the officials, and it was a pleader and "agitator", who saved the lives of the Sherbournes. At Gujranwala, the lawyers and the local leaders did their best to avert the *hartal* and rendered all possible help to pacify the crowd and make it disperse ; many of them actually put out the fire at some places, which the police had left to burn. At Gujrat, the prominent men, including several lawyers, were holding a conference with the District Magistrate to devise means to prevent possible disorder in their town, when the riot took place ; and thereafter they gave all possible assistance to the local authorities. At Lyallpur the local leaders, who were mainly pleaders, succeeded in keeping the people quiet; and there was no disorder. But at all these places, the local leaders were arrested, prosecuted and many of them convicted on one pretext or another. At Amritsar, S, Gurdial Singh Salaria, Barrister-at-Law, who had tried to disperse the mob on the bridge at great personal risk, was arrested and prosecuted for waging war against the King. Several other prominent barristers and pleaders, who had helped the authorities, were arrested and tried on similar charges ; and all the lawyers were enrolled as special constables. At Lahore, the pleaders and barristers, who had kept the people in check and did their utmost to have the shops re-opened, were arrested or deported and tried on a charge of waging war against the King for the very acts which they had done at the request of the officials and for their help. At Kasur, a large number of pleaders were arrested, including the gentleman who had saved the lives of the Sherbournes, his fault being that he had influence with the mob as the Sherbournes were saved at his intercession. All the leaders of Gujranwala were arrested and tried for waging war against the King, and some of them, who were pouring water on the fire, were accused of having thrown oil instead of water. The pleaders of Gujrat, who were with the District Magistrate when the so-called disturbance took place, were arrested and placed on their trial for waging war against the King. The pleaders of Lyallpur, were treated in a similar manner. Though everywhere the educated community as a whole assisted the officials during the distrubances, yet the rigours of martial law were visited on it with a redoubled force, because political life had to be completely crushed. For the same reason, the lawyers as a class were falsely accused of having taken a leading part in the disorders and were subjected to every species of hardship, persecution and indignity. The educated community has always been an eyesore with Sir Michael O'Dwyer on account of its political activity. Being the greatest sinners in this respect, the lawyers came in for a larger share of Sir Michael O'Dwyer's wrath. But in spite of every effort by the police to fasten the responsibility for the disorders on the educated classes in general and the lawyers in particular, not a single man of education has been proved to have participated in actual violence during the disturbances ; and the town of Lahore, which is the educational centre of the Punjab and where the educated classes preponderate, remained free from all disorder.

The Arya Samaj

The Arya Samaj was founded about half a century ago as a protest against the inertia and rigid prejudices of orthodox Hinduism. It represents the advanced wing of the Hindu religion and has always stood for social and religious reform. As the Samaj was a new sect, it had to launch a strong propaganda against the tenets of Christianity, Sikhism, Islam and orthodox Hinduism, which it has ruthlessly carried on ever since its inception. Partly by reason of its strenuous propaganda and great educational work and partly on account of the inherent soundness of most of its principles, the Samaj has obtained a large number of adherents, most of whom are earnest and devoted workers in its cause and occupy prominent positions in society. The marvellous success of the Samaj and its Anti-Christian, Anti-Hindu, Anti-Sikh and Anti-Islamic propaganda have turned the Government officials and a large section of the general public against it. Lala Lajpat Rai in his book, "The Arya Samaj," says:—

> "The foreign rulers of India have never been quite happy about the Arya Samaj. They have always disliked its independence of tone and its propaganda of self-confidence, self-help and self-reliance. The national side of its activities has aroused their antipathy They cannot

look with favour on an indigenous movement which according to them, can do big things without their help and guidance, and which has established a sort of Government within the Government. The progress it has made, the hold which it has established for itself on the minds of the people, the popularity which it has won in spite of its heterodoxy and its inconoclasm among the Hindus, the influence which it possesses, the immense 'go' which characterises it in all its doings, the national spirit which it has aroused and developed among the Hindus, the ready self-sacrifice of its members, the independence of their tone, and the rapidity with which the movement has spread throughout India, and last, but not the least, the spirit of criticism which it generates, have won for it the suspicion of the ruling bureacracy. This suspicion has more than once brought on its members the wrath of the authorities, in the shape of deportations, prosecutions, dismissals, etc."

For these reasons, the Samaj and its members have always been suspected and considered to be anti-government. The Samaj has been called a political body and openly accused of concealing its real intentions under the cloak of religious and social reform. The Punjab being the stronghold of the Samaj, and the Government of the Province having always possessed an unenviable reputation for its repressive policy, the Aryas in the Punjab have suffered a good deal for their religious beliefs. From 1907 to 1910, the officials in the Punjab persecuted the members of the Samaj in every possible way. In several cases, Government servants were asked to resign their membership of the Samaj if they wanted to continue in Government service. On their refusal to repudiate their religious faith, many of them were dismissed outright and the promotion of others was stopped. The Government servants and students were prohibited from attending the meetings of the Samaj, at which only religious sermons were given. The names of the members of the Samaj were entered in the police registers and their movements were watched; and the leaders of the sect were shadowed from place to place by the Criminal Investigation Department. This espionage was, however, discontinued after a time, as even the fertile genius of the Indian Police failed to make out a case against the Samaj as a body. In the Census Report of the United Provinces for 1901, Mr. Blunt, I.C.S., observed:—

> "There is, of course, no doubt whatever that the Samaj doctrine has a patriotic side... The Arya doctrine and the Arya education alike 'Sing the glories of ancient India,' and by so doing arouse the national pride of its disciples, who are made to feel that their country's history is not a tale of continuous humiliation. Patriotism and politics are not synonymous, but the arousing of an interest in national affairs is a natural result of arousing national pride. Moreover, the type of man to whom the Arya doctrine appeals is also the type of man to whom politics appeals, *viz.*, the educated man who desires his country's progress.... It is not therefore surprising that there are politicians among the Arya Samaj. But it is impossible to deduce from this that the Arya Samaj, as a whole, is a political body. From the first the Samaj has consistently affirmed that it is not concerned with politics, has laid down this principle in various rules, has discouraged its members from taking part in them and disavowed their actions in express terms when they needed disavowal."

In his Census Report for the Punjab for 1891, Sir Edward Maclagan (then Mr. Maclagan, I.C.S.), the present Lieutenant-Governor of the Punjab, said:—

> "The fact that the Aryas are mainly recruited from one class and that the Samaj possesses a very complete organisation of its own has laid it open to the charge of supporting as a body the proclivites of a large section of its members; but the Samaj as such is not a political but a religious body."

Sir Michael O'Dwyer, however, was not the man who could unlearn anything, or cast aside any suspicion of sedition or partiality for politics, however unfounded the suspicion may be. It is needless to say that the Samaj had no hand in the present disorders, and there is not the slightest evidence to connect it or its members as such with the crimes committed at the various places. But in the Report of the Punjab Government, an attempt is made to connect the Samaj with the so-called rebellion. Dealing with the events at Gujranwala, it is stated that "members of the Arya Samaj community were everywhere prominent in the movement." About Wazirabad the Report says, "The Arya Samaj element was again prominent in the disturbances." About Hafizabad, the Report states, "The agitation..... appears to have been largely due to the influence of members of the Arya Samaj community." Dealing with the causes of the trouble at Malakwal, the Report says that the place was visited by "two Arya Samaj lecturers..... who gave an inflammatory lecture" and excited the inhabitants to wage war. About Lyallpur, it is stated in the Report, that "That moving spirits in the agitation were mainly Hindus, and among them the Arya Samajists were conspicuous for their acitivity." These and other insinuations in the Report, whose publication was perhaps not foreseen by its authors, furnish a clear index to the views of the Government and its attitude about the Samaj. The result was that the members of the Samaj as such were terrorised and persecuted at many places by the officials who were entrusted with the administration of martial law. It is unnecessary to point out that the statements of official witnesses before Lord Hunter's Enquiry Committee, as well as the trials held by the Commissions, entirely disproved the assumption that the Samaj was connected with the recent disorders.

Real nature of the disorder

In India even the serpent is worshipped, and the Indian is the most forgiving person in the world; but Sir Michael O'Dwyer's oppressive regime alienated the sympathies of all classes and his attempt to throttle a peaceful agitation exasperated the long suffering people. The involuntary outburst of the feeling of indignation which the people had suppressed for a long time did not betoken a rebellious intent. The irresponsible acts of infuriated mobs, which can be swayed and moved to action by a little suggestion of a single mischievous person, cannot serve as an index to the deliberate feelings and opinions of a whole population; nor can the excesses of a demented mob be held correctly to reflect the better judgement of even the men comprising it. The so-called rebellion in the Punjab consisted in a number of riots at different places on different dates, to which a very small number of the disreputable and unruly elements of the population were driven in a moment of temporary excitement under circumstances which have already been related. The object of these riots, if they can be said to have an object, was not to subvert the Government. Not a single fire-arm was used anywhere by any private individual during these riots. What to say of anarchists, even the ordinary dacoits apparently do not find it difficult to procure and use fire-arms or manufacture bombs for their nefarious purposes. Thousands of persons in the Punjab possess arms, and it should not have been difficult for the supposed rebels to have stolen a number of them, if they really intended to wage a war of independence against the British Government in India. It is simply preposterous to imagine that the so-called rebels relied on their sticks to subvert the British rule, or that the civil authorities were rendered helpless at the sight of sticks and brickbats. In order to justify the declaration of martial law the civil authorities at Amritsar, Lahore and Gujranwala pleaded before Lord Hunter's Enquiry Committee that the situation was beyond their control. But the authorities did not as a rule try to prevent the action of the mob, when it was actually engaged in acts of violence; and wherever they tried to check the mob, they were successful. Everywhere the mobs voluntarily dispersed after their passions had cooled down; and there was no further disorder. If the people had broken out in open rebellion against the Crown, and if the authorities had become powerless, order could not have been automatically restored at all the places where there were riots without any action by the police or the military. Everywhere the military came upon the scene after the violence of the mobs had ceased, and order had been restored. If it was a rebellion, and the rebels had wrested the power from the civil authorities, one should have expected some sort of a struggle between the military and the rebels before the latter were vanquished. But nowhere was there a recrudescence of disorder, and the people did not raise their little finger to resist the grave injustice and tyranny which was practised in the name of law and order, and which by itself would have created a revolt in any other country of the world. At every place where there was a disturbance, perfect quiet prevailed after a few hours' rioting; and the authorities were able to make arrests immediately after the riots without the slightest resistance. There was no continuity of action on the part of the so-called rebels; and no connection has been established between the outbreaks of disorder at different places. The Government has failed to establish that there was an organisation behind the disorders, or even that they were deliberate and premeditated. There was no revolutionary crime in the Punjab before the so-called rebellion; and the riots themselves proved the unmistakable loyalty of the people. The Indians of all classes rendered the most valuable help to the authorities, and sometimes even at great personal risk saved European lives and property; and the vast majority of the population did not take part in the disorder. Even the Government of Sir Micheal O'Dwyer was compelled to acknowledge the loyal services of the Indians in an official communique which was issued on April 26th, the opening words of which are as follows:—

> "Many instances have come to the notice of the Lieutenant-Governor in which loyal Indians of all classes have rendered active assistance, often at risk to themselves, in protecting British Officers, soldiers, ladies and children who were attacked or threatened by the mobs at Amritsar, Kasur and elsewhere in the recent disturbances."

Every act of violence was accompanied by some brave and unselfish deed of an Indian. Mr. and Mrs. Sherbourne and their children were saved by an Indian pleader. Lieutenant Tatam was protected against maltreatment from the mob by some Indian passengers. The lawyers and other popular leaders of Gujranwala helped in extinguishing the fire and dispersing the mobs at considerable personal risk. At Amritsar Mrs. Easdon was rescued and Miss Sherwood was resuscitated by Indians; and the Bank Managers, who were killed, had been bravely defended by the Indian staff of the Bank. In his speech at the annual general meeting of the Alliance Bank, which was held on the 11th August 1919, Mr. E.J. Buck, C.B.E., the Chairman of the Board of Directors, expressed the appreciation of the Bank for the loyalty of its Amritsar staff in the following words:—

> "The Indian Staff, seeing that Mr. Thomson declined to leave, did their best to protect him, and one of the subordinate members stood over his body defending it to the best of his ability from the blows that were showered on it. Many of these blows fell on this brave Indian,

who was badly hurt in his efforts to save his chief. It gave the Directors great satisfaction to record the appreciation of the excellent services rendered to the Bank by the loyal staff at Amritsar by granting them a special bonus of three months' pay."

The Indian army and the police remained loyal to a man. Not only that, but they consented to be used as blind instruments of official tyranny; and did not hesitate in the slightest degree to commit the manifold atrocities which they were ordered to perpetrate. The patience with which the people submitted to the atrocities perpetrated by the soldiery and the police during the martial law regime furnishes a clear proof, if proof were needed, of the abiding loyalty of the people and their unbounded faith in the humane and just principles of British rule in India.

The Government and the exponents of its views have not been consistent in their estimate of the situation. We have already seen in the previous chapter how the theory that there was a conspiracy behind the disturbances has been changing and shifting from time to time, as its supporters were compelled to leave one position after another, till at last it was smashed as the result of the cross-examination to which the discoverers of the imaginary conspiracy were subjected before Lord Hunter's Committee. The position of the Government with regard to the declaration that there was a state of rebellion has not been more consistent. If there had not been "open rebellion," martial law could not be proclaimed; but Sir Michael O'Dwyer's desire for vengeance had to be appeased. It was, therefore, declared in utter disregard of actual facts, that five districts of the Punjab were in a state of "open rebellion". The Amir was led to misjudge the nature and scope of the disorder in India by the proclamation and administration of martial law which very much resembled the administration of a newly occupied territory of the enemy, and actually believed that the people were in a state of rebellion. The Amir thought that this was his opportunity and invaded the Indian territories. He pleaded the so-called Indian rising as an excuse for his own; but the Government of India at once repudiated the suggestion.

In the course of his proclamation of May 10th, 1919, Lord Chelmsford denied the suggestion that there was a revolution in India in the following words:—

> "Evidence is in His Excellency's hands which shows that the Amir excuses his act of treachery by *pretending* that India is in a state of revolution which will react on his own country. The Amir has professed to his people that in India neither men's property* nor their religion is safe; that three men are forbidden to speak together;† that Muslims are excluded from their mosques‡ and Hindus from their temples. Every man in India knows that these statements are false. Relying on such misstatements the Amir has called on Hindus and Muslims alike to show him allegiance... Inspired by these *futile* hopes of seducing His Majesty's subjects from their allegiance, the Amir has already commenced military operations."

Similarly, when at the Peace Conference, Sardar Ali Ahmed Khan, the Chief Afghan delegate, excused the Afghan invasion on the plea that "owing to the intorduction of martial law and certain legislative measures by the British Government" there was a rebellion in India, and its spread to the Afghan frontier was feared, Sir Hamilton Grant rejected the suggestion with icy contempt and stated that there were merely "local disorders" in India.

An impartal examination of the events, as they actually happend, leads to the irresistible conclusion that the disturbances were not pre-arranged, that they were no more than local riots in which a small fraction of the population participated, that the civil authorities never lost control of the situation, that the motive of the rioters was not to subvert the British rule in India. and that the cause was not a propaganda of lawlessness but the indiscreet acts of the authorities.

---

* In most cases the Commissions ordered forfeiture of property belonging to the persons convicted by them. In several places, especially in the district of Gujranwala, property of persons was confiscated or destroyed, merely because they were not in their houses when the police or military went to arrest them. In almost all places, people where threatened with wholesale reprisals against their property on the flimsiest grounds.

† A martial law order of Colonel Frank Johnson made it an offence for more than two persons to walk together in the public streets of Lahore (*Vide* Appendix I, page 235, Order No. 12).

‡ The Badshahi Mosque had been closed under orders of the martial law authorsities.

CHAPTER III
The Reign of Terror

1—BEFORE MARTIAL LAW

AMRITSAR

The *raison d'être* of rebellion.

As has been pointed out in the previous chapter the civil authorities at Amritsar did not interfere with the rioters, and the mob was allowed to proceed unchecked in its mad career. The result was that five Europeans were most brutally murdered, one lady was assaulted and beaten in the most shameful manner and several lakhs worth of property was destroyed or looted. The town had been abandoned to the furious mob; and it is, indeed, surprising that more mischief was not done. After the mob disappeared, the local officials reappeared. But they could not realise, as nobody else could realise, that the mob was capable of working so much destruction within the brief space of a few hours. The position was serious. Europeans had been murdered; the English Banks had been looted and burnt; the public buildings had been set on fire; a European lady had been mercilessly beaten in the public streets—things, which had never happened before in the history of British rule in India. The local officials were terrified. How were they to explain their inactivity ? How were they to account for the fact that innocent European lives had been lost without the slightest attempt by the officials to save them ? The guardians of law and order were naturally averse to admit that they had miserably failed in their duty, after they had committed the grave blunder of provoking a peaceful crowd to violence. The only other course open to them was to magnify the nature of the disorder and ascribe it to a widespread conspiracy. The theroy of rebellion was, therefore, propounded. The local Government was naturally willing to accept this solution, as it had also to show that its action in deporting the Amritsar leaders was not responsible for the riots. Under these circumstances, the civil authorities could not but declare that they had lost control of the situation. This was duly done when on the night (about 10 p.m.) of the 10th April 400 reinforcements from Lahore reached Amritsar. The Commissioner of the Division, who had arrived in the afternoon, told the Officer Commanding the troops that he "was to consider himself in charge of the military situation and take whatever steps he thought necessary to re-establish civil control".

Desire for Vengeance.

The cruel and cowardly crimes that were committed at Amritsar sent a thrill of horror throughout the country; and Indians of all classes and creeds condemned the acts of their fellow-countrymen in the clearest terms. Both the European and the Indian communities were justly indignant, and demanded that the perpetrators of these crimes should be brought to justice. But a large number of Englishmen wanted not only justice but also vengeance. In the eyes of the vast majority of Englishmen in India, the life of an Englishman is sacrosanct, while the life of an Indian is even less valuable than the life of their pet dogs. The European officials at Amritsar, therefore, became irate at the murders of Europeans and wanted to wreak a terrible vengeance upon the people, who had dared to desecrate the sanctity of European life in India. The officials—both civil and military—wanted to make the retribution so swift and so terrible as to make it impossible for an Indian to look into an Englishman's face without terror. As some Englishmen had been murdered, a holocaust of "native" lives was wanted at Amritsar to teach the "natives" a lesson which they would not forget for generations. It was suggested and seriously considered by the local officials that the town of Amritsar should be bombarded with machine-guns; and it was openly stated by them that they would have at least a thousand Indian lives for every single European killed in the riots. But the proposal had to be dropped, as it was found impossible to bombard the town without hitting the

Golden Temple, the sacred seat of the Sikh religion, an injury to which might have created a real rebellion by subverting the loyalty of not only the Sikh and general population of the province but also of the Sikh armies. Though saner counsels prevailed and this specific project was given up, the hunger for vengeance remained.

The 11th April

On the 11th, as a preliminary to avenge the blood of innocent Europeans, the water and electric supplies of the Indian quarter of the town were cut off and were not restored until martial law armed the officials with more effective weapons of public chastisement. On the morning of the 11th, the dead bodies of the persons, who had died as the result of the firing on the previous day, had to be disposed of; and the authorities were told that the coffins of the dead were to be followed by a large number of persons. Thereupon, the District Magistrate issued the following order :—

> "The troops have orders to restore order in Amritsar and use all force necessary. No gatherings of persons nor processions of any sort will be allowed. *All gatherings will be fired on.* Respectable persons should keep indoors until order is restored. Dead may be carried out for burial or burning by parties of not more than eight at intervals of not less than 15 minutes by the Gheemandi, Lohgar, Khazana and Chatiwind Gates."
>
> "MILES IRVING,
> D.C.
> 11.4.19."

The people were naturally dissatisfied with this order, and some prominent citizens visited the Deputy Commissioner and after some difficulty got it modified. The European officials made no secret of their intention to take drastic steps to avenge the murder of Europeans if an opportunity presented itself. The order on modification took the following form :—

> "People will be allowed to bury their dead in number about 2,000 provided—
>
> "(1) Only Sultanwind and Chatiwind Gates used.
>
> "(2) All over by 2 p.m.
>
> "(3) At 2 p.m., warning by bugle.

"(4) After 15 minutes fire.

"(5) No lathis."

"Miles Irving.
11.4.19."

The language of both these orders clearly indicates that the authorities had made up their mind to fire upon the people on the slightest excuse, even if no violence was intended or committed by the crowd. The people, however, followed these orders and did not give the authorities any pretext to carry out their intentions. More reinforcements arrived from Jullundur during the course of the day, and troops were marched into the city. Police investigations into the riots of the previous day were also commenced. In the evening, the General Officer Commanding, Jullundur Brigade (Brigadier General R.E. Dyer, C.B.) reached Amritsar, and the administration of the town was handed over to him by Mr. Miles Irving, the Deputy Commissioner.

De facto Martial Law

The Deputy Commissioner had no authority in law to hand over the government of the town to General Dyer. All that the Criminal Procedure Code authorises the District Magistrate to do is to secure military aid to help the civil authority to disperse an unlawful assembly or to suppress disorder or riot. *De facto* martial law has no place in the Indian constitution. Martial law can be established in India only under the provisions of Regulation X of 1804† by order of the Governor-General in Council, or under an Ordinance of the Governor-General. But the Deputy Commissioner or the General did not ever communicate with the Lientenant-Governor and receive his sanction for placing Amritsar under martial law. Before Lord Hunter's Enquiry Committee the extraordinary nature of the situation was pleaded in defence of this illegal action; but the facts elicited during the enquiry have failed to make out even a plausible case for taking this drastic step. After the afternoon of the 10th, there was no further disturbance at Amritsar. The

† *Vide* Appendix I: pages 200—201.

orders of the Deputy Commissioner with regard to the burial and cremation of the dead had been obeyed; and police investigation into the riots had been commenced without any opposition from the people. Perfect quiet prevailed in the town. The troops had marched through the city both on the night of the 10th and in the afternoon of the 11th without any resistance or resentment by the people. There were no demonstrations in the town. And above all, up to the evening of the 11th disorder had not broken out anywhere else in the province. On the 10th and 11th, the Commissioner, who travelled four times between Lahore and Amritsar (a distance of about 150 miles in all) in his motor car and during these journeys several times stopped on the road to talk to the people and ascertain their feelings, had not noticed any indication of impending disorder, nor was he molested on the way. Under the circumstances, the Deputy Commissioner had no reasonable excuse, much less a justification, for abdicating his position and handing over his duties to the General. Even if it be conceded that there was reasonable apprehension of a renewal of disorder at Amritsar, the authorities had now sufficient forces at their command to cope with it. Besides, a fear of possible disorder cannot by any stretch of reasoning be held to be a sufficient justification for establishing martial law in direct contravention to the law of the land. The General admits in his statement before Lord Hunter's Enquiry Committee that he did not care to inquire into the condition of the town before he accepted the invitation of the Deputy Commissioner to step into his shoes. The whole thing was done in such a callous and light-hearted manner that it betokens either gross incompetence on the part of the civil authorities or a conspiracy of the civil and military officers to take vengeance on the people.

The 12th April

On the 12th April, General Dyer, with some troops, marched through the town and arrested about a dozen persons, who were suspected of having taken part in the riots; but there was no opposition or resentment shown by the people. On the

12th (or on the 11th, or the 13th) no proclamation was issued warning the people that the town had been brought under martial law and the will of the Officer Commanding was the supreme authority. However, in spite of this attempt at concealment of the real situation, and the deliberate omission of the authorities to warn the inhabitants of their duties and liabilities under the martial law, there was perfect quiet in the town and the authorities did not get an opportunity to wreak their vengeance on the population of the city. Hope deferred maketh the heart sick; and the authorities could no longer remain inactive and leave everything to a fortuitous opportunity, which had not appeared during the preceding 48 hours and the chance of whose appearance decreased with every passing hour. The authorities, therefore, decided not to wait any longer, but to boldly take the initiative. The proposed bombardment having been given up, the next best thing was to collect the "rebels" in mass formation and then to fire upon them and cause as many deaths as possible. This was the plan of the official conspirators. Hans Raj was to act as the decoy for this purpose than whom no better man could have been selected for this task.

Hans Raj.

Now, who is this Hans Raj? Hans Raj was a young man of about 23 years, who had passed the Matriculation Examination of the University in 1911; but though he was young in years, he was not young in the villainy of his character. During this brief space of seven years, he had worked in many capacities and was dismissed from several employments on charges which reflect little credit on his character. First of all, he was employed as a travelling ticket examiner on the North-Western Railway, from where he was dismissed for embezzling railway money. Then he took employment as a clerk with Lala Harnam Shah, Municipal Commissioner, Amritsar, but after a short time his services were dispensed with. He also served as a clerk to the Union Club, Amritsar, but was dismissed on a charge of defalcation of the money of the Club. After this, he took service with Sardar Seva

Singh, a banker at Amritsar; but had to give up this appointment as well after a service of two months. During this interval Hans Raj had also tried to make friends with the police officials, and get an appointment in the police. In this attempt he did not succeed; but seems to have been put on the waiting list and, as a preliminary, allowed to act as a secret agent of the C.I.D. Hans Raj was, therefore, a rudderless youth of an extremely dubious character who had no ostensible means of livelihood. Up to the beginning of February 1919, Hans Raj did not exhibit any political inclinations; but during the two months preceeding the disturbances, we find him attending every political meeting at Amritsar, and taking a keen interest in the platform-ticket agitation, as well as in the agitation against the Rowlatt Bill, both before and after it became law. We find him at every public meeting that was held during this period, the proceedings of which he seems to have noted with extraordinary care, as would appear from his statement before the Commission in the Amritsar Leaders' Case. He describes the proceedings of the several meetings in such minute detail, that the conclusion is irresistible that he was not there as a mere spectator. Hans Raj's activities were not confined to the public meetings alone. He became a frequent visitor to the houses of the public workers at Amritsar, and after some effort succeeded in cultivating their acquaintance. By his prompt willingness to perform such odd jobs as printing of notices and resolutions, making arrangements at public meetings and other work of a subordinate nature, he was able to delude the public men at Amritsar into the belief that he was an earnest fellow-worker. Gradually he wormed himself into their confidence; and after signing the *Satyagraha vow,* he was elected the Joint-Secretary of the *Satyagraha Sabha,* which was formed on the 8th April, and thus taken into the inner counsels of the "agitators." During the fortnight preceding the riots, he was always present at the house of one or the other of the political workers, offering to copy out the resolutions, draft the notices of public meetings and have them printed, to do the little writing work that was to be done and to perform any other work that might give him information of the inner working of the movement. During the *hartals*, the Rowlatt Act meetings and the Ram Naumi procession, he was always at the heels of Dr. Satyapal and Dr. Kitchlew. On the fateful morning of the 10th April, he accompanied Dr. Kitchlew to the Deputy Commissioner's house, lest he might stray away on the road; and after the deportations, we find the Deputy Commissioner hand over to him the letters of the deportees to their relations. He took back all the three letters after the addressees had read them. Of these, he returned two after carefully copying them, and retained the third in his possession. After the deportations, we find him in constant attendance upon Dr. Bashir, Ghulam Muhammad, Gurbakhsh Rai, Bugga Mal, S. Gurdial Singh, Dina Nath, Swami Anubhawa Nand and other persons who were subsequently prosecuted under martial law. He also states in his evidence that he was present at the scenes of the riots. During this period, he also took possession of the *Satyagraha* register. The events of 10th, 11th and 12th are described by him before the Commission in such detail, that one is bound to conclude that either they are a later fabrication, or else, if they are true, he was all along aware that he would have to relate them at a future date. The suddenness with which he plunged into the public movements of the town, the fact that he was not qualified by his character and antecedents to take an honest part in any public work, the great difference between his education and social position and that of the political workers upon whom he forced his constant presence and the fact that he had been following Dr. Kitchlew, Dr. Satyapal and other public men from place to place with such unfailing regularity—all these facts, joined with the circumstance that he was an aspirant after police service, lead to the unavoidable conclusion that he was a secret spy of the police, who was introduced into the camp of the "agitators" with the object of watching and reporting their movements and actions. Such was the man who arranged the meeting at the Jallianwala Bagh, and by false pretences induced thousands of persons to assemble there. The conduct of Hans Raj after the Jallianwala Bagh meeting strengthens the conclusion that he was a secret agent of the police. After the massacre at the Jallianwala Bagh, his task seems to have been finished; and he managed to get fever on the morning of the 14th. On the 16th, he was arrested by the police; and four days later, became the chief approver in the Amritsar Leaders' Case. This is how he describes this apparent somersault in his statement before the Martial Law Commission :—

> "On my arrest was taken to fort, was kept with other persons arrested..... For four days there made no statement, was not questioned. No one said I was to be shot. I was then taken to Kotwali, and placed in lock-up. On reaching Kotwali I was asked to make a statement and I said I was ready to do so. I was put before a Magistrate and I made my statement..... After my statement I went to lock-up. No police officer spoke to me after that. When I made my statement I was not given a pardon. I was given a pardon on the 24th May."

Thus it was that the genuine patriot, the intrepid lieutenant of Dr. Kitchlew and Dr. Satyapal and the great leader of the Jallianwala Bagh, to whom General Dyer's bullets were "blank catridges," became an approver without the slightest persuasion or inducement, without any pressure or threats by the police, without even the promise of a pardon. Such selfless altruistic approvers are indeed a rare commodity. Who could have played the police spy to a greater perfection? It may also be mentioned that this prince of approvers was spirited away to Mesopotamia before Lord Hunter's Enquiry Committee commenced its proceedings at Lahore; and the learned Commissioners were deprived of his valuable statement, which was bound to prove a very instructive and interesting piece of evidence.

How the trap was laid.

On the evening of the 12th April, Hans Raj, the secret agent of the police, announced at a public meeting held at Dhab Khatikan, that on the following afternoon a meeting would be held in the Jallianwala Bagh at which Lala Kanhyia Lal, Vakil, would preside. Lala Kanhyia Lal is a veteran lawyer of Amritsar, whose name was used without his knowledge or permission to attract a large number of people to the Bagh. On the morning of the 13th at about 9-30, General Dyer with the District Magistrate, the Tahsildar, some Police Officers and a fairly large body of troops marched through a portion of the town, and, at intervals, the following proclamation was read out in the vernacular :—

> "I. It is hereby notified that no inhabitant of Amritsar is permitted to go out of the city in his own or in a hired conveyance or on foot without obtaining a pass from one of the under-mentioned officers :—
>
> (1) The Deputy Commissioner of Amritsar.
>
> (2) Mr. J. F. Rehill, Superintendent of Police, Amritsar.
>
> (3) Mr. Beckett, Assistant Commissioner, Amritsar. (Here follow names of 6 more officials).
>
> "2. No person residing in the city is permitted to leave his house after 8 p.m. Any person found in the street after 8 p.m. is *liable to be shot.*
>
> "3. No *procession* of any kind is permitted to parade the city or any part of the city or outside of it at any time. Any such procession, or gathering of 4 men, will be looked upon and treated as an unlawful assembly and dispersed by force of arms, *if necessary*.

This proclamation was read out only in a small portion of the town; and was heard by very few people, as the formidable procession of General Dyer scared away the inhabitants of the town. Even those who heard the proclamation could not understand its full significance, as its language was deliberately left vague. It appears that the General had learnt by the experience of the Deputy Commissioner, and did not believe in clear unequivocal warnings, which could have fulfilled the ostensible object at the expense of the underlying desire for revenge. On the 11th, the Deputy Commissioner had issued an unambiguous order, warning the people that after 2 p.m. they would be fired on; and the people had dispersed some time before the appointed hour. The General, however, did not want to take any risks on the 13th, and, therefore, he issued a misleading proclamation, which, while giving him a colourable excuse to shoot down the people, was not so definite and clear as to keep the people away from the Jallianwala Bagh. The natural meaning of the last part of the proclamation is, that any procession or gathering of four men in the public streets was to be dispersed by fire, if it was found *necessary* to take such an extreme step. The words "or gathering of 4 persons " seem to have been used in explanation of the word "procession"; and cannot be taken to apply to any collection of 4 men, who may find themselves together at any time or place and under any circumstances whatsoever. To say that the word "gathering" has no reference to the word "procession" would be to render the mere presence of 4 men at any place an unlawful assembly, even if it was a family gathering at the dinner table. No less vague and misleading were the words "if necessary". To a people living under a civilised and humane government, these words used in such a context could only mean that the authorities would resort to force, if the acts and nature of the assembly demanded it and if all other methods of dispersing it failed. The people did not know that the proclamation was a snare and was only a clever defence for the intended crime, every single detail of which had been worked out with extraordinary care. They could not believe from the misleading words of the proclamation, that the General would disperse a peaceful meeting by fire without warning. That these words were deliberately used to mislead the inhabitants of Amritsar is clear from the fact that out of the three proclamations or orders dealing with unlawful assemblies, the words *"if necessary"* are used only in the proclamation of the 13th. These words were not used in the order of the 11th, in which it was definitely stated that the crowd would be fired on after 2 p.m. On that day, the Deputy Commissioner expected a disobedience to his orders; and, therefore, did not disguise his intentions. Similarly, the words used by General Dyer in his Martial Law Order of 25th April were clear and definite. Paragraph 3 of the Order runs as follows:—

> "During the period of martial law, I prohibit all processions, meetings or other gatherings of more than 10 persons without my written authority, and any such meetings, gatherings or processions held in disobedience of this order will be broken up by force *without warning*."

Here, there is no attempt to disguise the intentions of the authorities by the use of vague and misleading expressions, because the General seriously wanted to prohibit meetings and processions. On the 13th, however, the General did not want the people to keep away from the meeting at the Jallianwala Bagh, because the thirst for vengeance had to be quenched in Indian blood. In the proclamation of the 13th itself, part second clearly states that persons who would be found outside their houses after 8 p.m. were "liable to be shot." The words are clear, because the General wanted the curfew hour to be strictly observed. Could not similar words have been used in the third, the fatal, part of the proclamation? The inference that the proclamation was never intended to stop the meeting at the Jallianwala Bagh is further strengthened by the fact that simultaneously or immediately after the General's proclamation, a boy was making an announcement in the streets of Amritsar, by beating an empty tin, that a meeting would be held at 4 p.m. at the Jallianwala Bagh. Unlike General Dyer's proclamation, this announcement was made in the whole of the town. No steps were taken by the authorities to stop this announcement, which must have occupied some hours. Nor were the people warned against acting upon what looked like an invitation to an innocent meeting. The first two parts of General Dyer's proclamation are also significant; and have a distinct connection with the Jallianwala massacre. The first part prohibits any one from leaving the town without a permit, which was intended to secure the attendance of the largest number of persons at the meeting of the evening. It may be noted that there was no similar restriction on persons entering Amritsar. The object of the curfew part of the proclamation was apparently to keep the dead and the wounded at the Bagh for at least one night. Had the curfew order a different object, it should have been withdrawn or modified for that night after the firing at the Bagh. It may be mentioned in this connection, that such orders were not issued at any other place, e g., at Gujranwala or Kasur, where equally grave riots had taken place and conditions similar to martial law prevailed. As already stated, this proclamation, of which the first two parts were calculated to make the intended massacre more extensive and brutal and the third part was deliberately misleading, was not read out in the greater portion of the town, nor were copies of it distributed among the people or posted at any public notice-board or any other place in the town. It has been stated before Lord Hunter's Enquiry Committee that as it was getting hot, the General returned to his headquarters at the Ram Bagh after about two hours' peregrinations in the city of "rebels." It would thus appear that the object of this proclamation was no more than to provide a plausible defence for the General, who had set up a death trap for the people of Amritsar. It is to be seen how far this clever defence avails him.

The meeting.

Hans Raj arrived early at the Jallianwala Bagh to make arrangements for the meeting, which consisted in putting up a wooden platform in the centre of the open space where the meeting was to be held. This was an important task, as he was to hide himself beneath this platform to keep out of the way of the bullets, which he knew or suspected would rain at the people in about a couple of hours. Soon after, the people began to assemble in large numbers. By those who were anxious to see a huge mass meeting at the Bagh, it had been falsely given out that the meeting was held under the auspices of the Chief Khalsa Diwan. Hans Raj had also announced, as mentioned above, that Lala Kanhiya Lal, an old and respected resident of Amritsar, was to preside at the meeting. The big Baisakhi Horse Fair, which is attended by thousands of villagers, was also closed at about 2 P.M. that day for no ostensible reason†, and these people could not easily leave Amritsar on account of the blockade which had been established by the General's order. It would thus appear, that every means was adopted to swell the

† "The large crowds of villagers which had assembled for the Baisakhi Horse Fair on the 10th did not as a whole take any part in the disorder" (Punjab Government Report).

number of the audience. The result was that about 25 thousand persons assembled at the Jallianwala Bagh. The audience included a large number of villagers, who had gone to Amritsar for the Baisakhi and were naturally anxious to see a meeting of the citizens. The Punjab Government admits in its Report that, "There were a considerable number of peasants present at the Jallianwala Bagh meeting of the 13th, but they were there for other than political reasons." There were also a large number of children and boys of tender years, who were playing about in the Bagh or were taken to the meeting by their unsuspecting relations. The people were unarmed and only a few had even sticks with them. It has been practically admitted by General Dyer in his evidence before Lord Hunter's Enquiry Committee that a large number of the persons, who had assembled at the Bagh, might have been ignorant of his proclamation.

The Massacre

Ever since General Dyer arrived at Amritsar, he was preparing his forces for the great hour of vengeance. He told Lord Hunter's Enquiry Committee that one of his first acts on taking over the administration of Amritsar was to reorganise the troops, reduce the strength of pickets and keep a strong "striking force" in reserve for a suitable opportunity. At about 12.15 P.M., General Dyer received definite information that the Jallianwala Bagh meeting was likely to be a grand success, as it had been advertised throughout the town without any interference. The General immediately set about organising his forces. In answer to Lord Hunter's awkward question, as to why he did not take measures to prevent the crowd from assembling, the General referred to his misleading and sham proclamation of the morning and replied, "I went there as soon as I could. I had to organise my forces, to think the matter out..... I had to organise my forces, I had to make up my mind what forces I was going to leave behind and where to post pickets..... If they were going to meet, I was going as fast as I could....." The General occupied four hours in the disposition of his forces and the pleasant occupation of making up his mind to shoot down the "rebels." At about 4 P.M., Mr. Rehill, the Superintendent of Police, went to the General and informed him that the meeting was an accomplished fact. The General was overjoyed at this announcement, and he tells the Committee, "My plans were complete *then* and I marched off towards the city soon after." The General took with him "every available man after providing for other things," and liesurely proceeded towards the Jallianwala Bagh at "ordinary walking pace." As the General had been telling the Committee that the meeting was convened and attended by rebels and was fraught with great danger, Lord Hunter naturally put to him the following question :— "You did not consider there was any necessity for proceeding with any extra expedition?" The General's reply is significant:— "No Sir. It was very hot. We went at usual pace of marching." Of course, the General could not admit that there was no need for hurry, as everything had already been pre-arranged and Hans Raj was sure to keep the intended victims on the spot till the General's army arrived to reap their harvest of blood. It may be mentioned here that about a quarter of an hour before the General reached the Bagh, aeroplanes had been sent on to reconnoitre the situation, and that this was presumably a prearranged signal for the police officials to leave the Bagh. It is significant that out of the thousands of persons who were killed or wounded at the Bagh, there was not one who belonged to the police or the Criminal Investigation Department. The General arrived at the Bagh with 40 Gurkhas armed with *kukris* (knives), 25 Sikhs and 25 Gurkhas, who were all armed with rifles. He had also two armoured cars with machine guns, which he was not destined to use on account of the narrowness of the entrance. The General reached the Bagh at about 5 or 5.15 P.M. and immediately occupied a strategic position, which does great credit to his military skill, and is a clear proof of the fact that every single detail had been thought out beforehand with a good deal of care. There must, however, be a few defects even in the most skillfully planned actions; and in the famous battle at the Jallianwala Bagh, the General had overlooked the fact that the lane, through which he had to lead his army against the "enemy," was not broad enough to admit the armoured cars. This certainly reduced the number of casualties that he succeeded in inflicting on the "enemy"; but the General with heroic patience put up with this hardship, and did not order the widening of the lane by pulling down or bombarding the adjoining houses. Both when the aeroplanes started hovering over the Bagh and when the General with his forces arrived, the people rose to leave the place; but Hans Raj, who was in possession of the meeting, kept them there by asking them not to be afraid and assuring them that the *sircar* would not fire on a peaceful meeting. When the soldiers fired their first shots, he told the running people to stay on the pretext that the shots were blank. The bravery with which the General fought the forces of the "rebels" can best be described in his own words, which he used in reply to the various inconvenient and impertinent questions of some of the inquisitive and ungrateful members of Lord Hunter's Enquiry Committee, who did not seem to appreciate the great and unique services rendered by him to the Empire :—

Lord Hunter :— I think you entered by the narrow entrance that leads into the Jallianwala Bagh?

General :— Yes.

Lord Hunter :— You had left your motor cars behind?

General :— Yes.

Lord Hunter :— Did you have the Gurkhas who were armed with kukris or they were left at the back?

General :— They had come into the Bagh.

Lord Hunter :— Then you had 40 Gurkhas and two columns of 25 men each, armed with rifles?

General :— Yes.

Lord Hunter :— You said you deployed 25 soldiers to the right and 25 to the left. *i.e.*, on the high ground on the north side of the rectangular space?

General :— Yes.

Lord Hunter :— That is a very convenient piece of land ?

General :— Very.

Lord Hunter :— There are very few entrances and exits?

General :—Yes. I think one wide, and there might have been 2 or 3 small exits.....

Lord Hunter :— When you got into the Bagh, what did you do?

General :— I opened fire.

Lord Hunter :— At once?

General :— Immediately. I had thought about the matter, and don't imagine it took me more than 30 seconds to make up my mind as to what my duty was.

Lord Hunter :— As regards the crowd, what was it doing?

General :— Well, they were holding a meeting. There was a man in the centre of the place on something raised. His arms were moving about. He was evidently addressing.

Lord Hunter :— So far as you knew was there anything occurring, except this man addressing?

General :— No, I could not see anything beyond that.

. . . .

Lord Hunter :— Before you dispersed the crowd, had the crowd taken any action at all?

General :— No Sir. They had run away, a few of them.

Lord Hunter :— Martial Law had not been proclaimed. Before you took that step, which was a serious step, did you not consider as to the propriety of consulting the Deputy Commissioner who was the civil authority responsible for the order of the city?

General :— There was not any Deputy Commissioner to consult at the time. I did not think it *wise* to ask anybody further.....

. . . .

Lord Hunter :— In firing, was it your object to disperse?

General :— No Sir. I was going to fire until they dispersed.

Lord Hunter :— Did the crowd at once start to disperse as soon as you fired?

General :— Immediately.

Lord Hunter :— Did you continue firing?

General :— Yes.

Lord Hunter :— After the crowd indicated it was going to disperse, why did you not stop?

General :— I thought it my duty to go on until it dispersed. If I fired a little, I should be wrong in firing at all.

Lord Hunter :— For what length of time did the firing go on?

General :— It might have been 10 minutes, it might have been less. I think it was probably less from the number of rounds that were fired.

Lord Hunter :— So far as you could see, had the crowd sticks in their hands?

General :— I could not say that they all had. I presume that a number had sticks.....

. . . .

Lord Hunter :— What reason had you to suppose that if you had ordered the assembly to leave the Bagh, they would not have done so without the necessity of your firing and continual firing for any length of time?

General :— *Yes, I think it quite possible that I could have dispersed them perhaps even without firing.*

Lord Hunter :— Why did you not have recourse to that?

General :— They would have all come back and laughed at me, and I should have made what I considered a fool of myself.

. . . .

Lord Hunter :— The crowd was very dense?

General :— Very dense.

Lord Hunter :— It was unlikely that a man shooting into the crowd would miss?

General :— No, except in certain circumstances. As they were running, a certain number of men were hit..... In the centre of the square the crowd was very dense. There as a man directed his fire, he should not miss.

. . . .

Lord Hunter :— As regards the removal of the wounded, were you in a position to render any aid?

General :— No Sir, not there. I should have given aid afterwards, if they asked for it. It was then not my duty to render aid. It was a medical question.

Lord Hunter :— Next day, you issued a proclamation with reference to the burying of the dead in these terms :— "The inhabitants may burn or bury their dead as they please. There must be no demonstrations of any kind."—That was the order?

General :— Yes, Sir.

* * * * * * * * * * *

Justice Rankin :— You thought it necessary to take action on the analogy of a state of war?

General :— Quite so. I looked upon these people who had rebelled as enemies of the Crown.

. . . .

Justice Rankin :— With reference to the proclamation that you took round prohibiting meetings, etc., what I am putting to you is that at this time the population of Amritsar presumably did not know much about martial law?

General :— No.

Justice Rankin :— They were entitled to, were they not, to some sort of definite warning from you to the effect that there had been no proclamation of martial law and that *de facto* martial law existed?

General :— I do not know whether I said this. I know I issued a proclamation, and I think everybody knew that martial law had taken the place of civil law to all intents and purposes, that I was in command and the military law was in force.

Justice Rankin :— You thought that going round with your troops and beating the drum would bring it home to them?

General :— I thought a number of people would know that I had taken over the law, that it had been handed over to me and that military law was in force.

. . . .

Justice Rankin :— On the march (to the Bagh) you came to the conclusion that if there was really a meeting the right thing was to open fire straightway?

General :— *Yes. I had made up my mind. I was only wondering when the actual time came I would fire or not.*

. . . .

Justice Rankin :— You commenced firing the moment you got your men in position?

General :— Yes.

Justice Rankin :— And the crowd began to go away and you continued firing?

General :— Yes.

Justice Rankin :— As a matter of fact, you continued firing until ammunition was running short?

General :— That is right.

Justice Rankin :— I also gather that the crowd was making for some of the entrances.

General :— Yes.

Justice Rankin :— I take it that towards these exits the crowd was rather thick than at other places?

General :— Yes.

Justice Rankin :— I gather from your statement that from time to time you checked your fire and directed it upon places where the crowd was thickest?

General :— Yes, that is so.

Justice Rankin :— And that for the reasons you explained, not because they were not going fast but because you had made up your mind to punish them for having assembled?

General :— It is quite right.

* * * * * * * * * * *

Sir C. L. Setalvad :— When you arrived there (the Bagh) you were not able to take the armoured cars in because the passage was too narrow?

General :— Yes.

Sir C. L. Setalvad :— Supposing the passage was sufficient to allow the armoured cars to go in, you would have opened fire with the machine-guns?

General :— I think the probability is, yes.

Sir C. L. Setalvad :— You did not open fire by the machine-guns by accident because they could not be got in?

General :— Yes. If they could be got in the probability would be that I would open fire with the machine-guns straight.

. . . .

Sir C. L. Setalvad :— Your idea was, as I put it to you, to strike terror?

General :— Call it what you like, I was going to punish them.

Sir C. L. Setalvad :— Producing sufficient moral effect not only on those persons but more specially throughout the Punjab—that was your view?

General :— I wanted to reduce the number of rebels.

Sir C. L. Setalvad :— You thought it would be a right thing in order to save the British *Raj*—That is what you thought?

General :— Yes. I was going to reduce the *morale of the enemy.* If they were going to fight me, they were rebels, and I was going to shoot them.

. . . .

Sir C. L. Setalvad :— Did it occur to you that you were really doing great disservice by driving discontent?

General :— No, I thought it was my duty to do it at the same time..... and any man, any reasonable being with a sense of justice, would see that I was doing a merciful act, and that they ought to be thankful to me for doing it.

Sir C. L. Setalvad :— But did this aspect of the matter strike you at all?

General :— Never. *I thought it would do a jolly lot of good to the people.*

. . . .

Sir C. L. Setalvad :— After firing, did you take any measures for the relief of the wounded?

General :— Do you mean immediately after ?

Sir C. L. Setalvad :— Yes.

General :— No, certainly not. It was not my duty. *It was not my job*. The hospitals were open. They could go there but they did not, because they thought they would be arrested.

* * * * * * * * * * *

Pt. J. Narain :— On the night of the 13th, you went inside the city to see if your curfew order was obeyed or not?

General :— That is so.

Pt. J. Narain :— And you found that your order was obeyed?

General :— That is quite correct.

Pt. J. Narain :— And you intended that that order of yours should be obeyed?

General :— If I gave an order, I intended that it should be obeyed.

The remorseless pride, the inhuman relish and the callous impudence, with which General Dyer recounted the story of his savage butchery at the Bagh, aggravates his crime; and the defiant cynicism, with which he described the details of his diabolical crime, is a clear proof of the fact that the massacre was not a thoughtless act of an over-zealous official, but was the outcome of the deliberate desire to teach the inhabitants of Amritsar a terrible lesson for having killed Europeans, and to create a widespread feeling of terror among the Indian population of the province. Every single detail of this cold and calculated massacre points to the fact that vengeance and frightfulness was the object, with which this crime was planned and carried out; and the General stands condemned out of his own mouth. The people were deliberately kept in ignorance of the fact that the town had been placed under martial law. The proclamation prohibiting meetings was not read in many parts of the town; and it is admitted that many of those present at the Bagh were not aware even of the existence of such a proclamation. No steps were taken to prevent the assembling of the people at the Bagh, though the meeting had been publicly announced twenty-four hours before it took place, and the General had four clear hours for that purpose. When the General was informed that the people had actually assembled, he started for the Bagh with machine guns and 90 soldiers. When he arrived at the Bagh, the people were peacefully listening to a lecture; there is not the slightest imputation that the speech was seditious or likely to incite the audience to violence. The General says that he had marched to the Bagh with the intention of shooting the people down, regardless of the fact that no violence was attempted or done by the crowd. That was why he had not brought any Civil Magistrate with him; nor did he consider it *wise* to consult any local official, because he did not want to run the risk of getting a negative advice. As soon as the General arrived, the people began to run away; but the General immediately opened fire. No warning of any kind was given to the people; nor were they ordered to disperse. The crowd was unarmed, and the General admits that he could have dispersed it without firing. But the demeanour of the crowd was irrelevant to the intentions of the General; and the massacre was not the result of anything that the people were actually doing at that moment. The crowd had begun to leave the meeting when they saw the General's forces enter the Bagh; and the movement towards the exits became general as soon as the firing began. The General did not stop the firing, but from time to time checked his fire and redirected it towards the exits where the crowd was the thickest. The people continued to run towards the two or three narrow exits, which were the only outlets from the Bagh; and the General continued to shoot, till at last the ammunition was exhausted. Many were shot down while attempting to scale the walls of the Bagh and jump over to the other side, while many others were wounded and died on account of suffocation caused by the heap of bodies under which they were buried. In all, one thousand six hundred and fifty rounds were fired; and according to the General's computation three or four persons could have been killed or wounded by each bullet, which were directed towards those points where the crowd was the thickest. According to the official estimate at least 500 persons were killed; and in order to calculate the number of the wounded, the General asks us to multiply this figure by three. The non-official inquiry has estimated the casualties at 1,000 killed and 3,000 wounded. The fact that out of a mass of about 25 thousand people only four thousand were killed or wounded does not reflect any discredit on the General or his soldiers. The General was the unfortunate victim of a serious miscalculation. He had intended to supplement the rifle fire with machine-guns; but they could not be got into the Bagh, and this item on the programme had to be omitted. After exhausting the ammunition, the General left the Bagh with his triumphant army, without giving a moment's thought to the thousands of persons, including many boys and children, who had been killed or, what was worse, were wounded in the massacre. The General refused to send for a doctor and attend to their injuries on the plea that it was not a "military" but a "medical" question. The General excuses his conduct in leaving thousands of persons, who were dead or were undergoing the agonies of death, to provide a feast for kites and vultures, because, according to this flower of the British Army, it was not his "job" to make ambulance arrangements for the treatment of the wounded or for the disposal of the bodies of those who had died, hundreds of whom were strangers to Amritsar and had been brought to that cursed town by an inexorable fate. Shylock also refused to call in a surgeon to stop the wounds which he was going to inflict on Antonio, because it was not so nominated in the bond. But it is quite possible that the Jew would have relented, after he had actually received his pound of flesh; but such was not the case with this gallant son of Mars. As if all this was not sufficient, the General went out at 9 o'clock in the night to satisfy himself that in obedience to his curfew order the people were all in their houses, and the dead and the dying were left unattended in the Bagh. Human ferocity could go no further.

The motive

In his frantic efforts to justify the savage butchery of his ghastly crime, the General has hit upon queer explanations. The General told Lord Hunter's Committee that all through the 12th and the 13th he was "constantly hearing rumours and messages" from the neighbourhood that the situation was growing more serious every moment. Both in his report, which, by the way, he wrote out "many months later," as well as in his statement before Lord Hunter's Committee, the General says that among the places where disorder had broken out and from where he had received messages, were Dhariwal, Gurdaspur, Tarn Taran, Kasur, Lahore and Hafizabad. The General's defence, therefore, is that the Jallianwala massacre was caused with a view to "make a wide impression throughout the Punjab". It is admitted by the General that this defence was put up by him many months later when he was writing his report, after the massacre had evoked a universal condemnation throughout the country. The very nature of the justification pleaded by the General shows that it was an after-thought. On the afternoon of April 13th, the General did not know that the Government of India would declare a state of "open rebellion" in several districts of the Punjab and would establish martial law; nor were there any indications on the 13th of the various outrages which followed. There was no rebellion till that date, and the question of preventing it did not arise. The six places from where the General says that he had received "rumours and messages" indicating a rapidly developing rebellion are not in the neighbourhood of Amritsar as stated by the General. All the places named by the General are situated at long distances from Amritsar. Dhariwal is situated at a distance of 35 miles, Gurdaspur 45 miles, Kasur 55 miles, Lahore 33 miles and Hafizabad about 140 miles from Amritsar. It is, therefore, not true to state that any of these places are in the neighbourhood of Amritsar. Of the six places mentioned by the General, there was no disorder or even a breach of the public peace at Dhariwal and Gurdaspur; nor was martial law proclaimed at these places. At Tarn Taran and Lahore there was no violence or disturbance by the people; and there was not the slightest injury to life and property at these places, which could have agitated General Dyer's mind. The riot at Hafizabad took place on the 14th and the mental balance of the General could not have been upset by the assault on Lieutenant Tatam, unless, of course, the General is also gifted with occasional glimpses into the future. Kasur was the only place where there was disorder on the 12th; and the regrettable murder of two British soldiers by the mob at Kasur might have heightened the General's hunger for vengeance. But we have been repeatedly told by the officials that in those days communications had been seriously interrupted, and it was almost impossible for them to communicate with each other. If that is a fact, it is not probable that the General would be aware, on the afternoon of the 13th, of the occurrence at Kasur which took place only about 24 hours earlier, especially because Kasur was not in the district of Amritsar and there was no official necessity of sending an urgent message to the General merely for his personal information. The mere inclusion of Hafizabad in the list of places from where the General claims to have received "rumours and messages" vitiates the whole statement, and undeniably proves that it is a later fabrication. Even if it were based on facts, the justification pleaded by the General in his defence is simply preposterous. The General was a mere usurper, who had assumed control of the town of Amritsar because of the actual or pretended weakness of the civil authorities. He had no business to rely on "rumours and messages," and shoot down the citizens of Amritsar, because there was disorder at places situated fifty miles away from it. If, as he desires, the Jallianwala massacre is to be judged by its effect, then also the General stands condemned. The thousands of persons, who were present at the Jallianwala Bagh, had come from all over the Punjab to Amritsar for the Baisakhi fair, and they carried the harrowing tale of the General's barbarity to the furthest corners of the province. There were strong rumours throughout the province that the Golden Temple had been bombarded and thousands of persons had been massacred at Amritsar. As has already been shown in the previous chapter, the Jallianwala massacre is responsible for many of the outrages committed after the 13th. In the second place, the General pleaded before Lord Hunter's Committee that he proceeded "on the analogy of a state of war" and "looked upon those people who had rebelled (the audience at the Jallianwala meeting) as enemies of the Crown". He further told the committee, "They were rebels and I must not treat them with gloves on. I was going to give them a lesson.......I wanted to reduce the number of the rebels..........I thought it would do a jolly lot of good to the people." If this is a true statement of the mental condition of the General, then he was labouring under a most lamentable hallucination, which can only be explained by the fact that his intellect was darkened and his conscience blinded by a mad desire for vengeance. Were the General a German officer and Amritsar a town in Belgium, his name would undoubtedly have found a prominent place in the list of the war-criminals. The General further tells the Committee that he felt that martial law had been flouted and that it was his duty to "immediately disperse by rifle fire". The General has admitted that his original intention was to use machine guns, that the people had not been informed of the existence of martial law, that they were not engaged in violence, that no warning was given to the crowd before he opened fire, that the firing was continued for about ten minutes after the crowd had begun to disperse, that the bullets were directed to places where the crowd was the thickest; and that his object was to "reduce the number of the rebels". Under these circumstances, even if it be admitted that martial law was not illegally brought into force at Amritsar, the General's action cannot be justified, because one of the elementary rules, if not the only safeguard, of martial law is that no more force should be used than is absolutely essential. There is a difference between martial law as it is known to the civilised world and sheer unmitigated butchery. Lastly, the General says that he could have dispersed the crowd without resorting to fire; but he did not do so, because the people would have laughed at him and he would have made a fool of himself. Now, after the massacre the General would certainly not be remembered as a fool but a murderer by history; nor need he be afraid of the mirth and laughter of the people. The thousands of widows and orphans, whose husbands and fathers met their tragic deaths at the Jallianwala Bagh without even a loving hand to close their dying eyes, will not know what it is to smile for many a long day. And if that was the object of General Dyer's he would indeed be the happiest man in the world.

Gujranwala District

Bombing from aeroplanes.

After indulging in the wanton acts of destruction described in the previous chapter the mob voluntarily dispersed at about 1.30 P.M., after which there was no further disorder at Gujranwala. But the District Magistrate had telephoned to Lahore for assistance; and a rumour had also reached the Lieutenant-Governor that his trusted lieutenant Col. O'Brien had been murdered by the Gujranwala mob. The result was that three aeroplanes were despatched from Lahore. The first aeroplane reached Gujranwala at 3.10 p.m.; and commenced its work ten minutes after its arrival. This aeroplane dropped 8 bombs and fired about 260 rounds from the machine-gun with which it was provided. Out of these, only 3 bombs were dropped at the town of Gujranwala and about 180 rounds were fired into the town; the remaining bombs and bullets were used on the neighbouring villages, where there was absolutely no distubance. Two of these bombs were dropped in close proximity to a mosque; and one bomb was dropped on the hostel of the Khalsa High School, which injured a student and some other inmates. The second aeroplane arrived at 3.25 p.m. and fired about 700 rounds from its machine-gun. The third aeroplane neither dropped bombs nor fired its machine-gun. There were in all about 40 casualties including 12 killed; and among those who were killed were at least one woman and child, and some boys. The fact that 8 bombs and about one thousands rounds of machine-gun fire were not able to do more damage clearly proves that the aeroplanes did not encounter any crowd and had no occasion to use their ammunition on large assemblies of men, otherwise there should have been more casualties to their credit. How far it is permissible to use aeroplanes and machine-guns to bomb and bombard unarmed citizens, who are not engaged in any act of violence, is a question which does not admit of two replies. If the dropping of bombs upon unarmed citizens in London by a belligerent power in time of actual warfare was a crime against humanity, still more reprehensible is the bombing of one's own subjects in times of peace. In this behalf, the following dialogue which occurred in the House of Commons on December 3rd, 1919, may be quoted:—

Lieut. Commander Kenworthy :— Asked the Secretary of State for India whether warning is given in time to allow the removal of women, children, and other non-combatants before bombing raids by aeroplane are carried out on frontier towns and villages?

The Secretary of State for India (Mr. Montagu):— Warning was given to the Wazirs amd Mahsuds, after they had rejected our terms, that they would be subjected to bombing from the air, after time had been allowed for the removal of women and children.

Lieut. Commander Kenworthy:—Is this the practice always followed in these operations?

Sir J. D. Rees:— And how long are the combatants likely to wait after this warning?

Mr. Montagu:— I think there is great objection to the use of aeroplanes for bombing women and children, and if the desired military results can be obtained without that, so much the better.

Lieut. Commander Kenworthy:— But have we always followed this humane practice?

Mr. Montagu:— So far as my memory serves me, since aeroplanes have been invented for bombing purposes this is the first time they have been used on the North West Frontier, and I am sure hon. Members will be glad it bas been found possible to give the warning.

No warning was, however, given to the inhabitants of Gujranwala and the neighbouring villages, before the aeroplanes commenced their operation; and when the people started to run to places of refuge they were shot down. Even the courtesy extended to frontier tribesmen was denied to peaceful British subjects. That the object of the bombing operations was not to disperse any crowd or prevent disorder is further proved by the fact that on the 15th of April also an aeroplane was sent down from Lahore which bombed a village outside the town.

The arrests.

In order further to terrorise the people of Gujranwala, Col. O'Brien on the morning of the 15th arrested no less than 22 respectable citizens of the town including several barristers and pleaders, admittedly without having any tangible evidence against any of them. Many of these gentlemen had rendered valuable help to the authorities on the previous day; but this was completely ignored, because they had participated in the agitation against the Rowlatt Act. These persons were arrested as they were found; and some of them, who were only half clad, were not allowed time even to put on the clothes. They were all handcuffed in pairs and chained together; in order to ridicule the Hindu-Mahommedan fraternisations of the 6th of April, the prisoners were so arranged that as far as possible each pair contained a Hindu and a Mahommedan. Accompanied by a large body of troops, all the prisoners were taken to the station and made to stand in the sun for some time. After about half-an-hour, a sort of procession was formed with the prisoners in the middle, the police and the military round about and an aeroplane hovering above. Thus the prisoners were marched at a rapid speed through the main streets of the town. In order to expedite the show and to further humiliate the prisoners, they were made to run at several places on the route. After about two hours the procession was taken back to the railway station, from where the prisoners were despatched in an open truck to Lahore.

Bombardment of villages.

Several hours after the mob at Chuharkana had dispersed after looting and burning the railway station, an armoured train with machine-guns, which had been despatched from Lahore, reached the station. After nightfall, the train was taken along the railway line and under instructions from Rai Sahib Lala Sri Ram Sud (Sub-divisional Officer at Shekhupura) some villages were bombarded without the slightest justification. The object was not to disperse any unlawful assembly, because there was none in existence. As the result of this indiscriminate bombardment, several persons were killed and wounded, whose exact number is not known. From Lala Sri Ram Sud's evidence before Lord Hunter's Committee no intelligent explanation of this wanton destruction of life and property can be gathered, except that the bombardment was intended to strike terror among the villagers.

2—MARTIAL LAW

Proclamation of Martial Law

The period of martial law.

Martial law was established in the districts of Amritsar and Lahore on the 15th April, in the district of Gujranwala on the 16th April, in the district of Gujrat on the 19th April and in the district of Lyallpur on the 24th April. Martial law was withdrawn from certain portions of these districts by orders, dated the 28th May and 9th June; and was completely removed from all parts of these districts on the 25th August. Martial law was withdrawn from the district of Gujrat on May 28th. The town of Lahore remained under martial law till the midnight of the 11th June; and the towns of Amritsar, Kasur, Gujranwala. Wazirabad, Akalgarh, Ramnagar, Hafizabad, Sangla, Chuharkana and Lyallpur remained under martial law till midnight of the 9th June. All railway lands situated in all these five districts remained subject to martial law till the 25th August.

Applicability of Martial Law.

No Government, unless it chooses to abdicate its power and renounce its duties, can afford to allow rebellion and disorder to appear or continue unchecked for any length of time. It is the paramount duty of every Government to maintain law and order; and the Government which does not employ all means in its power to suppress disorder fails in one of its primary duties. It is, therefore, a universally accepted doctrine of constitutional law and practice that if there is a foreign invasion, or rebellion, cr riots or insurrection amounting to rebellion, and the stability of the Government is theatened and the civil law proves powerless to cope with disorder, it is the clear duty of Government to suspend the civil law and establish martial law to restore peace and order. Martial law, which is really the negation of law, is, therefore, an extreme step which the Government should take only when all other means of restoring order fail; and as soon as disorder has been suppressed, martial law should cease. Just as when there is grave and imminent danger to life or property, an individual is entitled to ignore the ordinary provisions of law and do acts which would otherwise be criminal offences, in the same way, a Government may, when its very existence is threatened, resort to acts which would not be covered by the ordinary law of the land. But in both cases, the danger must be grave and imminent, and must be a real one; the justification for ignoring or superseding the ordinary rules of law ceases with the danger which gave rise to it; and the ordinary rules of law should not be violated to a greater extent or, in other words, no more force should be used, than is absolutely necessary. It must, further, be proved in justification of the individual or the State, as the case may be, that the use of legal force had failed to meet the exigencies of the situation; and that the safety of the individual or the State could not be ensured and maintained under the ordinary law. Martial law, in other words, is the exercise of illegal force by Government to suppress rebellion or disorder amounting to rebellion, in case the power vested in the Government by ordinary law is found to be insufficient for that purpose. In India, only the Governor-General in Council is empowered to establish martial law in times of war or rebellion.

Place of martial law in Indian polity.

Martial law can be established in India under the Bengal State Offences Regulation (X of 1804), which contains the following provision:—

"The Governor-General in Council is hereby declared to be empowered to suspend, or to direct any public authority or officer to order the suspension of, wholly or partially, the functions of the ordinary Criminal Courts of Judicature, within any zillah, district, city, or other place, within any part of the British territories subject to the government of Presidency of Fort William, and to establish martial law therein, for any period of time *while* the British Government in India shall be engaged in war with any native or other power, as well as *during* the existence of open rebellion against the authority of the Government, in any part of the territories aforesaid; and also to direct the immediate trial, by courts martial, of all persons owing allegience to the British Government, either in the consequence of their having been born, or of being residents within its territories and under its protection, who shall be taken in arms in open hostility to the British Government, or in the act of

> opposing by force of arms the authority of the same, or in the actual commission of any overt act of rebellion against the State, or in the act of openly aiding and abetting the enemies of the British Government within any part of the said territories."

It would thus appear that martial law can be established in any part of British India *while* the Government is at war with any native or other power or "*during* the existence of open rebellion against the authority of the Government," which means that as soon as the war ceases or the "open rebellion" is suppressed, martial law is *ipso facto* withdrawn. It was under this Regulation that martial law was proclaimed in the Punjab; and, therefore, it is by reference to the provisions of this Regulation that the legality and propriety of the proclamation of martial law and its continuation for more than four months is to be judged. The Governor-General might, perhaps, have been perfectly within his powers to have proclaimed martial law by an Ordinance under section 72 of the Government of India Act; but this was not what he did. The ordinance-making power of the Governor-General was requisitioned only for the purpose of providing for the constitution of Commissions for the trial of persons who had committed certain offences within a certain period, and for the mode of such trials; but the proclamation of martial law itself was under the Regulation quoted above, which is the authority cited by the Government of India in the Orders by which martial law was declared.* In order, therefore, to judge of the legality and propriety of the proclamation of martial law and its continued operation in the Punjab, we must confine our attention to the Regulation and see whether its requirements have been fulfilled.

Justification for the delaration of martial law.

As stated above, martial law can be established in India only under the Bengal State Offences Regulation, *during* the existence of open rebellion. It is, therefore, necessary under the provisions of the Regulation that "a state of open rebellion against the authority of Government" should exist

---

* For text of Orders declaring martial law, see Appendix I, pages 209-212.

not only when martial law is proclaimed but also that the rebellion should continue to exist during the whole of the period of martial law. The Regulation empowers the Governor-General in Council to "establish," which means to proclaim and continue, martial law only during the period of the rebellion. In other words, the Government of India has no authority under the Regulation to establish martial law for any period of time, during the whole or any part of which the rebellion does not exist. It is, therefore, incumbent on the Government to prove not merely that there was disorder in certain parts of the Punjab on certain dates, but also that the disorder amounted to "open rebellion against the authority of the Government," which existed on the date when martial law was proclaimed and lasted during the whole of the period for which martial law was established. Therefore, the question whether the disorder or riots in the Punjab ever amounted to "open rebellion" is not strictly relevant to the question whether martial law was properly established. We have to see whether "open rebellion" existed in the different areas in which martial law was proclaimed on the dates when martial was proclaimed, and whether the rebellion lasted right up to the 25th August. It is admitted in the Punjab Government Report that "actual disturbance was over" and everything was quiet, as General Dyer puts it, when martial law was proclaimed in the district of Amritsar. In the district of Lahore there was no disturbance or disorder. At Gujranwala, the disturbance was over before the proclamation of martial law. In Lyallpur, the public peace was never disturbed; and it is admitted in the Official Report that, "disturbances had actually *ceased* when the proclamation was made, and the presence of the moveable column had secured the district from any serious apprehension of the recrudescence of disorder." In other words, there was neither disorder nor even an apprehension of disorder, when martial law was proclaimed in this district. The Superintendent of Police of Lyallpur has admitted before Lord Hunter's Committee that it was not absolutely necessary to establish martial law in his district. At Gujrat there was never a serious disorder and the Punjab Government admits that "all active disturbance had ceased, when martial law was declared by Government on the evening of the 19th." The Deputy Commissioner of Gujrat was taken aback with surprise when he was informed of the order declaring martial law in his district. He refused to believe such a thing; and actually wired to the local Government to ascertain if there was not a mistake, and if it was not the Gujrat in Bombay, where martial law was meant to be proclaimed. The following is the telegram which the Deputy Commissioner, Mr. H. S. Williamson sent to the Government on April 20th :—

> "Surprised to be informed by Government that martial law has been extended to Gujrat. This district is quiet. General, Brigade Jhelum, has received no orders and agrees with me that martial law is not necessary."

On receipt of the reply that the Deputy Commissioner should obey the order, he proclaimed martial law. But only a few days later, he recommended to the Lieutenant-Governor that martial law be withdrawn from his district. We have already seen that the disorder, such as it was, never amounted to "open rebellion"; but whatever its nature or extent, it had ceased in each district before the proclamation of martial law.

Continuation of martial law.

If the declaration of martial law against unarmed civilian population at a time when there was no disorder, much less an "open rebellion," was unjustifiable, much more so was the continued operation of martial law for more than sixteen weeks. Sir Michael O'Dwyer in his proclamation of the 26th April admits that disorder had been suppressed but pleads that it was necessary to continue martial law to bring offenders to justice. Other official declarations also seek to justify the continuance of martial law on that ground. But that was a hollow excuse and is not supported by constitutional law or practice. Martial law may be used to suppress disorder; but not to punish those who took part in it, after order has been restored. All the constitutional lawyers and the highest legal authorities are agreed on this point. To quote only one, Chief Justice Cockburn, in the course of one of his most famous judgements observes:

> "If it be true that you can apply martial law for the purpose of suppressing rebellion, it is equally certain that you cannot bring men to trial for treason under martial law after a rebellion has been suppressed. It is well established according to the admission of every body, even of those who go the farthest in upholding martial law, that the only justification of it is founded on the assumption of an absolute necessity–a necessity paramount to all law, and which lest the commonwealth perishes, authorises this arbitrary and despotic mode of proceeding, but it never has been said or thought, except perhaps by King Henry VII, that martial law could be resorted to when all the evils of rebellion have passed away, and order and tranquillity had been restored, for the mere purpose of trying to punish persons whom there was no longer any sufficient cause for withdrawing from the ordinary tribunals and the ordinary law."

Apart from the illegality of the continuation of martial law merely for the purpose of withdrawing the criminals from the ordinary courts of justice, it is not clear how the continued operation of martial law could have facilitated the trials. The crawling order, the curfew order, the *salaming* order, the public floggings, the regulation of prices, the wholesale persecution of students, and the various other atrocities which were perpetrated under the cloak of martial law cannot by any stretch of imagination be held to have had any effect on the trial of the criminals, unless the object of all these measures was to terrorise the whole population and thereby facilitate the manufacture of false evidence against the accused. The object, or at any rate the effect, of the continued operation of martial law for more than four months after the last act of violence was committed was to humiliate and terrorise the people, to bring home to their minds the might of the Government by subjecting them to grave hardship and suffering and to impress upon them the terrible results of touching a European in India. It is not possible to explain the continuation of martial law for such a long period on any other basis. The reason for the continuance of martial law could not be the suppression of disorder, for no disorder existed; nor could it be the speedy trial of offenders, as the trials continued under the Martial Law (Trials Continuance) Ordinance (No. VI of 1919) even after martial law had been withdrawn. Could not this or a similar Ordinance have been issued a week after the declaration of martial law?

The Afghan campaign.

The Afghan campaign is put forward as another argument for the cotinuation of martial law in the Punjab. But the Government has admitted that order had been completely restored, and martial law had been in operation for several days when the war was declared. It is further admitted that the Indians had no sympathy with the Amir and there was no likelihood of their aiding the enemy. Sir Hamilton Grant, in the course of his speech at the Afghan Peace Conference, said:

> "Of the motives that prompted the Amir and his advisers I need not speak. Suffice it to say, that they had made two serious mistakes in their calculations. In the first place, they expected that the Hindus and Moslems of Northern India, already, *so they had been told,* in open mutiny, to rise with one accord to welcome an Afghan invasion. In the second place they expected a complete rebellion by all our tribes along the frontier. In both they were disappointed. Such local disorders, serious though they were, as had taken place in India had already been quelled. The vastly preponderating loyalty of India had reasserted itself. From the start it was clear that nothing could be more abominable in the eyes of both Hindu and Moslem than the prospect of an Afghan inroad. Indeed the Amir's action was from the outset condemned by all classes throughout India."

Under these circumstances, the Afghan campaign cannot be held to be an excuse for the prolongation of martial law in districts situated at a distance of hundreds of miles from the actual scene of warfare. In fact, the Afghan campaign had the effect of rallying the people to the side of Government and offers of men and money reached the Government from all parts of the Punjab. Even General Dyer admitted in his evidence before Lord Hunter's Enquiry Committee, that ten thousand Sikhs offered their services to him for the Afghan war.

Other Reasons.

The largest number of official witnesses before Lord Hunter's Committee have sought to justify the continued operation of martial law on the ground that the people were "sullen." Pressed further as to what they meant by the word sullen, the witnesses gave the highly illuminating reply that the people were "truculent." Did the Government officials expect the people to be dancing with joy over the measures adopted by Government to suppress an imaginary rising? Was it expected that the people would be jubilant over the massacre at the Jallianwala Bagh, the public floggings, the crawling, the bombing from aeroplanes, the bombardments by machine-guns, and the arrests, deportations, trials and convictions of innocent persons? These measures might, perhaps, have rendered the European population happy; but the Indians could not have been expected to share their felicity. Another argument urged in favour of the continuation of martial law after order had been completely restored is that it did not cause any harm to anybody. General Dyer is the chief exponent of this remarkable piece of reasoning. This is what he said before Lord Hunter's Enquiry Committee:

Lord Hunter:—I see, in your report you say that the city assumed normal conditions (after the evening of the 13th April)?

General:—Yes Sir. There was absolutely no crime.

Lord Hunter:—If that is so, was it necessary that martial law should be proclaimed on the 15th.

General:—It was; martial law had been in existence before it was proclaimed. As they were getting better, I relaxed the conditions.

Lord Hunter:—Martial Law had *de facto* been in existence from your arrival?

General:—Absolutely, Sir. It had the same effect.

. . . .

Sir C.L. Setalvad:—"After the 13th the city was the pattern of law and order,"—that applies to a period subsequent to the disturbances?

General:—Yes.

Sir C.L. Setalvad:—Can you tell us what the need of continuing martial law was over the period it was in fact continued?

General:—No harm would be done. It was very justly administered, and if I overlooked in any way to take it off when it was necessary it was not my job. When they told me it was to be off, it was off.

Sir C.L. Setalvad:—It was continued because no harm was done and it was justly administered?

General:—Yes.

Sir C.L. Setalvad:—But there was no particular necessity of continuing it?

> *General:*—Law and order had come back. It got better and better. There was a period when martial law was not necessary, but it did not continue for all too long. That is all.

No comment is necessary on this argument. Its absurdity is too obvious to require a demonstration. But all the same, it reveals the mentality of the men who were at the helm of affairs during the martial law regime. They were content to continue the hardships and sufferings of the people for any length of time, merely because the martial law was, in their opinion, justly administered. Disregard of the constitutional rights and liberties of His Majesty's Indian subjects and the contempt for the ordinary law of the land could not reach a higher limit.

Retrospective operation of martial law.

The fact that martial law was given a retrospective effect and acts done on or after the 30th of March were brought under the purview of martial law Commissions, is a clear proof of the fact that the object of the Government in declaring and continuing martial law was not to suppress disorder but to punish the "agitators". No act of violence was committed in the Punjab between the 30th of March and the 10th of April, still the Martial Law (Further Extension) Ordinance (No. IV of 1919) extended the jurisdiction of the Commissions to try persons accused of having committed any offence during this period, in order that the leaders of public opinion in the Punjab, who had carried on a peaceful and constitutional agitation against the Rowlatt Act, might be dealt with under martial law. Most of these leaders were, therefore, sentenced to long terms of imprisonment by the Commissions, and Sir Michael O'Dwyer succeeded in making short work of the hated "agitators". But the nemesis was not far behind. The Government had to release them after an incarceration of not even as many weeks as the number of years to which they were sentenced.

The position of Civil Authority.

As has already been stated, the civil power was never overpowered or rendered incapable of performing its duties. All that martial law accomplished was a change of names and methods, and the shifting of responsibility from the civil to the military authorities. A military officer was placed in charge of each district, who carried on his campaign of oppression on the advice and instigation of the chief civil officer stationed there, who in his turn took his cue from Sir Michael O'Dwyer. Deputy Commissioners and other Magistrates became Area Officers; civil judges were appointed to the martial law Commissions; the legal remembrancer to the Punjab Government became the Convening Authority; and the police carried on its work as before, with this difference that when any person was to be arrested or any house to be searched, the warrant, if any, was signed by the military officer and a couple of soldiers in uniform accompanied the police on such errands. Rumour goes so far, that in certain instances blank warrants, signed by the commanding officers, were made available to the police officials, in order to minimise delay. The indefatigable C.I.D. was also, if possible, more active than in normal times, and had really a roaring time under martial law.

The Double Government.

Martial law is proclaimed when the civil authority is paralysed; and ordinarily the civil government must cease with the declaration of martial law. But in the Punjab the civil power never lost control of the situation; and the declaration of martial law did not in fact substitute military rule for the civil administration of the five districts which were placed under martial law. In spite of the fact that martial law was in force, the civil officers continued to exercise authority independently of the military, which was not only an anomaly but an illegality. The establishment of martial law could only mean that the ordinary law of the land was suspended and the administration of the areas affected was handed over to the military. In other words, the declaration of martial law should have divested the Commissioner, the Deputy Commissioner, the Tahsildar, the Magistrate and all other civil officers of their authority; and as long as martial law was in operation they could not legally exercise any authority which they did not derive under martial law by order of the military commander. The Civil Magistrates, as such, had no power to exercise their usual jurisdiction as long as martial law was in force; and all convictions and sentences of their courts as well as all the proceedings of other Civil Courts were illegal and *ultra vires*. It cannot be pleaded that martial law was only partially introduced and restricted to the trial of only certain cases arising out of the disorders, because as a matter of fact the operation of martial law was not synonymous with the mere trial of certain persons for certain offences. The administrators of martial law assumed the complete control of the areas placed under their jurisdiction. They created new courts and promulgated new laws, violations of which were punished under martial law. They commandeered the properties of the inhabitants, regulated the prices, governed the police, controlled the movements of the people, interned and imprisoned persons, and otherwise exercised complete dominion over the proclaimed areas. But side by side with the military government, which was not subject to any restrictions, the executive and judicial civil officers also continued their usual work, because in point of fact the civil power had never been paralysed. Thus there was a double government, which was obviously illegal.

Punjab's solitary position.

The dreaded prospect of a revolution may justify resort to martial law, as might an insurrection or riot amounting to rebellion; but it has been laid down by all constitutional lawyers that no more force should be used in the suppression of disorder than is necessary, and that martial law should cease *ipso facto* on the restoration of order. This principle was strictly followed at Viramgaum and Ahmedabad where there had been more serious riots than at Amritsar, Kasur or Gujranwala. The Government of Bombay did not think it necessary to employ the methods followed in the Punjab in those places. Nor did the Chief Commissioner of Delhi declare martial law, in spite of the fact that the so-called disorder at Delhi was more serious than the riots at Lahore, Gujrat or Lyallpur. The Punjab Government was, therefore, naturally uneasy at its solitary position and made frantic efforts to have martial law introduced at other places. Sir Michael O'Dwyer discovered that a state of "open rebellion" existed in the neighbouring province and naively recommended that martial law should be proclaimed in the Imperial City; but the Chief Commissioner of Delhi, in spite of the fact that he had been for some years the Chief Secretary to the Punjab Government, refused to come to the rescue of his late chief and questioned the truth of the discovery. This cruel refusal to believe in the sovereign virtues of martial law irritated the Punjab Government; and inspired articles appeared in the *Civil and Military Gazette,* condemning the weakness of the Government of India in not forcing martial law upon the Delhi Government. In its leading article of the 2nd April, entitled "A Government that Governs," this journal, after praising Sir Michael O'Dwyer's strong administration, declared :

> "We know what the danger was from which we have been saved by the drastic action of the Punjab Government. We should have more confidence in the outlook if Government of India showed more of the spirit of Sir Michael O'Dwyer and could ensure equally firm and resolute action being taken by other local administrations whose handling of the situation is at present anything but firm."

Three days later, the same paper wrote another leading article entitled "The Weak Spot" in which it accused the Delhi authorities of refusing "to arm themselves with adequate powers." The following are the closing words of the article :

> "In Delhi itself the position continues uncertain. Optimistically worded reports speak of the city as quiet and normal, but it is obvious to the meanest intelligence that the authorities are very far from having the situation completely under control. Delhi was the scene of the first outbreak of violence, and the disorderly elements which were responsible for that outbreak obviously stand in need of a much sterner lesson than has yet been administered to them. Delhi stood alone in India in witnessing the extraordinary spectacle of the authorities parleying with the leaders of the agitation, while a threatening and turbulent mob gathered round the very building where the conference was going on. Such a course of procedure would argue dangerous weakness even in the case of a purely local disturbance, but where

the disturbance has assumed the proportions of a widespread and organised conspiracy against the peace and order of the State, such weakness in the administration becomes criminal folly. Knowing the composition of the Delhi administration, we cannot for a moment believe that the policy which it is pursuing is one of its own seeking. The inference is obvious that its hands are tied by instructions from higher authority. It is time that the Government of India realised that it cannot meet a danger like the present with half measures. It has acknowledged the need for drastic measures in the Punjab, and it cannot in reason or justice expect Delhi to save itself by half-hearted palliatives instead. The danger to be met in Delhi is precisely similar in origin and nature to that which is being met and overcome in the Punjab. Delhi is still to all intents and purposes a part of the Punjab, and the influence it exerts over the adjoining districts is very great, and the failure to vindicate the authority of the Government in the capital is bound to react most prejudicially on the state of affairs in our own province."

But these attempts failed to produce the intended effect, and the Government of India, as well as the Chief Commissioner of Delhi, persisted in their "criminal folly" of not administering the "sterner lesson" to the people of Delhi. For once, Lord Chelmsford refused to be deluded by the sophistries of Sir Michael O'Dwyer, because His Excellency had correct information about the situation at Delhi. In the passage quoted above, the semi-official organ of the Punjab Government, to carry its point, has admitted the undeniable truth that the situation at Delhi was "precisely similar in origin and nature to that... in the Punjab." From this it follows, that if martial law was not necessary in Delhi, it was equally unnecessary in the Punjab, and that its proclamation in the latter was entirely due to the man who was unfortunately at the head of its administration.

Responsibility for proclamation of martial law.

The various communications sent by Sir Michael O'Dwyer to the Government of India, on the basis of which martial law was declared in the various districts, have not been made public, except the following message, which the Hon'ble Sir William Vincent read out to the Imperial Legislative Council in the course of his final speech on the motion for leave to introduce the Indemnity Bill:—

"Railway stations between Kasur and Amritsar looted, British soldier killed. Two British officers injured at Kasur. Bands of rebels reported on the move. Kasur treasury attacked; state of open rebellion exists in parts of the districts of Lahore and Amritsar. Lieutenant-Governor with the concurrence of the General Officer Commanding the 16th Division and Chief Justice of the High Court requests the Governor-General in Council to direct him to suspend the functions of the ordinary criminal courts in Amritsar and Lahore districts and establish martial law therein and direct the trial of offenders under section 2 of Regulation X of 1804. Situation critical. Moveable column starts marching from Ferozpur to Amritsar through worst tract with guns tomorrow."

The Government of India received this message on the 13th April by wireless; and it was probably on the basis of this communication that the Governor-General in Council sanctioned martial law for the districts of Lahore and Amritsar. There can be no doubt that the statements contained in this message are a gross exaggeration of actual facts. There are no less than fourteen railway stations between Amritsar and Kasur; out of which no station was burnt or looted except Bhagtanwala which is a part of Amritsar and was attacked by a portion of the rioters on the 10th April. The attack on the Kasur treasury was repulsed by a few shots from the police, after which the mob dispersed and the police made several arrests without any resistance by the mob. The imaginary "band of rebels" were neither stationary nor "on the move"; and no evidence has been produced by the Government either before Lord Hunter's Enquiry Committee or before the Commissions of the existence or movements of these bands. The statement that part of the districts of Lahore and Amritsar were in a state of "open rebellion" is a mere assertion which, as we have already seen, is not supported by actual facts. The march of the moveable column with guns might have had a salutary effect on the people; but it does not prove the existence of a "state of open rebellion." Though the statements contained in this message were incorrect, the Government was bound to act upon them and cannot be blamed for having sanctioned the declaration of martial law on the recommendation of the Punjab Government conveyed in such terms. Sir William Vincent is right in saying that no "officer would have dared to take the responsibility of not accepting a recommendation of that character." It was, however, the clear duty of the Government of India, after they had declared martial law, to examine the facts for themselves and decide whether the martial law should be continued or not. The Viceroy, instead of having an unbounded faith in Sir Michael O'Dwyer, might have gone to the Punjab to see things for himself and obtain a direct knowledge of the rebellion that was said to be in existence in that province. It is not known as to what, if any, measures were adopted by the Government of India to have first-hand information of the state of affairs in the Punjab. But, in any case, the Government of India have not alleged that they were misled by the Punjab Government; and it must, therefore, be concluded that Lord Chelmsford shares with Sir Michael O'Dwyer the responsibility for continuing martial law in the Punjab for such a long time after the disorder, such as it was, had been completely suppressed.

Administration of Martial Law

Flogging.

Among the horrors, sufferings and indignities to which the people were subjected under the martial law, public flogging was perhaps the most sickening. In order to realise the barbarity of this inhuman form of punishment one has to witness it, as thousands of persons did during the martial law days. The victim was stripped bare of his clothes in the public gaze and was tied to the triangle. Then the man, who had to administer the lashes, came running from a distance and dealt the blow with all the force he could command. After the first or the second stroke, the unfortunate victim burst forth into loud shrieks of agony. Bleading started on the second or the third stripe; but the required number of lashes had to be completed. The man who had to do the flogging was required to put forth every ounce of his energy in the blows which he administered, so that after two or three runs he was exhausted and took rest, which were moments of indescribable torture to the bleeding victim. If the prisoner was a small boy or had a weak constitution, he collapsed; and the bleeding, the pain, and the dread of the coming lashes rendered him unconscious. But the remainder of the torture could not be inflicted, while the victim was not able to feel the anguish and the humiliation of the operation; and he was revived by sprinkling cold water on his face or pouring it into his mouth. In some cases, the prisoner became unconscious and was revived more than once before the flogging was completed. After the required number of strokes had been administered, the victim, who was by that time profusely bleeding, was taken down from the triangle and dragged to the jail, if he had also to undergo a term of imprisonment, or was given over to his relatives or friends. In almost all cases, the unfortunate victim of this atrocious treatment was not able to walk; and if he was a stranger to the place, he was left at the spot where he was lashed with nobody to look after him, until, perhaps, after some hours, some person out of charity secretly gave him food and succour. The wounds which resulted from this inhuman punishment took several days to heal; and in many cases the doctors, out of fear of the military authorities, refused to treat them. In almost every case the wounds left permanent scars on the body of the man who was subjected to this terrible punishment. Flogging was administered for the most trivial faults and the minor breaches of martial law orders. If a man failed to salute a European to the latter's satisfaction, or if he was found in a public street during the prohibited hours, or if he was suspected of selling milk or vegetables at higher rates, or if he otherwise incurred the displeasure of a military officer or soldier, he was summarily senteced to be whipped. The public exhibitions of this Russian form of punishment became so dreadful, that many persons offered to pay heavy fines or be imprisoned, rather than be subjected to the cruel punishment of whipping; but their offers were rejected with disdain by the Area Officers, who sentenced them. At first, everywhere floggings took place in the public streets; but, later on, when there was a great outcry all over the country against this barbarous practice, the triangles were transferred to semi-public places. Lashing people in the public streets is a barbarity which is a remnant of the middle ages and was considered to have passed away with the Russian autocracy; but General Dyer, in his statement before Lord Hunter's Enquiry Committee, is not ashamed to admire it as an efficient and deterrent form of punishment. This is what he says:—

Justice Rankin:—You said that whipping is the ordinary punishment under martial law?

General:—Yes, under martial law.

Justice Rankin:—I gather that was adopted in Amritsar?

General:—Yes.

Justice Rankin:—What is the authority for saying that because martial law was instituted in the city the ordinary punishment for minor offences is the sentence of whipping?

General:—It is the custom, I presume.

Justice Rankin:—In the Indian Army whipping continues as a recognised punishment?

General:—It has practically disapppeared. Martial law wants speedy punishment and that is why whipping came in under martial law.

Justice Rankin:—What else can be said for it as a punishment for the Civilian who has broken a martial law proclamation or committed a minor offence, except that it is a speedier punishment?

General:—I think that is about the greatest advantage. You have not to have a large number of officers and courts. A Provost-Marshal is appointed, he gives the order and all is over.

Justice Rankin:—On the other hand, there is this disadvantage that it is a humiliating punishment?

General:—Yes, it is humiliating.

Justice Rankin:—You do not believe that it was inflicted in fact upon people of respectable classes.

General:—I do not think I have said that.

Justice Rankin:—As far as you are concerned, there ought to be no discrimination?

General:—If they are guilty under martial law, they ought to be punished.

Justice Rankin:—Under martial law there were a great many proclamations issued every other day. It might easily be that a respectable person would commit an offence against these proclamations?

General:—They should not do things which would bring them under martial law.

In reply to the questions put by Lord Hunter, the General supported public floggings, and said that they were calculated to "make a good impression" on the "rebels". In the opinion of Col. Frank Johnson, flogging was the "kindliest method of punishment," and was necessary to "terrorise" the people. He preferred flogging to imprisonment, because "the jail is an extraordinarily comfortable place." Such being the views of the military officers who were charged with the duty of administering martial law, it was but natural that more than a thousand persons were subjected to the degrading punishment of flogging, the majority of whom were lashed in public. At a public exhibition of flogging at Kasur, Captain Doveton summoned the prostitutes of that town to witness the ghastly sight. The lawyers of Amritsar were also made to witness the flogging of two persons at the Ram Bagh. The administrators of martial law made such a lavish use of the barbarous and inhuman punishment of whipping, that the people were sickened with loathing and horror; and if that was the motive of the gallant gentlemen to whom the onerous task of suppressing the imaginary rebellion was entrusted, it must be admitted that they were eminently successful.

Crawling.

Miss Sherwood was assaulted and beaten by a portion of the Amritsar mob on the 10th April, five days before the declaration of martial law. There can be no doubt that this shameful act deserved the greatest censure and its perpetrators ought to have been awarded exemplary punishment. Eight persons were tried for this assault by the martial law Commission presided over by Mr. Justice Leslie Jones, all of whom were convicted of waging war against the King and sentenced to death and forefeiture of property, except one who was only sentenced to transportation for life and forfeiture on account of his being a mere boy. But these persons could not be convicted before the 31st May, as some sort of an investigation, trial and other needless formalities had to be gone through. General Dyer could not wait for such a long time; nor could he expect the whole town to be convicted and sentenced by even the martial law Commissions. He, therefore, decided to take his own measures according to martial law. He searched his brain for a suitable punishment, as he told Lord Hunter's Committee; or as General Hudson puts it, he wanted to do something to strike the imagination of the people. After about one week's labours, the General's brain brought forth the crawling order, which he had not even the time to reduce to writing, as in his case there was no interval between thought and action. But to the question whether he could remember the language of the order, the General gave the following reply to Lord Hunter's Committee:—"As far as I remember, I merely said that this street must be blocked at both ends; that no Indian must be allowed to go through; and that if he did go through, he must go through on all fours. That 'all fours' by some means which I cannot explain was interpreted into crawling. My order said 'on all fours'." Whether the General wanted the people to go on all fours or to crawl through the street, which is about 150 yards in length, is a matter for mere academic discussion; but the fact remains that the soldiers interpreted the order as directing them to make the people crawl through the whole length of the street. It is also significant that this order was never promulgated; but was at once brought into operation without any previous notice to the inhabitants of Amritsar. The order remained in force from the 19th to the 25th April; and during this week pickets of British soldiers were posted at both ends of the street from 6 am. to 8 pm., which was the curfew hour. All persons who lived in the crawling street, or had to pass it, were made to crawl after the manner of worms and reptiles. There were no exceptions. Even a blind man had to go through the operation. The old and the young, the rich and the poor, the thin and the fat all had to submit to this atrocious order. If by any chance, the unfortunate victim of General Dyer's idea of the sacredness of woman's person lifted his knees or back and raised himself 'on all fours' to avoid the dirt or rubbish which was lying about in the lane, which was not in this respect different from other Indian streets, he was struck down to the ground with the rifle butts of the soldiers and made to continue the crawling. It is needless to say that the people who lived in the street, which is a very thickly populated part of the town, were put to the greatest hardship which in case of several of them amounted to the most cruel torture. Apart from the indescribable humiliation and mental anguish to which they were put, their houses remained uncleaned and unscavenged for full one week, because the sweeper could not crawl with his broom and basket of filth; and their families had to starve for want of provisions. The persons, who were suffering from any disease, remained without medical aid, as the doctors would not crawl to their patients. It is not difficult to imagine the sufferings and hardships of the residents of the crawling lane; and no normal person would try to minimise them. But the General gave a further proof of the depravity of his mind by denying that his order could have caused any appreciable inconvenience to anybody. This is what he says: "I do not think it caused very great inconvenience. If they had suffered a little, it would be no harm under martial law." To the question whether the assailants of Miss Sherwood lived in the crawling lane, the General replied, "No. But I had erected a platform there in the middle of the street and thought, when I got these men who had beaten her, I would lash them down. I meant to lash them." As already mentioned, the crawling order remained in force for one week, during which, according to official testimony, fifty persons were made to crawl. This number includes a batch of persons, who were subjected to this operation by the police and the military for not properly *salaming* General Dyer. This is how the General describes the occurrence:—"Those who were impertient and were arrested by me were by some *accident* sent back to that street where my pickets were. My sergeant said, 'You crawl, that is the order.' And they had to crawl." Another batch of prisoners was also brought by the police to the street by *accident* and made to crawl, because, as the General puts it, his sergeant said, "The order is to crawl, you crawl." The actual number of persons who had to crawl through the street is much more than fifty, which includes only those who were taken to the place in custody for that purpose. General Dyer further told Lord Hunter's Committee that the order was withdrawn by him not of his own accord but under instructions from the higher authorities. In his defence he pleads that after lashing down the persons accused of the assault on Miss Sherwood in the crawling lane, he should have revoked the order, but he forgot to do so for no less than four days till he received orders from his superiors. The same story is to be found in the books of history about Siraj-ud-Daula who is said to have forgotten all about his prisoners in the Black Hole of Calcutta, until he woke up to realise the full enormity of his crime. Verily, great minds behave alike. The whole history of the administration of martial law in the Punjab may be summed up in the crawling order. The barbarity, the vindictiveness, the utter disregard of the liberty, the feelings and the self respect of the people, and the absence of all discrimination between the guilty and the innocent in the attempt to terrorise and humiliate the whole Indian population of the affected area—;are all present in the crawling order and the manner in which it was worked.

The students.

The students of the Schools and Colleges in the Punjab are just like the students in any other country; and have always been considered to be well-behaved and law-abiding. During the war, they did much useful work to help the Government. Hundreds of students of the Lahore Colleges toured through villages, lecturing upon the blessings of the British Raj, collecting war loans, contradicting false rumours and trying to obtain recruits for the army. A large number of the university students joined the Indian Defence Force; and raised from among theselves a Signal Company for service in the war, which did splendid work in Mesopotamia and elsewhere.

The Education Commissioner acknowledges the useful work of the students in his report on Indian Education for 1917-18 in the following words:—

> "Punjab colleges and schools also invested six lakhs in the war loan and subscribed a lakh and a half for objects connected with the war. In addition, they obtained by their efforts other recruits and subscriptions."

But all these services were forgotten, because a few students joined in the demonstrations against the Rowlatt Act and absented themselves from their lectures on one or two days during the *hartal*. This impulsive behaviour of a very small minority of the students was treated as it ought to have been treated by most of the principals; and no serious notice was taken of it. The administrators of martial law, however, detected sedition and rebellion in the conduct of the students and decided to give them a stern lesson. Thousands of the students of Lahore colleges were forced to attend roll-calls before the military officers four times a day for three weeks immediately before their examinations. The students of certain colleges had to walk no less than 16 miles every day for this purpose, which, according to Col. Johnson, had the effect of keeping them "physically fit." In order to ensure that every student walked these long distances in the burning sun, their bicycles were commandeered under martial law. This slow torture went on until Col. Johnson succeeded in coercing the principals of the various colleges into punishing a large number of their students. The principals who did not readily obey the orders of the Colonel by punishing an adequate number of students were threatened with the closing down of their colleges under martial law. In this manner, more than a thousand of the college students were awarded heavy punishments, which included expulsion from the University, rustication for a number of years, disqualification to appear in the approaching examinations, heavy fines and securities for good behaviour. It is needless to say that these students were not punished on any evidence or adequate inquiry but were simply picked out to make up the required number. The colonel was not contented with this *tour de force;* but extended his activities to the professors as well. He convicted and sentenced the principal of the Dyal Singh College to three months' imprisonment or a fine of Rs. 250, because an objectionable poem was said to have been exhibited on some part of the college buildings and the staff was not able to discover its author. The principal was not released, till the fine was paid up. After some days the fine was refunded, because the required number of students of the college had been punished and it was ascertained that the poem was posted on the walls of the building by an agent of the police. About 500 students and professors of the Sanatana Dharam College were arrested and interned in the Fort, because a martial law notice exhibited on the outer walls of the college hostel was torn or disfigured by an unknown person. This is how the incident is described by Col. Johnson before Lord Hunter's Enquiry Committee:—

Sir C.L. Setalvad:—The notice stuck on the outer walls of this college was torn down by someone?

Col. Johnson:—That was the information laid before me, not by the police, but by somebody.

Q.—Is it true that all the students of the hostel of the college were arrested?

A.—I ordered that every male found on the premises should be arrested.

Q.—How many were arrested?

A.—Five hundred.

Q.—Five hundred students were arrested for this notice being damaged?

A.—And the professors too.

Q.—All of them so arrested were marched to the Fort which is three miles away from the College?

A.—Quite.

Q.—And during this march, they were ordered to carry their beddings on their shoulders or on their heads?

A.—If they wanted to carry their beddings, they could.

. . . .

Q.—On a Lahore summer day?

A.—It was a May day.

Q.—It was very hot in Lahore?

A.—Yes.

Q.—All these 500 students and professors were marched a distance of three miles?

A.—Quite.

Q.—And they were kept under orders in the Fort?

A.—Yes, that is so.

Q.—How long were they kept there?

A.—I think one day. I beg your pardon, two days.

. . . . . .

Q.—Your frame of mind, then, colonel, was as you indicated in your report, that you were waiting for an opportunity to bring home to them the power of Martial Law?

A.—That is so.

Q.—You were longing for such an opportunity?

A.—Only in the interets of the people themselves.

Q.—I do not suggest that it was not in their interest. It may or may not be, but you were longing for an opportunity to show the might of Martial Law?

A.—Quite.

Q.—You got that opportunity?

A.—And I took it.

Q.—And you took it and marched these 500 students to the Fort in the hot sun?

A.—That is so.

Q.—And you still maintain, that was a proper exercise of your authority?

A.—Absolutely, *I will do it again tomorrow*, if circumstances require.

While Col. Johnson was having a busy time with the students of Lahore, it should not be imagined that the martial law administrators of other areas were idle. Col. Macrae of Kasur went much further. He collected the boys of the two local schools; and selected three from each, who appeared to him to be the strongest and the healthiest of the whole lot. These six boys were then whipped in public, in order that the other students might be inspired with a proper awe of authority. It is not alleged that these boys had committed any offence. Mr. Marsden, the Sub-Divisional Officer at Kasur, admitted before Lord Hunter's Enquiry Committee that "there was no particular object" in lashing these boys. At various places, the school boys, including children, had to attend three or four times a day to salute the Union Jack; and Mr. Bosworth Smith made an improvement on this practice in the area under his control. He also made the boys repeat the following formula:— "Sir we have committed no crime, nor shall we do anything wrong in future. I repent, I repent, I repent." Many of these boys were of tender years and suffered a good deal from walking long distances in the hot sun for their attendances; and several of them fell ill. It is also stated that some died as the result of these roll-calls. It is needless to point out that the campaign against students, which was so relentlessly carried on at almost all the places, was the most unfortunate feature of the administration of martial law, as it was calculated to create bitterness in the flexible minds of the younger generation. The saddest mistake which a government can commit is to implant the seed of resentment and anti-government feeling in the minds of the future citizens of the country over which it governs.

Arrests under martial law.

The police had a very busy time during the martial law regime; and it may be safely said that so many persons were arrested during the first month of martial law as have not been arrested in any single year in normal times. The people were arrested in their thousands without any substantial evidence against them; and in almost all cases investigation, such as it was, followed and not preceded these arrests. The arrests were made on charges ranging from a breach of a martial law order to murder or the waging of war, or on no charge whatever. In certain places, the arrests were made in such a promiscuous manner that no man considered himself safe. The faintest suspicion of having taken part at a Rowlatt Act meeting, or of having promoted the *hartal*, or of being present on any occasion when the police fired on the mob, was held a sufficient justification for an immediate arrest and detention for an indefinite period pending inquiry. In order further to terrorise the people, the persons arrested were put to the utmost humiliation and hardship. No spectacle was more distressing, or more shameful for the people as well as the Government, than to see men of light and leading, pleaders, barristers, bankers, wealthy merchants and other respectable and law-abiding citizens, being handcuffed and paraded in the public streets and made the object of vindictive ridicule by misguided officials, for having organised or suspected to have organised the *hartals* and public meetings against the Rowlatt Act. The number of prisoners was so great that they could not be accommodated in the jails and temporary arrangements were made to lodge them. At Kasur a huge "prisoners' cage" was erected and at Amritsar a temporary shed was constructed in the Fort. The more educated and high-placed was the prisoner, the greater were the indignities that were heaped on him. The educated persons were kept in solitary cells and subjected to the greatest hardship; and the accommodation being utterly inadequate, all the prisoners were lodged in complete disregard of the requirements of sanitation. It is alleged that the prisoners who were kept in the Amritsar Fort were made to run and skip in their chains to provide fun for the European women, who were staying there under orders of the officer commanding. Justice demands that no person should be deemed guilty without a full and fair trial. It, therefore, follows that no one should be punished or made to suffer any hardship or the least avoidable inconvenience, much less wanton indignities and humiliations, until an offence is legally proved against him. But under martial law there was no difference between convicted and under-trial prisoners.

Investigation.

During the martial law days at least ten thousand persons were arrested, out of whom about three thousand were placed on their trial on charges ranging from failing to salute a European to murder and conspiracy to wage war; and the rest were released after longer or shorter periods of detention without any trial or their even being informed of the charges against them. It was impossible for the police to properly and honestly investigate these thousands of cases during a few weeks' time. It was, therefore, natural for the police to replace inquiry by torture and honest investigation by corrupt practices. Evidence of a convincing kind has been placed before the public which conclusively proves that the most cruel and shameless methods of torture were used by the police to obtain confessions and evidence. In some instances, this torture took the most indecent and brutal forms. Cases have been brought to light in which it is publicly alleged that responsible police officials at Amritsar drove sticks into the vaginas and anus of persons to make them confess. In one case, it is alleged that urine was forced into the mouth of a man, when all other means of compelling him to make a false statement had failed. In view of the fact that the martial law courts were prepared to convict the accused on the flimsiest evidence, these barbarous practices of the police strengthen the conclusion that the persons who were arrested and tried were perfectly innocent. In some cases, the flying columns beat the villagers to extort confessions or obtain evidence. At least one such case has been admitted by the Punjab Government, as would appear from the following passage in the Official Report:—

> "On this date (18th April) the flying column visited Narwar and Jallo. Local infomation asserted that the persons who had burnt Wagha Station came mainly from the former village, and as the village headman and others refused to produce any evidence as to the persons culpable, the officer in charge of the column ordered three headmen and four others to be beaten by a cavalry sowar. The zaildar, two headmen and five others were subsequently arrested. The column then returned to Lahore."

In other words, seven men were beaten, and eight were arrested and removed from the village, because evidence of the identity of certain unknown offenders was not forthcoming. It must, however, be stated that the complaints of torture are mainly confined to the police of Amritsar and Gujranwala; and the former seems to be the greater sinner in this respect. No allegations of torture have been publicly made against the police forces in the districts of Lahore, Gujrat and Lyallpur, and particularly the conduct of the Lahore police has remained free from all reproach in this matter. No illegal means were adopted by the police officers at Lahore to secure evidence; and the investigations into the martial law cases were carried on just as they would have been under normal conditions.

Bribery.

The tone of the Indian police has undoubtedly improved in recent years; but there are still a large number of men in the police, whose honesty is not above reproach. Even in normal times, such men do not lose an opportunity to extort money from their unfortunate victims. But in the weeks that followed the riots, when the reign of law was abrogated and martial law stalked abroad claiming its victims by thousands, and the police was given a free hand to arrest and prosecute thousands of persons on the thinnest evidence, if any, the lower police officials grew bold and squeezed out as much money as they could from the persons against whom they could get up a suspicion of having taken part in the agitation or the riots that followed it. The reign of terror to which the declaration of martial law gave birth was their life's opportunity, and the corrupt officials of the police naturally made the most of it. The Amritsar police was again the greatest sinner in this respect; and the charges publicly made against some of the police officials are so serious and definite that the inactivity of the Government in this matter is nothing short of a scandal. It is true that the administrators of martial law were anxious to suppress corruption, but at a time when the whole population was terror-stricken and the police diaries were treated as holy scriptures by the officials, the people were naturally averse to make complaints against the police. Now that normal conditions have returned, it is the clear duty of the Government to sift the allegations that have been publicly made against the rectitude of the police. In this matter, again it must be acknowledged that the police at Lahore has on the whole remained clean, though several persons were arrested without sufficient cause and released without a trial after long terms of detention in the Fort or the jail.

Constitution and Procedure of the Commissions.

Under the provisions of the Martial Law Ordinance (No. 1 of 1919) Sir Michael O'Dwyer appointed four Commissions to try persons under martial law. These Commissions were invested with the powers of a general court-martial under the Indian Army Act, 1911; and there was no appeal from their findings or sentences. There was no necessity to establish these Commissions, as the High Court and all the ordinary criminal courts were open and working as usual. Originally the jurisdiction of the Commissions was restricted to the trial of persons who were actually taken in arms in open hostility to the Government or were arrested in an overt act of rebellion as specified in the Bengal State Offences Regulation; but this did not suit Sir Michael O'Dwyer, who wanted to send the whole gang of "agitators" to jail through the instrumentality of these Commissions. The Governor-General was, therefore, persuaded to issue another Ordinance called the Martial Law (Further Extension) Ordinance (No. IV of 1919) by virtue of which the Commissions were authorised to try all persons accused of any offence whatever committed on or after the 30th March 1919. This enabled the local Government to try by court-martial persons who had not taken an actual part in the disorders and whose only fault was their participation in the agitation against the Rowlatt Act at a time when there was no disturbance and nobody anticipated the subsequent happenings. While the Ordinance No. IV had given retrospective jurisdiction to the Commissions, the Martial Law (Trials Continuance) Ordinance (No. VI of 1919) kept alive the jurisdiction of the Commissions even after the withdrawal of martial law; and provided for the continuance of the trials though martial law was no longer in force. The Martial Law Ordinance (No. 1 of 1919) also authorised the Commissions to adopt a summary procedure in certain cases, in which, in the opinion of the convening authority, a summary trial was necessary in the interests of public safety. Though this provision was only permissive in its character, and in spite of the fact that the proceedings were conducted *in camera* and were not allowed to be reported in every case without a single exception the Commissions held summary trials to the prejudice of the accused; even Khuda Bakhsh, a Sub-Inspector of Police, who was accused of extortion was summarily tried in the interests of public safety. The truth of the matter is that the Commissioners did not want to have a full and faithful record of the proceedings, nor did they like to give more time to a case than could be helped. Whenever the counsel for the accused requested the Commission to take down any part of the statement of a witness, which it was thought would be of help to the accused, the invariable reply was that the record was merely for the information of the Commissioners and the statement in question would not serve any useful purpose.

The Trials.

In all, 114 cases were dealt with by the Commissions, and the number of persons tried by them was 852, of whom 581 were convicted. Of the persons convicted 108 were sentenced to death and forfeiture of property, and 265 to transportation for life with forfeiture. In every case, the Commissions took judicial notice of the fact that a state of open rebellion existed in the districts where martial law had been proclaimed, because the executive Government had declared that it was so; and on that assumption they convicted persons, who were alleged to have taken part in minor riots, or in cutting a telegraph wire or removing a piece of railway line, or to have thrown a brickbat at a police officer, of waging war against the King, and sentenced them to death or transportation for life with forfeiture of property. The executive officers of the Government, on the other hand, argue that the existence of a state of open rebellion is proved, because the Commissions have come to that conclusion. Thus the argument proceeds in a vicious circle, and nobody is any the wiser for it. Because the existence of rebellion was unjustly presumed by the Commissions without any proof whatever, they convicted persons charged with the most minor offences of waging war; and the heartless and tyrannical sentences passed by these Commissions are sought to be justified on the ground that the rigours of the Penal Code have been complied with. If the only excuse of inflicting life sentences on hundreds of persons, who were accused of assaulting a European or breaking the window pane of a railway carriage, is that this is the least punishment prescribed by the Penal Code, then the sooner the law is amended the better it is for all concerned. The Commissioners had a fixed idea in their minds that all acts were to be interpreted by them as waging war against the King; but this process of the Procrustes bed was not the only harmful feature of these Commisions. The accused, who found themselves arraigned in these tribunals, had very little chance of an acquittal. The presumption was always against the accused; and the defence evidence was in most cases dismissed with the curt remark that it was "worthless." In a word, these Commissions were the twentieth century incarnations of the courts of the Inquisition or the Star Chamber, with whose proceedings they had a marked affinity. The trials were to all intents and purposes held *in camera,* the accused were not allowed to be represented by counsel of their own choice, the judges were free to record as much or as little of the evidence as they desired, the witnesses cited for the defence were summoned or refused at the pleasure of the court or the convening authority, the counsel and witnesses who had the misfortune to appear for the accused were severely rebuked whenever they happened to say anything unpleasant to the court; in short, a speedy conviction was their watchword and terror their effect. At a time when the whole population was demoralised and terror-stricken, it was easy for the police to fabricate false evidence and extremely difficult, if not impossible, for the accused to get witnesses to tell the truth in their defence. But even in these circumstances, whenever the accused was able to produce valuable evidence in his favour the equanimity of the judges was sure to be disturbed. They either took the witness to task while his statement was being recorded, or tried to discredit him in their judgement. For instance, in the Lahore Leaders' Case several respectable witnesses proved that the *hartal* would have broken up even without the declaration of martial law, and that the accused and others were doing their best to have the shops reopened, a fact which was prejudicial to the prosecution. Several respectable witnesses had also deposed to the loyalty of the accused and gave evidence to prove their desire to prevent disorder. This enraged the Commissioners, and after accusing many of them of perjury, they indulged in the following remarks which had no relevance to the case against the accused:—

> "Mr Shafi and the *reis* class generally are, no doubt, prominent professionally or socially and a number of them are, of course, members of the Legislative Councils. It does not, however, follow that they are persons of influence in Lahore. On the contrary, there is ample evidence of a convincing kind that the people of the city regard them as time-servers and title-hunters and dislike them accordingly. It is clear, too, that other politicians look upon them as men who can be led though they cannot lead. Thus in his speech of the 4th of February, as reported in the *Tribune* of the 7th, a passage which provoked loud and prolonged applause, Gokal Chand did not hesitate to tell even Mr. Shafi and Sir Zulfikar Ali Khan that if they supported the Rowlatt Bills they would be regarded as enemies of their country and India would know the reason why. We do not propose to discuss Mr. Shafi's reasons for voting against the Bill, but we should not be surprised, if threats of this kind were not wholly without the effect intended and it may well be that such orders to toe the line had something to say to the complete unanimity on which Mr. Shafi dilated in his speech in Council."

The recording of full evidence was, of course, a useless burdening of the file as there was to be no appeal; but even the writing of a full judgement or analysing the evidence produced on both sides was deemed a waste of so much valuable time of the august Commissioners, in which they could have brought the light of their legal knowledge and high attainments to bear on the numerous other dark episodes of the rebellion. Speed being the essence of the justice administered under martial law, in some cases the Commissioners proceeded to pronounce orders even without waiting for the answers to interrogatories issued to witnesses cited for the defence. For instance, in the Gujranwala leaders' case, Lala Jagan Nath, who pleaded *alibi*, was convicted and sentenced by the Commissioners before they had received replies to the interrogatories that they had issued, which on their receipt clearly proved from the records of a State in Khatiawar that the accused could not be present at

Gujranwala when he was alleged to have entered into a criminal conspiracy with the other co-accused. Isolated acts of injustice there must always be, even in the best regulated society; but under martial law oppressive sentences and unjust convictions were the order of the day.

Summary Courts.

In addition to the four Commissions, the General Officers Commanding and Sir Micheal O'Dwyer had set up a large number of drumhead courts-martial, whose constitution was perfectly illegal, as the provisions of neither the Indian Army Act nor the martial law ordinances had been fulfilled. These courts-martial consisted of single military officers or civil magistrates; and a network of these courts was spread all over the martial law districts. These courts-martial tried no less than 1437 men, out of whom 1179 were convicted. The maximum sentence which these courts could award was 2 years' imprisonment or Rs. 1,000 fine or 30 stripes; and in a large number of cases all these punishments were combined and a cumulative sentence was passed against the person accused. The offences tried by these courts were mostly minor breaches of the martial law regulations of the General Officers Commanding or the orders of the martial law administrators of the different areas. But a large number of offences against the Penal Code were also tried by these courts. In several cases the accused were sentenced to severe sentences of flogging or fine on such flimsy charges as "showing disrespect to a European," "failing to *salam* a European Officer," "act to the prejudice of good order," "discourtesy to a European," and so on. These courts made the most lavish use of whipping and did not pay the least regard to the principles of justice or humanity. A big marriage party, consisting of about 30 persons, was arrested while the marriage ceremony was being performed, and placed on its trial before a court-martial at Lahore on the charge of constituting an unlawful assembly. The court promptly convicted the accused, including the bridegroom and the priest, and sentenced them to fine and whipping. This was not the only case in which the members of a marriage party were tried and convicted. Like the Commissions speed was the primary consideration with these courts; and the accused were put up for trial before them in large batches, in some cases of more than a hundred and were summarily disposed of at a single sitting. These courts perpetrated such glaring abortions of justice, that in some cases they passed even the bounds of decency; and compared to many of them the Commissions were palladiums of justice. In several cases, the courts refused to record the evidence of the defence witnesses who were present at the trial; and as a rule the accused were not represented by counsel, as their presence at the trials was met by a burst of indignation from several of the officers who constituted these courts. In several instances, the witnesses who gave evidence for the defence were harassed and prosecuted by the police on one pretext or another; and in some cases the courts did not even record the evidence or the judgement but only pronounced the sentence. Any serious attempt by the accused to defend himself was in several cases treated as an aggravation of the alleged offence, and at least one officer, Mr. Bosworth Smith, managed to extort confessions from a very large number of persons tried by him. In this matter it must be admitted that both the conduct and the sentences of the military officers, who presided at some of these courts-martial, were not so brutal as those of several of the civil magistrates; but even in the case of those military officers who wanted to be just there must have been unconscious miscarriage of justice, as most of them were not accustomed to weigh evidence or try judicial cases. As a rule, the object of most of the officers appointed to these courts was not to administer justice but to overawe and humiliate the people. To quote only one instance, Captain Doveton of Kasur had passed a general order that persons convicted by him should put their foreheads on the ground and make a deep obeisance to him before departing from the holy precincts of the sacred temple of justice of which he was the presiding deity. The nearest approach to the justice administered by these courts-martial is to be found in the stories that we read about the rough and ready methods of dealing out justice adopted by Tamerlane and Changes Khan, without the caprices of generosity which marked the latter.

Exclusion of lawyers.

It has always been the proud boast of British justice that every facility is afforded to the accused to establish his innocence; and English judges have always treated the counsel appearing for the defence with courtesy and fairness. This principle is so firmly rooted in the British system of judicial administration, that even in times of the greatest national crises it has been scrupulously followed. For instance, Viscount Reading, the Lord Chief Justice of England, made the following remarks during the trial of Roger Casement:—

> "There are some persons who, perhaps a little thoughtlessly, are inclined to rebel against the notion that a member of the English bar, or members of it, should be found to defend a prisoner on a charge of treason against the British State. I need not tell you I am sure, gentlemen, that if any one has those thoughts in his mind he has but a poor conception of the high obligation and responsibility of the bar of England. It is the proud privilege of the bar of England that it is ready to come into Court and to defend a person accused, however grave the charge may be. In this case, speaking for my learned brothers and myself, we are indebted to counsel for the defence for the assistance they have given us in the trial of this case; and I have no doubt you must feel equally indebted. It is a great benefit in the trial of a case, more particularly of this importance, that you should feel as we feel, that everything possible that could be urged on behalf of the defence has been said in this case after much thought, much study, much deliberation....."*

In India things are different. On account of the combination of the executive and judicial services, the courts have not the proper respect for forms of law which they should have; and as often as not, the lower judiciary treats lawyers as an inevitable nuisance. It was, therefore, natural that the unmitigated despotism of martial law should have revealed the judiciary in its true colours. The conditions of trials held under martial law were highly prejudicial to

---

* Trial of Sir Roger Casement," edited by G. H. Knott, (Butterworth & Co. pp. 178-179).

the person accused, who was generally considered to be guilty unless he proved himself to be innocent. The judges were prejudiced, the witnesses were terror-stricken, the police was corrupt and, to crown all, the accused were deprived of adequate legal help. The general demoralisation was so complete that counsel were not be had for love or money. Many prominent members of the bar were in hourly peril of arrest, because they had been participating in the public movements of the province; while those who had no such fear were afraid of incurring the displeasure of the authorities by defending persons who were alleged to have waged war against the King. Under these circumstances, the persons, who could afford it retained eminent advocates of other provinces for their defence. Mr. Kalinath Roy, editor of the *Tribune,* retained Mr. Eardly Norton, the well-known advocate of the Calcutta High Court, who promptly communicated with the Commission, which was convened for Mr. Roy's case, and requested the trial to be adjourned for his convenience. The Commission acceeded to this request, and postponed the case for a few days. In the meantime, the accused in the Lahore Leaders' Case also retained several leading lawyers of other provinces including some European barristers. The authorities did not want to take any avoidable risks in these trials; and on the day when the Commission was convened for the trial of the Lahore Leaders, the General Officers Commanding issued orders* prohibiting the entry of legal practitioners of other provinces into the martial law areas. The Punjab Government stated that this prohibition was due to the apprehension that the outside lawyers would revive the agitation and disturb the tranquillity of the districts in rebellion. Major-General Beynon, who issued the orders, denies the statement. He told Lord Hunter's Enquiry Committee that that was not the object. According to him, he issued the order because there was no military necessity for allowing lawyers of other provinces to enter the martial

* For text of the Order, see Appendix I, page 285.

law area. There is no doubt that the prohibition was illegal. Section 4 of the Martial Law Ordinance (No. 1 of 1919) laid down that the Commissions were to follow in all matters the procedure prescribed by or under the Indian Army Act, 1911. The Rules framed under this Act definitely recognise the right of the person accused to be defended by counsel of his own choice. Rule 22 of the Indian Army Act provides that "an accused person for whose trial a court-martial has been ordered shall be afforded proper opportunity of preparing his defence, and shall be allowed free communication with his witnesses, and with *any* friend or legal adviser whom he may wish to consult." Rule 81 goes further and provides that "at any general or district court-martial, an accused person may have a person to assist him during the trial, whether a legal adviser or any other person". Rule 87, further, provides that "neither the prosecutor nor the accused has any right to object to any counsel if properly qualified"; and according to this Rule, "counsel shall be deemed properly qualified if he is a legal practitioner authorised to practise with right of audience in a court of Sessions in British India." In the face of these Rules, the illegality of the order of prohibition is obvious. The plea that the order was issued to prevent the ingress of persons who might have created an agitation is falsified by the statement of Major-General Beynon before Lord Hunter's Committee, and seems to be only a clumsy after-thought. At a time when meetings were prohibited, the newspapers were pre-censored, the whole population was terror sticken, when even more than two men could not walk abreast in the public streets, it is inconceivable that any agitation against the Government could have been started in the province. The fact that some European barristers were also prohibited from entering the martial law areas gives the direct lie to these apprehensions. The real object of the ban on outside lawyers was to conceal the ugly practices of the martial law authorities from the prying eyes of outsiders; and to deprive the accused of the opportunity of putting up an efficient defence. This view is strengthened by the fact that similar restrictions were imposed as between the different martial law districts. A large number of the prominent lawyers of Lyallpur having been arrested, the martial law administrator of that district had prohibited the admission into his district of lawyers belonging to any other district of the Punjab. Thus there was another sanctum within the sanctum; and a Vakil of the Lahore High Court was actually arrested and convicted for appearing in a Lyallpur Court in complete ignorance of this order.

Special Features.

Never in the history of our connection with England has the fact of our being a subject race been so offensively brought home to us, as in the terrible months of martial law. The German atrocities against Belgium were surpassed both in their ingenuity and ferocity by the cruel wrongs inflicted on the people of the Punjab by the administrators of martial law. At *Amritsar,* people were arrested and flogged for not properly *salaming* the Europeans, and were collected in batches and taught the intricacies of the military salute; indiscriminate arrests, public whippings and the torture and bribery by the police went on unchecked from week to week; and no less than ninety-three lawyers were enrolled as special constables, in spite of the fact that ample police and military forces were available, and those pleaders and barristers were insulted, ill-treated and made to work like coolies, presumably to humiliate them and prevent their taking up martial law cases. At *Lahore,* Lieut. Col. Frank Johnson reigned supreme; and took full advantage of the training he had picked up during his administration of martial law in Bechuanaland. Public whippings were held for the edification and moral improvement of the people; the Badshahi Mosque was closed up; the motor cars, bicycles, tongas, carriages and electric lights and fans belonging to Indians were commandeered in their thousands and given over to Europeans for use to teach the people a lesson; a marriage party was treated as an unlawful assembly and flogged; more than two Indians were prohibited to walk abreast "on any constructed or clearly defined pavement or side-walk" as this was considered likely to ruffle the feelings of the European pedestrians and lead to a breach of the peace by them. It was made illegal for any Indian "to carry or be found in possession of an instrument known as a *lathi* (stick)"; the traders and shop-keepers were punished for having observed the *hartals* by being forced to sell their goods at prices fixed by the colonel; and thousands of students were harassed and punished for no known offence, as already described. The administration of martial law was most intensive at Lahore; and more than 60 martial law orders were promulgated which restricted the liberties of the people in every conceivable way. On the night when martial law was going to be withdrawn, a Magistrate went to the houses of all persons where copies of these orders were exhibited and insisted on their being burnt in his presence, without leaving any trace behind, as if the Government was ashamed of them. *Kasur* was in the hands of Captain Doveton, who possessed the gift of imagination in a remarkable degree. He ordered the looting and burning of the property of persons who were absent when the arresting parties went to their houses; the whole male population of the town was made to attend at the Railway Station on more than one day for purposes of a so-called identification parade; certain railway clerks were tortured to give false evidence; six school boys were publicly flogged, admittedly for no fault of theirs; and all persons convicted by the Captain were made to lie down on the ground in front of him and rub their foreheads at his feet. These and other orders, which were similar to those issued at other places, made the people Captain Doveton's "willing slaves", as he puts it in his report. Captain Doveton made full use of the proposition that "Martial Law is the will of the military commander;" and in the plentitude of his power, ordered people to mark time, climb ladders, dance with fools-caps on, rub their noses on the ground, skip for varying periods of time without a break, and so on. Respectable citizens were made to perform these antics by way of military punishments, as even the summary procedure of martial law was irksome to this imaginative officer; and to quote Mr. Marsden, the Sub-Divisional Officer at Kasur, he "did not like to go through the formalities of trial and sentence." In addition to the fancy punishments mentioned above, the captain ordered certain *Sadhus* to be white-washed. He also, by way of punishment, made a person write a poem in praise of the great qualities of head and heart possessed by the Captain. The administration of martial law was carried on in the most brutal and inhuman form in the *Gujranwala district,* which was divided up between Lieut-Col O'Brien and Mr. Bosworth Smith, than whom no more cruel officers could have been found in the whole of the Punjab. At Gujranwala a large number of persons were made to clean the drains in the *bazaar,* although the municipal sweepers had already cleaned them. At Wazirabad the *salaaming* order took a more ferocious form than elsewhere; and the persons who were considered to have violated this order were tied with their turbans and dragged to the military camp, where they were flogged or thrashed. One man was made to kiss the shoes of an officer, because his *salaam* had not been noticed. Butter was regularly collected for the troops without payment; and the curfew order, the no-travelling order, the flag saluting order and many other orders were in vogue at Wazirabad as at other places. The property of S. Jamait Singh, a wealthy citizen of Wazirabad, was confiscated, and his family, including women and children, was turned out of his house without even being allowed to put on proper clothes, because he was not present at Wazirabad when the police wanted him. On April 18th, a detachment of British soldiers surrounded the village of Nizamabad and looted the shops. For about a fortnight, the whole male population of the village had to attend the police station and remain there from seven in the morning till eight in the evening. A large number of persons were arrested and those against whom no evidence could be got up were released by Lieut-Col. O'Brien after being made to rub their noses on the ground before him. Under orders of Lieut-Col. O'Brien the people of Akalgarh were made to repair the road leading to the Dak Bungalow, so that his motor car might run smoothly over it. An exhibition of machine-gun fire was also held at the people's expense to terrorise them and to facilitate the fabrication of false evidence. At Ramnagar also, Lieut-Col. O'Brien made a large number of arrested persons rub their noses in the dust, before they were released. At Sangla, a demonstration with a machine-gun and Lewis gun firing was held, and the whole population was turned out of the village to witness it; for some days all inhabitants had to attend roll calls at the police station; provisions were taken away by soldiers without payment; and respectable men were forced to pull *pankhas* for the officers. The relations of the suspected persons, who were absent from the village, were arrested and detained as hostages. At Chuharkana, the soldiers looted the village, the provisions were commandeered without payment, the crops of several persons were confiscated, and for several days no one was allowed to reap the harvests which were ripe for the sickle. At Mahnianwala, soldiers promiscuously shot down the people on the 19th April; and afterwards there were wholesale arrests. Mr. Bosworth Smith beat the women of the whole village out of their houses, paraded them all in front of him, unveiled their faces with his stick, and used the most unmentionable language, calling them contemptible flies (*Gandi Makkhi*), bitches, she-asses, swine and worse things; and addressed them in the following terms:—"You were in the same beds with your husbands, why did you not prevent them from going out to do mischief." Mr. Bosworth Smith himself beat several persons with sticks in order to make them give false evidence. At Sheikhupura, almost all the pleaders were arrested, and released without trial after about 6 weeks' detention. These persons were paraded in handcuffs and chains throughout the town both after the arrest and before their release. An exhibition of machine-gun bombardment was also held here. The whole male population above the age of 10 years was made to sweep a large area of land, simply with a view to humiliate them. Provisions were commandeered without payment. Mr. Bosworth Smith collected all the people and made them stand in the sun. He then delivered to them a lecture on the Indian pleaders who, he said, were cheats and should be treated by the agriculturists as their dependents and menials (*kamins*). After these remarks, he abused the whole audience by calling them "Swine, *Gandi makkhi* (contemptible flies), *kala log* (niggers), *Sab ek rang ka*" (all of one colour) and so on; and took them to task for having rebelled against the Government by closing their shops. S. Gauhar Singh, a retired Inspector of Police, who had been arrested as a hostage for his sons and whose property had been confiscated on that account, was also paraded bare-headed, bare-footed and handcuffed before the audience. Except the above characteristics, the administration of martial law was conducted on the same lines in every district. The curfew order, the *salaaming* order, the order regulating prices of fruits, vegetables, milk and other provisions, the order prohibiting more than a certain number of persons to assemble, the order prohibiting travelling except by permission, the roll-calls of students, the order directing the pleaders and other "agitators" to guard martial law notices, stuck up at their houses, on pain of severe punishment in case any such notice be defaced or damaged, the confiscation or destruction of the property of persons who were for any reason absent from their village or town when the police wanted them, and the order directing the arrest and detention of the relations of such accused persons as hostages—these and similar other orders were the same all over the martial law areas. Racial discrimination was the keynote of all these orders; the orders relating to *salaaming*, motor cars, bicycles, possession of sticks, curfew, unlawful assemblies, walking on the public streets, travelling and so on, were all applicable to Indians as such, the Europeans being expressly or impliedly excluded from their operation. As would appear from the facts mentioned above, the atrocities perpetrated by the civil and military officers under the cloak of martial law were not in the nature of casual or inevitable excesses committed in the process of restoring order; but they were committed in cold blood, and flowed from the deliberate intention to strike terror in the minds of the people, to teach them a terrible lesson and to kill out political life in the Punjab by terrorising and humiliating the whole population. The actual operation and working of martial law was based on the threefold object of vengeance, striking a widespread terror and punishing the agitators.

CONCLUSION

If the recent disorders unmistakeably proved anything it was the utter failure of repression. Sir Michael O'Dwyer's theory of Government miserably failed in the Punjab; and, on his own showing, led an unarmed and admittedly loyal population to rise in open rebellion against his authority. The regime of blood and iron, which was inaugurated by martial law, further proved that a policy of repression weakens the prestige of Government and makes martyrs of the persons who are unjustly made to suffer. Every person, of whatever position in life, who was imprisoned under martial law, has been feted and hailed as a hero and patriot on his release, which has naturally led him to believe that he has done something to merit the acclamations of the people. It is indeed a sad state of things that the measure of a man's sincerity, patriotism and ability is the extent to which he is chastised by the Government. Such a state of affairs is injurious both to the Government and the people; and the Government should realise that repression carried beyond a certain point becomes its own antidote just as at a certain stage pain becomes its own anodyne. Every wise Government should see that that limit is not crossed.

By a century and a half of just and beneficent rule, the love and gratitude for the British nation has so deeply been rooted in the Indian hearts, that it is impossible to seduce the Indians from their loyalty to the British throne by the brief reign of terror, which was carried on in the Punjab under martial law. But every loyal citizen is horrified at the atrocities perpetrated by some of the officers of the Crown under the cloak of martial law, and is distressed to see that acts were done in the name of peace and order, of which every civilised Government should be ashamed; and the vehemence with which these acts have been criticised is the measure of the love and esteem in which the British Government is held in India. Had such acts been everyday occurrences, had the whole purpose and the policy of British rule in India not been sound and honourable, the horrors of martial law would not have caused so much pain and indignation throughout the country nor would they have produced so insistent a demand for reparation.

The honour and loyalty of the Punjab have been mercilessly traduced, her intelligentsia have been persecuted, harassed and dishonoured, her manhood has been disgraced, her people have been subjected to various forms of humiliation and suffering and hundreds of her innocent citizens have been massacred. She wants justice and reparation. The bitter memories of the last year can be obliterated, only if a full measure of justice is done to the people, and those responsible for bringing the Government into disrepute by their vindictive and cruel methods are brought to trial in an impartial tribunal. All reforms are futile, while fundamental human rights are not guaranteed to the Indians. No constitutional reforms would avail, if it remains possible for the officials to repeat the dark deeds of the last year. We want an assurance, both for our own sake and for the sake of England, that such cruel and inhuman acts will never again tarnish the fair name of Great Britain in this country. It is not a question of vengeance or retribution, it is a question of our future security and England's honour and reputation. The long history of British rule in the various parts of the Empire does not reveal a single instance in which the British nation has deliberately pursued a policy of tyranny and injustice, though there have been temporary lapses from the high ideals of Imperial justice, which British statesmen have always followed. It is, therefore, as much necessary for India as for England to demand a just and noble standard of conduct on the part of British officers all over the world, in order that the honour of England may not be sullied and the great and well-deserved reputation for upholding the principles of justice, liberty and Imperial rectitude, which she has acquired among the nations of the world, may not be irretrievably lost.

The mistakes were both on the side of the people and the Government, and everything should be done to soften the bitter memories of the last year. We are told that a new era is about to open in the history of our connection with England. It is but proper that the spacious days, that are promised to us, should begin with a clean slate and that all rankling sense of injustice over the past acts of the Government or its officials should disappear, without leaving the slightest trail behind. Let us enter upon the era of peaceful reconstruction with mutual confidence and goodwill; and let not the dawn of the new era be darkened with the clouds of suspicion or distrust.

APPENDIX I

Martial Law Ordinances, and other Notifications, etc.

A—REGULATION X OF 1804

A REGULATION *for declaring the Powers of the Governor-General in Council to provide for the immediate Punishment of certain Offences against the State by the Sentence of Court Martial:* PASSED *by the Governor-General in Council on the 14h December, 1804.*

1. WHEREAS, during wars in which the British Government has been engaged against certain of the native powers of India, certain persons owing allegiance to the British Government have borne arms in open hostility to the authority of the same and have abetted and aided the enemy, and have committed acts of violence and outrage against the lives and properties of the subjects of the said Government; and whereas it may be expedient that, during the existence of any war in which the British Government in India may be engaged with any power whatever as well as during the existence of open rebellion against the authority of the Government, in any part of the British territories subject to the Government of the Presidency of Fort William, the Governor-General in Council should declare and establish martial law within any part of the territories aforesaid, for the safety of the British possessions and for the security of the lives and property of the inhabitants thereof, by the immediate punishment of persons owing allegiance to the British Government who may be taken in arms, in open hostility to the said Government, or in the actual commission of any overt act of rebellion against the authority of the same, or in the act of openly aiding and abetting the enemies of the British Government within any part of the territories above specified: the following Regulation has been enacted by the Governor-General in Council, to be in force throughout the British territories immediately subject to the Government of the Presidency of Fort William, from the date of its promulgation.

2. The Governor-General in Council is hereby declared to be empowered to suspend, or to direct any public authority or officer to

order the suspension of wholly or partially, the functions of the ordinary Criminal Courts of Judicature within any zillah, district, city, or other place, within any part of the British territories subject to the Government of the Presidency of Fort William, and to establish martial law therein, for any period of time while the British Government in India shall be engaged in war with any native or other power, as well as during the existence of open rebellion against the authority of the Government, in any part of the territories aforesaid; and also to direct the immediate trial, by courts martial, of all persons owing allegiance to the British Government, either in consequence of their having been born or of their being residents within its territories and under its protection, who shall be taken in arms in open hostility to the British Government, or in the act of opposing by force of arms the authority of the same, or in the actual commission of any overt act of rebellion against the state, or in the act of openly aiding and abetting the enemies of the British Government within any part of the said territories.

3. It is hereby further declared that any person born or residing under the protection of the British Government within the territories aforesaid, and consequently owing allegiance to the said Government, who, in violation of the obligation of such allegiance, shall be guilty of any of the crimes specified in the preceding Section, and who shall be convicted thereof by the sentence of a court martial, during the suspension of the functions of the ordinary Criminal Courts of Judicature and the establishment of martial law, shall be liable to the immediate punishment of death, and shall suffer the same accordingly, by being hung by the neck till he is dead. All persons who shall, in such cases, be adjudged by a court martial to be guilty of any of the crimes specified in this Regulation, shall also forfeit to the British Government all property and effects, real and personal, which they shall have possessed within its territories at the time when the crime of which they may be convicted shall have been committed.

4. The Governor-General in Council shall not be precluded by this Regulation from causing persons charged with any of the offences described in the present Regulation to be brought to trial, at any time, before the ordinary Courts of Judicature, instead of causing such persons to be tried by courts martial, in any cases wherein the later mode of trial shall not appear to be indispensably necessary.

B—ORDINANCES

(I)—The Martial Law Ordinance 1919

Simla, the 14th April 1919

An Ordinance to provide for the trial of persons charged with offences under the Bengal State Offences Regulation, 1804

WHEREAS the Governor-General is satisfied that a state of open rebellion against the authority of the Government exists in certain parts of the Province of the Punjab :

And WHEREAS the Governor-General in Council has in exercise of the powers conferred by section 2 of the Bengal State Offences Regulation, 1804, suspended in respect of offences described in the said Regulation with which any person of the classes therein referred to may be charged, the functions of the ordinary Courts of Judicature within the districts of Lahore and Amritsar in the aforesaid Province and has established martial law in the said districts and has directed the immediate trial by courts-martial of all persons charged with such offences :

And WHEREAS an emergency has arisen which makes it expedient to provide that such trials shall be held in the manner and by the tribunals hereinafter provided :

Now, THEREFORE, the Governor-General in exercise of the power conferred by section 72 of the Government of India Act, 1915, is pleased to make and promulgate the following Ordinance :—

ORDINANCE NO. 1 OF 1919

Short title and commencement.

1. (*1*) This Ordinance may be called the Martial Law Ordinance 1919.

(*2*) It shall come into operation at midnight between the 15th and the 16th April 1919.

Trials under Regulation X of 1804 to be held by commissions

2. (*1*) Every trial held under the Bengal State Offences Regulation, 1804, (hereinafter called the said Regulation) shall, instead of being held by a court-martial, be held by a commission consisting of three persons appointed in this behalf by the Local Government.

(*2*) The Local Government may appoint as many commissions for this purpose as it may deem expedient.

(*3*) At least two members of every such commission shall be persons who have served as Sessions Judges or Additional Sessions Judges for a period of not less than three years, or persons qualified under section 101 of the Government of India Act, 1915, for appointment as Judges of a High Court. The Local Government shall nominate one of the members of the commission to be President thereof.

Convening authority.

3. A commission shall be convened by the Local Government or by such officer as the Local Government may authorise in this behalf.

Powers and procedure of commissions.

4. A commission shall have all the powers of a general court-martial under the Indian Army Act, 1911, and shall, subject to the provisions of this Ordinance, in all matters follow so far as may be the procedure regulating trials by such courts martial prescribed by or under the said Act;

Provided that where, in the opinion of the convening authority, a summary trial is necessary in the interests of the public safety, such authority may direct that the commission shall follow that procedure prescribed for a summary general court-martial by or under the said Act, and the commission shall so far as may be and subject to the provisions of the Ordinance, follow such procedure accordingly;

Provided further, that sections 78, 80 and 82, of the said Act shall not apply to any trial under this Ordinance.

Confirmation of finding and sentence unnecessary.

5. The finding and sentence of a commission shall not be subject to confirmation by any authority.

Saving of proceedings of courts martial already begun.

6. Nothing in this Ordinance shall affect any trial held or begun to be held by court-martial under the said Regulation prior to the commencement of this Ordinance.

Retrospective effect.

7. Save as provided by section 6, the provisions of this Ordinance shall apply to all persons referred to in the said Regulation who are charged with any of the offences therein described, committed on or after the 13th April, 1919.

CHELMSFORD,

Viceroy and Governor-General

(2)—The Martial Law (Extension) Ordinance, 1919

Simla, the 16th April, 1919

An Ordinance to extend the operation of the Martial Law Ordinance, 1919

WHEREAS the Governor-General is satisfied that a state of open rebellion against the authority of the Government exists in certain parts of the Punjab:

And WHEREAS the Governor-General in Council has in exercise of the powers conferred by section 2 of the Bengal State Offences Regulation, 1804, suspended, in respect of offences described in the said Regulation with which any person of the classes therein referred to may be charged, the functions of the ordinary Courts of Judicature within the district of Gujranwala in the aforesaid province, and has established martial law in the said district, and has directed the immediate trial by courts-martial of all such persons charged with such offences :

AND WHEREAS an emergency has arisen which makes it expedient to provide that such trials shall be held in the manner and by the tribunals provided in the Martial Law Ordinance, 1919, and also to provide for the same matter in any other area in which by order of the Governor-General in Council the provisions of the aforesaid Regulation may be brought into operation :

Now, THEREFORE, the Governor-General in exercise of the power conferred by section 72 of the Government of India Act, 1915 is pleased to make and promulgate the following Ordinance :

ORDINANCE No. 11 OF 1919

Short title

1. This Ordinance may be called the Martial Law (Extension) Ordinance, 1919.

Provisions of the Martial Law Ordinance, 1919, to apply in the district of Gujranwala.

2. With effect from midnight between the 16th and 17th April, 1919, the provisions of section 2 to 6 of the Martial Law Ordinance, 1919, shall apply to the trial of all persons in the district of Gujranwala in the province of the Punjab of the classes referred to in the Bengal State Offences Regulation, 1804, who may be charged with any of the offences therein described, committed on or after the 15th April 1919.

3. Where, after the commencement of this Ordinance, the Governor-General in Council, in exercise of the powers conferred by section 2 of the Bengal State Offences Regulation, 1804, suspends in respect of offences described in the said Regulation with which any person of the classes therein referred to may be charged, the functions of the ordinary Courts of Judicature within any area and establishes martial law therein, and directs the immediate trial by courts-martial of all such persons charged with such offences, the Governor-General in Council may by order in writing declare that the provisions of section 2 to 5 of the Martial Law Ordinance, 1919, shall apply to such trials in the said area.

Power to apply the provisions of the Martial Law Ordinance, 1919, in any area in which Regulation X of 1804 is in operation.

CHELMSFORD,
Viceroy and Governor-General

(3)—The Martial Law (Sentences) Ordinance, 1919

Simla, the 18th April 1919

An Ordinance to provide that persons convicted of any of the crimes specified in the Bengal State Offences Regulation, 1804, shall be punishable with penalties other than those provided in the said Regulation:—

WHEREAS an emergency has arisen which renders it necessary to provide that persons convicted of any of the crimes specified in the Bengal State Offences Regulation, 1804, shall be punishable with penalties other than those provided in the said Regulation.

Now, therefore, in exercise of the power conferred by section 72 of the Government of India Act, 1915, the Governor-General is pleased to make and promulgate the following Ordinance :—

ORDINANCE No. 111 OF 1919

Short title

1. This Ordinance may be called the Martial Law (Sentences) Ordinance, 1919.

Provisions for Punishments in case of convictions under Regulation X of 1804

2. Notwithstanding anything contained in section 3 of the Bengal State Offences Regulation, 1804.

(*a*) Any court-martial or any commission appointed and convened under the Martial Law Ordinance, 1919, may, when convicting any person of any of the crimes specified in the said regulation, sentence such person to transportation for life or for any period not less than ten years or to rigorous imprisonment for a term which shall not be less than seven years and shall not exceed fourteen years;

(*b*) No person so convicted shall be liable to forfeiture of property as provided in the said Regulation unless such court or commission so directs.

CHELMSFORD,
Viceroy and Governor-General

(4)—The Martial Law (Further Extension) Ordinance, 1919

Simla, the 21st April 1919

An Ordinance further to extend the application of the Martial Law Ordinance, 1919

WHEREAS an emergency has arisen which renders it necessary to provide that commissions appointed under the Martial Law Ordinance, 1919, shall have power to try persons and offences other than those specified in the said Ordinance :

Now, therefore, in exercise of the power conferred by section 72 of the Government of India Act, 1915, the Governor-General is pleased to make and promulgate the following Ordinance :—

ORDINANCE No. IV OF 1919.

Short title

1. This Ordinance may be called the Martial Law (Further Extension) Ordinance, 1919.

Commissions under Martial Law Ordinance, 1919, to try such cases as the Local Government may direct.

2. Notwithstanding anything contained in the Martial Law Ordinance, 1919, the Local Government may by general or special order, direct that any commission appointed under the said Ordinance shall try any person charged with any offence committed on or after the 30th March, 1919, and thereupon the provisions of the said Ordinance shall apply to such trials accordingly, and a commission may pass in respect of any such offence any sentence authorised by law.

CHELMSFORD,
Viceroy and Governor-General

(5)—The Martial Law (Trials Continuance) Ordinance, 1919

Simla, the 27th May 1919.

An Ordinance to provide for the continuance of trials held by commissions and summary courts under Martial Law.

WHEREAS in exercise of the power conferred by section 2 of the Bengal State Offences Regulation, 1804, the Governor-General in Council has been pleased to issue orders suspending in certain districts of the Punjab the functions of the ordinary criminal Courts of Judicature in so far as the trial of persons of the classes referred to in the said Regulation charged with the offences therein described is concerned, and to establish martial law in the said districts;

AND WHEREAS the Governor-General has been pleased to make provision by the Martial Law Ordinance, 1919, and by the Martial Law (Extension) Ordinance, 1919, for the holding of such trials by commissions;

AND WHEREAS the Governor-General in Council has further been pleased in exercise of the powers conferred by the aforesaid Regulation to suspend the functions of the ordinary criminal Courts of Judicature in the said districts in so far as trials held by commissions in accordance with the provisions of the Martial Law (Further Extension) Ordinance, 1919, are concerned;

AND WHEREAS an emergency has arisen which renders it necessary to provide for the continuance and completion of all such trials pending before the said commissions at the time of the cancellation of the said orders and for other matters in connection therewith;

Now, therefore, the Governor-General in exercise of the power conferred by section 72 of the Government of India Act, 1915, is pleased to make and promulgate the following Ordinance :—

ORDINANCE No. VI OF 1919.

Short title.

1. This Ordinance may be called the Martial Law (Trials Continuance) Ordinance, 1919.

Continuance of trials after the cancellation of orders establishing martial law.

2. When an order under section 2 of the Bengal State Offences Regulation, 1804, suspending the functions of the ordinary criminal courts in any district has been cancelled and martial law has ceased to operate, every trial which may at

the time of such cancellation be pending before any commission appointed as a result of such order under the Martial Law Ordiance, 1919, shall be continued by such a commission, and any person accused in any such trial may be convicted and sentenced and any such sentence shall be carried into execution, as if such order had not been cancelled.

Explanation :—A trial for the purposes of which an order has been made convening a commission under either the Martial Law Ordinance, 1919, or the Martial Law (Further Extension) Ordinance, 1919, shall be deemed to be a trial pending before such commission within the meaning of this section.

Provision for trials pending before summary courts on cessation of martial law.

3. Notwithstanding that the functions of the ordinary criminal courts have been suspended in any district and that a trial has commenced before a summary court other than an ordinary criminal court, such trial shall, when the summary court ceases by reason of the cessation of martial law to exercise jurisdiction therein, be continued before any competent criminal court which would have had jurisdiction therein save for the existence of martial law, and such court may act on the evidence recorded by the summary court or partly recorded by such court and partly recorded by itself, or it may resummon the witnesses and recommence the trial :

Provided that the accused may at the commencement of the proceedings before the second court demand that the witnesses or any of them be resummoned and reheard:

Provided further that nothing in this section shall be deemed to apply to the trial of an offence which is not punishable under any law for the time being in force.

CHELMSFORD,
Viceroy and Governor-General.

C—ORDERS DECLARING MARTIAL LAW

(1)—Lahore and Amritsar

Whereas the Governor-General in Council is satisfied that a state of open rebellion against the authority of the Government exists in the districts of Lahore and Amritsar in the Province of the Punjab;

Now, therefore, in exercise of the powers conferred by section 2 of the Bengal State Offences Regulation, 1804, the Governor-General in Council is hereby pleased to suspend the functions of the ordinary criminal courts within those districts in so far as the trials of persons of the classes referred to in the said Regulation, taken in arms in open hostility to the British Government, or in the act of opposing by force of arms the authority of the same, or in the actual commission of any overt act of rebellion against the State, or in the act of openly aiding and abetting the enemies of the British Government within the said districts, is concerned, and to establish Martial Law within the said districts.

The Governor-General in Council is also pleased to direct the immediate trial by courts-martial of all persons owing allegiance to the British Government, either in consequence of their having been born, or of their being residents, within its territories and under its protection, who shall be taken in arms in open hostility to the British Government or in the act of opposing by force of arms the authority of the same, or in the actual commission of any overt act of rebellion against the State, or in the act of openly aiding and abetting the enemies of the British Government within any part of the said districts.

J. H. DUBOULAY,

Secretary to the Government of India,

Dated 13th April 1919. *Home Department.*

(2)—Gujranwala

Whereas the Governor-General in Council is satisfied that a state of open rebellion against the authority of the Government exists in the district of Gujranwala in the Province of the Punjab;

Now, therefore, in exercise of the powers conferred by section 2 of the Bengal State Offences Regulation, 1804, the Governor-General in Council is hereby pleased to suspend the functions of the ordinary criminal courts within that district in so far as the trial of persons of the classes referred to in the said Regulation, taken in arms in open hostility to the British Government, or in act of opposing by force of arms the authority of the same, or in the actual commission of any overt act of rebellion against the State, or in the act of openly aiding and abetting the enemies of the British Government within the said district, is concerned, and to establish Martial Law within the said district.

The Governor-General in Council is also pleased to direct the immediate trial by court-martial of all persons owing allegiance to the British Government either in consequence of their having been born, or of their being residents, within its territories and under its protection, who shall be taken in arms in open hostility to the British Government, or in the act of opposing by force of arms the authority of the same or in the actual commission of any overt act of rebellion against the State, or in the act of openly aiding and abetting the enemies of the British government within any part of the said district.

J. H. DUBOULAY,

Secretary to the Government of India,

Simla, the 15th April 1919. *Home Department*

(3)—Gujrat

Whereas the Governor-General in Council has issued an order under section 2 of the Bengal State Offences Regulation, 1804, suspending the functions of the ordinary criminal courts within the district of Gujrat in the Province of the Punjab in so far as the trial of persons of the classes referred to in the said Regulation, taken in arms in open hostility to the British Government, or in the act of opposing by force of arms the authority of the same, or in the actual commission of any overt act of rebellion against the State, or in the act of openly aiding and abetting the enemies of the British Government within the said district, is concerned, and to establish Martial Law within the said district; and has also been pleased to direct the immediate trial of all persons owing allegiance to the British Government, either in consequence of their having been born, or of their being residents, within its territories and under its protection, who shall be taken in arms in open hostility to the British Government, or in the act of opposing by force of arms the authority of the same, or in the actual commission of any overt act of rebellion against the State, or in the act of openly aiding and abetting the enemies of the British Government within any part of the said district.

The Governor-General in Council is hereby pleased to declare the provisions of section 2 to 5 of the Martial Law Ordinance, 1919, shall apply to such trials in the said area.

J. H. DUBOULAY,

Secretary to the Government of India.

Simla, the 19th April 1919.

(4)—Martial Law (Further Extension) Ordinance Applied.

Whereas the Governor-General in Council is satisfied that a state of open rebellion exists in the districts of Lahore, Amritsar, Gujranwala, and Gujrat in the Province of the Punjab;

Now, therefore, in exercise of the powers conferred by section 2 of the Bengal State Offences Regulation, 1804, and in extension of the orders suspending in the said districts the functions of the ordinary criminal courts in so far as the trial of persons of the classes referred to in the said Regulation charged with the offences therein described is concerned, the Governor-General in Council is hereby pleased further to suspend the functions of the ordinary criminal courts in these districts in so far as trials held before commissions in accordance with the provisions of the Martial Law (Further Extension) Ordinance, 1919, are concerned.

J. H. DUBOULAY,

Secretary to the Government of India.

Simla, the 22nd April 1919.

(5)—Lyallpur

Whereas the Governor-General in Council is satisfied that a state of open rebellion exists in the district of Lyallpur in the Province of the Punjab;

Now, therefore, in exercise of the powers conferred by section 2 of the Bengal State Offences Regulation, 1804, the Governor-General in Council is hereby pleased to suspend the functions of the ordinary criminal courts of judicature in the said district:—

(a) in so far as the trial of persons of the classes referred to in the said Regulation, taken in arms in open hostility to the British Government, or in the actual commission of any overt act of rebellion against the State, or in the act of openly aiding and abetting the enemies of the British Government within any part of the said district is concerned, and

(b) in so far as trials held before commissions in accordance with the provisions of the Martial Law (Further Extension) Ordinance, 1919, are concerned.

The Governor-General in Council is further pleased to establish Martial Law in the said district, and also to direct the immediate trial by courts-martial of all persons owing allegiance to the British Government either in consequence of their having been born or of their being residents, within its territories and under its protection, who shall be taken in arms in open hostility to the British Government, or in the act of opposing by force of arms the authority of the same or in the actual commission any overt act of rebellion against the State, or in the act of openly aiding and abetting the enemies of the British Government within any part of the said district.

J. H. DuBOULAY,

Secretary to the Government of India.

Dated: Simla, 22nd April 1919.

(6)—Martial Law Ordinance Applied

Whereas the Governor-General in Council has in exercise of the powers conferred by section 2 of the Bengal State Offences Regulation, 1804, suspended in respect of offences described in the said Regulation with which any person of the classes herein referred to may be charged the functions of the ordinary criminal courts of judicature within the district of Lyallpur in the province of the Punjab, and, has established Martial Law in the said district and has directed the immediate trial by courts-martial of all such persons charged with such offences;

Now, therefore, the Governor-General in Council, in exercise of the powers conferred by section 3 of the Martial Law (Extension) Ordinance, 1919, is pleased to declare that the provisions of sections 2 to 5 of the Martial Law Ordinance, 1919, shall apply to such trials in the said district.

J. H. DuBOULAY,

Dated: Simla, 22nd April 1919. *Secretary to the Government of India.*

D—MARTIAL LAW REGULATIONS

Proclamation by G O C

WHEREAS Martial Law has been proclaimed and is in force in the districts of Lahore, Amritsar and Gujranwala, it is hereby notified that until further intimation, the following Regulations will be enforced within the limits of the 16th Indian Division in all places to which Martial Law has been or may be extended :—

No. 1—Law and Tribunals

Martial Law has been declared subject to—

(*a*) the maintenance of ordinary courts for ordinary offences and

(*b*) the establishment under the Martial Law Ordinance, 1919, of Special Tribunals for offences specified in section 2 of the Bengal State Offences Regulation, 1804.

The result of the establishment of Martial Law is that, subject to the said Ordinance, plenary power is vested in the General Officer Commanding the Division of prescribing offences, penalties, courts and procedure in regard to all matters connected with or arising out of the present disturbances and of taking all measures and issuing all orders that he may deem necessary for the suppression of these disturbances. In the excercise of these powers the General Officer Commanding the Division is pleased to declare that a breach of any of the Regulations Nos. 2-15 below, shall be deemed to be an offence.

No. 2—Offences

No person shall—

Rebellion (*a*) be actively in arms against His Majesty, or

Aiding rebels. (*b*) directly incite others to take up arms against His Majesty, or

(*c*) actively aid or assist the rebels, or

Endangering public safety. (d) commit any overt act by which the safety of His Majesty's Forces or subjects is endangered.

No. 3

Assisting or harbouring rebels.

No person shall assist or harbour rebels by giving them information, or by supplying them with shelter, food, drink, money, clothes, arms, ammunition, stores, forage, or means of conveyance, or by assisting them in any way to evade apprehension.

No. 4

Every person—

Failing to report rebels.

(*a*) who receives information of gatherings or intended gatherings of rebels, or

(*b*) who knows or has reason to believe that any of his relatives or dependents have joined or are about to join the rebels,

shall without delay give full information thereof to the nearest Military or Civil authority.

No. 5

Seditious language and publications.

1. No person shall make use of any language with the intention either:—

(*a*) of raising or fomenting disaffection among His Majesty's subjects, or

(*b*) of promoting hostility between different classes of such subjects.

2. No person shall print, publish, circulate or have in his possession any publications containing seditious articles or articles likely to promote disaffection or bad feeling.

No. 6

Protection of Railways. Canals and Telegraphs.

No person shall (*a*) in any way interfere with the working of the railways or canals, (*b*) damage or tamper with any material or property connected with railways and canals, (*c*) damage or interfere with telegraph or telephone lines or apparatus or wireless telegraph installation, (*d*) tap with the intention of reading off messages any telegraph or telephone lines.

The attempt to commit or the abetment of any breach of this regulation shall be punished as a breach of the regulation.

No. 7

Control of Transport.

1. No person shall save under a proper permit, have in his possession any motor vehicle.

2. Every person using any such vehicle shall pass any guard or sentry at a speed not exceeding 6 miles an hour and shall stop the car if so ordered by any guard or sentry, and shall carry on such a vehicle a suitable light between the hours of sunset and sunrise.

These Regulations do not apply to Civil Officers of Government or to members of His Majesty's forces (Naval, Military or Air Force, Indian Defence Force or Police) in respect of any vehicles lawfully issued to them as such officers or members.

No. 8

Control of travelling and movements.

No person shall, save under such conditions as may be prescribed, enter or leave this area, or move to and fro within it.

No. 9

Control of meetings.

No person shall, save under a proper permit, convene or attend any meeting of more than five persons, except in the case of—

(*a*) a meeting *bona fide* held for religious purposes in an authorised place of worship,

(*b*) a meeting of Municipal Committee or any other similar public body,

(*c*) a meeting of persons residing in one house and gathering in such house.

No. 10

Escaping

No person shall—

(*a*) escape or attempt to escape from any prison or other custody in which he is for the time being confined or restrained under Martial Law, or

(*b*) abet any other person in escaping or attempting to escape from any such prison or custody.

No. 11

Disobeying and obstructing Officers

No person shall—

(*a*) disobey or neglect to obey any order given by any Military or Civil Officer in the execution of his duty when administering Martial Law, or

(*b*) obstruct, impede, or interfere in any manner with any Military or Civil Officer or other person who is carrying out the orders of any authority administering Martial Law, or who is otherwise acting in the execution of his duty under Martial Law.

No. 12

False news and

No person shall disseminate false intelligence which he knows to be false, or spread reports calculated to create alarm or despondency.

No. 13

Defacing Martial Law notice.

No person shall destroy, deface, or in any way tamper with any notice exhibited under Martial Law while such notice is in force.

No. 14

Production of permits

Every person shall, when required to do so, give his correct name and address and produce his permit or pass to any Military or Civil Officer acting under the authority of these Regulations or to any soldier, volunter, or policeman in uniform.

No. 15

Miscellaneous offences.

No person shall commit any act, or be guilty of any omission—

(*a*) which is to the prejudice of good order of the public safety, or

(*b*) which is calculated to mislead, or hamper the movement of, or imperil the success of His Majesty's Forces.

No. 16—Penalties

Any person who contravenes any of the foregoing Regulations 2—15 (inclusive) shall be liable to trial by an officer authorised to dispose of an offence summarily under Martial Law. Such an officer may sentence an offender to imprisonment, rigorous or simple, which may extend to two years, or to fine not exceeding Rs. 1,000 or to both, and to six months' imprisonment in default of payment of fine, and may also inflict whipping in addition to, or in lieu of, any other punishment which he is empowered to inflict.

No. 17—Arrest and Trials

(*a*) For every offence against these Regulations the offender may be arrested with or without warrant from any officer authorised to dispose of offences. For minor offences against these Regulations the offender will not necessarily be arrested but may be summoned to appear before such officer.

(*b*) Whenever a person is summoned to appear or is arrested under Martial Law, the charge against him shall without unnecessary delay be investigated by an officer authorised to dispose of an offence summarily under Martial Law or by some officer deputed by him and not under the rank of Captain or, at his request, by a Civil Magistrate or by the police.

(*c*) The investigating officer will dismiss a charge brought before him if in his opinion the evidence does not show that some offence under Martial Law has been committed, or if in his discretion he thinks the charge ought not to be proceeded with.

(*d*) At the conclusion of the hearing, if the investigating officer is of opinion that the charge ought to be proceeded with, he shall without unnecessary delay either—

(*i*) dispose of the case summarily, or

(*ii*) in cases where he considers that the offence calls for a more severe punishment than he is empowered to inflict, refer the case to the Legal Remembrancer to the Punjab Government who, after considering the evidence, will decide whether to convene a Commission under the Martial Law Ordinance, 1919, for the disposal of the case or whether it should be remanded to the officer referring it for disposal or to any other officer exercising powers under these Regulations, or

(*iii*) remand the accused in custody while futher enquiries are being made.

In case (*iii*), if within reasonable time sufficient evidence is not forthcoming the accused person shall be discharged.

No. 18 — Officers authorised to dispose of offences summarily under Martial Law

The districts in which Martial Law has been declared shall be divided up into areas and for each such area an officer or officers will be authorised to dispose of offences summarily under Martial Law. Such officers shall be known as Area Officers.

In addition to the Area Officer every officer commanding a station or regiment, every Field Officer and every officer nominated by a General Officer Commanding a Brigade, by the Officer commanading

Lahore Civil Area or by the Local Government, is hereby authorised to dispose of offences summarily under Martial Law.

W. G. L. BEYNON, K.C.I.E., C. B. D. S. O,
MAJOR GENERAL,
Commanding the 16th Indian Division

The 19th April 1919 J. P. THOMPSON,
Chief Secretary to Government, Punjab.

AMENDMENT

The following amendment to the above Proclamation was published under date April 21st :—

Regulation No. 8 in Martial Law Proclamation of the 19th of April is hereby amended as follows :—

8. Where any orders have been issued regarding the control of travelling and movements, no person shall enter or leave the area to which Martial Law has been extended or move to and fro within it, in contravention of such orders.

Note — A similar Proclamation and a similar amendment were issued by Major General Sir C.M. Dobell, K.C.B., C.M.G., D.S.O. Commanding the 2nd (Rawalpindi) Division, bearing dates April 20th and April 21st respectively with reference to the District of Gujrat and places within the limits of that Division to which Martial Law had been or might to extended.

E—MARTIAL LAW COURTS

(1)—Commissions

Under section 2 of the Martial Law (Further Extension) Ordinance, 1919, the Lieutenant-Governor hereby directs that all persons charged with offences connected with the recent disturbances and committed on or after the 30th March, 1919, and before the dates of the Martial Law Proclamation issued by the General Officer Commanding 16th Indian Division and the General Officer Commanding 2nd (Rawalpindi) Division, respectively, in the Districts of Lahore, Amritsar, Gujranwala or Gujrat, shall be tried by one or other of the Commissions appointed in accordance with the Martial Law Ordinance 1919 under Notification No. 10527, date April 18th, 1919 or by any such Commission which may hereafter be appointed:—*Punjab Gazette Notification No. 11091 dated 23.4.19.*

Under section 2 (2) of the Martial Law Ordinance, 1919, the Lieutenant-Governor is pleased to appoint the following Commissions for the purpose of holding trials under section 2 (1) of the said Ordinance :—(1) The Hon. Mr. Justice Leslie-Jones; Mr. M.H. Harrison, I. C. S., District and Sessions Judge; S. Din Muhammad, Extra Assistant Commissioner; (2), Lieutenant-Colonel A. A. Irvine, C.I.E., District and Sessions Judge; Mr. F. W. Kennaway, District and Sessions Judge; Mr. I.C. Lall. Under section 2 (3) of the Martial Law Ordinance, 1919, the Lieutenant-Governor is pleased to appoint the Hon. Mr. Justice Leslie-Jones and Lieutenant-Colonel Irvine to be Presidents of the above-mentioned Commissions respectively.—*Punjab Gazette Notification No. 10527 dated 18.4.19.*

Under section 2 (2) of the Martial Law Ordinance, 1919, the Lieutenant-Governor is pleased to appoint the following Commission for the purposes of holding trials under section 2 (1) of the said Ordinance :— Mr. N. H. Prenter, I.C.S , District and Sessions Judge; Mr. S.S. Harris, formerly District and Sessions Judge, and Major P.W. Elliot, 20th D.C.O. Infantry. Under section 2 (3) of the Martial Law Ordinance 1919, the Lieutenant-Governor is pleased to appoint Mr. N. H. Prenter to be President of the above-mentioned Commission.—*Punjab Gazette Notification No.12341½ dated 5-5-19.*

Under section 2 (2) of the Martial Law Ordinance, 1919, the Lieutenant. Governor is pleased to appoint the following Commission for the purpose of holding trials under section 2 (1) of the said Ordinance :—The Hon. Mr. Justice Broadway; A.H. Brasher, Esq., I. C. S., District and Sessions Judge; and Khan Bahadur Shaikh Rahim Bukhsh. Under section 2 (3) of the Martial Law Ordinance, 1919, the Lieutenant-Governor is pleased to appoint the Hon. Mr. Justice Broadway to be President of the above-mentioned Commission.—*Punjab Gazette, May 20th.*

(2)—Area Officers

In continuation of and in modification of No. 11091, dated the 23rd April, 1919, the Lieutenant-Governor hereby directs that nothing in the said notification shall be deemed to prevent the trial of any persons charged with an offence (1) other than one which is shown in column 8 Schedule II, Code of Criminal Procedure, 1898 as triable exclusively by the Court of Sessions, (2) which is connected with the recent disturbances; and (3) was committed on or after the 30th March 1919, and before the dates of the Martial Law Proclamations issued by the General Officer Commanding 16th (Indian) Division, on the 19th April, 1919, and the General Officer Commanding, 2nd (Rawalpind) Division, respectively, in the districts of Lahore, Amritsar, Gujranwala or Gujrat, or before the 22nd April in the District of Lyallpur by a summary Court appointed under order dated 5th, May 1919, issued by the General Officer Commanding, the 2nd (Rawalpindi) Division.—*Punjab Government Notification No.* 12612 *(Home, Judicial) Dated May* 8, 1919.

(Punjab Government Notification No. 12341A, Military, dated the 5th May, 1919)

The following order of the General Officer Commanding, 16th Indian Division, is published for information.

1. I hereby appoint the officers specified below to be summary courts for the trial of minor offences connected with or arising out of the recent disturbances and committed on or after the 30th of March and before the date of my proclamation of the 19th April or, in the case of the Lyallpur district, before the 22nd April. The officers hereby appointed shall have jurisdiction within the areas in which Martial Law has been proclaimed within the limits of the 16th Indian Division in respect of such offences as were committed or triable within the areas in which Martial Law has been proclaimed within the limits of the 16th Indian Division.

2. Such courts (*a*) shall only take cognisance of cases sent for trial by the Police, (*b*) shall not try any person for any act which is not an offence under the ordinary law, (*c*) shall not try any person for any offence which is shown as triable exclusively by the court of session in column 8 of schedule II of the Criminal Procedure Code 1898, (*d*) shall not in respect of any offence pass any sentence which is not authorised by the ordinary law for that offence (see column 7 of schedule II aforesaid and also the Indian Whipping Act, 1909); and (*e*) shall not in respect of any offence pass any sentence which could not be passed by a Ist class Magistrate (see section 32 of the Code of Criminal Procedure, 1898).

3. The finding and sentences of such courts shall not be subject to confirmation by any authority, nor shall any appeal or application for revision lie in respect of them.

Schedule of Officers Appointed to be Summary Courts.

(1) All officers who have been or shall hereafter be nominated by the Lieutenant-Governor in the exercise of powers conferred by General Officer Commanding the 16th Indian Division to dispose of offences against the regulations contained in the proclamation issued by the said General Officer summarily under Martial Law.

(2) Khan Bahadur Shaikh Rahim Bukhsh, Director of Land Records.

(3) Mr. A. L. Hoyle, I.C.S., Lyallpur.

(4) Mr. J. D. Penny, I.C.S., Sheikhupura.

(5) Mr. F. W. Phillips, Honorary Magistrate, Lyallpur.

(6) All Cantonment Magistrates.

Note.—A *similar order of the General Officer Commanding 2nd (Rawalpindi) Division was published in which the same officers were oppointed to be summary courts within the areas in which Martial Law had been proclaimed within the limits of the 2nd Division.*

(*Punjab Government Notification No.* 10657 *Home—Military, dated the 20th April,* 1919).

It is hereby notified that the General Officer Commanding the 16th Indian Division has divided the portion of his command in which Martial Law has been proclaimed into three Areas, in accordance with Regulation No. 18 of the Proclamation of April 19th, as follows :—

(*a*) Amritsar Area comprising civil district of Amritsar.

(*b*) Lahore Area comprising the civil district of Lahore exclusive of Lahore Civil Area.

(c) Lahore Civil Area comprising the Municipality of Lahore. Mughalpura and all other places between the River Ravi and the Lahore Branch of Upper Bari Doab Canal, within a 3-mile radius of the Telegraph Office, Lahore.

2. He has further been pleased to authorize the following officers as Area Officers to dispose of offences summarily under Martial Law in the said Areas :—

Major S. R. Shirley M. C. 54th Sikhs, in the Amritsar Area.

Major H. A. Murray, 35th Sikhs, in the Lahore Area, and

(*a*) Lieutenant-Colonel the Hon'ble W.F.J. North, Somerset Light Infantry,

(*b*) Major E. C. Barnes, 19th Punjabis,

(*c*) Major J. C. Hunter, Superintendent, Carriage and Wagon Department, North-Western Railway.

} In the Lahore Civil Area.

A Punjab Government Notification dated the 4th May, 1919, says.—

It is hereby notified that the General Officer Commanding, 2nd (Rawalpindi) Division, has divided the portion of his command in which Martial Law has been proclaimed into the following areas, in accordance with Regulation No. 18 of the Proclamation of the 20th April, 1919 :—

(1) Gujranwala area comprising the Gujranwala Tahsil.

(2) Wazirabad area comprising the Wazirabad Tahsil.

(3) Khangah Dogran and Sharakpur area comprising Khangah Dogran and Sharakpur Tahsils.

(4) Hafizabad area comprising Hafizabad Tahsil.

(5) Gujrat and Kharian area comprising Gujrat and Kharian Tahsils.

(6) Phalia area comprising Phalia Tahsil.

(7) Lyallpur area comprising the Lyallpur district.

2. He has futher been pleased to authorise the following officers as Area Officers to dispose of offences against the Proclamation of 20th April, summarily under Martial Law in the said area :—

(1) Lieutenant-Colonel A. J. O'Brien, C.I.E., C.B.E., in the Gujranwala Area.

(2) Major C. W. J. Smith, D.S.O., 54th Sikhs, in the Wazirabad Area.

(3) Mr. B. N. Bosworth-Smith in the Khangah Dogran and Sharakpur Area.

(4) Captain W. J. Cole, Supply and Transport Corps, in the Hafizabad Area.

(5) Lieutenant-Colonel C. S. Browne, 37th Dogras, in the Gujrat and Kharian Areas.

(6) Lieutenant-Colonel S. D. Grant, V. C., 5th Gurkha Rifles, in the Phalia Area.

(7) Mr. G. F. de Montmorency, C. I. E., and Lieutenant-Colonel G. F. Hodgson, D. S. O., in the Lyallpur Area.

It is hereby notified in the exercise of his powers under Regulation 18 of the Proclamation of the General Officer Commanding, the 2nd (Rawalpindi) Division, dated the 20th April, 1919, the General Officer Commanding, the Wazirabad Brigade, has nominated the following officers to dispose of offences against the proclamation of 20th April, 1919, summarily under Martial Law :— Captain T. P Wheatley, Ist Garrison Battalion, Yorkshire Regiment; Captain W. J. Cole, Supply and Transport Corps; and Captain J S. L. Ewing, M. C., 19th Lancers, in the Gujranwala Area.

(Punjab Government Notification No. 10658, *Military, dated the 20th April,* 1919.*)*

In exercise of the powers conferred by Regulation No. 18 of the Proclamation issued by the General Officer Commanding the 16th Indian Division, dated the 19th April 1919, the Lieutenant-Governor hereby nominates the following officers to dispose of offences against the Regulations contained in the said Proclamation summarily under Martial Law where such offences have been committed within the areas in which Martial Law has been proclaimed within the limits of the 16th Indian Division :—

Mr. A. J. W. Kitchin, C.I.E., Commissioner, Lahore.

Mr. Miles Irving, Deputy Commissioner, Amritsar.

Mr. G.D. Rudkin, Joint Deputy Commissioner, Amritsar.

Mr. F. H. Puckle, Assistant Commissioner, Amritsar.

With effect from the date of their assuming charge of their appointments.

Mr. H. Fyson, Deputy Commissioner, Lahore.

Major M. L. Ferrar, Joint Deputy Commissioner, Lahore

With effect from the date of his taking charge of his

Lieutenant-Colonel A.J. O'Brien, C.I.E., C.B.E., Deputy Commissioner Gujranwala.

Mr. B. N. Bosworth Smith, Joint Deputy Commissioner, Gujranwala.

With effect from the date of his taking over charge.

Mr. A. A. McC. Mitchell, Assistant Commissioner, Lahore.

Mr. P. Marsden, Assistant Commissioner, Sub-Divisional Officer, Kasur.

Mr. F. B. Wace, Assistant Commissioner, Gujranwala.

Mr. S. M. Jacob, Director of Agriculture.

Mr. R. B. Beckett, Assistant Commissioner, Amritsar.

Mr. F. A. Connor, Extra Assistant Commissioner, Amritsar.

Mr. J. E. Keough, Extra Assistant Commissioner, Lahore.

Mr. E. A. Penhearow, Extra Assistant Commissioner, Lahore.

The following *Punjab Gazette* Extraordinary dated April 23rd 1919, was issued :— In exercise of the powers conferred by the Proclamation issued by the General Commanding the 2nd (Rawalpindi) Division, dated the 20th of April, 1919, the Lieutenant Governor hereby nominates the following officers to dispose of offences against the Regulations contained in the said Proclamation summarily under Martial Law where such offences have been committed within the areas in which Martial Law has been proclaimed within the limits of the 2nd Rawalpindi Division :—

The Hon. Mr. C. J. Halifax C. B. E., Commissioner, Rawalpindi.

Lieutenant-Colonel A. J. O'Brien, C. B. E., C. I. E. Deputy Commissioner, Gujranwala.

Mr. B. N. Bosworth-Smith, Joint Deputy Commissioner, Gujranwala;

Mr. B. Wace, Assistant Commissioner, Gujranwala;

Mr. S. M. Jacob, Director of Agriculture;

Mr. H. S. Williamson, Deputy Commissioner, Gujrat.

(*The Punjab Government Notification No.* 1113, *Military, dated April* 23*rd,* 1919.)

With reference to Home Department notification No. 10657, dated the 20th of April, it is hereby notified that the General Officer Commanding the 16th Indian Division has been pleased to authorise the following officer as Area Officer to dispose of offences summarily under Martial Law in the Lahore Area :—

Captain A. C. Doveton, 30th Punjabis.

The following *Punjab Gazette* Extraordinary was issued on the 24th April 1919 :— In exercise of powers conferred by Regulation 18 of the Proclamation issued by the General Officer Commanding the 16th Indian Division dated the 19th April, 1919, and by Regulation 18 of the Proclamation issued by the General Officer Commanding the 2nd (Rawalpindi) Division, dated the 20th of April 1919, the Lieutenant-Governor hereby nominates the following officers to dispose of offences against the Regulations contained in the said Proclamations summarily under Martial Law within the areas in the Lyallpur District in which Martial Law has been proclaimed within limits of the 16th Indian Division and the 2nd Rawalpindi Division respectively :—

Lieutenant-Colonel C. Powney Thompson, Commissioner, Multan; and

Mr. G.F. deMontmorency, Deputy Commissioner.

A Punjab Government notification, dated 4th May (Military) says:—

"It is hereby notified that in the exercise of his powers under Regulation No. 18 of the Proclamation of the General Officer Commanding, the 2nd (Rawalpindi) Division, dated the 20th April 1919, the General Officer Commanding, the Wazirabad Brigade, has nominated the following officers to dispose of offences against the Proclamation of 20 April, 1919, summarily under Martial Law:—

Captain T. P. Wheatley, Ist Garrison Battalion, Yorkshire Regiment.

Captain W. J. Cole, Supply and Transport Corps, and

Captain J. S. L. Ewing, M. C., 19th Lancers, in the Gujranwala Area,"

With reference to Notification No. 10657—Home–Military, dated the 20th April, 1919, it is hereby notified that the General Officer Commanding the 16th Indian Division has authorised the following officers as Area Officers to dispose of offences against the Regulations contained in the Proclamation issued by the said General Officer Commanding summarily under Martial Law :—

Mr. F. B. R. Spencer, Cantonment Magistrate, *vice* Major H. A. Murray, 35th Sikhs; Khan Bahadur Sheikh Rahim Bakhsh, Director of Records, in the Lahore Area—*Punjab Gazette Extraordinary of May, 7th, 1919.*

F—MARTIAL LAW NOTICES ISSUED AT LAHORE

NOTICE

All private car owners must produce their cars at the Punjab Club at 2 P.M. To-day Wednesday or as soon after as they see this notice.

By order,
F. JOHNSON,
Lieut.-Colonel,
Commanding Civil Station.

Lahore, 15th April, 1919.

No. 1

Whereas the Government of India has for good reasons proclaimed Martial Law in the districts of Lahore and Amritsar; and

Whereas superior Military authority has appointed me to command troops and administer Martial Law in a portion of the Lahore District, now known as the "Lahore Civil" command whose boundaries may be described as follows :—

The Civil Lines;

The Municipality and City of Lahore;

The Fort;

The Mogulpura Works;

and any other area not included in the above between the Ravi River and Lahore Branch of the Bari Doab Canal inclusive within three miles of the Central Telegraph Office, Lahore;

And whereas Martial Law may be briefly described as the will of the Military Commander in enforcing law, order and public safety:

I make known to all concerned that until further orders by me the following will be strictly carried out :—

1. At 20-00 hours each evening a gun will be fired from the Fort, and from that signal till 05-00 hours on the following morning no person other than a European or a person in possession of a Military permit signed by me or on my behalf will be permitted to leave his or her house or compound or the building in which he or she may be at 20 hours. During these prohibited hours no person other than those excepted above will be permitted to use the streets or roads,

and any person found disobeying this order will be arrested, and if any attempt is made to evade or resist that person will be liable to be shot.

This and all other orders, which from time to time I may deem necessary to make, will be issued on my behalf from the Water-Works Station in the City, whither every Ward will keep at least four representatives from 6 A.M. till 17.00 hours daily to learn what orders, if any, are issued and to convey such orders to the inhabitants of their respective Wards. The onus of ascertaining the orders issued by me will rest on the people through their representatives.

2. Loyal and law-abiding persons have nothing to fear from the exercise of Martial Law.

3. In order to protect that lives of His Majesty's Soldiers and Police under my command, I make known that if any firearm is discharged or bombs thrown at them the most drastic reprisals will instantly be made against property surrounding the scene of the outrage. Therefore it behoves all loyal inhabitants to see to it that no evil-disposed *agitator* is allowed on his premises.

4. During the period of Martial Law I prohibit all processions, meetings or other gatherings of more than 10 persons without my written authority, and any such meetings, gatherings or processions held in disobedience of this order will be broken up by force without warning.

5. I forbid any person to offer violence or cause obstruction to any person desirous of opening his shop or conducting his business or proceeding to his work or business. Any person contravening this order will be arrested, tried by a Summary Court and be liable to be shot.

6. At present the City of Lahore enjoys the advantage of electric lights and a water-supply; but the continuance of these supplies will depend on the good behaviour of the inhabitants and their prompt obedience to my orders.

FRANK JOHNSON, LIEUT.-COL.,
2-6 Battalion, Royal Sussex Regiment,
Commanding Lahore (Civil) Area.

Head Quarters, Punjab Club;
Lahore, 15th April, 1919.

No. 2

All tongas and tum-tums whether licensed for hire or otherwise will be delivered up to the Military Officer appointed for the purpose at the Punjab Light Horse ground by 17-00 to-day—Tuesday, 15th April. Drivers will receive pay and horses be rationed.

FRANK JOHNSON LIEUT.-COL.,
Commanding Lahore (Civil) Area.

No. 3

All motor cars or vehicles of any description will be delivered to the Military Officer appointed for that purpose at the Punjab Club by 17-00 this day.

FRANK JOHNSON, LIEUT.-COL.,
Commanding Lahore (Civil) Area.

No. 4

By virtue of the powers vested in me, I have prohibited the issue of Third or Intermediate Class tickets at all Railway Stations in the Lahore Civil Command except only in the case of servants travelling with their European Master or servants or others in the employ of the Government.

FRANK JOHNSON, LIEUT.-COL.,
Commanding Lahore (Civil) Area.

Headquarters, Punjab Club.
Time : 22-00 hours.
Lahore, 15th April, 1919.

No. 5

Whereas, from information received by me, it would appear that shops, generally known as Langars, for the sale of cooked food are used for the purpose of illegal meetings and for the dissemination of seditious propaganda, and whereas I notice that all other shops (particularly in Lahore City) have been closed as part of an organised demonstration against His Majesty's Government; now therefore, by virtue of the powers vested in me under Martial Law, I order that all such Langars or shops for the sale of cooked food in the Lahore Civil Area, except such as may be granted an exemption in writing by me, shall close and cease to trade by 10-00 hours to-morrow, Wednesday, 16th April, 1919.

Disobedience to this order will result in the confiscation of the contents of such shop, and the arrest and trial by summary procedure of the owner or owners.

FRANK JOHNSON, Lieut.-Col.,
Commanding Lahore (Civil) Area.

Headquarters, Punjab Club, Lahore.
Time : 23-00 hours
15th April, 1919.

No. 6

Whereas I have reason to believe that certain munshis, agents, dalals and chuprassees employed by legal practitioners in Lahore, are engaged in disseminating seditious propaganda, therefore by virtue of the powers vested in me under Martial Law, I make the following Order :—

(1) No such munshi, agent, dalal or chuprassee shall leave the Lahore Civil Command without a permit signed by me or on my behalf.

(2) Every legal practitioner resident in this Command will submit to me through the Deputy Commissioner of Lahore by 16-00 hours to-day a complete list of every munshi, agent dalal or chuprassee directly employed by him.

FRANK JOHNSON, Lieut.-Col.,
Commanding Lahore (Civil) Area.

Headquarters, Punjab Club, Lahore
Time : 08-00 hours.
Lahore, 16th April 1919.

No. 7

Whereas I have reason to believe that certain students of the D. A. V. College in Lahore are engaged in spreading seditious propaganda directed against His Majesty's Government, and whereas I deem it expedient in the interests of the preservation of law and order to restrict the activities of such students, I make the following order :—

All students of the said College now in this Command Area will report themselves to the Officer Commanding Troops at the Bradlaugh Hall daily at the hours specified below and remain there until the roll of such students has been called by the Principal or some other

Officer approved by me acting on his behalf, and until they have been dismissed by the Officer Commanding Troops at Bradlaugh Hall.

07.00 hours.
11.00 hours.
15.00 hours.
19.30 hours.

Headquarters, Punjab Club, Lahore.
Time : 08.00 hours. FRANK JOHNSON, LIEUT.-COL.,
16*th April,* 1919. *Commanding Lahore (Civil) Area.*

No. 8

Whereas some evilly disposed persons have torn down or defaced notices and orders which I have caused to be exhibited for the information and good government of the people in the Lahore (Civil) Command.

In future all orders that I have to issue under martial law will be handed to such owners of property as I may select, and it will be the duty of such owners of property, to exhibit and keep exhibited and undamaged, in the position on their property selected by me, all such orders.

The duty of protecting such orders will therefore devolve on the owners of property and failure to ensure the proper protection and continued exhibition of my orders will result in severe punishment.

Similarly I hold responsible the owner of any property on which seditious or any other notices, proclamations or writing not authorized by me are exhibited.

FRANK JOHNSON, LIEUT.-COL.,
Commanding Lahore (Civil) Area.

Headquarters, Punjab Club, Lahore.
April, 16th 1919.

No. 9

WHEREAS the leaders of the people whom I summoned to meet me yesterday have not kept their promise to arrange for my orders to be communicated to the people in their respective wards; AND WHEREAS, I deem it expedient for the sake of the people themselves that they should not be exposed to the risk of disobeying my orders through the neglect of their own leaders.

NOW THEREFORE I give notice that copies of all orders and notices issued by me under Martial Law will be exhibited at the following places :—

[Here follows a list of forty names].

No. 9 (*Revised.*)

WHEREAS, it has been found expedient to revise Martial Law Order No. 9.

NOW THEREFORE, I give notice that copies of all Orders and Notices issued by me under Martial Law will be exhibited at the following places :—

Inside the City

1. House of Mehta Amin Chand, Pleader, Gali Bhaddar Kali, Wachowali.
2. House of Dr. Khalifa Shuja-ud-Din, Bar-at-Law, Kucha Tirgaran, inside Mochi Gate.
3. Baitak of Suba, Contractor, Wazir Khan's Chauk.
4. House of Dr. Nihal Chand, Sikri, Wachowali.
5. House of Jai Gopal Tandon, Manager, *Punjabi* Press, inside Shahalmi Gate.
6. Shop of Fazal Din, Book-seller, Kashmiri Bazar.
7. House of Lala Kanshi Ram, Kapur, Works Reservoir.
8. House of Lala Sardari Lal, Vaid, Gumti Bazar.
9. House of Lala Kidar Nath, Contractor, Niween Gali, Sathan.
10. House of Badshah, son of Nur Din, Lakkar Mandi.
11. Shop of B. Hira Singh, Turiwalla, Hira Mandi.
12. House of Mohna, Saraf, Sua Bazar.
13. House of Lala Sundar Das, Bar-at-Law, inside Shahalmi Gate, Papar Mandi.
14. House of Thakur Sukh Ram Das, Editor, *Rajput Gazette*, Mohalla Purbian, Mochi Gate.
15. House of Lala Kanshi Ram Khosla, Editor, *Bulletin,* Chuni Mandi.
16. House of Pandit Chuni Lal, Vaid, near Bhairo Asthan.
17. House of Pandit Jewan Lal, Pensioner, Chauk Matti.
18. Shop of Bhagat Ram, Puri, Sudesh Vastu Stores, Sutar Mandi.
19. Shop of Jaggan Nath, son of Govind Ram, Attar, Rang Mahal.
20. Shop of Dayalu, Halwai, Neewan Katra, Akbari Mandi.

Outside the City

1. House of Dr. G.C. Naurang, Bar-at-Law, McLeod Road.
2. House of L. Dharam Das, Suri, Pleader, Maclagan Road.
3. House of L. Rattan Chand, Gowalmandi.
4. House of the Hon'ble K. B. Mian Fazal-i-Hussain, Bar-at-Law, Lytton Road.
5. House of Pir Taj-ud-din, Bar-at-Law, Empress Road.
6. House of L. Govardhan Das, Agent, Insurance Company, Gowalmandi.
7. House of L. Durga Das, Pleader, Circular Road, outside Lohari Gate.
8. Office of Mr. Nanak Chand, Bar-at-Law, Anarkali.
9. Shop of Lala Dhani Ram, Bhalla, Hindu Boot House, Anarkali.
10. Shop of Lala Durga Das, Cheap John, Anarkali.
11. Junction of Mall and McLeod Road.
12. Charing Cross.
13. Chauk New Kotwali.
14. House of S. K. Mukerji, Pleader, near Nila Gumbaz, Chauk Anarkali.
15. Shop of Amolak Ram, the Swadeshi Stores, Anarkali.
16. House of Mr. H. Beechey, Bar-at-Law, Fane Road.
17. House of Bakhshi Tek Chand, Pleader, Fane Road.
18. House of Lala Piari Mohan, B. A., Pleader, Bans Mandi.
19. D. A. V. College, Boarding Houses (Superintendent).
20. Law College Boarding Houses and Hostels (Superintendent).
21. Government College Boarding Houses (Superintendent).
22. Medical College Boarding Houses (Superintendent).
23. Dayal Singh College Boarding Houses (Superintendent).
24. Khalsa Boarding House, near Veterinary Hospital (Superintendent).
25. Forman Christian College Boarding Houses (Superintendent).
26. Vedic Ashram Boarding House (Superintendent).
27. Viram Ashram Brahmo-Samaj Boarding House (Superintendent).
28. Islamia College Boarding House (Superintendent).
29. Veterinary College Boarding House (Superintendent).
30. Rajput Boarding House (Superintendent).

31. Central Training College Boarding House (Superintendent).
32. Central Model School Boarding House (Superintendent).
33. Sardar Partap Singh, Boarding House (Superintendent).
34. Sanatan Dharm Boarding House (Superintendent).
35. D. A. V. School Boarding House (Superintendent).
36. Agarwal Ashram Boarding House (Superintendent).
37. Arts School Boarding House (Superintendent).

FRANK JOHNSON, LIEUT.-COL.,
Commanding Lahore (Civil) Area.

Headquarters, Punjab Club :
Lahore, 20th April, 1919.

No. 10

WHEREAS practically every shop, factory and business establishment in the Area under my Command has been closed in accordance with the *hartal* or compulsory closure of business directed against His Majesty's Government.

AND WHEREAS the continuance of such *hartal* is detrimental to the peace, good order and governance of the said Area.

AND WHEREAS I consider it advisable to limit from time to time the effect of such *hartal*.

NOW THEREFORE by virtue of the powers conferred on me by Martial Law, I make the following order, namely :—

By 14-00 hours to-morrow (Thursday), 17th day of April 1919, every shop and business establishment in the quarter generally known as Anarkali Bazar will open and carry on its business and each occupier of such shop or business premises will exercise his skilled trade or calling in exactly the same manner as he or they did before the creation of the said *hartal*.

And I warn all concerned that disobedience of this order without valid reason will result in the immediate opening by me of such shops or business premises by force, and that any resultant loss arising out of such forcible opening will rest on the owners or occupiers of such shops or businesses.

FRANK JOHNSON, LIEUT.-COL.
Commanding Lahore (Civil) Area.

Head-Quarters, Punjab Club,
Time : 22-00 hours.
Lahore, 16th April, 1919.

No. 11

WHEREAS I think it advisable to take such steps as I think necessary for the prevention of violence and the preservation of good order, more particularly for the prevention of injury to His Majesty's Soldiers and Police, as well as to all law-abiding citizens in the Area under my Command, I make the following order :—

From and after the promulgation of this order it shall be illegal for any male person to carry or be found in possession of an instrument known as a *lathi*.

All persons disobeying this order will be arrested, tried by summary proceedings and punished under the powers conferred on me by Martial Law.

FRANK JOHNSON, LIEUT.-COL.

Head Quarters, Punjab Club, Lahore *Commanding Lahore (Civil) Area.*
Time : 22-00 hours.
Lahore, 16th April, 1919.

No. 12

WHEREAS I deem it expedient to take further steps for the prevention of violence and intimidation and for the maintenance of good order in the area under my Command, I make the following order :—

From and after the promulgation of this Order it shall be unlawful for more than two persons to walk abreast on any constructed or clearly defined pavement or side-walk in such Area, and disobedience to this Order will be punished by all such special powers as are conferred on me by Martial Law.

FRANK JOHNSON, LIEUT.-COL.,

Head-Quarters, Punjab Club, Lahore. *Commanding Lahore (Civil) Area.*
Time : 22-00 hours.
16th April, 1919.

Notice to Motorists.

A picket is stationed at the Ferozpur Road, cross roads leading into Lahore Cantonment, and cars must stop there otherwise they will be fired upon.

FRANK JOHNSON, LIEUT.-COL.,

Headquarters, Punjab Club, Lahore *Commanding Lahore (Civil) Area.*
Time : 11-10 hours.
17th April, 1919.

No. 13

WHEREAS information laid before me shows that a Martial Law Notice issued by me and posted by my Order on a property known as the SANATAN DHARAM COLLEGE HOSTEL ON BAHAWALPUR ROAD, has been torn or otherwise defaced, in contravention of my Martial Law Notice No. 8.

NOW THEREFORE by virtue of the powers vested in me under Martial Law, I order the immediate arrest of all male persons domiciled in the said Hostel and their internment in the Lahore Fort pending my further Orders as to their trial or other disposal.

FRANK JOHNSON, LIEUT.-COL.,
Headquarters, Punjab Club, Lahore *Commanding Lahore (Civil) Area.*
Time : 15.25 hours.
17th April, 1919.

No. 14

WHEREAS practically every shop and business establishment in the area under my Command has been closed in accordance with the *hartal* or organized closure of business directed against His Majesty's Government.

AND WHEREAS the continuance or resumption of such *hartal* is detrimental to the good order and governance of the said Area.

AND WHEREAS I deem it expedient to cause the said *hartal* to entirely cease.

NOW THEREFORE by virtue of the powers vested in me by Martial Law, I make the following order, namely :—

By 10-00 hours to-morrow (Friday), the 18th day of April 1919, every shop and business establishment (except only *langars* referred to in Martial Law Notice No. 5, dated 15th April, 1919) in the Area under my Command shall open and carry on its business and thereafter daily shall continue to keep open and carry on its business during the usual hours, up to 20-00 hours, in exactly the same manner as before the creation of the said *hartal*.

And likewise I order that every skilled or other worker will, from 10-00 hours to-morrow, resume and continue during the usual hours his ordinary trade, work or calling.

And I warn all concerned that if at 10-00 hours to-morrow, or at any subsequent time, I find this Order has been without good and valid reason disobeyed, the persons concerned will be arrested and tried under the summary procedure of Martial Law, and shops so closed will be opened and kept open by force, and any resultant loss arising from such forcible openings will rest on the owners and on occupiers concerned.

And I further warn all concerned that this Order must be strictly obeyed in spirit as well as in letter, that is to say, that to open a shop and then refuse to sell goods and to charge an exorbitant or prohibitive rate, will be deemed a contravention of this Order.

FRANK JOHNSON, LIEUT.-COL.,

Headquarters, Punjab Club *Commanding Lahore (Civil) Area.*

Time : 10-10 hours.

Lahore, 17th April, 1919.

No. 15

WHEREAS it has come to my knowledge that the present state of unrest is being added to and encouraged by the spreading of false, inaccurate or exaggerated reports of rumours.

NOW THEREFORE by virtue of the powers vested in me by Martial Law I give notice that *any person* found guilty of publishing, spreading or repeating false, inaccurate or exaggerated reports in connection with the Military or political situation will be arrested and summarily dealt with under Martial Law.

FRANK JOHNSON, LIEUT.-COL.,

Headquarters, Punjab Club, *Commanding Lahore (Civil) Area.*

Time : 10-20 hours.

Lahore, 16th April, 1919.

No. 16

WHEREAS I have reason to believe that certain students of the Dyal Singh College in Lahore are engaged in spreading seditious propaganda directed against His Majesty's Government and whereas I deem it expedient in the interests of the preservation of law and order to restrict the activities of such students, I make the following Order :—

All students of the said College now in this Command Area will report themselves to the Officer Commanding Troops at the Telegraph Office daily at the hours specified below and remain there until the roll of such students has been called by the Principal or some other

Officer approved by me acting on his behalf, and until they have been dismissed by the Officer Commanding Troops at the Telegraph Office.

07.00 hours.
11.00 hours.
15.00 hours.
19.00 hours.

First parade at 11.00 hours on 19th April, 1919. Headquarters, Punjab Club.

FRANK JOHNSON, LIEUT.-COL.,

Time : 16-00 hours.

Lahore, 18th April, 1919. *Commanding Lahore (Civil) Area.*

NOTICE

It is hereby notified that applications for Night and Railway Passes will be attended to only at the following hours :—

From 10.00 to 13.00 hours, and
From 14.00 to 17.00 hours.

Headquarters, Punjab Club.

D. VANRENEN, MAJOR.
Staff Officer,

Lahore, 18th April, 1919. *Lahore (Civil) Command.*

MEMORANDUM TO OFFICERS COMMANDING UNITS AND DETACHMENTS, POLICE OFFICERS AND MAGISTRATES

(1) In order to prevent the occurrence of regrettable incidents it must be clearly understood that the existence of Martial Law neither necessitates nor justifies the committal of excesses either in—

(*a*) the maintenance of order;

(*b*) in enforcing obedience to Martial Law Regulations;

nor (*c*) in the infliction of punishment.

(2) The guiding principle to be borne in mind is that the force required in (*a*) and (*b*) and the ensuing punishment should never exceed the immediate necessities of the case.

(3) The punishment of whipping in particular, whilst probably the most efficacious and convenient method of summarily dealing with most minor breaches of Martial Law Regulations, requires tact and commonsense in its infliction. Under no circumstances should

old or feeble men be flogged, and the social status of the offender also needs consideration.

(4) It cannot be too clearly impressed on all ranks that the temporary supersession of the ordinary process of Civil Law by the introduction of Martial Law, does not mean that justice ceases to be administered; on the contrary, the suspension of the usual safeguards makes it doubly imperative that all concerned should bear in mind that it is "up to them" to see that justice, and not irresponsible violence, is administered.

(5) When in any case Officers or Magistrates acting on my behalf are doubtful as to the suitable punishment to be inflicted, the case can always be remanded and the question referred to me. In nearly all cases this can be done by telephone, obviating any delay.

(6) Nothing in the above is to be read as weakening the hands of all responsible for strictly maintaining good order and enforcing Martial Law Regulations.

FRANK JOHNSON, LIEUT.-COL.,
Commanding Lahore (Civil) Area.

Headquarters, Punjab Club,
Time : 08-00 hours.
Lahore, 18th April, 1919.

No. 17

WHEREAS it is deemed desirable to provide for the better mobility of His Majesty's Troops in the Area under my Command (and in those adjacent thereto).

NOW THEREFORE by virtue of the powers vested in me by Martial Law, I make the following orders :—

1. From and after this date no motor nor pedal-driven cycle shall leave the area under my Command without a permit signed by me or on my behalf.

2. All owners of motor and other cycles shall, when ordered to do so by me, whether by notice addressed to them personally, or as residents in certain districts or areas, or members of certain institutions, trades, or callings, deliver all cycles owned or possessed by them to the Officer appointed to receive them on my behalf, at the place and by the hour stated in such Notices which will be published from day to day in (amongst other places) the "Civil and Military Gazette."

3. And I further order that every motor cycle in the Area under my Command, other than those the *bona fide* property of Government or a Gazetted Officer be delivered to me or the officers appointed by me at the Cinema in McLeod Road between 08-00 and 13-00 hours on Monday, 21st April, 1919, and thereafter it will be a contravention of Martial Law for any person, other than those excepted in this paragraph or holding exemption certificates signed on my behalf, to be found in possession of a motor-cycle whether in runing order or otherwise.

4. And I further order that all pedal-driven cycles in possession of students on the rolls of the D.A.V., Sanatan Dharam and Dyal Singh Colleges, be delivered to the Officer appointed by me at the Bradlaugh Hall between 09-00 and 13-00 hours on Monday, 21st April, 1919, and thereafter it will be a contravention of Martial Law for any student of the said Colleges to ride or be in possession of a cycle.

And I warn all concerned that failure to comply with this Order, or tampering with any cycle to impair its immediate usefulness, will result in severe penalties under Martial Law.

FRANK JOHNSON, Lieut.-Col.,
Commanding Lahore (Civil) Area.

Headquarters, Punjab Club,
Time : 22-15 hours.
Lahore, 19th April, 1919.

No. 18

SURRENDER OF FIREARMS AND AMMUNITION

Whereas it has come to my knowledge that a number of persons in the Area under my Command are in possession of firearms and ammunition, by virtue of exemption, licence or otherwise.

And Whereas I deem it desirable in the interests of the safety of His Majesty's Troops and Police and for the prevention of disorder and violence, to take steps to ensure that such arms should not pass by theft or otherwise, into the possession of those who might use them unlawfully.

Now therefore by virtue of the powers vested in me by Martial Law I do make the following Order, that is to say :—

Any person in possession of any arms or ammunition, ordered by me or by any Officer, Magistrate, Soldier or Policeman acting on my behalf, to surrender for safe custody, such arms and ammunition shall deliver them to me at the place and by the hour mentioned in such Order.

And for the purpose of this Order, every Military or Police Officer, Magistrate, Soldier and Policeman shall be deemed to be acting on my behalf.

And I warn all concerned that disobedience of this Order will be summarily dealt with by me under Martial Law.

FRANK JOHNSON, LIEUT.-COL.,
Commanding Lahore (Civil) Area.

Headquarters, Punjab Club,
Time : 12-30 hours.
Lahore, 20th April, 1919.

No. 19

WHEREAS the services of motor drivers are immediately needed,

NOW, THEREFORE, by virtue of the powers vested in me by Martial Law, I make the following order, that is to say :—

By 10-00 hours to-morrow, the 22nd day of April, 1919, every licensed motor driver, other than a European or a person at present engaged as driver of a commandeered or exempted car, will report himself to Major Lindsay Smith, at the Transport Park, Punjab Light Horse Ground.

All drivers so reporting will either be registered or engaged. The latter will receive current rates of pay.

FRANK JOHNSON, LIEUT.-COL.,
Commanding Lahore (Civil) Area.

Headquarters, Punjab Club,
Time : 08-35 hours.
Lahore, 21st April, 1919.

No. 20

WHEREAS on the 15th day of April, 1919, in order to minimise the work of the Troops and Police, and the better to maintain public order and safety in the Area under my Command, by Martial Law Notice No. 1. I forbade certain classes of the inhabitants of the said Area to leave their houses or be in the public streets or roads, between 20-00 hours and 05-00 hours daily.

AND WHEREAS as this and other orders issued by me have been carried out to my satisfaction, I am desirous of removing as far as possible, restrictions which interfere with the religious exercises of certain classes of the inhabitants.

Now, THEREFORE, I order and direct that so long as the inhabitants of the area under my Command continue faithfully to obey all orders issued by me in the cause of public order and safety, the hours during which the streets, etc., are closed shall be between 21-00 hours, and 05-00 hours, and this alteration shall come into operation at 21-00 hours to-morrow, the 22nd day of April, 1919.

Headquarters, Punjab Club, FRANK JOHNSON, LIEUT.-COL.,
Time : 10-55 hours. *Commanding Lahore (Civil) Area.*
Lahore, 21st April, 1919.

No. 21

TO OWNERS OF CYCLES.

In continuation of paragraph 2 of Martial Law Notice No. 17, dated 19th April, 1919, by virtue of the powers vested in me by Martial Law, I order that—

All pedal-driven cycles (save and except such as are the *bona fide* property of Government) owned or possessed by persons, other than Europeans, residing in the district hereinafter described, shall be delivered to the Officer appointed by me at the Cinema McLeod Road, between the hours of 09-00 and 16-00 to-morrow (Tuesday) the 22nd day of April, 1919.

And therefore, it will be a contravention of Martial Law for any such person to be in possession of a cycle unless accompanied by a Certificate of Exemption from military service signed on my behalf.

DISTRICT AFFECTED

That portion of the area under my Command that lies South of the City Boundaries and the Ravi River exclusive, and North or West of the following roads inclusive :—

Chamberlain Road from the Mochi Gate, thence by Thornton Road, Nabha Road and Edward Road to the junction of Cust and Multan Roads.

Headquarters, Punjab Club, FRANK JOHNSON, LIEUT.-COL.,
Lahore, 21st April, 1919. *Commanding Lahore (Civil Area).*

No. 22

TO OWNERS OF CYCLES

In further continuation of paragraph 2. Martial Law Order 17, dated 19th April, 1919, by virtue of the powers vested in me by Martial Law, I order that—

All pedal-driven cycles (save and except such as are the *bona-fide* property of Government) owned or possessed by persons other than Europeans, residing in the district hereinafter described, shall be delivered to the Officer appointed by me at the Fort between the hours of 09-00 and 16-00 to-morrow (Wednesday) the 23rd day of April, 1919.

And thereafter it will be a contravention of Martial Law for any such person to be in possession of a cycle unless accompanied by a cerficate of exemption from Military Service signed on my behalf.

For the purposes of this Order, all cycles owned or ridden in the course of duty by Officers or servants of the Government shall be deemed to be the property of Government and therefore exempt from the order.

DISTRICT AFFECTED.

That portion of the Area under my Command known as the "City."

Headquarters, Punjab Club,
Time : 08-55 hours.
Lahore, 22nd April, 1919.

FRANK JOHNSON, LIEUT.-COL.,
Commanding Lahore (Civil) Area.

RAILWAY PERMITS

1. Notice is hereby given that permits to obtain Third and Intermediate Class Railway Tickets at the Stations in this Area, *viz.*, Lahore Junction and Badami Bagh, can only be obtained on personal application to the Assistant Inspector-General, Railway Police, near Lahore Junction Station or at Command Headquarters, Punjab Club, between 10.00 and 17.00 hours.

STREET PASSES

2. Applications for permits to be in the streets during prohibited hours can be obtained at Command Headquarters, Punjab Club, or from the Deputy Commissioner, Lahore (Town Hall Office).

3. All Secretaries of Government and Heads of Government Departments are authorized to issue such passes to their own employees. Books of Passes can be obtained on application to the Deputy Commissioner.

D. VANRENEN, MAJOR.
STAFF OFFIÇER,
Lahore (Civil) Command.

Headquarters, Punjab Club,
Lahore, 22nd April, 1919.

No. 23

WHEREAS it was not possible to receive, inspect and issue receipts for all pedal driven cycles surrendered in accordance with Martial Law Order No. 21 of 21st April, 1919, during the hours specified in the said order.

Now, therefore, I order that all persons residing in the area defined in the said order will deliver cycles in their possession to the Officer, appointed by me at the Cinema in McLeod Road, between 09-00 and 16-00 hours to-morrow (Thursday) the 24th day of April, 1919.

Headquarters, Punjab Club, FRANK JOHNSON, LIEUT.-COL.,
Lahore, 23rd April, 1919. *Commanding Lahore (Civil) Area.*

No. 24

WHEREAS I deem it expedient to make provision for the preservation of health and the greater comfort of British troops stationed in the Area under my command.

AND WHEREAS a number of electric fans and lights are required in the buildings in which some of such troops are quartered.

NOW, THEREFORE, by virtue of the powers vested in me by Martial Law, I authorize any officer appointed by me for that purpose to enter any college, public building, hostel, hotel, private or other residence or building and remove such number of electric lights and fans required for the purpose aforesaid.

And any attempt to obstruct such removal, or to hide, or to damage or to impare the immediate efficiency of any such fans or lights, will be summarily dealt with under Martial Law.

But nothing in this order shall authorize the removal of any fan or light from a room usually inhabited by a woman.

Headquarters, Punjab Club, FRANK JOHNSON, LIEUT.-COL.,
Time : 07-25 hours, *Commanding Lahore (Civil) Area.*
Lahore, 23rd April, 1919.

No. 25

WHEREAS it was not possible to receive, inspect and issue receipts for all pedal-driven cycles surrendered in accordance with Martial

Law Order No. 22 of 22nd April, 1919, during the hours specified in the said Order.

NOW, THEREFORE, I order that all persons residing in the Area defined in the said Order, that is to say, "THE CITY," will deliver cycles in their possession to the officer appointed by me at the Fort between 09-00 and 16-00 hours to-morrow, Friday, the 25th day of April, 1919.

Headquarters, Punjab Club, FRANK JOHNSON, LIEUT.-COL.,
Time : 07-40 hours. *Commanding Lahore (Civil) Area.*
Lahore, 24th April, 1919.

No. 26

WHEREAS I deem it necessary to take steps for the more complete control of horse drawn vehicles licensed to ply for hire in the Area under my Command, and in order to lessen the chance of further loss and inconvenience to the public by reason of any *Hartal* or refusal to ply for hire.

NOW, THEREFORE, by virtue of the powers vested in me by Martial Law, I order that on and after Monday, the 28th day of April, 1919, no landau, gharry, tonga or tum-tum shall ply for hire in the Area under my Command unless in possession of a permit signed by me or by an Officer acting on my behalf, which permit will be issued on payment shown in the schedule published below.

And I further order that the driver of every such licensed vehicle shall also be in possession of a military permit to drive such vehicle, for which a charge of Rs. 3 will be made.

All vehicles and drivers must obtain the necessary licenses and permits from Major Lindsay Smith, at the Transport Park, Punjab Light Horse Ground between 09-00 and 17-00 hours on the 25th, 26th and 27th days of April, 1919, and failure to obtain such licenses and permits will be dealt with as a breach of Martial Law.

Headquarters, Punjab Club, FRANK JOHNSON, LIEUT.-COL.
Lahore, 24th April, 1919. *Commanding Lahore (Civil) Area.*

SCALE OF CHARGES FOR MILITARY PERMITS TO PLY FOR HIRE AND DRIVE LICENSED VEHICLES

Class				Fee Rs.	A.	P.
1st (Landaus)	...	...	...	6	0	0
2nd (Gharries)	...	...	...	5	0	0
3rd (Tongas) A	...	...	...	3	8	0
3rd (Tongas) B	...	...	...	3	0	0
4th (Tum-tum)	...	...	...	2	0	0
Drivers' Permits	...	...	...	1	8	0

No. 27

WHEREAS, from information laid before me, I have reason to believe that a large number of students at the King Edward Medical College, Lahore, have openly given expression to seditious sentiments and cries.

AND WHEREAS, I deem it expedient to limit the mischievous activities of such students.

NOW, THEREFORE, by virtue of the powers vested in me by Martial Law, I make the following Orders :—

1. No student on the rolls of the said College at present residing in the Area under my Command shall leave such area without a permit signed by me or on my behalf.

2. All students of Ist, 2nd, 3rd and 4th years of the M.B.B.S. Class of the said College now residing in the Area under my Command, save and except those as to whose loyalty I am satisfied and to whom, on the recommendation of the Principal, I may grant exemption, will, from the promulgation of this Order, report themselves to the Officer Commanding Troops at Patiala House daily at the hours specified below, and remain there until the roll of such students has been called by an Officer appointed by the Principal and approved by me and until, they have been dismissed by the Officer Commanding Troops at Patiala House :—

07-00 hours.
11-00 hours.
15-00 hours.
19-00 hours.

Note.—4th year students are exempted from attendance at the 07-00 hours roll-call.

3. At 11-00 hours to-morrow (Saturday) the 26th day of April, 1919, in lieu of the roll-call at Patiala House, such roll-call will take place at the Fort, Lahore, and every such student in possession of a cycle will there and at that hour deliver it to the officer appointed by me, and thereafter during the continuance of Martial Law or until such time as I may rescind or modify this Order, any such student in possession of a cycle shall be deemed to have contravened Martial Law.

And I warn all such students that absence from any roll-call, without reasonable excuse, will be severely punished.

Headquarters, Punjab Club, FRANK JOHNSON, LIEUT.-COL.,
Time : 07-40 hours. *Commanding Lahore (Civil) Area.*
Lahore, 25th April, 1919.

No. 28

WHEREAS on the 23rd instant some evilly disposed person set fire to the contents of a pillar letter-box, causing loss and inconvenience to the public.

AND WHEREAS such offence can at present only be dealt with under process of Civil Law.

NOW, THEREFORE, by virtue of the powers vested in me under Martial Law, I hereby order that damage or attempted damage to or theft of any postal matter or Post Office property in the Area under my Command, shall be deemed to be an offence under Martial Law, punishable with all the certainty, celerity and severity of such Law.

FRANK JOHNSON, LIEUT.-COL.,
Commanding Lahore (Civil) Area.

Headquarters, Punjab Club,
Time : 08-50 hours.
Lahore, 25th April, 1919.

No. 29

WHEREAS by Martial Law Order No. 14, of 17th April, 1919, I warned dealers in the Area under my Command against charging exorbitant prices for their goods.

AND WHEREAS I find that the current retail price for *Atta* is as much as 5½ seers per rupee, whilst *Atta* can be purchased by retail shopkeepers at Rs. 5-13-0 per maund, so that such shopkeepers are making a profit of about Re. 1-7-4 per maund which is approximately equivalent to 25 per cent. *per diem*.

AND WHEREAS I deem such profit to be exorbitant and unlawful, and further that it is necessary to protect the people from the hardship and injustice of such exorbitant price :

NOW, THEREFORE, by virtue of the powers vested in me by Martial Law, I shall from time to time fix and determine the prices at which the necessaries of life shall be sold.

And I now order that—

From and after 17-00 hours this day and until further notice, it shall be a contravention of Martial Law, for any dealer in *Atta* to:—

(1) refuse to sell *Atta* when requested to do so, and

(2) to supply less than 6½ (six-and-a-half) seers per rupee (which will allow such retail dealer the excellent profit of annas 5/5½ per maund or say 5 per cent *per diem* on his capital involved).

And so that no retail dealer in *Atta* shall be able to plead, as an excuse for contravention of this Order, his inability to purchase *Atta* at the wholesale price named above, I give notice that on application being made to the Officer appointed by me for that purpose, *viz*., the Director of Civil Supplies, whose office is with that of the Director of Agriculture near the Civil Secretariat, he will give all necessary information and facilities to enable such retail shopkeepers to supply themselves with *Atta* at the said wholesale price, *viz*., Rs. 5-13-0 per maund.

And I warn all concerned that any disobedience of this Order will result in prompt and severe punishment under Martial Law.

FRANK JOHNSON, LIEUT.-COL.,
Commanding Lahore (Civil) Area.

Headquarters, Punjab Club,
Time : 10-50 hours.
Lahore, 25th April, 1919.

No. 30

WHEREAS it has been proved to me that certain students in Lahore Colleges are in the habit of defacing with obscene and filthy comments pictures appearing in illustrated papers of members of His Majesty's Naval and Military Forces, Civil or other Services.

AND WHEREAS such obscene and filthy comments are calculated

to promote disaffection and bad feeling, and to be prejudicial to good order.

NOW, THEREFORE, I warn all concerned that it shall be deemed to be a contravention of Martial Law, for any person to deface or mark any picture or letterpress purporting to represent or refer to British subjects by signs, drawings or words calculated to bring contempt, ridicule or dislike on such British subjects.

And such prohibition is also extended to the use of words, signs or gestures directed at, addressed or referring to any such British subjects.

And I shall hold responsible for such outrages on illustrations all who are inmates, owners and (or) occupiers, students and teachers, of the premises in which such damaged or defaced picture or literature is discovered.

FRANK JOHNSON, LIEUT.-COL.,
Commanding Lahore (Civil) Area.

Headquarters, Punjab Club,
Time : 17-50 hours.
Lahore, 25th April, 1919.

No. 31

WHEREAS by Martial Law Order No 14 of 17th April, 1919, I warned dealers in the Area under my Command against charging exorbitant prices for their goods.

AND WHEREAS I deem the present prices charged for milk, *viz.*

3 Annas per seer for cow's milk, and
4 " " " " buffalo's milk

to be unjustifiable, exorbitant, and to press heavily on the poorer people.

NOW, THEREFORE, by virtue of the powers vested in me by Martial Law, I order that, from and after 17-00 hours this day and until further notice, it shall be a contravention of Martial Law for any person who yesterday was a dealer in milk—

(1) to refuse to sell milk when in possession of milk and requested to do so;

(2) to adulterate milk, or

(3) to charge more than Annas 2½ per seer for cow's milk and
Annas 3 " " " " buffalo's milk.

And I warn all concerned that any disobedience of this Order will result in prompt and severe punishment under Martial Law.

FRANK JOHNSON, LIEUT.-COL.,
Commanding Lahore (Civil) Area.

Headquarters, Punjab Club,
Time : 06-40 hours.
Lahore, 27th April, 1919.

No. 32

WHEREAS by Martial Law Order No. 14 of 17th April 1919, I warned dealers in the Area under my Command against charging exorbitant prices for their goods.

AND WHEREAS I find that Khewra salt can be laid down in this Area at an inclusive cost of Rs. 1-12-0 per maund, whilst the people are made to pay Annas 1-6 per seer or Rs. 3-12-0 per maund, producing a profit which is exorbitant and unlawful.

NOW, THEREFORE, by virtue of the powers vested in me by Martial Law I order that from 14-00 hours to-morrow, Wednesday, 30th April, salt other than imported table salt, shall be supplied at a price not exceeding Anna One (A. I) per seer, a price which I shall shortly further reduce after I consider sufficient time has been allowed to enable small dealers holding stocks purchased at high rates to dispose of or reduce such stocks.

And I further order that from and after 14-00 hours to-morrow, not less than 7¾ seers of wheat shall be supplied for a rupee.

And I warn all concerned that—

(*a*) all those who to-day are selling salt or wheat must continue to do so but at the new prices.

(*b*) adulteration or short measure of all articles, whether a "controlled" article, like *Atta*, Milk, Salt and Wheat, or otherwise, will be deemed an offence against Martial Law and dealt with by me accordingly.

And finally I warn all concerned that unless the present unjustifiable prices, particularly of the necessaries of life, are at once materially reduced, I shall gradually fix the price of every article.

FRANK JOHNSON, LIEUT.-COL.,
Commanding Lahore (Civil) Area.

Headquarters, Punjab Club,
Time : 15-10 hours,
Lahore, 29th April, 1919.

No. 33

WHEREAS it has come to my knowledge that attempts are frequently made to extort money from persons with a view to either saving them from penalties for intentional or other breaches of Martial Law, or for the purpose of removing them from the restrictive incidence of such Martial or other Laws ;

AND WHEREAS I deem such conduct gravely detrimental to the good order and governance of the Area under my Command ;

I THEREFORE, by virtue of the powers vested in me under Martial Law Regulation No. 15, declare that it is an offence under Martial Law for any person in the said Area to offer or receive money or other valuable consideration, or to act as agent or "go-between" in any transaction or proposed transaction by virtue of which the person paying such money or giving such consideration expects, or is promised, to evade any penalties or proceedings or to obtain any benefit of any kind whatsoever under Martial or other Laws, or Orders.

And I warn all concerned that any person convicted of any breach of this Order in the said Area is liable to two years' imprisonment or fine and whipping.

FRANK JOHNSON, LIEUT.-COL.,
Commanding Lahore (Civil) Area.

Headquarters, Punjab Club,
Time : 17-15 hours.
Lahore, 2nd May, 1919.

No. 34

WHEREAS I have trustworthy information that certain dealers in wheat in the Area under my Command are evading Martial Law Order No. 32, dated 29th April 1919, and refusing to sell wheat at the price fixed by me on the ground that their supply of wheat is exhausted;

AND WHEREAS I have reason to believe that certain of the said dealers on the contrary have secret stores of wheat;

NOW, THEREFORE, by virtue of the powers vested in me by Martial Law, I make the following order :—

Every trader, banker, bunnia or other person in the said Area who owns or possesses, directly or indirectly, wheat exceeding 5 maunds in weight shall render to me in writing (enclosed in an envelope marked "Wheat") by 09-00 hours on the 7th day of May, 1919, a return showing the total quantity of wheat owned or possessed by him.

And so that no person intending to evade this Order may subsequently, when faced with the consequences of such evasion, complain that he was unaware of the procedure to be adopted by me;

I warn all concerned that as soon as possible after the hour named for the rendering of the said Returns, I shall cause them to be published, and at the same time offer substantial rewards for information that will lead to the conviction of any person failing to submit or submitting an inaccurate Return.

And such reward will be paid by the person disobeying this Order in addition to such other punishment as by virtue of Martial Law, I am empowered to impose.

And I further warn would-be infromers of the consequences of wilfully giving me false information.

Headquarters, Punjab Club. FRANK JOHNSON, Lieut.-Col.,
Lahore, 5th May, 1919. *Commanding Lahore (Civil) Area.*

NOTICE.

The public are hereby informed that a limited number of Hackney Carriages are plying for hire between 21-00 and 5-00 hours. These may be obtained at Shibbu Mal's Sarai, near Faletti's Hotel, Telephone No. 71; and the Hackney Carriage Stand on the Cooper Road, Telephone No. 142.

Persons other than Europeans making use of such Hackney Carriages must themselves be in possession of a permit entitling them to be out after 21-00 hours.

FRANK JOHNSON, Lieut.-Col.,
Lahore, 4th May, 1919. *Commanding Lahore (Civil) Area.*
Headquarters, Punjab Club.

No. 35

Whereas by Martial Law Order No. 14 of 17th April, 1919, I warned dealers in the Area under my Command against charging exorbitant prices for their goods;

And whereas on the 1st May I met at the Town Hall, Lahore, a large number of growers of, and wholesale and retail dealers in, vegetables, discussed the costs of production, transport and selling, pointed out the present unjustifiable prices of many vegetables particularly those that form part of the necessaries of life of the poorer classes, and finally gave the said producers and dealers three days in which to reduce their prices;

AND WHEREAS I find that no notice has been taken of my request for a reduction in the said prices;

NOW, THEREFORE, by virtue of the powers vested in me by Martial Law I make the following Order, that is to say :—

From 04-00 hours on Wednesday, the 7th day of May, 1919, it shall be a contravention of Martial Law for any dealer or other person in the Area under my Command, to charge or attempt to charge more than the prices shown below.

And any person found guilty of contravening this Order will be severely punished.

NAME OF VEGETABLE			MAXIMUM RETAIL PRICE.		
Bangan	...	...	As. 1	6	per seer.
Jinde	...	...	" 3	0	"
Bhindi tori	...	...	" 4	6	"
Karele	...	...	" 6	0	"
Tori (green)	...	...	" 2	6	"
Tomatoes	...	...	" 3	0	"
Kadu (ghia)	...	...	" 0	6	each.
Cabbages	...	...	" 0	9	"
Onions (dry)	...	...	" 0	9	per seer
" (green)	...	...	" 0	6	"
Potatoes	...	...	" 1	3	"
Peas	...	...	" 5	0	"
Sag	...	...	" 1	3	"
Kadu (Pahari)	...	...	" 0	9	each.
Khera	...	...	" 0	3	"
Kakri	...	...	" 0	3	"

FRANK JOHNSON, LIEUT.-COL.,
Commanding Lahore (Civil) Area.

Headquarters, Punjab Club,
Time : 15-20 hours.
Lahore, 5th May, 1919.

No. 36

WHEREAS by Martial Law Order No. 27 of the 25th April, 1919, I ordered certain action to be taken against all students on the rolls of the King Edward Medical College, Lahore, on account of the

AND WHEREAS the Principal of the said College has now reported to me that he has inflicted the following punishments, that is to say:—

(1) To be forthwith expelled from and permanently removed from the rolls of the College :—

1.	Qasuri Lal	...	First year student.
2.	Nank Chand Kapur	...	Second year student.
3.	Hans Raj Madan	...	Third year student.
4.	Jagat Ram Bhatia	...	Do.
5.	Gian Chand Bhatia	...	Fourth year student.
6.	Gopal Singh Chowla	...	Do.
7.	Lal Singh Sahotra	...	Do.
8.	Pran Nath	...	Do.
9.	Parma Nand	...	Do.
10.	Hans Raj Chhibber	...	Do.

(2) To suffer the loss of one (1) year's seniority :—

1.	Kulwant Rai	...	First year student.
2.	Jagrinda Singh	...	Do.
3.	Kanhya Lal Bhambri	...	Second year student.
4.	Lakshmi Narain	...	Do.
5.	Gurbakhsh Rai Dhamrati	...	Do.
6.	Shamsher Singh	...	Third year student.
7.	Kishori Lal	...	Fourth year student.
8.	Amolak Ram Mehta	...	Do.
9.	Hira Lal Sachdeva	...	Do.

(3) To forfeit their scholarships :—

1.	Qasuri Lal	...	First year student.
2.	Kulwant Rai	...	Do.
3.	Jagat Ram Bhatia	...	Third year student.
4.	Shamsher Singh	...	Do.
5.	Kishori Lal	...	Fourth year student.
6.	Amolak Ram Mehta	...	Do.

(4) To have their scholarships suspended for three months :—

1.	Mohan Lal	...	First year student.
2.	Parma Nand Bhatia	...	Do.
3.	Fakhur-ud-Din	...	Do.

4.	Ram Lal Ubroi	...	Do.
5.	Ch. Hakim Din	...	Second year student.
6.	Jagat Ram Sahai	...	Do.
7.	Amar Nath Chopra	...	Do.
8.	Jhangi Ram	...	Do.
9.	Mokham Chand	...	Third year student.
10.	Sh. Muhammad Yusuf	...	Do.
11.	Hukam Chand Gupta	...	Do.
12.	Bhagwant Kishori Sikand	...	Do.
13.	Vaishnu Das Kashyap	...	Fourth year student.
14.	Jagan Nath Chopra	...	Do.
15.	Daulat Ram Mehta	...	Do.
16.	Har Bhajan Singh	...	Do.

AND WHEREAS I consider the aforesaid punishments, although very merciful, to be sufficient to restrain the remaining and future students from being misled into disloyal and seditious action;

I direct that adequate disciplinary action having thus been taken against the College, from the promulgation of this Order the students shall be relieved of restrictions and liabilities imposed by Martial Law Order No. 27.

Headquarters, Punjab Club, Time : 22.50 hours. *Lahore, 5th May, 1919.*

FRANK JOHNSON, LIEUT.-COL., *Commanding Lahore (Civil) Area.*

No. 37

WHEREAS by Martial law Order No. 14 of the 17th April 1919, I warned all dealers in the Area under my Command against charging exorbitant prices for their goods;

AND WHEREAS many complaints having been made to me concerning the present price of Mutton and Goatflesh, I made and caused to be made exhaustive enquiries into the working of the meat trade in this Area.

AND WHEREAS, as a result of such enquires I find that a profit of about Rs. 3¼ is being made on an ontlay of Rs. 8½ which I deem to be unjustifiable.

NOW, THEREFORE, by virtue of the powers vested in me by Martial Law I make the following Order :—

From 05-00 hours on Friday, the 9th day of May, 1919, it shall be a contravention of Martial Law, for any Butcher or dealer in meat to charge or attempt to charge more than the following prices :—

Mutton	per seer 6 annas.
Goat flesh	" " 5 "

And being confident that a sufficiency of live animals can be obtained at a price to yield the butcher a reasonable profit on the basis of the above price.

I warn all concerned that it will be an offence against Martial Law for any person, who during the past week has generally dealt in meat, to refuse, without valid reason, to sell meat at the price now fixed when called upon to do so.

FRANK JOHNSON, Lieut.-Col.,
Headquarters, Punjab Club, *Commanding Lahore (Civil) Area.*
Time : 13-10 hours.
Lahore, 7th May, 1919.

No. 38

In accordance with the notice contained in Martial Law Order No. 34 of 5th May, 1919, I publish below the returns rendered to me as to stock of wheat held in the Area under my Command :—

And I further give notice that a reward varying in accordance with the magnitude of the mis-statements proved, but in no case less than Rs. 50 nor more than Rs. 500, will be paid to any person giving information which leads to the conviction of a person who has failed to render a return (or rendered one containing materially inaccurate figures) in response to Martial Law Order No. 34.

[Altogether 96 returns were made representing well over 22,000 maunds of wheat.]

FRANK JOHNSON, Lieut.-Col.,
Headquarters, Punjab Club, *Commanding Lahore (Civil) Area.*
Time : 12-10 hours.
Lahore, 7th May, 1919.

No. 39

Whereas my attention has been drawn to the rising price of Gram;

And whereas I have reason to believe that certain dealers in the Area under my Command are holding secret stores of Gram, the price of which is thereby artificially inflated;

NOW, THEREFORE, by virtue of the powers vested in me by Martial Law, I make the following Order :—

Every trader, banker, bunnia, or other person in the said Area who owns or possesses, directly or indirectly, Gram exceeding 5 maunds in weight, shall render to me in writing (enclosed in an envelope marked "Gram") by 09-00 hours on the 11th day of May, 1919, a Return showing the total quantity of Gram owned or possessed by him.

And so that no person intending to evade this Order may subsequently, when faced with the consequences of such evasion, complain that he was unaware of the procedure to be adopted by me.

I warn all concerned that as soon as possible after the hour named for the rendering of the said Returns, I shall cause them to be published, and at the same time offer substantial rewards for information that will lead to the conviction of any person failing to submit or submitting an inaccurate Return.

And such reward will be paid by the person disobeying this Order, in addition to such other punishment as, by virtue of Martial Law, I am empowered to impose.

And I further warn would-be informers of the consequences of giving me false information.

Headquarters, Punjab Club,
Time : 13-40 hours.
Lahore, 7th May, 1919.

FRANK JOHNSON,
Lieutenant-Colonel,
Commanding Lahore (Civil) Area.

No. 40

WHEREAS representations have been made to me regarding the hardship suffered by the poorer classes of the people owing to the present high prices of cotton cloth;

AND WHEREAS I find that the Cloth Merchants in the Area under my Command, with the hope and intention of enriching themselves, have purchased large stocks of cotton goods at high prices, and are now faced with a loss owing to the fall in the price of such goods in the markets of the world;

AND WHEREAS I find such Merchants are naturally opposed to the introduction of cheaper cloths until such time as their present stocks are exhausted;

AND WHEREAS the Government of India, studying the interest of the poorer people, did by the Cotton Cloth Act of 1918, secure a certain percentage of the output of all Cotton Mills in India at a low rate;

AND WHEREAS I find that such cheap cotton cloth, known as "Standard" cloth is not at present available to the people of Lahore;

AND WHEREAS the Director of Civil Supplies, acting for me, has obtained a sufficient quantity of such Standard cloth, and I deem it preferable to persuade the ordinary Cloth Merchants to deal in such cloth rather than open Government shops for that purpose;

Now, therefore, by virtue of the powers vested in me by Martial Law, I order the Cloth Merchants named below to stock and sell Standard cloth from 10-00 hours on Tuesday, 13th day of May 1919, at the price of Annas six (6) Pies nine (9) per yard, a rate which I have satisfied myself will leave a reasonable profit to the seller;

And further, that it shall be deemed a contravention of Martial Law if more than 12 yards are sold to any one purchaser, or if any person, having purchased such cloth from one of the Merchants referred to, re-sells it.

I further order each of the said Merchants to report themselves, either personally or by representative, to the Textile Assistant to the Director Industries at the Government Central Weavery, Old Police Lines, Sheranwala Gate, Lahore, between 07-00 and 14-00 hours on Monday, 12th May, 1919, with Rs. 493-6-6 in cash with which to purchase and take delivery of one bale containing about 1, 368 yards of the said cloth.

NAMES AND ADDRESSES OF MERCHANTS SELECTED FOR THE SALE OF CHEAP CLOTH.

[*30 in number*]

Headquarters, Punjab Club,
Time : 11-10 hours.
Lahore, 9th May, 1919.

FRANK JOHNSON,
Lieutenant-Colonel,
Commanding Lahore (Civil) Area.

No. 41

WHEREAS by Martial Law Order No. 35, of the 5th May, 1919, I fixed the maximum retail prices of certain vegetables ;

AND WHEREAS, I now find that certain of such prices can be still further reduced in the interest of the consumer without being unjust to the producer or seller.

NOW, THEREFORE, by virtue of the powers vested in me by Martial Law, I order that after 05-00 hours on Saturday, 10th May, 1919, it shall be a contravention of Martial Law, to charge or attempt to charge more than the prices set forth below for the following vegetables, viz :—

		RS.	A.	P.	
Baingan	... ...	0	1	0	per seer.
Bhindi Tori	... ...	0	4	0	Ditto
Karele	... ...	0	4	0	Ditto
Onions, dry (other than Karachi)	...	0	0	9	Ditto
Sag	... ...	0	0	9	Ditto
Kadu (Pahari)	... ...	0	0	6	each

And with those exceptions all the prices fixed in my said Martial Law Order No. 35 of 5th May, 1919, remain in force until further orders.

FRANK JOHNSON, LIEUT.-COL.,
Commanding Lahore (Civil) Area.

Headquarters, Punjab Club,
Time: 12-45 hours.
Lahore, 9th May, 1919.

No. 42

WHEREAS the Amir of Afghanistan has seen fit to take certain hostile action against the Government of His Majesty the King Emperor;

AND WHEREAS I deem it desirable to take steps to ascertain the names and business of all subjects of the said Amir, who may be in the Area under my Command;

NOW, THEREFORE, by virtue of the powers vested in me under Martial Law, I make the following Orders:—

(1) No Afghan subject shall leave the Area under my Command without my written permission.

(2) Every Afghan subject (except women and children accompanying husband or parents) now in the Area under my Command shall present himself for registration at the Headquarters of this Area between 09-00 hours to-morrow (Sunday), the 11th day of May, 1919, and 17-00 hours on Monday, the 12th day of May, 1919.

(3) From and including Tuesday, the 13th day of May 1919, it shall be an offence against Martial Law, for any person to harbour or assist in any way an Afghan subject not in possession of a Certificate of Registration signed by me or on my behalf.

And I further declare that should any person know of the existence of any unregistered Afghan subject in the Area under my Command, and fail to report such knowledge to me immediately, such person shall be deemed to have contravened Martial law, and be dealt with accordingly.

FRANK JOHNSON, LIEUT.-COL.,
Commanding Lahore (Civil) Area.

Headquarters, Punjab Club,
Lahore, 10th May, 1919.

No. 43

WHEREAS by Martial Law Order No. 15 of 18 April, 1919, I warned all people in the Area under my Command to refrain from spreading false, inaccurate or exaggerated reports or rumours in connection with the military or political situation;

AND WHEREAS I find rumours as false as they are stupid being circulated in the said Area in connection with events now taking place in or on the borders of Afghanistan, I deem it desirable to repeat my warning of the 18th April as to the severity of punishment that will be inflicted on any persons inventing, repeating or giving currency to false, inaccurate, or stupid rumours, particularly in connection with Afghanistan;

And so that no person shall be able to plead that he must listen to such rumours or remain in ignorance of passing events, I give notice that all communiques issued by the Government contain true and authentic news, and that all such communiques may be seen in the *Civil & Military Gazette* and *Haq*.

FRANK JOHNSON, LIEUT.-COL.,
Commanding Lahore (Civil) Area.

Headquarters, Punjab Club,
Time: 16-45 hours.
Lahore, 10th May, 1919.

No. 44

WHEREAS by various Martial Law Orders I ordered certain action to be taken with a view to restraining the seditious activities of the students of certain Colleges;

AND WHEREAS the Principals of some of the Colleges of Lahore have now reported to me that they have inflicted the following punishments, that is to say :—

1—DYAL SINGH COLLEGE

(*a*) Expulsion from the College :—

(i) Kundan Lal	...	Fourth year student.
(ii) Basti Ram	...	Third year student.
(iii) Bua Datt	...	Second year student.
(iv) Sukha Ram	...	Do.
(v) Ram Rattan	...	First year student.
(vi) Dewan Chand	...	Do.
(vii) Hazari Lal	...	Second year student.

(*b*) To rusticate for one year :—

(i) Bansi Lal	...	Fourth year student.
(ii) Khazan Chand	...	Do.
(iii) Chiragh Din	...	Second year student.
(iv) Asa Nand	...	Do.
(v) Dharam Singh		First year student.

(*c*) To be put back by one year :—

(i) Daulat Rai	...	Fourth year student.
(ii) Gokal Chand	...	Do.
(iii) Mohar Chand	...	First year student.
(iv) Dina Nath	...	Do.
(v) Purshottam Lal	...	Do.
(vi) Piare Lal	...	Do.
(vii) Balkishan	...	Do.
(viii) Guli Chand	...	Do.
(ix) Durga Prasad	...	First year student.
(x) Sant Ram	...	Do.
(xi) Salig Ram	...	Do.
(xii) Bhagwan Das	...	Do.
(xiii) Ishar Das	...	Do.
(xiv) Pralhad Chand	...	Do.

(*d*) To be suspended for three months:—

(i) Shinghar Singh	...	First year student.
(ii) Kidar Ishwar	...	Do.
(iii) Harnam Lal	...	Do.
(iv) Roop Chand	...	Do.

(*e*) To be deprived of their Scholarships for three months :—

(i) Dina Nath ... First year student.
(ii) Guli Chand ... Do.

(*f*) Fined Rs. 20 each :—

(i) Baij Nath ... Fourth year student.
(ii) Kishan Lal ... Do.
(iii) Ishar Das ... Do.
(iv) Kishan Chand ... Do.
(v) Ram Nath Sithi ... Second year student.
(vi) Dina Nath ... Do.

(*g*) Fined Rs. 10 each ... 219 students.

(*h*) To find security of Rs. 25 each ... 245 students.

(*i*) All students who failed to appear for examination on the 11th April, 1919, to be declared to have failed in the subjects of such examination.

2—Sanatana Dharma College

(*a*) To find security of Rs. 20 each ... 18 students.
(*b*) " " Rs. 10 " ... 53 students.
(*c*) " " Rs. 5 " ... 7 students.

Note—the students of this College were also interned for a period in the Fort.

3—Forman Christian College

(*a*) Expelled :—

(i) D. D. Chopra ... 6th year student.

(*b*) Rusticated for one year :—

(i) Manzur Hasan Khan ... 3rd year student.
(ii) Mohd. Hashim Khan ... Do.

(*c*) Detained for one year and not allowed to live in any hostel belonging to the College :—

(i) Sher Singh ... 6th year student.

(*d*) Detained for one year :—

(i) Karam Singh ... 3rd year student.
(ii) Rallia Ram ... 4rd year student.

(*e*) Fined Rs. 25 each :—

(i) Gujjar Mall ... 4rd year student.
(ii) Balbir Singh ... Do.

(*f*) Fined Rs. 10 each :—

(i)	Hari Singh	...	3rd year student.
(ii)	Munir-ud-Din	...	Do.
(iii)	H. R. K. Dogra	...	Do.

(*g*) Every resident of a hostel of the College, who did not attend the College on the 11th and 12th April without due reason, find Rs. 5 each.

4—DAYANAND ANGLO-VEDIC COLLEGE

(*a*) Expulsion (not in future to enter any College of the University):—

(i)	Sita Ram Aggarwal	...	3rd year student.
(ii)	Gian Chand Sangari	...	Do.
(iii)	J. S. Talwar	...	Do.
(iv)	Sada Nand	...	Do.
(v)	Gurdas Ram Anand	...	3rd year student.
(vi)	Som Dutt	...	Do.
(vii)	Mela Ram Sehgal	...	Do.
(viii)	Ram Nath	...	Do.
(ix)	Durga Dutt	...	Do.
(x)	Ram Rakha Bawa	...	Do.

(*b*) Rustication for one year :—

(i)	Vidya Sagar	...	3rd year student.
(ii)	Kundan Lal	...	1st year student.
(iii)	Sarv Mittra	...	3rd year student.
(iv)	Achint Ram	...	Do.
(v)	Chaman Lal	...	1st year student.

(*c*) To be put back one year :—

(i)	Keshori Lal	...	3rd year student.
(ii)	Dukh Bhajan Lal	...	Do.
(iii)	Hari Kishan	...	Do.
(iv)	Jagan Nath Deora	...	Do.
(v)	Indar Singh	...	Do.
(vi)	Jamna Das	...	Do.
(vii)	Bashambar Nath Basin	...	Do.
(viii)	Haveli Ram	...	1st year student.
(ix)	Bhagat Ram	...	Do.
(x)	Dhunda Mal	...	Do.

(xi)	Ganesh Das Dhawan	...	Do.
(xii)	Basheshar Nath	...	Do.
(xiii)	Munshi Ram	...	Do.
(xiv)	Som Dutt Sharma	...	3rd year student.
(xv)	Jamna Das	...	Do.

(*d*) Will not be permitted to rejoin the College to prepare for any subsequent examination :—

(i)	Bhim Sen Prashar	...	2nd year student.
(ii)	Ram Prashad	...	Do.
(iii)	Charan Das	...	4th year student.
(iv)	Pindi Das	...	2nd year student.
(v)	Abnashi Ram	...	Do.
(vi)	Bishan Das Chopra	...	4th year student.

(*e*) Forfeiture of scholarships and stipends:—

(i)	Gian Chand Sangari	...	3rd year student.
(ii)	Sita Ram Aggarwal	...	Do.
(iii)	Haveli Ram	...	1st year student.
(iv)	Ram Rakha	...	Do.
(v)	Din Dyal	...	Do.
(vi)	Ram Chand	...	3rd year student.
(vii)	Shiv Prashad	...	Do.
(viii)	Ram Karn	...	1st year student.
(ix)	Behari Lal	...	Do.
(x)	Khushi Ram	...	Do.

(*f*) To deposit security of Rs. 50 each ... 112 students.

(*g*) To pay fine of Rs. 10 each ... 270 students.

AND WHEREAS considering the aforesaid punishments, although very lenient and merciful, to be sufficient to restrain students in the future from being misled into disloyal and seditious action, I direct that, adequate disciplinary action having thus been taken, all restrictions imposed on certain students by Martial Law Orders No. 7 of 16th April, 1919, and No. 16 of 18th April, 1919, are cancelled from this date.

But in order, however, to minimise the chances of students being led or leading others astray, I Order that every student on the roll of a College in Lahore shall not reside, without my written permission, in any other place than in the Area under my Command or his registered home.

Headquarters, Punjab Club, FRANK JOHNSON, LIEUT.-COL.,
Lahore, 12th May, 1919. *Commanding Lahore (Civil) Area.*

No. 45

WHEREAS on the 15th day of April, 1919, in order to minimise the work of the Troops and Police and the better to maintain public order and safety in the area under my command, by Martial Law Notice No. 1, I forbade certain classes of the inhabitants of the said area to leave their houses or be in the public streets or roads between 20-00 hours and 05-00 hours daily;

AND WHEREAS by Martial Law Order No. 20 of 21st April, I substituted 21-00 hours for 20-00 hours laid down in the said Martial Law Order No. 1;

AND WHEREAS orders issued by me under Martial Law having been generally obeyed to my satisfaction, I am desirous of still further limiting the restrictions I deemed it necessary to impose on the movements of the people during the hours of darkness;

NOW, THEREFORE, I order and direct that subject to the continued good conduct of the people, the hours during which the streets, etc., are closed, shall be between 22-00 hours 05-00 hours and this alteration shall come into force at 22-00 hours on 13th day of May, 1919.

Headquarters, Punjab Club, FRANK JOHNSON, LIEUT.-COL.,
Time : hours. *Commanding Lahore (Civil) Area.*
Lahore, 12th May, 1919.

No. 46

WHEREAS by Martial Law Orders No. 36 of 5th May, 1919, and No. 44 of 12th May, 1919, I have caused to be made known the punishments inflicted by the Principals of various Colleges on certain of their students.

NOW THEREFORE, I set forth below details of the punishments which have been inflicted by the Principals of certain other Colleges in the Area under my Command, in order that present and future students may be warned thereby of the certainty with which punishment, imposed in these cases with the utmost mercy, follows participation in disloyal and seditious occurrences:—

1—GOVERNMENT COLLEGE

(*a*) Expulsion—Not in future to enter any College of the University :—

(i)	Jiwan Lal Gauba	...	1st year student.
(ii)	Nand Lal Saighal	...	2nd year student.
(iii)	Nand Lal Dhal	...	Do.
(iv)	Kartar Singh Bhalla	...	Do.
(v)	Jagat Ram Sethi	...	3rd year student.
(vi)	Ghazanfar Ali Khan	...	4th year student.

(*b*) Having completed their courses for the examinations, will not be taken back afterwards, either for the same examination if they fail, or for a higher one if they pass :—

(i)	Balwant Rai	...	2nd year student.
(ii)	Amrit Lal	...	Do.
(iii)	Hari Datt	...	4th year student.
(iv)	Parkash Chandra	...	Do.
(v)	Chuni Lal Nayar	...	Do.
(vi)	Kishen Dyal Kapur	...	Do.

(*c*) Rustication for one year:—

(i)	Brahma Vallabh	...	1st year student.
(ii)	Jawahir Singh	...	Do.
(iii)	Sant Singh	...	Do.
(iv)	Kishen Chand	...	Do.
(v)	Prahlad Varma	...	Do.
(vi)	Mehdi Hassan	...	Do.

(*d*) Forfeiture of scholarships:—

(i)	Hans Raj	...	1st year student.
(ii)	Sardari Lal Malhotra	...	Do.
(iii)	Viyas Dev	...	Do.
(iv)	Rajendar Nath	...	Do.
(v)	Mohammad Musa Khan	...	Do.
(vi)	Jagat Singh	...	Do.
(vii)	Ajodhya Lal	...	Do.
(viii)	Arjan Dev	...	Do.
(ix)	Des Raj	...	Do.
(x)	Nazir Ahmad	...	Do.

(xi)	Mohammad Sharif	...	Do.
(xii)	Hari Chand	...	Do.
(xiii)	Abdul Khaliq	...	Do.
(xiv)	Kishen Chand	...	Do.
(xv)	Sardari Lal Jain	...	Do.

(*e*) Forfeiture of half-fee concessions:—

(i)	Gopal Das	...	1st year student.
(ii)	Sardari Lal	...	Do.
(iii)	Devi Singh Lehre	...	Do.
(iv)	Hari Chand	...	Do.
(v)	Bishen Das	...	Do.

2—LAW COLLEGE

(*a*) To be put back for one year:—

(i)	Guru Das Sani	...	L. L. B. Class.
(ii)	Ram Rang Trikha	...	Do.
(iii)	Sada Lal	...	Do.
(iv)	Brij Lal Syal	...	F. E. L. Class.
(v)	Bal Dev	...	Do.
(vi)	Kanad Dev Sondhi	...	Do.
(vii)	Ram Saran Sharma	...	Do.

(*b*) Fined Rs. 10 each ... 38 students.
(nearly all of L.L.B Class)

(*c*) Fined Rs. 5 each ... 58 students.
of the L.L.B. and F. E. L. Class

(*d*) Fined Rs. 3 each ... 28 students.
of the F. E. L. Class

Headquarters, Punjab Club,
Time: 11-35 hours.
Lahore, 13th May, 1919.

FRANK JOHNSON, LIEUT.-COL.
Commanding Lahore (Civil) Area.

No. 47

WHEREAS I published in Martial Law Order No. 38, the Returns rendered to me as to stocks of Wheat held in the area under my Command on the morning of the 7th May, 1919:

AND WHEREAS certain persons, against whom action has been taken, failed to render their returns by the hour named;

Now, therefore I publish below the Returns received from those persons:—

[16 *in number.*]

Headquarters, Punjab Club,
Time : 14-30 hours
Lahore, 14th May, 1919.

FRANK JOHNSON, Lieut.-Col.,
Commanding Lahore (Civil) Area.

No. 48

In accordance with the Notice contained in Martial Law Order No. 39 of 8th May, 1919, I publish below the Returns rendered to me as to stocks of Gram in the Area under my Command :—

[*Altogether 55 Returns were rendered representıng Gram aggregating well ovr 25,000 Mds.*]

Headquarters, Punjab Club,
Time : 16-10 hours.
Lahore, 14th May, 1919.

FRANK JOHNSON, Lieut.-Col.,
Commanding Lahore (Civil) Area.

Martial Law Notice

(1) With reference to Martial Law Order No. 34 of 5th May, 1919, it is notified for information that Returns are not required of Wheat coming into possession of persons subsequent to 7th May, 1919.

(2) It is also notified that there is no intention of commandeering Wheat and that there is no restriction whatever on the amount of wheat which may be held in stock.

(3) Drastic steps are being taken to stamp out the habit of adulterating Milk and other food, and all concerned are notified that heavy penalties will invariably be imposed on conviction.

Headquarters, Punjab Club,
Time : 16.30 hours.
Lahore, 14th May, 1919.

E.C. BARNES, Major.
for Lieutenant-Colonel,
Commanding Lahore (Civil) Area.

No. 49

Whereas the behaviour of the people in the Area under my Command renders it possible to modify and/or annul various Martial Law Orders which from time to time I deemed necessary to issue and impose in the interests of order and public safety :

Now, therefore, I make the following Orders :—

(1) Martial Law Orders No. 6 and 12 of 16th April, 1919, are cancelled from this hour.

(2) Martial Law Order No. 1 (i) of 15th April, 1919, and No. 45 of 12th May, 1919, are still further modified so that after 22-00 hours on the 16th May, 1919, it shall be lawful to be in the streets and roads at all hours except only those between 22-00 hours and 04-00 hours inclusive.

(3) Martial Law Order No. 1 (4) of 15th April 1919, and Section 9 of Proclamation, dated 19th April, 1919, are so modified that the processions and gatherings in connection with *bona-fide* religious services, weddings, funerals or circumcision of children, shall be lawful without my written permission, provided always that such processions or gatherings do not exceed 100 persons in all and are not accompanied by any band or music.

In announcing these first relaxations of Martial Law Orders I warn all concerned that these concessions must not be misinterpreted as a sign of the weakening of Martial Law, which will still be applied with all swiftness and severity against those engaged in seditious propaganda or in attempting to aid the King's enemies;

And in particular I warn traders and bunnias that I am determined with all the power vested in me under Martial Law, to protect the people in the Area under my Command in the matter of adulteration of foods, or refusing to sell the necessaries of life at the reasonable prices I have fixed or may hereafter fix.

Headquarters, Punjab Club, FRANK JOHNSON, LIEUT.-COL.,
Time : 16-10 hours. *Commanding Lahore (Civil) Area.*
Lahore, 15th May, 1919.

No. 50

WHEREAS this is the Mahomedan Festival known as Shabrat when those of that faith usually visit their mosques during the hours of the night.

And being desirous that the necessities of Martial Law should interfere as little as possible with the religious exercises of the people in the Area under my Command.

NOW, THEREFORE, I give Notice that during to-night, the night of 15-16th May, Mahomedans wishing to visit their mosques may do so at any hour without let or hindrance, notwithstanding any Martial Law Order to the contrary.

But nothing in this Order shall be construed as permitting the opening of the Badshahi Masjid which remains closed pending the receipt of guarantees against its future misuse, nor the use of fireworks, nor does it refer to any other period than the night specified.

Headquarters, Punjab Club, FRANK JOHNSON, LIEUT.-COL.,
Time : 11-25 hours. *Commanding Lahore (Civil) Area.*
Lahore, 15th May, 1919.

No. 51

WHEREAS, a complete list of occupiers or owners of all buildings in the Area under my Command is to be prepared;

NOW, THEREFORE, by virtue of the powers vested in me by Martial Law I issue the following Orders:—

(1) The entire Area has been divided into 24 blocks.

(2) Each block has been put in charge of a separate *Patwari* to prepare the required list.

(3) It will be the duty of the *Patwari* to give 24 hours' previous general notice to the occupiers and owners of the particular part or locality of his block which he proposes to do each day.

(4) It will be the duty of each occupier or owner of the house or area in the locality about which a general notice has been issued to be present in person or by proxy at his place and furnish or cause to be furnished to the *Patwari* on his arrival the following information, i.e.:—

(i) His name, occupation and full address.

(ii) Annual rent of the house or part of the house or of the area occupied by him.

(iii) If a house or a part of a house or area is occupied by the owner or is occupied free of rent, he will state the annual rental value of the same, having regard to the cost of the building and the rents prevailing in the locality.

(iv) Furnish any other information necessary for the correct preparation of the required list.

And I warn all concerned that failure to comply with this Order or to furnish wrong information will result in severe punishment under Martial Law.

Headquarters, Punjab Club, FRANK JOHNSON, LIEUT.-COL.,
Time : 10-20 hours. *Commanding, Lahore (Civil) Area.*
Lahore, 17th May, 1919.

No. 52

WHEREAS, by Martial Law Orders No. 35 of 5th May, 1919, and No. 41 of 9th May, 1919, I fixed the maximum retail prices of certain vegetables;

AND WHEREAS, I now find that certain of such prices can be still further reduced in the interests of the consumer without injustice to either producer or seller;

NOW, THEREFORE, by virtue of the powers vested in me by Martial Law, I order that after 05-00 hours on Monday, 19th May, 1919, it shall be a contravention of Martial Law, to charge or attempt to charge more than the prices set forth below for the following vegetables, *viz.*:—

Name of Vegetable	*Maximum Retail Price*			
	Rs.	*A.*	*P.*	
Baingan	0	0	6	per seer.
Bhindi, Tori	0	3	0	per seer.
Karele	0	2	6	per seer.
Tori (green)	0	1	6	per seer.
Kadu (Ghia)	0	0	3	each.
Kadu (Pahari)	0	0	3	each.

Headquarters, Punjab Club, FRANK JOHNSON, LIEUT.-COL.,
Time : 12-25 hours. *Commanding, Lahore (Civil) Area.*
Lahore, 17th May, 1919.

No. 53

WHEREAS, owing to the misuse of the BADSHAHI MOSQUE by Mahomedans and Hindus as a meeting-place for the furtherance of seditious agitation, a misuse which constituted a danger to the peace, I by virtue not only of the powers conferred on me by Martial Law, but also by the right to deny access to the said Mosque vested for ever in the Commandant of Lahore on the 10th day of June 1856, when the said Mosque was, on certain conditions, given back to the

Mahomedan community, deemed it necessary to use and did so close and deny access to the said Mosque;

AND WHEREAS I have now received from a Committee of leading Mahomedans satisfactory guarantees and assurances against the future misuse of the said Mosque;

NOW, THEREFORE, I order that from the date hereof, all Mahomedans shall have access to the said BADSHAHI MASJID without let or hindrance and shall continue to have the free and undisturbed use of the said Mosque on original conditions.

Headquarters, Punjab Club, FRANK JOHNSON, LIEUT.-COL.,
Time : 13-45 hours. *Commanding Lahore (Civil) Area.*
Lahore, 20th May, 1919.

NOTICE

It is notified for the information of all concerned that the Office of the Lahore (Civil) Area has been transferred to Faletti's Hotel, (Telephone No. 92).

FRANK JOHNSON, LIEUT.-COL.,
Commanding Lahore (Civil) Area.

No. 54

WHEREAS it has been brought to my notice that excessive waste of water is taking place, both in the City and Civil Station of Lahore, where, owing to the present disturbances, the Government of the Punjab and many troops have to reside;

AND WHEREAS I have satisfied myself (*a*) that the four million gallons of water per diem now being supplied are more than sufficient for the needs of all, and (b) that the present supply cannot be increased at present;

NOW, THEREFORE, by virtue of the powers vested in me by Martial Law, I Order that after 12-00 hours tomorrow, the 24th day of May, 1919, it shall be deemed a contravention of Martial Law for any person or persons to waste or misuse the pipe supply of water.

FRANK JOHNSON, LIEUT.-COL.,
Headquarters, Faletti's Hotel, *Commanding Lahore (Civil) Area.*
Time : 13-10 hours.
Lahore, 23rd May, 1919.

No. 55

WHEREAS, I have received information that certain persons have insisted on being driven in Tongas retained for Military Services, and in some cases have actually assaulted the drivers who rightly refused to accept such persons as "fares";

AND WHEREAS all such Tongas in Military Services can be readily distinguished by the letter and number painted on the dash board;

NOW, THEREFORE, by virtue of the power vested in me under Martial Law, I declare that it shall be a contravention of such Law for any person to induce by threats, bribes or otherwise, any driver of Tonga in Military employ to ply for hire or neglect the work which he may be ordered to perform.

Headquarters, Faletti's Hotel, FRANK JOHNSON, LIEUT.-COL.,
Time : 15-45 hours. *Commanding Lahore (Civil) Area.*
Lahore, 23rd May, 1919.

No. 56

WHEREAS the Hindu Festival known as Bhadrakali, takes place on Sunday next, the 25th day of May, 1919, when people of the Hindu faith usually gather together for the purpose of worship at the Bhadrakali Temple in Lahore City;

And being desirous that the necessities of Martial Law should interfere as little as possible with the religious exercises of the people in the Area under my Command;

NOW, THEREFORE, I give Notice that during the night of Sunday next, i.e., the night of 25th-26th May 1919, the inhabitants of this Area may be out in the streets until 23-00 hours.

But nothing in this Order shall be construed as permitting the use of fireworks, nor does it refer to any other period than the night specified.

Headquarters, Faletti's Hotel, FRANK JOHNSON, LIEUT.-COL.,
Time : 07-15 hours. *Commanding Lahore (Civil) Area.*
Lahore, 24th May, 1919.

No. 57

WHEREAS, His Honour the Lieutenant-Governor Sir Michael O'Dwyer, K.C.I.E., K.C.S.I., has been pleased to express his wish that any restrictions imposed by the necessities of Martial Law, which might interfere with the religious observances of the people in the

Area under my Command, may be reduced to the minimum demanded by the Military situation.

AND WHEREAS the representatives of the Mohamedan community have petitioned me that from the commencement of the RAMZAN, the "Curfew" hours may be reduced to from 23-00 hours to 02-30 hours.

NOW, THEREFORE, seeing the excellent manner in which all Martial Law Orders have been obeyed in the Area under my Command, I make the following order, that is to say:—

With effect from 23-00 hours on Tuesday, the 27th day of May, 1919, until further Notice, Martial Law Order No. 1 (1) of the 15th April, 1919, and all subsequent modifications of such Order, are cancelled, and it shall only be unlawful for the persons referred to in such Order to be outside their houses or compounds between 23-59 hours (Midnight) and 02-00 hours.

Headquarters, Faletti's Hotel, FRANK JOHNSON, LIEUT.-COL.,
Time : 07-30 hours. *Commanding Lahore (Civil) Area.*
Lahore, 24th May, 1919.

No. 58

WHEREAS by Martial Law Order No. 29. dated 25th April 1919, I fixed the maximum retail price of ATTA at 6½ seers per rupee, and by Martial Law Order No. 32, dated 29th April, 1919, the maximum retail price of WHEAT at 7¾ seers per rupee;

AND WHEREAS the prices of the said commodities have risen since the above mentioned Orders were issued;

NOW THEREFORE, by virtue of the powers vested in me by Martial Law, I order that from and after 14-00 hours on the 30th day of May, 1919.

(*a*) not less than 6¼ (six and a quarter) seers of Atta shall be supplied for a Rupee, and

(*b*) not less than 7 (seven) seers of WHEAT shall be supplied for a Rupee.

And I warn all concerned that the other provisions of Martial Law Order Nos. 29 and 32 are still applicable and in force, and that any contravention thereof or of this Order will be dealt with summarily under Martial Law.

Headquarters, Faletti's Hotel, FRANK JOHNSON, LIEUT.-COL.,
Time : 11-55 hours. *Commanding Lahore (Civil) Area.*
Lahore, 28th May, 1919.

No. 59

WHEREAS the Mahomedan Mela known as PAR-KA-MELA takes place on the 14th and 15th June, 1919, when certain Mahomedans gather together at the Tomb of JAHANGIR at Shahdara, near Lahore;

And being desirous that the necessities of Martial Law should interfere as little as possible with such Melas;

NOW, THEREFORE, I give notice that for the period of the two days mentioned above, persons may gather together at the said JAHANGIR'S TOMB according to custom, and such persons attending the said Mela are permitted to be out of their houses during prohibited hours of the two nights in question, *i.e.*, the nights of the 14th-15th and 15th-16th June, 1919.

W.J.W. BRACKENBURY, LIEUT.-COL.,
Commanding Lahore (Civil) Area.

Headquarters, Faletti's Hotel,
Time : 12-30 hours.
Lahore, 31st May, 1919.

No. 60

WHEREAS Martial Law Orders No. 29 of 25th April, 1919, No. 32 of 29th April, 1919, and No. 58 of 28th May, 1919, were issued with a view to protect the public from the hardship and injustice of the exorbitant prices of WHEAT and ATTA;

AND WHEREAS it has now been represented to me that the necessity for fixing the prices of these two articles no longer exists;

NOW, THEREFORE, by virtue of the powers vested in me by Martial Law, I deem it advisable to suspend Martial Law Order No. 58, which fixed the prices of WHEAT and ATTA;

But I warn all dealers in these articles that the refusal to sell either WHEAT or ATTA shall continue to be a contravention of Martial Law, and will be dealt with as heretofore.

In order to further encourage dealers to import WHEAT, ATTA and GRAM into Lahore I direct the Municipality to refrain, for a period of ten days from this date, from levying octroi on WHEAT, ATTA or GRAM.

W.J.W. BRACKENBURY, LIEUT.-COL.,
Commanding Lahore (Civil) Area.

Headquarters, Faletti's Hotel,
Time : 16-15 hours.
Lahore, 2nd June, 1919.

No. 61

WHEREAS by Martial Law Orders No. 35, dated 5th May, 1919, and No. 52, dated 17th May, 1919, the maximum retail prices of certain vegetables were fixed under Martial Law;

AND, WHEREAS, I now deem it expedient to further amend such prices;

NOW, THEREFORE, by virtue of the powers vested in me under Martial Law, and notwithstanding anything contained in the aforesaid Martial Law Orders to the contrary, I ORDER THAT from 05-00 hours on the 5th June, 1919, it shall be a contravention of Martial Law to charge or attempt to charge more than the prices set forth below for the following vegetables, *viz.* :—

			Rs.	A.	P.	
Bhindi Tori	...	...	0	2	3	per seer
Karele	...	...	0	1	0	"
Tomatoes	...	...	0	1	0	"
Potatoes	...	...	0	1	6	"

W.J.W. BRACKENBURY, LIEUT.-COL.,

Headquarters, Faletti's Hotel, *Commanding Lahore (Civil) Area.*
Time : 15-30 hours.
Lahore, 3rd June, 1919.

No. 62

WHEREAS it has been represented to me that the wholesale price charged for Khewra Salt is exorbitant, and unjustifiable ;

AND WHEREAS I find that, as set forth in Martial Law Order No. 32, dated 29th April, 1919, Khewra Salt can be laid down in this Area at an inclusive cost of Rs. 1-12-0 per maund;

NOW, THEREFORE, by virtue of the powers vested in me by Martial Law, I order that from 18-00 hours to-morrow, Wednesday 4th June, 1919, salt other than imported table salt, shall be supplied to any purchaser of ten maunds or over at any one time and under any one transaction, at a price not exceeding Rs. 2-4-0 per maund.

And I warn all concerned that all those who are to-day selling salt wholesale shall countinue to do so at the new price and under the new conditions;

And I further warn all concerned that Martial Law Order No. 32, dated 29th April, 1919, insofar as it refers to salt remains unaffected by this Order except in regard to the purchase price of quantities of salt ten maunds or more in weight.

W.J.W. BRACKENBURY, LIEUT.-COL.,
Headquarters, Faletti's Hotel, *Commanding Lahore (Civil) Area.*
Time : 16-15 hours.
Lahore, 3rd June, 1919.

No. 63

WHEREAS by Martial Law Order No. 24, dated 23rd April, 1919, I took over a number of electric fans and lights;

AND WHEREAS I now deem it expedient to return them (or their value) to their owners;

NOW, THEREFORE, by virtue of the powers vested in me by Martial Law, I order all such owners to present themselves at Faletti's Hotel, Lahore, between the hours of 09-00 and 11-00 on Monday, the 9th June, 1919, to receive back their electric lights and fans (or their value);

And I warn all owners that should they fail, without sufficient reason, to so present themselves at the place and time mentioned in this Order, the electric lights and fans will remain in my charge at owner's risk, and I will not be further responsible.

W.J.W. BRACKENBURY, LIEUT.-COL.,
Headquarters, Faletti's Hotel, *Commanding Lahore (Civil) Area.*
Time : 12-10 hours.
Lahore, 6th June, 1919.

No. 64

WHEREAS by Martial Law Order Nos. 17, 21, 22 and 23 I ordered all pedal-driven bicycles to be delivered over to me;

AND WHEREAS I now deem it expedient to return all bicycles to their owners;

NOW, THEREFORE, by virtue of the powers vested in me by Martial Law, I order all owners to present themselves at the Cinema, McLeod Road, on any day between the hours of 07-00 and 19-00 but before noon on the 9th June 1919, to receive their bicycles.

And I warn all owners that bicycles not claimed before noon on the 9th June 1919, will remain in my charge but at owner's risk, and I will not be further responsible for the same.

Unless claimed within a further period of 48 hours *i.e.*, before noon on the 11th June, 1919, the bicycles will be handed over to the Superintendent of Police.

W.J.W. BRACKENBURY, LIEUT.-COL.,

Headquarters, Faletti's Hotel, *Commanding Lahore (Civil) Area.*
Time : 12-20 hours.
Lahore, 6th June, 1919.

NOTICE

Notice is hereby given that all temporary owners of commandeered bicycles allotted to them by the military authorities are to return same before 10-00 hours on Monday, 9th June, to the N. C. O. in charge of bicycles, Empire Cinema, Lahore.

Headquarters, Faletti's Hotel, W. D. BACON, Lieutenant,
Lahore, 6th June, 1919. *Staff Officer,*
Lahore (Civil) Area.

G—MISCELLANEOUS

(1)—Government of India Resolution on the Situation

The following resolution of the Government of India, in the Home Department, was published in a *Gazette of India Extraordinary* dated April 14th, 1919 :—

The present situation arising out of the agitation against the Anarchical and Revolutionary Crimes Act (commonly called the Rowlatt Act) renders it imperative on the Governor-General in Council to define the attitude of Government on the subject of that agitation and the serious disorders which have resulted therefrom, and to indicate the nature of the concerted action which it is now necessary to take for the preservation of law and order.

When the Bill was under discussion its opponents publicly stated that if it passed into law a campaign of agitation against it on a scale hitherto unattained would be organised throughout India, and a section of them indicated that they would support that campaign by resort to what is known as passive resistance. No one cognizant of the conditions of India could have been ignorant at the time of the dangers of initiating a widespread movement of this nature. They were clearly pointed out by many public men of moderate views and the representatives of Government did not fail during the debates on the Bill to emphasise the serious consequences to the public peace which would follow, from an agitation such as was then threatened. The warnings were unheeded, and to the agitation which has succeeded the passing of the Act must be directly attributed the open breaches of the public peace, the defiance of authority and the criminal attacks on life and property which have lately been witnessed in certain parts of India.

The agitation has followed a double line of action, namely, direct criticism of the Act by means of public speeches and publications and the initiation of the threatened movement of passive resistance. The latter movement was ushered in by a demonstration consisting of the observance of a day of fasting and the closing of the shops and places of business. Such a demonstration was not in itself illegal; but there is ample evidence to prove that in more than one place those locally responsible for its organisation overstepped the limits of lawful persuasion and resorted to direct interference with the business of many who were not interested in the movement, and to forcible obstruction of the traffic in the public streets.

But the indirect consequences of this aspect of the agitation have been for more mischievous in that it promoted a sense of unrest and of excitement which was bound to react and has reacted on the more ignorant and inflammable section of the population. The campaign has involved in many quarters the use of the most flagrant misrepresentations regarding the character of the Act. It is clear that large number of ignorant people have been deliberately led to believe that the new law gives the police unfettered authority to interfere with public meetings, not only of a political but of a religious and social nature, and to arrest summarily persons engaged in political work, and that it empowers the executive authorities to imprison without trial any person criticising the action of Government.

The Governor-General in Council thinks it necessary to reiterate here the following salient facts concerning this act. It is specially directed against revolutionary and anarchical crime and can only be brought into force in any locality when it has been proved to the satisfaction of the Governor-General in Council that such crime or movements tending to such crime exist. It has not, so far, been brought into operation in any part of India. Its first part merely provides for speedy trial of certain grave offences. In the second and third parts provision is made for preventive action (similar to but much more restricted in scope than that now provided by the rules under the Defence of India Act) against persons suspected of revolutionary or anarchical crime. Action cannot, however, be taken against any individual without the previous order of the local Government. There is nothing, therefore, which can justify the widespread rumours, for which the promoters of the agitation must be held responsible, that unusual or even extended powers have been given to the police, nor is there anything which need cause fear or apprehension to any person other than the revolutionary or the anarchist. Not only do the terms of the Act definitely exclude its use in any case not falling within the definition of anarchical or revolutionary conspiracy, but Government has given the most categorical pledge (which the Governor-General in Council takes this opportunity to reiterate) that the tenor and intention of the Act will be scrupulously safeguarded should occasion arise to put it into operation.

The Governor-General in Council considers it unnecessary to detail here the deplorable occurrences resulting from the agitation against this Act. The offences which have occurred at Delhi, Calcutta, Bombay and Lahore have one common feature—the unprovoked attempt of violent and unruly mobs to hamper or obstruct those charged with the duty of maintaining order in public places. At Amritsar and Ahmedabad they have taken a far graver form—a murderous attack on defenceless individuals and a wholesale and wanton destruction of private and public property. The Governor-General in Council thinks it right to state that at Amritsar the loss of life might have been greater but for the protection afforded by unofficial Indians to those who were threatened by the mob and he takes this opportunity of expressing the gratitude of Government for this conspicuous example of loyalty and humane feeling.

It remains for the Governor-General in Council to assert in the clearest manner the intention of Government to prevent by all means, however drastic, the recurrence of these excesses. He will not hesitate to employ the ample military resources at his disposal to suppress organised outrage, rioting or concerted opposition to the maintenance of law and order and has already sanctioned the application of the State Offences Regulation, 1804, in a modified form to certain districts of the Punjab. He will further use all preventive measures provided by the Statutes to check disorder at its source and in Regulation 3 of 1818, and the corresponding regulations applicable to Bombay and Madras, and in the Rules under the Defence of India Act he has powers which will enable him to deal effectively with those who promote disorder. He has sanctioned the extension of the provisions of the Seditious Meetings Act to the districts of Lahore and Amritsar in the Punjab and will authorise a similar extension to other areas in which local Governments see reason to require it. The Police Act of 1881 enables a local Government to quarter additional police on any locality which is guilty of organised offences against the public peace, at the charge of the inhabitants, and to levy from the latter compensation for those who have suffered from injury to their property. The Governor-General in Council will advise local Governments to make a free use of these provisions where necessary.

The Governor-General in Council feels that many of those who inaugurated this agitation must regret the lamentable consequences which have ensued—the loss of life and property and damage to the reputation of India. He now appeals to all loyal subjects of the Crown and to all those who have an interest in the maintenance of law and the protection of property, both to dissociate themselves publicly from the movement and to exert themselves in quieting unrest and preventing disorder. To all those who render such assistance to the cause of the public and the State and to those servants of Government who are charged with the onerous responsibility of suppressing excesses against public peace and tranquility the Governor-General in Council extends the fullest assurance of countenance and support.

(2)—Proclamation by Lieutenant-Governor

In view of the persistence of false rumours as to the acts and policy of Government spread by evil-minded persons in order to create alarm and hostility to Government among the ignorant and credulous, prompt measures must be taken by all officials of Government and by all law-abiding and respectable persons to contradict such rumours. People can be assured on the following points among others :—

(1) Government has no intention of interfering in any way with the customs of the people as regards births, deaths, marriages or in any other respects, nor is it in contemplation to levy any fees on these occasions.

(2) No extra taxation of any kind is proposed except an income-tax on *sahukars* and traders who have made Rs. 30,000 or more in a year out of war profits. Even this extra income tax is only temporary and for war expenses.

(3) On the other hand, incomes between Rs. 1,000 and Rs. 3,000 have been entirely exempted from income-tax this year. Agricultural income is still as before exempt from all income-tax.

(4) No alteration whatever has been made in the land revenue, cesses or water rates.

(5) No interference whatever is intended with standing crops and with rights in land.

(6) No interference whatever has been made or proposed in existing rights of inheritance.

(7) No damage whatever has been done to the Darbar Sahib at Amritsar, where prayers and ceremonies go on as usual.

(8) No alteration whatever has been made in the existing orders which allow the wearing of *kirpans* by Sikhs.

(9) The Army was enlisted for the period of the war and for six months after the war, and to keep that promise and to release zamindars to return to their villages, the troops are being demobilised as quickly as possible.

(10) The police have been given no fresh powers whatsoever.

(11) Every one is recommended to read the Rowlatt Act, and it will be seen that all rumours about it are false. Copies are being distributed in large numbers.

(12) Public meetings cannot be held without permission in six districts of the Punjab because of the present unrest. Those districts are Lahore, Amritsar, Jullundur, Gujranwala, Lyallpur and Multan. But even in those districts there are no restrictious on family or purely religious gatherings.

(13) Martial Law has been proclaimed in the districts of Lahore, Amritsar, Gujranwala, Gujrat and Lyallpur, where heinous offences have been committed, where murders and arson have taken place and where railway and telegraph lines have been interfered with. Where Martial Law has been proclaimed restrictions have been imposed for the protection of the public. Trains do not run at night and 3rd and intermediate class tickets are issued only on permits. These restrictions are only temporary, and they will be removed as soon as possible and as soon as all classes of the people again become law-abiding and peaceful.

(14) The statement that there is any connection between Martial Law and the Rowlatt Act is absolutely false, as anyone can see by reading the Rowlatt Act.

(15) Martial Law will not be extended to any district in which there is no disorder. But if people listen to false rumours now contradicted authoritatively and rise in rebellion and disorder, they must expect to find Martial Law applied to them.

(16) People who spread or who repeat false rumours should not be listened to, but should be arrested and should be made over to those in authority.

(17) People should remember how in the past, and especially during the war, they have been deceived by false rumours. The people of the Punjab are now learning how baseless these rumours have

been. Order has been restored almost everywhere by the prompt action of the troops—British and Indian—whom the mischief-makers attempted to malign, and by the loyal cooperation of the great mass of the rural population. Existing precautions must however be retained, at least till all criminals are brought to justice. For this purpose tribunals are now sitting. The Lieutenant-Governor counts on the assistance of all loyal citizens in restoring the good name of the province, which has been sullied by recent events in certain districts.

(18) Finally, he assures them that there has been no change whatever in the policy of the Sirkar, which is now and always to protect the peaceable and to punish criminals who disturb the peace. All persons should therefore go about their lawful business as usual and should rest assured that they are under the protection of the King-Emperor.

M. F. O'DWYER,

Lahore, April 26, 1919. *Lieutenant-Governor of the Punjab*

(3)—The land of *Salaaming*

Military Officers and British soldiers were very particular to be *properly* saluted by all who came across them during the Martial Law days. Those who did not salute them or did so in a manner which did not satisfy the soldiers and officers were flogged or beaten. The following is a specimen of the orders issued on the subject :—

NOTICE NO. 2 (LYALLPUR)

"Whereas it has come to my notice that certain inhabitants of the Lyallpur district are habitually exhibiting a lack of respect for Gazetted European or Civil and Military Officers of His Majesty's Services, thereby failing to maintain the dignity of the Government, I hereby order that the inhabitants of the Lyallpur district shall accord to all such officers whenever met the salutation usually accorded to Indian gentlemen of high social position in accordance with the custom of India. That is to say, persons riding on animals or on or in wheeled conveyances will alight, persons carrying open and raised umbrellas shall lower them, and all persons shall salute or '*salaam*' with the hand.

C.G. HODGSON, LIEUT. COL.,

24th April 1919. *Area Officer, Lyallpur."*

(4)—Arrest Without Warrant

It is notified that in exercise of the powers conferred by Rule 12-AA of the Defence of India (Consolidation) Rules, 1915, the Lieutenant-Governor is pleased to authorize all District Magistrates and Superintendents of Police to arrest without warrant any person against whom a reasonable suspicion exists that he is promoting or assisting to promote rebellion against the authority of the Government. —*C. & M.G., May* 11, 1919.

(5)—Ban on Lawyers

The following proclamation has been issued by Major-General Sir W. G. L. Beynon K.C.I.E., C.B., D.S.O., Commanding 16th Indian Division :— Notice is hereby given to all whom it may concern that legal practitioners, whose ordinary place of business is outside the Punjab, will not be allowed to enter the Martial Law area included in the limits of the 16th Indian Division, without the permission of the Administrator of Martial Law. A similar proclamation has been issued by Major-General Sir C.M. Dobell, K.C.B., C.M.G., D.S.O., Commanding the 2nd (Rawalpindi) Division, with reference to the Martial Law area included in the limits of the 2nd Division. —*C. & M.G. May,* 17, 1919.

H—WITHDRAWAL OF MARTIAL LAW

(1)

The following order was issued by the Government of India. Home Department, on May 28, 1919 :—

ORDER

In exercise of the powers conferred by section 2 of the Bengal State Offences Regulation, 1804, the Governor-General in Council is pleased to cancel the orders of the Government of India in the Home Department, dated the 13th of April 1919, the 15th of April 1919, the 19th of April 1919 and the 22nd of April 1919, which were published with the notifications of the Punjab Government Nos. 11877, 11878, 11879, and 11880, dated the 1st May 1919, suspending the functions of the ordinary criminal courts of judicature and establishing Martial Law within the districts of Lahore, Amritsar, Gujranwala and Gujrat, in the province of the Punjab, except in so far as the said orders apply to the areas specified in the second column of the following table :—

District	*Area*
Lahore	(1) The Lahore Civil Area as defined in Punjab Government Notification, Home (Military), No. 10657, dated the 20th of April 1919.
	(2) The Lahore Cantonment.
	(3) The Kasur Municipality.
	(4) All Railway lands.
Amritsar	(1) Amritsar Municipality.
	(2) Amritsar Cantonment.
	(3) The portion of Mauza Amritsar not included in (1) and (2)
	(4) Mauza Kot Saiyid Mahmud.
	(5) All Railway lands.

District	Area
Gujranwala	(1) Gujranwala Municipality.
	(2) Wazirabad Municipality.
	(3) Akalgarh Notified Area.
	(4) Ramnagar Notified Area.
	(5) Hafizabad Notified Area.
	(6) Sangla Notified Area.
	(7) Chuharkana Mandi Notified Area.
	(8) All Railway lands.
Gujrat	(1) all Railway lands.

(2)

The following order was issued by the Government of India, Home Department (Political), on the 9th of June, 1919 :—

ORDER

In exercise of the powers conferred by section 2 of the Bengal State Offences Regulation, 1804, and in continuation of the Order passed on the 28th of May 1919, the Governor-General in Council is pleased to cancel the orders of the Government of India in the Home Department, dated the 13th of April 1919, the 15th of April 1919 and the 22nd of April 1919, which were published with notification of the Punjab Government Nos. 11877, 11878, 11880, 11881 and 11882, dated the 1st May 1919, suspending the functions of the ordinary criminal courts of judicature and establishing Martial Law within the districts of Lahore, Amritsar, Gujranwala, Gujrat and Lyallpur, in the Province of the Punjab, in so for as the said orders apply to the areas specified in the second column of following table and from the date and time mentioned in the third column of the same :

Provided that nothing in this Order shall apply to any railway lands situated in the areas so specified.

District	Area	Time
Lahore	1. The Lahore Civil area as defined in Punjab Government Notification Home (Military) No 10657 dated the 20th April 1919.	Wednesday, the 11th June 1919 at 12 midnight.
	2. The Lahore Cantonment	Ditto ditto
	3. The Kasur Municipality	Monday, the 9th June 1919, at 12 midnight.

Amritsar	1. The Amritsar Municipality	Ditto	ditto
	2. Amritsar Cantonment	Ditto	ditto
	3. The portion of Mauza	Ditto	ditto
	Amritsar not included in (1) and (2)	Ditto	ditto
	4. Mauza Kot Saiyid Mahmad	Ditto	ditto
Gujranwala	1. Gujranwala Municipality	Ditto	ditto
	2. Wazirabad Municipality	Ditto	ditto
	3. Akalgarh Notified Area	Ditto	ditto
	4. Ramnagar Notified Area	Ditto	ditto
	5. Hafizabad Notified Area	Ditto	ditto
	6. Sangla Notified Area	Ditto	ditto
	7. Chuharkana Notified Area	Ditto	ditto
Layallpur	The whole district.		

(Government of India Order No. 1816, Home, dated Simla, August 25, 1919)

(3)

In exercise of the powers conferred by section 2 of the Bengal State Offences Regulation, 1804 and in continuation of the Orders passed on the 28th of May, 1919, and the 9th June, 1919, the 15th April, 1919, the 19th April, 1919 and the 22nd April, 1919 which were published with thenotifications of the Punjab Government Nos. 11877, 11878, 11879, 11880, 11881, 11882, dated the 1st May, 1919, suspending the functions of the ordinary criminal courts of judicature and establishing martial law with in the districts of Lahore, Amritsar, Gujranwala, Gujrat and Lyallpur in so far as the said orders apply to the railway lands situated within those districts.

APPENDIX II
Judgments of Martial Law Commissions*

"In England, the getting up a false case against an innocent man is a comparatively rare thing. In India, it may almost be called one of the customs of the country. If you want to spite your enemy, or to revenge some injury to yourself or your family, one of the most ordinary means of doing it is to bring a false charge. There are always professional witnesses to be had, who would join in such a conspiracy for the sake of a few annas; and it sometimes happens, that the police themselves are engaged as the chief actors in making these abominable charges".— The Right Hon. Sir Richard Garth, Q.C., Late Chief Justice of Bengal.

[Under section 2 (2) of the Martial Law Ordinance, 1919, the Lieutenant-Governor of the Punjab appointed the following four commissions for the purpose of holding trials under section 2 (I) of the said Ordinance:—(1) The Hon'ble Mr. Justice Leslie Jones—*President*; Mr. M. H. Harrison, I.C.S., District and Sessions Judge; S. Din Muhammad, Extra Assistant Commissioner. (2) Lieutenant Colonel A. A. Irvine C.I.E., District and Sessions Judge— *President*; Mr. F. W. Kennaway, District and Sessions Judge; Mr. I.C. Lall. (3) Mr. N.H. Prenter, I.C.S., District and Sessions Judge— *President*; Mr. S.S. Harris, formerly District and Sessions Judge; Major P. W. Elliott, 20th D. C. O. Infantry. (4) The Hon'ble Mr. Justice A. B. Broadway— *President*; Mr. A. H. Brasher, I.C.S., District and Sessions Judge; Khan Bahadur Sheikh Rahim Bakhsh. These Commissions dealt with 114 cases and the number of persons tried by them was 853, of whom 581 were convicted.]

1—BADSHAHI MOSQUE CASE (LAHORE)
(Mr. Justice Leslie Jones' Commission)

The evidence for the defence is worthless. Judicial notice is taken of the fact that there was already a state of rebellion in existence on the 12th of April. On that date a meeting with political objects was held in the Badshahi Mosque, Lahore. It was to be addressed by

---

* Schedules annexed to the judgments have been omitted; but details of sentences passed by Commissions and the reductions made in them by the Government may be ascertained from *Supplement I* at toe end of the book.

leading Hindus. Many Hindus were present and many people armed with sticks. Maulvi Abdul Hai having recognised Ch. Ali Gauhar, a C. I. D. Inspector, who was present in plain clothes, made an inflammatory speech against the C. I. D. in general, saying that no progress with their objects was possible until the C. I. D. were eliminated, and pointed out Ali Gauhar as an object of immediate attack. Mr. Abdul Hai and the other accused then set upon Ali Gauhar, who was beaten with stricks on the body. His assailants had him at their mercy but did not kill him. Followed by the mob he was chased to his house, where he shut himself in. There were shouts of "burn the house" and the door was entered, but the mob did not proceed to extremes. Ali Gauhar's *pagri* was afterwards burnt in the mosque.

Having regard to the state of rebellion which was in existence, the Court hold that in the circumstances the attack on Ali Gauhar, because he was an official of the C. I. D., was an overt act of waging war (see the judgment in the Supplementary Lahore Conspiracy case). There was double object of punishing a C. I. D. official as such and for securing freedom for seditious objects. Abdul Hai is acquitted on the charge under sections 302, 115, I. P. C. because the interpretation which he intended to be put on his words is open to question. All the accused are convicted and sentenced as shown in the annexed schedule to transportation for life and forfeiture of their property, that being the minimum sentence admissible by law.

Accused No. 1, Abdul Hai, was primarily responsible, and it is clear that he has tampered with students. Of the other accused, Bashir Ahmad (No. 2) was in close attendence upon Abdul Hai, and it was Bhagat Ram who burnt Ali Gauhar's *pagri* in the mosque. Labhu Ram (No. 6) is a man of some education who has been to England. At the other end of the scale are two young men, Muni Lal and Feroz Din, aged 21 and 18 respectively. The Court recommend the question of sentences in respect of the prisoners other than Abdul Hai, (No. 1) for the consideration of Government.

2—CROWN *Versus* BALWANT SINGH (LAHORE)

(Mr. Justice Leslie Jones' Commission)

The accused, Balwant Singh, a Ramdasia Sikh, is now a khalasi in the 24th N. W. R. Rifles. On the evening of the 11th of April, 1919, he shouted in the Badshahi Mosque a false story that Indian regiments had mutinied in Lahore Cantonment and were marching on Amritsar and Lahore. He also stated that they had killed about

200-250 British soldiers, and that he himself had killed six. He claimed to be a soldier and was dressed as one. He was garlanded and carried in triumph to the pulpit of the mosque, where he was called upon to make a speech. This he was unable to do and he shortly afterwards disappeared.

The Court hold that he committed an offence under section 121, I. P. C.

The offence is of a most serious character, but the prisoner is a man of no position or influence, and as he did not attempt to translate words into action and the only advice he gave was to go and meet persons who were not coming, he is sentenced as in the annexed schedule.

3—DANDA FAUJ CASE (LAHORE)

(Mr. Justice Leslie Jones' Commission)

The evidence for the defence as to facts is worthless.

Chanan Din, No. I, organised and led a band which called itself the "Danda Fauj," and armed with sticks paraded the streets of Lahore on the evening of the 11th and the morning of 12th April, *i.e.,* at the time when the state of rebellion was already in existence. They marched two deep carrying their sticks as if they were rifles at the slope or trail. At constant halts, they knelt, by numbers, as if in a firing position. On numerous occasions Chanan Din made inflammatory speeches proclaiming that he and his band were rebels and looked, not to His Majesty the King, but to Germany, Turkey and Kabul as their suzerains. He invoked the assistance of God and of these powers to overthrow the British Government. He also made reference to the Rowlatt Bill.

Chanan Din's speeches were applauded by the mob, and the Fauj, as it passed along, was joined by recruits who were supplied with sticks. One of the persons, who, knowing the assembly to be unlawful, supplied sticks, was Sita Ram, No. 7. *No real violence was attempted or committed.*

The evidence against Sham Das, No. 8, who was charged with the same action as that of Sita Ram, is insufficient, and he is acquitted.

Chanan Din, No. I, the principal offender, has already been convicted in the case of Crown *v.* Abdul Hai, etc. Of the other accused Qamar Din and Prem Narain, Nos. 2 and 3, were the most prominent.

Lal Din, No. 5, is given the benefit of previous loyal conduct.

Bashir, No. 4, is a youth of only 16 years. The sentences are as in the schedule annexed.

4—EXTORTION CASE (LAHORE)

(Mr. Justice Leslie Jones' Commission)

Bulaqi Shah and his son, Ram Lal, are rich money-lenders who closed their establishment during the *hartal*. Khuda Bakhsh, Sub-Inspector (No. 1) reported on the 20th April that Bulaqi Shah was encouraging the *hartal*. Next day Ram Lal was told by Ahmad Din (No. 2) that Khuda Bakhsh had a warrant against Bulaqi Shah which could be suppressed on payment. Ram Lal reported the matter, and Munshi Abdul Samad Khan, a Magistrate, was present in concealment at a meeting between the money-lenders and Ahmad Din which took place at 7 p.m. It was arranged that Rs. 300 should be paid next day to Khuda Bakhsh. The following morning Ram Lal visited Khuda Bakhsh, who sent Ahmad Din and Allah Din (No. 3) with him to collect the money at Bulaqi Shah's house, where another Magistrate, Sheikh Rahim Bakhsh was in concealment. The Magistrate arrested Ahmad Din and Allah Din as soon as the money was paid.

There is no evidence to justify the conviction of Allah Din, who acted in igorance under the orders of Khuda Bakhsh. He is therefore acquitted.

The facts against Khuda Bakhsh are clear, and Ahmad Din, (No. 2) was in his full confidence.

Khuda Bakhsh is not guilty under section 384, I. P. C. as extortion was not complete, and on that charge he is acquitted, but both he and Ahmad Din are found guilty under other charges framed against them, and are sentenced as in the scheduled annexed.

5—KASUR CASE

(Lieut-Col. Irvine's Commission)

The 15 accused before us are charged under sections 121, 148, 302-149, 326-149, I.P.C. On April 12th at Kasur, a mob, excited by speeches addressed to them on that and the previous day, invaded and wrecked the railway station, attacked an in-coming train, murdered two warrant officers (Master Gunner Mallett and Conductor Selby), assaulted and injured two officers (Capt. Limby, R. E. and Lieut Munro of the XVII Royal Regiment), and Corporals Battson and Gringham of the Queen's Regiment, assaulted Mr. and Mrs. Sherbourne of the Railway Department, all of whom were travelling in the train, burnt the Post Office and Munsif's Court, attacked the Tahsil, and were finally dispersed by fire from the police.

The speakers who incited the outbreak do not appear to be before us, but we note the sinister feature that the violence of the mob was directed against the wearers of His Majesty's uniform, and against the property of Government.

We have taken judicial notice of, and have not required evidence on, the existence of a state of insurrection at Kasur on April 12.

After careful consideration of all the evidence we have acquitted Gian Das, accused No. 15, and have convicted each of the remaining accused of an offence under section 121, I P. C., namely the offence of waging war against the King.

We sentence them as under:—

To death:— Chuni Lal, No. 1; Bir Singh, No. 2; Budha, No. 3; Gaman, No. 4; Daulat Khan, No. 6; Labhu, No. 7; Charan Das, No. 8; Sohna No. 9; Bulanda, No.10; Kamal Din, No. 12; and Jamal Din, No. 13, (eleven in all).

Bir Singh, No. 2; Gaman, No. 4; Daulat Khan, No. 6; Labhu, No. 7; Bulanda, No. 10; and Jamal Din, No. 13; were wounded by the fire of the police. Jamal Din is identified as having been with the mob from the beginning and the rest were prominent in the commission of the outrages. Budha, No. 3, was one of the leaders, and Charan Das, No. 8, and Sohna, No. 9, were conspicuous in the attack on Capt. Limby and Lieut Munro.

Chuni Lal, accused No. 1, and Kamal Din, accused No. 12 were among the leaders and, so far as the actual offence of waging war is concerned, nothing less than the capital sentence would be justified in the case of each of these accused. They were, however, prevailed upon to spare Mr. and Mrs. Sherbourne and their children, and eventually even assisted them to escape to a place of safety. For this reason and also on the ground of their youth we append to the sentences on Chuni Lal and Kamal Din a recommendation to mercy.

To transportation for life:—Jowala, No. 5; Hira. No. 11; Bura, No. 14.

None of these three appears to have taken a very prominent part and Jowala and Bura are youths of 19 and 18 years of age respectively; we have, therefore, refrained from inflicting the capital sentence upon them. In the case of all the accused who have been convicted we direct the forfeiture of such property liable to forfeiture as each was possessed of at the time of the commission of the offence. We have considered it unnecessary to record findings upon the other charges against the convicts.

We commend to the notice of Government the conduct of Mr. Khair Din, Examiner of accounts, to whose intervention and protection the escape of Mr. and Mrs. Sherbourne and their children was due.

6—NATIONAL BANK LOOT CASE (AMRITSAR)

Crown Vs. Ramzan and 3 others

(Lieut.-Col. Irvine's Commission)

On April the 17th at 3.30 p.m., the police, acting on information received, raided a house at Amritsar, and found the accused, who are Kashmiris and live together all in one room, in possession of a quantity of piece-goods and cotton which have been proved to be the property of the National Bank, and which had been buried under the earthen floor of the room. They were at once arrested. There is no evidence for the defence, which is a mere denial of the charge in each case. We register a conviction against each of the accused under section 412, I. P. C. We sentence Ramzan and Muhamadu to seven years' rigorous imprisonment each, while Guffar and Ahmad may, on account of their youth, undergo the lesser sentence of five years' rigorous imprisonment each.

7—NATIONAL BANK LOOT CASE (AMRITSAR)

Crown vs. Ghafar Bat and 3 others

(Lieut.- Col. Irvine's Commission)

On April the 17th at 4 p.m., the police, acting on information received, raided a house at Amritsar, and found the accused, who are Kashmiris and live together in one house, in possession of a quantity of piece-goods and yarn, which have been proved to be the property of the National Bank. They were at once arrested. There is no evidence for the defence of accused No. 1 to 3, who merely deny the charge in each case.

We register a conviction against each of the accused under Section 412, I.P.C., and sentence them to seven years' rigorous imprisonment each.

Judgement pronounced.

The property found may be made over to a properly accredited representative of the National Bank.

8—NATIONAL BANK LOOT CASE (AMRITSAR)

Crown vs. Manohar and 9 others

(Lieut-Col. Irvine's Commission)

On April 17th at 2-45 p.m. the police, acting on information received, raided a house in Amritsar and found the accused in possession of a quantity of piece-goods, proved to have been the property of the National Bank; they were at once arrested. The defence is absolutely worthless. Each accused has been sentenced to seven years' rigorous imprisonment, except Khalik, accused No. 2, who on account of his youth (he being about 17 years of age) has been sentenced to five years' rigorous imprisonment only. The convictions have been registered under section 412, I.P.C. The property found to be made over to a properly accredited representative of the National Bank.

9—NATIONAL BANK LOOT CASE (AMRITSAR)

Crown verus Kaman and 15 others

(Lieut-Col. Irvine's Commission)

On April the 17th at 2 p.m., the police, acting on information received raided a house reputed to be a gambling den in Amritsar, and found the accused all in one room in possession of a quantity of piece-goods which have been proved to be the property of the National Bank, and which they were apparently in the act of dividing. They were at once arrested. The defence is absolutely worthless.

Abdu (accused No. 6) states that he had come from Dera Ghazi Khan on April the 16th, and was merely in the house by chance; he describes himself as a resident of Dera Ghazi Khan, and merely a casual visitor to Amritsar. His witnesses who were called from Dera Ghazi Khan have not come; but the *Chaudhri* of the Katra states that he knows the man well, and that he is a permanent resident of Amritsar. The Sub-Inspector confirms this. The Inspector also states that this accused made no mention of his having come from Dera Ghazi Khan when the police questioned him. We and the defence

Counsel satisfied ourselves as to this from the police diaries. This defence in fact, was only put at the last moment, and was not mentioned in the statement which this accused made to the Court. We consequently reject his plea.

There is no reason to differentiate in the matter of punishment. Each accused has been sentenced to seven years' rigorous imprisonment, and the convictions have been registered under section 412, I.P.C.

The property found may be made over to a properly accredicted representative of the National Bank.

10—NATIONAL BANK LOOT CASE (AMRITSAR)

Crown Vs. Muhammadu and 2 others

(Lieut-Col. Irvine's Commission)

On April the 17th, between 4 and 5 p.m., the police, acting on information received, raided a house at Amritsar, and found the accused, who are Kashmiris and live together, all in one *baithak*, in possession of a quantity of piece-goods and yarn which have been proved to be the property of the National Bank. They were at once arrested. There is no evidence for the defence of the accused, who merely deny the charge in each case, and say that the property was being kept by them for some neighbours. We cannot accept the uncorroborated statement of the accused.

We register a conviction against each of the accused under section 412, I.P.C. and sentence them to seven years' rigorous imprisonment each.

Judgement pronounced.

The property found may be made over to a properly accredited representative of the National Bank.

11—NATIONAL BANK LOOT CASE (AMRITSAR)

Crown *Vs.* Mahaja

(Lieut-Col. Irvine's Commission)

On April the 17th, between 4 and 5 pm., the police acting on information received raided a house at Amritsar, and found the accused alone in this house, which belongs to him, in possession of a quantity of piece-goods which have been proved to be the property of the National Bank. He was at once arrested. There no evidence for the defence of the accused, who merely denies that he was present. We cannot accept the uncorroborated statement of the accused.

We register a conviction against him under section 412, I.P.C., and sentence him to seven years' rigorous imprisonment.

Judgement pronounced.

The property found may be made over to a properly accredited representative of the National Bank.

12—NATIONAL BANK LOOT CASE (AMRITSAR)

Crown Vs. Fazl Din

(Lieut-Col. Irvine's Commission)

On April the 17th, at about 5 p.m., the police, acting on information received, raided a house at Amritsar, and found the accused in the upper storey, which was in his occupation, in possession of a quantity of piece-goods which have been proved to be the property of the National Bank. The accused was the only male present; there were women and children besides. He was at once arrested. In defence the accused says that part of the cloth produced belongs to him; the Bank's representative does not claim the pieces in bundle B, but only those in bundle A, which the accused says he knows nothing about. The accused was caught in the act of burning a quantity of cloth (in *thans*) and his guilt admits of no doubt.

We register a conviction against him under section 412, I.P.C. and sentence him to seven years' rigorous imprisonment.

Judgement pronounced.

The property found may be made over to a properly accredited representative of the National Bank.

13—NATIONAL BANK LOOT CASE (AMRITSAR)

Crown Vs. Allah Rakha

(Lieut-Col. Irvine's Commission)

On April the 17th at about 5 p.m., the police, acting on information received, raided a house at Amritsar, and found the accused with one woman in this house, which belongs to him, in possession of a quantity of piece-goods, which have been proved to be the property of the National Bank. He was at once arrested. The accused denies that he was present, or that the house belongs to him, and adds that his mother was the real criminal. His witnesses are useless, and the Court does not consider that his plea is sustainable.

We register a conviction against him under section 412, I.P.C., and sentence him to seven years' rigorous imprisonment.

Judgement pronounced.

The property found may be made over to a properly accredited representative of the National Bank.

14—CROWN *Versus* MOTI RAM (LAHORE)

(Sedition and attempt to seduce Police)

Moti Ram, the accused in this case, was charged with an offence under Rule 24-29 of the Defence of India Rules, to which a charge under section 124-A, I.P.C., was subsequently added.

An armed guard of police under the command of Mr. Gray, Reserve Inspector, was proceeding from the Anarkali Police Station to the Lohari Gate. A crowd was collected near the Lohari Gate, and the accused in a frenized state and bare-headed shouted out several times to the police: *"Tum hamare bhai ho, hamare sath shahid ho."* The use of these words by the accused is positively sworn to by the witnesses, including Mr. Gray himself, who at once arrested the accused.

The defence is only as to character, and has no effect upon the case.

Counsel of the accused admits the commission of an offence under Rule 24 of the Defence of India Rules, but contends that the facts do not warrant a conviction under section 124-A, I.P.C. We do not agree. The date of the occurrence was the 11th of April, 1919 and the time about 8 a.m. We cannot imagine any more flagrant example of an attempt to excite disaffection (which words include disloyalty and all feelings of enmity) against Government, than the use of the words which we have quoted addressed to armed police in the presence of a mob. The obvious intention of the accused was to excite such disaffection as would seduce the police from their duty and induce them to join the mob against the Government. In the circumstances, the invitation to armed police to become martyrs was an offence of the greatest gravity, and, but for the staunchness which the police displayed, might well have led to a very serious catastrophe.

For these reasons, we convict the accused on both charges, and sentence him to transportation for life.

15—LAHORE UPPER MALL RIOT CASE

(Mr. Justice Leslie Jones' Commission)

The news of the detention of Gandhi and that of the rebellion at Amritsar reached Lahore on the afternoon of the 10th April. Telegrams giving some details of what had happened at Amritsar were received between 3 and 4 p.m. and their contents became public property. Towards evening a large and excited mob collected in Lahore city. Leaflets were distributed to it and some of its members were heard shouting both in English and in vernacular that Amritsar had been taken and the situation was well in hand in Lahore as three gates were already held and a fourth would soon be closed. Headed by a man carrying a black flag, the mob proceeded with shouts of "Gandhi ki jai" and "Shaukat Ali ki jai" from the Lahori Gate through Anarkali to the Upper Mall. Some of its members entered the compound of the Government Telegraph Office but turned back on seeing a detachment of the Royal Sussex which were guarding the building with fixed bayonets. By the time the mob had got as far as the Lawrence Statue, it numbered some thousands. There it was intercepted by two Indian Police Officers, with a handful of armed constables who were brought up at the double from Anarkali Police Station through the High Court grounds. These police lined the road in front of the mob but they were pressed back for a distane of about 200 yards as far as the Soldiers' Club. It was then getting dusk.

At this juncture Mr. Fyson, the District Magistrate, Mr. Cocks, D.I.G., C.I.D., and Mr. Clarke, D.S.P. arrived on the spot. Mr. Fyson ordered the mob to retire but they pressed round him. One of them seized him by the shoulder from behind and they began to go through the thin line of police. They also attempted to get round them by going through the compound of the Soldiers' Club. After some minutes, Mr. Fyson, who, owing to the uproar, had difficulty in making himself heard, ordered the police to withdraw a little further up the Mall in order to prevent them being overwhelmed by the mob and then as there was no other means of stopping its progress gave the order to fire. About a dozen rounds were fired and then the mob was pressed slowly back to the city. Near the Bank of Bengal, Mr. Clarke was thrown down but his assailant escaped.

It is beyond doubt that the Lahore mob which marched on the

Civil Station of Lahore was actuated by the same motives as that of Amritsar. It was essentially part of the same insurrection, and it was fully aware of what had happened in the neighbouring town the same day. It was rapidly becoming more threatening, and had already displayed its contempt of the authority and person of the District Magistrate. A collision was inevitable and had the mob proceeded a little further up the Mall it would have found a supply of deadly weapons ready to hand. Had it not been checked where it was there was the gravest danger that it would have hurried on, in the confusion and darkness, to the commission of awful crimes.

In ordinary circumstances the offences actually committed would not have amounted to more than rioting, but this occurrence cannot be viewed as a detached and independent incident. It was plainly a part and parcel of the rebellion which had already broken out.

We find, therefore, that offences under section 121, I.P.C., as well as under section 147, I.P.C., were committed.

There are only four accused. Of these Ahmad Din, No. 1, a Jat, aged 40, is an illiterate mineral water and ice vendor who made himself prominent as the bearer of the black flag. Ata Muhammad, No. 2, aged 25, is a book-seller who has been given a very good previous character by Mrs. Richards, wife of the Professor of English at the Islamia College, Barkat Ram, No. 3, aged 20, is a Telegraph Clerk, and Feroze Din, No. 4, aged 20, is the fireman of a Municipal Road Engine.

Accused Nos. 2 to 4 were all hit with buckshot and we have no doubt that they had all joined the mob.

They are convicted and sentenced as in the schedule annexed. But the question of their sentences will be referred for the consideration of Government.

16—GUJRAT CASE

(Mr. Justice Leslie-Jones' Commission)

This judgement deals with cases Nos. 5 and 7 both relating to the outbreak at Gujrat.

On the morning of the 14th April after the news of the rising in Gujranwala had been received, seditious notices were posted in Gujrat announcing a rebellion and *Hartal* and warning Europeans that if they were not careful they would be murdered. The shops were closed the same day, and a mob, shouting the usual cries, promenaded the city.

On the morning of the 15th the rioters reassembled, bareheaded, with a black flag and a picture of Gandhi. They then proceeded to the Mission High School and when the Head Master refused to close it, broke in, smashed the windows and furniture, and closed it forcibly. The city was again promenaded, and in the afternoon the mob marched, smashing lamps on its way, to the Railway Station, where it at once proceeded to wreck the telephone and telegraph instruments, and to burn the papers in the Booking Office. At this jucture the reserve police guard arrived, and fired under the orders of the Senior Subordinate Judge, who, with other officials, had already tried in vain to disperse the mob. No one was injured probably because the police fired high deliberately. A number of arrests were made on the spot and others afterwards.

So far as the general facts are concerned the cases are simple enough, but the matter is different as regards individuals. In some instances there is no evidences which, even if believed, would justify conviction, and in some others the evidence is very thin. In a good many more personal and party animosities have clearly played a very large part. Much of the evidence, even that of officials, is tainted in this way, and there has also been some deliberate perjury. We do not intend to discuss individual cases, but for various reasons we are not satisfied of the guilt of the following, who are, therefore, acquitted:—

Case No. 5—Kundan Lal (No. 7), Mahtab (No. 10), Tarlok Nath (No. 14), Mul Raj (No. 20), Guru Das (No. 22), Feroz Ali (No. 23), Tarlok Nath (No. 24), Prithi Raj (No. 23), Rahmat (No. 26), Fazal (No. 27), Hargopal (No. 28), Tara Chand (No. 29), Bhagwan (No. 30), Lal (No. 31), and Girdhari (No. 32).

In Case No. 7—Nand Lal (No. 1), Diwan Chand (No. 2), Ram Chand (No. 3), and Fazal (No. 4).

The remaining accused, Ghulam Nabi (No. 1), Peshawari Lal (No. 2), Abdul Shakur (No. 3), Najam Din (No. 4), Ghulam Muhammad (No. 5), Fakir Muhammad (No. 6), Kidar Nath (No. 8), Arura (No. 9), Ranjah (No. 11), Kali Das (No. 12), Tofail (No. 13), Devi (No. 15), Fakira (No. 16), Raja Ram (No. 17), Amar Nath (No. 18), Sadhu Singh (No. 19) and Ghulam Hussain (No. 21) are convicted and sentenced as shown in the schedule annexed. Of these Najam Din (No. 4), Arura (No. 9), Ranjha (No. 11) and Ghulal Hussain (No. 21), were the most prominent. The question of the sentences of the prisoners will be referred for the consideration of Government.

17—JALALPUR JATTAN RIOT CASE (GUJRAT)

We have before us 16 accused variously charged under sections 121, 147, 124-A, 323 and 146-149 I.P.C.

This case relates to the proceedings of April 15 and 16 at Jalalpur Jattan, a township some nine miles from Gujrat in the Gujrat District. There was a *hartal* on the 15th but apparently little else. On the 16th the Municipal Committee met in the morning to concert measures for dealing with possible disorder. They were too late. Hardly had they met when a mob invaded the room, snatched off the turbans of the members and impelled them from the building. Outside speeches were made against the Government and the Rowlatt Act, and the mob then moved off in two bodies, one to the Post Office and the other to the Mission School, where, however, no damage was done beyond the breaking of a few windows at the school by some boys, and the movement then subsided. The people who are mainly Kashmiris were obviously not prepared to go to extremes; and the efforts of the chief agitators met with no more than the success above described.

Although we cannot regard the occurrence as very serious—for the occasion seems to have been taken rather to emphasise the mob's antipathy to the Municipal Committee—yet the object of the leaders was undoubtedly to excite disaffection against Government. We are unable to find that war was actually waged or that the actions of the mob ever amounted to insurrection.

The evidence against the majority of the accused is unsatisfactory. The fact that the town is a hot-bed of partnership and petty faction has tainted so much of the evidence given that we have found the case unproved as against nine of the accused, who have consequently been acquitted. Of the remainder Abdul Rashid (accused No. 7), an Islamia School teacher since dismissed, was the worst offender. It is unanimously agreed that he uttered violent abuse of Government and was the most prominent of the leaders. That he was an organiser is shown by Exhibits P.A. and P.B., papers proved to be in his house. Abdul Aziz (accused No. 6) was another leader. Mahma (or Muhammad Din) accused No. 11, assaulted Muhammad Shah, Honorary Sanitary Inspector, who had been an energetic recruiter. Sardara (accused No. 12), assaulted Muhammad Shah and is uniformly named as an active member of the mob. Ihsan Ali carried a black flag and blew a horn; but otherwise does not appear to have taken a conspicuous part. The case of Nand Lal (accused No. 4), presents difficulty and we have decided to give him the benefit of the doubt; he is acquitted.

As to the law applicable we have already indicated that no offence under section 121, I.P.C., has been made out. We register the convictions of Abdul Rashid (No. 7), and Abdul Aziz (No. 6), under section 124-A, I.P.C., and of Ihsan Ali, Mahma and Sardara under sections 124-A-149, I.P.C., and sentence them as follows:

Abdul Rashid, (No. 7) transportation for 14 years.

Abdul Aziz (No. 6), transportation for 10 years.

Ihsan Ali (No. 8), Mahma, (No. 11) Sardara (No. 12), rigorous imprisonment for three years each.

It is unnecessary to come to a finding on the other charges.

Sentences pronounced on the above-named convicts. The case of Ghulam Muhammad (No. 17), who was arrested subsequently to the others, is postponed for production of defence evidence on the 15th of May, 1919.

18—NATIONAL BANK LOOT CASE (AMRITSAR)

Crown Vs. Kesho Ram

Kesho Ram, Brahmin, aged 25, Commission Agent of Patti, was arrested on the night of the 10th April in possession of about 50 yards of high quality cloth looted from National Bank at Amritsar that afternoon. There is practically no defence, and the case is clearly proved. Sentence—seven years' rigorous imprisonment under section 412, I.P.C.

The property to be delivered to an accredicted representative of the National Bank.

19—NATIONAL BANK LOOT CASE (AMRITSAR)

Crown Vs. Mehr Din

Mehr Din aged 45, Lohar, by occupation beggar, was caught on the night of the 18th April in possession of a quantity of cloth which had been looted from the National Bank on the 10th April. The case is clear. But the cloth in question was probably a part of that thrown out into the streets by the original dacoits or receiver on the 18th

April when the searches had begun. The accused, who is a person of somewhat feeble intellect, is convicted under Section 412, I.P.C. and sentenced to two years' rigorous imprisonment.

The property to be delivered to an accredited representative of the National Bank.

20—NATIONAL BANK LOOT CASE (AMRITSAR)

Crown Vs. Ali Mohammad

Ali Mohammad, son of Rukan Din, servant of a skin merchant, 40 years, of Amritsar, was found in possession of a large quantity of cloth etc., looted from the National Bank at Amritsar on the 10th April. The case is clear. He is convicted under Section 412, I.P.C., and sentenced to seven years' rigorous imprisonment.

The property to be delivered to an accredited representative of the National Bank.

21—NATIONAL BANK LOOT CASE (AMRITSAR)

Crown Vs. Khuda Bakhsh

Khuda Bakhsh, aged 45, Rajput, carrier, was found in possession of a quantity of cotton and chintz which was looted from the National Bank on the 10th April. The case is clear. He is convicted under Section 412, I.P.C., and sentenced to seven years' rigorous imprisonment.

Property to be delivered to an accredited representative of the National Bank.

22—NATIONAL BANK LOOT CASE (AMRITSAR)

Crown Vs. Nizam Din

Nizam Din, Sheikh, baker, aged 50, was found in possession of a large quantity of various kinds of cloth, wool and lace which had been looted from the National Bank at Amritsar on the 10th April. The case is clearly proved. Accused is convicted under Section 412, I.P.C., and is sentenced to seven years' rigorous imprisonment.

Property to be delivered to an accredited representative of the National Bank.

23—NATIONAL BANK LOOT CASE (AMRITSAR)

Crown Vs. Hussain Bakhsh

Hussain Bakhsh, mason, an old man of 70, is charged with being in possession, on the 17th April, of a few skeins and cotton yarn looted from the National Bank of Amritsar on the 10th April. It is very probable that the skeins were so stolen but they are not identifiable and we doubt if the accused had buried them as alleged. He is acquitted.

24—NATIONAL BANK LOOT CASE (AMRITSAR)

Crown Vs. Feroz Din

Feroz, Mashki, aged 20 of Amritsar, was found in possession of cloth, chintz, vaseline bottles and 50 wrist watches looted from the National Bank at Amritsar on 10th April. The case is clear. He is convicted under Section 412, I.P.C., and sentenced to seven years' rigorous imprisonment.

The property to be delivered to an accredited representative of the National Bank.

25—AULAKH CASE (GUJRANWALA)

(Lieut-Col. Irvine's Commission)

The eight accused are charged under sections 147, 435, 436-149 and 124-A-149, I.P.C., to which charges under section 121, I.P.C., were subsequently added.

On April 16th in the large Jat village of Aulakh in the Gujranwala district there was an insurrection in which the *patwarkhana*, containing valuable revenue records of six villages, was burnt to the ground. The eight accused have been proved to be the incendiaries, and they were headed by the two *lambardars,* Ganda Singh and Makhan Singh (accused Nos. 1 and 2), and Singhara Singh (accused No. 3). The accused violently prevented any attempt to put out the fire, and gave vent to treasonable cries announcing that Lahore, Amritsar and Chuharkana had been burnt; that the British *Raj* was extinct; that they were now rulers and that by burning the records, the Jats would get their land back; they also threatened that any supporters of Government would be thrown on the fire. The arrival of the patrol of Sh. Rahmat Ullah (P.W.I.) was fortunately sufficient to prevent the spread of disorder.

We consider that these actions clearly constitute the waging of war, the defence of *alibi* and enmity made in each case is absurd, and we convict all the accused accordingly of an offence under section 121, I.P.C. We note that the name of Gian Singh (accused No. 7) does not occur in the F.I.R. made the same evening by the patwari, but that official was clearly in a most perturbed state of mind. Gian Singh was named next morning; there is no special reason why he should have been implicated falsely, and we are satisfied that Gian Singh is guilty.

Only two punishments are provided for the offence—death or transportation for life; it is necessary to discriminate between the two sets of accused, namely, Ganda Singh and Makhan Singh, lambardars (accused Nos. 1 and 2) with Singhara (accused No. 3) who actually set fire to his own turban to start the conflagration and whose guilt we place on a par with that of the other two, and the remaining accused who joined the above-named three leaders. The two *lambardars,* who from their position could and should have checked any such outbreak of violence, yet were the actual leaders, are, in our opinion, guilty of a crime of the utmost gravity; their action in a strong Jat village like Aulakh might have had the most serious consequences and have caused a general rising in the whole countryside: their object is plainly indicated by the attack on the *patwarkhana* and revenue records as the symbols of Government authority in their village. It was only the absence of any but most feeble opposition that prevented the outbreak from being accompanied by murder. Not only therefore as a deterrent but also because we think the crime merits the extreme penalty provided for the offence, we sentence Ganda Singh, Makhan Singh and Singhara Singh to death. Although Ganda Singh has given his age as 70 years he is plainly not nearly so old as this: he is probably not more than 55. The remaining accused are sentenced to the lesser of the two penalties provided—that is to say, to transportation for life. It is unnecessary to record any finding on the other charges. We further direct that all property liable to forfeiture of which the accused were possessed at the time of the commission of the offence shall be forfeited to Government.

Judgement pronounced.

We invite the attention of Government to the action of Bulaqi, the third *lambardar,* who refused to join the conspiracy and endeavoured to send information to the thana. The *Patwari,* Diwan Chand, also behaved well. Further inquiry might reveal the names of others whose attitude or action may have merited recognition.

26—LOHARI GATE RIOT CASE (LAHORE)

We have before us nine persons accused of offences under sections 121, 147 and 152-149, I.P.C. The occurrences which form the subject of the charges constitute a continuance of the riot of April 10th on the Lahore Mall. That has already been dealt with judicially in another place. When the mob was driven back from the Mall it did not dissolve but was slowly pushed by a small force of police into the Nila Gumbaz Chauk and up the Anarkali towards the Lohari Gate. There it was reinforced by a crowd issuing from the City, and the police, under Mr. Clarke, D.S.P., were held up at a point a little short of the cross-road where the Circular Road cuts across the Anarkali. Mr. Broadway, S.P., came up with a small body of police and cavalry but even so the forces of order were unable to disperse the mob which showered brickbats upon the police and sowars. Two or three rounds of buckshot fired at the roofs of some houses from which the shower of missiles was most persistent failed to do more than check the attack from that quarter. A message brought Mr. Fyson, D.C., to the spot. He went forward into the crowd and endeavoured to reason with P. Rambhaj Datt or L. Duni Chand (he does not remember which) who were there, but all efforts to disperse the mob failed, and at last some half-a-dozen rounds of buckshot were fired. The mob was then dispersed without further firing.

We have acquitted Jiwan Lal (No. 7) and Feroz Din (No. 9), giving them the benefit of the doubt, and have convicted the remaining accused, all of whom were wounded by buck-shot, and of whose participation there is no doubt. That the offence committed was that of waging war needs no demonstration, and we register the convictions accordingly under section 121 I.P.C., ignoring the charges under the other sections. The capital sentence is not required, and the only other punishment allowed by the law is that of transportation for life. To this we sentence the remaining accused named hereunder, but in each case a recommendation for reduction of sentence will be made to the local Government.

1. Mahtab, 2. Abdul Rahim, 3. Bishan Chand, 4. Fazal Hussain, 5. Jadu Mal, 6. Ghulam Muhammad, 7. Shiv Das.

Such property as was in the possession of each of the convicts at the time of the commission of the offence, and as is liable to forfeiture, will be forfeited to the Crown.

We commend to the notice of Government the admirable conduct of all concerned in dealing with the mob.

27—GUMANPURA RAILWAY DERAILMENT CASE

(Amritsar District)

On the evening of the 12th April, Lal Singh (No. 1) Lambardar of Sanghna, a village some four or five miles to the west of Amritsar, visited the neighbouring villages of Gumanpura and Basarke, where he described the insurrections in the city; urged that everyone should rise to help, and that the railway line should be cut. He then returned to his own village. Later in the evening a meeting was held at Basarke under the guidance of Ishar Singh, (No. 2), and Inayat (No. 3), who declared that the British Government had been overthrown, and it was decided to follow the advice of Lal Singh and to cut the railway line which runs close by. A considerable body of men at once set out to accomplish this purpose. Willing assistance was obtained from two Gangmen, Jhanda (No. 14) and Jhanda (No. 15), who provided the tools and unscrewed the fish-plates. Two whole sections of the Up and Down lines were, with their sleepers, bodily removed leaving parallel gaps 30 feet long. The gang then went home. It was fortunate that the goods train from Amritsar was the first to arrive. The engine and eight wagons were derailed, but, as prompt information was wired to Amritsar, there was no further damage.

There are 16 accused. Against Amin Chand (No. 10) there is no evidence. Against Sadr Din (No. 4), Dogar (No. 11) and Ujagar Singh (No. 16) the evidence is not strong enough to warrant conviction. These four accused are, therefore, acquitted.

Of the rest Lal Singh (No. 1) is the only accused who has been charged by the Convening Officer under section 121, I.P.C. It was he who first incited the countryside to rise, and suggested the cutting of the line; and although by a fortnate chance no one was killed, the most likely result of his suggestion was a heavy loss of innocent lives. Plainly his object was not merely to derail a goods train. There had been no previous breaches of the line the railway were not on their guard, and in the case of a fast passenger train disaster would have been almost inevitable. Of this he must have been fully aware. His case is in no way improved by the fact that having originated the crime he was not present at its commission, and in our opinion he is by far the worst offender. He is sentenced to be hanged by his neck until he is dead, and to forfeiture to Government of such of his property as is liable to confiscation.

The remaining accused are sentenced as in the schedule annexed. In awarding sentences the age, social position, occupation and prominence of each have been taken into consideration.

[Sentences—Lal Singh, *lambardar,* sentenced to death and forfeiture of property; Ishar Singh, Inayat, Wasakhi, Lachman, Jhanda (14) and Jhanda (15) sentenced to transportation for life; Din and Buta Singh to ten years' rigorous imprisonment; Bishan Singh, Buta and Kishan Singh to seven years' rigorous imprisonment.]

28—AKALGARH RIOT CASE

(GUJRANWALA DISTRICT)

In this case the first six accused stand charged with offences under Sections 121, 124-A, 147, 426, 431, 435, 149 and 506 I.P.C., and the remaining accused, Nos. 7 to 30, with offences under Sections 121, 147, 435, 124-A—149, 431 and 426 I.P.C. Akalgarh is a small town in the Gujranwala district. There was the usual *hartal* there on April 6th, 14th and 15th, but only the occurrences of the last two dates are made the subject of the charges. The first six accused enforced the *hartal* with threats; meetings were held and a mob collected and roamed about between the Railway Station and the town with cries of "*Gandhi ki jai*" and "*hai hai Rowlatt Bill.*" Only passive resistance and *hartal* appear to have been advocated, however, until the 15th, when Bishen Das (No. 2) and Sohan Singh (No. 5) who had gone to Wazirabad to obtain information returned with the news of the happenings at Gujranwala, and upbraided the people with having done nothing at Akalgarh. That night feeble attempts were made to set fire to a couple of bridges on the line, the glass of a signal was broken and an insulator smashed. This mischief appears to have been done by boys, amongst whom were Utma (No. 7) and Dulla (No. 10), who are said to have broken the insulator only but the evidence against the rest of accused, Nos. 7 to 30 is uncertain and unreliable. The fact is that the leaders Nos. 1 to 6 were able to obtain only lukewarm support and the people were not prepared to go to extremes. The mob, never a large one, was kept off the station premises without difficulty and its proceedings were a mere parody of rebellion.

We acquit accused Nos. 11 to 30, we convict Utma (No. 7) and Dulla (No. 10) of mischief only under section 421, I.P.C. They are, however, mere boys of 15 years of age, and were incited by others; whipping would therefore be a suitable punishment but as they have been in custody for three weeks, we consider that they have already suffered sufficiently and we order them to be imprisoned until the rising of the Court only.

We convict Nos. 1 to 6, namely Badri Nath, Bishan Das, Gokal Chand, Bishambar Das, Sohan Singh and Ishar Das, of criminal intimidation under section 506, I.P.C., and sentence each to one year's rigorous imprisonment, and a fine of Rs. 100, or in default, three months' additional rigorous imprisonment. We also convict Bishan Dass (No. 2) and Sohan Singh (No. 5) of sedition under Section 124-A, and impose on each of them a sentence of one year's rigorous imprisonment, the sentences to run consecutively in each case.

29—KHEM KARN STATION CASE

(Mr. Justice Leslie Jones' Commission)

Khem Karn is a railway station about eight miles from Kasur on the line to Patti. The Kasur riot took place on the 12th of April, and on the same day at 3.45 p.m. the station staff of Khem Karn were informed that the telegraph wire had been cut. Immediately after, two men Arjan Singh and Maulu came into the station and demanded to know why the train had not arrived. (One of them Maulu, had been seen in Kasur the same morning amongst the rioters). They were joined by some 15 to 20 others, most of whom carried sticks, and the general attitude of the gathering was so threatening that the three members of the station staff fled from the office. In response to the alarm given by them some cultivators came to their assistance, and the rioters made off as fast as they could, dropping some of the booty as they went.

The damage done consisted of the removal of the telegraph instruments and other railway property, some bedding and personal property of the staff, the theft of Rs. 15 from the till and the breaking of the lamp-room door, from which a tin of oil was removed. Had timely assistance not been available it was the obvious intention of the rioters to set fire to the furniture and possibly to the building.

We find that the offence of dacoity has been established and convict 5 of the 11 accused who have been clearly identified—including the two ring-leaders, Arjan Singh and Maulu. These two are sentenced to transportation for life and the others to terms of imprisonment as stated in the schedule, the distinction drawn between Jamu and the other two being, that while they are menials he is a zemindar.

The remaining six accused are acquitted. There is no evidence whatever against Teju and that against the remainder is insufficient.

30—NATIONAL BANK LOOT CASE (AMRITSAR)

(Crown *Vs.* Gyan Das Faqir)

Gyan Das Faqir, aged 18, pleads guilty of being in dishonest possession of a small quantity of cloth which he picked up in the street, knowing it to have been stolen from the National Bank of India at Amritsar. He is convicted under section 412, I.P.C. We think he should be whipped, but as we are not authorised to inflict that punishment we sentence him to six months' rigorous imprisonment. The property will be delivered to an accredited representative of the National Bank of India at Amritsar.

31—HIRA MANDI CASE (LAHORE)

(Lieut-Col. Irvine's Commission)

Owing to the serious state of disorder existing in Lahore it was decided on April 11, 1919, to occupy certain points in the city by picquets of police and troops. To carry out this decision a force assembled at the Railway Station on the morning of April 12th, and proceeded through the Delhi Gate and up the Hira Mandi. On reaching the entrance to the Tibbi Bazar, this force which was accompanied by Civil, Military and Police Officers found itself so hampered by a large and unruly mob, which had collected in its rear, that it faced about and endeavoured to disperse the mob by pushing it back along the Hira Mandi. It reached the turning leading to the Badshahi Mosque and was there held up by the crowd which had assumed a very menacing attitude. Constant warnings had been addressed to the mob to induce it to disperse and at the turning final efforts were made to do this by peaceful means. These failed and the order to fire was given by the Deputy Commissioner. Not more than 8 rounds were fired by the police—the troops were not called upon to do so—and this quieted the mob sufficiently to allow of its being then dispersed without the use of further force.

Of the 16 accused now before us charged with offences under sections 121, 147 and 124-A, 152/149 I.P.C., no less than 14 were wounded by buckshot. Of the remaining two unwounded accused, we are not satisfied with the evidence against one, Muni Lal (No. 14 and acquit him accordingly; but the other Feroz Din (No.15) was arrested on the spot, and we find him, together with 14 wounded accused, guilty of an offence under section 121, I. P. C. The defence of all accused is that they were innocent bystanders, or passers-by, but in no case is this supported by convincing evidence.

None, with the possible exception of Feroz Din (No.15), appears to have been among the leaders, and as regards Feroz Din (No.15), although he is alleged to have been prominent in this and other disorders (he has been convicted in the Badshahi Mosque case and acquitted in the Lohari Gate case) there is insufficient evidence to justify that conclusion in the present case. In sentencing the convicts Nos. 1 to 13, 15 and 16 to the lesser penalty of transportation for life which we hereby do, we shall also recommend all for reduction of this sentence.

All property which was in the possession of each of the convicts at the time of the commission of the offence and is liable to forfeiture will be forfeited to the Crown.

32—NATIONAL BANK LOOT CASE

(Amritsar)

Crown *Vs.* Santa Singh

(Mr. Justice Leslie-Jones' Commission)

Santa Singh barber, of Tehra Kalan, aged 25, pleads guilty to the possession of property which he knew to have been stolen from the National Bank at Amritsar. He is sentenced to five years' rigorous imprisonment.

33—NATIONAL BANK LOOT CASE

(AMRITSAR)

Crown *Vs.* Sardara

(Mr. Justice Leslie-Jones' Commission)

Sardara, son of Dula, Rajput, aged 25, of Tehra Kalan, in Amritsar, pleads guilty to the possession of a quantity of cloth which he knew to have been stolen from the National Bank at Amritsar. In the circumstances he is sentenced to five years' rigorous imprisonment.

34—NATIONAL BANK LOOT CASE

(AMRITSAR)

Crown *Vs.* Mehr Din and another

(Mr. Justice Leslie-Jones' Commission)

Mehr Din pleads guilty of being in possession of a quantity of property which he knew to have been stolen from the National Bank at Amritsar. In the circumstances he is sentenced to five years' rigorous imprisonment. His co-accused, Shera, is found not guilty and acquitted.

35—NATIONAL BANK LOOT CASE

(AMRITSAR)

Crown *Vs.* Kirpa

(Mr. Justice Leslie-Jones' Commission)

Kirpa, son of Parema, aged 13, pleads guilty of being in possession of property, which he knew to have been stolen from the National Bank at Amritsar. He is sentenced to 15 stripes as a juvenile offender.

36—NATIONAL BANK LOOT CASE

(AMRITSAR)

Crown *Vs.* Kashmiri Lal

(Mr Justice Leslie-Jones' Commission)

Kashmiri Lal, son of Gandu Ram, Brahmin, aged 22, pleads guilty of being in possession of a quantity of cloth which he knew to have been stolen from the National Bank of India at Amritsar. The circumstances of the case having been considered, he is sentenced to five years' rigorous imprisonment.

37—NATIONAL BANK LOOT CASE

(AMRITSAR)

Crown *Vs.* Maya Ram

(Mr. Justice Leslie-Jones' Commission)

Maya Ram, aged 18, Brahmin, sometime driver, pleads guilty to being in possession of certain cloth which he knew to have been stolen from the National Bank at Amritsar. He is sentenced to two years' rigorous imprisonment.

38—NATIONAL BANK LOOT CASE

(AMRITSAR)

Crown *Vs.* Mahanna

(Mr. Justice Leslie-Jones' Commission)

Mahanna, son of Nur Din, aged 15, Arain, pleads guilty to being in possession of certain cloth which he knew to have been stolen from the National Bank at Amritsar. He is sentenced to 15 stripes as a juvenile offender.

39—HAFIZABAD CASE—(GUJRANWALA DISTRICT)

(Mr. H. Prenter's Commission)

Nineteen persons have been charged before us under sections 121, 147, 307, 436, 149, Indian Penal Code. An outrage occurred on the 14th April, 1919, at Hafizabad railway station (Gujranwala District) which has been clearly shown by the evidence to have had close connection with the riots in Lahore and other places. Meetings were held in Hafizabad in which not only was the Rowlatt Bill condemned but a strong action was urged upon the crowd in emulation of what had taken place elsewhere. On the morning of the 14th one of these meetings was held near the railway station and after the orators had incited the crowd to take immediate and vigorous steps to overthrow the Government by raising as much opposition to it as possible, some of the leading participants in the meeting called attention to the fact that the train was coming in. The train passed close by the mob who immediately said that a Ist class compartment was occupied by a Military Officer in uniform who had a child with him. The mob straightway rushed into the station and without hesitation made an attack upon the Ist class carriage. Lieutenant

Tatam (the officer in question) had taken the precaution of shutting and bolting the doors and windows. The mob broke in all the windows and shutters on the platform side with sticks and stones and endeavoured to hit the occupants. The latter withdrew into the bathroom, the window of which looked out on the offside of the train. The crowd (or some of them) then went to that side and broke the bathroom window and threw stones at the Europeans. In the meanwhile three Indian gentlemen with the greatest bravery and a sense of the seriousness of the situation tried to keep the crowd in hand. They also sent word to the Assistant Station Master to have the train started. This was done about eight minutes after its arrival and the train steamed out followed by a chorus of jeers and a final volley of brickbats. Lieutenant Tatam and the child escaped without injury. There can be no doubt but that the whole series of acts amounted to "waging war against the King." In this connection it is worth noting that on that day and on the previous day the crowd had marched about waving a black flag. They were incited by the orators to take active steps against the Government and the assault upon the train and upon the European officer were undoubtedly steps taken in furtherance of the common design. It is true that, thanks to the intervention of the Indian gentlemen already mentioned and to the departure of the train before the due time, not very much damage was done. But the intention of the mob is beyond doubt—namely, to attack the Government as represented by the officer, and but for the fortunate accidents we have alluded to Lieutenant Tatam and the child would have been killed. The lack of success was partly due to the fact that one of the leaders, Muhammad Din, changed his mind and tried to allay the storm be had assisted in raising. The pusillanimity of the mob owing to the lack of a vigorous leader does not in our opinion seriously lessen their guilt. We find that all who took part in the assault are guilty under section 121, Indian Penal Code. It remains only to record our finding as to whether the 19 accused persons were satisfactorily proved to have been active members of the mob. We find that the existence of certain intrigues and hostilities between the witnesses identifying certain of the accused, and those accused themselves, throws considerable doubt on the alleged guilt of Faqir Chand (No. 9), Abdulla (No. 13), and

Kartar Singh (No. 14). Karam Singh (No. 17) was present, but he seems to have been a mere spectator. We therefore acquit these four persons. All the rest were active participants in the assault.

Accused No. 1, Mangal Sen, was one of the ring-leaders. He carried the flag and he was foremost in the assault. Accused No. 2, Gujrati, was the principal orator who incited the crowd to war, and he was, moreover an active assailant. Kesar Mal, accused No. 3, was so prominent amongst the leaders and so eager to get at Lieutenant Tatam that he wounded himself on the glass of the carriage windows. Karm Chand No. 19, was peculiarly guilty. He brought down the news of the Lahore riot. He gave a most garbled account of it and by representing that the Lahore crowd had succeeded in beating the military he gave the Hafizabad crowd reason to believe that their insurrection would be successful. We think that these four men deserve the extreme penalty.

As regards the remainder we think that they should get the benefit of their own cowardice. Possibly their cowardice in itself indicates a slackening of efforts. They, in our opinion, will be sufficiently punished by a sentence of transportation. In convicting and passing sentence on the accused we note that accused, No. 4 is a youth and on this account we recommend him to mercy as we think that a term of five years' imprisonment would suit his case. Similarly we recommend No. 6 Jiwan Singh to mercy (in the shape of five years' sentence) as there is evidence that at times he is insane and thus liable to be carried away in a moment of excitement. The sentences awarded by us are contained in the accompanying schedule and we direct that all the property belonging to these convicted persons that is liable to forfeiture is to be forfeited to Government.

Sardar Karm Singh and Sardar Amar Singh, two of the Indian gentlemen who intervened, were passengers in the train. Bashir Hayat was on the spot and he also came to Lieutenant Tatam's assistance. The action of these gentlemen is worthy of the highest praise.

Sentences of death having been pronounced on accused No. 1, 2, 3, and 19, we direct that the executions do take place on the 24th May, 1919, (Saturday).

40—NIZAMABAD RIOT CASE
(GUJRANWALA DISTRICT)
(Mr. H. Prenter's Commission)

On 14th April, the serious outbreak of rioting took place in Gujranwala in which much damage was done by the mob and the authority of Government was openly defied. News of this quickly spread to the neighbouring town of Wazirabad and large crowds were addressed by various orators. It was determined to have a *hartal* on the next day and accordingly at an early hour a mob, led by Muhammad Hussain, Basheshar Nath and Din Muhammad, went through the city commanding shopkeepers to shut their shops. They went also to the Jubilee High School and after a display of violence they compelled the head master to close the school. Thus began a day of rioting, mischief, arson and dacoity, with the result that 19 persons have been placed before us for trial on charges under sections 121, 147, 436, 395, 149, and 412, I.P.C., and 13 others on charges under section 147, 395 and 412, I.P.C. The evidence as to what was done by the mob is exceedingly strong and clear.

The mob having closed the school tried to break out in one or two directions, but were headed off by a few troopers and their officer and ultimately they went along the railway line leading towards Gujranwala. First they came to a level crossing and then they smashed the gates, put the bars into some huts belonging to the railway and used as residence by the coolies, and then set fire to the huts. Having demolished this portion of the railway property they went further along the line to a railway bridge. This they broke up as well as they were able with crowbars with which they had armed themselves at the huts. Finding this procedure too slow they set fire to the bridge. At this point they found themselves within reach of the house belonging to the Rev. Grahame Bailey, a Church of Scotland Missionary. The ring leaders suggested that they should go and burn it. Some of the mob demurred saying that Mr. Bailey was an Irishman and therefore against the Government, but the more violent elements in the crowd prevailed and the whole body (with one or two exceptions) marched on the house. Fortunately Mr. Bailey and his family had been removed to Wazirabad on the previous afternoon by the military who had been expecting trouble. On reaching the house they were met by Mr. Bailey's servants who begged them to spare the house.

The servants were brutally commanded to go unless they wished to be burnt along with the house. A desperate scene of rioting and looting was witnessed, the house was thoroughly ransacked for treasure and then it was set ablaze. Damage to the extent of Rs. 40,000 is said to have been caused, and Mr. Bailey states that this does not include the cost of the house itself. Sated with their work, and probably anxious to dispose of their ill-gotten gains, the mob then dispersed. In the meanwhile the inhabitants of the neighbouring village of Wairoke had come to the spot, and the sight of so much abandoned loot proving too much for them they picked up what the rioters had left and decamped with it to their houses.

We are satisfied that the conduct of the crowd, which is proved beyond question, shows that this day of rioting was not the work of chance thieves or dacoits. The mob stirred by the news of the armed rebellion in Gujranwala plainly determined not to be left behind and they accordingly with deliberation set out in strength, to do all that was in their power to damage the Government. They destroyed or attempted to destroy every sort of Government property on which they could lay their hands, and the breaking of the railway line by the burning of a bridge links up their efforts with similar acts in other parts of the district. Finally they saw the house of Mr. Bailey and it is impossible not to believe that the burning of this home was an act of defiance of the Government and not one of enmity to Mr. Bailey who is deservedly most popular is this part of the Punjab. We are satisfied that it is because he was a white man, and not because of anything personal, that his house was destroyed. The mob therefore all along acted in a pre-concerted and deliberate way and were guilty of "waging war against the King." All who took active part in the operations are guilty of an offence punishable under section 121, I.P.C.

The evidence is given in such detail that it is possible to differentiate between the individual accused persons. For instance, it is clear beyond doubt that the ring-leaders were Muhammad Hussain (No. 1), Basheshar Nath (accused No. 2), Din Muhammad (accused No. 3) and Amar Singh (accuced No. 16). These were the men who led the mob successively to the school, to the level-crossing, to the bridge, and to Mr. Bailey's house, and these were the men who truculently ordered Mr. Bailey's servants to leave unless they wished to be burnt and who were most active in the burning and looting of the house.

Muhammad Hussain (No. 5), Abdul Rahman (No. 6), Abdullah (No. 7), Muhammad Hussain (No. 8), Allah Ditta (No. 11), Allah Ditta (No. 13), Abdul Karim (No. 15), and Nizam Din (No. 19)— all took a very active part in the destruction of the level-crossing gates, the huts, the bridge, and Mr. Bailey's house, but they were clearly acting under the leadership of the other four. Ata Ullah (No. 17) joined in the destruction of the gates, the hut and the bridge, but there is no evidence that he went to Mr. Bailey's house, and it is quite possible that finding that the mob were going to extreme lengths in their warfare against Government, he thought it wiser to dissociate himself from his companions. We have given him the benefit of this doubt and have found him guilty on the lesser charge of mischief under section 436, I.P.C. Muhammad Azim (No. 4), Rahmat (No. 9), Abdul Razaq (No. 10), and Ahmad (No. 14) are mere boys and cannot have intended to wage war. We have convicted them under section 495, I.P.C., and there is no doubt about their having taken part in the looting of the house. Abdul Wahib (No. 12) and Muhammad Hussain (No. 20) we have acquitted as the evidence against them was slight; they also are very young boys. Accused No. 18, Ahmad Din, was not put on his trial as the police have not as yet procured sufficient evidence about him.

As regards the rest of the accused, after careful scrutiny of the evidence we formed the opinion that (with the exception of three) they were not proved guilty of any offence. What happened was that seeing the house in flames they came to the spot and made off with such articles as the rioters had dropped or abandoned in their flight. Possibly the sight of the loot led them astray, but it appears that after a few hours' reflection they thought better of it and they collected most of their takings and stored them with Wilayat Shah (accused No. 21), the *Pir* of the village, and told Mr. Bailey's *khansama* what they had done. When the police arrived the missing articles were promptly given up. We think that they were moved by affection for Mr. Bailey and that they are entitled to a *locus poenitentieo*. We have therefore acquitted all except three.

Sardara (No. 22), Hazura (No. 23) and Ilahi Bakhsh (No. 24) are undoubtedly guilty of retaining property that had been taken by the dacoits from the house. Sardara and Ilahi Bakhsh actually broke open a box and stole the contents, whilst Hazura made off with a bundle of clothes. We think that Sardara should be dealt with sternly as he is the *lambardar* of the village, and that Hazura who did not take such leading part should be treated with some lenience. We convict all three under section 412, I.P.C. In all cases the defence evidence was quite worthless. We convict Nos. 1, 2, 3, 5, 6, 7, 8, 11, 13, 15, 16 and 19 under section 121, I.P.C., and Nos. 4, 9, 10 and 14 under section 395, I.P.C., No. 17 under section 436, I.P.C., Nos. 22, 23 and 24 under section 412, I.P.C.; and we acquit Nos. 12, 20, 21, 25, 26, 27, 28, 29, 30, 31, 32 and 33. We award sentences as given in the annexed schedule. All those convicted under section 121, I.P.C., are to have their property (liable to forfeiture) forfeited to Government.

[Sentences—Four accused Muhammad Hussain, Basheshar Nath, Din Muhammad and Amar Singh were sentenced to death and foreiture of property, eight to transportation for life and forfeiture of property; two to ten years' rigorous imprisonment, one to 7 years' and one to 5 years' rigorous imprisonment, four to 20 stripes, and 12 were acquitted.]

41—GUJRAT RIOT SUPPLEMENTARY CASE

(Mr. H. Prenter's Commission)

Two of the absconding accused in the Crown *versus* Ghulam Nabi and others of Gujrat tried by the Hon. Mr. Leslie Jones' Commission on 2nd May, 1919, in connection with the wrecking of the railway Station at Gujrat on 15th April last (Case No. 5 of 1919) have been arrested and put before us for trial. The evidence satisfies us that the mob were waging war against the King and did so with considerable effect. The evidence further proves satisfactorily that Tarlok Nath and Narinjan Das were active members of the mob throughout the day and took part in several acts of violence. They also incited their comrades by inflammatory remarks and speeches. They are guilty under section 121, I.P.C., and we convict them accordingly. We sentence them to transportation for life and direct that such of their property as is liable to forfeiture be forfeited to Government.

42—RIGO BRIDGE CASE (AMRITSAR)

(Lt.-Col. Irvine's Commission)

Sergeant Rowlands was brutally murdered near the Rigo Bridge at Amritsar at about 2 p.m. on April 10th. He appears to have gone to the city and to have been endeavouring to make his way back to the Fort when he found the city in an uproar. His skull was fractured in three places; the injuries were caused by blows from a heavy blunt weapon. Both accused subsequently boasted of their crime. Accused No. 1 is amply identified by independent witnesses, and accused No. 2 made a confession which was duly recorded by a 1st class Magistrate on April 14th. The weapon put in is a straining screw, and was discovered in consequence of information furnished by accused No. 1 himself who used it on the deceased. Accused No. 2 is said to have had a stick, but there is no evidence that he actually struck the deceased; he is, however, equally guilty of offences under sections 121 and 302 Indian Penal Code, of which we find both accused guilty.

The sentence in each case will be one of death and forfeiture of such property as each was possessed of at the time of the commission of the offence and as is liable to forfeiture.

43—SANGLA HILL CASE

Attempt to murder Mr. Wale

(Mr. H. Prenter's Commission)

Harnam Singh has been placed before us charged under section 307, I.P.C., of having attempted to murder Mr. Wale, of the Telegraph Department at Sangla Hill. The evidence shows that this was an isolated occurrence—an attack by a fanatic upon an officer of the Government. The identity of the accused has been fully proved. The attack was a very murderous one and Mr. Wale saved himself only by firing upon his assailant. There is no doubt as to the intention to murder. The defence evidence is worthless. We convict Harnam Singh, under section 307, I.P.C., and sentence him to transportation for life.

44—BHAGTANWALA CASE (AMRITSAR)

(Lt.-Col. Irvine's Commission)

On the afternoon of 10th April, a mob sacked the Post Office near the Golden Temple at Amritsar, collected and burnt all Government property in it, but refrained from setting fire to the building as it was privately owned The mob moved on to Bhagtanwala Railway Station, a mile distant, where they cut the telegraph wires, looted the godown and set the station building on fire.

The 15 persons brought before us were accused of having been concerned in one or other or both of these affairs, and have been charged with various offences under sections 121, 147, 395, 436 and 412, I.P.C.

We acquit accused Nos. 12 and 15, Buti and Khuda Bakhsh, *alias* Billa, against whom we think the evidence is insufficient. Against Gama (No. 11) an offence under section 412, I.P.C., only has been made out, and in convicting him under that section, we sentence him to five years' rigorous imprisonment.

The remainder have, we consider, been satisfactorily proved to have committed the offence of waging war under section 121, I.P.C., and we sentence each to transportation for life, namely:—

Nizam Din, *alias* Dado, No. 1, Chagha, No. 2, Habib, No. 3, Shamman, No. 4, Dilli, No. 5, Pira, No. 6, Manni, No. 7, Gurdit Singh, No. 8, Lal, No. 9, Majha, No. 10, Mahna, No. 13, and Dadu, No. 14.

As required by law, we further direct that all such property as was owned by each of these convicts and as is subject to forfeiture shall be forfeited to Government.

The first five of these were leaders and were in both affairs; their sentences require no commutation. As regards the rest, recommendations to mercy will be made.

45—THE "TRIBUNE" CASE

(Lt.-Col. Irvine's Commission)

The accused, Kali Nath Roy, was the editor of the "Tribune", a daily newspaper published at Lahore, with a circulation of from 4,500 to 5,000 copies. He is charged with offences under section 124-A of the Indian Penal Code and Rule 25 of the Defence of India Consolidation Rules, in that he, at Lahore, on the 3rd, 4th, 6th, 8th, 9th, 10th and 11th of April, 1919, "uttered sedition by written words, and published by written words false reports which he had no reasonable grounds to believe to be true, and which were likely to cause fear and alarm to the public, and promote feelings of enmity and hatred among His Majesty's subjects."

He has pleaded not guilty to these charges, and has put in a lengthy written statement, attached to which is a copy of an equally lengthy representation and apology addressed to the Lieutenant-Governor of the Punjab.

It is impossible to compress within the limits of the brief judgement, which is all that is within the scope of the instructions issued to this Commission, a full explication of all the matters which we have had to consider, but we shall endeavour to leave no point unmentioned even as we have left no point advanced unconsidered.

Before taking up our discussion of the articles which form the basis of the charges we may first refer briefly to the general law on the subject of sedition.

Among the Indian rulings consulted by us are: I.L.R. XX All. 55 (Amba Parshad's case); 27 P. R. 1914 (the "Zamindar" case); 15 P. R. of 1915 (the "Sher-i-Punjab" case); I.L.R. XXXII Bom. 112 (Tilak's case); I.L.R. XXII Bom. 152 (the "Pratod" case); 15 Cal. W.N. 141 (the "Karmayogin" case).

These judgements are easily available and we refrain from quoting from them here, but among the English rulings, (some of which incidentally supply powerful commentaries on the employment of the *hartal* and *Satyagraha* methods in general) are "Q. *v.* John Collins"— 3 S.T. 1149— and "Q. *v.* Sir Francis Burdett," from which we permit ourselves to extract the following pertinent observations. In the first of these, in commenting on the words used in connection with the arrest of Dr. Taylor, Littledale J. said:—You will have to consider whether this publication was or was not a calm and temperate discussion of the events which had occurred"— and "the people have a right to discuss any grievances that they may have to complain of; but they must not do it in a way to excite tumult."

In Q. *v.* Sir Francis Burdett—I, S.T.I, the words of Best J. were:—"The liberty of the Press is this, that you may communicate any information that you think proper to communicate by print, that you may point to Government their errors and endeavour to convince them their system of policy is wrong and attended with disadvantage to the country, and that another system of politics would be attended with benefit... But the question always is as to the manner. A question is made whether they show an intention to instruct by appealing to the judgement or to irritate and excite to sedition, in other words, whether they appeal to the sense or the passions."

In dealing with the articles of the charge we have carefully considered each of them as a whole, as well as the particular passages on which the prosecution have relied. We have endeavoured to divorce no portion from its context and, where the defence has relied on other articles or passages as explaining the meaning of articles in the charge, we have considered them together. We have borne in mind the particular points urged by counsel for the defence, namely—that the accused is a Bengali, not knowing the vernacular or the temper of the Punjab people well; his work in connection with the War Publicity Committee and so forth; that he is a "journalist", and that the Oriental style of writing may be considered somewhat florid and inflated. We have taken into account the time and place of the writings: the circumstances under which they were written, the sections of the public which the paper would reach, and the class of reader to which they were addressed. We have paid special attention to the ruling reported in 15 Cal. W.N. 141 (cited for the defence)—the "Karmayogin" case—(*vide* also Rattan Lal, 1909 edition p. 185); in which it was laid down that, though the "state of the country" must be taken into consideration, it would not entitle a court to convert an article, not falling within the mischief aimed at by section 124-A into one that does, (p. 155); in other words that it is necessary to find that an article is *per se* seditious.

We have considered the definitions of "disaffection," as compared with mere "disapprobation", as discussed by high authority: and to such articles concerned with the charge as might be held merely to express disapprobation we shall not here refer.

We have had to guard ourselves against the view that wild and inflammatory writing, published at a time of great popular excitement, can be explained away as "mere rhetoric," we cannot entirely ignore the events which occurred on or about the dates of these articles; and while realising that "intention" is the essence of an offence under section 124-A, I.P.C., we remember the *dictum* that "a man must be taken to intend the natural consequences of what he has done."

With all these considerations before us we may now state the general reasoning on which we have decided to convict the accused under section 124-A, I.P.C.

Although there is much which in unexceptional in the writings of the accused, yet there is also much that, in our opinion, undoubtedly tends and was intended to promote disaffection, and we hold strongly that the former cannot either excuse the latter or show that the meaning and intention of the articles and passages, to which we shall refer more particularly below, were other than appear on the face of them. Explanations, all more or less ingenious, have been offered of those articles and passages; and some of these we have accepted, but of others we would say generally that we find ourselves unable to carry the process far enough to exonerate the accused. It is unfortunate, to say the least of it, that so much and such elaborate explanation of words, of which the ostensible meaning is plain, should be required.

The line generally adopted by the defence in respect of any words complained of has been to say :— "We admit that, on the face of them, these words are open to objection; but look at some subsequent words in the same article, or even look at another article in the same issue, where we have given expression to sentiments of an entirely different nature. You must read the former in the light of the latter."

This is fallacious reasoning. When the meaning of a passage is obscure, or it admits of more than one meaning, it is then legitimate to read such passage in the light of another; but when there is no obscurity and the meaning of the passage is plain, this method of reasoning cannot be employed. You may reconcile apparent, but you cannot reconcile real, inconsistencies.

Again, when a public speaker makes two statements, or gives two pieces of advice, which are inconsistent with each other, and one of which is seditious and one not so, it is possible to call upon the speaker himself to make his choice and to abide by one or the other. But when a public writer in his newspaper makes two statements, or gives two pieces of advice, which are inconsistent with each other, and one of which is seditious and one not so, it is the reader who has to choose and, if he believes the seditious statement or acts upon the seditious advice, the editor cannot escape responsibility by subsequently pointing to the statement of advice which is not seditious. To hold otherwise would make the law relating to libel or sedition a dead letter by providing the would-be-libeller or seditionist with an open and easy escape from the consequences of his words. In the matter of sedition, the part of a journalistic Janus is one which no man can reasonably claim to play.

We now discuss the passages and articles in respect of which a conviction must be registered. We take these in chronological order.

First comes that of the 6th April, 1919. *"Prayer at the Juma Masjid"*. It is a news paragraph from a correspondent containing reference to the Delhi Martyrs. The Government *communique*, dated the 3rd April, had been published in the *"Tribune"* on the 5th April. The accused, in his written statement, has admitted the use of the word "Martyrs" to be "unfortunate" and "a mistake;" but in the issue of the 8th we find a front-page paragraph headed *"The Delhi Tragedy.—A Memorial Fund,"* and in the same issue we have a telegram (dated Delhi, April 6th, and published in the issue dated April, 8th) from a correspondent, bearing the editorial heading *"Memorial to Delhi Martyrs."* A fund had been started in Delhi called the "Relief and Memorial Fund for the dead and wounded in the Delhi Tragedy". The accused chose to emphasise the Memorial for Martyrs and not the Relief, and the inference from this is plain.

The next article is *"A Feature of yesterday's Demonstration"* in the issue of the 8th April in which occurs a passage of which the obvious meaning is that Government had been endeavouring to "dupe" the people.

Then comes, in the issue of April 8th, some particularly indefensible writing in the article entitled *"Action against Dr. Kitchlew and others."*—and we consider along with it the article *"Action under the Defence of India Act"* in the issue of April 11th. In these articles the editor has definitely asserted that the action of the "Punjab Government was both unjust and unwarranted"; and in the latter article it is said that "the Punjab Government has exposed itself to the general criticism at the bar of public opinion." We bear in mind how soon after the appearance of these articles the serious outbreak took place in Amritsar; and also the appropriate remarks on the subject of the Cawnpore mosque incident in P. R. 27 (Criml.) of 1914 (the "Zemindar" case). We are unable to accept the explanation that these articles were unobjectionable, because it was only intended to protest against the use of the Defence of India Act, as being a War measure. Apart from the fact that the Act is still in operation, there is no defence for the violence of the language used, and for the assumption that unwarranted action had been taken.

The leading article of the 9th April, is headed *"The Delhi Tragedy"*. Much of it is couched in what we consider indefensible language; all sorts of allegations are made against the authorities; and, in spite of the publication of the Government *communique* on April 5th, Swami Shradhanand's version of the Delhi incident (containing mention of "savage and inhuman" firing and so forth) is put forward as not having yet been "contradicted by any authority, whose contradiction would carry weight." In connection with this article we have considered the relevant observations in P. R. 15, (Criml.) of 1915, and I.L.R. XXII Bom. 112—and we are unable to accept as of any weight the argument that, on the 5th April, the "Leader" newspaper, with a much less careful, edited version of the Swami's story, had reached Lahore, and that consequently there was no objection to the publication of the "*Tribune*" article. The defect in this reasoning is too patent to require explication.

Lastly, we have the leading article in the issue of the 9th April, entitled "*Blazing Indiscretion*." The general tone of this article may be gathered from the head-line. With attacks on public servants in their private capacity we have nothing to do; but this was an attack on the Head of a Province in his public capacity, written at a time (one day before the trouble at Amritsar and Lahore) when, as was categorically stated by the accused in this very article, the atmosphere was "highly surcharged" and the "public mind" was "in a state of unusual excitement." That this state of mind was well realised by the accused we further see from the leading article of the 11th April, already referred to, which contains the statement that "the public have passed and are passing through a period of unusual excitement," and which further criticizes in no measured terms the action taken at Amritsar under the Defence of India Act.

Articles of later date cited by the defence, and written after it had obviously been realised by the accused that matters had gone too far, cannot avail him, nor can the opinions expressed in the "*Servant of India*" (issues of April 24th and May 1st) to the effect that the accused is "one of the most level-headed men in the country" and "a law-abiding citizen."

We convict the accused under section 124-A, I. P. C., in respect of all the articles and passages discussed above.

As regards the charge under Rule 25 of the Defence of India Consolidation Rules, it is quite arguable that a conviction should rightly be had in respect to the publication of "What Swami Shradhanand saw" in the issue of April 3rd, but in view of the conviction already registered under the ordinary law as contained in section 124-A, I.P.C., we do not deem it necessary to proceed further with the charge under the special enactment.

On the question of sentence, we do not think that transportation would be suitable in the present case : the maximum term of imprisonment allowed under the section is three years, and, after taking everything into consideration, we sentence the accused to two years' rigorous imprisonment together with a fine of Rs. 1,000 or in default, six months' further rigorous imprisonment.

46—AMRITSAR ASSAULT CASE

Attempt to kill Miss Sherwood

(MR. JUSTICE LESLIE-JONES' COMMISSION)

Miss Sherwood is a middle-aged lady, who was Superintendent of the Mission School in Amritsar. She is also a Lady Doctor, and as such has spent many years working in the city where she was greatly respected.

Her story is briefly that about 1 o'clock on the 10th of April, when she was bicycling from one of her schools to another she encountered a mob which raised cries of "*kill her, she is English.*" She wheeled round and tried to escape, but took a wrong turning and had to retrace her steps. She reached a lane where she was well-known, and thought she would be safe, but the mob overtook her and she was also attacked from the front. Being hit on the head with sticks she fell down but got up and ran a little way where she was again felled, being struck with sticks even when she was on the ground. Again she got up and tried to enter a house, but the door was slammed in her face. Falling from exhaustion she again struggled to get up but everything seemed to get dark and she thought she had become blind.

The evidence deals only with a part of what occurred. The witnesses, who are particularly good and have been entirely unshaken in cross-examination, prove that towards the end of the chase she was seized by Ahmad Din, No. 7, who seized her dress and threw her down. His brother, Jila, No. 8 pulled off her hat. Then Mangtu, No. 3, Mela, No. 4, Mangta *alias* Giddar, No. 5, and Lal Chand, No. 6, struck her with their fists. She got up and staggered on till Wilayati, No. 2, caught her by her hair, and having knocked her down took off his shoe and gave her five or six blows on the head. She got up and struggled a little further, until she was finally knocked down by Sunder Singh, No. 1, who struck her on the head with his *lathi*.

On this, the savage mob which had been shouting "*Victory to Kitchlu,*" raised the cry of "*she is dead,*" and then passed on.

Miss Sherwood was afterwards picked up by some Hindu shopkeepers, who took her to a temporary refuge. She was conveyed out of the city in the evening where the doctor who then attended her thought that she was still bleeding profusely from the scalp which was extensively wounded. If she had not been treated then her injuries would probably have been fatal. She has since gone to England in a critical condition.

The mob which chased and attacked Miss Sherwood was one of those which were attacking Europeans because they were Europeans, and the city was at the time in the full swing of murderous rebellion.

All the accused are convicted of the offences with which they are charged.

Some of the prisoners are youths, but at least one of them Wilayati, No. 2, was among the most brutal of a mob whose cruelty it would be difficult to surpass. The crime committed was far worse than most murders, and although Government may perhaps, in the case of some of these offenders, be pleased to exercise its prerogative of mercy, we, as Court of Justice, are not prepared to distinguish, except in the case of Jila, No. 8, who is much younger than the rest. The sentences are as in the schedule annexed. Jila, we consider, should be sent to a reformatory.

[*Sentences*—Seven of the accused, Sundar Singh, Wilayati, Mangtu, Mela, Mangta, Lal Chand and Ahmad, were sentenced to death and forfeiture of property. The eighth Jila, was sentenced to transportation for life and forfeiture.]

47—NATIONAL BANK MURDER CASE
(AMRITSAR)
(Lt.-Col. Irvine's Commission)

On April 10th, 1919, about noon, after the arrest of Kitchlew and Satyapal, disorder broke out in Amritsar, in the course of which an attempt was made to invade the Civil Station by a mob which had to be turned back by fire from troops and police. Shortly after this a mob attacked the National Bank situated in the city, brutally murdered Mr. Stewart, Manager, and Mr. Scott, Assistant Manager, sacked and burnt the Bank and looted the godown which contained cloth and goods to the value of several lakhs of rupees. The Chartered and Alliance Banks were subsequently sacked. A Mission Hall Church and the Religious Book Society's Depot were also attacked and burnt by the mob. There was no reason why these institutions should have been singled out by the mob or their leaders except that, as the evidence shows, they were out to destroy the visible manifestation of British connection with the country.

It is unnecessary to labour the point that the salient offence committed in connection with the attack on the National Bank, the facts of which form the main basis of the present charges, was one falling under section 121, I.P.C., and we have only to consider which of the 21 accused now before us were concerned in that attack. Certain of the accused could also be convicted under section 302, I.P.C., but we see no necessity to discriminate, more especially as in circumstances like those before us, there is only one possible penalty for the offence or offences committed.

We are not entirely satisfied that Ghulam Hasan *Pherna* (15), was in the actual attack on the Bank, but he is proved to have been found in possession of property looted therefrom. We convict him and sentence him to 7 years' rigorous imprisonment under section 412, I.P.C. As regards the remaining 20 accused we are clear that they each took an active part in the attack on the Bank. In convicting all of them of an offence under section 121, I.P.C., we would only note that Rattan Chand or Rattu (1) and Bhugga (2) were ringleaders, and initiated the outbreak with most significant promptitude, as soon as the news of the deportation of Kitchlew and Satyapal, whose lieutenants they are called, became known. We therefore, sentence each of the remaining 20 accused, as set out in the schedule, to death and to the forfeiture of such property as was owned by him at the time of the commission of the offence and as is liable to forfeiture.

We consider the conduct of Muhammad Hussain, P.W. 3, was very creditable throughout.

48—KASUR SUPPLEMENTARY CASE

(Lt.-Col. Irvine's Commission)

On April 12th, at Kasur, a mob, excited by speeches addressed to it on that and the previous day, invaded and wrecked the Railway Station, attacked an incoming train, murdered two warrant officers (Master Gunner Mallet and Conductor Selby), assaulted and injured two officers (Captain Limby, R.E., and Lieut. Munro of the XVIIth

Loyal Regiment) and Corporals Battson and Gringham of the Queen's Regiment, assaulted Mr. and Mrs. Sherbourne of the Railway Department—all of whom were travelling in the train, burnt the Post Office and Munsif's Court, endeavoured to free prisoners in the lock-up and in the Thana, attacked the Tahsil, and was finally dispersed by fire from the Police. The violence of the mob was directed against the wearers of His Majesty's uniform and against the property of Government, and the existence of a state of insurrection at Kasur requires no demonstration.

We have already on April 30th last dealt with fifteen persons who were concerned in one or other of the different phases of the outbreak and we have now had before us forty-nine persons similarly charged. The evidence of the approver has been accepted by us as substantially correct, but we have required corroboration of his evidence as against each accused before registering a conviction.

By order, dated 24th May, 1919, we have acquitted accused Nos. 3, 10, 13, 16, 17, 19, 20, 21, 25, 26, 27, 28, 30, 31, 32, 44, 46 and 49, against whom the prosecution evidence produced in Court was plainly inadequate. Of the remainder we also acquit Nos. 23, 24, 40, 42, and 45, not being satisfied that any charge against them has been sufficiently proved. We convict the remaining accused, all under section 121, Indian Penal Code, and sentence them as under:—

1. Nadir Ali Shah and 2, Dhani Ram—These men were manifestly leaders and fully deserve the sentence of death which we hereby pass upon them.

4. Chiragh Din—There is overwhelming identification of this accused, but he is a mere boy of sixteen years of age and the sentence of transportation for life, which is the only sentence save that of death which we can pass upon him, will be accompanied by a recommendation to mercy.

5. Allah Din, *alias* Dina, was positively identified by Mr. Sherbourne as a man who actually struck at him: the Naib Tahsildar also identified him: we pass sentence of death.

6. Rehlu, is fully identified by six witnesses as having been prominent in the attack on the Sub-Divisional Officer's Court. We pass sentence of death, but on account of youth add a recommendation to mercy : his age is twenty-four.

7. Piran Ditta, is fully recognised as having been with Rehlu No.

6, he too is sentenced to death, also with a recommendation to mercy on account of youth—he is twenty-two years of age.

8. Ram Saran Das is amply identified but is a youth of eighteen; sentenced to transportation for life, which will be accompanied by a recommendation to mercy.

9. Khushi Muhammad, son of Ilahi Bakhsh: is positively identified by Corporal Battson (whose refusal to be positive about any accused in the former case impressed us very favourably) by P. W. 12 and P. W. 28. His age is eighteen years only and we sentence him to transportation for life accompanied by a recommendation to mercy.

11. Nath Ram, is fully identified by the approver and by witnesses whom we consider reliable. The approver says that he was in the mob which pursued the Europeans at the Railway Station. We sentence him to death.

12. Diwan, is identified as having struck one of the Corporals: he is a youth and we think transportation for life will suffice instead of inflicting the death sentence.

14. Farzand, amply identified: he was at the Post Office and also attacked the train. The sentence on him is death.

15. Khuda Dad, is recognised by the Naib-Tahsildar and Munsiff as having been prominent ; he was also seen looting the station. The sentence is death.

18. Panna Lal, identified by Corporal Battson and others; he was a passenger by the train and joined the mob when it was stopped at the distant signal. He is young and we sentence him to transportation for life accompanied by a recommendation to mercy.

22. Ganda Singh, is well identified by the Inspector of Works (P. W. 42) and another witness. We sentence him to death.

29. Bishan Singh, was wounded and is clearly guilty, but he is a boy of seventeen years of age and we sentence him to transportation for life with a recommendation to mercy.

33. Jiwan Singh, we place reliance upon the evidence of the *Lambardar* Bahadur Singh (P. W. 46) who impressed us very favourably, and he is corroborated by P. W. 47. The part taken by this man does not seem to have been prominent and we think that a sentence of transportation for life will suffice.

34. Khushal Singh, is sixty-five years of age, a feeble old man. But he was aggressive and we find him guilty. In convicting him and

passing sentence of transportation for life we add to it a recommendation to mercy.

35. Hira Singh, his case is stronger than that of Khushal Singh and in sentencing him to transportation for life we are not prepared to recommend to mercy.

36. Mahnga, has a bayonet wound received in the Tahsil, but we are not satisfied that he was at the station : we sentence him to transportation for life.

37. Santa Singh, is identified beyond all doubt and was present both in the attack on the Tahsil and at the City Thana. The sentence is death.

38. Pira, was caught begging in Lahore Bazar concealed under a *burkha* and with a number of tickets looted from Kasur Station in his possession: before us he has refused to call evidence and poses as of weak intellect. He answers questions intelligently, however, and is plainly not insane. Sentence, transportation for life, coupled with a recommendation to mercy.

39. Ali Muhammad, is an octroi muharrir and was undoubtedly involved. He is only twenty-two years of age and we sentence him to transportation for life.

41. Tirath Ram is fully identified and took a prominent part. We sentence him to death.

47. Kheta Ram, was at the station when the warrant officers were murdered. Sentence, death.

48. Allah Bakhsh, also was in the assault on the warrant officers and he too is sentenced to death.

In each case the sentence, as required by law, is accompanied by an order that all such property as was possessed by each accused at the time of the commission of the offence and as is liable to forfeiture, shall be forfeited to Government.

The approver Gul Muhammad is discharged.

49—AMRITSAR (MRS. EASDON'S) CASE

(Mr. Justice Leslie-Jones' Commission)

Satyapal and Kitchlew were arrested in Amritsar on the 10th April, and in consequence, a *hartal* commenced at about midday. Crowds began to parade the streets and the position became serious near the Municipal Zenana Hospital when wounded men were brought for treatment to Kidar Nath's dispensary opposite. Mrs.

Easdon, the lady doctor in charge, sent away all her out-patients, ordered the hospital to be locked, and endeavoured to reassure her in-patients. She thought of trying to escape herself but was warned that it would be impossible to do so both by her chaprasi, Hussain Bakhsh, and by Mr. Lewis (a cousin of Mrs. Benjamin, Sub-Assistant Surgeon in the hospital) who had come especially to advise Mrs. Easdon to hide and to warn her that nobody could come to her assistance. It is said that having done so he left "to do some urgent work." Mrs. Easdon, who was thus left without any protection, except her chaprasi and her female hospital staff, listened to the shouts of the angry mob increasing, and heard cries that Europeans had been murdered. She had the main door locked; ordered Mussammat Mathri, *Dai*, to be sure to lock her door, which was still open; and then went to the upper storey from which she watched the mob outside. On being told by the hospital servants that she must hide herself as the mob wanted to kill her, she ran to the quarters of Mrs. Benjamin at the other end of the hospital.

Shortly afterwards, Mrs. Benjamin, whom she had sent downstairs to get some milk, rushed back with the appalling news that, assisted by Mussammat Mathri, the armed mob succeeded in getting into the hospital and that her life was in imminent danger. Mrs. Easdon had just had time to hide herself a few steps down an adjoining staircase when the mob, which had failed to find her downstairs, rushed up into Mrs. Benjamin's room and demanded to know where she was. Mrs. Benjamin, terrified though she was, swore that Mrs. Easdon had left the hospital but the mob was not satisfied and in the endeavour to find Mrs. Easdon broke open and searched all the cupboards and boxes in Mrs. Benjamin's quarters. Mrs. Easdon who was within a few feet of them, could hear all that occurred.

When the mob got back to the entrance of the hospital Mst. Mathri informed them that Mrs. Easdon was still inside. The search for her began again but by that time she had hidden herself in a latrine on the roof. Before the mob could find her, the news arrived of the burning of the National Bank and, in the hope of loot, the would be murderers dispersed.

Hussain Bakhsh Chaprasi, who had behaved loyally and bravely throughout, then got out of the hospital and returned with a "burka" and a pair of Indian paijamas. Disguised in these and, having blackened her feet with ink, Mrs. Easdon escaped by a back way to the house of Muhammad Sharif, Sub-Inspector of Police, who gave her an asylum. She had spent about three hours in the hospital since the mob had first begun to collect.

There are 16 accused. Of these Muhammad Amin No. 13 is a pleader, whose house is close to the hospital, and Muhammad Jamil No. 14 is his brother. Muhammad Amin was under great obligations to Mrs. Easdon, who had attended all his family with great kindness and skill, and he was on very friendly terms with her. He had seen her on the roof of the hospital when the mob was being collected and he could not but have heard the shouts when Mrs. Benjamin's room was being ransacked. Nevertheless he had preferred to return to his own house and to stay there leaving Mrs. Easdon to her fate. Even when the mob had left the hospital he did not go to her assistance. However, on the statement of Mrs. Easdon, as it now stands, there is no evidence against him of actual abetment and we must acquit both him and his brother, Muhammad Jamil, though their inhuman conduct and base ingratitude have disgraced them for all time.

Accused Nos. 3, 5, 6, 7, 8, 9 and 10 are also acquitted for the reason that the evidence of their participation is not sufficiently reliable to warrant a conviction.

Of the remainder, Muhammad Sadiq No. 11, though there is no evidence that he actually entered the hospital, was the man who collected the mob for the attack on it. The sole object was to kill Mrs. Easdon, as being a European.

Muhammad Askram No. 15, who is the son of Muhammad Amin, and a student at a Mission School, was a ring-leader of the mob inside the hospital and it was he who made the most persistent enquiries as to where Mrs. Easdon was to be found. Against Mahesha No. 1, Harnamoo No. 2, Karim Bakhsh No. 4 and Gama No. 12 there is ample and satisfactory evidence.

Nos. 1, 2, 4, 11, 12, and 15 are all convicted and sentenced to death and to forfeiture.

Mst. Mathri, No. 16, the disloyal assistant who enabled the mob to enter the hospital, and sent them back for their second search, is convicted and sentenced to transportation for life and to forfeiture.

50—CHARTERED BANK CASE (AMRITSAR)

After sacking the National Bank a party of the disorderly mob in Amritsar attacked the Chartered Bank, broke the windows, set fire to doors and chicks, threw the books outside and smashed the furniture and fittings but were able to find little of value. The Kotwali, with a D. S. P., Inspector, three sub-inspectors and a hundred constables was only 40 yards away and after the mob had been at its work of destruction for half an hour a body of 25 constables under a sub-inspector was sent across to the Bank. Even so they were fortunately in time to save the manager, Mr. Thomson, and Assistant Manager Mr. Ross, against whom the mob had been uttering threats, but who had remained hidden in an upper storey of the building while the mob was occupied below. The sub-inspector tells us that he threatened the mob with his revolver, but it is significant, in view of what happened at the other Banks, that mere threats were sufficient and the police appeared.

Three of the eleven persons originally accused have already been convicted in previous cases and have not been placed before us. Eight are left : of these we are not satisfied that, Abdul Aziz (5), Sultan Muhammad (6) and Gaman Mashki (8) are guilty and we acquit them. The guilt of the remaining five (1) Ibrahim, (2) Gaman Dhobi, (3) Nabi, (4) Ghauns, (7) Sadhu Singh, we consider adequately proved and we convict them, accordingly of an offence under section 121, I. P. C. None of these men were leaders, they are all of low status and appear to have taken subordinate parts. We sentence each, therefore, to transportation for life together with forfeiture of such property as was owned by each at the time of the commission of the offence and as is liable to forfeiture.

A recommendation to mercy will be made on behalf of Ghauns (4) aged 18, on the ground of his youth.

51—THE "PRATAP" CASE

(Mr. H. Prenter's Commission)

L. Radha Kishen is the editor of a newspaper called the "Pratap" published at Lahore. He has been placed before us for trial on a charge framed under Rule 25 of the Defence of India Act, in that on the 2nd, 3rd, and 5th of April, he published in that newspaper (and circulated) "false statements and reports which he had no reasonable ground to believe to be true with intent to cause fear and alarm to the public". The prosecution have proved that he published and circulated the following statements relating to the events which occurred at Delhi on 30th March:—

1. "By the evening of 31st March, forty Hindus and Mussalmans had been killed."

2. "It cannot be denied that most who were killed or wounded were innocent."

3. "The apprehension of a breach of the peace was not so great as to necessitate firing.........and..........the people threw stones and brickbats at the time when the authorities had already taken the initiative."

The prosecution have also established that each of these statements is false. (1) Since 30th March altogether 10 persons only have died as a result of the injuries received. (2) The persons killed were members of a violent and dangerous mob which had made several savage attacks upon the police and military. (3) The military and police did not fire until a very serious breach of the peace had actually taken place, and the statement of Mr. Jeffreys (P. W. 1) which stands entirely unrefuted shows clearly that had not the Additional District Magistrate ordered the police to fire very great damage to life and property would have taken place.

Lala Radha Kishen's defence consisted of a long written statement and of the evidence of one witness. This evidence clearly proves that Lala Radha Kishen's sole authority for the statement that forty had been killed by 31st March, was a postcard received by a friend of his from a person who had chanced to visit Delhi on the 30th. Lala Radha Kishen had therefore no reasonable grounds for believing the statement to be true. He rushed into print without taking the least trouble to ascertain whether this wild rumour was true or not. Without going into the question whether he intended to cause fear and alarm to the public, we are satisfied that the false statements did actually cause fear and alarm to the public. All the agruments addressed to us by counsel were quite wide of the mark. We are not concerned with the abstract question of how much liberty the press should enjoy. We have simply to see whether Rule 25 has been broken. It is no defence to say that other papers published much more alarming accounts of the Delhi riots, nor can we hold it a valid defence to show that on the 4th April, L. Radha Kishen published the official *communique* and admitted that there was no confirmation of the news that 40 had been killed. We have taken this half-hearted recantation into account in awarding sentence. We find L. Radha Kishen guilty of the offence with which he has been charged, and we convict him accordingly. We sentence him to undergo 18 months' rigorous imprisonment and to pay a fine of Rs. 500, or, in default, undergo a further period of six months' rigorous imprisonment.

52—ROBINSON MURDER CASE (AMRITSAR)

(Lt.-Col. Irvine's Commission)

When the mob at Amritsar was repulsed from the Civil Lines at the foot bridge over the railway on April 10th, 1919, part of the crowd turned towards the goods-shed and there caught and brutally murdered Guard Robinson.

Of the three men now before us, we are not satisfied that the prosecution has made out a case against the cartmen, Gulam Qadir (1) and Gullu (2), we have acquitted them accordingly.

The third accused, Kanhiya, *alias* Gayu, is, we think, proved to have been one of men from among the mob who actually struck Guard Robinson : we find him guilty of an offence under Section 121/302, I. P. C., and sentence him to death, together with forfeiture of such property as was owned by him at the time of the commission of the offence and as is liable to forfeiture.

53—WAGAH DERAILMENT CASE

(LAHORE DISTRICT)

(Lt.-Col. Irvine's Commission)

At the Bisakhi fair held at Maniala village in the Lahore district on April 13th, an impromptu meeting was held, speeches were made attacking Government, and a rising was advocated. That night, in consequence of this conspiracy, Wagah Railway Station was sacked and burnt, telegraph wires were cut, a length of line was taken up and an armoured train was consequently detrailed, but there was fortunately no loss of life ; the attack was directed solely against Government.

Forty-four men from different villages have been placed before us in connection with the conspiracy at Maniala and the events of Wagha station. Although no doubt some plot was hatched at Maniala, the actual evidence of what was said and by whom is so unsatisfactory, vague and indefinite that we cannot safely find any one guilty of the specific offence provided for by section 124-A, I. P. C. For the rest we have to depend on the evidence of two approvers, one of whom, Satar, we are not prepared to believe. The other, Shahabu, is more trustworthy, but we have decided to require corroboration of his statement as against any one accused before convicting. There is very little corroboration forthcoming, and it is plain that witnesses who know the facts will not come forward. We find only the following: Sulakhan Singh, son of Fauja Singh (1); Vir Singh, son of Thakur Singh (16); Uttam Singh, son of Thakur Singh (20); Joti Singh, son of Lal Singh (22)—guilty, in each case, of an offence under section 121, I. P. C., and sentence all four to transportation for life together with forfeiture of such property as was owned by each at the time of the commission of the offence and is liable to forfeiture.

Sulakhan Singh (1) is a havildar in the—and he was the leader both at Maniala and in the attack on Wagha. He has an exemplary conduct sheet for his 14 years' service and some remarks about him by the Officer Commanding the Depot of the regiment have been put before us. We find it difficult to account for his behaviour of 13th April, and in deciding not to sentence him to death, we have had regard to his past record. As the leader has been sentenced only to the lesser penalty of transportation for life, this is also the sentence which we have pronounced on the remaining accused. The two approvers are discharged.

54—SUPPLEMENTARY GUJRANWALA CASE
(Mr. H. Prenter's Commission)

A third batch consisting of 19 persons has been put up before us for trial under sections 121, 147, 124-A, 152, 395, 436, I.P.C., section 25, Act XIII of 1885, section 149, I.P.C. As we have remarked in our previous judgments (e.g. No. 8, of 1919) in connection with the Gujranwala riots of April 14th, there is no doubt but that the mob was waging war against the King. We have now only to see which of the accused have been prove to have taken an active share in the doings of the mob. We consider that the evidence against the following is insufficient, *viz.*, Nos. 5, 6, 10, 12, 13 and 15 and we accordingly acquit them. We do not find that any of the persons before us today were actual leaders of the mob. Several of the real leaders have already been tried, convicted and sentenced. The present case relates chiefly to the rank and file of the rioters. At the same time we find that certain members of this batch were much more active than the others, as they were seen at several of the places where most of the damage was done. Nos. 1, 2, 4, 7, 8, 9, 11, 14, 17, 18 and 19 are of this sort. Accused Nos. 3 and 16 were not quite so active, but they were undoubtedly members of the mob which waged war against the

King. No. 17, Anant Ram, made a strenuous effort to show that he was present at the railway station as a benevolent person who was trying to feed some poor and hungry passengers. We do not doubt that he was engaged in this work, but the evidence as to his inciting the mob to violence by shouting the usual war cries, and as to his being present in a number of danger-spots throughout the day convinces us that he was carried away by his feelings of hatred towards Government and that he did engage in the waging of war. He kept well in the background where danger might have been incurred. In short he seems to us to belong to the dangerous class of passive resisters, whose passivity changes into activity either in a moment of excitement or when no personal risk is to be feared.

We convict Nos. 1, 2, 3, 4, 7, 8, 9, 11, 14, 16, 18, and 19, under section 121, I.P. Code and sentence each to transportation for life and direct that the property of each, so far as is liable to forfeiture, be forfeited to Government. We recommend Nos. 3 and 16 to mercy as we consider that sentence of 10 years' rigorous imprisonment would suffice.

55—DHABAN SINGH RIOT CASE
(GUJRANWALA DISTRICT)
(Mr. H. Prenter's Commission)

The railway station of Dhabansingh, Gujranwala district, was attacked by a large mob at 4 o'clock on the morning of the 16th April. The office was burned, the safes were looted, and some goods belonging to the travelling public were stolen. Earlier in the night the same mob had burned a railway bridge over the canal at a distance of a mile and a half from the station, had removed two pairs of rails from the permanent way and had severed the telegraph wires in many places. This mob began to collect in the village of Nawan Pind, having been harangued by Gyan Singh and then some of the leaders went to another village, Manawala, and gathered many recruits from it. A considerable number of these rioters have been tried and convicted by special magistrates, and now eleven persons considered to be the ringleaders have been placed before us for trial, charged under sections 121, 147, 124-A, 395, 436, 140, I.P.C.

There is good evidence to show that the leaders incited the mob to cut the railway line for the express purpose of preventing the passage of troops, and we have no doubt but that the waging of war was the prime object of the rioters. It only remains to be seen which of these persons were actually engaged in the operations and to find out which of them were the leaders.

The evidence is overwhelming against every one of the accused as to their having taken a most active part in all that was done that night. There is a remarkable lack of even the ordinary enmities that sometimes induce witnesses to make false statements, and all the defence evidence was more than usually worthless. We convict each of the accused under section 121, I.P.C. Gyan Singh No. 8, was undoubtedly the moving spirit of the mob. It was he who preached war in Nawan Pind, and he was one of the two Kambohs who went as emissaries to Manawala village to collect recruits. We regard him as a dangerous man and we sentence him to death. We sentence all the others to transportation for life. We direct that such of the property of each as is liable to forfeiture be forfeited to Government.

56—CHHEHARTA CASE
(Amritsar District)
(Lt.-Col. Irvine's Commission)

On the night of April 10th, 1919, the Railway Station of Chheharta in Amritsar District was attacked by a mob of villagers; they only broke the lamps on the station itself and then proceeded to break open and loot a goods train which was standing in the yard. None of the twenty accused is identified as having been present on the spot but stolen property was recovered from all except No. 15, Bichattar Singh, who is acquitted. As regards the rest, we have a number of confessions but we do not lay much stress on them as they were made after the property had been recovered, and we are not impressed with the evidence of the very ordinary persons put in to testify that they saw certain of accused either going in or coming from the station.

We, therefore, think it safest to register convictions under section 412, I.P.C., only against these 19 accused. The sentences detailed in full in the schedule, will be as under:—

Imprisonment till the rising of the Court in the case of No. 16, who is a mere boy and was apparetly given a *than* of cloth by one of the looters: this he threw into a *khola* and gave up directly the police appeared.

Three years' rigorous imprisonment each in the case of Nos. 9, 11 and 19.

Five years' rigorous imprisonment each in the case of Nos. 2 and 5.

Seven years' rigorous imprisonment each for the remainder.

The lesser sentences are imposed on the ground of the youth of the offenders.

We note that there is no evidence whatsoever against Bichattar Singh (15), a retired Police Sub-Inspector, who so far as appears from the record, actually advised the mob to leave the station alone: we find it difficult to understand why he was charged at all and the reasons he has advanced have led us to refer the matter separately to the proper authority.

57—GUJRANWALA LEADERS' CASE

(Mr. Justice Broadway's Commission)

Fifteen persons have been charged before us under sections 121, 121-A, 124-A, 147, I.P.C., 124-A, 323, 436, 506, I.P.C., section 126, Railway Act, section 25, Act XIII of 1885, sections 109, 120, and 149, I.P.C., in connection with a serious outbreak that occurred at Gujranwala on the 14th April, 1919.

It has been proved that on that date, a general *hartal* took place at Gujranwala; a mob proceeded to the Station at about 7.45 a.m. and stopped a train that was about to start to Wazirabad, passengers were prevented from travelling and the guard and driver were assaulted; a bridge near the Gurukul on the Wazirabad side was set on fire; telegraph and telephone wires were cut and the Kachhi Bridge on the Lahore side was also set ablaze and the permanent way was damaged, thus practically isolating Gujranwala. Mr. Heron, Superintendent of Police, and the Police, and the Police were assaulted and forced to fire on their assailants. In the meantime, a crowd had collected at an open space outside the house of Amar Nath, accused (1) where a meeting was held, and when the crowd increased in numbers, an adjournment was made to a place in the city called the Niyain, where this meeting was continued. At these meetings various speeches were made, reference being made to the Rowlatt Act—Gandhi—and the need for Hindu and Mahomedan unity, while incidents that had taken place in Lahore were also emphasised. While the meeting at the Niyain was in progress, news was received there that some of the mob had been wounded—thereupon the crowd proceeded towards the Civil Station. The Post Office, Tehsil, Dak Bungalow, Courts and Church were set on fire, and an attack was made on the Jail, the Railway Station was burnt and the Goods Shed looted, damage being done to rolling stock as well. All these acts were directed against Government and Europeans, no property belonging to an Indian being in any way touched.

These acts undoubtedly constitute a determined and deliberate waging of war, and we hold accordingly.

The case for the prosecution is that the present accused were members of conspiracy entered into with the object of over-awing Government in connection with the Rowlatt Act and had agreed to carry out their object by the commission of the acts described above.

It is alleged that the people of Gujranwala knew little and cared less about the Rowlatt Act and that on the 4th April, certain of the accused decided to start an agitation against this act on the same lines as had been adopted in other parts of the country at the instance of Gandhi: a mass meeting was accordingly convened and held on the evening of the 5th April, when the Rowlatt Act was condemned, the Delhi incidents were referred to, and the people were asked to hold a *hartal* on the 6th April.

The proposed *hartal* was held accordingly and passed off without the occurrence of any untoward incidents.

On the 10th April, disturbances occurred in Amritsar and Lahore. Brij Bhushan Bhagat, a Barrister-at-Law and one of the leading agitators, went to Lahore on the 11th and discovered that a relative of his had been wounded in the riots at that place. This information was published by him on the 12th April, and advantage was taken of a meeting of the "District Congress Committee", held that evening at the house of Amar Nath, accused (1), to propose a second *hartal*. After this meeting, on the evening of the 12th and during the day of the 13th, certain of the accused in consultation with Bhagat agreed that they should follow the example set at Amritsar—burning bridges and cutting telegraph wires.

A private meeting was held in the evening of the 13th at which these matters were considered, and it was decided to hold a *hartal* on the following day and to arrange for the burning of bridges and cutting of telegraph wires, with the result already stated above. In addition to the statement of the approver Bhagat, there is ample evidence in support of these allegations which we consider established beyond doubt and we hold that the outrages committed on the 14th April, were directly due to the conspiracy entered into on the 12th and 13th.

We are not, however, satisfied, in this case, that prior to the 12th April, any indictable conspiracy had come into existence, and therefore feel constrained to acquit those of the accused who are shown only to have taken part in the proceedings prior to that date.

Turning to the individual cases:—

Amar Nath, accused I, was one of the originators of the agitation against the Rowlatt Act and also took part in the meeting on the 13th, and agreed to and approved of the commission of the proposed acts of violence. He was one of the principal leaders throughout. He spoke at both the meetings on the 14th, drawing particular attention to one of the persons injured in the Lahore riots in such a manner as to inflame the minds of his audience. We find him guilty under section 121, I.P.C.

Mangal Sen, accused 2, was one of the speakers at the meeting on the 5th April, and drew special attention to the Delhi incidents, making an impassioned speech. He was at the meeting on the 13th April, which was held at his house, and though, as stated by the approver, he at first objected to the proposed acts of violence, he ultimately agreed to give his support. He spoke at the meeting outside Amar Nath accused (1)'s house on the 14th arousing resentment against Government. We find him guilty under section 121, I.P.C.

Hakim Rai, accused 3, was chairman at the meeting of the 5th and was also at the meeting of the 13th, but we are not satisfied that he was present when it was agreed to commit acts of violence. He does not appear to have taken any serious part in the incidents on the 14th such as would render him criminally liable. We give him the benefit of the doubt, and acquit him.

Labh Singh, accused 4, took an active part in the inception of the agitation against the Rowlatt Act and was present at the meetings of the 12th and 13. On the latter date he is said to have at first opposed the commission of acts of violence but finally agreed. He was seen in several places with the mob on the 14th, but appears to have rendered assistance to the authorities on that date. We find him guilty under section 121, I.P.C.

Matiullah, accused 5, was one of the conveners of the meeting of the 5th April, though he was not present at it. He was also at the meeting of the 12th and, though he did not attend the meeting of the 13th, we are satisfied that he on other occasions agreed to the commission of acts of violence. On the 14th, he spoke at the meeting outside Amar Nath (1)'s house on Hindu and Mahomedan unity and was also at the Niyain meeting. We find him guilty under section 121, I.P.C.

Sarab Dyal, accused 6, was one of the conveners of the meeting of the 5th April, and seconded a resolution. He was also at the meeting of the 12th as well as that on the 13th. On the 14th he attended at the Niyain meeting but did not speak. We find him guilty under section 121, I.P.C.

Lal Khan, accused 7, spoke at the meeting outside Amar Nath accused (1)'s house on the 14th but does not appear to have taken any active part in the previous proceedings and we are not satisfied that his words amounted to an abetment of waging war. We accordingly acquit him.

Din Muhammad, accused 8, had apparently no knowledge of what had been going on prior to the 14th April, (*vide* approver). On the 14th April, although he addressed the meeting outside the house of Amar Nath, accused 1, he appears to have been rendering assistance to the authorities—helping to put out the fire at the Gurukul bridge and endeavouring to lead sections of the mob back into the city. His speech on Hindu and Mahomedan unity at such a juncture gives rise to a certain amount of suspicion but we think that he is entitled to the benefit of the doubt, and we accordingly acquit him.

Abdur Rahman, accused 9, was one of the conveners of the meeting of the 5th and spoke in place of Matiullah (5), but there is practically nothing else against him, and we acquit him.

Jagan Nath, accused 10, had the notice convening the meeting of the 5th printed in Lahore and was present at the meeting. He denies his presence at the meetings of the 12th and 13th, but we have no hestitation in holding that he was present at both, and that his defence evidence is worthless. There is ample evidence to show that on the 14th April, he took a very active part in having the shops closed. We are satisfied of his guilt, and convict him under section 121, I.P.C.

Mohan Lal, accused 11, was one of the conveners of the meeting of the 5th which he attended. He was also present at the meetings on the 12th and 13th and afterwards told the approver that he had arranged for the cutting of the telegraph wires. He was very prominent in the various events of the 14th April, and we are convinced that he acted as a leader throughout. He was riding dressed in khaki—forcing people to close their shops—at the station preventing passengers from travellng. He was one of those who dragged the driver from the engine. Afterwards he was seen going towards the Gurukul with the mob that set fire to the bridge there, and was also seen leading the mob back towards the station. Later he was seen in the mob that burnt the Dak Bungalow, etc. His guilt has been clearly established, and we convict him under section 121, I.P.C.

Mela Ram, accused 12, was one of the conveners of the meeting of the 5th April, and spoke at it. He was not at the meetings of the 12th and 13th. We are not satisfied that he took any part in what occurred on the 14th and acquit him.

Chuni Lal, accused 13, was at the meetings of the 4th and 5th April, and spoke at the latter on the Delhi incidents of which he claimed to be an eye-witness. He did not attend the meetings of the 12th and 13th, but we are satisfied that he agreed with Bhagat to set fire to bridges. He was at the meeting at the Niyain on the 14th and was one of those who prevented passengers from travelling by train, and was later one of those who threw stones at the Police at the Railway Station. He was also in the mob that set fire to the Post Office and Dak Bungalow. We find him guilty under section 121, I.P.C.

Bihari Lal, accused 14, is the brother of Mohan Lal (11). He was among those who prevented passengers from travelling, and was seen with the mob that set fire to the Gurukul Bridge. He was also seen in the mob that burnt the Dak Bungalow. We find him guilty under section 121, I.P.C.

Haveli Ram, accused 15, was one of the conveners of the meeting of the 5th April, and attended it. He was at the meeting of the 13th, and on the 14th was seen preventing passengers from travelling. He was one of those who threw stones at the Police and was in the mob at the Post Office which was ablaze. We find him guilty under section 121, I.P.C.

Of the accused we have found guilty, Amar Nath (1) and Mohan Lal (11) took the most active part throughout. Amar Nath's speeches on the 14th, made at a time when violence had actually been used and the minds of the people were already inflamed, were calculated to incite them to the commission of still further outrages. Mohan Lal was most active in leading the mob, and we therefore sentence both Amar Nath and Mohan Lal to death. We sentence the other convicted persons to transportation for life.

In the case of all the persons convicted, we further direct that such property belonging to each of them as is liable to forfeiture shall be forfeited to the Crown.

The sentences passed on Labh Singh, Matiullah and Sarab Dyal are the least we are empowered to inflict. We would, however, recommend them to the clemency of Government as we consider that Matiullah and Sarab Dyal were not prepared to go to quite such extremes as their co-conspirators, while Labh Singh evidently repented of his action and endeavoured to render assistance to the authorities.

58—AMRITSAR GIRLS' SCHOOL CASE

(Lt.-Col. Irvine's Commission)

Among the outrages committed in Amritsar on 10th April, 1919, the mob attacked and fired the Girls' Mission School, fortunately without discovering the four lady missionaries, who had been hidden by the staff. Mr. Marshall, Police Inspector, had a picquet close by and hearing of the attack on the school hastened there with half his picquet: the mob thereupon fled.

Of the nine men originally charged before us, one Muhammadi was withdrawn as he had already been convicted and sentenced in another case, and we have consequently tried only eight. Of these two have been acquitted as the evidence against them was inadequate.

Against the remaining six there is ample evidence and we convict them accordingly of an offence under section 121, I.P.C., namely:—(1) Imam Din, (2) Fazal Din, (3) Muhammad Sultan, (4) Abdur Rahman *alias* Manna, (6) Nanak Chand, (7) Ismail *alias* Phila.

In none of these cases do we consider that a death sentence is called for and we sentence each to transportation for life together with, as required by law, the forfeiture of such property as was owned by each at the time of the commission of the offence, and as is liable to forfeiture. The three last named accused are young and will be recommended for reduction of sentence.

MALAKWAL CASES (59, 60, 61 AND 62)

(Mr. H. Prenter's Commission)

In connection with seditious meetings at Malakwal (Gujrat District) followed by a plot to damage the railway lines and derail trains (which proved successful) four batches of accused persons have been placed before us for trial on various charges. With the consent of all the accused we heard the evidence against all concurrently, but we have kept the cases distinct. Five persons were charged in the first batch, six in the second, nine in the third and nine in the fourth. With regard to the first batch, Nos. 1 and 2 were charged under section 124-A, I.P.C., and rules 24 and 25, D. of I., and Nos. 3, 4 and 5 under rules 24 and 25, D. of I. We have found the evidence against Nos. 3, 4 and 5 rather weak and we accordingly acquit them. Bhog Raj, accused No. 1, is a stranger to Malakwal and the evidence proves beyond doubt that he went to that town for the express purpose not only of bringing the Government into hatred, but of exciting the inhabitants to actual waging of war. The substance of his speeches has been given by several witnesses whom we see no reason to disbelieve. Accused No. 2, Ram Chandra, is a professional agitator who goes about exciting people by his songs. At Malakwal he sang hymns in Sanskrit and lest any should not understand he accompanied his singing with a running commentary in Urdu. His comments on the Rowlatt Bill exceeded all reasonable bounds, and his language was clearly within the limits of section 124-A. We convict accused Nos. 1 and 2 under that section and sentence them to transportation for life.

As regards the second case all the accused were charged merely under section 147, and as we consider that the rioting, if any, was exceedingly trivial, we acquit them. With regard to these persons and also those acquitted in the first case we note that they are employees of the railway and their action in "striking" though it led to no serious stoppage of work and as far as we can see to no dislocation of traffic, yet it seems to us worthy of being dealt with by departmental inquiry. Their acquittal in these cases does not in any way absolve them from responsibility for disobedience of orders.

The third and fourth cases differ from the others considerably. The meetings held on 15th and 16th April, in Malakwal seem fortunately to have had little or no effect upon the general public, and there was no rioting and extremely little disturbance but a small band of conspirators was encouraged by the speeches and by events that had occurred in neighbouring places and they determined to wage active war against the Government. A small party went on the night of the 16th to the railway line and cut some telegraph wires, and were then joined by some firemen and shunters from the railway station and together these two parties removed a pair of rails. They then dispersed and the damage to the lines was not noticed until the following morning, when a passenger train was derailed. Two persons were killed in the wreck and several were injured. In case No. 3 the accused have been charged under sections 147, 25, Act XIII of 1885, section 149, I.P.C., except No. 6 (Allah Din) who was charged with abetment of these offences. We find that the following persons were of the party that cut the telegraph wires and we convict them under section 25, Act XIII of 1885:—Nos. 1, 2, 5, 6, 7, 8 and 9. We sentence them to six months' rigorous imprisonment each. We acquit Nos. 3 and 4. We have dealt with this case leniently because those who were especially active have been convicted in the fourth case, and the remainder seem to us to have joined in this offence in a very half-hearted fashion. Allah Din was merely the instigator and possibly he wished his followers to do a minimum of damage.

In the fourth case the accused are charged under sections 121, 147, 126 Railway Act and 302, I.P.C., 149, I.P.C. We find that the body of men who damaged the railway lines were undoubtedly guilty of waging war against the King. The intention was to render the passage of troops impossible and to put a stop to the work of Government. As regards No. 3 (Mangal Sen) we find that the evidence is to a certain extent tainted. We give him the benefit of the doubt and acquit him.

Accused No. 1 and accused 5 were undoubtedly the leaders. Raja Ram (No. 1) was the leader of the wire-cutting party and he induced some of that party to join in damaging the line. Sarwar (No. 5) was the leader of the gang that came from the Railway Station. We think they deserve the extreme penalty. The action of this band of conspirators resulted in the death of two persons. The remaining accused, Nos. 2, 4, 6, 7, 8 and 9 were merely the rank and file. We convict Nos. 1, 2, 4, 5, 6, 7, 8 and 9 under section 121, and sentence No. 1 (Raja Ram) and No. 5 (Sarwar) to death. We sentence Nos. 2, 4, 6, 7, 8 and 9 to transportation for life. We direct that such property of accused Nos. 1, 2, 4, 5, 6, 7, 8 and 9 as is liable to forfeiture be forfeited to Government. We note that Raja Ram, Karam Chand, Daulat Ram and Multani have been convicted in two cases and we order that their sentences run concurrently. We recommend Multani and Daulat Ram to mercy on account of their youth as we think that 10 years' rigorous imprisonment would suit the case.

The approver Ghulam Ali may be set at liberty.

63—SUPPLEMENTARY HAFIZABAD CASE

(Mr. H. Prenter's Commission)

In connection with the rioters who attacked Lieutenant Tatam at Hafizabad Railway Station on 14th April, we have found that they were guilty of waging war. A second batch has now been put before us who are alleged to have been active members of the mob. No. 7 has already been convicted under section 121 for waging war on the 15th and has been sentenced to transportation for life. The P.P. withdrew the case against him accordingly. We find the evidence very weak against Nos. 1, 3, 4, 5, 6, 8 and 9 and we accordingly acquit them. There remains only the case of No. 2, Hari Singh. We have good independent evidence that he was one of the mob that attacked Lieutenant Tatam and we have held that this mob's intention was to wage war against Government and that they did so by attacking a military officer. We, therefore, convict Hari Singh under section 121, Indian Penal Code, and sentence him to transportation for life. We direct that such of his property as is liable to forfeiture be forfeited to Government. We note that he was not a ringleader.

64—SUPPLEMENTARY NATIONAL BANK MURDER CASE (AMRITSAR)

(Mr. H. Prenter's Commission)

The Amritsar riot cases have been tried by another Commission. One Jai Ram Singh has been all along noted as an absconder and a reward was promised for his arrest. He was arrested on 3rd June, 1919, and has now been placed before us for trial under sections 121, 147, 302-149, Indian Penal Code.

Quite apart from the evidence of the approver, it has been fully proved by thoroughly independent evidence that Jai Ram Singh was the actual leader of the mob that attacked the National Bank on 12th April, 1919. That mob not only burned and looted the Bank but also murdered Mr. Stewart and Mr. Scott. We find him guilty under section 121, Indian Penal Code and sentence him to death. We direct that such of his property as is liable to forfeiture be forfeited to Government.

65—SUPPLEMENTARY KASUR CASE

(Mr. H. Prenter's Commission)

In connection with the rioting at Kasur Railway Station on 12th April, 1919, a large number of men have been convicted under section 121 by the 1st and 2nd Commissions (see cases Nos. 2 and 32) and now 3 persons have been put before us charged under sections 121, 148, 302, 326, 149, I.P.C., as having been members of the mob. Lieutenant Monro very definitely recognized accused No. 2 as the instigator of the band of persons who attacked him. We think that it would be dangerous to rely on his unsupported evidence as to the identity of this instigator and cannot hold it proved that accused No. 2 was the actual leader of the assault. But we have no doubt that he was one of the mob who attacked the train and killed 2 Europeans and wounded several others.

Accused No. 1 was also a member of this mob. We convict both of these persons under section 121, I.P. Code, and sentence them to death. Accused No. 3 was one of the mob that attacked the Tahsil. He was wounded in the firing that took place. We convict him under section 121, I.P.C., and sentence him to transportation for life. We direct that such of the property of each accused as is liable to forfeiture be forfeited to Government.

66—MOMAN STATION CASE

(Mr. H. Prenter's Commission)

On the night of 15th April, the Railway Station of Moman was attacked by a mob of some 60 or 70, who first warned the railway staff to go away as the station was going to be burned, and then proceeded very methodically to set fire to all the station buildings. Prior to this Harnam Singh had gone round to some of the neighbouring villages preaching open war against the Government and collecting recruits. Three persons, Harnam Singh, Banta Singh and Mian Singh, have been put before us for trial under sections 121, 147, 436, 395, 149, I.P.C., as having been the ring-leaders. There is not the least doubt but that Harnam Singh was the moving spirit. A few days ago he was convicted under section 307, I.P.C., for having made a determined attempt on the life of Mr. Wale at Sangla Hill Station on the 16th April. He is undoubtedly guilty under section 121, I.P.C., and convicting him under that section we sentence him to death.

Banta Singh and Mian Singh were ring-leaders to a lesser extent, and we must give them the credit of not having damaged the railway line. Mian Singh put up an elaborate *alibi* in defence, which we have examined carefully and found to be quite untrue. We convict them under section 121, I.P.C., and sentence them to transportation for life. As regards all three we direct that such property of each as is liable to forfeiture be forfeited to Government.

67—AMRITSAR LEADERS' CASE*

(Mr. Justice Broadway's Commission)

(*a*) Precis of the Case

For sometime past, certain persons in Amritsar—several of whom undoubtedly formed their revolutionary ideas during their visits to Germany and other places in Europe, or were members of the notorious defunct Shining Club—have cherished hostile intentions against the British Government, and have sedulously endeavoured to instil the poison in their minds into the hearts of others. These persons have never failed to seize every possible occasion to spread the idea, which they fostered among the public. Meetings were called on every possible opportunity, *e.g.*, on the subject of the issue of platform tickets, on the question of the preservation of the Muhammadan holy places, on the matter of the opening of grain shops, even on the petty complaints of students, etc., etc., at which, under their guidance, the discussions at once assumed a political trend. Under the pretext of holding meetings to protest against the passing of the Rowlatt Act, they succeeded in rousing popular feeling to such a high pitch, by their inflammatory and seditious speeches, that the Ram Naumi festival—on the 9th April, 1919—a purely Hindu religious festival, was converted into a political demonstration, with the result that, when Government found themselves obliged at this juncture to order the deportation of Drs. Kitchlew and Satyapal, their propaganda resulted in an open rebellion and rising against Government.

* The Court was convened on the 2nd of June, 1919. The case started on the 9th of June, 1919, and closed on the 29th of June, 1919. Judgment delivered on the 5th of July, 1919.

The serious excesses commited in Amritsar on the 10th April, 1919, are too well known to need recapitulation in detail; public buildings were sacked and burnt, railway lines and bridges destroyed and damaged, telegraph communications interrupted, and innocent Europeans brutally assaulted and murdered.

The accused named in the attached list having been found mainly responsible for all that has occurred are herewith sent up to stand their trial.

(*b*) Supplementary Precis of the Case

The facts of the case are that a criminal conspiracy was formed in Amritsar, in conjunction with conspirators elsewhere, to overawe Government and secure the abandonment of the Rowlatt Act.

The accused before the Commission were members of that conspiracy from the 30th March onwards up to the dates specified in the respective charges.

The conspiracy was formed prior to the 30th March, but inasmuch as the Commission is not competent to try offences committed before that date acts of the conspirators prior thereto will be proved simply to show the nature of the conspiracy and continuity of conduct. In pursuit of the objects of this conspiracy, a series of public meetings were held on 31st January, 5th February, 9th February, 11th February, 12th February, 21st February, 22nd February, 28th February, 23rd March, 29th March, 30th March, 6th April, 12th April and 13th April, attended and addressed by various of the conspirators in some of which sedition was uttered and the waging of war abetted.

In addition, the conspirators, or some of them, published a newspaper called the *Waqt,* which in pursuit of the objects of the conspiracy, published sedition and criminal incitements.

On 6th April, a general strike was proclaimed and subsequently also a general strike was proclaimed and maintained. On 6th and 8th April, secret societies were established, and on 9th violent and seditious demonstrations were made against Government.

Certain of the conspirators were restricted between the 2nd and 5th April and two were deported on the 10th April, and thereupon, under the instigation of accused Nos. 1 and 2, some of the conspirators and others, in pursuit of the objects of the conspiracy, broke out and waged war against the King on the 10th April; and remained in a state of war up to and including the 13th April.

Events subsequent to 13th April, are not charged against the accused.

During the period from 10th to 13th April, Europeans were murdered and assaulted by members of the conspiracy; banks were sacked and burnt; the Railway Station at Amritsar was partly sacked, and several other buildings were also sacked, much property destroyed: and the City of Amritsar was held by the conspirators in open defience of King's authority.

The principal specific facts which will be proved against each particular accused indicating his connection with and activities in the conspiracy are as follow: This list must not be taken as exclusive, as it may be deemed advisable to prove further other facts.

Saif-ud-Din Kitchlew, Accused No. 1

1. Speaker at the meeting of 31st January on "Constantinople Chala."

2. Speaker at meeting of 5th February, (Rowlatt Bill meeting)—Slightly inflamed speech.

3. Speaker at platform ticket meeting of 5th February—speech petulant in character, described by *Aror Bans* as "passionate"—passages of an exciting character.

4. Speaker at National Library meeting of 9th February: Chairman of meeting; advised boycott.

5. Speaker at platform ticket meeting on 11th February—somewhat excitable speech.

6. Speaker at Muhammadan trade meeting on 12th February; seized opportunity to incite against Government.

7. Speaker at Muhammadan meeting of 21st February, *re* Ansari's speech—virulent effort to inflame religious feeling; inciting to force veiledly.

8. Speaker at Annual Muhammadan Education Commitee on 22nd February; tried to introduce political matter into speech, but was stopped.

9. Speaker at grain-shops meeting on 26th February; tried to use it for political purposes.

10. Speaker at Rowlatt Bill protest meeting of 28th February—excitable speech.

11. Speaker at protest meeting at Lahore on 14th March—excitable speech.

12. Speaker at Rowlatt Bill protest meeting of 23rd March—highly inflammatory and dangerous.

13. Convener of, and speaker at, protest meeting of 29th March—excessively inflammatory and seditious.

14. Convener of the protest meeting of 30th March. President also—inflammatory speech; resulting in restriction order.

15. Spoke at two meetings in Jullundur on 1st and 2nd April in inflammatory manner.

16. Advocated incitement of villagers and the preparation and use of bombs.

17. Attended several secret meetings at own house between 30th March and 10th April, in which there were discussions as to creating trouble on the frontier and in villages, burning of European bungalows and murders of Europeans, boycott of courts and British trade and the spreading of false rumours.

18. One of conspirators who decided on 5th April, 1919, to have *hartal* on 6th and hold meeting of 6th.

19. Stopped cricket match on 6th as part of *hartal*.

20. Attended Home Rule *Satyagraha* meeting on 6th at own house.

21. Attended meeting of 8th April, to organize fraternization during Ram Naumi and spoke on subject; and subscribed for purpose. Made President of Satyagraha Sabha.

22. Opened house for recording vows of *Satyagraha* on 9th and arranged for printing of forms.

Joined Ram Naumi demonstrations, shouting political cries, garlanded by mob, and started procession off. Held meeting in Guru Bazar to discuss situation. Proclaimed "Shanshah Kitchlew."

23. Held violent secret meeting at own house on evening of 9th.

24. Deported on morning of 10th; gave instructions to followers to create disturbance and take revenge.

Satyapal, Accused No. 2

1. Speaker at first Rowlatt Bill meeting on 5th February, 1919; spoke in inflammatory fashion.

2. Speaker at first platform ticket meeting on 5th February, 1919, displaying bitter racial feeling.

3. Wrote on 12th February, 1919, to Mr. Bennet threatening, "you will witness in the city discontent and agitation the like of which you have never witnessed."

(*Note*:—Determined attempt to murder Mr. Bennett was made on 10th April, 1919).

4. Speaker at second platform ticket meeting on 11th February, 1919—highly inflammatory speech, full of intense racial feeling.

5. Wrote hysterical and abusive letter on 17th February, to Traffic Manager, North-Western Railway, threatening discontent, disaffection and agitation: and published this letter broadcast on 20th February.

6. Spoke at Muhammaden Education Meeting of 22nd February, somewhat bitter tone.

7. Spoke at grain shops meeting on 26th February, but not objectionably—tried to restrain Kitchlew.

8. Speaker at Rowlatt Bill protest meeting on 28th February; portions of speech inflammatory of racial feeling.

9. Speaker at Rowlatt Bill protest meeting on 23rd March—speech vitriolic and inflammatory in highest degree. Served with restriction order in consequence on 31st March.

10. Speaker at Rate-payers' meeting on the 23rd March—meeting to protest against official chairman of Municipal Committee.

11. Speaker at protest meeting of 29th March—seditious and inflammatory in the extreme. Convener of protest meeting.

12. Convener of protest meeting of 30th March.

13. Writer of seditious article in the *Partab*.

14. Attended several meetings at house of No. 1 between 30th March and 10th April in which there were discussions as to creating trouble on the Frontier and in villages, burning European bungalows and murdering Europeans, boycott of courts and British goods, and the spreading of false rumours.

15. Attended Home Rule *Satyagraha* meeting at house of No. 1.

16. Attended secret meeting on 8th April, 1919, to organize fraternization during Ram Naumi.

17. Joined Ram Naumi procession on 9th April, 1919, and distributed sweet-meats at common *chhabil* to mob. Joined meeting in Guru Bazar to discuss situation.

18. Deported on morning of 10th and gave instructions to followers to create disturbance and take revenge.

Badr-ul-Islam Khan, Accused No. 3

1. Speaker at Rowlatt Bill protest meeting of 28th February—inflammatory and inciting racial feeling.

2. Chairman at Rowlatt Bill protest meeting on 23rd March, but is not reported as speaking.

3. Chairman of gigantic meeting of 6th April—the last before the outbreak, but appears, both at beginning and end of meeting, to have advised the preservation of order.

4. Attended several meetings at house of No. 1 between 30th March, and 10th April, in which there were discussions as to creating trouble on the Frontier and in villages; burning European bungalows and murdering Europeans, boycott of courts and British trade and spreading false rumours.

5. One of the conspirators who arranged on 5th April, 1919, to hold *hartal* on 6th April, 1919, and the meeting of 6th.

6. Attended secret meeting on 8th April, 1919, to organize franternization during Ram Naumi and spoke on subject.

Hafiz Muhammad Bashir, Accused No. 4

1. Speaker at meeting of 31st January—speech not reported.

2. Speaker at meeting of 5th February—speech not reported.

3. Speaker at meeting of 12th February—speech not objectionable.

4. Speaker at meeting of 21st February—speech not objectionable.

5. Appears to have taken command when Nos. 1, 2, 5, 8, 9 restricted; convened meeting for 2nd April, recited inflammatory poem there.

6. Recited inflammatory poem in meeting of 6th April; moved harmless resolution.

7. As (14) against accused No. 2.

8. One of conspirators who arranged on 5th April, 1919, to hold *hartal* on 6th April, 1919, and meeting of 6th.

9. Attended Home Rule *Satyagraha* meeting on 7th April, 1919, at house of No. 1.

10. Attended secret meeting on 8th April, 1919, to organize fraternization during Ram Naumi; and spoke in seditious and violent

manner. Made Secretary of Satyagraha Sabha and proposed political processions, driving of internees round city to incite populace.

11. Headed a big mob on 9th April, 1919, in Guru Bazar and harangued them in violent terms.

12. Attended violent secret meeting at accused No. 1's house on 9th and spoke in an extremely violent fashion.

13. On receipt of news of deportations, swore to endure Government tyranny no longer. Proclaimed *hartal* on 10th and sent Rattan Chand to demand release of Nos. 1 and 2. Joined mob returning from Civil Lines at National Bank and incited it to take revenge. Present at sack of Bank.

14. Went to mob at Khairdin's mosque on 10th and incited it to further violence; then paraded on horseback through city with accused No. 7. Went on to own house where inflammatory speeches delivered to mob and deputed Chaudhri Bugga to form volunteer patrols for the night.

15. On 11th addressed mob at Khairdin's mosque in inflammatory fashion; advised mob to disobey Deputy Commissioner's order *re* removal of bodies and led tumultuous mob with bodies to graveyard.

16. On evening of 11th refused to stop *hartal* unless Nos. 1 and 2 were liberated and an amnesty granted with reference to affairs on 10th.

17. At meeting of conspirators on 12th where public meeting suggested and proposed collection of arms.

18. Ordered the meeting at Jalyanwala Bagh for 13th, did not attend himself. Insisted on meeting after proclamation of Martial Law.

Kotu Mal, Accused No. 5

1. Speaker at Rowlatt Bill meeting of 5th February—of a somewhat inflammatory nature.

2. Speaker at National Library meeting of 9th February, and subscribed Rs. 50 per mensem "to coach the masses in politics."

3. Speaker at grain-shops meeting of 26th February—slightly intemperate.

4. Speaker at Rowlatt Bill protest meeting of 28th February—not very objectionable.

5. Chairman for short period at Rowlatt Bill meeting of 23rd March.

6. Speaker at rate-payers' meeting of 23rd March: Chairman also—poor report.

7. Convener of protest meeting of 29th March: also spoke; but not much in his speech.

8. Convener of protest meeting of 30th March: prayed in a most inflammatory manner; resulting in restriction order.

9. As (14) against accused No. 2.

10. Attended Home Rule *Satyagraha* meeting on 7th April, 1919, at house of No. 1.

11. Attended secret meeting on 8th April, 1919, to organize fraternization during Ram Naumi.

Narain Das, Khanna, Accused No. 6

1. Present at meeting of 21st January.

2. Speaker at first meeting (Rowlatt Bill) on 5th February—speech not reported.

3. Speaker at Rowlatt Bill meeting of 26th February; advocating following the lines of Bengali agitation.

4. Convener of protest meeting of 30th March—does not appear to have spoken.

5. Convener of protest meeting of 30th March.

6. Speaker at meeting of 6th April, but speech not reported.

7. Originally proposed starting the *Waqt*.

8. As (14) against accused (2).

9. Deputed to arrange for causing trouble on Frontier—treasurer and collector of the Anna Fund of conspiracy.

10. One of conspirators who arranged on 5th April, 1919, to hold *hartal* and big meeting of 6th.

11. On 11th accompanied funeral procession from Khairdin's mosque.

Gurdial Singh, Accused No. 8

1. Speaker at protest meeting of 6th April, but speech not reported.

2. One of conspirators who arranged on 5th April to hold *hartal* and big meeting of 6th.

3. On 10th joined mob at Khairdin's mosque and said had been with mob at Railway bridge inciting them on. Paraded thereafter

with No. 4 on horesback through city. Went on to house of accused No. 4 and delivered inflammatory speech to mob outside in evening.

Anubhawa Nand, Accused No. 8

1. Speaker at protest meeting of 30th March—highly seditious and inflammatory, resulting in restriction order.

2. As (14) against accused No. 2.

3. Attended Home Rule *Satyagraha* meeting at house of No. 1 on 7th April, 1919.

4. Attended secret meeting on 8th April, 1919, to organize fraternization during Ram Naumi and spoke on subject.

5. Drafted *Satyagraha* and Home Rule League vow on 9th.

6. Joined meeting in Guru Bazar on 9th to discuss situation.

7. On 10th approved of murders, etc., and went to house of No. 4 in evening where addressed mob in inflammatory fashion.

8. At meeting of conspirators on 12th suggested public meeting. At this time collection of arms proposed.

9. Interviewed No. 4 on 13th *re* meeting.

Dina Nath, Accused No. 9

1. Editor of the *Waqt:* writer of a series of inflammatory articles therein and publisher of violent cartoons.

2. Speaker at Rowlatt Bill protest meeting on 23rd March—highly seditious speech.

3. Speaker at Rate-payers' meeting on 23rd March—poor report.

4. Speaker at protest meeting on 29th March—very seditious and inciting racial feeling.

5. Speaker at protest meeting on 30th March—highly seditious and inciting racial feeling, resulting in restriction order.

6. Spoke in inflammatory manner at two meetings in Jullundur on 1st and 2nd April.

7. As (14) against accused No. 2.

8. Stopped cricket match on 6th as part of *hartal.*

9. Attended Home Rule *Satyagraha* meeting at house of No. 1 on 7th April, 1919.

10. Attended secret meeting on 8th April, 1919 to organize fraternization during Ram Naumi and spoke on subject.

Joined Ram Naumi demonstration shouting political cries, was garlanded by throng and started procession off.

Joined No. 2 in distributing sweetmeats to mob at common *chhabil.*

Joined meeting in Guru Bazar to discuss situation.

11. Attended violent secret meeting on evening of 9th in house of accused No. 1.

12. No trace of his activities on 10th.

13. On 11th accompanied No. 4 to Khairdin's mosque and addressed mob there in inflammatory manner; and joined funeral procession; supported No. 4 in refusing to stop *hartal,* except on condition of liberation of No. 1 and 2 and amnesty for 10th.

Gurbakhsh Rai, Accused No. 10

1. Speaker at Rowlatt Bill protest meeting of 23rd March, but was inaudible.

2. Speaker at meeting on 12th April, at Hindu Sabha School; exhorted audience not to obey Government and proposed a fresh *hartal.*

3. As (14) against accused No. 2.

4. Joined mob sacking the Chartered Bank on 10th April, and went and reported to accused No. 4; went with No. 4 to incite mob at Khairdin's mosque; proceeded to house of No. 1 where violent speeches delivered to crowd.

5. At meeting of conspirators on 12th where public meeting and collection of arms proposed.

6. Attended and spoke at the meeting of 13th. Advised crowd not to disperse when ordered by military.

Ghulam Nabi, Accused No. 11

1. As (14) against accused No. 2.

2. Attended Home Rule *Satyagraha* meeting at house of No. 1 on 7th April, 1919.

3. Attended secret meeting on 8th April, 1919, to organize fraternization during Ram Naumi.

4. Organized body of boys dressed as Turkish soldiers with black crescent flag for Ram Naumi on 9th.

5. On 11th accompanied funeral procession from Khairdin's mosque.

6. At meeting of conspirators on 12th when public meeting and collection of arms were proposed—suggested collection of arms.

Ghulam Muhammad, Accused No. 12

1. Recited inflammatory poem in meeting of 30th March.

2. Recited inflammatory poem in meeting of 6th April.

3. As (14) against accused No. 2.

4. Attended Home Rule *Satyagraha* meeting at house of No. 1 on 7th April, 1919.

5. Attended secret meeting on 8th April, 1919 to organize fraternization during Ram Naumi and spoke on subject.

6. Arranged on 9th April, 1919 for printing of *Satyagraha* and Home Rule League vows. Joined Ram Naumi demonstration. Joined meeting in Guru Bazar to discuss situation.

7. Attended violent secret meeting on evening of 9th in house of accused No. 1 and recited highly inflammatory verses.

8. On 10th joined mob attacking Chartered Bank and told No. 4 he was sorry he had arrived too late at the National Bank. Went with No. 4 to incite mob at Khairdin's mosque to further violence; and returned to No. 4's house where inflammatory speeches were addressed to mob.

9. Delivered on 11th inflammatory poem to mob at Khairdin's mosque and accompanied funeral procession.

Supported No. 4 in refusing to stop *hartal* except on condition of liberation of Nos. 1 and 2 and amnesty for 10th.

10. At meeting of conspirators on 12th where public meeting and collection of arms proposed.

Abdul Aziz, Accused No. 13

1. On 11th offered to take the *Satyagraha* vow.

2. At meeting of conspirators on 12th when suggested public meeting should be held, accused proposed collection of arms.

3. On 13th took *Satyagraha* vow. Went to see accused No. 4 who directed public meeting should be held in Jalyanwala Bagh. Was present and spoke at this meeting, which was broken up by military.

Muhammad Ismail, Accused No. 14

1. Recited inflammatory poem in meeting of 6th April.

2. As (14) against accused No. 2.

3. Composed seditious verses, placarded throughout city on 9th.

Moti Ram Mehra, Accused No. 15

1. Convener of protest meeting of 29th March, but does not appear to have spoken.

2. Convener of protest meeting of 30th March.

3. As (14) against accused No. 2.

4. Deputed to arrange for causing trouble on the Frontier. Treasurer of, and collector for, Anna Fund of conspirators.

The following co-conspirators have been indicted separately for waging war and murder on 10th April.

A brief summary of their activities is attached for reference.

Rattan Chand

1. Recited poem at meeting of 30th March.

2. Speaker at meeting of 6th April.

3. One of conspirators who arranged on 5th April, to hold *hartal* and big meeting on 6th.

4. Headed the Ram Naumi demonstration on 9th and opened common *chhabil* for mob.

5. Headed mob on 10th going to Civil Lines under instructions of accused No. 4 to demand release of accused No. 1 and 2 : led mob back when fired on into city. Sack of Post Office, present and a participator in murders at Banks.

6. Accompanied funeral procession on 11th from Khairdin's mosque. Supported accused No. 4 in refusing to stop *hartal* except on condition of liberation of accused Nos. 1 and 2 and amnesty for 10th.

Chaudhri Bugga Mal

1. Financed the *Waqt*.

2. One of conspirators who arranged on 5th April, 1919, to hold *hartal* and big meeting on 6th. Arranged for drum beaters to announce *hartal*.

3. Used threats to secure *hartal* on 6th.

4. Headed Ram Naumi demonstration on 9th. Led part of mob on to Guru Bazar. Joined meeting in Guru Bazar to discuss situation.

5. Attended violent secret meeting on evening of 9th in house of accused No. 1.

6. Headed mob on 10th going to Civil Lines to demand release

of accused Nos. 1 and 2; led mob back when fired on into city. Sack of Post Office and present at Bank murders.

Reported to accused No. 4 and went with him to incite mob at Khairdin's mosque to further violence.

Returned to house of accused No. 4 and addressed mob outside in violent manner. Deputed to form volunteer patrols for city at night.

7. On 11th accompanied funeral procession from Khairdin's mosque. Supported accused No. 4 in refusing to stop *hartal* unless accused Nos. 1 and 2 were liberated and amnesty for 10th given.

A number of other conspirators have been separately indicted for various offences including murder, waging war, sedition and arson, and convicted.

The following minor conspirators to whom reference will be made in evidence have been sent for trial before summary Courts:—

1. Nur-ul-Hassan,
2. Abdul Wahid,
3. Dhaja Nand.
4. Girdhari Lal,

} Mainly engaged in reciting seditious poems in one or other of meetings.

(c) Judgment

Dr. Saif-ud-Din Kitchlew, Dr. Satyapal, Badar-ul-Islam Ali Khan, Muhammad Bashir, Kotu Mal, Narain Dass Khanna, Gurdial Singh, Anubhawa Nand, Dina Nath, Gurbakhsh Rai, Ghulam Nabi, Ghulam Muhammad, Abdul Aziz, Mohammad Ismail, and Moti Ram Mehra, fifteen persons in all, have been sent up for trial charged with offences under sections 121-A, 121, $\frac{124-A, 396, 147, 302, 326, 506, 426}{120-B}$ and 124-A, 147, $\frac{436, 302}{109}$, 506, I.P.C. in connection with the recent disturbances in Amritsar.

The allegation against these fifteen persons is that they were the leaders of the whole movement which culminated, on the 10th April, in acts of waging war.

Briefly stated the case for the prosecution is that a criminal conspiracy was formed in Amritsar, in conjunction with conspirators elsewhere, to overawe Government and secure the abandonment of the Rowlatt Acts; that this criminal conspiracy was in existence on the 30th March, 1919; and that these fifteen persons were then members of, or subsequently (up to the 13th April, 1919) joined it.

The events that occurred at Amritsar on the 10th April, last are too well known to require any detailed description. Drs Kitchlew and Satyapal, accused 1 and 2, were deported at 10 a.m. on that date—the news of their deportation was quickly taken to the city; a *hartal* was promptly organised and a mob started to go to the Deputy Commissioner's bungalow in the Civil Station to demand the release of the two deportees.

At the railway footbridge this mob was met by a small picquet of troops. The mob attacked this picquet with stones and brick-bats and had driven it back some 100 yards or so when Mr. Connor, Additional District Magistrate, arrived on the scene. He endeavoured to stop the mob but failed, and ordered the picquet to fire. This checked the mob and soon after the picquet was reinforced by Mr. Plomer, D.S.P., with a *posse* of armed Police.

A section of this mob attacked the Railway Goods-shed, murdered Guard Robinson and assaulted Mr. Bennett, Station Superintendent. Near the Rego Bridge Sergeant Rowlands, Cantonment Electrician, was brutally beaten to death and the telegraph office was attacked—other sections of the mob attempted to force their way over the Railway Road Bridge and the District Magistrate was compelled to give orders to fire on them.

In the city the National Bank was burnt and looted—Messrs. Stewart and Scott being murdered. The Alliance Bank was sacked and Mr. Thompson murdered, and attack was made on the Chartered Bank. The Religious Book Society's Book Depot, the Town Hall and the Indian Christian Church were burnt. Attacks were made on the Normal Girls' School and the Zenana Hospital, the Lady Doctor Mrs. Easdon having a narrow escape while Miss Sherwood was brutally and badly beaten.

The city itself was in the hands of the insurgents till the 13th April. That these acts constituted a deliberate and most determined waging of war cannot be disputed. Indeed the learned Counsel for the accused made no attempt at urging that war was not waged, and we have no hesitation in holding that war was waged on the 10th April.

Mr. Hassan Imam, who addressed us on behalf of all the accused with the exception of Narain Dass Khanna, accused 6, and Gurdial Singh, accused 7, filed an application objecting to the jurisdiction of the Court. He did not, however, address us at any length in support of this application and the impression we received was that he did not seriously press it. In any event we are unable to see any force in the objection. Mr. Hassan Imam next read out extracts from the speeches made by various non-official members of the Imperial Legislative Council during the debate on the Rowlatt Bill and contended that nothing in the speeches alleged to have been made by his clients approached the virulence and invective with which the non-official members of the Council had condemned the proposed measures, while His Excellency the Viceroy had neither reproved, censured nor ruled out of order any of the said members. He contended that the members of the Imperial Legislative Council were really on trial.

Whether, or not, the said non-official members of Council are in any way responsible for the action of the accused, is a matter that is not before us and with which we are in no way concerned. We think, however, that there is force in Mr. Herbert's contention that speeches made in a solemn assembly and addressed to gentlemen of high intellectual abilities, cannot be compared with or put in the same category as speeches (even if more moderate in tone) made at meetings at which the audience consisted in the main of persons of little or no education, and in which appeals were made not to the *minds* but to the *passions* of such audiences.

Beyond eulogising these speeches or of the non-official members in most eloquent terms Mr. Hassan Imam did not say very much.

He scarcely discussed the law involved in the case and only dealt briefly with the individual cases against his clients. He did, however, attack the statement of P. W. I. Hans Raj (an approver) and gave the usual warnings as to the danger of accepting the evidence of an accomplice without corroboration on material points. With regard to the statement of this witness, we say, at once, that, after giving our most careful consideration to his statement before us, and one made by him as a confession before Mr. Seymour, Magistrate 1st Class, on the 23rd and 24th April, (brought on to the record at the instance of Satyapal, accused 2) and after bearing in mind the warnings referred to above we have arrived at the conclusion that Hans Raj has endeavoured to tell his story as fully as he was capable of doing and has not deliberately made any false statement. That he has been occasionally confused is apparent but this is not surprising, considering the number of persons he had to deal with (a good many more than the accused in this case) and we have given the accused concerned the fullest benefit of any such confusion of idea, dates or names.

In the main details of his story, we regard him as worthy of credence. Not a single one of these accused has been able to show any valid reasons why Hans Raj should falsely implicate him and we have no hesitation in holding that the attempt made to prove him to be a misappropriator of money and drunkard and debauchee have signally failed. The defence obviously tried to prove too much and their witnesses on this point we regard as utterly worthless.

In addition to the oral evidence the prosecution have placed on record reports of speeches made by the various accused at various meetings held between the 31st January, 1919, and 6th April, 1919. No charge has been laid in reference to the speeches made prior to the 30th March, 1919—they have, however, been referred to as showing that the accused or some of them have been systematically doing their utmost to bring the Government, established by law in British India, into hatred and contempt and have convened meetings on any and every pretext, at which, while the object of the particular meeting was by no means objectionable, advantage has been taken to sow the seed of sedition in the minds of the people. In this judgment, it is not necessary to refer in detail to the various speeches in question. Suffice it to say that we are satisfied that the speeches were calculated to bring, and were made with the intention of bringing, the Government established by law in British India into hatred and contempt, and that there was a Criminal Conspiracy (which was in existence on the 30th March) having as its object the dissemination of sedition.

For the prosecution it is alleged that the object of this Criminal Conspiracy was to overcome the Government and bring about the abandonment of the Rowlatt Bill, and, if we were to accept the statement of the approver Hans Raj on the point, the matter would be clear enough—for he says that the "passive resistance" or *Satyagraha* movement was a mere cloak for active resistance and that violence was contemplated by the conspirators. It may be that this is true but inasmuch as this statement does not appear in the confession made by him on the 23rd and 24th April, we think it would not be safe to take it into account as against the accused persons. We, therefore, hold that the object of the Criminal Conspiracy was the dissemination of sedition.

Now the speeches at the various meetings dwelt constantly on the tyranny of Government and its harsh and repressive measures favouring the British at the expense of the Indians. Hindus and Mahomedans were called on to unite, so as to present a joint front to the Government particularly in respect of the Rowlatt Acts.

We entirely agree with Mr. Hassan Imam that Hindu and Mahomedan unity is a thing to be desired and worked for—if the object, however, is that they should unite in order to be one in their hatred and contempt for Government, *such an object* must be admitted to be reprehensible.

There can be no doubt that one of the objects for creating "contempt" for Government was to prepare the minds of the people for the reception of the *Satyagraha* movement—for "contempt" for a Government may induce people to defy its mandates and the *Satyagraha* vow clearly shows that laws passed by Government are to be disobeyed. Mr. Hassan Imam admitted that if two or more persons agreed to take this vow they became guilty of an offence under Section 120-A, I. P. C. That the result of the speeches at these various meetings was to rouse excitement in the people was admitted by Mr. Aziz Ahmad who, in the course of his able address on behalf of Gurdial Singh, accused 7, contended that the outbreak on the 10th April was due to the deportation of two of the "idols of the people" at a time when excitement was daily increasing.

We think this view is correct and that the disturbances of the 10th April, were indeed the result of this excitement which had been created and fed by certain members of the Criminal Conspiracy. Ex P. 44 a manuscript notice affixed to the Clock Tower on the 6th April, shows that some at least of the populace had been roused to such a pitch as to call on their fellow citizens "to die and kill." How far each of the accused can be held responsible for the disturbances is, however, another matter and we, therefore, proceed to take up the individual cases.

Before doing so we should state that at none of the various meetings were the Rowlatt Bill or Acts explained to the people present and on one occasion when a request was made that it should be translated, the President, a Barrister, said it was a difficult task but one which Dina Nath, accused 9, would perform—Dina Nath, accused 9, spoke after this but did not offer any explanation or translate the measures. Indeed, throughout the trial he has maintained that he knew no English!

Further, at all the meetings the people were given to understand that the Rowlatt Acts were actually in force in Amritsar and throughout India.

Coming now to the case of :—

Accused No. 1.—Dr. Saif-ud-Din Kitchlew—We find that he was undoubtedly known to Hans Raj, approver. He has been concerned in practically every meeting at Amritsar since the 31st January, 1919, and was a prominent figure at the meetings at Jullundur on the 1st and 2nd of April, 1919. His speeches were undoubtedly seditious and calculated to bring Government into hatred and contempt. Indeed two of his own witnesses characterise the speeches made by him at Jullundar as inflammatory.

We are, however, unable to see that he actually incited people to wage war. As we have said above we think it safer not to accept Hans Raj's statement that Dr. Kitchlew told him on the morning of the 10th to take revenge. Similarly we find that no mention was made by Hans Raj in his confession of the very important meeting on the 30th March, at this accused's house and we therefore feel constrained to rule out that portion of his evidence. We think it has been proved that meetings were held on the 7th and 8th April, at Dr. Kitchlew's house. There is direct corroboration of the meeting of the 8th, at the same time no agreement to wage war appears to have been arrived at these meetings. He was treated as a popular hero on the 9th at the Ram Naumi and was clearly regarded as a leader. He was present at the meeting on the night of the 9th April, at his house at which there was some discussion regarding the use of force but Hans Raj states that Dr. Kitchlew protested by reminding Bashir (4) of his vow. He undoubtedly was a prominent figure in the *Satyagraha* movement, the headquarters of which were at his house, and he also organised both the *hartals* on the 30th March, and 6th April, 1919, and was instrumental in stopping the Cricket Match on the morning of the 6th April. We find him guilty of being a member of a Criminal Conspiracy under Section 124-A, 124-A/120-B, I. P. C. His offence is an extremely serious one and we feel that the only sentence we can pass is that of transportation for life and we direct accordingly.

Accused No. 2—Dr. Satyapal—The case against Dr. Satyapal is very similar to that against Dr. Kitchlew. He started the platform ticket agitation—legitimate in itself—but used by him and his fellow conspirators to further the objects of the Conspiracy. The letters which he addressed to the Railway authorities in this connection were extremely intemperate. Until he was restricted he was a prominent figure at most of the meetings at which his speeches were as seditious as those made by Dr. Kitchlew. He was one of the conveners of the meeting of the 30th March, but did not attend it owing to his having been restricted. He continued a member of the conspiracy, being present at the meetings of the leaders on the 7th and 8th April, at Dr. Kitchlew's house. He has no enmity of any kind with Hans Raj and his assertion that Hans Raj's social position was so low that he did not associate with him is manifestly absurd. It is clear that he was regarded in the same light as Dr. Kitchlew as a popular hero and he shared the honours accorded to Dr. Kitchlew at the Ram Naumi. We find him guilty under Section 124-A/120-B I. P. C., and sentence him to transportation for life.

Accused No. 3—Badrul Islam Ali Khan—There is no doubt that this accused was present at the meeting of 28th February, 23rd March and 6th April, 1919. Hans Raj names him as one of those present on the 5th April, at the cricket match and on the 8th April, at the leaders' meeting. He was not, however, mentioned in the confession as present on the 8th April, at the leaders' meeting. His speeches at the meetings were moderate. We are inclined to think that the members of conspiracy were endeavouring to get him to join them but we are not satisfied that he did actually join. We give him the benefit of the doubt and acquit him.

Accused No. 4—Dr. Muhammad Bashir—This accused was present at several of the meetings and was clearly a member of the Criminal Conspiracy. He took a prominent part in the Ram Naumi procession and addressed Dr. Kitchlew in the Guru Bazar in inflammatory terms. He was at the meetings at Dr. Kitchlew's house on the 7th, 8th, and 9th April. On the 10th April it was from him that Hans Raj and others took their orders. He was present at the attack on the National Bank and incited the mob to take revenge for those injured by the firing. The evidence of Kesho Ram and Dholan Dass as well as that of Hans Raj leave no room for doubt that he was regarded as a leader by the people from the 10th onwards. He was prominent in insisting on the funeral procession proceeding to the Jalyanwala Bagh on the 11th, and when Kesho Ram and others summoned him he refused to go and insisted on their coming to his house where Ratto and Bugga also attended. He also organised the meeting on the 13th April, though he did not attend. We regard his defence as worthless and have no doubt that he was a member of the Criminal Conspiracy and that he also waged war and we find him guilty under Section 124-A, and 121 I. P. C. We can see no justification for passing any sentence other than the extreme one and sentence him to death. Such property as belongs to him and is liable to forfeiture will be forfeited to the Crown.

*Accused No. 5—Kotu Mal—*He was present at most of the meetings, including that at Dr. Kitchlew's house on the 8th April. His speech at the meeting of the 5th February clearly indicated his seditious views, and his subsequent activities satisfy us in that he was acting in concert with Drs. Kitchlew and Satyapal. His defence evidence does not help him and we find him guilty under Section 124-A/120-B, Indian Penal Code. We think he played a minor part and that a severe sentence is not called for. We, accordingly, sentence him to 3 years' rigorous imprisonment including three months' solitary confinement.

*Accused No. 6—Narain Dass Khanna—*This accused was present at most of the meetings and was a convener of some. He interested himself in trying to get the *Waqt* printed, showing his connection with Dina Nath, accused 9. According to the approver he took an active part in proclaiming the *hartal* of the 6th April, on the evening of the 5th. Mr. Puri laid great stress on the defence produced as to Narain Dass being at a Lodge meeting from 6.15 p.m. to 10 p.m. on the 5th. We see no reason to doubt the correctness in the main of this defence evidence, but do not regard it as seriously affecting the statement of Hans Raj, for in his confession Hans Raj does not say that Narain Dass actually took part in the proclamation work and we think he is making a mistake in the statement before us. We may say that we do not believe he went to the Lodge meeting at 5.30 p.m. He is alleged to have been deputed to spread sedition on the Frontier at a meeting on the 30th March. We have, however, already given our reasons for ruling out this portion of the approver's statement. He was present at the meeting of the 6th April. We believe he was a member of the Criminal Conspiracy, but we are not satisfied that he took any part in the events subsequent to the 9th April, and convict him under Section 124-A/120-B, Indian Penal Code, sentencing him, as in the case of Kotu Mal (5), to 3 years' rigorous imprisonment, including 3 months' solitary confinement.

Accused No. 7—Gurdial Singh—This accused was present at the meeting of the 6th April, but we are not satisfied that he joined the conspiracy. His actions on the 10th April, as deposed to by the Deputy Commissioner, indicate that he was supporting the authorities to the best of his power and at some risk to himself. Hans Raj does not attribute any acts to him, merely saying that Gurdial Singh had told Bashir (4) that he had done what he could on the 10th. Mr. Herbert did not press the case against him and we acquit him.

Accused No. 8—Anu Bhawa Anand—This accused appears to have come to Amritsar towards the end of March and was at the meeting of the 30th March at which he delivered an inflammatory and seditious speech, which resulted in his being restricted. He was present at the meetings of the 7th and 8th April at Dr. Kitchlew's house and was with Dr. Kitchlew in the Guru Bazar on the 9th April. His connection with the Conspiracy is we consider perfectly clear. According to the statement of the approver this accused was consulted by him and others and expressed his approval of the murders of Europeans committed on the 10th. He also suggested a meeting on the 12th April, as a means of keeping up the excitement and translated certain resolutions it was proposed to put before this meeting. On the 13th April, he is said to have provided a "Vow" form signed by Abdul Aziz. We see no reason for disbelieving Hans Raj whose statements with regard to this accused have been consistent throughout. No sort of enmity has been alleged, and his defence evidence is of no value. We find him guilty under section 124-A/120-B and 121 I.P.C., and sentence him to transportation for life, directing that such property as belongs to him and is liable to forfeiture be forfeited to the Crown.

Accused No. 9—Dina Nath—In addition to the evidence of the approver there is abundant evidence to show that the accused was a member of the Criminal Conspiracy. He was undoubtedly very closely connected with the publication of the "*Waqt*", a vernacular newspaper, which we consider was the organ of the conspiracy. He was present at most of the meetings and his speeches were invariably seditious. While his cartoons and letter press in the "Waqt" were clearly intended to create hatred and contempt for Government. He was present at the meetings on the 7th and 8th April, and was with Dr. Kitchlew on the 9th April. On the 11th he is said to have delivered an inflammatory speech at Khair Din's Mosque. He was at Bashir (4)'s house when Kesho Ram and Dholan Dass went there, and was one of those who did not support the proposal made by Kesho Ram and others to end the *hartal*. His defence evidence does not help him. Indeed one of his witnesses says that Dina Nath's character is not above suspicion. Having regard to his activities in connection with the object of the Conspirary and after the 10th April, we think that he is guilty of an offence under section 121, I.P.C., as well as under section 124-A/124-B I.P.C., and we sentence him to transportation for life and direct that such property as belongs to him and is liable to forfeiture be forfeited to the Crown.

Accused No. 10—Dr. Gurbakhsh Rai—This accused was present at the meeting of the 23rd March, but was not present at any of the other meetings. On the 10th April, he was seen by the approver near the Chartered Bank and went with him to the house of Bashir (4). He admits having drafted resolutions Ex. P. 8 for the meeting on the 12th at which he also spoke using violent language. He also was present and spoke at the meeting of the 13th which was dispersed by the Military. A number of "Vow" forms were found on the search of his house. His close connection with Hans Raj is shown by the recovery of Ex. P. 8 (Resolutions) from Hans Raj, and the approver is also corroborated as to this accused's presence at the meeting of the 13th. His defence is worthless.

We find him guilty under sections 124-A/120-B, and 121, I.P.C., and sentence him to transportation for life directing that such property as belongs to him and is liable to forfeiture be forfeited to the Crown.

Accused No. 11—Ghulam Nabi—The statement of Hans Raj made before us is not quite consistent with the confession so far as this accused is concerned. Though not impressed by his defence evidence, we have doubts as to his complicity in the conspiracy and the events that followed. Giving him the benefit of these doubts, we acquit him.

Accused No. 12—Ghulam Muhammad—In addition to the approver's evidence, there is ample material to show that this accused was a member of the Criminal Conspiracy. He was at the meetings of the 30th March, and 6th April, and at Dr. Kitchlew's house on 8th April. He was with Hans Raj on the 9th as well as at the Guru Bazar with Dr. Kitchlew. He was also at Dr. Kitchlew's house on the evening of the 9th. On the 10th April, he met Hans Raj near the house of Chartered Bank and accompanied him and

Gurbakhsh Rai to the Bashir (4). He made an inflammatory speech at Khair Din's Mosque on the 11th and took part in arranging the meeting of the 12th. His defence evidence is worthless. We find him guilty under section 124-A/120-B and section 121 I.P.C., and sentence him to transportation for life and direct that such property as belongs to him and is liable to forfeiture be forfeited to the Crown.

Accused No. 13—Abdul Aziz—This accused first appears on the scene on the 11th April, when he is said to have met Hans Raj and expressed a desire to take the "Vow." He also took part on the 12th in arranging for the meeting of that day—and took the "Vow" at the house of Anu Bhawa Anand (8). He was present at the meeting of the 13th as to which Hans Raj is corroborated by the boy Brij Lal (P.W. 52) whose evidence we regard as reliable. He spoke at this meeting in support of Resolution 2 of Ex. P. 8. As we are bound to take judicial notice of the fact that a state of rebellion existed at Amritsar at the time, as declared by the Governor-General, we find him technically guilty of an offence under section 121, I.P.C., and are forced to sentence him to transportation for life with forfeiture of such property belonging to him as is liable to forfeiture. We, however, recommend him most strongly to the clemency of Government as we are of opinion that a very light sentence would suffice.

Accused No. 14—Muhammad Ismail—This accused recited a poem at the meeting of April the 6th, which we, however, do not regard as of any serious import. He is alleged to have been present at the meetings of the 7th and 8th April, but we are not satisfied as to his having been there, inasmuch as he was not mentioned in Hans Raj's confession. We acquit him.

Accused No. 15—Moti Ram, Mehra—This accused is alleged to have convened the meetings of the 29th and 30th March. He also is said to have been present at the meetings of the leaders at Dr. Kitchlew's house on the evening of the 30th March, when he was deputed to go to the Frontier. As to this, however, we have already ruled out the approver's statement, and we think that there may be some doubt as to the identity of this accused.

We, accordingly, acquit him.

68—LAHORE LEADERS' CASE*

(Mr. Justice Leslie-Jones' Commission)

(*a*) First Precis of Lahore Case

The accused before the Commission are eleven in number, namely:—

1. Lala Harkishen Lal.
2. Pandit Rambhaj Datt.
3. Lala Duni Chand.
4. Lala Dharam Das Suri.
5. Doctor Gokal Chand Naurang.
6. Lala Mathra Pershad.
7. M. Habibullah Khan.
8. Karam Chand Hateshi.
9. S. Mohsin Shah.
10. M. Allah Din.
11. Mota Singh.

A measure for dealing with the apprehension and trial of persons accused of anarchical and revolutionary crime, when a state of such crime was considered to exist, based on the recommendations of the Rowlatt Commission, was under the consideration of the Government of India.

This measure was introduced into the Imperial Council on the 6th February, 1919.

In order, by the show of agitation against the measure, to induce the Government of India to withdraw it, certain of the accused conspired with others to hold a protest meeting in Lahore on February 4th.

This meeting was convened by the accused, Rambhaj Datt and Duni Chand, was attended by the accused Dharam Das Suri, Rambhaj Datt, Duni Chand, Gokal Chand, Habibullah and S. Mohsin Shah and was addressed among others by the accused Rambhaj Datt, Dharm Das Suri, Gokal Chand, Habibullah and S. Mohsin Shah. In the course of their speeches, in order to excite hostility against the measure and against Government, the accused uttered sedition and spread false reports as to the nature and objects of the said measure.

While the said measure was under the consideration of the Imperial Council and in order to increase the hostility against Government, certain of the accused with others conspired to hold another meeting on the 9th March in Lahore.

* The Court was convened on the 14th of May, 1919. The case started on the 17th of May, 1919, and closed on the 24th of June, 1919. Judgment delivered on the 5th of July, 1919.

This meeting was convened by accused Duni Chand, attended by accused Rambhaj Datt, Duni Chand, Dharm Das Suri, Gokal Chand and Habibullah Khan, and seditious addresses and false reports as to the nature and object of the said measure were given and circulated by the accused Rambhaj Datt, Gokal Chand and Habibullah Khan.

The measure, commonly known as the Rowlatt Bill, was passed by the Imperial Council on 18th March, 1919.

Thereupon a general conspiracy was formed by persons outside the Punjab with whom the accused associated to hold tumultuous meetings and to ordain a general strike with the intention and object of inflaming popular feeling against Government, and to so overawe it as to try and induce the vetoing of the measure.

Accordingly, throughout India and in the Punjab in particular the said conspirators including the accused declared a general strike, commonly known as a *hartal,* to take place on the 30th March, intending thereby to induce disorder, paralyse the economic life of the country and excite disaffection and hatred towards Government.

To give effect to this general strike, efforts were made by threats and persuasions and deliberate misrepresentations of the scope and objects of the measure to induce shopkeepers to close their shops and workmen, servants and others to cease work, and further mass meetings were to be held to excite disaffection and hatred against Government.

The methods of this general strike were euphemistically called "Passive Resistance."

In accordance with the plans of this general conspiracy a mass meeting was convened for the 30th March in Lahore by the accused, Duni Chand, Rambhaj Datt, Gokal Chand Naurang and Habibullah Khan and a general strike ordained.

In obedience to instructions from conspirators outside the Punjab, this mass meeting and general strike was postponed until the 6th April.

A fresh mass meeting for the same object and with the same intention was convened by the accused, Harkishen Lal, Rambhaj Datt, Duni Chand, Dharam Das Suri, Gokal Chand, among others for the 6th April, in the Bradlaugh Hall. The said mass meeting was attended by Rambhaj Datt, Dharam Das Suri, Gokal Chand, Mathra Pershad, Habibullah Khan and Karam Chand Hiteshi, and addresses of an inflammatory and seditious nature further misrepresenting the scope and objects of the Rowlatt Act were delivered by the accused Rambhaj Datt, Dharm Das Suri, Gokal Chand, Mathra Pershad, Habibulla Khan and Karam Chand Hiteshi, with the intention of exciting disaffection and hostility against the Government and with the knowledge that such incitement would lead to disorder, rioting, and the waging of war against the King.

Prohibitions against the holding of processions with a view to preserve the peace were issued by the Superintendent of Police, Lahore. In spite of these prohibitions, mobs of an unruly, tempestuous and riotous nature with inflammatory flags and other symbols marched to the Bradlaugh Hall with the active connivance and encouragement of certain of the accused.

Inside and outside the Bradlaugh Hall seditious and inflammatory cries were uttered. British Officers in uniform and other Europeans were openly insulted by members of the riotous assembly and the mob was complimented on its "orderly?" behaviour by the accused Habibullah Khan.

As a result of the incitements conveyed in the speeches of the accused above mentioned and others, members of the said assembly on dispersal paraded through a part of Lahore in a riotous, tumultuous and seditious manner.

On the 9th April, in pursuance of the conspiracy to excite disaffection and feelings of enmity against Government and on the occasion of the Ram Naumi procession the accused Rambhaj Datt, Gokal Chand, Dharam Das Suri, and Duni Chand and others encouraged the fraternization of Hindus and Mohammadans against the Government as by law established.

On the 10th April, the Government of the Punjab, with a view to maintaining peace and order, prevented the ingress of one of the conspirators by name Gandhi into the province and on the same date ordered the deportation of two other conspirators from Amritsar by name Kitchlew and Satyapal. These precautionary measures of Government for the preservation of peace and order were seized upon by the conspirators as a signal to wage war against the King.

In Amritsar, Europeans were brutally murdered, their property burnt and otherwise looted and destroyed. In Lahore, on the receipt of the news and in conjunction with the rising in Amritsar and elsewhere large mobs incited by the previous seditious and inflammatory utterances and acts of the accused and others rose in rebellion against the King. Acts of war were committed on the Upper Mall, in Landa Bazar, at Mochi Gate and at the Lahori Gate and the mobs waging war were dispersed by firing. On the 10th during the riots on the Mall the accused Duni Chand demanded the liberation of one prisoner arrested.

Among the persons conspicuous at the Lohari Gate were the accused Rambhaj Datt and Duni Chand, and at Mochi Gate accused S. Mohsin Shah.

On the 11th April, in pursuance of the object of the conspiracy a general strike or *hartal* was again proclaimed, which continued for some days. On the same day rioters and seditious mobs paraded the city of Lahore in a posture of war and inflammatory notices were posted throughout the city.

A tumultous, riotous and seditious mob assembled at the Badshahi mosque. The said mob included the accused Rambhaj Datt, Duni Chand, Harkishen Lal, Dharam Das Suri, Gokal Chand Naurang, S. Mohsin Shah, M. Allah Din and Mota Singh, and was addressed in a seditious and inflammatory manner by the accused M. Allah Din, Mota Singh and Rambhaj Datt. On the proposal of Duni Chand and Rambhaj Datt the said mob elected a Committee of a revolutionary character to conduct a general strike, control the revolutionary movement, and to advise those in rebellion and hostility to the King as to the line of action which should be adopted.

The said revolutionary Committee included the following accused:—Harkishen Lal, Duni Chand, Dharam Das Suri, Gokal Chand Naurang, Habibullah Khan, S. Mohsin Shah, M. Allah Din and Mota Singh; and a subscription of Rs. 1000 was made by Harkishen Lal for the purpose of a general strike and *Langars* were opened for the free rationing of the revolutionary mobs. The said Committee further attempted to dictate terms to Government as a condition upon which they would declare a cessation of the general strike and rebellion, and particularly Rambhaj Datt and Duni Chand attempted to make terms.

At the end of this gathering crowds walked the city shouting seditious words, destroying portraits of the King and Queen and announcing that the King was dead.

On the 12th April rioters' mob assembled near the Fort.

A meeting of rioters at the instance of the accused Rambhaj Datt and Duni Chand assembled in the Badshahi mosque. This riotous and seditious meeting assaulted Inspector Chaudhri Ali Gauhar. It was addressed in a seditious and inflammatory manner by Rambhaj Datt and Duni Chand, and a new Committee was formed including the accused Harkishen Lal, Rambhaj Datt, Duni Chand, Dharam Das Suri, Gokal Chand, Habibullah Khan, Mohsin Shah for the same purpose as the committee of the 11th.

On the same day Gokal Chand, Rambhaj Datt and Duni Chand dictated terms to Government for the stoppage of the general strike and rebellion and insulted loyal citizens.

The riotous and seditious mob, on leaving the Badshahi mosque, attacked forces of His Majesty at Hira Mandi and were dispersed.

Order was partially restored by the Military occupation of the city on the 12th and 13th April.

(*b*) Second Precis of Lahore Case

In continuation of my note of 5th instant in connection with the request of the accused in the Lahore Conspiracy Case to have the charges against them made more explicit, as they profess some inability to understand the charges as framed, I have the honour to forward herewith the following statement of the principal particular acts committed by each accused, indicating his connection with the conspiracy of which he was a member between the 30th March and 13th April, and indicating in what way he furthered the objects of the conspiracy, the objects of that conspiracy being:—

(a) to obtain the repeal of the Rowlatt Act by illegal and criminal means;

(b) to wage war against the King;

(c) to commit other criminal offences as indicated in the charges against the accused.

In re Harkishen Lal:—

(1) Convener of meeting on the 6th April in Bradlaugh Hall;

(2) Present in tumultuous meeting in Badshahi Mosque on 11th April;

In *re* Appointed a member of the Popular Revolutionary Committee.

Subscribed Rs. 1,000 to the funds for the maintenance of a General Strike.

(3) Appointed member of new Revolutionary Committee at Badshahi Mosque on 12th April.

(4) Present in tumultuous and inflammatory gathering in Town Hall on 13th April.

In re Rambhaj Datt (accused No. 2):—

(1) Advertised as speaker for meeting of 4th February.

(2) Speaker at such meeting in inflammatory fashion.

(2) Speaker at meeting of 9th March, advocating passive resistance in inflammatory manner.

(4) Convener of meeting for 30th March.

(5) Convener of meeting for 6th April; chairman of such meeting and addressed it in inflammatory manner.

(6) Took part in the Ram Naumi procession on the 9th April, for political purposes.

(7) Was member of a tumultuous mob waging war against the King at Lahori Gate on 10th April.

(8) Addressed tumultuous mob in dangerously inflammatory fashion at Badshahi Mosque on the 11th April. Dictated terms to Government on which order would be restored.

Asked mob to reassemble on 12th.

(9) Addressed mob in inflammatory fashion on 12th April, in Badshahi Mosque. Appointed member of the new Revolutionary Committee on 12th and dictated the terms of the revolutionists on which order would be restored.

(10) Took active part in tumultuous and inflammatory gathering in Town Hall on 13th April.

In re Duni Chand (accused No. 3):—

(1) Convener of meeting of 4th February.

(2) Speaker at such meeting, but nothing to show he spoke objectionably.

(3) Convener of meeting of 9th March and present.

(4) Convener of meeting of 30th March.

(5) Convener of meeting of 6th April; insulted police officers present.

(6) Induced several persons to join in a general strike on 6th April.

(7) Took part in Ram Naumi procession on 9th April for seditious propaganda.

(8) Was member of tumultuous mob waging war against the King at Lahori Gate on 10th April.

(9) Participated in tumultuous gathering in Badshahi Mosque on 11th April, and was appointed member of the Revolutionary Committee. Was one of the persons who dictated terms to Government.

(10) Convened tumultuous meeting at Badshahi Mosque on 12th, addressed it, made member of new Revolutionary Committee and again dictated terms to Government.

(11) Took active part in tumultuous and inflammatory gathering in Town Hall on 13th April.

In re Dharam Das Suri (accused No. 4):—

(1) Advertised as speaker for meeting of 4th February, and addressed same in a somewhat inflammatory manner.

(2) Present at meeting of 9th March.

(3) Convened meeting for 6th April; speaker and mover of a most inflammatory resolution. Insulting to Police Officers present.

(4) Present in tumultuous gathering in Badshahi Mosque on 11th April, and was appointed member of the Revolutionary Committee.

(5) Appointed member of new Revolutionary Committee on 12th April.

(6) Took active part in tumultuous and inflammatory gathering in Town Hall on 12th April.

In re Gokal Chand Naurang (accused No. 5):—

(1) Advertised speaker of meeting of 4th February; Speaker, and in parts of speech gave vent to intemperate and inflammatory utterances.

(2) Speaker in meeting of 9th March; not particularly objectionable in speech, but moved resolution inclined to incite.

(3) Convened meeting for 30th March.

(4) Convened meeting for 6th April, and spoke in inflammatory manner. Appeared to play a double part with crowd of which he was a leader and over which he had a great influence.

(5) Made member of Revolutionary Committee at Badshahi Mosque on 11th April.

(6) Made member of Revolutionary Committee at Badshahi Mosque on 12th April.

(7) Representative of revolutionists on 12th April and dictated terms of peace to authorities.

(8) Took active part in tumultuous and inflammatory gathering in Town Hall on 13th April.

In re Mathra Parshad (accused No. 6):—

(1) Attended meeting of 6th April and recited an exceptionally inflammatory poem.

In re Habibullah Khan (accused No. 7):—

(1) Advertised as speaker for 4th February, moved resolution.

(2) Present at meeting of 9th March; spoke shortly, but in very violent fashion.

(3) Convened meeting for 30th March.

(4) Present at meeting of 6th April, and openly encouraged defiance of law by congratulating mob on its procession conducted in defiance of prohibition.

(5) Made member of Revolutionary Committee on 11th April.

(6) Made member of Revolutionary Committee on 12th April.

In re Karam Chand Hateshi (accused No. 8):—

(1) Attended meeting of 6th April and gave utterance to a very inflammatory poem.

(2) Urged servants, etc., to strike against working for Europeans.

In re S. Mohsin Shah (accused No. 9):—

(1) Advertised speaker for 4th February and attended meeting.

(2) Attended meeting of 6th April; addressed overflow audience in inflammatory manner.

(3) Was member of riotous mob at Mochi Gate on 10th April.

(4) Attended Badshahi Mosque meeting on 11th April supporting accused No. 2 and made member of Revolutionary Committee.

(5) Made member of Revolutionary Committee on 12th April.

In re Maulvi Allah Din (accused No. 10):—

(1) Attended Badshahi Mosque meeting on 11th and addressed crowd in inflammatory fashion.

(2) Took active part in tumultuous gathering of 13th April in Town Hall.

In re Mota Singh (accused No. 11):—

(1) Delivered inflammatory speech in Badshahi Mosque on 11th April, and made member of Revolutionary Committee.

T.P. ELLIS

The 7th June 1919.

In reply to the reverse, the precis of the case gives in detail the particular acts against the accused, and it is difficult to understand what further details are required by the accused.

It may be explained to the accused that they are charged with Criminal Conspiracy.

Such a conspiracy existed before the 30th March, but inasmuch as the commissions are not empowered to try offences committed prior to 30th March, acts committed by them in the course of such conspiracy are not *charged* against them. They are charged only with the acts they each committed during the period between the 30th March and 13th April, and acts prior to or subsequent to that period are being proved merely to establish the continuity of their conduct.

The primary object of this conspiracy was to secure the repeal of the Rowlatt Act by illegal means, which is an offence under Section 120-A (2); the accused before the commission are, however, alleged to have proceeded further than this, and to have conspired either among themselves or with others within the conspiracy to:—

(a) procure the repeal of the Rowlatt Act by *criminal* means.

(b) commit a series of Criminal Acts, such as sedition, etc.

(c) to Wage War against the King.

These said conspiracies are punishable under Sections 120-B and 121-A, Indian Penal Code.

In addition thereto, the accused are alleged to have committed or abetted certain Criminal Acts, and to have taken certain action in pursuit of the objects of such conspiracies.

The charges have been so framed as to indicate the dates on which each accused committed such criminal acts or took such action in pursuit of the conspiracy during the period between the 30th March and 13th April.

Being members of a conspiracy, each accused is responsible for the acts of every other conspirator, whether before the Commission or not, committed in pursuit of the common object of the conspiracy, whether they were committed prior to or subsequent to the date on which such accused joined the conspiracy or did any act in pursuance of the common objects of the conspiracy.

In order to enable the accused to understand the individual case against each, a statement of the criminal acts and other actions against each will be forwarded at the earliest opportunity.

It must be distinctly understood, however, that the charge against each accused is not limited to the particular acts committed by himself, but extends to all acts committed by other conspirators in the pursuit of the common object; and that even if it be found that the particular acts of an accused are not in themselves criminal, he is responsible for the criminal acts of others in the conspiracy and committed in pursuit of the object of each conspiracy.

T.P. ELLIS

The 5th June, 1919.

(c) Judgment

Hitherto in dealing with cases under the Ordinances of 1919, we have confined ourselves to brief recitals of the facts as found. We think, however, that although not bound by law to write any judgment it is only right that we should deal at some length with the present case, and this because the trial and arguments have lasted well over a month, some 700 witnesses have been examined, and many questions of law and fact are involved of which the bare decision, if unsupported by some detailed explanation, might hardly be considered sufficient. Our views on certain questions of jurisdiction which have been raised will be found on the record.

In Lahore the public agitation against the Rowlatt Bills began with a protest meeting held at the Bradlaugh Hall on the 4th of February 1919. This was organised by the Indian Association and convened by Duni Chand, the Secretary. Speeches were made by Mr. Manohar Lal, Rambhaj Dutt, Gokal Chand, Dharm Das and others.

The second Bill was referred to Select Committee on the 10th of February, and on the 1st of March Mr. Gandhi published his manifesto including his *Satyagraha* vow. A second protest meeting was then held at the Bradlaugh Hall on the 9th of March. Dr. Kitchlew of Amritsar, Rambaj Dutt, Gokal Chand, Mr. Saunders and Habibullah addressed the meeting. The second Bill was passed on the 18th of March and on the 26th Mr. Gandhi's message of the 23rd was published in Lahore. This was the message which advocated fasting and suspension of business on the 30th. A third protest meeting was accordingly fixed for that day, but was not held as the date of the demonstration was postponed by Mr. Gandhi to the 6th of April. A *hartal,* however, was observed in Delhi on the 30th and in the riot which ensued the mob had to be fired upon and some lives were lost. On the 6th of April there was a complete *hartal* in Lahore, extending even to Muzang and Baghbanpura. As a natural consequence and, in spite of the fact that processions had been forbidden, a crowd collected and threatened to become unmanageable. The authorities had the situation in hand and nothing serious happened. The advertised meeting was held in the Bradlaugh Hall that afternoon and was addressed by several speakers including Rambhaj Dutt and Gokal Chand. Great pains had been taken to popularise this meeting, the names of 30 conveners had been advertised, and the number of those attending was so great that an overflow meeting had to be held outside.

Business was resumed as usual on the 7th. On the 9th of April the annaul Ram Naumi procession was held, at which speeches were made advocating Hindu and Muhammadan unity. On the afternoon of the 10th, news arrived of the Amritsar disturbances and the murder of Europeans, and also of Mr. Gandhi's arrest. A fresh *hartal* was started at once. On the evening of the 10th, a large mob advanced down the Mall and had to be dispersed by firing both on the Mall and at the Lahori Gate. On the morning of the 11th, a mass meeting of Hindus and Musalmans was held in the Badshahi Mosque, and when this broke up in the evening, it degenerated into a disorderly and mischievous rabble and marched through the streets shouting among other cries that the King was dead and destroying pictures of Their Majesties. On the 12th, the crowd once more assembled in the Badshahi Mosque and began the proceedings by driving out and beating an Inspector of the C.I.D., who was fortunate to escape with his life. After listening to some speeches and electing a committee, they marched through the city and came into conflict with the authorities at the Hira Mandi and had to be dispersed by firing.

The remaining incidents relate to various meetings and committees concerning the *hartal,* which continued in Anarkali until the 17th and in the city until the 18th when it was finally ended by orders passed under Martial Law.

Such are the main facts and the prosecution sets out to combine and connect these facts with the accused in such a way as to show that there was a conspiracy to secure the repeal of the Rowlatt Act by criminal means. The defence has asked us to believe that there was no sort of organization of the *hartal,* and that every individual shop-keeper in Lahore, Muzang and Baghbanpura decided of his own accord that he must close his shop as a protest. As disproving this contention, Exhibit p. 28 removed from the Gumti Bazar on the 3rd of April, is produced to show that pressure was being brought to bear in the city. It runs as follows:—

"Consider a while"

"If the mountain of calamity be about to fall on your motherland, and you do not render a bit of assistance to your country—who would be such a wretch as would not join in the mournful state of his country by closing his shop and observing a fast this (next) Sunday.

"May God cast them into Hell who do not close their business this (next) Sunday, and do not keep a fast."

Similar and much more violent posters are produced which were found in various parts of the city between the 3rd and 5th, four having been so found on the 6th and one of these at the Bradlaugh Hall. This is Exhibit P. 18.

"1. That which we apprehended has happened. The future of India in falling has assumed the form of the Rowlatt Bill.

"2. There is confusion in every town, province and throughout the Empire. Is this the law or the tremor of an earthquake?

"3. To practise tyranny and to give it the name of love, what a fine trick is this of the civilization of the West!

"4. This pitcher of the East was full of the honey of loyalty, and now its sweetness has become bitter to the British.

"5. Muhammadans and Hindus raised a thousand cries and lamentations, but could not cure Government of its obduracy.

"6. Their arguments had no effect on Vincent though Jinnah much beat his face and Sapru struck his head a great deal.

"7. In vain have we rubbed our foreheads for years in the Council Chamber. Now we are going to search for Gandhi's threshold."

Considerable reliance is placed on the fact that 16,000 copies of Gandhi's message were ordered by the Indian Association, to which several of the accused belong, and of which Duni Chand is the Secretary, and also on the fact that, as explained by Jaigopal Tandan, D. W. 22, copies of this message were "published broadcast" in the city. These, it is urged, must have been the copies ordered by the Association. It is contended that the *hartal* was far from being spontaneous, and that this is shown not only by the evidence of witnesses for the prosecution but also by the naive admissions of some of the witnesses for the defence such as that of D. W. 52.—"I have no notion who Gandhi is. He has cost me my livelihood." The *hartal* having thus been brought about and a large crowd having collected in the Bradlaugh Hall, speeches were made which, it is urged, were calculated to inflame the gathering, whose temper is shown by the hissing of C.I.D. officers, the perpetual shouting of "Gandhi ki Jai," "Shahidan-i-Delhi ki Jai," Tilak ki Jai," and "*Hartal* karne walon ki Jai." A resolution was proposed expressing sympathy "with the innocent persons shot without justification" at Delhi. Rambhaj Dutt, the President, who presumably voiced the views of those, who had organised, and of those, who attended the meeting, preached the observance of the *hartal* and explained that it was a deliberate threat to Government, or to use his own words that it meant "Saying to our rulers, Remove our sufferings or we close our shops, suspend our business and we ourselves starve." The meeting broke up before sunset and is said to have proceeded to the city crying "Hai Hai Rowlatt Bill" and "Hai Hai George mar giya." On the way it burnt explanatory copies of the Rowlatt Act, which had been distributed by the Publicity Committee.

While the temper of the people was still in a dangerous condition, the annual Ram Naumi procession was held and largely attended by Muhammadans. Speeches were made in which stress was laid on Hindu-Muhammadan unity. On this occasion this laudable object can, it is urged, have only been preached as meaning unity against the Government. Several of the accused joined in the procession and three made speeches.

On the following day, the news of the Amritsar outrages and of the arrest of Mr. Gandhi arrived. Shops were shut and crowds insisted on their being shut and this, it is said, was the natural development of the foregoing agitation in support of Mr. Gandhi's crusade. In the same way the rabble, which advanced down the Mall and had to be twice fired upon, was the natural result of the campaign organised and started by these men.

On the following day, an enormous crowd of Hindus and Muhammadans collected in the Shahi Mosque inside the gate of which a banner was hung bearing the inscription "The King who practises tyranny cuts his own roots underneath". This meeting of 25,000 people had been organised, it is said, by the conspirators as is shown by the speech of Rambhaj Dutt telling the crowd at the Lahori Gate on the 10th to disperse but to come to the mosque on the following day. Whether these men were asked to go by the Deputy Commissioner to put an end to the mass meeting or not, it is urged that they most certainly did not attempt to do so but deliberately promoted and continued the *hartal* and collected money for *langar khanas* (free kitchens) to ensure that continuance. The crowd was addressed from the pulpit by Rambhaj Dutt and others and was told to stand and face death if necessary and to come to the mosque on the following day. After the speech of Rambhaj Dutt a railway khalasi, named Balwant Singh, was carried into the mosque shouting that there had been a mutiny in cantonments, and that he had killed a number of British soldiers with his own hand. He was followed by Harkishen Lal, Duni Chand and Dharam Das, who were carried to the pulpit on the shoulders of the people. More speeches were made and a committee of management for the *hartal* was elected. As the result of this orgy of mob oratory, the rabble left the mosque headed by hooligans carrying sticks and marched through the city shouting seditious cries and destroying pictures of Their Majesties. On the following day the mob reassembled, as arranged by Duni Chand, and the proccedings were even more lawless than before. An Inspector of the C.I.D. was beaten and driven out and when Duni Chand and his party arrived speeches were again made from the pulpit by non-Muslims and a fresh committee was elected to deal with the question of the *hartal*.

The view taken of these meetings by orthodox Muhammadans is well expressed by the Hon'ble Khan Bahadur Fazal Hussain, no less a person than the Secretary of the Muslim League, who describes them as "sacrilege." Nawab Sir Zulfikar Ali Khan also states that this is the first mass meeting which has ever been held to his knowledge in the Shahi mosque. The position, therefore, it is urged, became more clearly defined than ever. The accused who had stage managed and directed the demonstration had openly shown their hand. They had been acclaimed by the populace as leaders, they had invited the citizens of Lahore to repeat the outrage of the 11th by desecrating once more the Shahi mosque on the 12th and this invitation had been accepted. The natural consequence, therefore, was that Mr. Shafi and other gentlemen on being called upon to assist the Government on the 12th turned to these leaders and craved their help and co-operation. As leaders they then laid down the terms on which they were prepared to put an end to the *hartal* and these conditions, after some modification, were taken by Mr. Shafi and others to the Chief Secretary. It was understood that the result of Mr. Shafi's interview would be conveyed to them at Duni Chand's house. This was done, and on this occasion Harkishen Lal is said to have abused Nawab Fateh Ali Khan for warning the public in a letter to the press of the dangers of *hartal* and passive resistance.

In the meantime the mob had left the Shahi mosque in the same state of tumultuous disorder as on the previous day, and on reaching the Hira Mandi came into conflict with the authorities and had to be fired upon before it would disperse.

The following day, the 13th, the principal accused attended by invitation a meeting with the Deputy Commissioner at the Town Hall, and there one Allah Din, a stranger from Hoshiarpur, was put forward by Duni Chand to inflame the feelings of those present by giving a lurid account of what he said was happening in the city. When the Deputy Commissioner arrived he was openly accused of "*Be-imani*" (breach of faith) in sending troops into the city.

Conditions were again laid down, the attitude of the conspirators being that of people who could close the *hartal* if they chose, and the meeting broke up without anything having been achieved. Subsequently the Deputy Commissioner explained to them that Martial Law would have to be introduced if the existing state of things continued. Another meeting was then held at Duni Chand's house and a small committee of six decided to advise the people to end the *hartal*. The prosecution is uncertain whether that decision was promoted by fear of Martial Law or by a desire to throw dust in the eyes of the authorities. When the decision was announced, it may have been unfavourably received by some of the mob waiting outside, but the leaders never told the people that Martial Law would follow and their story of a projected house-to-house visitation, which was stopped by a shower of rain, does not indicate serious effort. On the following morning, the three most prominent accused were deported.

It is pointed out, therefore, how up to the evening of the 13th the members of this conspiracy ruled the situation, spoke and acted as the rulers of that situation, dictated terms, objected to the conduct of the authorities, brought about various outrages and kept alive the general strike. It is not urged that all the accused were originally members of the conspiracy but that each and every one sooner or later joined the conspiracy and, either by word or deed, furthered its objects by speaking sedition or by such acts as the opening of *langar khanas.*

The accused fall into two groups. The first and infinitely the more important which is alleged to have formed the original conspiracy and is frequently referred to as the "lawyer accused," consists of five senior members of the Lahore Bar, being three Barristers and two Pleaders, accused Nos. 1 to 5, and two junior members, Mohsin Shah and Habibullah, Nos. 9 and 7, the latter a young man who was but recently enrolled. The second group consists of men who are said to have joined later. Doctor Karam Chand Hateshi, No. 8, is a well known medical practitioner of Lahore, who recited a poem of his own composition both inside and outside the Bradlaugh Hall on the 6th and opened a *langar khana* at his own expense on the 11th. Beyond these two acts, he is not shown as having joined or assisted the main body of the accused. Mathra Parshad, No. 6, an intinerant minstrel employed by the Arya Samaj, recited a poem on the 6th, taken from the Delhi paper "*Vijai*". Allah Din, No. 10, a mechanic from Hoshiarpur, who has recently come to Lahore, is alleged by the prosecution to have made three violent speeches: at the Badshahi Mosque on the 11th, Duni Chand's house on the 12th and the Town Hall on the 13th. Mota Singh, No. 11, is shown to have made a speech on the 11th in the Badshahi Mosque. He alone pleads an *alibi* and produces evidence to show that on the 11th he was in his school in Patiala, and that there must, therefore, have been a mistake in identity. Allah Din denies having been at Duni Chand's house on the 12th and, with this exception, he, Mathra Parshad and Karam Chand all admit having made speeches or recited poems on the occasions alleged, but they urge that these have been wrongly reported, and anyhow that what they said was in no way seditious or objectionable. Doctor Karam Chand adds that the opening of his *langar khana* was a spontaneous, independent, act of charity, and that he never had any sort of connection with any promoter or preacher of the *hartal*.

Those who are accused of having originated the conspiracy fall again into two sub-groups, the "principal accused" Nos. 1 to 5 and the "minor accused" Nos. 7 and 9. The defence of all seven, as opposed to those, who are said to have joined later, is a categorical denial, supported by the evidence of a large number of witnesses, of having either promoted or encouraged the agitation. They plead that they consistently helped the authorities, exercised a soothing and calming influence on the populace, endeavoured to get the *hartal* stopped, and on certain definite occasions succeeded in averting disturbances and induced the people to behave themselves. In the first place, they deny the authenticity of the order for the 16,000 copies of Gandhi's message and point to the absence of any direct evidence that these copies, by whomsoever they may have been ordered, were ever distributed. They admit that, being politically minded and members of the Indian Association, they have voiced their heartfelt conviction of the radical unsoundness and undersirability of the Rowlatt legislation, but they urge that, in doing so, they have but followed the example of all the members of the Viceroy's Council and have never exceeded the limits of legitimate criticism. As showing their anxiety to keep the agitation within proper bounds they prove that at a disscusion with the Deputy Commissioner one of them offered to cancel the meeting of the 6th altogether, and again that Gokal Chand, a prominent member and speaker, at an association meeting of the 4th opposed the holding of the meeting of the 6th and when he was over-ruled by the majority, asked to have his name removed from the list of conveners. His subsequent attendence is explained as due to a desire to help the police in getting the meeting dispersed before sunset and this more expecially because he had thrice succeeded in inducing the crowd to retire earlier in the day. Evidence is produced to show that, when the C.I.D. officers were hissed, he rebuked the gathering, and this unfortunate incident is described as a mere isolated act of bad manners on the part of an irresponsible minority. (No explanation is offered of the fact that Duni Chand, who does not deny that he received the letter asking him to make arrangements, deliberately led these officers into the body of the Hall though he knew that there were no arrangements, and that the crowd had already made a demonstration against the European wife of Mr. Jai Gopal.) Great stress is laid on the fact that the notice of this meeting contained no mention of the *hartal,* which had been advertised and was expected to begin before the hour fixed for the meeting; and the speeches in support of the *hartal* more especially that of Chaudhari Rambhaj Dutt are explained in the same way as those of the minor accused.

Many witnesses are produced to show that the Ram Naumi was celebrated as usual by the ordinary religious procession; that Hindu and Muhammadan unity was preached as a religious duty. Dharm Das and Mohsin Shah being among the speakers, and that as soon as the mob tried to break away from religion to politics and cried "Gandhi ki Jai" Gokal Chand rebuked the people and did so with the best results. In the same way all connection with the *hartal* of the 10th is stoutly denied, and this is explained to have been an orderly and spontaneous expression of pious grief by the citizens of Lahore on hearing the news of Gandhi's arrest. Two incidents are relied on as contradicting the theory of the prosecution that the outbreak on the Mall was brought about by the accused, and these are: offer made by Duni Chand to assist after the firing had taken place, and the speech by Rambhaj Dutt near the Lohari Gate, in which he is said to have confined himself to begging the rioters to return to the city. It is urged that on the 11th, it was at the wish of the Deputy Commissioner that accused Nos. 1 to 5 and No. 9 visited the Shahi Mosque, and the speeches made are described as calculated to soothe the people and close the *hartal*. The opening of the subscription for *langar khanas* is denied. It is admitted that a subscription of Rs. 1,000 was offered, though never paid, by Harkishen Lal; but this offer, it is said, was made only on condition that the *hartal* was closed and with the object of financing a subsequent campaign of constitutional agitation. All connection with the *langar khanas* is also denied and these, it is urged, were the outcome of the spontaneous charity of humane citizens, who could not see poor people starve, however misguided they might be. It might further have been pointed out that it was perhaps hardly for these accused, of whom the majority are Hindu lawyers, to put an end to the desecration of the Badshahi mosque when the members of the committee of management and the Musalman *Raises,* who must have known what was happening, saw fit to take no action, but, even if this be admitted, the question remains whether these persons, as alleged, actively encouraged and promoted the rioting and the sacrilege. The attendance of some of the accused on the 12th was again prompted, it is said, by a desire to help Government, and the meaning of the formation of a committee to consider the alternatives of continuance and cessation is said to be that a bald announcement of the real intention of ending the *hartal* at all costs would have been unfavourably received.

The principal accused explain how they were called into consultation by Mr. Shafi on the 12th, and how they agreed with him and other leading citizens on the action to be taken and the conditions to be laid down. They add, that the fact that all these gentlemen and title-holders agreed with them shows that the advice was moderate and sound. If Rambhaj Dutt on his arrival used angry and excited language to anybody, it was only in consequence of a carriage accident; and, in the same way, if Harkishen Lal later abused Nawab Fateh Ali Khan in a private house, it was a matter to be settled by the gentlemen concerned, and is certainly no evidence of a criminal conspiracy. Exception is taken to the evidence of the use of the word "*Be-imani*" on the 13th to the Deputy Commissioner, and it is pointed out that, at the worst, there was difference of opinion between him and some of the accused.

The separate incidents brought forward to show that the accused loyally assisted the authorities on every possible occasion are as follows:—

Duni Chand wrote to the students and others coming from the Ravi on the 6th, and told them not to hold a procession. On the same day, Gokal Chand three times succeeded in turning back the mob and preventing it from breaking out upon the Mall, and this he did at the special request of the police. The same afternoon, it is said, he rebuked the crowd at the Bradlaugh Hall and stopped the demonstration against the C.I.D. Officers. On the 9th, he controlled the mob and prevented the use of political cries at the Ram Naumi procession. On the 10th, Duni Chand offered his assistance after the firing on the Mall, and, later, Rambhaj Dutt tried to induce the mob at the Lohari Gate to return to the city. Mohsin Shah succeeded in doing so at the Mochi Gate; and finally Harkishen Lal gave excellent and prudent advice to the Deputy Commissioner as shown by witnesses, D.W. 10 and D.W. 31. This is said to have been not that the bodies of those killed in the riots should be returned as demanded by the mob, but that they should either be returned or disposed of.

The case for the defence, therefore, may be described as taking each separate incident and treating it as such, apart from all that occurred before or after. The importance of each adverse detail is then minimised, or an innocent explanation is tendered, which might very often be entertained and accepted were it possible to treat such incidents separately.

The case for the Crown, on the other hand, consists of collecting various facts and incidents and urging that the combined effect of such facts is sufficient to establish a strong and convincing case. Reliance is often placed by both sides on the same incidents. The defence shows that on certain occasions some of the accused did assist or did offer to try and assist the autorities. The prosecution, on the other hand, points to the same incidents as showing what great authority these people had, and it endeavours to establish that not only did they abstain from doing their duty but that they deliberately fanned the flames and excited the passions of their ignorant followers.

In order to clear the ground, it is desirable to discuss first the position which is held in Lahore by accused No. 1 to 5 i.e., the five Hindu Lawyers. There is a large body of evidence that they are in no sense leaders of the people; that they have no influence in the city, and that when some of them went there to induce the people to open their shops they were greeted with such cries as, "We did not close our shops for you and we will not open them for you". We have even been told that though these accused were powerless to end the *hartal*, Mr. Shafi and his friends would have had no difficulty in doing so had they really tried. In his arguments, Mr. Hassan Imam has left this part of the evidence severely alone, and has contented himself with saying that though some of these accused are leading men not only in Lahore but in India, leading men merely voice and do not lead public opinion, and that in any case his clients are in no sense leaders of the shopkeeping class.

Now it is true that in a letter published in the *Civil and Military Gazette* of May 11th, the Hon'ble Rai Bahadur Bakhshi Sohan Lal, who is a member of what has hitherto been described as the moderate party, advanced a claim that he with Raja Narendra Nath, the Hon'ble Rai Bahadur Ramsaran Das, the Hon'ble Mian Muhammad Shafi, the Hon'ble Sir Zulfikar Ali Khan and others had brought about the ending of the second *hartal;* that their influence had already borne fruit in the city on the 16th and was merely assisted by the action taken under Martial Law which "expedited" the conclusion of the *hartal*. This letter has never been publicly repudiated by any of those on whose behalf the claim was made, but it is sufficient to say that it is established both by the prosecution and the defence that the conclusion of the *hartal* was due solely to the orders passed under Martial Law. Mr. Shafi and the *rais* class generally are, no doubt, prominent professionally or socially and a number of them are, of course, members of the Legislative Councils. It does not, however, follow that they are persons of influence in Lahore. On the contrary, there is ample evidence of a convincing kind that the people of the city regard them as time-servers and title-hunters and dislike them accordingly. It is clear, too, that other politicans look upon them as men who can be led though they cannot lead. Thus in his speech of the 4th of February, as reported in the *Tribune* of the 7th, a passage which provoked loud and prolonged applause, Gokal Chand did not hesitate to tell even Mr. Shafi and Sir Zulfikar Ali Khan that if they supported the Rowlatt Bills they would be regarded as enemies of their country and India would know the reason why. We do not propose to discuss Mr. Shafi's reasons for voting against the Bills, but we should not be surprised, if threats of this kind were not wholly without the effect intended, and it may well be that such orders to toe the line had something to say to the complete unanimity on which Mr. Shafi dilated in his speech in Council.

Mr. Shafi has told us that on the 15th of March the moderate party issued from Delhi a manifesto in which they deprecated passive resistance as preached by Mr. Gandhi. Mr. Shafi had himself spoken in Council on these lines and we fully believe that he meant what he said, but, though he must soon have discovered the futility of the Delhi manifesto, neither he nor any of his friends, with the solitary exception of Nawab Fateh Ali Khan, made the slightest effort to check the propaganda which were being preached in the city of Lahore.

Again, while it appears to us to be quite possible that most of these gentlemen may not have wished to prevent the *hartal* of the 6th, we have no doubt that they did not approve of the *hartal* of the 10th, and would have stopped it if they could. Nevertheless, when asked by Government to help, it never occurred to them to go straight to the city and to make a direct appeal to the people. They assembled a few leading shopkeepers at the house of Mr. Muhammad Naki, but were at once referred by these shopkeepers to Harkishen Lal, Rambhaj Dutt and Duni Chand, who were described by name as the leaders. After that, all that Mr. Shafi and his friends attempted to do was to try and make terms with the leaders, whom they clearly regarded as controlling the situation; and they of all people were in a position to know. Mr. Fyson, the Deputy Commissioner, also so regarded them, and he has told us that some of them spoke to him as persons of authority with power to end the *hartal* if their terms were granted.

The accused have made a great point of the fact that Mr. Shafi and his friends agreed to the terms drawn up on the 12th of April and represented their own agreement to the Chief Secretary. Probably, however, that position was forced upon them by the unpleasant alternative of confessing complete impotence to Government and at the same time incurring still greater unpopularity in the city. It cannot have been altogether pleasant for Raja Narindra Nath to have to admit to us the small esteem in which he and his friends are held, but he has done so fully. He has told us that it would have been quite useless for any of the moderates to hold a meeting or to say a word in defence of Government, because only those who attack Government can get a hearing; that when he went into the city on 12th he would not have dared to explain the Rowlatt Act, and that when he went there again with the Hon'ble Rai Bahadur Ramsaran Das they were both taunted by the crowd as beneficiaries of Government. So too, Rai Bahadur Ramsaran Das himself was quite unable to keep his works open during the second *hartal,* and Mr. Shafi had to submit to a protracted *hartal* in his own ancestral village of Baghbanpura. Neither he, nor Sir Zulfikar Ali Khan, though they are on the Managing Committee of the Badshahi Mosque, attempted to prevent the sacrilege of the 11th or 12th. There are many other indications of the dislike, with which any one who is suspected of friendliness towards Government is received in Lahore City, but we will not labour the matter further. The point is that if the accused can produce a seemingly respectable witness D.W.II- 273 to testify to the enormous influence of Mr. Shafi, etc., and at the same time to state that even if the accused had been ten times more numerous than they were they would not have been able to exercise the slightest influence in the city of Lahore, they can produce evidence in support of any allegation which it may suit them to put forward from time to time. Mr. Ganpat Rai, as counsel for his brother Duni Chand, has twice told us that he could if necessary, produce the whole of Lahore city to give testimony, and for all practical purposes he has justified his claim by producing hundreds of schooled witnesses, for whom no falsehood is too extravagant and no fabrication too absurd. It is sufficient to give a few instances.

Having produced evidence to show that the *hartal* of the 11th was spontaneous, the defence follows this up with a large number of witnesses who say that the *hartal* continued on the 11th because the people were afraid that they would be shot if they left their houses. Nevertheless, on that very day a crowd of some 25,000 people admittedly assembled in the Badshahi mosque and afterwards behaved as if they were masters of Lahore.

So too, we have numerous statements that there was never any idea of opposition to Government, and this, in spite of the riot on the Upper Mall, the incident of Balwant Singh, the attack on the C.I.D. Inspector, the *Danda Fauj*, the destruction of pictures of Their Majesties, the shouts of "*Hai George mar giya*," and contents of the *Danda Akhbar*, Exh. P. 25, which we here append as indicating the prevalent temper of the mob, for it is by the most violent that mobs are swayed.

"NOTICE"

"*Mr. Shaukat Ali ki jai.*

"*Mahatma Gandhi ki jai.*

"DANDA AKHBAR.

"*First event*—When Mahatma Gandhi arrived at Palwal, the English monkey informed him that his entry into the Punjab was forbidden, and that he should please go back. He replied that he would never go back, then that pig monkey arrested him. Reports of his arrest reached here at once.

"*Second event*—When the news reached Amritsar, the *Danda Fauj* of the brave Sikhs set fire to the Bank, the Railway Station and Electric Power House. They cut the telegraph wires and removed the railway line. The *Danda Fauj* of Amritsar bravely killed a number of European monkeys and their Sikh Regiments have revolted and deserted. O Hindu, Muhammadan and Sikh brethren, enlist at once in the *Danda* Army, and fight with bravery against the English monkeys. God will grant you Victory. Do not apprehend that God does not help us. Cast away such a notion out of your heart. God helps us at all times and hours. Conquer the English monkeys with bravery. God will grant Victory. Leave off dealings with the Englishmen, close offices and workshops. Fight on! This is the command of Mahatma Gandhi.

"Third event—O Hindu, Muhammadan and Sikh brethren, do you know of the incident that took place at the Mall Road on the night of the 10th April? The Hindus and Muhammadans who were martyred that day were your own and they sacrificed their lives. Does not this incident excite you? What is the reason? Were not those who were made martyrs in Hira Mandi on the 12th April your own brethren, and died at the hands of the tyrants? Does the Prophet of God command you not to fight against the tyrant? No, never, Prophet himself fought, and has commanded us too to destroy the tyrants as he did. Should we not be ashamed of ourselves that while the tyrant is up to all sorts of cruelty, we are sitting quiet? O Hindu, Muhammadan and Sikh brethren, raise the cry of *Allah Akbar* and kill the *Kafirs*. Get ready soon, for the war and God will grant Victory to India very soon. Fight with enthusiasm and enlist yourselves in the *Danda* Army."

Signatures, to the notice:— "Servant of the Nation.

"DANDA AKHBAR.

"Hindus, Muhammadans and Sikhs".

We have even had witnesses who are prepared to swear that though it is stated by the defence that the people were afraid of leaving their houses, shouts of "Victory to Government" resounded through the streets of the city.

Then, too, we have the mass of testimony that the suspension of business was not compulsory. Leaving aside the statements of other witnesses for the defence, who closed their shops on the 11th, when they saw the crowds coming, and the pressure which must unquestionably have been used before all the small shopkeepers with perishable goods could be induced to close, there is plenty of evidence of a reliable character to show what really happened. Schools and public offices were forcibly shut, gates were picketed to prevent clerks going to work and no tonga-drivers were able to ply until they had first removed their license numbers. We had even witnesses who could swear that clerks stayed away from office merely because they wanted a holiday, and one of those who pretended to this knowledge was a tinker in the Kasera bazar.

In this connection, we may refer to the statement of the Hon'ble Rai Bahadur Bakhshi Sohan Lal, D. W. III-147. In his examination-in-chief, he had said all and perhaps more than he could have been expected to say, including a statement that the principal accused are all loyal ; but when questioned by the court as to his grounds for saying in his letter in the *"Civil and Military Gasette"* that compulsion was used, he mentioned amongst other things that a barrister named Behari Lal had complained to him of being stopped by a mob and asked to join it. At the next hearing the barrister in question, D. W. III-260, came to swear that he never said anything of the kind, and that Bakhshi Sohan Lal was a liar. We have no doubt that Bakhshi Sohan Lal's statement on this particular point was quite true, but nothing could show more conclusively the influence which some of these accused must possess.

Mr. Hassan Imam in arguing the case evidently felt that much of the evidence or the defence was too indigestible for serious discussion, and he confined himself in the main to the statements of witnesses for the prosecution which, he remarked, are replete with evidence showing the innocence of the accused.

In a sense that remark is true enough. In face of the general feeling against Government but few people can have been willing to give evidence for the prosecution, and some of those who were produced to give formal evidence, or evidence of a kind they could hardly avoid, discovered themselves as partisans for the defence as soon as their cross-examination began. Thus Mr. Hassan Imam was able to make great play with the statement of Piara Mohan, P. W. 27, a Vakil, who gave evidence against some of the lesser accused. He proved himself the staunchest friend of the principal accused, and besides being a convener of the meeting of the 6th, he had accompanied some of them to the Badshahi Mosque. There are several other instances.

Mr. Hassan Imam, however, was also able to claim considerable help from the statements of men like Mr. Shafi, and his argument was that if such obviously whole-hearted supporters of Government give any evidence which tells in favour of the accused that part of their evidence at least must be unquestionably true.

That is not the view we take, and we consider it necessary to speak plainly about this matter. One of the most important pieces of evidence against Harkishen Lal is the matter of his subscription of Rs. 1000 to the *langer khanas*. Whatever may be the merits of Harkishen Lal's action in this matter, and it will be discussed later, there is no doubt that these shops were the creatures of the *hartal* and were intended to prolong it. Yet both Ramsaran Das, P. W. 7, who was otherwise in our opinion one of the most straighforward of the witnesses for the prosecution, and Lala Karam Chand, an honorary magistrate and a member of the municipality, fell into line with many of the defence witnesses in telling us that the *langar khanas* had nothing to do with the *hartal*. We do not think it is necessary to give other instances, but we must state our considered opinion that many witnesses of high social standing have been guilty to a greater or less degree, if not always of bald falsehood, at least of *toning* down parts of their evidence, though not always the same parts, and have been prompted to do so either by sympathy or fear.

We make no doubt that when witnesses of this class told us that they asked some of the principal accused to help because they were recognised as leaders and had been nominated by the shopkeepers to voice the views of the city, they were merely stating a fact which at that stage of the case it had not even occurred to any one to contest. At the time when they gave their evidence, the point with the defence was, not whether the men named were leaders but whether they had been named or not, and even when at a subsequent stage of the case they came to regard their description of leaders as disadvantageous, they were never able to make any reasonable suggestion as to other persons who might be expected to lead the shopkeepers and were thus driven to their foolish assertion that Mr. Shafi and his friends could have ended the *hartal*.

The causes of their influence are obvious enough. The five Hindu lawyer accused are all men who have taken a prominent part in public affairs of various kinds. Duni Chand in particular is the Secretary of the All-India Arorbans Association, a body with a large following among the shopkeeper class, and he has long been a leading member of the municipality. They are all leading members of the Indian Association, a body which is constantly engaged in that highly-spiced criticism of Government which so appeals to the multitude. There is ample evidence that these men were regarded as leaders by all with whom they came in contact. The Deputy

Commissioner so regarded them, and so did the members of the moderate party. At the private meetings, the richer shopkeepers referred to them for guidance, and in the mosque the populace placed all decisions in their hands. In this connection Exh. P. 20, one of the seditious posters "How our leaders have departed" is not without interest; and we notice that in one of their own Exhibit D. I.-3 the *Desh* newspaper actually used the word "leaders" in referring to them. So too, they regarded themselves. Gokul Chand actually produced a witness to prove that he had lost influence through his alleged opposition to the holding of the meeting of the 6th of April, but he demonstrated it most effectually on that day; and according to his own account, Rambhaj Dutt was able to move a mob of which the Deputy Commissioner and the Police could make no hand. Throughout the proceedings their role of leadership is the same and recognised by all, and their actions, in whatever light they are viewed, are inconsistent with anything else.

For reasons which will appear later we do not intend to discuss in much detail the meetings and the agitation which led up to the first *hartal* of the 6th of April; but as we have heard a great deal on the subject, we think it desirable to state what our conclusions are.

There may perhaps have been some few persons who believed that the Rowlatt Bills, if enacted, were liable to abuse, and doubtless a good many more were roused to oposition by the speeches in the Imperial Council and the campaign in the press, but the bulk of the city population do not read newspapers and would have remained in complete ignorance, not merely of the objections to the Bills but even of their existence, unless other steps had been taken to educate them.

The unanimity which had been announced and was required had to be preached, and preached it was with a very considerable measure of success. But even of the educated few hardly any one appears to have read or considered the Bills for himself, and it was not the business of any one to combat all or any of the lies and misrepresentations which were in circulation.

It is true, that at one meeting Gokul Chand did give reasons of a legal and technical kind for his objections to the first of the two Bills; but the class of persons, who attended the Lahore meetings, did not go there to hear legal arguments and did not carry them away. What they learnt generally was that in spite of the opposition of the whole of India and in particular of a saint named Gandhi, who, they were taught to believe, was the Rishi of the Hindus and the Wali of the Muhammadans, an alien Government was trying to pass and eventually did pass an exceedingly harsh law which threatened the liberties of the humblest individuals; and that unless all classes and religions united against the Government, there was no hope of averting the imminent peril. This teaching was enforced with all the arts of demagogues, who were unsparing in their abuse of a Government, which, they said, was meting out tyranny in return for loyalty and sacrifice. Such speeches fell on the ears of ready listeners, some of whom, deliberately or otherwise, must have retailed a still more garbled version of the iniquities of Government. As the result, the catch phrase *"Na Vakil na dalil na appeal"* was on many lips; and it was commonly believed that all and sundry, though innocent of all crime, could be arrested at the will of the police and condemned without trial, that all assemblies of more than 3 or 4 people would be prohibited, and that in some mysterious way even the women and children would be made to suffer.

It was not possible, nor indeed would it have been worth our while, to examine all the hundreds of defence witnesses concerning their knowledge of Gandhi and of the Rowlatt Act, but we tested that of a good many. Most of them knew nothing more of Gandhi than his name, or of the Rowlatt Act than that it was said to be a harsh law, but some did not even know that. Yet nearly all the witnesses of the class to which we refer, and they were very numerous, are men who said that they closed their shops on the 6th on account of the Rowlatt Act and Gandhi's message, and closed them again on the 10th because news had come of Gandhi's arrest.

In face of the evidence before us, it is ridiculous to argue that the people of Lahore generally were influenced by their knowledge of the history of Mr. Gandhi's fights for liberty or the fineness of his character. It is true that during the months of March and April his name must by constant use have become familiar to most, but few indeed had heard more than the vaguest report of his holiness and patriotism.

Nevertheless, in spite of the general ignorance that prevailed, in one way or another, by means of meetings and other propaganda, a sufficient number of people had been taught enough (the truth of what they learnt being immaterial) to form a numerous and noisy faction which was only too ready to carry out the wishes of those who desired to procure the repeal of the Act.

Those of the accused who are concerned in earlier events, all assert that they did nothing either to compel or to persuade the *hartal* of the 6th. Of compulsion by the accused on either occasion we have no evidence. On the 6th at least the use of force was generally unnecessary as the *hartal* was pre-arranged. The positive oral evidence that some of the accused, *viz*, Harkishen Lal and Duni Chand, visited the city on the 5th with the object of persuading the people not to open their shops on the following day has been subjected to much criticism, but it is very likely that it is true. For the purposes of this case, however, it does not in the least matter whether it is true or not. It is impossible that a complete *hartal* could have been organised without persuasion from persons other than those who did not themselves know why they should close their shops, and there is no difficulty in tracing the source from which the persuasion came.

We see from the evidence of Amar Nath, P. W. 4, that Duni Chand was claiming a right of persuasion from the Deputy Commissioner, and it has actually been urged that Ex. D. II-1 is proof that the Deputy Commissioner himself gave his approval to use persuasion up to the evening of the 5th, though no longer. (See also in this connection the written statement of Rambhaj Dutt, accused No. 2, and the evidence of Dina Nath, D. W. 21.) The accused have urged the omission from Ex. P. 15 (the notice for the meeting of the 6th of April) of all reference to suspension of business, as proof that they did not wish even to recommend a *hartal*. But, as already mentioned, we have it from Jai Gopal Tandon, D. W. 22, that Mr. Gandhi's message was published broadcast through Lahore. We attach no importance to the inability of the prosecution to show that the 16000 copies of this message were paid for. The books of the Indian Association have been suppressed and the leaflets were certainly ordered by them. From this we may safely conclude, in spite of the contention that the opposition to the Act in Lahore was due not to the accused, who lacked influence to promote it, but only to the campaign in the press, that the accused themselves were regarding the press as a very inadequate organ for advertisement and that they did distribute the copies.

It is futile again to contend that there was nothing unusual about the Ram Naumi procession. There are of course many witnesses for the defence who stated this, but as already pointed out they stuck at nothing, and we fully believe the statements of Jawahir Lal, P. W. 12, and Muhammad Shah, P. W. 14, which show that it was of a highly seditious and inflammatory character.

The *hartal* of the 10th of April was certainly spontaneous in the sense that it started as soon as the news arrived of Gandhi's detention; and we have no evidence, on which we would care to rely, that it was initiated by visits to the city of any of the accused. It is not indeed likely that many of the shopkeepers wished to close their shops, but crowds began to collect and to tell them that they must do so. Those addressed obeyed, and the others rapidly followed their example.

Nor have we any evidence that any of the accused instigated the mob to proceed up the Mall.

Mr. Hassan Imam has contended that, as none of the Members of the Imperial Council were called to order by the President and some of the speakers were even complimented by the Home Member, the Council speeches must have been unobjectionable and that, as the speeches made in Lahore were no stronger than some of those made in Council, it is ridiculous to found charges of sedition on the speeches in the Bradlaugh Hall. Without entering into any comparison of the two sets of speeches, we need only remark that, in our opinion, some of the Council speeches, though they are published in the Gazette and are for sale to the public, might, if repeated in a heated atmosphere, easily excite disaffection towards Government. The influence of such speeches on the Lahore orators has been strongly marked.

Of the violent character of some of the Lahore speeches there is no room for doubt, and the reports on which the prosecution rely are, in our opinion, quite accurate enough for conviction of sedition against certain individuals. In this case, however, we are not entitled to convict persons except of offences committed collectively or as the result of conspiracy; and, as we think it an over-statement of the case to say that there was a conspiracy to "commit sedition" on the 6th April, we consider that the charges of sedition based on what occurred before the time of the second *hartal* must fall to the ground.

We have had some difficulty in following Mr. Hassan Imam through his discourse on the subject of passive resistance. He referred to a speech on the subject of Indians in South Africa, in which Lord Hardinge expressed what appeared to be an unqualified approval of passive resistance as practised by Mr. Gandhi in South Africa. Possibly the passive resistance of a minority in South Africa is less dangerous than a country like India where resistance to the law is never likely to be passive for long, once the passions of a credulous populace have been stirred up by sedition and the dissemination of wilful lies. In any case, two blacks do not make one white.

Mr. Gandhi, we are informed, though he is still at liberty, has been personally practising resistance to the law regarding proscribed literature. In Lahore, none of the accused got so far as that. Some of them no doubt recommended Mr. Gandhi's teaching for adoption; but, although at the invitation of Rambhaj Dutt at the meeting of the 9th of March the majority of the audience stood up together to signify their willingness to take the vow, no one actually took it. It is impossible in practice to resist the Rowlatt Act passively except by becoming an anarchist, and though at a later stage—*vide* Ex. P. 22, people were recommended to resist taxation, at the meetings under consideration it was never decided what laws should be passively resisted. We are, moreover, convinced that one at least of the accused was actually anxious to avoid starting a campaign of this kind.

Again, it is not in itself an offence to persuade people to suspend business. No doubt, after what had occurred at Delhi on the 30th of March, the accused must have known that a general *hartal* was likely to lead to rioting; but it cannot, we think, be fairly said that they intended that offences should be committed on the 6th of April, and if they did not, they do not appear to be criminally liable (in this connection see the case of Lord George Gordon, 13 State Trials).

We are, therefore, of the opinion that as regards these points also the charges must fail, and perhaps it is just as well that we are not obliged to convict in Lahore men who up to the time of the second *hartal* had done no more than others had accomplished with impunity elsewhere.

We may add that in the Gujranwala case the Commission presided over by Mr. Justice Broadway appears to have arrived at the same conclusion.

Whatever their earlier intentions may have been, on the evening of the 10th of April at least it must have become clear to all concerned that their agitation had resulted in a dangerous ourbreak. Open rebellion and murder had occurred in Amritsar; and if in Lahore it had not been possible by the prompt employment of military force to push the mob back to the city, like causes would most probably have been followed by like effects.

We have ourselves held in another case that the riot on the Upper Mall on that date amounted to an offence under Section 121, Indian Penal Code, and another Commission has come to the same conclusion in regard to the riots at the Lohari Gate.

It was obvious that unless the *hartal* ended at once further discontent, tumult, and outrage must necessarily result; and it was the plain duty of every loyal subject to do all that lay in his power to quell the excitement and to get the people back as soon as possible to peaceful employment. On no one did this duty lie more heavily than on those, who by their speeches and influence had created the danger.

This indeed is what the accused claim to have done; but though, in order to prevent a collision at that particular moment, Rambhaj Dutt did no doubt try to get the people to retire through the Lohari Gate, he certainly did not advise them to end the *hartal*. We have no hesitation in believing the statement of Maratab Ali Shah, P. W. 29, that even while telling them to retire he also told them to assemble the next day in the Badshahi Mosque. This meeting was certainly pre-arranged and no other explanation of its origin has been offered. Over the gate-way there was a flag with a seditious inscription and Hindus and Muhammadans alike had gathered together to the number of some 25,000. Never before has a joint meeting of a political character been held in the building.

Rambhaj Dutt of course attended this meeting, but his explanation is that he and others did so at the suggestion of the Deputy Commissioner, Mr. Fyson, and then only in order to assist in allaying the excitement and stop what was going on. Mr. Fyson himself does not remember having given any such instructions, and we think it probable that he did not do more than ask them to end the *hartal* and explain why the dead bodies could not be returned. But granting that he did so, Rambhaj Dutt did not carry out his instructions. The two best accounts of what occurred are contained in the statement of Jiwan Lal, P. W. 26, and in the report, Ex. P. 62, which was prepared by Hari Mohan Chatterjee, P. W. 28, for the Associated Press in India. The last named was the best witness who appeared before us throughout the course of this trial.

Rambhaj Dutt proceeded to address the gathering from the pulpit of the mosque. He no doubt appealed to the young men not to cause provocation or to resort to violence and probably also he advised them not to go on the Mall, but any communications which the Deputy Commissioner had asked him to make were given by him as the orders of the Deputy Commissioner and not as his own advice, and at the time he posed as a man who was himself not unlikely to be going to his death. He claimed that the firing at the Lohari Gate was unjustifiable, because the people who were fired upon were already moving off, and he urged that it was their duty to stand when fired upon and not to retreat. He referred, moreover, to an expected decision of a Satyagraha Committee that the orders of the police and other laws should be disobeyed even if death was involved; and he called upon the mob to continue and make permanent the union which had been displayed that day. In fact, instead of doing anything to allay the prevailing excitement, his speech was of a highly inflammatory character; and so far from telling the people that the *hartal* must be discontinued unconditionally, he informed them that the decision on that point would be referred to a committee.

Then, according to the statement of his own witness, Khan Bahadur Mian Siraj Din, Honorary Magistrate, and member of the Lahore Municipality, D. W. II-17, he went back and told Mr. Broadway, the Superintendent of Police, that he had persuaded the people to depart to their homes and not to form processions in the streets.

Shortly after his departure from the mosque, there occurred the incident of the arrival of Balwant Singh, which indicates clearly the excited condition of the mob, whose passions Rambhaj Dutt claims to have allayed. This took place during the course of what is described as the violent speech made by another of the accused Allah Din, No. 10, towards the end of which Duni Chand arrived upon the scene in the company of Harkishen Lal, Dharam Das and Piyare Mohan, P. W. 27.

Duni Chand too claims that he only went to the mosque, because he had been informed by his brother, Ganpat Rai, D. W. 114, that the Deputy Commissioner wished him to do so. The same witness states that it was Duni Chand's own idea to take Harkishen Lal with him, though it is not explained why he should have wished this, if Harkishen Lal is a man of no influence or popularity. The mob evidently thought otherwise, for not only Duni Chand, but his friends, Harkishen Lal and Dharam Das, were carried in triumph to the pulpit of the mosque. A committee was then formed at the suggestion of Duni Chand for the purpose of collecting funds to feed and help the poor during the period of the strike and for this object Harkishen Lal promised a subscription of Rs. 1000.

The fact that he offered to subscribe this sum is not denied, and the story that the offer was made only on condition that the people opened their shops first and then only to provide the expenses for constitutional agitation against the Rowlatt Act and for a memorial to His Majesty the King, is pure invention. There is no reference to anything of the kind in the very accurate report, Ex. P. 62, and the object plainly was to keep the *hartal* going, for if it ended, there would have been no need for the free distribution of food. Jiwan Lal has told us that before the meeting dispersed it was decided that the *hartal* should be continued, and that there should be another meeting in the mosque on the following day; and the impression which Hari Mohan Chatterjee took away with him was that the *hartal* was intended to continue for another week.

After the meeting dispersed a procession, led by men armed with *lathis*, went through the city with shouts of *"Delhi ke Shahidon ki Jai"* and *"Amritsar ke Shahidon ki Jai"* and yelling *"Hai Hai George Mar gaya"* destroyed such pictures of Their Majesties as were found on the way.

We have no doubt that all the speeches made on this occasion were both calculated and intended to make matters worse than they were already and they were eminently successful in achieving their object.

We are then told, however, that on that very night a number of persons, including of the accused, Harkishen Lal, Duni Chand Gokal Chand, Habibullah, Dharam Das Suri and Rambhaj Dutt, drew up a manifesto (*vide* Ex. D. I-I) beginning with the later and more pacific message of Gandhi and ending with their own advice in the following words:—

> "In compliance with the above-mentioned order of Mahatma Gandhi, it is our duty to exercise peace and patience at every step. The Lahore public have, in a manner worthy of their dignity, expressed their grief and sympathy over Mahatma Gandhi's arrest and their protest against the Rowlatt Act. The authorities have been now fully informed of the intentions and wishes of the public. We, therefore, request the public to resume their business as usual and keep up the further effort and struggle that is necessary in the city and outside the city through committees.

"We pray to the God of Universe that He may crown your intentions with success."

In face of what had just occurred it appears to us to be very unlikely that this manifesto was drawn up as early as 11th April, seeing that while recommending the continuance of the struggle against the Rowlatt Act by means of committees, it nevertheless advised an immediate resumption of business. The only evidence we have about it, which can be described as in any way reliable, is contained in the statement of Raja Narendra Nath, D. W. II-6, who said that on the evening of the 11th he had been told, that a manifesto of this kind was under preparation, not that it had been actually prepared. In any case, even if it can be believed that for the moment somewhat wiser counsels had prevailed, they were speedily abandoned. The statement of the printer, Dina Nath D. W. 21, who has been put forward to relate the reasons why it was not printed, is pure rubbish; and it is obvious, that had the signatories so desired, they could have got their manifesto printed and issued immediately, if not from the *Desh* press, then from some other.

We are by no means sure that this manifesto was not drawn up at some later stage of the proceedings, and then only with the object of providing exculpatory evidence.

The second meeting, which had already been arranged, took place in the Badshahi Mosque next morning. The temper of the crowd, which had assembled, is shown by the attack on Inspector Ali Gauhar, P. W. 46, of the C. I. D., while the mob were awaiting the arrival of the principal agitators. The story of Rambhaj Dutt, Harkishen Lal and Duni Chand is, that they had learnt accidentally of this second meeting and had gone to the mosque in order to do what they could in order to assist the Government. They did nothing of the kind. Rambhaj Dutt again exhorted the people to face death with fortitude.

By this time, there must of course have been many people who were suffering loss of business or even actual want and the question whether the *hartal* should be continued or not was certainly reopened. This led to the election of another committee to decide this particular question and to tell the Mohalla Chaudhries what they were to do. Among the members of this committee were Rambhaj Dutt, Harkishen Lal and Duni Chand, and it was Rambhaj Dutt who put the names to the vote by acclamation. The story of Ghulam Hussain Shah, P. W. 40, is on this point borne out by the report of Hari Mohan

Chatterjee, Ex. P. 63, and we have no doubt that it is correct. The defence has not thought fit to produce any evidence concerning what occurred on this occasion. The names of a few unpopular persons, including that of the Hon'ble Rai Bahadur Ram Saran Das, were rejected by the mob, and it is quite certain that these three accused had not proposed unconditional surrender. What occurred on this occasion emphasises what we have already said regarding the worthlessness of the manifesto, Ex. D. I-1.

Not long after the mob left the mosque, it had a collision with the Police and Military at the Hira Mandi, and the Police were ordered to fire. This affair has been the subject of another trial by the second Commission. Some details of what occurred are given in Ex. P. 63.

It was after this, that the meeting at Mr. Shafi's house was held. According to Mr. Shafi, Duni Chand and Gokal Chand expressed the view that their influence with the public was exaggerated and that, owing to the firing which had just taken place, people were more excited than before. They said, therefore, that unless the Government was prepared to make certain concessions, they doubted if the people would listen to them. The conditions which Duni Chand suggested were the repeal of the Rowlatt Act and the release of Mr. Gandhi. Nawab Fateh Ali Khan, however, includes the demands for the release of every one arrested at Amritsar and the removal of the Military from Lahore. When they were told that some of these conditions were impracticable, they agreed to (1) the withdrawal of the Military, (2) the restoration of dead and wounded, (3) the release on bail of all persons arrested, and (4) the formation of a committee to advise Government and to maintain order.

When Rambhaj Dutt arrived and heard the conditions, he was very excited and reiterated the demands for the repeal of the Rowlatt Act, the free entry of Mr. Gandhi into the Punjab, and the release of Kitchlew and Satyapal; but in spite of his objections, the conditions as originally drawn up were agreed upon. We do not believe that his excitement was due to his horse having shied.

The contention for the accused generally is that they knew that unless such concessions were granted the people would not be willing to end the *hartal*, though they themselves, if they had had the power, would have been quite ready to end it unconditionally.

It is, however, quite clear from the evidence that this was not their attitude at the time. They were objecting to having the *hartal* stopped until what they regarded as the grievances of the people were removed. They had just received a mandate from those assembled in the Badshahi Mosque to decide whether the *hartal* should be ended or not, and there is no evidence that anything has been said about conditions. The conditions, therefore, embodied their own ideas of what it was right to demand; and the plain fact is that they were quite unwilling even to attempt to end the *hartal*, unless they could go back with proof of a triumph over Government. There had been some shopkeepers there, but they took no part in the discussion.

Mr. Shafi and some of his friends, after learning the Government was not prepared to accept the conditions which had been laid down, repaired to the house of Duni Chand, where a Committee was sitting. Mr. Shafi was invited to address it; but after he had spoken, Allah Din, accused No. 10, got up and said that the Government had been guilty of a breach of faith in sending troops into the city, that innocent persons had been killed, and that unless the Rowlatt Act was repealed and Gandhi released there was no use expecting people to reopen their shops. Rambhaj Dutt and Harkishen Lal were both present. When Nawab Fateh Ali Khan came into the room, he was roundly abused by Harkishen Lal for having written a letter published in the "Civil and Military Gazette" on the 5th of April, in which he condemned passive resistance and the proposed *hartal* of the 6th. It is impossible to understand why, if Harkishen Lal was at this time willing to do all that he could to help Government, he should have made this letter a basis of attack. Duni Chand's party were not prepared to yield from the position they had already taken, but it was arranged that another meeting should be held in the Town Hall next morning.

This meeting was held in the presence of the Deputy Commissioner. It is over-stating the case to term it tumultuous, or to make it the basis of charges. Accused Nos. 1 to 5 and Allah Din, No. 10, were all present. Allah Din made a speech similar to that which he had made on the previous day, and he was supported by Rambhaj Dutt, both of them accusing the Deputy Commissioner of having broken faith in sending troops into the city. It is quite possible that Mr. Fyson had said something which Rambhaj Dutt either misunderstood or chose to misunderstand, but it is immaterial. The point is that Duni Chand's party at this meeting were no more willing than they had been before to try and end the *hartal* unless Government was first prepared to climb down.

Subsequently some of the accused were summoned by the Deputy Commissioner to his tent at the Telegraph Office, where he read to them some portions of Bengal Regulation X of 1804, and told them that unless the *hartal* was stopped Martial Law would be introduced. Mr. Fyson was not inviting legal opinions, but Rambhaj Dutt showed his continued recalcitrance by objecting that the Regulation could not be applied.

The same afternoon, another meeting was held at Duni Chand's. house. The best accounts which we have of this meeting are from Shuja-ud-din, Barrister, D. W. 8, and Feroz Din, Barrister, D. W. 116. Six persons—Duni Chand, Harkishen Lal, Gokal Chand and Mohsin Shah with the two witnesses—were elected to a sub-committee, which was to decide whether the *hartal* should come to an end. There were no shopkeepers on the committee, but apparently some of them were invited to give their opinion. The decision was in favour of an unconditional surrender, though, according to Feroz Din, Duni Chand at first objected and was unwilling to take any steps to persuade the people. It is said, and there is a great deal of evidence to that effect, that when the decision was announced by Rambhaj Dutt, the leaders were accused of truckling to Government. They, then, according to their own account, decided to visit the shopkeepers in the town, but gave up this idea as the rain came on. The more probable theory is that finding the decision unpopular they were unwilling to press it, for on the same evening Gokal Chand and Duni Chand again approached the Deputy Commissioner with a request for a concession, *viz*, the withdrawal of the troops. The people were never informed by them, that the authorities had decided to introduce Martial Law if the *hartal* did not end.

Next morning, accused Nos. 1, 2 and 3 were deported; but the *hartal* did not come to an end, until the 18th and then only by the military order.

It is hardly profitable to discuss whether or not the principal accused could have ended the *hartal* on the 13th, though we think that they might perhaps have done so if they had subordinated their own popularity to the public good, had been straightforward with the people and had really tried to get the saner elements of the city on their side.

That they could have done so on the 11th and again on the 12th, we make no doubt. We are not, however, going to convict anyone merely for failing to use his influence on the right side, even though we may consider that by doing so they could have restored peace in the city; and for a like reason were do not regard as a proper subject of a charge the action of any of the accused in laying down to Government the condition, on which they were prepared to assist. No doubt they were morally bound to help unconditionally, but they were not legally bound to do so and their omission was not in itself an offence. Their attitude in that matter is of course good evidence of their intentions; but so far as charges are concerned, we shall confine ourselves to criminal acts of a positive kind.

In doing so, however, we must, as even Mr. Hassan Imam has conceded, take judicial notice of the state of rebellion which existed on the 10th of April onwards. It has not been argued before us that the acts in the Badshahi Mosque attributed by the prosecution to some of the accused would, if proved, fall short of offences under section 121, Indian Penal Code, and of their extreme gravity there can be no doubt. After weighing all the evidence, we are of opinion that the prosecution has established that there was an active conspiracy in Lahore to bring about the repeal of the Rowlatt Act by criminal means, namely, by waging war against the King, and that in furtherance thereof war was waged from the 11th onwards. These men knew, none better, that the state of rebellion was largely due to their own efforts, and that Lahore was one of the principal centres from which disaffection and open defiance of Government were spreading through the Punjab. The mere fact that owing to the rapid assumption of military control no serious damage was done in Lahore itself is to our minds quite immaterial. The results of their efforts were not confined to Lahore; and if in order to overawe Government into the repeal of the Act, they did what lay in their power to produce further excitement and outrage, they must take the consequences.

Before proceeding to discuss the case of each individual accused, it is necessary to remark that all of them, according to their station in life, have been able to produce testimonials, from more or less eminent members of society, to their moderation and loyalty. These they could doubtless have multiplied as often as they wished.

Some of them, again, have been able to show that in recent times they have not merely prayed for the success of the British

Arms, but have advocated War Loans, helped in recruitment, and have even "given" relatives to the Indian Defence Force or clerks for Mesopotamia. Perhaps all of these efforts were not very valuable, and it has to be remembered that some of the accused are men who are always in the lime-light, but we have no doubt that every one of them, however much he might dislike the existing Government, at least preferred it to prospects of German rule. None of these things, however really affect the matter before us. It is on the evidence of their actions in this case that the accused must be judged.

Harkishen Lal (No. 1).—Much stress is laid on statements by men like Mr. Shafi and Sir Zulfikar Ali Khan that this accused has taken no part in politics for several years past. These gentlemen were evidently misinformed. Harkishen Lal is not a frequent speaker on public platforms, but he is nevertheless an active politician—*vide* the statement of Barkat Ali, D. W. IX 3—and was recently elected a member of a deputation to proceed to England. He is President of the Indian Association, and though he did not attend it, he was one of the conveners of the meeting of the 6th April. We have no doubt that throughout he was in the full confidence of Rambhaj Dutt and Duni Chand. He was acting in close co-operation with them on the 11th, 12th and 13th April, was present at both the meetings in the Badshahi Mosque, and his general attitude is shown by his unprovoked attack on Nawab Fateh Ali Khan. There is no need to recapitulate what we have said about his promised subscription to the *hartal*.

Rambhaj Dutt (No. 2) was the chief spokesman of the conspiracy. As early as the 4th February; he made a seditious speech in which he foreshadowed the same fate for England as had befallen Germany. On the 6th April, he preached the *hartal* and the need of undergoing suffering, an idea which he further developed and amplified in subsequent speeches. On the 10th of April at the Lohari Gate he invited the mob to the Badshahi Mosque; and on the following day, he made a violent and inflammatory speech and incited the people to stand firm and be shot. On the 12th, he again enlarged upon the same text. We find that he has throughout been one of the moving spirits in the conspiracy.

Duni Chand (No. 3) was the chief organiser, as opposed to the chief spokesman of the conspiracy. As Secretary of the Indian

Association, he arranged the earlier meetings of protest. His influence in the city is proved to be infinitely greater than that of any of his companions. He attended the meeting of the 11th of April at the Badshahi Mosque and took the leading part in the appointment of a committee to continue the *hartal,* and in the raising of subscriptions for *langar khanas.* When the meeting broke up, he invited the mob to come again next day and he came himself with Rambhaj Dutt and Harkishen Lal. On the 13th at the Town Hall he deliberately put forward Allah Din, a stranger and mob orator, to tell the meeting what was happening in the city. This man had spoken on the 11th at the mosque and on the 12th at Duni Chand's own house and had no qualification for the task beyond the violence of his language. Duni Chand further threatened the authorities with the possibility of a riot, as the consequence of not acceding to his request for the release on bail of Moti Ram, and behaved throughout as an acknowledged leader; considering what had happened and was happening, the one incident of calling the meeting of the 12th in the Shahi Mosque, which he must have known would end in bloodshed, would be sufficient in itself for a conviction of waging war, and taken with the remainder of the evidence it established beyond doubt that Duni Chand was a most active member of the conspiracy.

Dharam Das (No. 4) is an irresponsible and excitable fanatic, who does not appear to be taken very seriously by most people. He is deeply interested in philanthropic and religious movements and is a prominent preacher of the Brahmo Samaj. On the 4th February he made an intemperate and incoherent speech at the Bradlaugh Hall, and he accompanied Duni Chand and Harkishen Lal to the Shahi Mosque on the 11th April, but he did not go again on the 12th. Considering the peculiar temperament of this man and his incessant pursuit of notoriety, as evidenced by his frequent speeches at all sorts of meetings, we think that the most favourable interpretation of his conduct must be accepted. In spite of his love of public speaking, he took no part in the proceedings on the 11th and he abstained from accompanying Duni Chand and Harkishen Lal to the meeting, which he knew would take place on the following day. This we believe to mean that he did not know the grave nature of the situation until he arrived at the mosque on the 11th, and that on realising what was happening he deliberately refrained from further action.

Gokal Chand (No.5) took an active part in the earlier stages of the agitation, and we are not satisfied with his explanation of his conduct at the meeting of the 6th April. His conviction, however, depends on the part played by him in the later events. It had already been explained that we do not regard participation in the meeting at Mr. Shafi's house on the 12th as a criminal act. His did not attend either of the mosque meetings and his election to committees in his absence is no proof of his intent to wage war. Possibly, his absence was due only to an instinct of self-preservation; but on the 6th April when matters looked serious, he used his influence on the right side; and on the whole we think that the facts point to the conclusion that he was averse to open defiance of authority, and that it was for this reason that he did not join in instigating the populace to prolong the *hartal*.

Mathra Parshad (No. 6) is a peripatetic minstrel. On the 6th April he recited a poem, of which the general tone and one line in particular were seditious, but he had no connection with the events after that date.

Habibullah (No. 7) is a young man of good family and some property, who was probably drawn into this agitation by mere desire for notoriety. He would have been much better advised to leave politics alone, but the case against him is largely based on misconceptions. His speech on the 9th March was in support of a compromise designed to avoid the *Satyagraha* vow, and that of the 6th April has been misinterpreted by the prosecution as the result of a mistake which is now admitted. He did not attend the mosque meetings and he was not responsible for his election to the *hartal* committees. Indeed after the 9th April he took no part in any of the proceedings.

Karam Chand (No. 8) recited on the 6th April a seditious poem which did not lose its general character by the mere insertion of certain complimentary references to the Secretary of State. We cannot, however, convict him in this trial of an isolated act of sedition at that stage. We distrust the evidence that he attempted to prevent dhobis from doing their work, and the only other point against him is that he maintained a *langar khana* on the 11th and the 12th in the Dhobi mandi, which is at some distance from the city. There is, however, reliable evidence that this kitchen was not used by the city roughs, and it was closed as soon as Government had made arrangements for the provision of supplies. Karam Chand is undoubtedly a man of charitable disposition which he has often shown in a practical way, and it is certain that he entertained no animosity towards Europeans. His recitation may have been a mere poetical extravagance, and in our opinion his *langar khana* was not intended to prolong the *hartal*.

Mohsin Shah (No. 9) is a member of the provincial Muslim League. We do not trust the evidence that he joined the mob on the 10th April and prefer his explanation as more likely to be true. The only real point against him is his attendance on the 11th at the Badshahi Mosque, where he went with Rambhaj Dutt, knowing that Mr. Fyson had sent them, if not to the mosque itself, at least to make certain communications to the populace. We are not sure that he knew what Rambhaj Dutt was going to do; and afterwards, when called upon to assist his leader, he seems to have been too frightened to open his mouth. He was not present when he was elected to the *hartal* committee and he did not return to the mosque next day. He does not appear in any of the other proceedings except those of the 13th, when he voted for unconditional surrender, and the indications are that he did not wish to provoke further resistance.

Allah Din (No. 10) was present on the 11th of April in the Badshahi mosque, where he made an inflammatory speech. His connection with the principal accused is shown by his presence on the 12th at Duni Chand's house, where he made another violent harangue, a performance which he repeated at Duni Chand's suggestion on the 13th in the Town Hall. We have no doubt that he was a member of the conspiracy and committed an act of waging war.

Mota Singh (No. 11) made a seditious speech in the Badshahi mosque on the 11th April. He is a school master from Patiala and denies that he was in Lahore that day. We find that it is fully established that he was, and that it was he and none other who made the speech in question and this after he had realised the nature of the gathering. Had he taken no part in the proceedings, it might be held that he only joined the mass meeting out of curiosity; but as soon as he made seditious speech himself, he thereby associated himself with the other speakers and by that act joined the conspiracy and committed an act of waging war.

We convict Harkishen Lal, Rambhaj Dutt, Duni Chand, Allah

Din and Mota Singh under sections 121 and 121A, Indian Penal Code, and sentence them to transportation for life and forfeiture. We do not consider it necessary to recorded finding on other charges.

Allah Din and Mota Singh are minor offenders, and had it been in our power we should in their cases have awarded much lighter sentences.

If there is any excuse for the other convicts it can only in the encouragement, direct or indirect, which they received from Delhi and Bombay.

The remaining accused are acquitted.

APPENDIX III
Proceedings in Privy Council

(I)—Amritsar National Bank Murder Case

(a) Text of Petition

The following is the full text of the petition of appeal to the Privy Council on behalf of Bugga, Rattan Chand, Ghulam Hassan, (son of Ida), Faqir, Asadulla, Karam Chand, Karm Bakhsh, Manohar Singh, Muhammadi, Jani, Nizam, Feroze, Chiragh, Sadru, Ghulam Hassan (son of Makhan), Inayat, Ghulam Rasul, Harnam Singh, Mehr Sain, Sandhi, and Roshan, petitioners, *Versus* the King-Emperor, opposite party :—

To the King's Most Excellent Majesty in Council, the humble petition of the petitioners above-named sheweth :—

1. Your petitioners, 21 in number, are native British subjects living at Amritsar in the Punjab who have been sentenced to death, with the exception of your petitioner Ghulam Hassan (No. 15) who has been sentenced to seven years' rigorous imprisonment under Martial Law by a Special Commission purporting to exercise the powers of a Summary General Court-Martial. Your petitioners, however, are not soldiers or subject to Military Law and desire to obtain special leave to appeal from the sentences pronounced upon them in the circumstances following.

2. On the 10th April, 1919, a riot took place in the city of Amritsar. The riot was over by the evening of that day. None of your petitioners were taken in arms or taken in the actual commission of any overt act of rebellion or otherwise taken in the act within the meaning of paragraph I of Regulation X of 1804, which Regulation confers powers to provide for the immediate punishment of the offences therein specified by sentence of Court-Martial. By Act IV of 1872, passed by the Governor-General of India in Council, Section 3, Regulation X of 1804 is declared to be in force, but this Regulation only confers powers to punish civilian inhabitants by sentence of Court-Martial within the limits above indicated and your petitioners, therefore, did not fall within it.

3. On the contrary your petitioners were arrested while peaceably occupied at their homes or otherwise, some days after the riot was

over. No copy of the charges against them is available but the accusation against your petitioners was that of committing an offence under Section 121 and other Sections of the Indian Penal Code (Act XLV of 1860). Section 121 is as follows :—

> 'Whoever wages war against the Queen, or attempts to wage such war, or abets the waging of such war, shall be punished with death, or transportation for life and shall forfeit all his property.'

Offences against the Indian Penal Code are to be tried by the Criminal Courts referred to in Section 28 of the Code of Criminal Procedure (Act V of 1898) and no jurisdiction to try by Court-Martial is thereby conferred.

4. On April 14, 1919, the Governor-General of India, purporting to act under Section 72 of the Government of India Act 1915, made the Martial Law Ordinance No. I of 1919 which came into operation at midnight on the 15th April, 1919. Ordinance No.I is as follows :—

[*For text of the Ordinance No. 1 of 1919, see Appendix I, Pages 202-203, Ante*]

5. It will be observed that Ordinance No. I was given a retrospective effect, but it only applied to offences committed on or after the 13th April 1919. Inasmuch as the accusation against your petitioners was of offences committed on the 10th April, 1919, Martial Law Ordinance No. I had no application to them.

6. As a matter of fact, perfect order had been restored in the city of Amritsar by the 15th April 1919. The Civil, Criminal and other Courts throughout continued to administer justice in the ordinary course without any interruption and there was in fact no ground for having recourse to Martial Law or to exceptional tribunals on the ground that the Ordinary Courts were not discharging their functions. Nevertheless, your petitioners were not brought before the Ordinary Courts of the country.

7. On April 21st, 1919, the Governor-General of India purporting to act under Section 72 of the Government of India Act, 1915, made a further Ordinance No. 4 of 1919, which is in terms following :—

[*For text of Ordinance No. 4 of 1919, see Appendix I, Page 206, Ante*].

8. It will be observed that this later made ordinance does not purport to suspend the operation or sittings of the Ordinary Courts.

Its principal object appears to be to extend the retrospective operation of Ordinance No.2 so as to cover offences of still earlier date.

9. Your petitioners were tried by a Commission presided over by a Military Officer purporting to be appointed under Ordinance No. 1 of 1919, with the powers of a Summary General Court-Martial and sitting at Lahore on the 29th May, 1919, and the following days. Your petitioners were prevented by a summary order of the Military Authorities which prohibited all persons from entering the area in which Martial Law had been proclaimed from obtaining the assistance of Counsel engaged by them. Your petitioners are of right entitled to be defended by Counsel under the provisions of Section 340 of the Code of Criminal Procedure (Act V of 1898) and your petitioners' defence was therefore seriously prejudiced.

10. On June 2, 1919, the said Commission purported to convict your petitioners, of offences under Section 121 of the Indian Penal Code and passed sentences of death and confiscation of your petitioners' property. The judgment of the Commission marked 'A' is attached hereto.

11. Your petitioners submit that the said Commission had no jurisdiction to try your petitioners for the offences under Section 121 of the Indian Penal Code or for any other offence under the Ordinances above mentioned, and that the Ordinary Courts were the only Courts which had jurisdiction to try your petitioners for any offence alleged to have been committed by them on April 10, 1919.

12. Section 72 of the Government of India Act 1915 confers upon the Governor-General a power to make Ordinances in cases of emergency but the power of making Ordinances under that Section is subject to the restrictions set out in Section 65 Sub-section 2, and your petitioners contend that the law and constitution therein referred to, upon which their allegiance depends, is violated and set at naught by depriving them of a proper trial with full means of defence before Courts constituted for that purpose.

13. Your petitioners further contend that, inasmuch as Regulation X of 1804 deals solely with certain offences therein specified when committed by persons who are taken in the act of committing them, the Commission appointed under Ordinance No. 1 of 1919 is in any case limited by this jurisdiction to trial of offences of this character, and that upon its true construction Ordinance No. 4 of 1919, while increasing the retrospective effect of Ordinance No. 1, does not validly

confer a jurisdiction to deal with offences of another kind. If any other construction is adopted your petitioners contend that Ordinance No. 4 and also Ordinance No. 1 are *ultra vires* and unconstitutional.

14. Your petitioners further contend that it is not competent to the Governor-General to confer upon a new tribunal such as the said Commission a jurisdiction to try accused persons on the charge of having committed certain acts before the said Commission was created, and that a Court-Martial or other exceptional tribunal substituted for it cannot lawfully and constitutionally deal with such cases inasmuch as proclamation of Martial Law itself cannot have a retrospective effect.

15. Your petitioners further submit that there was no evidence to warrant the conviction of your petitioners on the charges made against them, and that they are entitled to be pronounced innocent of the charges, and that a grave denial of justice has been perpetrated.

16. The present petition has been prepared on the materials which have already reached this country from India but these materials have only arrived at the last moment and may not be complete so that your petitioners desire to reserve the right to urge further objections to the validity of the proceedings and the jurisdiction of the Court when the complete record is available. Your petitioners therefore humbly pray that your most Excellent Majesty in Council will be pleased to order that your petitioners shall have special leave to appeal from the said order of conviction and sentences dated the 2nd June, 1919, of the said Commission, and that the said Commissioners may be ordered to transmit forthwith the transcript of all proceedings and evidence of the said trial to the registrar of the Privy Council or for such other order as to your Majesty may seem just and proper.

And your petitioners will ever pray, &c.

'A'

[*Here follows a copy of the judgment in this case, for which see Appendix II, Page 329-330, ante.*]

(*b*) *The Proceedings*

In the Privy Council before the Rt. Hon. Viscount Haldane, the Rt. Hon. Lord Buckmaster and the Rt. Hon. Lord Atkinson.

Between Bugga and others, (Petitioners) *Versus* the King-Emperor, (Respondent), on appeal from the Martial Law Commissioners at Lahore.

The Rt. Hon. Sir John Simon, K. C. and Mr. B. Dube, instructed by Messrs. Barrow, Rogers and Nevill, appeared for the Petitioners.

Sir Erle Richards, K. C., and Mr. Kenworthy Browne, instructed by the Solicitor, India Office, appeared for the Respondent.

Sir John Simon's Argument

Sir John Simon :—My Lords, this is petition of twenty-one subjects of the King, Natives of India, who have been sentenced, as regards twenty of them, to death, as regards the other one, to seven years' rigorous imprisonment, by a Special Commission, which is purporting to exercise the powers of a Summary General Court-Martial.

Sir Erle Richards :—The death sentence has been commuted in fifteen cases.

Sir John Simon :—I did not know that that was the case. I suppose it has been commuted to penal servitude for life.

Sir Erle Richards :—I do not know.

Sir John Simon :—At any rate, the remaining prisoners are still under sentence of death.

Viscount Haldane :—How many are still under sentence of death?

Sir John Simon :—Five, at any rate, are still under sentence of death.

Sir Erle Richards :—I have not been able to ascertain exactly how many. Certainly two are. There is a doubt about three others on the cables. Fifteen have certainly had their sentences commuted.

Viscount Haldane :—However, it is a very serious matter?

Sir John Simon :—Yes, my Lord, in any view. The matter is not only very grave for these persons, but it is a matter, I think, of some constitutional importance, and though the materials on which this petition has been drawn have, as I gather is also the case with my learned friend, been derived largely by cable, and therefore may be a little fragmentary, I think I shall be able with confidence to put the outline of the matter strictly before your Lordships. If your Lordships would be good enough to take the petition, I have had it drawn in a way which I think will most clearly indicate what the points are. In the first paragraph we set out that the petitioners, 21 in number, are native British subjects, living at Amritsar in the Punjab, who have been sentenced to death, with the exception of your petitioner, Ghulam Hussan (No. 15) who has been sentenced to seven years' rigorous imprisonment under Martial Law by a Special Commission purporting to exercise the powers of a Summary Court-Martial. Your petitioners, however, are not soldiers or subject to Military Law, and desire to obtain special leave to appeal from the sentences pronounced upon them in the circumstances following. On the 10th April, 1919, there was a riot in the City of Amritsar.

Viscount Haldane :—A question may arise as to the powers of the General Summary Court-Martial.

Sir John Simon :—Yes.

Viscount Haldane :—And a question may arise whether the Sovereign in Council would review the proceedings of a General Court-Martial. I have never heard of it being done.

Sir John Simon :—I think we shall have to go through the story. I quite agree that may be a question. That particular point may be avoided by saying that this Special Commission, though it really derives its authority, if it has any, from a Regulation which provides for the trial of persons by Court-Martial, is nonetheless composed of not three soldiers but one soldier and two civilians.

Viscount Haldane :—What arrested my attention was something rather in your favour; that it is purporting to exercise the power of a Summary General Court-Martial.

Sir John Simon :—Yes.

Viscount Haldane :—It may be still a court with the powers of a Court-Martial ?

Sir John Simon :—That I think, putting it roughly, will turn out to be the position, but nonetheless my clients are in the position of persons who have been dealt with under the conditions of Martial Law. "On 10th April, 1919, riot took place in the City of Amritsar. The riot was over by the evening of that day. None of your petitioners were taken in arms, or taken in the actual commission of any overt act of rebellion, or otherwise taken in the act within the meaning of paragraph 1 of Regulation X of 1804"—It will be necessary to look at that Regulation—"which Regulation confers powers to provide for the immediate punishment of the offences therein specified by sentence of Court-Martial. By Act IV of 1872, passed by the Governor-General of India-in-Council, Section 3, Regulation X of 1804, is declared to be in force"—this was in the Punjab—"but this Regulation only confers power to punish civilian inhabitants by sentence of Court-Martial within the limits above indicated, and your petitioners therefore did not fall within it." The point is this. Under Regulation X of 1804, which has just been given a continuing legislative operation it has been pointed out by a learned commentator and I think will be probably accepted as correct, that paragraph 2 of the Regulation is really strictly limited to cases in which the civilian is really taken in *flagrante delicto*.

Viscount Haldane :—That is the Regulation of 1804 ?

Sir John Simon :—Yes. May I read the recital first ? I will read the first paragraph, which is really the recital: "Whereas during wars in which the British Government has been engaged against certain of the native powers of India, certain persons owing allegiance to the British Government have borne arms in open hostility to the authority of the same, and have abetted and aided the enemy, and have committed acts of violence and outrage against the lives and properties of the subjects of the said Government; and whereas it may be expedient that during the existence of any war in which the British Government may be engaged with any power whatever, as well as during the existence of open rebellion against authority of the Government"—we are coming to a document which was issued by the Governor-General, in which he recites that in his judgment open rebellion had occurred— "in any part of the British territories subject to the Government of the Presidency of Fort William, the Governor-General should declare and establish Martial Law within any part of the territories aforesaid for the safety of the British possessions and for the security of the lives and property of the inhabitants thereof, by the immediate punishment of persons owing allegiance to the British Government who may be taken in arms, in open hostility to the said Government, or in the actual commission"—that means who are taken in the actual commission—"of any overt act of rebellion against the authority of the same, or in the act"—this is to say, who may be taken in the act—"of openly aiding and abetting the enemies of the British Government within any part of the territories above specified, the following Regulation has been enacted by the Governor-General in Council to be in force throughout the British territories immediately subject to the Government of the Presidency of Fort William from the date of its promulgation." Then Section 2 : "The Governor-General in Council is hereby empowered to suspend or to direct any Public Authority or Officer to order the suspension of, wholly or partially, the functions of the ordinary Criminal Courts of Judicature within any zilla, district, city or other place, within any part of the British territories subject to the Government of the Presidency of Fort William and to establish Martial

Law therein, for any period of time while the British Government in India shall be engaged in War with any native or other power"—of course that is not this case—"as well as during the existence"—I lay particular stress on "during the existence"—"of open rebellion against the authority of the Government, in any part of the territories aforesaid, and also to direct immediate trial by Courts-Martial of all persons owing allegiance to the British Government, either in consequence of their having been born, or of their being residents, within its territories and under its protection"—these 21 persons are certainly British subjects, and owe allegiance—"who shall be taken in arms in open hostility to the British Government, or in the act of opposing by force of arms the authority of the same or in the actual commission of any overt act of rebellion against the State, or in the act of openly aiding and abetting the enemies of the British Government within any part of the said territories." On that I make these two comments: first that the persons who are contingently subject of such a mode of trial are all persons who are taken in *flagrante delicto,* and none of these 21 persons is in that position.

Viscount Haldane :— Or in the act of openly aiding or abetting the enemy.

Sir John Simon :—Yes, but *taken* governs all. These persons were not *taken* in the commission of any overt act at all. They were at their homes five or six days afterwards when they were arrested. The other point I make on Section 2 is this. Your Lordship notices that it is introduced by the power of the Governor-General, in the case of an open rebellion, to suspend wholly or partially the functions of the ordinary Criminal Courts of Judicature, and to establish Martial Law therein. The two things are related, and the scheme of this power, therefore is : first, it is limited to persons who are taken in *flagrante delicto*; and secondly, the extent to which you set up an exceptional tribunal is precisely the same, is co-extensive with, the suspension, for the time being, of the ordinary Courts for dealing with such cases, and that, of course, is quite consistent with the well-understood theory in our constitution here at home that in time of actual necessity, when the immediate necessity is to deal with persons who are actually found in a state of rebellion, it may be that on the principle of some sort of law of necessity......

Viscount Haldane :— Martial Law is not law. It is this : that the Commander-in-Chief supersedes all the Courts. He in the exercise of his power tries them by Court-Martial.

Sir John Simon :—Yes, I am only anxious to show the limitation of that. Your Lordships will take it from me, perhaps without reading it, that there is a legislative provision.

Viscount Haldane :—He may partially suspend. He may allow the Civil Courts to proceed in certain cases. A State can do anything. This is not quite consistent with the real theory of Martial Law. The Governor can do things which are analogous to Martial Law.

Sir John Simon :—Yes.

Viscount Haldane :—There was a case before this Board which I argued, and argued unsuccessfully, on appeal against the sentence of a Court-Martial in South Africa, in which Lord Halsbury gave a famous definition.

Sir John Simon :—Yes. It is a matter which has been the subject of much discussion since.

Viscount Haldane :—There it was held that Martial Law had survived the hostilities, I think.

Sir John Simon :—Not quite. At present I am not proposing to argue the matter, but to put before your Lordships in order five or six matters.

Lord Buckmaster :—It sets up a special tribunal and imposes on that tribunal the obligation of passing one sentence, and one sentence only, on the people who are brought before it.

Sir John Simon :—May I go on with my argument—though we may have to return to the consideration of the constitutional aspect of this ? I had the South African case in my mind. I am pointing out that in paragraph 2 we say : Here is Regulation X of 1804, and on the true construction of the Regulation it is limited to the case of persons who are taken in the act of doing a number of specified things. It is confirmed by legislative provision of 1872.

Viscount Haldane :—There is a remarkable provision in Section 4 which says that the Governor-General may direct people to be tried before the Ordinary Courts notwithstanding all this which by hypothesis would supersede it.

Sir John Simon :—Yes it is curious.

Viscount Haldane :—I do not suppose you are going to argue that the Governor-General could not get himself empowered to do all these things by the Indian Legislature.

Sir John Simon :—That is not the point I am going to make at all. Your Lordships will come to the point.

Viscount Haldane :—I only wanted to clear it out of the way.

Sir John Simon :—Your Lordships will understand that it will be important for the moment to see what is the extent to which Regulation of 1804 can go. I make the point that the Special Tribunal exceeded its powers. Then paragraph 3 :—

"On the contrary, your petitioners were arrested while peaceably occupied at their homes, or otherwise, some days after the riot was over." It is perfectly plain that they were not taken in the act of anything. "No copy of the charges against them is available, but the accusation against your petitioners was that of committing an offence under section 121, and other sections of the Indian Penal Code (Act XLV of 1860). Section 121 is as follows :— 'Whoever wages war against the Queen, or attempts to wage war, or abets the waging of such war, shall be punished with death, or transportation for life, and shall forfeit all his property.' Offences against the Indian Penal Code are to be tried by the Criminal Courts referred to in section 28 of the Code of Criminal Procedure (Act V of 1898), and no jurisdiction to try by Court-Martial is thereby conferred." Now we come to the special provision :—"On April 14th, 1919"— that is, four days after the riot was over—"the Governor-General of India purporting to act under Section 72 of the Government of India Act 1915"— the case I have to present to the Board largely turns on considering that section and the related sections—"made the Martial Law Ordinance No. 1, which came into operation at midnight on the 15th April, 1919."— Then we have set it out in extenso, and I will read it : "Whereas the Governor-General is satisfied that a state of open rebellion against the authority of the Government exists in certain parts of the province of the Punjab." The reason, no doubt, why that is recited is because Section 72 confers certain powers upon the Governor-General to make ordinances in cases of emergency. Again, Your Lordship will remember that in Regulation X of 1804 there had been a reference to cases where it might be expedient during the existence of open rebellion to make certain provisions. So it recites:— "Whereas the Governor-General is satisfied that a state of open rebellion against the authority of the Government exists in certain parts of the province of the Punjab, and whereas the Governor-General in Council has in exercise of the powers conferred by Section 2 of the Bengal State Offences Regulation 1804"—that is the one Your Lordships have just looked at—"suspended in respect of offences described in the said Regulation, with which any person of the classes therein referred to may be charged, the functions of the Ordinary Courts of Judicature within the districts of Lahore and Amritsar in the aforesaid provinces, and has established Martial Law in the said districts"—that is the first half of Section, 2, which I have just read to Your Lordships—"and has directed the immediate trial by Courts-Martial of all such persons charged with such offences"—those offences must necessarily be offences that you are taken in the act of committing.—"And whereas an emergency has arisen which makes it expedient to provide that such trials shall be held in the manner, and by the tribunals hereinafter provided. Now therefore the Governor-General in Council in exercise of the powers, conferred by Section 72 of the Government of India Act, 1915, is pleased to make and promulgate the following:—Ordinance No. 1, of 1919. (1) This Ordinance may be called the Martial Law Ordinance, 1919"—If the name has anything to do with it, there is no doubt what it is.—"(2) It shall come into operation at midnight between the 15th and 16th April, 1919. Every trial held under the Bengal State Offences Regulation, 1804"—that is Regulation X of 1804—"shall, instead of being held by a Court-Martial, be held by a Commission consisting of three persons appointed on this behalf by the local Government." The President is a Military Officer, and the two others are Civilians.

Sir Erle Richards :—May I say this. I do not think my friend knows the practice in the Punjab. It is true the President was in the Army to start with, but Your Lordships are probably aware that in the Punjab Civil Service they take into their employ a number of Military Officers. It was an old practice that began in troubled times. This gentleman has for 25 years been a Civil servant, and for a long time he has been acting as Sessions Judge.

Viscount Haldane :—Does he maintain his Military rank?

Sir Erle Richards :—Yes, he is a Major or a Colonel. It is a question that has been much discussed; whether they ought not to abandon their Military rank on going on to the Bench.

Sir John Simon :—I am obliged to my friend for his explanation. I was not aware of it. "The local Government may appoint"— that means the Government of the Punjab—"as many commissions for this purpose as it may deem expedient. At least two members of every such Commission shall be persons who have served as Sessions Judges, or Additional Sessions Judges, for a period of not less than three years, or persons qualified under Section 101 of the Government of India Act, 1915 for appointments as Judges of a High Court. The local Government shall nominate one of the members of the Commission to be President thereof. A Commission shall be convened by the local Government, or by such officer as the local Government may authorize in this behalf. A Commission shall have all the powers of a General Court-Martial under the Indian Army Act, 1911"—I know Lord Haldane is specially familiar with this subject matter.

Viscount Haldane :—It is a very different thing from a District Court-Martial.

Sir John Simon :—Yes. There are four kinds of Courts-Martial in the Indian Army system : a General Court-Martial, a Summary Court-Martial, a District Court-Martial and a Summary General Court-Martial.

Viscount Haldane :—Is there a Judge Advocate in India who reviews the decision of Courts-Martial ?

Sir John Simon :—There is an express provision here that they are not to be reviewed.

Viscount Haldane :—A Court-Martial goes up for review to the Judge Advocate. That is the safeguard in Courts-Martial, and here one would expect to see that there was some one who advised the Governor-General separately.

Sir John Simon :—I think it is clear by inference, from paragraph 5 of the Ordinance—"The finding and sentence of a Commission shall not be subject to confirmation by any Authority."

Sir Erle Richards :—The confirmation of a Court-Martial is necessary under the Army Act. That is to take these proceedings out of the provisions of the Army Act.

Viscount Haldane :—Under the Indian Army Act confirmation is required; is that confirmation by the Judge Advocate ?

Sir John Simon :—I think not: "The findings and sentences of General Courts-Martial may be"—I think that really means must be—"confirmed by the Commander-in-Chief in India or by any officer empowered in this behalf by the warrant of the Commander-in-Chief in India." I do not think there is a Judge Advocate.

Lord Buckmaster :—That means confirmation is necessary and those are the people who exercise the power ?

Sir John Simon :—Yes.

Sir Erle Richards :—There is a Judge Advocate.

Viscount Haldane :—In time of war the power is handed over to the Commander-in-Chief, and it may be that in India they have taken the situation as more approximating to war than peace, and have handed it over to the Commander-in-Chief, in which case it is natural that they should say that no confirmation is required.

Sir John Simon :—It remains to be seen whether it cannot be reviewed by the Privy Council.

Lord Buckmaster :—Does this Ordinance do more than create a Court under the provisions of the Regulation of 1804, to exercise the powers that are there conferred ?

Sir John Simon :—I do not think it does, but I point out in the paragraph immediately following after I have set out in this document that this Ordinance would not have touched me at all, it is because it did not touch me that they made another Ordinance and tried to bring me in.

Lord Buckmaster :—You would not be hurt by this Ordinance.

Sir John Simon :—No. Will Your Lordships look at paragraph 7: "Save as provided by Section 6, the provisions of this Ordinance shall apply to all persons referred to in the said Regulation". My first way of putting it is, that I am not a person referred to in the Regulation.

Viscount Haldane :—Your alleged offence was on the 10th April.

Sir John Simon :—I am not on the question of date for the moment, though it is a second reason. I am not a person who has been *taken* in the act of open rebellion or anything whatever. I have been dealt with by this summary procedure although any case against me is an inferential case depending upon evidence, and not upon the fact that I was seen there with arms in my hands taking part in the actual violence.

Viscount Haldane :—Your first point is, this tribunal does not suit your case.

Sir John Simon :—Yes.

Viscount Haldane :—Your second point I suppose is on the dates.

Sir John Simon :—Yes, in any case my offence was an offence on the 10th April, whereas this was to be limited to persons who are charged with any of the offences therein described committed on and after the 13th April.

Viscount Haldane :—I do not think any presumption should be made against the power of the Legislature to say that an offence really committed is to by tried not be such and such a Court, but by such and such another.

Sir John Simon :—It is only one of the points I am going to develop in a moment.

Lord Buckmaster :—The point applies to the second Ordinance as well.

Sir John Simon :—Yes. I have not read paragraph 4. Will Your Lordships look at that ? After providing that it is to have the power of General Court-Martial under the Indian Army Act, 1911, and "shall, subject to the provisions of this Ordinance, in all matters follow so far as may be the procedure regulating trials by such Courts-Martial prescribed by or under the said Act," it goes on : "provided that where, in the opinion of the convening authority, a summary trial is necessary in the interests of public safety."—I have some difficulty in seeing how a summary trial could be necessary in my case, it appears now it was a little too summary—"such authority may direct that the Commission shall follow the procedure prescribed for a Summary General Court-Martial by or under the said Act, and the Commission shall so far as may be and subject to the provisions of this Ordinance follow such procedure accordingly." Then it says that Sections 78, 80 and 82 of the Act are not to apply. I will tell Your Lordships what they are. Section 78 of the Indian Army Act is the Section which provides that every Court-Martial shall be attended by a Judge-Advocate or somebody nominated by him, that is to say, a man who knows something about the way in which to present a case. This is explicity removed from its application. Then Section 80 is a provision which entitles the accused to be asked whether he objects to be tried by a member of the tribunal. All that right of objection by the accused is removed. Then Section 82 is the provision that there is to be an oath of the President and Members before they try the prisoners.

So far I could not be hurt though, as I have pointed out in my paragraph 5, "It will be observed that this Ordinance No. 1 was given a retrospective effect, but it only applied to offences committed on or before the 13th April, 1919. Inasmuch as the accusation against your petitioners was of offences committed on the 10th April, 1919, Martial Law Ordinance No. 1 had no application to them (6) As a matter of fact, perfect order had been restored in the city of Amritsar by the 15th April, 1919. The Civil, Criminal, and other Courts throughout continued to administer justice in the ordinary course without any interruption, and there was in fact no ground for having recourse to Martial Law or to exceptional tribunals on the ground that the ordinary Courts were not discharging their functions. Nevertheless, your petitioners were not brought before the ordinary Courts of the country."—Then in paragraph 7 we say,—"On April 21st, 1919, the Governor-General of India, purporting to act under Section 72 of the Government of India Act, 1915, made a further Ordinance No. IV of 1919, which is in terms following : 'Simla, the 21st April, 1919. An Ordinance further to extend the application of the Martial Law Ordinance 1919. Whereas an emergency has arisen which renders it necessary to provide that commissions appointed under the Martial Law Ordinance 1919"—that is No. 1, which your Lordships have just had—'shall have power to try persons and offences other than those specified in the said Ordinance. Now, therefore, in exercise of the power conferred by Section 72 of the Government of India Act, 1915, the Governor-General is pleased to make and promulgate the following Ordinance :— No. IV of 1919. 1. This Ordinance may be called the Martial Law (Further Extension) Ordinance, 1919. 2. Notwithstanding anything contained in the Martial Law Ordinance 1919, the local Government may by general or special order direct that any commission appointed under the said Ordinance shall try any person charged with any offence committed on or after the 30th March, 1919'—that is moving the date back, and it says 'any offence'; a question will arise as to what is the true construction of that—'and thereupon the provisions of the said Ordinance shall apply to such trials accordingly, and a commission may pass in respect of any such offence any sentence authorized by law'."

Lord Buckmaster :—"Any offence" must be an offence as defined by the Regulation of 1804.

Sir John Simon :—I venture to think so.

Lord Buckmaster :—That brings it back to the same position as the other.

Sir John Simon :—If I am right in that view, which I submit with some confidence, that is a conclusive objection to the regularity of this proceeding. It has been treated as though it has conferred upon this special commission the right to try a man for obtaining credit when he is a bankrupt or any other crime in the calendar, and I venture to think it does not do anything of the sort.

Lord Buckmaster :—If you once depart from the Regulation of 1804, there are no limits.

Sir John Simon :—That is what I mean. "8. It will be observed that this later made Ordinance does not purport to suspend the operation or sittings of the Ordinary Courts." Section 2 is a thing which has two limbs : Its principal object appears to be to extend the retrospective operation of Ordinance No. 1 so as to cover offences of still earlier date. "9. Your petitioners were tried by a Commission presided over by a military officer."—I quite accept what my learned friend, Sir Erle Richard says : I call him a military officer, but I gather he will also be in the Permanent Civilian Service.

Sir Erle Richards :—He is a Sessions Judge, I think.

Sir John Simon :—"With the powers of a Summary General Court-Martial and sitting at Lahore on the 29th May, 1919, and the following days."

Your Lordships notice that this was more than a month after the Second Ordinance—"Your petitioners were prevented by a summary order of the Military authorities which prohibited all persons from entering the area in which Martial Law had been proclaimed from obtaining the assistance of Counsel."

Viscount Haldane :—If you are tried by court-martial you are not entitled to be defended by Counsel.

Sir John Simon :—I put it in the form of a dilemma. I say either I am entitled to be tried as a person who is being tried under martial law, in which case I have some very serious objections to raise, or else I am being tried by something which is not Martial Law, in which case I am entitled to Counsel—one or the other.

Viscount Haldane :—It may be the true construction is this, that is a civilian tribunal which has all the powers of a court-martial, including the power to say the prisoners can have a prisoner's friend.

Sir Erle Richards :—I do not understand my friend to say that the prisoners were not defended by Counsel. The burden of their grievance is that they were not allowed to have certain Counsel up from Bengal. My instructions are that they were defended by Counsel. At any rate, they could have got Counsel in Lahore. They wanted Counsel from Bengal and there were particular reasons why they wanted particular persons, but there was an order of the military authorities at the time that no persons from Bengal were to come into the Punjab.

Sir John Simon :—I rather infer that they got some professional assistance; but it was not the professional assistance they wanted.

Viscount Haldane :—However, there is another answer, that the Military authorities had made an order that nobody was to come from Bengal into the Punjab.

Sir John Simon :—Then paragraph 10 : "On June 2nd, 1919, the said Commission purported to convict your petitioners of offences under section 121 of the Indian Penal Code and passed sentences of death and confiscation of your petitioners' property." I do not think your Lordships need look at the judgment for the moment. I wanted to put my points in order. Before I set them out would your Lordships look at Section 72 of the Government of India Act, 1915. There is nothing new in it but it will be convenient to look at it. The Governor-General purports to be making these Ordinances under Section 72. "The Governor-General may, in cases of emergency, make and promulgate ordinances for the peace and good government of British India or any part thereof and any ordinance so made shall, for the space of not more than six months from its promulgation, have the like force of law as an Act passed by the Governor-General in Legislative Council"—these are important words—"but the power of making ordinances under this section is subject to the like restrictions as the power of the Governor-General and the Legislative Council to make laws". Therefore, one asks oneself where shall one find the restrictions on the power of the Governor-General and the Legislative Council to make laws. You will find that in Section 65, sub-section 2, which contains a provision which is not by any means new, which has more than once been commented on and expounded, and which is really the protection for constitutional liberty in India. It is this: "Provided, that the Governor-General in Legislative Council has not, unless expressly so authorized by Act of Parliament, power to make any law repealing or affecting (i) any act of Parliament passed after the year one thousand eight hundred and sixty and extending to British India (including the Army Act and any Act amending the same); or (ii) any Act of Parliament enabling the Secretary of State in Council to raise money in the United Kingdom for the Government of India; and has not power to make any law affecting the authority of Parliament, or any part of the unwritten laws or constitution of the United Kingdom of Great Britain and Ireland, whereon may depend in any degree the allegiance of any person to the Crown of the United Kingdom, or affecting the sovereignty or dominion of the Crown over any part of British India."

I submit it has already been so construed in India that what that refers to is this : it is a principle which is as old as Calvin's case. Allegiance and protection are reciprocally due from the subject and the Crown and the constitutional laws that provide for the liberty of the subject are the *quid pro quo* for the duty of allegiance. This is precisely the constitutional proposition which in a very famous passage Chief Justice Cockburn expounded in his charge to the Jury in the Jamaica Riots Case, the Queen *Vs*. Nelson. He there explains exactly the same proposition. He says that the reason why it is not constitutional to put civilians upon trial by Court-Martial is this. Your Lordships remember that Nelson and the other accused persons had sat upon the Court-Martial and sentenced somebody to death and he was shot, and they were subsequently tried for murder in this country. He points out, "the reason why a civilian cannot be put on trial by Court-Martial, among other things, is precisely because you get the allegiance of persons to the Crown in a reciprocal relation with the constitutional guarantee of a regular trial in the ordinary Courts of Law." It is rather interesting to notice that Chief Justice Cockburn anticipates, or at any rate speaks in exactly the same terms as Regulation X of 1804. He says, "Nothing that I am saying applies to the case where a man is taken with arms in his hands in the midst of a violent disturbance." He points out, "in a case such as that it may well be that apart from any application of law the authorities, not because they are applying any law but because they are dealing with it from the necessities of the case, may have to shoot him out of hand." He is pointing out that there is this relation between allegiance on the one hand and constitutional protection on the other, and apparently that is exactly what is meant here when the Governor-General is given certain very extreme powers. You see how extreme they are, because Regulation X itself gives a very remarkable power; but it is not a power that can be exceeded. Those words are to be given a meaning.

Viscount Haldane :—Is the Queen *Vs*. Nelson reported in the Law Reports?

Sir John Simon :—I have here from the Inner Temple Library Chief Justice Cockburn's charge to the Jury, with some comments by Mr. Finlay, whose book is of great interest. I rather think your Lordship referred to it when you applied for leave to appeal in the South African case. I want to read two or three short passages.

Lord Buckmaster :—I am always afraid that in fixing my attention too closely upon one point I may prevent my mind from grasping the real value of the others. Up to the moment, it seems to me that the real point in this petition is this, that the Governor-General exercised powers conferred by the statute of 1804, and that he was entitled to do so.

Sir John Simon :—Certainly.

Lord Buckmaster :—The Order that he issued was an Order which purported in terms to relate and to relate only to those offences that were prescribed in the Regulation of 1804.

Sir John Simon :—Yes.

Lord Buckmaster :—The subsequent Ordinance that was issued did nothing except that it caused previous Ordinance to have a retrospective effect.

Sir John Simon :—Yes.

Lord Buckmaster :—You say the Regulation of 1804 has no application to you because according to its true construction the man must either be taken in arms or in an overt act of rebellion or an act of openly aiding and abetting the enemies of the British Government. You say none of those circumstances apply to your clients?

Sir John Simon :—That is so. I agree to have rather moved from one point to the other. Before I submit what is really a separate ground, the ground of Section 72, may I just a little expound the point which Lord Buckmaster has referred to. I want to point out that one has in these matters to be candid, just as candid when one is opposed as when one is applying *ex parte*. It is a possible contention that Ordinance No. IV, the amending Ordinance, not merely increases the retrospective effect, goes back to an earlier date, but that the reference to any offence brings in any offence in the calendar of criminal law. On that I make submission that it is not so, and I point out this special reason why it could not be so.

Lord Buckmaster :—It is only the offences therein described.

Sir John Simon :—Yes, and there is this further reason. It is a direction that a Commission appointed under Ordinance No. 1 is to have certain powers. You see what the Commission under Ordinance No. 1 is : It is a Commission that is appointed to exercise the same functions as a Court-Martial would exercise under Regulation X, and, therefore, the two things will not fit. You get a Commission which is not rightly described, if it is really to be regarded as authorised to run over the whole body of the Indian Penal Code.

Lord Buckmaster :—It is not any offence; it is any of the offences described in the previous Regulation.

Sir John Simon :—Yes.

Lord Atkinson :—It alters the date, but not the kind of offence.

Sir John Simon :—That is what I feel. Therefore I am in this opinion, that no single one of these 21 cases, whatever may be said against the men and whatever the evidence may have been about which I know very little, was a case of a man being taken in the act there described. It would follow, if that construction was right, that there has been here a very grave misunderstanding of the Commission's powers.

Lord Buckmaster :—Is there any reference in the Second Ordinance that was issued except the reference in Section 2, to any offence?

Sir John Simon :—I have the advantage of having an alternative case. I am confining myself, and it is much better to do so, to the first way of putting it, which is the way Lord Buckmaster is now putting it to me. In that connection, may I give your Lordships one other reference, a reference which I venture to think is of very great interest. I owe this to the researches of my friend Mr. Dube. I have here a book which I have also got from the Inner Temple Library called Hough's Practice of Courts-Martial. Captain Hough was a Deputy Judge Advocate General. This book was published at Calcutta in 1834.

Viscount Haldane :—This is with regard to Indian Courts-Martial.

Sir John Simon :—Yes.

Viscount Haldane :—I have never heard of this book.

Sir John Simon :—It is a book of great interest, 1834, is after Regulation X of 1804. It is pointed out by my learned friend that on page 345 of that book there is extracted an extremely interesting document which is addressed to the Secretary to the Government, the Judicial Department by the Advocate General of that time, a gentleman named Mr. Spankie, relative to the Native Detachment Courts-Martial at Cuttack from 14th September 1817 to 4th March 1818. He extracts the report there named. What the Advocate General is saying is this. "(1). It appears from the documents referred to that Martial Law was put in force under the orders of Government by virtue of Regulation X of 1804. (2). The preamble of the Regulation states that it may be expedient, in certain cases therein mentioned, that 'the Governor-General in Council should declare and establish martial law for the safety of the British possesssions, etc., by the immediate punishment of persons owing allegiance to the British Government who may be taken in arms, in open hostility to the said Government, or in the actual commission of any overt act of rebellion against the authority of the same, or in the act of openly aiding and abetting the enemies of the British Government within any part of the territories above specified.' (3). This enacting part conformable to the object developed in the preamble enacts". Then he sets it out. Then he makes this comment.

"Four overt acts are enumerated, and it seems to me quite clear that the word *taken* in the first, must, on necessary construction, be carried forward and annexed to each member of the sentence containing the description of the overt act."

Viscount Haldane :—Which section is he quoting there?

Sir John Simon :—Section 2. He says the word "taken" is mentioned in the first of the four overt acts. He says, it "must on necessary construction be carried forward and annexed to each member of the sentence containing the description of the overt act." Then he says : "Here the circumstances in which the Courts-Martial are to have authority to try are clearly marked and defined. The criminal must be taken in open acts of the treasonable and rebellious description mentioned. It seems to me also liable to some doubt whether the fourth overt act specified in the Regulation does not mean an aiding and abetting of such enemies of the British Government as are contemplated both in the preamble and in section 2—enemies with which the British Government may be engaged in war,—not the rebels with arms in their hands. If there could be any doubt of the extent of the authority and jurisdiction of the Courts-Martial under Regulation X of 1804, it would be removed by the instruction of 11th April, 1805, communicated for their guidance to the authorities in Cuttack during the late disturbances. These instructions, (paragraph 4) say 'If any person or persons charged with any of the overt acts of rebellion specified in Regulation X of 1804, shall be apprehended by any Military Officer when not in the actual commission of offences of that description they are to be delivered over by the Military to the Civil Power.'

The Courts-Martial in Cuttack do not appear to have considered themselves as at all confined to the cases of prisoners taken in *flagrante delicto* or even to traitorous and rebellious acts of the specific quality stated in the Regulation. They seem to have acted as if they had possessed an unqualified jurisdiction over all treasonable and rebellious acts without limitation of time, place or circumstance. The charge (conforming as in all limited jurisdiction it ought to the cases in which the jurisdiction is given) does not state the circumstance of the criminal being *taken* in the fact, or that it was in some open act of the treasonable, rebellious quality which alone the Court-Martial could lawfully try." Then he proceeds to discuss the cases. I am anxious to take the same points here.

Viscount Haldane :—To sum that up, the word 'taken' governs. Your case is that he must be *taken*?

Sir John Simon :—Yes.

Viscount Haldane :—Do you say *'taken in arms'*?

Sir John Simon :—I think the construction is fairly clear.

Viscount Haldane :—You say they must be *taken in arms*?

Sir John Simon :—There are four cases. The first is that they should he *taken* in arms; the second case is *taken* in the act of opposing by force of arms; the third is *taken* in the actual commission of any overt act of rebellion; and the fourth is *taken* in the act of openly aiding and abetting the enemy. That is not what happened here.

Lord Buckmaster :—In order to be quite clear about the effect of the second Ordinance, is not this worthy of note, that either it must be strictly limited to the offences under the Regulation of 1804, or it must have an indefinite application?

Sir John Simon :—Yes.

Lord Buckmaster :—Under the Regulation of 1804, the powers conferred by which are the powers that the Commissioners are to exercise and nothing else as far as I can see, there is only one sentence, death.

Sir John Simon :—Yes.

Lord Buckmaster :—If, therefore, this were to refer to any offence, it would mean that if you caught a boy doing something silly in the street, you would have no alternative but to sentence him to death and to leave it in the power of the Viceroy to exercise the King's clemency to reprieve him from a sentence which obviously could not be executed. That seems to be a patent reason why the second Ordinance can only relate to the offences mentioned in the first.

Sir John Simon :—I accept all that. It is right to point out, of course, that the second Ordinance does enact that the Commission may pass in respect of any such offence any sentence authorised by law, but the only sentence that is really authorised by law is death. That is one way I put it. Though I am not attempting to discuss the matter, I want to point out that I have a second alternative which I venture to submit is just as powerful, and it is this. I impeach the authority of the Governor-General in Council to pass such an Ordinance as No. IV, if it has any wider construction than that. Supposing against me, on its true construction Ordinance No. IV does cover an offence which is against paragraph 121 of the Code, I think it will turn out that these men were arraigned simply on a charge of breaking paragraph 121 of the Code, in which case they are entitled to say these whole proceedings are *coram non judice*. The three judges are sitting there with limited jurisdiction and they seem to have thought they could try these people for ordinary murder. That would be conclusive answer. But it is said, on its true construction the Governor-General in Council in an emergency has power to pass an Ordinance which will empower a jurisdiction wider than Regulation X of 1804, then I say, granted that is so there may be such cases, but it cannot take the form of a proceeding against a man for what is in effect a breach of allegiance, while at the same time refusing to give him the constitutional protection which the law provides.

The constitutional protection which the law provides is as old as the Petition of Rights. This is the very thing which our ancestors insisted upon. I have traced it back a long way and the meaning of it is that although in times of emergency the Governor-General has very important powers which no loyal British subject would in any way seek unduly to cut down, still those powers are by the express terms of the statute limited by reference to Section 65 Sub-section 2, and Section 65 Sub-section 2 is a section which says that the unwritten laws and constitution of the United Kingdom of Great Britain and Ireland whereon may depend the allegiance of any person cannot in any way be affected. This has been raised in India. Your Lordships will find an interesting discussion on that in the 6th volume of the Bengal Law Reports. It is a case of *in re* Ameer Khan, Mr. Justice Norman says at page 452: "Now if it be true as laid down in Calvin's case, that *protection trehit subjectionem et subjectio protectionem,* that allegiance and protection are reciprocally due from the subject and the Sovereign, it is evident that the strict observance of the laws which provide for such liberty and security ensures faithful and loving allegiance of subjects. The infraction of such laws may be carried to such an extent as to give rise to the right of self-defence on the part of the subject, a right, which, says Sir Michael Foster, 'the law of nature giveth, and no law of society hath taken away.' No man can study the history of England or can read the great judgment passed by the High Court of Parliament by the Bill of Rights on King James, II, without seeing that on the faithful observance by the Sovereign of the unwritten laws and constitution of the United Kingdom, as contained in the great Charter and other acts which I have mentioned, depend in no small degree the allegiance of the subject. It would be a startling thing to find that rights of so sacred a character could be taken away by an act of the subordinate legislature.

Viscount Haldane :—My criticism upon that is that it is so general and vague that there is hardly a thing in our constitution that would not come against this. Does not that mean the power of the Crown with regard to naturalisation and with regard to the denial to a man of his specific rights as a British subject ?

Sir Erle Richards :—Your Lordships may remember that this argument was before the Board very recently in the case of Mrs. Besant.

Viscount Haldane :—Did Lord Phillimore in his judgment say anything about it ?

Sir Erle Richards :—There is a passage in 46 Indian Appeals.

Viscount Haldane :—Lord Phillimore gave a very elaborate judgment.

Sir Erle Richards :—Yes. May I read one passage on this point? Mrs. Besant had raised the point in regard to the Press Act. Lord Phillimore giving the reasons of the Board said "It was contended in the High Court and before this Board that it was beyond the competency of the Indian Legislature to enact Section 23 and possibly even to enact the Press Act. This argument which was mainly founded upon the language of Mr. Justice Norman in the case of Ameer Khan (6th Bengal Law Reports at page 451), received some encouragement from the O.C.J. But their Lordships find themselves unable to appreciate it."

Viscount Haldane :—The Press Act was an Act interfering with the liberty of the subject simply.

Sir Erle Richards :—Yes.

Viscount Haldane :—I want to see how allegiance comes in here. What this Act does is to set up a special tribunal.

Sir John Simon :—I think it is rather more than that. I should submit that it would be strictly correct to say that it is part of the constitution and indeed part of the unwritten law of the Kingdom upon which allegiance depends at any rate in some degree that subjects should be tried in the ordinary course of law and that civilians should not be submitted to the tender mercies of what is in effect a Court-Martial.

Viscount Haldane :—What connection has that with allegiance except that it may shake the allegiance ?

Sir John Simon :—That is the connection.

Viscount Haldane :—To that extent every change of law does.

Lord Atkinson :—Supposing there is a statute making a certain thing a crime that was not a crime before ?

Sir John Simon :—That would be an example.

Viscount Haldane :—It is done daily in this country. Look at the Children's Act, for instance. Parents were put under restrictions with regard to their children.

Sir John Simon :—May I read one or two passages from Chief Justice Cockburn's charge, which has been referred to already ? They do bear very directly on the point I am making. I am merely selecting two or three passages because Your Lordships do not want the whole matter argued out now. On page 29, Chief Justice Cockburn is addressing the jury in these terms : "But on the other hand, I think it impossible to entertain a shadow of doubt that these proceedings were utterly illegal. If it be true that you can apply Martial Law for the purpose of suppressing rebellion, it is equally certain that you cannot bring men to trial for treason under Martial Law after a rebellion has been suppsressed. It is well established according to the admission of everybody, even of those who go the farthest in upholding Martial Law, that the only justification of it is founded on the assumption of an absolute necessity—a necessity paramount to all law and which, lest the commonwealth should perish, authorises this arbitrary and despotic mode of proceeding; but it never has been said or thought except perhaps by King Henry VII that Martial Law could be resorted to when all the evils of rebellion have passed away and order and tranquility had been restored for the mere purpose of trying to punish persons whom there was no longer any sufficient cause for withdrawing from the ordinary tribunals and the ordinary law."

The other passage which I have noted is on page 47, where the Chief Justice says. "I have now gone through the history of this country so far as relates to Martial Law. I believe I have mentioned every instance in which Martial Law has ever been proclaimed or been referred to. But I own that on this point I speak with considerable diffidence, for I cannot claim to have made history my special study, and my researches on this particular matter have necessarily been confined to the intervals of constant and severe judicial labour and historians may therefore very likely be aware of facts which have escaped me; but so far as I have been able to discover no such thing as Martial Law has ever been put in force in this country against civilians for the purpose of putting down rebellion."

There are other passages which I need not trouble about now. My other point is a good one, but I do certainly desire to have the opportunity of developing as I think it might be developed, the argument that supposing it could not said......

Lord Buckmaster :—It is much more serious thing than the other.

Sir John Simon :—It is, supposing it might be said that the second of those Ordinances, so far as its true construction goes, confers upon this wholly exceptional tribunal a power to sentence people to death because at some previous date it is said that there is evidence to show that they took part in a disturbance, then I do most respectfully submit that a subordinate legislature which is given certain limited powers by the Government of India Act has no power to do any such thing.

Viscount Haldane :—I do not know what Sir Erle Richards is going to contend. Subject to that, my impression is that the second of those Ordinances merely dealt with the offences cognizable under the Commission set up by the first Ordinance and that it did not set up a new set of offences. Is it your case that it did, Sir Erle Richards ?

Sir Erle Richards :—The view that I shall present is that the first of those Ordinances did not enlarge the nature of the offences, but the second one did.

Lord Buckmaster :—Your case is that 'any offence,' there means any offence of any sort or kind.

Sir John Simon :—Then Your Lordships appreciate I am relying upon my second string. I can see if that argument was ever likely to prevail, I should be in a strong position for saying there is plainly a limit put by the constitition of India upon the powers of the Governor-General in case of emergency to promulgate ordinances. This is the limit. It is not competent to the Governor-General, because there is an emergency, to provide three Judges nominated by a District Government to try a small boy for stealing an apple and sentence him to death.

Viscount Haldane :—I think you have a strong argument for saying that the construction of the second one is one which excludes it. If it was intended to give any such power as that, the second Ordinance is far from clear : "Notwithstanding anything contained in the Martial Law Ordinance, 1919, the local Government may, by general or special order, direct that any Commission appointed under the said Ordinance shall try any person charged with any offence committed on or after the 30th March, 1919." Are not these offences *ejusdem generie* with the offences cognizable under the other one ?

Sir John Simon :—I think so. This greatly strengthens the argument that the amending Ordinance is dealing with a Commission already constituted.

Viscount Haldane :—It may be, the view of the Government of India is that they wish the question raised and argued; but if they wish to raise any thing so big that a boy may be tried and sentenced to death for stealing an apple, one would have thought they would have put it in explicit terms.

Lord Atkinson :—If it is not confined to the earlier offences, it extends to any offence.

Sir John Simon :—Yes. I submit that at any rate it is in the circumstances not right that these very severe penalties in the case of some of these men who, in spite of the remission in the case of others, are still under sentence of death should be imposed and carried out. We were under the severest restriction of time. We were told if we did not get leave to appeal to-day, the sentence would be carried out.

Viscount Haldane :—Let us separate the points. The first is that the offences are limited to the offences cognizable under the first of the two Ordinances.

Sir John Simon :—Yes, and in that connection I put it, that when arrested these men were peaceable at heir homes. They were not taken in *flagrante delicto* in any sense. Secondly, I may point out that if upon any proper construction the Ordinances under which this alleged jurisdiction had been conferred on this tribunal is so wide as to deal with other offences, it must deal with any and every offence which by general or special order the local Government chooses to direct the Commission to deal with. That is exactly the thing which the Petition of Rights says cannot be done. It is almost in these words. The Petition of rights says that the Authorities, the Crown, the Executive, have directed Commissions to try persons for various offences and it proceeds to set out that that was unconstitutional and contrary to law, and that is the thing which as long ago as 1628 was declared to be a breach on the part of the Executive of the duty of protection which is correlative with allegiance. I submit on its true construction the second Ordinance merely carried the time further back. May I call attention to the other points I make ? I also make this point. I submit, that an exceptional Tribunal cannot be substituted for the ordinary law here, so that it can deal with retrospective matters, among other things for this reason that a Proclamation of Martial Law itself cannot have any retrospective effect. Chief Justice Cockburn points out in his charge to the jury, to which I have referred. A Proclamation of Martial Law may by way of warning have an operative effect from the time of the Proclamation, but it cannot in itself confer jurisdiction which did not exist before to deal with matters which have already passed.

Viscount Haldane :—Let us suppose the construction were this, that the powers are the existing powers which are simply handed to the Commission to apply; the offences are not new offences but only the mode of trial is new and exceptional. The Viceroy sets up this Tribunal, and he says it is to try people for all offences committed since a certain date in March.

Sir John Simon :—It is a separate point, and not a point necessary for me at this stage but it is a point I want to save because when one reads Regulation X of 1804, a question will arise as to what is the meaning of conferring jurisdiction upon a special Tribunal to deal with persons who shall be taken in arms. It may be that the meaning of it is that you are to suspend the ordinary law. There might be a Proclamation warning every body that a very exceptional situation had arisen, and then saying that anybody who is taken with arms in their hands or is in open rebellion is going to be dealt with by drum-head Court-Martial. It is a very different proposition to say that a Proclamation could be made saying that something that a man did three days ago was going to be dealt with by an exceptional Tribunal. I have raised I think sufficient grounds for the purposes of to-day.

Lord Buckmaster :—I suppose there will be this answer on your first point. They are going to say that the second Ordinance was passed under the Statute of 1915, and that they did not attempt to rely upon the power given by the 1804 Regulation as they did in the first, and secondly, they must have intended to cover something which the first Ordinance did not cover.

Sir John Simon :—Yes.

Lord Buckmaster :—What do you say to that ?

Sir John Simon :—I say first of all the amending Ordinance, No.4, the Martial Law Amending Ordinance, is in terms dealing with a Commission appointed under Martial Law Ordinance No. 1.

Viscount Haldane :—And it is to extend its application ?

Sir John Simon :—Yes. You must therefore say : What Commission is this about which you are speaking ? You find it is a Commission which is given a jurisdiction subject to a limit of date within the ambit of Regulation No. X of 1804.

Lord Buckmaster :—That is not quite what is in my mind. I think what can be said against you is this : If the object of this second Ordinance was merely to make the first Ordinance retrospective, it would not be necessary to invoke the powers conferred by Section 72 of the Act.

Sir John Simon :—It has been done in both cases. The same thing has been done. It gets rid of that difficulty. There is no question that it is done under Section 72.

Sir Erle Richards :—The Governor-General can only make Ordinances under that section.

Lord Atkinson :—The first Ordinance comes into operation on the 15th and 16th April, and it takes cognizance of all offences committed after the 13th April.

Sir John Simon :—Yes. The only other thing I wanted to mention is this : Sometimes when petitioners are able to get leave to appeal from Your Lordships they are limited to the grounds which they indicated in their petition. I hope that Your Lordships, if you are minded, after hearing the argument, to give leave, will not limit me in that way, because really the matter has come to our knowledge very recently. We are dealing with fragmentary materials, and we should go into the matter more fully if Your Lordships give leave, and put forward any further grounds which occurred to us.

(*Counsel and parties are ordered to withdraw and after a short time are called in again*).

Viscount Haldane :—Sir Erle, as at present advised, there is one point on which their Lordships want you to satisfy them that there has been no miscarriage of justice, that is that the second Ordinance enlarges the powers under the first, because if the powers under the first are not enlarged they do not extend the time unless a person is taken in the act. Will you confine yourself to that point ? Really, it is a very formidable point. If we give leave to appeal here, we should not be able to confine, or think it right to confine, the appellants with regard to the other points which come in incidentally, although it may be that we should not have given leave on those points.

Sir Erle Richards' Argument

Sir Erle Richards appearing on behalf of the Secretary of State :— I am very well aware of the very great importance of this point, because these are not the only men who have been sentenced by this sort of Tribunal. There was a very general rising in the Punjab, and a number of Europeans were murdered. I want Your Lordships to remember that it is a matter of great importance.

Viscount Haldane :—We realise that.

Sir Erle Richards :—Everybody who has been convicted would then have a right of appeal to this Board.

Lord Buckmaster :—No, only the people who have been convicted when they have been seized otherwise than *flagrante delicto*.

Sir Erle Richards :—That is a large number.

Viscount Haldane :—All we can do is to look at the Ordinances.

Sir Erle Richards :—It is really such an extremely short point that I do not want to press it, if Your Lordships think there is a case to be argued; but the arguments I shall advance, if this case is to be argued in detail, are these.

Lord Atkinson :—In its terms, Ordinance IV extends to everything. It can never have been intended to extend to everything. You must look for some restriction and the only place you find it, as it seems to me, is in the Regulation of 1804.

Sir Erle Richards :—May I put it in this way ?

Lord Atkinson :—Where do you find the restriction ? It cannot be intended to extend to every crime.

Lord Buckmaster :—What you want is to avoid the Board expressing any definite opinion if we thought it was a proper case for argument on appeal.

Sir Erle Richards :—I do want to put the sort of arguments, that I shall advance before Your Lordships. I think the whole thing turns upon this Ordinance. We are not dealing with Martial Law but a statutory enactment.

Viscount Haldane :—In a most significant way, the Governor-General in Council has referred to the Bengal State Regulation of 1804. It would have been perfectly open to him to have said—"Under my powers of 1915, I make a new Ordinance" instead of which he says, "I refer to the Bengal Regulation".

Sir Erle Richards :—May I read this last Ordinance because I think it turns largely upon that. It is very short. It begins in this way : "Whereas an emergency has arisen which renders it necessary to provide that Commissions appointed under the Martial Law Ordinance 1919 shall have power to try persons and offences other than those specified in the said Ordinance."

Viscount Haldane :—The purpose is established by the fact that the persons charged with offences were to be persons charged with offences committed after April 12.

Sir Erle Richards :—I submit the ordinary way to construe it would be that "every person" means persons other than those taken in the act, and so forth.

Viscount Haldane :—If the Governor-General made such a revolutionary change in the law, and said that everybody was to be tried for stealing a pair of boots or getting drunk in the streets before this Commission by Martial Law, would not he have said so ?

Sir Erle Richards :—I do not think the Ordinance gives that power at all. If your Lordship would look at paragraph 2, what it says is this : "Notwithstanding anything contained in the Martial Law Ordinance 1919, the local Government may, by general or special order, direct that any Commission appointed under the said Ordinance shall try any person charged with any offence committed on or after the 30th March, 1919." That is the thing which is to be found all through the Indian legislation. You give the local Government the power of sending offences for trial to this Commission.

Viscount Haldane :—The Criminal Law is the same all over India: there is a general Code for the Criminal Law which is applicable to India generally. Is it not very extraordinary, if there is to be a change in the nature of the Courts, that it should go over to the local Government ?

Sir Erle Richards :—No, I think not. I could find cases where there are exceptional things to be dealt with and the local Government is given the power of deciding whether those cases should be exceptionally dealt with.

Viscount Haldane :—This is much wider; this is saying that the local Government shall have the power to direct that a man charged with the offence of embezzlement is to be tried by Court-Martial. I should have thought they would have said so if that was intended. It is a matter of very high policy to give that power to the local Government. I am only referring to one of the possibilities of the system.

Sir Erle Richards :—It is from the point of view of the Indian State, because possibilities of the construction are that the change to the local Government was meant to prevent these offences being submitted to this Special Tribunal. All through the Indian Statute books you find this sort of discretion vested in the local Government. The local Government has authorised the trial of any person before this Commission. You may say it is a wide power, but it is not an unreasonable power, because the Lieutenant-Governor will settle whether the case is a proper one to be tried or not. That, I submit, is not an unreasonable construction.

Lord Atkinson :—It is an authorised provision ?

Sir Erle Richards :—If it is a statute it is authorised. I will deal with that point in a moment. The Indian legislative body has ample power to make these provisions. I think I can satisfy your Lordships on that point.

Viscount Haldane :—It is worded in such a way as to be susceptible of two constructions, and to my mind the limited construction is just as natural for the words as the wider one. That being so, the change purported to be made points to the limited construction.

Sir Erle Richards :—At this stage I do not want to prolong the argument.

Viscount Haldane :—I am very anxious that this Board should not express any definite view on it, but leave it perfectly open. Do you not think under the circumstances that as there is great doubt about the matters it had better be brought here ?

Sir Erle Richards :—If your Lordship thinks there is great doubt, I shall not say anything further about it.

May I say one word upon the other aspect of the case, and only one word ? That argument on the construction of the section has been advanced in many cases; but it has never received any support in India, except in Mr. Justice Norman's judgment, and that was upset by the Court of Appeal although they decided the case on another point.

Viscount Haldane :—I can understand the objection to giving leave to appeal to raise that question; and if it stood alone, it would be possible that we should have given leave on it, but if this case comes here, of course consistently with the proper administration of justice we should allow them to raise it; but we are not encouraging it.

Sir Erle Richards :—I am obliged to your Lordship. This is a question which does not affect only these Courts during the war. From 1915 there have been a large number of these bodies. This body is one of many such bodies which have been sitting continuously under an Act called the Defence of India Act. It would attack a great deal that has been done in India for many years past.

Viscount Haldane :—We should not give leave upon that point.

Sir Erle Richards :—I am obliged to your Lordship. I derive encouragement from that expression of opinion. May I add one word ? It is open to my friend to raise questions upon the facts in this sense, that he may point out that there was some mistake of law. That, of course, will be open to him. I would only ask on behalf of the Secretary of State, that we may have reasonable notice of the points that my friend intends to raise, because it may be necessary for us to give evidence.

Viscount Haldane :—You will give that undertaking, Sir John ?

Sir John Simon :—Certainly. I am sorry I cannot indicate more precisely now what my points will be, but my friend knows that we are acting under a severe restriction as to time.

Sir Erle Richards :—I am not complaining, because I have not the record, and I know nothing about what happend below.

The Judgment

Viscount Haldane :—We think under the circumstances it is right that there should be leave to appeal. This Board, as we have often said, is not a Court of Criminal Appeal, but there is a class of cases which is generally defined as the class of cases which falls within the category of what the Board laid down in *Dillet's Case,* in which they do advise the Sovereign to interfere where there has been a miscarriage of justice, referred for its meaning to the fundamental principles of justice; for instance, if there has been anything *coram non judice,* that is a case in point. If the argument that has been addressed to us here is right, the case has been *coram non judice.* There is one point, at any rate, on which we think that there is a serious point to argue, without expressing any opinion upon it; and that is that the second Ordinance has not extended the scope of the first Ordinance and the first Ordinance is limited to cases,where the defendant is taken *flagrante delicto*. There are other points besides that; there is the question of whether this could have retrospective action; that is quite another point. Then there is the question as to allegiance, to which reference has been made. I do not say whether we should have given leave to appeal on these points; as regards the allegiance I think we should have been reluctant to do so, but it must be open to the appellants, when they come here, to argue these points. We do not express any opinion except that we think that within the principles of Dillet's Case we are bound to advise the Sovereign that there should be a scrutiny of what has happened with a view to ascertaining whether there has been a miscarriage of fundamental principles of justice.

Lord Buckmaster :—I hope nothing I have said will be taken as expressing any considered opinion.

Sir John Simon :—We quite understand that.

Sir Erle Richards :—That will be taken as applying to anything that may have been said of the other point I have taken.

(2)—Mr. Kali Nath Roy's Case*

The following is a report of the proceedings in the Privy Council in Mr. Kalinath Roy's case :—

Present :—Viscount Haldane, Lord Dunedin, Lord Atkinson, and Lord Sumner.

Kalinath Roy (Petitioner), *Versus* the King-Emperor (Respondent).

Petition for Special Leave to Appeal from the Martial Law Commission at Lahore.

Counsel for the Petitioner :— Mr. Dube, instructed by Mr. H. S. L. Polak.

Counsel for the Respondent :— Mr. Kenworthy Browne, instructed by the Solicitor, India Office.

Mr. Dube :—My Lords, this is an application for special leave to appeal from a conviction by the Martial Law Commission under Section 124-A of the Indian Penal Code. In paragraph 2 of the petition, your Lordships will notice that the articles in connection with which the petitioner was charged were dated 3rd, 4th, 6th, 8th 9th, 10th and 11th April, 1919. They were articles in the *Tribune,* a paper of which the petitioner is editor. Under the first Ordinance of 1919, the Governor-General of India may set up a tribunal under Martial Law to try the offences under Regulation X of 1804. Two of your Lordships are aware that in a previous application for leave to appeal the question was raised that the Martial Law Commission has no jurisdiction, except in those cases in which the persons were taken in the act. May I draw your Lordships' attention to Regulation X of 1804, which makes it quite clear :— "Whereas during wars in which the British Government has been engaged against certain of the Native powers of India, certain persons owing allegiance to the British Government have borne arms in open hostility to the authority of the same, and have abetted and aided the enemy, and have committed acts of violence and outrage against the lives and properties of the said Government; and whereas it may be expedient that, during the existence of any war in which the British Government in India may be engaged with any power whatever, as well as during the existence of open rebellion against the authority of the Government in any part of the British territories subject to the Government of the

*For the Judgment of Martial Law Commission in this case, see Appendix II, Pages 322-328, *ante*.

Presidency of Fort William, the Governor-General in Council should declare and establish Martial Law within any part of the territories aforesaid for the safety of the British possessions and for the security of the lives and property of the inhabitants thereof, by the immediate punishment of persons owing allegiance to the British Government who may be *taken* in arms, in open hostility to the said Government, or in the actual commission of any overt act of rebellion against the authority of the same or in the act of openly aiding and abetting the enemies of the British Government within any part of the territories above specified; the following Regulation has been enacted by the Governor-General in Council, to be in force throughout the British territories immediately subject to the Government of the Presidency of Fort William from the date of its promulgation." Section 2 of the Regulation enacts in the same terms. Your Lordships will notice that it is persons who shall be taken in arms in open hostility to the British Government. Ordinance No. 1 of 1919 was passed under Section 72 of the Government of India Act, 1915. Your Lordships will notice that that Ordinance by Section 7 provides : "Save as provided by Section 6, provisions of this Ordinance shall apply to all persons referred to in the said Regulation who are charged with any of the offences therein described committed on or after the 13th April, 1919."

Viscount Haldane :—Where are the limiting words of the Judicial power of the Commission ? It has the power of a General Court-Martial. That we understand. Where are the words which limit their jurisdiction to what is prescribed in the Regulation of 1804 ?

Mr. Dube :—It says in the preamble of the Ordinance : "And whereas the Governor-General in Council has in exercise of the powers conferred by Section 2 of the Bengal State Offences Regulation, 1804." That is on page 1 of the petition. The submission of the petitioner is, that the power of the Governor-General is to pass this Ordinance in respect of the offences contemplated by Section 2 of Regulation X of 1804.

Viscount Haldane :—You say it is limited to what you have read ?

Mr. Dube :—It is limited to what is provided for by Section 2.

Viscount Haldane :—Mr. Browne, what is the point of Government of India upon this ? This is one of the grounds, on which we gave leave to appeal in the other case last week ?

Mr. Kenworthy Browne :—The question of the right constitution of the Court arises in this case practically in the same form as it did in the other case.

Viscount Haldane :—It is really the same question.

Mr. Kenworthy Browne :—It does not assume exactly the same form, but practically it is the same.

Lord Atkinson :—Do you not think it is very difficult to distinguish between the two cases ?

Mr. Kenworthy Browne :—Yes, subject to one question of fact which I want to submit. This man was convicted on 28th May, and was sentenced to two years' imprisonment. That sentence was reduced to three months' imprisonment, and will expire before the matter comes before your Lordships. I thought it right to bring that matter to your Lordships' notice, especially having in mind certain observations by Lord Cairns in a case that presents certain points of resemblance to this which I propose to your Lordships.

Lord Dunedin :—I think it is better that the matter should be brought up here. You want a decision on it ?

Mr. Kenworthy Browne :—We shall get the decision in the other case.

Lord Dunedin :—I know nothing about facts, but assuming this man was guilty of seditious writing, I think it is very advisable that he should be punished, whether he comes under the words of this Act or not. If he can get out of it, the sooner there is new legislation to provide for it the better.

Viscount Haldane :—Mr. Dube, your client may have committed no offence so far as this Regulation is concerned, but that he may be guilty under another Act.

Mr. Dube :—My client submits that he is triable by the general Courts of the country.

Viscount Haldane :—I think under these circumstances we had better give leave to appeal. We do not give it on any question of fact, but only on the question of whether the trial was *coram non judice*.

Mr. Kenworthy Browne :—I thought it right to bring that circumstance to your Lordship's notice.

Mr. Dube :—Your Lordships will not preclude me from arguing on the appeal, that the articles complained of offered no ground for the suggestion that they are seditious.

Viscount Haldane :—Quite so.

Mr. Dube :—If your Lordship pleases.

(3)—Lahore Leaders' Case*

The Petition of Lala Harkishen Lal and others for Special Leave to Appeal from Martial Law Commissioners at Lahore was heard in the Privy Council on Tuesday, the 21st October, 1919.

The Rt. Hon. Lord Shaw of Dunfermline, the Rt. Hon. Lord Phillimore, the Rt. Hon. Sir John Edge, the Rt. Hon. Ameer Ali and the Rt. Hon. Sir Lawrence Jenkins were present.

The Rt. Hon. Sir John Simon, K. C., and Mr. Dube (instructed by Messrs. Barrow, Rogers and Nevill), appeared for the Petitioners.

Mr. Kenworthy Browne (instructed by the Solicitor, India Office) appeared for the Respondent.

Sir John Simon :—My Lords, I appear with my friend, Mr. Dube, in support of this petition for special leave to appeal. It is a petition by five Indian British subjects living in Lahore. I ought to tell your Lordships at once that the main ground upon which they ask for special leave to appeal, is a ground which has already been declared by your Lordships' Board more than once within the last few months to be a sufficient ground. The matter first came before the Privy Council on 23rd July, 1919, before a Board which consisted of Lord Haldane, Lord Buckmaster and Lord Atkinson. It happens that the Board as constituted to-day does not contain any of those three learned Lords. In that case, the petition was the petition of a series of British subjects, the first of whom was named Bugga. The main point which we took—there may be other points—is the same as the point I would take to-day. To put it in a few sentences, it is this. The submission which we make is that the conviction which has been pronounced is *coram non judice*. These five men, for whom I appear to-day, have been convicted both of sedition and of waging war under sections of the Indian Penal Code, not before the duly constituted Criminal Court, which would entertain charges under those sections of the Criminal Code, but under a Special Tribunal which, in view of the disturbed state of this part of India had been set up, or was purported to have been set up, by Ordinance passed by the Governor-General-in-Council. The point which we took before Lord Haldane in July last on an exactly similar issue was this : that the second of those two Ordinances has been framed under a complete

---

*For the Judgment of Martial Law Commission in this case, see Appendix II, pages 364—418, *ante*.

misapprehension as to the true extent to which this special power can be exercised by a Special Tribunal. Your Lordships will remember that under the Bengal Regulation of 1804, it is possible upon a proclamation of Martial Law in Bengal, and it has since been extended to other parts of India, to constitute a Special Tribunal which may validly try persons who are taken in *flagrante delicto*. The whole point of it is, that the Ordinance is one which points to offences committed by persons who are taken in the actual commission of those offences, taken in actual rebellion, and so on. The point which we took in July last on behalf of Bugga and the others was that presumably under some misapprehension, the Special Tribunal which had been set up was purporting to sentence people who had never been taken in *flagrante delicto* at all, but was acting as though it was a Court-Martial authorised by the Law of India to try persons on evidence, from which it was sought to draw the inference that in fact they had been concerned in these outbreaks and outrages. We contended that that was wholly contrary to the true view of the powers which the tribunal had, or indeed the powers which the Legislature in India would have to exercise, and, secondly, after that had been explained, Lord Haldane said—Lord Buckmaster also made a number of observations—that certainly there must be leave to appeal granted. Lord Haldane said—"We think under the circumstances it is right that there should be leave to appeal. This Board, as we have often said, is not a Court of Criminal Appeal, but there is a class of cases which is generally defined as the class of cases which falls within the category of what the Board laid down in Dillet's Case in which they do advise the Sovereign to interfere where there has been a miscarriage of justice referred for its meaning to the fundamental principles of justice ; for instance, if there has been anything *coram non judice,* that is a case in point. If the argument that has been addressed to us here is right, the case has been *coram non judice*. There is one point, at any rate, on which we think that there is a serious point to argue, without expressing any opinion upon it, and that is that the second Ordinance"—I will explain in a moment what is meant by this— "has not extended the scope of the first Ordinance, and that the first Ordinance is limited to cases where the Defendant is taken in *flagrante delicto*." I must explain the matter a little more in detail. The position is this. These men were charged with having committed these serious offences, sedition and the like on dates—it is material to notice the dates—which range from, I think, 6th April to 12th April. The latest date charged is 12th April, and no doubt in point of date that is quite accurate. Normally speaking, anybody who commits the offence of sedition on 12th April, has to be tried in India by the ordinary constitutional process before a Criminal Court. At a later date there was enacted Martial Law Ordinance No. 1. Your Lordships have it in a form of an exhibit marked A, which is described as: "An Ordinance to provide for the trial of persons charged with offences under the Bengal State Offences Regulation, 1804." Stopping there for a moment, since the Bengal State Offences Regulation, 1804, is limited to cases where persons are taken with arms in their hands, the first Ordinance would not touch my client, because, he was arrested long afterwards in a different part of India. Your Lordships will see it recites : "And whereas the Governor-General-in-Council has in exercise of the powers conferred by Section 2 of the Bengal State Offences Regulation, 1804, suspended in respect of offences described in the said Regulation." That is the Regulation of 1804, and your Lordships will see it is the offence of being "taken in arms in open hostility to the British Government, or in the act of opposing by force of arms the authority of the same, or in actual commission"—that is taken in the actual commission—"of any overt act of rebellion against the State or in the act"—that again is taken in the act—"of openly aiding and abetting the enemies of the British Government."

Therefore, that Regulation of 1804 is one which does after a proclamation of Martial Law justify a wholly abnormal Tribunal constituted for the purpose of administering Military Justice, or as it is called, Martial Law, whatever Martial Law is, because you are dealing with people who are taken in the offence. That is all this first Ordinance has done.

Lord Phillimore :— What do you say to the end of Section 2 of the Regulation of 1804 ? If it covers the same ground I think the language is wider there : "And also to direct the immediate trial, by Courts-Martial, of all persons owing allegiance to the British Government,"—I omit the next words—"who shall be taken in arms in open hostility to the British Government, or in the act of opposing by force of arms the authority of the same, or in the actual commission of any overt act of rebellion against the State, or in the act of openly aiding and abetting the enemies of the British Government within any part of the said territories." Those seem rather stronger words than the other words.

Sir John Simon :— Be it so, but they would not be large enough to cover the case of a person who is taken long after. I am pointing out that Ordinance No. 1 could not touch me, because the charge which was made against me is not within Section 2 of the Bengal State Offences Regulation, 1804, at all. Not only so, but your Lordships will observe in Section I of the Ordinance it provides: "This Ordinance may be called the Martial Law Ordinance, 1919." Then it says : "It shall come into operation at midnight between the 15th and the 16th, April, 1919." Therefore, not only of course is the whole subject-matter as regards the kind of crime to be investigated, one which is not wide enough to cover the offences which these people are said to have committed, but since everything they did was finished and done with by 12th April, this first Ordinance in any case would not do much then. Thereupon, at a later stage there was a second Ordinance No. 4, which reads as follows : "Whereas an emergency has arisen" and so on. One of the points about this is that on the face of it it is retrospective : "Notwithstanding anything contained in the Martial Law Ordinance 1919, the Local Government may, by general or special order, direct that any Commission appointed under the said Ordinance"—that is the Commission to try people who have been *taken* in the act—"shall try any person charged with any offence committed on or after 30th March, 1919." Our submission before the Board in July last was, that on its true construction this second Ordinance, which I have just read, no doubt places the date further back, but it does not upon its true construction confer upon the Court-Martial the right to try a boy for stealing apples, or for any other crime in the Calendar; but as regards the kind of offence that the Tribunal has to deal with, the kind of offence is still the offence that was to be dealt with in the earlier Ordinance, and all that it does, and purports to do is, to give a jurisdiction for trying persons who were proved, or said, to have committed offences which fall within the definition in the Regulation of 1804. It has been treated as though the effect of the second Ordinance was to give this Court-Martial jurisdiction to try people for offences under the Indian Penal Code of different sort and kind. Your Lordships will see from the shorthand notes that the matter was fully discussed—I submit, I am in as quite strong a position as the other petitioners were.

Lord Shaw of Dunfermline :— It is desirable in these cases that nothing shall fall from us except what is absolutely necessary. Mr. Kenworthy Browne, would your assent to the proposition that the main ground of argument submitted to this Board and assented to as giving reasons for leave to appeal is a ground which occurs in the present case ?

Mr. Kenworthy Browne :— Yes, my Lord, I do.

Sir John Simon :— Then that really is all I need say. Really the matter was recognised on the previous occasion by those representating the Government of India. Sir Erle Richards on the previous occasion, speaking on behalf of the Government of India, said, "I want your Lordships to remember that it is a matter of great importance. (Viscount Haldane). We realise that. (Sir Erle Richards). Everybody who has been convicted would then have a right of appeal to this Board. (Lord Buckmaster) No. Only the people who have been convicted when they have been seized otherwise than in *flagrante delicto*." That is exactly my case. What I ask for, therefore, is leave to appeal, though this is a criminal matter, to the King in Council. I understand that the first case in which we got leave to appeal is one which will shortly come before this Board ; and if I am given leave to appeal in the present case then I shall be in a position to promptly take advantage of the decision in the first case if the decision in the first case should be in favour of the accused persons, otherwise these people will be detained and have to begin after the first case has been decided.

Lord Shaw of Dunfermline :—Before you conclude, Sir John, would you give us your view on this alternative, namely, on the assumption that you are correct, and that must be taken to be so, because Mr. Kenworthy Browne has assented to your view.

Sir John Simon :—Yes, my Lord, I am obliged to my friend.

Lord Shaw of Dunfermline :—As a matter of procedure, would it make any difference to these accused until the trial of Bugga Case ?

Sir John Simon :—I would put it in this way, I should submit that the proper course, with great respect to the Board, would be, in the first place, to give me special leave to appeal. That puts me before the King. Then if those representing the Government of India are prepared to undertake that the Bugga Case, as far as they are concerned, shall be brought on as rapidly as possible, as I assume it will be, and secondly, in the event of the decision being, that the trial was *coram non judice*, that thereupon they will co-operate to get these other convictions quashed forthwith, I shall be content. I should not in the meantime think it right that one should begin to accumulate all the material and evidence, and all the rest of it, for making up a Record, but one has to remember that these people are in fact in custody serving a sentence, and, therefore I must be assured that the executive who otherwise I understand would not be in a position to let them out—I want the conviction quashed not a pardon—will be prepared to act upon the decision in the Bugga Case if it is in my favour, for the advantage of these other people, the appeals coming on without any opposition and the appeals being allowed. There are two steps, of course. I have first to get over the difficulty that generally speaking the King in Council does not give leave to appeal in a Criminal Case. That is the first step. That step, I submit, I am entitled to take to-day. But if I am to go on and say, now that I have got leave to appeal to the Privy Council, I am entitled without delay to have the Record made up, to have the exhibits and all that, I think it would be unreasonable. I have said the right course was, the authorities acquiescing, on leave being given, to undertake before the Board first that the Bugga Case should come on as promptly as possible, and secondly, as soon as that is decided, if it is decided in favour of the appellants, that they will cooperate to bring on these other appeals which will then be open.

Lord Phillimore :—You are asking, not only for leave to appeal, but to put them on further terms. You cannot ask that to-day.

Sir John Simon :—I only mean this, my Lord. If I get leave to appeal and nothing more is said, then I shall be entitled under the order which the Board will make, to say to the authorities, please collect the Record and send it over and so on, I want to get ready. I hope I may be able to avoid that.

Lord Shaw of Dunfermline :—Mr. Kenworthy Browne, the demand made here on behalf of these persons is a demand or right to be released. They cannot be released except by a Government act of clemency, unless they are released in course of law. They demand to be released in course of law, and it occurs to some of us, it occurs to me, that even although the Bugga Case were held to be in point and to rule this, they could not obtain their legal release as a right except the stage is traversed of their getting leave to appeal. Unless they got leave to appeal, they are not in forum to ask any advice from this Board to His Majesty, and therefore, after all it does seem to me, if you are agreed upon the facts and the binding authority one way or another of the Bugga Case to be of advantage to postpone the getting of leave to appeal, we should be glad to hear you.

Mr. Kenworthy Browne :— My Lords, I have only one word to say about that. Apparently there is no reason why the Bugga Case should not be disposed of this sitting. I have made enquiries about it from the point of view of the India Office, and it is more than likely that the case be put down, if your Lordships permit it, before the end of the present sitting. If that is taking a too hopeful view, it will certainly be set down at the beginning of next sittings. Meanwhile there are these three cases, and I am told there are a great many more, two dozen has been suggested to me as a number, that are coming on.

Sir Ameer Ali :— They are all on the same basis ?

Mr. Kenworthy Browne :— Yes, I am taking the same point, namely, that the Ordinance of 1919 is limited by the terms of the Regulation of 1804, which is a point to be argued if your Lordships were to direct that these applications should stand over until the main question is settled, which I hope it will be quite soon, then the position will be that a great deal of expense will be saved, a great deal of time will be saved, and the labour of the preparation of all these numerous records will be saved. That really is the only point.

Lord Phillimore :— I have been thinking that it would be putting the appellants to unnecessary expense as well as the Government of India, if we were to grant leave now. One would expect all the other two dozen people to apply for leave to appeal, and there would be the expense of a great number of petitions of course and in due course of law they must not merely have their petitions but they must have their appeals. There will be a petition, a case for appeal, a case on the other side, and a formal hearing and a decision. Whereas, supposing the Government take the reasonable course, if this first case goes against them, of immediately submitting to any short form of quashing the convictions, a great deal of expense to the country and to the appellants would be saved.

Mr. Kenworthy Browne :— My submission to your Lordships, as I have said, is that the matter should stand over in order to save expense and trouble.

Mr. Ameer Ali :— I thought you did not want any of the expenses to be incurred on these records.

Lord Shaw of Dunfermline :— Your object, Sir John, is to obtain a *locus standi* to come before the King.

Mr. Kenworthy Browne :— Sir John Simon has made his position quite clear. May I make my position clear My suggestion is only for a saving of time, expense and labour.

Sir John Simon :— Then I have not made my position clear. My position is nothing to do with that. My position is to draw this distinction. The first step is that I should be within the ear of the Court, and I can only be in that position if they have granted me special leave to appeal. Until then, the Court knows nothing of me. I am asking to be before the Court. There is no expense involved in saying that. If it stopped there, the Order which the Privy Council would make would be wider and would include a direction to prepare the Record. I quite agree with my friend that one ought to take steps that will avoid the expense, I think quite unnecessary, of getting together records and printing them.

Lord Shaw of Dunfermline :— You would assent to that, Mr. Kenworthy Browne ?

Mr. Kenworthy Browne :— Certainly.

Lord Phillimore :— I am afraid you have misunderstood my point altogether.

Sir John Simon :— I do not know any method, speaking subject to correction, by which when a Subject of the King has been sentenced to a term of imprisonment he can be put in the position of a person who has not been put in prison, except it be by his conviction quashed. We are not content to receive a pardon from the Crown. We do not want a pardon. We want it to be stated that we have never been convicted, and I know of no method by which it can be done except by the Order of the Privy Council. I hope to get that Order.

Lord Phillimore :—That means that every one of them will come here. There are three sets of Petitioners here. Everyone else who has been convicted must come here, and not merely get leave to appeal but put in a Petition of Appeal, lodge a case, and get a decision. That seems to be appalling.

Sir John Simon—It would be, but my own impression is that assuming the Government of India as Respondents, already being before the Board, are prepared to co-operate those steps, which I perfectly agree are appalling steps, can be simplified, and shortened to a very great extent. It is presumably entirely within your Lordships' powers to say, as soon as the Bugga Case has been decided, if it has been decided in favour of the Subject, we are going to put all these other cases in which leave has been granted on this same point into the list tomorrow, though none of them will require a case to be signed, or a reply to be made, because, we know the situation, and we are then with the assent of the Government of India going to quash all those convictions. That is all I want, but your Lordships cannot do that, if I am not.

Sir John Edge:—We could only do that after the Appeals have been admitted. If your Appeal is admitted before us, then on the argument of the first case we can advise the King to quash the other convictions.

Sir John Simon:—I want to come in at the door.

Mr. Ameer Ali:—You want a *locus standi?*

Sir John Simon:—Yes. We will not put any expense on the Country.

Lord Phillimore:—Am I not right in thinking that you have, accoding to the ordinary procedure, first to get leave to appeal, then secondly to file a Petition of Appeal to bring your case on—you may never use your leave—and then thirdly, in the ordinary course file your case ? I appreciate that we can dispense with Cases, but I do not think we can dispense with a Petition of Appeal as apart from a Petition for leave to Appeal.

Sir John Simon:—I think your Lordship is quite right.

Lord Shaw of Dunfermline:—I think that must be so.

Lord Phillimore:—And the cases must be signed by the parties, and so on. Then it might mean, if that procedure was to be taken, at least a Petition of Appeal must be presented on behalf of each of these Appellants. I should have thought it might be cut much shorter by the Government eventually undertaking to release all these people.

Sir John Simon:—How can they do that ? Assuming that A.B. has been committed to a gaoler upon the order of an Authority purporting to be a Court, the method by which the gaoler opens the door and lets him out is, he can only be let out by one of two methods, either that the Crown in India in the exercise of the prerogative of mercy grants his release.

Sir John Edge:—You do not ask for that ?

Sir John Simon:—No. The other : that a superior Court of Appeal quashes the conviction.

Lord Phillimore:—You are speaking with great forgetfulness of what has happened in England. How many people who were hunger-strikers have been let out without pardon by simple executive acts?

Sir John Simon:—I thought there was a cat-and-mouse Act which specially provided for it.

Lord Phillimore:—Before that Act it was constantly done.

Sir John Simon:—I think if your Lordships look into it, you will find that everyone of those persons in point of form gets a conditional pardon.

Lord Shaw of Dunfermline:—We must keep in view the fact, that there are no doubt possibly other cases to come before us; but the position today is that you ask for leave to appeal as of right, founded upon authority, and I think you must assent to what Lord Phillimore says, that it is highly desirable not to allow that leave with expenses to the other side.

Sir John Simon:—I entirely agree, my Lord.

Lord Shaw of Dunfermline:—Your expense is your own affair; but that the Government of India should be put to expense, we should all agree, should be avoided if possible. On the other hand, you must observe Lord Phillimore's point. It is this, Leave is only an allowance to you to come here *in forum.* Once you are *in forum,* you can only arrive into the forum by coming in by your Petition of Appeal, and naturally it will follow that though it may mean a short summary simple affair, you would present your Petitions of Appeal.

Sir John Simon:—I ask for the assurance which I understand my friend is in a position to give.

Mr. Kenworthy Browne:—I do not know what assurance my friend requires.

Sir John Simon:—I want to make it quite plain that if I offer, if the Tribunal thinks it right to direct, that after I file my Petition of Appeal I should hold my hand, and that therefore there should be no printing of the records in those cases, in the meantime that the Government of India will cooperate as far as in them lies to bring on this hearing without formal Cases, as soon as the Bugga case is decided, otherwise, I should want to get all the documents ready, which would be most unreasonable.

Lord Shaw of Dunfermline:—I think the position is quite clear. Mr. Kenworthy Browne does not differ, and nobody differs, on the merits of this. The thing is to do it in the most appropiate way, or the most convenient way. What you want to do is to get these Appellants in *pari passu* with the Bugga Case to the extent of being before this Board, but *quoad ultra* no expense could be incurred; and it goes without saying that in the interests of all parties, the trial of that most important case should be hastened.

Mr. Kenworthy Browne:—Certainly my Lord, there will be no delay on the part of the Government. Certainly, I can give an undertaking as to that.

Sir John Edge:—If the result of the first is to decide that there was jurisdiction to try these men and to commit them, would all the Appeals fail ?

Sir John Simon:—I am not prepared to say that, because I do not know. Lord Haldane on the previous occasion was careful to guard the interests of the Appellants, because he said:—"We are satisfied that we ought to give special leave to appeal on those points" which he indicated, but he said, "there may be other grounds, there is one, for example, whether an Ordinance of this kind can be retrospective in its true operation, and there may be other points" and he said, "We will leave the Petitioners open to take other points, but the ground upon which we give them leave to Appeal, to come here, is this point."

Sir John Edge—I suppose in those other cases, the facts would not be disputed as to what part the Petitioners took in the proceedings ?

Sir John Simon:—I do not think so. In the present case, I am quite certain they would not.

Lord Phillimore:—Is there anything in the present case that distinguishes it from the Bugga Case. Have you any advantages that Bugga had not ?

Sir John Simon:—The actual charge in the Bugga Case was of taking part in the Amritsar riots. In the present case it is not a charge of riot, it is a charge of sedition, and a charge of making war against the King. I have not really addressed my mind to the question.

Lord Shaw of Dunfermiline:—It is very desirable not to go into it.

Sir John Simon:—If your Lordships grant leave to Appeal, the form of Order which is issued from the Department here is an order which directs the parties with reasonable promptitude to prepare their record. Sometimes, people do not take advantage of that; but that does not alter the fact that the direction is given.

(Counsel and parties are ordered to withdraw, and after a short time are again called in)

Lord Shaw of Dunfermline:—Their Lordships will humbly advise His Majesty that leave to Appeal should be granted in this case. The Order to be pronounced will be the same, as that announced in what is admitted to be the precedent, the case of Bugga. With regard to what follows, their Lordships desire to say almost nothing except to say that should it be ultimately held that Bugga's Case covers the present case no unnecessary expense or circuitous procedure should take place in this present Appeal. No doubt *pro forma* a Petition of Appeal will be necessary, but the parties will judge whether anything else will be required to enable the precedent of the Bugga case to be instantly applied on its merits when these are reached.

APPENDIX IV
Martial Law & Its Applicability

(1)—Applicability of Regulation X of 1804

Towards the end of the year 1817, Martial Law was established at Cuttack and a large number of persons were tried and convicted by Courts-Martial constituted under Regulation X of 1804, the trials being in many respects similar to those that were held a century later in the Punjab under the Martial Law Ordinance of 1919. Mr. R. Spankie, the Advocate-General of Bengal at that time, impeached the legality of those trials on almost the same grounds as are being urged against the Punjab trials. The following is the opinion of Serjeant Spankie on the trials held at Cuttack:—

Rebellion in East Indies

To W.B. Bayley, Esqr. Secretary to Government, Judicial Department,—*From* Advocate-General Spankie,—relating to native Detachment Courts-Martial in Cuttack, 17th September, 1817 to 4th March, 1818.

Sir,—I have the honour to acknowledge the receipt of your letter of the 14th instant transmitting, by direction of the Hon. the Vice-President in Council, various documents respecting the cases of certain prisoners, tried by Court-Martial in Cuttack; and in reply, I have to request that you will lay before the Hon. the Vice-President in Council the opinion I have formed upon the subject.

1. It appears by the document referred to that *Martial Law* was put in force under the orders of Government by virtue of Regulation X of 1804.

2. The preamble of the Regulation states, "that it may be expedient, in certain cases therein mentioned, that the Governor-General in Council should declare and establish Martial Law for the safety of the British Possessions and etc., by the *immediate* punishment of persons owing allegiance to the British Government, who may be *taken* in arms in *open* hostility to the said Government, or in the actual commission of any overt act of rebellion against the authority of the same, or in the *act* of *openly* aiding and abetting the enemies of the British Government within any part of the territtories above specified."

3. This enacting part conformably to the object developed in the preamble, enacts (Sect. 2). "That the Governor-General in Council shall be empowered, among other things, to direct the immediate trial by Courts-Martial of all persons owing allegiance, and who shall be *taken* in arms, in *open* hostility to the British Government, or in the act of opposing by force of arms the authority of the same, or in the *actual* commission of an *overt* act of rebellion against the State, or in the act of *openly* aiding and abetting the enemies of the British Government."

4. Four overt acts are enumerated, and it seems to me clear that the word *taken,* in the first, must, in necessary construction, be carried forward and annexed to each member of the sentence containing the description of the overt act; indeed, the sentence would not make sense without it.

5. Here the circumstances in which Courts-Martial are to have an authority to try are clearly marked and defined. The criminals must be *taken* in open acts of the treasonable and rebellious descriptions mentioned.

6. It seems to me also liable to some doubt, whether the fourth overt act specified in the Regulation does not mean an aiding and abetting of such enemies of the British Government as are contemplated both in the preamble and in Sec.2—enemies, with which the British Government may be engaged in war, not rebels with arms in their hands.

7. If there could be any doubt of the extent of the authority and jurisdiction of the Courts-Martial under Regulation X of 1804, it would be removed by the instructions of 11th April, 1805, communicated for their guidance to the authorities in Cuttack during the late disturbances. These instructions (paragraph 4) say:—"If any person or persons, charged with any of the overt acts of rebellion specified in Regulation X of 1804, shall be apprehended by any *military* officer, when not in the *actual commission* of offences of that description, they are to be delivered over by the military to the civil power."

9. The Courts-Martial in Cuttack do not appear to have considered themselves as at all confined to the cases of prisoners taken *flagrante delicto,* or even to traitorous and rebellious acts of the specific quality stated in the Regulation. They seem to have acted as if they had possessed an unqualified jurisdiction over all treasonable and

rebellious acts, without limitation of time, place, or circumstance. The charge (confirming as in all limited jurisdictions, it ought, to the cases in which the jurisdiction is given) does not state the circumstance of the criminal being *taken* in the fact, or that it was in some open act of the treasonable rebellious quality which alone the Court-Martial could lawfully try.

10. The first case is "for rebellion against the British Government by being seized with arms in the house."

11. The court find him guilty of a breach of allegiance to the British Government. *Sentence.*—Four years' imprisonment in the convicts' gaol at Cuttack.

12. The prisoner is acquitted of *rebellion*—the only part of the charge made a crime under the Regulation.

13. The next case—'1st. Being seized with arms in his house. 2nd. Deputing four Suwars to find out whether Atchet, Piddam was off his guard. 3rd. Having in possession four orders signed by the chieftain of the rebels addressed to various parts of the Dendmals. 4th. For preventing the well-affected inhabitants from returning to their allegiance to British Government, by threatening them with death. 5th. Alarming the inhabitants of the Dendmals which had just returned to a state of tranquillity by creating and circulating false reports of its being the intention of the chieftain of the rebels (Jugbundoo Bryadhun) to attack this post with fourteen pieces of cannon and 4,000 or 5,000 men; by which means he prevented the remaining few from returning to their allegiance.'

14. Found guilty of the 2nd, 3rd and 4th charges, acquitted of the 5th, on revision, guilty of the fifth (paragraph 15).

16. The fifth charge, the same as the preceding. No. 'open overt' acts, as specified in the Regulation.

17. The next case.—'For having taken up arms and aided and abetted in a rebellion against the State.'

18. Found guilty and sentenced to be hanged.

19. Here the court who finds the prisoner guilty, or (in the words of the charge) would have been justified and bound to find him guilty of having taken up arms at any time, or having aided and abetted in any manner, which such court might have construed to be aiding and abetting at any time, without the qualification of the prisoner being taken in the 'actual' commission of any crime or in any 'open' act of the description specified in the Regulation.

20. The next case—'For high treason, for aiding and abetting the insurgents in this district, in one or either of following instances:— Ist. For adhering to and accompanying the insurgents in this district. 2nd. For selling a quantity of salt belonging to Government and defrauding Government of the same. 3rd. For collecting the money in the neighbourhood from the cultivators for the insurgents and for being in the capacity of a collector on the part of Jugbundoo, at the same time he was seized.'

21. Guilty of first charge; acquitted of the second charge; on the third, acquitted of collecting money from the cultivators, but guilty of the rest of the charge. *Sentence*—to be hanged.

22. The second charge is a mere fraud. The aiding and abetting which amounted to treason or rebellion were not well defined. Acquitted of collecting money from the cultivators, but guilty of being a collector on the part of Jugbundoo "at the time 'he' (not distinguishing whether 'he' refers to the prisoner or Jugbundoo) was seized."

23. It is doubtful whether this prisoner was guilty of any offence. He certainly is not charged with being taken in the 'actual' commission of any offence or of the open overt act specified in the Regulation.

24 – 25. The next case is—'Ist. For aiding or joining in a rebellion against the legal authorities of the State between the month of March 1817, and the present period. 2nd. For joining or following the rebel chief Kurna kun Purraun Gooroo, sometime during the above mentioned period.'

26. Acquitted of the first; guilty of the second charge. Sentence—to be hanged.

27. Second prisoner acquitted.

28. Third prisoner charged—'For aiding, abetting or joining in a rebellion against the legal authorities of the State, between the month of March 1817, and the present period.'

29. Guilty, to be hanged.—(Three other cases the same).

34. No *taking* specified, though the Court may have received evidence of what they consider aiding, abetting or joining, at any time whatsoever from the 17th March, 1817.

35. The last case.

36. Charge the same.

37. Guilty, to be hanged.

38. Same remark as to those immediately preceding.

39. The whole of the proceedings and sentences illegal.

40. The manifest intention of Government in its legislative capacity was, that none but cases of the simplest and most obviously criminal nature should be the subject of trial by the courts-martial; the fact, whether a person was *taken* in the actual commission of an overt act of rebellion, or *taken* in the act of *openly* aiding and abetting the enemies of the State or taken in *open* hostility, might safely be tried by such courts; and such a provision for trial was calculated to prevent *military* severity in the field becoming absolute *massacre.* But all complex cases depending upon circumstantial proof, and requiring either a long examination of facts or a discriminating inference from facts in themselves equivocal were purposely withdrawn from the cognizance of these tribunals. It never was intended that courts-martial should try, as those have done, acts, even of criminal nature, in which the prisoner was not *taken* and unless the acts were open overt acts and of the most material palpable quality.

41. To guard against a dangerous usurpation of authority, the charge should have stated the prisoner was *taken in the actual commission of some open overt act* of the description specified in the Regulation; for without such limitation, the court-martial is let in to try all manner of *traitrous, treasonable,* and *rebellious* acts direct or indirect. It does not appear that the distinctions required both by the regulations and by the positive instructions of Government have been at all regarded in practice.

42. Some of the cases exhibited instances of laxity in the charge, and indeed in the conception of the nature of the crime which sufficiently evince the danger that would ensue if the courts were not to be most strictly limited, both as to the extent of their authority and the defined quality of the offence submitted to them.

43. It is impossible, though I think it is not either morally or legally to be presumed in the present case, that some of the prisoners tried may have been *taken* in the fact, as required by the Regulation. But, on the face of the proceedings, the sentences are wholly *illegal* and I think, that no punishment whatever can legally be inflicted upon them. Indeed, they are so utterly void that the prisoners, if they be guilty and if it be thought advisable, might still be prosecuted before the criminal courts of ordinary jurisdiction. The humanity of

the Commander-in-Chief* and the military commissioner† of the district has led them to *commute* all sentences by which death was to be inflicted; so that if the proceedings be irregular, the consequences are not irreparable.

44. The proceedings of those courts-martial appear to be in some other respects irregular and seem to indicate a misapprehension of their proper functions and jurisdiction.

45. The object of Martial Law in the trial of offenders under it, is justly stated in the Regulation X of 1804, to be *immediate punishment* for the "*safety of the British Possessions and for the security of the lives and property* of the inhabitants thereof." It is, in fact, the law of social defence, superseding under the pressure, and therefore under the justification of an extreme necessity, the ordinary forms of justice. Courts-Martial under Martial-Law, or rather during the suspension of Law, are invested with the power of administering that prompt and speedy justice in cases presumed to be clearly and indisputably of the highest species of guilt. The object is self preservation by the terror and the example of speedy justice; but courts-martial which condemn to imprisonment and hard labour belie the necessity, under which alone the jurisdiction of Courts Martial can lawfully exist in civil society.

46. I would not be understood to mean that the superior military authorities may not properly commute the punishment of death in cases in which, in the first heat and danger of *rebellion,* sentence of death has been given by a court-martial. It seems important, however, that the court-martial itself should be confined to cases of the most obvious and dangerous criminality, admitting as far as they are concerned but of one sentence. It is essential to preserve the distinction of crimes and the character of the jurisdiction, and that the lenity of the tribunal should not become an argument for the unnecessary employment of it.

47. In all the cases above considered there appears no reason why the criminals might not have been sent before the ordinary courts agreeably to the expressed directions and instructions of Government. It seems desirable that the attention of the military authorities should be drawn to the distinctions laid down in

---

* Marquis of Hastings.

† Lieutenant-General Sir G. Mastindell, K.C.B.

Regulation X and in the instructions of Government as long as the existence of Martial Law is found necessary.

48. The proceedings and sentences of the courts-martial are *illegal;* and `I conceive that, as a court of law in reviewing the proceedings of interior jurisdictions sets aside the *whole* where error, and particularly want of jurisdiction, manifestly appear, the Supreme Government exercising the same functions of review and control, must quash the whole of the illegal proceedings and cannot consider them the foundation of any lawful punishment at all.

R. SPANKIE,

Fort William. 27th April, 1818. *Advocate-General.*

(2)—Martial Law in the Punjab

By

Sir P. S. Sivaswamy Aiyer, K. C. S. I., C. I. E.

(*From the Servant of India, dated the 5th June, 1919*).

While the administration of martial law in the Punjab has been widely discussed in the press, the legal aspects of the subject have received comparatively little attention from the public. It is neither practicable nor desirable to go into the merits of any individual case, but it is worth while considering the scope and effect of the regulations and ordinances under which action has been taken and the powers of the Crown and the military authorities, apart from any specific enactments.

The regulation under which martial law has been introduced in the Punjab is the Bengal State Offences Regulation, 1804, which has been declared to be in force in the Punjab by section 3 of the Punjab Laws Act, 1872. Section 2 of this regulation empowers the Governor-General-in-Council to suspend or direct the suspension of, wholly or partially, the functions of the ordinary criminal courts and to establish martial law therein during the existence of any war or open rebellion against the authority of the Government and also to direct the immediate trial by courts-martial of all persons owing allegiance to the British Government, who may be guilty of certain offences. The only offences which can be taken cognizance of are those specified in the second paragraph of section 2. The persons who can be tried by courts-martial under this regulation are subjects of the British Government who shall be *taken*.

1. in arms in open hostility to the British Government; or
2. in the act of opposing by force of arms the authority of the Government; or
3. in the actual commission of any overt act of rebellion against the State; or
4. in the act of openly aiding and abetting the enemies of the British Government within any part of the territories in question.

The punishments provided by section 3 are death and forfeiture of property. Having regard to the severity of the punishments provided and the language of Sections 1 and 2 and the whole scheme of the regulation, there can be no doubt as to the correctness of the opinion of Advocate-General Spankie that the manifest intention of the Regulation was, that none but cases of the simplest and most obviously criminal nature should be the subject of trial by the courts-martial, that only persons who were *taken* in the actual commission of overt acts of rebellion or hostility should be tried by such courts, and that complex cases depending upon circumstantial proof and requiring either a long examination of facts, or a discriminating inference from facts, in themselves equivocal, were purposely withdrawn from the cognizance of these tribunals. Where persons concerned in acts of rebellion were not taken in the actual commission of the offences specified in the Regulation, the intention of the legislature evidently was that they should be handed over to the civil power for trial by the ordinary criminal courts, as will appear from the instructions issued by the Governor-General on the 11th April, 1805, (See Harrington's Bengal Regulations, Edn of 1821, p. 350).

The Martial Law Ordinance—1 of 1919, recites that the functions of the ordinary criminal courts have been suspended in respect of the offences described in section 2 of the Regulation, and provides for trial in respect of such offences being held by commissions of three persons appointed by the local Government instead of by court-martial. The object of this substitution was presumably to secure the presence in the tribunal of Judges in the civil employ of the Government. As a consequence of this constitution of the tribunal, the right of the accused to challenge the members of the tribunal has been excluded, and the necessity for confirmation of the finding and sentence as required by sections 94 and 98 of the Army Act has also been provided against. Though this Ordinance came into force at mid-night on the 15th April, 1919, it was expressly rendered applicable to all persons referred to in Regulation 10 of 1804, who were charged with any of the offences therein described committed on or after the 13th April, 1919. The question has been raised in some quarters whether the Ordinance is valid, insofar as it purports to give retrospective effect. To the mind of a lawyer there can be on doubt as to the validity of an express provision of this sort. Though the inclination of the courts would be against the retrospective operation of penal laws in cases in which the language of the statute admits of reasonable doubt, there can be no question as to the validity of an express provision for giving retrospective effect. The only offences which can be taken cognizance of by the commissions under this ordinance are those described in section 2 of the Regulation above referred to. It is not every offence under Chapter VI of the Penal Code that could be brought under this ordinance, section 124-A dealing with sedition, would fall outside the class of offences described in the regulation; so also offences under section 129. Whether offences under section 121-A or 123 of the Penal Code could be taken cognizance of or not under the Martial Law Ordinance would depend upon the circumstances of the case. The Martial Law Ordinance does not authorise the military authorities to enact rules or regulations or to create any new offences in respect of infringement of any rules or orders, which may be issued by them. Whether, apart from the provisions of the Martial Law Ordinance, the Crown or the military authorities have any power to issue such regulations and how breaches of such regulations may be punished are distinct questions, which will be examined later on. As regards the sentences which may be imposed by a commission constituted under this ordinance, they could not pass any sentence except that of capital punishment, and forfeiture of the property of the person convicted was an automatic and necessary result of the conviction under section 3 of the regulation. To obviate this hardship, the Martial Law (sentences) Ordinance was issued on the 18th April, 1919, and it enabled the tribunals to pass any sentence of transportation for life or for any period not less than 10 years or of rigorous imprisonment for a term of not less than 7 and not more than 14 years, and it further provided that forfeiture of property should not follow a conviction automatically, but only when so directed by the court or commission. The only other ordinance which it is necessary to notice is the Martial Law (further extension) Ordinance, which was passed on the 21st April, 1919. This ordinance gives an extraordinary extension to the scope of the Martial Law Ordinance 1 of 1919. Whereas by the first Ordinance only persons charged with the offences described in section 2 of the regulation could be tried, the further ordinance provides for the trial of any person charged with any offence committed on or after the 30th March, 1919. It may be anything punishable under the Indian Penal Code or, for the matter of that, even under a special or a local law. The offence may be simple trespass, defamation, bigamy or nuisance. It need not involve the safety of the British possessions or the security of the lives and property of the inhabitants.* Of course,

* For a contrary view as to the interpretation of this Ordinance, see *Appendix III,* Sir John Simon's argument in the Amritsar National Bank Murder Appeal before the Privy Council.

it is not at all likely that such cases will be actually tried by the commission, for this extended jurisdiction of the commissions is made dependent upon a general or special order to be issued by the local Government and they are not likely to refer ordinary cases not connected, in their opinion, however directly or indirectly, with the recent disturbances. The provision is referred to here merely for the purpose of showing how entirely it is left to the local Government to displace the ordinary criminal courts and introduce the procedure of courts-martial. Under the regulation it is, no doubt, open to the Governor-General-in-Council to direct any public authority to order suspension of the ordinary criminal courts, wholly or partially, but the extent to which such suspension of the ordinary criminal courts may take place, may be gathered from the general scheme of the regulation. The suspension of the functions of the ordinary criminal courts and the exercise of jurisdiction by courts-martial constituted under the regulation are co-extensive. Inasmuch as the jurisdiction of courts-martial under section 2 of the regulation is confined to the four classes of crimes described therein, which are all more or less overt acts of hostility (or rebellion) to the State, the functions of the ordinary criminal courts cannot also be suspended to any greater extent, except as regards these crimes, Even in respect of the crimes specified, the regulation (section 4) displays a solicitude to avoid the institution of courts-martial, except where trial by them appears to be indispensably necessary. In view of the facts that martial law was established in exercise of the powers conferred by section 2 of the regulation, that the procedure of courts-martial was also introduced in exercise of the same powers, that the commissions appointed under the Martial Law Ordinance are only a convenient substitute for the tribunals prescribed by the Indian Army Act of 1911, and that the procedure to be followed by these commissions is the procedure prescribed for courts-martial by the Indian Army Act, the legality of the extension of the scope of the martial law ordinance to persons other than those referred to in Regulation X of 1804, and other than those subject to the Indian Army Act and to all kinds of offences, even those not falling under the Regulation or the Army Act, appears extremely doubtful. In passing it may be observed that a sentence of whipping would not be a legal punishment either under Regulation X of 1804, or under the Martial Law (sentences) Ordinance of 1919, or under the Army Act. Though corporal punishment is permitted under the Army Act, it is only in respect of persons subject to the Act and under the rank of warrant officer. Any sentence of corporal punishment can only be justified under the ordinary criminal law. It is conceivable that a military officer charged with the duty of suppressing a rebellion may have to resort to corporal punishment, but it can only be inflicted as a matter of unavoidable military necessity and not under the show of any legal trial.

It may perhaps be argued that, notwithstanding the fact that Ordinance IV of 1919 was intended to extend the scope of the martial law ordinance, which was brought into existence under the conditions described in Regulation 10 of 1804, it is open to the Governor-General to do anything he may please in the exercise of his powers under Section 72 of the Government of India Act, 1915. Under this section the Governor-General may, in cases of emergency, make and promulgate ordinances for the peace and good government of British India or any part thereof; and any ordinance so made has, for the space of not more than six months, the same force of law as an act passed by him in Legislative Council. The power is subject to the same restrictions and disallowance as an act of the Indian Legislative Council. It may be said that the ordinance-making power of the Governor-General is practically unlimited and that it is legally open to him to suspend all courts or to abolish the Evidence Act or to order any and every offender to be tried by courts-martial. There are, however, two conditions laid down in the section, that it must be a case of emergency and that the ordinance must be for the peace and good government of the country. Whether in the existing circumstances in the Punjab the ordinary criminal courts should be regarded as unfit for bringing offenders to justice, or whether it is indispensable for the peace and good government of the province that their functions should be suspended and offenders should be tried by the procedure of courts-martial, is a question of fact upon which a divergence of views may be reasonably possible; and it would be a matter for regret if the Government were not guided by the same solicitude for preserving the jurisdiction of the ordinary criminal courts as is apparent in Regulation 10 of 1804. *Prima facie*, one would be inclined to think that this unlimited delegation to the local Government of the power to suspend the functions of the ordinary criminal courts in respect of offences outstrips the necessities of the case. It seems a reasonable view to take that the power conferred by Section 72 of the Government of India Act represents the prerogative of the Crown, which has been defined as the residue of discretionary authority, which at any given time is legally left in the hands of the Crown, or, in other words, the Executive Government, and that the exercise of the emergency power under Section 72 should, in practice if not in theory, be guided by the same considerations and limitations as the exercise of the prerogative by the Crown under similar circumstances in England.

The circumstances under which Martial Law may be proclaimed in the case of a rebellion, the significance of the proclamation and the validity of measures taken upon such proclamation have been discussed by eminent text-writers, and the weight of authority is in favour of the view that, while it is the duty and the prerogative of the Crown to suppress revolts and it is also competent to employ military force so far as may be necessary for the purpose, it is illegal for the Crown to resort to Martial Law for the purpose of punishing offenders. In his History of the Criminal Law of England, Mr. Justice Stephen sums up the result of his discussion on pages 215 and 216 of Volume I as follows :—

(i) Martial Law is the assumption by officers of the Crown of absolute power exercised by military force for the suppression of an insurrection and the restoration of order and lawful authority.

(ii) The officers of the Crown are justified in any exertion of physical force extending to the destruction of life and property to any extent and in any manner that may be required for the purpose. They are not justified in the use of cruel and excessive means, but are liable civilly or criminally for such excess. They are not justified in inflicting punishment after the resistance is suppressed and after the ordinary courts of justice can be re-opened.

(iii) The courts-martial by which martial law is administered are not, properly speaking, courts-martial or courts at all. They are merely committees formed for the purpose of carrying into execution the discretionary power assumed by the Government.

It may be taken as settled law in England that if in the suppression of a rebellion and the effort to restore peace and order, any subjects of the Crown are punished or put to death by a trial under court-martial, such punishment may be challenged in the ordinary courts after the restoration of order and can only be justified on the ground of necessity which must be proved as a fact. Necessity is the measure of duration and extent of the force to be employed. The fact that the summary execution of rebels, whose crimes can be punished by the ordinary courts of law, may check the spread of treason does not show that the execution is necessary or legal. (See Appendix, Note X on Martial Law, Dicey's "Law of the Constitution," 7th edition, pages 538 to 554). In opposition to the view put forward by Professor Dicey, it is urged by Sir Erle Richards that inasmuch as military operation cannot be conducted in time of war or rebellion without interference with rights of property and person and such interference is according to the authorities not contrary to law, it follows that the interference must include also the right of trial and the infliction of punishment. (See Law Quarterly Review, Vol. XVIII, page 139). The conclusion deduced from the premises is, by no means, necessary. Sir Erle Richards assumes that if a Commanding Officer has the power of controlling the movements of the civil population, he must also have the power of punishing those who are guilty of a breach of his order. An infringement of the orders of the military authorities may be either an offence or not an offence. If it is not an offence, the civil courts cannot punish and the military authorities also should not interfere by way of punishment. Sir Erle Richards does not sufficiently distinguish between the nature of the coercive measures, which may be taken to prevent a breach or avert its consequences and, the measures necessary by way of punishment for a breach. The former class of powers must necessarily vest in the military authorities, but the latter power is not so vested. The necessity for the trial and punishment of civilians by the military authorities may conceivably exist in some cases; as, for instance, where it is impossible for the ordinary civil courts to exercise their functions. But, even in such cases, the correct view to take is put forward by Mr. Justice Stephen that the courts-martial are merely committees formed for the purpose of carrying into execution the discretionary power of the Crown. The case of Wright *Vs.* Fitz Gerald, 27 State Trials, page 765, is opposed to the contention of Sir Erle Richards, who relies chiefly upon the decision of the Privy Council in *Ex-parte* Marais (1902), A.C. 109. This decision has been canvassed at length by several critics, and the most acceptable view is that the courts will not and cannot interfere with actual military operations or while war is actually raging entertain proceedings against military men and others for acts done under the so-called martial law. The judgment of the Privy Council asserts nothing as to the jurisdiction of the courts when peace is restored in respect of acts done during time of war and eminent jurists have held that even in time of war the exercise of jurisdiction by the ordinary courts is rather rendered impossible than superseded (See Dicey's "Law of the Constitution," 7th edition, page 546). With reference to this case of *Ex-parte* Marais, the remarks in note (*d*) on page 403 of Vol. 6 of Halsbury's "Laws of England" are of interest, when it is remembered that the judgment of the Privy Council was delivered by Lord Halsbury. Here it is said, it is doubtful how far sentences of fine and imprisonment passed by courts-martial upon civilians would be valid in law after the war or insurrection is over. According to Sir Frederick Pollock, the only point decided by *Ex-parte* Marais, was that the absence of visible disorder and the continued sitting of the courts are not conclusive evidence of a state of peace. Sir Frederick Pollock holds the view that the justification of any particular act done in a state of war is ultimately examinable in the ordinary courts, and that a person justifying his act must show not merely that he acted in good faith, but also that there was reasonable and probable cause according to the apparent urgency of the circumstances. (See Law Quarterly Review, Vol. XVIII, pages 156 to 158). Sir Frederick Pollock's view is criticised at length by Professor Dicey at pages 551 to 554 of note X in the Appendix to his "Law of the Constitution." The difference between the two eminent jurists consists in this : that the test proposed by Frederick Pollock would justify acts not dictated by immediate necessity, while according to Professor Dicey and a number of other jurists immediate necessity is the sole ground of justification.

It will be clear from the foregoing statement that in England there cannot at common law be any supersession of the civil courts by the exercise of the prerogative of the Crown. If, however, the disturbance of the country renders it imposible for the ordinary courts of law to sit or enforce the execution of their judgments, in such cases martial law is indulged rather than allowed as a law, and it is a rude substitute for the ordinary courts. In the language of Sir James Mackintosh, while the laws are silenced by the noise of arms the rulers of the armed force must punish as equitably as they can those crimes which threaten their own safety and that of society, but no longer. While the closure of the courts owing to the impossibility of exercising their functions is a reason for indulging martial law, the fact that the Courts may be actually sitting is not *conclusive* evidence of a state of peace. The ordinary courts of justice may, as a matter of fact, will be exercising their functions as a matter of sufferance by the military authorities. (See *Ex-parte* Marais, 1902, Appeal cases 109; Elphinstone *Vs.* Bedree Chand, I Knapp, P. C. 316).

Applying these principles to the case of the Punjab, could it be said that it was impossible for the ordinary courts to sit or exercise their functions, or that if they did it was only by sufferance of the military authorities. There is nothing to show this. It does not appear that the establishment of martial law in respect of offences other than those specified in Regulation 10 of 1804, was called for by the impossibility of the ordinary courts exercising their functions. The fact that trial by courts-martial is bound to be swifter or would serve as an example of terror to others and to keep the rest in due awe and obedience is not a sufficient justification in policy for the establishment of martial law. Even taking it for granted that the establishment of martial law was originally justified, the question whether the state of open rebellion or such circumstances as justified the introduction of martial law have continued in existence so as to justify the continuance of martial law, is also a question of fact.

One question which naturally arises with reference to the administration of martial law is, whether the Crown or the military authorities have any power at common law to create any new offences. According to the law in England, they clearly do not possess any such power. Where it is necessary to enable the military authorities to issue any rules or regulations affecting civilians and where it is necessary to treat any infringements as offences, the practice in England has been to confer such powers by statute; witness, for instance, the English Defence of the Realm Consolidation Act, 1914, 5. Geo. 5, Chapter 8. Section 1 of the statute expressly confers power to issue regulations and authorise trial and punishment by courts-martial. It will be interesting to note that by the Defence of the Realm Amendment Act, 1915, 5, Geo. 5, Chapter 34. Section I, any person not subject to the Naval Discipline Act or to military law, who is alleged to be guilty of an offence against any regulations made under the Defence of the Realm Consolidation Act, 1914, is entitled to be tried by a civil court with a jury instead of being tried by courts-martial.

The officer administering martial law in Lahore has issued a large number of proclamations partaking of the character of regulations and providing for the trial and punishment of persons guilty of an infringement of these regulations. These proclamations merely recite that the Government of India have proclaimed martial law, and that superior military authority has appointed him to administer martial law. No other source of authority is quoted, and while the officer in charge was entitled to take measures reasonably necessary for the safety and peace of the area under his command, he had, to all appearance, no valid authority empowering him to create any new offences or to try and punish civilians for infringements of his regulations. The Government of India, no doubt, are empowered by the Defence of India Act, IV of 1915, Section 2, to make rules for securing the public safety and the defence of British India and to create offences in respect of contraventions of such rules, but it does not appear that the Governor-General-in-Council has any power to delegate his powers under Section (2) to the military authorities. We do not know whether the officer administering martial law tried and punished any persons for infringements of his regulations, but if he did his proceedings cannot be treated as *ipso facto* valid. A perusal of the different orders passed by him also creates a doubt whether they were called for by the military necessities of the situation or by a desire to strike fear into the minds of the inhabitants by a show of exuberant severity or to secure certain conveniences for the public or particular sections thereof which would have been secured by the civil Government. Whatever might have been the reason of the regulations, any infringement of them could not be an offence unless it was one under some other law.

(3)—Legality of Courts of Area Officers

(By Syed Hasan Imam)

The question put to me is whether the Summary Courts in the district of Lyallpur under the order of Major-General Beynon for trial of offences constituted in connection with the recent events, were properly constituted in accordance with either the Ordinances issued by the Viceroy or the Indian Army Act.

The last Ordinance issued by the Viceroy is Ordinance No. VI called "The Martial Law (Trials Continuance) Ordinance, 1919". In giving my opinion, I must mention that while I have had the advantage of examining Ordinances 1, 2, 3, 4 and 6, I have not found Ordinance V in either the book called "The Martial Law in the Punjab," prepared for private use by Mr. Shaik Umar Baksh or in any of the issues of "The Independent" or the "Civil and Military Gazette" or in any other paper. Subject to what may be contained in Ordinance V, I proceed to give my opinion upon the constitution of the Summary Courts in the light of the provisions of Ordinances I, II, III, IV and VI and the Indian Army Act (Act VIII of 1911).

In Ordinance I, Section 2, it is laid down that every trial held under the Bengal State Offences Regulation, 1804, shall instead of being held by a Court-Martial be held by a Commission consisting of three persons appointed in this behalf by the Local Government; and the Local Government may appoint as many Commissions for this purpose as it may deem expedient. In Section 4 it is laid down that a Commission shall have all the powers of a General Court-Martial under the Indian Army Act and shall, subject to the provisions of this Ordinance, in all matters follow so far as may be, the procedure regulating trials by such Courts-Martial prescribed by or under the Act, provided that where in the opinion of the convening authority, summary trial is necessary in the interests of the public safety such authority may direct that the Commission shall follow the procedure prescribed for a Summary General Court-Martial by or under the said Act, and the Commission shall so far as may be and subject to the provisions of this Ordinance, follow such procedure accordingly.

Ordinance II merely extends the application of Sections 2 to 6 of Ordinance I to trial of persons in the district of Gujranwala.

Ordinance III merely deals with the question of sentences.

Ordinance IV merely authorises a Commission appointed under

Ordinance I to try persons charged with any offence committed on or after the 30th March, 1919.

Ordinance VI authorises the continuance of trials even after the cancellation of orders establishing Martial Law; and it provides that in cases of trials commenced before a Summary Court other than an Ordinary Criminal Court they shall, when the Summary Court ceases by reason of the cessation of Martial Law to exercise jurisdiction therein, be continued before any competent Criminal Court which would have had jurisdiction therein save for the existence of Martial Law. I find that in none of the Ordinances mentioned above is there any mention of the constitution of Summary Courts such as seem to have been established by the order of Major-General Beynon, dated the 5th May, 1919.

Major-General Beynon promulgated an order appointing certain officers to be Summary Courts for the trial of minor offences connected with or arising out of the recent disturbances and committed on or after the 30th March, 1919. According to that order such courts could only take cognizance of cases sent for trial by the Police and could not, in respect of any offence, pass any sentence which was not authorised by the ordinary law for that offence, and could not in respect of any offence pass any sentence which could not be passed by a first class Magistrate. The order further declares that the findings and sentences of such Courts shall not be subject to confirmation by any authority, nor shall any appeal or application for revision lie in respect of them. The officers appointed by Major-General Beynon were mostly officers of civil employee holding no military rank.

Under Section 53 of the Indian Army Act there are four kinds of Courts-Martial, namely, (1) General Courts-Martial, (2) District Courts-Martial, (3) Summary General Courts-Martial and (4) Summary Courts-Martial. A General Courts-Martial is to consist of at least seven officers; but when so many officers are not available, it would be permissible to have at least five officers to preside over the General Court-Martial. A District Court-Martial, under Sec. 58 of the Indian Army Act must consist of not less than three officers. A Summary General Court-Martial must also consist of not less than three officers as laid down in Section 68 of the Indian Army Act. The only Court-Martial that can be presided over by a single officer is the Summary Court-Martial.

Section 64 of the Indian Army Act runs thus :—

(1) "A Summary Court-Martial may be held (a) by the Commanding Officer of any Corps or Detachment of His Majesty's Indian Forces or of any detachment of these forces, (b) by the Commanding Officer of any British Corps or detachment to which details subject to this Act are attached. (2) At every Summary Court-Martial the officer holding the trial shall alone constitute the Court, but the proceedings shall be attended throughout by two other officers who shall not as such, be so affirmed."

It is quite clear, therefore, that the Summary Courts created by Major-General Beynon by his order of the 5th May, were no Courts as such, either under the Ordinances, I, II, III, IV and VI or under the Indian Army Act. If Ordinance V, which I have not been able to trace, makes any provision for the creation of Summary Courts, Major-General Beynon might or might not have been within his powers to create such Courts; but in the absence of Ordinance V, I am unable to pronounce an opinion thereon. But under the Ordinances I, II, III, IV and VI and the Indian Army Act, I have no doubt that Major-General Beynon had no authority to constitute Summary Courts, such as he did.

(4)—What is Martial Law

(From Encyclopaedia of the Laws of England, Vol. VIII)

Martial Law orginally meant the law administered in the Court of Earl Marshal by the constable and marshal, over troops in actual service, whether in the realm or without, and accordingly it used to be written "Marshal law" and we retain the form in Judge-Marshal and provost-marshal; but in Courts-Martial and martial law the changed form is in use. Martial Law then was what is now known as Military Law. The law which had thus been used for the government of armies in the field was frequently made use of by the sovereigns before Charles I, and by that king to punish subjects in rebellion. Commissions were issued, as is recited in the Petition of Right (3 Chas. I.C.I.), to certain persons to proceed in particular cases "according to the justice of martial law," and thereby persons had been put to death who, if deserving death, ought to have been tried in the ordinary way while others pleading privilege, had escaped. Such Commissions were declared to be wholly and directly contrary to the laws and statutes of the realm, and accordingly it was provided that no such Commission should in future be issued. Ths suspension of the ordinary laws of the land, and the temporary government of a country, or portions of it, by Military Tribunals, is the second and proper meaning of the term Martial Law. It is in this sense that most writers on the constitution and the army speak of Martial Law as being unknown to English jurisprudence, and as having no place in the institutions of the country.

Military Law providing for the discipline of the army is sometimes called Martial Law, and that of course takes its place in the institutions of the country. So also Martial Law is used here as a compendious term for the Common Law right of the Crown and its representatives, to repel force by force, in the case of invasion, insurrection, or riot, and to act against rebels as if they were foreign invaders, in order to put down the disturbances, although the parties afterwards must be tried by the ordinary courts, and all officers who may have used excessive and unnecessary force may be liable themselves to be called to answer for their acts.

P·ıt the truly distinctive use of the term "Martial Law" is the suspension of the ordinary law and its substitution by the law of Military Tribunals set over all the population of a district, and no provision is made for that in the English constitution, which is called the "state of siege" on the continent of Europe, where the Civil Law is suspended for the time being, or made subordinate to the Millitary, and the place or district is put under the authority of the Military power. Yet it is in similar circumstances to those in which the state of siege is proclaimed that the English proclamations of Martial Law, as they are called, have from time to time taken place in our history. Whatever may be the true meaning of this, and whatever the legal effect, it is certain that it has been left without specific definition, and it is not regulated by known limitations as is the case in the countries just mentioned.

There shall not be substituted Military Tribunals for the punishment of rebels or rioters after the suppression of disturbances by the Military, is quite clear. When peace has become established, all wrong-doers must be handed over to the Civil power, since it is illegal to resort to Martial Law as a special mode of punishing rebellion. On the other hand, whatever powers may be necessary for suppressing the rebellion and restoring order, whatever physical force is required to be used for that purpose, even to the destruction of life and property to any extent, may be justified by the Military authorities. But this does not imply that wanton and excessive means beyond those absolutely necessary are justifiable. If such are used, the Military are responsible, both civilly and criminally, as if there had been no proclamation of Martial Law, and like other citizens. But it seems clear also that amongst the methods employed for suppressing a rebellion, as distinct from punishment after the rising has been put down and the ordinary courts of justice are available, is that of holding inquiries and inflicting such punishment as may be necessary to attain the sole object the Military Law has in view, *viz.*, the suppression of the disturbances and establishment of the ordinary course of things.

The late Sir James Fitz-James Stephen, in the *History of the Criminal Law*, Vol. I, 721 p, speaking of the Military Courts held for such a purpose, points out that they are not Courts-Martial properly speaking, but Committees for deciding on the excercise of the discretionary power of the Military. The officers are not administering a Law but doing acts which must be supposed to be for suppressing the rebellion; and the holding of the inquiry is a means of showing that they are acting in good faith, they are not protected as if they were performing judicial acts on Courts-Martial, properly so called, under the Army Act; and they remain personally liable if they take any proceedings through such a Court or Committee in excess of what is necessary for suppressing the rebellion. The distinction between such a Court and one held after the restoration of peace is exemplified by the case of *Wolfe Tone* (27 St. Tri, 614), who, having taken part in 1798 in a French invasion in aid of rebellion in Ireland, was captured when the French surrendered, and therefore after the suppression of the rebellion was accomplished. A Court-Martial sentenced him to death, but the Court of King's Bench caused him to be released on a *habeas corpus*.

Something more than this is claimed by those writers who assert that the proclamation of Martial Law is the assertion of some prerogative power of the Crown distinct from its Common Law right of calling upon all citizens to assist, by the use of necessary physical force, in suppressing rebellion. Within the realm, it is admitted that the Petition of Right forbids the issuing of Commissions for holding tribunals by Court-Martial after the rebellion is suppressed; but it is affirmed that except to his extent, the prerogative exists, both within the realm and in the dominions outside the realm of England, as it did before in the case of war and of rebellion. Lord Blackburn in his charge to the grand jury in the case of *R. Vs. Eyre* 1867, (Finlason's Report, pp. 70, 71), puts this claim on behalf of the Crown thus "That whilst the insurrection existed, pending the insurrection, and, for a short time afterwards, the Crown had, and *de facto* exercised, the power to proclaim Martial Law, in the sense of using summary proceedings to punish the insurgents, and to check and stop the spread of the rebellion by summary proceedings against the insurgents, so as, to adopt a modern phrase, 'to stamp out the rebellion!' " Upon this he observed, "Now no doubt the extent to which the Crown had power to do that has never yet been decided. It has never come to be decided what this precise power is". Nothing has occurred since then to settle the law more definitely; and the best opinion seems to be that Martial Law, as it is known in England, is only another name for the Common Law duty incumbent on all citizens to put down rebellion by all possible means.

It is to be noted that the proclamations of Martial Law which have been made in the 18th century, and within the present century, do not proceed upon this asserted prerogative power, and do not assume to set up the "state of siege," but merely justify the use of arms against rebels; and after the suppression of the insurrection Acts of Indemnity have always been passed for the purpose of indemnifying those responsible for carrying out repressive measures, unless they can be shown to have acted maliciously and oppressively, in excess of the requirements of the position. In a despatch published in Clode, *Military Forces of the Crown,* Vol. II, p. 511, in respect of an Indemnity Act passed by the Legislature of St. Vincent in 1862, it is said: "The first clause declares the proclamation of Martial Law to have been '*lawfully issued*'; but this is not the fact, and ought not have been so declared. In proclaiming Martial Law the executive authority in fact declares itself obliged, for the protection of the community, to neglect law, trusting to the legislature to relieve all who, in obedience to the constituted authority, may have acted in defence of the public safety, from the consequences of having acted unlawfully. The proclamation was right and necessary but it was not strictly lawful."

(5)—The Jamaica Rebellion

(a) The rebellion in Jamaica and the consequent declaration of Martial Law with special reference to the case of George William Gordon, a coloured member of the House Assembly

(*Extracts from "A Treatise on Martial Law." By Finlason*)

The Governor could only act upon the representations he received, and the first official account was from the "Custos" of the Parish who would answer to the Lord Lieutenant of a country, who wrote to the Governor, describing a desperate outrage upon justice and informing him of the apprehensions entertained of an attack from the rebels and requesting the assistance of a Military Force, stating that the Civil Force was quite inadequate. The account showed what evidently was a designed and deliberate outrage, with the intention of resisting justice. Upon receiving this account, the Governor at once demanded Military assistance in aid of the Civil Force, and for the protection of the magistracy; which, however, so speedy was the progress of the insurgents from riot to open rebellion, was too late to prevent a sanguinary attack upon the magistracy, and a small Civil and Military force they had for their protection.—(Pages, 115-116).

When, therefore, next day he received intelligence of the dreadful massacre which had occurred and found that the blacks had risen in rebellion and that it was expected that they were preparing to advance in a career of plunder and murder, he at once saw that it was a case with which it was impossible for the small Military Force then at his command to cope without declaring Martial Law; and accordingly he at once summoned a Council with whose concurrence, as they were unanimously of the same opinion, it was resolved to declare Martial Law; and accordingly next day it was declared under statutable authority.—(P. 125-126).

On the second day after the outbreak of the rebellion into insurrection, Martial Law was declared in the disturbed district, by which it was declared that the Military Forces should have all power of exercising the rights of belligerents against such of the inhabitants as the Military might consider opposed to the Government, and to the peaceable and well-disposed subjects.—(P. 127).

The Commander-in-Chief having chosen a superior officer to command as Brigadier in the field, gave him general but no special instructions, but considering him as well informed as himself as to the state of affairs, left him and the officers under him, to carry on the Military operations according to his own judgment, giving them no particular directions as to the mode of carrying out Martial Law, beyond general directions to capture rebels and dipose of them summarily according to their deserts.

The general principle was laid down by the Commander-in-Chief, that rebels were to be captured; that if they were guilty and taken red-handed under circumstances which made their guilt clear, they were to suffer summary justice, but if this guilt was doubtful, they were to be released, and this was interpreted by the General in active command to mean that all ringleaders or those who were found in arms were to be summarily dealt with, whether or not found actually engaged in conflict or attack—as being in arms not on the side of the Crown, was a clear act of rebellion.—(Pages 138-139).

On the third day after the declaration of Martial Law the General in Command of the forces on service sent a despatch to the Commander-in-Chief and through him to the Governor disclosing that Courts-Martial had been held for the trial of prisoners and that a number had been convicted and executed for active participation in the rebellion, and the acts of murder by which it had been commenced prior to the declaration of Martial Law. And this course had the assent of the Commander-in-Chief and the Governor-General.—(Pages 148-149).

Very soon after the Military operations commenced, the officer in command of a principal detachment informed the Commander-in-Chief that he was necessarily embarrassed by the large number of prisoners whom he hesitated to execute and of course could not retain; and the substance of the directions he received was that he should execute all whose complicity in the rebellion was clear, inflict minor punishments for mere acts of plunder and release the rest, and the General in actual command approved of a similar proceeding.—(Page 150).

Within a week after the rebellion broke out, the Governor, anxious to unite conciliation with terror and prepare the way for a termination of Martial Law, proposed the consideration of an amnesty excepting actual murderers, but his Council were of opinion that it was far too soon to think of it and that it would not be safe to do so until more troops had arrived.—(Page 161).

It was at this point in the case that the prisoner, supposed to be the real author of the rebellion, was ordered by the Governor to be arrested out of the district in which Martial Law was declared and to be taken to the district with a view to his trial.—(Page 176).

The Governor in a despatch* which he wrote immediately afterwards to the Secretary of State, set forth grounds and reasons on which he had ordered the arrest and avowed his responsibility for it—that is for the act of arrest and the removal of the prisoner in custody into the proclaimed district upon the charge of having caused or incited to the rebellion there.—(Page 176).

The question whether there was evidence on which any charge could be framed which would be cognizable under Martial Law, was deemed to be one purely Military and resting with the Military Commanders to determine. The General in command considered the evidence with a view to determine it and convened the Court and controlled the proceedings.

So it was the Military Commander who framed the charges on which the prisoner was tried, the twofold charge of treason and sedition and the charge of complicity with the rebels or in other words conspiring with them to incite the blacks to rebellion. The first was in substance a charge of actually engaging in or raising the rebellion—the other charge of conspiring with the ringleaders, both charge equally capital, under Martial Law.

The charges against the prisoners therefore were in substance rebellion, and conspiracy to incite to rebellion, that is, rebellion generally, not necessarily the particular insurrection. Nor would it necessarily involve an actual intent to raise such an insurrection as had burst forth.—(Pages 190-191).

The result of the Court-Martial was that Gordon was found guilty and sentenced to be hanged.

---

* Despatch of Governor Eyre, dated 20th October :— There was one very important point to be decided upon. Throughout my tour I found everywhere the most unmistakable evidence that Mr. George William Gordon, a Coloured Member of the House of Assembly, had not only been mixed up in the matter, but was himself through his own misrepresentations and seditious language addressed to the ignorant black people, the chief cause and origin of the whole rebellion. Mr Gordon was now in Kingston and it became necessary to decide.

The Commander-in-Chief having received the report of the proceedings, sent it to the Governor* without any disapproval.

The Secretary of State on receipt of the Governor's despatch reporting the breaking out of the rebellion and acquainting him with the measures which had been taken to suppress the insurrection and prevent its spreading wrote a despatch conveying general approval of the measures thus taken, but reserving a more particular expression of opinion and pointing out that passages in the Military reports required explanation. The same despatch, however, contained passages which while recognizing the humanity, and propriety, on the score of humanity, not less than policy, of measures of severity for the suppression of the rebellion, indicated a desire for explanation of certain general statements in the despatches, and which were supposed to indicate that those measures had been carried further than necessary, and for satisfactory evidence that this had not been so.—(Pages 232-233).

At the same time in a separate despatch, the Secretary of State desired to be furnished with the evidence in the case of the person who had been executed as the author of the rebellion and to be informed whether the Governor's approval of the execution "rested on evidence of the prisoner's participation in the insurrection itself or the lesser offence of seditious language, *calculated but not intended*

---

what action should be taken with regard to him. Having obtained a depositon on oath that certain seditious printed notices had been sent through the Post Office, directed in his handwriting to the parties who have been leaders in the rebellion, I at once called upon the *Custos* to issue a warrant and capture him. For sometime he managed to evade capture; but finding that sooner or later it was inevitable, he proceeded to the house of General O'Connor and there gave himself up. I at once had him placed on board the Wolverine for safe custody and conveyance to Morant Bay. Great difference of opinion prevailed in Kingston as to the policy of taking Mr. Gordon. Nearly all coincided in believing him to be the occasion of the rebellion and that he ought to be taken; but many of the inhabitants were under considerable apprehension that his capture might lead to an immediate outbreak in Kingston itself. I did not share in this feeling. Moreover considering it right in the abstract, and desirable as a matter of policy that whilst the poor black men who had been misled were undergoing condign punishment, the chief instigator of all the evil should not go unpunished, I at once took upon myself the responsibility of the capture.—(176).

* His Excellency returned the documents with this letter:— King's House October 22, 1866—Sir—I have the honour to acknowledge.

to produce rebellion;" and he also desired explanation of Gordon's removal from a district not under Martial Law into the proclaimed district for trial under Martial Law.—(Pages 236-237).

The official despatch from the Commander-in-Chief to the Secretary of State for War contained a serious charge against the Governor of having "crowded the camps with political prisoners and rebels, captured in districts not under Martial Law and whom the Governor desired to have tried by Martial Law," that is, as the Commander-in-Chief represented, illegally. Upon these official representations, the Secretary of State addressed to the Governor another despatch enclosing them and containing more specific and categorical demands for information as to the number of persons killed, either in the field or by sentence of Court-Martial and under what circumstances in each class of cases.—(Pages 243-244).

On this a Royal Commission of Enquiry was appointed.

The Commission was in short a species of Court of Enquiry, a kind of investigation which, for upwards of a century, the Crown has been accustomed to institute, not with any judicial character, but for the *purpose of informing its own conscience* as to the conduct of its officers in public and military capacities, in cases where it does not appear that there are sufficient grounds for Courts-Martial or for any criminal proceeding.—(Page 257).

The object and scope of the enquiry were clearly and concisely indicated by the Secretary of State in his letter to the Head Commissioner on the occasion of his appointment and were declared distinctly to be to "enquire into the origin, nature and circumstances of the recent disturbance and into the measures taken in the course

---

receipt of your communication dated today, transmitting for my information copy of a despatch received at noon this day, from Brigadier-General Nelson with proceedings of a Court-Martial on G. W. Gordon and other documents which you requested me, after perusal, to return to you with as little delay as possible. I have duly read the papers referred to and I fully concur in the justice of the sentence and the policy of carrying it into effect. There can be little doubt, I think, whatever Mr. Gordon's intention may have been, it is entirely due to his agitation, bad advice and seditious language amongst the peasantry of this colony, that the rebellion broke out and the massacre of so many gentlemen and the destruction of so much property ensued. It will be remembered also by Your Excellency that colonel commanding another force in the field has reported that he has sufficient evidence to justify the execution of Mr. Gordon.

of their repression"; the basis of the enquiry being also stated to be the despatches already addressed to the Governor, containing the demands for information required by Her Majesty's Government.—(Pages 259-260).

There was abundant evidence that there was diffused among the negro population deep-rooted impressions and ideas as to emancipation, especially as to its involving their right to the back or waste lands, without payment of rent and there was also ample evidence to connect it with the present rebellion.

That the real origin of the disturbances was agrarian discontent and the desire among the peasantry for the acquisition of land and a notion which had been imposed into their minds that emancipation involved their title to the lands, was proved by the entire evidence as to the language of the ringleaders and in the opinion of the most intelligent and impartial persons who heard the whole of the evidence, it was the impression it conveyed.—(Page 272).

There was abundant evidence that there had been a system of agitation calculated to incite the blacks to rise in rebellion and every possible effort used to make them believe themselves oppressed and to excite their feelings of animosity to the utmost against the white race. And that the leaders perfectly well knew that the course they were taking must lead to anarchy and rebellion and were warned of it, and persisted.—(Pages 274-275).

Evidence was likewise given that the character of the black pupulation was such, from ignorance and credulity and excitability, that agitation and disaffection were calculated to work far more

---

This latter evidence too is quite unconnected with that adduced before the Court-Martial, and has not been under consideration at all—I believe that, were condign punishment to fall only on the ignorant people who have been misled into rebellion and the educated coloured man who led to that rebellion to escape, a very unfortunate impression would be produced upon the public mind which in the present state of the colony might lead to very serious results. It is only by making it plain to the entire population that the guilty agitator and user of seditious language will meet the same punishment as the uneducated fools whom he misleads, that we can hope to check and put down the spirit of disloyalty and disaffection, already so rife in the land, and which may at any moment occasion in other parishes outrages similar to those which have recently occurred in St. Thomas in the East. I received Your Excellency's letter at 4.30 p.m. and I return the documents contained in it without delay as requested, I have & c, E. Eyre—(Pages 198-199).

serious mischief and cause far more imminent peril than might result in a colder or more reasonable race; and that in the opinion of those who were best acquainted with them, from long residence in the island, in such a state of disaffection, a spark would be sufficient to cause a flame of insurrection through the island even without any premeditation or actual combination.—(Page 277).

There was positive evidence, confirmed by a great deal of circumstantial evidence, that the attacks on the Police in the district had been deliberately arranged by the leaders of the rebellion, and this only a week before the outbreak; and that all that followed was in consequence of these deliberate arrangements.—(Page 280).

That the massacre, which was the outbreak of the rebellion, was deliberate and designed, was proved not only by the words and acts of the open and acting leaders, but by the knowledge of others—the more secret leaders at a distance—as to what was about to occur and warning given to intended victims.

It was proved that many of the prisoners, executed under martial law, declared with their dying breath, that the two men executed as the secret and active leaders of the rebellion had brought them to that end, which was naturally enough regarded at the time as sufficient ground for suspicion.—(Pages 282-283).

Evidence was given as to the circumstances of the disturbances; and the circumstances under which martial law was declared. For the first ten days after the outbreak of the rebellion, the utmost alarm and consternation prevailed through the eastern and central parts of the island, especially the eastern, where the insurrection had broken out; the whites were driven in numbers, from their residences, forced to seek safety in flight, and it was not until after the lapse of a fortnight, and after energetic military measures, that anything like confidence began to be restored.—(Pages 289-290).

Evidence was also taken as to the local extent of martial law, or the district as to which it was declared and applied; and it appeared that the Commander-in-Chief was always of opinion that the entire island should be declared; but that the Governor was of opinion that it should be confined to the district in which the actual outbreak of rebellion had taken place, and that, on grounds of public convenience, the principal city should be excepted.

Reason of policy and public convenience having prevented the Governor from putting that city under martial law, the Governor avowed that he had taken upon himself the responsibility of directing the arrest of several persons there, for supposed complicity in the rebellion; and he stated the grounds and reasons upon which he took those measures; which were the only, or the principal active operative measures, he took personally, upon his own responsibility.—(Pages 298-300).

The military officers, it appeared, endeavoured to the utmost in carrying out martial law, to apply it only to *hostility*, and to distinguish between that and mere felony, not connected with, or necessarily involving, hostility or rebellion. But, on the other hand, in a warfare against rebels, who waged *their* warfare against the loyal subjects of the Crown, not in an honorable and regular way, but by felonious acts of arson and devastation—they did not consider that the only evidence of hostility was the use of arms.

It must be clearly kept in mind that, at common law, the military could not lawfully kill or inflict sentence of death, even in cases of men, not only found in arms, but even in cases of those found in the *act* of felonious outrage, unless the infliction of death was *necessary* to *prevent* the act of outrage, or to prevent the escape of the felon, or unless it occurred in the encounter with a felonious or rebellious body. And, therefore, martial law would be required to authorise even the execution of those found in arms, or with arms in their hands, or even taken in the act of arson or murder. On the other hand, in the view of the military authorities, the severities of martial law were not restricted to such cases, although, by military usage, the power of instant execution, without enquiry, might be so restricted.

The officers stated, moreover, as they had in their reports, the circumstances of embarrassment under which they soon found themselves placed by the accumulation of prisoners, and the difficulty, or rather practical impossibility of guarding them, and the consequent necessity of dealing summarily with them in some way, upon summary enquiry, which is one of the primary and main difficulties to be met with by martial law, when the number of prisoners is far too great to be dealt with in the ordinary way, and they can only, from the nature of the case, be dealt with summarily.—(Pages 347-349).

The Commissioners entered particularly into the case of Gordon, the person who had been, by order of the Governor, arrested in the place excepted out of the declared district, and sent into it, with a view to his trial, if there should, in the opinion of the General-in-Command, be sufficient evidence to warrant it. For that arrest and removal, no doubt, he was responsible, and they conducted his examination, evidently with a view to the propriety of the measure, and not merely with reference to its legality, as to which, indeed, many of the topics they entered into would be irrelevent.—(Pages 392-393).

As regarded the arrest and removal of the prisoner, for which alone the Governor was responsible, evidence was entered into, as to whether the facts justified him, morally as well as legally; and as to this, persons in the highest position, and of the best means of information, firmly believed the prisoner to be the author of the rebellion; and, on the other hand, there was sworn evidence of an act of seditious incitement in the declared district, for which he was liable to be tried there, and nowhere else.—(Page 395).

The only grounds on which the fairness of the trial was attempted to be impeached was the omission of the court to adjourn, in order to allow the prisoner the opportunity of trying to produce some witness to prove something to explain matters entirely collateral, and, indeed, comparatively immaterial, on which he had produced a witness who did not support his statement, and upon this, it appeared, that he did not himself ask for adjournment.

This could hardly affect the substantial question, which was, whether he had a fair trial. The Commissioners entered, it is true, also, into other matters, and into the non-observance of the legal rules of evidence, as to the reception of depositions of absent witnesses, or of oral evidence of the contents of written documents, and the like; but this, it is to be presumed, was not upon the view that these rules are obligatory upon drumhead courts-martial, under martial law, but with a view to ascertain how far their non-observance was wilful and intentional, or had operated, in the particular case, substantial injustice. (Pages 404-405).

The Commissioners took great care to enquire whether any substantial injustice or injury had been done to the prisoner by the receiving these depositions; and with this view they had before them the witnesses whose depositions had been received, and examined them, and allowed them to be cross-examined, and, beyond all doubt, they adhered to their depositions, and were not shaken in the least.—(Page 407).

It is to be observed here, that the great object of martial law being to admit of more prompt and speedy deterrent measures than can be attained at common law, it would make it of no avail, if those strict rules of evidence were to be observed, the effect of which must necessarily be to interpose great delay, while the legal evidence is being obtained. Thus, to procure the attendance of witnesses at a distance, would cause a delay of several days; and the very necessity for martial law, a present emergency, would render such delay inadmissible. It would have necessitated a postponement of the trial.

The great question, both moral and legal, was, whether the prisoner had had a fair trial, and this, it was clear, he had.

That is, he heard the evidence given against him; anything he had to say upon it, either in the way of cross examination or observation, was listened to; he was heard patiently in his own defence and any witness he had he was allowed to examine in his defence.—(Pages 408-409).

Before stating the report of the Royal Commissioners, so far as it bore on the subject of martial law, it may be well to refer to its terms and its recitals. The Commission recited :—"That it is alleged that great disaffection prevailed in the island, and that evil-disposed persons had concerted the destruction of other subjects therein. That grievous disturbances had broken out in the island and had been suppressed, and that the said disturbances and suppression had been attended with great loss of life, and, it is alleged, that excessive and unlawful severity had been used in such suppression. And that it greatly concerns us that full and impartial enquiry should be made into the origin, nature, and circumstances of the said disturbances, and with respect to the measures adopted for the suppression of the same, and the conduct of those engaged in such suppression."

The Commissioners, after sitting in Jamaica for many weeks, and taking the evidence of hundreds of witnesses, agreed to a Report, which, while entering into many particular cases, and details, not necessary to enter into here, contained much general matter, very valuable for future guidance, especially as it was adopted by the Crown.—(Pages 418 and 419).

(b) Case *and* Joint Opinion *of* Mr. Edward James, Q. C. *and* Mr. Fitzjames Stephen, Q.C., *on Martial Law, with reference to the Jamaica Insurrection, 1866*

(From "Cases and Opinions on Constitutional Law" by William Forsyth—Appendix, Pages 551-563.).

Case submitted by the Jamaica Committee :—The Committee desires to be advised what steps are open to them to assist their fellow-subjects in Jamaica to obtain the protection of the law; and, if the law has been broken, to bring the guilty parties to justice; and also what steps are open to them, as Englishmen, to vindicate constitutional law and order, if constitutional law and order have been illegally set aside by the local Government in Jamaica.

With this are sent copies of the despatch from Governor Eyre to Mr. Secretary Cardwell, on the 20th of October, 1865, and also of the Address of the Governor to the Jamaica House of Legislature, at the annual meeting which took place on the 7th of November. Copies are also sent of such reports of the military officers as have appeared in the papers.

Considering for the present nothing but these official documents, and taking for granted that the statements they contain are all true, counsel is requested to advise :

1. What is the meaning of the term "martial law," and what is the legal effect of a proclamation of martial law ?

2. Are there grounds for concluding that Governor Eyre has acted illegally and criminally in the mode in which he states that he has proclaimed and enforced martial law, and especially in removing the Hon. G. W. Gordon from Kingston to Morant Bay, and there handing him over to Brigadier-General Nelson, to be tried by court-martial ?

3. Could Mr. Gordon be legally convicted and punished by court-martial for any act done prior to the proclamation of martial law, or for any act done beyond the boundaries of the proclaimed district?

4. Are officers acting in enforcing martial law exempt form all control beyond the instructions they receive from their superior officers? If not, are there any principles acknowledged by martial law, or by the British Constitution, which would render it illegal— (*a*) to continue for several days shooting down men, and flogging men, women and children, and burning their habitations, in the absence of the appearance of organized resistance; (*b*) to inflict punishment without or before trial; (*c*) to inflict punishment for the

purpose of obtaining evidence; (*d*) to inflict death for or on the evidence of looks or gestures ?

5. In case Governor Eyre or his subordinate officers have been guilty of illegal acts in the course of the late proceedings in Jamaica, what are the proper modes of bringing them to trial for such illegal acts ?

6. Are any and (if any) what, proceedings for the above purpose open to private persons in this country ?

7. The last question has reference to a bill of indemnity, if one should be passed by the Jamaica Legislature.

<u>*Opinion*</u>—The questions asked in this Case all depend more or less upon the general question, "What is the nature of martial law, and what power does it confer?" We will, therefore, state our view of this subject before answering the specific questions asked, and we must do so at some length, on account both of the importance and the obscurity of the subject. The expression "martial law" has been used at different times in four different senses, each of which must be carefully distinguished from the others :—

1. In very early times various systems of law co-existed in this country—as the common law, the ecclesiastical law, the law of the Court of Admiralty, &c. One of these was the law martial, exercised by the constable and marshal over troops in actual service, and especially on foreign service. As to this, *see* an essay on the "Laws of War," by Professor Montague Bernard, in the "Oxford Essays" for 1856.

2. The existence of this system in cases of foreign service or actual warfare, appears to have led to attempts on the parts of various sovereigns to introduce the same system in times of peace on emergencies, and especially for the punishment of breaches of the peace. This was declared to be illegal by the Petition of Right, as we shall show more fully immediately. (*See* Hallam's "Constitutional History," vol. I., p. 240, 7th edition, ch. v., near the beginning.)

3. When standing armies were introduced, the powers of the constable and marshal fell into disuse, and the discipline of the army was provided for by annual Mutiny Acts, which provide express regulations for the purpose. These regulations form a code, which is sometimes called martial, but more properly military law. (Grant and Gould 2 H. Blackstone, 69).

4. Although martial law in sense (1) is obsolete, being superseded

by military law, and in sense (2) is declared by the Petition of Right to be illegal, the expression has survived, and has been applied (as we think, inaccurately and improperly) to a very different thing—namely, to the common-law right of the Crown and its representatives to repel force by force in the case of invasion or insurrection. We shall proceed to develop and illustrate this view of the subject.

The provisions of the Petition of Right on Martial Law (3 Car. I., c. I.), are contained in ss. 7, 8, 9, 10. These sections recite that commissions under the Great Seal had lately been issued to certain persons to proceed in particular cases "according to the justice of martial law;" and that thereby persons had been put to death who, if deserving of death, ought to have been tried in the ordinary way, whilst others, pleading privilege, had escaped. Such commissions are then declared to be illegal; and it is provided that henceforth no commissions of like nature may issue forth to any person or persons whatsoever.

The commissions themselves explain the nature of the system which the Petition of Right prohibited. Three, which were issued shortly before it passed, are given in 17 "Rymer's Foedera" (pp. 43, 246, 647). They are dated respectively 24th November, 1617; 20th July, 1620; 30th December, 1624. The first is a commission to certain persons for the government of Wales and the counties of Worcester, Hereford and Shropshire. It directs them to call out the array of the county, and then proceeds to direct them to lead the array—

"As well against all and singular our enemies, as also against all and singular rebells, traytors, and other offenders and their adherents, against us our Crowne and dignitie, with the said principalitie and dominions of North Wales and South Wales, the marches of the same, and counties and places aforesaid, and with the said traytors and rebells from tyme to tyme to fight, and them to invade, resist, suppresse, subdue, slay, kill, and put to execution of death, by all ways and means, from tyme to tyme by your discretion.

"And further to doe, execute, and use against the said enemies, traytors, rebells, and such other like offenders and their adherents afore-mentioned, from tyme to tyme as necessitie shall require, by your discretion, the law called the martiall lawe according to the law martiall, and of such offenders apprehended or being brought in subjection, to save whom you shall think good to be saved, and to slay, destroie, and put to execution of death, such and as many of them as you shall think meete by your good discretion, to be put to death."

The second empowers Sir Robert Maunsel to govern the crews of certain ships intended for the suppression of piracy, and gives him "full powers to execute and take away their life, or any member, in form and order of martial law."

The third is a commission to the Mayor of Dover, and others, reciting that certain troops, then at Dover, were licentious, and empowering them—

"To proceed according to the justice of martial law against such soldiers with any of our lists aforesaid, and other dissolute persons joining with them, or any of them, as during such time as any of our said troops or companies of soldiers shall remain or abide there, and not be transported thence, shall, within any of the places or precincts aforesaid, at any time after the publication of this our commission, commit any robberies, felonies, mutinies, or other outrages or misdemeanors, which by the martial law should or ought to be punished with death, and by such summary course and order as is agreeable to martial law, and as is used in armies in time of war, to proceed to the trial and condemnation of such delinquents and offenders, and them cause to be executed and put to death according to the law martial, for an example of terror to others, and to keep the rest in due awe and obedience."

The distinctive feature of all these commissions is, that they authorise not merely the suppression of revolts by military force, which is undoubtedly legal, but the subsequent punishment of offenders by illegal tribunals, which is the practice forbidden by the Petition of Right. In illustration of this we may compare the proceedings described in Governor Eyre's despatch with the course taken by a Lieutenant-general and his Provost-marshal in the reign of Queen Elizabeth, under one of the commissions declared to be illegal by the Petition of Right. In 1569 the Earls of Northumberland and Westmoreland had risen and besieged and taken Barnard Castle, and committed other acts of open treasonable warfare. The rising took place, and was suppressed, in the course of the month of December. The Earl of Sussex received from the Queen a commission, evidently similar to the one already cited, and appointed Sir George Bower his Provost-marshal. Sir George Bower made a circuit through Durham and Yorkshire, between the 2nd and the 20th of January, 1569, and executed at various places 600 persons. (Sharpe's

"Memorials of the Rebellion," No. 1569, pp. 99, 113, 121, 133, 140, 143, 153, 163.)

It appears from Governor Eyre's despatch, passing by earlier portions, which contain instances of acts done by the so-called courts-martial susceptible perhaps of a construction different from those which follow, that at daybreak on Monday, the 16th of October (paragraph 41), the last definite act of violence mentioned having taken place on the 15th (*see* paragraph 33), a court-martial sat to try prisoners, and twenty-seven were found guilty and hung. By the 18th (paragraph 55), many rebels had been captured, and several courts-martial had been held and capital punishment inflicted. On the 19th (paragraph 57), all was going on well in camp, more rebels had been captured or shot. Afterwards, on the 23rd of October, Mr. Gordon was hung. As Governor Eyre mentioned no acts of violence subsequent to that above referred to, it would appear that these executions were punishments for past offences, and not acts required for the suppression of open insurrection. The measures adopted thus resemble those taken by Sir George Bower, in 1569, under the authority of the commission declared illegal by the Petition of Right. As to the legal character of such punishments, Lord Coke observes (3rd Inst., c. 7, p. 52): "If a lieutenant, or other that hath commission of martial authority in time of peace, hang, or otherwise execute any man by colour of martial law, this is murder; for this is against Magna Charta, c. 29." (*See* too Hale, Hist. C. L. 34.)

These authorities appear to show that it is illegal for the Crown to resort to martial law as a special mode of punishing rebellion.

We now proceed to consider the authorities which look in the other direction. In 1799, an Act of the Irish Parliament (39 Geo. 3, c. 11) was passed, the effect of which was to put the parts of the country which were still in rebellion under military command, according to a system therein described. The preamble states that the rebellion had been already suppressed, and it sets forth that on the 24th of May, 1798, Lord Camden did, by and under the advice of the Privy Council, issue his orders to all general officers commanding his Majesty's forces, to punish all persons acting, ordering, or in any way assisting in the said rebellion, according to martial law, either by death or otherwise, as to them should seem expedient, and did by his proclamation of the same date ratify the same. It further goes on to recite, that "by the wise and salutary exercise of his Majesty's undoubted prerogative in executing martial law, for defeating and dispersing such armed and rebellious force, and in bringing diverse rebels and traitors to punishment in the most speedy and summary manner, the peace of the kingdom has been so far restored as to permit the course of the comman law partially to take place," &c. And in the body of the Act (section 6) there is contained a proviso that "nothing in this Act shall be construed to abridge or diminish the undoubted prerogative of His Majesty, for the public safety, to resort to the exercise of martial law against open enemies or traitors."

It is impossible to suppose that such a declaration as this should operate as a repeal of the Petition of Right as regarded Ireland, though the language of the two Acts appears to be conflicting. As, however, it merely declares an "undoubted prerogative of the Crown," it cannot refer to what the Petition of Right expressly denied to exist, and therefore it must probably be construed to mean only that the Crown has an undoubted prerogative to attack an army of rebels by regular forces under military law, conducting themselves as armies in the field usually do. This construction is strengthened by the fact that traitors are coupled with open enemies. Now, the force used against an invading army is used for the purpose, not of punishment, but of conquest, and thus the words in the Irish Act would mean only that the Crown has an undoubted prerogative to carry on war against an army of rebels, as it would against an invading army, and to inflict upon them such punishment as might be necessary to suppress the rebellion, and to restore the peace, and to permit the common law to take effect.

As soon, however, as the actual conflict was at an end, it would be the duty of the military authorities to hand over their prisoners to the civil powers. This was affirmed by the case of Wolfe Tone, who, having been captured when the French surrendered, was sent up to Dublin Barracks, tried by a court-martial, and sentenced to death. The Court of King's Bench immediately granted a *habeas corpus* and directed the sheriff to take into custody the Provost-marshal and officers in charge, and to see that Mr. Tone was not executed (27 St. Tr. 624-5). No doubt many Military executions took place during the Irish rebellion, but an Act of Indemnity was passed in respect to them, and it must also be remembered that by the laws of war (which are a branch of morals rather than of law proper and prevail not over soldiers, but as between contending armies), many severities may be justified, such as the refusal of quarter, and the putting to death of soldiers who surrender at discretion; and thus, in a war like that in 1798, much might be done which might pass under the name of martial law, but which in reality would be no more than incidents of ordinary warfare conducted with unusual rigour.

Another argument is drawn from the annual Mutiny Acts. They contain a declaration that "no man can be forejudged of life or limb, or subjected to any punishment within this realm by martial law, in time of peace." This has been construed to imply that in times of war or disturbance martial law is legal. As to this, however, it must be remembered that in its original meaning, the phrase "martial law" included what we now understand by military law, and that one principal object of the commissions declared to be illegal by the Petition of Right, was the creation of military tribunals without Parliamentary authority. Hence the words "in peace," which were not in the first Mutiny Act, probably mean that standing armies and military courts were, in time of peace, illegal, except in so far as they were expressly authorised by Parliament.

The whole doctrine of martial law was discussed at great length before a committee of the House of Commons, which sat in the year 1849, to inquire into certain transactions which had taken place at Ceylon. Sir David Dundas, then Judge Advocate General, explained his view upon the subject at length, and was closely examined upon it by Sir Robert Peel, Mr. Gladstone, and others. The following answers, amongst others, throw much light on the subject :—

"5437. The proclamation of martial law is a notice, to all those to whom the proclamation is addressed, that there is now another measure of law and another mode of proceeding than there was before that proclamation."

"5459. If a Governor fairly and truly believes that the civil and military power which is with him, and such assistance as he might derive from the sound-hearted part of the Queen's subjects, is not enough to save the life of the community, and to suppress the disorder, it is his duty to suppress by this (*i. e.,* by martial law) or any other means.

"5476. (Sir Robert Peel.) A wise and courageous man, responsible for the safety of a colony, would take the law into his own hands, and make a law for the occasion rather than submit to anarchy ?— *A.* I think that a wise and courageous man would, if necessary, make a law to his own hands, but he would much rather take a law which is already made; and I believe the law of England is, that a Governor, like the Crown, has vested in him the right, where the necessity arises, of judging of it, and being responsible for his work afterwards, so to deal with the laws as to supersede them all, and to proclaim martial law for the safety of the colony.

"5477. (In answer to Mr. Gladstone.) I say he is responsible, just as I am responsible for shooting a man on the King's highway who comes to rob me. If I mistake my man, and have not, in the opinion of the judge and jury who try me, an answer to give, I am responsible.

"5506. My notion is, that martial law is a rule of necessity, and that when it is executed by men empowered to do so, and they act honestly, rigorously, and vigorously, and with as much humanity as the case will permit, in discharge of their duty, they have done that which every good citizen is bound to do."

Martial law has, accordingly, been proclaimed in several colonies—viz., at the Cape of Good Hope, in Ceylon, in Jamaica, and in Demerara.

The views thus expressed by Sir David Dundas appear to us to be substantially correct. According to them the words "martial law," as used in the expression "proclaiming martial law," might be defined as the assumption for a certain time, by the officers of the Crown, of absolute power, exercised by military force, for the purpose of suppressing an insurrection or resisting an invasion. The "proclamation" of martial law, in this sense, would be only a notice to all whom it might concern that such a course was about to be taken. We do not think it is possible to distinguish martial law, thus described and explained, from the common-law duty which is incumbent on every man, and especially on every magistrate, to use any degree of physical force that may be required for the suppression of a violent insurrection, and which is incumbent as well on soldiers as on civilians, the soldiers retaining during such service their special military obligations. (On this subject *see* Lord Chief Justice Tindal's Charge to the Grand Jury of Bristol, in 1832, quoted in I Russ. on Cr. 286 n.) Thus, for instance, we apprehend that if martial law had been proclaimed in London in 1780, such a proclamation would have made no difference whatever in the duties of the troops or the liabilities of the rioters. Without any such proclamation the troops were entitled, and bound, to destroy life and property to any extent which might be necessary to restore order. It is difficult to see what further authority they could have had, except that of punishing the offenders afterwards, and this is expressly forbidden by the Petition of Right.

We may sum up our view of martial law in general in the following propositions :—

1. Martial law is the assumption by the officers of the Crown of absolute power, exercised by military force, for the suppression of an insurrection, and the restoration of order and lawful authority.

2. The officers of the Crown are justified in any exertion of physical force, extending to the destruction of life and property to any extent, and in any manner that may be required for this purpose. They are not justified in the use of excessive or cruel means, but are liable civilly or criminally for such excess. They are not justified in inflicting punishment after resistance is suppressed, and after the ordinary courts of justice can be reopened. The principle by which their responsibility is measured is well expressed in the case of *Wright* v. *Fitzgerald,* 27 St. Tr. p. 65. Mons. Wright was a French master of Clonmel, who, after the suppression of the Irish rebellion, in 1798, brought an action against Mr. Fitzgerald, the sheriff of Tipperary, for having cruelly flogged him without due inquiry. Martial law was in full force at that time, and an Act of Indemnity had been passed, to excuse all breaches of the law committed in the suppression of the rebellion. In summing up, Justice Chamberlain, with whom Lord Yelverton agreed, said :—

"The jury were not to imagine that the Legislature, by enabling magistrates to justify under the Indemnity Bill, had released them from the feelings of humanity, or permitted them wantonly to exercise power, even though it were to put down rebellion. They expected that in all cases there should be a grave and serious examination into the conduct of the supposed criminal, and every act should show a mind intent to discover guilt, not to inflict torture. By examination or trial he did not mean that sort of examination and trial which they were now engaged in, but such examination and trial—the best the nature of the case and existing circumstances should allow of. That this must have been the intention of the Legislature was manifest from the expression 'magistrates and all other persons,' which provide that as every man, whether magistrate or not, was authorized to suppress rebellion, and was to be justified by that law for his acts, it is required that he should not exceed the necessity which gave him that power, and that he should show in his justification that he had used every possible means to ascertain the guilt which he had punished; and, above all, no deviation from the common principles of humanity should appear in his conduct."

Mons. Wright recovered £500 damages; and when Mr. Fitzgerald applied to the Irish Parliament for an indemnity, he could not get one.

3. The courts-martial, as they are called, by which martial law in this sense of the word is administered, are not, properly speaking, courts-martial or courts at all. They are mere committees formed for the purpose of carrying into execution the discretionary power assumed by the Government. On the one hand, they are not obliged to proceed in the manner pointed out by the Mutiny Act and Articles of War. On the other hand, if they do so proceed, they are not protected by them as the members of a real court-martial might be, except in so far as such proceedings are evidence of good faith. They are justified in doing, with any forms and in any manner, whatever is necessary to suppress insurrection, and to restore peace and the authority of the law. They are personally liable for any acts which they may commit in excess of that power, even if they act in strict accordance with the Mutiny Act and Articles of War.

Such, in general, we take to be the nature of martial law.

We now proceed to examine the Act of the Jamaica Legislature under which Governor Eyre appears to have acted, as we presume, regularly.

The Act is 9 Vict. cap. 30, and is a consolidation of the laws relating to militia. The sections bearing on the subject of martial law are as follows: Sect. 95 constitutes a body called a council of war; sect. 96 is in these words; "And whereas the appearance of public danger, by invasion or otherwise, may sometimes make the imposition of martial law necessary, yet, as from experience of the mischief and calamities attending it, it must ever by considered as one of the greatest of evils : Be it therefore enacted, that it shall not in the future be declared or imposed but by the opinion and advice of a council of war, consisting as aforesaid, and that at the end of thirty days from the time of such martial law being declared, it shall *ipso facto* determine, unless continued by the advice of a council of war as aforesaid." Sect. 97 empowers the governor, with such advice as aforesaid, to declare particular districts to be under martial law, and to except others. Sect. 117 says that "This Act shall continue to be in force notwithstanding and during martial law."

It is a grave question whether, if this Act be considered to confer upon Governor Eyre any other power than he already possessed at common law, the Act itself would be valid. The powers of the Jamaica Legislature are derived, not from Parliament, but from Royal Commission. As the Crown cannot authorize legislation inconsistent with the law of England, it could not authorize the Jamaica Legislature to confer upon the Governor, or anyone else, powers inconsistent with the provisions of the Petition of Right. It is indeed provided by 28 & 29 Vict. c 63, ss. 1, 2, and 3, that no colonial law shall be deemed to be void on the ground of repugnancy to the law of England, unless it is repugnant to the provisions of any Act of Parliament applicable to any such colony by express words or necessary intendment. We apprehend, however, that if the Act of the Jamaica Legislature be construed as authorizing or recognizing anything declared illegal by the Petition of Right, it is repugnant to a provision of an Act of Parliament extending by necessary intendment to the colony of Jamaica.

It appears, however, that the Act does not create any new power, but only limits the existing power, and provides regulations under which it is to be exercised. It provides that the Governor shall not proclaim martial law without the advice and consent of a council of war, constituted in a certain way, and that when proclaimed it shall expire, *ipso facto,* in thirty days. It also provides that its operation may be limited (as in the present case it was) to certain districts.

We now proceed to the consideration of the specific questions contained in the case :—

2 and 3. The legality of the conduct pursued towards Mr. Gordon depends, according to the principles stated above, on the question whether it was necessary for the suppression of open force, and the restoration of legal authority, to put him to death. We see nothing whatever in Governor Eyre's despatch which affords any ground for thinking that such could have been the case. The fact that Kingston was exempted from martial law shows conclusively, as against Governor Eyre, that in his opinion no necessity for the assumption of arbitrary power existed then and there. The fact that Mr. Gordon was in lawful custody shows that he was at all events disabled from doing further mischief, however guilty he might previously have been. It would perhaps be too much to say that no conceivable state of things could justify the treatment which he received, but no such facts are mentioned in Governor Eyre's despatch. As to the legal

power of the officers sitting as a court-martial at Morant Bay, we are of opinion that they had no powers at all as a court-martial, and that they could justify the execution of Mr. Gordon only if, and in so far as they could show that, that step was immediately and unavoidably necessary for the preservation of peace and the restoration of order. They had no right whatever to punish him for treason, even if he had committed it. Their province was to suppress force by force, not to punish crime.

4. This question is answered in our introductory observations. Cases might be imagined in which some of the acts specified might be justified. In a case, for instance, where the loyal part of the population were (as in the case of the Indian Mutiny) greatly outnumbered by a rebellious population, measures of excessive severity might be absolutely essential to the restoration of the power of the law; but this would be a case, not of punishment, but of self-preservation. No facts stated in Governor Eyre's despatch appear to us to show any sort of reason for such conduct in Jamaica.

5. They may be indicated in Middlesex under the provisions of 42 Geo, 3, c. 85. See, too, 24 & 25 Vict. c. 100, s. 9. They may also be impeached in Parliament.

6. Any person in this country may prefer a bill of indictment.

7. This is a question of great difficulty. As Governor Eyre's consent would be necessary to such an Act, and as he could not pardon himself, we are inclined to think that such an Act would be no answer to an indictment in England. Besides this, if Governor Eyre has committed any crime at all, it is a crime against the law of England. Whilst Governor, he could not be made criminally responsible in Jamaica (*Mostyn* v. *Fabrigas,* I Smith's "Leading Cases," p. 543, 4th ed.). It is not competent to the Legislature of Jamaica to pardon crimes committed against the laws of England.

To obviate all difficulty, we should advise that if such an Act were passed, a petition should be presented to Her Majesty, praying her to refer to the Judicial Committee of the Privy Council the question whether the Act ought to be disallowed and that the petitioner might be permitted to show cause by counsel why it should be disallowed. Unless and until they are disallowed by the Queen, the Acts of the Jamaica Legislature are valid.

EDWARD JAMES.

Temple, January 13, 1866. J. FITZJAMES STEPHEN.

(c) Extracts from the despatch, dated the 18th June, 1866, of Mr. Cardwell,

the Secretary of State for Colonies, on the findings of the Jamaica Commission

"In the conclusions at which you have arrived Her Majesty's Government generally concur. Though the original design for the overthrow of constituted authority was confined to a small portion of the parish of St. Thomas-in-the-East, yet there can now be no doubt that the disturbances there had their origin in a planned resistance to that authority. It is further evident, looking to the singular rapidity with which disorder spread over an extensive tract of country, and to the state of excitement prevailing in other parts of the island, that the ultimate defeat of the insurgents would have been attended with a still more fearful loss of life and property had they been permitted to obtain a more than momentary success. Under these circumstances, Governor Eyre fully deserves all the commendation which you have bestowed upon the skill, promptitude, and vigour, which he manifested during the early stages of the insurrection, to the exercise of which qualities on his part you justly attribute in a great degree its speedy termination. As regards the proclamation of Martial Law under the Island Act of 1844, Her Majesty's Government agree with you that the Council of War had good reason for the advice which they gave, and the Governor was well justified in acting upon that advice. Her Majesty's Government agree in your conclusion that the military and naval operations were prompt and judicious; and considering the large share personally taken by Governor Eyre in the direction of those operations, they attribute to him a large share also of the credit which is due for their success. The addresses of the Legislative Council, of the House of Assembly, of the various parishes of the island, and of others, testify the sense generally entertained by the white and coloured inhabitants of their obligation to Governor Eyre for the promptitude and vigour of those measures.....

"On the other hand, however, it must he borne in mind that martial law, and the execution of capital sentences under martial law, continued for the full period of a month authorised by the statute, although after the few first days of the insurrection no serious outrages were committed by the insurgents, nor was any resistance offered to the troops. As early as the 27th October, Governor Eyre wrote to me that on the 20th he had left Morant Bay, satisfied that the rebellion was got under; and on the 30th, a fortnight before the actual expiration of martial law, it was formally stated in the proclamation of amnesty that the wicked rebellion lately existing in certain parts of the county of Surry had been subdued; that the chief instigators thereof, and actors therein, had been visited with the punishment due to their heinous offences; and that the Governor was certified (? satisfied) that the inhabitants of the district lately in rebellion were desirous to return to their allegiance.....

"You have justly observed how much easier it is to decide such questions after than before the event, and that sometimes the success of the measures adopted for the prevention of an evil deprives the authors of those measures of the evidence they would otherwise have had of their necessity. Yet, upon a full review of all the circumstances of the case, Her Majesty's Government cannot but agree with the conclusion of your report, 'that by the continuance of martial law in its full force to the extreme limit of its statutory operation, the people were deprived for longer than the necessary period of the great constitutional privileges by which the security of life and property is provided for.' They also agree with you that, if not from the date of the apprehension and execution of Bogle, at least from the time at which the reinforcements from Nassau and Barbadoes had arrived, and the amnesty was proclaimed, 'there could have been no necessity for that promptitude in the execution of the law which almost precluded a calm inquiry into each man's guilt or innocence'; and that 'directions might and ought to have been given, that courts-martial should discontinue their sittings. The prisoners in custody might well have been handed over for trial by the ordinary tribunals.....

"That I may do full justice to the reasons which induced him to consider desirable the continuance of martial law, I will transcribe them in his own words. In answer of your question, No. 46,634, he says:— 'I now give the reasons which induced me to think that martial law should be continued. They are very short:—I. In order to deal summarily with the cases excepted from the operations of the amnesty, many of the parties being as guilty as those tried by courts-martial previous to the amnesty, and there being no valid reason why they should not be dealt with in the same manner. 2. To preserve peace and good order in the districts where the rebellion had existed, and to afford time to reorganise the civil institutions. The custos, the magistrates, the clergy, and other principal inhabitants had been killed, wounded, or driven away. The Inspector of Police had been killed, and the force became disorganised and demoralised. The court-house itself was burnt to the ground. It was impossible to re-establish civil institutions and relations at such a juncture, or with a sufficient time being allowed for reconstruction and for the return of magistrates, clergy, and other inhabitants who were compelled to fly during the rebellion. I think that is one very important reason why it was impossible to have suspended Martial Law.'

"And in answer to your next question, 46,635 :—'What, in your opinion, would have been the evils that would have arisen from taking that particular course on the 30th of October?', he proceeds:—'3rdly. It was important that for some short time longer at least the Government should continue martial law to operate as an example and a warning *in terrorem* over the disaffected of other districts, without the necessity of imposing it in those districts. 4thly. The indication which the continuance of martial law in the county of Surry for some days after the amnesty gave of the determination of the Government to deal promptly and decisively with persons guilty of rebellion, or the concomitant crimes of murder and arson, was the most efficacious step it could take to overawe the evil-disposed in other parts of the colony, and thereby prevent any rising amongst the negro population of the districts where disaffection and seditious tendencies were known to exist.' Those were the four principal reasons which operated with the Government at the time.....

"It remains, at present, to consider the conclusions at which we have arrived with respect to the continuance of Martial Law in its full force, to the extreme limit of its statutory operation, and to the excessive nature of the punishments inflicted. In reviewing this painful portion of the case, the greatest consideration is due to a Governor placed in the circumstances in which Governor Eyre was placed. The suddenness of the insurrection; the uncertainty of its possible extent; its avowed character as a contest of colour; the atrocities committed at its first outbreak; the great disparity in numbers between the white and the black populations; the real dangers and the vague alarms by which he was on every side surrounded; the inadequacy of the force at his command to secure superiority in every district; the exaggerated statements which reached him continually from distant parts of the island; the vicinity of Hayti, and the fact that a civil war was at the time going on in that country;—all these circumstances tended to impress his mind with a conviction that the worst consequences were to be apprehended from the slightest appearance of indecision. Nor must it be forgotten that he resisted the proposal urgently made to him by the custos and the magistrates to proclaim Kingston, that he refused to accede to the suggestion of Colonel Whitfield to proclaim the parishes of Trelawney, St. James'. Hanover and Westmoreland; or to that of Major General O'Connor, who thought that from the first the whole island ought to have been placed under martial law; and that in respect both to the assistance offered by the Governor of Cuba and to the summoning of British troops from Halifax, Nova Scotia, he showed himself superior to feelings of alarm expressed and entertained by those around him.....

"It may, indeed, be admitted that, as you have said, the Government would have incurred a serious responsibility, if, with the information before them, they had thrown away the advantage of the terror which the very name of martial law was calculated to inspire; but it appears from the summary of the sentences by courts-martial appended to your report, that the numbers executed must have included many who were neither ringleaders of the insurrection nor participators in actual murder or outrage of the like atrocity; while for the wholesale flogging and burning of houses, the circumstances of the case do not appear to furnish any justification. Future good government is not the object of martial law. Example and punishments are not its objects: its severities can only be justified when and so far as they are absolutely necessary for the immediate re-establishment of the public safety. Her Majesty's Government have learnt rather with regret than with surprise, as the result of your careful examination of the proceedings, that while in the great majority of the cases the evidence seems to have been unobjectionable in character, and quite sufficient to justify the finding of the court, and the account given by the more trustworthy witnesses as to the manner and deportment of the members of the Courts was decidedly favourable, yet you have been compelled also to call attention to some cases in which either the finding or the sentence was not justified by any evidence appearing on the face of the proceedings; and to other cases, of which the evidence allowed to be given was of a most objectionable description; and again to others, in which the sentences seem to have been wholly disproportioned to the offences charged.....

"Her Majesty's Government have arrived at this conviction with the deepest concern. They are desirous of recognising every consideration which can extenuate the condemnation it necessarily involves. But their anxiety must be to prevent the recurrence in any future case of proceedings like those which they now deplore. It appears to them to be evident that, even in the first excitement of the disturbances, and still more at some later period, if martial law was allowed to continue, instructions ought to have been issued to the officers to whom the actual conduct of the operations was entrusted which would have rendered such an abuse of power impossible. They agree entirely in the words which you have adopted, etc., (quoting the words already cited).....

"I think it is due to Mr. Eyre that I should accompany this observation by the statement that, in the instructions to Colonial Governors, no reference is made to the possible occurrence of such an emergency as that in which he was placed. How far it may be possible to frame general instructions which might assist the Governor in the case of future disturbances arising in any colony, is a subject which will receive careful consideration at the hands of Her Majesty's Government.....

"It appears that Mr. Eyre was only very generally informed of the measures actually taken. In his first despatches in reply to my enquiries, he said that whilst all the general arrangements for the suppression and punishment of the rebellion were made under his immediate direction, the subordinate details, and the internal management of the districts under martial law, including the appointment of courts-martial, the trial of prisoners, the approval of sentences, and the carrying out of such sentences, rested entirely with the military authorities, were reported to the General in Command, and only partially came under his own notice in a general manner; and in his despatch of April 5, he further says:—'Having been personally present in the eastern district up to 20th October, and considering that one of the chief grounds stated for the appointment of a commission of enquiry was an allegation of excessive and unlawful severity, I think it right to mention that no such cases came under my own observation, nor were any brought to my notice, or any complaints made to me against the officers in command during the whole period of Martial Law'; and he then proceeds to relate instances in which abuse had subsequently come to his knowledge, and in which he had taken measures for punishment or for enquiry. With respect to the measures of severity to which I have above referred, you have not imputed, and Her Majesty's Government do not impute, to Mr. Eyre any personal cognizance, at the time, of those measures, but they feel strongly that, when a Governor has been compelled to proclaim martial law, it is his bounden duty to restrain within the narrowest possible limits the severities incident to that law, and, for that purpose, to keep himself constantly informed of what is taking place under it. In the first alarm of such a disturbance, it cannot be expected that it will be possible for him to restrain all persons, acting under martial law, within the bounds which his own discretion would prescribe; but if it were deemed necessary to continue martial law, it was the duty of the Governor to inform himself of the character of the proceedings taken, and to put an end to all proceedings which were not absolutely necessary, and therefore justifiable on the ground of necessity. Her Majesty's Government cannot, therefore, hold the Governor of the colony irresponsible, either for the continuance or for the excessive severity of those measures.....

"In his first despatch Governor Eyre directed the especial attention of Her Majesty's Government to the case of Mr. Gordon, who had been arrested at Kingston, where martial law did not prevail, had been carried to Morant Bay, tried by court-martial at that place, condemned, and executed. To all the circumstances of this case you have given great attention, and have reported your opinion that 'the evidence, oral and documentary, appears to be wholly insufficient to establish the charge upon which the prisoner took his trial.' In this conclusion Her Majesty's Government concur. They have not forgotten that, while Governor Eyre at first exempted Kingston, on grounds of public policy, from the proclamation of martial law, he had it in his power, and would have exercised that power, to issue a new proclamation, if he had thought it necessary to do so, before arresting Mr. Gordon. They have duly weighed the reasons which he has assigned for the course which he pursued, namely, 'that, considering it right in the abstract, and desirable as a matter of policy, that whilst the poor black men who had been misled were undergoing condign punishment, the chief instigator of all the evils should not go unpunished he at once took upon himself the responsibility of the capture; and that, having seen the proceedings of the court, he concurred both in the justice of the sentence, and of the policy of carrying it into effect, regarding it as absolutely necessary for the future security of Jamaica, that condign punishment should be inflicted upon those through whose seditious acts and language the rebellion had originated.' But it is evident that such considerations ought to be admitted with great hesitation. If lightly accepted, they would be liable to great abuse, and cases like the present, instead of being regarded as warnings, might become precedent for future action.....

"In the present case, not only has the necessity of the course adopted not been proved, but it appears from the evidence of Mr. Westmoreland, one of the executive Committee, that he suggested at the time that Mr. Gordon, who had been placed on board the Wolverine, should be reserved for trial by a regular tribunal, with all the means of defence secured by the ordinary process of law to every subject of the Queen. This, in the judgment of Her Majesty's Government, would have been the proper course. Considerations of public safety justified the arrest of Mr. Gordon. His removal on board the Wolverine would have been judicious; but his trial by Court Martial, and his execution by virtue of the sentence of that court, are events which her Majesty's Government cannot but deplore and condemn.....

"Her Majesty's Government have been advised, by the law officers of the Crown, that the effect of the Indemnity Act will not be to cover acts done, either by the Governor or by subordinate officers, unless they are such as (in the case of the Governor) he may have reasonably, and in good faith, considered to be proper for the purpose of putting an end to the insurrection, or such as (in case of subordinates) have been done under, and in conformity with, the orders of superior authority, or (if done without such orders) have been done in good faith, and under a belief, reasonably entertained, that they were proper for the suppression of the insurrection, and for the preservation of the public peace of the islands. As regards all acts done by or under military authority, Her Majesty's Government are advised that the proclamation of martial law, under the Islands Statute of 1844, operated within the proclaimed district to give as complete an indemnity as the Indemnity Act itself. But—1. For any acts done beyond the proclaimed district, the authority of the Act of 1844, and of the proclamation, is inapplicable. 2. Civilians who may have acted *bona fide* for the suppression of the rebellion, although without military authority, would have a protection secured to them by the Indemnity Act, which they might not obtain from the mere operation of martial law. 3. Under the Indemnity Act, the certificate of the

Governor is conclusive for the protection of subordinates. I have already directed you, and your own judgment doubtless would have led you to the same conclusion, how careful you must be in giving these certificates; and, with this precaution taken, Her Majesty's Government have determined that the Act of Indemnity ought be left to its operation.....

"On my own part, I have to request that you will cause careful investigation to be made, in those cases of civilians which appear to require it, with a view to such further proceedings as may be requisite and just. It will not be desirable to keep alive in the colony the heartburnings connected with these lamentable occurrences, by any very minute endeavour to punish every act which may now be the subject of regret. But great offences ought to be punished. I rely on your Government to accomplish this necessary object, and shall expect to receive a full report of the measures which have been taken with that view. You will, of course, be very careful not to give certificates under the Indemnity Act, in any cases in which there is reasonable ground to question the propriety of giving them....."

(6)—Martial Law and the Constitution of England

(From "Constitutional Law of England" by E.W. Ridges)

Conclusions as to Martial Law by Prerogative. From consideration, of the authorities on martial law in connection with prerogative, the following deductions may be made:—

(1) The Crown's prerogative to declare martial law does not exist in time of peace; its extent in time of war, if it exists at all, has never been judically determined, but the only excuse for its exercise is the necessity occasioned by an actual state of war, or rebellion or insurrection amounting to war.

(2) Its exercise must cease with the necessity which gave rise to it, and the civil courts will grant a *habeas corpus* in the case of persons detained in military custody for acts done after the war, insurrection or rebellion is over. (Wolfe Tone's Case).

(3) The extent of the Crown's prerogative being uncertain, the Government would either obtain Parliamentary sanction for its exercise, or Acts of indemnity would be passed.

(4) There seems no reason why, supposing the same necessity to exist, martial law should not be proclaimed in England, as well as in the colonies or Ireland; but in this case the Government would probably be particularly careful to obtain the sanction of Parliament.

(5) Where a state of war actually exists and is recognized by the courts, the latter, even though they may be still sitting for some purposes, have no jurisdiction over the actions of the military authorities (*ex parte* Marais). But it seems doubtful whether sentences of fine or imprisonment would be valid without confirmation by Parliament.

(7)—Suppression of Riots by the Military

Opinion of the Attorney-General Sir John S. Copley, on the authority of the military to take away life in suppression of a riot in the island of Barbadoes.

Lincoln's Inn, January 18, 1824.

My Lord,—I have had the honour to receive your Lordship's letter, dated the 6th instant, transmitting to me therewith a letter from Governor Sir Henry Warde, dated Barbadoes, the 4th of November last, together with a memorial from the Council of that island, requesting the opinion of the law officers of the Crown upon the question therein stated, *viz.*, "Whether there is any statute passed before the settlement of that island in the year 1625, which authorises the military, acting under the magistrate for the suppression of a riot, to take the life of rioters, if such a measure should be necessary, and, if not, is such a proceeding sanctioned by the common law of England."

Your Lordship also enclosed despatches from the Governor reporting the occurrences which had lately taken place in the island, and which had given rise to the present application. And your Lordship was pleased to state that you had received his Majesty's commands to desire that I would take the papers into consideration, and report to your Lordship as speedily as possible, for his Majesty's information, what instructions it might, in my opinion, be proper to transmit to the Governor upon the case stated.

In obedience to the commands of his Majesty, I have taken the papers as speedily as possible into my consideration, and beg leave to report to your Lordship that there is no statute passed before the settlement of the island of Barbadoes in the year 1625 and now in force, of the nature above alluded to; but by the common law the military may effectively act under the direction of the civil power in the suppression of the riots. The Late Chief Justice Mansfield, in the case of *Burdett* V. *Abbott*, in the Exchequer Chamber (4 Taunt. Repp. 449), in speaking upon this subject, observes that a "strange mistaken notion had got abroad, that because men were soldiers they ceased to be citizens. A soldier (he adds) is gifted with all the rights of other citizens, and is bound to all the duties of other citizens, and he is as much bound to prevent a breach of the peace or a felony as any other citizen. This notion is the more extraordinary, because formerly the *posse comitatus,* which was the strength to prevent felonies, must in a great proportion have consisted of military tenants who held lands by the tenure of military service. If it is necessary for the purpose of preventing mischief, or for the execution of law, it is not only the right of soldiers, but it is their duty, to exert themselves in assisting the execution of a legal process, or to prevent any crime or mischief being committed. It is therefore highly important that the mistake should be corrected which supposes that an Englishman, by taking upon him the additional character of a soldier, puts off any of the rights and duties of an Englishman." Soldiers, when called upon and required to aid the civil magistrate in apprehending or opposing persons engaged in a riot, will be justified in using the force necessary for that purpose; any excess will be illegal and for such excess the soldier, as well as the mere citizen, will be responsible. In this respect the law as applicable to both classes is the same. If, in executing the commands of the magistrate, opposition is made by the rioters, force may be opposed to force; but the same rule still applies, *viz.*, that the extent of the force used must be regulated by the necessity of the occasion. The excess only is illegal. If the military, in obeying the lawful commands of the magistrate, be so assailed that resistance cannot be effectually made without sacrificing the lives of the rioters, they would in law be justified in so doing. It is obvious, therefore, that each case must depend upon its own circumstances, and the only rule that can be given is that the force, to be legal and justifiable, must in every instance, as far as the infirmity of human passion will admit, be governed by what the necessity of the particular occasion may require.

I beg leave to suggest that it will be proper to direct the Governor to take especial care that a magistrate be present when the military are called out for the purpose of suppressing a riot, and that they act in his aid and by his command. Temper and coolness upon such occasions, and forbearance as for as it can be exercised consistently with the public safety, cannot be too strongly recommended.

To Karl Bathurst. J. S. COPLEY
&c, &c.

APPENDIX V

The Indemnity Act

(1)—Indemnity Act, 1860

Act XXXIV of 1860

RECEIVED THE G.G.'S. ASSENT ON THE 2ND AUGUST 1860

An Act to indemnify Officers of Government and other persons in respect of fines and contributions levied, and acts done by them during the late disturbances.

Preamble

WHEREAS fines and penalties have been imposed and levied by officers of Government in respect of acts committed during the late disturbances; and whereas assessments and contributions have been made and collected for the recónstruction or repairs of public buildings destroyed or injured during the same period and for other purposes; and whereas it is expedient to indemnify all officers of Government and other persons acting under the authority of officers of Government from any penalties or proceedings to which they may have rendered themselves liable since the tenth day of May 1857 in respect of the said fines, penalties, assessments, and contributions, and of any other acts which may have been done by them, and which have been or shall be ratified by the Executive Government, and to confirm and make valid the levy of the said fines, penalties, assessments, and contributions, and the said acts; It is enacted as follows :—

Indemnity in respect of fines, penalties, etc., imposed since 10th May, 1857.

1. All fines, penalties, assessments, and contributions imposed since the tenth day of May 1857 in respect of the destruction or injury of Government or other property, or on any other account connected with the late disturbances, by any officer of Government, or by any person acting under the authority of an officer of Government, shall be deemed to have been duly imposed and levied if the same shall have been levied in pursuance of an order of Government or shall have been or shall be ratified by the Executive Government; and all officers of Government and all persons acting under their authority are hereby indemnified and discharged from liability in respect of any such fines, penalties, assessments, and contributions, and levying the same, and no suit or proceeding shall be commenced or prosecuted in respect thereof:

Provided that nothing in this Act shall authorize the levy of any fine, penalty, assessment, or contribution not already levied.

Proviso.

2. All acts done since the tenth day of May 1857 in connection with the late disturbances by officers of Government, or by persons acting under their authority or otherwise, in pursuance of an order of Government, or which shall have been or shall be ratified by the Executive Government, are hereby confirmed and made valid; and all such officers of Government and persons as aforesaid are hereby indemnified and discharged from liability in respect of such acts.

Indemnity for certain acts done since 10th May 1857.

(2)—Text of the Indemnity Bill, 1919

The following is the full text of the Bill to indemnify officers of Government and other persons in respect of certain acts done under Martial Law and to provide for other matters in connection therewith:—

Whereas owing to recent disorders in certain districts in the Punjab and in other parts of India it has been necessary for the purposes of maintaining or restoring order to resort to Martial Law;

And whereas it is expedient to indemnify officers of Government and other persons in respect of acts, matters and things ordered or done, or purporting to have been ordered or done, for the purpose of maintaining or restoring order, provided that such acts, matters or things were ordered or done in good faith and in a reasonable belief that they were necessary for the said purpose;

And whereas certain persons have been convicted by courts and other authorities constituted or appointed under Martial Law and it is expedient to confirm and provide for the continuance of sentences passed by such courts or authorities ;

It is hereby enacted as follows :

(1) This Act may be called the Indemnity Act, 1919.

(2) No suit or other legal proceeding whatsoever, whether civil or criminal, shall lie in any court of law against any officer of Government, whether civil or military, or against any other person acting under the orders of any such officer for on account of or in respect of any act, matter or thing ordered or done or purporting to have been ordered or done for the purpose of maintaining or restoring order in any part of British India, on or after the 30th of March 1919, and before the commencement of this Act by any such officer or person; provided that such officer or person has acted in good faith and in a reasonable belief that his action was necessary for the said purposes; and if any such proceeding has been instituted before the passing of this Act it is hereby discharged.

(3) For the purposes of Section 2 a certificate of a Secretary to Government that any act was done under the orders of an officer of Government shall be conclusive proof thereof, and all actions taken for the aforesaid purposes shall be deemed to have been taken in good faith and in a reasonable belief that they were necessary therefor unless the contrary is proved.

(4) Every person confined under and by virtue of any sentence

passed by a court or other authority constituted or appointed under Martial Law and acting in a judicial capacity shall be deemed to have been lawfully confined and shall continue liable to confinement until the expiration of such sentence, or until released by the Governor-General in Council or otherwise discharged by lawful authority.

(5) Where under Martial Law the property of any person has been taken or used by any officer of Government whether civil or military, the Governor-General in Council shall pay to such person a reasonable compensation for any loss immediately attributable to such taking or using to be assessed upon failure of agreement by a person holding judicial office, not inferior to that of District Judge, to be appointed by the Government in this behalf.

(6) Nothing in this Act shall (*a*) apply to any sentence passed or punishment inflicted by or under the orders of any Commission appointed under the Martial Law Ordinance, 1919, (*b*) be deemed to bar a full and unqualified exercise of his Majesty's pleasure in receiving or rejecting appeals to His Majesty in Council or to affect any question or matter to be decided therein or (*c*) prevent the institution of proceedings by or on behalf of Government against any person in respect of any matter whatsoever.

(3)—The Indemnity Act, 1919

(Received the assent of the Governor-General on the 25th September, 1919)

ACT NO. XXVII OF 1919

An Act to indemnify officers of Government and other persons in respect of certain Acts done under Martial Law, and to provide for other matters in connection therewith.

WHEREAS owing to the recent disorders in certain districts in the Punjab and in other parts of India, martial law has been enforced;

And whereas it is expedient to indemnify officers of Government and other persons in respect of acts, matters and things ordered or done or purporting to have been ordered or done for the purpose of maintaining or restoring order, provided that such acts, matters or things were ordered or done in good faith and in a reasonable belief that they were necessary for the said purposes;

And whereas certain persons have been convicted by courts and other authorities constituted or appointed under martial law, and it is expedient to confirm and provide for the continuance of certain sentences passed by such courts or authorities;

It is hereby enacted as follows :—

Short title

1. This Act may be called the Indemnity Act, 1919.

Indemnity of Government officers and other persons for certain acts.

2. No suit or other legal proceeding whatsoever, whether civil or criminal, shall lie in any court of law against any officer of Government, whether civil or military, or against any other person acting under the orders of any such officer for or on account of or in respect of any act, matter or thing ordered or done, or purporting to have been ordered or done, for the purpose of maintaining or restoring order in any part of British India where martial law was enforced, on or after the 30th of March, 1919, and before the 26th of August 1919 by any such officer or person; provided that such officer or person has acted in good faith and in a reasonable belief that his action was necessary for the said purposes;

And if any such proceeding has been instituted before the passing of this Act it is hereby discharged.

Rules of evidence.

3. For the purposes of section 2 a certificate of a Secretary to Government that any act was done under the orders of an officer of Government shall be

conclusive proof thereof, and all action taken for the aforesaid purposes shall be deemed to have been taken in good faith and in a reasonable belief that it was necessary therefor unless the contrary is proved.

Confirmation and continuance of martial law sentence.

4. Every person confined under and by virtue of any sentence passed by a court or other authority constituted or appointed under martial law and acting in a judicial capacity shall be deemed to have been lawfully confined and shall continue liable to confinement until the expiration of such sentence, or until released by the Governor-General in Council or otherwise discharged by lawful authority.

Compensation in respect of loss attributable to certain acts.

5. Where under martial law the property of any person has been taken or used by any officer of Government, whether civil or military, the Governor-General in Council shall pay to such person reasonable compensation for any loss immediately attributable to such taking or using, to be assessed upon failure of agreement by a person holding judicial office not inferior to that of a District Judge to be appointed by the Government in this behalf.

Savings.

6. Nothing in this Act shall—

(*a*) apply to any sentence passed or punishment inflicted by or under the order of any Commission appointed under the Martial Law Ordinance, 1919.

(*b*) be deemed to bar a full and unqualified exercise of His Majesty's pleasure in receiving or rejecting appeals to His Majesty in Council or to affect any question or matter to be decided therein, or

(*c*) prevent the institution of proceedings by or on behalf of the Government against any person in respect of any matter whatsoever.

(4)—Act of Indemnity

(A NOTE BY MR. C. R. DAS)

The recent announcement by His Excellency, the Viceroy, makes it incumbent on us to examine the nature and limits of an Act of Indemnity. It has been asserted by the Anglo-Indian Press that the promulgation of Martial Law is invariably followed, when Martial Law comes to an end, by an Act of Indemnity. It is necessary to dispose of this fiction at the very outset. The Duke of Newcastle, when Colonial Secretary, objected to the statement in the Colonial Act of Indemnity passed after the existence of Martial Law in St. Vincent in 1862 that "the proclamation of Martial Law had been lawfully issued" on the ground that "the proclamation was right and necessary, but was not strictly lawful, and to declare it so would be to endanger a most important constitutional principle. In proclaiming Martial Law, the executive authority in fact declares itself obliged, for the protection of the community, to neglect the law, trusting to the Legislature to relieve all who in obedience to constituted authority may have acted in the defence of the public safety from the consequence of so doing. The Indemnity contained in the second clause is too wide. It would enable a person to escape punishment for the most wanton and unjustifiable acts, even to homicide, if it could be shown that he had been in any wise engaged in suppressing or endeavouring to suppress the insurrection." (Code 11, 511.) So in 1867 Lord Carnarvon, when Colonial Secretary, refused to recommend for the royal assent an enactment of Antigua, making it usual for the Government to proclaim Martial Law. Mr. G. C. Phillimore, an accomplished writer on the subject, said in a paper which he contributed to the journal of comparative legislation that "Colonial Secretaries have frequently refused to recommend for the royal assent Colonial Acts of Indemnity." Indeed, the traditional attitude of the Colonial Office may be seen from the following circular letter, which was issued to the Governors of Colonies:—

"An enactment which purports to invest the Executive Government with permanent power of suspending the ordinary law of the Colony, of removing the known safeguards of life and property, and legalising in advance such measures as may be deemed conductive to order by the military officers charged with the suppression of disturbances, is entirely at variance with the spirit of English Law. If its existence can in any way be justified, it can only be because there exists such a state of established insecurity as renders it necessary, for the safety and confidence of the well-disposed, that in times of national emergency the Government shall possess this extraordinary facility for the suppression of armed rebellion; but, whatever apprehensions or disturbances may exist in any of Her Majesty's Colonies, it is certain that no such chronic insecurity prevails in any of them, and in no colony therefore should the power be given by the present law to the Governor of Antigua be suffered to continue. . . . . In giving you these instructions, Her Majesty's Government must not be supposed to convey an absolute prohibition of all recourse to Martial Law under stress of great emergencies, and in anticipation of an Act of Indemnity. The justification, however, of such a step must rest on the pressure of the moment; and the Governor cannot by any instructions be relieved from the obligation of deciding for himself under that pressure whether the responsibility of proclaiming Martial Law, is or is not greater than refraining from doing so." (Code 11, 667).

No reasonable person will deny that in an emergency, when the whole fabric of Government is threatened, the State is entitled to protect itself by having recourse to Martial Law. When there is no order, there can be no law, and the only law that will guide the persons in authority is the law of necessity. Just as necessity justifies Martial Law, so it must justify the duration of it and the methods adopted for administering Martial Law. And when it has been established (but not before) that this supreme and paramount necessity did exist and that the methods adopted were not in excess of what was strictly necessary for restoring peace and the authority of law, the State is entitled and even bound to protect its servants by passing an Act of Indemnity. The true scope of an Act of Indemnity is to legalise that which was illegal, but which was necessary for the restoration of law and order. "It seems to be plainly within the competence of the Legislature" said Willes, J., in the celebrated case of Phillips V. Eyre (L. R. 6, Q. B. 1 at 17), "which could have authorized by antecedent legislation the acts done as necessary or proper for preserving the public peace, upon a due consideration of the circumstances to adopt and ratify like acts, when done, or, in the language of the law under consideration, to enact that they shall be 'made and declared lawful and confirmed.' Such is the effect of the Act of Indemnity in question."

The power of a Legislature to pass an Act of Indemnity is

therefore undoubted, but it is a power which can only be exercised when two essential conditions have been satisfied, namely, first, that there was a supreme and paramount necessity which justified the promulgation of Martial Law and, secondly, that excesses of authority were not committed in the administration of Martial Law. Indeed the Acts of Indemnity in England have always been purposely framed so as to give Parliamentary sanction only to such acts as have *bona fides* and of necessity been done to meet the demands of the emergency justifying the proclamation of Martial Law; and it has been held that such an Act, as invariably framed in England, does not protect persons who have been exercising Martial Law from criminal liability for any excess of authority committed by them, on the ground that these are not justified by necessity. See Wright V. Fitzgerald, 27, State Trials, p. 765.

It will be necessary to take an Act of Indemnity passed by the British Parliament to illustrate my meaning. After the rising of 1715, the British Parliament passed an Act of Indemnity "to indemnify such persons who have acted in defence of His Majesty's person and Government, and for the preservation of the public peace of the kingdom" and it provided as follows:— "Whereas in the year of our Lord one thousand seven hundred and fifteen, as well in the time of, as before the unnatural Rebellion, which begun in or about the months of September or October in the same year, divers Lord-Lieutenants, Deputy-Lieutenants, Justices of the Peace, Mayors, Bailiffs of Corporations, Constables and other officers and persons well-affected to His Majesty and His Government, in order to preserve our ancient happy establishment, and the peace of this Kingdom, and suppress and put an end to the said rebellion, apprehended and put into custody, and imprisoned several criminals and several persons, who they suspected, might disturb the public peace, or foment or promote riots, tumults, rebellions, or evil designs against the Government, and also seized and used several horses, arms and other things, and also pressed divers horses, carts and carriages for the service of the public; and did for the purposes aforesaid enter into the houses and possessions of several persons; and did quarter and cause to be quartered divers soldiers and others in the houses of divers persons; and did divers acts which would not be justified by the strict forms of law, *and yet were necessary, and so much for the service of the public, that they ought to be justified by Act of Parliament,* and the persons by whom they were transacted ought to be indemnified; be it therefore enacted, all personal actions, etc., *for anything done in order to suppress the Rebellion in* 1715 *shall be discharged."*

It is manifest from a mere perusal of this Statute that the two essential conditions for an Act of Indemnity are, first, that the acts done were necessary and for the service of the public; and secondly, that the acts done were in order to suppress the rebellion and not in excess of what was strictly necessary to suppress the rebellion. As regards the first condition, there can be no doubt. As regards the second, the weighty observations of Mr. Justice Chamberlain in his charge to the jury in the case of Wright V. Fitzgerald (27, State Trials, pp. 765 at 766) may be cited; "It is required," said His Lordship, "that he should not exceed the necessity which gave him the power; and that he should show, in his justification, that he had used every possible means to ascertain the guilt which he had punished; and, above all, no deviation from the common principles of humanity should appear in his conduct."

The principles being well-established, it is necessary next to enquire whether it is possible for the Indian legislature to declare, before the Committee appointed by the Governor-General-in-Council has reported to that Council, first, that there was a justifying necessity for the promulgation of Martial Law; and, secondly, that the acts done in the administration of Martial Law were not in excess of their powers. His Excellency in his recent speech in the Council said: "After disorders involving great upheaval of normal conditions, such an enquiry as I have just announced is one inevitable consequence. The second and no less necessary sequel is the passing of an Act indemnifying these officers of the Government, who were called upon to undertake the onerous and ungrateful task of restoring order, and the validating of such acts as the stress of circumstances required. Whatever the findings of the Commission may be, such a measure would be necessary, and in justice to our officers, we are bound to indemnify them at the earliest convenient moment."

I quite agree that an enquiry is inevitable after the recent events in the Punjab, but I would add that such an enquiry in the past has always included an enquiry into the necessity of Martial Law and that the enquiry has always been held by the British Parliament and not by the Government responsible for the promulgation of Martial Law. I will give two instances. The Ceylon rising of 1845 led to the appointment of a Committee of the House of Commons to enquire into the proceedings under Martial Law, before which the

Judge-Advocate-General, Sir David Dundas, gave evidence. After the period of Martial Law in Jamaica, a Parliamentary Commission was sent to the island which, after an exhaustive investigation into all the circumstances of the execution of Martial Law, reported that the declaration of Martial Law was justifiable, the proceedings were rebellious and of deep design, and that the Commissioners fully approved of the conduct of the Governors and officers in the prompt measures which ? they have been that Martial Law was continued longer than was necessary, and the punishments that were inflicted were excessive in the later stages, and that much that was lamentable might have been avoided if clear and precise instruction had been given for the regulation of those engaged in suppressing the rebellion and as regards Gordon, (who was shot after a trial by Court-Martial) they were of opinion that the express evidence forthcoming did not appear to be sufficient to establish the charge against him, and that there was no widespread conspiracy to which he was privy. On these findings, which were concurred in by Mr. Cardwell, the Colonial Secretary, criminal proceedings were brought by the Crown against Governor Eyre and General Nelson.

I ask, is there any precedent for a Committee of Enquiry being appointed by a Government responsible for the promulgation of Martial Law. The question at issue is, did the Government of India act rightly or with discretion in promulgating Martial Law in the Punjab. The Government of India concedes that an enquiry is necessary, but says, "we shall ourselves, appoint the Committee of Enquiry and the Committee of Enquiry must report to us." We are now told that the Government of India will merely act as the Post Office and that the report will really be considered by the Secretary of State for India. That may be so, and it must be admitted that this is a distinct improvement. But the procedure adopted by the Government will still prevent the British Parliament from effectively having its voice heard on the report of the Committee and suggesting such measures as ought to be taken on the report.

In the second place, is it open to the Committee on the terms of reference to find that there was no justification at all for the promulgation of Martial Law or that, if there was such a justification, it was continued longer than was necessary and that the punishments that were inflicted were excessive, and that, as regards persons or some of them or any of them who have been excecuted or imprisoned in the administration of Martial Law, the express evidence forthcoming did not appear to be sufficient to establish the charges against these persons or some of them or any of them and that there was no widespread conspiracy to which they or some of them or any of them were or was privies or privy ?

If it is not open to the Committee to arrive at these findings, then the terms of reference are clearly defective, and the enquiry itself will constitute one of those melancholy jokes which the Government of India knows how to perpetrate. But on a careful reading of the speech of the Viceroy and from the fact that the Government has refused to answer some of the most pertinent questions put by Pundit Madan Mohan Malaviya on the ground that they will form the subject of investigation by the Committee, it will appear that the Committee will have power to go into the whole question relating to the necessity for, and the administration of, Martial Law in the Punjab. If this view be correct, is it open to the Government of India to solemnly declare in their Bill of Indemnity that there was necessity for the promulgation of Martial Law in the Punjab (such a declaration being a necessary declaration in every Act of Indemnity) when it is open to the Committee to come to an exactly opposite conclusion? Is it open to the Government of India to solemnly indemnify all persons who have taken part in the administration of Martial Law in the Punjab, when it is open to the Committee to come to the conclusion that excesses have been committed in the administration of Martial Law and that the express evidence forthcoming did not appear to be sufficient to establish the charges against some of the persons who have been executed or imprisoned by those responsible for the Martial Law administration? In my view only one answer can be given to these questions.

Two courses, and only two, were open to the Government of India. They might have taken up the position that there was complete justification for the promulgation, duration, and administration of Martial Law. They might have said, "we have satisfied ourselves that there was overwhelming necessity for Martial Law and for the methods that were adopted for administering it, and we decline to have our administration enquired into by any Committee whatever." That position would have been politically indefensible, but bureaucratically unassailable; but still it was open to them to take up this position. If they had taken up this position, it was not only entitled to, but indeed bound in honour at once to pass an Act of Indemnity, the conditions precedent for such an Act being shown to exist so far as the Government of India is concerned. But this is not the position that has been taken up by Government. It does indeed protest that there was complete justification for Martial Law and the administration thereof; but it concedes and invites an enquiry into the whole question relating to the recent events in the Punjab. It concedes therefore (if I have correctly understood the function of the Committee) that it will be open to the Committee to differ completely from the advice of the Government of India. What justification is there for the Government to proceed with an Indemnity Bill at this stage, before the Committee has made its report to the Government of India ?

The view which I earnestly press upon the Government of India is this : The true scope of the Act of Indemnity is to legalise illegalities only when it has been shown that there was paramount necessity in the perpetration of these illegalities and only so much illegality (and not one jot or iota more) as was essentially necessary in the circumstances. You may say, but, if you take up that position, then dismiss the Committee which you yourself have set up in utter disregard of every constitutional precedent and not, as courageous men, on your own responsibility. But it is not fair to the country, it is not fair to the Committee, it is not fair to yourselves to appoint a Committee and then proceed to deliver the following message to the Committee through the instrumentality of an Act of Indemnity. "If you agree with us, well and good. If not, so much the worse for your verdict, because we have formed our opinion on the materials before us and we decline altogether to consider your verdict."

(5)—The Punjab Indemnity Bill

SOME SUGGESTIONS FOR AMENDMENT

(By Sir P. S. Sivaswami Aiyer)

A few days ago, the suggestion was made by the Madras Liberal League, that if the Government considered it necessary to pass a measure immediately for the protection of officers and other persons against legal proceedings at the instance of persons aggrieved by the administration of martial law, their objects might be temporarily but effectively attained by passing an Act suspending all actions and proceedings by persons aggrieved, and the running of limitation against them, pending the inquiry by the Commission and the disposal of the appeals by the Privy Council. The Legislative Council would then be in possession of all the circumstances of the case and be able to pass a final Indemnity Bill adapted to the requirements of public interest and justice. But, as unfortunately, there is no chance of this course being adopted, it is necessary to scrutinise the language of the Bill and suggest such amendments as may now appear to us to be necessary. The Bill was published here on the 15th instant, and it was stated that it would be introduced yesterday or to-day and passed into law on the 24th instant. The interval allowed to the country for the study of the Bill and making representations thereon is altogether insufficient, and the haste with which it is being rushed through in the Council is, to say the least, indecent, more especially when, so far as the public are aware, not even a single suit has been instituted against any officer up to this moment.

The following few suggestions for the amendment of the Bill are the result of such consideration as I have been able to give to the language of the Bill.

Preamble—Wherever the words "maintaining or restoring order" occur, it is necessary that the words "maintaining or" should be deleted. It is well established that martial law can be introduced only during a state of actual war, insurrection or rebellion, that the moment this state of things comes to an end the application of martial law ceases to have any justification, and that it cannot be resorted to for the purpose of bringing offenders to trial and punishment. The resort to martial law, for the purpose of *maintaining order* as distinguished from the *restoration of order* is not justified.

Clause 2—The words "acting under the orders of any such officer" are much too wide and should be restricted. As the clause stands, it would cover an order given by the humblest policeman. The general rule of liability in regard to subordinates is, that they are protected if they act under the orders of a person, whom they are generally bound by the rules of their service to obey, and the orders are of a kind which that person is generally authorised to give, and the particular order is not *necessarily* or *manifestly* unlawful. As regards outsiders, too, though they are bound in certain cases to assist authorities in the suppression of disorder there are obvious limits to the plea of obedience to the orders of officials. It is, therefore, necessary to restrict and define 'the officers or class of officers whose orders should be allowed to be set up as a plea. In regard to the purposes for which action may have been taken, the words "maintaining or restoring order" should be replaced by the words "suppressing insurrection and restoring order." The words "in any part of British India" should be qualified by the addition of the words "in which martial law was proclaimed after March, 1919." After the words "that his action was necessary for the said purpose," the words "and without needless severity" should be inserted. Even the introduction of martial law does not justify the resort to needless measures of severity or release an officer from the feelings of humanity.

Clause 3—There is no need for making the certificate of a Secretary to the Government *conclusive* proof of the fact that an act was done under the orders of an officer of Government. The certificate of the Secretary is likely to be based, in most cases, upon information subsequently derived and possibly not accurate; and though there are precedents in favour of investing the certificate with conclusive effect, it is desirable to provide for its being merely presumptive evidence liable to be rebutted. While it is necessary to protect acts done under authority given at the time, there is no need to protect acts done originally without any authority.

Clause 4—The whole of this clause may well be deleted. So far as the officer acting in a judicial capacity is concerned, he is already provided for by clause (2). As regards the operation of sentences passed by such officers, it must be remembered that the introduction of martial law by the Governor-General was in the exercise of statutory powers and not in the exercise of the prerogative of the Crown. If the courts or other authorities referred to were appointed under the Martial Law Ordinances, there is no need for legalising their existence, and this is the reason for the saving clause contained in Clause (6) sub-clause (*a*) of the Bill. If the courts or other authorities referred to in Clause (4) were not appointed under the Martial Law Ordinance, but otherwise, it could only be in exercise of the powers conferred by the prerogative. But of any intention to resort to this prerogative, there is no evidence. Even if it should be supposed that consistently with the indemnity conferred on the officers purporting to act in a judicial capacity the sentence of confinement inflicted by them should be legalised, there is no necessity for the provision that the persons confined should be declared legally liable to serve the remainder of their terms of imprisonment. It is also necessary that if the confinement is to be declared to have been lawful, it should have been under a sentence passed in accordance with the principles of natural justice and for offences either under the Penal Code or under some special or local law. A sentence imposed in respect of something which is not an offence at all under any such law, but in respect of an infraction of some rule passed by the martial law officer, would be *prima facie* null and void and should not be legalised; and even if policy requires the legalisation of such confinement in the past, it would be absurd to legislate for its future operation. Supposing, for instance, that there was a rule that every Indian meeting an European in the streets should salute him, and a sentence of imprisonment was imposed for failure to comply with the rule, it would be absurd to legalise such a sentence. The alternative amendments required in the case of *Clause (4)* are:—

(1) That the whole clause should be deleted; and

(2) That if the whole clause is not deleted, all the words following "shall be deemed to have been lawfully confined" should be deleted; and

(3) The addition after the words "shall be deemed to have been lawfully confined" of a proviso to the following effect "provided that the sentence shall have been passed in respect of some offence under the Penal Code or some special or local law and in accordance with the principles of natural justice."

Clause 6—Sub-clause (3) of the saving clause is quite superfluous. It would, on the other hand, be useful and desirable to insert a sub-clause providing that nothing under the Act shall be deemed to restrict or interfere with the inquiry by the Committee into the need for the introduction of Martial Law or its continuance, the manner in which it has been administered and the conduct of the officials responsible for the introduction, continuance or administration of Martial Law.

—*"New India."*

(6)—The Indemnity Bill

(By Sir Narayan Chandavarkar)

Surprise is expressed in some quarters that Indian politicians of all shades of opinion have opposed the decision of the Government of India to introduce an Indemnity Bill in the Imperial Legislative Council at the earliest convenient moment for the purpose of indemnifying all the officers in respect of their acts in connection with the recent disturbances. Moderate politicians are once again charged with joining and placating Extemists in this opposition. The authority of the constitutional lawyer, A V. Dicey, is cited in support of the principle and policy of the measure.

But here is what Mr. Dicey says in his book called "A Leap in the Dark":—

"Of all the laws which a Legislature can pass, an Act of Indemnity is the most likely to produce injustice. It is, on the face of it, the legalisation of illegality, the hope of it encourages acts of vigour, but it also encourages violations of laws and of humanity. The tale of flogging Fitzgerald in Ireland, or the history of Governor Eyre in Jamaica, is sufficient to remind us of the deeds of lawlessness and cruelty, which in a period of civil conflict may be inspired by recklessness or panic and may be pardoned by the retrospective sympathy or partisanship of a terror-striken or vindictive legislature."

Further on, he writes:—

"An *ex post facto* law is the instrument, which a legislature is most apt to use for punishing the unpopular use of legal rights. There is not a landlord, there is not a magistrate, there is not a constable in Ireland, who may not tremble in fear of *ex post facto* legislation. There is no reason, as far as the Home Rule Bill goes, why the gaoler who kept Mr. William O'Brien in prison, or the warders who attempted to pull off his breeches, should not be rendered legally liable to punishment for their offences against the unwritten law of Irish sedition. No such monstrosity of legal inequity will, it may be said, be produced. I admit this. But the very object of prohibitions" (against the passing of an *ex post facto* law) "is the prevention of outrageous injustice. The wise founders of the United States prohibited to Congress and to every State legislature the passing of *ex post facto* legislation."

The principle of an Indemnity Act is generally understood to be this: Where Government are compelled to adopt extreme measures to cope with and put down disturbances of an extraordinary character amounting to rebellion, and when the ordinary law is inadequate for the purpose and martial law becomes necessary, policy and practice require the passing of an Indemnity Act to protect themselves and their officers against liability for any mistakes or excesses committed in the *bona-fide* exercise of their extraordinary powers. The principle of such legislation underlies, for instance, the Judicial Officers' Act, which provides that Judges are absolutely protected from all liability in respect of their decisions, when those decisions relate to matters within the jurisdiction of the judge concerned, and that a Judge is also so protected in respect of decisions relating to matters outside his jurisdiction, if the decisions in such matters were passed *bona-fide* and not from any by-motive, such as malice.

That principle is regarded as applying to the officers, who carry out the orders of Government in coping with lawlessness by means of martial law on the ground usually assigned, that they have a moral and also legal claim to be indemnified against acts committed *bona-fide*, and not from any by-motive, in exercise of their jurisdiction under martial law. They can claim no such right in respect of acts committed perversely or recklessly, perversity and recklessness being evidence presumptive of by-motives and malice.

So much for the constitutional aspect of the question.

Now as to its application to H. E. the Viceroy's two announcements (1) that an Indemnity Bill will be introduced "at the earliest convenient moment" into the Imperial Legislative Council, and (2) that a Commission has been appointed to enquire into the causes of, and the measures adopted regarding, the recent disturbances.

Mr. Dicey's opinion quoted above from his booklet, "A Leap in the Dark," published in 1893, examined into "the leading principles" of the Irish Home Rule Bill, officially styled "The Irish Government Act, 1893," introduced in that year in Parliament.

In Mr. Dicey's opinion, one serious defect of that Bill was that its provisions relating to the restrictions on and safeguards against the legislative power of the contemplated Irish Parliament, "contain no prohibition against the passing of an Act of Indemnity" by that Parliament. Such a prohibition was, he thought, necessary, because:—

"Circumstances no doubt may arise in Ireland, as in other countries, under which the maintenance of order or the protection of life may excuse or require deviation from the strict rules of legality. But the question, whether these circumstances have arisen, will always be decided far more justly by the Parliament at Westminster than it can be decided by the Parliament at Dublin. Can anyone really maintain that a Parliament in which Mr. Healy, or, for that matter, Col. Saunderson might be leader, would be as fair a tribunal as a Parliament under the guidance of Mr. Gladstone or Lord Salisbury for determining whether an officer, who, acting under the direction of the Irish Government and with a view to maintain order at Belfast or Dublin, should have put an agitator or conspirator to death without due trial, had or had not done his duty?"

Apply that to India, substitute "India" for Ireland, and Simla for Dublin and so on in the passage above, and it ought to follow, on Mr. Dicey's high authority as a constitutional lawyer of acknowledged repute, that not the Indian Legislature but the British Parliament ought to pass an Indemnity Act, if after having considered whether circumstances necessitating it have arisen, it concludes that they have. Whether those circumstances have arisen can be settled by Parliament, only after Commission appointed by the Crown on its behalf has enquired and reported the results of its enquiry to the Crown for consideration by Parliament.

That is the sound constitutional principle and policy supported by the high authority of Mr. Dicey. It justifies the substantially unanimous Indian protest against—(1) the appointment of the Commission of Enquiry by the Government of India instead of by the Crown and (2) the introduction of an Indemnity Bill into the Imperial Legislative Council in India.

That protest is against what one might well call, adopting Mr. Dicey's phrase, "a leap in the dark."—*The Indian Social Reformer.*

THE PUNJAB "REBELLION" OF 1919 AND HOW IT WAS SUPPRESSED

THE PUNJAB "REBELLION" OF 1919

AND HOW IT WAS SUPPRESSED

AN ACCOUNT OF THE PUNJAB DISORDERS AND THE WORKING OF MARTIAL LAW

(In Two Volumes)

By
PANDIT PEARAY MOHAN

With a Foreword by
LALA LAJPAT RAI

Introduction to new edition by
BIPAN CHANDRA

Editor
RAVI M. BAKAYA

Volume II

GYAN PUBLISHING HOUSE
NEW DELHI-110002

First published in 1920
Original title
**AN IMAGINARY REBELLION:
AND HOW IT WAS SUPPRESSED**
AN ACCOUNT OF THE PUNJAB DISORDERS
AND THE WORKING OF MARTIAL LAW

ISBN : 81-212-0671-5 (Set)
ISBN : 81-212-0688-X (Vol. II)

First Reprint in 1999 by
Gyan Publishing House,
5, Ansari Road, Darya Ganj
New Delhi-110002

Laser Typesetting at A.S. Printers, Delhi

Printed at Chawla Offset Printers, Delhi

CONTENTS

APPENDIX VI

PAGE

Punjab Disturbances and Imperial Legislative Council

Amendments

APPENDIX VII

Miscellaneous

Supplement I

Supplement II—Omitted for want of space

APPENDIX VI
Punjab Disturbances and Imperial Legislative Council

(1)—Hon'ble Pandit Malaviya's Questions

The Hon'ble Pandit Madan Mohan Malaviya gave notice of the following questions, which he wanted to ask at the Simla session of the Imperial Legislative Council, which was held in September, 1919. With the exception of a few minor questions, all the others were disallowed by His Excellency the President on the plea that the Hunter Committee would investigate the whole matter. It is interesting to note, that the Hunter Committee did not record any evidence on most of the matters contained in these questions. The questions are given below:—

I—Will the Government be pleased to lay on the table a statement showing:—

(a) The number of persons actually arrested and detained in custody in connection with the recent disturbances in the Punjab, classified according to town or village, and showing the names, parentage, caste, profession and place of residence of the persons arrested or detained;

(b) The number of persons out the above list who were actually put on trial;

(i) before the Commissions constituted under the Martial Law Ordinance of 1919 promulgated by the Governor-General;

(ii) before the Summary Court established under the orders of the General-Officers Commanding the Lahore and Rawalpindi Divisions;

(iii) before the Area Officers constituted by or in virtue of the powers conferred by the General Officers Commanding the Lahore and Rawalpindi Divisions for offences against the Proclamation issued on the 19th April, 1919, (Notification No. 10,766 of Home Department Military, dated 21st April, 1919);

(iv) before the ordinary municipal courts in districts where Martial Law was not declared; and

(v) before the Special Tribunal constituted under the Defence of India Act;

(c) number of persons convicted out of those mentioned in clause (b), and the offence or offences of which they were convicted, and the sentences passed in each case;

(d) the number of persons discharged or acquitted out of these mentioned above in clause (b);

(e) the number of persons arrested but released.

II—Will the Government be pleased to lay on the table a statement giving the following particulars regarding all cases tried by the Summary Courts established by the General Officers Commanding the Lahore and Rawalpindi Divisions and also by the Area Officers appointed under Notification mentioned in Q I. (b) iii:

(a) The total number of cases decided by each of the said courts and officers from day to day;

(b) The number of cases in which summaries or memoranda of evidence and reasons for findings arrived at were recorded;

(c) The number of cases in which only reasons for findings arrived at were recorded;

(d) The number of cases in which no summary or memorandum of evidence, nor any reasons for the findings arrived at, were recorded, and

(e) The number of cases in which the record does not show even the offence charged.

III—Will the Government be pleased to lay on the table a statement showing:—

(a) The number of applications for copies of judgments and evidences and other proceedings of the Summary Courts and of the courts of the Area Officers made on behalf of the persons convicted, to the Legal Remembrancer, the District Magistrates, Martial Law Administrators and other civil or military authorities;

(b) The number of cases in which copies have been supplied; and

(c) The number of cases in which such copies have been refused and the reasons for such refusal.

IV—Will the Government be pleased to lay on the table a statement showing:—

(a) The number of persons flogged in each town or village within the martial law area in the Punjab, whether,

(1) Under Martial Law,

(i) on conviction, or

(ii) without conviction

or

(2) under the Ordinary Criminal Law during the period in which Martial Law was in force, giving names, parentage, age, caste, profession and residence of the persons flogged;

(b) The offence for which each such person was convicted and the name and designation of the officer who passed the order;

(c) The number of stripes inflicted on each such person; and

(d) the name of the locality where the flogging was administered.

V—Will the Government be pleased to state:—

(a) the number of persons who were sent under the martial law to the Central Jail, Lahore, to be flogged there, and were actually flogged;

(b) the authority under whose orders they were so flogged; and

(c) whether there is a record of all such cases of flogging. If there is, will the Government be pleased to lay it on the table?

VI—Will the Government be pleased to give the names, ages and other particulars of persons who were flogged on being arrested and subsequently put on trial in what is known as the Sherwood case of Amritsar?

VII—Will the Government be pleased to lay on the table lists of persons who, after being sentenced by Martial Law Commissioners or other Martial Law officers, were

(a) executed,

(b) tranported,

(c) confined in the Lahore Central and Borstal Jails and various District Jails in the Punjab?

VIII—Will the Government be pleased to lay on the table a statement, showing the total number of persons who were (1) killed or (2) died of wounds, or (3) were wounded but recovered during the recent disturbances in the Punjab, giving the names, parentage and other particulars and specifying the place where each person was killed or wounded?

IX—(a) Will the Government be pleased to state how many people were (1) killed and (2) wounded by the firing that took place on

(i) the Upper Mall, Lahore, on the 10th April,

(ii) outside the Lohari Gate on the 10th April,

(iii) in the Hira Mandi Chauk on the 12th April ?

(*b*) Will the Government be pleased further to state the number of persons injured, if any, among the Police or the Military, specifying the nature of their injuries received in the places and on the occasions mentioned above ?

X—Will the Government be pleased to state what steps were taken by the Police or the Military to disperse the crowd in the three places mentioned in the preceding question, before they resorted to firing; also to state what was the immediate cause, which necessitated the firing on each occasion ?

XI—Will the Government be pleased to state, if it is a fact that some of the wounded on the Upper Mall, Lahore, who had been taken possession of by' the Police, were removed to the Charing Cross Police Station and not to the hospital which was nearer, and that some out of this number died at the Police Station, without any medical aid ? Will the Government be pleased to state the number of persons, who so died at the Police Station, with their names and other particulars ?

XII—Will the Government be pleased to state:—(a) Whether orders had been issued at the end of March or the beginning of April, 1919, against Dr. Satyapal and Dr. Kitchlew of Amritsar, under the Defence of India Act, requiring them to abstain from addressing public meetings and whether these gentlemen had submitted to those orders?

(b) If so, what was the reason for deporting these gentlemen on the 10th of April ?

XIII—Will the Government be pleased to state if it is a fact that the Government apprehended public excitement at the deportation of Dr. Kitchlew and Dr. Satyapal and for that reason picqueted the carriage-overbridge with the Military or mounted Police ?

XIV—Will the Government be pleased to state if it is a fact that on the morning of the 10th April, business in Amritsar was going on as usual till the news of the deportation spread through the city, when all shops were suddenly closed in consequence thereof?

XV—Is it a fact that after the shops were closed ; an unarmed crowd started from the city to go to the house of the Deputy Commissioner to urge the release of the deportees and on the route passed by the National Bank, the Alliance and the Chartered Banks, the Church, the Town Hall and other public buildings without making any attempt at mischief ?

XVI—Is it a fact that the progress of the crowd towards the Deputy Commissioner's bungalow was barred by the picquet mentioned above, which fired upon the crowd ? If so, what was the immediate occasion for the firing ?

XVII—Will the Government be pleased to state—

(a) The number of times the crowd was fired upon at the foot and carriage-overbridges at Amritsar on 10th April ?

(b) Is it a fact that no violence against person or property was committed by any section of the crowd till after they had been fired upon ?

XVIII—Will the Government be pleased to state—

(a) Whether any proclamation prohibiting meetings under the Seditious Meetings Act was issued on or before the 13th April, 1919, at Amritsar ? If so, at what time, in what manner, and in what parts of the city was it published ?

(b) If no such proclamation was published, will the Government be pleased to state if there was any prohibition of meetings by any other authority on or before the 13th April and, if so, when, under what law, and by whom such prohibition was issued, and in what parts of the city and in what manner it was published ?

XIX—Will the Government be pleased to lay on the table a plan of the Jallianwala Bagh, where a large number of people were shot, while assembled at a meeting, on the 13th April, 1919, drawn to scale, and showing

(a) all the entrances and exits to the Bagh;

(b) the height of the houses and the walls surrounding the Bagh;

(c) the spot where the Military were posted at the time of the firing on the 13th and its height above the ground where the people were assembled;

(d) the position of the armoured car posted in or near the Bagh on that day; and

(e) the position of the audience and their distance from the firing party.

XX—Will the Government be pleased to state what was the number of persons assembled at the Jallianwala Bagh on the 13th April at the time they were fired upon?

XXI—Will the Government be pleased to state—

(a) How and when and by whom the meeting at the Jallianwala Bagh held on the 13th April was advertised in the city?

(b) When did the authorities come to know that such meeting was going to be held ?

(c) What steps, if any, were taken by the authorities to make it known to the persons assembling that the meeting was prohibited.

(d) When did the people begin to assemble in the said Bagh ?

(e) At what time did the proceedings begin and how long did they continue before the arrival of the Military ?

(f) Whether there was any reconnoitering by aeroplane over the Jallianwala Bagh at the time the meeting was going on and before the Military arrived ?

(g) What steps, if any, were taken by the authorities to disperse the meeting from the time the people began to assemble to the time when the Military arrived ?

(h) At what time did the Military arrive on the scene and how long after did they open fire on the crowd ?

(i) What was the strength of the Military, what was their equipment and who were the officers in command ?

(f) Did any, and if so, which magistrate or other responsible civil officer accompany the Military to the garden or was present there at the time of the firing ?

(k) By whose orders were the military sent there, and with what instructions, if any ?

(l) Were the people assembled entirely unarmed and were there also a number of children among them ?

(m) Was the order to fire given by any magistrate or did the Military act on their own initiative ?

(n) Did the officer, who ordered the firing, warn the people assembled, and give them time to disperse before giving the order?

(o) How long did the firing last and how many rounds were fired ? What was the nature of the ammunition used ? What was the total number of bullets actually fired ?

(p) What was the total number of persons (i) killed (ii) wounded, who subsequently died, and (iii) wounded who recovered, at Jallianwala Bagh together with their names, parentage, age, residence and other particulars ?

(q) Whether there were any ambulance or first-aid arrangements previously made by the authorities for the wounded, on the spot ? If not, were any steps taken, after the firing for the disposal of the dead bodies and the treatment of the wounded ?

(r) Of the persons wounded at the garden, how many were admitted to any hospital ?

(s) Was any order in force at Amritsar on the 13th April last, prohibiting people from leaving the houses after 8 p.m. ?

(t) How long after the firing was the Bagh cleared of all corpses and by what agency ?

(u) Will the Government be pleased to state if some of the bodies of the dead and the wounded lying overnight in the garden were mutilated and despoiled of their valuables during the night ?

(v) Will the Government be pleased to state whether any boys or children were shot or otherwise killed or injured at the Jallianwala Bagh on the 13th of April, 1919; and if so, will the Government be pleased to give a list of the children, stating their names, ages, etc. ?

XXII—Will the Government be pleased to state whether there were any casualties among people, who were in the houses or streets in the neighbourhood of the Jallianwala Bagh, when the firing took place there on the 13th of April ? If so, will the Government be pleased to state the names, age and other particulars of the sufferers?

XXIII—Will the Government be pleased to state if any steps were taken by the authorities, and if so, when, to ascertain the names and prepare a list of all the persons killed and wounded in the Jallianwala Bagh ?

XXIV—Is it a fact that the 13th of April was the Baisakhi festival (New Year's day) on which the biggest *mela* in the province is held at Amritsar, which is attended by thousands of persons from all parts of the province ? Will the Government be pleased to state if a large number of such persons from outside were also present in the meeting at the Jallianwala Bagh on that day ? If so, what steps were taken and when, to trace out the casualties among them ?

XXV—Will the Government be pleased to lay on the table a statement giving the names of persons who were wounded at the Jallianwala Bagh, who have been prosecuted and convicted or discharged, stating in cases of conviction, the offence or offences with which they were charged and the punishments awarded to them ?

XXVI—Will the Government be pleased to lay on the table copies of all orders, proclamations, posters, notifications and notices issued—

(a) by the administrators of Martial Law in the Punjab in their respective areas,

(b) by civil authorities in the same areas during the operation of Martial Law, and

(c) by civil authorities after the withdrawal of Martial Law notifying that certain acts by the civil population will be treated as offences, and dealt with by Military Officers ?

XXVII—(a) Will the Government be pleased to state if it is a fact that in the lane known as *Dogglan-ki-gali* in the quarters known as *Kauriyan-wala Khuh*, where Miss Sherwood was assaulted, every Indian, irrespective of age or position in life, wishing to pass through the lane, was made to crawl on his belly through the whole length of the lane and British soldiers were posted from morning to 8 p.m. to enforce the observance of this order ?

(b) Whether, as a consequence of the enforcement of this order, houses in the lane remained unscavenged for many days ?

XXVIII—Will the Government be pleased to state—

(a) If all the legal practitioners of Amritsar, nearly one hundred in number, were compulsorily enrolled as special constables, and irrespective of age and physical fitness, were not only made to patrol the city for nearly a month, but also required to walk several times a day to a place outside the city, to answer to roll call.

(b) Were they allowed to attend to their professional duties during the period ?

(c) Is it also a fact that those lawyers were made to fetch and carry tables, chairs, etc., for Europeans ?

(d) Is it also a fact that the said lawyers were all summoned and made to stand in rows in front of the flogging stand ; and that two persons were actually flogged in their presence ?

XXIX—(a) Will the Government be pleased to state if it is a fact, that the electric and water-supply of the city of Amritsar, exclusive of the Civil Lines, was cut off for four or five days, about the 12th of April last ?

(b) Is it also a fact that a large number of wells in the city of Amritsar had been closed in recent years, when Mr. King was Deputy Commissioner there ?

XXX—Will the Government be pleased to state—

(a) If it is a fact, that several very respectable under-trial prisoners, including bankers, lawyers and doctors, of Amritsar, were hand-cuffed in pairs and confined for several days in an open racket court in April last, at a time when it was hot during the day and cold during the night.

(b) Whether they remained so hand-cuffed continuously for all the 24 hours of the day for several days together, and whether they had to eat, drink, sleep and attend to the calls of nature while so hand-cuffed in pairs ?

(c) Whether the said prisoners were subsequently removed to cells in the forts, and kept there so hand-cuffed ? If so, what were the dimensions of such cells and the number of prisoners confined in each ?

XXXI—Will the Government be pleased to place on the table a plan drawn to scale, of the town of Gujranwala and of Gharjak, Bhagawanpura, Dhulla and other neighbouring villages thereof, where bombs were dropped or machine-guns were used, showing—

(a) the situation of the properties to which damage was done by the mob on 14th April, last;

(b) houses actually occupied on the 14th and 15th April by the Europeans; and

(c) the spots where bombs were dropped or to which machine-gun fire was directed, indicating in each case whether it was part of a house or other building or on open space ?

XXXII—Will the Government be pleased to state -

(a) How many aeroplanes were sent from Lahore to Gujranwala on 14th April, 1919, and by whose order ?

(b) How many of these aeroplanes were equipped with machine-guns or armament of other kinds ?

(c) How many bombs were dropped from these aeroplanes and how many shots fired from machine or other guns ?

(d) What was the total number of casualties due to such bombing or firing, giving the names and other particulars, of the persons wounded or killed ?

(e) Whether any bombs were thrown or shots fired from aeroplanes at any place in Gujranwala town or in neighbouring villages on any date after the 14th April ? If so, how many and where ?

XXXIII—Will the Government be pleased to state the sex, ages, designations and other particulars of Europeans who were in Gujranwala town at the time of the arrival of the aeroplanes on the 14th April.

XXXIV. Will the Government be pleased to state the names and places, if any, in the Gujranwala district other than the town of Gujranwala and its neighbourhood, where any firing was resorted to by the police or the military ? If so, will the Government state the nature of arms and amunition used in each place and the number of casualties with names and other particulars.

XXXV. Will the Government be pleased to state.

(a) If it is a fact that on the 15th April last, Col. O'Brien, Deputy Commissioner of Gujranwala, with strong body of police and European soldiers and with an armoured-car, marched to the house of Lala Melaram, B.A., LL. B., Pleader ; and arrested and hand-cuffed him and took him away without allowing him to dress himself or to speak to his family ?

(b) Whether the party then met Mr. Labh Singh, M.A., (Cantab), Barrister-at-Law, and arrested and hand-cuffed him and chained him with Lala Melaram ?

(c) Whether the party then proceeded to the houses of twenty other gentlemen, (pleaders, bankers and other respectable citizens) and arrested and hand-cuffed and chained them all together ?

(d) Whether the persons so arrested and chained together were marched to the city two and two headed by a Hindu and a Mahomedan to ridicule Hindu and Mahomedan unity, as was stated at the time by Col. O'Brien ?

(e) Whether, under the orders of Col. O'Brien, two Municipal Commissioners walked in front of the procession thus formed and pointed to the aeroplanes hovering overhead, kept on shouting to the people to make way for the prisoners on pain of being bombed or shot down ?

(f) Whether, after being thus paraded through the principal streets of the town, the prisoners were taken to the Railway Station and put into an open coal truck, which was guarded by a number of European soldiers with fixed bayonets, and by an armoured-engine, with a gun directed towards the prisoners ?

(g) Whether the prisoners were not allowed to leave their places even for the purposes of attending to the calls of nature : and whether some gentlemen had to relieve themselves where they were huddled together ?

(h) Whether, on reaching the Lahore Railway Station, and before being removed to the jail, the prisoners were kept for about ten hours, along with thirty other prisoners, in a room which opened by means of an iron-barred and impanelled door into another room which was used as latrine ?

XXXVI. Will the Government be pleased to state whether a number of pleaders and other respectable citizens in the town of Shekhupura, in the district of Gujranwala, were arrested and treated in a manner similar to that adopted at Gujranwala and were subjected to similar inconveniences and indignities when being taken to Lahore?

XXXVII. Will Government be pleased to state, whether almost the entire population of the town of Shekhupura above the age of 10 years, irrespective of rank or social position, was summoned by Mr. Bosworth Smith, I.C.S., Joint Deputy Commissioner and one of the Martial Law Officers, and made to sweep a large open piece of ground?

XXXVIII. Is the Government aware, that a marriage party of certain Mahomedans of village Rajgarh within the Municipal limits of Lahore was arrested, and the members thereof were convicted by Mr. E.A. Penhearow, one of the Martial Law Officers at Lahore ?

If so, will the Government be pleased to state.

(a) the number of persons tried and convicted ;

(b) whether the bridegroom and the Mullah Priest were also among the accused ?

(c) the offence for which they were arrested and tried ; and

(d) the sentences passed upon each person.

XXXIX. Will the Government be pleased to lay on the table the correspondence which passed between it and the Punjab Government leading to the declaration of Martial Law in the Punjab ?

XL. Will the Government be pleased to State—

(a) the facts and circumstances, which in its opinion constituted a state of open rebellion against the authority of the Government in certain parts of the province of the Punjab, within the meaning of Regulation X of 1804, on the date on which Ordinance I of 1919 was promulgated by the Governor-General; and,

(b) the date or dates, up to which sach state of open rebellion continued in each part of Punjab, to which the said Ordinance had been applied ?

XLI. Will the Government be pleased to state—

(a) Whether a number of barristers, pleaders and other respectable persons of Gurdaspar district, where martial law was never proclaimed, were arrested on or about the 2nd May, 1919, brought in hand-cuffs to Lahore, confind in the Central Jail there and released at Gurdaspur on the 8th July without trial, after having been kept in solitary cells for most of the period ?

(b) If so, will the Government be pleased to give the names and other particulars of the persons arrested and state the reasons for their arrest and the law under which they were detained in custody without trial for such a long time ?

XLII. Is it also a fact, that at the time of the release of the Gurdaspur lawyers referred to in the preceding question, the District Magistrate of Gurdaspur, Mr. Harcourt, I.C.S., expressed his regret in open Court, that Government had taken no action against them, and told them that he, however, was taking steps to move the High Court at Lahore to proceed against them under the Legal Practitioners Act?

XLIII. Will the Government be pleased to state—

(a) Whether General Dyer visited Gurdaspur on the 18th April, 1919, and held a Darbar in the Government School Hall, to which lawyers, honorary magistrates, government servants, bankers, traders, Zamindars, Lambardars etc., were invited by the Deputy Commissioner ?

(b) Was the hall guarded by the military with armoured cars and machine-gun ?

(c) Did General Dyer address the audience as *Budmashes* and use other insulting language ?

XLIV. Did General Dyer address similar remarks to a similar meeting at the town of Batala, in the district of Gurdaspur ?

XLV. (a) Is it a fact that Sarder Gauhar Singh, a retired Inspector of Police of Sheikhupura, was arrested and sent to the Central Jail at Lahore, as a hostage for his three sons, named Amar Singh, Atma Singh and Santokh Singh, the last aged 16 years, who were wanted by the police but could not be found at the time in the station ?

(b) Is it also a fact that though he has been released, a report has been made by the executive authorities, recommending forfeiture of his pension !

XLVI. Will the Government be pleased to state—

(a) If it is a fact, that the Gujranwala police proceeded to the town of Hafizabad with a warrant for the arrest of 121 persons, containing neither the names nor the descriptions of the persons to be arrested, and that the said police did arrest 121 residents of Hafizabad under the said warrant.

(b) Will the Government be pleased to place on the table a statement giving the names and other particulars of the persons so arrested, the dates of their release and of conviction, the offence or offences for which they were arrested or convicted and the sentences awarded to those convicted ?

XLVII. Has the attention of the Government been drawn to a letter published in the *Leader* newspaper of Allahabad, dated the 14th August, 1919, and signed 'Justice,' detailing the humiliation to which the people of Hafizabad were subjected during the martial-law period, in particular, that school children and even infants of four or five years of age had to be present at the roll call twice a day before a military officer ?

XLVIII. Will the Government be pleased to state, if it is a fact that certain District Officers or their subordinates in the Punjab have imposed and collected, by coercion and threats, large sums of money as fines from several villages and small towns for their alleged misdeeds during the recent disturbances ? If so, will the Government be pleased to make a detailed statement, showing the amount so collected from each village or town, the law under which, and the authority under whose orders, the money was so collected and the manner in which it was disposed of ?

XLIX. Will the Government be pleased to state.

(a) Whether on the 14th April last, a bomb was thrown from an aeroplane at the Khalsa High School Boarding-house at Gujranwala, which is situated at a distance of over a mile from the buildings against which any violence had been committed and the places where any mob had collected ?

(b) Did the bomb burst and injure the platforms and some of the walls of the premises ?

(c) Were over 150 students present at the time in the boarding-house ?

(d) Is it a fact that shots were fired from one of the aeroplanes and injured a *halwai*, who had a shop on the premises ?

L. Will the Government be pleased to state, whether Lala Dhanpat Rai, a Pleader of Kasur, aged over 70 years, was arrested on the 15th April, four days after the riot that took place there, hand-cuffed and marched to the Railway Station, surrounded by a strong military guard with fixed bayonets, and from there taken to the Lahore Jail, where he was kept for nearly two months and then released without any charge or trial ?

LI. Will the Government be pleased to state, if amongst others, Maulvi Ghulam Mohi-ud-Din, Pleader of Kasur (who had last year been publicly rewarded for his services in connection with the war) and Maulvi Abdul Qadir, a Senior Pleader of Kasur, were arrested and kept in confinement for some weeks in an improvised lock-up near the railway station, and were then released without any charge or trial ?

LII. Will the Government be pleased to state, if it is a fact that three gallows were erected in a public place at Kasur, and were not taken down till after several days ? If so, what was the object with which they were so put up ?

LIII. Will the Government be pleased to state, if it is a fact that several school boys at Kasur were flogged, and if so, to state their names, ages and other particulars, together with the number of stripes administered in each case and the offence for which the boys were so punished ?

LIV. Will the Government be pleased to state, if it is a fact that during the martial-law period, permits to travel were refused to several pleaders of Kasur, who had to attend to their cases before ordinary municipal courts at the headquarters of the district, *viz*., Lahore ?

LV. Will the Government be pleased to state, if it is a fact that on or about the Ist of May, 1919, practically the whole population of the town of Kasur, was summoned to the Railway Station for the purpose of identification, and that they were made to stand bareheaded, exposed to the sun, for six hours or so ? Is it also a fact, that while the male population was thus withdrawn from the town, several houses were searched by the military or the police accompanied by the Ward Member, and that, in some cases, even the *Zenana* apartments were entered in search of possible hiders ?

LVI. Will the Government be pleased to state why, Mr. Manohar Lal, M.A., (Cantab), Bar-at-Law, formerly Minto Professor of Economics at the University of Calcutta and now a prominent member of the Lahore Bar and a syndic of the Punjab University, was arrested on the 18th April, 1919, and kept in jail for nearly a month, including one week of solitary confinement ?

LVII. Will the Government be pleased to state, if it is a fact that on the date Mr. Manoharlal was arrested, his bungalow was locked and sealed by the police and his wife and children turned out and obliged to live in one of the out-houses used as servants' quarters, until the bungalow had been searched about a week later ?

LVIIL. Will the Government be pleased to state.

(a) Why Rai Sahib Seth Ram Prasad, Municipal Commissioner, and one of the largest house proprietors and bankers of Lahore, was arrested in April last and marched in hand-cuffs to the Central Jail, a distance of nearly three miles, kept in solitary confinement, and then released without trial after several weeks ?

(b) Will the Government be pleased to state the sums subscribed by him and his son towards the war loans and war charities, and other services rendered by him during the war ?

LIX. Will the Government be pleased to state if the following incidents connected with the arrests and detention without trial, of Lala Ratanchand, Secretary of the Punjab Provincial Congress Committee, and Lala Dhaniram Bhalla, a merchant of Anarkali, Lahore, are correct ? A letter from the Deputy Commissioner of Lahore was received by Lala Ratanchand, on the 19th of April, asking him to produce his carriage before the Martial Law Officer-in-charge of the Transport. Lala Ratanchand immediately wrote in reply that he had never possessed and was not then in possession of any carriage at all. In spite of this on the 20th of April he was sent for by the Deputy Commissioner and asked why he had failed to produce his carriage. Lala Ratanchand explained that he had no carriage at all. After further questions, his statement to this effect was recorded by the Deputy Commissioner, and he was allowed to go.

On the evening of the 22nd at about 8.30 p.m., Lala Ratanchand was arrested by a police inspector and taken to the police station, where he was told that the reason for his arrest was his failure to produce a carriage in accordance with the orders of the Deputy Commissioner. On his again representing the facts of the case, the police officer had enquiries made from Lala Ratanchand's neighbours and relations, and after having satisfied himself, he released him.

In the afternoon of the 24th April, the Superintendent of Police, C.I.D., went to his house with a military guard in motar-car and arrested Lala Ratanchand again and took him to the Delhi Gate Police Station, while he was under high fever. Here, Lala Ratanchand

and Lala Dharamdas Suri, Vakil, High Court and Lala Dhaniram Bhalla, who had also, in the meanwhile been arrested, were surrounded by about a hundred European and Indian soldiers, with fixed bayonets and made to walk through the city to the Fort, a distance of about a mile, where they were confined. Here Lala Ratanchand and Lala Dhaniram were kept for fifty days during which time no statement was ever taken from them, nor were they ever told for what offence and under what law they had been arrested and detained.

LX. Will the Government be pleased to state the circumstances, under which the following persons were arrested and released without trial after being kept in custody for several days.

1. Lala Dunichand, piece-goods merchant, Bazaz Hatta, Lahore.

2. Lala Vaid Raj Sardarilal, Managing-Director, Ayurvedic and Pharmaceutical Company Ltd., Lahore.

3. Sardar Wadhawa Singh, dealer in perfumes, and jams, Lahore.

4. Lala Amirchand, proprietor, Swadeshi Stores, Anarkali, Lahore.

5. Lala Jagannath, Secretary, Arya Samaj, Wachhowali, Lahore.

6. Lala Hiralal Kapur of the *Punjab Samachar*, Lahore.

7. Lala Kaluram Kohli, proprietor, Simla Hindu Hotel, Lahore.

8. Lala Diwanchand, proprietor, West End House, Lahore, (arrested at his shop at Amritsar).

9. Lala Mohanlal *Saraf*, Banker, Suha Bazar, Lahore.

10. Lala Kishenchand, carpet-merchant, Lahore.

11. Lala Saligram, proprietor, Aror Bans Press, Lahore.

12. Lala Rajaram, jeweller, Bazaz Hatta, Lahore.

13. Lala Daulatram, goldsmith, Gumti Bazar, Lahore.

14. Mistri Karimbaksh, gas-contractor, Gumti Bazar Lahore.

15. Pandit Amarnath Sharma, estate-agent, Jauri Mauri, Lahore.

16. Lala Chunilal, shopkeeper, Moti Bazar, Lahore.

17. Sirdar Mohan Singh, hardware merchant, Dabbi Bazar, Lahore.

18. Lala Hemraj, banker and landed proprietor, Shahdara.

19. Mian Sirdar Mohammed, *alias* Saradara Munshi, Shahdara.

20. Mian Siraj Din, Munshi, Shahdara.

21. Mian Nurdin, *alias* Madha, Mochi Gate, Lahore.

22. Mian Zahur Din, son of Nurdin, house-proprietor, Rang Mahal Bazar, Lahore.

23. Lala Jagannath, cloth merchant, Bazaz Hatta, Lahore.

24. Lala Desraj, stamp-vendor and deed-writer, Bazaz Hatta, Lahore.

25. Lala Mulk Raj, shopkeeper and chaudhri of Gumti Bazar, Lahore.

26. Badshah, *bhusawala*, Bhati Gate, Lahore.

27. Malha Khan, *alias* Malha, *Halwai*, Delhi Gate, Lahore,

28. Mian Shadi Khan, *kakezai*, Mohalla Kalal, Lahore.

29. Mian Ibrahim Khan, cloth-merchant, Lohari Mandi, Lahore.

30. Pandit Jairam Das, Kucha Kaghzian, Machhi Hatta, Lahore.

31. Lala Jairam Das Khatri.

32. Pandit Hukumal, son of Pandit Thakur Das, Wachhowali, Lahore.

33. Lala Beliram of the firm of Ganeshdas-Shankerdas, Bazaz Hatta, Lahore.

34. Mian Rajdin, unbrella-maker, Dabbi Bazar, Lahore.

35. Mian Muhammad Hassan, son of Shadi Khan, *Kakezai*, Mohalla Kalal, Lahore.

36. Mian Jalal Din, son of Azizuddin, Shopkeeper, Akbari Mandi, Lahore.

37. Swami Sevanand, physician-in-charge of the Ramkrishna Charitable Dispensary, Sutar Mandi, Lahore.

38. Lala Ganeshdas, merchant, Bazaz Hatta, Lahore ; and

39. Tarachand, barber, Wachhowali, Lahore.

LXI. Will the Government be pleased to state if Dr. Kedar Nath of Amritsar, a retired Civil Surgeon, aged 60 years, who had been invalided in 1909 on account of heart troubles, was arrested and hand-cuffed and marched through the streets with 62 other prisoners to the Jail, and kept in confinement for a fortnight with two other prisoners, in a cell which was meant for one person only, and then released without trial ? If so, for what offence ?

LXII. Will the Government be pleased to state.

(a) If it is a fact, that martial law notices were posted at the houses and shops of a number of people at Lahore with directions that the occupants must guard the posters, and that if they were damaged, torn or disfigured, the occupants would be severely punished under Martial Law.

(b) Is it a fact, that mostly the people, who had taken part in public movements or had any interest in any of the persons arrested, were selected for this form of harassment ?

LXIII. Will the Government be pleased to state, if it is a fact that even after the arrest of the persons at whose houses the martial-law notices were posted at Lahore, martial law authorities continued to post such notices at their houses, making the members of their families responsible for duly exhibiting and protecting them, thus forcing them to keep anxious and continuous personal watch over the said posters ?

LXIV. Will the Government be pleased to lay on the table a statement showing the number of persons punished for tampering with the martial-law posters, giving in each case the name, age and parentage, etc., of the said persons and the punishment inflicted upon them ?

LXV. Will the Government be pleased to state if it is a fact that—

(a) the name of the Sanatan Dharma College Hostel, Lahore, was not included in the first published list of places at which martial law notices were to be exhibited ;

(b) That, notwithstanding this, some posters were put up on the boundary wall of the hostel without intimation to the college authorities or the inmates of the hostel ;

(c) That one of the posters was torn by some unknown person, whose identity has not yet been discovered and on this all the students in the hostel were called by the martial law authorities and were marched in the sun carrying their bedding on their shoulders to the Fort, a distance of nearly three miles, and interned there in a body;

(d) That the students were not released until the Principal and the President of the Committee of the College gave an undertaking on the following day to the authorities to be personally responsible for the proper exhibition and safety of the notices ?

LXVI. Will the Government be pleased to state if it is a fact that—

(a) One morning, during the martial-law period, the Principal of the Dyalsingh College, Lahore, was served with an order of the Administrator of Martial Law, Commanding Lahore Civil Area, to the effect that it had been reported to him that a certain objectionable poster had been found put up on the outer wall of the College premises and had been removed by the police and brought to his notice, and that if the College authorities did not find the writer and report him before 12 noon the same day, drastic measures would be taken against all concerned with the College ;

(b) On this, the trustees (Raja Narendra Nath, M.A., once Commissioner of Lahore, Rai Bahadur Sundardas Suri, M.A., and Lala Shiv Dayal, M.A., retired Inspectors of School and Lala Kunwar Sain, M.A., Barrister-at-Law and Principal, Law College) and the staff made a careful inquiry and came to the conclusion that none of the students of the College was the writer of the notice ;

(c) That meanwhile Col. Frank Johnson, the Martial Law Administrator, arrived there in person and it was pointed out to him that there were no signs on the wall at all to indicate that the poster in question had been nailed or posted there. But he replied, pointing his finger to a certain spot on the wall, that he decided that it had been posted at that spot ;

(d) That the next day the Principal was sent for at the Martial-Law Head-quarters and was informed that he must pay a fine of Rs. 250 or in default undergo three months' imprisonment and then he was taken in a motor-car to the College with two soldiers, with fixed bayonets, and was released on payment of the fine to the latter;

(e) That from that time onwards, the students began to keep careful secret watch all round the extensive college and hostel premises day and night in batches and kept a regular diary ;

(f) That after a few weeks' continuous watch and ward, the batch of students on guard at the time caught hold of a person red-handed trying to put up on the College wall a spurious poster, and were about to take him before the martial-law authorities when several other persons arrived on the scene and rescued the offender, saying that they belonged to the police and would themselves take him before the Martial Law Officers ;

(g) That on this incident being brought to the notice of the martial-law authorities by the Principal, the fine which had been previously imposed on him was remitted ?

Will the Government be pleased to give the name and other particulars of the offender, and state what action, if any, has been taken against him ?

LXVII. Will the Government be pleased to state—

(a) If it is a fact that all the students of the D.A.V., Dayalsingh and the Medical Colleges at Lahore were required to attend roll-calls before military officers, when they were made to stand in the sun, guarded by the Military with fixed bayonets, and that this process was continued for three weeks, immediately preceding the University Examination.

(b) Is it also a fact, that in the case of the King Edward Medical College, the total distance which the students were made to traverse on foot in the summer heat for attending the roll-call, amounted to not less than 16 miles a day ?

(c) Is it a fact, that some students actually fainted while going to, attending or returning from such roll-call parades and that thereupon a nearer place was fixed for taking the roll-call ?

LXVIII. Will the Government be pleased to state, if it is a fact that the principals of certain colleges in Lahore were coerced by the Martial Law Administrator to inflict very severe punishments on a certain percentage of their students, without regard to any evidence of their guilt ? If so, will the Government be pleased to lay on the table all the orders issued by the Martial Law Administrator and all the correspondence relating to this matter between him and the Principals of the said colleges ?

LXIX. Will the Government be pleased to state how many motor-cars, cycles, carriages, bicycles, electric fans, lamps and telephones were commandeered from the inhabitants of Lahore and what was the military necessity justifying such a course ?

LXX. Is it a fact, that most of the Europeans whose motor-cars had been commandeered were supplied by the military authorities with conveyances commandeered from Indian gentlemen ?

LXXI. (a) Will the Government be pleased to give the names and addresses of all the residents and institutions, from whose premises electric fans, lights, and phones were removed ?

(b) Have the fans, lights, telephones so commandeered been in all cases returned to their respective owners since the withdrawal of martial law ? If not, why ?

LXXII. Will the Government be pleased to state if it is a fact, that electric fans and lamps were removed by the martial law authorities from places of worship, like the temples of the Brahmo Samaj and Arya Samaj, thus hurting the feelings of and causing discomfort to the worshippers ? And is it a fact that in spite of representations having been made both to military and civil authorities, these fans and lamps have not yet been returned ?

LXXIII. Is the Government aware that in some cases tried by martial law officers, specially towards the close of the martial-law period, the accused were convicted without the whole of the defence evidence being heard, even though witnesses were present in Court on the ground of want of time, e.g., in the case of Lala Gurdasram and Lala Shivaram, Pleaders of Hafizabad, in the district of Gujranwala, who were sentenced to two years' rigorous imprisonment each by Mr. Wace, I.C.S. ?

LXXIV. Will the Government be pleased to state if it is a fact—

(a) That Ramlok, son of Daulatram, aged 17 years, a student of the Government High School, Lyallpur, was arrested on the 25th April, and having been detained in police custody for 3 weeks was released for want of evidence against him ;

(b) That several days after his release, his father Daulatram appeared as a defence witness for one Ramditta and deposed that the police had asked Ram Ditta to turn an approver but he had refused to do so ;

(c) That on this, his son Ramlok was re-arrested on the following day and put on his trial for the very same offences, for which he had been arrested and released before ;

(d) That the trial of Ramlok was fixed for the 9th and 10th June, but, as martial law was going to be withdrawn at mid-night on the 9th June, the trial was accelerated to the 5th June, without any previous intimation having been given to the accused or to his father; and

(e) That the accused was tried and sentenced to one year and seven months' rigorous imprisonment for offences under Section 147, 426 and 506, Indian Penal Code by Mr. A.L. Hoyle, I.C.S., officer presiding over Summary Courts under Martial Law, without any chance being given to him to produce his defence ?

LXXV. Will the Government be pleased to state if it is a fact— (a) that one Bhagwan Singh, a meat-seller of Lyallpur was arrested on the 6th June last and placed before the Martial Law Summary Court on the 7th June ; (b) that, on the 8th June, part of the evidence was heard and the case was adjourned ; (c) that, as the Martial Law was to be withdrawn at midnight on the 9th June, the case was taken up at 11 o'clock that night, without any opportunity being given to his counsel to be present, and the accused was sentenced to three months' rigorous imprisonment ?

LXXVI. Is the Government aware, that in some cases tried by the Martial Law Commissions constituted under Ordinance No. 1 of 1919 no record of evidence of witnesses either for the prosecution or the defence has at all been made, nor judgments recorded, though heavy sentences have been awarded, e.g. (a) the case of Crown *versus* Fazla son of Umardin, Kakazi convicted under Section 124-A, and sentenced to transportation for life by the Commission presided over by Lt. Col. Irvine on the 26th of April, 1919, and (b) trials Nos 20 and 21 of Hansraj and Hariram of Amritsar before the Commission presided over by the Hon Mr. Justice Leslie-Jones, I.C.S., Judge of the High Court of Judicature at Lahore, convicting the aforesaid persons to 7 years' rigorous imprisonment each under Section 412 I.P.C. ?

LXXVII. Is the Government aware, that in several cases tried by the Martial Law Commissions constituted under Ordinance No. 1 of 1919, examination of outside witnesses for the defence was refused except by interrogatories; and when in pursuance of this order of the Commission, interrogartories were actually put in, they were referred by the Commission to the convening authority, who disallowed such as he did not think proper, without hearing the accused or his counsel in contravention of the provisions of Section 85 (7) of the Indian Army Act ?

LXXVIII. Is the Government aware that in several instances the convening authority refused to issue interrogatories for examination of defence witnesses, unless money was deposited by the accused to defray the expenses thereof.

LXXIX—(a) Is the Government aware that in the trial known as the Gujranwala Leaders' Case, held before the Commission presided over by the Hon. Mr. Justice Broadway, a Judge of the High Court of Judicature at Lahore, one of the accused Jagannath who wanted to establish an *alibi* by production of State records and other evidence from Kathiawar, was ordered to deposit Rs. 250 before the interrogatories could be issued ?

(b) Is the Government also aware that though Jagannath did deposit the above sum and interrogatories were actually issued, the learned Commissioners delivered judgment, convicting Jagannath and sentencing him to transportation for life and forfeiture of property, without waiting for the return of the interrogatories in spite of the written and oral protest of his counsel ?

LXXX. Will the Government be pleased to state if it is a fact that in the case known as the Lahore Conspiracy case (King-Emperor *vs.* Harkishen Lal, etc.) tried by the Commission presided over by the Hon. Mr. Justice Leslie-Jones, I.C.S., though the Public Prosecutor was present throughout the trial to conduct the case on behalf of the Crown, the cross-examination of the defence witnesses was conducted by the commissioners themselves and the Public Prosecutor put only half-a-dozen questions to 2 out of more than 600 witnesses examined for the defence, thus depriving the defence of the right of re-examination ?

LXXXI—Will the Government be pleased to state :—

(a) Whether it is a fact that the convening authority issued written orders which were exhibited in the court-room prohibiting the taking of short-hand notes of proceedings before the Commission, even when an undertaking was offered on behalf of the accused that such notes would be used solely for the purposes of the cases and would not be published ?

(b) Is it also a fact, that on protest being made by defence counsel that the convening authority had no power to pass such an order, the Commission presided over by the Hon. Mr. Justice Leslie-Jones, I.C.S., expressed its inability to interfere with the order of the convening authority ?

LXXXII. (a) Will the Government be pleased to state the grounds on which the Martial Law Authorities prohibited the entry of counsel from outside the Punjab into the Martial Law area ?

(b) Will the Government be pleased to state if Sir Erle Richards, Senior Counsel for the Secretary of State for India, who opposed the application of Ratanchand and Choudhry Bugga for special leave to appeal to the Privy Council, was right in stating that the prohibition was confined to persons coming from Bengal ?

(c) Is it a fact that besides Mr. Eardley Norton, Mr. J.N. Roy, Mr. B. Chakravarti, Mr. Gregory, Mr. Langford James, Mr. C. R. Dass, Mr. B. C. Chatterji of Calcutta Bar, permission to appear before the Martial Law Commission at Lahore was refused to the Hon. Pandit Motilal Nehru of the Allahabad High Court, Mr. Syed Hasan Imam of the Patna High Court and Sir Chimanlal Setalvad and Mr. Azad of the Bombay Bar ?

LXXXIII. Is the Government aware that the Administrator of Martial Law at Lyallpur issued an order prohibiting the entry into that district of legal practitioners who ordinarily practise in the districts in the Punjab, other than Lyallpur ?

LXXXIV. Is the Government aware (a) that Maulvi Muharram Ali Chishti, a Vakil of the High Court at Lahore, who was unaware of the order referred to in the preceding question, appeared in the last week of May before the Sessions Judge at Lyallpur in an ordinary criminal case (No. 116 of 1919) , without any objection being raised by any one to his entry in the district; (b) that about a fortnight later, on the 11th June, two days after the Martial Law had been withdrawn from Lyallpur and on the day on which it was to be withdrawn from Lahore, Mr. Moharram Ali Chishti was arrested by the Lahore Police and placed before Major Ferrar, one of the Martial Law Officers at Lahore, on the charge of having acted in contravention of the order referred to above, and fined Rs. 100.

LXXXV. Will the Government be pleased to state (a) the reason why permission to enter the Martial Law area was refused to Mr. C.F. Andrews, who had been appointed as the representative of several leading Indian papers ; and (b) why later on, when Mr. Andrews was coming to Lahore on his own account, he was taken out of the train at Amritsar Railway Station, detained there for several hours and finally sent back out of the province ?

LXXXVI. Will the Government be pleased to state :—

(a) If it is a fact that after the declaration of Martial Law at Lahore, no Indian was allowed to travel by train either from or to Lahore, without a special permit granted to him by the Martial Law Authorities ?

(b) Whether, as a matter of fact, such permits were granted to Indians only on the recommendation of a European or Anglo-Indian, irrespective of his position in life ?

LXXXVII—Will the Government be pleased to state if it is a fact that the Hon. Khan Bahadur Mian Muhammad Shafi, C.I.E., at that time a member of the Viceroy's Legislative Council and President of the High Court Bar Association, Lahore, asked for a permit for his agent to enable the latter to travel to his lands in the Montgomery district, and that this application was refused ?

LXXXVIII. Will the Government be pleased to state if one of the orders issued by the Martial Law Authorities at various places in the

Punjab, was that every Indian of whatever status in life must *salam* every European ? If so, will the Government be pleased to state:—

(a) The areas, in which such orders were issued and enforced ?

(b) The number of persons arrested and punished for infringement of such order ; and

(c) The names, ages and occupations of persons, who were flogged for breach of this order and the number of stripes inflicted in such cases ?

LXXXIX. Will the Government be pleased to state, if it is a fact that one Gopaldas, son of Deviditta Mal, caste Arora, of Akalgarh, who was a telegraph peon at Lyallpur during the Martial Lal days, was arrested for not *salaming* a European officer to whom he had gone to deliver a telegram, and that he was given five stripes for it in jail, although he protested that he had actually *salamed* the officer and was willing to do so again ?

XC. Is it a fact that in some districts in the Punjab, where Martial Law was in force, orders were issued that every Indian, driving in a carriage or riding a horse, must get down when he passed by a European, and further that Indians carrying open unbrellas must close and lower them when they met a European ?

XCI. (a) Will the Government be pleased to lay on the table a statement, showing the number, names and other particulars of persons, if any, who have been arrested, detained, tried and punished on the Railway Stations by the Martial Law Officers since the withdrawal of Martial Law from the districts in which those stations are situated ?

(b) If so, will the Government be pleased to state what is the nature of the punishment inflicted in each case ?

XCII. Will the Government be pleased to state if there is any reason for the continuance of Martial Law on the Railway Stations in the Punjab ? Is the Government aware that such continuance of Martial Law exposes Indians to unecessary humiliations and hardships, and causes needless irritation ?

(2)—Viceroy's Speech

In the course of his opening speech at the meeting of the Imperial Legislative Council; held on the 3rd of September, 1919, His Excellency the Viceroy said :-

* * * *

"Another personality we shall miss is that of Sir C. Sankaran Nair. Sir Sankaran Nair felt it incumbent on himself to resign his office. His reasons for resigning were honourable to himself and I thoroughly appreciated them, but as the relations between colleagues in a Government are necessarily of a private nature I do not propose to discuss them".....

* * * *

"Since the close of the last session, there have been events of a grave character disturbing the peace and tranquillity of this country, and I cannot pass them over without mention. Last session certain Hon. Members during the passage of the Rowlatt Bill gave me warnings, of an almost minatory character, that if that Bill were passed into law there would be agitation of a serious nature. I think, Hon. Members will realise that no Government could deviate from a policy, which it regarded as essential, on account of any threat of agitation. However, there were those who thought that it was necessary to make good this threat; and as a consequence, the deplorable events occurred which are to be the subject of an enquiry. It is not my intention to discuss these events but I would point out this, that it is easy to minimise their gravity after the disorders have been put down. No one, who had the responsibility of dealing with them, is likely to forget the issue which they had to face. Murder and arson were committed, telegraph wires were cut, railway lines were torn up, and for some days my only sure communication with the Government of the Punjab was by means of wireless. Ocular proof of the gravity of the situation, with which we were then faced and of the damage done, is still manifest in many of the districts which suffered, and to any one who would attempt to minimise the trouble I would say : go into these districts, and see for yourself the wastages of senseless destruction which are still there. The policy of my Government was clearly set out in our resolution of April 14th. I promised support to the head of each Local Government for such measures as he thought it might be necessary to take, and that support was given unwaveringly throughout. No one deplores more than I the need there was for stern action, but the result of our prompt measures was that the disorders were quelled and peace restored. It is my desire now, and it is that of His Honour the Lieutenant-Governor of the Punjab, to exercise clemency towards the unfortunate, misguided men who were led away by 'some educated and clever man or men,' to use Mr. Gandhi's words, to commit outrages. For some time past, Sir Edward Maclagan has been busily engaged in reviewing the sentences passed and in every case possible he has tempered justice with mercy. For those cases which have come before the Government of India, I have no hesitation in claiming that they received the most careful consideration, and that orders were passed with the greatest possible despatch.

"For some time past my Government has been in correspondence with the Secretary of State upon the question of an enquiry into these disorders. We have both been anxious to settle this question as quickly as possible, but an announcement has been delayed largely by the difficulty of procuring the services of a suitable chairman. It was only on Saturday last that I heard that Lord Hunter had agreed to come to India in that capacity. The Committee is now complete and will consist of the Chairman, Lord Hunter, formerly the Solicitor General for Scotland, and the following members : (1) The Hon. Mr. Justice Rankin, (2) The Hon. Mr. Rice. (3) Major-General Sir George Barrow, (4) Sir Chiman Lal Setalvad and (5) Sahibzada Sultan Ahmad. Their instruction will be to inquire into, and to report to the Governor-General in Council, regarding the causes of, and the measures taken to cope with, the recent disorders in Delhi, the Punjab and Bombay Presidency. The proceedings of the Committee will ordinarily be public, but the Chairman will have authority to direct them to be held *in camera*, when he considers that the public interests so require. It is hoped that the Committee will begin its sessions next month. The members have a difficult task before them and I trust that people of all classes of opinion will do nothing to add to their difficulties by the needless importation of irrelevant or intentionally inflammable material.

"After disorders involving a great upheaval of normal conditions, such an enquiry as I have just announced is one inevitable consequence. The second and no less necessary sequel is the passing of an act indemnifying those officers of the Government, who were called upon to undertake the onerous and ungrateful task of restoring order, and the validating of such acts as the stress of circumstances required. Whatever the findings of the Commission may be, such a measure would be necessary; and in justice to our officers, we are bound to indemnify them at the earliest convenient moment........"

* * * *

(3)—From Proceedings of Meeting held on September 10, 1919

(A) Questions and Answers

The Hon'ble Rao Bahadur B. N. Sarma asked :—

4. "On what date did Sir Edward Maclagan arrive in India in April, and what were the reasons, if any, that prevented his taking over charge of the administration of the Punjab at once ?"

The Hon'ble Sir William Vincent replied :-

"Sir Edward Maclagan landed at Bombay on 21st April, 1919. In view of recent events in the Punjab, the Government of India considered it desirable to place him on special duty to assist the Lieutenant-Governor at a time when the burden of administration was peculiarly heavy. This arrangement continued till 26th May 1919, when Sir Michael O'Dwyer's term of office expired in the ordinary course."

* * * *

The Hon'ble Rao Bahadur B. N. Sarma asked :-

10. " (1) How many persons were tried in the Punjab by the Special Martial Law tribunals, and how many of them were sentenced (a) to death, (b) to transportation for life, (c) to imprisonment exceeding three years, and (d) to forfeiture of property ?

(2) How many such persons have appealed or applied for mercy; and have all such petitions been disposed of by the authorities before the death sentences were executed ?

(3) How many of those sentenced to death have been executed?

(4) In how many cases of persons convicted by the Martial Law tribunals have (a) the sentences been reduced, and (b) orders of foreiture of property been cancelled ?"

The Hon'ble Sir William Vincent replied :-

"(1) 852 persons were tried,

(a) 108 were sentenced to death.

(b) 265 to transportation for life.

(c) 104 to imprisonment exceeding three years.

(d) 356 to forfeiture of property.

The Hon'ble Member's attention is drawn to the provisions of Section 121 of the Indian Penal Code, under which most of these persons were convicted. The minimum sentence which can be imposed under that section is transportation for life and forfeiture of property.

2. All persons sentenced to death submitted petitions to Government, and the petitions of all the 18 persons who have been executed were duly considered before execution. The Government of India are not aware how many petitions have been presented in non-capital cases, but all cases have been reviewed by the Local Government whether petitions were presented or not.

3. 18 persons have been executed.

4. (a) 488 sentences have been reduced.

(b) 332 sentences of forfeiture have been remitted : and in ten other cases the sentences have not been enforced."

* * * *

The Hon'ble Rao Bahadur B. N. Sarma asked :-

14. "(a) Was any difference made between the Indian and European edited newspapers of the Punjab regarding the publication of news during the late disturbances and, if so, why ? (b) What control, if any, was exercised by the Government of India over the Punjab Government in this matter ?"

The Hon'ble Sir William Vincent replied :-

" The Government of India are informed that the publication of all news relating to the disorders in the Punjab was subjected to precensorship without any such discrimination as is suggested. The Government of India passed no orders on the subject."

* * * *

The Hon'ble Pandit Madan Mohan Malaviya asked :-

40. "Will Government be pleased to lay on the table a statement showing—

(a) the number of persons actually arrested and detained in custody in connection with the recent disturbances in the Punjab, classified according to town or village and showing the names, parentage, caste, profession and place of residence of the persons arrested or detained ;

(b) the number of persons out of the above list who were actually put on tarial—

(i) before the Commission constituted under the Martial Law Ordinance of 1919 promulgated by the Governor-General ;

(ii) before the Summary Courts established under the orders of the General Officers Commanding the Lahore and Rawalpindi Divisions;

(iii) before the Area Officers constituted by or in virtue of the powers conferred by the General Officer Commanding the

Lahore and Rawalpindi Divisions for offences against the Proclamation issued on the 19th April 1919. (Notification No. 10766 of Home Department, Military, dated 21st April 1919);

(iv) before the ordinary Municipal Courts in districts where Martial Law was not declared ; and

(v) before the Special Tribunal constituted under the Defence of India Act ;

(c) the number of persons convicted out of those mentioned above in part (b) and the offence or offences of which they were convicted and the sentences passed in each case ;

(d) the number of persons discharged or acquitted out of those mentioned above in part (b) ;

(c) the number of persons arrested but released without trial ?"

The Hon'ble Sir William Vincent replied :-

"(a) the information is not available.

(b) The following are the figures reported. It is possible that some small modifications may be found necessary.

(i) 852.

(ii) 1437.

(iii) 564 (included in (ii)).

(iv) 13.

(v) 56.

(c)

(i) 581.

(ii) 1179.

(iii) 495 (included in (ii)).

(iv) 11.

(v) 21.

(d)

(i) 271.

(ii) 258.

(iii) 69 (included in (ii)).

(iv) 2.

(v) 35.

For details as to sentences and convictions attention is invited to the statements* placed on the table.

---

* Not included in the proccedings published in the Gazette. See *Supplements I and II*.

(e) No information is available."

The Hon'ble Pandit Madan Mohan Malaviya:—"My Lord, with regard to the answer of the Hon'ble Member respecting part (a) of this question, namely, that the information is not available, am I to understand that the number of persons actually arrested and detained in custody in connection with the recent disturbances in the Punjab is not known to the Government ?"

The Hon'ble Sir William Vincent:—"That is correct. The number of persons arrested is not known to the Government of India."

The Hon'ble Pandit Madan Mohan Malaviya:—"May I request that the Government will be pleased to ask for that information and lay it on the table at the next meeting of the Council?"

The Hon'ble Sir William Vincent:—"I ask for notice of that question."

The Hon'ble Pandit Madan Mohan Malaviya:—"Then my Lord, with regard to part (e) the Hon'ble Member says that no information is available as regards the number of persons arrested but released without trial. Will the Government be pleased to ask for this information also and lay it on the table at the next meeting of the Council ?"

The Hon'ble Sir William Vincent :-" My Lord, these are really questions more for the local Council than for us ; but we have met the Hon'ble Member as far as we have information. If the Hon'ble Member so desires, I will attempt to have the information collected."

The Hon'ble Pandit Madan Mohan Malaviya asked :-

41. " Will Government be pleased to lay on the table a statement giving the following particulars regarding all cases tried by the Summary Courts established by the General Officers Commanding the Lahore and Rawalpindi Divisions and also by the Area Officers appointed under Notification No. 10766 of the Home Department, Military, dated 21st April, 1919 :-

(a) the total number of cases decided by each of the said Courts and officers from day to day ;

(b) the number of cases in which summaries or memoranda of evidence and reasons for findings arrived at were recorded ;

(c) the number of cases in which only reasons for findings arrived at were recorded ;

(d) the number of cases in which no summary or memorandum of evidence, nor any reasons for the findings arrived at was recorded; and

(e) the number of cases in which the record does not show even the offence charged ?"

The Hon'ble Sir William Vincent replied :—

"(a) Attention is invited to the statement placed on the table.*

(b) (c) and (d). From the material at present available Government are not in a position to give accurate information on this point.

(e) None."

The Hon'ble Pandit Madan Mohan Malaviya :— " My Lord, I beg here also to ask a supplementary question, and I may with Your Lordship's permission say here that the local Council is not sitting, and that is why it has become necessary for me to ask so many questions here. With regard to the answer to parts (b), (c) and (d), that from the material at present available Government are not in a position to give accurate information on this point, namely, as to the number of cases in which summaries or memoranda of evidence and reasons for findings were recorded, etc. will the Government be pleased to ask for such information and lay it on the table at the next meeting of the Council ?"

The Hon'ble Sir William Vincent :— " I will ask for the information, but I cannot undertake to lay it on the table at the next meeting of the Council."

The Hon'ble Pandit Madan Mohan Malaviya asked :-

42. " Will Government be pleased to lay on the table a statement showing—

(a) the number of applications for copies of judgments and evidence taken and other proceedings of the Summary Courts and of the Courts of the Area Officers in cases arising out of the recent disturbances in the Punjab made on behalf of the persons convicted, to the Legal Remembrancer, the District Magistrates, Martial Law Administrators and other Civil or Military Authorities ;

(b) the number of cases in which copies have been supplied ; and

(c) the number of cases in which such copies have been refused and the reasons for such refusal ?"

The Hon'ble Sir William Vincent replied :—

"The Legal Remembrancer to the Punjab Government received some three or four applications for copies of proceedings of the

---

* Not included in the proccedings published in the Gazette. See *Supplement II*.

Summary Courts, but as the records of these cases were not in his office, he returned them to the applicants. The information about the other authorities mentioned is not available."

The Hon'ble Pandit Madan Mohan Malaviya :— " I beg to ask, my Lord, if the Legal Remembrancer informed the applicants where they could obtain copies of the judgments ?"

The Hon'ble Sir William Vincent :— " I have no information on the point. The Legal Remembrancer is an officer of the Provincial Government."

The Hon'ble Pandit Madan Mohan Malaviya asked :—

43. " (a) How many people were (a) killed and (b) wounded by the firing that took place on—

(i) The Upper Mall, Lahore, on the 10th April,

(ii) outside the Lohari Gate on the 10th April,

(iii) in the Hira Mandi Chauk on the 12th April ?

(b) What was the number of persons injured, if any, among the Police and the Military, specifying the nature of their injuries, in the places and on the occasions mentioned above ?"

The Hon'ble Sir William Vincent replied :—

"The figures are given below —

(i) *Upper Mall.*

(a) I killed.

(b) 7 wounded.

(ii) *Lohari Gate.*

(a) 3 killed.

(b) 12 wounded.

(iii) *Hira Mandi.*

(a) 2 killed.

(b) 27 wounded.

No Military or Police Officer was killed at these places, but in every case there were assaults on Magistrates, on the Police or on the troops. "

The Hon'ble Pandit Madan Mohan Malaviya :— " I beg to ask if the Government will be pleased to state the details of these assaults on Magistrates, Police and the troops."

The Hon'ble Sir William Vincent :— " The details of these assaults will be placed before the Committee of Inquiry which will be appointed by the Government of India."

The Hon'ble Pandit Madan Mohan Malaviya asked :—

44. " Will Government be pleased to lay on the table a statement showing the total number of persons who were (1) killed, or (2) died of wounds, or (3) were wounded but recovered, during the recent disturbances in the Punjab, giving the names, parentage and other particulars, and specifying the place where each person was killed or wounded ?

The Hon'ble Sir William Vincent replied :—

"The numbers killed in each district so far as has been ascertained were as follows :-

Lahore	....	.....	.....	14
Amritsar	.....	.....	.....	301
Gujranwala	.....	.....	....	17
Gujrat	.....	....	....	2
		Total	...	334

Further information is not available."

The Hon'ble Pandit Madan Mohan Malaviya :— "May I ask if the Government is aware that the popular estimate of the numbers killed at Amritsar is over a thousand ?"

The Hon'ble Sir William Vincent :— " I am aware that exaggerated accounts of the casualties at Amritsar are prevalent. The figures which I have given are those which we have been able to ascertain from the Local Government."

The Hon'ble Pandit Madan Mohan Malaviya asked :—

45. "Will Government be pleased to lay on the table lists of persons who after being sentenced by Martial Law Commissioners or other Martial Law Officers in connection with the recent disturbances were—

(a) executed,

(b) transported, or

(c) confined in the Lahore Central and Borstal Jails and various District Jails in the Punjab ?"

The Hon'ble Sir William Vincent replied :—

"The figures asked for are given below :

(a) 18 persons.

(b) 26 "

(c) The number of persons in the Punjab Jails are distributed as under :

Multan District Jail	...	...	30
Multan Central Jail	...	...	79
Jullundur District Jail	...	...	29
Amritsar	...	...	1
Ludhiana	...	...	15
Lyallpur	...	...	50
Ferozepore	...	...	41
Campbellpur District Jail	...	...	3
Dhariwal Jail	...	...	11
Lahore Borstal Jail	...	...	189
Lahore Central Jail	...	...	503
Gujranwala District Jail	...	...	41
Sialkot " "	...	...	26
Montgomery " "	...	...	34
Rawalpindi " "	...	...	149
Shahpur " "	...	...	4
Delhi " "	...	...	6
Gurdaspur " "	...	...	18
	Total	...	1,229"

The Hon'ble Pandit Madan Mohan Malaviya asked :—

46. "Will Government be pleased to give the names, ages, and other particulars of persons, if any, who were flogged on being arrested and subsequently put on their trial in what is known as the Sherwood case of Amritsar ?"

The Hon'ble Sir William Vincents replied :—

"Six of the persons accused of the assault on Miss Sherwood were convicted of disorderly conduct while in custody and were sentenced on conviction by a Summary Court to two years' imprisonment and whipping. These offences were entirely separate from the assault on Miss Sherwood. Futher details are not available."

The Hon'ble Pandit Madan Mohan Malaviya asked :—

47. "(1) Will Government be pleased to state—

(a) the number of persons, if any, who were sent under Martial Law to the Central Jail, Lahore, to be flogged there and were actually flogged;

(b) the authority under whose orders they were so flogged ; and

(c) whether there is a record of all such cases of flogging?

(2) If there is such a record, will Government be pleased to lay it on the table?"

The Hon'ble Sir William Vincent replied :—

"(a) Number of persons actually flogged 58

(b) Authority under whose orders they were flogged—

By Deputy Commissioner, Lahore	... ...	7
By Officer Commanding, Lahore Civil Area	...	31
By First Class Magistrates	... ...	12
By Martial Law Commissions	... ...	8
Total	...	58

(c) There is a record in the Lahore Central Jail, but it is not proposed to lay it on the table."

The Hon'ble Pandit Madan Mohan Malaviya :—"May I ask the reason why?"

The Hon'ble Sir William Vincent:— "The Government of India do not think that any useful purpose will be served by laying this information on the table."

The Hon'ble Pandit Madan Mohan Malaviya asked:—

48. "Will Government be pleased to lay on the table a statement showing—

(a) the number of persons flogged in connection with the recent disturbances in each town or village within the Martial Law Area in the Punjab, whether :—

(1) under Martial Law,

(i) on conviction, or

(ii) without conviction; or

(2) under the ordinary criminal law during the period in which Martial Law was in force,

giving names, parentage, age, caste, profession and residence of the persons flogged,

(b) the offence for which each such person was convicted and the name and designation of the officer who passed the order :

(c) the number of stripes inflicted on each such person ; and

(d) the name of the locality where the flogging was administered?"

The Hon'ble Sir William Vincent replied :—

"The detailed statements already placed on the table give some of the information the Hon'ble Member wants. Further information is not available."

(*B*)-Resolution *re* Appointment of Commission to Inquire into Recent Disturbances in the Punjab

The Hon'ble Pandit Madan Mohan Malaviya :—"My Lord, before the announcement was made by your Excellency on the 3rd instant that a Committtee of Inquiry was going to be appointed, I had given notice of the Resolution which stands in my name on the agenda of today. In view of that announcement, it has become necessary. . . . . ."

The Hon'ble Sir George Lowndes :—"My Lord, I rise to a point of order. The rules require that any Member moving a Resolution should move the Resolution first and not make his speech first."

The President :—"That is so."

The Hon'ble Pandit Madan Mohan Malaviya :—"I will follow the technical rule, my Lord, but I thought there was reason in the circumstances of the case to justify a deviation. I will read the Resolution. My Lord, the Resolution of which I have given notice and which stands on the paper runs as follows. . . . . . ."

The Hon'ble Sir William Vincent :—"The Hon'ble Member must move his Resolution first."

The Hon'ble Pandit Madan Mohan Malaviya :—"I understand the meaning of the word 'move' and the duty that rests upon me in moving the Resolution. I am not bound to use the word 'move' in moving the Resolution, and if Hon'ble Members will have a little patience, I shall show them that I am moving the Resolution. May I proceed now, my Lord?"

The President :—"Yes."

The Hon'ble Pandit Madan Mohan Malaviya :—"Thank you, my Lord.

"My Lord, the Resolution of which I have given notice and which stands on the agenda runs as follows :—

> 'This Council recommends to the Governor-General in Council that he should request His Majesty's Government to appoint without further delay a Commission consisting of gentlemen unconnected with the Indian administration to inquire into (*a*) the causes of the recent disturbances in the Punjab, and (*b*) the propriety of the measures adopted in dealing with them, and to vest the said Commission with legal authority to annul or modify sentences passed by the Martial Law Commissions or by Magistrates specially

empowered to deal summarily with cases alleged to have been connected with the said disturbances.'

"My Lord, before placing my reasons for this Resolution before the Council I should like to refer to the circumstances, to the events, which have happened since notice was given of this Resolution. Those events are very well known to the Council, and they are that on the 3rd of this month your Excellency was pleased to announce that the Government had decided to appoint a Committee of Inquiry to investigate the recent occurrences in the Punjab. It becomes necessary for me, therefore, before formally moving the Resolution. . . . . . ."

The President :—"The Hon'ble Member must understand that he is moving the Resolution. Though he has not used the word 'move', I can only take it that he has moved it."

The Hon'ble Pandit Madan Mohan Malaviya :—"Certainly, I used the words 'before formally moveing it.' This may come at the end of the speech instead of coming at the beginning."

The President :—"All right ; the Hon'ble Member must understand that he has moved the Resolution."

The Hon'ble Pandit Madan Mohan Malaviya :—"Yes, my Lord. Your Excellency was pleased to announce on Saturday—my Lord, if I may say one thing with great respect, it is that the rules of Council are meant to enable us to proceed in a reasonable manner, and where reason demands that a change should be made, I think I am entitled to place the matter before your Excellency as President of this Council, to consider and rule upon. Now, my Lord, the Resolution of which I gave notice has become dead, dead as Queen Anne, by reason of the fact that on the 3rd instant, your Excellency was pleased to announce that the Government had decided to appoint a Committee of Inquiry to investigate the Punjab affairs. I beg, therefore, in view of that fact, to ask for your Excellency's leave to amend the Resolution in the form of which I have given notice to the Legislative Department. It runs, my Lord, as follows :—'That this Council recommends to the Governor-General in Council, that he should recommend to His Majesty's Secretary of State. . . . ."

The Hon'ble Sir William Vincent :—"My Lord, may I rise to a point of order. The Hon'ble Member is now proposing an amendment to a Resolution which he has never moved, at least sometimes he says he has moved it, at other times he says he has not. I am entitled to three day's notice of any amendment proposed and I take objection to the amendment."

The Hon'ble Pandit Madan Mohan Malaviya :—"Under the rules of this Council as I understand them, when the President of the Council expresses an opinion about a matter of fact, that is loyally accepted by every Member of this Council. Your Excellency having said that I had moved the Resolution, which I quite readily accepted, I submit the Hon'ble Member is out of order in saying I had not moved the Resolution. . . . ."

The President :—"The point of substance which the Hon'ble Member must take and which the Hon'ble the Home Member has pointed out is that if a copy of an amendment has not been sent to the Secretary at least three clear days before the date fixed for the discussion of the Resolution, any member may object to the moving of the amendment. That is the point he has taken; the other was, I think, a slap at the Hon'ble Member which perhaps the Hon'ble Member had deserved, perhaps he had not. That is the point which the Hon'ble the Home Member has put before me, and on that point I must rule that the Hon'ble the Home Member has a perfect right to object to the moving of such an amendment. As the Hon'ble Member is aware, this Resolution of his has been before the Council for a large number of days. My speech was made on September the 3rd, just a week ago. If the Hon'ble Member had given notice the day following that he regarded his Resolution as dead, dead as Queen Anne, and that he wished to put in an amended Resolution, then it would have been open to me—and I should have looked upon it favourably— it would have been open to me to allow him to amend or substitute another Resolution. But what did the Hon'ble Member do? At 7.30 last night I received a letter which had been written by him requesting to be allowed to substitute one Resolution for another. I do not think that this is a reasonable notice to give to Hon'ble Members here who have prepared themselves to meet the Resolution of the Hon'ble Member, and therefore I have no choice, as far as I can see, but to say that the Hon'ble Member must comply in this case with the rule, especially in a matter of such paramount importance."

The Hon'ble Pandit Madan Mohan Malaviya :—"My Lord, I bow to your Excellency's ruling. In so far as the question of notice is concerned, I quite see that the Hon'ble Member can insist on his three days' notice. But. My Lord, if that is the only difficulty, as my object is to get this matter considered by this Council properly, I should request your Excellency to allow me to keep back this matter and allow the Hon'ble Member to have ample notice of this Resolution. I am sorry I could not send notice of this earlier because the matter, as your Excellency has recognised, is of great importance, and I had to consult friends as to what course I should adopt. I came to the conclusion to which I did in consultation with several friends only last evening and took the earliest opportunity to intimate the fact to the Secretary of the Legislative Department. I am not entitled to go on with this matter unless your Excellency should permit me to do so. I therefore put two propositions for your Excellency's consideration. One is, your Excellency may allow me, if the Hon'ble Member waives his objection, to proceed with the matter and dispose of it. The second is, that if that is not to be, then as only one part of my Resolution is dead as Queen Anne, and the other parts are not, it will be my duty to proceed to discuss the Resolution. I will take either course. I have no wish to spend one minute more of this Council's time or my time than is necessary. If my Hon'ble friend wants notice, I am willing that this matter should come up after the three days' notice....."

The Hon'ble Sir William Vincent :—"May I speak on a point of order?"

The President :—"Yes, on a point of order."

The Hon'ble Sir William Vincent :—"I put it to your Lordship that a Member is not entitled to amend his own Resolution. An amendment must come from somebody else. If the Hon'ble Member seeks to substitute a new Resolution of his own, I am entitled to the full fifteen days' notice."

The President :—"I think that is quite clear that if he substitutes one Resolution for another, he must give the usual time, which is fifteen days' notice."

The Hon'ble Pandit Madan Mohan Malaviya :—"My Lord, I exactly used the word 'substitute' in the letter which I sent to the Secretary in which I requested that in view of the fact that a Committee had already been appointed to inquire into the measures taken, His Excellency the President might allow me to substitute the amended Resolution in place of the one of which I had given notice. I have complied with that requirement, but of course if your Excellency rules that I should give fifteen days' notice of it, I will, with your Excellency's permission, now give notice of it. I shall wait until fifteen days are over, in which case I understand that your Excellency will be pleased to allow me to discuss this substituted Resolution. . . . ."

The President :—"I cannot give the Hon'ble Member any such promise. The Hon'ble Member's Resolution will then have to take its place in the list of Resolutions suggested to this Council. The Hon'ble Member's Resolution has been given special priority in this case and put on the first day devoted to Resolutions, but the Hon'ble Member now wishes not to move that particular Resolution, and his Resolution, if he wishes to substitute another one, must take its chance with the other Resolutions."

The Hon'ble Pandit Madan Mohan Malaviya :—"In that case, I beg leave to proceed with the Resolution of which I have given notice. My Lord, the reasons which led me to give notice of the Resolution which stands upon the paper, it is hardly necessary for me to repeat. The Government, His Majesty's Government and the Government of India, acting together have recognised that the events which have recently taken place in the Punjab have been of so unfortunate and so grave a character that a Committee of Inquiry should be instituted in order to inquire into them. That having been done, my Lord, it becomes unnecessary for me to either go into those unfortunate events or to draw any inferences which should support such a request as is contained in the Resolution. But before proceeding further, as it is the first opportunity when this melancholy affair comes up before the Council, I wish to say with regard to the occurrences in the Punjab that every one of us, Indians in this Council, and indeed I may say I speak in this matter on behalf of all Indians whether in this Council or outside, deplores the distressing events that took place in the Punjab. My Lord, I do not agree with those who think that the Rowlatt Act agitation was responsible for those events. Nor do I agree with those who think that the *Satyagraha* movement was responsible for any evil results. The fact remains undisputed and undisputable that the great *Satyagraha* day—the 6th of April, 1919—passed off throughout the country without a single untoward incident. I believe that if some of those who were in power and whose duty it was to keep law and order, had not mismanaged the situation none of the distressing events which we deplore would have occurred. In refering to those events, my object is not to raise a controversy on them, but to express my deep sorrow that they should have happened. I deplore the desecration that was committed on places of worship and the destruction of public buildings. I deplore more deeply the greater desecration which was committed on the living temples of God, on human beings, whether British or Indian, who were destroyed in a fit of fury or without any justification. My Lord, I mourn the death of the seven Europeans who were killed in these disturbances. I grieve for them, as I would grieve for the death of my dearest and nearest. I mourn also the death of those several hundreds of persons—their number has been stated by the Government to-day to be more than 300, and it is believed by the public to be more than a thousand—I grieve for the deaths of those who fell victims to the fury or the indiscretion of those who were charged with suppressing disorder. My Lord, as I have said, it is a sad thing to reflect that any places of worship were desecrated. I am a Hindu, but I never pass by a mosque or a church without paying it that silent reverence which is due to every place of worship. But, my Lord, places of worship are after all made by men; if they are destroyed man can remake them. But a man is a temple created by God, and all of us, men, Governors, Kings and administrators, cannot even if we combined, re-build one single human temple if it has been destroyed by the hands of man or beast. I am therefore grieved beyond expression to think of the appalling number of deaths which have been caused, but I will say no more about it at present. My object to-day is merely to express my sorrow for what has happened. It is not my object to apportion blame, whether one brother was to blame for it or another, it is equally a matter of pain to me. I have not any idea here of apportioning blame or desiring that blame should be fixed upon one rather than upon another. I only refer to these unfortunate events to remind you that very distressing things have happened, and it is right, and the Government have held that it is right that they should be inquired into and their repetition made impossible.

"My Lord, while referring to these events in the Punjab, I wish also to say that it is a matter of real regret to me that I should have to raise questions relating to them at a time when Sir Edward Maclagan has assumed charge of the Government of the Punjab. His kindly and generous nature has inspired respect for him throughout the province and throughout the country, and the Punjab in its hour of distress honoured him by calling for him as a saviour. It was a cruel fate which kept him from the people of the Punjab and the people of the Punjab from him. It is a real regret to me, entertaining the respect which I do for him, that I should have to raise these questions at a time when he is the responsible head of the Punjab Administration, and my regret is not quite shaken off by the thought that he was not responsible for the events to which attention is to be drawn and which happened at a time when he was not in charge. My Lord, I also want to say that it is far from my object to impute blame wholesale to the members of the Punjab service. On the contrary, it gives me pleasure to acknowledge that at a time when some members of that service did commit what the people consider to be great wrongs, there were several members of the same service whom the people esteemed and respected and were grateful to for having kept their heads cool and their districts calm. It is not my object to attack either the Punjab administration or the services as a whole. It is my object as a humble subject of the King and as a humble servant of the people to draw attention to events which require looking into. It is for this reason that, distressed by the delay which was caused in the announcement regarding the appointment of a Committee of Inquiry, I gave notice of the Resolution which stands on the paper.

"My Lord, as I have said before, it is not necessary for me now to justify the Resolution. The Government have thought it necessary to appoint a Committee of Inquiry. They have considered the situation to be so grave as to call for the appointment of a Committee of a very important character. Lord Hunter is to preside over it ; several important gentlemen are to be members of it. Why then, it may be asked, is it necessary for me to take up the time of this Council by pressing this Resolution ? The reason, my Lord, is this : As the expression of opinions through the press and associations has made it clear, the public are dissappointed with the constitution of the Committee. Your Excellency must have noted, and other members of the Government must have noted, the chorus of dissatisfaction and disappointment with which the announcement has been received by the Indian papers. The '*Leader*,' a leading organ of sound moderate opinion, has expressed itself in unequivocal terms. It has said that the Committee will not command confidence. The reasons it has urged are, first of all, that the Indian element on it is very week. Secondly, that the Committee is to report to the Viceroy who has been so much identified with the Punjab policy. And thirdly, that 'the terms of reference do not empower the Committee to go into individual cases.' It has concluded by saying : 'To say that the people will be keenly disappointed with the constitution and terms of reference of the Committee is only to express very mildly the effect they will produce.' Similarly, the '*Bengalee*' and other leading organs of public opinion have expressed themselves dissatisfied with the constitution of the Committee and its terms of reference. My object here is not to attack anybody, not to impute any motives to any one, not to cast any reflections upon any officer of Government, but humbly to draw attention to the reasons which justify this dissatisfaction and disappointment and which should lead the Government to reconsider the matter.

"I will take up the first point with regard to the report being made to the Viceroy. My Lord, I speak with the utmost respect without any thesire to say anything personal, and I shall be sorry if any remarks of mine in any way, either directly or indirectly, indicate any want of respect for the head of the Government or for the Government of India. My Lord, the Committee is to inquire into events which have happened in the Punjab with which the Government of India are closely identified. My Lord, it was the Government of India, or, If you please, the Governor-General in Council, who declared that there was a state of open rebellion in Lahore and Amritsar. That was the starting point of the chapter of troubles. It was the Governor-General who promulgated Martial Law Ordinances. It was the Governor-General in Council who supported and sustained the late Lieutenant-Governor of the Punjab, Sir Michael O'Dwyer, in carrying on the martial law administration there. It was the Governor-General in Council who accepted the resignation of Sir Sankaran Nair, which as a protest, a most emphatic protest, against martial law. . . . ."

The President :—"Order, order. What authority has the Hon'ble Member for making that statement. I told the Council in my speech the other day that Sir Sankaran Nair had not given out publicly his reasons for resigning, and that any commnications he had made were entirely private as between colleages."

The Hon'ble Pandit Madan Mohan Malaviya :—"I beg your Lordship's pardon, my Lord. It has been said in the papers that Sir Sankaran Nair resigned on account of the administration of martial law in the Punjab. If I have erred in saying this, I beg your Excellency to pardon me.

"Now, my Lord, these are facts of such an important character that there is a feeling in the public mind that the Committee of Inquiry ought to report not to the Governor-General in Council, but to His Majesty's Secretary of State for India. I disclaim, my Lord, any idea of suggesting that the Governor-General in Council will not deal fairly and squarely with the Report of the Committee. Personally, I have not the least doubt that every member of the Government will give it his best and most impartial consideration and arrive at conclusions which justice and honour should dictate. But, my Lord, in this matter the Government has to pay heed to the public opinion of the country, and, in view of the events which have happened, the public clearly feel that it would be right, it would be more satisfactory, if the Report went to the Secretary of State for India. This is a view which I consider it my duty to commend to the consideration both of your Excellency's Government and of the Secretary of State. It is not, I repeat, that I make any insinuation or any suggestion, or that I personally have any doubt about how the matter will be dealt with by the Governor-General in Council. But it is my duty to draw attention to the public opinion of the country which is voiced by papers of the standing of the '*Leader*' and the '*Bengalee*,' as well as other organs of Indian public opinion, all of which want this matter to be re-considered.

"I will now come to the next point by reason of which I consider that this Committee is defective and unsatisfactory, and that is the personnel of the Committee. The Committee consists of six members including the President. Four of these are Europeans and only two are Indians. Now, my Lord, I would not have raised the question of Indians and Europeans, were it not that the Government have themselves raised it by proposing such a Committee as they have done.

"My Lord, it is deplorable that seven European lives were lost, but your Lordship is also aware from the answers given to-day by Hon'ble the Home Member that several hundreds of Indian lives have been lost ; and several hundreds of barristers and vakils, merchants and bankers, and other respectable Indians are rotting in the jails of the Punjab, as the list laid before the Council by the Home Member discloses. Several hundreds of Indians have been subjected to indignities which should have been inconceivable. When the Indian members and the Indian public cry for an inquiry into such a state of affairs, one should expect that the Government would appoint a larger number of Indians on the Committee of Inquiry than of non-Indians. Instead of doing that, if the Government had put the number even as equal, it would have given more satisfaction. But they have not done this either.

"My Lord, here again I do not mean for a moment to insinuate that any member of the Committee will look at these questions from a racial point of view. I personally believe that every one of the members will act honestly and impartially as a gentleman, and I have no fear, not the remotest fear, in my mind that these gentlemen will not act impartially and justly ; but how does the constitution of the Committee appear to the general public ? Four of its members are Europeans. They ask why should there be four Europeans as members and why only two Indians ? Are not Indians more concerned in this matter than Europeans ? The matter ought not to be regarded in any racial light, but it ought to be looked at from the point of view of the persons, whose fates are to be tried or whose interests are at stake, who would naturally desire in a matter like this to see that the jury consists of persons in whom they have confidence. The Indian public do not know sufficiently about some of the members who have been appointed on the Committee. They know only of some ; and by reason of want of knowledge of the qualifications and character of some of the members, they do not feel the same confidence that they would if they had found in the Committee the names of some of those with whom they are acquainted, whom they respect and honour, and in whom they have confidence. For this reason, my Lord, the constitution of the Committee is defective, and I certainly say that it would have been wiser on the part of the Government if they had at least made the number of Indian and European members equal. It is even now possible for the Government to equalise the number by appointing a third Indian member. There are a number of gentlemen available in the country, both among Indian Judges and Indian public men, any one of whom, who enjoys the confidence of the public, might be appointed without any disadvantage to any interest. My Lord, it is in this respect that the constitution of the Committee is considered to be defective. I will not dwell upon the personal merits of any individual, as I have said I have absolute confidence that every member of the Committee will look at the questions in a straight way like a gentleman and come to conclusions which truth and justice and honour dictate.

"My Lord, why has the Government appointed this Committee?

It has appointed it, in the first place, to redress wrongs which, it must be satisfied, have been inflicted ; and, in the second place, to satisfy public opinion which has been outraged by the events which have taken place. Now, if the public is to be satisfied, if that is the object of appointing this Committee of Inquiry, I submit with great respect that the Government would be wise in appointing a third Indian as member of this Committee, and I hope it will.

"My Lord, the third respect in which the Committee is unsatisfactory is that the terms of reference are not sufficient. Your Excellency has seen from the answers given by the Home Member what sad havoc has been played with the liberty and honour of a number of His Majesty's subjects. Now, my Lord, even if their Lordships of the Privy Council hold that there was no justification for introducing martial law in the Punjab, even if they sweep aside all the proceedings of the martial law commissions and martial law officers, what would be the position ? They will only deal with the appeals of those individuals who have gone up to the Privy Council; they will not be able to touch the cases of the vast number of men who have not appealed and who probably will not be able to appeal to the Privy Council. My Lord, the Committee of Inquiry will be an executive body ; it can only make recommendations. In the Resolution I have suggested the Commission will be vested with legal authority to deal with, to annul or modify sentences. But it is the convictions which have to be set aside. My Lord, I have reflected that this cannot be done by a Commission or Committee unless it is constituted into a Court, for which either this Council should pass an Act constituting it as a judicial tribunal, or Parliament should do so. In the absence of such a constitution of a judicial tribunal, the Commission or Committee can only make recommendations which may be dealt with by the executive Government. Now, the Governor-General in Council or the Secretary of State can, as executive officers, wipe out the sentences of any individual ; but, my Lord, neither the Secretary of State nor the Governor-General in Council has any authority to set aside any of the convictions ; and, my Lord, if the convictions remain, can any of these men be happy to think that the stain of having waged war against the King will remain on their forehead for ever ? My Lord, comparatively the sentences do not mean so much. What matters most to every decent citizen, to every loyal subject, to every gentleman, is that his honour should remain stainless, that the stain which has been cast upon his honour shall be completely wiped off. Now, my Lord, as matters stand in the British Empire at present, that can only be done by His Majesty's Privy Council. I submit, therefore, that the reference to the Committee of Inquiry is insufficient and incomplete, and that they should be asked to recommend, if they should think it fit, to His Majesty in Council that the convictions by the martial law commissions and martial law officers and tribunals specially empowered to deal summarily with cases of persons alleged to have been connected with the said disturbances should be annulled. I, therefore, ... "

The Hon'ble Sir William Vincent :—"May I rise to a point of order ? The Hon'ble Member is doing exactly what he said he would not do, that is, moving an amended Resolution."

The President :—"I should like the Hon'ble Member to show how what he is saying now in the course of his arguments comes within the Resolution which stands on the paper."

The Hon'ble Pandit Madan Mohan Malaviya :—"My Lord, it will be quite clear in a minute. If the Hon'ble the Home Member had not interrupted me, he would have heard it by this time. My Lord, my Resolution says that :—

> 'This Council recommends to the Governor-General in Council that he should request His Majesty's Government to appoint without further delay a Commission consisting of gentlemen unconnected with the Indian administration.'

To support it I have to show that the Committee of Inquiry which has been announced is defective, and that the terms of reference are insufficient, and I have been endeavouring in my humble way to show it. I am surprised that this should not have been clear to the Hon'ble the Home Member. I will proceed more rapidly because I fear my end is approaching. My Lord, I have drawn attention to three circumstances by reason of which I am not satisfied with the proposed Committee of Inquiry ; and by reason of which I humbly urge that this Council should recommend to the Governor-General in Council that he should request His Majesty's Government that a Commission should be appointed by them to investigate the Punjab occurrences, and that the terms of reference should be laid down as I have suggested.

"Now, my Lord, if this is done, what will be the result ? The result will be that your Excellency's Government will satisfy Indian public opinion. I assure your Excellency that my countrymen are not unreasonable ; my experience, extending over forty years, of public life in this country, has convinced me that there has not been one single occasion, when if the Government has been in the right, the people have not recognised that they were right ; and I believe that in the interests of the good name of the Government, in the interests of justice, in the interests of truth, nothing in more desirable than that the inquiry which the Government have recognised as necessary should be conducted by men who satisfy public opinion, by men who would inspire confidence in the public mind, and that the terms of reference should be such as would enable the Commission to wipe off any stain which has been cast on those concerned, if they should, after investigating the matter, come to the conclusion that it is right that it should be done and in order that the public feeling should be allayed.

"My Lord, it has distressed the people of the Punjab and of India that after the great war, after the loyal services rendered by the people of the Punjab, after the loyal services rendered by India—and we have been repeatedly told that the Punjab has borne the foremost share in the sacrifices made, and that her sacrifices have been appreciated by everybody who knows the fact—it has distressed us all to think that this province should be visited by such a terrible calamity, almost before the war has come to an end. The total number of persons who have been arrested has not been found out by the Government, though several months have passed ; yet the number that has been announced by the Hon'ble the Home Member is distressing to think of. I have visited the Lahore Central Jail and the Borstal Jail on three occasions, and I was grieved to find that men, good men, any of whom might get a seat in this Council, men as honourable as any member of this Council, were rotting in those jails for no fault of their own, for no guilt of thier own. I feel that this is a situation that calls for the most searching and impartial inquiry—an inquiry that should command complete public confidence, that would silence the tongue of calumny, silence false rumours and establish that Government does not favour anything except truth and justice; establish that the Government are as solicitous for the life and the honour of every single Indian subject of His Majesty, as they are of the life and honour of every European subject of His Majesty. This demands, my Lord, a commission of the character which I have indicated. It is for these reasons that I move this Resolution, being thoroughly dissatisfied with the constitution of the Committee as announced and with its terms of reference. I hope the Government will consider the matter in the light in which I have presented it. I have no wish to embarrass the Government. I tried to modify my Resolution, but I will not speak about it now. I have indicated in my speech measures which might make the Committee satisfactory. I have suggested a modification which will make it unnecessary for the Government entirely to remodel the Committee, by means of a reasonable addition in one respect, and a reasonable extension in another. As this does not evidently commend itself to your Excellency's Government, I must press for the acceptance of my Resolution that a Commission, not a Committee, should be constituted on the lines I have indicated, with the instructions which I have indicated, including the power to recommend that any conviction might be annulled."

His Honour the Lieutenant-Governor :—"My Lord, I should like with your permission, to make a few remarks before this debate comes to an end.

"In considering the steps which have been taken to deal with the recent disturbances, we must, I think, bear in mind the warning which your Excellency gave us at the first meeting of this Session against the tendency, now that the disturbances have been quelled, to minimise their gravity. I do not think that even while the disturbances were in progress people in other parts of India fully realised how extremely serious they were, and now that peace has been restored, there are a good many people inside the Province and outside it, who have persuaded themselves that nothing very serious occurred. I have had an opportunity of meeting the chief citizens of two of the towns in which the more serious disturbances occurred. On both occasions, I have had to bring to their memory the gravity of the danger through which they passed. If the disturbances had not been met, with the utmost rapidity, had they been allowed to proceed a little further than they did, the lives and property of all classes, more especially of the trading classes in the central Punjab, and possibly in other areas extending even beyond the Province, would have been in the most imminent danger. The Province has escaped, and very narrowly escaped, a most serious catastrophe.

"The Hon'ble Member has spoken a good deal about the sentences passed by martial law commissions. A good deal can be said about them, but I shall at present only say a few words in order to dispel any misapprehension there may be about the attitude which the Government has hitherto adopted in the matter. As regards the findings of these commissions, it must be remembered that they represent the opinion, the unanimous opinion, of three experienced officers, who had the accused and the witnesses before them and heard what had to be said on either side. It is only in cases where there is patent and incontestable evidence of error that findings of this kind can be upset by an executive authority, and although I have examined many cases, I have not found one in which I felt justified in impugning the substantial accuracy of the findings of the Court.

"As regards the sentences I think things are different. The Courts were in a great many cases bound by the law to pass the severest form of sentences. They were influenced in a large number of cases, and I think justifiably influenced, by a sense of the great danger to which the persons before them had so recently exposed the country. It is always open to the Government in such cases to adopt a more extended view and to look upon punishments with regard to their aggregate effect. Where it feels it can reduce the sentences without unduly weakening their deterrent influence, it is justified—and where the numbers concerned are considerable, it is more than justified—in ordering a reduction. The sentences passed on the *Ghadr* revolutionaries in 1915 were in this way reduced by my distinguished predecessor and in the case of such recent sentences as came before him before he left the country, he had himself ordered a considerable number of reductions. To what extent and at what time he would have conducted a general review of these sentences, if he had stayed in the country, I cannot say, but I have reason to believe that after a suitable interval had elapsed, a review would have been undertaken by him. I have myself found that it was possible to effect reductions very shortly after quiet was restored, and I recognised that in doing so I have undertaken a considerable risk. The reductions have, however, served to show that the Government in punishing disturbers of order has no desire to be oppressive or vindictive, and they have helped to ease the tension which has inevitably sprung from the events of April last. They have been made in the hope that the old feelings of confidence between the Government and the people which the sudden upheaval of last April had so violently interrupted might be restored, and if in this hope we are, as I trust we shall not be, disappointed, it will not be for want of anxious effort on the part of the Government.

"I would in all earnestness ask the Council to appreciate the attitude which the Government has adopted. We cannot let past outrages go unpunished, but we are doing what we can to restore good feeling, and to bring things back to normal and peaceful conditions, and the least we can ask from those who have the interests of the country at heart is that they should aid and not impede us in our task."

The Hon'ble Mr. W. E. Crum :—"My Lord, I stand here to-day as a representative elected by the Bengal Chamber of Commerce, but in speaking I speak not only for the Chamber but also for the great European community scattered throughout the provinces of India. And what is that community? It is a community as truly of the citizenship of India as any community in India. It has been said that we are simply foreigners who come to India to make what money we can in a few years out of the Indians and then go and spend it in England. My own position, my Lord, I will explain to the Council and ask them to judge. My father lived, worked and died in India. For twenty years I have worked in India. My children have been born in India, and I hope that my sons will come back and work in India. The money that I have inherited and the money which I have earned is all invested in India's trade and commerce, and as long as I live it will be so invested. And my position is simply that of many of the thousands of the European community who are scattered throughout India, and as such we claim citizenship of India and the right of protection. We are as solicitous for the future of India, for her material welfare and prosperity, as any other member of your Excellency's Council. But, my Lord, with regard to what has happened in the Punjab, it is we who are the aggrieved parties. The Hon'ble Pandit has told us, and I believe with all sincerity, how much he regrets the murders, the sacrilege of churches and the destruction of property which have taken place. But that does not alter the fact that these murders did take place, that churches were burnt, and that property belonging to Europeans was destroyed because it belonged to Europeans. And so, my Lord, we have the right not only to claim the protection of Government for those Europeans scattered all over India, but also must we be given some assurance that occurrences such as have happened in the Punjab will not happen again.

"My Lord, the Hon'ble Pandit paid a very just tribute to the good work which Sir Edward Maclagan is now doing in the Punjab. But I consider that India also should be thankful and should pay a tribute to his predecessor, sir Michael O'Dwyer because it was all important for India that at that very serious time she had in the Punjab a man of the courageous fearlessness, of the justice and of the determination of Sir Michael O'Dwyer, and on behalf of the European community, I wish to thank him for the prompt measures which he took in quelling the disturbances. And, further, I wish to thank those officials of the Punjab, both European and Indian, who did their duty and stuck to their posts when circumstances were so much against many of them.

"I should like to allude, my Lord, to the behaviour of His Majesty's Army in the Punjab. . . . . "

The Hon'ble Pandit Madan Mohan Malaviya :—"May I rise to a point of order, my Lord? I did not want to go into details regarding the work of His Majesty's forces in the Punjab, and I doubt whether any of the Hon'ble Member's remarks are pertinent here. I have avoided, so far as I could all reference to facts which are to be inquired into by the Committee of Inquiry (Laughter). . . . . . "

The President :—"It is impossible for me to hear what the Hon'ble Member is saying if his voice is drowned by laughter."

The Hon'ble Pandit Madan Mohan Malaviya :—"A little levity is sometimes unfortunately imported even into the most solemn discussions. I have avoided going into those facts of a cardinal character which would establish whether Sir Michael O'Dwyer was responsible for creating the serious time referred to by the Hon'ble Member or not, and whether His Majesty's forces had done well or not. I have avoided all reference to these details, and I would suggest that Hon'ble Members may discuss the Resolution on the grounds I have put forward. I think it would be unfair to the Committee of Inquiry to prejudge matters which have been referred to them, but I put this before your Excellency so that the blame for importing these matters into the discussion may not rest upon me."

The Hon'ble Mr. W.E. Crum :—"My Lord, I think also that the thanks of my community are due to His Majesty's Army in India, both European, Sikh, Muhammadan and Gurkha, who in spite of the greatest provocation behaved with a restraint and discipline which will be a model to the Army in India for ever afterwards.

"Now, my Lord, I cannot help thinking that instead of the Hon'ble Pandit having moved this Resolution that I should have moved it as a member of the European community, and it seems to me that the wording of the Resolution is wrong. The Resolution asks for the annulment and modification of sentences on those who have already been convicted of murder, arson and sacrilege. My Lord, rather surely should the Resolution have asked that reparation should be made for the lives that have been lost and the properties that have been destroyed, and I would ask that in the terms of reference to the Committee of Inquiry which your Lordship has appointed, there should be included the question of reparation for those who have suffered, the question of who is to pay for this reparation, and the question as to how the scattered European community is to be safeguarded in the future. My Lord, I would go further, and ask that as this is a matter which concerns my community so deeply, your Excellency may be pleased to add to this Committee a member of the non-official European Community. My Lord, the Committee consists of two eminent Judges, a member of your Excellency's Government, a distinguished soldier and two members of the Indian Community. All that I ask is, that we non-official Europeans should also be represented, and since the Hon'ble Mover of the Resolution has asked that the Commission should consist of gentlemen unconnected with the Indian administration, I think that he at least can take no objection to my request."

The Hon'ble Maharaja Sir Manindra Chandra Nandi :— "My Lord, I think I would be failing in my duty if I were not to speak a few words in connection with the present Resolution. It is the barest truth to say that the recent happenings in the Punjab have grieved people all over India. The loyal and law-abiding section of the Indian Community very much deplores the excesses committed by the mob in this province. But there is also a strong feeling, even among the most considerate and sober-minded, that the retribution visited on the people of the Punjab has been unduly severe and undiscriminating. A policy of conciliation and clemency has no doubt been adopted lately, but it has not succeeded in appeasing the public mind altogether. It is a matter of satisfaction that, in response to the public demand for an inquiry, Government have thought fit to appoint a Committee, as was announced by your Excellency the other day. The personnel of the Committee seems, however, to admit of improvement, and I would implore your Excellency's Government to strengthen it by the addition of a few more non-official Indian members possessing public confidence. There is also a general desire that the terms of reference should be more comprehensive, so as to include individual cases. I venture to suggest that the disturbances in Calcutta should be included within the scope of this inquiry."

The Hon'ble Major Malik Sir Umar Hayat Khan :—"My Lord, the request for the Commission of Inquiry ought to have come from a Punjabi who knew all that happened in the Province and not from an outsider. We have sufficiently suffered from the help extended to us from other Provinces. Most of the well-wishers and inhabitants of our Province are against the holding of any inquiry whatsoever, as they feel it may pour oil on the fast dwindling fire, and even the private inquiry of some gentlemen was resented by the people when some of the newspapers voiced their feelings.

"I also hope that the element of the public men from outside would not be further added to the Commission of these inquiries to enhance our troubles. If any other Indian is to be added to meet the wishes of some of the Members, I suggest that he may be a Sikh from Punjab, as most of the disturbances took place in the area mostly inhabited by the Sikhs, and as there was a Hindu and a Muhammadan member already on the Commission, the appointment will be welcomed by that community. The appointment of a Punjabi with the knowledge of the language of the Province, as well as with the first-hand knowledge of affairs not dependent on the misleading reports and extremist papers, will be of much value to the Commission. As I had worked thoughout the disturbances as well as at the Frontier troubles, I wanted to deal at length about the close connection of the two and the origin and gravity of the situation, as well as the minute plans of those who wanted to prove their threats as genuine. I refrain from bringing forward any facts and reserve them for a future date when I hope to review the situation and try to prove what would have been the inevitable result if prompt measures had not immediately been taken."

*　　　　*　　　　*　　　　*

The Hon'ble Rao Bahadur B.N. Sarma :—"My Lord, your Excellency in your opening speech on the 3rd has rightly given us a warning that nothing that we may do either here or outside should create or embitter the feeling of the various communities in India, and in view of the appointment of the Commission which has been announced by your Excellency, I think it would not be pertinent to make any remarks in detail with regard to our views of the occurrences in the Punjab. But I should be failing in my duty if I did not express in the Council the views of a vast majority of my countrymen, educated as well as uneducated, with regard to the happenings in the Punjab in so far as they have a bearing upon the Resolution in question. Every one whom I have heard deplores greatly the excesses of the mob in the Punjab, the violence and distemper exhibited and the disastrous consequences to European life and property, and I associate myself with what has been said by the Hon'ble Pandit Malaviya with regard to the keen regret of the country as regards those occurrences. Whether some of the later occurrences, or even all those occurrences were not the result of some of the measures taken either then or a little while previously are questions which will come up before the Committee, and I therefore think it would not be right to express an opinion on that question.

"But with regard to the first part of the Resolution raised by my friend, there is something to be said and I hope your Excellency will not take us amiss when we express our view that it might have been desirable and even now would be desirable if a Commission from England, consisting it may be exclusively of Englishmen from there, were to inquire into these Punjab occurrences. Your Excellency will remember that a large part of the Indian public, while deploring the excesses, doubted and doubts whether the circumstances warranted the declaration of a state of war or open rebellion.

"The question is one which, I think, would have to be inquired into by the Committee and the views of the Government of India and the Resolution of the Government of India may have to be canvassed. We are thankful to your Excellency for taking the initiative and appointing this Committee, showing thereby complete confidence in your own honesty and integrity which nobody has ever doubted. But there are many who have doubted and still doubt on reasonable grounds as to whether the Government has not on one-sided reports been thrown into a state of panic and cast an unmerited slur upon the loyalty of vast sections of people in the Punjab and possibly elsewhere. Therefore, it would have been desirable if a Commission entirely unconnected with India, with fresh minds, had been appointed by His Majesty's Government at Home to inquire into these questions, because the questions relating to the Punjab are not, as my friend the Hon'ble Sir Umar Hayat Khan thought, connected only with the Punjab, but are of an all-India or imperial character. It is with great distress of mind and regret that I have to state that, rightly or wrongly—and I hope sincerely, that the Committee will find that the opinion is wrong—rightly or wrongly, there is an impression abroad that British justice has never sunk so low as during the past few months, and nothing has distressed us so much, because we, who believe in the continuance of the British connection with India, have set great store upon the prestige of the British race, upon their reputation for integrity and for justice; and it has saddened us that that tie was being weakened by the events which took place in the Punjab. It would have been well, therefore, if the Committee had consisted exclusively of Britishers fresh from England, and if the Commission had been appointed by the Government at Home to inquire into these questions and the Report had been made to His Majesty's Secretary of State. However, it may not be too late even now. The Government of India has shown its good faith in starting the inquiry itself, and there would be nothing to prevent them from asking His Majesty's Government to clear the doubts and fears of the Indian people. I was very glad to hear that my friend from Bengal owns his Indian citizenship. Nobody has ever doubted it. Nobody has ever doubted that there are large numbers of Britishers in India who are as proud of being Indian citizens as we are ourselves, and I agree with him that everything that is possible should be done to safeguard their lives and properties, especially as they are scattered all over India. But, my Lord, may I point out to the Council that what the people of India object to is not the swift, speedy, stern punishment of the offenders who are responsible for crimes, but to what they believe to be the use of Prussian methods of terrorism in order to inspire fear in the Indian mind when the European is approached. It is a continuance of that old spirit which we thought had ended and would end with the war that the Indian people fear so much; and if the European community does not back up the theories and doctrines supported by some of the Anglo-Indian papers and does not believe in methods of stern vengeance, I am sure everyone will cordially echo what was expressed by my friend the Hon'ble Mr. Crum. It is that question again which is one of the crucial questions which will have to be investigated by this Committee, the question, namely, not as to whether a few more than the really guilty had suffered or not—in every disturbance of this sort ideal justice cannot be dispensed and in administering speedy justice you must punish the innocent as well as the guilty—but the question is whether the methods that had been adopted were adopted with a view to mete out justice or perpetuate the old pernicious methods of upholding prestige even if terrorism has to be employed. I therefore think that Indian confidence in British justice and integrity might be greatly restored—and that is the real point to be gained now—by the appointment of such a Committee as has been prayed for by my friend the Hon'ble Pandit Madan Mohan Malaviya.

"Then, as regards the question as to whether the Committee should be invested with power to annul sentences, there are of course legal and technical difficulties no doubt, but it may be permissible to authorise the Committee to make recommendations in this respect. With due respect I venture to say that we who have been trained in the administration of justice and who have been assisting the administration of justice have looked in vain in what appeared in the newspapers as judgments in these cases, for materials to judge whether these sentences were right or wrong, whether the convictions were right or wrong, and in the few cases in which lengthy judgments have been written, I may venture to say that they have left majority of lawyers as well as non-lawyers unconvinced and they have been forced to the conclusion that it would have been impossible to expect a British Court of justice to convict men on such flimsy materials as apparently formed the basis of such judgments. I hope the Punjab Government and the Government of India had ampler materials than were furnished to the public, on which they could come to a decision as to whether the convictions were right or wrong. I hope one day the materials will be published and the public will be shown that they were absolutely in the wrong. But, so far as the materials in the hands of the public go, I can boldly state that, on the materials furnished and on the judgments, it would be impossible to justify any confidence in the conclusions, I would say, of the Hon'ble Judges who tried these cases. I am not going to impute motives. All of us are human; when we are perturbed by our feelings we are apt to have our judgments misled, and it may be therefore that in the disturbed Punjab of 1919 the atmosphere was too vitiated to permit correct conclusions to be come to. But the Government of India have materials, I hope, and, I think, it would not be wrong for us to recommend that this Committee should go into that question and make recommendations not simply as to whether the sentences should be reduced, but as to whether the convictions should be upheld. After all the Privy Council may be technical and justice may not be administered. I repeat again that the true foundation of the British connection lies in the confidence of the people in British methods, and I hope that in accepting a portion of the Resolution the Government would not be doing wrong in attempting to restore that confidence."

(4)—From Proceedings of Meeting held on September 12, 1919

Debate on Hon'ble Pandit Malaviya's Resolution—(*contd.*)

The President:— "The debate will be resumed on the Resolution moved by the Honb'le Pandit Malaviya."

The Hon'ble Mr. Kamini Kumar Chanda:—"My Lord, rising to speak on his Resolution at this stage I confess to a feeling of some embarrassment. There is so much to say that I really do not know where to begin, where to end, what to say or how much to say. Now, in spite of what has fallen from the lips of my Hon'ble and gallant friend sitting to my right (Hon'ble Sir Umar Hayat Khan) whose authority on military affairs in the Punjab no one for a moment will dispute, I feel constrained to say that one feels that recent happenings in the Punjab have been such as to make it impossible to believe that anything even making a near approach to them could happen under the British administration. I take it, my Lord, that my Hon'ble and gallant friend and gentlemen of his way of thinking believe that there was nothing to complain of about the treatment meted out to the people of the Punjab recently. But my Lord, on the other hand, I do not refer to the communications, the harrowing accounts, which some of us have been receiving first-hand from people living in the Punjab. Leave that alone. There is the resignation of Sir Sankaran Nair which the other day the Secretary of State told the House of Commons, as wired by Reuter, was due to his views with regard to Martial Law in....."

The President:—"Order, order. I stopped the Hon'ble Pandit when he referred to Sir Sankaran Nair's resignation. There is no official statement to which the Hon'ble Member can refer. The Hon'ble Member must leave the subject."

The Hon'ble Mr. Kamini Kumar Chanda:—"I bow to your Lordship's decision. I referred only to what was stated by the Secretary of State in Parliament. However, that is interpreted by the people differently and simply on that account, apart from other evidence, the people feel distressed about the Punjab. Then, my Lord, when a saintly character like Mr. C. F. Andrews was denied entry into the Punjab to see with his own eyes the state of things there, you cannot expect that that would have a reassuring effect upon the public mind that everything there would bear open scrutiny. Then there are the proclamations, notifications, ordinances, orders, I do not know by what name they are called, issuing from the martial law administration, some of which have seen the light of day and which fill the mind with amazement mingled with indignation. I am not surprised, my Lord, that my Hon'ble and gallant friend, the Hon'ble Major Malik Sir Umar Hayat Khan, Tiwana, not only sees nothing to object about the treatment of the Punjabis under martial law regime, but would resent any one from outside calling attention to what has been described by Sir Rabindranath Tagore, the poet and recluse who never mingles in politics, but felt constrained in his protest against the administration of martial law in the Punjab to request to be relieved of his knighthood, 'as a degradation not fit for human beings' under 'methods of administration without a parallel in the history of civilized nations.' I say, my Lord, I am not surprised at that attitude. The mentality is easily understandable. Then, my Lord, if even a tenth part of the allegations and suggestions, which the industry and devotion of the Hon'ble Pandit has formulated in a string of questions of the most searching character and which has found its way into the press, bears anything like semblance of truth in them, one would say that he would like to run away from this land and go into the jungles. I sincerely trust, my Lord, for the good name of the Government under which I am proud to live that my Hon'ble friend is mistaken. I sincerely trust these charges are untrue, but if true, my Lord, would they not constitute a very grave indictment against the administration of Sir Michael O'Dwyer, hardly less grave than the charges that were made against Warren Hastings ? My Lord, I humbly submit that these things must be refuted, must be disproved by the findings of an independent tribunal, whose verdict will carry universal assent. My Lord, it is hardly necessary to point out in the words of the Court of Directors of the East India Company that it is not enough that justice is done but the people should be made to realise, to feel, that justice is being done. The Government of India is responsible for ratifying the policy adopted by Sir Michael O'Dwyer, and it is a matter for grave regret that the Government do not see its way to have a Royal Commission to investigate these charges, a Commission whose verdict, whose decision, would carry infinitely greater weight than that of any Commission or Committee that may be appointed in this country. My Lord, in view of the fact that the policy that will have to come under the scrutiny of the

Committee is ultimately the policy of the Government of India, it can hardly he doubted that the finding of the Committee in so far as it may find in favour of that policy will not carry conviction if it has to report to the Government of India. On the other hand, my Lord, I fully realise that in view of the fact that your Excellency was pleased to announce the appointment of a Committee of Enquiry and the terms of reference to it, it is hardly likely that the Government will feel disposed to accept the suggestion of my Hon'ble friend to have another Commission.

"My Lord, I submit that under these circumstances it is very desirable to find a *via media*, and a practical solution would be to ask the Committee to report not to the Government of India but to the Secretary of State. The composition of the Committee should also be revised. It cannot be denied that the composition of the Committee has not evoked much enthusiasm in the country among the Indians. Of course, I do not speak about the Anglo-Indian press which in this matter does not count. My Hon'ble friend read extracts from the leading organs of what is known as the moderate party, and even they do not appear to be satisfied with the composition of the Committee. In the first place, the Indian element is hardly adequate. In a matter like this, I submit that the number of Indians should be equal to that of the Europeans. In the next place, as regards the personnel of this Committe, we see here as we saw in the case of the recent Reforms Committee that a Moslem member is drawn from one of the Indian States. I do not know if that means the introduction of a new policy. Without making any the slightest reflection in the remotest degree against the gentleman concerned, I submit that it is hardly right and fair to the great Moslem community to go out of British India to the Indian States, to make a selection of a Moslem member. I submit that this is a matter for your Excellency's consideration. I submit that in these circumstances the best thing would be to add another Indian member selected in such a manner as would give satisfaction to the Indian community. I do not know that any better selection could be made than one from the panel which my Hon'ble friend suggested in the revised Resolution which he wished to move but was not allowed to move. Say what you will, it is impossible to deny that the judgments or decisions, call them by the term judgments if you like, of the courts of martial law, which was described by Lord Haldane when dealing with applications to grant leave to appeal to the Privy Council from the martial law decisions, 'as a negation of law' have caused deep distress to the public that Indians of the Punjab who are held in high esteem for their character and position are branded as rebels. There may be technical difficulties in the way of a Committee going into these matters, but surely something can be devised if you really wish to bring peace to the land. The Hon'ble Pandit Malaviya suggested that there had been convictions without any record of any summary or any memorandum of evidence, convictions without reasons of decisions, cases without even disclosing the offences, cases taken up at midnight without giving due notice to the accused persons, their relations, friends or lawyers of the change of date, because martial law was going to expire after midnight In such cases the mind is distressed and unless you find some means by which these cases can be scrutinised, the grievance will remain. I really feel that there can be no real difficulty in finding a means, if you wish it. If you can have an Indemnifying Bill you may as well have some measure which will enable these cases being revised. A simple process would be to vest the Committee with power to investigate the cases, with power to investigate this matter, look into the judgments and then report to His Majesty in Council with recommendations for annulment of convictions. We are grateful to your Excellency and to His Honour Sir Edward Maclagan for acts of clemency in the wholesale reductions of sentences ordered. I do not know if the Government have seen an account given by a press correspondent of his interview with Kali Nath Rai after his release from jail. It appears therefrom that these acts of clemency failed to evoke any response in the hearts of the accused persons. It appears almost as a mockery to tell an innocent man that his sentence has been reduced or that he has been pardoned. In these cases what is prayed for is no clemency but justice, no favour but fair treatment. With these humble words, I support the Resolution of my learned friend."

The Hon'ble Sardar Sunder Singh Majithia:—"My Lord, I sincerely deplore the most unfortunate events that have happened in my province, and in view of the Committee of Inquiry that was announced by your Excellency in your Excellency's opening speech this Session on the 3rd September, and which I have no hesitation in saying will be welcomed by my follow-subjects in the Punjab, I think the Resolution of my Hon'ble friend is unnecessary, as the necessity of an inquiry which my Hon'ble friend wanted has already been conceded. I would, however, very strongly urge the addition of a third Indian member, from amongst the public men in India, on this Committee. I hope that if your Excellency's Government were to accede to this request, it will satisfy everybody.

"Your Excellency, as representing His Majesty the King-Emperor, is, I think, the right person to whom the report of this Committee should be submitted.

"One point more I would, however, suggest if the enquiry has to serve a useful purpose ; and that is, that an assurance should be given to the people who are to give evidence before this Committee that they will be fully protected from every sort of harassment from the underlings of the Police or otherwise.

"The need of an inquiry having been admitted and a Committee having been appointed. I would advise my Hon'ble friend, the mover, if it would not be wise to withdraw his motion."

The Hon'ble Raja Sir Rampal Singh:—"My Lord, I think I would be failing in my duty towards my country and its Government if I do not make a few observations in support of the Resolution that was moved by the Hon'ble Pandit Madan Mohan Malaviya. After the announcement made by your Excellency as to the appointment of the Committee and its personnel and the terms of reference, I thought it might not be of much avail to press the Resolution on the attention of the Government. But the exigencies of the situation require that the views of the non-official Members of this Council and of those whom they represent, may with advantage be put before the Government, with the object of impressing upon them the desirability of some modification in the constitution of the Committee and their terms of reference in order to restore confidence in the public mind which has got shattered in the sense of justice of the Government.

"With all the precautions that were taken to exclude the public from getting a glimpse of the terrible happenings in the Punjab, the country is full of all sorts of rumours which have created a widespread dissatisfaction, discontent and resentment. I have no direct knowledge of the disturbances and the manner in which the Punjab authorities quelled them, but the little that I could gather from the papers and other sources is enough to convince me that the stern measures adopted under the plea of restoring law and order were uncalled for, hasty, and out of all proportion to the gravity of the situation. Was the Government justified in declaring a state of open rebellion in the Punjab, I believe not. At a time when the

Government was entangled in the grip of bloody war, the Punjab showed by her enormous contributions in men and money, her sincere earnestness and loyal devotion to the cause of the Empire. How was it that a few months after the war, which had terminated in the much desired victory of the *Sarkar,* she got her head turned as to rebel against that very *Sarkar* ?

"It requires too great a stretch of one's imagination and too great a strain on one's credulousness to believe that a state of open rebellion did exist in the Punjab. However, if for argument's sake, it may be admitted that such a state of things did prevail there, was it justifiable for the authorities concerned not to have used proper and wise discretion in the exercise of the unrestricted powers that seem to have been bestowed upon them ? The seriousness of the recent Punjab affairs cannot be too highly exaggerated and a patient and impartial inquiry and the redress of the wrongs that might have been done can only clear the atmosphere and restore confidence in British justice. The times are changed. The moral sensibility of India has become very sensitive in sympathy with the modern standard, and so any miscarriage of justice or any high-handedness creates a feeling of alarm and resentment not only in the locality concerned, but throughout the length and breadth of the country.

"Political demonstrations, strikes and passive resistance are matters of common occurrence in modern political warfare in democratic countries. What wonder there is if India, walking on the footsteps of such countries and taking her lessons from the people who rule over her, indulges in similar movements. Never in those countries is a state of open rebellion declared, then why should India receive a different treatment at the hands of her Government? I admit the populace of this country is not as disciplined and orderly as of some of the European countries, and sometimes control over the mob is lost and most reprehensible excesses are committed which cannot be too highly deplored and condemned. No sane man can have the least sympathy with the culprits of such excesses. By all means they deserve the severest punishment which the Criminal Law provides. But, my Lord, to conclude from such excesses that the country is in a state of rebellion is nothing short of libel to the good name, reputation and honour of India. I, therefore, pray that the Government will be pleased to see their way to modify the constitution of the Committee and the terms of reference in such a manner as to secure the confidence of the country.

"My Lord, we are very keen on an inquiry to be made by an independent and impartial Committee having a sufficient number of Indians on it and commanding the confidence of the public. If the Punjab will be adjudged by such a tribunal to be guilty of rebellion against the Sovereign, I am sure she would willingly do the penances for her misdeeds and the people outside her limits will only pity her folly. But if the case is otherwise and there were potent provocative causes for the disturbances, the sin of defaming the name of India will fall on those who misled the Government of India into commiting this serious blunder."

The Hon'ble Mr. K. V. Rangaswamy Ayyangar:—"When I rise to say a few words on this occasion, I am not unmindful of your Excellency's advice not to accentuate the differences between the races by our speeches. Had the Government of the Punjab and the Imperial Government only cared for this principle not to stir up race hatred by unnecessary and unjust acts, there would have been no occasion for such an advice as came from your Excellency at the opening day to the Members here. As if those acts have not already created a feeling of estrangement, our speeches expressing the sentiments of the people are not going to create any new differences. Your Excellency also said on the opening day that the Government cannot deviate from the policy and all our talks and efforts to make the Government deviate from the policy were futile....."

The President:—"I never said anything of the sort, Mr. Ayyangar. Please quote me correctly if you quote me at all."

The Hon'ble Mr. K. V. Rangaswamy Ayyangar:—"Then I much regret. It is our duty to voice forth the sentiments of the people, and this makes me bold to say what I feel, and what the country feels, over the Punjab incidents.

"It was on the occasion of the Anniversary of the Durbar Day in 1912, the gravest act of treason was committed by some individual in throwing a bomb at no less a person than that most humane and just ruler Lord Hardinge. The then head of the Government did not commit any hasty action and pronounce martial law at Delhi and sack Delhi. There was even a talk that some military authority approached the Government for a similar proclaiming, but that it was not permitted. Thus the then rulers averted a great calamity that would have befallen India as it happened during recent times.

"Your Excellency had asked us to go and see the spot personally even now. No one denies there were certain rash acts committed by some stray individuals in tearing asunder the railway lines and telegraph wires and burning properties. The loss of innocent European lives is highly regrettable. By all means trace out the culprits and award them due sentences. But how could the British sense of justice suffer to see other than the real culprit pay the penalty ? The organisers of the meeting for the repeal of the Rowlatt Act should not have been held responsible for the rash acts of these stray individuals. Could the organisers of the Durbar Day in 1912 be court-martialled for the rash acts of the bomb-thrower on Lord Hardinge? Against such an act there have been demonstrations in the whole of India. But in the other parts of the country the authorities acted with calmness and prudence, while in the Punjab they immortalised themselves by interpreting constitutional agitation as 'open rebellion'. I have it on the authority of the moderate journal 'The Leader' that the Provincial Satrap of the Punjab is said to have declared his intention of taking a note of the Anti-Rowlatt agitation and Passive Resistance demonstration before there was any disturbance of peace. A meeting was held at Amritsar and the two leaders that took part in it were deported under the Regulation III of 1818. At Lahore on the 10th April, a small crowd passing through the street in an unoffensive manner was fired upon. Bombs were thrown from aeroplanes ; the authorities in the Punjab did not apprehend any rebellion ; and the martial law was not declared to quell any rebellion, but to teach a lesson to the political agitators what it is to mix up with politics. As a matter of fact, I was told by a respectable gentleman that an Englishman who wanted to enter the Punjab and make inquiries for himself was told by a very high authority that the people should be taught a lesson, as to how they would fare if they would molest any European. If it is asserted that martial law was introduced only after a serious rioting, it may be pertinently asked whether Martial Law Orders were not issued to the province of Delhi and parts of Bombay also. But for the tactful handling of the situation, Delhi, Bombay and Calcutta also should have shared the fate of the Punjab. What I want to point out is, that the Martial Law Orders were passed before there was rioting or rebellion; and without the martial law there would be restored quiet in the Punjab as in Delhi, Bombay and Calcutta. The measures adopted there are according to the judgments of persons who were in touch with the Punjab and gentlemen who cannot come to false conclusions, grossly illegal, excessive and wrong, and the reports conveyed in the papers about such atrocities as committed at Jallianwala Bagh and other places fill one's heart with horror and dismay. Other ways of teaching the people to look at a European with awe and respect should be resorted to, and the martial law is not at all the weapon for that purpose. The principles laid down for the promulgation of martial law do not at all seem to have been observed. 'The only principle on which the Law of England tolerates what is called martial law, is Necessity'. Every bad act in this world is only the result of hasty action; and hasty action should be questioned by an impartial Tribunal and retribution effected.

"The right Hon'ble Lord Sinha says, in the House of Lords, that it was not in the power of the tribunal to sentence these men, save for anything else than transportation for life and forfeiture of property. The Judges and the Tribunals, and the Right Hon'ble gentleman were convinced that the judgment is quite unjustified in the case of Hari Krishan Lal, and a lot of others, but yet they have to plead that it was not in their power to award just and deserving judgments. Why should we drag in a martial law and place these men for trial under Martial Law Tribunals when the ordinary courts were going, and then plead that it is not in our power to award just judgments? The judgment in the case of Hari Krishan Lal read together with the Amritsar one forms one of the saddest commentaries on British justice....."

The Hun'ble Sir William Vincent:—" May I rise to a point of order ? Is the Hon'ble Member in order in discussing a judgment which is now pending before the Privy Council ?"

The President:—"The Hon'ble Member is not in order. If the Hon'ble Member will look at Rule 3 (c) and at Rule 15 he will see that he is not in order in referring to any matter which is under adjudication by a court of law. Therefore he must not mention the matter at all."

The Hon'ble Mr. K. V. Rangaswamy Ayyangar:—"We want the Committee to inquire whether martial law was necessary and justified, and whether the findings of the Martial Law Courts, the severity and the cruelty of their sentences, were right. And if they were not right, what are the proceedings to be taken against the administrators and promulgators of martial law, and what is the compensation that is to be given to the innocent and injured ? Many adult earning members of large families were incapacitated and many died. The Committee should find out whether the shooting of the people was justified before there was any disorder and whether there were any disorders before fire was opened. It is to question the action of the Government of India, the Government of the Punjab, and the administrators of martial law, that we want the Commission of Inquiry. The Commission that we want should be unconnected with the Government of India, and it should be elected by the Non-official Members of this Council or nominated by His Majesty's Government. The Committee that has been appointed may carry out the orders, and act up to the terms of reference, of the Government of India. But what we the people of India want is, that an independent Committee should be constituted to find out how the wrongs done to the people may be rectified and compensated, and to devise means how such outrages will not be made possible to be repeated again by an easily excitable authority with an inflammable Press.

"It is unfortunate that of all the Provinces, the Punjab which has supplied so many recruits to the army, and on whose wheat the major portion of the life in the British Empire is sustained, should suffer this monstrous treatment. It was only the other day, in this very Council, that Sir Michael O'Dwyer wasted nearly an hour in praise of his province, the Punjab. The latest Administration Report also is very eulogistic of the Punjab services and loyalty. Then as the 'Modern Review' puts it, either those protestations were reprehensible untruth, or the province was suddenly converted to a mire of discontent on account of bad rule. Will the Committee be empowered to suggest how the authorities who were the cause of all this discontent, and those of them who were responsible for unnecessary harshness and cruelty, and those also who by corrupt practices became rich at the expense of the people, should be punished ?

"I am bringing to notice that such a thing has happened and I hope that the people will be treated with justice by the Committee of Inquiry."

* * * *

The Hon'ble Sir William Vincent:—"My Lord, I am afraid that the Hon'ble Member has been a little unlucky in his attempt to modify the terms of his Resolution, but if that is so, I think that many in this Council will agree that it is largely owing to his own fault. Since the Secretary of State's speech in the House of Commons, most people have been aware of the character of the inquiry which the Government of India proposed into these disorders, and certainly on the 3rd of this month it was quite obvious what the intentions of the Government of India and the Secretary of State were. The Hon'ble Member at that time, although there was sufficient interval between that date and the 10th, did not give us any notice of any amended form of Resolution until the very last moment, and it is reasonable to assume or conclude—and the conclusion is fortified by what I have heard here during this debate—that one of the reasons which led him to this modificaion of his Resolution was that he could find no support for it in its original form, or no adequate support. The Hon'ble Member has evaded the difficulty by some very clever manoeavring ; and he really made a speech which covered all the points in the amended Resolution, although nominally moving the original one. But even then, I think, the Council will realise that he has got himself into a pretty fair muddle at the end. I have not heard one speech from any Hon'ble Member who has been able to support the Resolution in its entirety in its present form. I have heard various suggestions of different kinds from Hon'ble Members. The Hon'ble and gallant Member, Sir Umar Hayat Khan suggested the addition, I think, of a Punjabi, if any one was added to the Committee. The Hon'ble Mr. Crum said 'You should add another European to the Committee'. Mr. Sarma, who is generally a whole-hearted supporter of the Hon'ble mover, said, 'I really cannot support the last part of this Resolution' but other measures to revise sentences should be taken. My Lord, I think it will be obvious to this Council that it is quite impossible for me to announce the decision of Government on any of these new suggestions at a moment's notice. The constitution and terms of reference of this Committee have been settled after very careful consideration and prolonged consultation with the Secretary of State, and Hon'ble Members will themselves realise that it is quite impossible for me to answer these questions off hand. What we all want is an impartial inquiry into this matter which will result in the ascertainment of the facts. The Government deplores as much as the Hon'ble Member does the loss of life that has occurred during these recent disorders. We cannot agree with him, however, that it is a matter of the number so much as of the manner in which and the reasons for which these men and women unfortunately met their death....."

The Hon'ble Pandit Madan Mohan Malaviya:—"No 'women'."

The Hon'ble Sir William Vincent:—"But, my Lord, I do think there is some cause for complaint....."

The Hon'ble Pandit Madan Mohan Malaviya:—May I interrupt my Hon'ble friend ? The Hon'ble Member said 'women'; has any woman met her death in these events ?"

The Hon'ble Sir William Vincent:—I did not say death, my Lord, or if I did I made a mistake. One woman was however treated with the greatest indignity and left for dead ; I do not know if that will satisfy the Hon'ble Member. But what I was trying to say was that, while the Hon'ble Member and others have deplored these dreadful happenings, there has been in some quarters, a tendency unfairly to minimise them. If I may cite a very prominent example I could not do better than quote the Hon'ble Mr. Ayyangar. It is my misfortune, my Lord, that the Hon'ble Member cannot hear what I say, charm I never so wisely, so that if I address myself to this point it is not in the hope of convincing him. But what I take exception to is his minimising of these events and calling them 'rash acts.' He referred to injuries and the deaths, murders or some words of that kind, of Indians but not one word of what happened to the outrages on those unfortunate Europeans. Now, I have no desire whatever to excite prejudice in this matter, and if other Hon'ble Members had followed the example of the Hon'ble mover it would have been possible for me to avoid reference to details to a great extent. But I do deprecate any such minimissing of terrible incidents. We have, for instance, the case of this lady, Miss Sherwood, to whom I referred just now. Now what are the facts in regard to this unfortunate woman? She had worked for years in this country as a doctor, a perfectly inoffensive woman, respected, as I understand, by all. She was attacked by a mob of people which knocked her down six times, beat her with shoes, struck her with *lathis* and left her for dead. This is described at a meeting of the All-India Home Rule League, of which I believe the Hon'ble mover is a member....."

The Hon'ble Pandit Madan Mohan Malaviya:—"I am President of the All India Congress Committee."

The Hon'ble Sir Willian Vincent:—"Am I to understand the Hon'ble Member is not a member of the Home Rule League? However, that outrage was described at a meeting of this body as a petty assault. Now I put it to the Council that that is not a fair description....."

The Hon'ble Pandit Madan Mohan Malaviya:—"May I know which body described it as a petty assault ?"

The Hon'ble Sir William Vincent:—"My Lord, may I be allowed to continue my speech without these constant interruptions?"

The President:—"This Hon'ble Member will have an opportunity of replying later, and I think he should allow the Hon'ble the Home Member to continue without interrupting him."

The Hon'ble Pandit Madan Mohan Malaviya:—"My Lord, may I submit that in Parliament questions are asked as the discussion is going on. These questions cannot be asked at the end of a speech."

The Hon'ble Sir William Vicent:—"My Lord, may I ask that the time for which the Hon'ble Member interrupts me may be deducted from the period which I am allowed.

"Then, my Lord, there is another class of men who deplore the occurrence—gentlemen, who protest their horror and indignation really as a prelude or as an introduction to deprecating any effective measures being taken to suppress disorders. No attempt, my Lord, was made by gentlemen of this category in any way to stop the false reports about the Rowlatt Act or to quell the disturbances.

"But, my Lord, while I mention these men, it would be ungrateful and unfair of me if I were not also to refer to the services of other Indians, some of whom are in this Council now. I include my Hon'ble and gallant friend Sir Umar Hayat Khan Tiwana, Sardar Sunder Singh and many other members of the Punjab whom it would be invidious to mention, who not only sought to assist Government in this time of trouble, but did everything they could to allay the disorders and further, my Lord, did what was necessary—that which, thank God, has not been necessary since 1857—to save European lives from murder and outrage at the hands of the mob. To them the thanks of Government, as we said in a Resolution at the time, the greatest thanks of Government as are deservedly due. I am anxious, my Lord, not to enter into these matters because I do not seek in any way to prejudice this inquiry. I want, as I have said before, to deal with the proposal which is actually before this Council. There have been modifications of the Resolution suggested, on which I can, as I have explained, express no opinion. They are matters on which the collective counsels of the Government of India must necessarily be taken, and on which consultation with the Secretary of State will in some cases at least also be necessary. I trust, therefore, that Hon'ble Members will not press me on points which are not directly before them as part of this Resolution. The proposal before Council is in the first place for the appointment of a Royal Commission. May I point out that the only authority which can constitute a Royal Commission is His Majesty's Government. Now, His Majesty's Government is represented by the Secretary of State so far as India is concerned. The constitution and scope of the present Committee has been settled after prolonged consultation with him and it is, I submit, idle now to ask us, the Government of India having decided the constitution of that Committee, to re-open the matter with him. The Secretary of State, who is his Majesty's representative, has accepted our view that the present form of inquiry is adequate. If any motion for a Royal Commission is now to be made, I submit that it should be made in the House of Commons. But, when he was making the motion, although that is part of the Resolution, the Hon'ble Member did not suggest that the inquiry should be by Royal Commission or that the Committee should be so appointed, but he suggested that certain members should be added to it and that the Committee should report direct to the Secretary of State. There are various arguments which will, I think, commend themselves to reasonable members of the Council why the Government of India should only appoint a Committee to report to itself. The Government of India cannot say to a Committee 'you are to report to His Majesty or to the Secretary of State or any authority but itself.' Of course, in the normal course of things, the report of this Committee will be forwarded by the Government of India to the Secretary of State and will be laid undoubtedly in the ultimate resort before His Majesty's Government. But the authority who appoints a Committee of this kind must, according to ordinary procedure, require that Committee to report to itself. There is, however, really a very much larger question of principle involved. The Government of India has certain statutory responsibilities for the peace and good government of this country, and it cannot divest itself of those responsibilities save for very cogent reasons. To do so would be tantamount to an admission that the Government is not competent to fulfil its proper functions, that it is unworthy of the confidence of His Majesty's Government and that it is unable to discharge its duties towards its own officers. That is a position which, I think, although some members of the Council may wish it, the majority will, I hope, not approve. The idea underlying the proposals is that the Government/of India is on its trial. My Lord, that is a position that the Government of India do not and cannot accept. Because certain persons have chosen to promote serious disorders in this country, because certain measures have been taken to quell those disorders, is the Government of India for that reason to divest itself of its responsibilities in a matter of this gravity ? There can be only one answer to a question of that kind. It is not reasonable that the Government should be required to take such a course, and if such a proposal is to be made, then the proper place in which to move it is another place.

"There remains this question, the third question, I think, of remission of sentences. My Lord, the sentences have been reviewed with the greatest care by the Local Government, and in many cases by the Government of India, and as admitted by many members of this Council clemency, great clemency, has been shown. It has indeed been alleged in some quarters that the clemency shown by the Government in this matter is an indication of weakness. That is a proposition which the Government of India do not for a moment support. They recognise that many of the unfortunate men who were concerned in these disorders were the dupes of others; the disorders are now over and the desire of the Government is that normal conditions should return. My Lord, I confess that one is not much encouraged in the exercise of clemency by language such as that used by the Hon'ble Mr. Chanda, but such language will of course not deter the Government of India from continuing in that course which it conceives to be right and just.

"The Hon'ble mover suggested that it was necessary that the report, so far as sentences are concerned, should be made to His Majesty in Council because otherwise the guilt of these men could not be wiped off, that they could not be purged of the stain that lay on them by reason of the convictions. At least that is what I understood. I think there is some misapprehension on that matter, because your Excellency has in the matter delegated to you exactly the same powers of pardon as those which are exerciseable by His Majesty. This, therefore, is a reason which will not really hold water.

"The Hon'ble mover in his opening speech admitted, in the most candid manner, his full confidence that your Excellency and your Excellency's Government would deal with this matter with justice and integrity. He could say nothing himself against the personnel of the Committee and admitted that it really would deal with the inquiry justly, impartially and fairly. I tried to take the words down and I believe I am substantially correct. Now, my Lord, if that is so, is there any reason for changing the whole of the personnel of this Committee? Is there any reason why, if this Government is, as the Hon'ble mover says, anxious to act with the utmost fairness, why we should divest ourselves of our responsibility in this matter or that the Committee should report direct to His Majesty's Government? The inquiry will, as is already known, be as far as possible public, and it is our intention, unless there is some unforeseen reason to the contrary, to publish the final report. The personnel of the Committee is such that it must, in spite of what has been said, command very considerable confidence. There are certain additions proposed to which I have already adverted, but to which I can at the present moment make no definite answer. But I want to assure the Council of this, that the desire of the Government is one and one only, that there may be an impartial inquiry into these disorders, that the truth may be ascertained, and that what is possible may be done to restore normal conditions, to allay racial feeling and restore the country to peace and quiet."

The Hon'ble Sir Dinshaw Wacha:—"Your Lordship, in a controversy on a subject of the character which is now under discussion by the Council, it is very natural that sentiments, feelings, suspicions, imagination and one thing or another of a kindred character should always be mixed up. It is quite natural; and it is only human that in such a controversy there shall be extreme views. It is also natural that there should be moderate views as well. Human nature being what it is, I am not at all surprised that one set of controversialists have gone to one extreme and another set of controversialists to another extreme. The pendulum swings from one end to the other. There is no golden mean, as it were, where the whole controversy might be balanced, as we could balance a pair of scales, and come to a right judgment on the subject. That being the situation, my Lord, I am very sorry that the controversy has assumed a kind of character here which is undesirable. But I do believe that what the Hon'ble the Home Member, who has taken the wind out of my sails in some respects, has already said on the subject I may observe that after what the Hon'ble Sir William Vincent has said on the questions raised by the motion of my friend, Hon'ble Pandit Malaviya, it is very necessary that we should calmly consider the matter and have a balance of mind so adjusted as to arrive at a very correct decision on this Resolution. In this matter, I believe that it is always the case that where passions and prejudices and feelings are excited there is not, what you might call, 'clear thinking'. Clear thinking requires clear grasp of facts; and as far as facts are concerned I find, of course, that facts have been adduced by more than one speaker, which may or may not be right The merits of the question will be decided by a Committee of Inquiry which has already been appointed. That Committee will really be the tribunal which will go into the correctness of facts, which will inform us exactly what are and what are not facts. Personally, speaking for myself, I am not aware of what the actual facts are and what are not. In Bombay, I read a variety of papers and heard a variety of 'facts' from persons who said they had had facts on first-hand information received from people in the Punjab who knew what the course of events was. Still, after all, we, Indians, are the persons who have asked for the inquiry. The Government has rightly responded to the request of the public, and, of course, asked the Secretary of State to appoint a Committee of Inquiry. That Committee has already been appointed. Therefore, the only thing now left to us, is to suspend our judgment and see what the inquiry does, what the facts elicited are, what the situation was like, and await their final conclusions. As far as their judgment is concerned I have certainly no fear on the subject. I have, as my friend Pandit Malaviya has said, firm faith in the integrity and impartiality of the tribunal itself; and I have also large and firm faith in the sense of British justice. British justice may be erratic sometimes, as every human thing is; even the planets and constellations sometimes go out of their orbits. But still, if there is any prestige for the British Government in India, and if there is any love of British institutions, among Indians, it is certainly on account of the stern sense of British justice; and, I repeat, in that justice I have the firmest faith. That being the case, I will only say this: I appeal to my Hon'ble friend, Mr. Malaviya, to withdraw his Resolution; or if he cannot withdraw it, at any rate let him delete that part of it which goes before, and refer only to the request that there may be a third Indian member who commands the confidence of the public. Your Lordship, I may say this that I myself have felt, and so too my numerous friends in Bombay as well as my Association which has sent a telegram on the subject to the Home Member, that India would be quite satisfied, (so far as I have read the public papers of all sorts and shades of opinion), if a third Indian member enjoying public confidence is appointed. I appeal to your Lordship to intervene in the matter and request the Secretary of State in response to the prayer of the Indian public to appoint a third Indian member, and I think all controversy, all animated controversy, will be at an end. Everybody will be satisfied that a Committee of Inquiry, so constituted as to inspire full confidence, will do full justice to the responsible task entrusted to them. I cannot forget at the same time what my Hon'ble friend Mr. Crum said on this subject from his point of view. Europeans have also a large concern in this inquiry. If there is to be a third Indian member, why not also have a non-official European member, who will represent the non-official European point of view ? After all, the Committee, if constituted as now suggested, should inspire confidence, and it is to be hoped that they will come to a right decision. I respectfully request that your Lordship with your great authority will represent to the Secretary of State the feelings of the people on the subject. With these few words I resume my seat."

The Hon'ble Mr. Sachchidananda Sinha:—"My Lord, I desire to assure your Excellency that I have risen to speak on this Resolution with a sense of very great responsibility. I have had the privilege of addressing Viceroys in this Council on many previous occasions, but never have I addresed the Council on an occasion like this. I realise that feelings have been naturally roused on both sides, which have to some extent found expression in the Council. Far be it from me to say one word that would add to the tension of these feelings on either side, but I hope the few temperate observations I propose to make may be of some use in presuading your Lordship's Government to accept the very reasonable proposal that we have made jointly before the Council. Much has been said by previous speakers to represent the Indian point of view in regard to the situation in the Punjab, and the Hon'ble Mr. Crum has represented to your Lordship the view which our European fellow-subjects have taken in this matter. I would like to give the Hon'ble the Home Member and the Hon'ble Mr. Crum the assurance that I am not one of those who either minimise the gravity of the situation in the Punjab, or say a few words of sympathy by way of a prelude to making further demands. On the contrary, I frankly confess that I am ashamed of the doings of such of my countrymen in the Punjab as had any hand in killing Europeans, or in injuring them or destroying their property, for they had not only harmed Europeans, but injured us also in the matter of our demands for the rights and privileges that we legitimately claim as British subjects in this country. We are all against mob-rule. I, therefore, claim that I am not at all minimising the gravity of the situation. In fact, I go further. I heard with surprise the Hon'ble Mr Crum say that because a few Europeans had suffered or lost their lives, therefore he felt that he and the Europeans were the aggrieved party.

"I venture to say that it seems to me to be putting the case at rather a low level. Whether the people who lost their lives, through the action of the mob, be Europeans or Indians, so long as they are our fellow-subjects, of whatever nationality, all British subjects are the aggrieved party. I claim that I feel it as much as the Hon'ble Mr. Crum that my European fellow-subjects should have lost their lives through the action of the mob. At the same time, while candidly admitting that, I would like to lay before your Lordship the Indian point of view. To put it in a short sentence the Indian point of view is this: that although the Government were fully justified in resorting to all effective measures for the purpose of re-establishing law and order, their action went far beyond the requirements of the case. In fact, in the name of law and order things were perpetrated which cannot be justified in the light of that high standard of British justice with which we have been long associated in this country. That, in short, is our point of view. If your Lordship will permit me, I will read out a sentence from a well-known Anglo-Indian paper, the *'Madras Mail.'* Coming from an adversary, its admission is very valuable. It says in its leading article in a recent issue :—

> 'We are quite convinced that Indian sentiment has been genuinely and deeply stirred by the events in the Punjab, and that, however much capital may be made out of that affair by factious individuals ever on the lookout to villify the *British Raj*, there is a substantial body of loyal and moderate opinion which has been shocked by what it regards as an outrage upon Indian fellow countrymen.'

"My Lord, I submit that in this one short sentence the leading Anglo-Indian paper of Madras summarises and sums up correctly the Indian point of view. My Lord, it is very desirable, therefore, that the Committee which has been constituted should be one which will be able to inspire confidence in the public mind. I do not wish to take up the time of the Council in discussing whether it would have been of greater advantage if this Committee had been a Royal Commission, reporting to His Majesty's Government through the Secretary of State, but I desire to say that in asking for the Royal Commission there is no such feeling as the Hon'ble the Home Member spoke of, namely, that we desire to place the Government of India on their trial. The Hon'ble the Home Member shakes his hand to imply that he refuses to accept my statement, I can assure him....."

The Hon'ble Sir William Vincent:—"That was not intended."

The Hon'ble Mr Sachchidananda Sinha:—"I can assure him,

speaking with the full weight of responsibility, that it is far from our desire to place the Government of India on their trial. I remember my late lamented leader, Mr. Gokhale, declare on a memorable occasion in this Council that he could not defeat the Government if he would as the prestige of the Government of India was such a valuable asset to our progress. For similar reasons we do not desire to place the Government of India on their trial. But the real point is this. The Government of India are believed to have been associated too closely with the policy pursued in the Punjab by Sir Michael O'Dwyer. I hope I shall quote your Lordship correctly and shall not make the mistake as the Hon'ble Mr. Ayyangar did. Your Excellency said in your opening address on the 3rd of this month:—'I promised support to the head of each Local Government for such measures as he thought it might be necessary to take, and that support was given unwaveringly throughout.' Now, I am far from suggesting that your Lordship was not justified in taking the line of action you did. I am fully aware of the fact that your Lordship appreciates and realised your responsibilities in this grave matter. I merely submit that the people naturally believe that when that was the view of the Government of India, and they took such action as they did in pursuance of it, the people are not wrong in assuming that the Government of India were too closely associated and identified with the policy pursued in the Punjab. And the reason why we press for a Royal Commission is, that we believe that all human beings, howsoever exalted their position, are liable to be influenced in their action and judgment by an inherent unconscious bias. When the Government of India have admittedly made themselves responsible for the policy of the Punjab Government, we believe that your Lordship's Government will not be in so good a position for appreciating the evidence and of passing judgment in the matter, as another independent body would be. However, the Hon'ble the Home Member says that it is too late now to bring up the proposal and it could only be done in the House of Commons. I do not think I personally can bring it up in the House of Commons, and there is not time enough for us to get it done, as the committee will be coming out soon. That is why we are concentrating our efforts and pressing for an additional Indian member on the Committee. In spite of what the Hon'ble the Home Member said, it is a fact that the Committee, as at present constituted, does not find favour with the bulk of the people I am sorry to say...."

The Hon'ble Sir William Vincent:—"The Hon'ble Member is wrong."

The Hon'ble Mr. Sachchidananda Sinha:—"I can assure your Lordship that so far as Indian public opinion has found expression in the press, the constitution of the Committee has been found to be wholly unsatisfactory, and I find that the *Times of India*, which says that the constitution of the Committee should satisfy all reasonable persons, goes on in the next breath to say that it would like one more member on it. That is a sample of the reasonableness of persons who say in one breath that they accept the constitution of the Committee and in the next that they would like to have one more. That shows that all parties in this country are more or less dissatisfied with the constitution of the Committee. Now I am not going to make any personal observations about the personnel of the Committee, but I would point out that out of the six members of the Committee no less, my Lord, than five are officials, Indian or European, and I believe that there is only one non-official, Sir Chimanlal Setalvad. It is not a matter of race or nationality, but I maintain that when there are no less than five officials and but one non-official on the Committee, it is bound to find very little favour with the public. I, therefore, submit that on this particular matter, the members of this Council who have spoken so far—the Hon'ble Sir Dinshaw Wacha, the Hon'ble the Raja Saheb of Kanika, the Hon'ble Sardar Sundar Singh Majithia and others—all agree that your Lordship should move in the matter and give us at least one more non-official Indian member to satisfy the public demand. Speaking for myself, if your Lordship's Government thinks that there should be added to the Committee a non-official European member also, as the Hon'ble Mr. Crum suggested, I have no objection to it. I venture to hope, my Lord, that in the few observations I have made, I have said nothing to rouse feelings on either side, and that they will, therefore, carry weight with your Lordship's Government. I hope that they will be pleased to consider sympathetically the proposal in regard, at any rate, to adding one more non-official Indian member to this Committee. If that is done, I think the Committee's Report may satisfy the public in a larger measure and carry more weight than it otherwise would."

The Hon'ble Mr. N.F. Paton:—"My Lord, as the Hon'ble the Home Member has said, the object of this Commission is to arrive at the truth in regard to the very deplorable occurrences that took place in the Pubjab, and I think that if the widest satisfaction is to be got from the findings of this Commission, it is necessary that the greatest possible confidence should be reposed in it from the start.

"On behalf of the non-official European community, I beg your Excellency's Government to consider the suggestion made by my Hon'ble friend Sir Dinshaw Wacha and by the Hon'ble Mr. Sinha, that there should be nominated on this Committee not only another Indian representative but a representative of the non-official European community as well."

The Hon'ble Pandit Madan Mohan Malaviya:—"My Lord, I am indebted to your Lordship for many things and have to thank you for many kind acts. But throughout the period during which I have had the privilege of being known to you, I have never had occasion to be more thankful to you than when you did not allow me to substitute the Resolution which I wanted to substitute for the one that stands on the paper. My Lord, Simla is one of the worst places that could be selected by the Government of India for its headquarters. Matters of the gravest importance are being dealt with by the Government of India, and we are so far removed from the places where the millions dwell that it is practically impossible for any man like me to know what the currents of public opinion in the country are until perhaps it becomes too late. I gave notice of my intention to substitute a Resolution which your Lordship very kindly disallowed, because in the solitude of Simla and with such support as I could find here, I thought it was best in the circumstances of the situation to substitute the Resolution which I intended to substitute for the one which is on the paper. But from the communications which I have now received from my friends in the country and from the comments which have been published in the press, I find that had I done so I should have exposed myself to their condemnation, because, my Lord, there is one strong chorus of disapproval of the constitution of the proposed Committee, and there is one strong desire that not a Committee, but a Commission should be appointed to inquire into the occurrences in the Punjab. When a gentleman of the position, the weight and experience of Sir Narayan Chandavarkar, once a Chief Justice of Bombay and of Indore, a gentleman known for his moderate views, also says that a Royal Commission should be appointed, when he too expresses dissatisfaction with the constitution of the Committee which has been announced, I submit, my Lord, that a strong case is made out for a re-consideration of the matter.

The press, the Indian press, is almost unanimous in expressing its disapproval of the constitution of the Committee. I do not wish to take up the time of the Council by reading many opinions, because I have to say much. I would invite your Lordship's attention, and the attention of the Government, to what the *Tribune*, the *Bengalee*, the *Bombay Chronicle*, the *Hindu*, the *Independent*, the *Leader* and several other papers have said. That being so, my Lord, I find that I was mistaken in trying to substitute the Resolution which I wanted to substitute for the one before the Council. I am thankful also to find that I was mistaken, because the Hon'ble the Home Member said in one of his answers yesterday that the Government of India is going to appoint a Committee, and I take it therefore that the Committee has not yet been appointed, and that this is just the time when my Resolution should come up before your Excellency's Government for reconsideration.

"Now, my Lord, before proceeding further, I wish to say that the subject matter of my Resolution requires calm consideration, and I wish every one will approach it in a solemn spirit of responsibility. The matter is too sacred, far too serious, to permit of any party or racial considerations to be brought in. And here I may say once more that there is no man living who can feel more deeply sorry than I do for the loss of Mr. Stewart of the National Bank at Amritsar and of other Europeans who were killed there. In talking about the unhappy incidents of Amritsar to friends in Bombay, Poona and Calcutta, I have everywhere expressed deep sorrow that a gentleman so popular as Mr. Stewart was in Amritsar should have been laid low by the hand of some person in a fit of wickedness. My Lord, six other Europeans lost their lives in these disturbances, and I grieve for every one of them. I should be ashamed, I should not be worthy of my religion, if I made any distinction between a European and an Indian where human life was concerned. When the Hon'ble the Home Member referred to the case of Miss Sherwood, he forgot that there were many of us Indians who felt the same grief at the ill-treatment offered to her, as we would have felt if similar ill-treatment had been offered to our own dear sister or mother. But that should not lead any one of us to overlook or minimise the wrongs done to Indians. I ask every Anglo-Indian friend, ask every Anglo-Indian brother and sister, to approach the question in a solemn spirit, and I am sure that when the facts are known, there will not be a single Anglo-Indian man or woman in India, may I go further and say, there will not be a man or woman in the British Empire, who will not feel sorry for the things which have happened and who would not be in sympathy with the object of my Resolution and the proposals which I lay before Government. My Lord, I had no wish to enter here into the details of the harrowing tale of what has happened. I little expected that the Hon'ble the Home Member, himself a previous Judge of the High Court, would import into the discussion of my Resolution irrelevant matters of detail which I had clearly stated ought to be kept out of it.

"I had said that I would not go into details, because the Government of India recognised the need and importance of an inquiry. But the speech which the Home Member has made compels me, in order that nobody should be under a misapprehension, to tell your Lordship and this Council, and through this Council the country and the Empire, that at least 300 and odd human lives were destroyed in the Jallianwala Bagh, under circumstances which will not bear examination when the facts are known. I hold in my hand letters telling me of the deaths of numerous boys who had gone to the Jallianwala Bagh. One of these boys was Abdul Karim, aged 16 years, who passed the last matriculation examination in the first division, the result of which was published after the boy died. He was shot in three places, on his thigh, his chest and his head and expired instantaneously there. I hold in my hand a photograph of another boy named Madan Mohan, aged 13, son of Dr. Mani Ram Dentist, who was shot in the head and died instantaneously. My Lord, let me read this letter from the bereaved father which he addressed to the Health Officer, Amritsar. He says :—

'As desired in the official notification, I give below a brief account of the tragic death of my son Madan Mohan which occurred in Jallianwala Bagh on 13th April last. The delay in submitting this information is due to my absence from Amritsar to Mussoorie hills.

'Jallianwala Bagh is at a distance of about 3 minutes' walk and is the only open place near my house which is opposite to Clock Tower. My son Madan Mohan, aged about 13 years (born on 27th Baisakh 1962), along with his playmates used to visit this open square for play almost daily. On 13th April last, he went there as usual and met his tragic end, having been shot on the head which fractured his skull, he bled and died instantaneously. I with eight or nine others had to search for about half an hour till I could pick up his corpse as it was mixed up with hundreds of dead bodies lying in heaps there, who met their respective ends under circumstances well known. This is how my innocent child of innocent age was murdered by those who allege they acted in the name of Justice, Law and Order, but behaved in a grossly un-British manner.'

"My Lord, I could mention many other equally distressing cases, I have been twice to the Jallianwala Bagh. The walls around it still speak of the murders that were committed there, of the volleys of service bullets that were fired at the people who were assembled at a meeting, who had no arms, who were not making any protest against anything, but were sitting down to hear a lecture. According to the official statement made yesterday, 300 of such men were massacred there. Perhaps, when the inquiry proceeds further, it will be found that the popular estimate that over 1,000 were killed is nearer the truth.

"Now, my Lord, I want the Government to realise the intensity of the feeling of Indians, and I should say they should be the feelings of every human, man and woman, in regard to the circumstances. I impute no blame here to any individual. I have avoided trying to apportion blame. I deplore the event. Whether it was a British officer who was guilty of this massacre of innocents, or an Indian, it is to me a matter of equal sadness and sorrow. It can give me no pleasure to think that any British fellow-subject of mine should have been led by those who were in power, or by his own ignorance or error, to commit any such foul deeds as the people say have been committed. But I do think, my Lord, that the facts which have been stated are grave enough to call for a most impartial and most searching inquiry on the part of His Majesty' Government. I do not know of any event, since the advent of British rule in India, more melancholy, more calculated to distress man than these events of Amritsar, and I therefore say that it is the duty of Government to institute an independent inquiry which will bring out all the real facts. When the facts have been found, I have no doubt that my British fellow-subjects, like any other decent people will call for justice, not with any desire for vengeance, but with the desire that the calls of humanity should be met, the calls of Justice should be satisfied. I regret to say that in his attempt to minimise the value of the proposal I have put forward that the inquiry should be by a Royal Commission, the Home

Member understated the facts. He showed that he does not yet realise the enormity of the evil that has been wrought; that he does not yet feel that, holding the office of the Home Member, he ought to stand forward to plead for justice in the case of every single subject of His Majesty who met with death in these tragic times in the Punjab.

"My Lord, if we ask for a Royal Commission, it is not out of any disrespect to your Excellency or to any member of your Excellency's Government. I shall be sorry if any word which I utter should indicate the smallest disrespect to any member of the Government. But, my Lord, what are the facts ? I ask the Government to look at them in a calm dispassionate manner. Mr. Sinha has referred to some of them. You have to deal with public opinion, and the public feel, by reason of the acts committed during the last few months, that the Government of India having been closely identified with the policy pursued in the Punjab, it ought not, in fairness, in propriety, to deal with the report which will be submitted by the Committee of Inquiry into Punjab affairs. My Lord, if the Government of India will appoint this Committee, that fact will no doubt lead naturally to the conclusion that the report should come to the Government of India. I quite agree with the Home Member there. But it is exactly because it is desired that the report should not be dealt with by the Government of India, that it is urged that the Government of India should not appoint the Committee. I quite agree with the Hon'ble the Home Member that if the Government of India does appoint the Committee, the report should come to it. That is why, holding the view I hold, I have urged in my Resolution that the Governor General in Council should request His Majesty's Government to appoint a Commission. I did not use the word 'Royal' before 'Commission,' because I thought it would be understood by everybody familiar with the work of the Government here and in England that, when I said that His Majesty's Government should appoint a Commission, it meant a Royal Commission. Now, my Lord, Commissions and Committees are appointed with a certain purpose. When there was a great outcry about nationalisation in England in March 1919 and a Commission was to be appointed, the *'New Statesman'* speaking of its Report, said :—

> 'And, human nature being as it is, the character of that report depends, almost entirely, on the way in which the Commission is constituted, on which Mr. Lloyd George's final decision will not be known until this article is in the press.

The Prime Minister has, therefore, in the matter, during these very days, the gravest of responsibilities. He can appoint members, whom the public will accept as quite a good choice, from whom he can confidently expect one report; or he may choose other members, equally acceptable to the public, from whom he will expect another report. What is vital is to get a report that will prevent the strike. Which report is Mr. Lloyd George selecting the members for ?'

"It is vital here to get a report which will state the truth in regard in the occurrences in the Punjab.

"Now, my Lord, if the Government of India are going to appoint the Committee, naturally the public ask what has the Committee to inquire into? Obviously, it has to begin with inquiring into the truth or otherwise of the declaration of open rebellion in Lahore. That was not an act of the Local Government, that was an act of your Excellency's Government and all that followed thereafter—the establishment of martial law and its maintenance in spite of the protests, of the press and the public—is all what the Government of India are responsible for, with which they have been closely, sadly too closely, identified. My Lord, your Lordship has desired that a reference should not be made to the reason for the resignation of Sir Sankaran Nair : but when I referred to it the other day, I mentioned that the reason for it had got into the papers; and to-day, I have got in my hand the Debates of the House of Commons which show that a question was put about it by Colonel Wedgewood, in answer to which Mr. Montagu said—'I have no official information, but understand that Sir Sankaran Nair resigned because he differed from his colleagues in the question of continuing martial law in the Punjab.' Now, my Lord, it is no good running away from facts.

'Our acts our angels are, or good or ill,
Our fatal shadows that walk by us still.'

"If the Government of India or the Governor General in Council declared that there was open rebellion in Lahore and Amritsar, if the Governor General in Council gave his authority for the establishment of martial law in Lahore, Amritsar and other places, if the Governor General in Council maintained martial law when there were protests from all quarters that it should be ended, if the Governor General in Council, on the protest of a colleague that martial law should cease in the Punjab, accepted his resignation and allowed martial law to continue in the Punjab, then, my Lord, you ought to pardon those who think and say that the Government of India is too closely indentified with the policy pursued in the Punjab to take an impartial view of the matters with which the Committee will have to deal, though their bias may be, will be unconscious.

"Lastly, my Lord, there is your Excellency's speech of the 3rd of September. I speak with great respect, but I beg your Lordship and the Government to practise a little introspection on a solemn occasion like this and to reflect whether those who are urging, respectfully urging, that the Committee should not report to your Excellency's Government, are wrong when they find that even in that speech your Lordship showed a very firm attitude in support of what has been done. These are the reasons, my Lord, which have led the public to ask that the Government of India should not appoint the Committee of Inquiry; these are the reasons which justify my Resolution in asking your Excellency's Government to ask His Majesty's Government to appoint a Commission. The Hon'ble the Home Member tries to meet me by saying that the Secretary of State has been consulted. 'It is in consultation *with* him, said he that 'the Committee is going to be appointed.' My Lord, I do not want the Committee to be appointed in consultation *with* the Secretary of State. I want the Committee to be appointed *by* him, in order that the report should go *to* him and therefore be laid at His Majesty's feet.

"My Lord, I will now come to the question of the constitution of the Committee. I beg your Excellency to consider whether public opinion is not justified in expressing disapproval of its constitution. I fear, my Lord, I am exceeding my time. If your Lordship will, in view of the peculiar circumstances permit me to go on, I will....."

The President:—"I have no wish to stop the Hon'ble member, but I think that five minutes ought to see the end of his speech. He has already exceeded his time."

The Hon'ble Pandit Madan Mohan Malaviya:—"Thank you, my Lord. The constitution of the Committee is open to exception. As I said on the first occasion, I do not make the smallest insinuation against the impartiality of any member of the Committee, but not knowing some of the gentlemen who have been nominated the public are sceptical about them. And I am bound to place the public view before this Council and the Government. My Lord, I hope the Hon'ble Mr. Rice will absolutely excuse me if I refer to him by name. The objection is that an additional Secretary to the Government of India in the Home Department should be appointed by the Government of India to a Committee of Inquiry which is to enquire into matters with which the Government of India is identified. I refer to it to show that the Government themselves are to blame for the criticism which is being hurled at the constitution of the Committee.

"Now, my Lord, I will make one suggestion, the Commission which I would suggest should be one consisting of, say, Lord Haldane, Viscount Esher and Sir Lawrence Jenkins, or I should like to have a Commission consisting of Mr. Austen Chamberlain an *ex*-Secretary of State for India, and Lord Hardinge and Lord Curzon, *ex*-Governors General of India. My Lord, I suggest such a Commission as it will command confidence all round. Speaking of Lord Hardinge I am reminded as one speaker has already said that he passed through more strenuous times in India than any predecessor of his had known, and let us hope any successor will know. He very narrowly escaped death at the hands of a villain, and yet, my Lord, the first thing he uttered to Sir Guy Fleetwood Wilson—when he saw him after the bomb had struck him—and I heard it from Sir Guy's own lips, was 'No change of policy, Wilson' ; and Sir Guy Fleetwood Wilson replied 'No change of policy, your Excellency.' Martial law was not then declared and people were not subjected to any of the troubles they have had to suffer in the Punjab. Lord Hardinge knew the people, he loved them, and I could not suggest a better name for the Commission. Then, I suggest Mr. Austen Chamberlain. We have not had the honour of welcoming him in India, but we have faith in him as an English gentleman that he will do the right thing if he presided over the Commission. And I name Lord Curzon, because I have confidence that, if Lord Curzon came out and inquired into all that happened, he would not spare the wrong doers and the public would be satisfied with his verdict. I place before the Government the option of one of these two Committees. I do not ask for the inclusion of a single Indian name, and I am sure that, if it were necessary, a hundred platforms would support my view and make it clear that the public will be quite satisfied if we had a Commission of the kind I have suggested.

"But, my Lord, if you will not have a Commission of that kind, then you must recognise the justice of putting on the proposed Committee at least one more Indian, not a safe man whose views will not come into conflict with the views of the Government, but a gentleman who enjoys the confidence of the public, and who may be supposed to represent the opposition. 'Ditcher', writing in *'Capital'* has done me the honour of suggesting that I should be placed on the Committee. My Lord, I suggest a better name. I know many facts about the occurrences in the Punjab. I venture to think that I know more facts about these distressing events than probably any member of the Government, either the Government of India or the Government of the Punjab does; but there is one gentleman who knows more about them, and that is my esteemed friend the Hon'ble Pandit Moti Lal Nehru, Advocate of the Allahabad High Court. He has, my Lord, at the sacrifice of a fee a thousand rupees a day, laboured for many days in the Punjab sifting out facts, and gathering evidence. He is in possession of a volume of facts which will be of great help to the Committee. I suggest that as Mr. Montagu appointed Lord Sydenham to the Joint Committee, so your Excellency's Government may appoint Pandit Moti Lal Nehru, a clear-headed advocate and a sound lawyer, as a member of the Committee. If he is not acceptable, then I would suggest that Justice Sir Abdur Rahim may be so appointed. My Lord, these are suggestions which, I hope, the Government will consider.

"I will now deal with the remarks....."

The President:—"The Hon'ble member has been speaking already five minutes over the allotted time, and I think that he ought to observe the rules."

The Hon'ble Pandit Madan Mohan Malaviya:—"May I have a few minutes more ?"

The President:—"I gave the Hon'ble member five minutes, and those five minutes are already up."

The Hon'ble Pandit Madan Mohan Malaviya:—"Would your Lordship kindly allow me a few minutes more?"

The President:—"How many minutes more?"

The Hon'ble Pandit Madan Mohan Malaviya:—"Five, if you please, my Lord."

The President:—"I will give you five minutes."

The Hon'ble Pandit Madan Mohan Malaviya:—"Thank you, my Lord. I just want to advert to a few other remarks which have fallen from some Hon'ble members in the course of the debate. I will first refer to what Sir Umar Hayat Khan said. He expressed almost a resentment that some of us from outside the Punjab should have gone to that province. I think he will not find anybody in the Punjab to support that view. If he went there, my Lord, I think, he would find that the work of the *Seva Samiti*, and the work of Pandit Moti Lal Nehru and myself has met with the hearty appreciation of a vast body of our fellowmen; he would find that three hundred and odd families of those who had either been killed or had otherwise suffered, or been deprived of liberty were being relieved by the agency of the *Seva Samiti*, of which I have the honour to be the President and Pandit Moti Lal Nehru, the Vice-President. He would also find that we have helped many persons to have their appeals filed before the Privy Council. I should not have referred to these matters were it not for the fact that, while he himself was not able to render any assistance to the people of the Punjab in their distress, he should yet make it a grievance that some people from outside the province went there to render such assistance. We do not regard ourselves as outsiders. We consider every countryman of ours, wherever he may be, as a countryman.

"Then, my Lord, with regard to the remarks of the Hon'ble Mr. Crum, I would say this that we have absolutely no racial feeling in this matter. I desire and expect that Anglo-Indians and Indians should co-operate in this matter to find out the truth, and I support the suggestion he made that it should be an instruction to the Committee that they should recommend what reparation should be made to those or their relations who suffered during these tragic disturbances. As regards his suggestion that there should be an Anglo-Indian member added to the Committee, I have not the least objection to it either. But, my Lord, I do take exception to what he said regarding an assurance being given to the scattered European community that it shall be safeguarded in future. My Lord, the community as a whole, Indian, and European, has to be safeguarded in future. The reason why these five Europeans met with their untimely end, will probably be known when the Committee of Inquiry will report. It will probably be found that the Indians were to blame, but that provocation had been given to them which led to the unfortunate, deplorable, detestable crimes which some of them committed. Before the crimes were committed, some Indian lives had been destroyed by the firing that took place at the railway bridge at Amritsar. The Deputy Commissioner of Amritsar deposed in one of the cases which was tried by one of the Martial Law Commissions, that he had found no evidence to show that any excesses had been committed by the mob before the firing took place.

"Lastly, my Lord, I wish to say a few words about some of the remarks of His Honour Sir Edward Maclagan. I need hardly again protest my deep respect for His Honour. But, while I feel grateful that he has shown consideration in many respects to those who are at present locked up in His Majesty's jails, I regret to think that he fails to realise that no reduction of sentences, that no such amelioration of the hard conditions of jail life as he has been good enough to bring about, can relieve those who are unjustly suffering imprisonment of the poignant grief which they feel every moment of their existence in the jail. I would ask His Honour seriously to think whether any mitigation of sentence or relief given in the manner indicated above, can obliterate the sorrow, the indescribable grief of those who are at present unjustly locked up and are undergoing imprisonment in the jails of the Punjab. My Lord, I think His Honour said that he would not disturb the findings of the Commissions. Probably he felt that he could not. But, my Lord, most of the 1,500 men who are locked up in the jails ought to be as free as we sitting here to-day are. I request, therefore, that whether the Committee of Inquiry comes four weeks hence or earlier, your Excellency's Government and His Honour the Lieutenant-Governor of the Punjab should seriously consider whether on such security or securities, personal or pecuniary or both, as may seem to him adequate, those men who have not been concerned in arson, or murder or pillage should not be released, both in order that pending the result of the inquiry, they may not suffer further unnecessary imprisonment, and in order that they should be able to give evidence before the Committee and have their case properly put before it, I earnestly hope the Government will be pleased to consider this suggestion."

The Hon'ble Sir William Vincent :—"My Lord, the Hon'ble Mover has complained that by reason of his solitude in Simla and of his inability to consult his colleagues he was not able to modify his Resolution earlier. If that is so, my Lord, the Hon'ble Memer has been much maligned. The general impression is that he has been having daily consultation with non-official members, that he has interviewed them one after another. Hon'ble members will know if this is correct as not, and also whether he has not taken every opportunity of ascertaining what their views are. I have been told in fact that there is no legitimate measure for winning support for his

Resolution which he has not taken and his complaint that the Resolution was not amended because of his being unable to consult his colleagues is not one therefore....."

(*The Hon'ble Pandit Madan Mohan Malaviya here got up to intervene.*)

The President :—"Order, order, the Hon'ble Member has already taken up the time of the Council."

The Hon'ble Pandit Madan Mohan Malaviya :—"I only want to correct a statement of fact. I did consult some Members and it was only after consulting them that I sent in notice of the amendment."

The Hon'ble Sir William Vincent :—"My Lord, I find it a little difficult to proceed if I am subjected to these constant interruptions. I have allowed a great many statements of the Hon'ble Member, even some which I considered to be misstatements, to go unchallenged, and I ask for some consideration from the Hon'ble Member.

"There is another point in the Hon'ble Mover's reply to which I wish to draw attention, and that is, the question of minimising the character of the disorders and outrage. I again ask the Hon'ble Member how the attacks on these unfortunate non-officials can possibly be justified. There may be questions as to the propriety of the action taken by the troops and police on particular occasions, but I have never yet heard any suggestion that these attacks on these private individuals were not absolutely unprovoked attacks on perfectly harmless people not connected with the Government at all; attacks on the conduct of officials are another matter, but these bank managers who were murdered were not officials of any kind, and I think that it is unfair even to insinuate in this Council that there was any justification for the murders of these unfortunate men—murders which the Hon'ble Member regrets so greatly and at the same time attempts in a manner to justify—perhaps 'justify' is too hard a word, I ought not to use it, but murders at any rate in regard to which he pleads extenuating circumstances when he says that after the inquiry is made it will be found that the victims were also a good deal in fault. I suggest that this is prejudicing the inquiry in an eminently unfair manner.

"Similarly, I refer to his observations about the Jallianwala Bagh. That is a matter which will come up before the Committee. If it is found that there was no justification for the firing, then will be the time to decide what action should be taken; but I ask this Council now not to prejudge any individual or any officer of Government in this matter. The Hon'ble Mr. Chanda, if I may say so, took up very nearly the same line as the Hon'ble Mover, and in my humble judgment, there were other members of this Council including Mr. Ayyangar who spoke, not as if they wanted an inquiry, but as if they really wanted this Council to prejudge the case to create an atmosphere against the Government, to induce a feeling of prejudice and bias in the minds of Hon'ble Members, and in fact to condemn in advance those into whose conduct they were professing to ask for an inquiry. That is an attitude which, I think, is unfair to those whose conduct is impugned.

"There is only one other remark that I have to make. It was said that there were great protests at the time against the imposition of martial law. My Lord, the position is really this; there is now a tendency to minimise the disturbances, to make out that they were much less serious than they actually were. The gravity of the situation in April last is now forgotten. At this time there was a general feeling of great apprehension throughout the whole of India; there was no word of protest at all; it was some time afterwards that we first heard of these protests. When the disorder was at its height we were asked to suppress it firmly. When this was done, men, in some case those very men who asked us to deal with it at the time, turned round on the authorities. A few years ago when there were disturbances in Bihar and the Government failed to take sufficiently drastic action to meet with the approval of certain papers, they were blamed for not doing more, for not having taken sufficiently severe measures. In the present case there was a crisis of the first magnitude, our officers were called upon to arrive at important decisions at a moment's notice, very momentous decisions on which the peace of the country depended; at the time they were acclaimed and applauded by many for having saved the country. Now, my Lord, that the danger is past, there is an attempt to turn on them and to protest that their conduct was cruel and unreasonably severe.

"My Lord, there is only one final point that I wish to mention with regard to a remark of the Hon'ble Mr. Sinha. He said that the Hon'ble the Home Member had maintained a non-possumus attitude, I think that this was the expression that was used, in regard to certain modifications which have been proposed. My Lord, if that was the impression which I created, I can only regret it. What I wished to convey was that a number of new suggestions had been pressed on Government, in regard to which it was impossible for an individual member of this Government to express an opinion, and that therefore I could make no statement on these suggestions. If that, my Lord, is taking up a non-possumus attitude, then I must plead guilty. But I think a fairer and broader interpretation might well be placed upon my words."

The Hon'ble Sir Dinshaw Wacha :—"May I make a suggestion, my Lord, that the Resolution be divided into two and put separately?"

The President :—"I think we have discussed the Resolution as a whole, and I shall put it as a whole."

The Resolution was put and negatived.

In the course of the debate on the Hon'ble Mr. Chanda's Resolution *re* Inquiry into firing upon crowds at Calcutta, the Hon'ble Major Malik Sir Umar Hayat Khan Tiwana made the following remarks:—

The Hon'ble Major Malik Sir Umar Hayat Khan :—"My Lord, up to a certain extent I will support the Hon'ble gentleman on my left and the case is this. I think, wherever these disturbances took place, whether in Calcutta, in Delhi or in the Punjab, the origin of all of them was the same, and if the same Committee were to make inquiries they would find that all these disturbances were connected. This, I think, would help the inquiry to a very great extent and if inquiries were made in Calcutta by the same Committee, it would be much better. I am very glad that the Hon'ble gentleman read through all those papers, by which I have been able to find out that exactly what was happening in Calcutta happened, I believe, in Delhi as well as in the Punjab. That also shows, that as the origin of these disturbances is one, the same Committee should investigate into them. There have been differences between what happened in the Punjab and in Calcutta and Delhi, but this is due to the fact that there are certain peculiarities in the Punjab. It is the home of soldiers, it is the home of brave men, and when they are excited naturally they do certain things which other people do not, and if there were any difference between the happenings in the Punjab and elsewhere, it is due to this fact. Then many other things have been said by my Hon'ble friend such as the words used, namely, *'Gandhi ji ki jai.'* Well, the same words were used everywhere which again shows that the origin was one and the same. As he said, the boys were taught first to begin because it was considered that nobody would fire on them. That was the kind of thing which was done everywhere, so that it looks as if the people who started this were at one place and they planned these things and then sent out orders all round, so as to be obeyed. In the same way the time which was chosen synchronised. It was a very bad time and it was chosen when big fairs were being held not only in one part of the country but all over the country, where not only people from the cities but people from outside attended. It was considered that if such a propaganda was started in the cities, those men would go into the country and induce the country people to join. It would have been a very serious thing for the Punjab if this had happened, because the country is the place from where the soldiers are recruited. It was thought that the soldiers would join, but these men had been in France and elsewhere and they knew what our Government was and how strong it was. That was why they did not join. But if this plot had been properly planned out, and the soldiers had been fools enough to join in it, there would have been very great difficulty, because, being the hot weather, the only troops available would have been the English and the Gurkhas, who cannot fight so well at that time of the year. Again, it is known that Kabul only joined because men were sent there. If anything had happened to the soldiers and, if the enemy from outside had come into India, I do not know how difficult would have been the situation thus created; nothing could have been worse....."

The Hon'ble Pandit Madan Mohan Malaviya :—"May I rise to point of order? Is my friend the Hon'ble Member in order in talking of these things on this Resolution?"

The President :—"I presume he is leading up to some point."

The Hon'ble Major Malik Sir Umar Hayat Khan :—"I am referring to these things simply to show that there were differences in the Punjab. The differences were due to the peculiar circumstances of the Punjab. I want to show that the origin of the disturbances in Calcutta, Delhi, Hyderabad and all these places was the same; there were these differences in the Punjab, while in other places, the people being more learned adopted a different course. I only want to show that, as the circumstances were one, the same Committee ought to be asked to investigate into the happenings in Calcutta.

* * * * *

(5)—From Proceedings of Meeting held on September 18, 1919

The Indemnity Bill

The Hon'ble Sir William Vincent :—"My Lord, I move for leave to introduce a Bill to indemnify officers of Government and other persons in respect of certain acts done under martial law, and to provide for other matters in connection therewith. This measure, my Lord, has been the subject of so much discussion both in the Press and by other competent authorities, that I think I ought to set out to the Council in some detail the reasons that have led the Government to introduce the Bill at this moment and to explain *seriatim* the effect of, at any rate, the more important clauses of the Bill; and I will ask Hon'ble Members to listen to me as carefully as they can, to follow in particular the detailed statement of the effect of the clauses, to view this matter without any kind of bias and to get rid of any misapprehension as to the intentions of Government or as to the meaning of the Act, which may have been created by writings or speeches outside this Council.

"My Lord, wherever martial law is declared, as it was recently in the Punjab, it inevitably follows that speedy and decisive action has to be taken by the executive officers of Government for the restoration of order. Not only does this responsibility lie directly on the supreme military commander, but also on those who are subordinate to him: that is, he gives orders which he thinks necessary, and it is their bounden duty to carry out those orders. It follows that frequently action which is just and proper, though not necessarily legal, is taken by these authorities.

"They cannot possibly wait in such circumstances to examine the law and see whether what they propose to do is strictly legal or not; delay at such a time is fatal. The authorities and the officers concerned have to act at once. Indeed, the very meaning of martial law is, that it confers powers to maintain order at any cost, that may be necessary, of life or property. That is the essence, as I understand it, of martial law. Such conduct will in some cases necessarily involve an infringement of the personal rights of individuals, either of their liberty or their rights in regard to property; and when martial law expires, an Indemnity Act of some character is the inevitable consequence. I think members in this Council will realise that if such an Indemnity Act is not passed, no officer charged with the very irksome and responsible duty of restoring order will ever act with the confidence that is really essential for the effective handling of the situation. If he has to wait, to hesitate, to examine the law, to consult legal authorities here and there, the time for action may be gone, and the very mischief he seeks to stop develop to a dangerous degree. That such an Indemnity Act is the normal consequence of any period of martial law is, I believe, accepted by all constitutional writers. I do not wish to weary the Council by citations from a number of these, but I will content myself with one :—

> 'If at a period of national danger a breach of the law is demanded, if not by absolute necessity yet by stress of political expediency, the law breaker whether he be a General or other servant of the Crown who acts *bona fide* solely with a view to public interest may confidently count on protection by an Act of Indemnity. . . . .
>
> 'Statutes of this description have been invariably, or almost invariably, passed after the determination of a period of civil war or disturbance and the very object is to protect officers and others who in the interests of their country have in time of common danger pursued an illegal course of conduct.'

"These quotations are from one of the greatest writers on Constitutional Law, Dicey. In fact, we know that whenever there has been an insurrection or civil war or invasion by a foreign power, Acts of this character have invariably been passed. There was one in England after the insurrection of 1715, again after 1745; we had one in this country after 1857, and more than one instance of such Acts is to be found in the various Colonial Legislatures, including the Legislature of South Africa. Further than this, when a military officer is acting under the stress of such circumstances, in a crisis of great magnitude, it is essential that he must have behind him some sanction to enforce his orders; reference to ordinary Courts in such cases is impracticable. It would involve delay which would be fatal to the very object he has in view. Consequently summary measures, often stern and always of a very speedy character, are necessary if order is to be restored. There are some who think that these summary orders necessarily connote injustice and an undue degree of harshness, but it is not correct to think that this is either the practice or the intention of many commanders. I should like to cite from the Martial Law Regulations passed in Lahore on this point. This is an order by Col. Frank Johnson, a somewhat well-known name.

> 'In order to prevent the occurrence of regrettable incidents, it must be clearly understood that the institution of summary law neither necessitates nor justifies the committal of excesses, either in the maintenance of order or in enforcing obedience of martial regulations or the infliction of punishment. It cannot be too clearly impressed upon all ranks that temporary

supersession of the ordinary process of civil law by the introduction of summary law does not mean that justice ceases to be administered; on the contrary, the suspension of the usual safeguards make it doubly imperative that all concerned should bear in mind that it is up to them to see that justice and not irresponsible violence is administered.'*

"It is however essential that the military authorities in such cases should have power to come to swift decisions of a most important character; power to take prompt action on all matters affecting the State; power to punish summarily and effectively those who endanger the peace.

"My Lord, it may be said that martial law was not necessary in the Punjab and that the Government made a mistake in proclaiming it. I do not seek to argue that point now. I believe that any such course would be unfair to those concerned, primarily or indirectly concerned, until the evidence of the facts has been recorded by the Committee of Inquiry. The decision on that matter must rest with the Committee in a great measure and after their report has been received, with other authorities. But, irrespective of this question, the position of our officers must be protected. I do not know if I make myself clear on that point. What I wish to say is this, whether martial law was necessary or not, our officers, our subordinate officers were bound to carry out their duties, and to give effect to the orders given them and they cannot be penalised on that account. I think the case has been very clearly put on this point by a writer in, I think, the '*Civil and Military Gazette*' recently. He called himself 'An Indian Student of constitutional law' or by some such title. I commend that article to the consideration of Members of this Council. It appears to me to put the case for an Indemnifying Act both impartially and fairly.

"So far I have been dealing with the part of this Bill which deals with indemnifying officers of Government. The second part deals with the validating to a certain extent of a number of sentences which have been passed. I shall explain this in detail later, but it is clear, as I said before, that where military officers are given power to issue certain orders, it is essential that they should also have authority to enforce those orders. There must be some sanction behind them, some power of enforcing order speedily and effectively and in

* For full text of this order, see Appendix I, pp. 238-239, *ante*.

many cases—in fact I believe this is the normal course—summary Courts are appointed to administer justice in such circumstances. They do not deal normally with all criminal cases, but only with cases arising out of a breach of military regulations or cases connected with the disturbances, and I believe I am right, so far as the Punjab is concerned, in saying that the duties of the summary Courts were confined to this class of cases; but I speak subject to correction on this matter. It is sometimes supposed that these summary Courts, however, dealt only with petty offences, such as breaches of military law regulations. That is an entirely incorrect assumption, and if Hon'ble Members will see the statement* that, I think, was laid on the table here recently, if not I will have it so placed, they will see that the summary Courts dealt with many offences of great gravity, such as arson, theft, rioting, breaches of the Railway Act—and they are really very serious—and offences under the Telegraph Act, which really meant the endangering of all communications both between the Local Government and their officers and between the Government of India and the Local Government. Many of these men are now under confinement, and I want to make it clear to the Council that, unless their confinement is now ratified in some manner, then the continued detention of these men in jail is illegal. In fact from the date on which martial law expired our only justification for retaining these men in custody was our intention to introduce an Act of this character at the earliest opportunity.

"My Lord, I will now, if I may, proceed to explain the Bill clause by clause. I will not deal with clause 1, which is of no great importance, but proceed at once to clause 2. That clause indemnifies any officer of Government, whether civil or military, from any action civil or criminal, in respect of any matter or thing done for the purpose of maintaining or restoring order. But I want Hon'ble Members to read and fully consider the effect of the proviso to that clause 'provided that such officer or person has acted in good faith and in a reasonable belief that his action was necessary for the said purposes.' Those are really the governing words of the clause. I think I have already said, or at any rate I say now, that this Bill will in no way forestall the inquiry by the Committee, and I will proceed to justify that statement. I do not think that any member of this Council will for a moment suppose that the Committee of Inquiry, which

---

* See *Supplement II.*

assesses the blame for these disturbances, will recommend any form of punishment for any officer of Government who has acted *bona fide* and in a reasonable belief that what he did was necessary. Further, in any case the report of the Committee is not affected by this Bill. This Bill protects officers against proceedings in the Courts of Justice. The report of this Committee, whatever be its value, will in no sense be evidence for the purposes of any such cases; that is a matter which can only be decided on evidence in the Courts. The Government of India have decided, for the satisfaction of their own conscience and to meet the public demand, to appoint a Committee to inquire into these disturbances, and their action on the report of that Committee will not be limited or barred by this Act in any way. This Bill simply deals with suits and legal proceedings, and really all that it seeks to do is to protect from legal proceedings *bona fide* action taken with a reasonable belief that it was necessary to suppress disorder, and not any action taken *mala fide* or without good reason. We make no attempt by this Bill at any rate to protect officers who have been guilty of excesses which cannot be justified by the terms of this proviso. Now I myself shall be much surprised and disappointed if the Council will not give protection to officers for actions of this character, actions which are morally right though they may be legally wrong, that is, actions for which no strict legal justification can be made out. If this Council says that in a time of this character when the country was in great disorder—and I put it very mildly—officers who acting on the understanding that martial law had been proclaimed by an authority which is superior to them, over whose actions they have no control, if officers acting on that assumption and acting *bona fide* and perfectly reasonably are not to be protected by Government, then the future prospect of Government officers is very serious. How can any member of this Council expect an officer to act confidently, firmly and decisively, if he knows that this Legislative Council and the Government will repudiate his action at the first opportunity? Is he not entitled to come down here and say: 'I have done what I was told. I have acted perfectly reasonably, I have acted fairly, I have acted *bona fide;* now give me that protection which I am entitled to by all constitutional practice.' My Lord, in a Resolution published by this Government some time ago, I think during the period of the disturbances, we solemnly promised that we would afford all those charged with the onerous duty of restoring order our full countenance and support, and it is in fulfilment of that promise that I now come to this Council and ask Hon'ble Members to ratify what we then promised, believing that that is a just and honourable course which must commend itself to all Members here. As I said before, I conceive it to be impossible that the Committee should censure anyone who is not guilty, who has acted *bona fide* and in a reasonable belief, that his action was necessary, and the report of the Committee will not and cannot affect the liability of officers of Government in the Courts of law. That is the reason, my Lord, why I say that this Bill, which merely seeeks to protect those who have done their duty, in no way forestalls the report of inquiry by this Committee.

"I now come on to section 3; and this is a section which, I am afraid, I shall have to explain at some length, because there exists considerable misapprehension about it. Section 3 says:

> 'For the purposes of section 2 a certificate of Secretary to Government that any act was done under the order of an officer of Government shall be conclusive proof thereof, and all action taken for the aforesaid purposes shall be deemed to have been taken in good faith and in a reasonable belief that it was necessary therefor unless the contrary is proved.'

"Now a certificate of a Secretary to Government only proves, and the Hon'ble the Law Member will bear me out here, that the act was done under the orders of an officer of Government. Many private individuals during these recent disturbances have assisted Government in various ways, many indeed have been of the greatest assistance to the authorities; and all that this portion of the clause says is, that if any man acted under the orders of an officer of Government and can get a certificate to that effect, thus far and no further is that certificate conclusive proof of that fact. The question of *bona fides,* as I understand the Bill, is a matter for the Court entirely. That is, a man will go to the Court and it will be for the Court to say, whether his action was *bona fide* and reasonable, and what fairer proposition could be put to this Council? When a man goes down the Court shall have power to say, 'yes, you did so and so, whether it was reasonable or not, that shall be judged by one of the Government judges acting in his judicial capacity.' My Lord, if there is any cause of complaint in this matter, it might well be on the side of Government officers that the Bill does not go far enough, and if Hon'ble Members will look to the Act of 1860, which was passed after the Mutiny, they will see that the provisions of that Act went very much further than this, and that when a Secretary to Government there ratified the conduct of an officer, this ratification absolved the man altogether from any possibility of a suit; that is the kind of certificate which apparently some Hon'ble Members think that this Bill provides. It does not. If this Bill had come on for consideration after the Commission of Inquiry, after the whole of these matters had been investigated, it might have been possible to frame it in that way. It is true, however, that this clause does go thus far, that it provides that 'all action taken for the aforesaid purposes' that is for restoring order, 'shall be deemed to have been taken in good faith and in a reasonable belief that it was necessary therefor unless the contrary is proved.'

"My Lord, is a Government officer to be denied even that protection, that he shall be presumed to have acted in good faith, that he shall be presumed to be innocent until he is proved to be guilty! Is that much to ask from this Council? Is that a reasonable request, or is it not? I believe also that a clause of this kind is a normal condition—I speak again subject to correction—of many Indemnity Bills of this character.

"My Lord, I now pass on to clause 4, which sanctions the retention in custody of persons convicted by summary Courts. I have explained to this Council that many of these men have been convicted of serious offences; that they are in reality dangerous criminals whom it would be most unsafe to release wholesale upon the countryside. I believe—I have been told this by the Punjab Government also—that any such release would not be compatible with the public safety. But I ask Members of Council to read this clause again with clause 6. Clause 4 says: 'that every person confined under or by virtue of a sentence passed by a Court, or any other officer acting in a judicial capacity shall be deemed to have been lawfully confined and shall continue so until discharged by lawful order or released by order of the Governor General in Council.' Clause 6, however, again limits that and restricts the operation of that clause. First of all it says:—

> 'Nothing in this Act shall apply to any sentence passed or punishment inflicted by or under the orders of any Commission appointed under the Martial Law Ordinance, 1919.'

"Members of this Council are aware that various persons who have been convicted by the Commissioners appointed under this Ordinance have appealed to the Privy Council. It would obviously be improper for us to attempt in any way by an Act now to invalidate the actions of those Commissioners. The sentences depend for their validity upon Ordinances already passed. I do not propose to discuss the question of these Ordinances here for one moment, nor would it be relevant to this discussion. All I wish to point out is, that this Bill in no way affects sentences by Commissioners appointed under the Ordinances. Then there is a second limitation, that the Bill in no way prejudices the right of any person who thinks he has been dealt with unjustly to appeal to the Privy Council from sentences of these summary Courts. There is no intention, even if there were the power, of which there may be some doubt, of interfering with that right. Any man who has been convicted by one of these summary Courts is at liberty to go and seek for leave to appeal to the Privy Council just as if this Bill had not been passed. I tried to make that clear because it has been suggested that in some way the action of this Government, in introducing this Bill, is intended to prejudice the authority and power of the Judicial Committee. It is quite clear to my mind that it is not so. It has been our deliberate intention to make that abundantly manifest to every reasonable man. At the same time, my Lord, I do admit that there are many men in this country, perfectly loyal citizens, men of weight and authority, who have grave apprehensions and felt great uneasiness as to many of these convictions. We believe that many of these apprehensions are ill-founded, but still there is no getting over the fact that there is this sense of uneasiness as to the correctness of all these convictions. That apprehension has been alleviated to a considerable extent, but not removed, by the admitted clemency of His Honour the Lieutenant-Governor, and the debate on the Resolution to appoint a Committee to investigate these occurrences indicated—I think, on the part of many Members not hostile to this Government, not unreasonably opposed to everything we do, but Members who are ready to co-operate with Government in this matter, in all matters, and who really seek to do what is right—uneasiness in the mind of many Members of this Council and a feeling that some of these sentences had not been examined with sufficient care; and there was further indication of that feeling in the proposal made for revising the terms of reference to the Committee. I think Hon'ble Members will remember the various suggestions. Well, to meet these apprehensions the Government of India have decided to have all these cases examined and revised by two Judges of the High Court, one being an Indian and one being a European, in order that they may recommend to His Excellency the Viceroy or the Governor General in Council, as the case may be, through the Local Government, such action as they think fit, either in the direction of remitting or commuting sentences, or any other course they may think desirable, having regard to the circumstances of the case. My Lord, it is the desire of the Government of India that full justice should be done in this matter. They are as anxious as any Member of this Council that innocent men should not be detained in jail. One point, however, I have not made clear, and that is, that our intention is that only the cases of those men who remain under sentences should normally be inquired into by these Judges, though they will also deal with any other cases which may specifically be referred to them by His Excellency or the Government of India.

"Now, I do hope that this will meet the approval of Council and indicate the desire of Government to prevent injustice. I believe that such a Tribunal as we propose, being composed of judicial officers, will be far more effective for the purpose of seeing that justice is done than any Committee of Inquiry which may be appointed to investigate the general occurrences. For, not only will the officers have the advantage of judicial experience, but, by reason of their being on the spot, they can begin the work immediately and directly. So that I hope the matter will be dealt with with reasonable expedition.

"There is only one other clause in the Bill, clause 5, to which I need draw attention, and that provides for the payment of compensation where the property of any person has been commandeered by the military authorities. Members of this Council are aware that when martial law is declared and when the military authorities take over control, they frequently have to, and frequently do, commandeer property for their own use, if such action is in the public interests necessary. All that this clause proposes is, that the Government should pay compensation for such commandeering and provides the means by which the compensation may be assessed.

"My Lord, summarising what I have said, I want to make one of two points quite clear. First, this Bill is the inevitable consequence of martial law. Whether martial law was necessary or not, we must at least protect our officers. The Bill will not in any way forestall the decision of the Committee of Inquiry. The indemnity of officers is limited, and reasonably limited, to those who have acted *bona fide,* the question of *bona fides* will be decided by the Courts, and the validating clause, to which I have referred already, does not affect either any case tried by the Commissions or any right of appeal to the Privy Council. Further, in order to prevent any injustice, and, so far as we are able, to enable us to exercise clemency, so far as is compatible with the public safety, we will have the cases of the men convicted by these summary Courts and still in jail revised by two of the best judicial authorities that we can procure. My Lord, I contend that this is a reasonable Bill, a Bill of the most moderate character, and that it only affords such protection as it is essential for us to give to our officers, which they have a right to demand of us and which it is our paramount duty to give them. I may be asked why the Bill is introduced at this session. Indeed, I promised the Council to explain this, and, having regard to what your Excellency said, if I am only to speak once both on the Bill and the amendment, save for my right of reply, I ought to explain now why the Bill is introduced at the present juncture. The reason is very simple. If it is not passed now, if it is not brought into effect now, then our officers, officers who, *ex hypothesi*, have behaved fairly and properly, will be left liable to suits at the instigation of any malicious person. Is that reasonable, is that fair? I may be told that no suits will be brought in the immediate future. My Lord, suits might be brought, might even be decreed against them before any Bill was brought forward in this Council, not against men who have acted *mala fide*, but against those who have merely done their duty with the greatest care and in the most reasonable manner. I say to this Council that that is a position to which no reasonable man here can ask us to submit our officers. Many of the men against whom suits might be brought, against whom action might be taken, may have gone from this country. Should they be left with this sword of Damocles hanging over them although they have done nothing to deserve it? Is that fair? Then, there is another point. If this Council does not validate the detention in jail of these criminals, to whom I referred just now, then we shall have at once to release the whole number of these dangerous offenders on the world. I have told you that we have consulted the Punjab Government on this matter, and they were definitely of opinion that such a release was not compatible with the public safety. The men are not convicted of minor petty offences at all; they are men who were engaged in the burning and looting of stations, in the attacks on railway lines and in the cutting of telegraph wires, guilty of theft and very many of them of arson. They are a class of men who cannot be released with safety at present, and I submit that this Council will be well advised if they do not ask us to release them. My Lord, looking round the Council here, I see many members who have large vested interests in the country. I should like to know how long they would retain their property, their wealth or even their lives if the forces of disorder were once to break loose in this country. I ask the Members of this Council to look at the question in that light. Is it not their bounden duty to afford protection to those who have undertaken terrible responsibilities in times of difficulty and done their duty *bona fide* and honestly? That is the question that I put to each Member here. I want them to visualise what the position of an officer of Government in such circumstances is. Take the case of a young military officer. He does not know whether martial law has been rightly or wrongly proclaimed. His one object is to perform his duty, to do it fairly and honestly. He is told that the country is in disorder and that his duty is to suppress it. He tries in a reasonable and fair way to carry out what he believes to be his duty, and then, when he comes to this Council for protection, my Lord, are we to say, 'No, we cannot give it to you until an inquiry has taken place,' or 'Postpone it till some other day.' I do not hope and trust that this Council will not endorse any such monstrous proposition. It is often assumed that it is only Europeans and Government that are interested in the maintenance of order. Hon'ble Members know that that is not so. Once rioting breaks out, who are the people who suffer? At least some Hon'ble Members of this Council know that they would be the first—their whole existence depends on the maintenance of law and order in this country. And how can they expect, how can any Member of this Council expect, military officers of Government to do their duty unless they receive reasonable support? A military officer is in a position of peculiar difficulty. If he does not suppress disorders, he is liable to censure, blame and punishment at the hands of his superior officers. If he does not take adequate measures, he may be removed from his office. Why, even civil officers in England have been held to blame for action of that kind. Take the case of the Mayor of Bristol. After the Bristol riots he was accused of failing to do his duty in not having taken adequate measures to quell the disorders and he was prosecuted. But, apart from his personal responsibility, every officer of Government in this country is responsible under the system of administration for the lives and property of many hundreds and thousands living under his charge. Let each Member visualise to himself what his position would be faced with these difficulties, often with insufficient forces at his disposal to cope with disorders, doing what he thinks to be his duty, acting according as God gives him to see the right, and then being penalised and held liable to prosecution and persecution afterwards for no reason whatsoever.

"My Lord, I have spoken with some heat because I want to make it plain that I conceive that refusal to grant the limited protection which we ask for our officers would be a gross injustice to those whom we have solemnly undertaken to protect.

"My Lord, I have attempted throughout my speech to say nothing that can in any way prejudice the result of the inquiry by the Commission. I have dealt solely with principles, not with particular actions. Whether any particular action was reprehensible, whether it was right or whether it was wrong, is not a matter which comes within the scope of the Bill. That is a matter either for the Committee of Inquiry and subsequent action by Government or for decision by the Courts. I have endeavoured throughout my speech to avoid saying anything which may prejudice the inquiry. I have also endeavoured, and I hope successfully, to avoid saying anything which might promote racial ill-feeling, and I would ask Hon'ble Members who follow me, so far as they are able, to follow the same course, remembering always how far the deliberate promotion of racial feeling—no, I will cancel that word 'deliberate,' for I do not wish to excite any bitterness myself—I will say ill-feeling has been responsible for the deplorable loss of life, and for the terrible happenings in this country. I would ask each Member of this Council, in speaking to this motion, to realise that any intemperate language of his which may revive or promote such ill-feeling is a great danger and to remember that the man who uses it is rendering a real disservice to this country and is pursuing a course of conduct the dangers of which, in present circumstances, it is difficult to overestimate."

The Hon'ble Mr. Kamini Kumar Chanda :—"My Lord, may I respectfully inquire of the Hon'ble the Home Member if this committee of judges will go into the question of convictions also and not only of the sentences?"

The President :—"I certainly did not catch what the Hon'ble Member was saying."

The Hon'ble Mr. Kamini Kumar Chanda :—"I beg to inquire, my Lord, whether this committee. . . . . . "

The President :—"More slowly, please."

The Hon'ble Mr. Kamini Kumar Chanda :—"Whether this committee of judges will go into the question of convictions or only of sentences?"

The Hon'ble Sir William Vincent :—"If it will make any difference to the Hon'ble Member's amendment, I shall be very glad to give this information."

The Hon'ble Mr. Kamini Kumar Chanda :—"My Lord, I beg to move this amendment which stands in my name and it reads as follows:—

> 'That the consideration of the motion do stand over till after the submission of the report of the Committee of Inquiry into the Punjab affairs.'

"My Lord, I wish at the outset to assure your Excellency and the Council that I have not taken upon myself to move this amendment with a light heart. I have listened to the very impressive and very weighty utterance of the Hon'ble the Home Member, and I am aware that your Excellency's Government is convinced of the imperative necessity, according to their information, of this legislation; and if I move this amendment, not to oppose the passing of this Bill, but for the purpose of postponing its consideration now, I can assure the Council that it is due to an impelling sense of duty. I have given the matter my most serious and, I may add, anxious consideration, and I felt it to be my duty to place this amendment before the Council. In doing so, regard being had to the considerations which the Hon'ble the Home Member has so impressively and eloquently pleaded for, in proposing my amendment in view of the circumstances, I propose to avoid, as far as possible, all debatable matters. Of course a certain amount of controversy and dispute is inevitable; I shall try to minimise it. There are so many matters to speak about and there is no time limit, and there might be a temptation to go on for a long time, but, my Lord, I shall try to be very brief; and for this purpose I do not propose to go into any individual cases about which it is charged that the administration of martial law has been guilty of excesses. There is one other remark which I wish to submit before I go into my motion. My Lord, it is a matter of great regret to us, I consider it almost as an irony of fate, that this painful episode in the administration of the Punjab Government should have to be discussed after His Honour Sir Edward Maclagan has assumed charge of the province. We know that in the short time he has been in charge of the province he has endeared himself not only to the province but to the country as a whole. It is well-known that every one heaved a sigh of relief when His Honour was able to take charge of the province. I am sure His Honour will understand that in bringing this matter at this stage, after His Honour has been in charge of the province, it is only from a painful sense of duty that we do so.

"Now, coming to the amendment, I may say at once that I agree to the general proposition which has been stated by the Hon'ble the Home Member, and which is also mentioned in the Statement of Objects and Reasons of the Bill, namely, that after a period of martial law such legislation is inevitable. In fact, I think the Hon'ble Member might go further and say with Professor Dicey, whom he has quoted, that in England such legislation is undertaken before the suspension of the Habeas Corpus Acts runs out. That is so in England; but, my Lord, my submission is this that the cases are not really analogous; the conditions obtaining in England are not the same as in this country. In England, it is well-known that it is the British Parliament with whom rests the question of the suspension of the Habeas Corpus Acts. Here under the Statute, it is your Excellency in Council who have to declare martial law. Therefore, the necessity which might exist in England for an Act of this kind does not necessarily exist in this country. Now, that apart, if we inquire as to why it is usual that in England suspensions of the Habeas Corpus Acts are always as a matter of course followed by a Validating Act, we shall see that that is because there has been up to now no case where the question of the necessity of the suspension of Habeas Corpus Acts has been raised. It has always been accepted that there was clear necessity. Where there is undisputed necessity for the declaration of martial law or suspension of the Habeas Corpus Acts, of course the Validating or Indemnity Bill will follow as a matter of course. But, my Lord, here the case is different. Here it has been denied, it has been disputed that there was any necessity for this declaration of martial law. The public have complained that martial law was declared on insufficient, inadequate grounds; that there are grave doubts whether under the existing conditions it could be legally done, and that there have been excesses under that declaration. In view of all this that differentiates the case of India from that of England, I say, my Lord, that the question as to why, while I do admit that a validating or indemnity Bill follows as a matter of course the declaration of martial law or suspension of the Habeas Corpus Acts, I oppose this motion or rather move that this motion do stand over, does not arise. If the question can arise, my Lord, I submit the answer has been given to this by the Government themselves. I do not think there has been any case anywhere where there has been an inquiry about the necessity of martial law. I do not think there has been any case in India where a Committee of Inquiry was appointed to discuss and to investigate the necessity or legality of a declaration of martial law, but here the question was raised and the Government of India accepted straightway the challenge as it were, and appointed a Committee of Inquiry to go into these matters. I submit, my Lord, that that has made all the difference. No doubt the composition of the Committee and the terms of reference do not fully satisfy the public demand; but that is another matter. Now, my Lord, what are the scope and the functions of this Committee of Inquiry? We learned from your Excellency's speech on the 3rd that the Committee of Inquiry was to inquire into and report about, among other things, the measures taken to cope with the disorders in the Punjab. What were the measures that were adopted in the Punjab? It is no other than the delaration of martial law. The question that arises is, whether there was any necessity for that declaration, whether it was proper to declare martial law, whether under the conditions obtaining at the time there was legal power to declare martial law, and whether it has been carried out properly. These are questions, my Lord, that this Committee will have to decide. Now what is the reason, the justice, the necessity for this Bill? If we look to the Preamble of the Bill we see it is stated :—

> 'Whereas owing to the recent disorders in certain districts in the Punjab and in other parts of India, it has been necessary for the purpose of maintaining or restoring order to resort to martial law.'

'Resort to martial law.' These, my Lord, are the very matters which this Committee of Inquiry will have to go into and report on; that is the basis of this Bill. I submit that that can hardly be fair. I submit that having referred this matter for inquiry by this Committee, the Government of India have divested themselves for the moment of the power of going into this matter. If you go on with this Bill then what is there remaining for the Committee to go into? What will remain, if you now assume that there was necessity for martial law, what would remain for the Committee to inquire into, whether there was any necessity for martial law? But we are told by the passing of this Bill, that there was a necessity for the declaration of martial law. This is surely prejudging the question, it is tying the hands of the Committee, it is not fair. My submission is that on this ground you are prejudging the question. The Committee are in possession of the seizin, as lawyers call it, of this matter. This Council has no jurisdiction to go into the matter at this stage. Of course as the matter has been referred to the Committee, it would not be right for the Council now to go into the question, as to whether the declaration was necessary or legal, or whether it was properly carried out. My submission is this that, in view of this and in view of the complaint that martial law was improperly and illegally declared, I think we ought to state the case on which this demand is made. My Lord, what is the law under which this martial law has been declared? It is the Bengal State Offences Regulation, X of 1804. What are the conditions under which this Regulation can be enforced? The Preamble says that there are two conditions, in the first place, it must appear that the British Government is at war with any other power, or that there was a state of open rebellion in the country. These are the two conditions which give jurisdiction to the Government to enforce this Regulation in any place it wishes. Nobody will contend for a moment that at the time this declaration was made, the British Government was at war with any other power. Then we have to fall back upon the second condition, namely, that there was a state of open rebellion in the country. On what is this condition based? What is the proof that there was open rebellion in the country at the time? My Lord, it is well known that after the Rowlatt Bill was passed in the teeth of opposition from the Indian members of this Council and the country, Mr. Gandhi, as a last resort, declared *Satyagraha* or passive resistance. We need not go into the question, whether it was wise or not; it is a fact that he did so and the 6th of April was appointed as the *Satyagraha* day, to be observed in the country as a day of humiliation and prayer on which all business was to be suspended. We know that that was done in the country and that there was no disturbance anywhere. Now what about the Punjab? Was there any response in the Punjab to this appeal of Mr. Gandhi's? Now, before going into the question, I may tell the Council that on the 7th April His Honour the Lieutenant-Governor, Sir Michael O'Dwyer, held a Durbar and delivered a speech in the course of which he said 'From the Prince's palace down to the peasant's hut I find I can meet

Punjabis of whatever class or condition without any suspicion or mischief.' That was on the 7th April. Surely this language could not have been used by the ruler of the Province if there was anything like rebellion there. It is inconceivable that such language could have been employed if there was anyhing indicating in the remotest degree that there was rebellion in the province, not only at that time but even a week after when martial law was declared. But what happened when this appeal of Mr. Gandhi was published, how was it received in the province? There is an account published in the *Civil and Military Gazette,* a newspaper which is not as a rule friendly to Indian aspirations and public movements. It is there stated that between 1 and 2 P.M., crowds had collected in the city and moved towards the Bradlaugh Hall where a meeting took place to protest against the Rowlatt Bills. This meeting was held between 5 and 6 P.M., the proceedings were orderly and no disturbances occurred in the city or outside the hall. Then what took place at Lahore on the 6th of April?

"We find, moreover, my Lord, that it was not only at Lahore, but at Ferozepore, Gurdaspore, Hissar, Jullundur, Mooltan, Muzzaferpore, Rohtak, Sialkot and Simla, that demonstrations and *hartals* were observed but there were no disturbances. Is that the sign of open rebellion which somebody seems to have discovered in the Punjab? I think, my Lord, in a sense it might be said to be rebellion. We know that Sir Michael O'Dwyer was in the habit, both in season and out of season, somewhat aggressively, of priding himself that his province was the quietest, the most loyal and the most well-behaved of all the provinces in India and from which he was able to drive out the disease known as political agitation. Now these demonstrations in their intensity and widespread character must have shocked His Honour, awakened to a grim and unpalatable reality and forced the realisation, to him most unwelcome, that his province was going to be infected, converted to evil ways of the other and vicious provinces. We get an insight, we get some glimpse into his inner thoughts, if we turn to the speech of His Honour which he delivered at the Durbar the following morning when he said this: 'that the British Government which has crushed foreign foes and quelled internal rebellion could afford to despise political agitators.' Now what was the occasion for this remark, my Lord? I say that explains the psychology of the subsequent orders and proceedings. Well, I might point out that there were not only these demonstrations in utter defiance of his wishes, almost as a challenge to him, but what is more, the horror of horrors, there was at the time going to grow up what is called the Hindu-Moslem fraternisation. We read in the *Civil and Military Gazette* on the 9th April: 'At Lahore there was procession held accompanied by extraordinary scenes of Hindu-Moslem fraternisation. In Amritsar, the procession showed similar scenes of Hindu-Moslem fraternisation, speeches were delivered and votes of sympathy were passed with the Delhi martyrs.' It is exceedingly significant that that was placed as a piece of evidence in a case before the Martial Law Courts as evidence of rebellion. My Lord, this state of things, these demonstrations and *hartals* and these scenes of Hindu-Moslem fraternization certainly were very uncomfortable, and it was felt that something must be done, some steps should be taken to nip in the bud the incipient rebellion in the Province, and we find that the first overt act in this campaign against political agitation was that on that very night Mr. Gandhi, who was then on his way to Delhi on a peaceful mission, was obstructed under the orders of His Honour the Lieutenant Governor at a small station called Kosi, which is in the Punjab territory, and turned back and was escorted to Mr. Gandhi's province, Bombay. Well, that was wired all over the country as the arrest of Mr. Gandhi. What was the result? We know there have been very unfortunate happenings throughout the country. Now, my Lord, it is usual for the Anglo-Indian papers to put down these happenings to agitation against the Rowlatt Act. My submission is, my Lord, that the Rowlatt Act can no more be held responsible for these happenings than the action of Sir Michael O'Dwyer, which was described by Mr. Kali Nath Roy as an act of 'blazing indiscretion' for which he was sent to jail for three years. Well, my Lord, let us see what happened in the Punjab. I say the news of the arrest of Mr. Gandhi was received at Lahore on the afternoon of the 10th. Let us see what happened there. But there is a difficulty here to find out what happened. On the following morning, the 11th, Sir Michael O'Dwyer acting under the Defence of India Rules, passed an order muzzling the Indian press, prohibiting the publication of any account of what took place on the previous day. Now why this anxiety to keep the outside world in the dark as to the happenings at Lahore on the 10th? Therefore, the public outside Lahore, we, had to rely on the Government Communiques and the accounts given in the Anglo-Indian press, for the events that took place at Lahore and other places on the 10th. Of course, the Anglo-

Indian press were evidently able to be above the orders of Government with regard to the publication of accounts of any events. The Government Communique is this: This is dated the 12th April:

> 'Lahore. The shops in the city and its vicinity were closed and a noisy crowd endeavoured to force its way towards the Civil Lines. This Crowd was met with a small police detachment near the High Court, and on its refusal to abandon its progress was dispersed, under the orders of the District Magistrate by musket fire. At a later hour in the evening, the police were again compelled to fire on a disorderly crowd which attacked them with missiles in the vicinity of the Lohari Gate. Two persons were killed in the day's firing and about four others wounded.'

"These are the words of the Government Communique, and the account that was published in the *Civil and Military Gazette* was this:—

> 'A crowd collected in the bazar which rapidly grew and started coming down Anarkali. Then the mob which had assumed a very threatening attitude proceeded down the Mall. By this time, the police were out in force, and a party of them stopped the mob. The Deputy Commissioner then arrived, and seeing the seriousness of the situation and the impossibility of stopping the mob by any other means gave the order to fire. This produced some result, for the crowd went back and were forced up Anarkali Bazaar. Then they formed at the top of the Bazaar where they had to be dispersed again by fire..... The arrangements throughout were in the hands of the civil authorities as, thanks to their immediate and effective action, the necessity did not arise to ask the military to take charge.'

"But the *Pioneer* went one better and in its account on the 13th it says :—

> 'The European residents, already disturbed by the news from Amritsar, had to face a serious situation created by an infuriated mob which was bent on mischief. *Large forces of military and the police promptly dealt with the outbreak, and on more than one occasion had to fire on the mobs.* Strong action resulted in the restoration of order and the city is now being patrolled..... Buckshot cartridges were used.'

"But on the following day, it says :—

'Buckshot was supplied to the police, *except for 5 rounds of ball issued by mistake.*'

"On the 20th there was another Government Communique to contradict what appeared in the *Leader* about this, and this is what is said :—

'The facts are that despite orders previously promulgated forbidding processions, a large crowd, probably of some thousands, marched from the city up the Mall, forcing back a small body of police which tried to bar their progress. The crowd consisted of city rif-raff and students, but the latter were grown up and not boys. The crowd was making its way to the civil station and would undoubtedly have committed excesses such as marked the Amritsar occurrences, had it been allowed access to the European quarters.'

"These are all the accounts published by Government and the Anglo-Indian papers of the occurrences in Lahore on the 10th. What do they say? Never mind for the present that there are serious contradictions. Take the account substantially as it stands. I ought to mention, my Lord, that there is another fact. The *Civil and Military Gazette* on the 16th of May stated that the Deputy Superintendent of Police was struck on his head which had to be bandaged. Now it is remarkable that this incident is not mentioned in the Government Communiques, nor in the Associated Press telegram. As a matter of fact, this police officer was struck, his head was broken, there was a split. How is it that this incident does not find a place in the Government Communiques? The fact of the matter is that, as was discovered by the *Civil and Military Gazette* later, it was 'caused by a policeman by mistake' and not by the mob, that is why it was not mentioned by the Government Communique. Now take the accounts as they stand, what do we find? That a mob, unarmed, it must be remembered, unarmed, 'of city riff-raff and students,' to quote the words of the Government Communique, were making their way from the city towards the Mall. What happened? It does not appear that any serious attempt was made to persuade the mob to go back, that civil force was attempted. But from a sense of panic, the order to fire was given and there were casualties. What did they do? It is not stated anywhere that they did any injury to any one or destroyed property on their journey from the city to the Mall. It was asserted in the latest Government Communique that they would have done mischief, but why is this assumed, it is not stated that up to then anything was done by that mob. Well, what were the objectives of the mob? Was an inquiry made to find out why this mob was proceeding towards the Mall? It was unarmed it must be remembered. Well if the object was to do any wrong, to break the law, is it conceivable that 'this riff-raff and students' would go unarmed, or would refrain from doing anything in the city or in their journey up the Mall? No inquiry was made as to why they were journeying to the Civil Lines. If an inquiry had been made it would have been found that their object was nothing more than to interview His Honour himself and to intercede with him and ask him to withdraw that order against Mr. Gandhi. But what happened? This march of the unarmed mob of city 'rif-raffs and students' was the first overt act of rebellion. Anyhow, my Lord, whatever happened then, it was put down in the course of an hour, if it was a rebellion, it was quieted in an hour's time. We read in the Government Communique 'that by 8 p.m., the city was quiet; after that time no further disturbance occurred.' Thus in an hour's time this rebellion was put down.

"Then what happened on the following day, on the 11th? We find again from the Government Communique that on the 11th everything was quiet. Well, is that a sign, my Lord, of any rebellion at Lahore at the time? The solitary instance mentioned is that a mob of some three or four hundred people, unarmed, 'city rif-raff and students', were proceeding towards the Mall, and assuming that they were rioters, they met with their deserts because they were fired on by the armed police and there were some casualties, but after that everything was quiet and there was nothing on the following day. Then, on the 12th, what happened? On the 12th the Government Communique says :—

> 'On the morning of the 12th troops passed through Lahore city and occupied certain commanding points. At one point only the crowd *obstructed the passage* of the troops and brickbats were thrown. The police accompanying the march, under the orders of the District Magistrate, dispersed the crowd, two being killed and as many were wounded.'

"And the *Civil and Military Gazette* on the 13th says :—

> 'The rendezvous for the march of troops and police through the Lahore city was the cross roads outside the railway station at 9-15 a.m. The crowd in front of the fort in Minto Park had

to be forced back and the cavalry dispersed it without using their lances. The crowd, however, came in again behind *in rear of the cavalry* and the Deputy Commissioner ordered a detachment of police to get behind the cavalry and fire.'

"And there was an Associated Press telegram which says that 'more than a dozen had been wounded, some of them having received serious wounds. One of them who received 9 wounds on the chest died this afternoon. Nearly 10,000 people attended his funeral. The deceased was a student of the 4th year class and had come here to sit for the University examination.'

"Now, my Lord, as to the assumption that brickbats were thrown at the military, as stated in this Communique, it will be seen, neither the *Civil and Military Gazatte* nor the Associated Press telegram corroborates this. However, assuming that this was done, would that constitute rebellion, or would that make it a clear sign or proof that there was rebellion in the city so that you would have to declare martial law? Has it been inquired into by whom and under what circumstances these brickbats were thrown? There is a discrepancy again. One account says the cavalry were obstructed in front and brickbats were thrown, whereas another account says that when they passed through the city the mob came behind and threw brickbats. However, leave that alone. Does that alone constitute a state of rebellion in the city?

"My Lord, I have tried my best to see if there was any other case of rowdyism. I said there was no account published in the Indian papers or any other information than the Government Communiques and the accounts in the Anglo-Indian papers and there is no allegation of any of this unlawful act anywhere.

"My Lord, beyond these two incidents, one on the 10th and one on the 12th, I have not come across anything mentioned in the papers, as having taken place in Lahore. Well, I should feel grateful if the Hon'ble the Home Member will inform the Council if there was any other occurrence in Lahore, which justified the Government in declaring martial law. After this, my Lord, on the 14th, martial law was declared. We do not find on what grounds this order was based. Of course, attempts were made by interpellations in this Council to find out the grounds in justification of martial law, but they have not been answered. Martial law came into force at midnight between the 15th and 16th. Several days later, by another Ordinance, No. IV, this martial law was given retrospective effect so as to cover everything that was done from the 30th of March. My Lord, it is a serious question as to whether this can be done under the law. The matter has been placed before the Privy Council in the appeals which have been admitted, and we shall know the decision of their Lordships. Another question, my Lord, in this connection is, whether this could legally be done. We find, my Lord, that Lord Wellesley, in whose time this State Offences Regulation of 1804 was passed, issued instructions for the guidance of the Local Governments and therein it was stated (Circular of the Marquis of Wellesley, dated the 11th April 1805). 'Even if a person or persons charged with any overt acts of rebellion specified in Regulation X of 1804 shall be apprehended by any military officer, when not in the actual commission of offences of that description, they are to be delivered by the military to the civil power.' That was laid down in the Instrument of Instructions regarding this Regulation, and the Regulation itself shows that only charges against persons caught in *flagrante delicto*, that is red-handed, could be tried by martial law, and that was expressly declared in the Instrumant of Instructions. Furthermore, my Lord, it appears that the Government of Bengal consulted the Advocate General, Mr. Spankie,* at the time, and his opinion was to the same effect. Now, my Lord, this question becomes a serious one as to whether retrospective effect could be given to this Regulation by Ordinance No. IV. My submission is that here also the matter is before the Privy Council which has got seizin of the matter, and if you ask this Council now to decide, it would be wrong; you cannot go into this before their Lordships have decided the question as to whether martial law was rightly or lawfully given retrospective effect to by Ordinance No. IV. And this Bill is based upon the assumption that the order was legal, because it is stated in the Bill that anything done between the 30th of March and the date of the passing of this Bill will be protected. Therefore, my Lord, taking all these questions into account, it would not be right to ask this Council to pass this Bill at this time. We must wait for the finding of the Committee, we must wait for the decision of the Privy Council on the questions raised as to the legality of the promulgation of martial law and the giving of retrospective effect to it. Well, let this Committee have a free hand to go into the matter, sift out facts, find out what was done, and then it will be time enough to go into the question of protecting the officers of

* See Appendix IV, pages 468-474, *ante*.

Government who had carried out the instructions under martial law. The Hon'ble the Home Member has raised the point that, even assuming that martial law was not properly or legally promulgated, the question of protecting the officers of Government remains, because it is no fault of theirs that they were called upon to carry out these orders. Now, my Lord, everything depends upon what the orders were and how they were carried out. You cannot say beforehand that you will pass a general law that every officer is protected for anything he did under any order given. Well, so far as that matter goes, that is already provided for under the existing law. Under the Penal Code if a public servant carries out an order given by a superior, whether legal or illegal, how far he is bound to carry it out is provided for in the general law. If the Committee finds out any specific instances not covered by the existing law, then it will be time enough to consider how far that law has to be supplemented. My submission is that at present we have got a general law. Then, my Lord, even in England instances have occurred where officers commanding the military have had to undergo prosecution for excess of zeal in discharging their duty when their services were requisitioned. In connection with the riots in County Clare in Ireland in 1852, a jury brought in a verdict of guilty of murder against the soldiers who had fired on a mob, but for which they would have lost their own lives. So, I submit, my Lord, that it is premature now to consider this point. The whole thing will depend upon what orders were given, how those orders were carried out. At present all that we need consider is provided for in the general law.

"Then, the other point raised by the Hon'ble Sir Willaim Vincent is that, if you are to wait, there will be actions brought against Government officers and they may be decreed. My submission on this is that it is purely imaginary. If any action is to be brought by any man for damages against any officer of Government for anything done during the time martial law was in force, we know that probably at first notice will be given to Government or the Government officer concerned, and atfer the expiry of the statutory period only can a suit be filed. Then, assuming that no notice is given but suit filed, the mere fact that a suit is filed need not frighten us. Civil suits, it is well known, are not disposed of as expeditiously as criminal cases. Well, a plaint is filed, then a date will be fixed for the defendant to enter appearance and file his written statement. I do not know what the practice in the Punjab is, but I know in Bengal and Assam no date is fixed earlier than three weeks' time. Well, my Lord, if the defendant has to enter appearance before the Council meets the next time, surely the Courts concerned would be bound to grant postponement for filing written statements in such contingencies. Usually, you find in civil cases, two or four months, or even one year has been given for filing written statements in complicated cases. And in a case of this kind no Court will refuse to grant time for adjournment till the next Session of this Council at any rate. From now till the Delhi Session there is only (?) time. First notice will have to be given two months before any suit is filed, and even after the suit is filed, you will get ample time to have the case adjourned till the meeting of the Delhi Session of this Council. Even if that is not enough you can easily provide for it in various other ways. You can pass the Bill in the Delhi Session and give it a retrospective effect so that it will cover any suit or action that may have been filed already. You can do more; you can have some provision suspending all these actions in the meantime, till the Council meets at Delhi. Apart from the questions arising from the fact that a Committee of Inquiry has been appointed, I think we should consider that public discussions of the happenings in the Punjab are bound to create some bad blood and should, if possible, be avoided, and that can be avoided if the Council does not rush through with this Bill now. Let the Committee inquire, find out the facts, sift out the facts, and then we can see how far officers ought to be protected, and how far there ought to be an Indemnifying Act. These are my submissions on which I respectfully venture to think that this Bill ought not to be passed at this stage. I spoke only of Lahore, but the same considerations apply as regards other places. With these remarks I place the amendment before the Council."

The Hon'ble Sardar Sundar Singh Majithia:—"My Lord, I must confess that some of us, non-official members, who are not well versed in legal technicalities—being laymen so far as law is concerned—are placed in a very awkward position when they are required to assent to a measure like the one we are discussing to-day and for the introduction of which leave has been asked by the Hon'ble the Home Member. Persons like myself feel the weight of responsibility very heavy; I cannot say for others, but for myself I have felt very keenly. We have, as dutiful subjects of the King-Emperor, a duty to His Majesty the King-Emperor and to the Government established under law in this country; but, on the other hand, being representatives on this Council of the people we owe a duty to our fellow subjects which we have to discharge to the best of our abilities. I can assure your Lordship that I have been feeling this responsibility very keenly and the tension on my feelings for the past few days has been very very great. Under such circumstances, one could only bow before the All Omnipotent for light being granted for guidance in the path which may be the right path.

"When I first heard of the Indemnity Bill, I was under the impression that we were to be asked to indemnify all actions of Government officers, whether they were done in good faith or not. Till I had seen the Bill, I was under this impression and as such I felt that I could not give support to such a measure, knowing as I do some of the inconveniences and indignities that some of my countrymen have suffered during the currency of the martial law in my province. I have not the remotest inclination to defend those who have broken the law, and I have no hesitation in saying that no Government can afford to let such actions go unpunished. No man who loves peace and order could possibly side with such people who break the law and commit atrocities which cause feelings of horror and contempt in the minds of right-thinking and law-abiding persons. But, on the other hand, one cannot shut one's eyes to some of the doings in my province. My Lord, this, however, is not the place to talk of those things. So I would not touch that point at all, as I believe and as I think that they are to be sifted into by the Committee of Inquiry that has been appointed by your Excellency. On the other hand, I would not withhold protection to those officers of Government who have done their duty during these trying times conscientiously, and whose actions have been taken in good faith and in a reasonable belief that they were necessary for the maintenance of law and order in the country. I understand that after martial law an indemnifying measure has always been enacted. Such a measure was passed in 1860 in India. I am not a lawyer, but I am told that that measure was of a more severe nature and went much further than the one introduced to-day. I am also told that indemnifying measures have been passed in other countries also, such as South Africa and nearer home at Ceylon. I would therefore be prepared to give my assent to the measure before us to-day; but I want to be assured fully that Government has no intention to afford protection to those who have acted against the strictest sense of justice and against good faith. Though personally I have no doubt on this point and I am sanguine that Government have no intention of that sort, but an assurance of this nature will satisfy public opinion in the country. One thing more, before I give my assent to the measure before the Council. I would like Government to agree and concede that all cases tried under martial law will further be examined and that wherever injustice is found to have been done, those who are detained in jails will be given their liberty. I am glad that the point has been conceded and that two High Court Judges will revise these judgments and I thank Government for this. I have no wish to ask any leniency for those who have committed atrocities; but on the report of the Committee of Inquiry I would suggest that amnesty be granted, as I think that many of these unfortunate persons have in the heat of the roused feelings been led astray from paths of righteousness and of their duty as law-abiding citizens of the Empire. With this assurance that the Act does not white-wash all actions done in bad faith as against good faith, and with the promise of a further reconsideration of the cases tried by martial law courts, I would give my assent to the measure before the Council. I have avoided making any mention of the unfortunate happenings in my province as this Council Chamber is not now the right place for these to be ventilated. They are in a way *sub-judice* and till the report of the Committee of Inquiry is published, we must suspend our judgments. The other day I asked for an assurance for the protection of persons who come to tender evidence before this Committee of Inquiry. I understand that the Home Member is willing to give that assurance and that steps will be taken to duly proclaim this to the people. I would, therefore, beg my Hon'ble friends and colleagues to refrain from bringing in matters which are now in the province of the Committee of Inquiry to inquire into and sift."

The Hon'ble Pandit Madan Mohan Malaviya :—"My Lord, the measure which the Hon'ble the Home Member has asked for leave to introduce is one of the most important measures which have ever been proposed by the British Government in this country, and it calls for very careful consideration. My Lord, the Hon'ble the Home Member has said that where there is disorder and it has been found necessary to proclaim martial law, certain acts have had to be done which may not be strictly justified in law, but may be morally defensible, and that an Indemnity Act almost as a natural consequence followed. Now, my Lord, the Hon'ble Member having raised the question, as it was necessary for him to raise, under what circumstances martial law should be introduced and under what circumstances an Indemnifying Bill or Act is permissible or justifiable, it is necessary for us to go somewhat into this question. I am not going far into the earlier Acts; I shall start with the period mentioned by the Hon'ble the Home Member, the year 1715. Members of this Council will remember that that was the year in which James the Pretender came over to England, and wanted to wrest the throne of England. Six thousand Highlanders from Scotland joined his forces and there was a regular invasion, an invasion in which there was regular warfare, there were not merely riots and tumults, but actual war waged against the Crown of England. The Pretender was defeated and it was necessary to justify the acts which had been committed in the suppression of that rebellion; it was in these circumstances that Parliament passed an enactment, like this, Chapter 39 of George I says:—

> 'An Act to indemnify such persons who have acted in defence of his Majesty's person and Government and for the preservation of the public peace of this Kingdom in and about the time of the late unnatural rebellion from vexatious suits and prosecutions. And whereas in the year of our Lord 1715 as well as in the time of, as before the unnatural rebellion, which begun in or about the months of September or October in the same year. And whereas divers Lord Lieutenants, Deputy Lieutenants, Justices of the Peace, the Mayors, Bailiffs of Corporations, Constables and other officers and persons well affected to His Majesty and his Government, in order to preserve our present happy establishment and the peace of this Kingdom and to suppress and to put an end to the said rebellion, apprehended and put into custody and imprisoned several criminals and several persons who they suspected might disturb the publick peace or foment or promote riots, tumults, rebellions or evil designs against the Government; and also seized and used several horses, arms and other things and also pressed divers horses, carts and carriages for the services of the publick; and did for the purposes aforesaid enter into the houses and possessions of several persons and did quarter and cause to be quartered divers soldiers and others in the houses of divers persons; and did divers acts which could not be justified by the strict forms of law *and yet were necessary and so much for the service of the publick that*

they ought to be justified by Act of Parliament and the persons by whom they were transacted ought to be indemnified.

'Be it therefore enacted.' etc.

"Now, my Lord, your Lordship will see and the Council will see that the essential point of this enactment is that there was a rebellion which had to be suppressed and put an end to. Secondly, that Parliament expresses itself satisfied that the acts which had been done and which could not be justified by the strict forms of law were yet necessary and that they ought to be justified by an Act of Parliament, and that the persons who committed them ought to be indemnified. That establishes the cardinal principle which underlies legislation of the character which is now before the Council. It is a principle which was re-enacted in 1745. There was a second Pretender, the late Pretender's son Charles Edward. He tried to invade England—that was in 1745. This time again 6,000 Highlanders joined his forces and later on the number rose to 9,000. There were regular pitched battles fought. Several members of the Scottish peerage and others joined the rebellion. There was regular war and the King's loyal subjects fought against the enemies of the King and defeated them. That was in 1745. It was necessary after the rebellion had been suppressed to introduce an Act of Indemnity. This Act, Chapter 20 of George II, ran as follows :—

> 'An Act to indemnify persons who have acted in defence of His Majesty's person and Government and for the preservation of the publick peace during the time of the late unnatural rebellion and sheriffs and others who have suffered escapes occasioned thereby from vexatious suits and prosecutions.
>
> 'Whereas during the unnatural rebellion which began in or about the months of July or August in 1745 and still continues, divers Lieutenants, Deputy Lieutenants, Justices of the Peace, Mayors, Bailiffs of Corporations, Constables, and other officers and persons well affected to His Majesty and his Government, in order to preserve our present happy establishment and the peace of this Kingdom and to suppress and to put an end to the said rebellion, apprehended and put into custody and imprisoned or caused to be apprehended, put into custody and imprisoned several criminals and several persons who they suspected might disturb the publick peace or foment or promote riots, tumults, rebellions or evil designs against the Government; and also seized and used several

horses, arms and other things and also pressed divers horses, carts and carriages for the services of the publick and did for the purposes aforesaid enter into the houses and possessions of several persons and did quarter and cause to be quartered divers soldiers and others in the houses of divers persons; and did divers acts which could not be justified by the strict forms of law *and yet were necessary and so much for the service of the publick that they ought to be justified* by Act of Parliament and the persons by whom they were transacted ought to be indemnified.

'And whereas divers sheriffs, gaolers and other persons may be or are in danger of being sued, indicted, prosecuted or proceeded against by reason of escapes of prisoners let out or discharged by the persons engaged in the said rebellion.

'Be it therefore enacted.....'

"Here again the Council will note that the essential point in the preamble is that it was necessary to suppress and put an end to the rebellion and Parliament was satisfied that acts had been performed that were not strictly according to law, acts which were not only necessary but it was necessary that the servants of the public ought to be justified by an act of Parliament. Now, my Lord, the third time that the English Parliament passed an Indemnity Act was in 1706; that was in connection with the Lord George Gordon riots. This was not a rebellion against the King by enemies of Great Britain, but this time the Catholic Relief Bill having been passed certain section of Protestants in England could not bear the idea that it should be on the Statute-book, and they constituted a strong party and presented a petition to Parliament signed by 120,000 persons asking for the repeal of the Act. They went and invaded the Houses of Parliament. Sixty thousand persons were there, and the riot had to be suppressed. After the riot had been suppressed, Lord George Gordon escaped but others got the punishment which the law considered fit for them, but after the riots had been suppressed an Act of Indemnity was passed. That was in the year 1780. The Act ran as follows:—

'Chap. LXIII, Geo. III. An Act to indemnify such persons as have acted in the suppression of the late Riots and Tumults in and about the Cities of London and Westminster, and Borough of Southwark and for the preservation of the publick peace.'

"Now the preamble recited:—

'Whereas on the second day of June, in the year one thousand seven hundred and eighty a great number of disorderly persons assembled themselves together, in a riotous and tumultuous manner, near to both Houses of Parliament, and possessed themselves of the Avenues leading to the same, the said Houses being then sitting, and there committed great Acts of Outrage and Violence to many of His Majesty's subjects; and afterwards proceeded to attack the Houses of some of the Publick Ministers, of Foreign Princes and States, residing at His Majesty's Court, and to break into the Chapels belonging to such Publick Ministers, and to set Fire thereto, and continued riotously and tumultuously assembled for several Days and Nights; and during that Time attacked and set Fire to the Gaol of Newgate, the King's Bench Prison, the Prison of the Fleet, and set at liberty the prisoners therein respectively confined, and broke other Gaols and Prisons, and set at liberty the prisoners confined therein, and set fire to, and pulled down, the Dwelling houses of divers of His Majesty's peaceable subjects, in several Parts in and about the Cities of London and Westminster, and Borough of Southwark, and burnt and consumed the Materials and Furniture of the same, and did other Acts of Outrage and Violence; and whereas divers Magistrates and others have exerted themselves for the suppression of the said Riots and Tumults, and for putting an End to the said Outrages, and for restoring and preserving the Publick Peace, and on the Occasions, and for the Purposes aforesaid, have done divers Acts which cannot be justified by the strict Forms of Law, and yet, were necessary, and so much for the Preservation of the Lives and Properties of His Majesty's Subjects, and the Publick Safety and Peace, that they ought to be justified by Act of Parliament, and the Persons by whom they were transacted ought to be indemnified; be it therefore enacted.....'

"Now, my Lord, these enactments clearly lay down that the legislative body which is to give its sanction to the acts which were performed during a time of trouble were necessary for the suppression of a rebellion or riot which amounted to rebellion and that they were so very necessary that the legislative body ought to justify them and indemnify those who had taken part in them. It is not every ordinary riot which would come in the category of the riots mentioned there. It must be a riot which, as Lord Halsbury points out in his article on the Laws of England, must be a riot or rebellion amounting to war. This is what he says in Volume VI of the Laws of England:—

'As the source and fountain of justice, the Crown may issue such Commissions to administer the law as are warranted by the common or statute law. But it may not, without authority, establish Courts to administer any but the common law, and it may not, it is said, grant the right to hold a court of equity. The Crown may not issue Commissions in time of peace to try civilians by martial law; but when a state of actual war, or of insurrection, riot or rebellion amounting to war exists, the Corwn and its officers may use the amount of force necessary in the circumstances to restore order, and this use of force is sometimes termed martial law. When once this state of actual war exists, the Civil Courts have no authority to call in question the actions of the military authorities, but the powers of the military authorities cease and those of the Civil Courts are resumed *ipso facto* with the termination of the disorder.'

"My Lord, the point on which I wish to lay stress is that there must be either a rebellion or insurrection or a riot amounting to war to justify resort to martial law. These are the general principles which the Laws of England have laid down. So far as India is concerned, the matter rests on a more definite footing. The Government of India is empowered under Regulation X of 1804 to establish martial law in certain circumstances. Now it is essential to draw attention to the language of that Regulation, because your Lordship professedly acted under that Regulation in declaring martial law in the Punjab. My Lord, that Regulation was passed in 1804, and it ought to be remembered that it was passed at a time when the British Government was trying to establish its power in this country, when there were many small States trying to prevent its establishment of power in this country. That was the period during which this Regulation was passed. Little did I think, my Lord, I venture to say, that the authors of this Regulation had imagined that this Regulation would be resorted to in the Year of Grace 1919 after the great war had been won. However, the Regulation is as follows:—

'Whereas, during wars in which the British Government

has been engaged against certain of the native powers of India, certain persons owing allegiance to the British Government have borne arms in open hostility to the authority of the same and have abetted and aided the enemy, and have committed acts of violence and outrage against the lives and properties of the subjects of the said Government; and whereas it may be expedient that during the existence of any war in which the British Government in India may be engaged with any power whatever, as well as during the existence of open rebellion against the authority of the Government in any part of the British territories subject to the Government of the presidency of Fort William, the Governor-General in Council shall declare and establish Martial Law within any part of the territories aforesaid for the safety of the British possessions, and for the security of the lives and property of the inhabitants thereof, by the immediate punishment of persons owing allegiance to the British Government who may be taken in arms, in open hostility to the said Government, or in the actual commission of any overt act of rebellion against the authority of the same, or in the act of openly aiding or abetting the enemies of the British Government within any part of the territories above-specified the following Regulation has been enacted by the Governor General in Council to be in force throughout the British territories immediately subject to the Government of the presidency of Fort William from the date of its promulgation.'

"Now, my Lord, it is clear that this Regulation can only be justly put into force when there is either a war or open rebellion against the authority of the Government. Your Lordship in establishing martial law by the notification, dated Simla, the 14th April 1919, consequently said that:—

'Whereas the Governor General is satisfied that a state of open rebellion against the authority of the Government exists in certain parts of the province of the Punjab; now, therefore, in exercise of the power conferred on him he is pleased to make and promulgate the following Ordinance.....'

"Now, my Lord, section 2 of the Bengal State Regulation provided that where the Governor General was so satisfied it was open to him to establish martial law, and that section also repeated that it was during the existence of open rebellion against the authority of the Government, or who may have borne arms in open hostility to Government that martial law should be established. In the notification dated the 14th April, 1919, your Lordship was satisfied that a state of open rebellion against the authority of the Government existed in certain parts of the province of the Punjab. Now, my Lord, the public have not been told what were the circumstancs which constituted a state of open rebellion in Lahore. I gave notice of certain questions and I wanted to find out what it was that constituted a state of open rebellion. But unfortunately the Government told me that the questions could not be answered in view of the fact that an inquiry had been ordered and that it would not be in the interests of the public that these questions should be answered. Now, my Lord, I submit that it was essential, and it is still essential, first to inform the Council, when the Executive Government have come to the Legislative Council to ask for their support to ratify acts which are done under the Ordinance promulgated by the Governor General or the Governor General in Council, what were the circumstances under which martial law was proclaimed. I asked whether the Government would be pleased to lay on the table the correspondence which passed between them and the Punjab Government leading to the declaration of martial law in the Punjab. I also asked whether the Government would be pleased to state the facts and circumstances which, in its opinion, constituted a state of open rebellion against the authority of the Government in certain parts of the Province of the Punjab within the meaning of Regulation X of 1804 between the date on which the Ordinance was promulgaed by the Governor General and the date on which open rebellion was declared to exist in the part of the Punjab to which the Ordinance had been applied. I am sure your Excellency will recognise that these question sought to do nothing except what was right in the circumstances. I had heard that the *Pioneer* had proclaimed that an Indemnifying Bill was going to be introduced to this Council, and I gave notice of a question an answer to which it would be necessary to have in order that I should be able....."

The Hon'ble Sir William Vincent :—"My Lord, may I rise to a point of order? Is it in accordance with the practice in this Council for an Hon'ble Member to refer in public to a question which has been disallowed? Is it not a fact that he Hon'ble Member has been reprimanded for doing this on a previous occasion?"

The Hon'ble Pandit Madan Mohan Malaviya :—"My Lord, I do not know of a reprimand and I do not recognise any such reprimand. I am entitled on a Bill before the Council to draw attention to every fact in the Council. I was perfectly right, I submit, to do what I did.

"Now, my Lord, I asked for information, and, as I said before, in answer to my question I was informed that the Government could not answer these questions and numerous other questions of which I had given notice, as a Committee of Inquiry had been constituted or was going to be constituted and these matters would be dealt with by it. Now, my Lord, I would not complain of these questions not being answered, if the Government also recognised the fairness, the wisdom of staying its hand until these facts had been placed before the Committee of Inquiry, and until the public had come to know of them. Your Lordship will kindly remember that since this unfortunate declaration of open rebellion in the Punjab, which among other evils contributed to the Afghan war, since the declaration of this open rebellion and the establishment of martial law in the Punjab, the Punjab Government shut the rest of India and the world out from all knowledge of the events which were happening in the Punjab. My Lord, not only were individuals not permitted to go in and expose the events that were takng place there to the light of day, but even the representatives of many respectable well established leading papers in the country, and a man, himself a man of peace and of humanity, Mr. C.F. Andrews, when he asked permission—I hear a little laughter. My Lord, I do not know what the laughter is about. If it is to say that Mr. Andrews is not a man of peace and humanity, I am sorry for those who think so. Now, my Lord, I saw a man of Mr. Andrew's antecedents and character, devoted to the service of his fellow men, who goes to different parts of the world in order to serve his fellow men, who was appointed as the representative of several leading papers who sought permission to go to the Punjab, even after he had paid a visit to Simla and was on his way to Lahore, was stopped at Amritsar and disgracefully dealt with and turned back from the Punjab. Now, my Lord, other papers were not allowed to send their representatives to the Province and other public men were not allowed to go there. The result was that we did not know what had happened. From the information that we had, the All-India Congress Committee met and sent a long cablegram to His Majesty's Secretary of State in which they drew attention to the seriousness of the situation.

"Now, my Lord, in that cablegram the All-India Congress Committee, which met on the 20th and 21st of April at Bombay, passed among others the following resolutions:—

'Resolved that the All-India Congress Committee deplores and condemns all acts of violence against person and property, which were recently committed at Amritsar, Ahmedabad, Viramgaum and other places, and appeals to the people to maintain law and order and to help in the restoration of public tranquillity; and it urges upon the Government to deal with the situation in a sympathetic and conciliatory manner immediately reversing the present policy of repression.

'Resolved that the All-India Congress Committee places on record its strong condemnation of orders passed under the Defence of India Act by the Government of the Punjab, Administrator of Delhi and by the Government of India against a person of such well-known noble character and antecedents as Mr. M. K. Gandhi. The Committtee cannot help feeling that, if these orders had not been passed, some of the regrettable events which followed them, may not have happened. The Committee requests the Government of India to withdraw its own order and to ask the Local Governments in question to do the same.'

"Then, my Lord, there was a cablegram which I sent to His Majesty's Premier and to the Secretary of State for India. I will read it as it stands without articles, etc.

'All-India Congress Committee desire most earnestly to represent to His Majesty's Government intense gravity of present situation in India, real causes and need for change of policy pursued at present. While deploring and condemning popular excesses which have occurred in some parts of country and which popular leaders have everywhere used their influence not unsuccessfully to restrain, Committee urge impartial consideration of circumstances which have so aggravated and embittered feelings of people throughout country as to make such outbreaks possible. Resolution of Government of India, dated 14th instant, describing present situation as arising out of Rowlatt Act agitation makes only partial statement of case. Undoubtedly intense universal bitterness of opposition to Rowlatt Act forced through legislature by official votes against unanimous protest of all non-Indian members and in face of unparalleled opposition throughout country was immediate cause of recent popular peaceful demonstrations but subsequent excesses were provoked by needless and unjustifiable action of Government of India, and Punjab and Delhi Governments against so revered a personality as that of Mr. Gandhi and against other popular leaders. For complete understanding, however, of present discontent and its causes other important factors must be considered.'

Then, my Lord, after dealing with the causes which included India's services during the war, and the attitude of European and Anglo-Indian officials towards the Reforms and the fate of Turkey and the Rowlatt Bills, the Committee went on to say:—

'In such circumstances the two Rowlatt Bills were introduced and the principal one forced through Council in spite of unanimous opposition of non-official Indian members, appeal for postponements and reconsideration and warnings of agitation that would inevitably follow throughout country which was stirred by this measure and uncompromising attitude of Government in degree unparalleled in history of country. Committee here cannot enter in detail as to justifiable apprehensions caused by passing into law of this Act.

'They are content to represent that it is total distortion of facts that an agitation against a measure placed on Statute-book in time of peace depriving subjects under any circumstances of sacred right of free and open trial and otherwise restricting fundamental liberties and depriving accused persons of normal and essential safeguards designed for protection of innocent persons should be regarded as an unreal agitation engineered by political agitators for their own ends. Committee have no authority to discuss merits of passive resistance movement led by Mr. Gandhi but would emphasise that nothing but feeling of high-souled patriotism and intense realisation of injustice involved in passing of this measure could have actuated man of his saintly character and noble record. Committee submit that so far as facts are publicly known no violence had anywhere been committed by the people until after the arbitrary restrictions placed on Gandhi's movements leading to his arrest and forcible deportation without any announcement about his destination while he was on his way to Delhi with object of pacifying people after unfortunate episode there on March 30th. Grave allegations were made that authorities in Delhi unjustifiably fired on crowds killing and wounding several. Government of India have ignored demands for inquiry into this and have published *ex parte* statement of Local Government exonerating local authorities on unconvincing statements. Had Gandhi been allowed to proceed Delhi Committee believe he would have restored normal conditions. Government on contrary by his arrest and deportation provoked outbreaks in Ahmedabad and Viramgaum. Outbreak had become imminent in Bombay also, but it was averted by wise action of authorities in restraining police and Military and efforts of Gandhi and other leaders pacified people and restored quiet.

'Committee invite attention to the contrast between the rapidity with which tranquillity was restored in Ahmedabad by presence of Gandhi, his co-operation along with that of other leaders with authorities and continuance of disorders in Punjab where reckless and horrible methods of repression under Martial Law such as public flogging of citizens in streets, dropping of bombs from aeroplanes, wholesale firing on people assembled in streets, have been resorted to. These methods of repression have created horror and resentment throughout country.

'Committee recognise need for strong measures to deal with popular violence where occurring and popular leaders and bodies and all public men are ready to co-operate with Government in putting down popular excesses and violent movements against authority, but use of such methods as have been in force in Punjab antagonise feeling of people towards Government and sow seeds of bitterness and distrust.

'Committee most earnestly urge His Majesty's Government to intervene and put an end to these methods, and to order the appointment of commission of officials and non-officials to investigate causes of discontent and allegations of excesses by authorities in repressing popular outbreaks.'

"My Lord, that was submitted on the 28th of April this year and it prayed that the Government should appoint an early Commission.

'Committee strongly urge His Majesty's Government to consider that popular discontent has been provoked by causes set forth above. At Amritsar disturbances followed immediately on Sir Michael O'Dwyer's action in arresting and deporting Dr. Kitchlew and Dr. Satyapal. Committee most earnestly represent that situation cannot be dealt with alone by repression and attitude of sternness towards people displayed in Resolution of Indian Government of 14th instant which gives free hand to Local Governments to employ every weapon in armoury of repression and is sadly lacking in spirit of conciliation. Situation calls for highest statesmanship which will deal with it in spirit which animated British Government and Indian people in their recent struggle for maintenance of liberty and freedom of peoples from despotic domination and not in a mood of ruthlesss repression.

All-India Congress Committee feel that they can appeal with confidence in His Majesty's Ministers to consider this representation with sympathy and to take definite steps forthwith to reverse the policy of repression and to satisfy Indian feeling with regard to the Muhammadan question, the reforms and repeal of Rowlatt Act. Committee respectfully submit this action alone will secure real peace and contentment in the land.' "

(At this stage the Council adjourned for Lunch).

The Hon'ble Pandit Madan Mohan Malaviya:—"My Lord, the point to which I was drawing attention when the Council rose was whether there was open rebellion in Amritsar and Lahore and certain parts of the Punjab when this notification was published. Because, my Lord, the Bill starts with saying, it assumes, that there was open rebellion and all the acts which took place subsequent to the declaration that there was a state of open rebellion are based upon and flow from it, so to say. Now, my Lord, I have drawn attention to the general situation which existed in the Punjab and the country at about the time when this declaration was made. I have drawn attention to it in order that a bird's-eye view may be presented of the situation as a whole, and I have shown that the All-India Congress Committee drew the attention of Government to the fact that the disorders which had taken place had their origin not in anything in the attitude of the people so much as in the attitude of the authorities who had to deal with the people. Now, my Lord, I want to enter somewhat in detail into the circumstances which existed then. I consider it essential to do so in order that this cardinal fact, this key stone of this whole unfortunate edifice, which constituted the establishment of martial law and its result, should be fairly and squarely fixed at its proper place.

"Now, what happened was, my Lord, that in the last Session of this Council the Rowlatt Bill was introduced. That Bill was opposed practically unanimously by all the Indian members, and Government was urged to postpone legislation until another Session. The Government did not see fit to yield to that request. Agitation followed in the country and that agitation took one particular shape by the suggestion of Mr. Gandhi. That shape was that the people should express their dissatisfaction with the carrying out of the Rowlatt Act against the wishes of the people by observing a day of humiliation and prayer. My Lord, it is a pity that this action of Mr. Gandhi was not appreciated by all the Local Governments equally well; there were some, I am thankful to say, which appreciated it at its proper estimate and allowed the people to express their injured feelings in the way Mr. Gandhi had suggested. As a result of that suggestion, on the 30th March last a *hartal* was observed, that is, a general closing of the shops was observed at certain places and also at Delhi. At Delhi somewhat unfortunate events took place. Some people tried to put pressure upon some confectioners at the railway station to persuade them to close their business that day, and a crowd assembled, and what took place there led to firing. I do not want to go into greater detail in regard to this matter, but I want to indicate the general fact that the mob was there and as a consequence of what happened, the firing that took place, people's minds were more embittered. That was the first blunder committed. Then, my Lord, a second time firing took place at Delhi and that also gave cause for more resentment. But notwithstanding this unfortunate firing and the loss of life, and the wounds which it inflicted upon some of the people, it is a fact, which cannot be gainsaid, that the 6th April 1919, which was the great *Satyagraha* day throughout the whole country, was observed throughout the country peacefully. No untoward incident has yet been alleged to have occurred during the observance of that *Satyagraha* day. Now, what, my Lord, was the *Satyagraha* day? Hindus and Mussalmans, and Indian Christians, and generally the whole Indian community agreed unanimously to abstain from doing any business that day, closed all their business shops, undergoing a great deal of loss in order to show the general resentment of the Indian community at the attitude of Government, and as a step which might persuade the Government to reconsider their position. Now, my Lord, that passed off well, as I say, and Local Governments other than the Punjab Government did not find in the demonstrations that took place any occasion for embarking upon a policy of repression. But not so the Government of the Punjab as it was then constituted. On the 3rd and 5th April, the Government of the Punjab issued orders against Dr. Satyapal and Dr. Kitchlew forbidding them from making speeches in public. These two gentlemen submitted to that order and nothing untoward happened in Amritsar in consequence thereof. The 6th of April was observed as a *Satyagraha* day in Amritsar, as well as in other places, and the day passed off peacefully there too. Three days after, there was the *Ram Navami* procession in Amritsar, that is the day on which Rama's birth is celebrated. It is a great day with the Hindus, but this time Muhammadans and Hindus united with each other in celebrating that day. That is to say, Muhammadans came forward to express their full fellow-feeling with the Hindus in observing that day, and there were great processions in Amritsar, and the Deputy Commissioner of Amritsar witnessed these processions from the Allahabad Bank, where he was, I am told, sitting at the time. My Lord, there is absolutely nothing against the Government in that procession. I am told that while the people shouted out *Hindu Mussalman ki jai* and *Mahatma Gandhi ki jai* they also shouted out *King Emperor ki jai*; it was a perfectly loyal demonstration and had absolutely nothing to do with any political feeling.

"But there was one feeling which is very important and which has its political value, and that was that Hindus and Muhammadans acted towards each other in a friendly way in which they had never before in the history of Amritsar. Ordinary observances and caste restrictions and rules were put aside and their fraternising was a matter upon which every reasonable man, every God-loving man and man-loving man ought to rejoice. But on the following day at about 10.30 a.m. these two gentlemen, Dr. Satyapal and Dr. Kitchlew, were ordered to be deported from Amritsar. Nothing had happened up to the moment of their deportation which the public is aware of which would justify that order. They had been told to abstain from speaking in public; they had submitted to that order; nothing untoward had happened, there was no agitation which might endanger the public peace in Amritsar; and yet the Punjab Government thought it fit to issue this order of deportation against two men who were at the moment idolised by the people because they were honest and honourable men and the people felt that the orders were unjust orders.

"Now, my Lord, that was the second blunder committed in Amritsar. And what was the attitude that was behind that blunder? While other Local Governments noted the fact that public feeling was incensed against the attitude o the Government in the matter of the Rowlatt Bill, they thought it fit to allow that feeling to have its free and full expression.

"The Lieutenant-Governor of the Punjab, on the other hand, thought he must teach a lesson to those who were agitating. In a speech delivered from his seat in the Legislative Council he threatened action and also expressed his dissatisfaction. He said he would take very severe action and that threat he carried out unfortunately in the order of deportation. What happened? Before news of deportion was received business was going on as usual at Amritsar, banks were open, other public offices were open, in fact business men were transacting business as usual. When the news arrived there was a general feeling of resentment and sorrow. Shops were closed in a short time. At that time Mr. John, the Municipal Engineer, cycled through the city. He found people doing their business as usual, there was nothing to give any indication that trouble was coming, and when he passed through the crowds no one noticed him. He found crowds passing the National Bank, and the Chartered Bank, as also the Town Hall and other public buildings. The crowd went in the direction of the Deputy Commissioner's bungalow, as has been stated in the evidence of officials as well as non-officials, their object was to go to the Deputy Commissioner and to request that these men, Doctors Satyapal and Kitchlew, should be released. Up to then the mob showed no signs of mischief; they passed several public buildings without any thought of injuring them. When they reached the Amritsar foot-bridge they found that a military picket barred their proceeding further in the direction of the civil station. Now, at that place the mob was fired upon; they were at that time unarmed; I am told that they did not even have a stick in their hands; I am told that there was no attitude of defiance or violence and at that time it is possible that the mob might have been gently pressed back, gently and firmly pressed back. It was then that firing was resorted to and, as a consequence the people became incensed, and that some persons then died and some were wounded. News was taken to the city; this fostered the resentment of the people. Firing was resorted to a second time near this bridge and more persons were killed. The Deputy Commissioner, in his own statement, says that before firing took place the mob did not commit any excesses. I have evidence to show that violence was not done before the shots were fired. Now, my Lord, Mr. Miles Irving, the Deputy Commissioner, says that the worst that he expected from the deputation was a disorderly demonstration at his house. It is alleged on the side of the people that if this firing had not been resorted to, and if more restraint had been exercised, all the evils that followed might not have taken place. My Lord, what happened was deplorable. Infuriated by having some of the mob killed or wounded, a portion of the mob went back to the city saying, 'they have killed some of our men, let us fight them.' Up to that time the evidence proves that no harm was done, the mob then rushed back to where fuel is stacked, I have myself seen the stack of wood, they picked up pieces of wood near the railings and then lost their temper, returned and committed the foul murders that they did. I submit that these are the circumstances which we should bear in mind in considering what happened. I need not of course express my sorrow for the lives lost; every decent man must regret the fact that Mr. Stuart and Mr. Robinson and that other Europeans at the railway station were killed. The whole unfortunate affair was finished in the course of two hours. The report in the *Civil and Military Gaztte* says that at 5.30 p.m. all was quiet. I shall not go into the question whether the firing was justified or not, but I would draw attention to the fact that the firing having taken place, and the mob having become infuriated, it went into the city to revenge itself by taking the lives of five European fellow-brethren. In a couple of hours all was quiet at Amritsar. There was no trouble on the 11th. The people brought back the corpses, the Hindus and the Moslems decided that they should accompany the corpses in honour of the men and buried or burnt them according to their religion. They finished the whole job before 9 or 10. Thousands of people came out to accompany the bier of the unfortunate men who had been killed, and yet not a single untoward incident occurred in Amritsar. After having buried or burnt the corpses the people came back to the city and all was quiet. On the 12th again all was quiet at Amritsar. On the 13th the Seditious Meetings Act was proclaimed in Amritsar. Upto that time all was quiet. I should like any member on behalf of the Government to cite one single fact or circumstance which would show that after 5.30 on the 10th April, when these unfortunate deaths took place, at the railway station and banks, that there was a single incident at Amritsar which could by any stretch of imagination be construed into open rebellion. My Lord, what happened on the 13th? It is distressing to think of. On the evening of the 12th a certain number of persons tried to have a meeting held in a certain place in the city, very few people attended, but it was announced at the meeting that a meeting would be held on the following day at Jallianwala Bagh. This is a place which is surrounded on all sides by houses, there are three or four exits to it, the biggest is on one side and the smaller exits are not larger than the doors of this hall. I am told that between 16,000 and 20,000 persons assembled there. It was given out that Lala Kanhaya Lal, a very old esteemed pleader of Amritsar, would preside. Lala Kanhaya Lal told me personally that he never was approached and that he never gave his consent to preside, that this was falsely given out.

"That was a ruse to draw the people to the meeting. Hearing that a man of his position and respectability was going to preside, many people came to attend the meeting. That day also happened to be my Lord, the *Bysakhi* day.

"The *Bysakhi* day is one of the most important days in Amritsar, and on that day one of the biggest *melas* is held there. People come to Amritsar for the *mela* from long distances, not only from the interior parts of Amritsar, but from long distances, from Rawalpindi and Peshawar. A number of Sikhs and Jats had come to Amritsar for the *Bysakhi* day. These people not knowing that meetings had been prohibited assembled in the Jallianwala Bagh in large numbers, I am told they numbered about 20,000. The *Civil and Military Gazette* states in its report that the people numbered about 6,000. But whatever the number may be the gathering was certainly a very large one. My Lord, when the meeting had assembled, when several thousands of people had assembled, an aeroplane passed over the place where the meeting was to be held, and within half on hour or so of this, came the troops, and while the people were sitting down to hear the lecture which was being delivered by one of the men, the troops came and fired upon the people—and the people say, without giving them any warning or any time to run away from the meeting. Now, my Lord, it has been stated by the Hon'ble the Home Member, that 'the number of persons who had been killed there has been traced to 300.' But from a letter received this morning by me from a friend, I am informed, that the number of deaths which have been traced already amounts to 530 killed and 190 wounded, and among the 530 killed, he gives me the names of 42 boys whose ages range as follows: 1 from 7 months, who was being carried by his father to the place, to 15, 17, 18, 14 and one of 4 years, more than one of 12 years, several of 14 years and several of 15 years. These are the names of the boys who were killed at this meeting. The names of many others might be forthcoming, but even if this list is final as I very much wish and hope it may be, even, then, my Lord, the number is appalling to think of and it is also horrible to think of the fact that people assembled at a meeting sitting down to hear a lecture should be fired upon by His Majesty's troops, and when they were running for their lives they should still be fired upon, and that so many of them should be killed in a few minutes' time. Now, my Lord, I should like the Hon'ble the Home Member with all his reading of history to cite one instance so horrible to think of as the one like the Jallianwala Bagh, and to tell me if any Government has attempted to pass an Indemnifying Bill to justify anything approaching the deeds that were perpetrated in the Jallianwala Bagh.

"My Lord, I will go back to Lahore for a moment. I will come back afterwards to the events that followed at Amritsar. But let me say here that even after this butchery in the Jallianwala Bagh—and the Bagh is now called the bloody Bagh—even after this the people did not show the smallest sign of committing any violence. They submitted to these atrocities, they calmly resigned themselves to it and there is not one single incident mentioned which would justify anybody to describe the state of things in Amritsar, even after that event and before it was proclaimed that there was a rebellion in Amritsar, as an act of violence or hostility to Government. This was, my Lord, on the 13th of April. On the same day by a notification, to which I have already referred, it was declared that a state of open rebellion against the authority of the Government existed in certain parts of the Punjab, and by an Ordinance this was extended to Lahore and Amritsar, which were the first which came in for the operation of this declaration. Now, I submit, my Lord, with great respect, there is nothing I know of, and I have taken pains to verify the facts, to justify the declaration that there was a state of open rebellion in Amritsar on the day that your Lordship was advised that there was rebellion. I will go back to

Lahore. Lahore observed the 6th of April as a *Satyagraha* day. The day passed off peacefully. Up to the 10th no untoward event happened in Lahore either. On the 10th owing to the news of Dr. Satyapal and Dr. Kitchlew having been deported, there was all this trouble in Amritsar. The same day news was received in Lahore that Mr. Gandhi had been arrested, and deported to a place unknown, I mean to say, the place where he was deported was not announced. Now, my Lord, Mr. Gandhi, as is probably known, not only to my Indian friends but to every gentleman in this country, or at least ought to be known, is a gentleman who is held in the highest reverence by millions of people. By his saintly character, by his desire not to hurt any fellow-man, by his desire to stand up for truth, justice and humanity, he has established himself in the affections and reverence of the people to an extent which is not enjoyed by any other of my fellow countrymen. Mr. Gandhi having been responsible for the *Satyagraha* day being observed, he had to issue instructions that the day should be observed without any violence, without causing hurt to any fellow-men; but certain unhappy events to which I have already referred having taken place at Delhi, public sentiment having been roused by these events, Mr. Gandhi was coming to Delhi to quiet the people and to see that feeling should not be further embittered. While he was on his way to Delhi the Government of India was advised to issue an order confining him to Bombay, and the Government of the Punjab and the Delhi administration issued orders prohibiting him from entering the Punjab and Delhi. My Lord, that was a gratuitous insult offered to Mr. Gandhi. Any Government ought to feel honoured by the presence of a man like Mr. Gandhi within its own jurisdiction, and in asking Mr. Gandhi to keep out from the Punjab and the Delhi province, the administrations of those places showed that they did not like the broadminded view which those at the head of administrations are expected to take in such matters. Well, the result was that as the news was received that Mr. Gandhi had been arrested and deported, the temper of the people was tried. At Lahore, a mob gathered and they were going towards the Government House towards the Upper Mall, in order, I am told, to go up to Government House to make a representation. They passed several European buildings; they passed several European gentlemen without showing the smallest sign of any desire to hurt anybody. The Europeans who have their shops on the Upper Mall did not find any of their shops injured, not even a pane injured. When they were on the Upper Mall at one place the police wanted to prohibit them from going any further and wanted to turn them back. They did not like to be turned back, but eventually they agreed and they did turn back, and their attitude in going back shows that if firing had not been resorted to, there would have been no evil consequence resulting from the presence of the mob at that place for a little while. A little gentle persuasion, a little firmer attitude, if need he, would have succeeded, that is the belief of a lot of people. Now, my Lord, that having happened, when the mob were going back near Anarkali, they were fired upon and certain persons lost their lives. This enraged public feeling, but what happened? I ask your Lordship to note that there is no people on earth that I know of, that I have read of, or heard of, who would have shown their law-abiding character better than did the people of Lahore and Delhi where the firing had been resorted to. They did not do any anything, they went back to their homes. It was all quiet at 8 o'clock. Before the people had returned to their homes, Government House had been seized by panic. Messages were sent to the troops to be in readiness and to take up positions. Ladies in the Club and other places were told to hurry back home. Several of them did, but at 8 o'clock all was quiet, and those ladies who had gone to Government House were permitted to go back to their homes. The people did not do anything to justify the panic. The whole thing was over in a short time. Whether the firing was justified or not, leaving that question apart, the whole thing was over within an hour and a half or two hours, and there was quiet in the city, and that same day the Lieutenant-Governor was entertained at a party. That was on the 10th. What happened on the 11th? The people here again asked that they should be allowed to carry their dead in procession, and they performed the ceremonies that they had to, but nothing further happened. On the 12th there was a meeting at the Badshahi Mosque. The people had assembled there to express their regret at what had happened, the shops continued to be closed, but no harm was being done to anybody except the poor men, who were suffering for want of food, and Lala Harkishen Lal, to his honour it may be mentioned, said he would subscribe Rs. 1000 to help to keep the people from starvation. At that meeting there was a Criminal Investigation Department man who went into the meeting and expressed sentiments which people resented. This man was roughly treated, his *pugree* was thrown aside, but afterwards the meeting passed off quietly; nothing more happened. When the people were going back they say thay passed the troops and they say there was something which led the troops to fire. Again some cf the people were injured, some killed. Now, my Lord, what happened afterwards? Even after this unfortunate incident the people kept quiet. There was nothing, not a flower-pot injured in Lahore, not a pane of glass broken by the people—I did not hear what the Hon'ble the Law Member said....."

The Hon'ble Sir George Lowndes:—"The Hon'ble Member was not intended to hear."

The Hon'ble Pandit Madan Mohan Malaviya—"The noise was so great I thought something was said for me."

The President:—"I am sure the Hon'ble the Law Member would have got up in his place if he had wished to put any question; that is the usual course."

The Hon'ble Pandit Madan Mohan Malaviya:—"Now, my Lord, what are the incidents which the Hon'ble the Home Member, or anybody supporting the Bill, would expect as happening between the evening of 10th and midnight of the 15th which would justify a declaration that there was a state of open rebellion in Lahore? The Law Member has not uttered one word to justify that view. Now I submit that there was nothing; that the people were living quietly; that whatever action had been taken by the Government in the shape of placing the military and police in positions and everything else was done and there was quiet in Lahore. Whether the quiet was due to the action taken by Government or whether it was due to the innate good sense of the people is a matter which I will not go into. Any way the result was there. There was quiet in Lahore, and all the panic which resulted in ladies being frightened into leaving Lahore and being sent up to hills seems to be utterly unjustifiable. My Lord, up to the 15th then if this was the state of Lahore and Amritsar, how is this Council being asked to assume that there was a state of open rebellion in those places? Why should this sweeping Indemnifying Bill be put before this Council and the Council asked to support it? Let me refer to a few other incidents that happened in the Punjab. It is said that this open rebellion was to be found in other places in a few days. But, my Lord, note the sequence of events. This was up to the 10th of April. I have shown that on the 10th of April what happened at Amritsar was due to the deportation of Dr. Satyapal and Dr. Kitchlew, and after the 10th to the news of the arrest and deportation of Mr. Gandhi and possibly also, though I cannot say, my Lord, to the receipt of the news of what had happened at Amritsar. Now beyond that we have nothing to show that there was a state of rebellion in those places. And what is the next place to which I should invite attention? It is Gujranwala. Gujranwala kept quiet. Up to the 13th we did not hear of any untoward incident there. They had held a meeting; they had observed the *Satyagraha* day; they had shown their opposition to the Rowlatt Act, but nothing further had happened. It was on the 14th, when the news of the Jallianwala Bagh massacre reached Gujranwala that the people committed some excesses. But let me tell you what they did. 'There was a complete and spontaneous *hartal* in the whole town; everything went off orderly and everything was perfectly quiet in the town,' as the judgment in the Pleader's case shows. Then, my Lord, on the 13th as the news of the arrest of Mr. Gandhi had reached the town and the citizens were thinking of observing a *hartal* on the 14th, the matter of holding a meeting in case of the proposed *hartal* was considered at an informal meeting at the house of Diwan Mangal Sen. Please note, my Lord, what happened. Diwan Mangal Sen, one of the most esteemed men in Gujranwala, who had made his contributions to His Majesty's Government during the war, and considerable contributions too, along with many other respectable men, were hauled up and tried as persons who had waged war against the King. On the 12th when they met to consider the matter, after having decided what they would do, they informed the authorities that the people had decided to close business on the 14th. Mirza Sultan Ahmed, the acting Deputy Commissioner, issued instructions to the Municipal Commissioners asking them to see that everything remained quiet on the 14th. They did not do so in a surreptitious way.

"They did all in a fair, frank and open manner and there was nothing wrong which they had to conceal. The proceedings of the meeting of the Municipal Commissioners and the conversations which took place with the Deputy Commissioner are, I understand, on the record.

"Now the morning of the 14th of April opened well. All was quiet. There was complete spontaneous *hartal* throughout the city on this day. A big *Bysakhi* day was held at Wazirabad which is visited by numerous people from Gujranwala and other places. Hence there was a tremendous rush for Wazirabad in the 7.30 train. Booking was therefore stopped and many people were thus kept back. Out of this arose a general feeling to the effect that either all or none should go to the fair at Wazirabad. The train moved and in the rush the guard was stopped from getting into his compartment. As the guard was left behind, the train stopped at the distant signal. The mob at the station rushed towards the train and succeeded in getting out of the train many of the people. The mob asked the driver to come down and the driver did so. There was thus nobody in charge of the engine. Some of the mischievous hooligans then took some burning charcoal from the engine and set fire to old rejected sleepers lying near the Gurukula bridge. The happenings were purely accidental, being due to the mischief of these very few people and were not at all premeditated. It is worthy of note that no damage at all was done to the bridge and the train passed away safely after some delay. Now, my Lord, as the mob was returning from the Gurukula bridge *via* the Grand Trunk Road, which runs parallel to the railway lines, it was increased by handreds of other people from the town and the railway station. The news was on every lip that a slaughtered calf was hung up from a girder on the railway bridge on the Lahore side. Hindu and Muhammadan relations were perfectly friendly at the time, and people therefore suspected that this was the work of the C. I. D. This idea gained strength from the fact that there is a large number of Hindu temples in that vicinity. The effect of this idea was most unfortunate on the public. Munshi Din Muhamad, a local pleader and a Muhammadan leader, declared that it could not be the work of Muhammadans and that he would himself remove the carcase. This convinced the public that it was not the work of any Muhammadan acting on his own behalf and that it was the work of some police underlings. the excitement reached a very high pitch when people who had seen a slaughtered pig on the other side of the station gave this news to the mob. The mob had now reached the place where the slaughtered calf was hung up. Mr. Heron, the Superintendent of Police, had also reached the place. Some of the enraged mob caught Mr. Heron and managed to throw him down and snatched away his pistol. This they did because they thought the police underlings had done the mischief to which I have referred. These young men were however calmed down by Mr. Din Muhamad, who persuaded them to leave Mr. Heron alone and to give him back his pistol. When Mr. Heron had thus received his pistol he fired on the mob, particularly on those young men who had given it back to him. Now several persons were wounded—*vide* page 32 'Punjab Disturbances,' published under the authority of Government. Thereupon, the excitement was fanned into a flame. The crowd then returned to the railway station and demanded the blood of Mr. Heron who had so unjusty fired upon them, and one of the men who was so wounded died the following day. The huge crowd faced the police, the municipal Commissioners and the magistrates who had all arrived at the railway station, for more than two hours, the Grand Trunk Road alone separating the two. The mob continued to yell, tremendously enraged at the spilling of innocent blood. Mr. Heron wanted to open fire on the mob, although the magistrates and the municipal commissioners were doing their utmost to push the mob back into the town. The latter had just succeeded in persuading some people to go back when a shot was fired—accidentally or deliberately I cannot say—by a police constable. This fanned the flame again into a fire. The crowd, which had so far been passive and sullen, now got enormously enraged at this. They swelled in number. Mr. Heron gave the order to fire. Fire was consequently opened and many casualties occurred. Thereupon the excited mob resorted to many acts of incendiarism, burning the post office, the dak bungalow, the tahsildar's and the Honorary Benches' Courts, a block of the district courts, the railway godown, and the church. This again is vouched for in the 'Punjab Disturbances' published under authority. . . . ."

The Hon'ble Mr. J.P. Thompson:—"What authority has the Hon'ble Member for saying that the pamphlet entitled 'The Punjab Disturbances' was published under the authority of the Punjab Government?"

The Hon'ble Pandit Madan Mohan Malaviya:—"Is that not so? It is compiled from the 'Civil and Military Gazette,' second edition. Does my Hon'ble friend say that it is not published by the authority of the Punjab Government?"

The Hon'ble Mr. J.P. Thompson:—"The cover states by whom it was published."

The Hon'ble Pandit Madan Mohan Malaviya:—"My Lord, if Mr. Thompson will not give me a direct answer I am sorry I cannot say more. I was told it was an authoritative publication. If it is not, I am sorry for the statement, but he ought to tell me whether it was or was not. We want facts. It contains many official Communiques.

"Now, my Lord, the people who were wounded by the firing of Mr. Heron at the Siddhan bridge where the slaughtered calf was hung up were taken through the bazaar to Niyanin where an open air meeting was all the time being held to keep the public engaged. At this meeting, speeches on Hindu-Muhammadan unity were delivered, and the people were advised to be calm, *vide* instruction given to the Manager of the Islamia School by the acting Deputy Commissioner to deliver a lecture at the meeting. The Manager's statement in the Pleaders' case will be quite sufficient for that purpose. The point I am coming to is that this was all the trouble, the regrettable, unfortunate trouble. But it was all over by about 3 p.m. Morever, there had been no riots in the city proper. The people had kept perfectly quiet in the city, and all these events occurred in the civil station outside the Circular Road. Between 3 and 4 p.m., just about the time when, as was said in the *Civil and Military Gazette* report, the crowd was dispersing, aeroplanes arrived. Now, my Lord, the crowd had dispersed and the remnants of the crowds were dispersing when the aeroplanes arrived and bombs were dropped from the aeroplanes in several places. I have seen several of the places where these bombs were dropped, and I have learnt on the spot that several lives were lost, five in one place and two in another. When the crowd had dispered or was going back, I should like the Council to be informed where was the necessity for dropping bombs from aeroplanes upon the town of Gujranwala? It was not in one place that bombs were dropped but in many places, and in places in the centre of the inhabited parts of the city which was all surrounded by houses. One bomb was also dropped in the boarding house of the Khalsa High School, where 160 boys were about the place at the time.

"Bombs were also dropped in the suburbs of Gujranwala where the mob had committed no excesses, and also outside the town of Gujranwala over the house of Lala Amar Nath, pleader, one of the secretaries of the Home Rule League. A bomb was also dropped in another village close by, where I am told, a woman and child were killed by it. Now, my Lord, I should like anybody to tell me what earthly justification there could be for the dropping of half a dozen or may be more, I cannot say, bombs from aeroplanes over the people of Gujranwala when the mob had dispersed or was dispersing. This happened on the 14th. Everything was then quiet in the town, and a bomb was dropped again in Gujranwala on the morning of the 15th. I should like to know what justification can be pleaded for these actions. Now, my Lord, in spite of all this the people kept quiet. There was no rising of the people, there was no violence committed by the people. What little happened near the railway station was under the circumstances which I have mentioned to you. One European gentleman, an engineer, I think, was living about a mile or so away, I cannot give the exact distance, but sufficiently far away from the scene where the mob had committed any excesses. There was no danger to European life and no insult to any European lady. Why then was this bombing resorted to? My Lord, I should like here to know what was there in the state of Gujranwala to justify the declaration, to bring it in the category of places where there was proclaimed to be a state of open rebellion?

"Now, it is noteworthy, and I wish the Council to note that the events which took place at Kasur, the regrettable murder of two Europeans there and the cutting of telegraph wires in some places, the derailment of trains here and there; these are the events which took place. The papers gave a list of them and you know them. These unfortunate regrettable events took place subsequent to the 10th of April, when a wrong had been done, when as the people believed an unjustifiable wrong had been done to a number of members of the public by the firing that was resorted to at Amritsar. My Lord, you must make allowances, take note, I mean to say, of the circumstances which surround the case, and the fact that these events took place in these places after the deplorable occurrences at Amritsar is a circumstance to be taken into account. I do not want to extenuate the evil that was wrought. I deplore it, but I think it will not be right, it would not be just to exclude from one's consideration the sequence of events in order in judging where how much blame ought to be allotted to one or other party or to certain parties. Now, my Lord, I leave the main incidents so far as they affect the questions of a state of open rebellion at that. I would now invite your Lordship's attention to the second important part. What I have said has reference to the statement in the preamble of the Bill that 'owing to recent disorders in certain districts in the Punjab and other parts of India, it has been necessary for the purpose of maintaining and restoring order to resort to Martial Law.' I respectfully question the correctness, the truth, of this statement, and I submit that if the Council is not placed in possession of facts that may be in the possession of Government, if the Council is not placed in possession of facts which would justify the statement that there was open rebellion in Amritsar, Lahore and other places, this preamble of the Bill ought not to stand where it does.

"Then, my Lord, the second point to which I would invite attention is, in the preamble also. It says that it was necessary for the purpose of maintaining and restoring order to resort to martial law. Now, my Lord, what are the facts? I have submitted that all was quiet at Amritsar at about 5.30 or so on the afternoon of the regrettable day when several European and Indian lives were lost. On the 11th and 12th there was no violence on the part of the people. On the 13th the violence that took place was on the part of some of the authorities and not of the people. Beyond the 13th nothing took place on the part of the people. How was it necessary, then for the purpose of maintaining or restoring order to resort to martial law? Order had been restored; the passions, the regrettable passions which had led to certain crimes, had been exhausted, had exhausted themselves. The people felt that there was nothing more to be concerned about. There is one important circumstance to which I will draw attention in this connection. The Hon'ble the Home Member made a fervent appeal to those of my friends who have been blessed with large stakes in the country to reflect what would be their fates and the fates of their property if law and order were not to be preserved. Let me tell the Hon'ble Member and all who may wish to know it that the police in Amritsar was practically absent after these disorders and that the people themselves organised parties and kept watch and ward over the city and very few unfortunate events occurred; I believe that none occurred at all, so far as I am told. The people finding that the police were not doing their duty in keeping watch and ward and giving protection, organised themselves into parties and protected their town from any mischief either within or from outside. I submit, therefore, that the statement that it was necessary for the purposes of maintaining or restoring order to resort to martial law is not correct, so far as Amritsar is concerned.

"Now, let me come to Lahore. Is it correct in the case of Lahore? I have submitted that while Lahore had a large European population neither at the time of the trouble on the 10th nor at any other time was any European in danger of his life or of his liberty. It is said, as was pointed out by Mr. Chanda, several days after the events that a European police officer had received a hurt and that his head had to be bandaged, but it was also stated that the hurt had been caused to him by a policeman. That being so, my Lord, I ask every member of this Council to call for information which would convince him that there was any danger which any reasonable man—men who are overtaken by cowardice or who have a craven fear, an indefinable fear may run into panic—but I should like to know any circumstances which could have led any decent man, European or Indian, to think that his life or honour was in danger in Lahore during the days between the 10th and 15th April, when it was declared that Lahore was in a state of open rebellion. I submit it was not. I submit that it is to the credit of Lahore that though these unfortunate events, shooting of some innocent persons had occurred, it kept its head cool and it did not give its fellow-citizens, its European fellow-citizens, men or women, any cause to think ill of the people of Lahore. It did not give any fellowman among Europeans any cause to adopt an attitude of resentment much less of vindictiveness towards any fellowman, and yet, my Lord, it was declared that Lahore was in a state of rebellion. I submit it was not, and that is a cardinal point in dealing with this Bill.

"My Lord, what are the orders that were issued under martial law, which even by the wildest stretch of the imagination can be said to have been demanded for maintaining or restoring order? What are the facts which made it necessary to issue the orders for maintaining or restoring order in Lahore? I gave notice, my Lord, I tried to elicit facts by a string of questions; unfortunately as I have said before Government has not thought fit to answer them, and I take it, I am entitled to take it by implication, that they have admitted the truth of it; at any rate until on behalf of Government facts contrary to those implied in my questions are stated, I am entitled in dealing with a matter of such grave importance as this Bill to assume that the truth of those statements cannot be impeached. Now, my Lord, what are the martial law orders that were issued? Before I proceed further I should like to refer to the particular martial law order to which the Hon'ble the Home Member drew attention. If in the light of subsequent events the spirit of that order had been observed, we would not now be discussing this Bill to-day. But unfortunately the acts carried out went far beyond and greatly against the spirit of that order. The first question to which I shall draw attention is that of flogging. How many persons were flogged and for what offences? I have looked into the question and

I find that there is a provision that flogging should not be one of the punishments to be inflicted by the Martial Law Commissions. If I am right, and I think I am right, then it is regrettable that flogging was resorted to the extent it was during the continuance of martial law at Lahore, Amritsar and other places. My Lord, can anyone tell me that it was necessary to resort to flogging in order to maintain order or to restore order? With the ample military resources of the Empire to which your Lordship referred in your speech on the 3rd instant, did the Government stand in any danger of having their authority upset if they did not resort to this vile form of inflicting punishment on a fellow-man. I should like to know what justification can be pleaded for the flogging that was resorted to in various places. My Lord, leading men were arrested in Amritsar. I will refer to the orders as I find them in order to save time.

"My Lord, I asked the Government to be pleased to lay on the table copies of orders and proclamations, posters, notifications and notices issued by the administrators of martial law in the Punjab....."

The President:—"Order! Order!! The Hon'ble Member is entirely out of order. He knows perfectly well that this is a question he put forward to me as President to be allowed or disallowed. I disallowed it for reasons which appear on the face of the rules in regard to the asking of questions. The Hon'ble Member knows perfectly well that no discussion in Council can be permitted in respect of any order of the President under rule 7 or rule 8. I cannot allow the Hon'ble Member to proceed with what is really a discussion of my orders in regard to that matter."

The Hon'ble Pandit Madan Mohan Malaviya:—"Thank you, my Lord, I did not propose to discuss your Lordship's order. I wanted information and I was going to explain why I have not got it."

The President:—"You proposed to discuss it in another way."

The Hon'ble Pandit Madan Mohan Malaviya:—"True, indirectly that would be the result, my Lord."

The President:—"Quite so. I am glad that the Hon'ble Member has made that admission. That is exactly what he is aiming at, and I do not intend to permit it."

The Hon'ble Pandit Madan Mohan Malaviya:—"My Lord, the propriety of your disallowing the question was not the point I had in mind; what I wished to explain was, that I was not able to refer to proclamations, etc., which had been issued. I hope, my Lord, that you will feel that that is the correct explanation. I am in the unfortunate position that in discussing a Bill of this comprehensive character which deals with martial law I have to refer to martial law notifications, etc., and if I refer to the difficulties in which I am placed I have not the remotest idea, my Lord, directly or indirectly, of making a reference to the propriety of your disallowing my question. Many martial law orders and notices were issued. I am unfortunately not in a position to place them all before the Council, because I have not got them. I shall try to show that all could not possibly be justified on the ground that they were necessary for the purpose of maintaining or restoring order. That is the point on which I am asking the attention of the Council. Let me refer to one. I am told that in a lane known as the *Duglan-ki-Gali* Lane* every Indian irrespective of age or position had to pass through crawling on his belly the whole length of the lane. British soldiers were placed there to see that the order was obeyed. I should like to know if this was necessary for the purpose of maintaining law and order? Then, my Lord, the electric lighting and the water-supply of the whole of the city of Amritsar including the civil lines was cut off for four or five days from the 12th of April last. It is also a fact that a large number of wells in the city of Amritsar had been closed when Mr. King was Deputy Commissioner, because he thought that the water of the wells was not healthy. By the shutting off of electricity and water supply much hardship was inflicted on the people. I should like to know how this was necessary in order to maintain order or to restore order? Then, my Lord, it is said that a number of people, very respectable people, including bankers, lawyers and doctors, were kept handcuffed in pairs for several days. They were kept in an open racket court, where it was very hot in the day, and very cold at night. They were kept handcuffed continuously for 24 hours of the day for several days together and they had to eat, drink, sleep and attend to the calls of nature whilst handcuffed in pairs. I should like to know if it was necessary for the maintenance of law and order to issue such orders or carry out anything of that sort? Further, I am told that when on the 15th April the aeroplanes did their work and frightened the people of Gujranwala as they did, there was not the smallest suggestion that there was any spirit of rebellion or resistance in the town.

---

* In Amritsar.

"The Deputy Commissioner of Gujranwala, with a strong body of police and European soldiers and with an armoured car marched to the house of Lala Mela Ram, B.A., L.L.B., pleader, and arrested and handcuffed him and took him away, without allowing him to dress himself or to speak to his family. The party then met Mr. Labhsing, M. A. (Cantab), Barrister-at-law, and arrested and handcuffed him and chained him with Lala Mela Ram. They proceeded to the houses of twenty other gentlemen (pleaders, bankers and other respectable citizens) and arrested and handcuffed and chained them all together. The persons so arrested and chained together were marched to the city, two and two, headed by a Hindu and a Mahomedan, to ridicule Hindu and Mahomedan unity as was stated at the time by Colonal O'Brien. Two Municipal Commissioners under the order of Colonel O'Brien walked in front of the procession thus formed and pointing to the aeroplanes hovering overhead kept on shouting to Indian people to make way for the prisoners on pain of being bombed or shot down. After being thus paraded through the principal streets of the town the prisoners were taken to the railway station and put into an open coal-truck which was guarded by a number of European soldiers with fixed bayonets and by an armoured engine with a gun directed towards the prisoners. The prisoners were not allowed to leave their places even for the purposes of attending the calls of nature, and some to these gentlemen had to be there and to suffer all the trouble in the condition they were. My Lord, I am further told that on reaching Lahore railway station and before being removed to the jail, the prisoners were kept for about ten hours along with thirty other prisoners in a room which opened by means of an iron-barred and panelled door into another room which was used as a latrine My Lord, I am told that a number of pleaders and other respectable citizens in the town of Shekhupura in the District of Gujranwala, were arrested and treated in a manner similar to that adopted at Gujranwala and were subjected to similar inconveniences and indignities when being taken to Lahore. I am told further that almost the entire population of the town of Shekhupura above the age of 10 years, irrespective of rank or social position, was summoned by Mr. Bosworth Smith, I.C.S. Joint Deputy Commissioner and one of the Martial Law Officers, and made to sweep a large open piece of ground. I am told, further, my Lord, that a large marriage party of certain Mahomedans of the village of Rajgarh within the Municipal limits of Lahore was arrested and the members thereof were convicted by one of the Martial Law Officers. My Lord, these are some of the allegations which have been made in regard to the unfortunate events at Amritsar and Gujranwala. I should like to know which of these punishments was necessary for the purpose of maintaining or restoring order. Now, my Lord, I will draw the attention of the Council to some more facts, to give them an idea of the indignities perpetrated in other parts. I will draw the attention of the Council to the allegation, among others that Moulvie Gholam Mohi-ud-din, pleader of Kasur, who had last year been publicly rewarded for his services in connection with the War and Maulvie Abdul Qadir, a senior pleader of Kasur, were arrested and kept in confinement for some weeks in an improvised lock-up near the railway station, and were then released without any charge or trial. I am told that several school boys at Kasur were flogged, and I should like to know how that was necessary for the purpose of maintaining law and order. My Lord, it has been stated, and the facts cannot be denied, that Mr. Manoharlal, M. A. (Cantab), Bar-at-law, formerly Minto-Professor of Economics at the University of Calcutta and now a prominent member of the Lahore Bar, and a Syndic of the Punjab University, was arrested and kept in jail for nearly a month, including one week of solitary confinement. Will anybody tell me why it was necessary to put this respectable gentleman to this indignity? Will anybody tell me why this gentleman was arrested? I am told his whole sin was that he happened to be one of the trustees of the *Tribune* paper which had enraged some of the officials, particularly the head of the Punjab Government. For the crime of being a trustee of a paper which was edited by a gentleman whose name was known and whose articles have been pronounced by most competent and sober Indians to have been written very carefully, this respectable gentleman, a member of the Bar and a Minto-Professor, was subjected to this indignity. I should like to know from the Council's own lips how much indignity was inflicted upon him and how much hardship he suffered. I should like to know why this was done? Then Rai Saheb Seth Ram Pershad, a Municipal Commissioner in Lahore, one of the largest house proprietors and bankers of Lahore, was arrested in April last and marched in handcuffs to the Central Jail, a distance of nearly three miles, kept in solitary confinement, and then released without trial after several weeks. Does the Hon'ble the Home Member ask the Council to indemnify those officers who inflicted these indescribable indignities upon their fellowmen as respectable as any Member of this Council? Does the Hon'ble the Home Member mean to ask the Council to indemnify officers against such acts? My Lord, the list is long. I do not wish to take up the time of the Council unnecessarily except to the extent that it may be necessary to impress upon every member of this Council the necessity of examining carefully the provisions in the Bill and the proposal which is now before the Council before giving its assent. My Lord, there is a case from Amritsar, of Dr. Kedar Nath, a retired Civil Surgeon, aged 60 years, who had been invalided in 1909 on account of heart troubles; he was arrested and handcuffed and marched through the streets with 62 other prisoners to the jail and kept in confinement for a fortnight with two other prisoners in a cell which was meant for one person and then released without trial. Now, martial law notices were posted at the houses and shops of a number of people at Lahore with directions that the occupant must guard the posters, and that if they were damaged, torn or disfigured, the occupants would be severely punished under martial law. My Lord, one of these persons, an English lady, the wife of Pir Taj Din, herself told me that she had to keep a watch to see that the posters stuck to their house were not damaged or torn so that she and her husband might not come in trouble, and all this trouble could not be prevented by the fact of her being an English woman. I should like to know why it was necessary to subject respectable people to all this hardship and indignity?

"My Lord, the manner in which the students were dealt with can be gleaned from another incident to which I will call the attention of the Council. The students of Lahore have been wronged beyond expression, and I should like to know how it was necessary for the maintenance of law and for restoring order to deal with the students in the manner that was done. All the students of the Dayanand Anglo-Vedic College, the Dyal Singh College, Lahore, and the Medical College at Lahore were required to attend roll-calls before military officers when they were made to stand in the sun guarded by the military with fixed bayonets and this process was continued for three weeks immediately preceding their University examinations.

"In the case of the King Edward Medical College, the total distance which the students were made to traverse on foot in the summer heat for attending the roll call, amounted to not less than 16 miles a day. Some students actually fainted while going to, attending, or returning from, such roll-call parades and it was after that that a nearer place was fixed for taking the roll-call. My Lord, the Principals of certain Colleges in Lahore were coerced by the Martial Law Administrator to inflict very severe punishments on a certain percentage of their students without regard to any evidence of their guilt. Some of them were expelled, some were rusticated, some were sent down one year, and I am told that a number of students were fined. I am told that the total number of students who have been subjected to this injustice and wrong is about a thousand. I should like to know how this was necessary to maintain order.

"My Lord, it has been alleged by some of those who were tried that in the cases tried by some of the officers who were empowered to deal with these cases, especially toward the close of the martial law period, the accused were convicted without the whole of the defence evidence being heard, even though witnesses were present, on the ground of want of time. For instance, in the case of Lala Gurdasram and Lala Shivaram, pleaders of Hafizabad in the District of Gujranwala, who were sentenced to two years' rigorous imprisonment each by Mr. Wace, I. C. S. My Lord, a student, Ramlok, son of Daulatram, aged 17 years, was arrested on the 25th April, and having been detained in police custody for three weeks, was released for want of evidence against him. Several days after his release, his father Daulatram appeared as a defence witness for one Ram Ditta and deposed that the police had asked Ram Ditta to turn an approver but he had refused to do so. On this his son Ramlok was re-arrested on the following day and put on his trial for the very same offences for which he had been arrested and released before. The trial of Ramlok was fixed for the 9th and 10th June but as martial law was going to be withdrawn at midnight on the 9th June, the trial was accelerated to the 5th June without any previous intimation having been given to the accused or to his father. The accused was tried and sentenced to one year and seven months' rigorous imprisonment for offences under sections 147, 426 and 506, Indian Penal Code, by Mr. A.L. Hoyle, I. C. S., officer presiding over summary courts under martial law, without any chance being given to him to produce his defence.

"And, my Lord, one Bhagwansingh, a meat-seller of Lyallpur was arrested on the 6th June last and placed before the Martial Law Summary Court on the 7th June; on the 8th June part of the evidence was heard, and the case was adjourned; but as martial law was to be withdrawn at midnight on the 9th June, the case was taken up at 11 o'clock that night without any opportunity being given to his counsel to be present, and the accused was sentenced to three months' rigorous imprisonment.

"My Lord, in some of the cases tried by the Martial Law Commissions constituted under Ordinance No. 1 of 1919, no record of evidence of witnesses, either for the prosecution or the defence, has at all been made, nor judgments recorded, though heavy sentences have been awarded. For example, the case of Crown *versus* Fazla, son of Umar Din Kakezai, convicted under section 124-A, and sentenced to transportation for life by the Commission presided over by Lieutenant-Colonel Irvine, on the 26th of April 1919, and trials Nos. 20 and 21 of Hansraj and Hariram of Amritsar, before the Commission presided over by the Hon'ble Mr. Justice Leslie-Jones, I.C.S., Judge of the High Court of Judicature at Lahore, convicting the aforesaid persons to seven years' rigorous imprisonment each under section 412, Indian Penal Code. Now, my Lord, in several other cases examination of outside witnesses for the defence was refused except by interrogatories. In some, no one would like to believe it, but in some cases even the offence with which a man is charged has not been mentioned. I hold in my hand a copy of an order with findings, dated 26th May 1919, passed in the Court of A.L. Hoyle, Esquire, Magistrate, 1st Class, of the Lyallpur district at Lyallpur, in Martial Law Cases held at Lyallpur, for Dijkote Tehsil, Lyallpur.

It says:—

'Finding—All accused guilty.

'Penalty or disposal:—

'Accused No. 1, Basant Ram, 2 years' rigorous imprisonment,

'Accused No. 2, Charan Dass, 9 months' rigorous imprisonment,

'No. 3, Jawanda Ram, 9 months' rigorous imprisonment,

'No. 4, Bhagat Singh, 6 months' rigorous imprisonment,

(Sd) A. L. HOYLE
Summary Court

"My Lord, this is the way in which people have been deprived of their honour and liberty. Is it meant that these cases shall be indemnified?

"There is another copy of an order, dated 28th May 1919, with finding, passed in the Court of the same gentleman. Mr. A.L. Hoyle, Magistrate, 1st Class, at Lyallpur.

'Finding.

'Accused 1 to 12 each guilty of rioting (section 147, Indian Penal Code) and offence under section 25 of the Telegraph Act, accused 13, 14, 16 guilty under section 147, Indian Penal Code, accused 15, 17, 18 doubtful.

'Penalty or disposal.

'Accused Sita Ram (1) 2 years' rigorous imprisonment for each offence, accused Ram Dutt 6 months' rigorous imprisonment for rioting, 18 months' rigorous imprisonment for the offence under section 25, Telegraph Act, Amar Nath (2) Kesar Mall, Gyan Chand, Amar Nath (6), Agya Ram, Kaka Ram, Hari Chand, Divan Chand, Girdhari, Sita Ram (12), 6 months' rigorous imprisonment for rioting and 1 year's rigorous imprisonment under section 25, Telegraph Act. All sentences consecutive.

'Kesar Singh, Teja Singh and Bhag Singh 3 months' rigorous imprisonment, Nand Singh, Balwant Singh and Jaimal Singh acquitted.'

"Now my Lord, this is the way in which havoc has been made of the liberty and honour of many fellow subjects of ours.

"My Lord, there are other instances to some of which I must invite attention. An order was issued that every Indian who should pass by a European must salaam, and in some places they were told that they must get down from a carriage if they were driving at the time. In several instances unfortunately several Indians were flogged or otherwise punished for not salaaming to Europeans and not carrying out this martial law order. In one case one Gopaldas, son of Deviditta Mal, caste Arora, of Akalgarh, who was a telegraph peon at Lyallpur during the martial law days was arrested for not salaaming a European officer to whom he had gone to deliver a telegram and that he was given five stripes for it in jail, although he protested that he had actually salaamed the officer and was willing to do so again. I should like to know, my Lord, if this was necessary in order to maintain law and order. In some of the districts where martial law was in force orders were issued that every Indian driving in a carriage or riding a horse must get down when he passed by a European and, further, that Indians carrying open umbrellas must close and lower them when they met a European.

"My Lord, the evil was not confined to these few places and these few cases to which I have drawn attention. There has been much more injustice done and I shall draw attention to one of these that occurred in Ramnagar. I am reading from the Judgment at Ramnagar, my Lord. There were 28 persons accused. No untoward event happened at Ramnagar at any time.

"When the news of Gandhi's arrest reached there, I am told that a few boys expressed their mourning for the event and went to bathe in a river in the locality....."

The Hon'ble Sir William Vincent:—"May I inquire, my Lord, if this is the Ramnagar where the King's effigy was burnt?"

The Hon'ble Pandit Madan Mohan Malaviya:—"This was alleged, but it was an untruth."

The Hon'ble Sir William Vincent:—"I only wanted to know, my Lord."

The Hon'ble Pandit Madan Mohan Malaviya:—"My Lord, my friend thought that he had scored a great point in mentioning that. I have not less respect for His Majesty the King-Emperor than the Hon'ble Sir William Vincent has, but I will show to your Lordship and to the Council that an untrue story was concocted and had to be abandoned, and that the facts would not justify the punishment which was inflicted upon the people. Now, my Lord, at Ramnagar, on the 15th instant, a certain number of boys met together and expressed their grief or resentment, whichever you please, at the arrest of Mr. Gandhi and the Rowlatt Act. They went and had a bath in the river which runs through the locality. The event passed off, no notice was taken of it, and it was reported that there was quiet in Ramnagar. A few days afterwards the Deputy Commissioner, Colonel O'Brien I think it was, went there, certain instructions were given and the Revenue Assistant called a meeting of the citizens of Ramnagar and arrested four men. Several days afterwards, I think it was on the 12th of May or the 28th May, I do not exactly remember which, 23 or 24 other persons were got hold of and also *challaned*. Another man was subsequently arrested, and so the party was made up to 28. The charge against them was that they had burnt the effigy of the King. I will read the judgment to your Lordship. It says:—

'Bhagwan Dass, Kapur Chand and Barkat Ali are eye-witnesses to the fact that a mob of Hindus, in whom the 28 accused were included, burnt the effigy of King George on the bank of a creek of the Chenab near the town of Ramnagar and then marched back through the town. The leader in this was Hari Singh Giani, Headmaster, who produced a small effigy which he burnt on a funeral pyre on the bank and throughout acted as crier, while others answered as chorus. The cry raised was *Rowlatt Bill Kala Bill Marya* (and His Majesty's name is brought in and abused). 'The Rowlatt Bill, Black Bill is dead' (and abuse of the King-Emperor). The ashes were cast into the river by Hari Singh and most people bathed as purification. Other witnesses, one Hindu and several Muhammadans, give evidence that Hari Singh Giani, Daulat Ram, Balmokand, Karam Chand and Gobind Sahai organised a *hartal* on the afternoon of the 15th and had called all the Hindus to a meeting near the river. On their return they came through the town headed by Hari Singh as crier, shouting out *Rowlatt Bill Kala Bill Marya* (the Rowlatt Bill, the Black Bill, is dead, and abusing His Majesty—I am translating the words I do not wish to utter them). The crowds are said to have consisted of about 200; but all three principal witnesses united in naming the 28 accused. Some named others but these have been weeded out where not corroborated. The witness who saw the crowd return also named the accused though one or two were doubtful in the case of 5 or 6. . . . .

'All the accused plead not guilty. Most of them call witnesses for good character or for *alibis* of no value. It is noticeable that witnesses for the defence do their best to prove their own absence during the period of the alleged offence, which suggests that they are not prepared to deny that such a thing took place. . . . .

'Of the defence witnesses worth noticing, those for Balmokand tried to prove an *alibi* for him in Gujranwala. He himself claimed to be in Gujranwala up to 1.30 on the 15th.

. . . .

'Other witnesses speak of having met Balmokand on the road. But they avoid arguments which might agree and be tested on cross-examination. On the other hand, it is shown by evidence that Balmokand rode off from Gujranwala and passed Manchor, 3 miles from Ramnagar, at midday on the 15th. . . . .

'It is indisputable that the affair of burning the King-Emperor (he says burning the King-Emperor but he evidently means the effigy of the King-Emperor) took place. There certainly was a *hartal* and the people went to the river. Although a few witnesses for the defence try to declare that there was no *hartal* ever, this is disproved by the first report when it was known that anything more serious had happened and also by the anxiety of the majority of the defence witnesses to prove their own absence. The evidence that the King-Emperor was burnt in effigy by Hari Singh with the plaudits of the mob sitting round him is also ample. Two Hindus and one Muhammadan gave evidence to this, as also to the casting of the ashes into the river and the purification of Hindus by bathing. Many more witnesses prove the return of the party through the town with Hari Singh chanting in front *Rowlatt Bill Kala Bill Marya,* etc. The case did not come to light for a week and could not be investigated till later, but this was due to the absorption of all officials in the outrages elsewhere and the Sub-Inspector in those of Akalgarh. The story is not one that would have been invented. I find that the case has been well sifted and that the 28 accused are proved by the evidence of the prosecution to have been there.....

'The offence is so gross that the accused are lucky in not having been sent up to a Tribunal. Hence the maximum imprisonment must be inflicted on almost all Many of the accused are wealthy and heavy fines are very suitable. I sentence them as under:—

1. Daulat Ram,
2. Balmokand,
3. Karam Chand,
4. Gobind Sahai,
5. Hari Singh,

to rigorous imprisonment for two years, of which three months to be in solitary confinement and to pay fines of rupees one thousand each, or in default rigorous imprisonmemt for six months in addition.'

"Now, my Lord, the people say that if there was a fair trial it would have been established that this story was entirely untrue, and that they did not burn the effigy of the King-Emperor. Now, these people, as the judgment says, were wealthy and respectable, and for that reason they are sentenced to such heavy punishment and such large fines, which, in the case of such people, is a very serious matter. These respectable people had no reason to indulge in such foolish and wicked mischief, but you subject them to trial in a summary court, where their honour is concerned, and you do not give them an opportunity to establish their innocence, and they are sentenced to two years' rigorous imprisonment. These are the cases in which the Bill seeks that the sentences shall be confirmed. I submit, my Lord, that nothing could be a grosser wrong than to ask the Legislative Council to confirm sentences of this nature, where men have not been given an opportunity to have their defence properly put and where they have not been given an opportunity to appeal to a higher tribunal.

"Now, my Lord, I will not deal with any more cases. I think what I have submitted is suffiient to show how great is the need for having the facts of these unfortunate times sifted and well established before an Indemnifying Bill should be dealt with by this Council. As I have submitted before, there are two points essential in asking for an Indemnifying Act. One is, that there should have been either open rebellion or war against the King or riots or insurrection which amounted to war, which it was necessary to suppress; and secondly, even if such a necessity was shown to have arisen it should be further shown that the acts done were such as, in the language of the three Statutes which I quoted, were not only necessary but so much for the benefit of the public, that those acts ought to be justified by the Legislature, and that the officers who did them ought to be Indemnified. I submit, my Lord, that this has not been shown to be the case. Now, the Hon'ble the Home Member tells us that the question whether martial law was necessary will be discussed and settled by the Committee of Inquiry, but he says, 'Go further. Take the fact that martial law was declared. Then I ask you to consider the case, the position, the pitiable position, of those officers who were ordered or directed or commanded to do certain acts. We promised them in our Resolution of the 14th of April 1919 that we would give them our ample support. We are bound in honour to protect them from the results of actions which they undertook upon that assurance'. My Lord, that is begging the whole question. If you are not right in giving them that assurance, that assurance will not stand them in good stead. You ask that the Council should pass this indemnifying measure, and yet you say that the question whether martial law was necessary or not shall be determined by the Committee of Inquiry. I submit that this is a preposterous position to take before this Council. If the Bill is passed, what will be the effect of the decision by the Committee of Inquiry as to whether there was open rebellion in Lahore or Amritsar or not? In the quotation to which I have referred Earl Halsbury has made it clear that the Crown may not issue commissions in times of peace to try civilians by martial law; but when a state of actual war, or of insurrection, riot or rebellion amounting to war exists, the Crown and its officers may use the amount of force necessary in the circumstances to restore order.

"The cardinal point, therefore, is, whether there were circumstances which justified the declaration of martial law. You cannot go on to deal with this Bill without first dealing with that cardinal point. If you think that you owe it in courtesy to the Committee of Inquiry which you have constituted to leave the decision on that important matter to them, I say in fairness to every one concerned, including the Government, stay your hand, do not proceed with this Bill. Wait for the result of that inquiry. Let the facts be sifted out and when the facts have been sifted out, indemnify officers for all acts done in good faith with reasonable care and caution, for restoring order or maintaining it, wherever it might have been necessary. No sensible man would for a moment object to His Majesty's officers or those acting under their instructions being indemnified and protected against the consequences of acts done by them in good faith with reasonable care and caution in circumstances where the existence of martial law could be justified. But where the existence of martial law is not justified, where the very foundation upon which martial law rests is non-existent, I submit, that the officers who took certain steps against their fellow men have to take their chance of having their cases adjudged and determined in the light of equity and justice by ordinary courts in the country.

"Now, my Lord, the Hon'ble the Home Member said he did not want to prejudice the inquiry that the committee is going to make. But I am sorry to think that though he may never have meant it, his observations read outside this Council and in England will leave only one impression. If the object was to prejudice the inquiry, his speech could not be better framed than it was. My Lord, the Hon'ble the Home Member in effect said, 'Well, I do not want to go into the facts—that is a matter for the Committee of Inquiry. But the Committee of Inquiry are not going to censure any man for performing any act in good faith.' What is this, my Lord? Why raise the question now? When you say the Committee of Inquiry is not going to pass any censure upon any officer of Government for certain things, are you leaving the Committee quite free to do what they may think fit? Either leave the matter fairly to the Committee's decision, or say frankly, as you have the power to say it that you do not want any inquiry into these dark deeds and that you want to throw a veil over them. Throw it if you can; of course in this country you can do it, but perhaps the fear of the English public and Parliament might deter you from doing so. In that case I say wait, do not proceed with this Bill until you have the report of the Committee of Inquiry. The Committee of Inquiry will certainly be prejudiced if they read the speech of the Hon'ble the Home Member. They might well take it as their instructions from the Government, because the Hon'ble the Home Member represents your Excellency's Government in all these matters, even more perhaps than your Excellency does. I venture to say that the public will consider it very wrong on the part of the representative of the Government to give expression to the opinions and remarks to which the Hon'ble Member has given expression to-day. The Hon'ble Member also said that he did not want to prejudice any decision that the Privy Council may think it fit to pass on any of the appeals before them and pointed to a provision in the Bill, expressly guarding against the effect of this Bill upon any judgments which the Privy Council may wish to pronounce. But, my Lord, if you indemnify acts in the manner in which you are doing with the provisions in this present Bill, well may their Lordships of the Privy Council complain that you have done what no ordinary citizen is expected to do, namely, to pronounce judgment on some important aspects of the case before they have had time to deal with them.

"My Lord, I wish here to make it clear that I have done all that I could as an individual member of this Council to postpone the discussion of questions of fact and law relating to the events that have occurred. I gave notice of questions—I do not refer to them now—I am only showing how I gave notice of these questions with a view to elicit facts which might postpone the introduction of the Bill. Most Indian members of this Council, if not all, were anxious and they expressed their desire to the representatives of Government that the introduction of this Bill might be delayed until the Committee of Inquiry had submitted their Report. My Lord, we are not anxious for any particular verdict. God knows I am not anxious that the fault or guilt shall fall upon any particular individual. I only want the facts to be proved; I want that the facts being proved whosoever may have been responsible for acts which cannot be justified or excused should stand a trial before the public opinion of this country and the public opinion of the High Court of England. We think that when you have appointed a Committee of Inquiry to go into those facts, it is only fair that a discussion of facts which the committee has to deal with or the law which the committee may have to consider should be avoided. I should have been glad to avoid such a discussion but it has been forced upon me and I wish this to stand on the record of the proceedings of this Council. But, my Lord, now that this Bill has been introduced, we are compelled to refer to the events which have led to its introduction. The souls of those who died at Amritsar and other places, appeal to us to point out to your Excellency's Government the facts which are of a cardinal character, of vital importance, for a consideration of this Bill. The men who have lost their sons, those who have lost their brothers, the women who have lost their husbands, the mothers who have lost their sons, who are mourning the deaths of the relations who have met an untimely end, they plead through us for the most careful consideration of the whole affair. They plead that no decision should be arrived at and that no Act should be passed which would prejudice a proper consideration of their case. The Government cannot say that the delay of a few months will really prejudice their position. If the Hon'ble the Home Member, advised by the Hon'ble the Law Member, felt that if a Bill like this is not passed, every moment of the detention of numerous persons who have been condemned by the Martial Law Commissions and the Martial Law Summary Courts to imprisonment is unjustifiable, why did the Government not introduce the Bill earlier? Why did they not call a meeting of the Legislative Council earlier to deal with this matter? If they have allowed so much time to pass, if it is only now when public opinion is forcing attention to what has happened in the manner in which it is doing, that they now feel that they must have an Act to safeguard their officers, I say let them wait another few months until the Committee have reported.

"My Lord, there is a provision in the Bill giving retrospective effect to it. That provision might be of use to those who want this Bill at once in order to prevent the evil which may result to any officer by a suit having been instituted against him. I do not know of any case which has been instituted. The Punjab has been frightened beyond description; the Punjabis have been terrorised in a manner in which the people of no part of the country were terrorised ever before. In spite of the presence of Sir Edward Maclagan in the Punjab, that terror has not yet entirely been removed from the minds of the people. In this state of things they cannot be anxious, I do not know that many are anxious, to institute any suits for damages. I do not know that any suits have been instituted and that many are anxious to rush forward with cases into the Courts. All that they desire at present is, that what has happened should be established beyond doubt. It will be time then to consider for them what they should do. Indeed, after the Committee has reported they might well expect the Government to take such action as the Government might think fit, against such officers as may have been shown to have acted in an unjustifiable manner. Where the number of persons to whom injury has been done is so large and many of them are poor, you cannot expect that they will be able, that many of them will be able, to seek redress and to obtain it. It is only if the conscience of the Government, to which the Hon'ble the Home Member referred, if the conscience of the Government should be stirred by the recommendations of the Committee of Inquiry, if the Government should think that they owe it to His Majesty's Government and to the name of Britain and to British justice, that they should bring certain persons, they may be Indians, they may be Europeans, who have been guilty of inexcusable wrong-doing, to justice, it is only then there would be a chance of justice being done.

"My Lord, all these considerations support the view that the Government should not be in a hurry to proceed with the Bill.

"Having said this much on the general aspect of the Bill I shall now address myself to some of its provisions and to the remarks which the Hon'ble the Home Member made in regard to them. The Hon'ble the Home Member said that, when martial law is introduced, the officers of Government have not time to wait to examine things, that they must take prompt action, that they may perform acts which are illegal, but so long as they perform acts which are moral and proper they should be protected. From what I have said it will appear that it is very important to find out which acts come under that category, *viz.*, acts which though not legal are right and proper. Then he said that an Indemnity Bill of some character is the inevitable sequel to the introduction of martial law. I agree that an Indemnity Act of a certain character may be inevitable, but this involves two important questions. What are the circumstances in which an Indemnity Act is passed? And what should be its nature? The Hon'ble the Home Member quoted Dicey. He says that the time for which an Indemnity Act is passed must be one of national danger. I have shown that there was no national danger. In a few cases individuals lost their reason, were carried away by passion and committed deplorable acts, but we cannot say that these constituted national danger. My Lord, in this connection I wish to draw attention to the contrast to which reference was made in the cablegram of the Indian National Congress to which I alluded before in Council. At the time there was trouble at Lahore there was also trouble at Ahmedabad and Viramgam. His Excellency the Governor of Bombay allowed Mr. Gandhi to go to Ahmedabad and see the people and to work freely among them. He was able to quiet them, and also to censure them for the outrages they had committed. Martial law was gone in a few days. That was all that was needed at places like Amritsar and Lahore at the utmost. I say there was no justification for martial law in Amritsar, because it was stated to be quiet after 5.30 p.m., on the 10th of April. But assuming that there was justification for martial law on the 10th April, it should have been withdrawn by the 12th or 13th. The action taken in Ahmedabad forms a happy contrast and affords an instructive lesson in the light of what has happened here. The Hon'ble the Home Member says that there must be a period of national danger when martial law is introduced. I agree with him, but I submit that there was not a period of national danger in the Punjab to justify the introduction of martial law. The other point that he referred to when quoting from Dicey was, that the acts done must be *bona fide* and solely in the public interest. It is only in such cases that the persons can be indemnified. In view of all that I have said, I ask the Council to judge, whether a Bill of such a sweeping character as is before the Council, should be passed when the allegations which have been put forward on behalf of the people have yet to be ascertained. Then the Hon'ble the Home Member referred to various Colonial

Legislatures including the South African which have passed Indemnity Acts.

"I may mention here that members of this Council are put to great inconvenience for want of a good library for ourselves. We have at times to borrow books, not only from the library of the Legislative Department which perhaps causes them a little inconvenience, but also to get books from distant places in order to carry on our work. I am indebted for a copy of the Cape of Good Hope Act to the Hon'ble the Law Member, who lent it to me at my request. The absence of a good library hampers our work; if we had such a library we might be able to save much of the time of the Council and our own.

The Cape of Good Hope Act shows that a Commission consisting of the Lord Chief Justice of England, General Ardagh and Judge Bigham of His Majesty's High Court was appointed to inquire into the administration of martial law during the period of the Boer War. It would support what I said in regard to the constitution and powers of a commission of enquiry on a previous Resolution. Now to come to this Act, VI of 1900. This was passed while the Boer war was going on. It set out the circumstances under which the Act was introduced. It was to punish those persons who had taken up arms against Her Majesty the Queen or otherwise assisted her enemies. It was for the suppression of hostilities and for the maintenance of good order. My Lord, this Act cannot afford any parallel for the legislation which is now under consideration. The Act passed in 1902, No. 4 of 1902, is also important. It was an Act to indemnify the Governor of the Colony and the officer commanding His Majesty's forces in the Colony and all persons acting under their authority and in good faith, in regard to acts done or committed during the existence of martial law, to validate certain sentences passed by courts-martial or military courts and to confer certain powers on commissioners inquiring as to and reporting on such sentences being still unexpired. And it promised indemnity in respect of certain acts, matters and things whatsoever that were ordered as necessary for the suppression of hostilities or the establishment and maintenance of good order and government in or for the public safety of the Colony between certain dates.

"Now, my Lord, I submit that here again it had reference to the suppression of hostilities or the establishment of good order and government. It has to be shown that this was necessary.

"Secondly, my Lord, this Act which, I think, has been taken as a model for the Bill which is now before the Council points out that it is only acts done or committed during the existence of martial law which can be indemnified. The Bill in the Statement of Objects and Reasons does say that 'the object of the Bill is to indemnify officers of Government and other persons for acts done *bona fide* in the course of martial law during the recent disorders, and to provide for the continuance of the sentences passed by courts established under martial law.' But, the Council will see that the provisions of the Bill go far beyond it. Whether this was deliberate or unintentional, I cannot say, but the Council will see that the Bill says in clauses 2 'No suit or other legal proceedings whatsoever, whether civil or criminal, shall lie in any court of law against any officer of Government, whether civil or military, or against any other person acting under the orders of any such officer for or on account of or in respect of any act, matter or thing ordered or done or purporting to have been ordered or done for the purpose of maintaining or restoring order in any part of British India on or after the 30th of March 1919 and before the commencement of this Act.'

"Now, my Lord, as we all know martial law came into force in Lahore and Amritsar, at midnight of the 15th or rather at 12 o'clock of the night between the 15th and the 16th. By what justification then can events which took place from the 30th March to the date on which martial law was proclaimed be included within the scope of the Bill, I am unable to understand. Ordinarily such a Bill should be confined to the period during which martial law prevailed, but this Bill goes beyond that period, and the second terminus which it fixes is the commencement of this Act. I should like to know what justification there is for that either.

"My Lord, the next point to which I would refer is this. The Bill seeks to indemnify officers against their acts, 'provided that such acts, matters or things were ordered or done in good faith and in a reasonable belief that they were necessary for the said purpose.' This, my Lord, is very objectionable. All that you ought to do is to indemnify officers for acts, which were done in good faith and were in fact reasonable, and necessary. If a man shoots his fellowman it is for him to show that he acted in a reasonable manner and in good faith. Now, is that man to be indemnified? In this matter I would draw attention to a few observations of Mr. Justice

Chamberlain in one of the State Trials which took place in 1799. It was the case, my Lord, of Wright *vs* Fitzgerald. Wright brought a suit against Fitzgerald for assault and battery. He had been flogged by the order of Fitzgerald, 50 lashes had been given to him and in addition 50 more. Now, in disposing of that case, Mr. Justice Chamberlain proceeded to charge the jury as follows:—'His Lordship said that the jury were not to imagine that the legislature, by enabling magistrates to justify under the Indemnity Bill, had released them from the feelings of humanity, or permitted them wantonly to exercise power, even though it were to put down rebellion. No, it expected that in all cases there should be a grave and serious examination into the conduct of the supposed criminal; and every act should show a mind intent to discover guilt, not to inflict torture. By examination or trial he did not mean that sort of examination and trial which they were then engaged in, but such examination and trial, the best the nature of the case and the existing circumstances would allow of.' That was what Mr. Justice Chamberlain said. He said that 'every man, whether Magistrate or not, was authorised to suppress rebellion, and was to be justified by that law for his acts, it is required, that he should not exceed the necessity which gave him the power; and that he should show in his justification, that he had used every possible means to ascertain the guilt which he had punished; and, above all, no deviation from the common principles of humanity should appear in his conduct.'

"My Lord, the Legislature is asked at this moment. . . . . ."

The Hon'ble Sir George Lowndes:—"Will the Hon'ble Member kindly give me the reference?"

The Hon'ble Pandit Madan Mohan Malaviya:—"It is State Trials, Vol. XXVII, 1820. Now, my Lord, I submit that in these remarks of Mr. Justice Chamberlain, we get a great guidance for our work in which the Council is asked to engage itself. We are not a Court sitting here to consider whether a person charged for having committed any particular act during the recent disturbances should have a decree passed against him or should be exempted. The Legislature is sitting at present to lay down the principles and the provisions under which the case of such a man should be tried and considered, and I submit, that the remarks of Mr. Justice Chamberlain are therefore of peculiar help and guidance to us.

"In the Bill what is provided is that—

'It is expedient to indemnify officers of Government and other persons in respect of acts, matters and things ordered or done or purporting to have been ordered or done for the purpose of maintaining or restoring order, provided that such acts, matters or things were ordered or done in good faith and in a reasonable belief that they were necessary for the said purposes.'

"Now, my Lord, my particular objection is to the expression 'in a reasonable belief.' I submit that as the Bill stands it would make it impossible for any plaintiff, ordinarily speaking, to succeed in any suit which he might institute against any individual who had wronged him. This becomes clear when you look at section 2, for it says that no suit shall lie against any officer of Government who may have done certain things, 'provided that such officer or person has acted in good faith and in a reasonable belief that his action was necessary for the said purposes.'

"Now, my Lord, I submit that even apart from the rules of evidence in section 3, to which I shall refer later, the officer whose action may be questioned must not only show, that he had done the act in good faith, but also that the act was necessary and that he had done it with reasonable and proper care and consideration. In the words of Justice Chamberlain, 'he should not have exceeded the necessity which gave him power. And no deviation from the common principles of humanity should appear in his conduct.' Now, I submit, my Lord, that the Bill goes much further than this and gives a measure of protection which is not justified by previous enactments, or by considerations of reason and justice. In the case, which I have quoted, the charge was that Wright had been wrongly flogged by Fitzgerald. Here we have many cases in which flogging was resorted to rather freely. In that case, in concluding the judgment of the case, Lord Yelverton, speaking of the defendant, for whom it had been pleaded that he had done many acts of loyalty, said: 'he had indeed manifested his loyalty most fully for he had written it in blood and imprinted his name on the plaintiff's back'. My Lord, here too the administrators of martial law had written their names in blood on the backs of many innocent fellow-subjects, and they should be allowed to ask those who so injured them to prove that they had acted with reasonable care and caution in the interests of public peace and good order, and without deviating from the common principles of humanity.

"My Lord, the provisions to which I have drawn attention become much more objectionable when you come to section 3 which says:—

> 'For the purpose of section 2 a certificate of a Secretary to Government that any act was done under the orders of an officer of Government shall be conclusive proof thereof, and all action taken for the aforesaid purpose shall be deemed to have been taken in good faith and in a reasonable belief that it was necessary therefor unless the contrary is proved.'

"My Lord, what is given with one hand is taken away by the other. Read with section 2 of the Bill, this section 3 practically shuts out all chance of success for any plaintiff who may wish to have a suit instituted, to have an injury done to him investigated. It says, that unless the contrary is proved, an action shall be deemed to have been taken in good faith and in a reasonable belief that it was necessary for the purpose of maintaining or restoring order. Let us assume—I may be doing an injustice to the gentleman, but I name him as an illustration—that Mr. Manohar Lal, Barrister-at-law, institutes a suit, brings an action for damages for the wrong done to him by his being confined in the manner in which he was confined, in a cell and otherwise. Why should he be asked to prove that the person who caused him the injury acted without good faith and without a reasonable belief that his confinement was necessary for any human purpose? Why should not the burden of proving that he acted in good faith and with reasonable care be cast upon the defendant? It ought to be sufficient for the purpose of a fair trial of a character like that in any Court that the plaintiff should state before the Court on oath the facts of the case, and if the facts of the case did not show that he was either a criminal or had been condemned, or that he was guilty of any act for which he should be locked up, then it should be for the defendant to establish that the facts were such that he could not but act in the manner in which he did, and that therefore he should be excused for having so acted. It is a double wrong, my Lord, a double wrong to plaintiffs, to persons who have been subjected to all these humiliations and wrongs, that they should be called upon to prove that those who oppressed them had acted without good faith and without reasonable belief. I submit, my Lord, that fairness demands that this clause should be deleted. It will be possible for anybody to think of having a chance of success in a suit for damage only if this should be deleted. To require the plaintiff to prove that the defendant has *not* acted in good faith and reasonable belief is entirely wrong. How can the plaintiff exercise an attribute of omniscience. How can he search into the heart of the defendant and show an intimacy with the motives of a stranger only known to him by his tyranny and oppression, and prove that the injury he received has been the consequence of a malicious intention? Motives can only be inferred from actions, and it is for the defendant to show that his motives were such as to justify his actions being excused. It will be impossible for the plaintiff to prove things specially within the knowledge of the defendant. I submit, therefore, that this section 3 of the Bill is open to grave objection, and that it takes away what the Bill appears to give in another section.

"Now, my Lord, there are other objections to which the Bill is open. I will go back to the preamble. It says:—

> 'Whereas owing to the recent disorders in certain districts in the Punjab and in other parts of India, it has been necessary for the purpose of maintaining or restoring order to resort to martial law.'

"I do not know how this wide wording will affect acts done in Delhi, for instance, and in Calcutta. The object of the Bill should be clear and the language that is used should be modified in order to make it clear. I am not sure, as the preamble stands, whether it does not also cover places where no martial law was established. Clearly it should not.

"Then, my Lord, I come to clause 4, confirmation and continuance of martial law sentences. The Bill provides that, 'Every person confined under and by virtue of any sentence passed by a court or other authority constituted or appointed under martial law and acting in a judicial capacity, shall be deemed to have been lawfully confined.' And, it goes on to say: 'and shall continue liable to confinement until the expiration of such sentence, or until released by the Governor-General in Council or otherwise discharged by lawful authority.'

"My Lord, I must say that this provision of the Bill has shocked me most. I think, my Lord, that the statement of the Hon'ble the Home Member made it clear that the Government of India are conscious that, unless an Indemnifying Bill of the nature now before the Council, that is to say, unless a legislative provision of the nature embodied in clause 4 is passed by this Council, the detention of men who have been sentenced by martial law courts will be illegal. I take it, my Lord, that that is the position. That being so, I submit it is wrong to these people that the help of the Legislature should be invoked, not for remitting or wiping off the convictions or sentences, but for confirming them and continuing them.

"My Lord, it seems to me that the Bill was not conceived with sufficient care and deliberation; that the various provisions which were necessary in the circumstances of the situation were not fully considered at one time. It seems to me that, even if the model of the Acts of South Africa had been kept fully before the Government, the Bill should have been drafted, might have been cast, in a different mould, might have consisted of different provisions. The Hon'ble the Home Member, and I suppose the Hon'ble the Law Member, perhaps on referring to the South Africa Act, Act IV of 1902 of the Cape of Good Hope, would have noticed that there was a provision made for a revision of the sentences of those who had been convicted or sentenced by the martial law authorities. Now, my Lord, it is perhaps to make up for that omission, that the Hon'ble the Home Member has today announced the decision of the Government of India that two Judges of the High Court will be appointed to revise the sentences passed by summary courts. I welcome that announcement so far as it goes, but it only strengthens my suspicion that the matter was not considered in all its aspects when the Bill was drafted. I would draw attention here to the provisions of the Act of the Cape of Good Hope. May I ask the Hon'ble the Law Member for a copy of that Act, Act IV of 1902?"

The Hon'ble Sir George Lowndes:—"It might save the Hon'ble Member trouble if I were to inform him that was not the Act which we took as a model at all, but the later Act of 1915, of which he does not appear to know."

The Hon'ble Pandit Madan Mohan Malaviya:—"I thank the Hon'ble the Law Member. I did not know of the Act of 1915 or, at any rate I did not remember it in the midst of the Statutes which were noted by my friends who have been working for me in this matter. But I am thankful to the Hon'ble the Law Member for informing me of it, and I shall feel thankful to him if he will let me have a copy of that Act also."

The Hon'ble Sir George Lowndes:—"Certainly, after the Hon'ble Member has finished."

The Hon'ble Pandit Madan Mohan Malaviya:—"My friend the Law Member, need not be so afraid of letting me look at the Act before I finish, for I might find some help from it. However, I shall be content for such courtesy as he thinks fit to extend to me.

"Now, my Lord, this Act, Act IV of 1902, contained important provisions regarding the confirmation of sentences passed by military courts, but it also contained provision for the revision of sentences. I beg to draw your Lordship's attention and the attention of the Council to this provision. The Act declared that—

'The several sentences pronounced by Courts-Martial constituted and convened by proper authority, and holden in districts of this Colony in which martial law was proclaimed or imposed, and during the existence thereof, upon persons not ordinarily subject to Military Law tried by such Courts for acts of high treason, murder, or for all or any other crimes of offences whatsoever, or for all or any contraventions of any Regulations expressed or purporting to be issued under martial law and commonly termed Martial Law Regulations are hereby confirmed; and all such persons confined in any prisons or other legal places of confinement within the Colony under or by virtue of such sentences shall be deemed to have been and to be legally confined there, and shall continue to be so confined there or elsewhere, as the Governor may direct, until the expiration of the sentences respectively passed upon them or until they are discharged by lawful authority, and such sentences shall be deemed to be sentences duly passed by duly and legally constituted Courts of this Colony....'

"The second part of this section goes on to say:—

'Each and all of the officers of the prisons or other legal places of confinement mentioned in the preceding sub-section who have, or had, at any time in good faith received into, or kept in confinement any of the persons mentioned in the said preceding sub-section shall be deemed for all purposes to have acted legally.'

"And the third part is also important. It went on to say:—

'All persons in this Colony who have been deported without the limits thereof under and by virtue of any of the foregoing sentences referred to in the preceding sub-section shall be deemed to have been and to be legally deported without the limits of this Colony, and such acts or cases of deportation as aforesaid shall be deemed to be among, and shall be included under, the acts, matters and things referred to in the second section of this Act.'

"Now, my Lord, in reading these provisions, it should be remembered that it was in consequence of the Boer War that it had become necessary to proclaim martial law in South Africa. The object of these provisions no doubt was to legalise the sentences which had been passed but there was the important fact that there was a war waged against the Queen. It was necessary under those circumstances to confirm the sentences, particularly in the case of persons not ordinarily subject to military law tried by martial law courts for acts of treason, murder or for other crimes or offences or for any contraventions of any Regulations expressed or purporting to be issued under martial law and commonly termed Martial Law Regulations. For the same reason it was necessary to enact that the punishments which had been inflicted should be regarded as legal and that a suit should not lie against persons because they had confined rebels in imprisonment or deported them. Your Lordship will have noted that in section 2 jailors are indemnified, and in part 3 certain acts are validated and, therefore, I submit, the object was more to legalise the acts which had been done and the punishments which had been suffered and which might be suffered as a matter of necessity until they were remedied later on. But this was accompanied, my Lord, if not preceded by a very salutary provision. Your Lordship will be pleased to note that while this general Indemnity Act was passed on the 15th September 1902, a Commission was appointed on the 2nd of August 1902. Edward VII, by the Grace of God of the United Kingdom of Great Britain and Ireland, appointed a Commission. Its terms of reference were incorporated in the first schedule of the Bill. It was not an extraneous announcement like what the Hon'ble the Home Member has made today that the Government of India would be pleased to appoint two High Court judges to revise sentences passed by Summary Courts and here I may say that the public have come, my Lord, not to have the same confidence in High Courts after the troubles in the Punjab. My Lord, this ought to be a part of the Bill so that the public might know that there is sufficient and adequate provision made for a revision of all sentences passed by martial law courts and authorities.

"The first Schedule, my Lord, to the Cape of Good Hope Act sets out the Commission passed under the Royal Sign Manual and Signet appointing the Right Hon'ble Baron Alverstone, Sir John Charles Bigham and Major-General Sir John Charles Ardagh, to be Commissioners to inquire into the sentences imposed by the military courts, established under martial law in the South African Colonies and Protectorates and appointing Gilbert Mellor, Esq., to be Secretary to the Commission. Your Lordship will see that the Lord Chief Justice of England was the president of the Commission and Justice Bigham 'one of the justices of our High Court of the justice' was a member and that General Sir John Charles Ardagh, K.C.I.E., was the other member. It is important to draw attention to certain provisions of this Schedule. It runs as follows:—

> 'Whereas in consequence of the war declared by the late Governments of the South African Republic and Orange Free State against Her late Majesty Queen Victoria, it became necessary to proclaim martial law in our colonies and protectorates in South Africa; and whereas certain persons have been by military courts established under martial law in the said colonies and protectorates sentenced to terms of penal servitude and of imprisonment and to the payment of fines and are now undergoing the said sentences and have not paid but are liable to pay the said fines;
>
> 'And whereas the aforesaid war having now ceased it is expedient that inquiry should be made with regard to the aforesaid sentences with a view to ascertaining whether we might properly and without danger to the public safety of our said colonies and protectorates extend our grace and mercy to any of such persons and where such sentences and any and which of them might properly be by us remitted or reduced;
>
> 'Now, know ye that we, considering the premises, and reposing great trust and confidence in your fidelity and discretion and integrity, do authorise and appoint you the said.... (three persons) to be our Commissioners to inquire into the said sentences imposed by military courts established under martial law in our said colonies and protectorates and with as little delay as possible to report to us in writing under your hands and seals respectively whether in the case of the said persons, and of which of them respectively, who

shall be at the date of your report then undergoing any such sentence or who shall not have paid but shall then be liable to pay any such fines, it is expedient, having regard to all the circumstances relating thereto, that such sentences or fines should be remitted or reduced.'

"Now, my Lord, your Lordship will please note that the Commission was 'to report with as little delay as possible.' That, my Lord, was incorporated as part of the Bill. I shall feel grateful to the Hon'ble the Law Member if he will kindly give me Act VI of 1900 also....."

The Hon'ble Sir George Lowndes:—"I was in hopes, my Lord, that I had not got it, but I have."

The Hon'ble Pandit Madan Mohan Malaviya:—"Now, my Lord, there is an important provision in this Act of 1900, to which I invite the attention of Council and the Government. My Lord, the whole attitude of the Government as disclosed in these two South-African enactments and as disclosed by the Bill presented to this Council shows, I am sorry to say, a regrettable difference. In this Act of 1900 (VI of 1900), there was a provision to confirm sentences, merely to legalise, as I have pointed out already, what has been done.

'All actions, indictments and legal proceedings whatsoever which might be brought or instituted in any of the courts of this colony against His Excellency the Governor of the Cape of Good Hope or the officer for the time being in command of His Majesty's Forces in this colony or against any person or persons acting under them or either of them respectively, in any command or capacity, civil or military, for or on account or in respect of any acts, matters, and things whatsoever in good faith advised, commanded, ordered, directed or done as necessary for the suppression of hostilities in or the maintenance of good order and government or for the public safety of this colony between the date of the commencement of a state of war between Her Majesty's Government and the Government of the South African Republic and Orange Free State and the date of the taking effect of this Act, shall be discharged and become and be made void.'

"Then, my Lord, it is laid down in section 5 that:—

'In all cases of convictions for high treason or other crimes of a political character during the period specified in section 1 of this Act, where such convictions have taken place before courts-martial or military courts constituted, convened and held as in the last preceding section set forth or where they have taken place before the ordinary criminal courts having jurisdiction over them, it shall be lawful for the Governor, should he consider that any such case would, had it been dealt with after the taking effect of this Act, have been a case proper for the consideration of the Commissioners appointed under section 33 hereof, to order that the said sentences imposed upon such persons shall be altered into the sentence laid down in section 50 of this Act. The person affected by any such sentence shall thereupon become liable to suffer the penalty imposed by the said fiftieth section and no other.'

"That is to say, a sentence under section 50 has been substituted for the one already imposed. Now section 50 says:—

'The said Commissioners shall, after hearing the evidence, if any for and against the accused, decide whether he is guilty or not of the charge brought against him, and in all cases in which an accused person shall be found guilty, the said Commissioners shall adjudge that he shall be, for the period of five years and no longer, disqualified from being registered as a voter or from voting for the election of members of Parliament, or of a Divisional or Municipal Council, or of a Village Management Board or from being or continuing to be a member of Parliament, or from holding any public office, or continuing upon the Commission of the Peace or from serving upon a Jury in civil or criminal cases, anything contained in any Law or Act of Parliament to the contrary notwithstanding; and thereupon such person shall be in Law absolutely disqualified, in regard to all the afore-mentioned matters and his name, if upon any existing voters' list, shall be and is hereby removed therefrom, and the vote of any such person given at any such election shall be null and void and may be struck out in any proceedings in which the result of such election is challenged in any competent court. Save as hereinafter provided the findings or decisions of the said Commissioners shall not be subject to appeal or to review by any Court whatever.'

"Now, my Lord, you will see what an important difference of outlook and aim these provisions of the Indemnifying Acts to which I am referring show as compared with the provisions of the Bill before us. My Lord, three High Commissions were appointed as part of the South-African Act, and they were given power to wipe off all other sentences in the case of persons found guilty of high treason or other crimes of a political character and to substitute a municipal disqualification. Therefore, it was not in ordinary trifling cases, cases of not *salaaming* a European, but it was in cases of convictions for high treason or for other crimes of a political character during the period of the war that this municipal disqualification was to be substituted as the only punishment.

"The other day, my Lord, I brought forward a Resolution and urged that the Government might consider the advisability of appointing a Committee of Inquiry (or the Commission which I suggested) being empowered where they thought fit to recommend to His Majesty's Privy Council that convictions by Martial Law Commissions and Martial Law Summary Courts might be annulled or modified. My Lord, this Act to which I make reference supplies further reason in support of my proposition. It is said by the Hon'ble the Home Member that the Government of India are going to appoint two High Court Judges to revise sentences passed by Summary Courts. My Lord, the Government of India cannot constitute a court. The Government of India cannot constitute a regular court. The Governor-General in Council can no doubt introduce martial law and constitute certain courts under martial law, but the Government of India cannot constitute a regular court.

"If these two High Court Judges are to revise certain martial law sentences, they will not be a court. They will only be advisers, very honourable advisers, of the Government of India in respect of the cases which the Government of India may deal with. But I submit with confidence, notwithstanding what the Hon'ble the Law Member may say to the contrary on this point, that the Government of India cannot by appointing two High Court Judges to revise sentences passed by martial law officers invest them with the authority of a legal court . . . ."

The Hon'ble Sir William Vincent:—"I never suggested anything of the kind."

The Hon'ble Pandit Madan Mohan Malaviya:—"I thank the Hon'ble the Home Member for removing my doubts on the point. I should like to know, then, what will be the position of the two Judges. I should feel grateful to the Hon'ble the Home Member if he will make the point clear. It will save time, I wish to know if they are merely to advise, whether their opinions will be merely recommendations to be considered by the executive Government or whether they will have power to wipe out convictions, or to remit or reduce entences. I should be very grateful if the Hon'ble the Home Member will enlighten me on that point."

(At this point the Hon'ble Mr. Malaviya resumed his seat).

The President:—"The Hon'ble Member will proceed with his speech."

The Hon'ble Pandit Madan Mohan Malaviya:—"My Lord, I take it, in the absence of any explanation from the Hon'ble the Home Member that the matter is left vague. I take it that in the absence of further information these two Judges will be merely advisers to the Government. I submit that that will not be a satisfactory position. Next, I should like the Government to consider the propriety of including in the terms of reference some direction such as that contained in section 50 of the Cape of Good Hope Act, to which I have referred. In view of what has been said and has not been contradicted or controverted, it is time for the Government of India to make up its mind to release the persons who are undergoing imprisonment from further humiliations and hardships. I submit that this is a suitable moment for the Government to consider this matter. If the Bill proceeds as it is then, I submit, the postition will be this. We do not know how long these High Court Judges may take to deal with the cases to be entrusted to them, the procedure has not been indicated, and therefore no one can form any idea of the time the revision will take. Till then, 'every person confined under and by virtue of any sentence passed by a court or other authority constituted or appointed under martial law and acting in a judicial capacity constituted shall be deemed to have been lawfully confined and shall continue liable to confinement until the expiration of such sentence or until released by the Governor-General in Council or otherwise discharged by lawful authority.' I submit that that is not a satisfactory postition, particularly in view of the remarks which the Hon'ble the Law Member made. He said he had consulted the Government of the Punjab, and it was of opinion that it would be dangerous to let off many of the men who were undergoing imprisonment at present and who were under sentences passed by martial law authorities. I would suggest that it should be pointed out to His Honour the Lieutenant-Governor of the Punjab that if there are persons who are considered dangerous, there are provisions under the existing enactments by which they can be taken up and judicially proceeded against and confined. There are many provisions under the existing enactments which enable the executive Government to proceed against person of doubtful or dangerous character and bind them over to keep the peace and to be of good behaviour. It is open to the Government to have them tried in the regular courts in the ordinary way. Great complaints have been made that these convictions and sentences are illegal. The Hon'ble the Home Member has practically admitted the truth of this contention and, unless some provision such as I am referring to is enacted, these unhappy men will continue in jail. That being the position, I submit that these men should at an early date be set free to enjoy the liberty to which they are entitled, and if they are not entitled to that liberty by reason of any act of wrong-doing the ordinary courts of law should be allowed to deal with them. I need hardly draw attention again to the remarks of Lord Halsbury, but it is my duty to refer to certain information which has been printed and reproduced in an excellent volume by Sheikh Nabi Bakhsh, a Vakil of the Punjab High Court. Your Lordship and the Council would have noted what Lord Halsbury states in his article on martial law in the 'Laws of England' that the powers of the military authorities cease, and those of the civil courts are resumed *ipso facto* on the termination of disorder. Disorder terminated long long ago in the Punjab and martial law was also discontinued partly in May and partly in June, and finally last month. I think it was about the 25th or 28th of August. Therefore, the course I am suggesting is the right course to be pursued; let there be such a provision enacted as that to which I have drawn attention, section 5 of the South Africa Act, to secure the early release of persons now undergoing imprisonment, unless it be a case of murder or arson; let even these men be proceeded against in the ordinary way. Give these men the right to choose in the matter, and some may not choose to have a fresh trial.

"My Lord, it is important to bear in mind the limitations of martial law. They have been very carefully explained in various places. For instance, Justice Sir James Fitz James Stephen, in his book on the History of Criminal Law of England, says: I will read only his summing up to save time. He says, 'I will sum up.....' "

The President:—"I understand it is your summing up also."

The Hon'ble Pandit Madan Mohan Malaviya:—"No my Lord, I am reading the summing up of Sir James Fitz James Stephen."

The President:—"All right, proceed."

The Hon'ble Pandit Madan Mohan Malaviya:—"He says:—

'I may sum up my view of martial law in general in the following propositions:—1. Martial law is the assumption by officers of the Crown of absolute power exercised by military force for the suppression of an insurrection and the restoration of order and lawful authority. 2. The Officers of the Crown are justified in any exertion of physical force, extending to the destruction of life and property to any extent, and in any manner that may be required for the purpose. They are not justified in the use of cruel and excessive means but are liable civilly or criminally for such excess. They are not justified in inflicting punishment after resistance is suppressed, and after the ordinary courts of justice can be re-opened. The principle by which their responsibility is measured is well expressed in the case of Wright *versus* Fitzgerald. Wright was a French Master of Clonmell who after the suppression of the Irish rebellion in 1798.....'

The President:—"The Hon'ble Member really must not repeat himself. We have already had the case of Wright *versus* Fitzgerald for half an hour."

The Hon'ble Pandit Mandan Mohan Malaviya:—"My Lord, I am quoting the summary of Sir James Fitz James Stephen....."

The President:—"I am quite aware of that. But we have all heard the case of Wright *verses* Fitzgerald for half an hour this afternoon, and I do not propose that we should hear it again."

The Hon'ble Pandit Madan Mohan Malaviya:—"Very well, my Lord. Then Sir James Fitz James Stephen proceeds to say:—

'3. The courts-martial, as they are called, by which martial law in this sense of the word is administered, are not properly speaking, courts-martial or courts at all. They are merely committees formed for the purpose of carrying into execution the discretionary power assumed by the Government. On the one hand, they are not obliged to proceed in the manner pointed out by the Mutiny Act and the Articles of War. On the other hand, if they do so proceed they are not protected by them as the member of a real court-martial might be, except in so far as such proceedings are evidence of good faith. They are justified in doing, with any forms and in any manner, whatever in necessary to suppress insurrection, and to restore peace and the authority of the law. They are personally liable for any acts which they may commit in excess of that power, even if they act in strict accordance with the Mutiny Act and the Articles of War.'*

"Therefore, my Lord, disorder having been suppressed and the ordinary courts of justice being at work, cases of persons who cannot be released entirely might well be referred to such courts. I will refer to one other opinion, namely, that of Mr. R. Spankie, a former Advocate-General of Bengal. Writing on the proceedings of a court-martial held under Regulation X of 1804 in April 1818, Mr. Spankie said :—

> 'The manifest intention of Government in its legislative capacity was, that none but cases of the simplest and most obviously criminal nature should be the subject of trial by the courts-martial; the fact, whether a person was taken in the actual commission of an overt act of rebellion, or taken in the act of openly aiding and abetting the enemies of the state or taken in open hostility, might safely be tried by such courts; and such a provision for trial was calculated to prevent military severity in the field becoming absolute massacre. But all complex cases depending upon circumstantial proof and requiring either a long examination of facts or a discriminating inference from facts in themselves equivocal were purposely withdrawn from the cognizance of these tribunals. It never was intended that courts-martial should try, as those have done, acts even of criminal nature, in which the prisoner was not taken and unless the acts were open overt acts and of the most material palpable quality.'†

"My Lord, for all the reasons I have stated, I submit that the provisions of the Bill as they stand are unsatisfactory, and leave

* For full text of Sir Fitzjames Stephen's remarks on the subject, see Appendix IV, pages 510-513, *ante*.

† For full text of Mr. Spankie's opinion, see Appendix IV, pages 468-474, *ante*.

should not be given to introduce it now and in its present form. Now, if the Bill is not introduced now, my Lord, and in its present form, as I have said before, not much harm will be done, and the Government will be in a much better position to deal with the matter after the report of the Committee of Inquiry. On the other hand, my Lord, grave injustice and disadvantage are likely to result if the Bill is passed at present. Of course, it is in the power of your Excellency's Government to pass the Bill. We know it. We have had recent experiences to convince us of it. You do command a large official majority in this Council. The representatives of the people are few, and several of these few are absent at present. But I submit, my Lord, in this matter it would be right and proper that your Excellency's Government should consider what the public opinion of the country is. (*The clock here struck six.*) Shall we stop now ?"

The President :—"Is the Hon'ble Member concluding his speech ?"

The Hon'ble Pandit Madan Mohan Malaviya :—"My Lord, I should like to conclude tomorrow."

The President :—"The Council will now adjourn till 11 o'clock tomorrow. We shall sit from 11 to half-past 1, and we shall sit again from 3 until we finish."

(6)—From Proceedings of Meeting held on September 19, 1919

The Indemnity Bill—(*contd.*)

The Hon'ble Pandit Madan Mohan Malaviya :—"My Lord, before I conclude I would like to draw attention to two other matters relating to the Bill which are to my mind of great importance. One is that section 6, the saving clause, says :—

> 'Nothing in this Act shall prevent the institution of proceedings by or on behalf of the Government against any person in respect of any matter whatsoever.'

"This no doubt reserves to the Government the right of instituting any proceedings by or on behalf of the Government against any person. But, the right of private individuals to bring any suit or to institute any legal proceedings against any individual is restricted by the provisions of clauses 2 and 3. Now, my Lord, I have already submitted that clause 2 of the Bill bars a suit. It says:—

> 'No suit or other legal proceeding whatsoever, whether civil or criminal, shall lie in any court of law against any officer of Government . . in respect of any act . . done . . for the purpose of maintaining or restoring order, *etc.*; provided that such officer or person has acted in good faith and in a reasonable belief that his action was necessary for the said purposes.'

"And then comes section 3 which says :—

> 'For the purposes of section 2 a certificate of a Secretary to Government that any act was done by the orders of any officer of Government shall be conclusive proof thereof, *etc.*, unless the contrary is proved.'

"Now, my Lord, the result of these two clauses taken together is, as I have submitted before, practically to make the chance of success for any private individual very small, and I submit this is not right. I want to illustrate how very unjustly the provisions of this Bill will operate to make it difficult for any individual, who may have been injured, to obtain justice. I would like to draw attention to one concrete case which occurred at Amritsar. That case is the case of Mr. Gurdial Singh Salariya, Barrister-at-law. This gentleman was in the District Court along with several others on the 10th of April, 1919, when he heard that there had been trouble owing to the deportations, and that the mob had been fired upon. He and other pleader friends consulted together and resolved to inform the Deputy Commissioner that they thought they might go and help, and with his consent, went to try and quiet the trouble. They did go there, and this gentleman and his friends who were with him laboured for a long while to quell the mob and to turn them back. He succeeded also to a large extent in sending back part of the mob from the railway overbridge, and, in order that he might do his work better, obtained the loan of a horse from a policeman with the help of the Deputy Commissioner and rode about appealing to people to go back. While he was doing this, the military fired upon the mob. There was a crowd near the overbridge; he found the military ready to fire and he shouted out at the top of his voice to stop. He requested the Deputy Commissioner to give him some time to persuade the crowd to go back, and, while he was doing so, they began to fire upon the crowd all at once without warning this gentleman that they were going to do so. Luckily, he escaped. The Deputy Commissioner in his statement before one of the Martial Law Commissions said that this gentleman, Mr. Gurdial Singh, 'went with his permission to push back the mob and that he was genuinely trying to do so.' He further said that 'owing to a dangerous rush of the crowd, it was necessary to fire, while Gurdial Singh was trying to keep them back, and that he had been pointed out to the soldiers as a friend He ran serious risk of being shot and deserves credit for having tried to quell the mob in a brave and determined manner.' This was the statement made by the Deputy Commissioner of Amritsar in the case when Mr. Gurdial Singh was tried. Now, my Lord, having done what he did to quell the mob, Mr. Gurdial Singh went home. This was on the 10th of April. On the 23rd of May, a policeman, a constable in white clothes, went to him in court and asked him to accompany him to the Kotwali, where he was wanted by the police. He went there and was placed before the Deputy Superintendent, I think. He was asked a few questions and was politely told that he was to go to jail where he was to be confined. Now, my Lord, this gentleman was kept in Amritsar for two days or so and then he was removed, handcuffed, to Lahore. On the morning of May the 26th, he was made to walk on foot from the railway station at Lahore to Montgomery Hall, and was kept there the whole day sitting on the ground. Then, my Lord, he was removed to the Central Jail and was put in an iron cage, seven feet by 20, although his guardian had paid Rs. 30 in order that he might be put in another place. He was removed the next morning to that other place but was not long there and was sent on to another jail.

"This gentleman was arrested on the 23rd, and was put on his trial on the charge of having taken part on the 5th April, 1919, to bring about *hartal* on the 6th. It was proved by the evidence of a surgeon, I think a civil surgeon, that he was lying ill at home on that day. The second charge against him was that he was a speaker at the meeting of the 6th April, the great *Satyagraha* day meeting. He did admit that he did take part, and all glory to him for having taken part in that meeting. The third charge against him was that he had incited the mob at the railway bridge on the 10th April, when he had, at the risk of his life, tried to send back the mob to the city, and further that he had on horseback gone down to the city and delivered an inflammable speech. Now, my Lord, as I have said before, the Deputy Commissioner was examined and he deposed to the fact that this gentleman had honestly endeavoured at the risk of his life to quell the mob, and to send them back to the city. The question put to the Deputy Commissioner was 'Do you know as a fact that Gurdial Singh Salariya did his best to keep the mob back on the 10th April 1919 ?' The answer was, 'Yes, this is the only conclusion to be drawn from the action I saw.' Then the question was. 'Did you actually see him shouting to and entreating the mob on the carriage-bridge to disperse ?' And the answer was, 'Yes, I remember him distinctly as he swarmed up a lamp post to address the crowd better.' Then he was asked, 'Did his attitude and efforts against the mob appear to you genuine ?' The answer was, 'Yes, I certainly think they were genuine.' Then again, 'Was Gurdial Singh in danger of being shot when he was roaming about facing the mob and telling them to get back and thus did real service ?' The answer was, 'Yes, owing to the dangerous rush of the crowd it was necessary to fire while he was trying to keep them back and though he had been pointed out to the soldiers as a friend he ran serious danger of being shot. He deserves credit for having tried to keep the crowd back in a brave and determined manner.' Now, my Lord, in spite of all that this gentleman had done, he was put on his trial and kept in jail from the 23rd May, for nearly a month and a half. He was subjected to all the indignities and to all the humiliation and trouble to which I have referred. In the judgment in his case the Martial Law Commission said: 'This accused was present at the meeting of the 6th April. (That of course was a crime in the eye of the Commission). But we are not satisfied that he had joined the conspiracy. His actions on the 10th April, as deposed to by the Deputy Commissioner indicate that he was supporting the authorities to the best of his powers and at some risk to himself. Hans Raj (the approver) does not attribute any acts to him, merely saying that Gurdial Singh had told Bashir that he had done what he could on the 10th. Mr. Herbert (the Crown Advocate) did not press the case against him and we acquit him.' Now, my Lord, I should like to ask what would be the position of Mr. Gurdial Singh if he was to seek some compensation, some remedy for the gross, unjustifiable wrong done to him ? Here is a man who at the risk of his life rendered service to the Government and the public at the time of the disorders. While the Deputy Commissioner and the police superintendent who saw him work at the railway bridge were still in Amritsar, this gentleman was arrested and *challanned* in a humiliating manner and kept in jail for a period of a month and a half, had to undergo all the anxiety, trouble and indignity and humiliation of arranging for his defence and had to thank God that he was acquitted after all. Is he, if this proposed Bill is passed, to be defeated in a suit, unless he can swear that there was in the minds of his assailants and persecutors a milicious intent? Or is it right that he should be able to go into the Court, state the facts and ask his persecutors to plead whatever excuse or justification they may have to plead for these acts ? Which will be the right course ? Which will be the fair procedure ? I submit, there can be only one answer. The gentleman has been obviously unanswerably wronged. You are by this Bill shutting him out from having a chance of success in a suit for damages, by the provisions you have incorporated in this Bill. He may go with his plaint into a Court, and the answer will be that no suit will lie unless it is proved by the plaintiff that the defendant had not acted in good faith and in a reasonable belief that the steps he had taken against the plaintiff were necessary for the purposes of maintaining or restoring order. I submit, my Lord, I cannot imagine a grosser perversion of what should be the right procedure than what is incorporated in this Bill. I have drawn attention to this case for two reasons, first, to emphasize that the provisions of section 2 and 3 are entirely unjust and ought to be entirely deleted, I mean the proviso to section 2 and the new rule of evidence incorporated in section 3. I have also referred to it to show that though clause 6 of the Bill saves to Government the power to proceed against any person against whom they may think it fit to, the case of private individuals who may wish to proceed against those who have harassed them or subjected them to oppression, has not been sufficiently taken care of. My Lord, it may be said that the Bill provides that the Government can proceed against any person in respect of any matter, and that it will be only reasonable to expect that in a case like the one I have mentioned the Law Member and the Home Member would advise the Government of India to institute a suit to find out who were the persons who were responsible for all the humiliation and indignity and suffering inflicted upon Mr. Gurdial Singh and to bring them to trial. That should ordinarily be the case, my Lord; but unfortunately, in the circumstances of the situation, it is not given to private individuals who have suffered to expect, to have a reasonable expectation, that such a course would be pursued. I regret to say it, but it is a fact which I ought to mention that, while I have heard much indignation expressed at the acts of lawlessness that were committed by some sections of the mob, I have not heard one word of sympathy from the Government benches with those who lost their lives, or with their relations or with others who have suffered in consequence of recent troubles, except with my European fellow-subjects for whom I share the sympathy with members of the Government. My Lord, it has been a sad thing for me to reflect that while such outrageous events have happened, while the casualties have been ascertained to the extent that has been done, there should not have been one word of sympathy, expressed on behalf of Government with these men who have suffered.....”

The Hon’ble Sir William Vincent :— “May I offer a word of explanation ? I said quite definitely in this Council that no one deplored the loss of life more than I did. It is unfair to say that I did not express any sympathy with those who suffered.”

The Hon’ble Pandit Madan Mohan Malaviya :—“My Lord, I take it, I will accept it, that the Hon’ble Member did mean to express sympathy with Indians.......”

The Hon’ble Sir William Vincent :—“Not only mean to, but I did do it.”

The Hon’ble Pandit Madan Mohan Malaviya :—“My Lord, I am glad to be assured, that the Hon’ble Member did express sympathy with Indians as well as Europeans who had suffered. But I still expected a more sympathetic attitude on the part of Government in order to give an assurance to the public that if there are any cases in which the facts found justify such a course, the Government will itself proceed to bring the offenders, the wrongdoers, the oppressors of His Majesty's subjects to trial.

"And this brings me to one other aspect of the question, and that is the question of compensation for the damages sustained by the people. In the Cape of Good Hope Act, VI of 1900, there is a whole chapter devoted to the provision for compensation for damages sustained by the people from military operations. Now, what does section 5 of the Bill before us provide ? It says—'Where under martial law the property of any person has been taken or used by any officer of Government, whether civil or military, the Governor-General in Council shall pay to such person reasonable compensation for any loss immediately attributable to such taking or using to be assessed upon failure of agreement by a person holding judicial office not inferior to that of a District Judge to be appointed by Government in this behalf.' My Lord, the Bill confines itself to compensation for loss of property used for military purposes. But what about the lives that have been lost in military operations ? Lives that are much more valuable than any property lost. I submit that the proper course would be to incorporate in this Bill a provision to the effect that a Committee should be constituted under this Act and it should have power to decide what compensation should be given to those who have suffered loss of life or limb, as well as to those who have suffered loss of property. In this respect the Bill is defective, and for this reason also I submit that the Government should reconsider the matter.

"The Council will have noted that my proposal is not that no Indemnity Bill should be introduced and passed, but that such a Bill should not be introduced at present, that it should be kept back until the Committee of inquiry has reported. I would point out that this is not such a wide suggestion as it may seem to some people. After the dark days of the Mutiny the Government was in no hurry to pass an Indemnity Act. The Indemnity Act was passed in the year 1860; it received the assent of the Government of India on the 2nd August, 1860; that is, two years after the mutiny had been suppressed. I submit, my Lord, that the Government would not be unwise, and that no interests would be jeopardised if the Government do not proceed with the Bill at present. I am strengthened in urging this before the Council by the reports which I have received, newspapers, telegrams and letters have been coming to me from different places expressing a deep sense of dissatisfaction among the general Indian public with the decision of the Government to proceed with this Indemnity Bill. I will read out a telegram I have received from Lahore. It runs—'Members of the Indian Association, Lahore, respectfully enter their emphatic protest against the statement made by the Hon'ble Malik Umar Hayat Khan at the recent meeting of the Imperial Legislative Council that the people of the Punjab do not want a Commission of Inquiry into the happenings of April last. As a matter of fact, the entire province demands a searching investigation by an imperial Commission, unconnected with the administration of the country; the fact that public meetings of protest cannot be held owing to Ordinances and official orders should not be misconstrued. They wish further to give expression to strongly-felt public opinion of the Punjab that passing of the proposed Bill at the present stage will not only be premature but also prejudicial to the conduct of proper inquiry. There will be ample time for enactment of a law for the protection of officials after the Commission of Inquiry has pronounced its verdict as to the necessity of a declaration of martial law and suggestions of measures and methods adopted in its working. The Punjab Association feel in any case that there is absolutely no necessity for validating sentences illegally passed by Martial Law Commissions and officers. They pray that the Government will be pleased to abandon the Bill at present.' This is one of several telegrams received, I also wish to show how the public opinion has expressed itself. Sir Narayan Chandavarkar, Vice-President of the National Liberal Association, cabled to the Secretary of State and to your Excellency a few days ago praying among other things that the Indemnity Bill should be abandoned at the present stage, as its necessity depends on the result of inquiry by the already appointed Commission. Then again, my Lord, 'Ditcher' in *Capital* has said that it is obvious that after the passing of the Indemnity Act the findings of the Committee will be of purely academic interest. The *Daily News* of London has observed in referring to the proposed Commission that 'the provision for a complete whitewashing of the official policy of the Punjab is made doubly certain by the resolve to protect officials by the Act of Indemnity before the inquiry is entered on. This policy, for which there is no defence, recalls the disastrous action taken after the Ceylon disturbances in the first year of the war. By such un-British tactics the British name is besmirched.' The Indian papers have almost without exception written strongly against the policy of proceeding with this Bill before the Committee has made its report. There is hardly time for me to refer to the opinions of the *Leader* the *Bombay Chronicle,* the *Nation,* the *Bengalee* and other papers. But I think it necessary to invite attention to a very valuable article from the pen of Sir Narayan Chandavarkar which has been published in the '*Indian Social Reformer.*' The other day the Hon'ble the Home Member relied upon a letter published by an anonymous 'Indian student of constitutional law' for support of his view in introducing this Indemnity Bill. I was rather taken aback; it seemed to me to be a great fall for the Hon'ble the Home Member of the Government of India to refer to an anonymous writer for support of the policy decided upon by the Government of India. However, that is the concern of the Hon'ble the Home Member. I now present to him a very valuable contribution to the discussion of this Bill, the opinion of a gentleman who has acted for years as an honoured Judge of the Bombay High Court, officiated for some time as Chief Justice of that Court and was also Chief Justice in Indore for several years. On important occasions he has laid the Government and the public of India under an obligation by expressing well-considered opinions on constitutional questions. Writing in the *Indian Social Reformer*, Sir Narayan Chandavarkar says.* 'Surprise is expressed in some quarters that Indian politicians of all shades of opinion have opposed the decision of the Government of India in introducing an Indemnity Act in the Imperial Legislative Council at the earliest convenient moment for indemnifying all the officers in respect of their acts in connection with the recent disturbances..... The authority of the constitutional lawyer, A. V. Dicey is cited in support of the principle and policy of the measure. But here is what Mr. Dicey says in his book, called *A leap in the dark.'* My Lord, I may mention that this book—'A leap in the dark'—was published in 1893. Its purport was to examine the leading principles of the Irish Home Rule Bill which was introduced in that year in Parliament. In Mr. Dicey's opinion one of the most important defects of the Bill was, that its provisions relating to the restrictions on and safeguards against the legislative power of the contemplated Irish Parliament contained no prohibition against the passing of an Act of Indemnity by that Parliament. Mr. Dicey said in that book :—

* See Appendix V, pages 541-543, *ante*.

'Of all the laws which a legislature can pass an Act of Indemnity is the most likely to produce injustice. It is on the face of it the legalisation of illegality, the hope of it encourages acts of vigour, but it also encourages violations of law and of humanity. The tale of flogging Fitzgerald in Ireland, or the history of Governor Eyre in Jamaica, is sufficient to remind us of the deeds of lawlessness and cruelty which in a period of civil conflict may be inspired by recklessness or panic and may be pardoned by the retrospective sympathy or partisanship of a terror-stricken or vindictive Legislature.'

"Further on he writes:—

'An *ex post facto* law is the instrument which a legislature is most apt to use for punishing the unpopular use of legal rights. There is not a landlord, there is not a magistrate, there is not a constable in Iraland who may not tremble in fear of *ex post facto* legislation. There is no reason, as far as the Home Rule Bill goes, why the gaoler who kept Mr. William O'Brien in prison or the warders who attempted to pull off his breeches, should not be rendered legally liable to punishment for their offences against the unwritten law of Irish sedition. No such monstrosity of legal inequity will, it may be said, be produced. I admit this, but the very object of prohibitions (against the passing of *an ex post facto* law) is the prevention of outrageous injustice. The wise founders of the United States prohibited to Congress and to every State legislature, the passing of *ex post facto* legislation.'

"My Lord, dealing with the particular Home Rule Bill and commenting upon the absence from it of a prohibition against the passing of an Indemnifying Act, Mr. Dicey said that it was necessary that there should be such a prohibition. He said :—

'Circumstances no doubt may arise in Ireland, as in other countries, under which the maintenance of order or the protection of life may excuse or require deviation from the strict rules of legality. But the question, whether these circumstances have arisen, will always be decided far more justly by the Parliament at Westminster than it can be decided by the Parliament at Dublin. Can anyone really maintain that a Parliament in which Mr. Healy, or for that matter, Colonel Saunderson might be leader, would be as fair a tribunal as a Parliament under the guidance of Mr. Gladstone or Lord

> Salisbury for determining whether an officer, who, acting under the directions of the Irish Government and with a view to maintain order at Belfast or Dublin, should have put an agitator or conspirator to death without due trial, had or had not done his duty.'

"My Lord, as Sir Narayan Chandavarkar says, substitute India for Ireland and substitute Simla for Dublin and so on, and it would appear that the passage applies very much to the proposal now before the Council. I submit that in view of these very weighty expressions of opinion, the Government would be wise in postponing action in this matter of an Indemnifying Bill. My Lord, it is open to the Government, it is in the power of the Government, as I said yesterday, to pass the Bill by the official majority which it commands. But I appeal to your Excellency to reconsider this question and not flout public opinion which has been so widely expressed in this matter. My Lord, it may be that the Government can carry on the administration of the country without paying heed to public opinion, but it is not the right thing to do so. The right thing to do is to act in accordance with the principles of justice for which the blood of Britons and of Indians was shed in the last great war, to do that which is right, to do that which truth, justice and honour demand; and in this matter truth, justice and honour demand that where so many deplorable acts have been committed, where so much illegality has been practised, where so many indignities have been offered, when there are such serious allegations regarding the action of His Majesty's officers, civil and military, when there are serious allegations regarding the attitude of the Government of India itself in the matter of the Punjab administration during the last few months, I submit, my Lord, that truth, justice and honour demand that you should stay your hand and to let this Bill lie over until the Committee of Inquiry has reported. When the Committee of Inquiry has submitted its report, I venture respectfully to say that the right course for the Government of India would be to submit that report to His Majesty's Government and to consult them, in view of the facts which will then be established, as to which acts of the officers of His Majesty's Government, civil or military, should be indemnified, and also as to what compensation should be offered on behalf of the public, that is, the Government, to those who have suffered unjustly during these disturbances and operations. I ask, my Lord, for an attitude of greater sympathy, an attitude of greater desire to do justice between man and man, between Indian and European, between one fellow subject and another, not in any vindictive spirit, not in any revengeful spirit, but purely with a desire that justice should be done, and that right should triumph. It is for these reasons, that I most earnestly appeal to your Excellency and to your Excellency's Government to reconsider the matter and not to proceed with this Bill. If this is done, my Lord, the whole country will feel grateful; both in England and in India public opinion will feel that your Excellency's Government have rightly considered the force and the weight of public opinion and respected it. My Lord, the mightiest Government has to bow to public opinion. It so happens that the public opinion in India is not powerful enough to make itself felt by Government, but, I submit, that we should guide overselves in such matters and on such occasions by what we find in England; and I venture to say with great respect that no Government in England would have dared to bring forward a Bill of this character in the circumstances which have been disclosed in this debate; and I, therefore, submit, my Lord, that though the Government here has the power, it ought not to exercise that power, and ought to wait until the Committee of Inquiry has reported. I make this appeal in the name of those who have lost their lives, in the name of those who have lost their limbs in these recent disturbances, in the name of those who have suffered indescribable indignities, in the name of those who are undergoing imprisonment at this moment unjustly in His Majesty's jails, in the name of those women who are mourning the loss of their husbands, their relations, or sons—in the name of all those, my Lord, I appeal to your Excellency's Government to stay the hand of Government and to wait for the Committee of Inquiry. When the Committee of Inquiry will have reported, both the Government and the public will be able clearly to see what are the facts, and what is the right course to pursue in those circumstances. Every reasonable man in this Council will then offer his support to the measure that may then be proposed.

"In view of these circumstances, my Lord, this is what the situation demands. I hope that your Excellency's Government will not judge this matter merely by the opinions of a few members who have the privilege of sitting in this Council. I hope, in deciding this matter, your Excellency will bear in mind the vast volume of Indian opinion outside this Council and also the opinion in England. If you will decide with due regard to that opinion, I have no doubt that your Excellency will come to only one conclusion, and that is, to postpone the introduction of this Bill till the Committee of Inquiry have reported."

The Hon'ble Mr. J. P. Thompson :—"With your Excellency's permission, I should like to make a few remarks on the amazing speech, to the last quarter of which we have just been privileged to listen. I do not propose to touch on the legal questions, or questions of constitutional law which have been raised by the Pandit. They will no doubt be dealt with by the Legal Member, if he thinks there is anything in them that merits a reply. Nor do I propose to deal with the details of the administration of martial law by military officers; that is a matter for one of my military colleagues to deal with. Nor again, shall I touch on the general questions or the justification for the introduction of martial law, the alleged provocative action of the Punjab Government in deporting Kitchlew and Satyapal and excluding Mr. Gandhi from the Punjab, or such other matters of general nature. I propose to confine myself to the specific allegations which have been made by the Pandit of misconduct and mal-administration on the part of civil officers who were responsible for the administration of justice during the period of martial law. Before I start with allegations made by the Hon'ble Pandit there were two remarks which fell from the speaker who preceded him which, I think, require a passing notice. The first point was the statement made by Mr. Chanda that on the 11th of April, orders were issued by the Punjab Government prohibiting the publication of any accounts in the newspapers. The order that was passed, my Lord, was an order requiring any newspaper, whether English or Indian, to submit any accounts which it proposed to publish of the events which had taken place for precensorship before publication. It was an order which, as I have said, applied both to the English and the Indian press, and there was nothing whatever to prevent any newspaper which desired honestly, and for the public good to publish true information from publishing it.

"The second point in Mr. Chanda's speech on which I wish to make an observation is, his allegation that it was out of revenge for the fraternisation between the Hindus and Muhammadans at the festival of *Ram Naumi* on the 9th of April, that Sir Michael O'Dwyer excluded Mr. Gandhi. Now, my Lord, I have the greatest admiration for Sir Michael O'Dwyer, but I do not think that any one here would claim for him that he was a prophet. The fraternisation at the *Ram Naumi* took place on the 9th of April; the orders for the exclusion of

Mr. Gandhi were passed, so far as I remember, some 48 hours before that fraternisation took place.

"I now come, my Lord, to the allegations which have been made by the Hon'ble Pandit. I am afraid my remarks must of necessity take rather a discursive form, but I do not see that I can deal with the allegations which have been made in any better form than by taking them in the order in which the Hon'ble Member has made them, and I think in all the cases with which I shall deal I shall be able to show the Council that the story which has been given by the Pandit is a distortion or an exaggeration, or a misunderstanding of the facts. The first case he mentioned was that of the exclusion of a gentleman from the Punjab who was so well-known that the Pandit could not even give us his correct name; he called him Mr. Hume. . . . ."

The Hon'ble Pandit Madan Mohan Malaviya :—"Mr. C.F. Andrews.

The Hon'ble Mr. J. P. Thompson :—"His real name was Mr. C. F. Andrews, but the Pandit called him Mr. Hume. Now, my Lord, the facts in regard to the exclusion of Mr. Andrews are these. On the 5th of May, the Punjab Government received a telegram from the editor of the *Independent* newspaper at Allahabad saying that he, along with the editors of the *Bengalee,* the *New India,* the *Amrita Bazar Patrika,* the *Hindu* and the *Leader* proposed to depute Mr. Andrews to the Punjab with a view to report to the Indian press on the condition of affairs in the Province with special reference to the administration of martial law. Now, my Lord, at the time when that request was made, two of the papers on whose behalf it was made had been excluded from the Province—one more of them has been excluded since—and almost all of them have distinguished themselves by the bitterness of their attacks on the Punjab Administration. Now, my Lord, I put it to the Council, if these papers wished to obtain the good offices of the Punjab Government with the military authorities in order to enable Mr. Andrews to enter the martial law area, was this quite the most tactful way of doing it ? Could the Punjab Government be expected to use their good offices on behalf of newspapers whose bitter criticism, whose unfair criticism of what had been done had earned for them exclusion from the Province ? I do not think there is a single Member here, my Lord, who will answer that question in the affirmative.

"I now pass on to the Pandit's allegations about the Jallianwala Bagh. I do not wish to dwell on this extremely painful incident, but I merely wish to offer one or two remarks in regard to the number of casualties. The Hon'ble Member has hinted that more than a thousand persons were killed there. He told us yesterday that his latest information was that 530 had been traced. Now my Lord, I daresay we shall never know the exact number of persons who met their deaths in that garden. But what the Punjab Government have done is this. We made a proclamation in Amritsar and in the surrounding villages inviting all persons who had any information in regard to the names of those who had met their deaths there to come forward and give that information to Government. We knew that private organisations were at work collecting information on the same subject. We gave instructions to the local authorities that they were to see that this proclamation was brought to the notice of those persons so that they might have no excuse for not coming forward and giving us any information that they possessed. I make no doubt, my Lord, that that proclamation also came to the notice of the Pandit. Our enquiries show that the total was 291, and I claim that any information which asks us to accept figures beyond this must he received with the gravest suspicion.

"I now come, my Lord, to the case of the Badshahi Masjid. In this case an Inspector of the C.I.D. was assaulted in the Badshahi Masjid in Lahore on the 12th April.

"The facts as given in the judgment are as follows :—

> 'On that day,'—on the 12th of April,—'a meeting with political objects was held in the Badshahi Mosque, Lahore, which was to be addressed by leading Hindus. Many Hindus were present and many people armed with sticks. Maulvi Abdul Hai, having recognised Chaudhri Ali Gauhar, C. I. D. Inspector, who was present in plain clothes, made an inflammatory speech against the C. I. D. in general, saying that no progress with their objects was possible until the C. I. D. were eliminated. He pointed out Ali Gauhar as an object of immediate attack and the others then set upon Ali Gauhar who was beaten with sticks on the body. His assailants had him at their mercy but did not kill him.'

"Now, what is the story to which the Hon'ble Member gives the weight of his authority, in regard to the origin of that attack. He tells us that that Inspector had drawn on himself the resentment of the crowd by certain remarks that he had made. I have before me my

Lord, the record of that case. I have been through the whole of the evidence from start to finish, and there is not a suggestion anywhere, neither in the statements of the witnesses for the prosecution nor in the statements of the witnesses for the defence, nor in the statements made by the accused themselves, nor is there any hint in the cross-examination of the witnesses for the prosecution, of this story which the Hon'ble Member has told us.

"Now my Lord, I do not wish to use hard words about the Pandit, but I put it to the Council that the suggestion that he has made is not one which comes within the limits of fair controversy, stretch them how far you will. In this Council, my Lord, we are all supposed to be Hon'ble Members. It is a title that is given to us on account of the position we occupy, and not with regard to the moral character of members who occupy that position. But I do claim, my Lord, that that title justifies the public in expecting from members who speak in this Council a standard of honour and fair dealing, straight dealing, which, I think, the Pandit has failed to reach in the present instance....."

The Hon'ble Pandit Madan Mohan Malaviya :—"I am sorry for that."

The Hon'ble Mr. J. P. Thompson :—"The next allegation with which I will deal is, one to the effect that the electric and water-supply of the whole city of Amritsar, exclusive of the Civil Lines, was cut off for about five days, about the 12th of April last, and that a large number of wells in the city of Amritsar had been closed under recent orders when Mr. King was Deputy Commissioner there. I understand that six wells were so closed. As regards the stoppage of the supply of electrocity, on the 10th of April the mob attacked the power-house and stopped the electric light plant working. On the 11th, they prevented repairs being done and power was cut off that evening by order of the General Officer Commanding and remained cut off until the 19th. As regards the water-supply, I am informed that on the night of the 10th the water-supply was cut off by the Municipal Engineer, as there was a rumour in the city that the supply had been poisoned, though who published that rumour I cannot say, but it was found necessary to shut off the supply again on the following day, and it remained shut off until the 14th by order of the General Officer Commanding.

"The next incident that the Hon'ble Member dealt with was another Amritsar incident. He told us that several very respectable people, undertrial prisoners, including bankers, lawyers, doctors and so on—the class of people, in brief, who always 'rot' when sent to jail—were handcuffed in pairs and confined for several days in the racket court at Amritsar where they were subjected to several kinds of inconvenience. Temporary arrangements were made for the confinement of prisoners in the racket court in Amritsar; they were provided as soon as possible with shelter, but they were not handcuffed, so I am informed, for more than two or three days. And the picture which the Hon'ble Member has drawn of the inconveniences to which they were put is very largely exaggerated. I would remind the Council that at the same time at which these honourable gentlemen were confined in the racket court, English women and children were also confined in the Fort because of the violence of people outside. They remained there some days deprived of all the comforts and conveniences that they had in their own houses, and in some cases without even the decencies of ordinary life. Is this Council going to condemn the temporary arrangements which were made for these respectable gentlemen of Amritsar, when it finds that English women and children were subjected to not dissimilar inconveniences within a few yards of the place where these people were confined ?

"I now come on, my Lord, to the case of Gujranwala. The Hon'ble Member told us that on the 15th of April last Colonel O'Brien, Deputy Commissioner of Gujranwala, with a strong body of police and soldiers and an armoured car marched round the city arresting people right and left; that the persons so arrested were chained together and marched to the city two-and-two, headed by a Hindu and a Muhammadan, with a view to ridiculing Hindu-Muhammadan unity, and that, 'in the words of Colonel O'Brien' two Municipal Commissioners marched in front of the procession so formed and, pointing to the aeroplanes hovering overhead, kept on shouting to the people to make way for the prisoners; and that, after having been paraded through the principal streets of the town, the prisoners were taken to the railway station and put into an open truck guarded by a number of European soldiers with fixed bayonets, and so on. Let me read to the Council a description which is based on information supplied by Colonel O'Brien himself to explain what it was that happened. I should tell the Council that the outbreak in Gujranwala in which such a vast amount of damage was done to Government property took place on the 14th. On the morning of the 15th, Colonel

O'Brien felt himself in a position to make arrests. He did not think it safe to lodge the prisoners in the local jail. In order to make certain that there would be no trouble, he asked by telephone that an aeroplane and special train should come out in the afternoon. It was essential that no warning should be given to those who were to be arrested. He laid his plans accordingly. A list was prepared and a route arranged. He then started with the police to make arrests, as well as a party of British soldiers to prevent resistance. There was no armoured car. Pleaders, Barristers and others believed to be concerned in the outrages were arrested and handcuffed. As the party pursued its route, a Muhammadan and a Hindu, both members of the Municipal Committee, went well in front to warn the people against resistance. There was no intention of ridiculing Hindu-Muhammadan unity, and, if a Hindu was linked with a Muhammadan, it was by accident and not by design. The party arrived at the station within a quarter of an hour of the time fixed to find that the only accommodation for the escort and the prisoners was an open truck. It was nearly 5 o'clock, the journey to Lahore would take two hours, and there was no time to be lost. It is possible that all concerned may have been put to some inconvenience. It is not alleged that there was anything more than this, and the essential thing was to get the prisoners into Lahore as soon as possible.

"The Hon'ble Member's statement went on to deal with what happened at Shekhupura, where, he said, Colonel O'Brien had committed very much the same atrocities. The arrests at Shekhupura were made with equal celerity, as he had to visit on the same day Chuharkhana, Moman, Dhaban Singh and Sangla, at all of which places outrages had occurred. The Shekhupura prisoners were taken to Lahore by an armoured train which Colonel O'Brien found at Chichoki Mallian.

"The next atrocities to which I turn were those which were committed at Kasur. Kasur is a small place about 35 miles from Lahore where two British warrant officers were killed on the 12th. I cannot lay my hands at this moment on the statement which was made by the Hon'ble Member in regard to the outrages on respectable person at Kasur; but it related, I remember, to two pleaders, Ghulam Mohiyuddin and Abdul Kadir; it was stated, if I remember aright—the Hon'ble Member will correct me if I am wrong—that these two persons were confined for a long period, many weeks, in a lock-up at the station. The facts as given by the Sub-divisional officer are as follows:—

'Ghulam Mohiyuddin and Abdul Kadir were arrested and were confined in the police station; and once or twice they were detained by the military in the temporary lock-up near the station when brought from the police station with other prisoners for evidence or identification. They were released after a few days at my request in my presence by the officer commanding when I had decided that the evidence as to their being rioters was not true.'

"The other Kasur case to which the Hon'ble Member referred was the case of certain boys who were said to have been flogged there. The story is true. Six boys, three of them belonging to the Municipal Board High School and three belonging to the Islamia School, were caned at Kasur. The headmaster of the Municipal Board High School had invoked military assistance to deal with the boys who had acted very insubordinately and joined hands with the pupils of the Islamia School. The officer commanding directed the headmaster to choose the worst offenders and sent them up for punishment. In addition, two school-boys sent by the commission for summary trial were caned—three strokes each—by the martial law officer after trial.

"The next case to which the Hon'ble Member referred was that of Mr. Manohar Lal, a distinguished graduate of Cambridge University and a barrister-at-law. He was one of the trustees of the *Tribune* as the Pandit told us, and the question had been raised as to whether, when the editor of the *Tribune* was being prosecuted, it would be possible to prosecute the trustees too, or at any rate the resident trustee who happened to be in Lahore at the time and was believed to have taken considerable interest in the management of the paper. It is true that Mr. Manohar Lal was arrested and that he remained in confinement for the space of about a month. It is not true, as the Hon'ble Member stated, that his family were kept out of his house for a week; his house naturally was locked up after his arrest, as it might have been necessary to make a search, but his family were allowed to return and did return, I understand, the very next day.

"The Hon'ble Pandit then went on to tell us that hardship was inflicted on respectable persons in connection with the custody of martial law notices. Now, my Lord, that is a matter which primarily concerns my Hon'ble friend on my left. But it is a matter of such vital importance to the civil population, that the meaning of these punishments, which were inflicted in regard to martial law notices and the procedure that was adopted in order to safeguard them, should be properly understood, that I make no apology for making a few remarks to the Council on the subject. Martial law notices are a most important part of the machinery of martial law. If you create new offences, you must advertise them; otherwise well meaning people have not a fair chance. The man who tears down a martial law notice may be the cause of an honest man being shot. When such notices were first put up, it was found that they were torn down and defaced. Colonel Johnson interviewed the leaders of the people and they promised to arrange for the publication of the orders in the different quarters of the city. They failed to fulfil their promise. Colonel Johnson accordingly decided to impose on selected owners of property the duty of protecting them. It is true that a number of persons connected with public movements or interested in persons who had been arrested were selected, because they were *prima facie* the persons in whose custody the notices would be safest. My Lord, I can say with regard to this policy that its success was ample justification for any hardships that might have been inflicted. After this class of property-owner had been made responsible for the safe custody of the notices, I believe hardly any were torn down or defaced.

"The Hon'ble Member then went on to state that in some cases tried by martial law officers, especially towards the close of the martial law period, the accused were convicted without the whole of the defence evidence being heard, and even that witnesses who were present in Court or attended the Court for that purpose were not heard. He gave the case of two pleadars, Lala Gurdasram and Lala Shivaram, of Hafizabad in the district of Gujranwala. Well, my Lord, I have not had time to make inquiries from each Deputy Commissioner as to what happened in his district, but I have made inquiries from the district in which this particular case occurred, and the answer I have received is as follows:—

> 'It is not the fact that martial law courts refused to hear witnesses for the defence who were present in court or attended the court for that purpose. In the case mentioned, as in some others, the court exercised its discretion in not summoning certain witnesses named by the accused when such witnesses lived in distant places and the accused could allege no real reason for producing them as witnesses and it appeared they were named as such merely for purposes of vexation and delay.'

"From Gujranwala, the Hon'ble Member went to Lyallpur and he stated that there was a man named Ram Lok at Lyallpur, son of one Daulat Ram, who was arrested on the 25th April, was detained in police custody for over three weeks and then released for want of evidence; that after his release his father appeared as a defence witness for one Ram Ditta and was asked to become approver but refused to do so; that on this his son Ram Lok was re-arrested on the following day for the offence for which he had been arrested and released before. He then went on to say that the trial was unduly expedited at the end owing to the approaching termination of martial law. Now, my Lord, Ram Lok was not arrested on the 25th April, he was arrested on the 28th May. He was not detained in custody for three weeks; he was convicted on the 5th of June. His arrest had nothing whatever to do with the evidence given by his father on behalf of Ram Ditta and indeed, the police at the time, I am assured, did not know what evidence his father had been giving in the case against Ram Ditta. Finally, my Lord, the accused pleaded guilty.

"The Hon'ble Member then went on to speak of men who had been sentenced to long terms of imprisonment without any evidence having been recorded or any judgment having been written. Well, I can quite understand the Hon'ble Member feeling a little bit disoriented when he deals with cases in which there are not full records. Full records are what he has been accustomed to, and it gives him something of a shock to find that a man has been sent to jail on a scanty record. I need hardly perhaps tell him that a scanty record does not mean scanty evidence; but it may be news to him to know that no court martial ever gives any reasons for its findings, and the procedure of these courts was much more that of courts-martial than of the ordinary courts of law. The particular cases which the Hon'ble Member has selected are not very fortunate ones. He has taken the case of a man named Fazla, *tongawala,* who, he says, was sentenced to transportation for life for waging war against the King, without any evidence being recorded.

"I have seen the record and the Judge's notes. Two sides of foolscap are covered with the notes....."

(At this point the Hon'ble Mr. Malaviya got up)

The President:—"Order, order. The Hon'ble Member must not interrupt. He has had his say and Mr. Thompson now has the ear of the house."

The Hon'ble Pandit Madan Mohan Malavia:—"The Hon'ble Member is wrong. I did not refer to the case of Fazla."

The Hon'ble Mr. J.P. Thompson:—"The record is in the possession of Sir William Vincent. I am certain of the facts I have stated.

"The other case the Hon'ble Member mentioned was that of Hari Ram and Hans Raj. These two men were prosecuted for being in possession of Amritsar loot. It is true that in this case no evidence was recorded, but it is not true that there was no judgment. There was a judgment, which sets out the facts of the case and the reasons for the finding.

"Then the Hon'ble Member passed on to a consideration of what is known as the *salaaming* order at Lyallpur. The justification for this order is not really a matter for me, but I happen to have the record of the case he referred to; so I think perhaps I am justified in making a few remarks about it. I do not wish to justify, it is no part of my business to justify, the infliction of sentences of flogging for the non-salaaming of British officers. But in the particular case which the Hon'ble Member mentioned, the man who was convicted had previously been warned that he was committing a breach of martial law in not *salaaming* British officers and the offence for which he was punished was his second offence.

"My Lord, the Hon'ble Member read out to the Council the judgment of Colonel O'Brien in the Ramnagar case, in which the King was burned in effigy. This case has engaged the attention of the Punjab Government. We made some further inquiries with a view to ascertaining whether the facts were as found. As the Council will gather from what the Hon'ble Member has said, the case is one which has attracted a certain amount of attention. The case was examined by two officers independently of Colonel O'Brien, and both reported, after going through the case, that there was no ground for distrusting the conclusions arrived at by the officer who had tried the case. The Hon'ble Member tells us that some of the accused were not arrested till the 28th May. He then said that the people were of such position that it was impossible for them to have committed the offences that were alleged against them. My Lord, we have adduced against the reasoned judgment of an officer who had heard the evidence, an officer of long experience, who must, I think, have been in charge of one district or other in the Punjab for nearly twenty years, we have adduced a misstatement and an opinion. I claim that

that is not sufficient to justify Government in remitting the punishment of these men.

"The last cases to which the Hon'ble Pandit referred were certain cases tried by Mr. Hoyle. He said that the particulars in the judgment were scanty. The records I hold in my hand (shown to Council). This is the record of one case, 5 pages of evidence written in a small hand, and this is the record of the other case, 8 pages of evidence. The cases tried by Mr. Hoyle were, as a general rule, tried with great care, and I should not be afraid to show the records to the most hostile critic.

"That concludes the examination of the detailed allegations of the Hon'ble Pandit. I trust I have succeeded in convincing the Council that the allegation made by the Pandit show a degree of credulity, not to say gullibility, lack of proportion and a power of closing his eyes to everything that can possibly be said on the other side, that justify me in saying that it is difficult any longer to have any confidence in his power to appreciate any political situation, or his willingness to admit that there is anything whatever to be said in favour of those who are unfortunate enough to differ from him. As regards the Hon'ble Pandit's credulity, I should like to tell the Council a story. The Pandit has recently been paying a number of visits to Amritsar, in the course of which he has been making those inquiries the valuable results of which he has indicated to the Council in his speech. During the course of one of these visits he paid a visit to the Jallianwala Bagh. After his visits there he reported to the Municipal Committee that there were corpses down the well and that they constituted a grave danger to the health of the locality. On examination it was found that he had mistaken an earthen pot for the head of the corpse and a bundle of cloth that had been looted for the body....."

The Hon'ble Pandit Madan Mohan Malaviya:—"There was one corpse, several of us saw it."

The Hon'ble Mr. J.P. Thompson:—"I adhere to my statement of fact. If the Hon'ble Member believed in his own story, I am sure he would have found one little minute during the 4½ hours he addressed the Council to bring in that picturesque touch. This is an example of the Hon'ble Pandit's credulity. He tells us that he had the evidence of two of his senses, his eyes and his nose, as regards the presence of the corpse. I ask the Council whether we are to take statements which he has only on hearsay and to rate them at any high value than the evidence of his own senses. I have mentioned this story because, I think, it is important for the Council to realise what a terrible enemy we have had to contend against in the rumours spread about the country during the past troublous months. I think it will help the Council to correlate the intelligence and mentality of the Hon'ble Pandit with that of the lower orders of the people among whom these rumours find credence and have currency. I should like to give the Council some examples of these rumours, because, I believe it is only in this way that it will understand what an unrivalled field the agitator in this country has if he chooses to set about sowing false rumours in the countryside. The rumours in regard to the Rowlatt Act are known to everybody here and I need not more than refer to them; such rumours as that no one should be allowed to possess more than 10 bighas of land, that 50 per cent of the produce was to be taken as Government dues, that no marriages were to be allowed until the parties had been examined by a Government medical officer and so on. I do not wish to say anything more about those rumours, nor do I wish to deal with those rumours which dealt with things which are not inherently impossible. For instance, there was a rumour going about which, I believe, found wide credence, that at one period of the disturbances a personal attack was made on Sir Michael O'Dwyer, and his Private Secretary drew out his revolver and shot not his assailant, but the Hon'ble Mian Mohammad Shafi. No, it is another kind of rumour to which I want to draw the attention of the Council. They illustrate better the difficulties of the situation with which we have to deal, rumours which savour of magic of faerie. We had stories that the Germans had signed the peace with an ink which would fade and that there would soon be no evidence that the treaty had been signed at all. We had stories that Mr. Gandhi was distributing magic emblems in the shape of miniature swords which would inspire the holders with an undying hatred against the British Government. We had stories that the Amir during the recent hostilities had called to his aid a regiment of paladins from Samarkand, against whom no mere human force could stand. But perhaps the most extraordinary of all rumours which got about was a rumour which gained wide credence in the district of Muzaffargarh. It is a district which lies along the Indus in the extreme south-west of the province. It is inhabited mainly by Mohammedans. A rumour got about that on the night of the *Shab-i-barat* all those who had died in the influenza epidemic at the last autumn would rise from their graves. The *Shab-i-barat* is the night on which Mahommedans believe that God records the actions which will be performed by all human beings in the coming year, and the names of all those who are to die or to be born. Pious Moslems keep awake all night in the hope of catching a glimpse of the glory of the Almighty. The rumour, as I said, spread and with it went an order to the women of the district that they should be ready that night in the graveyards with clothes for the dead, against their expected resurrection. The rumour was contradicted before the night arrived, but I believe that there were many poor women who watched by the graves that night, in the hope that at midnight the graves would open and their lost ones would rise again.

"I have nothing more to say, my Lord. I do not propose, as I told the Council, to deal with the question of the causes of the recent discontents. But there is one statement which I do not feel I can let pass unchallenged. The Hon'ble Mr. Chanda and the Hon'ble Pandit Malaviya have both told us that the *Satyagraha* movement was innocent in connection with these disturbances. My Lord, I should like to tell the Council a story. It came to my notice a few days ago in connection with an appeal for mercy for an unfortunate man who had been condemned to death. There were in Lahore two brothers, Indian Christians. They were both in service and they lived with their families in the same compound. The master of one of them went to Bombay and took his servant with him, and he went away leaving his wife and two little children, aged six and three, in charge of his brother. While he was away his wife died. His brother sent word to him to return. He was very poor and so borrowed a few rupees for the funeral in the absence of his brother. A few days later his brother returned. When he returned, it was the days of the *hartal* in Lahore, and the shops were all closed. He found both of his children ill; it was partly illness and partly starvation. Milk was what he wanted for them and milk he could not get. All day long he tried to obtain it, but without success. The shops were shut and none would sell. In the evening he returned in despair. Late at night his brother who had been out on the same errand like him returned with empty hands, and when he opened the door of the hut where the children slept, he found there two little bodies lying on the bed with their throats cut. At whose door, my Lord, will those two lives be laid?"

The Hon'ble Major Malik Sir Umar Hayat Khan:—"My Lord, a telegram has just been received, and I believe two or three pleaders sitting together have drafted it in the name of the whole of the Punjab to delay this Bill. Of course, all the other subjects of His Majesty who form about 99 per cent, have also to be kept in view. I had agreed, some of the members had agreed, if Government did not bring forward this Bill, to remain silent; but now that the Bill is before the Council, I wish to say what I originally wanted to.

"While welcoming the Bill which is a very ordinary measure and always follows disturbances and martial law, I am of opinion that it has come rather late, and now that it has come it should be passed at once. It is a good thing that hitherto no one has sued any of those subordinates who acted under orders of their superiors and who in turn acted with the best of intentions to speedily quell a fire, the flames of which would have spread to the rural population from which the Army is recruited and that, plus the Frontier troubles at a very critical time of the year, may have proved disastrous, for a while. I hope that the loyal soldiers and other officials will not be left a minute more without the protection of this most urgent Bill and that it will be passed into law.

"Before the Bill was introduced we had many consultations, and the main objections to the Bill were that it would prejudice the Committee of Inquiry and hamper its work and that the unwarranted acts of various individuals and officers would go unpunished. It looks as if the Government of India had deputed a spy with us because they have framed the Bill in such a way that they have met all the possible objections which one could raise. This could be seen from the Statement of Objects and Reasons where it is clearly pointed out that. 'It gives protection only to acts done in good faith and in a reasonable belief that they were necessary,' etc. It continues further:—'It thus leaves open the question of fact in any given case to be considered by the intended Committee of Inquiry, and does nothing to prejudice the Committee's findings or the action which Government may take upon its report.'

"Now coming to the preamble of the Bill in which it is said:—'It has been necessary for the purpose of restoring order to resort to martial law,' I would like to offer certain observations to show the state of various places in the province where martial law was necessary.

"Apart from the section which was responsible for the disturbances, the general population deplored it and positively knew that this was all due to an organised conspiracy, and it will not be out of place to quote a portion of the address presented by the Muhammadan community of the Punjab on the eve of Sir Michael's departure. this community forms the majority of the population. On that occasion representatives of nearly all the districts of the Punjab were present. It runs as follows :—

> 'Although towards the conclusion of your Honour's brilliant regime the enemies of law and order as a result of an organised conspiracy which may be the outcome of a foreign influence succeeded in deluding a section of the people into riots and disturbances, yet it is a standing tribute to your Honour's far-sighted statesmanship and firmness that the situation was soon got well in hand and by using the speedy and effective method of martial law peaceful life is once more possible for the law-abiding citizens of our chief towns.'

"Later on, when all the spiritual leaders met to condemn the action of the Amir of Afghanistan in declaring war against India, and thus naturally against His Majesty's Muhammadan subjects, and to say farewell to Sir Michael, they said :—

> 'We condemn the actions of those enemies of the country whose conspiracy has brought about disturbances in the country.'

"So from this it will be seen that the general public apart from evil-doers recognised that there was a conspiracy at the bottom of all these affairs.

"The Hon'ble the Home Member held an inquiry into the doings of the *Ghadr* Party, *i.e.*, those who wanted to bring about mutiny in the beginning of the war and what were their methods? They intended to cut the telegraph wires, break the railway lines, derail the trains and plunder the public, etc. What did the recent conspirators do? They took exactly the same line and the whole thing was very cleverly managed. Meetings were convened in the mosques to unite Muhammadans. It was known that the Muhammadans had strained feelings about the Turkish affairs, and if their mosques were bombed or fired upon, it would infuriate them. Such meetings were held in Delhi, Lahore and various other places. The same thing was planned in Amritsar with regard to the Sikhs, in which they succeeded to a good extent, and spread all sorts of rumours about the Durbar Sahib, the Golden Temple. But it was owing to the loyalty and far-sightedness of the Sikh nation, that their designs were frustrated. The similarity of action which I explained the other day in various centres at one and the same time illustrates that the origin was the same. The time of a great fair chosen to spread the propaganda with much ease was cleverly fixed where people from all the rural parts of the country assemble so that they may carry it with them to the villages. The columns of the extremist newspapers were engaged for propaganda, and though we may now satisfy ourselves that the editors of some such papers were punished, they had done their work.

"On the 5th of April last everything was so ripe that all sane thinkers knew the trouble had arrived. Though this was also known to the authorities and though some arrangements of police and troops were made as a safeguard, I am sorry to say the authorities were yet doing things in a half-hearted manner. Knowing that there would be trouble. I offered my services with my men and sowars to help the Police which were accepted, and from that time onward I continued to work throughout the disturbances helping the Police, the Publicity Board and the military authorities.

"From this it will be clear that everyone knew perfectly well the impending danger. Although the Lahore authorities prohibited the forming of any procession next day, the 6th of April, all such orders were disregarded and though the facts were reported and later on they saw it for themselves, they were weak in not enforcing their orders. This weakness so encouraged the mob that from that date onward no man with a title or one considered to be of the Government party could appear among the public. The war cries of *Hindoo Mussalman ki Jai* meant that both the communities had joined in a common cause by eating and drinking together. The excitement of the public went on increasing while the prestige of Government went on decreasing. When on the 10th things reached their climax, all this time the Punjab Government was hesitating and minimising the gravity of the situation.

"As the martial classes of the Punjab were about to give a farewell party to the Lieutenant-Governor, and as most of the leading men including the members of the Provincial Council were present, a deputation waited upon a high official to impress the delicacy of the situation just before disturbances had broken out. When the disturbances had broken out on the 10th, the Punjab Government summoned all the representatives of Lahore, as well as those of the other parts of the Province, to discuss the situation, and out of thirty or forty members representing all sections and classes, except two, were all unanimous in advising the Government to be firm and take strong and immediate action so that the disturbances would not spread to the rural areas. But I am sorry to say that the Punjab Government did not follow the advice and still hesitated to take any proper action. This was interpreted by the prople as inability of the Government to do anything, and disturbances at various places like Gujranwala, Kasur, etc., were the result. Had martial law been introduced earlier it would have saved many lives and disastrous results. I have dealt with this at some length to show the state of affairs. Most of the students who were approached by some of their teachers were wearing the black badges of martyrs and did not attend the schools and colleges. The Railway employees had also been approached and had struck work. Apart from the various strikes, a *Danda* Battalion with heavy clubs was in charge of Lahore city, who terrorized all the peace-loving people who wanted to assume normal conditions. Free food was supplied to all these and other evildoers, while the rest of the population could not get sufficient to eat, many having reached the point of starvation. The Council will have heard the sad story which Mr. Thompson has just related of those children who could not get food.

"A regular agency of exaggerated rumours against the Government was opened. The emissaries reached Peshawar and then further on to Kabul. This will prove, I hope, the necessity of the preamble of this Bill.

"It will be admitted on all hands that acts committed by the soldiers under order of their superior are *bona fide*. But if it may be considered that the higher officials are to be blamed for harshness I have already stated the case of some at Lahore for so delaying action.

"In Gujranwala, the rebels the whole day burnt building after building belonging to the Government as well as the records, church and station, and the authorities took no action till evening, when some aeroplanes turned up. If the night had fallen before their arrival none can foretell what would have happened during that time.

"The excuse that the local authorities have put forward at Gujranwala that they did not fire and allowed everything to be set on fire all the day long was that young children were put forward as a shield, and had they fired upon the mob the children would have been killed. But this was no novelty, as the same thing was tried at

Malakwal and even at Amritsar, which fact you would have heard and seen when a photo was shown in a debate the other I day. The law clearly provides in section 106 I. P. C. for it.

"Thus the authorities cannot hold it as a good excuse. It is said, one of the bombs was thrown intentionally on a Boarding House at Gujranwala, and the officer in the machine is accused for it. It will not be out of place if I say this from my experience that bombing by aeroplanes is not always very accurate and generally does not hit the target one wants to. At an Arab village we had a camp scattered in about a mile square. A famous Turk came to bomb us in an up-to-date German machine. In all his attempts he missed the whole camp and hit a mule at a good distance away from the camp.

"In many other places all the Government stacks of fodder were being burnt and all the grass preserves were used as common property. Even His Majesty's effigies were made and burnt.

"It was not only in Gujranwala that this was done, but I know of certain cases in Lahore where students and a few others did this. The evidence was not sufficient to prosecute, but it is a fact that this was done. All attempts were made to approach soldiers to detract them from their allegiance, but thanks to God, owing to their staunch devotion and loyalty as well as their knowledge of the strength of the British Arms, all attempts were frustrated on which mostly the conspirators depended and all their calculations went wrong as those of the Kaiser William, and law and order was restored. All of those who were trying to quell disturbances and at the same time had to meet the Frontier troubles, faced a critical situation, and no one for a moment could predict that all this dark cloud and storm would pass away in such a short time. So provision had to be made for all eventualities.

"If all this does not show that it was a conspiracy of waging war against the Crown and the necessity of martial law, no one can understand what more was needed.

"My Lord, when all are accusing the Punjab Government for hasty steps, we who know the facts complain of their over-cautiousness which has been mostly the cause of some of the mufassil disturbances and maintaining martial law for such a long time. Had martial law been introduced three days earlier, it would not have been necessary to continue it for more than a week or two, and there would have been no necessity of constituting courts under the law nor would so many people have gone to jails.

"My Lord, I have patiently heard my friend the Hon'ble Pandit Sahib, and I not only praise his endurance but congratulate him on his masterly speech in defence of those accused in the recent disturbances. It is simply natural, that in so doing he should advocate their cause and theirs only. But this in only one side of the shield. The accused that he has pleaded for are a fraction of a class which in itself is a fraction of the population of our province. The dumb masses of the rural population were never counted an asset in politics, but now they have become such so as to be reckoned. The acts of some of these criminals brought restrictions on the free movements of this overwhelming peace-loving population and the inconvenience that they had to undergo for the acts of the abovementioned few made them come out of their general silence. Their feelings could be only known to those who live among them and know their language. In the village *Daras* as well as in trains, abuses were levelled on the class which brought about the troubles in the Province, through which they were suffering so much. But as they do not possess an organ their prepondering voice is lost.

"Though a case has been made out minimising the gravity of the situation and certain challenges have been thrown out, I accept some. It has been said in the debate by my Hon'ble friend who sits on my left that the Government Communique said everything was quiet at Lahore.

"The feelings in Lahore, though were at the highest which could be ascertained from many acts, had to be minimised when a Communique for the general public in the Punjab was prepared. Any intimation of gravity to the public would have brought about disastrous results in the rural masses.

"There was a question of joint press telegram not coinciding with the Government Communique. The reason was that one of the criminals was responsible for so wrongly reporting, who has been brought to book and is now in jail.

"I would now like to state some questions of fact not in a form of speech but taking them one by one.

(1) It is said that of the cases where the Indemnity Act came into operation in England there were sixty thousand people who demonstrated against the Law. I can safely say that the mob in Lahore was well over a lakh and perhaps even two.

(2) It has been discussed that one of the acts to justify martial

law was in the case where jail-birds were set free. This was being attempted in Gujranwala that evening, if the aeroplanes would not have arrived.

(3) There is no denial about the fact that when the *Ghadr* Party started its operations there were widespread disturbances in the rural places like Jhang and Muzaffargarh, etc., and if not nipped in the bud by the Punjab Government, things might have resumed exactly the previous course even this time.

"Jhang and Muzaffargarh disturbances were in rural parts and it was possible that such could occur in that connection all over the country.

"On the 6th, many of the students in defiance of law went to the River Ravi and formed a procession which was strictly prohibited by the Government authorities. When I first met them, as I had volunteered to do, there was no policeman in uniform so as to stop them. Their demeanour in forcing the shops to be closed and keep away people from their business was such that it was essential that they should be forbidden to take part in politics, and I hope the authorities responsible will be called on for not exercising better control.

"During this time when there was a grave danger that the rural population might be affected, I was deputed to go to my district for two days. I found that a campaign of false statements was being carried out in trains as well as in the mufassil. Some of these were that Lahore and Amritsar were lost to the Government, and that they were rapidly losing other places, the army was out of hand and the Europeans were being killed wholesale. The rumour was that all the communications were being cut and parties had started for doing so in each district. In my district I had to raise within a day three hundred horsemen to look after a long Railway line and the authorities had to raise some more men to guard various other portions of the Railway line.

"A reserve had to be kept in hand at the Headquarters to rapidly move to any site of disturbances. It was owing to these precautions that nothing happened there and the same sort of measures had to be taken in nearly all the districts.

"It has been said that *Jai* of King-Emperor was also repeated by the mob. I am sorry to say that it was not the word *Jai* but it was '*Hai, Hai.*'

"From Delhi came letters and men to press on the shopkeepers to suspend business. Some of those who used to buy cloth from the big firms and were given latitude to pay money after it was sold, the demand came that if they would not suspend business they would be required to pay money immediately. If this was done their bankruptcy was sure and certain. Thus they were forced into the arena.

"Some poor men who were in debt to these people had also to join them.

"Then it is said that nothing serious happened in Lahore. The reason is that later on ample arrangements were made; the army was on the spot and the evil-doers were absolutely helpless to be able to do anything. As long as they were not checked some heads were being split in the language of my Hon'ble friend on my left.

"The Western Punjab next to the Frontier was so frightened by the disturbances in the east and declaration of war in the west, that they all collected to form organizations to save themselves.

"I only put forward these few remarks at the end to throw some light on the real state of things, and with these remarks I support the Bill."

*****

The Hon'ble Mr. W. E. Crum :—"My Lord, I rise with, no wish to prolong this discussion, but rather in the hope that what I have to say may possibly persuade members that there is very little use prolonging it and talking in the strain we have heard so far. The Hon'ble the Home Member in the speech with which he opened the discussion made the point very clear indeed, that we were here not to discuss the question as to whether martial law should or should not have been ordered, but that we were here to discuss the question as to whether those officers who have been acting under martial law and who have committed possible offences against civil law, as to whether Government who has promised those officers protection should protect them or not. Now, my Lord, the Hon'ble Mr. Chanda and the Hon'ble Pandit have spoken for a very long time in this Council, and for some time I was at pains to discover what the object of their speeches was. I do not think that they could possibly pretend that their intention was to persuade this Council that we were here for a discussion as to whether martial law was justified or not; and it seems to me that the only object and certainly the only effect that their speeches could have would be to persuade people outside this Council that Government had done wrong in ordering martial law, and therefore prejudicing not only the people, but also the Committee of Inquiry which is about to sit. Well, my Lord, they have had their answer. I doubt whether this Council has ever listened to a more convincing or a more crushing reply than that of the Hon'ble Mr. Thompson. The original speeches of the two Hon'ble Members and the reply will go out to India, and the original speeches and the reply will be weighed in the balance, and I should not at all be surprised if the Hon'ble Pandit was not sorry that he had ever touched upon the subject as to whether martial law should have been ordered or should not have been ordered.

"Now my Lord, there was one point which I must say puzzled me for a considerable time in the speeches of the Hon'ble Mr. Chanda and the Hon'ble Pandit, and that was the question as to what would happen to these officers of Government who had obeyed the orders of the Government and had thereby possibly exceeded civil law, if it was eventually decided that Government were wrong in ordering martial law, and therefore, if as I understood the Hon'ble Pandit to suggest, indemnification could not be allowed. As far as I could make out the Hon'ble Mr. Chanda made no reference to this subject. The Hon'ble Pandit said that these officers must take their chance.

"Now, my Lord, I can conceive of no more dishonest, no more ridiculous, no more piteous attitude for any one to take up than to suggest that, when Government had told its officers that they would be protected, they should not be protected, and to my mind it is upon his point, and this point alone, that the discussion to-day should continue. Government have said that they will protect their officers. Are Government going to protect them or not? I wonder if the Hon'ble Member realises, I wonder if other members of this Council realise what would happen to India, to any country, if when Government has given a promise it goes back upon that promise. The result would be nothing but chaos; from the highest officer in Government service down to the latest joined sepoy and the lowest village chowkidar, every one would be afraid to do his duty; and, my Lord, I do press this upon non-official members of this Council, that the point before them is that we are not here to discuss whether Government were right in ordering martial law or not, that we are not here to discuss whether this man was rightly put in prison or was not rightly put in prison, but that we are here only to discuss one point, namely, that Government have given a promise—are they to fulfil that promise or are they not?"

The Hon'ble Rai Sita Nath Ray Bahadur :—"My Lord, in rising to support the amendment proposed by my friend the Hon'ble Mr. Chanda, I have no desire to minimise the gravity of the situation caused by the recent events in the Punjab. But now that your Excellency's Government have been pleased to appoint a Commission to inquire into the matter, I fail to understand what harm will come if the introduction of the Bill is postponed till the Commission have submitted their report.

"I fully realise the paramount duty of Government to protect their servants who have acted under orders and acted *bona fide* and in good faith in the discharge of their duties. And had not the special circumstances in the Punjab and the popular demand induced Your Excellency's Government to appoint a Commission of Inquiry, I am sure my friend would not have been justified in pressing the amendment. But as matters stand, I think there will be no harm in acceding to his request. True, in the meantime suits may be instituted against Government officers. But suits of a contentious nature in which written statements have to be filed and witnesses examined cannot be disposed of before four or five months, *i.e.* before the Council meets at Delhi. Even if urgency is felt the Government of India which will move to Delhi in about a month's time can call an emergency meeting of the Council at Delhi and have the Bill passed into law. As the Bill is to have retrospective effect, the interests of the officers of Government will in no way be prejudiced by deferring the passing of the Bill till the Commission of Inquiry have submitted their report.

"I beg to reiterate that it is the paramount duty of Government to protect its officers who in an emergency are called upon to act and who act under orders and in the discharge of their duties, and I have no mind to say that Government should not protect its servants nor any mind to minimise the gravity of the situation created in the Punjab."

[*At this stage the Council adjourned for Lunch*]

The Hon'ble Mr. W. M. Hailey :—"My Lord, If I rise to address the Council it is not with any desire to add to the number of the Punjab champions. It is perfectly true that I have spent more than half of my official career in that province. I have every affection for it, I owe every obligation to it; but I have been away from it long enough, not to believe that the Punjab is always above criticism, just, my Lord, as I also possess a very strong disinclination to join that band of thinkers who seem to consider that everything that is done in the Punjab is wrong, and that the Punjab service must be inevitably and invariably condemned, without benefit of clergy.

"My Lord, I rise simply because I have had the opportunity of studying closely many of the facts in connection with these disturbances, and although I think the Council is very well able to judge of the value of the arguments adduced by the Hon'ble Pandit in defence of his case, yet there remain a number of facts, of which the Council should, I think, be put in a position to learn the truth. I hold they have not all been represented by the Hon'ble Pandit in their actual light, and that is my reason for rising to address the Council now. The first thing, my Lord, on which the Hon'ble Pandit dwelt at some length, and I take it that this was the salient point of his case, that martial law was unnecessary. If it was introduced without justification then, he argues that the whole case for this Bill falls to the ground. I take it and I think I have interpreted him rightly, that he holds that constitutional practice will alone justify the introduction of a Bill of this nature if martial law was in itself justifiable and introduced in a good cause. Now, he first of all drew a picture of what the state of things was before the 30th March. He said that nowhere at that time was there any inclination or any intention of rebellion. In fact, if I may say so, the only sinister aspect in the picture was a Government which persisted in passing the Black Act, and that there was somewhere in the dusty background of the north a reactionary Lieutenant-Governor who was determined to pounce upon and punish agitation. I think, my Lord, we must admit that those who originated the agitation which we hold led to these disturbances, those who originated that agitation, had no intention of producing rebellion. When in this Council we were threatened with an agitation which would disturb the good relations between the Government and the people, and when that threatened agitation was followed up in the Press and on platforms throughont the country, then I think those who promoted it had no idea of producing an open rebellion against the Crown. But I maintain they produced an atmosphere which was in itself dangerous and liable to bring about a rebellion. If they did so, it was not without warning from their own friends. As early as January last the *Bengalee* newspaper, and I quote the *Bengalee* because the Hon'ble Pandit also referred to it with approval, warned them that they were playing with fire. Later on, and I am glad to quote another of their friends, Mrs. Besant—even if she no longer ranks as such—warned them that an agitation of passive resistance would only lead to riot and bloodshed. Bengal, which knows something of the meaning of prolonged agitation, refused to have anything to do with the particular form of agitation which they originated and supported. I maintain, therefore, that those who promoted this agitation were fully warned of what was likely to happen, and I maintain that Government, if it had expected that trouble was likely to arise from that atmosphere, was justified in that expectation. However, the *hartal* came off in certain places of the Punjab on the 30th March, and I freely admit that up to that time there was no disorder. Now let me go to the second stage, that which ends on or about the 6th of April. There again there were nowhere signs of open disorder. It is true at Amritsar there were inflammatory posters put up, one of which called on the people to 'die and kill,' but the attitude of the crowds was not such as to lead anybody to suppose at that time that any disorder was contemplated. Now I go a step further, and I take the events that followed on the 6th April, the universal *hartal* of the 6th April. The Hon'ble Pandit has taken us in some detail into those events, and I must follow his narrative in detail. He first of all takes Amritsar, and he says that Amritsar was all peaceful, was all quiet, up to the 10th April and that subsequently if any trouble arose it was due to the action of Government in first of all forbidding Dr. Kitchlew and Dr. Satya Pal to speak in public, and in the second place, in deporting them. I realise the action of Government in deporting Dr. Kitchlew and Dr. Satya Pal needs justification. The justification is this. When subsequently a Martial Law Commission sat to decide the case of these gentlemen, it found that they had from the 30th March indulged in language which was not only likely but which was intended to bring the Government of the country into contempt. It found that on the 8th April, following the *hartal*, they had held private meetings, the sole object of which was to keep up the excitement. But what was the population in which the excitement was to be kept up, the population of the Central Punjab?

"I yield to no man in my admiration of the sterling, virile and martial qualities of the men of the Central Punjab. We owe much to those qualities in many a hard contest, but they have some of the defects of their virtues. When the Rowlatt Commission was writing of men of this class, it said that in their case the interval between thought and action was very short, and if once they gave way to the appeal of inflammatory addresses, they were likely to take speedy action such as would be subversive both of law and the future of the constitution. And these were the men among whom the excitement was to be kept alive. There were moreover local causes at work at Amritsar. That is to say, there had some time before been very keenly contested municipal elections, and the candidates and their enemies had engaged bands of hooligans, who, we know, were subsequently largely instrumental in perpetrating the atrocities on the 10th of April. There were besides a very large number of Kashmiri Muhammadans to whom vigorous appeals had been made to show sympathy for the cause of Turkey, and these appeals had not been without effect in inflaming their feelings. Now, a Government faced with a situation like that has to take its precautions. It would be blameworthy if it did not take such precautions and I maintain that anybody with a knowledge of administration, with an interest in the maintenance of law and order, could come to no other conclusion than that the men who were mainly instrumental in keeping alive that excitement should be removed from the scene of their activities. That decision was announced to the Deputy Commissioner on the evening of the 9th April. On the 10th morning, he took certain precautions. I do not desire to take up the time of the Council with too much detail, but I am obliged to follow the narrative of the Hon'ble Pandit in this respect. He was afraid of a demonstration by an excitable and inflammable people, a demonstration mainly directed towards the release of Dr. Satyapal and Dr. Kitchlew, and he therefore put out pickets to prevent the crowd from crossing into the civil lines. When the news of the deportation was known in the city, his anticipations were justified; a crowd collected and attempted to go to the civil lines, and it was at this point that the first conflict occurred. This is what happened. I think anybody would assume from the Hon'ble Pandit's narrative that this was more or less a peaceable crowd—I admit that it was unarmed—that it was a peaceable crowd and could have been dealt with by peaceable methods. The words at all events, I think, that he used were that all it required was a gentle pushing back. Now, my Lord, I daresay there are some here who have had some experience of crowds. If they have, they will bear me out when I say that, if you have a picket of a few mounted men, it is exceedingly difficult to indulge in moral suasion of that kind. At all events what happened was that, so far from the crowd being gently pushed back, they violently pushed the picket back. It was reinforced by a small body of infantry. When it was further pressed back, it was then, and then only, that the order was given by a First Class Magistrate to fire. Now that was the beginning of all the trouble, and the Hon'ble Pandit, I think, will have us believe that if that picket had not fired, none of the subsequent troubles of the Punjab would have ensued. I maintain that the subsequent events afford perfectly good evidence that something would have happened, if that picket quietly let the crowd go past. What did happen in Amritsar is unfortunately too well-known to everybody. And with every desire to avoid embittering feelings by reciting the events, I must refer to some portion of them. It was not only that Banks were burned, that Churches were burned, that a number of Europeans were murdered: it was not only that. The fact was that the whole thing was done with the utmost ferocity that Europeans were not only murdered but that indignities were heaped upon them. I do not say this with any desire to embitter feelings; I only say it as showing the temper that the crowd was in; I only say it as showing that even if that picket had not fired there, trouble would have arisen elsewhere. And it seems to me that it is unreasonable to say to this Council, that you must look on the previous provocation given to this crowd, as affording—I do not think the word 'justification' was used; I do not think the word 'palliation' was used—but I think it was said that you must look on the action of the picket's firing as some sort of explanation of the subsequent action of the crowd. Disorder did not stop there; and this is a dangerous feature to which I wish to call attention; it did not stop at murder and arson; it did not stop at showing the utmost cruelty to a woman and searching out another woman with every intention of murdering her. It did not stop there. The crowd went on afterwards seeking to destroy communications. It burned Bagtanwala station; it attacked and looted Cheharta Railway Station. I find it curious that the Hon'ble Pandit omitted to call any attention to this dangerous tendency of the crowd. The Hon'ble Pandit left Amritsar for a time and went to speak of Lahore. Now at Lahore he equally said that the atmosphere between the 6th and the 10th was quiet and peaceful, and the only reason that trouble arose in Lahore was that the Government excluded Mr. Gandhi from the Punjab. First, as to the exclusion of Mr. Gandhi from the Punjab. I think that also requires explanation, and, if possible, justification. I have described something of the atmosphere that there was in the

Punjab at the time, and the Hon'ble Mr. Thompson has referred to the extraordinary rumours which were set on foot regarding the operations of this Act. These were rumours which did not appeal primarily to educated people; the bulk of the rumours were such as appealed with exceptional force to the land-owning classes. He has told us, and there is every evidence to support what he said, that people were circulating rumours that the land-owning class was to lose its status; that men who had previously been proprietors were to become tenants; that land-revenue was to be raised; that produce was to be taken instead of cash; and these are exactly the type of rumours which are likely to produce among a vigorous population and cultivators trouble, the end of which no man can foresee. The population at large then had been told that the Act involved such consequences, and they had learnt that there was only one man in India that could help them in the situation. I do not think Mr. Gandhi was known personally in the Punjab, but he had acquired there the reputation, as somebody said (I think it is mentioned in one of the judgments), the reputation of a *rishi* and a *wali* I certainly have read one speech in which the coming of Mr. Gandhi was compared to the coming of Christ, to the coming of Muhammad and to the coming of Krishna. Now, that was the man who, if I should use the words of a speaker at Amritsar, was to break the power of the bureaucracy; that was the man around whom the whole of the agitation centred; that was the man who by his new device of passive resistance was to relieve the people of the burden with which they were threatened. They understood nothing of the real meaning of passive resistance. So little did they understand the meaning of this peaceful movement of Mr. Gandhi's that, as Mrs. Besant afterwards said, people who committed arson and assaulted women did so with the name of Mr. Gandhi upon their lips. We have been told—I have seen it stated in the newspapers—that Mr. Gandhi's action in coming to the Punjab was a peaceful one, that had he gone there he would have stilled all angry passions, and restored tranquillity. My Lord, I think I am right in saying that Mr. Gandhi could not even address Punjab crowd in a language which would be understood by them. How then was he to still those angry passions? What possible effect would Mr. Gandhi's arrival in the Punjab have had except to make people believe that there was truth in these sinister rumours, to make people believe that he had come there to continue the fight against Government? With a population such as that which I have described, a belief of that sort would have been bound to lead to fresh disaster. I maintain that no one with any feeling for the security of the Province could have safely allowed Mr. Gandhi to have arrived in the Punjab at that juncture.

"I have been obliged to interrupt the course of my narrative, and I will now continue it. The attitude of Lahore, the Hon'ble Pandit said, was open to no exception. There had been no trouble, there had been no disorder, everything was peaceful. Well, my Lord, a gentleman who was subsequently prosecuted, an editor of one of the newspapers, himself admitted that at this juncture the atmosphere was highly surcharged, and that the people at large were in a state of very unusual excitement. The Commission which subsequently sat to judge the facts, in what is known as 'the Lahore Leaders case,' were of opinion that the fraternisation at the Ram Naumi on the 9th was used for a seditious purpose. We know that Honorary Magistrates and members of the Municipal Committee, who were believed to have taken the part of Government and attempted to dissuade the people from closing their shops, were threatened; we know that many of them were practically confined to their houses. Then, again, we also know that the feeling of the people was being worked up by a variety of literature in the shape of posters. Let me proceed now to the actual incidents of the 10th. It has been very widely stated that all that the crowd intended to do, when it went up to the Upper Mall on the 10th, was to make a peaceful demonstration in front of Government House. It has been insinuated in various quarters that it was a small crowd of students. The best authority we have so far on the nature of the crowd and on the nature of what it did, is the judgment of the Commission. These Commissions may be attacked as having no legal authority, their sentences may be attacked as being too severe, but is this Council going to believe that these judicial officers would perjure themselves by misstating the facts on which they have founded their judgment? That is an impossible supposition. They state the case as follows, and I must quote at some length :—

"Towards evening a large and excited mob collected in Lahore City. Leaflets were distributed to it and some of its members were heard shouting both in English and in vernacular that Amritsar had been taken and the situation was well in hand in Lahore, as three gates were already held and a fourth would soon be closed. Headed by a man carrying a black flag, the mob proceeded with shouts of *Gandhi ki Jai,* and *Shaukat Ali ki Jai* from the Lohari Gate through Anarkali to the Upper Mall. Some of its members entered the compound of the Government Telegraph Office, but turned back on seeing a detachment of the Royal Sussex which were guarding the building with fixed bayonets. By the time the mob had got as far as the Lawrence Statue, it numbered some thousands. There it was intercepted by two Indian Police officers, with a handful of armed constables who were brought up at the double from Anarkali Police Station through the High Court grounds. These police lined the road in front of the mob but they were pressed back for a distance of about 200 yards as far as the Soldiers' Club. It was then getting dusk.

'At this juncture Mr. Fyson, the District Magistrate, Mr. Cocks, Deputy Inspector-General, Criminal Investigation Department, and Mr. Clarke, Deputy Superintendent of Police, arrived on the spot. Mr. Fyson ordered the mob to retire, but they pressed round him. One of them seized him by the shoulder from behind and they began to go through the thin line of police. They also attempted to get round them by going through the compound of the Soldiers' Club. After some minutes Mr. Fyson, who, owing to the uproar, had difficulty in making himself heard, ordered the police to withdraw a little further up the Mall in order to prevent them being overwhelmed by the mob, and then, as there was no other means of stopping its progress, gave the order to fire. About a dozen rounds were fired and then the mob was pressed slowly back to the city. Near the Bank of Bengal Mr. Clarke was thrown down, but his assailant escaped.'

And now comes what I consider the salient point of this judgment:—

'It is beyond doubt that the Lahore mob which marched on the Civil Station of Lahore was actuated by the same motives as that of Amritsar. It was essentially part of the same insurrection, and it was fully aware of what had happened to the neighbouring town the same day. It was rapidly becoming more threatening, and had already displayed its contempt of the authority and person of the District Magistrate. A collision was inevitable, and had the mob proceeded a little further up the Mall, it would have found a supply of deadly weapons ready to hand. Had it not been checked where it was, there was the gravest danger that it would have hurried on, in the confusion and darkness, to the commission of awful crimes.'

"That is the opinion of the Commission which had heard both sides of the case, and it is their deliberate opinion that, had the mob not been checked then, it would have committed grave disorders similar to those which occurred at Amritsar. There was a subsequent incident on the same day which the Hon'ble Pandit minimised in the same way as he minimised this. I find myself under the necessity of referring to this also at some length. I might say that the military had by this time arrived and were ready to assist the police.

'When the mob was driven back from the Mall it did not dissolve, but was slowly pushed back by a small force of police into the Nila Gumbaz Chauk and up the Anarkali towards the Lohari Gate. There it was reinforced by a crowd issuing from the city, and the police under Mr. Clarke, Deputy Superintendent of police, were held up at a point a little short of the cross-roads where the Circular Road cuts across the Anarkali. Mr. Broadway, Superintendent of Police, came up with a small body of police and cavalry, but even so the forces of order were unable to disperse the mob which showered brickbats upon the police and sowars. Two or three rounds of buckshot fired at the roofs of some houses from which the shower of missiles was most persistent failed to do more than check the attack from that quarter. A message brought Mr. Fyson, Deputy Commissioner, to the spot: he went forward into the crowd to reason with Pandit Rambhaj Dutt or Lala Duni Chand (he does not remember which) who were there, but all efforts to disperse the mob failed, and at last some half a dozen rounds of buckshot were fired. The mob was then dispersed without further firing.

'We commend to the notice of Government the admirable conduct of all concerned in dealing with the mob.'

"Now, those who listened yesterday to the description of this particular incident from the lips of the Hon'ble Mr. Chanda are at liberty to compare the two narratives and are at liberty to attach their own weight to the statements made by him. He dwelt on this incident at some length, based his description merely on certain statements in the newspapers. He did not refer to the judgment of the Commission, although he had then, I assume, in his possession a copy of it, because later on he alluded to it. Now those were the incidents of the 10th. By 8 o'clock, as the Hon'ble Pandit says, the troops were in the city, and everything was quiet on that night and during the 11th. So peaceful was the city, says the Hon'ble Pandit, 'that a meeting was held at the Badshahi mosque.'—I have his words here—'to express indignation at what had happened.' He merely mentions an incident on the 12th to which the Hon'ble Mr. Thompson also referred, namely that a C. I. D. Inspector, Ali Gauhar, was assaulted. Now what really happened was this. I take it from the reports of the various judgments of the Commission. On the 11th all shops were closed and an enormous crowd of Hindus and Muhammadans, said to number 25 thousand people, collected at the Badshahi mosque, inside which a banner was hung with the inscription 'The King who practises tyranny cuts his own roots underneath.' This is the meeting which the Hon'ble Pandit says passed over quietly. Well, let us see the facts. After the speech of Lala Rambhuj Dutt Chowdhry, an incident occurred which will show exactly what kind of meeting it was. This incident is described in the judgment of the Commission, dated the 29th April 1919. An ex-sepoy, named Balwant Singh, was brought in. He shouted a false story that Indian Regiments had mutinied in Lahore Cantonment and were marching on Amritsar and Lahore. He also stated that they had killed about 200-250 British soldiers and that he himself had killed six. He claimed to be a soldier and was dressed as one. He was garlanded and carried in triumph to the pulpit—he, a Sikh, was carried in triumph to the pulpit—of the mosque, and there he was called upon to make a speech. This he was unable to do and he shortly afterwards disappeared. Then, states the Commission, as a result of an orgy of oratory, the rabble left the mosque, led by hooligans who carried sticks and shouted seditious cries and destroyed pictures of His Majesty. The allusion to the band of hooligans requires some explanation. It was an organised body, described as follows by the Commission:—

> 'They marched two deep carrying their sticks as if they were rifles at the slope or trail. At constant halts they knelt, by numbers, as if in a firing position. On numerous occasions Chanan Din made inflammatory speeches proclaiming that he and his band were rebels and looked, not to His Majesty the King but to Germany, Turkey and Kabul as their suzerains.

He invoked the assistance of God and of these powers to overthrow the British Government. He also made reference to the Rowlatt Bill. Chanan Din's speeches were applauded by the mob, and the *Fauj,* as it passed along, was joined by recruits who were supplied with sticks.'

"Now, what were the feelings which actuated the people who got up this affair is very well shown by a poster, which, I will not say was issued on this date, but which certainly was issued either on this date or a day or two afterwards. I will read some extracts from it:—

'When Mahatma Gandhi arrived at Palwal, the English monkey informed him that his entry into the Punjab was forbidden, and that he should please go back. He replied that he would never go back; then that big monkey arrested him. Reports of his arrest reached here at once.'

"The first part is merely abuse—that matters little; but the second part is noteworthy.

'When the news reached Amritsar, the *Danda Fauj* of the brave Sikhs set fire to the Bank, the Railway Station and Electric Power House. They cut the telegraph wires and removed the railway line. The *Danda Fauj* of Amritsar bravely killed a number of European monkeys and their Sikh regiments have revolted and deserted. Oh Hindu, Muhammadan and Sikh brethren, enlist at once in the *Danda* Army, and fight with bravery against the English monkeys. God will grant you victory. Do not apprehend that God does not help us. Cast away such a notion out of your heart. God helps us at all times and hours. Conquer the English monkeys with bravery. God will grant victory. Leave off dealings with the Englishmen, close offices and workshops, fight on. This is the command of Mahatma Gandhi.'

"And there is a good deal more, very much to the same purport:—

'Oh Hindu, Muhammadan and Sikh brethren, do you know of the incident that took place at the Mall Road on the night of the 10th April? The Hindus and Muhammadans who were martyred that day were your own and they sacrificed their lives. Does not this incident excite you? What is the reason? Were not those who were made martyrs in Hira Mandi on the 12th April your own brethren, and died at the hands of the tyrants? Does the Prophet of God command you not to fight against the tyrant? No, never, the Prophet himself fought, and has commanded us too to destroy the tyrants as he did. Should we not be ashamed ourselves that while the tyrant is up to all sorts of cruelty, we are sitting quiet? Oh Hindu, Muhammadan and Sikh brethren, raise the cry of Allah Akber and kill the Kaffirs. Get ready soon for the War and God will grant victory to India very soon. Fight with enthusiasm and enlist youselves in the *Danda* Army'.

"The was the spirit which actuated this quiet and peaceable city on the 11th and 12th. But even if on the 11th and 12th there was nothing beyond what I have described in Lahore city itself, what about the state of Lahore district? On the 12th a violent outbreak occurred at the neighbouring town of Kasur, the headquarters of a sub-division in the Lahore district. The Kasur outbreak will be particularly interesting to Council because it had to be quelled entirely by Indian officers. What happened there? The crowd, excited, inflamed went to the railway station. It attacked a train in which there were a number of Europeans. It attacked, but fortunately did not injure owing to the bravery of an Indian gentleman, a European woman and her three children; but it killed two British warrant officers and injured two commissioned officers. In that case at least I claim that no one can say that there was either justification or 'explanation' for the violence of the mob; none of that crowd had been fired on by the police or military; the only firing was the discharge of the revolvers by the two unfortunate warrant officers when they were in danger of their lives. After murdering the two Europeans, the mob continued its course through the small town and burnt all the Government property that came within their reach. That is an incident which, I think, will disprove entirely any suggestion that the action of the crowds in the Punjab, where they broke out into violent excesses, was due to any sort of provocation or had any sort of justification.

"I have carried the narrative up to the 12th. The date is important because it was on the 13th that a reference was made to the Government of India on the subject of the declaration of martial law. I ask the Council to note the state of things in the Punjab as a whole on the 13th, when that question came up for consideration. You cannot take these incidents as isolated; you cannot say 'After all the military had got possession of Amritsar; there were large forces in Lahore; no further trouble was to be anticipated.' You cannot say that. You have got to look at what was happening not only in those two cities, not only at what had happened in Kasur, but at what was happening all round. It is very easy to sit in this Council Chamber, my Lord, in that atmosphere of protection of life and property which is the outcome of our rule; it is very easy to sit here and threaten us with agitation; it is equally easy, again, to sit here after the atmosphere of law and order has been restored and to minimise the magnitude of the events which took place in the Punjab. Some members of this Council may have fallen into the first mistake; I hope that none will fall into the second. Let me state, as briefly as I can, the nature of the problem as it presented itself to the Government of India when they decided to introduce martial law. There had been outrages at Amritsar, outrages which showed a strong and very bitter racial feeling. At Lahore the crowd had, at the Badshahi Mosque, openly welcomed the false news that the Sikhs had mutinied in Amritsar, had destroyed portraits of the King, had supported the formation of an organized force of hooligans, had attempted to force the closure of the railway workshops. At Kasur they had murdered Europeans and destroyed all the Government property within reach. But it goes further than that. Everywhere attacks had been made on the communications. Bhagtanwala station had been burnt, Cheharta station looted, Khem Karan and Patti stations had also been attacked, the communications had been so far impaired that, as your Excellency reminded us, it was impossible to communicate with Lahore from Simla except by means of wireless. There was every proof then that disorder was spreading outside the cities. In cities it is a comparatively simple problem to deal with disorder; you can send troops and isolate them; but when you have communications attacked, and the telegraphs cut all over the province, how are you to meet the situation? You are dealing with a warlike, virile, martial people, suddenly filled with a spirit of disorder. We know that in a number of villages in the Punjab the people had begun to believe that law and order had completely broken down. I would cite the case of the attack on the Treasury at Tarn Taran, attempt made by villagers on the line at Gumanpura, or better still the case in which a mob of villagers burnt the records at Aulakh, I maintain that, in the circumstances, there was every proof that rebellion had broken out, and not only broken out, but was spreading through the central Punjab. It was in these circumstances that your Excellency agreed to martial law. I will go further and say that you cannot judge of the justification of the order merely by the antecedent circumstances and facts; you ought to take into consideration also what happened immediately afterwards, since that also shows what the state of the Punjab was. The Hon'ble Pandit has referred to what happened at Gujranwala on the 14th, and as usual minimises the disorders that occurred there. He very unfairly, I think, tried to throw the greater part of the onus on the police officer in charge of the station; he said the subsequent disorders were due to the officer firing off his revolver. Will Council believe that before the revolver was fired two railway bridges had been set on fire, telegraphs cut and the Post Office also set on fire? He referred again to the hanging of a calf from the railway bridge, and he thought that the fact afforded some sort of explanation of what happened afterwards, since the public believed that the Criminal Investigation Department had done it. That suggestion caused at the time a ripple of laughter in Council, and I will therefore avoide criticising it. But, my Lord, when I hear him tell the story about this calf, and the pig said to have been killed near a mosque, I could not help thinking of the expression we so often use about a cock and a bull. There was no justification for the disorders and outrages that took place at Gujranwala, for they took place before the crowd was fired on at all. It was not, as he would have us believe, a fortuitous collection of schoolboys bent on wanton mischief that set fire to the railway bridges, nor was it a mere fortuitous collection of people that pulled up the permanent way or which deliberately cut the communications with Lahore. The firing by the police at Gujranwala did not result in many casualties; and it was fortunate perhaps in the circumstances, since this was a case in which a young officer, without any senior Magistrate to give him assistance, had to deal with matters on his own responsibility, and quell disorder which resulted in the burning of the railway station and a number of Government buildings, the burning of the church, and the looting of the goods shed where there were goods to the value of eight lakhs of rupees. I protest against the allegation that there was any explanation or justification in anything that that police officer did for the action of the mob. That was one instance of what happened on the 14th, and it was not an isolated instance. If disorder had stopped there, you might say that the declaration of martial law was hasty; but it did not stop there. I have the record here of a large number of cases showing the extent of the disorder and the danger to communications, though I will not venture to try the patience of the Council by reading them all. Let me finish the record of the 14th. On that day—the day of the trouble at Gujranwala—an attack was made on a European officer in the train at Hafizabad. Wires were cut near Batala in the Gurdaspur district, there was a strike on the Railway in Hissar district, workmen stoned the time-keeper's office at the Railway workshops at Lahore, telegraph wires were cut between Lahore and Amritsar, and an unlawful assembly, at which decision was taken to indulge in general looting, was held at Padhana. Down in the south there was a railway strike at Samasata, and the telegraph wires were cut. Up in north at Rawalpindi seditious notices were found posted calling on the people to rise during the night. At Rohtak there was a joint attack on the line by the mob and the railway staff, a railway bridge was damaged and attempts made to wreck a mail train. At Sialkot wires were cut between Sialkot and Wazirabad. Now I come to the 15th. At Gujrat a crowd attacked the Railway Station, and smashed the telegraph instruments; the police had to fire on the mob. At Malakwal junction in the same district a mob was only prevented from making trouble at the station by the presence of troops. In the Jhelum district a train was derailed on the main line at Kala. At Sialkot wires were again cut near Dhariwal. In Lahore District grass stacks were set on fire near Bhangali and Padri. At Hafizabad in the Gujranwala district the mob attempted to rescue men arrested damaging telegraph wires and the police had to fire on them. At Chuharkana, also in the Gujranwala district, the station was attacked, railway lines torn up, telegraphs cut and the station burnt and looted. The market was only saved from the mob by the arrival of an armoured train. Close by, the Dhaban Singh railway station was burnt and all the telegraph wires cut, and late at night the Moman station was burnt. At Wazirabad in the same district a mob pelted the troops at the station with stones, cut wires at the station, and then burnt the house of the Rev. Mr. Bayley, a missionary who had resided for very many years in the district and who (as the Commission stated in their judgment) was greatly respected by everybody; he was a linguist of wide renown, and the mob burned not only his property, but what was even more valuable, they burnt the records of many years' scientific labour. At Gojra in the Lyallpur district a mob endeavoured to get an engine-driver to refuse to start his train by telling him that the troops at Multan had mutinied. A number of telegraph wires were cut in Rohtak. At Sialkot, an attempt was made to fire a railway carriage in a siding. Let me go on to the 16th. In the Gujrat district a mob entered the Town Hall at Jalalpur Jatan, insulted the Municipal Commissioners and damaged the furniture, and at night the railway line was dismantled near Malakwal resulting in the derailment of a train next morning and the loss of two lives. In the Jhang district telegraph communication was interrupted between Jhang and Subhaga. In the Lahore district telegraph wires were cut at Changa Manga and Raewind. In Rawalpindi, telegraph wires were again cut. In Sialkot, the permanent way was attacked between Sialkot and Wazirabad and the wires cut. In the Gujranwala district all wires were cut near Sangla station and a murderous attack made on a European telegraph Inspector. Wires were cut in four other places on the Sangla-Shahdara line.

"I leave the 16th and come to the 17th. In the Gurdaspur district telegraph wires were cut between Chhaina and Dhariwal, and three other places, and telegraph wires were cut between Kaler Kalan and Kunja in the Jullundur district. In the Lahore district, near Jallo and Harbanspura, an attempt was made to derail a train by placing obstructions on the line. In the Lyallpur district a party proceeded to a neighbouring village and returned after breaking the telegraph insulators and cutting telegraph wires *en route*. At Lyallpur itself a stack of Government *bhoosa* valued at Rs. 50,000 was set on fire and burnt. In Rawalpindi, telegraph lines were interrupted near Gujar Khan. Trouble did not even stop on the 17th. On the 18th, in the Ferozepore district, obstructions were placed on the railway line; in the Gurdaspur district canal wires were again cut. In the Jullundur district Sidhwan flag-station was burnt. On the same day, the 18th, at Lyallpur, an attack on Moman Kanjan station was only interrupted by the arrival of troops, and a gang of villagers from a village colonised by Manjha Jat Sikh colonists, came out at night and tried to wreck the line between Toba Tek Singh and Jhaniwalla. Well, I fear, I have already wearied you by narrating this series of events, but it was essential in order to prove my point that I should bring them to the notice of the Council. It is impossible to allow any minimising of what happened in the Punjab between the dates I have mentioned. I maintain, and I repeat to the Council, that not only should we take into consideration what happened before the declaration of martial law, but we are entitled to quote as justification of our action what happened immediately afterwards as showing the real state of the province.

"Now I will not attempt to deal at any length with the legal aspect of the case. It was necessary, for the declaration of martial law under Regulation X of 1804, that there should be either war or open rebellion. I understand that jurists have differed as to what constitutes open rebellion, but, I believe, it is fully accepted that to establish the existence of war you do not need the existence of an army with all its paraphernalia. What is quite certain, and what, I think, I may with confidence place before the Council is this, that to justify a declaration of open rebellion, it certainly does not require the existence of an army or of an attack by armed forces. Why, the Hon'ble Pandit himself referred in the course of his speech yesterday to open rebellion in the Gordon riots. I maintain that the Gordon riots, which were treated by martial law, were in no wise as serious as what happened in the Punjab on the dates I have mentioned. There you had a case, and readers of 'Barnaby Rudge' will remember it well, in which crowds assembled more or less out of religious animosity, burnt chapels and ended up by burning distilleries; yet under the law of England it was held to justify the application of martial law; what is more, the action taken to suppress disorder was held to justify the application of an Indemnity Act. I put it to the Council that the justification necessary for Government to declare the existence of a state of rebellion, is a matter of common sense, and I maintain that the account which I have given of what happened in the Punjab in the middle of April would justify any Government in declaring that there was a state of rebellion in the Punjab. If the Council will agree with me that Government merely exercised ordinary common sense in making that declaration, then, I think, a great part of the Hon'ble Pandit's case falls to the ground.

"His contention was that if martial law was not justified, then an Indemnity or Validation Act is not justified. I maintain the state of things in the Punjab shows very clearly that martial law was justified, and it follows as a corollary that you must have an indemnity and that you must have a validation.

"My Lord, when I began to speak I intervened more or less as giving evidence of facts. But there is one other consideration which, before I sit down, I should like to put to the Council India is only now on the threshold of its political career, and it will not escape all the surging troubles which have come to the world since the war, since the beginning of unrest in the world at large. The officers of State, Indians as well as Europeans, and in the future probably more Indians than Europeans, will have to deal with those troubles. I have quoted to you one case at least in which an Indian officer, without any European support, had to deal with very serious trouble, the case at Kasur: there are other cases, such as that of Tarn Taran and Hafizabad. I ask the Council to reflect whether it is wise that officers of State, and particularly Indians, should feel that they are without support in dealing with troubles such as those I have enumerated. I feel myself the case of Indians to be infinitely harder in this respect than that of Europeans. They are liable to criticism of the most intimate nature, I mean in their families and in the circle of their friends. If they do anything which is thoroughly unpopular, they are liable to social and perhaps even to religious, ostracism. Is it right, is it fair, to hesitate for one second to give them support for the reasonable use of their discretion? I appeal to the Council to view this case with some sense of proportion, and with something of insight into the future. I appeal to it not to look at it in any spirit of partisanship. If I may, I should like to quote the words of one who, I think, was not less distinguished by patriotism and by love of his country than those who have been most keen in their attack on this Act in the last few days. Before the Hon'ble Mr. Sastri left Bombay, he spoke as follows:—

> 'At the same time he was one of those who believed that the Punjab Government had had good cause to use strong measures—perhaps the measures they had used were excessively strong, far stronger than the necessity of the case required—but they had had a case for the use of strong measures. No Government in the world, however mild or sympathetically disposed, would have sat quiet without using stringent measures to restore order when they had a mob sprinkling kerosene oil on buildings and burning them down, clubbing and burning Europeans to death. They were bound to render to Government the most cordial co-operation in bringing things once again to a normal state.'

"Now I quote those words, my Lord, because, I think, they show that an Indian public man, distinguished for his public spirit, can yet give Government its due, can yet recognise the gravity of the situation in the Punjab, and can retain his right of free criticism, without falling into the attitude of the persistent and unreasonable partisan. It is the spirit of that speech which I commend to the Council in dealing with this question."

The Hon'ble Mr. Sachchidananda Sinha :—"My Lord, in the course of the last few days I find I have been called upon to address this Council for the second time upon the Punjab affairs. On the first occasion it was due to the Resolution of my friend, the Hon'ble Pandit Malaviya, that I had to address this Council; now it is in connection with a Government Bill that I find I have again got to express my opinion. The Hon'ble the Home Member in introducing the Bill yesterday and asking for leave of this Council made a speech, which if I may say so without impertinence was free from any trace of bitterness or acerbity. If anything, it was a little unnecessarily forceful, due perhaps to his emotional Celtic temperament, but otherwise I have no grievance against it. And, I may say in justice to him that, in introducing the Bill his opening words were solicitious of the co-operation of non-official members of this Council, and he begged of us not to import into our speeches any needless acrimony or bitterness. I may venture to say, my Lord, that the Indian members who have so far spoken have, on the whole, adhered to the suggestion thrown out in such a friendly way by the Hon'ble the Home Member. But I wish I could say that the suggestion had been as well received and acted up to, in the spirit in which it was sought to be pressed, by the European members in this Council. I am sure I am voicing the unanimous opinion of almost all the Indian non-official members of your Lordship's Council when I say that the friendly admonition of the Hon'ble the Home Member was completely lost upon the Hon'ble Mr. Thompson, about which it will be necessary for me to say a few words later. But before I do so, I desire to express, if I may be allowed, my whole-hearted appreciation of the spirit underlying the Hon'ble Mr. Hailey's speech. Mr. Hailey has presented, it seems to me, the case for the Government in a spirit of such remarkable fairness and with such skilful advocacy as to carry conviction to a certain extent even to the minds of his opponents, and this is the highest compliment I can pay to him. If all speeches, my Lord, on the Government side were as fair and as skilful, I am sure the non-official members of this Council could be easily persuaded, even on most contentious matters to see, at least partially, eye to eye with the Government. But before I make my submissions to your Lordship in regard to the Bill and the reasons why, after most careful consideration, I have not been able to agree with the Hon'ble the Home Member as to the desirability of its introduction at the present moment, I should like to say and I am sure some of my European colleagues here, if not all, will agree with me—that the language which was indulged in this morning by the Hon'ble Mr. Thompson is to be strongly deprecated. Because we non-official members of the Council express opinions which may not suit the views and sentiments of our European colleagues, for them to indulge in the style and language and make personal attacks as did the Hon'ble Mr. Thompson on Mr. Malaviya, I submit, my Lord, with the greatest deference, is highly objectionable. Mr. Malaviya is a gentleman who is quite capable of defending himself : he will survive Mr. Thompson's attack, as he has done others in this Council and outside. He is a gentleman held in the highest esteem throughout the length and breadth of India for his devotion to the country, and however much you may differ from his views or his manner of presenting his case, there can be no justification for anybody to have made a personal attack on him as Mr. Thompson did this morning....."

The Hon'ble Mr. J. P. Thompson :—"My Lord, may I rise to a personal explanation? I did not attack the Hon'ble Pandit for his opinions, but for his statement of fact."

The Hon'ble Mr. Sachchidananda Sinha :—The Hon'ble Mr. Thompson told us—I quote his words—that he was a great admirer of Sir Michael O'Dwyer. Those who listened to his speech this morning hardly needed that assurance, for those who remember the famous speech of Sir Michael O'Dwyer in this Council must have felt satisfied that the Hon'ble Mr. Thompson's own way of handling facts is reminiscent of the methods of the late Lieutenant-Governor of the Punjab. When I find the Hon'ble Mr. Thompson charging the Hon'ble Pandit Madan Mohan Malaviya with distortion, exaggeration and misunderstanding, when I find him, again, charging Pandit Madan Mohan Malaviya with credulity, gullibility, a lack of the sense of proportion and the power of closing his eyes to the political situation, and when I find him subsequently winding up his peroration by saying that in intelligence and mentality he was correlated with the lower orders, I bespeak to these the attention of the Council and venture to ask whether it is a fair presentment of the case, or one that can be justified.

"Now, my Lord, I shall pass on to other matters. The Hon'ble Home Member was pleased to commend to the attention of this Council—and, I think, he particularly looked hard at me when he did so, as if he tried to stare me out of countenance—certain articles which had appeared in the *Civil and Military Gazette* of Lahore on this question by an anonymous scribe who signs himself as 'An Indian student of Constitutional Theory and Practice'—a rather long and pompous designation under which he takes shelter. The Hon'ble the Home Member asked us particularly to read those articles which, he said, put before us the whole case in defence of the Bill which we are now discussing. The Hon'ble the Member did not at the same time ask us to read a reply to those articles which appeared in the *Tribune* of Lahore. Perhaps he had not seen it himself. Now, this writer, my Lord, who has taken refuge in anonymity, says some very interesting things in his articles which have a bearing upon the point we are discussing now. I believe the Home Member asked us to read the articles for the reason that the writer says :—

> 'Indian publicists and Indian editors (I am afraid I come under both these categories) should have, therefore, no sort of quarrel or dispute with the coming Indemnity Bill. Any unreasoned or obstinate opposition will show how ill-equipped and ignorant of the very A B C of the constitution are our leaders in the Legislative Council and the writers in the Press.'

"I fear it was for this particular reason that the Hon'ble the Home Member commended the articles to our special attention. Further on, I find that this anonymous writer who comes to teach us the elementary principles of Constitutional law concludes by saying:—

> 'I also hope that the Indian members of the Imperial Legislative Council, and particularly the Hon'ble Mr. Malaviya on whom the mantle of the irreconcilable oppositionist seems by an irony of circumstances to have descended, will not fritter away their energy and their time in an unreasoned, purposeless and infructuous opposition to a constitutional practice that stands hallowed by the observance of centuries in democratic England itself.'

"Personally, my Lord, I shall be sorry, indeed, to waste a minute of my time in any unreasoned, purposeless or infructuous opposition to a Government measure. It has been my effort all my life to offer reasoned criticism and not to lead a purposeless, infructuous opposition. The writer seems to forget that, whatever weight of reason there may be on our side, any opposition here to a Government measure is bound to be, so far as we are concerned, infructuous, because, when the Government bring in a measure, there are behind the Front Government Benches the serried ranks and solid phalanx of our official friends, 35 strong, who sit here for the purpose of supporting the Government in any measure the latter like to bring in, whether it affects the European non-officials or the Indian.

Theirs not to reason why,
Theirs not to make reply,
Theirs but to vote and die.

"What is the good in a Council like this for any of us to try and persuade the Government? Once they have made up their minds that a measure has to be got through this Council, the old shibboleth of the responsibility for maintaining law and order being on the Government is trotted out and there are those 35 valiant soldiers to vote down any opposition that we may have to offer. Therefore, it is not for the purpose of carrying on any infructuous opposition that I have to place before your Lordship a few observations. The reason for it is this. Your Lordship's Government, as the Executive, have done certain things, have taken a certain line of action. Your Lordship's Government now come before this Council to ask the moral assent of the non-official members to the view taken by the Executive. If I am not asked for my moral assent, if the Government simply ignore me, I shall make no grievance of that. I shall not take up in that case a minute's time of this Council. But when the Hon'ble the Home Member gets up and puts forward reasons and arguments before me and asks me to give my moral assent—for my vote does not count for anything—then I am bound to examine his arguments and make my submissions as I conceive them to be.

"Coming, therefore, to the question of moral assent, my first submission is that in the preamble of this Act I find it stated—

> 'Whereas owing to the recent disturbances in certain districts in the Punjab and in other parts of India, it has been necessary for the purpose of restoring order to resort to martial law,' and so on and so forth.

"Now supposing the preamble had been worded like this:—'Whereas owing to the recent disturbances in certain districts in the Punjab and in other parts of India, the Governor-General in Council had deemed it right and proper to establish martial law therein', I would have had nothing to say against it. But when your Lordship's Government ask my assent to the declaration that it was necessary to proclaim martial law, I am entitled to say that, quite apart from whatever views I may hold, it will be prejudicing the work of the Committee your Lordship's Government have been pleased to constitute, if I were to give my assent now to this preamble as it stands. Therefore, quite apart from the facts as to what transpired in the Punjab—I have heard different versions of them; one was given by the Hon'ble Pandit Madan Mohan Malaviya who put forward the cases of those persons, subjects of His Majesty the King-Emperor, who are said to have grievances in the matter, while contrary versions have been given by Messrs. Thompson and Hailey who say that the facts are not exactly as the Hon'ble Pandit Madan Mohan Malaviya put before the Council—what I say is this. You have constituted a Committee to go into this matter, to analyse and sift the evidence and to come to certain conclusions. What will be the value of those conclusions if we now assent to this preamble that it was necessary for the Government to declare martial law? Therefore, my submission is, that by assenting now to this preamble the non-official members of this Council, whether Europeans or Indians, will be making the work of the Committee infructuous, and here I may be permitted to refer to one or two observations which were made....."

The Hon'ble Sir William Vincent :—"May I inquire, my Lord, with a view to shorten the debate, if the Hon'ble Member's objection to the Bill is confined to this statement in the preamble? Because, I may say now, my Lord, that Government are quite prepared to reconsider the question of this preamble."

The Hon'ble Mr. Sachchidananda Sinha :—"That, my Lord, is but one of my objections. That is No. 1. But certainly if this Government will meet us half-way, it will be of great importance. I hope the Hon'ble Member will agree to that alteration. Now, my Lord, when the Hon'ble the Home Member put that question, I was going to deal with one or two observations of my friend, the Hon'ble Mr. Crum. Without the least desire to cast any aspersion of even the mildest character on my esteemed friend, I do say that I can quite understand his difficulties in not being able to appreciate the points—the legal points—involved in this Bill. To him the matter of fact is that Government have done certain things; they gave certain promises to their officers, and why should not those promises be carried out by the Government? That is the way it strikes him and he, therefore, characterised the attitude of those who oppose this Bill at the present stage as dishonest, ridiculous and piteous—rather unnecessarily strong words those, for which there is no justification. He also said that it seemed to him that the only object of those persons who are offering opposition to this Bill is to persuade the public outside this

Council that the Government have done something wrong. Well, I desire to assure him that, far from that being the object of those of us whose misfortune it is to differ from the view of the Hon'ble the Home Member, we are trying to persuade the Government to do what we conceive to be right. That is my answer to the Hon'ble Mr. Crum. I think that in saying what he did he did a great injustice to us, who come here at the sacrifice of time, money and energy from different places in British India to serve our country to the best of our lights.

"Now, my Lord, this Bill deals, leaving the preamble alone, with martial law and indemnity, and to be able, therefore, to appreciate the points involved, we must have a clear notion of what these two are. I am aware that I am addressing the official benches and also the Hon'ble the Law Member, who is a great authority on the subject. But I make these submissions for his attention also. Now, what is martial law? Martial Law is defined, my Lord, in various standard works of legal literature; but I have no desire whatever to quote them. I shall only invite your Lordship's attention to what I find Lord Morley in his memorable 'Recollections' wrote to Lord Minto, when there was some talk of martial law being established a few years back. He said: 'Martial law is only a fine name for the suspension of all law.' And again; 'If you declare martial law in India, it will be a gigantic advertisement of national failure.' Well, it is not for me to say whether the declaration of martial law in the Punjab this year was or was not a gigantic advertisement of national failure on the part of British statesmanship; but we must remember that when we talk of martial law in the Punjab, it means that for the time being there was no law at all, that the whole legal machinery was suspended, and that, as a matter of fact, things were done which would never have been done otherwise than under the cloak of martial law. I shall now, with your Lordship's leave, read out one short passage from a judgment of Lord Chief Justice Cockburn in the well-known case of Phillips V. Eyre (4 Q. B. D. p. 225), to show what an act of indemnity really amounts to. He said: 'There can be no doubt that every so-called Indemnity Act involves a manifest violation of justice inasmuch as it deprives those who have suffered wrongs of their vested right to the redress which the law would otherwise afford them, and gives immunity to those who have inflicted those wrongs not at the expense of the community for whose alleged advantage the wrongful acts were done, but at the expense of individuals who, innocent possibly of all offences, have been subjected to injury and outrage, often of the most aggravated character. It is equally true, as was forcibly urged on us, that such legislation may be used to cover acts of the most tyrannical, arbitrary and merciless character, acts not capable of being justified or palliated even by the plea of necessity, but prompted to local passions, prejudices or fears, acts not done with the temper and judgment which those in authority are bound to bring to the exercise of so fearful a power, but characterised by reckless indifference to human suffering and utter disregard of the dictates of common humanity. On the other hand, however, it must not be forgotten that against any abuse of local legislative authority in such a case, protection is provided by the necessity of the assent of the Sovereign acting under the advice of Ministers, themselves responsible to Parliament.' Now, I can quite understand an Act of Indemnity not working unnecessary hardship on the subject population, where the measure is assented to by the Sovereign on the advice of his Ministers and with the assent of Parliament. But, here, my Lord, where the Government of India, the executive of the King-Emperor in this country, do certain things and then come and ask for the assent of this Council, with a standing official majority at their back, surely that cannot possibly convince the people that the action of the Government was right; and that the Government in asking this Council to pass this Bill will not be asking assent to a measure which might be of the most tyrannical and arbitrary character. That is the whole difficulty which we have to face in regard to this Bill; and that is why we have to be so very careful. Now, my Lord, apart from that, we find that in this Bill there are provisions of a very serious character, and it is, therefore, difficult for us to assent to the policy of this Bill. Take, my Lord, for instance, apart from the preamble, the provision in clause 2, which fixes the period of immunity from 'on or after the 30th of March 1919' and brings it down to the time when martial law had been completely withdrawn. In other words, by making this provision your Excellency's Government are asking our assent to give the operation of martial law retrospective effect. Now, this question was raised in the House of Commons in 1906 by Mr. Ramsay MacDonald who, your Lordship may remember, was appointed a member of the Royal Commission on Public Services in India by His Majesty's Government. I mention this fact so that it may not be said by the Hon'ble the Home Member in referring to Mr. Ramsay MacDonald; 'Oh, he is a crank,' and all that sort of thing. Well, he raised the question as to whether it was desirable to give retrospective effect in legislation of this kind to the administration of martial law. This is what he said: 'The second point was that this incident, the murder of two policemen, took place on the 8th February, and martial law was proclaimed on February the 9th; that the incident took place at a time when there was no martial law in the colony, at a time when the civil law was still in operation; yet the natives accused of the murder of the policemen were tried by martial law. Was martial law to be made retrospective in the future ? Bad as martial law undoubtedly was and unjustified as those were, as he thought, who declared it, ten thousand times more unjustifiable was it, that this negation of all law should be made retrospective and to cover acts committed previously to its being proclaimed.' The Right Hon'ble Mr. Winston Churchill who was called upon to defend the measure giving retrospective effect to it said this in reply: 'Martial law is no law at all. Martial law is brute force. The only restriction on martial law is, that no more force is used than necessary, and where more force is used than necessary, persons may afterwards be called to account unless covered by an Act of Indemnity. The Hon'ble Member for Leicester suggested that it was illegal to try these men by martial law for an offence committed before martial law was proclaimed. Of course, all martial law is illegal, and an attempt to introduce illegalities into martial law is like attempting to add salt water to the sea.' Now, under clause 2 it is proposed to give retrospective effect. The Hon'ble the Home Member advanced no sounder argument than did Mr. Churchill when he talked of adding salt water to the sea. Then, we find in clause 3 of the Bill that the ordinary rule of evidence is completely reversed, and we note that the burden of proof is cast on the plaintiff or the prosecutor....."

The Hon'ble Sir George Lowndes :—"I think the Hon'ble Member is making a mistake when he says that the burden is thrown on the prosecutor."

The President :—"I think it was a slip of the tongue."

The Hon'ble Mr. Sachchidananda Sinha :—"It is hard for your Excellency to realise what our difficulties are in speaking a foreign tongue in this Council. We are apt to make mistakes. Then, I find here further in one clause, that there is no limitation as to the places where officers are to be protected. I have no desire to take up any further the time of the Council, but my submission is that many cogent reasons have been advanced by us why your Lordship's Government should postpone the consideration of this measure. Firstly, by the words in the preamble we shall be nullifying the effect of the report of the Committee. We shall be calling upon them to assume that it was necessary to declare martial law. Now, Mr. Hailey may be satisfied as to that and Mr. Thompson also, who was Sir Michael O'Dwyer's right hand man. I daresay he is, but we naturally feel a certain amount of diffidence about this point. Secondly, I have shown that the Bill is open to great objection in the matter of giving retrospective effect. Your Lordship's Government are no doubt aware that since it was announced in the *Pioneer* of Allahabad that the Government were going to bring in an Indemnifying Bill, Indian public opinion has been roused. It has been insistent that this Bill should not be proceeded with at the present time. My Hon'ble friend, Mr. Malaviya, referred in some detail this morning to the strong volume of public opinion on this subject. He showed by quotations from a well-known London paper that public opinion, even in London, sees no justification for the Government's action in this matter. In India, I can assure your Lordship, almost every shade of public opinion, the so-called moderate and the so-called extremist, is unanimous in asking Government to forbear from pressing this Bill. Not only people of supposed advanced views, but even such a moderate man as Sir Narayan Chandavarkar, an ex-Chief Justice, whom, I believe, the Hon'ble the Home Member appointed last year as one of the advisers of Government....."

The Hon'ble Sir William Vincent :—"He was appointed by the Bengal Government."

The Hon'ble Mr. Sachchidananda Sinha :—"Then the Government of Bengal are entitled to praise for their choice in having appointed him as their adviser. I understand from the papers that even he sent to your Lordship a telegram asking your Excellency not to press this Bill at the present time. He has also written a long article in the *Indian Social Reformer* from which the Hon'ble Mr. Malaviya quoted certain passages. Now, my Lord, I do venture as a responsible adviser of your Government to say that it is not right for the Government of India to flout public opinion in this way and say to us: 'Oh, we are responsible for maintaining law and order, the responsibility is cast on us by Parliament, and we shall do what we think proper.' That, my Lord, is a wholly wrong attitude. Public opinion has got to be appreciated; it has got to be considered and given due weight to. We are apt to believe that public opinion came into existence in this country only with British rule, and that it came here along with certain other Western ideas. As a matter of fact, even in the early days people who had not acquired English education knew the value of public opinion. My Hon'ble friend Mr. Shafi will appreciate the well-known lines of the great Hindustani poet, *A'tash.*

'Sun to sahi Jehan men hai tera fisana kya
kahti hai tujhe khalk-e-khuda ghaebana kya'

which means 'do for God's sake listen to what people are saying about you and pay some respect to it.' That shows that public opinion was held in great respect even in earlier days. Therefore, I say, put off the Bill for two or three months. I understand the Committee will soon be out and will submit their report by the end of the year. Is there any advantage in pressing this matter at this stage notwithstanding public opinion to the contrary? I protest, my Lord, against the Government acting in defiance of public opinion; the result of such action in the past has been acerbity and ill-will on the part of His Majesty's Indian subjects. It is not desirable that the Government should repeat that experiment. I feel strongly that that would be a blunder. I do not want an indefinite postponement; if that was meant I should vote against it. I am in favour of a Bill of Indemnity—the only question is, should it be passed now, before the autumn session is over? I do hope your Lordship will take into your careful consideration the view I have put forward. A large number of Indian members of this Council, including the Hon'ble Maharaja of Kassimbazar and the Hon'ble Rai Sita Nath Ray, take the same view as I do. My Lord, your Government will be in a stronger position by listening to and accepting the suggestion we have jointly made."

*****

The Hon'ble Lieutenant-General Sir Havelock Hudson:—"My Lord, my only reason for intervening in this debate is to clear up one or two remarks which have been made by my Hon'ble friend the Pandit as regards the action of certain officers and others connected with the suppression of rebellion in Amritsar. I do not think the Hon'ble Member has given these events in their clear perspective, or in their proper perspective. The first event to which I shall refer is the Jallianwala Bagh, and in order to give the situation as it would appear to the Officer Commanding at Amritsar. I must ask your Lordship's permission briefly to state the situation at Amritsar on the 10th of April. We have the attempts of the crowd in the Civil Lines, the troops stoned and ordered, after due warning, to fire; the attack on the Telegraph Office; the Telegraph Master rescued by an Indian Officer when in the hands of the mob; the murder of a European guard at the goods station; the murders of the Manager and Assistant Manager of the National Bank; the murder of the Manager of the Alliance Bank; the attack on the Chartered Bank; firing of the Town Hall and its sub-post office; looting of other post offices; attack on the Zenana Hospital; the assault on Miss Sherwood; the burning of the Indian Christian Church, and attempt to fire the C. M. S. Girls' Normal School; the murder of a sergeant of the Military Works Department; a second attempt of the mob to break into the Civil Lines; troops again stoned and ordered to fire, later on towards nightfall systematic destruction of all lines of rail and telegraph communication; and, finally, the destruction of two small railway stations and the looting of a goods train.

"My Lord, does not this read rather like the preamble of the Indemnity Act on the Gordon riots of which the Hon'ble Pandit kindly made us a present? The above would be the situation as it would appear to an officer who found himself in a position such as confronted the General when he assumed command at Amritsar on the 11th April last. It will be realised, I think, that the situation was one of unexampled gravity. The Commissioner of the Division had definitely stated 'that the situation had passed out of his control,' that he must rely on the military authorities to restore order by the exercise of military force. The city was in the hands of an unruly mob; organised attacks had been made on Government property; Banks had been burned and looted; railway and telegraph communications had been interrupted; inflammatory posters inciting to 'die and kill' had previously been posted on the clock tower in the heart of the city, and the lives of Europeans had been taken in circumstances which I shall not describe in detail. It would be clear to the officer in command that the rebellion was not confined to Amritsar alone. He would be aware of the riots at Delhi and Lahore, and he would have had an opportunity of gauging the temper of the people by his personal observation. He would have been aware of the danger of the spread of rebellion into the surrounding districts. As an officer in a highly responsible position he would know that it was his duty to take all measures necessary to restore order, and that his actions would be judged by the measure of his success in so doing. He would also know that he would be held personally responsible for any action of his which might be considered to be in excess of the reasonable requirements of the situation. You cannot conceive that any officer, on whom such a responsibility had been thrown, would enter on his task in any spirit of light-heartedness; nor would an officer of his seniority and experience (he had 34 years' service) set about his task with a disregard of the sanctity of human life or with a desire to exact reprisals for the acts of rebellion which had already been committed. His first act would be to dispose his troops with a view to the protection of life and property. His second would be to warn the populace as to the result, if it became necessary, to use military force in the suppression of further disorder. These are the steps which were in fact taken by the officer in command at Amritsar.

"On the 11th and 12th he reorganised his troops and on the 12th he marched a column round and through the city in order that a display of force might have its effect on the minds of the populace. We have it on record that the bearing of the inhabitants was most insolent, and that many spat on the ground as the troops passed. From the shouts of the mob it was clear that they were in an entirely unrepentant spirit. No military force was used on this occasion, as the officer in command decided to issue proclamations as to his future intentions before employing such force. From a military point of view he would have been quite justified, I hold, in using force on that day, but the General Officer Commanding decided to pursue his policy of patience and conciliation. A proclamation was issued on the evening of the 12th and on the morning of the 13th April, the Officer Commanding marched with a body of troops through all the main streets of the city, and announced by beat of drum his intentions of using force should occasion arise. The people were permitted to collect in order to hear the proclamations.

"The announcement that unlawful assemblies would be dispersed by fire was received with jeers and cries, indicating that the mob had no belief in the sincerity of the warning given. While the troops were still in the city, information reached the Officer Commanding at about 12 o'clock that, in spite of his proclamation, a big meeting of rebels would be held at the Jallianwalla Bagh at 4.30 that afternoon. As this place had been used before for meetings, and as large assemblies had been addressed by the heads of the agitation on the 29th and 30th March, and the 2nd April, and as a dense mass meeting had assembled here on the 6th during the *hartal* and had listened to speeches intended to bring Government into hatred and contempt, it would have been clear to the officer in command that he might expect deliberate defiance of his orders. Now, he was well aware of the events of the 10th of April when the murders of Europeans and the attacks on property had been made and when the firing which had been employed to suppress these disorders had been totally inadequate. The Officer Commanding at Amritsar had to decide about midday on the 13th of April, how he would act if the projected meeting took place in direct defiance of his authority. After making dispositions for the safety of his command, he found that he had but a small striking force at his disposal. I believe the number was 25 men of one regiment and 25 men of two other regiments, belonging to the Indian Army, and, in addition, 40 Gurkhas armed with *kukris* only, and two armoured cars. Realising the gravity of the situation the officer commanding did not send, as he might have, a subaltern in charge of this small force. He realised that it was an occasion on which he, and he alone, must exercise the responsibility. He marched this force straight to the Jallianwala Bagh, leaving the armoured cars which he had also taken with him behind, because they could not get into the Bagh. On reaching the Bagh, his force was confronted by a vast assembly, some thousands strong, who were being harangued by a man who was standing on a raised platform. The Hon'ble Pandit would give us to believe that this was a fortuitous meeting of villagers and that they were listening to a lecture. That was not so in accordance with the facts, so far as I have been able to gather. It was clearly the duty of the Officer in Command to disperse this unlawful assembly. Realising the danger to his small force, unless he took immediate action, and being well aware of the inadequacy of the measures taken to restore order on the 10th of April, he ordered fire to be opened. The crowd was dispersed and the force was withdrawn. I have given the Council this narrative to show how the situation would be viewed by the soldier, and will content myself with saying that from a military point of view the sequence of events justified the exercise of military force, and that the object of its exercise was fully attained. Also, from a purely military point of view, the Officer in Command would have been gravely at fault had he permitted the elements of disorder to continue unchecked for one moment longer.

"The next point which I wish to turn to is another one to which reference has been made. It is the issue by the Officer in Command at Amritsar of orders that any persons who wished to pass the scene of the assault on Miss Sherwood should be made to crawl on their hands and knees. As this incident has been described at a meeting of the Bombay Provincial Congress Committee and All-India Home Rule League as a 'petty assault on a woman', I think it only right to remind this Council of what actually had occurred. In the first place, I would say that this is not merely an isolated instance of an attempt to assault European ladies. We have it on record that on the 10th of April the mob entered the Zenana Hospital in their endeavour to find the lady doctor in charge, who however escaped. After leaving the building the crowd again returned on information given by a disloyal servant, to search for her again, breaking open the rooms and cupboards in their search which was fortunately fruitless. On the same day, the mob attempted to set fire to the Church Missionary Society's Girls' Normal School, in which were four lady missionaries who remained hidden. I am sorry to have to refer in some detail to the assault on Miss Sherwood, but it is necessary, because I wish this Council to view the situation as the Officer Commanding on the spot must have viewed it. This lady had for many years been working in the city and was greatly respected; and the assault on her was characterised by extreme brutality. The following abridged account is taken from the judgment of the Commission which tried her assailants:—

> 'When she was bicycling from one of her schools to another, she encountered a mob which raised cries of 'kill her ! she is English.' She wheeled round and tried to escape but took a wrong turning and had to retrace her steps. She reached a lane where she was well-known and thought she would be safe, but the mob overtook her and she was also attacked from the front, being hit on the head with sticks. She fell down, but got up and ran a little way where she was again felled, being struck with sticks even when she was on the ground. Again, she got up and tried to enter a house but the door was slammed in her face. Falling from exhaustion she again struggled to get up, but everything seemed to get dark and she thought she had become blind.'*

"Her dress was seized, her hat was pulled off, she was struck with fists, she was caught by the hair and beaten on the head with shoes and was finally knocked down and struck on the head by a lathi. She suffered grave injuries to the scalp and was in a critical condition when she left for England.

* For full text of the judgment, see Appendix II, pages 328-329, *ante*.

"I feel sure that the Council will agree that it is not surprising that the Officer in Command took the view that some unusual measures were necessary to bring home to the mob that such acts of violence directed against defenceless women could not be tolerated. Something was required to strike the imagination and impress on all the determination of the military authorities to protect European women. This Council can readily understand how easily the feelings of soldiers would be outraged by acts of this nature and that they might be led to uncontrolled reprisals. Incidentally it is worthy of note in this connection that we have no charge against any of our soldiers during this rebellion. It is easy, my Lord, to criticise the orders issued by the Officer in Command at Amritsar, but the circumstances were altogether exceptional and the punishment, though humiliating, was not such as to cause danger to life or physical hurt. Except on one occasion when a body of prisoners were brought down the street in which Miss Sherwood had been assaulted, no compulsion was brought to bear on any individual to submit to the order. The order remained in force for a period of five days and there is good reason for the belief that, except for the party of prisoners already mentioned, those who were subjected to the order came voluntarily to submit to it for the sake of notoriety or martyrdom. One man after going down the street on his hands and knees three times had to be stopped giving further exhibitions.

"My Lord, the order was of course an unusual one and not one which might have been considered necessary by other officers in like circumstances. The Officer in Command at Amritsar will doubtless be prepared to justify his action should he be called upon to do so.

"The next point to which I wish to refer is, the use of aeroplanes at Gujranwala. I am not concerned in justifying to the Council the order given by responsible authority to send aeroplanes to Gujranwala on the 14th and 15th April. I merely wish to explain from the point of view of an officer who receives such orders, how he would act in aid of the civil power and for the protection of life and property when so ordered. The situation, as far as it was then known, would be explained to him and his action would be left to his discretion. In this particular instance information was received by the military authorities at Lahore that a mob had attacked the railway station at Gujranwala, had looted the goods shed and had set fire to the Tehsil, the Dak Bungalow, the court-house and the Church. It was known that there was only a small body of police at Gujranwala at the time and no troops. Owing to the interruption of communications, to despatch troops would have involved excessive delay. If any measure of protection were to be afforded in time, the use of aeroplanes provided the only possible solution. Well, I think, I must explain to the Council the limitations of aeroplanes when used for such a purpose. It is not possible for the pilot or observer to communicate with persons on the ground, either to obtain information or to issue warnings as to the measures he intends to adopt. In the first place, the noise of the engines precludes all verbal communication, and aeroplanes have not yet reached that development when they can hover in mid air. From their bird's eye view, the pilot and observer are able to ascertain that buildings are burning, that railway communications have been interrupted and trains destroyed, and that crowds are collected; they cannot easily discriminate between the innocent and the guilty; but on the other hand, from this bird's eye view the observer is able to get a much better idea of the general situation than an officer who is only on foot. When, however, it is clear from the nature of the damage that general rebellion is in progress it may be a reasonable assumption that the crowds are collected with criminal intent. The presence of an aeroplane over a crowd is in itself a warning to those engaged in disorder that they are likely to be taken to account unless they disperse; and the dropping of the first bomb (the effect of which is local but the noise of which is considerable) affords a further warning which can hardly be mistaken. It may of course be argued that a bomb cannot be dropped nor a machine gun fired from an aeroplane with any great degree of accuracy. This may be true, but when the mark aimed at is unlawful assembly it is not very material whether those in front or behind are made to sufler. It may be remembered that it is often just those persons who are most responsible for incitement to disorder who keep in the background and urge others forward to commit excesses. There is even a third category which never appears on the scene at all. Even admitted that the aeroplane in its present state of development is not an ideal instrument for enforcing order, still where as in the case of Gujranwala no other military assistance was available, we must not blame the Officer Commanding the aeroplane for the limitations of his machine. My Lord, my object in recounting to this Council in some detail the measures taken by the military authorities to reconstitute civil order out of the chaos produced by the state of rebellion, is to show that there is another side to the picture which is perhaps more apparent to the soldier than to the civilian critic. No more distasteful or responsible duty fails to the lot of the soldier than that which he is sometimes required to discharge in aid of the civil power. If his measures are too mild he fails in his duty. If they are deemed to be excessive, he is liable to be attacked as a cold-blooded murderer. His position is one demanding the highest degree of sympathy from all reasonable and right-minded citizens. He is frequently called upon to act on the spur of the moment in grave situations in which he intervenes, because all the other resources of civilisation failed. His actions are liable to be judged by *ex post facto* standards, and by persons who are in complete ignorance of the realities which he had to face. His good faith is liable to be impugned by the very persons connected with the organisation of the disorders which his action had foiled. There are those who will admit that a measure of force may have been necessary, but who cannot agree with the extent of the force employed. How can they be in a better position to judge of that than the officer on the spot? It must be remembered that when a rebellion has been started against the Government, it is tantamount to a declaration of war. War cannot be conducted in accordance with standards of humanity to which we are accustomed in peace. Should not officers, and men who through no choice of their own are called upon to discharge these distasteful duties, be in all fairness accorded that support which has been promised to them? My Lord, I feel before I conclude, I must make a reference to the amendment which the Hon'ble Mr. Chanda has proposed. I must confess that I heard this with some amazement. I suppose there is no class that has really suffered more by the disturbances in the Punjab than the forces of the Crown. Here they were at close of four years of war; most of them were looking forward to demobilization and their hard-earned leave and many of them to a return home. They were suddenly called on to perform what is the most distasteful duty, as I have said before, which soldiers are ever required to carry out. They had nothing to do with the outbreak of the disturbances or with the imposition of martial law. They only did their duty and, as a recognition, the Hon'ble Member suggests that Government should defer till some indefinite date the fulfilment of their promises of support. My Lord, it may be within the recollection of Members of this Council that Hon'ble Members both inside and outside this Chamber have repeatedly referred, and that with legitimate pride, to the services rendered by India and more especially the Indian Army. It was only last week that this Council listened to the Hon'ble Mr. Sarma's eloquent tribute to the services of that Army, and yet it is that very Army that the Hon'ble Mr. Chanda by his callous amendment to this Bill would leave in the lurch. For what effect would the amendment have if accepted? Officers and men would be liable to prosecution for any illegal act committed under martial law, and as martial law is in itself no law, all their acts under that law would be illegal. Actions for damages, for illegal arrest and a host of other charges could be preferred against them, and the question whether they acted in good faith would have no force with the courts which try their cases. My Lord, I think all soldiers would view with suspicion, if not horror, the airy suggestion that Mr. Chanda made that the actions would not come up at once, that they would be postponed for a month, then perhaps for two and then again for three months and so on indefinitely. The Manual of Military Law, which is the soldier's only guide, is silent as regards martial law; there is only one chapter in the whole of that book relating to martial law, but that chapter is written by Lord Thring, and there is one sentence in it, which is the soldier's sole guarantee, which I quote below: It runs as follows:—

> 'It is only necessary to add that, when a proclamation of martial law has been issued, any soldier who takes, in accordance with the official instructions laid down for the guidance of those administering martial law, such measures as he honestly thinks to be necessary for carrying to a successful issue the operation of restoring peace and preserving authority, may rely on any question as to the legality of his conduct being subsequently met by an Act of Indemnity.'

"The Government, my Lord, have taken the only honourable course and that is to introduce an Indemnity Bill on the earliest possible occasion. To have done otherwise would have been the negation of Government and repudiation of its obligations."

The Hon'ble Rao Bahadur B. N. Sarma:—"My Lord, I am glad before I vote I have had an opportunity of listening to the statement of the case on behalf of the Punjab Government and of the military authorities. It is a matter of very vital importance that we should look at the question impartially and dispassionately and not fall into the error of saying 'ditto' to whatever the people say, at the same time reviewing the course which the Government may ask the Council to ratify. What does the Bill ask us to do? In the first place, it asks us to state as legislative authority that martial law was necessary to restore order in the Punjab. I do not think that is open to argument. The second point is, we are asked to protect the civil and military officers who have acted under the orders of Government in accordance with the promises made to them that they would be protected in whatever they did recently for the purpose of carrying out what Government had in view. I may note in this connection, my Lord, that the Bill does not confine its operations to the events which have occurred after martial law had been declared. It relates to events which preceded the declaration of martial law in the various districts of the Punjab. Therefore, I may say at once that there is a complete answer that people can give to this Bill as it stands, namely, that it is not a Bill intended merely to carry out the promises which Government made to its officers after martial law had been declared, but also to ratify the action of the Military and Civil authorities in the suppression of these disorders before martial law had been declared. It is open to the Government to bring in a Bill for the purpose of giving protection to its Civil and Military officers as to what took place before martial law, I quarrel with the position. This is a vital point. Then clause 3 throws the onus on the people of saying that any particular act which Government wished to carry out was not *bona fide*. If the question stopped there, there might be something to be said for the Bill, but we are asked to go further. We are asked to say here whether we feel martial law was justified or not; whether martial law was kept in force longer than the necessity required; whether it was legal on the part of the Government; whether they were right in passing Ordinance No. V or not. In any event we are asked to ratify all the convictions and sentences of the Summary Courts in respect of which the public are not in a position to know whether justice has been done or not done, by reason either of the absence of the record or the absence of the full judgment. I ask the Council's attention especially to this aspect of the question, because had the Hon'ble Mr. Crum and those who followed him taken into consideration the fact that we are asked to keep in prison those who might have been wrongly convicted, convicted on the passion of the moment, the matter may have assumed a different aspect. I am one of those who believe that any disorder whatever should be sternly put down at the initial stage. I am not going to quarrel with any measures that Government thought necessary for this purpose. I go further and say that those responsible should be severely punished.

I go further and I agree with the Hon'ble the Home Member that, whether the Government were right or wrong, the officers who carried out their duties under the orders of Government, especially in a country like India, ought to be protected if they acted humanely and in accordance with the dictates of a civilised Government. There is no quarrel with the Government on that score, but, my Lord, I feel that the constitutional issues at stake in this controversy between the people and the Government are of such vital importance that we would do well to consider carefully before according sanction to this step. I understand there is justification for the belief held by the people, that if there is grave disorder, the Government are prepared to treat the people of India like cattle—no consideration is necessary so long as it is expedient to bring about peace and order and to protect the lives and property of Europeans. That, my Lord, is the issue that has been raised by this unhappy controversy, and it is therefore necessary to examine in detail whether these are real issues in sanctioning this Bill, and as to whether people are merely clamouring for the punishment of officers who have carried out their duties in a difficult time with reasonable precautions and regard to human life and suffering. It is not necessary in this case to consider whether some of the old dicta uttered by constitutional writers really justify Government in their action in declaring martial law necessary. On that basis I think people have some justification for thinking that in some of the occurrences, it may be riots and disorders, in the case of an unarmed mob, there was no justification for the employment of martial law. I am not going to take up the time of the Council longer, because whether martial law is employed or not, I take it that the civil power has every right and justification for asking the military and the police to come to its aid in suppressing disorders, and provided the duties are carried out *bona fide*, in good faith, and with due caution, there is no necessity for any mere technicalities; but on the question of constitution it has been said that martial law having been declared, it is necessary to introduce this Indemnifying Bill, but, I think, my Lord, it is necessary to state that in the view of many of us martial law was unnecessary and should not have been declared. In this connection, I would draw the attention of the Council to what Mr. Dicey says on this question. He says :—'The question for our consideration is, on what principle, and within what limits, does armed resistance to the authority of the Crown, either on the part of an invading army, or on the part of rebels or rioters, afford a legal justification for acts done in England by the Crown, its servants, or loyal citizens, which, but for the existence of war or insurrection, would be breaches of law.' Throughout the question is treated as one of civil war, and, I think, the essence of the whole thing is, whether a section of the population, whether large or small, resisted with arms the authority of the Crown.

"Now, my Lord, the second point to which I would invite the attention of the Council is, whether according to all writers on martial law, it is not considered to cease the moment the necessity ceases. I do not think there is any single writer who states that in order to prevent a future trouble, in order to prevent similar mishaps, in order to preserve order, even though the disorders have been suppressed, martial law can be continued especially during a time when civil courts are in working order. Therefore, my second point would be, my Lord, that after the 21st or 22nd of April when according to Press Communiques order had been restored in the Punjab, it was not right, it was not proper, for the Government to have continued martial law and to have created those tribunals to exercise jurisdiction in respect of all offences, whether those offences were committed or not. This has a vital bearing upon the question as to whether the Council will be justified in confirming the convictions and sentences passed by those tribunals, even though the Government have given us the assurance that they would be re-considered by two High Court Judges.

"Then the third point, my Lord, and what I look upon as the more important point, is this, and that is the moral aspect of the question. There are two theories of Government, one theory which attempts to employ only the civilized methods, however, long and protracted may be the struggle between the forces of order and disorder. And the other based upon the theory that in a country which is not thoroughly civilized, it is open to the Government to resort to terroristic methods if the object in view is an honest one, if the end to be achieved is the restoration of peace and order, and that it would not be wrong to humiliate a whole race, that it would not be wrong to subject them to indignity or to do whatever is necessary to terrorise or cow down the population if the object in view is to be achieved. My Lord, if the second theory is advocated, and that was the example that was set to us by some of the old sovereigns and perhaps it would be advocated even now by a few, but which has been repudiated most whole-heartedly by all civilized

Governments in the world, and for the suppression of which theory Great Britain herself has allowed herself to run into a debt of 8 thousand millions and the de-population of her fair provinces. The question, my Lord, now is as to whether any British officer of the Indian Government can be allowed to rule India on the second theory, because the view I take of the facts is that there are several British officers who are under the impression that so long as order and peace are restored, if a person believes that it is reasonable to do anything which attains that end, and if that theory is to be accepted, then certainly the Government are perfectly right in bringing forward clause 2 of the Bill. But if that theory is repudiated, as I hope it will be repudiated by every true Britisher and by the Government, then it seems to me, my Lord, that on the face of it, it is impossible to throw the onus upon the Punjab Public of proving that the several acts, both by the military and civil authorities, are acts, which can be justified by rules of morality or by rules of humanity. It is therefore I find it difficult to give my vote to this clause, although I agree that the officers are to be protected. It is necessary that my view, which I believe is also the view of a large section of the people, is open to criticism and it must be demolished if it is unfair, because it is the view held by a large section of the Indian population, and it is well that the hollowness of that view should be exposed in all its bareness in order that people may take a right view of the situation. My Lord, how do we look at the situation is this, and it is easier for me to do so because I am not hampered by some considerations which may hamper others. Although I objected to the Rowlatt Act, I never was in favour of an agitation on the lines of the *Satyagraha* movement. I was unpopular on that account, and therefore, I say I am able to speak with greater fulness than many others. But, my Lord, it must be said, that it was not the *Satyagraha* movement which was responsible for these unhappy events, although it was the occasion and although—here I agree with the Hon'ble Mr. Hailey—it created a certain atmosphere which led to these disturbances, it was not the real cause, but it was the unhappy view of the Punjab Government that the prestige of the British race should be upheld against the warlike races of the Punjab by methods which cannot be justified in other provinces. We find that on the 30th of March there was no disorder; on the 6th of April there was no disorder. I assume for argument's sake that Satyapal and Kitchlew were preaching sedition and were trying to bring about excitement. Was there anything to prevent the Government from arresting these men and putting them on their trial? There is nothing to which the Indian public submits so cheerfully and loyally as an open trial. It is this theory of keeping up prestige by deportations, by secret methods, which the public have been resenting, and it was the deportation of these two men, whatever action may have been justifiable against them, which was resented. That is the way in which we look at it. Well on the 10th some precautionary measures were taken. Assuming that the mob was unruly and assuming that it was incumbent on the officers to shoot some members of the mob, that would not afford any justification whatever for the lawless action of the mob after that. That is reprehensible and it ought to be put down with a stern hand. I agree with that also. But it affords an explanation of this tension between the British Government and the people on some subjects which has been produced, especially in the Punjab on account of the difficulties in that Province and other causes. It is that tension which led to this racial difficulty. When the mob thought that they were unjustly dealt with, they did not distinguish between the British citizens and the British Government or between individuals. It affords an explanation, as I have said, but no justification. And then followed the unhappy incidents of the mob on the 10th. Hon'ble members will notice that up to the evening of the 10th there was no unhappy incident in Lahore. Communications were interfered with for a little time, but there was time for the news from Amritsar to reach Lahore before the unhappy incidents in Lahore took place, and therefore—I will not say it is right—there are many people who believe that the unhappy incidents in Lahore were the result, the natural result of the provocation which was given to the British community by the savage doings of the mob in Amritsar on the morning of the 10th. Then a large number of Indian lives were sacrificed; it may have been right, I will not question that now. But, my Lord, I cannot help thinking that, after the explanation which was given by General Hudson, people would be willing to think that the Jallianwala episode was not the result of the unhappy tension and temporary dislocation of certain officers who wanted to show what their attack upon European lives would mean. I think it was by way of reprisals. The public will still unhappily continue to think that it was by way of reprisals, by way of revenge, and not for a possible violation or disobedience of the orders of the authorities in prohibiting a meeting. They think that was taken advantage of to teach the mob a lesson, because it is impossible for us to conceive that when men from all parts of the Punjab, Jats and other cultivators who had nothing to do with politics, were collected in large numbers for the *Bysakhi* fair, no precautions would be taken against shooting down such a large mob simply on account of the reason that it was a lawless mob which violated and disobeyed the injunctions of the Government. Hon'ble members will notice that it was only that morning that the Seditious Meetings Act was proclaimed to be in force. It was on the 13th morning. There was hardly time for the public to know that meetings were prohibited under that Act. But I should assume that a certain section of the people did know of the prohibition and in spite of the prohibition went there, and others gathered there from curiosity or because there happened to be a fair. But no explanation has been forthcoming to the effect that the mob resisted or did any act which justified the shooting down of any person. And what is more important to notice is, assuming, for argument's sake, that a few shots were thought to be necessary to cow down the people and send them away, there was no justification for shooting down 300, 500 or a thousand as is generally believed. That, my Lord, is the crux of the whole situation. There was one reference in General Hudson's speech which gives a partial support to this. The General Commanding felt that the punishment that was awarded on the 10th was not sufficient to teach the people a lesson; they were still continuing to be insulting, and therefore it might be, inasmuch as good order and peace were in his hands, he felt that a few more drastic measures had to be taken and hence this unhappy incident.

"I must meet a point raised by the Hon'ble Mr. Hailey, and that was in regard to the incident at Kasur. The incidents at Kasur on the 12th are partly explainable by the incidents at Amritsar on the 10th and the incidents at Lahore on the 10th. I am not justifying the acts of the mob; I am not in any way palliating what they have done; I am only suggesting that it is an explanation, but an explanation which would show that there was no rebellious tendency in the land, that it was only bitter resentment at the thought that British officers should have shot down Indians, and Indians thought it was unjustly done. I do not say, it was unjustly.

"Then what follows after the 13th ? I think the papers will show that the news reached Gujranwala before the 14th morning when a train was held up there. And it must be remembered that shopkeepers and all classes came to Amritsar for the *Bysakhi* fair from all parts of the Punjab and carried back reports, it may be exaggerated reports, of what had taken place in Jallianwala Bagh all over the Punjab, and there is nothing surprising in people becoming lawless suddenly when they felt that they were most inhumanly dealt with. I do not say it is a right feeling or a wrong feeling, but that is the feeling, and is there anything impossible in the view that with such inflammable material in the Punjab, as we are told, the mob should have behaved in that way? Then in Gujranwala we find, possibly after the spreading of this news, it is impossible to say without an inquiry, because there was time for the news to reach them, after the spreading of this news, we find all the incidents in Gujranwala taking place, the burning of the railway station and the other actions of the mob. Here, my Lord, I must as a Member of Legislative Council decline to sanction the action either of the civil authorities or the military authorities in using bombs and aeroplanes. Even in a state of war—but we are not concerned with that—at any rate in peaceful times, even with a lawless mob like that in Gujranwala, they are not justified. That is a doctrine to which we should not give our legislative sanction. It would be most mischievous and harmful and dangerous.

"And there seems to be absolutely no necessity for the authorities to have asked for this aeroplane to drop bombs not merely there but in adjoining villages and it can only be considered to be revengeful. Various issues of the *Civil and Military Gazette* of that date show that the mob were dispersing. General Hudson says 'How was the officer commanding to know whether the mob was dispersing or not?' Of course, if the civil authorities had given the military authorities the necessary sanction, I would not blame the military authorities. They have to support the civil authorities and their action might be justified. But, I think, the civil authorities do not give any explanation as to why they allowed the use of bombs or whether they sanctioned their use. And whatever may be the merits, as regards the action of the military authorities, the civil authorities cannot be exonerated in respect of this action. And this was done before martial law was proclaimed, so that the action of the officers who shot down people in Amritsar and Lahore and the action at the Jallianwala Bagh on the 13th and the action at Gujranwala before the proclamation of martial law, which was between the 15th and 17th—I speak subject to correction—would not come within the purview of this Act and within the preamble of this Act if you justly follow the procedure which has been followed in other countries by following up martial law with an Indemnity Bill. Therefore, I have to deal with this simply because the Government have asked this Council to give protection to officers who acted before martial law was proclaimed. Ordinarily, they are liable to be brought before the courts, the civil and military authorities would be liable to be brought before the civil Courts, and I do not know whether on previous occasions protection has been given—I am speaking subject to correction—but at any rate the preamble does not justify it. Now the action of the authorities in dropping bombs, if that is true, is a matter which I think cannot and ought not to be brought within the purview of this Act. The answer of the Hon'ble the Home Member may be 'Yes, but why argue this. We say if it is not done *bona fide* and in a reasonable belief to produce a particular result, the officers will be condemned by the Courts; we do not protect them.' But, my Lord, if the whole transaction from start to finish proceeds upon the basis that British officers are justified in humiliating the Indian public and in the employment of any means that may be necessary to bring about the desired result, if we accept that theory, what justification have we in allowing any British officer to be punished ? Therefore, we shall have to make up our minds as to that at the outset. Assuming that that was the belief of British officers, or of Indian officers for the matter of that, or of the Government for the matter of that, assuming that they felt that any humiliating action is justified, any drastic action is justified, in order to bring about the result, then all we can say is that we shall have nothing to do with the Bill. We can never subscribe to that doctrine. I argue simply because I believe that the Government would not subscribe to that doctrine, British officers would not subscribe to that doctrine and no Britisher would subscribe to that doctrine.

"Then, my Lord, we find that there were incidents on the 11th, 12th, 15th, 16th, 17th, and so on. May I say in this connection, my Lord, that I believe that the attempt to humiliate the educated classes has been indirectly responsible for these unhappy events. There is no going away from that point. Sir Michael O'Dwyer has told us, and in distinct terms, on more than one occasion that he did not believe in these mild methods, that he did not believe that the country is in a fit state for the introduction of any reforms on a reasonable scale. He has told us that the educated Indian is really a menace to the British Government....."

The Hon'ble Mr. W.M. Hailey :—"May I rise to a point of order ?"

The Hon'ble Rao Bahadur B. N. Sarma :—"I beg the pardon of the Council for using that. I meant a section of the educated community is really a menace to the British Government."

The Hon'ble Mr. W.M. Hailey :—"My Lord, I merely rose to a point of order. I desired to obtain some verification for the statement which the Hon'ble Mr. Sarma has made. He has now corrected it."

The Hon'ble Rao Bahadur B.N. Sarma :—"I think the speeches of Sir Michael O'Dwyer—I am not accusing him of dishonesty, I only mention his view, his honest view of what is right and proper—show that he thought that a section of the educated Indian public was pursuing a career which was ruinous to the Government as well as to the country, and there was no love lost between the Indian Press and himself. Bearing these facts in mind, and bearing in mind the fact that the Commissioners in their judgments looked upon various acts of these educated men as having brought about these results, there was nothing surprising in the action which was taken by the Punjab Government against various educated men, leaders in various cities, vakils and others, in handcuffing them and subjecting them to trial and punishment. There is nothing surprising in that. They may be justified in doing it, but I am bringing this out to show that that led to a storm of indignation throughout the province. If at a crisis like that the Government chooses to shoot down the mob, the Government chooses to punish all educated Indians, to humiliate them, to make every educated Indian *salaam* a European, to make them crawl on their bellies, I ask, my Lord, has not that very action produced the results which were meant to be remedied ? Therefore, here is an explanation, not a justification, for the action of the mob or for the action of the educated classes. If they went wrong throughout the Punjab there was a very good explanation for the occurrences. But, my Lord, it is not necessary to go at any greater length into what occurred in the Punjab, except by way of supporting my proposition that the whole of India feels that she has been disgraced. That is the feeling, my Lord, and I hope the Government will try to assuage that feeling and show that it is unjustified. Unfortunately, the whole of India feels that the Indian public have been grossly insulted by the authorities in the Punjab. Well, there may be some who are sceptical on the point, but, turning to the statement of trials by summary courts and area officers, in the districts of Lahore, Amritsar, Gujranwala, Gujrat and Lyallpur, I find a number of cases in which men have been whipped for not *salaaming* European officers. Well, take that for granted that it might have been done in a reasonable belief to teach the Indians a lesson. That is not the question at issue. The order should not discriminate between Indian and Indian because we are living in democratic times. But there was nothing to prevent the troops from whipping a High Court Judge for disobeying this order and refusing to *salaam* a European. Is it, therefore, wrong on the part of the Indian public to deeply resent this action of the authorities as being wholly unjustified, and as the Government of India ask us to ratify the convictions based upon such grossly uncivilized methods ? That is the point at issue, my Lord. If the Government say that these convictions would be set at naught, that the men would be released, then it might be quite a different thing. But we are asked by the Government of India to ratify the convictions of these men who have suffered gross indignity for opposing an illegal and inhuman ordinance passed by the military authorities. I therefore submit, my Lord, that as the Bill stands, it is self-condemned. We appeal to the moral convictions; of course we know perfectly well that legalities have not much force and validity in troublous times; but all authorities in England and elsewhere are agreed on this point, that moral considerations must prevail, that the officers who seek protection must appeal to morality and to say that they have behaved as humanly and in as civilized a manner as possible. I submit, my Lord, on behalf of the Indian public that it is impossible for them to ratify and sanction these convictions, if they have a spark of self-respect in them, if they have anything worth considering in them. I have already alluded to the fact, my Lord, that it is impossible, having regard to the events at Jallianwalla Bagh and elsewhere, to raise the presumption in the manner in which it is sought to raise it. I pray that the Government will deal only with cases which took place after the martial law ordinances were issued. Then that would exclude from the purview of our consideration a large number of actions which have to stand on their merits under the common law of the land. If they are to be brought in on the ground that the essence of martial law is a necessity and that those people are entitled to protection, then I humbly pray, my Lord, that the onus of having acted in good faith and in a reasonable manner should be laid upon them. I also ask, my Lord, as to why there is in this clause the phrase 'reasonable belief that those measures are necessary for the purpose of maintaining order, etc.,' in addition to the words *'bona fide'*? Hon'ble Members will see that it would be extremely difficult, if not impossible, for any plaintiff or any prosecutor to show that the officers who were concerned in the discharge of these duties did not believe them to be necessary. That would be an impossible position to take up. The only point would be as to whether they were reasonable in believing them to be necessary. But if it is the sentiment of the British public as voiced loudly by several European papers that they are very sorry that Sir Edward Maclagan should have pursued this clemency policy which is likely to mar all the good work done by his distinguished predecessor, when we see that that is the atmosphere, if I would think that this was the mentality at the time, that this was the atmosphere at the time, then I say, my Lord, it is necessary that we should carefully consider what they might consider to have been a reasonable belief that their actions were justified by necessity. But we, my Lord, as legislators, find absolute difficulty in ratifying any action which is based upon ideas of revenge, reprisals or upon methods which should not be pursued, which are acknowledged should not be pursued. That is my real difficulty. My real difficulty is not that I am unwilling to protect officers, even though the martial law proclamation and orders were wrong—even assuming that I am prepared to protect the officers, but not all officers who have acted in particular ways.

"I have only a few words to add with reference to clause 4, and that is this. Hon'ble members will find that these summary courts were established or have acted in exercise of powers granted to them by Ordinance IV. The Ordinance, my Lord, gives these tribunals power to deal with any offences whether they were connected with these troubles or not, any offences which occurred after the 30th March, in accordance with the law of the land, but I suppose following the procedure of Ordinance No. 1 of 1909 as far as may be....."

The Hon'ble Sir George Lowndes :—"I think the Hon'ble Member has made a verbal slip; that Ordinance has nothing whatever to do with summary courts; it deals only with commissions."

The Hon'ble Rao Bahadur B.N. Sarma :—"Or rather courts which were empowered to deal with cases just as summary courts-martial are empowered to do....."

The Hon'ble Sir George Lowndes :—"The Hon'ble member is, I think, mixing up two different things. Commissions were appointed under the first Ordinance, and under Ordinance No. 4 the

Commissions were entitled to try these persons. In addition there were summary courts appointed by the martial law authorities."

The Hon'ble Rao Bahadur B.N. Sarma :—"I shall be glad to proceed upon the footing that these courts should have followed the ordinary procedure and should have dealt with these cases and have ordered those punishments which are awardable under law. I have made a mistake. It is true that under the first Ordinance the Commission shall have all the powers of a general court-martial under the Indian Army Act, and shall, subject to the provisions of this Ordinance in all matters, follow so far as may be the procedure regulating trials by such courts-martial prescribed under the said Act. Provided that where in the opinion of the convening authority a summary trial is necessary in the interest of the public safety such authority may direct that the Commission shall follow the procedure prescribed for a summary general court-martial by or under the said Act, and the Commission shall, so far as may be and subject to the provisions of this Ordinance, follow such procedure accordingly. Provided further that sections 78, 80 and 82 of the said Act shall not apply to any trial under the Ordinance. Then this is the other Ordinance which I was referring to. 'This Ordinance may be called the Martial Law (Further Extension) Ordinance, 1919.' I shall be glad to hold the other view notwithstanding anything contained in the Martial Law Ordinance I of 1919. The Local Government may by general or special order direct that any commission appointed under the said Ordinance shall try any person charged with any offence committed on or after the 30th March, 1919. There is no limitation there. Thereupon the provisions of the said Ordinance shall apply to such trials accordingly and the Commission may pass in respect of any such offence any sentence authorised by law. I think, therefore, that it was competent to the officers who dealt with cases under this Ordinance to follow the procedure that was prescribed in Ordinance No. 1. Even in respect of trials which did not fall within Ordinance No. 1 but were matters under the Penal Code or which were taken up by the convening authority before these tribunals. However, that is a matter which I shall leave now. Hon'ble members turning to this statement will find that a very large number of convictions in accordance with this Ordinance were passed towards the end of April, the beginning of May, June and July. This was dated the 21st April when according to the Press Communiques order had been restored and everything was quiet, barring a few incidents here and there. I do not say that there was no fear of recurrence of these events, that is unnecessary for my argument; but the Press Communiques that were issued would show clearly..... I will take one.

"I take one. On the 22nd of April the following Press Communique was issued: 'Situation seems to be well in hand..... disturbances except the cutting of telegraph wires'. I am not going to argue that reports of disorders were not coming in, it is unnecessary to argue the point, there may have been disturbances, but all I can say is that the disturbances had been quelled by the 30th. My point is that martial law cannot be invoked and should not have been invoked after the 21st of April for the purpose of administering justice for the further prosecution of measures of Government—we are not concerned with them. My submission is that on the 21st or 22nd of April the ordinary courts should have been allowed to proceed. It may be said that if that were done it would not have been possible to get through the work expeditiously. There was nothing to prevent Government from appointing additional tribunals to deal with the offenders. I take strong exception to the ordinary safeguards which are open to the public being removed by executive action in a time of peace....."

The Hon'ble Mr. J. P. Thompson :—"My Lord, in the absence of Mr. Hailey, may I explain for the Hon'ble Member's information that disturbances were not over by the 20th of April ? There were several cases of cutting of telegraph wires."

The President :—"Order, order. The Hon'ble Members may rise to a point of order or for a personal explanation, and if Mr. Hailey is not here, Sir William Vincent who has yet to speak, can reply to the point."

The Hon'ble Rao Bahadur B. N. Sarma:—"Subject to correction, I should like to say that though these disturbances continued till May or June there was no justification for the continuance of martial law. It was not necessary for a sporadic disturbance. According to all constitutional writers this rebellion, which I am assuming for the sake of argument, would justify martial law coming to an end by the 21st or 22nd of April. Therefore, we need not ratify the action of the Executive Government in introducing a new procedure in removing the normal safeguards to which British Indian subjects of His Majesty are entitled. My submission is that the ordinary tribunals and normal procedure should have been followed. The judgments show that the normal procedure was not followed. There were 236 offences tried and my submission is that we as a legislature would not be justified in ratifying and validating all these convictions and sentences. Sir William Vincent had a very powerful argument in support of his position when he said that the Government of the Punjab felt that if these convictions are not upheld and if the men are let loose there will be no safety. Another argument was that if these men were tried over again this would lead to great public expense. My Lord, there is no escape from that. I do not want any man rightly convicted to escape, but Government could put these men on their trial in the ordinary courts and the public peace will not then be disturbed, people will have confidence that whatever may have been done in a time of panic, if done honestly and *bona fide*, Government rightly recognise any injustice that may have been committed and therefore will follow the normal procedure. Let the men be tried under the usual procedure, with the usual safeguards, a certain amount of money may have to be spent, but it would be usefully spent. There is no difficulty in the way of accepting the suggestion that has been thrown out that two High Court Judges, or ten High Court Judges should go into these sentences. My Lord, unless the Judges see the statements made by witnesses which have been recorded, I cannot see how the Judges are to deal with all the cases. I am sure where the records are full, it will be competent for the Judges to set aside these convictions or advise the Government of India to do so. But where we have only pencil notes or no notes of evidence or where the evidence is meagre, my submission is the Judges will not be able to remedy matters, in some instances at least, inasmuch as we know a record has not been kept. It is impossible for the Government of India to inspire public confidence, and I feel it would be well for the Government not to press for clause 4, asking us to ratify whatever has been done under martial law by these tribunals. My Lord, a word, I think, is necessary from me in addition to what the Hon'ble Mr. Sinha said in reference to what fell from Mr. Malaviya. I have aked for certain information to be given, and for the publication of certain correspondence. The Government felt very rightly that in the public interests this should not be disclosed. I cannot help thinking that in the interests of the public it should be disclosed, so that both the parties may be ready for the tribunal. I think it would be well if both parties should state their case so that the truth may come out; on the other hand, the view of Government may be justified on various points and the other people would not press it, so both parties would come prepared. In the absence of that information, and inasmuch as there is an uneasy feeling in certain sections, it was the duty of the Hon'ble Mr. Malaviya to bring forward the grievances of the people. This duty he has discharged, and we are grateful to him for it. I maintain that in regard to the statements made, no one would have been more happy than many of us if these facts were untrue. But beyond one or two statements of officials, namely, whether a C. I. D. officer had been murdered or European officials suffered some injury, I do not think there was any reply worth mentioning, but beyond one or two statements of an inconsequential nature, namely, as to whether a C. I. D. officer was insulted and as to whether particular European officers did not receive injury, I do not think on essential points there was any reply worth mentioning. That is a question, I suppose, of difference of opinion amongst the Council, but at any rate some of those points were not answered.

"Then, my Lord, ridicule is properly applicable to show up a man who makes pretensions which are absolutely unjustifiable. That is a perfectly legitimate weapon, but what was the occasion for the use of the strong language, that was employed in regard to the Hon'ble Pandit Malaviya ? The Hon'ble Pandit has kindly shown me the correspondence, and we find that, unless the Hon'ble Mr. Thompson made a personal inquiry into the question of a corpse that was found in the well, which has absolutely no political aspect, it is rather difficult to say who is in the wrong. The people think that the administrators of this land lend a ready ear to those who always flatter them, to the police and to other officials. That is the trouble. Now the Hon'ble Mr. Thompson takes up the position of a Municipal Commissioner and tells us that 12 or 13 others went to the well and found nothing and 8 days afterwards they found a corpse. Meanwhile, it would not have been possible for that corpse to have been removed. As a matter of fact even the Commissioners seem to have taken the pains to see what was there. I only allude to this to show, my Lord, that on such scanty materials Hon'ble Members of this Council do not deserve attack and they require protection. Of course the protection is both ways, but, I think, my Lord, the Hon'ble Members were perfectly right.

"My Lord, I have tried my level best to see whether I could support this Bill. I have some difficulties along with the Government in pressing for a complete postponement of this measure. It is true that the officials have to be protected. I agree with Sir Sivaswami

Iyer that it is incumbent upon the Government to bring in a Bill by way of a temporary measure to safeguard the interests of the officers who were employed in the work and protect them pending the result of an inquiry, before Government make up its mind as to how best to deal with these officers. That, no reasonable man can object to. But, my Lord, notwithstanding some safeguards, there is great danger in giving undue protection to these officers, some of whom do not at least deserve any protection, having regard to the events which have transpired. The officers, my Lord, were very anxious that their doings should not be known to the public. They shut out the general public from the Punjab; the Indian press in the Punjab was muzzled. Even Mr. Andrews who wanted to go here was prohibited. Under those circumstances, is it strange in our saying they should wait patiently until the general public has had an opportunity of judging as to what has actually transpired ? The officers did not want to take the public into their confidence, and therefore it is not unreasonable for us to ask that this measure should be postponed until the Committee of Inquiry has submitted its report; but I do not do even that, I ask the Government to give them temporary protection. But I cannot see my way either to ratify all these convictions and sentences or to give complete protection irrespective of the inquiry to every officer even subject to the safeguards mentioned."

The Hon'ble Sir George Lowndes :—"My Lord, this has been a day of telegrams and I should like to add my quota. I have received, as I am sure I ought to inform the Council, a telegram from the Wardha Home Rule League protesting against the introduction of this Bill. I have no doubt that this protest will meet with the consideration it deserves in this Council. The Hon'ble Pandit also referred to, and read out a telegram from, the Indian Association of Lahore. Members of this Government have also received the same telegram, but in their case it has not been signed, and it would be interesting if the Hon'ble Pandit could let us know by whom his copy is signed. The Secretary of that Association, I understand, is now confined in one of His Majesty's jails, and, I think, we ought to know who has signed it on his behalf. (*After a pause*). I do not think I need wait till the Hon'ble Pandit....."

The Hon'ble Pandit Madan Mohan Malaviya :—"Perhaps I have given it to the reporters. So far as I can remember, it was not signed, but I am sure it was signed. I can say, my Lord, that the Indian Association is an Association of long standing in Lahore. (*After* *a pause*). I have just got the original telegram. I had it in my pocket, I thought I had given it to the reporters and it had not come. The telegram is not signed."

The Hon'ble Sir George Lowndes :—"My Lord, I begin my remarks by saying that I regret very deeply the events which have happened in the Punjab and in other parts of India. No one deplores more than I do the loss of life, both Indian and European, which has occurred, and I would add no one deplores more than I do that it is in most cases the dupes who have suffered and the agitators behind them who have escaped. But my object in rising at this late hour in Council is not so much to express my regret, though I am glad to have the opportunity of doing so, but to deal as shortly as I can with the constitutional position of martial law in our polity in India.

"And I doubt if, with all that has been said, the real position has been explained to the Council. The Hon'ble Pandit, I think it was, on a previous occasion contented himself with saying, as has been repeated today, that martial law is the negation of law. But an epigram like that never can contain more than a germ of the truth, and it was hardly sufficient for the Hon'ble Pandit and other lawyers who have followed him to dismiss the whole subject of martial law as summed up in that short epigram. There is a great deal more behind it, which it is essential that we should consider in connection with this Bill. No doubt it is true in one sense that martial law is the negation of law, but in every civilized country in the world it steps into the place of the civil law when occasion requires. It is not only in our own Empire and in our own history that martial law has a definite place. It will be found in the constitution of pretty well every continental country of Europe. It is especially provided for in the French constitution and is there known as a 'state of siege,'—I am translating of course. It can be declared, in France, by the President on the advice of his Ministers if the Chamber is not sitting. In our own constitution it has been known from the very earliest days. But before I come to the historical side, which I shall deal with—as shortly as I can—I think I should explain the basis of it. The law of which it is said to be the negation is the thing that provides for normal conditions, but for normal conditions only. Abnormal conditions are left to be met by extraordinary measures. The Code of Criminal Procedure in this country provides for police measures to deal with riots. If they get beyond the police, the police can call in the military to their aid, but it is still the civil arm which is dealing with what has occurred, and the military are called in to their aid only. If matters go beyond this, charge must be taken completely by the military. The law does not attempt to provide further than that. Abnormal conditions have now arisen, and the enforcement of law and order is, and has to be, handed over to those who can do it by force of arms. The line, I think Hon'ble Members will agree, between riot and insurrection and revolution is a very thin one in every case. What is a riot this morning may be an insurrection this afternoon, and a revolution tomorrow. If you are unable to put it down at the outset, you may find that a fire has been lighted which all the fire-engines of the country cannot extinguish. It is that thin line which is the difficulty in all such cases. There is the line first of all between disturbances which the police can quell by themselves, and others for which they must call in the aid of the military, and there is the line between what the police aided by the military can deal with, and the situation that must be handed over entirely to the military arm. Once that last line is overstepped, it is no longer a mere riot, conditions are no longer normal; it is a case for what we have called martial law, that the name is a convenient one and no more, I quite agree. It arises only when the civil arm is no longer able to maintain order. That is why it is a negation of the civil law; it is a negation of the law because the law has failed, and for no other reason. Whatever we may like to call it, a rebellion or an insurrection,—whatever politicians in this country may like to call it— we have to deal with the facts, not with the words we use to describe them. The question we have to consider here is, whether at the time when martial law was put in force in India the situation was such that the civil authorities were unable to cope with it. Therefore, let us not quarrel over words or discuss the difference between rebellion, insurrection and revolution. The practical question before the Council is, whether there had arisen in the Punjab at this time a state of things with which the civil authorities were unable to deal. We have been told in this Council that no such state of things existed. I would much rather have left the question where my Hon'ble friend, Sir William Vincent, left it in his opening speech, not discussing whether it was necessary to proclaim martial law, but leaving that to be considered by the Commission. I would rather merely assume that martial law was declared, for, as my Hon'ble colleague put it, it follows essentially from that that there must be an act of indemnification and validation. Some Hon'ble Members, led by that redoubtable champion of the liberties of the people, who is still sitting here after his temporary disappearance, thought fit to go into all the happenings, for what purpose, I frankly say, I cannot conceive. What this Bill proposes is that only acts which were done *bona fide* and which were believed to be reasonably necessary for the restoration or maintenance of order are to be the subject of indemnification, or validated in part, nothing else. The Hon'ble Pandit spent some hours telling us of a number of acts that would not be covered by the Act. He went through the whole history of what had happened in his own way recounting to us a great number of things which he told us could not have been *bona fide* which could not have been necessary, and therefore, if I may say so, would not have been touched by this Act. What was his object, I repeat, I cannot conceive, unless possibly the time has come when it may be necessary for the Hon'ble Member again to seek re-election, and we may consider this as an election speech in which, *pace* Mr. Sinha, terminological inexactitudes are often thought to be excusable. But it was not only the Hon'ble Pandit, but other Hon'ble Members have taken up definitely the position that there was never any situation (I am not attempting to put it in their own words) with which the civil law could not have coped. We began the other day with my Hon'ble friend Raja Sir Rampal Singh, whose absence I greatly regret today, for I dislike criticising anyone in his absence, but he has, I may presume, thought it wise to beat a strategic retreat. The Hon'ble Raja Sir Rampal Singh, coming from the fastnesses of his ancestral castle in Oudh, said there was no rebellion, no insurrection—only a few little disturbances ! Of course, sitting at home in safety, it was quite easy for him to say to himself there is no fire going on; there is no trouble! If you are a long way away and your house is not in danger of the conflagration, it is easy to take up this attitude. I strongly suspect that my Hon'ble friend from Oudh did not want to see the fire and I suggest that the most charitable way of looking at his speech is that it was written for him by a friend.

"Then we have my Hon'ble friend Mr. Ayyangar who indeed is present, but whom I fear I shall not be able to make cognisant of my words at the moment. From the religious solitude of far Madras, he tells us again, that there was no rebellion, nothing serious was going on at all. I think the expression he used, so far as my memory serves me, was only 'a few rash acts' were committed in the Punjab.

"Then we come to my Hon'ble friend Mr. Chanda. He put it in the forefront of his argument that there was no rebellion there, nothing that the civil arm could not deal with. And where does the Hon'ble Mr. Chanda come from ? Assam ! He too has come from the confines of India to say there were no serious disturbances in the Punjab. Can nobody tell us any better than this? Are there no members here who belong to the Punjab, who have been in the middle of these disturbances, who know what happened, who have seen what happened ? There are surely many of them in this Council, but has anyone of them told us that there was no rebellion in the Punjab, that there was nothing that could not be put down by the civil arm ? Is it not an extraordinary fact that to find support for the opposite view you have to go to a member from Assam, a member from Madras—I am glad I do not have to speak in the plural of Madras—a member from the fastnesses of Oudh and, if I may say so, the self-constituted Special Commissioners from the United Provinces. Now, if other members of the services who sit here had not replied in detail to what I do not hesitate to call the monstrous statements of the Hon'ble Pandit, I should have taken some pains to reply to them in detail; but it is not necessary for me to do so now. Let me come now to the speeches of my Hon'ble friend Mr. Sarma and of my Hon'ble friend Mr. Sinha, who seems to think that we come here to talk about martial law and the doings in the Punjab with kid gloves on our tongues. I do not. Let us all say what we think. I shall not blame any Hon'ble Member who says what he really thinks, and surely in this Council I am entitled to say what I really think. But I will only say that the speech of my Hon'ble friend the Pandit was characterised by certain terminological inexactitudes, a phrase which has, I believe, parliamentary sanction. I have said that no member from the Punjab has come here to tell us that there was not a rebellion in the Punjab; I only use that word for convenience. But is there no one else to whom I can appeal who, at all events, does not bear the ticket of Government upon his back ? I seem to remember one Horniman as somewhat of an ally of the party which the Hon'ble Pandit, I believe, now leads. I have some recollection of a letter of his published in the newspapers. It did not seem to accord with the view which is taken by his lieutenant now. I have got the words here—the expression used by Mr. Horniman of *Bombay Chronicle* fame, if I mistake not, was 'the recent deplorable revolutionary outbreaks.' Then there was another stout ally, a former ally at all events of that same party, Mrs. Annie Besant, I am sure many Hon'ble Members in this Council will remember the words of wisdom that fell from her with regard to the situation in the Punjab. Let me remind them. I quote from her letter in the *Times of India* of the 19th of April 1919 :—

> 'I ventured to urge before this movement was started that its logical result was riot and bloodshed, and to point to the danger of a revolutionary movement here. Surely what had happened in Europe was warning enough and I even noted the elements here on which Bolshevist propaganda might work. Are there not in the Punjab signs of such a movement? The cutting of telegraph wires, the derailing of troop-trains, the burning of railway stations, the attacks on banks, the setting free of jail-birds, are not the actions of *Satyagrahis* nor even of casual rioters, but of revolutionaries.'

I understand that Mrs. Annie Besant has now been disowned as an ally of the party over which my Hon'ble friend the Pandit, now presides with such skill, but those were words coming from the very party of which the Hon'ble Pandit is now the lieutenant, and I doubt if there is any Member of this Council who, if the proposition is put in the way I have put it, namely, whether there was a situation with which the civil arm was unable to cope, could do otherwise than admit the fact.

"Let us get so far in the argument. Now the next question that arises—I am dealing largely with theory now—is, is it or is it not the duty of every stable Government to maintain law and order in the country? I might go a little further, and say, is it not the first duty of every stable Government to do this? There again I think that even the Hon'ble Pandit will not venture to answer me in the negative. If it is so, if it is the first duty of Government to maintain the public peace, if that is accepted, does it not follow essentially from that that the Government must have the power to do so? If it is necessary to go beyond what I call the civil arm and invoke the direct intervention of the military, the situation is that which we describe as martial law. If it is the duty of Government to do that, do not Hon'ble members think that it must follow that Government has the right to do it, and that there must be some sanction behind it? Writers on Constitutional Law have always struggled to find the sanction for martial law. There are three schools of thought which have existed in the past. The first school of thought, which has very much behind it historically, asserts that it is in the inherent power of the Crown to proclaim martial law. Let me not be misunderstood. I mean that if it is in the power of the Crown to put martial law in force, then the municipal courts are unable to take cognizance of cases arising out of it, because what has been done has been by the prerogative of the Crown. I say there is a great deal historically in favour of that view. I do not wish to trouble the Council at length with this, but I think it might interest Members to hear what such a great man as Pitt said in introducing the second Irish Indemnity Bill. He said:—'The Bill which I have to propose is not one to *enable* the Government of Ireland'—mark the word 'enable,' I am not merely emphasising it, it is in italics in the report—'to *enable* the Government in Ireland to declare martial law in districts where insurrection exists, for that is *a power* which His Majesty *already possesses*'. That is probably the *locus classicus* of the doctrine that it is a right and a power which the Crown inherently possesses, but it goes possibly a little further than that, because it has been recited that the Crown has that power in at least two Statutes which have been passed by Parliament, and therefore Parliament has at all events tacitly acquiesced in that doctrine. However many constitutional lawyers doubted whether the right of the Crown to enforce martial law could exist after the Constable's Court by which it was ordinarily enforced and by which trials were held had been abolished—and that was in the late Tudor times—and therefore they struggled to find a substitute for the prerogative of the Crown in the sanction of the Common Law itself which the opposite school always denied.

"Here again, I do not wish to labour the point. The argument was that the power, as we lawyers say, flowed from the duty, the duty connoted the power following the legal maxim '*necessitas, quod cogit, defendit*,' and there is a considerable school of thought who still maintain that position. But in more recent times another school of thought has taken what is possible a half way course and argues that though there may be a prerogative right in the Crown, though there may be a power under the common law to enforce martial law, the safer view at all events to take is that martial law should be followed by validation and indemnity. I think Hon'ble Members will see that this is common sense in many ways. After the disturbances have been put down, we do not want the battles fought all over again in the Courts; what we want is peace and quiet. For this reason the policy has always been to validate afterwards in order to prevent these discussions in the Courts when the crisis is over. That view certainly holds the field in modern times, namely, that though martial law may not be necessarily the negation of law, though it may have a foundation in the law, yet it undoubtedly takes the place of the ordinary civil law in abnormal circumstances, and therefore it is always desirable, always even necessary, for the reasons I have given, that a Validation or Indemnity Act should follow it. Hon'ble Members have referred, particularly Mr. Sarma, to the Regulation of 1804, under which martial law at all events in some districts was put in force. That Regulation, as no doubt Hon'ble Members will remember, gives to the Government powers to establish martial law and for trials to be held by courts-martial. Now, power to establish martial law is in itself statutory sanction for martial law; remember that 'martial law' means,—I need not cite again the quotation from Steven's History of Criminal Law, to which the Hon'ble Pandit has referred. Martial law means the military taking the place of the civil arm in order to enforce law and order. This power to establish martial law is derived from the Legislature in the case of the Regulation of 1804, and we have to read into the words 'martial law' the various things which it connotes, that is to say, if we have statutory power to establish martial law, that makes legal *ipso facto* every act which can be justified by martial law. We in India therefore are in the position of having statutory power to proclaim martial law though it none the less leads us to resort to indemnity. But martial law has not been enforced under the Statute in all districts. It has been enforced under the inherent power in other places. I need only refer to the case of Bombay which is probably not covered by the Bengal Regulation. But notwithstanding that we have statutory power to put martial law into force in some parts of India, it is none the less necessary, for the reasons I have already given, to have an Indemnifying and Validation Bill. This, if I may say so, is agreed to by every sensible Member of this Council. The only argument I have heard against it is that of the Members who said that there were no serious disturbances in the Punjab, and of those who said. 'By all means let us have an Indemnity Bill but not today.' Well, that it is necessary to have some Indemnity Act is beyond question. I will tell the Council in a moment what a length of precedent there is for it. But apart from its being strictly constitutional, I should like to put the question very plainly indeed to some of my Hon'ble friends in this Council, and I would appeal especially to my Hon'ble friend the Maharaja of Kassimbazar, whose speech indicated a somewhat hesitating acceptance of the proposals now before this Council. Do you or do you not want to be protected in your lives and property, whatever may happen in India? Do you wish the Government to do what I have spoken of as the first duty of the Government, namely, to protect your life and property? And that if they cannot do it through the Police, do you wish them to do it by the use of the Military? Let us have a plain answer to that question from anyone who is not prepared to agree to a Validating Bill. If you do not want it, tell the Government you do not want and the Government will not do it. Let me tell you this that if this Council will not indemnify the soldiers who had to enforce martial law in order to preserve the public peace, they will not willingly do it again. You cannot place these unpleasant duties on your officers and at the same time leave them, as Mr. Chanda suggests, at the mercy of the Courts. That is not the way to treat officers whom you have asked to protect your lives and property. You have got to indemnify them at the earliest possible opportunity, and unless, I say, you do that, they cannot be asked to take any risks in protecting you. Why should they ? Why should a man, in order to protect your life and property or to protect my life and property or anyone else's, do that which he knows may subject him to the direct penalties of the law? Remember when we talk of indemnifying officers, it is not the high officers of Government that you are asked to indemnify. It was the Gurkha soldiers who fired on the mob and, may be, killed people; it is the Indian soldiers and Indian officers whom you are asked to indemnify just as much as the British officers. Every soldier who fires according to orders and, may be, kills a person may be liable under the common law of the country to be indicted for murder. If my property is in danger, or my life is in danger from a mob, whether it be in Amritsar, Delhi or Lahore, can I ask the soldiers to fire upon the mob to protect me if I am not prepared to back them up afterwards by an Indemnity Act at the earliest possible opportunity? Surely not. Let Hon'ble Members come out into the open, let them say that they do not want to be protected, let them do what the Hon'ble Pandit suggested, constitute among themselves a body of watch and ward, let us get rid of the police....."

The Hon'ble Pandit Madan Mohan Malaviya :—"We do not want our lives to be protected at the expense of others."

The President :—"Order, order. The Hon'ble Member has had his say."

The Hon'ble Sir George Lowndes :—"I thank the Hon'ble Pandit. It reminds me of a statement once made by one of the most eminent Judges in India to counsel who protested against being interrupted. He said, do not worry, Mr. So-and-so; an interruption always shows me where the shoe pinches. . . . ."

(The Hon'ble Mr. Malaviya here rose to-interject a remark).

The President :—"The Hon'ble Member has for a long time been a Member of this Council and knows perfectly well what order means. I must ask him to observe order."

The Hon'ble Sir George Lowndes :—"It may interest the Council to hear that I had the curiosity to have looked up in our reports the number of interruptions recorded in this Council during the whole of last year. The total was 51. Of these, the Hon'ble Pandit was responsible for 29. It appears to me that he has had rather more than his due share.

"Now, I say if you want officers of Government and soldiers under their orders to protect the lives and property of people, you must be prepared to indemnify them. I say it is necessary, and in accordance with common sense, and that it is in accordance with the practice of hundreds of years in this great Empire to which we have the honour to belong. The limits are perfectly well understood. The limits within which indemnity will be given are the limits of good faith and doing that which is reasonably necessary.

"They are clearly laid down in every book on Constitutional Law. We are not asking Hon'ble Members in this Council to go beyond that. I shall show in a moment that we are not asking them to go nearly so far as has been done in some cases. If Hon'ble Members will look back to constitutional history, they will note that in the earliest days the turbulent Barons were controlled by martial law.

"In Wat Tyler's rebellion in the time of Richard II martial law was put in force, and though it was directly contrary to the terms of the Magna Charta, men who had taken part in that rebellion were tried by court-martial or even put to death without any legal form of trial at all. Coming on to later times we find martial law again put in force in Jack Cade's insurrection in Henry VI's reign. I do not want to go back for a precedent to ancient days. I only want to make it quite clear to the Council that the enforcement of martial law has been a part of the British constitution from the very beginnings from Norman times through Tudor times, down to the days of the Hanoverian House and on to the present day.

"When we come to the Georges, the questions involved are

probably more important, as we get the Acts which have already been referred to. I do not propose to refer to them in any detail except to correct certain inexactitudes which have crept into the Hon'ble Pandit's arguments with regard to them. We have first of all the 1715 Act to which my friend the Hon'ble Pandit referred. I regret to have to refer to it again, but with almost characteristic inexactitude the Hon'ble Pandit only read from the preamble of the Act and forgot to read the operative part of the Act. He told us that the Act did not do what as a matter of fact it does. One cannot always, I am afraid, collate from the preamble to an Act what is enacted by it. But let me read on after the long preamble—the enacting part is there. The only part which the Hon'ble Pandit did not read, as far as I remember, was this: 'All personal action, *etc.*, for anything done in order to suppress the Rebellion in 1716, shall be discharged. And if commenced again, the person sued may plead the General Issue, *etc.*, Double Costs.' But the preamble was the only part in which the Hon'ble Pandit was interested, because he preferred to. . . . . ."

The Hon'ble Pandit Madan Mohan Malaviya :—"May I rise to a point or order ?"

The President :—"On a point of order."

The Hon'ble Pandit Madan Mohan Malaviya :—"I want to explain that I was arguing on the preamble and it was not necessary for me to read the whole of the Act."

The Hon'ble Sir George Lowndes :—"Neither necessary, my Lord, nor advisable for my Hon'ble friend's arguments.

"I do not think I need say anything more about this. Hon'ble Members have heard the Act read, apart from the operative part, by my Hon'ble friend the Pandit.

"Next we come to the 1745 Act, and there again the Hon'ble Pandit's researches did not go far enough. The Hon'ble Pandit referred to 19, George III, Chapter XX, which was an Indemnity Act, and which was passed after the disturbances, but he apparently did not find out that before the rebellion began Parliament passed another Statute authorising martial law being put in force. Therefore, they began before the Pretender's invasion by authorising the putting in force of martial law, *i.e.*, you have got curiously enough, almost the same position which we have in India now, that is to say, they were allowed by Statute to establish martial law, as we are here, yet after it was all over they proceeded to indemnify by the Statute to which the Hon'ble Pandit referred. The Indemnity Act of 1745 is practically in the same terms as the one of 1715. The Hon'ble Pandit put forward a tentative argument with regard to these Acts that they can be no model for us because they were dealing with invasions from outside, 'rebellions' in what may be called the technical sense. He suggested that that was quite a different case. There, he said, 8,000 Scotsmen flocked to the Pretender's flag and there was a regular war. But I am afraid that argument is destroyed entirely by the next Act of 1780 which dealt with the Gordon riots—as the Gordon riots were nothing in the world if not a purely internal disturbance. My Hon'ble friend, Mr. Hailey, reminded you of their history—more Members of this Council will no doubt remember the story in 'Barnaby Rudge,' it was hardly more than a riot, but a riot in the morning which might have been a rebellion in the afternoon, and it had to be dealt with by martial law. In that case there was, I believe, no statutory power given to proclaim martial law; but, afterwards, Parliament granted an indemnity in respect of all the acts that were done. I may perhaps read from the Act of 1780 again. It is very interesting, because it shows how far Parliament went. After the part the Hon'ble Pandit cited, namely :—'Divers Acts which cannot be justified by the strict Forms of Law, and yet were necessary'—that is the part the Hon'ble Pandit read—it goes on 'That All Personal Actions and Suits, Indictments and Informations, which have been or shall be, commenced or prosecuted, and all Molestations, Prosecutions, Proceedings whatsoever, and Judgments thereupon (if any be), against the said Megistrates, or other Persons for, or by reason of any Act, Matter or Thing commanded or done on the Occasions, and for the Purposes aforesaid, or any of them before the twentieth day of June, one thousand seven hundred and eighty, shall be discharged and made void; and every Person, by whom any such Act, Matter or Thing, which shall have been commanded or done, before the said twenty-fourth Day of June, one thousand seven hundred and eighty shall be freed, acquitted and indemnified, as well against the King's Majesty. . . . . .'

"It will be seen that the Hon'ble Pandit was again somewhat inaccurate in saying that it had only a very limited application. It may seem so if you read only the preamble, but if you read the operative part of the Act, it indemnifies and makes good every act done by every person for the suppression of that rebellion.

"Well, let me continue the history as shortly as I can. We come next to the Irish trouble in 1798, which resulted in what is often called the Battle of Vinegar Hill.

"There, again, they not only had the Indemnity Act, 41 George III, C. 104, but Parliament gave before-hand power under Act 39, Geo. III, C. 11, to enforce martial law. So, again, the position was almost exactly what we have here. First of all, the power given by the Legislature to put martial law in force, and secondly, the indemnity for anything done under it. It is in connection with the 1798 rebellion in Ireland that the case of Wright and Fitzgerald arose. I think the Hon'ble Pandit referred to it, or, at all events, to the summing up of Mr. Justice Chamberlayne. It is a typical and illustrative case and, I think, the Council may like to know just a little bit more about it. Fitzgerald was a High Sheriff and Wright, as the Hon'ble Pandit told us, was a school master. Fitzgerald ordered Wright, at any rate according to the allegation, to be flogged with 500 stripes (they did not do things by half measures in those days), and he was flogged, and, according to the evidence, flogged in Fitzgerald's presence, under the most harrowing circumstances, circumstances, I may say, almost as harrowing as those which the Hon'ble Pandit, with such oratorical effect, described to us yesterday. The Judge summed up, as the Hon'ble Pandit has told the Council, there was a sympathetic Irish jury, and he was awarded £500 damages. The Hon'ble Pandit did not care to read any further than that. If he had looked on a little further, he would have seen that the case went on to the Court of Exchequer and was quashed and Fitzgerald, the High Sheriff, got his full costs. Therefore, the end was not quite where the Hon'ble Pandit left it. So much for Vinegar Hill and Wright and Fitzgerald.

"Now, let us pass on to 1803. Emmett's Insurrection it is usually called. That was a case which was curiously like the present one. A mob went about in Dublin killing everybody they met who did not belong to their persuasion. In a fit of what, I suppose, my Hon'ble friend Mr. Ayyangar would call rashness, or it may have been pleasantry, they killed the Lord Chief Justice. There was no time for Parliament to authorise the proclamation of martial law, but the Government put it in force and they passed the usual Indemnity Act, 43, George III, C. 117. I do not wish to speak about martial law in Ireland at this day, though it is a matter which touches us very nearly. Many Members of this Council may no doubt know that Ireland is at present under martial law, but they have not got to the indemnity stage yet. Let us now go to South Africa. I am only endeavouring to show the Council how entirely constitutional the putting in force of martial law is when the civil arm cannot cope with disturbances, and that in every case it is almost necessarily followed by an Indemnity Act at the earliest possible moment. In South Africa, the story begins with 1835; again in 1846, and again in 1850, martial law had to be put into effect; and in every case there was an Act of Indemnity passed by the local Legislature. The case, therefore, is in this respect nearer to our own. Then in 1900 and again in 1902 and again in 1914 in South Africa, we find martial law in force and Indemnity Acts passed which the Hon'ble Pandit has or would have referred to, if he had had the books. In 1900, there was Act VI of 1900 which was a full Indemnity Act, much fuller than this one. I think perhaps I may go into the terms of it very shortly. Hon'ble Members will find in that Act that very objectionable clause which, I think my Hon'ble friend Mr. Sarma, and, if I remember aright, Mr. Sinha, have referred to: 'every such act, matter or thing referred to in the preceding sections shall be presumed to have been advised, commanded, ordered, directed or done, as the case may be, in good faith, until the contrary shall be proved by the party complaining.' The terms are little wider than in our Bill. By that Act they indemnified people in respect of 'any acts, matters and things whatsoever in good faith advised, commanded, ordered, directed or done as necessary.' I draw attention to those words because, in drafting the Bill which is before the Council, we have had all these models before us, and what we have in the Bill about 'in the reasonable belief that it was necessary,' is merely a translation from the expression I have quoted which you find all through these recent South Africa Acts—I mean '*done as necessary*.' I think any lawyer will agree with me that 'done as necessary' means done in the belief that it was necessary. But in order that there should be no doubt about it, we have thought it was better to translate it into plainer language.

"When we come to the second of the more modern South Africa Acts, we find exactly the same words; it is to be an indemnity 'for or on account of or in respect of any acts, matters and things whatsoever in good faith advised, commanded, ordered, directed or done as necessary for the suppression of hostility and the establishment and maintenance of order.' Then, again there is exactly the same clause with regard to the presumption; 'every such act, matter or thing referred to in the preceding section shall be presumed to have been advised, commanded, ordered, directed or done, as the case may be, in good faith until the contrary is proved.'

"Let me for one moment discuss, if I can do so, the argument that has been raised on this. It has been suggested that we are doing something outrageous in providing in this Act that the onus of proving ill-faith is to be on the man who alleges. But is this not the essence of our criminal law? I may be wrong in thinking so, but this is why I ventured to interrupt my Hon'ble friend Mr. Sinha, who put forward, as I thought, the suggestion that it was not for the prosecution in criminal cases to prove intent or ill-faith. But, is it not the basis of the law which we have inherited from the British constitution, that you presume every man to be innocent until the contrary is proved? And does this go any further than that? At all events, it has been adopted in every modern Validation Act, and we have frankly followed on the same lines. I was asked by the Hon'ble Pandit whether I had taken the Act of 1906 for my model. I told him that the actual model was the most recent Act of all, the 1915 Act. I think probably the Council will agree with me that, so far as I am responsible for the drafting of any Bill, I follow the most recent model; and that is what I have done, though, as I said before, we have, I believe, examined every Indemnity Act we could get before we started to draft this Bill.

"Now as to Act XI of 1915, of which I am glad I was able to give my copy to the Hon'ble Pandit though I am afraid rather late. It provides that 'every act, matter or thing referred to in sub-section (1)'—the general words are in the previous section—'shall be presumed to have been advised, commanded, ordered, directed or done (as the case may be) in good faith until the contrary is alleged and proved by the party complaining.' We have that again. Then we have the specific provision with regard to sentences, which again I may read and, I think, Hon'ble Members will see that our Bill does not go nearly as far as this really.

> 'The several courts-martial and military and special tribunals constituted and convened by or on the authority of the Government or its officers during the period aforesaid for the trial and punishment of persons guilty of treasonable, seditious or rebellious conduct, or of persons subject to military law shall be deemed to have been constituted in accordance with law, and the several sentences pronounced by all such courts and tribunals, as well as by Magistrates' courts or

other inferior courts, for any contravention of, or failure to comply with, any law or statutory regulations known as martial law regulations, or any orders or instructions, given on the authority thereof, are hereby confirmed.'

Hon'ble Members will notice that we have not gone as far as that in our Bill. Sub-section (2) says :—

(2) 'Every person confined in any prison, gaol, lock-up, or in any other place whatever under and by virtue of any such sentence aforesaid shall continue liable to be confined therein or elsewhere as the Minister of Justice may direct, until the expiration of such sentence, or until released by the Governor-General in the exercise by him of the Royal mercy, or until otherwise discharged by lawful authority.'

(3) 'Every such sentence shall be deemed to be a sentence passed by a duly and legally constituted court of the Union, and shall be carried out or otherwise dealt with in the same manner as the sentences of such a court.'

Those are the material sections of the latest South African Act, and there is a great deal more in it that my Hon'ble friends will see follows largely the previous models of 1900 and 1902.

"Then if I may pass away from South Africa and follow up the other cases in which martial law has been proclaimed and followed by indemnity, we have the very well-known case of Jamaica in 1865. A long pamphlet dealing with all that happened has been published at the *Tribune* Office, an office, I think, not unknown to my Hon'ble friend the Pandit; and it was to me rather remarkable that he did not refer to the contents of that pamphlet in any way at all. Perhaps we should be glad he did not or he might have been addressing the Council till now. But there was much in that pamphlet which, I am sure, gave him food for reflection. It deals with the well-known case of Governor Eyre. He arrested a man called Gordon, who was believed to be the centre of the insurrection in Jamaica, outside the martial law area altogether, and executed him. An Indemnity Act was passed by the local Legislature, and then Gordon's widow came to England and prosecuted Eyre under an Act which allows Colonial Governors to be prosecuted in England, for the death of her husband, claiming damages. The case was a *cause celebre* at the time, and allegations much like those that have been made by the Hon'ble Pandit were made with regard to the doings in Jamaica. The case came before the Grand Jury. The Grand Jury were charged by one of the greatest of Judges, and they did as they were entitled to do, as men of common sense would do presumably in such a case, they threw the indictment out and there was an end of it; they would not allow it even to be tried. There was another case to which the Hon'ble Mr. Sinha, if I remember aright, referred in connection with the Jamaica riots. That was the case of Eyre and Phillips. But the sole question there was, whether Eyre the Governor was within the Indemnity or not; there was no other question concerned. My Hon'ble friend Mr. Sinha has referred to the report of the case in the Queen's Bench. I should have liked to refer to the report in the Court of Exchequer, but when I asked for the book, I found that the Hon'ble Pandit had unfortunately taken it away to the farthest end of Simla. It has now been given to me, but too late for me to quote. All I need point out is, that the only question before the Court was whether this case was covered by the Indemnity Act or not, whether an Indemnity Act passed by a local Council could indemnify its own Governor because he was a party to it. I am speaking from recollection, but, I think, the Hon'ble Mr. Sinha will agree that that was substantially the sole question decided in that case.

"Then let us come nearer home, to Ceylon. In Ceylon, they had martial law in 1848, and they had a local Indemnity Act there, but I am afraid I have not got it. The same thing happened in St. Vincent in 1862; martial law proclaimed and followed by an Indemnity Act. And as the Council have been told, in India, after the Mutiny, we had an Indemnity Act, Act XXXIV of 1860. It is rather material perhaps to refer to that Act because Hon'ble Members will at all events see that, in bringing this Bill before the Council, we have not gone as far as we might have. The Act of Indemnity of 1860 was in very wide terms. I need only read section 2, which is the martial one.

> 'All acts done since the tenth day of May, 1857, in connection with the late disturbances by officers of Government or by persons acting under their authority or otherwise, in pursuance of an order of Government, or which shall have been or shall be ratified by the Executive Government, are hereby confirmed'†

That meant that the Executive Government was made the sole arbiter as to whether a man was to be indemnified for a particular

† For full text of the Act, Appendix V, Pages 525—526, *ante*.

act or not. Surely we have got a good deal more liberal a measure here, in that we leave it to the Courts to decide whether any act complained of was done *bona fide* and in the reasonable belief that it was necessary for the suppression of disorder.

"With regard to the question of reasonable belief, which has been somewhat attacked, it may be useful to read to the Council what one of the greatest Lord Chancellors said in the House of Lords in a debate on the Gordon Riots in 1780. It appears to me very material on this point. Lord Thurlow was the Lord Chancellor at the time, and he came down from the Woolsak to address the House. Of course I am not going to read the whole speech, but only a very short passage. Hon'ble Members will remember that the Gordon Riots were purely civil disturbances. There was no case of an invasion from outside. The Gordon Riots were very similar to the present case. They were an attempt to overawe the Government and induce them to repeal the Catholic Disabilities Act which had recently been passed. The cry was 'No Popery' 'Repeal, repeal.' This was very much like the object of these disturbances in the Punjab which was to get this very timorous Government to repeal the Rowlatt Act. Lord Thurlow said:

> 'Under these circumstances it was, and after it had been in vain endeavoured to quell the riots by the intervention and authority of the civil power, that the Military were employed; and therefore, the case being so far similar to the Rebellion in 1715 and 1745, that there was an actual insurrection, that the laws of the land were trampled under foot, and the King's Government opposed. The military as well as everyone in a brown coat were justified in the commission of such trespasses and acts of homicide for the purpose of restoring the public peace as were justifiable in the year 1715, and in the year 1745.'

This disposes entirely of what I may call the argument of the Hon'ble Pandit that martial law is only applicable where there is a case of invasion. In the Gordon Riots the military and private persons were entitled to do everything that they were entitled to do in 1715, and in 1745, when martial law, as Hon'ble Members will remember, had actually been declared by Act of Parliament, though here it had not. I will continue my quotation 'to do everything that was justifiable in the years 1715 and 1745 for the purpose of putting an end to the rebellion then on foot in the Kingdom. Not that he meant to say that either soldiers individually or collectively any more than private persons might not in their endeavours to quell the outrages, etc., lately committed have been guilty of some things which, under a cool legal investigation would appear to be contrary to law and punishable either by the Common or Statute Law of the Realm, for, undoubtedly, in opposing, repressing, and quelling such daring outrages as had been perpetrated, the military, as well as individuals, must necessarily have been forced into excesses; but when the occasion was duly considered, and the extreme hurry and violent confusion in which all men who joined in restoring the public peace were obliged to act, those excesses would be seen to have been unavoidable, and to be the proper objects of an Act of Indemnity, but not an Act more necessary for the military than for other persons who had done as the military had done, and been instrumental in effecting that good purpose which the military had effected.'

"My Lord, I think three points emerge very clearly from this speech of Lord Thurlow. The first is, that the power of enforcing martial law where disturbances have gone beyond the civil arm is very akin to the result of self defence; it is so not in the case of soldiers only but of everybody else. Secondly, it shows that we should look at the acts done in the light in which the Council are asked to look at them under this Bill, namely, considering whether the persons who did them did them in good faith and in the reasonable belief that they were necessary. The third point is quite clear from what the Lord Chancellor says. In doing that we have to take into account the circumstances of the time, the excitement of the moment, and the unfortunate fact that the man may have no one to consult. These are the legitimate circumstances which have to be taken into account. That, I venture to submit, is very material. In this connection I draw the attention of Council to the fact that the Bill reserves power to Government to prosecute in any case where it may find it necessary. No one in dealing with this Bill has referred to that point. Clause 6 (*c*) runs 'Nothing in this Act shall prevent the institution of proceeding by or on behalf of the Government against any person in respect of any matter whatsoever.' Thus Government is not precluded from taking any action against an officer that is necessary. Then I draw altention to clause 6 (*b*), in which though we have confirmed sentences we have not gone nearly as far as was the case in the South Africa Acts. We have left the right of appeal to the Privy Council fully open. Under that clause if any appeal goes to the Privy Council, it will be decided as if this Act had not been passed. We cannot do more. If these sentences are monstrously unjust, if these tribunals have no jurisdiction, if there has been a denial of justice, if there has been a travesty of justice, (I believe I am correctly repeating expressions which have been used in this Council), the Courts are open and in England, the Privy Council will listen to any appeal on these grounds if a case can be made out. Years ago in Dillet's case it was laid down on what lines the Privy Council will hear appeals in criminal cases. If, as I say, there has been any denial of justice, we have left it open to the person aggrieved to go to the Privy Council. if there has not been a denial justice, surely the sentences must be confirmed.

"There is much I should like to say in answer to my Hon'ble friend Mr. Sinha and again in answer to the speech of my Hon'ble friend Mr. Sarma, but I am afraid that at this hour I must resist the temptation. However, I cannot help referring in conclusion to one dictum of my Hon'ble friend Mr. Sinha. He said 'what is the good of my trying to persuade the Government'; I think I may console myself with the retort. 'What is the good of my trying to persuade Mr Sinha?'"

* * * * * * * * * * *

The Hon'ble Sir William Vincent :—"My Lord, I do not know if I shall be in order if, before replying on this debate, I give to Council some new information, with reference to the Committee of Inquiry. I think the Council will be interested to know that the Secretary of State has now sanctioned the addition of one Indian and one European member to that Committee. This information has really no connection with the Bill, but it is a matter in which the Council is greatly interested.

"My Lord, when I closed my opening speech on this Bill, I said that I had avoided, as far as possible, prejudicing any question that would come before the Committee or saying anything that might provoke racial feeling. I believe it has generally been accepted by this Council that that was my attitude. But I was a little suprised to be accused by the Hon'ble Mr. Malaviya, of all people in this Council, of attempting to prejudice the work of the Committee and that, because I had ventured to put it to the Council—and I think Sir George Lowndes also said the same thing—that if the Committee of Inquiry appointed to inquire into this matter found that a man had acted reasonably and *bona fide,* I was quite sure they would not hold him in any way to blame. Well, after I spoke the Council heard the various statements made by the Hon'ble Member himself, attempts to create prejudice, to minimise various facts and to place before Council *ex parte* statements as to particular incidents on which it was suggested that this Council should condemn particular officers or particular actions. My Lord, the Hon'ble Member has received such severe. . . . ."

The Hon'ble Pandit Madan Mohan Malaviya :—"May I rise to a point of order, my Lord ?"

The President :—"Personal explanation or point of order ?"

The Hon'ble Pandit Madan Mohan Malaviya :—"A correction, my Lord."

The President :—"Personal explanation ?"

The Hon'ble Pandit Madan Mohan Malaviya :—"Exactly, my Lord. I never said that the Council should condemn any officer on *ex parte* statements. I said their action should be sifted by the Committee of Inquiry and then judgment pronounced."

The Hon'ble Sir William Vincent :—"My Lord, the Hon'ble Member has received such severe castigation from the Hon'ble the Law Member that it really would be an act of cruelty to say anything more of his speech. I can only say that, even if I had in any way been guilty of attempting to prejudice the decision on any point by the Committee or of creating an atmosphere of bias in respect of any matter, it would have been a case a Satan reproving the sin, for no man has been more guilty in that respect than the Hon'ble Member himself. But I leave it to Council to judge if I said anything which could prejudice the inquiry. My Lord, I regret very much, however, that an attempt has been made by the Hon'ble Member and by others to place particular incidents before the Council to make *ex parte* statements as to what happened on particular occasions, because I think that statements on the one side necessarily evoke from others contradiction, and that this Council was therefore placed in a very unfortunate position in regard to such incidents—incidents, of which as the Hon'ble Mr. Sinha said, the Council do not know much, of which they now have had stories from one side and stories from the other, and I feel that would have been much better if both sides had left all these incidents alone. Such a course would not have affected this Bill and Council have left the whole of the facts to the Committee of Inquiry to decide.

"I must, however, myself quite clearly disclaim any intention to justify any particular action. It was for instance suggested that I was attempting to indemnify officers who were concerned in the Jallianwala Bagh incident. My Lord, I had no such intention, nor can such an intention be deduced from the Bill. The question, whether these officers will be indemnified or not, will depend on the findings of Courts as to whether their action was *bona fide* and reasonable or not. I do not seek in any way to prejudge the point.

"In the course of the debate the Hon'ble Sir Dinshaw Wacha inquired whether the passing of this Bill would in any way affect the Committee of Inquiry. The answer has been given. The Committee of Inquiry is an administrative Committee. Its report will have no legal effect. The result will be, when it reports, that the opinions and recommendations will have to be decided by the authorities in order to see whether any person is to be punished or censured or commended administratively; but that has nothing whatever to do with the Courts. That Report will not be evidence in the Court. The legal liability of those concerned is a separate matter and can only be settled by either the common law or a Bill of this character.

"My Lord, it has been said that martial law was not necessary. I was anxious to abstain from expressing any view of the point at present; but as the subject has been dealt with at such length, I wish to add one word to the discussion, and that is to read the actual message—if I may with your Lordship's permission do so—on which the Government of India declared martial law. The Council have learned from Mr. Hailey's speech and from other Members all the incidents which preceded the 13th of April, and it is not necessary for me to reiterate them. Well, on that day, all other telegraphic communication being cut, we received the following message by wireless telegraph :—

> 'Railway stations between Kasur and Amritsar looted, British soldier killed.' (As a matter of fact there were two). 'Two British officers injured at Kasur.' (There were more people than two injured.) 'Bands of rebels reported on the move, Kasur treasury attacked; state of open rebellion exists in parts of the districts of Lahore and Amritsar. Lieutenant-Governor with the concurrence of the General Officer Commanding the 16th Division and Chief Justice of the High Court requests the Governor-General in Council to direct him to suspend the functions of the ordinary criminal courts in Amritsar and Lahore districts and establish martial law therein and direct the trial of offenders under section 2 of Regulation X of 1804.

Situation critical. Moveable column starts marching from Ferozepore to Amritsar through worst tract with guns tomorrow.'

"I want to put it to any Member of this Council whether, if he had been a Member of the Government of India at that time, with the information which is now before the Council, on receipt of a telegram of that kind, he would not have acted exactly as the Government of India did: if any officer would have dared to take the responsibility of not accepting a recommendation of that character. That is all, my Lord, on the question of martial law, but I think that this message adds to the information before the Council.

"My Lord, it has been said that this present Bill goes too far. I do not think it necessary for me in any way to discuss that point. It has been fully debated already by the Hon'ble the Law Member. Many detailed criticisms of various clauses were put forward which, if I may say so, appeared to me to be irrelevant in a debate of this character. We ought now really only to discuss the question as to whether an Indemnity Act of this character is necessary or not, and that is a question about which, I believe, nearly all the Members in this Council have been now convinced. It has been said, however, that we ought to postpone the Bill, because actions will not be brought at once, or if they are brought, postponement may be secured. Another suggestion was, 'you should bring the Act in now, but make it an Act which will only suspend civil or criminal proceedings against officers'. I would point out in answer to these suggestions that an action begun now may be decided before any Indemnity Act could be passed after the report of the Committee is received, and any lawyer member of this Council will know how difficult it would be to pass an Indemnity Act in regard to a suit either commenced or decreed. As to pending suits, is it fair that we should leave officers who, *ex hypothesi*, as I said before, have done their duty, with a possibility of being sued—or that we should say to them 'Well, you may be indemnified for doing what was right or you may not, we will tell you that six months later, when the Committee of Inquiry, which has nothing really whatever to do with your legal liabilities, has decided some other point.' I submit that is not a right position for Government to take.

"My Lord, there is only one other matter to which I wish to draw attention and that arises out of the remarks made by the Hon'ble Sardar Sundar Singh Majithia. He asked me to give him an assurance that those who gave evidence before the Committee would in no sense be harassed by the police. I am glad to give him that assurance, and I am quite sure that His Honour the Lieutenant-Governor will give full effect to it.

"Another point was that I was asked whether if the Committee should find that any officer of Government had been guilty of improper conduct, he would be punished. My Lord, I have already said that it is our hope that we may be able to publish the report of Committee, and it is certainly not our intention to treat the recommendations of this body as of no account in so far as we may accept their views. Any recommendations which they make will have to be considered, and such action as we think necessary will certainly by taken upon them."

The motion for postponement of the Bill was put and negatived.

The motion that leave be given to introduce the Bill was put and agreed to.

The Hon'ble Sir William Vincent :—"My Lord, I now introduce the Bill and move that the Bill, together with the statement of Objects and Reasons relating thereto, be published in the *Gazette of India* in English."

The motion was put and agreed to.

The Council then adjourned till Tuesday, the 23rd September, 1919, at 11 A.M.

(7)—From Proceedings of Meeting held on September 24, 1919

The Indemnity Bill—(*contd.*)

The Hon'ble Sir William Vincent:—"My Lord, I move that the Bill to indemnify officers of Government and other persons in respect of certain acts done under martial law, and to provide for other matters in connection therewith, be taken into consideration.

"The main principles of this Bill have been fully debated only a few days ago, and it would be idle for me now to waste the time of the Council by covering the same ground again. Such details as have been criticised by Hon'ble Members are the subject of amendments which are before the Council, and I need not address Council in regard to them at present."

The Hon'ble Pandit Madan Mohan Malaviya:—"My Lord, I beg to propose that the Bill be referred to a Select Committee. This is a very important Bill, my Lord, it involves very important questions of law, and, I submit, it is not a measure which should be hurried through the Council without its provisions being examined in a Select Committee. I suggest, my Lord, that the Select Committee should consist of the Hon'ble the Law Member, the Hon'ble the Home Member, the Hon'ble Sir Edward Maclagan, His Excellency the Commander-in-Chief, the Hon'ble Mr. Sarma, the Hon'ble the Maharaja of Kassimbazar, the Hon'ble Mr. Sinha, the Hon'ble Sardar Sundar Singh Majithia, the Hon'ble Mr. Crum and myself. There will be no harm, my Lord, if the Bill is delayed a little while; its provisions are so important that they ought to be examined in Select Committee. I, therefore, move that the Bill be referred to a Select Committee consisting of the Hon'ble Members whose names I have mentioned....."

The Hon'ble Sir William Vincent:—"Do I understand that the Hon'ble Member is moving an amendment to the motion?"

The President:—"Is the Hon'ble Member moving an amendment to the motion which is on the paper?"

The Hon'ble Pandit Madan Mohan Malaviya:—"My Lord, I have put forward what I had to say, I do not wish to add to or subtract from it."

The President:—"What I want the Hon'ble Member to give me a clear answer to is this. Is the Hon'ble Member putting forward an amendment to the motion which is on the paper?"

The Hon'ble Pandit Madan Mohan Malaviya:—"My Lord, I do not know whether I should call it a technical amendment. I am endeavouring on the motion before us to put forward the proposal that I have put forward, for the consideration of this Council. If a technical amendment is needed, my Lord, I will say that it is a technical amendment, but, I submit, that it is not necessary that there should be an amendment. On a motion made by the Hon'ble the Home Member, I am entitled to put forward the view I have done for the consideration of the Council."

The President:—"The Hon'ble Member is perfectly within his right to oppose a motion which is before the Council, but if the Hon'ble Member wishes to move an amendment, he must move it now. I take it from the Hon'ble Member that he is opposing the motion and not moving an amendment."

The Hon'ble Pandit Madan Mohan Malaviya:—"My Lord, if an amendment is the only proposition which is before the Council on a question like this, I put it forward as an amendment."

The Hon'ble Sir William Vincent:—"Then, my Lord, I take objection to the motion, on the ground that I have had no notice of the amendment."

The Hon'ble Pandit Madan Mohan Malaviya:—"I submit, my Lord, that the Rules do not require notice. I beg your Excellency to refer to the Rules."

The President:—"Will the Hon'ble Member refer me to the rule under which there is no necessity to give notice in the case of an amendment such as he proposes?"

The Hon'ble Pandit Madan Mohan Malaviya:—"I think, your Excellency, that the Member who objects should show under what rule it is necessary. If the Hon'ble the Secretary of the Council will send me a copy of the Rules, I will refer your Excellency to it."

The Hon'ble Sir George Lowndes:—"May I suggest that the practice here is, when we have got a motion before the Council, your Lordship as President has only that one motion to put to the Council. It is only if an amendment is moved to it, that your Excellency can put another motion to the Council. At present, there is only the one motion before the Council."

The President:—"It is true that, under rule 28, when a Bill is taken into consideration by the Council, any Member may propose an amendment of such a Bill of which three days' notice should be given. What the Hon'ble Member suggests is not an amendment of the Bill, and, I think, he is in order and the Hon'ble Member can move the amendment as he proposes. Do I understand the Hon'ble Member has moved the amendment?"

The Hon'ble Pandit Madan Mohan Malaviya:—"My Lord, I beg to move the amendment which I have placed before the Council."

The motion was put and negatived.

Then the motion that the Bill be taken into consideration was put and agreed to.

The Hon'ble Sir William Vincent:—"My Lord, I move as an amendment:—

'That in the preamble of the Bill for the words 'it has been necessary for the purpose of maintaining or restoring order to resort to martial law' the words 'martial law has been enforced' be substituted.'

"During the debate on this Bill it was apparent from the speeches of many Hon'ble Members that the recital in the preamble was interpreted by them as a quasi-admission that this Legislative Council accepted the view that the declaration of martial law was necessary; among other Members, my Hon'ble friend, Mr. Sinha, drew particular attention to this point. I then said that we would consider the question of amending the preamble, and the present amendment is proposed to give effect to that intention and to make it abundantly clear that there is nothing in the Bill which can in any way be interpreted as meaning that this Council has ratified or admitted the necessity for the enforcement of martial law.

"The amendment as proposed merely makes a statement of absolute fact, which no one can controvert, that martial law was enforced."

The motion was put and agreed to.

The Hon'ble Rao Bahadur B.N. Sarma:—"I think, my Lord, the 2nd* and 3rd* amendments on the list would fall to the ground having regard to the acceptance of the first."

The Hon'ble Rao Bahadur B.N. Sarma:—

*2. That for the first paragraph of the preamble the following be substituted, namely:—

'Whereas for the purpose of suppressing the recent disorders in certain districts of the Punjab and in other parts of India, and restoring order therein martial law has been resorted to.'

*3 'That the words 'maintaining or' in paragraph 1 of the preamble be omitted.'

The President:—"That is so No. 4† goes as well."

The Hon'ble Mr. Sachchidananda Sinha:—"My Lord, the amendment I propose is....."

The Hon'ble Sir William Vincent:—"My Lord, may I suggest that, with your Lordship's permission, the Hon'ble Mr. Sinha should take up this amendment, which is really a consequential one, along with a subsequent amendment of his."

The Hon'ble Mr. Sachchidananda Sinha:—"I shall do so with your Lordship's leave. I propose that—

'In the second clause of the preamble the word 'certain' be inserted between the words 'indemnify' and 'officers' and I also propose....."

The President:—"I think if the Hon'ble Member would postpone this until he comes to the clause, it will be more convenient to take it on the clause."

The Hon'ble Mr. Sachchidananda Sinha:—"I shall do so, my Lord, I now propose that in the same clause 2 of the preamble the words 'purporting to have been ordered or done' be omitted. The reasons for the proposal are these. Acts which are either done or ordered to be done for the purpose of maintaining or restoring order are acts which we can all understand. But it is difficult to understand acts to which the words in the preamble refer, namely, acts 'purporting to have been ordered or done'. As this might cause some confusion without any substantial object being gained, so far as I know, I propose that these words be omitted."

The Hon'ble Sir George Lowndes:—"My Lord, the Government are not prepared to accept this amendment. The words are perfectly innocent in themselves, and they appear in most of the idemnity clauses, which so often find a place in our Acts. The object is to avoid any dispute as to whether an act was actually done for a particular purpose or only intended so to be done though it may not have effected that purpose. Assuming that there is any question as to whether any act done in good faith and in the belief (we shall come to that point later) that it was necessary for a particular purpose, its justification ought not to depend upon whether as a matter of fact the purpose was attained; if it was intended to attain that purpose, the act ought to be covered by the Indemnity. When we come to the

† **The Hon'ble Mr. Malaviya:**—

4 'That in the first clause of the preamble the words 'maintaining or' be omitted.'

question of good faith, Hon'ble Members have got many amendments on the paper, and they may possibly succeed in striking out the words in that clause; if so, then it might be reasonable to omit these words; but we could not omit them at the present stage. It am quite willing, my Lord, to defer a vote on this amendment until we have done with the 'good faith' amendments, if my Hon'ble friend thinks there is any chance of their being carried; but I do not think there is any great chance of that."

The Hon'ble Mr. Sachchidananda Sinha:—"As to the question of any chance of our amendments being carried, I have not the slightest hope at all; I would not defer consideration on that account."

The motion was put and negatived.

The Hon'ble Pandit Madan Mohan Malaviya:—"My Lord, I beg to move 'that in the second clause of the preamble, the words 'maintaining or' be omitted. My Lord, it is an abnormal position to my mind for which no support is found in the ancient Statutes of Parliament, though it may be found in some of the more recent enactments in some of the Colonies that you should resort to martial law for maintaining order. Maintenance of order should be secured by the ordinary police assisted, when it may be necessary, by the military troops. I therefore submit that these two words 'maintaining or' should be omitted from the second clause of the preamble."

The Hon'ble Sir William Vincent:—"My Lord, I submit that it is essential that these words 'maintaining or' should be retained. It will be obvious to Members of this Council that once martial law is declared, or enforced, officers of the Government have not only to suppress active disorder, but they have to maintain order as well. For instance, my Lord, supposing there was a disorderly mob about to collect for some improper purpose, it would in such circumstances obviously be necessary for the military commander to issue orders prohibiting the assembly, and, if necessary, prevent such assembly by force. Otherwise indeed his position would be an impossible one; he would have to wait until mischief was begun and then begin to suppress it. It will be clear to the Council therefore, I hope, that the retention of these words is absolutely necessary."

The Hon'ble Rao Bahadur B.N. Sarma:—"My Lord, I think that the Hon'ble the Home Member might reconsider this question. His objection to Mr. Malaviya's amendment is, that during the suppression of a disorder, order has to be maintained; it can only be maintained under martial law, and consequently the words 'maintaining or' would be thoroughly appropriate, because there would otherwise be no one to maintain order during that period.

"What is mentioned here is 'or for the purposes', the general purposes, 'of maintaining or restoring order.' That raises a large question, namely, whether in future where disorders are to be suppressed martial law can continue for the general purpose of maintaining order, if the officers charged with the duty of suppressing disorders should be indemnified under this Act in respect of acts done after the disorders had been suppressed. My submission is, that this would lead to the acceptance by the Legislature of the principle that martial law can be resorted to by the Government for the purpose of maintaining order although they had suppressed disorders, and that any person who uses extreme measures thereafter for maintaining order should be protected. The ordinary law is, that the civil arm must meet all contingencies and maintain order once violent armed rebellion is suppressed. My submission is that we in this legislative assembly should not accept any other principle. I do not want to raise this question merely for an argumentative purpose. I submit that this Act will be quoted as a precedent. It may be open to a future Government, whenever a riot cannot be quelled, to have recourse to martial law. The police and the magistracy have the right to invite the co-operation of the military for the purpose of quelling a riot and all necessary force can be used; but the civil power and the military assisting it have to take cognisance of the fact that if unncessary force be used the officers would be liable to punishment. I do not think there have been any cases where the officers in such circumstances have been protected by an Indemnity Act. I will quote a passage from Dicey, showing that protection lasts only as long as the necessity lasts for suppressing disorder, but no longer. This is what Dicey says:—

> 'Martial law in the sense in which the expression is here used, means the power, right or duty of the Crown and its servants, or, in other words, the Government, to maintain public order, or in technical language the King's peace at whatever cost of blood or property may be in strictness necessary for that purpose. Hence, martial law comes into existence in times of invasion or insurrection where and in so far as the King's peace cannot be maintained by ordinary means, and owes its existence to urgent and paramount

> necessity. The point to be borne in mind is, that the power to exercise martial law which is not ill described by an expression known to the American Courts, namely, that of 'War power', as it originates in so, it is limited by the necessity of the case. The only principle on which the law of England tolerates what is called martial law is necessity, its introduction can only be justified by necessity; its continuance requires precisely the same justification of necessity and if it survives the necessity on which alone it rests for a single minute, it becomes instantly a mere exercise of lawless violence.'
>
> There are a number of other passages:—
>
> 'Such legal right to duty always lasts so long and so long only as the circumstances exist which necessitate the use of force.'

"My submission is that the Government would be right in asking for the protection of their officers during the suppression of the rebellion, and for the purpose of maintaining order during that period; but they cannot ask, and they should not ask this Council, for the acceptance of this novel principle that whenever order cannot be maintained by the police and the military force is used, its officers be indemnified. I, therefore, submit that the words 'maintaining or' should be omitted in the second paragraph of the preamble."

The Hon'ble Sir George Lowndes:—"My Lord, as I pointed out the other day, martial law steps in when the ordinary civil courts are unable, I use the words deliberately, to maintain order or to suppress disorder. The Hon'ble Pandit and the Hon'ble Mr. Sarma have suggested that the insertion of the word 'maintaining' created a new doctrine without a precedent. It is, if I may say so, nothing of the sort. It is inconceivable to me that Mr. Sarma should say this after reading the passage he did from Dicey. Let me read it again:—

> 'Hence martial law comes into existence in times of invasion or insurrection when, where, and in so far as the King's peace cannot be maintained by the ordinary means.'

The Hon'ble Pandit Madan Mohan Malaviya:—"What page?"

The Hon'ble Sir George Lowndes:—"My Lord, I decline to be interrupted by the Hon'ble Pandit. When the ordinary courts cannot maintain order or suppress disorder, you must have martial law. The maintenance of order is one of the definite objects with which martial law is put into force. The Hon'ble Pandit also said that there was no precedent for this, and yet during the past few days I have lent him and every Member of this Council who has asked for them, the South Africa Acts which are the latest examples of martial law and Idemnifying Acts. In each one of them you find that martial law was used for maintaining order. I will not trouble the Council with many extracts, I will read the first that comes to hand. Section 1 of the Act of 1900 says—my Hon'ble friend will find the same in them all—

> 'All·acts, matters and things whatsoever in good faith advised, commanded, ordered, directed or done, as necessary for the suppression of hostilities or the establishment and maintenance of good order and government.'

It is the same in most of the older Acts. We are introducing nothing new, nothing without precedent."

The Hon'ble Pandit Madan Mohan Malaviya:—"My Lord, the Hon'ble the Law Member quotes a sentence from Dicey in which he says that where order cannot be maintained by the civil courts martial law steps in. That is very different from saying that that sentence gives support to the proposition he advances. Our point is that you do not find this authority in the Acts of Parliament. You had some authority in the three Acts of South Africa but, my Lord, these three Acts of South Africa ought not to be a model as against the Acts of Parliament. I should like the Hon'ble the Law Member to quote any Act of Parliament in which for the purposes of maintaining order martial law has been justified. Then, my Lord, I gave a certain authority which the Hon'ble the Law Member will not disregard....."

The Hon'ble Sir George Lowndes:—"My Lord, may I interrupt?"

The Hon'ble Pandit Madan Mohan Malaviya:—"My Lord, I object."

The Hon'ble Sir George Lowndes:—"Very well. The Hon'ble Member does not want it. It is there."

The Hon'ble Pandit Madan Mohan Malaviya:—"The Hon'ble the Law Member was afraid to let me have the page of his quotation, which is the smallest courtesy that any Member of this Council is entitled to. We are coming to bad ways."

The President:—"I quite agree Will the Hon'ble Member proceed."

The Hon'ble Pandit Madan Mohan Malaviya:—"Thank you, my Lord.

"Now, the Earl of Halsbury in Vol. VI of the Laws of England says:—

> 'The Crown may not issue commissions in time of peace to try civilians by martial law: but when a state of actual war, or of insurrection, riot, or rebellion amounting to war exists, the Crown and its officers may use the amount of force necessary in the circumstances to restore order, and this use of force is sometimes termed martial law. When once this state of actual war exists, the Civil Courts have no authority to call in question the actions of the military authorities; but the powers of the military authorities cease and those of the Civil Courts are resumed *ipso facto* with the termination of the disorder.'

"I submit, my Lord, that this is an authority which the Hon'ble the Law Member cannot disregard or make light of, and it is entirely in support of the proposition which I have put before the Council, namely, that the words 'maintaining or' should be omitted from the second clause of the preamble."

The motion was put and negatived.

The Hon'ble Rao Bahadur B.N. Sarma:—My Lord, I beg to move that in paragraph 2 of the preamble the words 'in a reasonable belief that they were necessary' be omitted.

"My Lord, as far as I can see, the words used in all the enactments dealing with Acts to indemnify officers are 'done in good faith as necessary for the said purpose.' I have not been able to come across these additional words 'in a reasonable belief that they were necessary.' On that ground alone I might ask the Council to follow the precedents set to us by the Legislature of various countries and drop the words 'in a reasonable belief that they were necessary,' because they would lead to an inquiry of a somewhat elaborate character on which no safe conclusions can be come to. But I have a greater objection, and it is this. As the Bill stands, the person who comes into the Court to seek redress will have to show two things, first of all, that the act of which he complains was not done in good faith, and, secondly, that it was not done in a reasonable belief that the act was necessary for the purpose. I would first like to ask the Hon'ble the Law Member to explain clearly for what purpose these additional words have been used, and how they would not be covered by the same words 'good faith', and if some additional meaning is sought to be imported, what that additional meaning is. But as they stand, my difficulty is, the person aggrieved will have to prove two things instead of one thing which generally he is asked to do by almost every Legislature. Then with regard to the words 'reasonable belief'. Supposing a person has to show that an officer did not believe that an act was necessary, I think it is almost impossible for him to prove it. But you may say that the words 'reasonable belief and in good faith' are there. There, my Lord, comes in the difficulty. Supposing in a particular community there is a belief entertained that particular measures, however wrong they may be from the moral standpoint, are necessary for achieving a certain end. Now, taking the moral atmosphere of Germany, for instance, it was considered by all alike, professors, philosophers of law, philosophers of morality, by military men and in fact by all classes, that certain measures, which were condemned by the rest of humanity as non-civilized methods, could be employed. Well, if you are to judge a German officer labouring under that impression, could not these words 'reasonable belief' protect him, because he believed that they were necessary, the atmosphere in which he moved led him to believe that they were necessary also. Therefore, if you are to judge him by that standard, certainly he ought to be protected. Similarly, supposing the atmosphere in the Punjab in those days was such that the several gentlemen who were responsible felt that there must be a deviation, a departure from standards which are generally considered to be humane and civilized. I need hardly allude to the *Salaaming* order and several other orders that were passed to which allusion has already been made, because it will only tend to embitter feelings and do no good. There are certain orders which cannot be justified by any standard of morality. Now, supposing the officers, having regard to the mental atmosphere surrounding them, believed that those acts were necessary and reasonable, my Lord, will they be protected? I submit, an elaborate inquiry of that description might be opened, I will not say would be opened, but might be opened, if the various theories on which States like India are held and can be held in subjection are to be brought before the law courts. Therefore, there is no precedent for it; it might lead to various difficulties; and I, therefore, earnestly request that these words be omitted."

The Hon'ble Sir George Lowndes:—"My Lord, I regret I am unable either to omit these words or to explain any more clearly to my Hon'ble friend, Mr. Sarma, than I did on the last occasion, what the real intention and object of the words are. We had a clear admission of the propriety of this clause in his previous speech when he asked us to adopt the actual wording of the South Africa Acts, which the Hon'ble Pandit so violently disputed.

"I explained last time that the words 'in a reasonable belief that the acts were necessary' are only a translation from the wording of the South Africa Acts; we could, of course, use the actual words of the South Africa Acts, that is, acts 'done as necessary.' I think this means 'done as being necessary,' that is, the acts were so done because the men who did them believed that they were necessary. We do not stop there. We say 'reasonably believed' that they were necessary. We only propose to indemnify men, who had a reasonable belief that their acts were necessary. I am sure the Council will accept this as at all events a fair translation of the words which my Hon'ble friend Mr. Sarma would have preferred to have in the Bill.

"Then he talked about the mental atmosphere being immaterial. He forgot, I am sure, the question which I read from the speech of perhaps one of the greatest Lord Chancellors in the House of Lords. I quoted it at some length and I do not propose to read it again—it is here and my Hon'ble friend can see it if he wishes to. Lord Thurlow says that you must take into account the mental atmosphere, that you must consider the circumstances under which a man had to make up his mind as to what he should do in an extreme emergency, and if he made up his mind reasonably, you should not cosider *ex post facto* whether the acts he did were necessary. The real test should be whether he had a reasonable belief at the time that they were necessary, and did them in good faith. If Hon'ble Members are going to insert amendments like this in an Act which is intended to protect officers who did their duty in good faith under very trying circumstances, I say an Indemnity Act from this Council is not worth having."

The motion was put and negatived.

The Hon'ble Pandit Madan Mohan Malaviya:—"My Lord, I beg to propose that—

'In the second paragraph of the preamble for the words 'and in a reasonable belief that they were necessary for the said purposes', the following be substituted:—

'necessarily and properly, in furtherance and execution of the objects for which martial law was proclaimed as aforesaid.'

"My Lord, I have taken this clause from an Act of the laws of St. Vincent, Act No. 189 of 1862. After indemnifying certain officers against acts done by them during the prevalence of martial law, the Act proceeds—'provided always an indemnity hereby granted is granted on this supposition and condition that all such acts, matters and things shall have been done or shall be done *bona fide* necessarily and properly in furtherance and execution of the objects for which martial law was proclaimed as aforesaid.'

"Now, my Lord, I think that this is a much more reasonable provision to adopt, than the one that stands at present in the Bill. Here, you say that a man should have acted *bona fide,* that is, in good faith, and necessarily and properly. That would include a consideration of what humanity demands. That will include also that the thing should have been done to suppress disorder, and a reasonable belief will be implied in the phraseology I have suggested. He must act reasonably in finding out that it was necessary and in a proper way. I hope this amendment at least may find acceptance at the hands of Government."

The Hon'ble Sir George Lowndes:—"If I heard the Hon'ble Member aright he said he had taken these words from an Act of St. Vincent. That is no doubt out of compliment to the Hon'ble Member who is in charge of the Bill. I can see no other reason for his having done so. The Act of St. Vincent goes back to 1862, that is getting on to 60 years ago now, whereas we have tried to follow a more recent model. I have nothing really to add to what I said on the last amendment. The point is this, as I tried to explain, that we do not want in this Bill to make the test whether things were or were not in fact necessary. The fact that they were unnecessary, judged *ex post facto*, is not the test for indemnity in the case of acts done under these very difficult circumstances. What we have got to find is, whether they were reasonably believed to be necessary at the time, taking into account the conditions under which the men who did them had to act. We are not going to examine them on an *ex post facto* basis, or consider, looking back now when all is over, we think they were really necessary or not. That is not my idea of an Indemnity Act. I regret Government is not able to accept this amendment."

The Hon'ble Pandit Madan Mohan Malaviya:—"My Lord, we have had some novel arguments, but the most novel argument I have heard today is the argument of the Law Member that a thing is to be rejected because it is ancient. I fear much will have to be put aside in favour of modern ideas as to what should or should not be done. I take it that the fact that a thing is ancient is rather a recommendation. At any rate, I am prepared that the matter should be considered on its merits. Let us consider which is better, the provision which is now being proposed by the Government, the paraphrase of the words 'done as necessary' of the Acts of South Africa, or the language of the enactment from which I have borrowed my phraseology, namely, that the indemnity shall be granted upon this supposition that all such acts, matters or things shall be done *bona fide,* that is in good faith of course, necessarily and properly in furtherance and execution of the objects for which martial law was proclaimed as aforesaid.'

"If this phraseology is adopted, where it would be reasonable to extend indemnity it would be extended, but it would cut off a lot of other acts which may not have been done properly and which may not have been necessary. The Hon'ble the Law Member would not allow any discussion of the question whether certain acts were necessary or not by the phraseology which he has chosen to adopt. How is a man to know what the belief of a particular individual was when he was acting? If you put it on the ground that he should show whether the thing was necessary, that he should show that it was proper, then you are on solid ground, but you are in the regions of vagueness and uncertainty in putting in the phraseology that a thing should be done in a reasonable belief. I, therefore, hope that unless the Government can find some more substantial argument against my proposition than that it is somewhat ancient as compared to the provisions in the South Africa Acts, they will reconsider the position. This will mean a great change in the outlook of those who may be concerned with such cases. If you retain the phraseology 'in good faith and in a reasonable belief,' you make it a very difficult thing, if not a practical impossibility, for the plaintiff to establish a case for damages against a person who may have injured or oppressed him. He may come into the witness box and swear that he reasonably believed that this was necessary and that would be an obstacle. The Act even saves him the necessity of swearing even to that, because the third section of the Act says that, that will be presumed if a certificate has been obtained from a Secretary to Government. I therefore think we are carrying things too far if putting the provision in the present form, and if you accept my suggestion and substitute the words 'necessarily and properly in futherance and execution of the objects for which martial law was proclaimed,' you would leave a fair chance to plaintiffs to have the justice to which they may be entitled. I, therefore, press this amendment on the consideration of the Government."

The motion was put and negatived.

The Hon'ble Sir William Vincent:—"My Lord, may I again suggest that the Hon'ble Member should take up this amendment with his amendment No. 32. I would suggest, with your Lordship's permission, that it would be more convenient to the Council. The present is a consequential amendment on the later one."

The Hon'ble Rao Bahadur B.N. Sarma:—"I have no objection to that; even if No. 32 is rejected it comes to the same thing."

The President:—"No. 10* will stand over."

The Hon'ble Mr. Sachchidananda Sinha:—"My Lord, I move that—

> 'In clause 2 for the words 'any officer of Government whether Civil or Military,' the words 'any police officer of or below the rank of Assistant or Deputy Superintendent of Police and any soldier or non-commissioned officer of His Majesty's Army acting under the orders of their superior officers' be substituted.'

"My Lord, the reason for this amendment is obvious. In the course of his opening speech the Hon'ble the Home Member insisted repeatedly that if this Indemnity Act was not passed, it would be putting in a very serious predicament a large number of soldiers and inferior officers who had taken part in carrying out the orders of their superior officers. I, therefore, propose to limit this class by giving a definition of the officers concerned, as to who the officers will be who will be indemnified by this Act, for all acts done by them. As regards the superior officers, they will be under the common law protected for all acts done in good faith. But if it can be established that certain acts were done by them, or ordered by them not in good

---

* **The Hon'ble Mr. Sarma** :—10. 'That to paragraph 3 of the preamble, the following be added 'in certain cases and subject to the limitations specified herein below.'

faith, if they committed an atrocity or something that should not be done, the law will not protect them. For this reason I propose my amendment."

The Hon'ble Sir William Vincent:— "I think when I explain to the Council what the effect of this amendment would be, every Member of this Council, every reasonable Member, including the Hon'ble mover, will be convinced that it really is an impossible amendment for acceptance. Reading the amendment, it will be seen that it would limit the protection afforded by the Bill to the case of police officers and soldiers. Now, many other officers besides police officers have been engaged in the suppression of the disorders, officers both civil and military.

"I am, for instance, informed that *Tehsildars* and other revenue officers have been so used. There was also an Indian Sub-divisional Officer at Kasur and there was an Indian Deputy Commissioner in one district besides European Deputy Commissioners in other districts whose services were similarly used, and there is really no reason why the protection which is given to police officers should be refused to officers of this class. Then, again, in the case even of police officers, why is an Assistant or a Deputy Superintendent of Police to be exonerated for acts done in good faith, while a Superintendent of Police is not to receive the same protection? Is that fair, is that reasonable? Is there any reason for instance why Mr. Heron, Superintendent of Police in one of the districts, whose name I have heard quoted—I do not happen to know him myself—if he has acted *bona fide* and in the reasonable belief that his action was necessary, should not receive the protection of this Act? Is there any reason why a subaltern or commissioned officer of the Army who has had to take part in quelling these disorders and who would be excluded by this amendment, should not receive the benefit of the Act? I am sure, if he thinks over the effect of his proposal, that the Hon'ble Member will withdraw his amendment."

The Hon'ble Mr. Sachchidananda Sinha:—"I desire to say in reply that the reason why I framed the amendment in this way was that I considered that those officers who may be held to have initiated a certain policy should not receive the protection of the Indemnity Act unless, of course, they can show that their acts were done in good faith. That was the only principle on which I framed my amendment. I have nothing further to say."

The motion was put and negatived.

The President:—"With the rejection of that amendment the amendment to be moved by the Hon'ble Mr. Sinha, No. 5* on the paper, with regard to the preamble, will, of course, drop."

The Hon'ble Mr. Sachchidananda Sinha:—"My Lord, I move—

'That in clause 2 for the words 'person acting under the orders of any such officer' the words 'person acting under the orders of any Magistrate, police officer not below the rank of Deputy or Assistant Superintendent of Police, and any commissioned officer of His Majesty's Army' be substituted—

The reason for this amendment is that otherwise the private individual, for whose benefit this clause is intended, might plead that he did a certain act under the orders of a *chaukidar* or a constable. That would be certainly carrying, I would not say the joke too far, but the point too far, and, therefore, I have brought in these words to give some substance to the proposition that the officer concerned must be one of a certain standing and not anybody or everybody. On this ground I move my amendment."

The Hon'ble Sir William Vincent:—"This is an amendment of much the same character as the last one; the acceptance of it would involve this consequence, that any person acting under the orders of, say, an Inspector of Police—and I believe an Inspector of Police was actually the senior officer present at one place, Tarn Taran, though I have not verified this point—any person acting under the orders of an Inspector of Police would not be protected, however properly he had acted, however *bona fide* his action might have been. Again, there were many places in which non-commissioned officers of the Army were placed in positions of great responsibility. Is the man who obeyed, *bona fide*, the orders or of such an officer not to be protected, if he has acted properly? Was it his duty to ascertain the badges or rank of an officer giving the orders or to inquire of a Police officer 'What are you exactly? Are you an Inspector of Police or an Assistant Superintendent?' I do not think that this amendment will commend itself for one moment to this Council. And I again suggest to the Hon'ble Member that, instead of putting an amendment of this character to the vote, he should exercise a wise discretion and withdraw it."

---

* That in second clause of the preamble the word 'certain' is inserted between the words 'indemnify' and 'officers'. *Vide* page 840 *ante*.

The Hon'ble Mr. Sachchidananda Sinha:—"There is nothing to withdraw, the result will be the same. It will be defeated."

The motion was put and negatived.

The Hon'ble Mr. Sachchidananda Sinha:—"This* is practically the same as the last amendment which I moved (No. 12) and, as that was not accepted, it is no good pressing this."

The motion was by leave withdrawn.

The Hon'ble Mr. Sachchidananda Sinha:—"My Lord, I move that in clause 2 after the words 'British India' the words 'where martial law was established' be inserted.

"My Lord, I do hope that the Hon'ble the Home Member will see his away to accept this amendment, because it will bring the preamble into consonance with the section. The preamble very properly lays down:—

> 'Whereas owing to the recent disorders in certain districts in the Punjab and other parts of India, martial law has been enforced.'

In section 2 no such limitation is placed and the very general and wide words 'British India' are used. It might lead to some serious difficulty if this Act were applied in other places than the districts of the Punjab or certain other places specified in the preamble. Therefore, I think, the Government might see their way to accept my amendment that the words 'British India' should be limited by the words 'where martial law was established.' "

The Hon'ble Sir William Vincent :—"My Lord, I submit this is an unsound amendment. The use of words 'martial law was established' implies in some way that a proclamation of martial law or some formal action of that kind is necessary before martial law is enforced. That is however not the fact. A proclamation of martial law is only the means by which the fact of martial law being in force is made known to the public, I presume that the Hon'ble Member meant by the words 'martial law was established' that martial law had been proclaimed."

The Hon'ble Mr. Sachchidananda Sinha :—"I mean exactly what the Hon'ble Member meant by changing the preamble himself from the words 'it has been necessary for the purpose of maintaining order to resort to martial law' into the words 'martial law has been

---

* 13. 'That in clause 2 the words 'or purporting to have been ordered or done be omitted.'

enforced.' If he will accept same words in this clause, I shall be quite happy to withdraw the words of my amendment 'where martial law was established.'

The Hon'ble Sir William Vincent :—"Very well, my Lord. I am informed by my Hon'ble colleague the Law Member that the use of the words 'where martial law was enforced' is not open to objection, and I am prepared to accept the amendment as modified."

The Hon'ble Mr. Sachchidananda Sinha :—"I am very grateful to the Hon'ble the Home Member."

The amended motion was put and agreed to.

The Hon'ble Rao Bahadur B. N. Sarma :—"My Lord, I beg to move 'that in clause 2 for the words 'the 30th of March 1919' the words 'the proclamation of martial law therein' be substituted.'

"Then the clause will run :—

'No suit or other legal proceeding whatsoever, whether civil or criminal, shall lie in any court of law against any officer of Government, whether civil or military, or against any other person acting under the orders of any such officer for or on account of or in respect of any act, matter or thing ordered or done for the purpose of maintaining or restoring order in any part of British India where martial law was enforced on or after the proclamation of martial law therein, etc.'

"This is an important amendment. From the opening words of the Hon'ble the Home Member when speaking to the previous amendment, I can see in a way what the object of putting this particular date, the 30th of March 1919, is. Now, my Lord, we are here on a very important question as to whether this Indemnity Bill is to cover acts done when the civil power was in authority, but merely asked the military to aid it in suppressing disorder as it is entitled to do under the Criminal Procedure Code, or whether it is to be restricted to acts done by officers after the proclamation of martial law.

"In the former event we come to this that it is open to the executive Government to enable its officers, civil and military, to do whatever may be done during the operation of martial law even prior to the proclamation of martial law, when civil courts are sitting and in full assumption of authority, and indemnifying them thereafter. My Lord, I submit that is a very dangerous doctrine to lay down. It would be extremely mischievous if the civil authorities or the military authorities who assist them, during the time of peace when the civil authorities are in full direction of the maintenance of order, are to consider themselves as entitled to protection for their acts which are legally indefensible. It would lead to very grave consequences if officers, civil and military, were to be under that impression, or if any indulgence should be shown to the executive Government by protecting their officers in respect of acts which cannot be justified under the ordinary law of the land. I know there are certain passages which can be quoted in support of the position that martial law is after all a technical term for military law, which enforces order when there is grave necessity even though there may be no proclamation, and that proclamation might possibly be construed by constitutional writers as being intended for the protection of the public not to violate certain orders. But, my Lord, we sitting here as a Legislature, and knowing full well that the people have no real voice in the Government, should not allow the executive of the land to take such wide powers or allow executive officers in the country to believe that they can seek protection even for absolutely unjustifiable acts on theoretical grounds. I submit, therefore, that the definition of martial law put forward by constitutional writers tentatively should not be relied upon by the Government as justifying the insertion of the words '30th March 1919'. My Lord, this is a very important question, for the simple reason that martial law was confined chiefly to the province of the Punjab, though, I believe, it was in force in the Bombay presidency for a day or two and never in Delhi at all. It is admitted that before the 10th of April there was no collision between the military or the civil authorities and the people. Consequently, I cannot understand the reason for the insertion of the date 30th March. Martial law was proclaimed by His Excellency the Governor-General in Council only on the 14th; it might have been intended to be proclaimed a little earlier, but the earliest date was the 14th April 1919, so far as I can see. It is just prior to that period that various acts of a highly unjustifiable character according to the people were committed. I need hardly allude to the Jallianwala Bagh incident, the belly crawling incident or the aeroplane incident. Those were acts for which the civil and military authorities would have to justify themselves before the ordinary courts in the land in the usual way. To raise a presumption in those cases would be, my Lord, a violent confiscation of the rights of the subject. It may be that those officers can justify themselves before the Committee of Inquiry or before a judicial tribunal; but for us, my Lord, to raise a presumption in their favour on our present information, as this Bill proposes to do, would be absolutely unjustifiable and a travesty of justice. I think, on the other hand, as to the persons who have issued these orders, who have exercised those acts in a transparently high handed character absolutely—I do not want to prejudge matters one way or the other, but as things stand we have to go upon certain facts—I submit to enable those officers to reap the benefit of these provisions would be to ask the people to believe that the executive Government would do anything to protect its officers whatever may be their high-handedness, and however unjustifiable may be their acts. I hope and pray that the Government will have some regard for public sentiment and reestablish itself in the confidence of the people by showing clearly that it is immaterial how high the officer may be and that justice would be done. We were told that it was under the authority of the civil power that aeroplanes were used in Gujranwala, and that the incidents which occurred on the 13th April at Amritsar, were after the civil power acknowledged its inability to enforce order. Consequently, I think, it ought to be open to the judicial tribunals to go into the question as to whether by the constitutional law of the United Kingdom or India it is open to the civil power to employ aeroplanes under such circumstances or under any circumstances. My Lord, to take protection for all those acts which have been condemned in England even during the time of the war, would, I think, be going too far even in India. I hope, therefore, that the protection will be really given only in respect of acts done after martial law had been proclaimed and not a minute before. Let those officers, if any, be brought either by the Government or by the public before judicial tribunals in the ordinary course. It is perfectly open to them to show that they acted in good faith and in a reasonable belief that they were only maintaining or restoring order and justice, that the civil power had asked them and that the civil power was justified in asking them to do so. That is a question of fact, as has been proved by constitutional writers, which has to be determined by the judicial courts, namely, the justification of any particular act done in a state of war is ultimately examinable in the ordinary courts. But in the absence of an Indemnity Act the law goes so far as to say that the justification of any act is a question which can be brought up in a civil court. When the law is so stringent in the absence of an Indemnity Act, we ought to be very careful as to how far we interfere with the common law of the land and the statutory law of the land which lays down the policy for civil and military officers. There are the Criminal Procedure Code and the Indian Penal Code; there are various other penal laws which show clearly the limits within which officers should act during peace time, during the time the civil arm is supreme. No one will venture to say that the civil arm was not supreme before the proclamations. I, therefore, submit that the Council will see their way to accept my amendment which follows logically and as a natural consequence the acceptance of the principle that an Indemnity Bill follows the enforcement of martial law. The Hon'ble Sir William Vincent has told us in the beginning of his introductory speech in substance as follows 'Martial law has been proclaimed, people have acted on the faith of that; we have proclaimed on the 14th April or some such date that support will be given to every civil and military officer in enforcing order; and acting on the strength of that proclamation we are keeping our good faith with the officers who acted and here are Hon'ble Members opposing us.' My Lord, I am not referring at all to what has been done after that promise was held out. But that promise was made only on or after the 14th April. There is another point also. Various acts committed prior to the proclamation of martial law would come within the purview of this Act, if 30th March be taken into consideration. Even taking the theory that martial law really means law which the military would enforce when the civil arm is weak or unable to maintain order, even assuming that, my submission is that these proclamations were issued for the purpose of giving notice to the people. Even taking that doctrine, my submission is that the 30th March is absolutely unjustifiable, and I hope Government will be able to accept this amendment."

The Hon'ble Sir William Vincent :—"My Lord, the Hon'ble Member now proposes that the period prescribed in this clause for the protection of officers should begin from the proclamation of martial law. If Hon'ble Members will look down the list of amendments they will see, however, that he proposes that the termination of the period during which protection should be given should be the 23rd April, a date long before our notification withdrawing martial law was issued. The date of commencement is to be postponed and the last day up to which protection is to be given is to be antedated. But, my Lord, I want to pass to very much broader objections than this to the amendment. It is one of a series of amendments intended to whittle down the whole effect of this Act. General principles were discussed in great detail in this Council lately, and there was a general consensus of opinion that the principle of the Bill should be accepted; I think there were only three or four Hon'ble members who did not take that view. In such circumstances, it is a very common move to say, 'well, if we have to pass the Bill let us make it ineffective by a succession of amendments', and the present is one of the amendments intended to effect that object. My Lord, our view is that the whole of these disturbances are one connected whole; that they began with the disturbances of the 30th March at Delhi, and from that date onwards, from time to time, it was necessary to enforce martial law in different places. There was no definite proclamation of martial law in some places at all, nor is any proclamation the essence of the matter. The real question is, when was martial law actually enforced? The Hon'ble Member is aware of the weakness of his position when he said that various quotations would be made to prove that he was incorrect. I have a number of authorities on the point here. I will cite one, a quotation from the Law Quarterly Journal: Mr. Erle Richards, Lord Justice. 'A proclamation is not in any sense essential to the exercise of these powers; it is a convenient notification to the inhabitants that the Commander has assumed control of the district but in no way affects the legality or illegality of his action'. Then I will read a joint opinion by the Attorney-General and the Solicitor-General in regard to certain disturbances which arose in Canada. 'In any district in which by reason of armed bodies of inhabitants being engaged in insurrection the ordinary course of the law cannot be maintained, we are of opinion that the Governor may, even without any proclamation, proceed to put down the rebellion by force of arms.'

"There are numerous other authorities on the same question, and the law is perfectly clear. In fact, I am not aware that martial law was at any time proclaimed in the Bombay Presidency. If it was, I have not seen any notification, I speak subject to correction. If that is so the effect would be if the Hon'ble Member's amendment were accepted, that the officers of Government in Bombay in those places in which martial law was enforced would not get any protection at all under the Bill. There were also certain districts in the Punjab in which the military authorities had to take over control when the civil authorities were not able to cope with the situation, and where martial law was enforced long before it was formally proclaimed by the Government of India. Thus, in Amritsar, the local military authorities in order to preserve peace, had to take over the situation long before or at any rate sometime before martial law was proclaimed. The Hon'ble Member went on to say 'why were the ordinary laws, the Criminal Procedure Code and the Indian Penal Code not utilized?' 'Why did these gentlemen not look up these laws and act according to them?' That, my Lord, is exactly the position that I said in the opening debate was impossible. When there is serious disorder which the civil authorities are entirely unable to deal with, an insurrection against the King, is the officer who has to quell it to run and look up the Criminal Procedure Code or the Indian Penal Code, to discover if there is a section that will protect him before he takes effective action? Such a position is absurd.

"For these reasons, my Lord, it is impossible for the Government to accept the date of the proclamation of martial law as the date from which this clause of the Bill is to protect officers for *bona fide* action."

[At this stage the Council adjourned for Lunch till 3 p.m.]

The Hon'ble Pandit Madan Mohan Malaviya :—"My Lord, the position taken up by the Hon'ble the Home Member does not come on some of us as a surprise. Hitherto we understood that an Indemnifying Bill was to be introduced in the areas where martial law had been proclaimed and because martial law had been proclaimed. But now the position taken up by the Hon'ble the Home Member is that a proclamation of martial law is not essential, and that if the military take charge of a place where there has been a disturbance, that is sufficient to bring the area in which this happened within the operation of this Bill. My Lord, it is a dangerous extension. It is meant to cover cases which could not be justified without such extension, and it is a great wrong to those who suffered in those areas where martial law had not been proclaimed.

"My Lord, it is hopeless to expect that the Government will go back upon the position taken up by the Hon'ble the Home Member, but we feel that we must enter our protest against this departure. The Hon'ble the Home Member complained that the series of amendments which have been put forward by some of us had only one object, namely, to whittle down the Bill. My Lord, when we cannot entirely prevent the passing of the Bill the next best thing that we can do, is to minimise the evil which its provisions contain, to safeguard the interests of the public as much as we can, and to object to as many provisions as are clearly objectionable, and to endeavour to put in as many safeguards as we may be able to press upon the consideration of the Government. I do not think the complaint that has been made by the Hon'ble the Home Member is justified. I hope that if the Government cannot see their way to accept this amendment, they will at any rate recognise that we have reason on our side, and that they have the votes on their side."

The Hon'ble Rao Bahadur B.N. Sarma:—"My Lord, we still hope that the Hon'ble the Home Member will confine the operation of the Bill to areas where martial law had been proclaimed. The Hon'ble Pandit Malaviya has also referred to the very great danger of extending it to areas where the civil arm was exercising its jurisdiction, although the civil officers had to call in the aid of the military for the purposes of enforcing order, it being thought that the police were not able to cope with the evil. There seems to me, my Lord, another great danger, and that is this. It means that any Local Government without coming up here under the provisions of section 71 of the Government of India Act for the purpose of asking the Government of India to frame regulations for their presidencies when the ordinary law is not sufficient for the purpose, can, by virtue of the doctrine now enunciated practically extend martial law to any area within their jurisdiction the moment they feel that the civil power is temporarily unable to cope with disorder in any town or village. I think that was never intended by the constitution. Section 71 of the Government of India Act says 'that the Local Government of any part of British India to which this section for the time being applies may propose to the Governor-General in Council to draft any regulation for the peace and good government of that part with reasons for the proposed regulations.' The Government may or may not accept this proposal; that is quite a different matter. Here Hon'ble Members will see that the Punjab Government approached the Government of India....."

The Hon'ble Sir George Lowndes:—"My Lord, I must protest again at the Hon'ble Member solemnly quoting from the Regulation section of the Government of India Act which only applies to certain territories like the North-West Frontier. It has no application whatever to the Punjab, to Bombay, to Bengal or to any of the major Provinces."

The Hon'ble Rao Bahadur B.N. Sarma:—"There was a power, I know, by which the Presidency Governments were also empowered by Statute to approach the Government of India for aid where they felt the ordinary law was insufficient. My argument does not cease to have any force even if section 71 is inapplicable to this particular case. My argument is that whether the Regulation applies to this case or not, the new doctrine that martial law can be enforced by a Governor or the head of a province and people can be handed over to the tender mercies of the military who can frame new laws, new penalties and do anything they like the moment they feel that law and order cannot be temporarily coped with the aid of the civil force alone, is entirely a wrong doctrine. My point was that the law takes note of these difficulties where the civil arm is insufficient and makes it an incumbent duty upon the military officers to help the civil. But in all these cases, prior to the actual proclamation of martial law the civil power would be responsible and the ordinary law would guide the courts in deciding the legality of the actions of men who have acted during that period. Now the constitutional writers who refer to the fundamental basis of martial law merely refer to the common basis of the power of the Crown to enforce order whether martial law is proclaimed or not. They simply say that necessity is the basis of martial law. Ordinarily, therefore, even without the proclamation of martial law the civil power has got jurisdiction to arm itself for certain purposes to quell disorders, but only so much force as is necessary should be employed. Therefore, the fact that here is a common basis for the two does not, I submit, empower the executive Government to treat the two as exactly parallel and ask that the civil or the military officers who had exercised jurisdiction are entitled to seek the protection of an Indemnifying Act even before the proclamation of martial law. I would only suggest, if there be any difficulty about the fixing of dates, the words 'the enforcement of martial law' may be used so as to cover any difficulty, but I do not think that the real point would be met. But I throw out this suggestion to the Hon'ble the Home Member, because on a previous occasion instead of the words 'proclamation of martial law' he accepted the words 'enforcement of martial law.' Of course whether the words 'enforcement of martial law' would cover a particular case will be dealt with by the Tribunals when the cases come up."

The motion was put and negatived.

The Hon'ble Sir William Vincent:—"My Lord, I move 'that in clause 2 for the words 'the commencement of this Act' the words 'the 26th of August 1919' be substituted.'

"My Lord, when I moved for leave to introduce this Bill, this clause which extended the period during which special protection was afforded to our officers up to the commencement of the Act, was the subject of justifiable criticism. Since then I have again looked up the dates on which martial law was actually proclaimed and the dates on which it was withdrawn in the different areas. The dates on which it was proclaimed vary from the 13th April to, I think, the 22nd of April. The dates on which it was withdrawn vary from the 28th May to the 28th of August. I ought to explain, however, that after the 11th of June martial law was enforced only in railway lands in the Punjab, and that it was enforced there only by reason of the military requirements during the Afghan campaign. It was then obviously of paramount importance that military operations for the transport of troops and munitions should not be impeded by any disorders on the railway or by any interruptions of communications.

"The areas of the Punjab in which martial law was at the time in force were disturbed areas, and there was considerable risk of communications being interrupted if we relaxed military control of the railways: for that reason martial law was continued in the railway areas only up to midnight of the 25th of August this year, and that date has therefore been fixed upon now as a convenient date up to which the special protection afforded to our officers should be extended."

The Hon'ble Rao Bahadur B.N. Sarma:—"If this amendment is accepted my amendments entirely fall to the ground, because the amendments I have suggested, are that the operation of this Bill should be confined to the 23rd of April. The reason why I suggested the 23rd April was that, as far as I could gather from the Press Communiques which were quoted in the book 'Punjab Disturbances,' the disturbances ceased on that date. I see that there was real trouble with regard to railway and telegraph communications, wires being cut and so on, until about the 21st of April. I pointed out on a previous occasion that both the Communiques of April 22nd and May 2nd showed that the Province had quieted down, although it may be as a matter of precaution the military were there to see that no further disturbances broke out. The following Communique was issued:—'Lahore April 22nd, situation well in hand and reports of the districts contain no disturbing items except cutting of telegraph wires near Chakki bridge, Kangra District.'

"And then a Communique of May 2nd gives a list of all the occurrences with reference to the cutting of wires and the derailment of trains and so on, and as far as I could gather, the period that this covers is up to about the 21st of April. Later on, the Communique states:—'An account will subsequently be published of injury which has occurred since 21st April, but the operations of martial law had by that date already begun to have their effect, and subsequent interruptions were comparatively few.'

"I shall proceed on the basis that martial law had this effect, even assuming for argument's sake that there were a few interruptions later on.

"I have stated already the fact that martial law can be legally enforced only so long as there was necessity therefor and not one moment longer. It would be a usurpation of absolute power, an exercise of lawless law, if it is kept one moment longer. I realise that you may have to keep the force active in order to guard against a further recurrence of events, but my submission is that that would have to be done under the ordinary law of the land, and martial law proper would cease to have operation the moment the disturbances are quelled, and that is a very important doctrine to maintain in a country like India, because the executive are not really controlled by the Legislature, and it is necessary that they should be chary of any attempt to keep these lawless laws in operation one minute more than is absolutely necessary. I submit that any action that might have been taken by the Government subsequent to that should be considered as having been done under the ordinary law of the land, that is under the civil power, and should not be brought within the jurisdiction of the military courts. It is only for that purpose that I have brought in this amendment that martial law should, as martial law, be considered to have ceased on the 23rd of April for the purposes of this Bill."

The Hon'ble Sir William Vincent:—"I am glad at last to obtain an admission from the Hon'ble Mr. Sarma that up to the 23rd of April there was serious disorder, because for sometime in this Council a definite attempt was made to make out that nothing occurred at all but a little local rioting which was not of a serious character....."

The Hon'ble Rao Bahadur B.N. Sarma:—"May I say, I did not agree with the proposition; I assume it was so."

The Hon'ble Sir William Vincent:—"The Hon'ble Member may now use the word 'assume.' What he did do was to admit the fact and it is a great advance on previous statements. The Hon'ble Member went on to suggest that, at any rate, this violent form of disorder had ceased on the 23rd April. But, my Lord, I drew attention just now to the position of the Hon'ble Member in this matter. He did not wish clause (2) to take effect from the date on which the disorder began. Then he said 'No, you must stick to the date of your proclamation.' But when it is a question of determining the period during which protection by the Act should be afforded, he will not take the date on which the notification withdrawing martial law was issued. He says, 'No, you must come back to the actual facts, irrespective of the date on which martial law was withdrawn. And I maintain there was no disorder after the 23rd.' Well I suggest to the Council that this is not reasonable. Responsibility for declaring martial law rested with the Government of India, acting on the advice of the Local Government, and I read to this Council the telegram upon which we acted. The position then of our officers was this, they were aware that martial law was in force; they were, therefore, acting under orders. Provided that they acted *bona fide* and in a reasonable belief that their action was necessary, are they to be deprived of protection because Members of this Council may say the Government continued martial law too long, or are they not entitled to plead 'We were acting on the orders of the Government as set out in notifications which had been issued in the Gazette'? I want the Council, however, again to remember that we do not claim the protection of those men if they have acted *mala fide* or improperly; it is *bona fide* action taken in a reasonable belief that it was necessary alone that is protected. Now is it much to ask the Council to protect such men for such action during a period while the Government of India themselves rightly or wrongly declared that martial law was necessary? That is the point that I want to make to the Council. My Lord, it is often assumed that directly the military authorities have quelled the open disorder and disturbances with which they are called to deal, they must at once abrogate their authority to the civil authorities. I do not know how far that is good constitutional law, but there is good authority for the proposition that the actual presence of violent disorder is not essential to the continuance of martial law, and this had been laid down by no less an authority than Pollock, when he says 'that the absence of visible disorder and the continued sittings of the court even are not conclusive evidence of the state of peace.' There is another well-known case on the point from India in which, although the courts had been open for six months, the Privy Council held that the seizure of property by the military authorities on the plea that martial law was in force, was perfectly justifiable because the war had not at the time ceased. Further, as a matter of common sense, the fact is that once you have established martial law to quell an open insurrection, it would be the height of folly, and, I think, Hon'ble Members of this Council will agree with me, it would really be the height of folly to abrogate it unless you have some reason to believe that the civil authorities could control the situation if martial law was removed. If you thought that the position was such that the military authorities would have immediately to be called in again, it would be idle to stop martial law or make over control to the civil authority. Such conduct would be doubly unwise on an occasion like the present, when we were at war with a power on the frontier in close proximity to the Punjab. The date I propose for insertion in the clause, the 26th of August 1919, is actually the date on which the last notification withdrawing martial law was issued by the Government, and that is the reason for fixing that date in the Bill." *(After the Hon'ble Sir William Vincent had finished speaking, the Hon'ble Pandit Madan Mohan Malaviya rose).*

The President:—"Order, order. The Hon'ble Member has replied."

The Hon'ble Pandit Madan Mohan Malaviya:—"I was going to ask your Lordship whether I was entitled to speak, because the Hon'ble Mr. Sarma....."

The President:—"You should have taken the opportunity of speaking immediately after the Hon'ble Mr. Sarma.

"If this amendment of Sir William Vincent's is carried, it will involve the rejection of all† amendments down to amendment No. 22."

The motion was put and agreed to.

The Hon'ble Pandit Madan Mohan Malaviya:—"My Lord, I beg to move:—

'That in clause 2 for the words 'provided that such officer or person has acred in good faith and in a reasonable belief that his action was necessary for the said purposes' the following be substituted:—

'Provided always, that the indemnity hereby granted is granted upon this supposition and condition, that all such acts, matters and things shall have been done *bona fide*, necessarily and properly, and without needless severity, in furtherance and extension of the objects for which martial law was proclaimed as aforesaid.'

"My Lord, in speaking to a similar amendment earlier in the debate, I drew attention to the fact that I have taken the language of this amendment from the Act of St. Vincent. My Lord, in this particular amendment I have introduced four words which are not to be found there, namely, 'and without needless severity.' I submit, my Lord, that it is desirable that we should substitute the

---

†**The Hon'ble Mr. Sarma :—**

18. 'That in clause 2 for the words 'and before the commencement of this Act,' the words 'up to the 23rd April, 1919', be substituted.'

The Hon'ble Mr. Sarma :—

19. '*If amendment No. 18 be rejected.* That for the words 'and before the commencement of this Act,' the words 'until the suppression of the disorders' be substituted.'

The Hon'ble Mr. Sarma :—

20. '*If amendment Nos 18 and 19 be rejected.*That in cluase 2 for the words 'and before the commencement of this Act,' the words 'during the continuance thereof,' be substituted.'

The Hon'ble Mr. Sinha :—

21. 'That in clause 2 for the words from 'on or after the 30th March' to 'this Act' the words 'during the period when martial law was in force' be substituted.'

The Hon'ble Mr. Malaviya:—

22. 'That in clause 2 for the words 'on or after the 30th of March, and before the commencement of this Act', the words 'during the continuance of martial law' be sustituted.'

amendment which I propose, in order that it might be possible for those who have suffered to have redress of their grievances. This is a measure which is being passed without the report of the Committee of Inquiry which has been appointed being laid before this Council. That imposes upon this Council the duty of more closely examining the provisions of the Bill. My Lord, if the Bill is passed as the section stands, I submit it will be very difficult for any person who has been damaged or injured by the operation of martial law to obtain a redress of his grievances, and in support of the view which I have submitted to the Council, I would invite intention to the debate that took place in the House of Lords in 1818. An Indemnity Bill was to be introduced there, but before it was introduced a Committee of Inquiry had been appointed and had reported. In introducing the Bill the Duke of Montrose claimed that it was a corollary from that which had preceded it, namely, the suspension of the Habeas Corpus Act, and he urged that an Indemnity Bill was a necessary consequence of the suspension of that Act. This is the view which has been urged by the Hon'ble the Home Member and the Hon'ble the Law Member. We have been told repeatedly that an Indemnity Bill was an inevitable consequence to the introduction of martial law. Here, my Lord, what the Premier said on the discussion which was raised by Lord Lansdowne was that:—

> 'after such a report as that presented to Their Lordships by the Committee, a Bill of Indemnity seemed to follow as a measure due in justice to those who had been entrusted with the difficult task of carrying the act of suspension into execution.

And he said:—

> 'The Government were anxious to lay all the information with respect to their conduct before the Committee of the two Houses of Parliament in order that they know how they exercised the powers entrusted to them generally and particularly, and judge from that how far they were entitled to such protection as they now came forward to apply for. They did not ask for it as a necessary consequence of the suspension of the Habeas Corpus Act, but on the ground of the belief expressed by the Committee that the powers committed by Parliament to their discretion had not been abused. That and that alone was the ground upon which they stood before Parliament and the country. The Bill did

not follow as a matter of course. The conduct of Ministers had been referred to a Committee. From the report of the Committee it appeared that all the detentions which took place under the suspension were fully warranted by circumstances and, if Their Lordships had any confidence in that report, they must in justice and in fairness grant the protection the Bill now proposed.'

"Now, my Lord, let us see how these remarks have a bearing upon the proposal before us. Here martial law was proclaimed at a time somewhere between the 13th and 15th of April. This was continued up to the 26th of August. There have been many protests, many representations to Government, that the continuance, at any rate, of martial law was not justified, and it was on that ground that one of your Hon'ble Colleagues laid down the reins of his office. Now, my Lord, the Government have recognised the wisdom, the justice, of appointing a Committee of Inquiry to consider how far these matters, the complaints, were justified or well-founded. That Committee of Inquiry has not yet met. The complaints, the allegations, to which I drew attention are to be laid before that Committee and the Committee has to make its report. Assuming that the Committee come to the conclusion that the introduction of martial law was justified, the next question for them to consider and answer would be whether its continuance was justified, and, if so, up to what period of time, because every detention of every single individual—and I understand the number is over 1,000 of those who are at present in jails....."

The Hon'ble Sir William Vincent:—"My Lord, May I rise to a point of order, to inquire whether this is relevant to the particular amendment before the Council?"

The President (to the Hon'ble Pandit):—"Will you show me how it is relevant?"

The Hon'ble Pandit Madan Mohan Malaviya:—"In this way, my Lord, very easily. It is relevant to show that the language used in this section should be as I suggest, namely, that only acts done *bona fide,* necessary and properly, and without needless severity, should be indemnified. The object of my remarks is to show to your Lordship that it is yet a question for the Committee to consider whether the continuance of martial law and the detention of so many prisoners who have been detained in jail was necessary, whether it was proper and whether it was carried out without undue severity during the period up to which this martial law existed....."

(*The Hon'ble Sir William Vincent here rose again*).

The Hon'ble Pandit Madan Mohan Malaviya:—"May I finish my remarks; I am explaining the reasons why my speech is relevant to the amendment....."

The President:—"I hope you will give me some better reason, because, at present, I am not satisfied."

The Hon'ble Pandit Madan Mohan Malaviya:—"I am giving my reasons. It is for you, my Lord, to judge whether they are right or wrong. What I submit is that there are numerous persons who have been detained and who are undergoing imprisonment. In the case of many of these persons, they desire to bring suits to test the validity of the detentions. If the indemnity is granted in the general terms in which it is proposed in the Bill before us, it will be a very difficult thing for them to have a chance of proving their case. If the words which I suggest are substituted, namely, that it is only those acts which have been done *bona fide*, necessarily and without needless severity, that it is only such acts which will be indemnified, then, I submit, they will have a better chance of having redress of their grievances. That is the reason of my amendment....."

The President:—"If you confine your remarks to the matters and things that have been done *bona fide*, necessarily and properly, and without needless severity, you will be in order, but you will not be in order if you travel outside the discussion of those words."

The Hon'ble Pandit Madan Mohan Malaviya:—"Thank you, my Lord; I shall so confine myself.

"My Lord, from the statements laid on the table by the Hon'ble Home Member the other day in answer to some of my questions, Council will have seen what a large number of persons has been kept in imprisonment, and I submit that for them it will be easier to prove that certain acts were not done *bona fide* necessarily and properly and without needless severity than it would be for them to prove that certain acts were done in good faith in a reasonable belief that those acts were necessary. For these reasons, I commend this amendment to the consideration of the Council."

The Hon'ble Sir George Lowndes:—"My Lord, this amendment has really been discussed over and over again; and I have explained why we use the words 'acts done in good faith and in a reasonable belief that they were necessary.' It is no good my explaining them any more. If I explained the intention fifty times, the Hon'ble Pandit would not understand. There is no one so deaf as he who will not hear. The Hon'ble Pandit again cited the Act of St. Vincent, which is, I think, going back to an ancient and, if I may say so, an insignificant precedent. If the Hon'ble Pandit prefers the British Statutes, let us by all means go back to the precedent of 1780 under which all acts which were done for the suppression of rebellion were to be validated. That is the formula adopted there. If the Hon'ble Pandit thinks that it has the sanction of time, I am quite willing to follow it. We have tried to put before the Council a more modern formula and a reasonable limitation of both validation and indemnity by the clause proposed in this Bill. If the Council thinks otherwise by all means let us go back to the beginning; not to the St. Vincent Act, which is hardly a worthy precedent for this Council to copy—let us go back to the British Statutes of the end of the 18th century. I have explained over and over again why I personally prefer the drafting which has been adopted in this Bill, and, I think, it is clear why the Hon'ble Pandit objects to it. I submit the Council should not do anything of the sort."

The motion was put and negatived.

The Hon'ble Rao Bahadur B. N. Sarma:—My Lord, I move that in clause 2 for the concluding words 'it is hereby discharged' the words 'the provisions of this Act shall apply thereto' be substituted.'

It is a formal amendment which I have moved, that if there be any proceeding already pending, it should be open to the plaintiff or prosecutor to show that the officer did not act in good faith and in a reasonable belief, and I do not think the Hon'ble Member intends that an action should be dismissed without giving the party an opportunity. 'If any such proceeding has been instituted before the passing of this Act' are, I think, very wide terms; and that is the reason why I have brought forward this amendment. It is a mere formal amendment."

The Hon'ble Sir George Lowndes:—"My Lord, again, I am afraid, Government are unable to accept this amendment. The plain and simple words are 'it is hereby discharged'; those are the words which have been used in the Acts which we have copied—the South Africa Acts and others. The Council may also be interested to know the wording proposed in the Indemnity Act which is either now before Parliament or will very shortly be. It is a general Indemnity Act practically for the whole Empire in respect of things done during the war. The actual words which we have adopted are to be found in this the most recent piece of drafting available. The words there used are: 'If any such proceeding has been instituted, whether before or after the passing of the Act, it shall be discharged and made void'. We only go as far as 'discharged'; we do not think it necessary to put in the words 'made void.' I am not discussing the merits of the clause. I am only pointing out that we have followed the most modern form available."

The Hon'ble Rao Bahadur B. N. Sarma:—"My Lord, if the Hon'ble the Law Member had told me that if there be any proceeding instituted it would be governed by the provisions of this Bill and that the party would be entitled to show that the officer acted in bad faith or without reasonable belief, I would have been content. There is no use telling me that there are other Acts in which similar words were employed and that we are only following the modern drafting. The question is as to what by the use of this very wide language is intended. I do not think that it was the object to have all actions discussed apart from their merits, and therefore I brought in this amendment."

The Hon'ble Sir George Lowndes:—"My Lord, may I give the Hon'ble Mr. Sarma the fullest assurance that that is the intention. It is, I think, clear that that is the meaning of the words and nothing more."

The motion was put and negatived.

The President:—"The next three amendments are identical. The first is to be moved by Mr Sarma, the second* by Mr. Malaviya the third* by Mr Sinha. The fate of the three will be decided upon the first."

The Hon'ble Rao Bahadur B. N. Sarma:—"My Lord, I move 'that in clause 3, the words from 'and all action' to the end of the clause be omitted.' I did not intend to move this amendment if my amendment about 'reasonable belief' and about limiting the operation of this Bill to the period covered by the martial law proclamations

---

* **The Hon'ble Mr. Malaviya** :—

26. 'That in clause 3 the words from 'and all action' to the end of the clause be omitted.'

The Hon'ble Mr. Sinha:—

27. 'That in clause 3 the words from 'and all action taken' to the end of the clause be omitted.'

had been accepted, because I realised that during that period this presumption in respect of acts done by officers ought to be raised, namely, that they had acted in good faith, and it would be for the other party to show that the acts were not done in good faith, and all the precedents are in favour of that proposition. I need not go over the ground again covering the period before the actual proclamations and after the actual necessity, according to some others, had ceased. We cover the incidents in Amritsar and Gujranwala and other places which we feel justified in the extension of this presumption in favour of the officers. Those are the grounds upon which I rely for asking that these words should be deleted from this clause."

The Hon'ble Pandit Madan Mohan Malaviya:—"My Lord, I will add only a few words and two opinions to what has been said by Mr. Sarma in support of this amendment. We urge that the words which we have indicated should be omitted so that the onus of proof will not be thrown upon the plaintiff or complainant, to prove that the person who assailed his honour or his liberty did not act in good faith and reasonable belief. Now, my Lord, this is, in conformity with the Statutes of Parliament and the English opinion. I will cite two weighty opinions on the question.

"When the matter was being discussed in the House of Commons, Mr. John Stuart Mill said:—

'There may be a public necessity in the case of rebellion requiring that certain acts not justified by the ordinary law of the country should be done, but these acts should be acts of suppression and not of punishment. Now a point which has not been noticed and to which I attach the highest importance is this—that in a case of public necessity those who act upon it, and do under the supposed necessity that which they would not ordinarily be justified in doing should be amenable to the laws of their country for so doing. As in the case of killing any person in self-defence so in the case of putting any person to death in defence of the country, the person who does it ought to have the onus thrown upon him of satisfying the ordinary tribunals of the country that the necessity existed.

'What therefore we say does not exist, and ought not to exist, and which if it does not exist we should do our utmost to put an end to, is the idea that any proceeding such as a declaration of martial law, can or ought to exempt those who act upon it from amenability to the laws of the country. We contend that the law of necessity, of which nobody denies the existence, would justify the executive in doing things, if no such thing as martial law had ever been heard of, and that by using the term martial law you ought not to be able to get rid of all responsibility. We demand that the officers of Government of this country should not be able to escape or get out of the region and jurisdiction of the law; but, that whatever they do, if it be against the law, they should be compelled to justify. They must show the necessity which existed, not to the satisfaction of a court-martial merely, but of the regular tribunals of the country.'

"Now, my Lord, I submit that this weighty opinion should have some value with the Government of India. This was the opinion of a philosopher, a statesman and a legislator. Let me quote to Council the opinion of a Judge, Chief Justice Cockburn. In discussing an Indemnity Act he laid down in no equivocal terms that 'It should be confined to acts honestly done in the suppression of existing rebellion and under the pressure of the most urgent necessity. The present indemnity is confined to acts done in order to suppress the insurrection and rebellion and the plea contains consequently the necessary averments that the grievances complained of were committed during the continuance of the rebellion and were used for its suppression and were reasonably and in good faith considered by the defendant to be necessary for the purpose; and it will be incumbent on the defendant to make good these averments in order to support his plea.'

'My Lord, the Bill before us would make incumbent upon the defendant to support his plea and on the plaintiff the necessity of proving that the defendant had not acted in good faith and in the reasonable belief that his action was necessary for suppressing disorders. I submit that this is without justification and it is a pity to my mind that the Hon'ble the Law Member should have gone to the Legislature of South Africa for the clause which he has inserted in the Bill. I submit that we should adhere to the views expressed by John Stuart Mill and by Chief Justice Cockburn of leaving the onus on the person on whom it naturally and reasonably lies. Who can give evidence? The man who pleads good faith. Who can say he had a reasonable belief in a particular thing? The man who had that belief. Thus you are asking another man whom this person has assaulted or injured to give proof of the non-existence of good faith; of the non-existence of a reasonable belief. You are putting the cart before the horse; you are doing an injustice to those men who are seeking redress. I will quote the words of Lord Holland in a debate in 1818, regarding the suppression of disorder—

'After having mangled the limbs of a man without trial and without proof of guilt it was a horrible crime to deny him redress by passing an Act to protect his persecutor.'

"The Government, my Lord, are throwing upon the plaintiff the burden of proving what it is not reasonably possible for him to do."

The Hon'ble Mr. Saohchidananda Sinha:—"I should like to add a word in support of this amendment. I think it will be hard on the plaintiff or the prosecutor to have to prove his case, if the clause stands as it is. The Hon'ble the Law Member said the other day that in ordinary criminal cases the burden of proof is cast on the prosecutor. This is certainly true. But he will agree with me when I say that in criminal cases the prosecutor is discharged from responsibility when he has made out a *prima facie* case. When an accused person is put on his defence then the onus is shifted to him and he must then bring his conduct within the purview of any exception of the law. Similarly, I submit that to hold the plaintiff responsible to prove not only the want of good faith but also of the reasonableness of belief in the mind of the defendant would be certainly to place upon him a burden that he cannot possibly discharge."

The Hon'ble Mr. Shafi:—"My Lord, the amendment moved by my Hon'ble friends, everyone of whom belongs to the legal profession, raises a question of law of considerable importance and, with your permission, I propose to deal with it from the strictly legal point of view. At the very outset I wish to emphasize the fact that, in order to arrive at a correct conclussion with reference to this question, it is essential for Hon'ble Members to bear in mind what clause 3 exactly enacts. Now, even a cursory analysis of this clause will make it clear that it can be divided into two parts. The first portion of this clause relates to the evidential character of the Secretary's certificate in connection with the first issue in such cases, i.e., whether the action was performed under the orders of an officer of the Government. With reference to this portion of the clause, no

Hon'ble Member has raised any objection whatever, and I take it that this portion of the clause is acceptable to everyone of them. The clause then proceeds:—'and all action taken for the aforesaid purposes shall be deemed to have been taken in good faith and in reasonable belief that it was necessary therefor unless the contrary is proved.' In other words, the onus of proof of absence of good faith and of a reasonable belief will be on the plaintiff or prosecutor, as the case may be. This being so, the question arises whether the position which is embodied in this clause is a novel one, incapable of being supported either by general principles or by precedent, or is it a position which is justified by general principles as well as by authority. Now, my Lord, in the very remarkable address delivered by him the other day when the Hon'ble the Law Member made a comprehensive survey of the constitutional aspect of martial law, he cited precedent after precedent from various countries within the British Empire from which it was perfectly clear that whenever and wherever martial law had been introduced, it had invariably been followed by an Indemnity Act. Hon'ble Members will remember that he cited the corresponding clauses in these Indemnity Acts in order to show that in seeking to enact clause 3 we were not making any new departure. In ordinary circumstances a reference to that speech would have been quite sufficient to meet the situation, but on this occasion I propose, with your Excellency's permission, to go a little further in order to established three propositions. The first of these propositions is that the position which is enacted in the second portion of this clause is one which already finds place in more than one of the Acts which have been passed by the Indian Legislature; the second is that it is in perfect consonance with the statutory rules of evidence as obtaining in this country, and the third proposition is that it is justified by judicial authority. Now, turning to the first proposition, as far back as the year 1850, an Act was passed by the Indian Legislature in order to protect Judicial officers in respect of acts which may have been done without jurisdiction but in good faith, Act No. XVIII of 1850. To section 1 of that Act I beg your Excellency's permission to refer. This is what is laid down—

> 'No Judge, Magistrate, Justice of the Peace, Collector or other person acting judicially shall be liable to be sued in any Civil Court for any act done or ordered to be done by him in the discharge of his judicial duty whether or not within the limits of his jurisdiction; provided that he at the time in

good faith believed himself to have jurisdiction to do or order the act complained of.'

"Now, my Lord, in a leading case on this section their Lordships of the Privy Council in a judgment reported in 2, Moore's Indian Appeals, at page 293, laid down the following principle. I am afraid I must correct myself. This rule was not based on this particular section, but was based on the corresponding section in 21, Geo. III, cap. 70, sec. 24. Their Lordships held that the section protectiong the Provincial Magistrate in India from actions for any wrong or injury done by them in the exercise of their judicial offices does not. confer unlimited protection, but places them on the same footing as those in English Courts by a similar jurisdiction and only gives them an exemption from liability when acting *bona fide* in cases in which they have mistakenly acted without jurisdiction. Trespass will not lie against a judge for acting judicially but without jurisdiction unless he knew or had the means of knowing of the effect of jurisdiction, but now mark what follows 'and it lies upon the plaintiff in every such case to prove that fact.'

"Now, my Lord, the Hon'ble Pandit thought it was very extraordinary that the onus of proving the absence of good faith should be placed upon a plaintiff in a case such as this. Your Lordship will see that this is exactly what their Lordships of the Privy Council laid down in this ruling, *i.e.* that it will be for the plaintiff to prove that the Magistrate acted otherwise than in good faith in cases of this description.

"Turning now to section 43 of the Police Act, No. V of 1861, it enacts as follows :—

'When any action or prosecution shall be brought or any proceedings held against any police officer for any act done by him in such capacity, it shall be lawful for him to plead that such act was done by him under the authority of a warrant issued by a Magistrate. Such plea shall be proved by the production of the warrant directing, and purporting to be signed by such Magistrate and the defendant shall thereupon be entitled to a decree in his favour.'

"That is to say, under this enactment the mere production of the warrant directing the police officer to do a certain thing will entitle him to a verdict in his favour and a suit against him shall be dismissed.

"Now, your Lordship will see that the provision which I have just read out is analogous to the first part of clause 3, and if we had stopped at the end of the first part, we would have been perfectly justified in doing so, because there is the precedent of the Police Act in its favour; but in the present enactment, we do not stop there; we go on to say that the act must have been done in good faith and so on. Therefore, it is perfectly clear that the present Act is justified by the precedent of the Police Act also.

"Turning, my Lord, to the Statutory Rules of Evidence as obtaining in India, it seems to me that it is unquestionable that the onus of proof as laid down in the clause under discussion is in perfect consonance with the provisions of the Evidence Act. Let me in this connection invite the attention of the Council to two facts. The proceedings instituted by the person against whom action has been taken will either be criminal or civil. Now in criminal cases, it is one of the fundamental principles of criminal administration in all civilised countries, that the accused must be presumed to be innocent until his guilt is established by the prosecutor so that the onus of proof lies in every criminal case on the prosecutor to establish the guilt of the accused. No authority is required for this A. B. C. of Criminal Law, but if the Hon'ble Pandit who, I believe, has given up practice for a large number of years, requires an authority, I will only mention section 101 of the Indian Evidence Act and invite his attention to illustration A below that section :—

> 'A desires a court to give judgment that B shall be punished for a crime which A says B has committed. A must prove that B has committed the crime.'

And the onus of proof lies on the prosecutor.

"Now, my Lord, turning to cases of civil preceedings, section 102 of the Indian Evidence Act enacts as follows :—

> 'The burden of proof in a suit or proceeding lies on that person who would fail if no evidence at all were given on either side.'

"That is the general principle laid down in the Indian Evidence Act regarding the question of onus of proof. Now if in a civil suit a plaintiff were to come into court and ask for damages against the defendant officer of Government on the ground of certain action done by that officer, it is obvious that if no evidence were produced on either side, it is the plaintiff who must fail; his suit would naturally be dismissed if no evidence is produced on either side. And may I remind my three learned friends that this question is really concluded by authority. The case, which under these circumstances will be instituted, will be of the class of cases which are characterised as suits for damages for malicious prosecutions. It has been laid down by their Lordships of the Privy Council and by all the High Courts that even in cases where an accused person has been discharged or acquitted, whether in the original court or on appeal, when that person, in his own turn, comes into a civil court and asks for damages for malicious prosecution as against the prosecutor, he must, in spite of his discharge by the Criminal Court, establish three propositions. Firstly, that he was innocent of the crime with which he was charged, secondly, that the prosecution was malicious, and thirdly, and this is the most important point to which I wish to invite the attention of the Council, it is for the plaintiff to prove absence of reasonable and proper cause on the part of the defendant. That rule is obviously analogous to the rule which is embodied in the proposed clause. I need not cite in support of this position a long string of authority which can be cited. It is sufficient for me to invite attention to only two leading authorities on this position. The Privy Council judgment to Indian Law Reports, 25, Bombay, 322, Judgment by Lord MacNaughton, and the Calcutta High Court Judgment reported in Indian Law Reports, 28, Cal. 591, Judgment of Sir Francis Maclean, Chief Justice. Therefore, my Lord, I submit that, on the ground of judicial authority, on the ground of precedent, on the ground of statutory rules of evidence, the onus is rightly placed on the plaintiff or the prosecutor in this clause when he comes into court either claiming damages or charging the accused person with an offence under the criminal law of the land, and, I submit, therefore that the principle of onus laid down in this clause is not only not extraordinary, but is the rule which already prevails, and in consequence, we are not enacting anything new."

The Hon'ble Sir George Lowndes —"My Lord, this is not an amendment which Government can accept, and I am in some difficulty in dealing with it. My Hon'ble friend Mr. Sarma told the Council that he was willing to accept the position that it should be assumed that acts were done in good faith and were necessary until the contrary is proved in all cases of what I would call statutory law. But my Hon'ble friend would not apply the same rule to cases under non-statutory martial law. I am in a difficulty as to this, as

I do not understand his differentiation between the two. Then came the Hon'ble Pandit, who would not accept it at all. This is a case in which I am afraid the Vincent Act did not help the Hon'ble Pandit, and therefore we did not hear anything about it. The Hon'ble Pandit's argument was based on a passage which, I think, he quoted from a newspaper called the *Servant of India* referring to an argument by Chief Justice Cockburn, not as a Judge, I understand, but in a discussion on some Indemnity Bill of which the Hon'ble Member did not give us any particulars. As far as I know, an Indemnity Bill on the lines of Lord Cockburn's argument was never passed by Parliament....."

The Hon'ble Pandit Madan Mohan Malaviya :—"It was as a Judge that that remark was made by Lord Cockburn."

The Hon'ble Sir George Lowndes :—"I can carry it no further than the narrative in the *Servant of India* which I have before me. It refers to a remark by Lord Cockburn in discussing an Indemnity Bill. I know no more about it, nor, I think, does the Hon'ble Pandit.

The Hon'ble Pandit Madan Mohan Malaviya :—"May I mention that it will be found in 4 Queen's Bench Division, which is where I think that case was reported?"

The Hon'ble Sir George Lowndes :—"Again I say that, so far I know such an Indemnity Bill was never passed by Parliament. It was apparently a suggestion by an eminent authority as to what should be put into an Indemnity Bill, but the suggestion does not appear to have been carried into effect.

"I think the Council may be interested to hear a relevant clause of the general Indemnity Bill which is, I believe, now before Parliament.

"The clause provides, as our Bill does, for certificates that acts were done under authority and goes on to say that 'any such act, matter or thing done by or under the authority of such person shall be deemed to have been done in good faith unless the contrary is proved.'

"That is one of the terms of the Imperial Bill now before Parliament, and our clause follows it very closely."

The Hon'ble Mr. Rao Bahadur B. N. Sarma :—"My Lord, my Hon'ble friend Mr. Shafi has obliged us by discoursing upon the rules of evidence and upon the previous history of enactments with regard to the onus of proof. I do not think anybody here need be told that the plantiff or the prosecutor ought ordinarily to prove his case, that the actions of the accused or defendant infringe upon some legal right, some rule of law. That he has to do. But these general dicta are a little beside the point. What we are now concerned with here is that admittedly certain actions are in violation of the ordinary law of the land. Admitting that, the question is whether we are to give protection to officers violating the law on the ground that their acts are to be presumed to have been done in good faith for the purpose of carrying out the object of martial law. That is the real point. Therefore, in the absence of an Indemnity Bill like this, the onus would really lie upon the person pleading good faith in defence. I will only quote one passage—'A person who under martial law imprisons or kills British subjects in India must if he is to escape imprisonment, justify his conduct by proving its necessity.'

"Here what we say is, though as a matter of fact the act may not be necessary, we shall presume that the officer believed it to be necessary, and therefore we shall exempt him from punishment. Therefore I do not see how Mr. Shafi's remarks will help us. The question is are we as a Legislature to raise this presumption in favour of all acts, or only some or in favour of no acts? I took an intermediate position. It was necessary under the circumstances in which this Bill was brought in for Hon'ble Members to contend really that, in the absence of a clear proof of necessity, the onus should not be on the plaintiff, but even to an intermediate position objection has been taken by the Hon'ble Sir George Lowndes. Here we have two classes of cases; one class, in which martial law has been proclaimed and in respect of which there is some doubt. Then we have another to which the ordinary law should be applied and to protect which would be a violation of the constitution. Having regard to the facts which have been so far disclosed it would be a travesty of justice to presume good faith and reasonable belief, in favour of certain officers in respect of some of the incidents which occurred before the 14th and the 16th April, 1919. I suggested that therefore no presumption should be raised in respect of acts done before the proclamation of martial law, and after the necessity therefore had ceased in the eye of the law. Of course here we are not arguing before Judges on the question of presumptions and technicalities, we are arguing whether the course suggested by the Government is expedient; whether it is politically right, whether it would not be a dangerous precedent, when we know as a matter of fact that those presumptions are not justifiable in many cases as far as our present information goes."

The motion was put and negatived.

The Hon'ble Rao Bahadur B. N. Sarma :—"My Lord, I move that after the words 'and all action taken' in clause 3 the following be inserted:—'after the proclamation of martial law therein and during the continuance thereof.' I have really stated all my reasons with reference to this point in dealing with the previous amendment. I shall therefore not weary the Council by repeating them. I respectfully submit that a distinction must be drawn between acts committed before the proclamation of martial law and after its proclamation; and, I think, there would be grave disaffection felt by the public if Government should try to shield acts which *prima facie* must be assumed to be guilty."

The Hon'ble Sir William Vincent :—"My Lord, I have really nothing to add to what I have already said on this subject. I have explained that martial law was enforced before it was formally proclaimed in certain areas."

The motion was put and negatived.

The Hon'ble Pandit Madan Mohan Malaviya :—"My Lord, I beg to move 'that in clause 3 for the words from 'and all action' to the end of the clause the following be substituted :—

> 'and that every act, matter and thing shall be presumed to have been done, *bona fide*, necessarily and properly, until the contrary shall be made to appear by the party complaining.'"

The Hon'ble Sir George Lowndes :—"I think there is nothing more to be said on this point, and I shall not weary the Council by repeating my arguments."

The motion was put and negatived.

The Hon'ble Rao Bahadur B. N. Sarma :—"My Lord, I ask for the omission of clause 4. Clause 4 runs thus :—

> 'Every person confined under and by virtue of any sentence passed by a court or other authority constituted or appointed under martial law and acting in a judicial capacity shall be deemed to have been lawfully confined and shall continue liable to confinement until the expiration of such sentence, or until released by the Governor-General in Council or otherwise discharged by lawful authority.'

"Of course this is partly governed by clause 6, which says:—

"Nothing in this Act shall—

(*a*) apply to any sentence passed or punishment inflicted by or under the orders of any Commission appointed under the Martial Law Ordinance, 1919, or

(*b*) be deemed to bar a full and unqualified exercise of His Majesty's pleasure in receiving or rejecting appeals to His Majesty in Council or to affect any question or matter to be decided therein.'

"Therefore, one class of cases really goes out, namely, those that are covered by the judgments of the Commissions appointed under the Martial Law Ordinances. I dealt at some length before with my objections to this part of the Bill and I shall not repeat them again. I shall try to summarise the various points on which I based my argument in asking the Council not to accept these convictions and sentences as being right and as deserving of confirmation. The point that was made by the Hon'ble the Home Member for bringing in a clause of this description was that *prima facie,* these sentences might, after martial law ceased, be considered to be *ultra vires* and without jurisdiction. That, therefore, many persons might have to be released, and, inasmuch as inconvenient results would follow, an enactment of this description is absolutely necessary in the interests of peace and order. Well, the answer to that is twofold. First of all, you might bring up those offenders who the Government think are really guilty and deserving of further detention before the ordinary courts. The only question would be one of expense. They may be re-arrested, and put in jail pending trial, and the interests of peace and order would not suffer in the slightest degree. The only question would be as to whether public time and public money would not be wasted by pursuing such a course. Put shortly the point is whether, on the balance of convenience, we are to confirm these convictions following precedents, or, having regard to the special methods employed in the Punjab, we should insist upon the Government bringing up the cases again wholly or partially. Hon'ble Members will see that I have got another amendment to the effect, that, at any rate in cases not covered by the Indian Penal Code or any special or local law this clause should not be applied. The objections; my Lord, are these. Assume that there was a necessity for martial law. According to many of us that necessity began, if at all, on the 14th or 16th and ceased about the 23rd. If the above view be correct, it was wrong both on principle and the dictates of sound policy for the Government to have established tribunals or passed any Ordinance on the 21st for the purpose of dealing with the disturbances. The questions as to the interpretation and validity of these Ordinances, Nos. I and IV, how far they are applicable and as to whether they are applicable in cases governed by the Bengal Regulation only, are really before the Privy Council, but I submit on the question before the Legislative Council we are not hampered by considerations which might restrict the action of the Privy Council or of any duly constituted authority. The question, my Lord, is, was there any reason for the ordinary courts of the land not trying these offenders, and if special tribunals were rightly established, their not trying the offenders with the ordinary procedure observed, at any rate after the 21st? If Hon'ble Members turn to the statement of trials by summary courts and area officers in the districts of Lahore, Amritsar, Gujranwala, Gujrat and Lyallpur, Hon'ble Members will find that most if not all of these convictions were late in April, and in May, June, July, and on later dates. It may be argued that martial law cannot be said to be in force when the ordinary courts are sitting for administering the law, and all writers have held that that is one of the criteria. The judicial tribunals in the Punjab were administering justice ordinarily without any interference, I take it, after the 21st. If they were administering the law after the 21st or the 23rd, was there any necessity for depriving the citizens of the Punjab of the protection of the procedure which was guaranteed to them by the Legislature deliberately in enacting the Criminal Procedure Code and other laws? My submission, therefore, is that there was a violation of the fundamental principle of jurisprudence and violation of the protection given by the Legislature, when courts were constituted which could set at naught the ordinary procedure. This is my first and strong objection to our ratifying these convictions. Of course, if there was a state of war, if it was absolutely impossible for any court to sit and try cases, then certainly it would have been foolish on my part to say that the strict procedure of the Criminal Procedure Code should be adhered to. Necessity knows no law, and if the ordinary law courts cannot administer the law, there is no use of complaining that they did not. But here that was not the state of things. The courts were sitting, the courts were administering justice; there was absolutely nothing, therefore, to justify the depriving the citizens of the protection of the ordinary procedure. It is true that courts of three Judges have been appointed, but the ordinary right of appeal has been taken away. That is my second objection.

"There is a third objection, my Lord, and that is this. As things stand, in some cases the evidence was not clearly recorded; in other cases there are no clear judgments, so that it is absolutely impossible in a large number of cases—I will not say in all—for the Legislative Council, the Government or any Judges who may be appointed, to consider as to whether these decisions were rightly come to. There can be no scrurtiny, and therefore I submit as a matter of principle that there should be no confirmation of these sentences.

"Then, my Lord, there is another ground, and a stronger one. These martial law officers have issued various regulations the enforcement of which might or might not be justifiable during actual rebellion or the suppression thereof. But, I submit; it would not do for the Legislature sitting here deliberately to confirm sentences under martial law orders based on principles opposed to the ordinary notions of civilisation. The number of regulations apart from notices framed by these various officers and prescribing penalties was, I think, 15. Regulation 16 runs thus :—'Any person who contravenes any of the foregoing regulations shall be liable to trial by an officer authorised to dispose of an offence summarily under martial law, and such officer may sentence the offender to imprisonment, rigorous or simple, which may extend to two years or to fine not exceeding one thousand rupees or with both ..... and may also inflict whipping in addition to or in lieu of any other punishment which he is empowered to inflict.' I need hardly say that failure to *salaam* a European, discourtesy to a European officer and such like things had been made offences either by notice or by regulation. Therefore the point is that if by clause 3 you confirm the conviction—I know it has been confined only to cases where persons have been confined—if you confirm the conviction you necessarily ratify the legality of a provision which could inflict the punishment of whipping and other punishment upon any person guilty of any infraction of martial law. We are grateful to the Hon'ble the Home Member for confining clause 3 to cases of imprisoned persons, but I would ask him to see whether we are not, as a matter of fact, in confirming the validity of these convictions, really ratifying Regulation 16 covering them all and convictions passed under regulations which cannot, I think, be ratified by any Legislature. It may be that some of the regulations are perfectly unobjectionable; but here the officers in command went and multiplied martial law offences, created offences which were not known to the law of the land, and under a comprehensive code of punishments a person could be whipped and imprisoned for any offence and in confirming the rule which inflicts the penalty you validate that rule; that is my real difficulty. When the question of the amendment of the Army Act was under the consideration of this Council, I sought to move an amendment that the punishment of whipping should be abolished. His Excellency the Commander-in-Chief was so good as to sympathise with the object of my amendment .....”

The Hon'ble Sir George Lowndes :—“I rise to a point of order. I ask whether these remarks have anything to do with the clause of the Bill to which the Hon'ble Member has moved an amendment? It does not deal with convictions or the nature of the punishment; it only confirms sentences of confinement and nothing else.”

The Hon'ble Rao Bahadur B. N. Sarma :—“That is my real difficulty and I think that is no sufficient answer to my question. I find that in case No. 159 a person was thrashed and he was also remanded.....”

The Hon'ble Sir William Vincent :—“May I explain, my Lord, that this clause has nothing whatever to do with any sentence of whipping at all? I submit that the Hon'ble Member is out of order in attempting to create prejudice by bringing up this question of whipping.”

The President :—“The Hon'ble Member must confine himself to the clause he asks this Council to delete.”

The Hon'ble Rao Bahadur B. N. Sarma :—“No one would be more glad if it were possible.....”

The President :—“It is certainly possible.”

The Hon'ble Rao Bahadur B. N. Sarma :—“I shall then treat it as possible, because I take it that both the Hon'ble the Law Member and the Home Member do not want to uphold the legality of that rule. It may be legal or it may be illegal, that was just the point I was driving at. My real difficulty was that you would be indirectly ratifying that rule inasmuch as there were cases in which persons were remanded to custody and the punishment of whipping to which

I was alluding is provided for in the general penal clause. I know that any observation made by any Hon'ble Member in the course of the discussion would be absolutely irrelevant for the purpose of interpreting the Act when it comes up before the law courts; but I do not think that there is much use carrying the discussion further on this point.

"Then, my Lord, apart from that clause I would ask this Council to bear in mind that various offences had been created, such as selling foodstuffs, milk, etc., above controlled rates and so on, punishable in the same manner, and the preamble (paragraph 3.) was not limited in its operation as is clause 4 of the Bill. Of course it may be said that the operative part of an act is the thing that matters, and it is a perfectly sound argument; but I know the preamble is sometimes used in interpreting an Act. The preamble says—

> 'Whereas certain persons have been convicted by courts and other authorities constituted or appointed under martial law, and it is expedient to confirm and provide for the continuance of sentences passed by such courts or authorities.'

"It is very general; and, therefore, there is danger in wide interpretation of this clause and Regulation 16. I am glad to be told at any rate that no such use would be made of it and that it was not intended to cover that part of the Regulation which provides for the punishment of whipping, etc. I shall proceed, my Lord, on that assumption. Then the question is as to the various offences not known to the law which had been created by these martial law orders, and the various terms of imprisonment ranging up to two years, etc., inflicted under these. My submission is, would it be right for us as a Legislature to confirm these convictions without knowing more, especially when we know as a matter of fact that all the materials are not before anybody on which the rightness and appropriateness of the decisions may be examined. I, therefore, submit that this clause should be eliminated, and the ordinary procedure should be resorted to."

The Hon'ble Sir William Vincent :—"My Lord, I hope Hon'ble Members will not conclude from what the Hon'ble Mr. Sarma has said, that this clause involves the admission of the principles to which he has referred. It does not. He referred, for instance, to the sentences of whipping awarded by the military authorities for certain offences. Whatever may be the merits or demerits of such a form of punishment, every Member who reads the clause which is now under discussion will see that there is no reference in it to whipping at all, and that it does not justify such sentences. I suggest further that the introduction of the racial question and the mention of this form of punishment were made in order to create a prejudice in the minds of the Council. I can conceive of no other reason for the mention of these matters. My Lord, I have already in my opening speech explained to the best of my ability why we cannot accept this amendment. When martial law is introduced in a particular area, it is clearly necessary for the military authorities to have some means of enforcing their orders, of punishing summarily and speedily crimes directly connected with the disturbances and breaches of military regulations. I think that is a proposition that will be evident to everybody, and as a matter of fact. I believe that when martial law is enforced the normal procedure is to constitute some form of summary courts; if indeed such courts were not constituted, there would be no authority whatever which could enforce obedience of martial law regulations. Otherwise if the offender were sent to the civil courts they would say 'this is not an offence under the civil law or one of which we can take any cognizance whatever.' Many of the men sentenced by these summary courts were, as I explained to the Council before, convicted of very heinous crimes, such offences as arson, the possession of stolen property, the destruction of railway lines, etc. I am very anxious not to repeat what I have said already. A large number, about 90 per cent I believe —but I will not guarantee that statement—were tried before 1st class magistrates whose business it is normally to try similar offences. I have already given an undertaking to this Council, further—and I have already addressed the Punjab Government on the subject—that we will have the sentences of all these men revised by two High Court Judges. Further, those who have been convicted of offences which are really a violation of military regulations only, will be released by Government, provided that the facts found by the court are not such as to justify a conviction for an offence punishable under the ordinary law. I do not know if I make myself quite clear. There are a certain number of offenders who have been definitely convicted under various sections of the Indian Penal Code. There is another class of offenders who have been convicted of breaches of military regulations. In some of the latter cases the facts found would justify the conviction of these men under the ordinary criminal law. We have cases, for instance, of extortion; one man was convicted of extorting money from a townsman on threat of giving certain information to the Police. This is a conviction that might well have been had under section 384. There is another case of indecent assault on a woman in which the conviction was recorded as a breach of military regulations; then we have cases of injuries done to railways and telegraphs. In such cases although the convictions have been recorded as breaches of military regulations, these records will only be revised in the ordinary way. Where, however, the offence consists of violation of military regulations and the facts found do not constitute an offence under the ordinary law it is the intention of the Government—I gave the undertaking before and I give it again—to release the men immediately. I hope that will go some way towards Mr. Sarma. But the amendment he proposes goes a great deal further than this, and would mean that none of these sentences of imprisonment should be validated at all. My Lord, I do not know how the military Commander can do his duty without these sentences. If anybody is whipped a large section of public at once protests; 'what a scandal, what a barbrous thing?'

"What then is to be done with these offenders if they are not to be imprisoned or whipped? Fining would not meet the circumstances of many cases. I have explained that Summary Courts were absolutely necessary and that proceedings in the ordinary courts would in cases in which speedy measures were necessary be an impossibility. Where martial law has been in force it has been the practice to constitute these court, and it has been the practice to validate the sentences and the normal procedure to go very much further than the Bill which we have under consideration. Here, for instance, is the South Africa Act of 1915 which has been constantly quoted. It runs:—

> 'The several courts martial and military and special tribunals constituted and convened by or on behalf of the Government or its officers during the period aforesaid for the trial and punishment of persons guilty of treasonable, seditious or rebellious conduct or of persons subject to military law shall be deemed to have been constituted in accordance with law, and the several sentences...are hereby confirmed.'

And goes on:—

> 'Every person confined in any prison, gaol, lock-up, or in any other place whatsoever under and by virtue of any such sentence aforesaid shall continue liable to be confined therein.'

"The same provisons will be found in both the older South Africa Acts. In one of them there is a definite reference to offences which really consist of a breach of military regulations, the very class of offences to which the Hon'ble Member made a reference. Similarly, the Imperial Bill, which has now been quoted, says:—

'Any sentence passed, judgment given or order made by any military court (other than a court-martial constituted in pursuance of any Statute) in connection with the present war or by any court established for the administration of justice within any territory in the occupation of any of His Majesty's forces during such occupation or after such occupation has determined until the Court has been abolished or superseded by such lawfully constituted authority as may hereafter be established for the administration of such territory shall be deemed to be and always to have been valid.'

In asking the Council to adopt this clause we are not therefore departing from the normal procedure. It was, however, suggested in another part of the argument of the Hon'ble Mr. Sarma, if I understood him aright, the point raised was that the ordinary courts were sitting and it was therefore improper to resort to summary courts—....."

The Hon'ble Rao Bahadur B.N. Sarma:—"You could for the sake of the convenience of the administration multiply the officers, but the procedure would be the ordinary one."

The Hon'ble Sir William Vincent:—"That is much the same thing, but in any case wherever military courts of this character have been constituted, it has been the universal practice. I think, to adopt a summary form of procedure. In fact this is obviously necessary if justice is to be administerted quickly. In many cases where martial law has been established in the past, we know also that the Civil Courts have sat for the trial of ordinary offences concurrently with Military Courts specially constituted for the trial of offences connected with these disturbances. Finally, before I sit down, I want to point out two results of the adoption of this amendment. One is that Government would have to release a very large number of criminals, dangerous criminals, on to the country. That would be extremely unwise; and the second result would be that Council would deliberately put the Government in this position, that they would be liable to actions for wrongful imprisonment brought by a number of men who have done their best to destroy the safety of the State in a time of grave peril. That, I hope, this Council would not agree to."

The Hon'ble Rao Bahadur B.N. Sarma:—"My Lord, I am thankful to the Hon'ble the Home Member for his promise to release persons who were merely guilty of infraction of martial law regulations, and whose cases could not have been brought up under the criminal laws of the land. I think the people must be satisfied with that promise. But, my Lord, with regard to the question as to what effect it would have on public peace if a large number of people are released, I have already answered that; they may be brought before the ordinary courts. With regard to the cases of imprisonment, I still submit there is absolutely no information whatsoever as to why the ordinary courts were not allowed to proceed or the ordinary procedure was not followed, beyond the answer that military officers could not have done it. My reply to it, my Lord, is, that the courts specially constituted to try offences only on the ground of necessity might have followed the regular forms and should have followed the form in a time of peace when there was actually no rebellion. In the interests, my Lord, of persons who may have wrongly suffered as well as of the future, I think I must press this amendment."

The motion was put and negatived.

The Hon'ble Rao Bahadur B.N. Sarma:—"My Lord, having regard to the promise we have received. I shall not press the other two* amendments on the agenda, and I beg leave to withdraw them."

The motions were by leave withdrawn.

The Hon'ble Mr. Sachchidananda Sinha:—"My Lord, I propose 'that to clause 5 the following be added:—

'Such assessment by the said Judicial Officer shall be made pursuant to an inquiry conducted in the manner, so far as possible, laid down for the trial of suits in the Code of Civil Procedure.'

---

* **The Hon'ble Mr. Sarma:**—

32. '*That if amendment No. 31 be rejected* the words 'and shall continue liable to confinement until the expiration of such sentence or until released by the Governor-General in Council or otherwise discharged by lawful authority' in clause 4 be omitted.'

33. 'That to clause 4 the following be added:—

'Provided that no person shall continue liable to confinement after the date of commencement of this Act unless he shall have been convicted and sentenced for some offence under the Indian Penal Code or some special or local law in force before the establishment of martial law'

'An appeal shall lie to the High Court against such order of assessment in the manner provided for appeals from orders in the Code of Civil Procedure, the order passed by the High Court being final.'

"My Lord, this amendment does not touch at all even the fringe of the substantive provisions of the Bill. It only provides a machinery for the assessment being made, and as there is no provision of that character in this Bill, I think, my Lord, this amendment might be adopted with a view to provide a machinery for the purpose."

The Hon'ble Sir William Vincent:—"My Lord, the intention of the clause is to provide a summary remedy for persons who might consider themselves aggrieved owing to their properties having been commandeered by the military authorities. The Bill does not, as I understand, prevent a regular suit from being brought. Our intention is merely to provide a convenient remedy for the assessment of damages, and any one may seek redress in a law court. In those circumstances, if any person wishes to go to a law court and have a full trial, he may do so, but we do not think that it is desirable to prescribe the lengthy procedure of the Civil Court for an officer of the kind proposed. We do not either think it necessary to allow an appeal from proceedings of this character."

The Hon'ble Mr. Sachchidananda Sinha:—"My Lord, with regard to that part of the question which refers to appeals, I am prepared to withdraw it. But I think there should be some procedure laid down, and I have added the words 'so far as possible.' I do not, therefore, insist upon the trial being conducted in strict accordance with the Civil Procedure Code. I am prepared to withdraw the second clause about the appeal, to which the Hon'ble the Home Member objects."

The motion was put and negatived.

The President:—"I should have stated after Mr. Sarma withdrew his amendments just now, that amendment* No. 10 which stood on the agenda until these amendments were disposed of was of course dropped. It is consequential."

The Hon'ble Sir William Vincent:—"My Lord, may I point out that the same position arises with regard to an amendment of Mr. Sinha also?"

---

* 10. 'That to paragraph 3 of the preamble the following be added 'in certain cases and subject to the limitations specified herein below.'

The Hon'ble Rao Bahadur B.N. Sarma:—"My Lord, I submit that this should be accepted, because it refers to certain cases only. It refers to certain cases and subject to certain limitations only, and those words I would like to be added to paragraph 3 of the preamble."

The Hon'ble Sir William Vincent:—"If the Hon'ble Member wishes to move the amendment, I have no objection."

The President:—(To Rao Bahadur B.N. Sarma) "You move No. 10."

The Hon'ble Rao Bahadur B.N. Sarma:—"I think that will clear the position."

The President:—"Yes, Mr. Sarma is moving his amendment No. 10 which was held up until the other two amendments 32 and 33† were disposed of."

The Hon'ble Rao Bahadur B.N. Sarma:—"My Lord, the Act deals with only certain cases, and it imposes certain limitations. Clause 4 deals with the cases only of persons who were actually confined in prison, and in order to bring it into conformity with the other provisions, I propose that to paragraph 3 of the preamble the words 'in certain cases and subject to the limitations specified herein below' be added. I therefore hope that this amendment will be accepted."

The Hon'ble Sir William Vincent:—"My Lord, I may say at once that we have no objection whatever to the introduction of the words suggested by the Hon'ble Member if the insertion will please him, but they really do not make any difference in the effect of the Bill. As it will apparently gratify the Hon'ble Member, I am prepared to accept an amendment, substituting the words 'certain sentences' for the words 'sentences'."

The Hon'ble Rao Bahadur B.N. Sarma:—"It is not a matter of gratification, My Lord, but it is a question of some importance and I am glad that the Hon'ble the Home Member has accepted a modified form of my amendment."

The amended motion was put and agreed to.

The Hon'ble Pandit Madan Mohan Malaviya:—"My Lord, I beg to move 'that in clause 6, sub-clause (b) be omitted and the said sub-clause be inserted as a new clause 7, and that to the said new clause 7 the following be added:—

---

† Vide page 890.

'And any order made by His Majesty in Council on any appeal presented by any individual or individuals against any conviction or sentence passed by any tribunal constituted under martial law and acting in a judicial capacity or by Commissioners appointed under the Martial Law Ordinance, 1919, as to the legality, propriety or correctness of any conviction or sentence may be taken advantage of by any other person convicted by the tribunals or Commissioners aforementioned though he may not have appealed against his conviction or sentence to His Majesty in Council, if the grounds upon which any order of His Majesty in Council is based are common to or govern the case of such other persons, and the Governor General in Council shall be bound to act upon the reasons underlying the said order of His Majesty in Council in all cases governed by such order; and the High Court of Judicature established in the Province shall on an application made to that Court for that purpose decide whether any particular case is governed by the rule laid down or reasons underlying any order of His Majesty in Council.'

"My Lord, the object of my amendment should be obvious to everybody who has followed the debates during the last few days over the Punjab affairs. There is a large number of persons who have been arrested, detained, tried, convicted and are undergoing sentences. A few of these have appealed to His Majesty's Privy Council. An appeal to His Majesty in Privy Council is not an easy affair; it involves much expenditure, much local help, and everybody is not in a position to do so. Even if the public do extend their help to some persons, as I am thankful to say help has been extended to a number of persons to have their cases brought before His Majesty in Privy Council, the number of such cases will, I fear, be small. There will still be a large number of persons who will not be able to approach the Privy Council. The cases that have been tried, many of them might probably rest upon some common ground. At any rate it is expected that the decision of His Majesty in Council about certain poin*s will govern a number of cases, and the object of my amendment is that, where His Majesty in Council has considered the case and has expressed an opinion upon the matters involved in it, the benefit of that decision should be secured to such other persons who may have been tried by these martial law commissioners or summary courts and who may not have taken their case to the Privy Council.

My Lord, I hope that this will commend itself to the Government because it would be anomalous and deplorable that when His Majesty in Council has expressed an opinion upon points which affect the cases of other persons, they should not have the benefit of that decision. I do not think the Government would wish to contemplate that situation. I venture to think that in this matter, at any rate, the Government will be in sympathy with my amendment. The second clause which I have added, clause 7, lays down, in order to make assurance doubly sure, that the Governor General in Council should be bound by the decision of their Lordships in the Privy Council in such cases, and that they should be bound, on receipt of the order of His Majesty in Council in any particular case to take action on all such cases as may be affected by it. But my Lord, we are all human and there is no knowing whether a decision of the Government of India will satisfy the persons whose right or interests may be involved, and for that reason, as an assurance that everybody will have a chance of having the matter properly considered and decided, I have suggested that the High Court of Judicature established in the province should, on application made to that Court for that purpose, decide whether a particular case is governed by the rules laid down or the orders of His Majesty in Council. I hope the proposal will commend itself to Government."

The Hon'ble Mr. Sachchidananda Sinha :—"I should like to say one word, my Lord, in support of this proposal, which seems to me a very reasonable one. Otherwise, there will be great hardship entailed on a large number of people who cannot appeal to His Majesty in Council. Therefore, people here should be given the benefit of a Privy Council Judgment, if they move the High Court on the ground that the facts and circumstances in their cases are similar to those of the cases before the Privy Council, and obtain a favourable order therefrom."

The Hon'ble Rao Bahadur B. N. Sarma :—"My Lord, I have a similar amendment against my name. It is obviously just that if the grounds of decision upon which the Privy Council set aside a conviction are common, it should apply to similar cases, and the Government or the High Court should set aside those convictions and sentences also. Of course, if the grounds on which the Privy Council set aside these convictions are of a technical character, and not based upon merits, there is nothing to prevent the Government from bringing up the offenders before the regular courts for trial.

Therefore, the ground of convenience should not be for keeping those men in confinement, even though their cases may be really governed by the decision of the Privy Council."

The Hon'ble Sir William Vincent :—"My Lord, if Hon'ble Members will again read clause 6 of the Bill they will see that nothing in the Bill can affect trials by commissions. Sub-clause (a) of this clause runs as follows: 'Nothing in this Act shall apply to any sentence passed or punishment inflicted by or under the orders of any Commission appointed under the Martial Law Ordinance, 1919.'

"If Hon'ble Members will now turn to the amendment which is proposed in clause 6 by Mr. Malaviya, they will see that an important part of his amendment is entirely inconsistent with the sub-clause which I have just read. You cannot in one sub-clause of a Bill say that nothing in this Act shall affect trials before the Commissions, and in the next sub-clause go on to provide for such convictions and sentences. I do not know if I have made myself clear, but it seems to me that, as a matter of drafting and of principle, this is impossible. We are particularly anxious, and have been most careful throughout this Bill, to avoid any reference to these Commissions appointed under the Martial Law Ordinance, because we know that certain sentences from them are before the Privy Council on appeal, and it would be manifestly improper....."

The Hon'ble Pandit Madan Mohan Malaviya :—"My Lord, I do not want to stick to the actual wording of the amendment. If the Hon'ble Member will put it in a different form which will be acceptable, I shall be quite agreeable."

The Hon'ble Sir William Vincent :—"I am aware of the habit of the Hon'ble Member of putting a motion in an impossible form and then asking me at the last moment to put it into proper form. Well, I cannot do it at this juncture, he should have thought of this before. But I shall be able, I hope, to some extent at any rate, to meet the object which he has in view. I was for the moment trying to point out to the Council that it would be entirely inconsistent with the rest of the Bill if this amendment, as it is worded, was passed by the Council, and I cannot possibly undertake at a moment's notice to alter the amendment into a form in which it could be accepted. I have already accepted one amendment from Mr. Sinha to-day, and I am not at all sure that I was wise in doing so....."

The Hon'ble Mr. Sachchidananda Sinha :—"I can assure the Hon'ble Member he was."

The Hon'ble Sir William Vincent —"It may however meet the Hon'ble Member and others here if I explain that if there is a decision by the Privy Council in any appeal before them and any appellant is acquitted on grounds which affect the conviction of other persons who have not appealed, we shall certainly examine the cases, and if we are satisfied that the reasons set out in the Privy Council's judgment apply to any cases of the persons under confinement here, we shall give effect to the principles enunciated by the Privy Council. It follows necessarily, that if the men who have appealed to the Privy Council are acquitted on grounds which would apply to other cases, those who have not appealed will receive the benefit of the decision. But I want the Council to remember that the position of the persons to whom this Bill applies is entirely different from the position of persons tried by the Commissions. These men were tried by sammary courts appointed by the military authorities. The proclamation of martial law is a statutory authority vested in the Governor General in Council, I believe, and it seems to me that the validity of the sentences of summary courts depends upon entirely different grounds from those which form the basis of the decision of the Commissions. It is however quite possible that I may be wrong in this matter and, should the judgments of the Privy Council be decided on grounds which would indicate that the trial of these persons by summary courts was not justified, then certainly we shall have to take action to meet the decision of the Privy Council. I hope that this undertaking will meet, to some extent, the wishes of the Hon'ble Member."

The Hon'ble Pandit Madan Mohan Malaviya :—"Will the Government accept the last provision that 'the High Court of Judicature established in the province shall on an application made to that Court for that purpose decide whether any particular case is governed by the rule laid down or reasons underlying any order of His Majesty in Council?'"

The Hon'ble Sir William Vincent :—"I did not deal with that point by error, I ought to have done so. I am afraid the Government cannot accept this proposal. They do not intend to allow any appeal to the High Court from summary convictions by a military court. That is an entire negation of the principles on which martial law is administered. But I have given an undertaking as to the intentions of Government in this matter, and if we do not carry it out, there are many opportunities by which Hon'ble Members of this Council or any one else can make it incumbent on us to fulfil our undertaking."

The Hon'ble Pandit Madan Mohan Malaviya :—"My Lord, my amendment does not suggest that the High Court should hear appeals from the decisions of summary courts. All that I ask is that 'the High Court of Judicature established in the province shall on an application made to that Court for that purpose decide whether any particular case is governed by the rule laid down or reasons underlying any order of His Majesty in Council.' I wish the High Court to be empowered to deal with this on an application made to them, and I think that Government might see their way to accept this much.

"My Lord, as to the assurance given by the Hon'ble the Home Member, I am thankful for it. It is satisfactory, so far as it goes, and I hope that the public may not, as I fear the public may, have reason to regard that what should have been incorporated in the Bill was merely accepted as an assurance, and be disappointed again as they have been in the past. Your Lordship will remember, the Council will remember, that, in the matter of the Press Act, certain assurances were given by Government, but the public have had to complain that they were not carried out. Therefore, I propose this for the consideration of the Government when I suggest that the wording of clause 6 might be modified. I was under the impression that the Hon'ble the Home Member had thought of some changes in the wording which he might accept. Well, my Lord, the Bill is not to be referred to a Select Committee. The difficulty of drafting becomes very great and, in view of that difficulty, I am not surprised that the wording leaves much to be desired. But the principle of it being accepted, as the statement of the Hon'ble the Home Member shows, I hope the Government will accept the amendment as it stands."

The motion was put and negatived.

The President :—The rejection of that amendment will also dispose of Mr. Sarma's amendment* No. 37.

The Hon'ble Mr. Sarma :—

***37.** 'At the end of clause 6 add a new clause :—

'Any person convicted and sentenced by a Court or other authority constituted or appointed under martial law and acting in a judicial capacity, including commission issued under the Martial Law Ordinances of 1919 shall have the benefit of any order in Council regarding the legality, propriety or correctnesss of any conviction or sentence in an analogous case or cases in so far as the grounds of such order or decision may be applicable to him.

On application by any person convicted and sentenced as hereinbefore referred to, the High Court of the Province concerned shall determine whether the case of the applicant is governed by the decision of the Privy Council and pass such orders as it may deem fit.'

The Hon'ble Mr. Sachchidananda Sinha :—"My Lord, I move that in sub-clause (*c*) of clause 6 for the words 'against any person' the words 'against any officer of Government, Civil and Military, or any other person' be substituted.

"My Lord, the only reason for this is that the Hon'ble the Home Member explained that the Government wanted to reserve to themselves the right of proceeding against any officer, if that was necessary for the ends of justice. This amendment is intended to make that point clear."

The Hon'ble Sir William Vincent :—"My Lord, if there was anything in the amendment I should be very pleased to accept it, but it is really entirely unnecessary. It is the first time that I have ever heard that the word 'person' does not include an officer of Government."

The Hon'ble Mr. Sachchidananda Sinha :—"I wanted to be quite sure of that."

The Hon'ble Sir William Vincent :—"That is the advice I have received from the drafting Department."

The Hon'ble Mr. Sachchidananda Sinha :—"I beg to withdraw it, my lord."

The motion was by leave withdrawn.

The Hon'ble Rao Bahadur B. N. Sarma :—"My Lord, I beg to move the following amendment, 'that the following new clause be inserted as clause 7 :—

> 'This Act shall be in force till the Committee appointed by the Governor General in Council to inquire into the recent disorders makes its report and for a period of three months thereafter.'

"My Lord, I gave notice of this amendment to provide against a certain contingency. Unfortunately, that contingency has occurred. If my amendment that the Bill should be confined to what took place after the proclamation of martial law and during its continuance had been accepted, there might not have been very much necessity for this amendment. I shall not repeat the reasons which I have already urged for the acceptance of this amendment now. All that I shall say is that we meet all the objects which the Government have in view by accepting this clause. The Government asked 'are our officers to have the sword hanging over their heads until this inquiry is over?' We have given them protection; nobody can institute any suit against them. We have also provided for the legality of all convictions and sentences during a long period. But if the Committee of Inquiry should furnish ample grounds on various questions, as to the necessity for martial law being proclaimed or as to the conduct of particular persons, high or low, before the martial law was proclaimed or after it was proclaimed, it may be necessary both for the Government as well as for this Legislature to consider the question as to what protection should be afforded to those officers and to meet those contingencies. We have thrown the onus in all cases alike upon the prosecutor or the plaintiff, as the case may be. It may be that the Government or the Legislature would ask for a revision especially on the facts being ascertained by a public court of inquiry of the kind mentioned. Therefore, I submit, there are ample grounds for meeting the wishes of the people by accepting a clause of this description. We protect the officers of the Government, we provide for the legality of these trials to a certain extent, but, at the same time, the Government have appointed a Committee of Inquiry at the request of the people. That Committee of Inquiry would go necessarily into the kind of measures which were adopted by the martial law officers or others for the purpose of suppressing these disturbances, and, I think, a report of that description would help the solution of the difficulty. It may be that the Inquiry will show there was absolutely no necessity for it, and in that case everybody would be satisfied that the action of the Government was right. I hope, therefore, that this amendment may meet with some luck."

The Hon'ble Sir William Vincent :—"My Lord, there are more cogent reasons against accepting this amendment than arguments of mere convenience. It is true that many of us would be averse from going through all this troublesome discussion on the Bill again three or four months later; but the real objections to this amendment are more deeply-rooted, and, I myself am rather surprised that a gentleman who is a professional lawyer, as I understand, should have failed to realise that this passage of the Bill has absolutely no connection with the work of the Committee. The one principle upon which we have insisted and which has been accepted by this Council is, that the report of this Committee is an administrative matter; the

Committee will inquire into the conduct of officers from an administative point of view; their report will in any case only be considered by Government in deciding what the action of the administrative authorities is to be. This Bill deals with the question of legal liability of officers and others, and has nothing to do with the report of the Committee. Let us assume for one moment that the committee reported that a man was liable to censure or should be punished. Can it be supposed for one moment that that would affect his legal liability, that the report can be put in as evidence? Nothing of the kind. The two subjects are entirely distinct; the one deals with the administrative aspect of the action taken, and the other with the legal aspect of any case gone into by the Courts. It was for that reason that my Hon'ble friend, Sardar Sundar Singh, asked me whether, if the report of the Committee indicates that certain persons are liable to be censured, the Government would act on the report irrespective of the Bill, and I was able to give him an assurance that the passing of this Bill will not make any difference to that question at all.

"There is a further objection to the amendment, one of root principle, which has been discussed *ad nauseam* in this Council; it is this, that if the amendment were accepted our unfortunate officers would only obtain exemption from suit for a few months, and at the end of that time they would again become liable to suits (having had a short interregnum of peace), although they have acted *ex-hypothesi* properly and *bona fide*. A very similar question we discussed in the opening debate, and if this amendment is pressed to a division, I really do not believe that the Hon'ble Member will now receive more than one vote in support of his proposal."

The Hon'ble Rao Bahadur B. N. Sarma :—"My Lord, the Hon'ble the Home Member's arguments may be extremely convincing to him and to several others, but I may assure him that the matter does not admit of such a summary disposal. I never for a moment thought that the report of the committee would be evidence in any judicial tribunal, or that would necessarily completely govern the action either of the Government or of the Legislature. All that I said was that it would enable us to enact an Indemnity Bill that is suited to the occasion, which would satisfy the requirements of justice as well as the legitimate wishes of the people, while affording protection to those who really deserve it. We have had to proceed on assumptions to a very large extent in enacting this Bill. Ordinarily an Act of Indemnity would only follow martial law only if there was necessity for the enforcement of martial law. If an Indemnity Bill be not passed the questions whether there was necessity for the enforcement of martial law, whether there was a state of war, are questions of fact which would be adjudicated upon in a court of law. Therefore, we consented to the amendment moved by the Hon'ble the Home Member, because we felt that there were cogent reasons for an interim Act of this description. If there really was no necessity, then the question would stand upon the same footing as when the civil power takes the assistance of the military authorities for the purpose of protecting law and order, Of course, if the Legislature should still feel inclined to protect those officers even under those circumstances, it may do so; but it would not have much of a precedent in its favour. Therefore, my Lord, the decision of the Inquiry Committee would not be final and conclusive, but would help both the Government and the Legislature in arriving at sounder conclusions on questions of presumptions, on questions of fact, than they are in a position to do at present, when everything must be taken for granted one way or the other. Take, for instance, the actions about which so much reference has been made, on the 13th and 14th April. We are asked to presume good faith and reasonable belief. Would it not be more satisfactory to have the explanations of the officers themselves, to have the evidence before us that they were justified in doing what they did? If they were justified, then by all means protect them by a legislative enactment. Therefore, my Lord, it is not without very sound reasons that I have brought forward this amendment. What is the cry outside? What is the legitimate cry? It is that the Government have been hurrying through a Bill simply to protect their officers, many of whom do not deserve it. It may be that the Government should do something to protect their officers before they can quite make up their minds as to what they should ultimately do. But my submission is that that should only be temporary, and they should not ask the Council as they have asked, by means of a majority, to raise certain presumptions in the way they are doing; the Council might not have done it if they had the facts more clearly. That is the reason why I ask this Bill should be of a suspensory character, and

I have behind me the opinion of very eminent men outside the Council who have been connected with the administration. There is no necessity of giving any names; but they are people who are not likely to take irrational views of things. Therefore, here is no question for professional lawyer or non-professional men. Nobody could fall into the error that this committee's report would be evidence in any court of law, or that we should necessarily act upon it. All that I said and say still is that we would have better material upon which we can proceed before enacting a measure of this description, which is sure to create dissatisfaction everywhere and which has already created dissatisfaction."

The motion was put and negatived.

(8)—From Proceedings of Meeting held on September 25, 1919

The Indemnity Bill—(*contd.*)

The Hon'ble Sir William Vincent:—"My Lord, I move that the Bill to indemnify officers of Government and other persons in respect of certain acts done under martial law, and to provide for other matters in connection therewith, be passed, as amended by this Council. I think most Members of this Council are relieved at the conclusion of a somewhat long and troublesome debate, and I will not detain them long. The discussion of the Bill has necessarily involved references to subjects of considerable delicacy, upon which there is great feeling on the part of many Members of this Council, but nevertheless the Council may congratulate itself, on the whole, on the self-restraint that has been manifested in the course of the debate. There was, however, great feeling, as I said, on both sides, and despite obvious efforts at times, it has manifested itself to a considerable degree. Nor can there be any doubt that both Europeans and Indians are deeply moved by the recent occurrences. I am glad that in spite of all this nothing has prevented the Council from arriving at a perfectly just appreciation of the requirements of the case, and that Members have recognised, generally speaking, that this Bill is a necessary measure which deals with principles, and not with individual actions. It is for that reason I believe that the Bill, which I have had the honour to move before the Council, has met with such general approval, and as I am speaking on it, I think that the Council might like to know the views of one who has taken a great interest, both in these disorders and in the measures which have been taken to suppress them. I refer to Mr. Gandhi. There are different opinions about this gentleman. Some look on him as a dangerous crank with an extraordinary amount of that Scotch quality, a good conceit of himself. There are others, persons whose opinion is equally entitled to great weight, who believe him to be man of saint-like character, selfless disposition and almost superhuman insight. Mr. Montagu himself in a recent debate described him as a man of the highest motives and the finest character, a man who his worst enemy, if he has any enemies (he is very lucky if he has not), would agree is of the most disinterested ambitions it is possible to conceive. Well, my Lord, it is probable that a correct estimate of the character of Mr. Gandhi would lie between these various extremes, but I hope that the Council will not in any way acquire the impression that in offering these observations I am seeking to convey my own opinion about him, or the opinion of the Government. An expression of opinion would be improper. At the same time, there are certain characteristics in Mr. Gandhi which all will admit. He is not in any way predisposed to favour the policy of Government. That is certain. He has also got what is not very often found in this country, the full courage of his convictions. If he thinks anything he never hesitates to tell either the Government or any one else what his views are, and for that reason, I think, it would interest the Council to hear what a leading Indian of this position and character thinks about the Bill. So far as the question of indemnity is concerned, Mr. Gandhi would go very much further than we have done. He does not refer at all to *bona fide* or reasonable belief. He assumes these, and says—'I would therefore say that rather than complain that the Bill has been prematurely brought in, we should give our best attention to the provisions of the Bill. Thus, for instance, we would allow a provision to the effect that such officers as may have given orders of firing shall not be criminally triable for murder or civilly liable for damages.' Then be goes on to say that such officers, where in fault, should be dealt with administratively.

"Members of this Council will see that our Bill does not go nearly as far as that. In a later letter in which he answers various persons who have attacked the Bill he writes as follows:—I am quoting from 'Young India' of the 20th September, a paper which, I believe, is now controlled by Mr. Gandhi.

> 'I must respectfully dissent from the view that such a Bill can only be properly passed after a Commission has reported. I venture to submit that the Bill as published is almost harmless and it is a Bill we shall be bound to pass as it is even after the Commission has reported.'

"My Lord, that opinion, take it for what it is worth, I think, supports the view which the Government has put forward throughout this debate. The Hon'ble Mr. Madan Mohan Malaviya has repeatedly referred to Mr. Gandhi as an authority of the very greatest weight, to whose views the deepest consideration is due. Well, my Lord, may we hope that on this occasion he will concur in the views of the authority whom he so much reveres. At any rate, I put it to the Council that these letters are of interest and that they support the conclusions which we have always advocated in this Council, that this Bill is a necessary and harmless measure which in no way forestalls the report of the Commission."

The Hon'ble Pandit Madan Mohan Malaviya :—"My Lord, I regret I must oppose the motion that the Bill as amended be passed. I do so with all the responsibility which I feel rests upon me as an elected Member of this Council, and I do so after having heard the words of my esteemed friend Mr. Gandhi, to which reference has been made by the Hon'ble the Home Member.

"My Lord, the Bill has to be considered on its merits. Opinions for and against it have no doubt to be weighed, and the opinion of Mr. Gandhi is entitled to weight. I am glad that the Hon'ble the Home Member has paid a compliment to Mr. Gandhi and advised us to pay great heed to his opinion. I hope, after reading this opinion of Mr. Gandhi, he will advise the Government of India, in the first instance, not to delay cancelling the order which they have maintained against Mr. Gandhi for the last many months, confining him to the Bombay Presidency, and, secondly, I hope the Hon'ble the Home Member will advise the Punjab Government and the Delhi Administration to follow suit. My Lord, that should be the least evidence of the sincerity of the appreciation of the Hon'ble the Home Member of Mr. Gandhi's position.

"Coming to the question before us, I attach, as I have said, great weight to the opinion of Mr. Gandhi; but there is a higher authority to which I have to bow, and that is the conscience that sits within me; and that conscience tells me that the Bill ought not to be passed as it stands.

"Now, my Lord, I will make my position clear, and as briefly as I can. Your Lordship and the Council know, the whole country knows, that the Bill as it was drafted rested on the preamble wherein it was stated :—

> 'Whereas owing to the recent disorders in certain districts in the Punjab and in other parts of India, it has been necessary for the purpose of maintaining or restoring order to resort to martial law.'

"My Lord, that phraseology was in conformity with well-established precedents. But our complaint was that the phrase, 'as it has been necessary,' used in this preamble was not sufficient, and that the larger phraseology of the English Statutes, to which I drew attention, should have been employed. I did not refer to I William and Mary to which the Hon'ble the Law Member took us back, but, as he did refer to it, so far as I remember, I may say that the phraseology used therein also supports my contention. The preamble to that Act said :—

> 'Whereas about the time of His Majesty's enterprize divers Lords and Gentlemen well affected to their country did act as Lieutenants, etc., though not authorised thereunto, and did apprehend and put in custody criminal and suspected persons, and did seize horses, etc., in which proceedings some force or violence, or defect of form was unavoidable which in a time of peace would not have been warrantable, and divers matters and things have been done, *all of which were allowable and necessary in regard of the exigencies of public affairs and ought to be justified,* and the parties thereto indemnified, be it enacted therefore,' etc.

Mark the language 'all of which were allowable and necessary in regard of the exigencies of public affairs and ought to be justified.'

"That was, my Lord, in 1689. I will omit the intermediate Statutes and I will come to the Statutes of 1715 in which, as I reminded the Council, it was recited in the preamble, which is the most important part of an Indemnity Bill, that the Acts which that Statute sought to justify were done during the rebellion 'in order to preserve our present happy establishment and the peace of this Kingdom and to suppress and put an end to the said rebellion.' Here, my Lord, I will say parenthetically that I regret I was wrong in saying that there was no authority for the use of the words 'maintaining or' in the Bill in the earlier Statutes of the English Parliament. My friend the Hon'ble the Law Member was right and I was wrong. But, my Lord, the language that was used was employed to show that the maintenance of peace was necessary, because there had been a rebellion or an insurrection or riots amounting to war. Now, my Lord in the Statute of 1715, after reciting the acts which had been done, it was said that whereas 'certain persons had for the purposes aforesaid, namely, in order to preserve our present happy establishment and the peace of this Kingdom and to suppress and put an end to the said rebellion, did divers acts which could not be justified by the strict forms of law, and yet were necessary, and so much for the service of the public that they ought to be justified by Act of Parliament, and the persons by whom they were transacted ought to be indemnified, it should therefore be enacted,' etc. My Lord, my complaint was that while the draft of the Bill did use words in the preamble to show that the acts against which it was sought to indemnify officers were *necessary, i.e.,* that it was necessary to resort to martial law, the advisers of the Government had not seen fit to incorporate the next clause of these carlier Acts, that is, the one which said, that, besides being necessary, the acts were also 'so much for the service of the public that they ought to be justified by Act of Parliament.' My Lord, I need not refer to the other Statutes, namely, to those of 1745 and 1780; this is the phraseology that has been used in both of them. Now, my Lord, not only in the English Statutes but in the South African Statutes also, to which the Hon'ble the Law Member seems to have taken a great fancy, the language used was 'done as necessary for the suppression of hostility in or the maintenance of good order or government, or the public safety of this Colony.' That was in Act VI of 1900, when the Boer War was going on. So also in Act IV of 1902 the language used was 'done as necessary for the suppression of hostilities or the establishment and maintenance of good order and government, in or for the public safety of this Colony.' It will be clear, therefore, my Lord, that the keystone upon which the edifice of an Indemnity Bill rests in all these Statutes, whether of the English Parliament or of South Africa, has been the declaration by the Legislature that the acts which were done and which it was sought to justify and indemnify officers against, were acts necessary for the suppression of disorders or for the preservation of the public peace. Not only that, but the English Statutes go further and say that those acts should also have been so much for the service of the public that they ought to be justified by Act of Parliament.

"This view is supported by the opinions of some distinguished Members of the House of Lords in the debate of 1818 and by the opinion of John Stuart Mill, to which I invited attention yesterday. Now, my Lord, the position taken up by the Government in the Bill as it was introduced was that it was necessary to introduce martial law for restoring or maintaining order. What have the Government done? The Government have now taken out the words 'It has been necessary for the purpose of maintaining or restoring order to resort to martial law,' and have substituted therefor 'martial law has been enforced.' I say the Law Member and the Home Member have cut the ground from under their feet, and they have no legs to stand upon in this Council and ask that the Indemnity Bill should be passed. I should like the Hon'ble the Law Member, who is a very learned man and whose researches in law and history must be deep, to tell me of any instance where an Indemnity Bill has been put on the Statute-book of any country without its Parliament or legislative body being satisfied that the acts which had been done were necessary, just and proper . . . . . ."

The Hon'ble Sir George Lowndes:—"Does the Hon'ble Pandit really want me to tell him?"

The Hon'ble Pandit Madan Mohan Malaviya:—"I shall feel thankful to the Hon'ble the Law Member if he will do so."

The Hon'ble Sir George Lowndes:—"Will the Hon'ble Pandit look at the St. Vincent Act that he is so much in love with?"

The Hon'ble Pandit Madan Mohan Malaviya:—"I thank the Hon'ble the Law Member. The St. Vincent Act said: 'acts which had been done *bona fide*, necessarily and properly for the suppression of rebellion. The language used there is clear . . ."

The Hon'ble Sir George Lowndes:—"The Hon'ble Pandit must refer to the preamble; he is not reading from it now."

The Hon'ble Pandit Madan Mohan Malaviya:—"You have to take the preamble and the body of the Bill together. However, my Lord, without spending more time to look up that Act of St. Vincent—I have found the preamble of the amending Act, but the original Act I am not able to lay my hands upon just at this moment—I will say that I am glad to find a change in the attitude of the Hon'ble the Law Member towards the Act of St. Vincent. It was but yesterday that he held up that Act to ridicule, and today he cites it as an authority for the attitude now taken up by Government. What have things come to, my Lord? What a fall, what a sad fall? My Lord, if this is the position, I say the Government have to justify the introduction of this measure, and I submit that they have left no justification whatever for it now. My Lord, the whole situation has been altered by the modification which the Government have introduced; and I submit that on this ground alone, without raising any other point, I am entitled to ask that the Council should not pass this Bill. I submit that Government have to go further than what the preamble as it now stands lays down. It is not enough to say that, whereas martial law had been enforced certain acts done during the course of martial law should be justified and indemnified. It is not enough to say that. You must consider what the acts were;

and has it been shown that the acts done were such as ought to be justified and indemnified against? The other day I referred at some length to the many allegations on the part of the people who have suffered, that it was not necessary to introduce martial law. I have referred to many opinions expressed, and I will quote one more to-day. At the end of the debate the Hon'ble the Home Member read to the Council a telegram which the Government of India had received from the Punjab Government on the 13th April last asking that martial law should be introduced in Lahore, Amritsar and certain other parts of the Punjab. Now, my Lord, that telegram stated that certain unhappy events had happened on the 10th April at Amritsar and Lahore, and that two Europeans had been killed at Kasur on the 12th. My Lord, I submit that that telegram did not state the whole truth. It stated only a part of the truth, and did not supply all the material that was necessary in order to enable a sound judgment to be formed as to whether martial law should or should not be introduced. My Lord, as a matter of fact, we have indisputable evidence that on the evening of the 10th April after the temporary stir and disturbance and the firing on certain persons on the Upper Mall and at Anarkali Bazar, everything was quiet in Lahore. The then Lieutenant-Governor was entertained at the Government House at a party that evening only a little after that time, and the Lahore correspondent of the *Pioneer*, whose identity must be known, I think, to the Hon'ble Mr. Thompson, writing on the 20th of April (his letter was published in the *Pioneer* of April 25th) said as follows:—

> 'As a matter of fact when that evening was over (namely, the evening of the 10th April) no real anxiety remained.' No real anxiety remained though he adds—'although of course the rioters were still exercising their sway and on Friday, Saturday and Sunday business and ordinary administration was practically at a standstill.'

My Lord, I am sure the identity of this writer cannot be an unfathomable mystery to the officers of Government, and writing on the 20th April, this writer stated as a matter of fact that when that evening of the 10th April was over, there was no real anxiety left. That was the state of things in Lahore; and we have had in the official Communiques and the *Civil & Military Gazette* publications that after 5.30 p.m., there was quiet in Amritsar on the 10th of April. I submit, therefore, my Lord, that the telegram upon which the Hon'ble the Home Member has relied was not sufficient to justify the introduction of martial law. Nor did he say anything else to justify the introduction of martial law in Lahore and Amritsar and in several other parts of the Punjab. We have, on the other hand, allegations put forward after some inquiry which show that there was nothing to justify the introduction of martial law. It is one thing to call in the aid of the military to suppress disorder, and quite another thing to introduce martial law. There was trouble at Lahore, there was trouble at Amritsar and in certain other places. The civil authorities rightly called in the aid of the military when they thought that their forces might not be sufficient to quell the disturbances. That has been done on numerous occasions without martial law being introduced; that will be done and ought to be done when necessary. As the Hon'ble the Law Member told us in his exposition of the law, where the civil authority finds itself unable to cope with disturbances or to quell them, it is justified in calling in the aid of the military; and where both acting together fail to establish order or to quell the rebellion, it is then that civil authority would be justified in handing over their charge to the military. Now, I submit that the events which have been stated show that the first stage was reached, and that the second stage was not reached. That is to say, the civil authorities with the help of the military had restored quiet in Lahore and in Amritsar and in some other places, for instance, at Kasur, and that they succeeded in restoring quiet. And that therefore, it was not necessary to resort to the next step, namely to make over charge of the towns and the population to the will of the military officers.

"My Lord, of the many allegations that I put forward in support of my oppostion to the Bill, an attempt has been made to controvert only some and to qualify a few others. A partial attempt has been made to offer an explanation of some of the allegations of people who have suffered or of the relations of people who have suffered. Many have remained unanswered. As I said on the first day, the Government have not taken the opportunity which I offered to them of stating the facts of which they must have a better knowledge than other people. But the Government having refused to state the facts for the information of the Council, I submit, my Lord, I am entitled to assume the correctness of the allegations implied in my questions for the purposes of this debate. The Council will remember that I did not profess to have any personal knowledge of the martial law incidents. I put forward these allegations on the authority of partial investigation by myself and my friends. I put forward these allegations as they were vouched for by respectable persons in whose veracity and honour I have confidence. If any of the statements are incorrect, no one will be more happy than myself to be corrected. No one can be more sorry than I will be if statements in regard to which I may have been mistaken or misinformed remain uncontradicted. I, therefore, welcome any criticism which would throw light on the facts brought forward if they are incorrect, and I should be thankful to any gentlemen who supplied correct information. But what has been the case here? Let me examine some of the statements made by way of criticism of, or reply to, what I said. I will deal with the speeches of the Hon'ble Mr. Hailey, Mr. Thompson, General Havelock Hudson and Sir George Lowndes.

"My Lord, in the admirable statement which Mr. Hailey made on behalf of the Government, he wanted us to believe that the state of things in Lahore and in Amritsar and in other places in the Punjab, where martial law was introduced, was so horrible that Government could not but resort to martial law. He told us that the Rowlatt Act agitation had created an atmosphere that was surcharged with danger. He said that the *Satyagraha* movement had come in and spread in the Punjab. But, my Lord, the Rowlatt Act agitation was not confined to the cities of Lahore and Amritsar. The Hon'ble Mr. Hailey is well aware, even better than I am, that there was agitation against the Rowlatt Act throughout the Punjab. He is also aware, I presume, that the *Satyagraha* movement had spread to all parts of the Punjab; that, generally speaking, the 6th of April was observed as a *Satyagraha* day throughout that Province. He is aware that in none of these other numerous districts of the Punjab did the agitation against the Rowlatt Act or the *Satyagraha* movement lead to any stir or to any insurrection or rebellions movement. He is aware that there was no trouble whatever in any of these places. And no trouble arose in these places, for instance, in Jullundur and all the other districts of that division, because the authorities did not interfere intemperately, but interfered sympathetically with the movement. They wisely said 'let the people give vent to their feelings regarding the Rowlatt Act; let them observe the *Satyagraha* day as they like'. Here, in Simla, Mr. Tollinton, the Deputy Commissioner expressed sympathy with the attitude of the people in observing the *Satyagraha* day. On the day following they resumed their business in the ordinary way. I could name several other Punjab officials who acted in the same way; but perhaps I had better not, I am sure the Hon'ble Mr. Hailey being Additional Secretary to the Punjab Government must know that in many districts of the Punjab, where the Rowlatt Act agitation and the *Satyagraha* movement were as strong as in any other place, there was no trouble. I contend, therefore, that the circumstances to which the trouble owed its origin was the blazing indiscretion of the Punjab Government as it was then constituted, in having deported two such public men as Dr. Satyapal and Dr. Kitchlew. That was the root of the trouble.

"I need not repeat the sequence of events here. I submit that for a proper consideration of the question that is now before the Council, it is necessary for the Government to show that there was a clear necessity for the introduction of martial law. But it is not enough to show that the introduction of martial law was necessary. It may have been necessary, let us assume for argument's sake that it was necessary to introduce martial law in certain places at a certain time; the Government have to go further and to show that it was necessary to introduce it at midnight on the 15th of April; the Government have to show that it was necessary to introduce it in other parts of the Punjab and to maintain it up to the periods up to which it was maintained. I submit that this has not been shown by the Hon'ble Mr. Hailey. But I will not deal with the rest of Mr. Hailey's remarks, as I wish to compress my speech as much as possible. While Mr. Hailey has shown that these were anxious times in the Punjab and that the Government had to exercise vigilance, he has not shown that the situation was such that a sober-headed sympathetic Governor could not have managed it, without resorting to martial law and inflicting the many indignities and humiliations that were inflicted on the loyal prople of the Punjab. In contrast to this, I drew attention to what happened at Ahmedabad. Nobody on the official side has referred to it. Perhaps because it could not be referred to except to support what I have said. Trouble arose in Ahmedabad also, but it was completely got over in two days' time by the Government of Bombay allowing Mr. Gandhi to go to Ahmedabad and advise the people. A similar course could have been pursued at Lahore and Amritsar, and, if it was found necessary to introduce martial law, it should have been got rid of at the outside within four days or six days or a week. It was certainly not necessary to expose respectable people to all the indignities and humiliations to which they were exposed, and to keep up this state of things for the inordinate period of time for which it was kept up.

"I will next deal with the Hon'ble Mr. Thompson. Mr. Thompson was the Chief Secretary to the Government of Sir Michael O'Dwyer while martial law was enforced. I can quite understand that he feels he is personally on trial; and I can, therefore, excuse him for importing a great deal of the personal element and unnecessary heat into the statements he put before the Council. But, my Lord, when we calmly examine his statements what do they come to? As I said before I am never discomfited if any statement made by me in the Council or elsewhere should be found to be inaccurate. Therefore, I repeat that, if Mr. Thompson only gave me correct information in regard to incidents which I have mentioned, I should have whole-heartedly thanked him, however poignant might be my regret that I should have made an incorrect statement. Mr. Thompson stated that I had said that in the Badshahi mosque meeting a C. I. D. Inspector, Ali Gauhar, had made certain remarks which had caused resentment to the persons assembled there.

"He told us that he had the file of the case before him, and nowhere had it been stated in it that such a statement as I had made had been made, namely, that this Inspector had made certain remarks or said something which excited the people assembled there. For the benefit of Mr. Thompson and the Council, I beg to draw attention to the statement made on solemn affirmation by Inspector Ali Gauhar Khan, Criminal Investigation Department, himself in trial No. 1 of 1919 before the Martial Law Commission. He there stated:— 'We were in plain clothes in the mosque. There were several thousands of people in the mosque awaiting the people who were to address the meeting. Abdul Hai told me that he recognised me as a C. I. D. man, as my department had had him imprisoned for three months and put on security for three years. When I denied that I was a C. I. D. official, Abdul Hai went towards the pulpit and addressed the crowd saying 'the C. I. D. police had always been intruding in our meetings,' etc.

"Now, the man was a C. I D. official, and only when he denied it, Abdul Hai went to the pulpit and addressed the crowd saying that the C. I. D. police were always intruding in their meetings, etc.

"Now, my Lord, I am sure that Mr. Thompson would feel that my statement that the C. I. D. Inspector had made certain remarks which were resented by some persons at the meeting, was not altogether incorrect.

"I take the next point made by Mr. Thompson that relates to the incident regarding hand-cuffing in Amritsar. Mr. Thompson wanted the Council to believe that so far as he knew nobody had been hand-cuffed there. I hope I am repeating his words correctly. Speaking with reference to the hardships to which Indians had been subjected, he also spoke of the not dissimilar inconveniences to which certain European ladies and children who had been sent to the Fort had been subjected. Now, my Lord, I would place before the Council a statement on the subject, which I have in my hands of a Barrister-at-law who says: 'On the 21st morning I myself with Sheikh Mohamed Amin, pleader, his son and brother were taken to the Rambagh in a well-guarded *bund gari* and from thence ordered to be taken to the Fort. We four were there put in a cell hand-cuffed two together. In a corner of the cell was a little heap of parched gram and a bucket of water. In the afternoon we were taken out and marched in a file with a large number of Kashmiri coolies and others to the open square inside the Fort, all hand-cuffed, two together. There we had to march round and round with European ladies and gentlemen watching the show.' I suppose this was one of the inconveniences to which the European ladies and gentlemen were exposed in the Fort.

"Now, my Lord, I will take the next point. I referred to several cases of flogging. Mr. Thompson picked up one case and said, 'Oh, they were school boys; the Head Master had asked the Military to help him in maintaining discipline amongst students by flogging some.' He overlooks the fact that even that would not justify the flogging of the students by the Military people. And he has not a word to say regarding the many other cases of flogging which are mentioned in the statement which was laid on the table by the Hon'ble the Home Member in reply to a question which I put on the subject.

"Mr. Thompson next referred to Mr. Manohar Lal's case. My Lord, I had said in regard to Mr. Manohar Lal's case that his wife and children had been turned out and were obliged to live in one of the outhouses used as servants' quarters until the bungalow had been searched about a week later. I did not state the exact period, because I did not know it. Mr. Thompson in referring to it grew very angry, and said that the wife and children of this gentleman were allowed, so far as he was aware, to return to the bungalow the next day. Now, my Lord, I have ascertained the exact facts from Mr. Manohar Lal and from others who knew it. Mr. Manohar Lal's house was locked on the 18th. His wife, an invalid lady, was turned out of the house at once. She was compelled to live in one of the outhouses on the whole of the 18th, the whole of the 19th and until late in the evening of the 20th, when the search of the house had been completed. She had not any bedding to lie upon with her, she was not allowed to take anything out of the house. Her friends sent her bedding and food, and thus she lived in an outhouse in her invalid condition for three days. Now, my Lord, if my statement that it was about a week later that they were allowed to return to the house was incorrect, Mr. Thompson, in his capacity as Chief Secretary to the Punjab Government, should have told us what the exact period was and not fulminated that this was a very serious discrepancy.

"My Lord, I should not leave Mr. Manohar Lal's case without drawing your Excellency's attention to certain other remarks Mr. Thompson made about it. He said that Mr. Manohar Lal was a Trustee of the *Tribune*, and as such he was wont to take some interest in the paper. Mr. Thompson wanted the Council to think that that was a sufficient justification for the action that had been taken against him. I am not surprised, my Lord, that this view was put forward by Mr. Thompson, because in the letter, dated the 20th April which appeared in the *Pioneer* to which I have referred before, I find it stated:—

> 'Manohar Lal, the Trustee of the *Tribune* represents one of those cases which make one despair of educating on western lines. He gained a scholarship to England and at the 'Varsity' gained a brilliant reputation for economics. On his return to India, however, he failed to maintain the promise of his academic career, and while he always posed as an authority on education, he has done very little practically to utilise his own talents to their full extent.'

"My Lord, it is sad to find that with the writer of the letter in the *Pioneer* Mr. Thompson thinks that the mere fact of Mr. Manohar Lal's being a trustee of the *Tribune* was sufficient to put this distinguished scholar, not less distinguished than Mr. Thompson, to all the indignities, humiliation and suffering to which he and his wife were exposed!

"The next point I will deal with is the treatment of respectable citizens in Gujranwala. Mr. Thompson read what I thought was a letter from Colonel O'Brien giving his version of the affair. My Lord, he seemed, so far as I could make out, to question the correctness of the statement that a Hindu and a Mussalman were handcuffed together by deliberate design. He said that was accidental. My Lord, I refuse to take that statement as correct. I will quote from the correspondent of the *Pioneer* on this subject also, from a letter published in the paper of the 25th April. He said:—

'The outbreak in Gujranwala had almost a comic opera termination. Colonel O'Brien had handed over charge to Mirza Sultan Ahmed and was in Lahore when the news came in. He immediately hurried back to his former district, and after the immediate suppression of the riot he arrested eleven leaders (including one Mangal Sen, a local financial genius) marched them in procession through the city, accompanied by a detachment of the 26th Royal Sussex and headed by two City Fathers—a Hindu and Mussalman respectively—who under orders shouted out to their constituents not to misbehave themselves by acts of violence' 'This spectacle', says the learned and large-hearted correspodent of the *Pioneer*, 'this spectacle of Hindu-Mussalman unity must have been almost as impressive as the sight of Munshi Ram preaching in the Jumma Masjid at Delhi.'

I leave the Council to judge from this quotation what were the feelings of the men whom Mr. Thompson represents, in relation to this incident, and I ask the Council not to accept the statement read out by Mr. Thompson that it was merely by accident that a Hindu and a Mussalman were handcuffed together and marched in the disgraceful manner in which they were.

"My Lord, Mr. Thompson's next point related to my reference to trials in a summary way. I have said, that in certain cases notes of evidence had not been recorded. I did not say that in all cases notes had not been recorded. Mr. Thompson showed that he had before him several pages of notes of evidence in certain cases. That may be; I never said there were no notes of evidence taken in any case. What I did say was, that it had been alleged that notes of evidence had not been recorded in a certain number of cases. I also placed before the Council certified copies of judgments in two cases, in one of which I pointed out that even the offence with which the accused was charged was not mentioned. That was a case tried by Mr. Hoyle on the 26th of May, 1919. Mr. Thompson had not a word to say about it.

"My Lord, the next incident to which I referred, and to which Mr. Thompson also animadverted, was the Ramnagar case, where it is alleged that the King's effigy was burnt. Mr. Thompson failed to grasp my point and did not represent me correctly. My complaint was that here was a case in which respectable, probably the most respectable, Hindu citizens of Ramnagar, were charged with having burned the King's effigy. Their position and status in society, their wealth and character made it impossible for me to believe, and should make it impossible to be believed, that they would be guilty of such foolish and wicked mischief. Their complaint was that they had not had a public inquiry which they wanted. They had not had a regular inquiry, and they urged that if they had a regular inquiry, if they had an opportunity of appeal to a higher court, the facts would have been sifted and their innocence would have been established. They urged that the case was a trumped up one, without any foundation, and that they were entitled to have the matter regularly tried. There was no martial law necessity for trying this case in a summary way before any martial law tribunal, and my complaint was that by having been put before a martial law summary court for trial on such a charge, they were deprived of the opportunity they should have had to establish their innocence, and that they have been unjustly dealt with.

"My Lord, I must also say a word about the Lyallpur *bhusa* case. It has been said that at Lyallpur Rs. 60,000 worth of *bhusa* was set fire to by incendiaries. If this was so, it was of course a very serious mischief. But was it so? I hold in my hand a copy of an Order passed by the District Magistrate of Lyallpur on an Inquiry relating to this affair. Government had evidently asked him to report under section 15-A of the Police Act what compensation should be fixed upon for the burning of this *bhusa*. The case was taken up by Mr. G.F. deMontmorency, and the conclusion which he arrived at was, that the burning of the *bhusa* was not the result of incendiarism, committed by any of those who were believed to have taken part in the rioting, but that it was probably due to an accident. At any rate, he was unable to find that it was the act of any of those who were suspected of it. This is what he says:—

'The *bhusa* appears to have gone on fire between 8-15 p.m. and 8.45 p.m. The fire was noticed by the picket at about 8.40. . . . A few people from the factories, a few members of the Municipal Staff and the Storekeeper alluded to above were the only persons on the spot when I arrived. There was no information of any crowd having visited the stacks or of any single person having been seen near the stacks. The absence of the chaukidar seems to have been due to laziness, and not to have been arranged or premeditated. Neither patrol nor picket saw anything suspicious in the vicinity of the goodsyard. . . . A very exhaustive police inquiry was made; no trace of anything bearing on the burning of the *bhusa* came out. There were some approvers in the Lyallpur cases who were associates and in the secrets of those who were convicted in the Lyallpur disorders. None of these however had any information to give in regard to the burning of *bhusa* which does not seem to have formed part of the plans of their associates.

'There was a strong suspicion at the time that this was the work of an incendiary, because—

(1) similar acts had occurred elsewhere in connection with the disorders;

(2) a plot to burn *bhusa* had been alleged to exist at Toba Tek Singh;

(3) the fact that goods bad been moved from the goodsyard the day before.

'The police inquiry has failed to connect the burning of this *bhusa* with the act of any incendiary or with any riot or rioters. Those convicted in jail in Lyallpur disorders were questioned by me. They have now after conviction no object in concealing what they know and have given information on a number of other points, but none of them have any information to give about the *bhusa*.

'I have examined the theory of whether it was the act of some villager or villagers; but no clue has been obtained.'

The learned District Magistrate says that there had been several fires since April last due to cinders from chimneys, but he is not certain that this was due to that. In conclusion he says:—'I have been ubable to find anything except suspicion to point to this injury having arisen from riot and unlawful assembly within the area. I am therefore unable to make the assessment contemplated in section 15A (2) (c) of the Police Act'. So much for the burning of the *bhusa*. I hope that my Hon'ble friend will revise his opinion about this incident also.

"I will now come to the question of the number of deaths caused by the firing in Jallianwala Bagh. Mr. Thompson warned the Council against accepting the statement communicated to me on the day I spoke last on the subject that 530 deaths had been traced and that 192 persons had been found to have been wounded. With reference to the number of deaths, he told the Council that the Government has issued a proclamation to ascertain their number, and that the number which has been reported was 291. He further told us that the Government of the Punjab has adopted every means in their power to ascertain the number of deaths in question. He said:—

> 'A proclamation was made in Amritsar and the surrounding villages inviting all persons who had any information regarding the names of those who had met with death. Intructions were issued to the local authorities there to encourage men to come forward and give the information they possessed. Every possible step was taken in that direction. The result of the inquiry was that the total number of casualties amounted to 291, and any further number suggested by anybody must be taken with great discretion.'"

The Hon'ble Mr. J. P. Thompson:—"Suspicion was the word I used, my Lord."

The Hon'ble Pandit Madan Mohan Malaviya:—"He used the words 'great suspicion'; very well. But, my Lord, what are the actual facts? I have in my hand a letter which has been published by Mr. V. N. Tiwari, Honorary Secretary of the Seva Samiti, who has been working for some time in connection with the distribution of relief in Amritsar. He writes:—

> 'The number of killed so far known to us comes up to 530 including 60 who could not be traced and, unknown and unclaimed, were cremated by certain philanthopic gentlemen.'

"Now, my Lord, the representatives of the Seva Samiti went to Amritsar to distribute relief, and we set an inquiry on foot to find out who were the persons who had been killed or wounded in order to decide whom to give succour, and it was thus that we found out, by sending men round, the number of persons who had met with death or had been wounded. Our Secretary writes:—

> 'I have had to make from the day I came here strenuous efforts to ascertain the number of killed and wounded at the Jallianwala Bagh. The method pursued by our volunteers has been to go from house to house in the city of Amritsar, ascertaining the names not only of the killed, but also of the wounded. I further arranged to send out volunteers to visit every single village in the districts of Amritsar, Gurdaspur, Sialkot and Lahore, so that we might give relief to their dependents in case of want. We are also advertising in the Urdu and Gurmukhi papers of the Punjab asking people to communicate to the office the names and addresses of the killed and wounded'.

It is thus, my Lord, that the number, 530, was obtained. It was not an imaginary number. It was a number obtained with at least as much care, if not much greater care, as the number reported to the authorities at Amritsar. But, my Lord, to give the authorities at Amritsar their due, I do not think they have anywhere stated that they have received the last information about the number of deaths caused. So far as I remember, I think they said that up to the date on which they sent the information to the Government of India, the number of deaths reported was 291, and I think, It was so stated in the statement which was laid on the table. The Hon'ble Mr. Thompson need not, therefore, have asked the Council to receive the number, I stated 'with great suspicion.' Receive it with caution always, but you should not refuse to believe that a larger number of deaths may have occurred simply because the official sources have told you that the number was 291. I do not wish to add even one to the number of deaths that has been caused. I cannot. The number has to be found out. Let us combine to find out the truth and let us stand by the truth.

"Lastly, I will refer to the incident of the corpse in the Jallianwalla Bagh well. Here the Hon'ble Mr. Thompson excelled himself. Referring to my statement, he questioned its correctness and held it up as a test by which any allegations placed by me before the Council or the country should be judged. My Lord, I am compelled therefore for his benefit, as well as for the information of the Council, to refer to this unfortunate incident at some length. My Lord, my esteemed friends, Pandit Motilal Nehru, Swami Shraddhanand and myself, accompanied by several other gentlemen, went to the Jallianwala Bagh, to see the locality where the massacre of so many of our fellow-men had occurred. When we were there we looked into this well, and one of my friends noticed that there was what looked like a corpse in the well. A stone was thrown at it; the thing turned up and we saw it, and the stench was so great that we all moved back from the well. When we returned home, it struck me and one of my friends, that we should bring this fact to the notice of the Deputy Commissioner of Amritsar, merely from the point of view of the sanitation of the locality. There was absolutely no political meaning in my letter to the Chairman of the Municipal Board, and there was no point to be made against the Government, assuming, which would be a wicked assumption, that we were anxious to find out facts against the Government, with the desire of *budnaming* the Government. My Lord, as the fact of a corpse being in the well had come to our notice, we thought that, as a matter of humanity to the people who were living around, we should draw the attention of the authorities to it. I, therefore, wrote this letter to the Chairman of the Municipal Board:—

> 'I beg to draw your attention to the fact that there are still one or more corpses in the big well situate in the Jallianwala Bagh in a very advanced stage of decomposition. I visited the Bagh yesterday in the company of some friends, and we saw a corpse giving out an unbearable stench floating in the water. There are inhabited houses in the close vicinity of the well and, unless it is thoroughly cleansed and disinfected immediately, the health of the neighbourhood will suffer seriously.'

This letter was dated the 30th of June. On the 8th of July, I got a reply from the President of the Municipal Committee in which he said:—

> 'In reply to your letter of 30th June 1919 reporting the existence of corpses in a well in Bagh Jallianwala, I have the honour to say that the well was thoroughly dragged by divers in the presence of the Police and ten competent witnesses. No corpses or skeletons were found, the only things discovered were some pieces of cloth and an earthen pot.

'The well has been disused for some time, which doubtless accounts for the odour you noticed.'

"My Lord, I have to move about a good deal and could not reply to this letter till late in August, and then both my friend Pandit Motilal and I sent a letter to the Deputy Commissioner of Amritsar. In his letter my friend Pandit Motilal said:—

'The report made by his subordinates, I have no hesitation in saying, is a wholly perverted and false account of the incident.

'The Hon'ble Pandit Madan Mohan Malaviya and myself in company with other gentlemen of unimpeachable veracity have actually seen clearly and unmistakeably with our own eyes a dead human body in the well and no police *camouflage* will alter the fact. They may as well try to make out that no human lives were lost in the Jallianwala Bagh on the fateful afternoon of the 13th April.

'It is not my business to inquire by what legerdemain the putrid corpse came to be substituted by 'the loot from the National Bank,' and the only reason why I am troubling you with this letter is that you have by writing to me for information about bribery in the Police of Amritsar evinced a desire to take the people into your confidence, a desire which is highly valued by all public men in India. This incident will, however, show what use the underlings in office make of an honest endeavour on the part of the public to bring facts to the notice of the authorities and how ready the latter are to accept the garbled accounts of their subordinates in preference to authentic statements of facts made by persons of the position and standing of the Hon'ble Pandit Madan Mohan Malaviya. It also affords a sad commentary on the possibility of the much-talked of co-operation between officials and non-officials.'

"My Lord, I supplemented this with a short letter, I said:

'Pandit Motilal Nehru has now told you what he and I in the company of several gentlemen actually saw in the well at the Jallianwala Bagh, and the fact that some pieces of cloth and an earthen pot were found when 'the well was thoroughly dragged by divers in the presence of the Police and ten competent witnesses some days later seems to me wholly immaterial. That there was at least one corpse in the well when we visited it on the 29th June last can admit of no possible doubt and no length of disuse of the well can account for what we saw with our own eyes. I may add that our sense of smell is sufficiently developed to distinguish between the exhalations from a decomposing corpse and the odour of a disused well.'

"My Lord, the Deputy Commissioner of Amritsar acknowledged this letter thus:—

'I thank you for your letter of August 20th. Whatever may be the true facts of the case I think I could convince you, if you could spare time on one of your visits to Amritsar to see me, that my predecessor had as good reasons for supposing you were mistaken as to what you saw in the well as he had for thinking you were correct.'

This was a letter from a gentleman to another gentleman.

"Now, my Lord, I think the facts are sufficiently clear and I need not dilate upon them. Will anybody tell me that it is impossible that the corpse which we saw had been taken out of the well before the ten competent withesses had been summoned by the police to make a report such as was made? I leave it to every reasonable man to judge it for himself.

"Now, my Lord, I will not spend any more time upon the Hon'ble Mr. Thompson. I will only say this:—He is a junior member of this Council; I am a senior member of this Council, perhaps the most senior. My Lord, the traditions of this Council have been, the old traditions of this Council are, that we treat every member who enters our brotherhood as a gentleman. I hope, the Hon'ble Mr. Thompson will not compel us to depart from those traditions.

"I hope that now that I have told him the facts he will behave as a gentleman and withdraw the unworthy remarks with which he offended the dignity of this Council.

"My Lord, I will next deal with the remarks of General Sir Havelock Hudson *re* the incidents at the Jallianwala Bagh. My Lord, it is painful to me to have to refer to these incidents. I have not known in my reading of history anything more distressing to think of than those incidents. The General has tried to give an explanation. He has not controverted the facts, he has tried to give an explanation according to the facts supplied to him. I do not impute any personal misstatement to the General. He is an honourable soldier. He has spoken according to the brief supplied to him by those who were in a position to do so, or whose duty it was to do so. But judging from the allegations which have been made to me, allegations made in many cases by persons who were actually in the Jallianwala Bagh when this tragedy occurred, I am sorry to have to say that several of the statements supplied to the General are incorrect. My Lord, the General described to us, as far as he could, the state of mind in which the military officer, who was asked to co-operate with the civil authorities, would find himself. He said:—'When the military officer had reached the place his first care would be to dispose of his troops with a view to the protection of life and property; his second would be to warn the populace as to the result if it became necessary to resort to force in suppressing any attempt at rioting. These are the steps which were in fact taken by the Officer Commanding at Amritsar. On the 11th and 12th, he reorganised his troops and on the 12th he marched a column round and through the city in order that a display of force might have its effect on the minds of the populace. Then, my Lord, the General said that a proclamation was issued on the evening of the 12th; and on the morning of the 13th April, the Officer Commanding marched a body of troops through all the main streets of the city and announced by beat of drum his intention of using force should occasion arise. The people were permitted to collect in order to hear the proclamations. He then went on to say: 'While the troops were still in the city, information reached the Officer Commanding at about 12 o'clock that in spite of his proclamation a big meeting of rebels would be held at the Jallianwala Bagh at 4.30 in the afternoon.' Now, my Lord, a meeting was no doubt held, but were the men who assembled there rebels? It is a violation of truth to say that they were. I am not saying that the General has said it, he is repeating, I take it, what has been put into him. But I say, my Lord, it is an untruth, to say that the men who were assembled at the Jallianwala Bagh—unarmed inoffensive men, children of tender years and aged men, and the rest of them—that they were rebels. They showed nothing to justify the accusation that they were rebels. But let me proceed. The Officer Commanding received information at about 12 noon that a meeting would be held at 4.30. What did he do, my Lord? General Hudson says:—'As this place had been used before for meetings, and as large assemblies had been addressed by the heads of the agitators on the 29th March and 30th March and the 2nd April, and as a dense mass meeting had assembled here on the 6th during the *hartal* and had listened to speeches intended to bring Government into hatred and contempt, it would thus have been clear to the officer in command that he might expect deliberate defiance of his orders. Why should any such silly thing have been clear to the officer in command? Because certain meetings had been held in this place, because certain speeches had been delivered on another occasion, and because all that had been done peacefully and without giving rise to any violence or disorder, should not the officer in command have concluded that the meeting of the people which was to assemble would disperse as peacefully as similar meetings had done before? What was there to justify the view that he should expect a deliberate defiance of his orders? Even if he did come to such a conclusion, was it not his duty to see that sufficient warning was given to the people that if they did not disperse they would be shot at? No such warning was given. I submit, my Lord, that was a great, a most sinful and criminal dereliction of duty. And what does the General say, happened? The Officer Commanding at Amritsar had to decide about midday on the 13th April how he would act if the projected meeting took place in direct defiance of his authority. I say that the first thing that he ought to have done when he heard of the projected meeting was to communicate by beat of drum to the people that the meeting was prohibited, and that if they assembled in defiance of his order they would be dispersed by force. It is said that there was a proclamation made in some parts of Amritsar. The people allege, those who live there told me, that the proclamation was not made in all parts of the city, but only in certain parts, and that people in the other parts did not hear of it at all or they would not have gone to expose themselves to a risk of their lives.

"The next thing, my Lord, that the General has been made to put forward is equally unsatisfactory. He has said: 'The Officer Commanding at Amritsar had to decide about midday on the 13th April how he would act if the projected meeting took place in direct defiance of his authority. After making dispositions for the safety of his command, he found that he had but a small striking force at his disposal. Realising the gravity of the situation the Officer Commanding this small force (of 50 rifles and forty men armed with kukries only and two armoured cars), marched this force straight to the Jallianwala Bagh, leaving the armoured cars behind owing to the narrowness of streets. On reaching the Bagh his force was confronted by a vast assembly, some thousands strong, who were being harangued by a man who was standing on a raised platform.' Now, my Lord, was this force of 50 rifles and 40 men armed with kukries only such a despicable force as the General would have us believe? Was this force with all the munition it had at its disposal—I am told on the authority of a high official that 1700 service bullets were used there, another version being that 2800 had been used—such a despicable force that it could not face a few thousands of men who were utterly unarmed? Could it by any justification be said that this force was confronted by a force of some thousands strong, as one force is confronted by another force? I submit not. The General went on to say: 'Realising the danger it was clearly the duty of the officer to disperse this unlawful assembly.' Very well I will agree it was; then this duty could have been performed by simply proclaiming to the people that if they did not disperse they would be fired on. My Lord, I referred the other day to the Riot Act passed, I think, in the reign of George I. In that Act it is provided that after a proclamation has been read to a riotous assembly to disperse, an hour must elapse from the time of reading the proclamation, before the assembly should be fired on. That was a humane provision. Do not wait for an hour, if you think you must not; but most certainly you must make sure that the people have heard the proclamation and understood what the situation is; and if they continue to remain where they were then fire on them, but still not in a way to kill them but to impress them with the danger to which they are exposed and to make them run away from the place. But what was the course followed here. The General said: 'Realising the danger to his small force, unless he took immediate action, and being aware of the inadequacy of the measures taken to restore order on the 10th of April, he (the Officer Commanding) ordered fire to be opened. The crowd was dispersed and the force withdrew.'

"My Lord, what a chapter of woe is concealed between these two sentences. The people were fired on. They began to run for their lives to all the corners of the Jallianwala Bagh; and they were shot at, even when they were flying. I have seen the place, and people have told me that there were heaps of corpses piled one on the top of another. The people tried to climb over the walls to save themselves from the fire. They were not allowed to escape. I am told that there was a wall of corpses raised at more than one place in the Jallianwala

Bagh. I have seen a narrow lane, not wider than five feet, into which the people ran for their lives and were there shot at. I have seen a receptacle there which, it was said, was filled with the blood of those men who were killed or wounded. Was it necessary for dispersing the assembly, to shoot at people who were running for their lives? When the Officer Commanding had seen that the persons assembled were running away for their lives, was it necessary to continue the firing? Should he not have stopped it, at least then? It is well known to the military authorities, and to General Hudson, that a number of men had stretched themselves on the ground to escape being shot. One of these men told me that while he was lying so stretched on the ground, two shots passed over him and that the third hit him in the leg and has maimed him for life. Should not these facts have been disclosed by General Hudson when he was speaking on behalf of the Government, and should not some explanation be offered for them? My Lord, it was a most unjustifiable massacre of men which was made in the Jallianwala Bagh in the name of dispersing the assembly there. General Hudson spoke of this assembly as an organised rebellion. I do not know what to say about it. It is inexpressibly sad to hear any such expression used of men who had not the remotest idea of rebelling against the King. I have told the Council that there was one man in the assembly with a child of 7 months in his arms. There were a number of boys there of ages ranging from 12 to 18. I have seen some of the young men who were injured; I have talked to them. They did not go to the meeting with any idea or organised rebellion; they had no such idea. If they had any idea they would have gone there armed at least with *lathis*; they were entirely unarmed, innocent and helpless, and yet they were fired on. I will not attempt to characterise the whole sad affair. My feelings are too deep to permit of my doing so.

"I will now refer to the incident of people having been made to crawl on their hands and knees. I was shocked at the ripple of laughter which passed through some parts of the Council when it was told that several men had undertaken to do this voluntarily. I should like to know whether any Member of this Council would like to voluntarily perform that process in this room. I will say nothing more about it. But before I leave Amritsar, I should say a word about the stopping of the electric lights and the supply of water. As a sort of explanation, I could not regard it as a justification, it was said that there was a fear that the people were going to attack the water pump station. But it was not said that there was any attack really made. It was also said that there was rumour afloat in the city that the water had been poisoned, and so it was considered prudent to stop the supply. But the water was not stopped in the civil station, and if such a rumour had got about, should it not have been left to die of itself? Could not the residents of the city have been left to discard any such rumour if they had heard it? Was it not the best way to kill the rumour to let the people have the water to quench their thirst and be happy? I say this is the feeblest, flimsiest explanation that was ever offered. And then what about the electric light? Was any poison introduced in it? Why was it then cut off? I have never heard such flimsy arguments used in this Council ever before. I will now come to the Gujranwala incidents. I think I have made it clear that I have no complaint personally against General Hudson. I take it that he merely put forward the case which those who were responsible for supplying him with his brief, put in his hands. But I must point out that no case has been made out for the use of the aeroplanes in Gujranwala. It was said at the time in the *Civil and Military Gazette* that 'the crowds were giving up the contest' *i.e.* were dispersing 'when the aeroplanes arrived from Lahore'. Now if the crowds had begun to disperse when the aeroplanes arrived, where was the necessity for using them? Where was the necessity for inflicting several casualties by bombs and machine-guns? Where was the necessity of throwing bombs at places a mile and a half or two miles from the railway goods shed which had been set fire to? Where was the necessity of dropping bombs from aeroplanes in the villages of Gharjak, Bhagwanpur and Dhulla? The picture given of Gujranwala by General Hudson would make one think that there was a condition of war there. The difficulties of aiming from aeroplanes were brought into requisition and offered as some sort of explanation. Were there any sort of anti-aircraft machines at work at Gujranwala that the aeroplanes had to fly at great height and so missed their aims? I have been told that the bombs were dropped from no great height—perhaps from 100 feet at the outside. Would a bomb dropped from a height of 50, 60 or 100 feet fall half a mile or a mile away from the place where the object aimed at existed? The village Gharjak, which I visited, must be over a mile from the place where the crowd was assembled. I was told that there were some small children playing in the field where the bomb was dropped. It was mere luck that they were not hurt. I have seen the Khalsa Boarding House at Gujranwala; it is, I think, about a mile from the town proper. I have seen where a bomb fell in that institution. It was lucky that 160 students of the boarding house had just gone out of the hostel to see the aeroplanes, or some of them might have been done to death. I saw the injuries done to the walls by the missiles. In Dhulla, a woman and a child were killed. Was this, I ask, my Lord, necessary for maintaining or restoring order at Gujranwala? I submit not. As regards the plea for the soldier which General Hudson put forward with such pathos, I will deal with it later on. I have not less regard for a soldier's life, than General Hudson has; but things have to be seen in their true proportion. We have to see clearly what the duties and responsibilities of soldiers, as well as of civilians, are to the population at a time of disorder.

"I shall now deal with the speech of the Hon'ble the Law Member. He ridiculed the opposition to the Bill.

"He held up the Hon'ble Raja Sir Rampal Singh to ridicule and said that the speech which he delivered in this Council the other day was not written by him, but by some one else for him. My Lord, this statement was untrue, and it was a gratuitous insult offered to Raja Sir Rampal Singh. I knew that Raja Sir Rampal Singh is able to write his own speeches and does write his own speeches; and I wired to him asking him to come up here to be able to reply to the charge, but the Hon'ble Member evidently got my wire rather late. So he has wired to me; 'Wire too late cannot reach in time. Lowndes' attack unjustifiable and groundless; speech was written by me, contained my views, Government is wrong.'

"Now, my Lord, the next gentleman to be attacked was Mr. Sinha. If he had made a speech which met with the approval of the Hon'ble the Law Member, he would have had the honour of being quoted as Mrs. Besant, Mr. Horniman, Mr. Sastri and Mr. Gandhi have been quoted. But he had the misfortune to express opinions which were not acceptable to the Hon'ble the Law Member at the time, and my Lord, Mr. Sinha also came in for unjust criticism. So did my friend Mr. Chanda. I will not speak of myself for I take the criticisms of some Hon'ble Members on the Government side in a very calm and considerate manner. I know that it is a very unpleasant thing to speak the truth and even more unpleasant to hear the truth on occasions. But I try to put forward the truth according to my light. Perhaps I err sometimes in doing so. Perhaps

I err more than others. If so, I am sorry for it; but I put forward what I believe to be the truth whole-heartedly, and I shall continue to do so regardless of any frowns or criticisms from Government benches. The learned Law Member referred to us as gentleman who came from remote places—he said one came from his palace or fortress in Oudh—I do not remember the exact words he used."

The Hon'ble Mr. Sachchidananda Sinha:—"From the fastnesses of Oudh."

The Hon'ble Pandit Madan Mohan Malaviya:—"Yes, from the fastnesses of Oudh; another from Assam; a third from Bihar; and a fourth came from Allahabad and he said that not a single Punjab Member had asked that the Bill should be proceeded with. My Lord, you do a wrong to the people of the Punjab in not giving them an opportunity to elect their own representatives. You nominate such men as you like, and then you turn back upon them and say that the Members who are sitting here from the Punjab do not say that the Bill should not be proceeded with. I mean no disrespect to the Punjab member; but if you yourself shut the popular voice out of this Council, should you turn back and make use of that fact as an argument in support of your measures? Is this fair, my Lord? I say it is not. I know perhaps one Member from the Punjab is elected. But how many elected Members have you given to the Punjab? Let the people have the opportunity of returning those in whom they have confidence, and you will hear their opinions as freely expressed here as you hear the opinions of the people of the other provinces. My Lord, the Hon'ble the Law Member went on to quote Mrs. Besant, and Mr. Horniman—and when he had not the courtesy of putting a 'Mr.' before his name—and he or Mr. Hailey quoted Mr. Sastri. My Lord, I am sorry for the Hon'ble the Law Member that he should have to rely in support of the Bill before the Council on expressions of opinion by Mr. Horniman in his paper when the sad events of the Punjab were fresh and when it had not been investigated what the facts were;—when the Punjab Government supported by the Government of India would not allow the real facts of the situation to leak out from the Punjab, when people were taken aback by what had happened, but had had no time and opportunity to investigate the facts. Mrs. Besant stood in the same position. I am sure if the facts were known as they are known now, neither Mrs. Besant nor Mr. Horniman, nor Mr. Sastri would adhere to the opinions which they had expressed; the opinions they would now express would be very much modified in the light of the facts which have been published.

"Then, my Lord, my friend the Law Member went a little further and speaking with the air of a Dogberry dressed in a little brief authority, he spoke of us contemptuously as self-constituted Commissioners who went from Allahabad to the Punjab. Now, my Lord, let me tell the Hon'ble Member that we are not self-constituted Commissioners. The Congress, the last Congress, was attended at Delhi by nearly 5,400 delegates from all parts of India. According to a prescribed procedure it regularly appoints every year an All-India Congress Committee as its executive. This All India Congress Committee is representative of all sections of the people. In view of the recent events in the Punjab, this Committee met and considered the situation, and appointed a sub-committee—of which I have the honour to be ex-officio President and my esteemed friend the Hon'ble Pandit Motilal Nehru a member, and of which several other distinguished Congressmen are members—to arrange to help in the inquiry which the Government had said was going to be conducted. Now, my Lord, having been so commissioned, not by ourselves but by a very respectable body, from whom it is an honour to take a commission, we did spend some time in the Punjab. We investigated the facts; we visited the places where these sad events had happened; we saw with regret the signs of the fires that had been set to houses and Churches; we saw also with regret and pain the signs of the killing that had been resorted to in the Jallianwala Bagh; and we heard distressing accounts of other deaths which had been caused. My Lord, we did not publish any expression of our personal opinions on the situation, until we had visited these places and made inquiries. What was the next step I took? My Lord, I sent to the Government the result of my investigations, and the investigations of my colleagues, in the shape of a number of questions, and asked them to give us information on the various allegations that had been made to us.

"We thus placed the Government in the best position we could to know the facts, and if they did not know them, to inquire into them. And now that the Bill before us is being presented by Government, I feel it my duty to oppose the Bill on the ground that these allegations should be inquired into by the Committee that has been appointed before the Bill is passed. I have said in distinct terms more than once, as the report of my speech by the official reporters will show, that the facts have to be sifted. Let them be sifted by the Committee of Inquiry which you have appointed, and when we know what the facts are, then will be the time for the Government and the Council to sit down together and weigh what are the acts which should be justified by this Council; what are the acts among those which some people had unfortunately, in the performance of their duty, to commit, and against which they should be indemnified. That is the reason why I oppose the Bill. I have during these six weeks met a number of men of the Punjab, both among those who are enjoying their freedom as we do, and those who have unfortunately been deprived of their freedom and are shut up in His Majesty's jails. I have met a number of such people and ascertained facts first-hand from them, some of the facts from the lips of the men who are condemned to death and are passing anxious days to know what will happen to them. I have not put forward these facts lightly; I feel it my duty to bring these facts to the notice of Government. Even if I had not a commission from the Congress Committee, I should have been proud and thankful to have gone forward to the Punjab, as a self-constituted commissioner, to find out the wrongs that had been done to my fellow-men and to bring those wrongs to light. My Lord, I owe a duty to my fellow-men. When atrocities were perpetrated in Belgium, who constituted the Commission over which Lord Bryce presided? Did the Belgian Government constitute that Commission? No, so far as I remember, it was the then Premier of England who asked Lord Bryce and others to visit Belgium and to report upon the wrongs which it was said had been perpetrated. If the Government of India did not take the steps which they were bound in duty and in honour to take, if the Punjab Government did not take the steps which they were bound in honour and in duty to His Majesty the King-Emperor and the people to take, to ascertain the facts and to seek to have the proper remedies adopted, it was no sin on my part, nor on the part of my friend Pandit Moti Lal Nehru or my other fellow-workers, to go to the Punjab and to make such a sacrifice of our time and other advantages as was demanded by the situation in the cause of humanity. Now, my Lord, I appeal to all my friends, to all my friends, official as well as non-official, to look at the whole question in a fair manner. Speeches cannot explain away things. Let us combine to find out the facts. I have heard some very brilliant speeches made in this Council on these unhappy incidents; I heard these speeches applauded, loudly applauded, by those whose points of view coincided with those of the speakers. My Lord, I have been reminded of a few lines from Milton (quoted by a writer on the atrocities in Belgium), in which he draws a terrible imagery when he says of Nature:

'Only with speeches fair
She woos the gentle air
To hide her guilty front with innocent snow,
And on her naked shame
Pollute with sinful blame
The saintly veil of maiden white to throw;
Confounded that her Maker's eyes
Should look so near upon her foul deformities.'

"My Lord, I fear that even now some of my Hon'ble friends on the Government benches do not realise the enormity of the things that have been done. I appeal to them not to think of disposing of these by speeches, but to look closely into the facts, and if the truth be where the people allege it is, to accept the truth. George Herbert is one of your holiest of divines. He has been described as 'groaning and growing towards heaven.' He has beautifully expressed this sentiment, of which I make a present to my friends; not by way of taunt, the occasion is too serious for it; but in all humility and sincerity. Let the officers of Government and ourselves putting aside all small feeling of jealousy, all small feeling of racial bias, let the officers of Government and ourselves combine to find out the truth. Let the truth be established in order that justice may be done. George Herbert says:—

'If truth be with thy friend, be with them both.
Share in the Conquest, and confess a troth'

"If the truth is with my friends, who have put the opposite side, I say, my Lord, solemnly and deliberately, I shall bow to them and be grateful to them for establishing it. But if the truth be on the other side, for God's sake, for the sake of our fellow-men, for the sake of truth and justice, for the good name of the British Government, let it be found and established, and let the Council be then asked to determine what acts ought to be justified and indemnified.

"My Lord, there is only one other aspect of the question to which I have to draw attention. I am sorry I have not the strength in me at this moment to say all that I wish to say; but I cannot conclude—I shall not be doing my duty to this Council and to His Majesty, to whom I owe allegiance, if I were to conclude without making one more earnest and final effort to prevent the Government from committing the great mistake which they are going to commit if they accept this Bill. Among the arguments advanced by the Hon'ble Sir George lowndes, one was that an Indemnity Bill was a necessity. Your Lordship also was advised to say in your opening speech that, whatever the result of the inquiry, we were bound to protect our officers. My Lord, with great respect I beg to differ from that view. It is not correct to say that, whatever may be the result of the Inquiry, an Indemnity Bill must be passed. As Lord Alverstone said in a debate in 1818 in the House of Lords—from which I quoted yesterday—'a legislative assembly has to be satisfied whether the acts done were necessary and proper before it would indemnify those that committed those acts.'

"Now, my Lord, the rights of man do not depend upon any particular charter or constitution. 'The sacred rights of man,' as Alexander Hamilton has well put it, 'are not to be seached for in old parchments and musty records; they are written as with a sunbeam in the whole volume of human nature by the hand of Divinity itself and can never be erased by mortal power.' Among these is the right to protection of life and liberty. Every single individual, however humble he may be, can claim this right of his Government. His Majesty's Government have also promised this right to every individual among his subjects. Now, my Lord, if a man has been injured, if one has been deprived of his life or limb, or liberty or honour, he or his relations have a right to seek a redress of the wrong done. If you want that a person who has suffered loss of life, limb, liberty or honour should not be able to seek any redress against that loss, you must put it on some footing which will be understood and appreciated by him. Parliament can ascertain acts. The community, the public at large whom the Parliament or the Council represents, can take note of the events which happened, and of the circumstances in which they happened, and can say, that though certain wrongs were done yet in view of the situation, in view of the greatest good of the greatest number, those regrettable wrongs shall be excused. The individual acquiesces in that decision, he waives his right to sue his oppressor or assailant or those who injured him. That is done with the implied consent of the person who is vitally interested in the matter. Here you are asking us to assent to a Bill which seeks to justify acts which still require investigation, to indemnify officers against acts, the legality, the propriety, the humanity of which is still under consideration, still to be investigated. I submit, my Lord, it is an utterly wrong procedure that you are following. The keystone of an Indemnity Bill, as I have submitted, is that the introduction of martial law should have been necessary and for the benefit of the public. You have taken away that keystone and yet you want to pass the Bill. My Lord, it is not right to do so. Let me here quote to the Council the opinion of Sir James Macintosh cited at page 541 of Dicey's 'Law of the Constitution.' He says:—

'The only principle on which the law of England tolerates what is called Martial Law is necessity; its continuance requires precisely the same justification of necessity; and if it suvives, the necessity on which alone it exists for a single minute, it becomes instantly a mere exercise of lawless violence. When foreign invasion or Civil War renders it impossible for Courts of Law to sit, or to enforce the execution of their judgments, it becomes necessary to find some rude substitute for them, and to employ for that purpose the Military, which is the only remaining Force in the community. While the laws are silenced by the noise of arms, the rulers of Armed Force must punish, as equitably as they can, those crimes which threaten their own safety and that of society; *but no longer*'.

"My Lord, martial law was introduced at midnight between the 15th and 16th of April. This Bill seeks to justify and validate acts which were done before that date. It also seeks to justify and validate acts done during all the long period during which martial law was maintained. I submit, my Lord, there is no justification for the Council to pass such a Bill, to accept such a measure.

"My Lord, the Law Member dealt with many side-issues in his long and learned speech, but he did not reply to the main points raised by me, points which have become very much stronger by the alteration made by the Government in the preamble of the Bill. I submit, therefore, that the Government are not justified in proceeding with the Bill. I may here say that the learned Law member told the Council that the conviction in the case of Fitzgerald to which I had referred has neen quashed. I find on page 819, in column 820, of 27 State Trials of 1820 the following paragraph:—

'An application was made on the part of Fitzgerald in the Court of Exchequer to set aside the verdict obtained against him by Mr. Wright which was dismissed with full costs'."

The Hon'ble Sir George Lowndes:—"May I explain that that is the passage I quoted from, and it appears to me to be direct authority for the statement that the conviction was quashed?"

The Hon'ble Pandit Madan Mohan Malaviya:—"Here is the authority."

The Hon'ble Sir George Lowndes:—"The Hon'ble Member knows English. As I read the passage 'which' refers to the last substantive before it".

The Hon'ble Pandit Madan Mohan Malaviya:—"I will again read the passage and leave it to my Hon'ble friend who knows English better than I do to say what it means:—

> 'An application was made on the part of Fitzgerald in the Court of Exchequer to set aside the verdict obtained against him by Mr. Wright which was dismissed with full costs.'

"Now, my Lord, I will not detain the Council longer. I think what I have said is sufficient to show that the Council ought not to accept the motion of the Hon'ble the Home Member unless it is satisfied of the essential fact that there was an open rebellion, and that it was necessary to introduce martial law. This question remains to be determined by the Committee of Inquiry and therefore the Bill is premature.

"My Lord, the learned Law Member and the Hon'ble the Home Member spoke vehemently of the duty of protecting soldiers, policemen and other officers who had acted under the orders of Government. They urged that these at least should not suffer for any error of the Government of India. I submit that this is an entirely fallacious argument, opposed to the basic principles of the constitution. It is a well-settled principle that no order of a superior officer can protect or ought to protect a subordinate in his commission of any illegal acts. If a subordinate receives an order to do any illegal thing or act from his superior, it is his duty to disobey it. Even the King cannot give an order to do an illegal thing. In support of this view I would draw attention to a passage in Dicey at page 283. He says:—

> 'The legal dogma, as old at least as the time of Edward the Fourth, that, if any man arrest another without lawful warrant, even by the King's command, he shall not be excused, but shall be liable to an action for false imprisonment, is not

a special limitation imposed upon the royal prerogative, but the application to acts done under royal orders of that principle of individual responsiblity which run through the whole law of torts.'

"My Lord, the Governor General cannot claim to exercise a higher right than His Majesty the King does and in the case of a King, I may remind the Council that the promise given by Charles I to Strafford that 'not a hair of your head shall be touched by Parliament' was insufficient to protect that bureaucrat from the just anger of Parliament. The argument that the Council is bound in honour to protect its officers has also no force. The Council never made a promise to anybody to protect him. If the Executive made a promise, every officer ought to know the limitations on the power of the Executive, and I hope that one of the results of these deplorable incidents will be that soldiers and public officers will have learnt their duty to the people. If any officers of Government have acted in excess of their authority or without humanity, they ought to take their trial and answer a charge on that account. The Hon'ble the Law Member and the Hon'ble the Home Member specially mentioned the cases of soldiers called upon to protect the lives and property of civilians and said that if indemnity was not granted to them the soldiers would refuse in future to act. My Lord, I do not think that any such evil result will follow. I think the result that will follow will be a salutary one for the soldiers and for the civilians as well. The argument is an entirely fallacious one. Soldiers have a right, like other citizen, to repel force by force and to take all proper steps to protect life and property. But if soldiers were to kill men unarmed, unresisting, and disfigure, maim or cut down women and children, if unresisting men were cut down, whether by troops or not, it would be murder, for which the parties are liable to be tried by the laws of the country.' I refer my Hon'ble friend, the Law Member, to the case of R. *vs.* Burdett, 4 B. and Al. 323 at p. 327, where the Judgement of Bayley, J. from which I have quoted is given.

"But it is said that soldiers must obey orders given by their military officers on pain of being court-martialled. Here also the law is quite clear. Soldiers are bound to obey orders, but not illegal orders, which are manifestly and obviously illegal such as the order to fire at Jallianwala Bagh was. I shall again refer to Dicey who puts this view very clearly. He says at p. 299:—

'A soldier is bound to obey any lawful order which he

receives from his military superior. But a soldier cannot any more than a civilian avoid responsibility for breach of the law by pleading that he broke the law in *bona fide* obedience to the orders' (say) of the Commander-in-Chief. Hence the position of a soldier is in theory and may be in practice a difficult one. He may, as it has been well said, be liable to be shot by a Court-martial if he disobeys an order and to be hanged by a judge and jury if he obeys it. His situation and the line of his duty may be seen by considering how soldiers ought to act on such occasions.'

"Now, I will not quote further, though what follows is very important and throws valuable light upon the question raised by the Hon'ble the Law Member. The whole law has been very well summarised by Dicey at p. 302 of his valuable book. He says:—

'The hardship of a soldier's position resulting from this inconvenience is much diminished by the power of the Crown to nullify the effect of an unjust conviction by means of a pardon. While however, a soldier runs no substantial risk of punishment for obedience to orders which a man of common sense may honestly believe to involve no breach of law, he can under no circumstances escape the chance of his military conduct becoming the subject of inquiry before a civil tribunal, and cannot avoid liability on the ground of obedience to superior orders for any act which a man of ordinary sense must have known to be a crime'.

"I submit, my Lord, this places the legal aspect of the case in a thoroughly clear light. I will refer to only one other passage from a judgment of Justice Stephen which is found at p. 301 of Dicey's book, and which seems to me to be very apposite. It is this:—

'Soldiers might reasonably think that their officer had good grounds for ordering them to fire into a disorderly crowd which to them might not appear to be at that moment engaged in acts of dangerous violence, but soldiers could hardly suppose that their officer could have any good grounds for ordering them to fire a volley down a crowded street when no disturbance of any kind was either in progress or apprehended. The doctrine that a soldier is bound under all circumstances whatever to obey his superior officer would be fatal to military discipline itself, for it would justify the private in shooting the

Colonel by the orders of the Captain, or in deserting to the enemy on the field of battle on the order of his immediate superior. I think it is not less monstrous to suppose that superior orders would justify a soldier in the massacre of unoffending civilians in time of peace or in the exercise of inhuman cruelties such as the slaughter of women and children, during a rebellion.'

"I submit, therefore, with confidence, that the view put forward by the Hon'ble the Law Member is not the correct view of the law, and I submit that both on grounds of fact and law this Bill is premature. Let, my Lord, the Government and the country wait, therefore, for the result of the inquiry which the Secretary of State and your Excellency's Government have agreed to institute. On the results of that inquiry being known, let the matter be placed before this Council for further consideration, and let everybody concerned rest assured that every man will render all the reasonable support which ought to be given to soldiers and other public officers who have discharged their duty properly. I once more most earnestly request your Excellency not to proceed with this Bill and to let it stand over till the next Session in Delhi."

[At this stage the Council adjourned for Lunch till 3 p.m.]

The Hon'ble Mr. J. P. Thompson:—"I should be grateful, my Lord, to the Hon'ble Member for having given me such an easy task to deal with. If it is true that there are people from whom abuse is a compliment, I should thank the Hon'ble Member for the compliments he has showered on me. But I feel I do not deserve them. Tne heat with which he credited me was non-existent and many of the statements which he put into my month I never made.

"The first case that the Hon'ble Member dealt with was that of the Inspector who was assaulted in the Badshahi mosque at Lahore. He prefaced his remarks by telling us that he had sent in certain questions and that, as Government did not give him an answer to those questions, he felt justified in stating these questions to the Council in the form of facts. I should like to have heard from the Hon'ble Member, if he had been in his seat, whether the allegation against the Inspector was ever submitted in the form of a question. It it was, all I can say is that, to the best of my recollection, I have never seen it. I do not propose to deal with the quotation which he read out from the evidence of Inspector Ali Gauhar, because the ripple of laughter which went round the Council when the Hon'ble

Member read it showed me that I had already a verdict in my favour. The Hon'ble Member played his trump card and found he had revoked.

"The next case he dealt with was that of the persons confined in the racquet court at Amritsar. As regards this, I gave the facts as they were supplied to me. How far that explanation satisfies the Hon'ble Member or the Council is another question, but I pointed out, as the Council will remember, that if these gentlemen were subjected to hardships, there were European women and children suffering not dissimilar hardships within a very few yards of the place where they were confined.

"The next case to which the Hon'ble Pandit passed was that of the schoolboys who were flogged at Kasur. He complained, if I understood him aright, that I did not deal with many other cases of flogging. He left it to be inferred that a reference to these other cases had been contained in the question which had been disallowed and which he afterwards stated to the Council in the form of a narrative. I will read that question to the Council—'Will the Government be pleased to state if it is a fact that several schoolboys at Kasur were flogged and, if so, state their names, ages, and the number of stripes administered in each case and the offences for which they were punished.' I told him that three pupils of the Municipal Boarding School were caned and three of the Islamia school. This was done by way of school discipline. At the request of the Head Master, military aid had been invoked 'to deal with continuous insubordination on the part of the boys.' I am reading from the explanation submitted by the Sub-divisional Officer. That explained what had happened in the case of the schoolboys who had been caned at the request of the Head Master. I went on to say that two other schoolboys were sent by the Commission for summary trial and received there strokes of the cane after trial by the martial law officer. I ask the Council what other explantion I could give. So far as I am aware that explanation covers the cases of flogging of schoolboys at Kasur, and it was with the flogging of schoolboys at Kasur that the question put by the Hon'ble Member dealt.

"Then, my Lord, the Pandit went on to the case of Mr. Manohar Lal. He tells us, if I understood him aright, that Mr. Manohar Lal's house was locked up for several days and that his family were compelled to live in outhouses. The facts as I understand them, and I have received them from the officers at Lahore who are familiar with the case, are that, Mr. Manohar Lal was arrested on the 18th April. On the evening of that day, I think, the house was shut up by the Police. When they got there, they found his family moving into outhouses, thereby indicating that they had already received instructions from Mr. Manohar Lal as to what they were to do. The house was searched on the morning of the 19th and at 1 o'clock that day his family were permitted to return to the house.

"Then, my Lord, we come to the case of Gujranwala. On this as well as other cases, the Pandit quoted certain extracts from accounts which appeared in the *Civil and Military Gazette* and he appeared to be under the impression that there was something official about them. Hon'ble Members will recollect that at an early stage in the proceedings the Pandit quoted from a publication entitled 'Punjab disturbances' which was issued by the *Civil and Military Gazette* in respect of which he definitely alleged that the publication was one which was published under the authority of the Punjab Government. I corrected him, and he pretended not to be satisfied with my explanation, but I note he did not venture to quote it as a Government publication again. My Lord, as far as I can recall, the only connection that the Punjab Government had with the publication was to protest against the inclusion of certain of its contents. The Pandit read certain extracts from one of these articles which appeared in the *Civil and Military Gazette* on what happened at Gujranwala. The Council will remember that in his original speech he stated that respectable persons were chained together and were marched to the city two by two, headed by a Hindu and a Muhammadan 'with a view to ridicule Hindu and Muhammadan unity as was stated by Colonel O'Brien.' Now, my Lord, the passage which he quoted from the article after describing how persons had been marched through the city went on to say that this spectacle of Hindu and Muhammadan unity must have been most impressive. Would not anybody reading that article come to the conclusion that that was merely a comment of the writer? I do not see what justification the Pandit had for reading into the action of Colonel O'Brien, who was in charge of the arrest at Gujranwala, the sentiments supplied by the writer of the article in the *Civil and Military Gazette*.

"As regards the Ramnagar case I have nothing more to say. The Pandit gave no answer to the criticism which I passed on what he said at the time. All he had to offer us was the *a priori* argument that because these people were respectable they could never have taken part in such disreputable performances.

"The Hon'ble Pandit also attributed to me, if I understood him aright, certain remarks regarding the burning of a *bhusa* stack at Lyallpur. To the best of my belief, my Lord, I never touched on the incident of the burning of a *bhusa* stack at Lyallpur. I knew perfectly well what the facts were, and the Pandit, so far as I remember, asked no question about it. It is possible I think, that it was Mr. Hailey who in another connection mentioned the case of burning a *bhusa* stack at Lyallpur, but as I do not remember exactly in what connection he mentioned it, I am unable to say how far, from the point of view of the Pandit, that mention was justified.

"I now come, my Lord, to the case of the Jallianwala Bagh at Amritsar. The Pandit told us that he received a letter from a Mr. Tiwari, stating that 531 persons had been killed including 60 who had not been traced. He did not tell us how he came to include persons who had not been traced, but he said that 531 were killed.

"Now, my Lord, since I spoke on last Friday, another fact has come to my notice which makes it more probable perhaps than before that the details that we have got regarding the number of persons who were killed in Amritsar are very near the mark. I was informed only a few days ago by a very old resident of Amritsar that for every cemetery and every burning ground in Amritsar, there are sub-registrars who write down particulars of every corpse which is brought for disposal. Those returns are submitted to the Registrar and through him to the Health Officer. So that whether people report deaths or not there is this additional check, supplied by the cemeteries and burning grounds. I still claim, my Lord, that any deaths which were reported, which are considerably in excess of the number which we admit, namely 291, must be received with grave suspicion. I did not claim, and I do not claim now, that we know or ever shall know, the exact number of persons who were killed. But what I do say is, that the information that we have supplied is far and away the best information which is at present available, and that if the people who are collecting information for the Pandit have done their duty in responding to the invitation which was conveyed to them to give us any information which they might possess as to the number of persons who had been killed—I say that if they have done their duty—then our figures are as nearly complete as I or the Pandit can make them.

"As regards the corpse which the Pandit says he saw in the well, really the incident is hardly worth dealing with. But one thing is certain, and that is, that if there was a corpse down the well when the Pandit visited the place at the end of June, it was not the corpse of anybody who had been killed on the 13th of April. It is established by expert evidence that after 2½ months in the hot weather a corpse would be a mere collection of bones at the bottom of a well—so that as evidence of anything which had been in there from the time when the firing took place on April the 13th, there is nothing in it at all. But it does seem to me that when the Pandit wrote to the Municipal Committee saying that there were 'still' one or more corpses down the well, it was perfectly obvious that what he was doing was trying to create horror or pity in the minds of his hearers in connection with the incident of the Jallianwala Bagh. I leave the matter to the Council, but that conclusion appears to me to be irrefutable.

"The Pandit again talked of the desire for co-operation between officials and non-officials in connection with these disturbances. I have already given you one instance in which we had invited the co-operation of those who were collecting information in regard to the number of deaths in Jallianwala Bagh. The Pandit's assertion that the number of deaths is nearly double what we found after issuing that invitation is a strange comment on the degree of co-operation which has been offered by non-officials. I will give the Council another instance. There were, as the Pandit no doubt knows, a large number of serious allegations against the honesty of the police at Amritsar. It was said that many of them had made large sums. The Lieutenant-Governor was anxious that these allegations should be probed to the bottom, and instructions were issued that the local authorities should invite the co-operation of the Pandit and Pandit Motilal Nehru in finding out whether there was anything in them. Letters were written and the answers we received gave us no information at all. Whether any further answers have been sent since the two which I saw, I cannot say; but the first letters that were received gave us no information at all....."

The Hon'ble Pandit Madan Mohan Malaviya:—"I have seen no letter of the kind mentioned; nor has my friend Pandit Motilal Nehru received anything as far as I know."

The Hon'ble Mr. J. P. Thompson:—"The Hon'ble Member is certainly in a better position than I am to say whether he received a letter or not, but I understood a letter was sent to him and to

Pandit Motilal Nehru who was working in close co-operation with him, and the answer that was received was one which gave us no assistance at all. Whether a separate letter was sent to the Pandit or not seems to me to be really immaterial.

"The last specific allegation that the Pandit made was in regard to the cutting off of the electric lights and water-supply at Amritsar by order of the General Officer Commanding. It was not really for me to justify the action taken by the military authorities. But I gave the Council what I believed to be the facts, and here again it is for the Council to say whether they are satisfied with the explanation or not. But what I said, on the information supplied to me, was that on the 10th of April—I give it in rather greater detail—on the 10th of April two out of the three feeders which give energy to the city were damaged by the mob about 1 p.m. Later on at 2.30 p.m. the mob entered the power-house and stopped the whole plant. At 7 p.m. the one remaining feeder was started. On the 11th the mob prevented a mistri from mending the two damaged feeders. That evening the power was cut off the city altogether by order of the General Officer Commanding, and remained off till the 19th. In regard to the water-supply, I mentioned the story that the supply had been poisoned. But the water was turned on again early on the 11th after having been cut off on the evening of the 10th, and it was again cut off later on the 11th and remained off till the 14th. Those were the facts and that is the explanation. How far it is a justification it is for the Council to say. That completes, my Lord, the examination of the cases with which the Pandit has dealt.

"He then went on to give me a severe rebuke for transgressing, as he said, the traditions of this Council. I think if the Hon'ble Member had been familiar with the lighter forms of English literature and especially with the literature of the comic stage, he would have avoided the 'you're no gentleman' retort which usually comes from a housemaid caught out in an embarrassing situation. It is hardly worthy of the dignity of this Council.

"Towards the close of his speech the Hon'ble Member quoted some lines from Milton. It is quite in keeping, my Lord, with human nature for a disappointed man to seek refuge in great literature. His attack has failed all along the line, and I sympathise with him in his disappointment. Let me give him another quotation from the poem which, I think, perhaps describes his situation with some appropriateness:—

'The old Dragon under ground
In straiter limits bound,
Not half so far casts his usurped sway,
And wroth to see his kingdom fail,
Swinges the scaly horror of his folded tail.'

"My Lord, the lashing of the Pandit's tail is the measure of his disappointment.

"My Lord, I have nothing more to say. But with regard to what the Pandit has said about me, what I will say is this. What this Council values above all else, and what I trust it will always value is straightforwardness and simplicity of character. And I hope that, senior or junior, there will never be a lack of Members in this Council who will be ready to protest against perversions of truth and to stamp misrepresentations for what they are."

The Hon'ble Major Malik Sir Umar Hayat Khan:—"My Lord, allow me to congratulate the Hon'ble the Home Member on the skill with which he has piloted the ship of the Indemnity Bill through the storm of discussion, no doubt, with the help of the high-skilled Legal Engineer, the Law Member and cleverly manoeuvring it has saved it from the three pests, i. e., mine, torpedo and submarine, with not less than 38 attempts by them.

"After the complete victory of the Right the other day, the course of events was so changed that nearly all had joined the victorious camp except those whose business naturally it was not to do so and had to stick on, through thick and thin, to the opposite camp so as to justify themselves to be called 'public men.'

"Apart from few irreconcilables the majority of the population forming 90 per cent of the Punjab would welcome the Bill and thank the Government for so many gracious acts done during the period. The Martial Law Commissions of the Judges of the High Court and some other experienced men were provided to administer justice for the heinous crimes instead of first or second class Magistrates which was a great improvement on the ordinary machinery of justice. They acquitted large numbers of people who were guilty and convicted only those against whom there was sufficient evidence. The extraordinary kindness shown by His Honour the Lieutenant-Governor of the Punjab in commuting the sentences and their further reduction by your Excellency's Government has caused further satisfaction.

"Though in ordinary circumstances things would have ended here, it is gratifying that two Judges have been appointed to investigate into the cases in order to minutely sift the various facts over again which may be called an unprecedented kindness. In case the Privy Council accepts the appeals of the wealthier men who have approached it, the announcement by the Government that all the poorer accused will get the benefit of the above under the same circumstances is another thing of far-reaching importance. The Government has also kindly given assurances that no one appearing before the Committee will be liable to be molested by any authority or police, and their promise that all those will be released whose cases do not fall under the ordinary law, has further helped the accused. And last but not the least the grant of not only the one Indian member which was asked for but also the appointment of another Indian member in the shape of an Englishman. We call him Indian as his community has got vested rights in the country the welfare of which, I am sure, is the nearest to his heart.

"I think by all the above the Government has gone to an extent that no Government in history would have done so far for the breakers of law and order. I hope when all the above is finished, it will result in wholesale clemency except for some such whose release will amount to letting loose wolves in the flocks of sheep.

"My Lord, those of us who have been saved from a great catastrophe pray that Government will take precautions that such a thing may never recur, because if it again does so there is danger of its coming in a more complete form. This time those responsible for the Egyptian and Indian troubles and foreign invasion not being in possession of cables and having no proper communication have come one after the other and suppressed in detail but at some next time such may not be the case.

"I also hope that some battalions of Sappers and Pioneers will be trained to work as engine drivers and guards, etc., as this time the wholesale strike of the Railway employees was only just averted. Had it occurred as it was arranged transport of reinforcements, food-stuff and other provisions to the Frontier would have been greatly hampered.

"My Lord, there is a section which believes that this our august assembly was to an extent directly or indirectly responsible for the recent trouble by their utterances. One of the leading arguments of the Council in defence of some of the accused was that their inflammatory speeches for which they were being punished and which roused the public feelings for the acts committed did not go half the way as some of those delivered in your Excellency's presence, and people wonder whether there is any regulation which could be put in force to moderate such language and, if there is such, what is the cause that this remedy is not applied when certain portions of certain speeches reach the extent of creating hatred among the classes and go a long way to bring the Government established by law into contempt. I think all the above is being governed by the ordinary law of the land.

"The defence of a public prosecutor against the argument of Mr. Hussan Imam that such speeches in the Council were meant for a responsible class, while those of the accused were for the ordinary public, is a poor argument and falls to the ground as the next day a speech here is public property and the extremist papers, like one or two of those we have got in our province, intensify them by their comments on them.

"I have only put forward this as an appeal on behalf of the general rural public of the Province so that such happenings may not recur and the lives of the innocent people, English as well as Indians, may not be lost as well as those at the Frontier either in action, or through epidemics.

"My Lord, all arguments used to-day have been already put forward on the day when the Hon'ble Pandit Malaviya first spoke on this Bill, and though he does not believe in what the other people say, the others have the same right to say that they do not believe in the allegations that he has put forward. For instance, the Gujranwala case was discussed the other day. The railway line was broken and the police and other people at Gujranwala were absolutely helpless till the evening. If troops were sent from Lahore, it is such a long distance, that thay could not possibly have reached that day, nor could they come by train, as, I have already said, the railway line was broken. There was no other possible way to help the authorities at Gujranwala that day except by aeroplane. I hear the people were in the act of opening the prison and letting out all the prisoners when the aeroplanes arrived.

"About Lahore, it is said, my Lord, that everything was quiet. I wish my Hon'ble friend the Pandit Sahib was there at the time. Just as he has seen certain things and believes in them, I think he should also believe in us who saw that the conditions were such that if the military were not there, there would have been many other acts committed.

"As the military were there and suppressed the disturbance, we cannot say there was nothing. Of course nothing happened or could have happened because there was force to suppress it, but it was only that force which kept things quiet.

"With these few remarks, I hope the Bill will be passed."

The Hon'ble Mr. Sachchidananda Sinha:—"My Lord, I hope this unequal struggle between the official members and the non-official members of this Council will soon be over; for my part, I find it rather too trying for my nerves. The debate has been going on now for three or four days, and almost everything which could be said for or against the measure has been put forward by the advocates of the respective sides. It seems that at the end of the discussion we are as far off from coming to an agreement as we were when the Bill was introduced.

"The motion before the Council now is that the Bill be passed. Under ordinary circumstances I should have held it unjustifiable at this late hour to prolong the agony by making any lengthy observations, but the matter, my Lord, is of such great and grave importance, that I do not think I shall be justified in recording my vote without giving, howsoever briefly, my reasons for the action which I propose to take. When the Bill was introduced and leave was sought for its introduction, some of us felt compelled to oppose that. What has happened since then that the Hon'ble Member should feel justified in asking us to-day to give our assent to the Bill? We tried to improve the Bill to the best of our lights by sending in 38 amendments. Far from feeling grateful to us for trying to improve his Bill, the Hon'ble the Home Member, with that emotional Celtic temperament to which I referred the other day, actually charged us with trying to whittle down the Bill. That, my Lord, was the unkindest cut of all. When we come here to assist him with our experience, with our guidance, those are the thanks which we get in this Council. Now, lest your Lordship and the Council may think that in dilating at some length on the difficulties and the misfortunes of Indian non-official members of this Council, who have to oppose official views, I am at all exaggerating, I shall, with your Lordship's leave, read out two or three sentences, not from an Indian paper, moderate or extremist, but from a well-known Anglo-Indian paper of Calcutta, called *Looker-on*. This is what the writer in *Looker-on* says of our most piteous condition:—'I am always struck by the pathetic aspect of the incident when an Indian Councillor gets up on his hind legs'—those are his words, not mine—'and debates a motion eloquently and cheerfully, knowing all the while that the division which he has succeeded in forcing must go against him. It requires a certain amount of assurance, not to say spiritual pluck'—the words are 'spiritual pluck' not 'spirituous pluck'—'to do, as many Indian debaters do, without giving an unedifying exhibition of temper, spleen and despair'.

"Now, my Lord, under those circumstances, I am particularly grateful, speaking for myself, that of the 38 amendments which were moved by us the Hon'ble the Home Member was graciously pleased to accept one of mine. Afterwards, he made an observation, however, which deprived his action of its little grace, that he was not sure that he had been wise in accepting my amendment. I ventured to assure him then and there that this was the wisest act he had done, if not in his life, at least in the course of this debate. I am also grateful to him, my Lord, particularly, for accepting my suggestion in my opening speech and amending the words of the preamble by dropping the words 'that it was necessary to declare martial law' and putting in the words 'where martial law was enforced.' My Lord, did he suspect then that the Hon'ble Pandit would take advantage of that to build his argument on that, because he had withdrawn from that position of there being the necessity for martial law being declared, therefore the whole Bill must fall through? Well, my Lord, grateful as I am for these two acceptances on his part, I do not think that the rejection of our 37 amendments justifies him in asking me to give my moral assent to the Bill.

"My Lord, I shall, with your Lordship's leave, refer to one or two observations which have been made by official members in the course of the discussion. I shall first say a word about the incursion of the Hon'ble Mr. Shafi. I confess I do not understand what on earth made him intervene in this debate. I thought he was the Education Member, concerned with the carrying out of educational policy, with certain sanitary matters and possibly also with ecclesiastical affairs, but of this last I am not sure. What he has got to do with the declaration of martial law and an Indemnity Bill, I cannot for the life of me understand. I suppose he was most anxious to support the Government. I believe some of us, when we cross the floor from this side to that, undergo some sudden changes in our views and sentiments, and I dare say that is what made him support the Government. He did so, however, by reading out section 101 of the Evidence Act and sundry old reports of Privy Council cases, and he tried to teach us the A.B.C. of the law of evidence. He said it was surprising that we, lawyers in this Council, did not even know what he called the A.B.C. of that law and he tried to explain it to us as best he could. I was gratified, however, that he did not go on to the D.E.F. and the X.Y.Z., as, otherwise, we might have been here all night. He laid down the proposition that what appears in clause 3 of the Indemnity Bill in regard to the rule of evidence and the burden of proof is a most elementary principle to be found in all the laws and the prophets. Now, if that be so, and the Hon'ble Member's argument be sound, what is the good of having that specifically provided for in this Indemnity Bill at all? If that is the Common Law, if that is the Statute Law, if that is the Privy Council ruling, I suppose any court would act up to it without there being a specific provision. As, however, the Hon'ble the Law Member has taken particular care to put in that provision here, I have a suspicion that it is not after all such a small thing, a mere A. B. C., as the Hon'ble Mr. Shafi was anxious to make out.

"My Lord, I shall, with your Lordship's leave, refer to one or two observations of the Hon'ble the Law Member. I most gratefully acknowledge that, during the debates in this Council, he has been exceptionally kind and encouraging to me, and he has never said a word about me of which I need make any grievance. My friend the Hon'ble Pandit Madan Mohan Malaviya thought that I had been rather severely handled by the Hon'ble the Law Member on the last occasion; but in a debate, as in love and war, I think all is fair, and I make no grievance of that. But he did make one or two observations, not in regard to me personally, but in regard to certain matters, which I think need a reply. May I say that it seemed to me rather an ungracious act on the part of the Hon'ble the Law Member to have made certain adverse comments, in the absence of the Hon'ble Raja Sir Rampal Singh, about his speech, the more so as the Hon'ble Raja Sir Rampal Singh had made that speech not on the motion about the Indemnity Bill, but on a previous occasion in regard to the constitution of the Punjab Inquiry Committee? However, I felt gratified at this reference and the gratification was due to the fact that I did want that some official member of this Council should protest against speeches supposed to be written by friends, because I have a shrewd suspicion that as often as not the speeches made by some non-official members in the Council supporting Government are written by friends. Therefore, I am grateful to the Hon'ble the Law Member for raising the point; and, in future, when a suspicion crosses his mind that some speech on the Government side by a non-official member may have been written for him by a 'friend,' I hope he will not forget to take that fact into consideration in assessing the value of the speech.

"Now, my Lord, I was also amused, as one who is a lawyer by profession, to see the lengths to which some of us, even members of your Excellency's Executive Council, are driven in a debate when harassed from pillar to post, as happened to the Hon'ble the Law Member yesterday. When the Hon'ble Pandit Malaviya quoted once or twice from an Act of St. Vincent, the Hon'ble the Law Member pooh-poohed it, as if to refer to an Act of St. Vincent was something like *lese majeste* to Sir William Vincent; but to-day he himself, in reply to the Hon'ble Pandit, referred to the same Act, which he repudiated yesterday as something insignificant and worthless. That is all, my Lcrd, which I have to say in regard to the observations of the Hon'ble the Law Member.

"I shall now say something, my Lord, about the Hon'ble the Home Member's observation. I think it is but fair to say that his speeches in this Council on this rather controversial measure have been, on the whole, very conciliatory, indeed; and so far as I am personally concerned, I have got no grievance to make against the wording or the spirit of them. But I take exception not to his manner but to his matter. I confess I was very agreeably surprised this morning to hear him quote, of all persons, the great Indian leader, Mr. Gandhi. This was in the same strain in which the Hon'ble the Law Member quoted Mrs. Besant and Mr. Horniman. I do not know if he quoted Mr. Tilak; perhaps he did not. Well, Mr. Gandhi is certainly a gentleman whose observations are entitled ordinarily to the very greatest respect. But the Hon'ble the Home Member tries to make much of Mr. Gandhi's observations as in this particular instance they suit his purpose. It is, I presume, from *Young India* that he quoted this morning. Is he aware that in *Young India* Mr. Gandhi has been writing week in, week out, on the Punjab situation, taking up the case of each particular person convicted, and saying in terms absolutely unequivocal that there has been a great travesty of justice and that all these persons have been put to very great inconvenience and trouble by the arbitrary conduct of the officials? I only desire to say that I hope that these observations also of Mr. Gandhi will carry equal weight with the Hon'ble the Home Member, when he comes to deal with the cases of these persons.

"Now, my Lord, there is one thing more I would like to say. In my opening speech on this Bill, I said that the Indian view was that, whereas Government were fully justified in resorting to effective measures for putting down the riot or disturbance or rebellion, call it what you like, the steps taken for that purpose went far beyond the requirements of the situation, and that in the name of putting down the disturbances and maintaining or restoring order, measures were carried out which were oppressive and tyrannical. This, I said, was the Indian view. I sedulously refused to go, My Lord, into the facts of the case, and I assured you that I had kept an open mind on the subject. But I find that my friend, Mr. Malaviya, on the one side, and Mr. Hailey and Mr. Thompson and General Hudson on the other, have put forward in this Council different versions of the facts. I am now in a better position to make up my mind as to the facts, after having heard both sides. I listened very carefully, my Lord, to the statements of fact of these gentlemen, both on the last occasion and to-day; and making every allowance for an inherent, unconscious bias in my own mind as an Indian, I have tried to place myself in a detached position, and I venture to say that leaving aside every statement of the Hon'ble Pandit and accepting as gospel truth the statements made by the official members in the Council—Mr. Hailey, Mr. Thompson and General Hudson—there is, to my mind, a clear admission made by these gentlemen that things were done which, to use the mildest language, should not have been done. I shall not say one single word about the observations of Mr. Malaviya. I shall take it that they are incorrect and inaccurate. Let us, however, take the statements made here before your Lordship and this Council by Mr. Hailey, Mr. Thompson and General Hudson as the truth. I shall not traverse the ground in detail; but I shall take one or two instances and the explanations which the official members have offered to this Council. I hope every member of this Council will consider the matter apart from any ideas of race or nationality. Has Mr. Thompson's explanation satisfied the Council that the arrest of Mr. Manohar Lal, a Barrister-at-Law, late Minto Professor of Economics in Calcutta, a distinguished scholar, a favourite pupil of Professor Marshall of Cambridge, and his detention for, I believe, nearly a month, and then his being discharged without being brought to trial, was a right course to adopt? Mr. Thompson said, Mr. Manohar Lal was a trustee of the *Tribune*, and it was supposed that as a resident trustee in Lahore he had taken an active part in inspiring the writings in that paper. Well, now, I will ask 'Is it fair, is it right that because a man happens to be a resident trustee of a newspaper, assuming even that it is seditious, when once the editor has been brought to trial, the editor who alone was responsible before law, the trustee should be arrested and placed in detention for a month and then let go without any case being started against him?' I venture to submit, my Lord, any question of race or nationality apart, that that is not the way of treating a British subject. I am glad that Sir Micheal O'Dwyer did not go beyond arresting the resident trustee and did not order the arrest of the readers of the paper as well, because in that case I might have been arrested too as one of them. I am glad that he drew the line at the resident trustee and did not extend his order to the readers of the paper. I say that just to show, my Lord, that the explanation offered by Mr. Thompson does not satisfy me at all and I have given my reasons therefor.

"I shall now take an instance from the statement of General Hudson. Fortunately in his case I am in a better position, because I find that the *Civil and Military Gazette* has published what it calls 'the full text' of his speech. From this full text, I shall take up one point, namely the unfortunate assault on Miss Sherwood and the orders passed in consequence thereof. General Sir Havelock Hudson admitted 'the issue by the officer in command at Amritsar of orders that any persons who wished to pass the scene of the assault on Miss Sherwood should be made to crawl on their hands and knees,' as 'something was required to strike the imagination.' He continued, 'It is easy to criticize the orders issued by the officer in command at Amritsar, but the circumstances were altogether exceptional and the punishment though humiliating was not such as to cause danger to life or physical hurt.' And he then added. 'No compulsion was brought to bear on any individual to submit to the order. The order remained in force for a period of five days. There is good reason for the belief that except for the party of prisoners already mentioned, those who were subject to the order came voluntarily to submit to it for the sake of notoriety or martyrdom.' That is the explanation that the Hon'ble General Hudson gave. The facts are not denied. The Hon'ble Pandit Malaviya, who among his many virtues does not unfortunately possess the saving grace of humour, complained to the Council in tones of bitter anguish that when that was said by General Hudson a titter of laughter went round the Council. I should think that but for the restraining influence exercised by your Lordship's presence the Council would have indulged in a loud guffaw. Who could, my Lord, accept with equanimity the statement that human beings preferred to crawl on their hands and knees to obtain 'notoriety or martyrdom'? This was ordered, General Hudson said, to strike the imagination . . . ."

The Hon'ble Lieutenant-General Sir Havelock Hudson:—"I think the passage which was referred to as raising a loud guffaw was not that quoted by the Hon'ble Member. It was the one that the men went on their hands and knees that raised the titter."

The Hon'ble Mr. Sachchidananda Sinha:—"There was something about hands and knees."

The Hon'ble Lieutenant-General Sir Havelock Hudson:—"The person went three times on his hands and knees."

The Hon'ble Mr. Sachchidananda Sinha:—"My contention is that if this explanation did not evoke a loud guffaw, it should have done so. Now, my Lord, speaking seriously, I venture to ask the Council whether it is right to defend this action, whether His Majesty's Indian subjects should be made to crawl on their hands and knees because some other persons had been guilty of committing some nefarious deed. I ask whether such a thing should be sanctioned. Whatever the Hon'ble Pandit may have said, General Hudson said that that was done to strike the imagination! I do not know anything about striking the imagination; but what I do know and feel is, that those who were made to crawl on their hands and knees must have left the place with a bitter sense of rancour rankling in their hearts. If General Hudson meant that this may be called striking the imagination, all I can say is that when he joined the Army the imaginative literature of England lost a great deal.

"Thus there is no doubt, my Lord, that things have been done which should not have been done. My Lord, such being the case and the Government having withdrawn from the preamble the statement as to the necessity of the declaration of martial law, the question is whether the Bill should be passed. Nothing having happened since the introduction of the Bill to induce me to change my mind about it, I believe I am justified in voting against it. Your Lordship will remember that on the last occasion when I ventured to take up the time of the Council, I maintained that public opinion was insistent that the Bill should be either withdrawn or put off for some time. Now when I refer to public opinion, I am afraid of a recurrence of what happened then. The Hon'ble Mr. Macpherson, in the course of his manuscript eloquence, said that, I represented only a small section of the Bihar and Orissa public, while he himself represented a large one. But as I explained the other day, when I talked of Indian public opinion I referred to the classes who alone can at present speak out their minds. I shall not, however, refer on this occasion to Indian public opinion; if I did so, I could show that Sir Sivaswami Iyer, who was a member of the Madras Executive Council, has been publishing articles in various papers strongly opposing the passage of the Bill at the present moment. I shall, with your Lordship's permission, quote some passages from an article in a well-known paper—the *Indian Daily News*. The articles is from the pen of one who has himself been a high official, and has acted as Standing Counsel to the Government of India. The paper is owned and edited by Mr. Graham, and the article in question shows how this debate has struck the mind of an independent European in this country. This is what he says:—

> 'The debate now proceeding at Simla is a fair sample of the way India has been governed in the past. The Government adopt an attitude and defend that attitude to the last gasp. Thay accept nothing, listen to nothing and decline to budge. They do not listen to Mr. Crum or Mr. Sarma or the 'resuscitated' Pandit. They get the Associated Press to give a full account of Sir William Vincent's 'testy' speech as *Capital* calls it, which is in their opinion so convincing that it has only to be read to be accepted as Gospel. Of course it is not, for it is merely an angry gabble, but Simla sticks to its opinion and lives on.'

I omit the concluding words of the sentence for fear they may be considered unparliamentary. The writer then proceeds as follows:—

> 'The main fact that strikes one reading the debate now proceeding about the Indemnity Bill is that the bureaucracy

and the Government of India are playing the same old game, namely, absolute inability to yield to suggestion, to accept compromise, and eagerness to play all the trumps, which they have dealt themselves. This is the spirit that invited the Reforms, this imperviousness to reason, this contempt for opposition and this extreme use of every controversial weapon they had helped themselves to in the past. This debate has once more shown the Government of India in its obdurate and obstinate condition and in its best form of stolid opposition.'

I do not say, my Lord, that I accept every word of it, but it shows how this debate strikes a European critic of the Government, a man who has occupied the high position of Standing Counsel in the Calcutta High Court. Therefore, my Lord, I venture to submit that we are not so unjustified, as some of the official members would like to make out, in asking your Lordship's Government to postpone this measure for the time being, at any rate till the Punjab Inquiry Committee submits its report. But as your Lordship's Government are unwilling to accede to our request, I feel justified in recording my vote against the Hon'ble Member's motion that the Bill be passed."

The Hon'ble Sir George Lowndes:—"My Lord, if the only speech against the Bill to-day had been that of the Hon'ble Mr. Sinha, it would not have been necessary for me to trouble the Council for long. His speech was made in the lighter vein that I am afraid carries us a very little way. But we have had a long and powerful speech from his leader Pandit Malaviya. He gave us a bountiful display to-day, but we sitting in this Council Chamber cannot be swayed by beautiful words or impressive sentences.

"We are here as the responsible Government of a great country, and we have got to carry on that Government not with our hearts but with our heads. I will only say for myself—it may be a rash thing to say—that not one word of that extremely eloquent speech carried conviction to my mind. I said on the last occasion when I addressed this Council, that it was necessary for the Hon'ble Pandit as a preliminary to certain proceedings outside this Council to make a great display, and it may be that that is again the explanation of the necessity for it to-day. But I venture to suggest that nine-tenths of what my Hon'ble friend said had no bearing whatsoever on the question before this Council. Let me reiterate it again. It has been said, almost to weariness already, that what we are considering here is not whether acts which are alleged to have been unnecessary, which are alleged to be *mala fide*, are to be protected, but whether indemnity is to be granted in respect of acts which were *bona fide* and which are held to have been necessary. It is no good to get up and reel out a string of so-called facts which the speaker pretends are outside the principle of the Bill. If they are, we are not concerned with them. They will be judged in another place. What we are concerned with here is simply the case of a man who has acted *bona fide* as a servant of Government or under the orders of a servant of Government. If he has done what was necessary for the maintenance or restoration of order, is he to be indemnified? I venture to think that I did not exaggerate when I said that nine-tenths of the Hon'ble Pandit's speech had nothing whatever to do with that point. But here again, as on a previous occasion, I am glad to be able to follow the lead of my hon'ble friend Mr. Sinha, and I need do no more than quote his words, which I hope, I have taken down accurately. 'I shall not say a word about Mr. Malaviya's statements. I shall take them all as inaccurate.' Those are the words which Mr. Sinha used just before he sat down and they suit me down to the ground.

"But let me turn to one or two arguments in the remaining tenth of the speech which, I think, necessitate some answer. There were in the Hon'ble Pandit's speech, many, no doubt unconscious, perversions of fact. Let me refer to one of them at least. The Hon'ble Pandit said that the Bill seeks to validate all the acts that were done—he put it in two parts—prior to the 13th April and subsequent to the time when the disturbances had ceased. But this Council has been told over and over again that we are not proposing to validate any of those acts. It was, if I may say so, a confusion which has run through the Hon'ble Pandit's mind from the very commencement of this debate, a confusion between validation and indemnity. I explained just now what the proposed indemnity is and how far it goes. Validation is something quite different. The English Acts which my Hon'ble friend has quoted; the South African Acts which he quoted, validate all acts which were done under Martial Law. We do not propose to do this. Validation in this Bill, let me repeat once more, is confined to the validation of the sentences of men who are now in jail and whom we, as a responsible Government, consider that we cannot in the public interest release. That is the utmost extent to which validation goes under this Act, and it is no good to try and pervert facts and put forward to the public that we are trying to validate every act which has been done under Martial law; to say so is a perversion of facts....."

(Here the Hon'ble Pandit got up to interrupt the Hon'ble the Law Member).

The President:—"The Council has listened to the Hon'ble Member with unexampled patience. It is now his business to exercise that same patience towards the Hon'ble the Law Member."

The Hon'ble Pandit Madan Mohan Malaviya:—"May I explain a fact?"

The President:—"I think the Hon'ble Pandit has had 6½ hours of this Council's time and should now let the Hon'ble the Law Member have a little time of the Council."

The Hon'ble Sir George Lowndes:—"Let me explain another thing which seems not to have struck the minds of many lawyers in this Council. My Hon'ble friend Mr. Sinha suggested that he knew all about law and there was no necessity for my Hon'ble Colleague in this Council to lecture him—I think that was the word he used—on the law. I do not doubt that my Hon'ble friend knows all about it; though it is sometimes convenient to forget what one knows. Now let me remind him what is the position with regard to validation. We propose to indemnify only the officers of Government against the consequences of acts they have done, and not to validate the acts themselves. We leave any remedy there may be against Government entirely open. If there is any complaint to be made in a civil action, any claim to damages open, let the man who complains sue Government, let him take his chance in the courts; we all know how the Government is sued—in the name of the Secretary of State. Have we attempted by this Bill to preclude actions against the Secretary of State? Are not we responsible? Have not we from the very first as a Government taken responsibility for what we have thought to be necessary? Any act that has been done unjustly, contrary to orders, *mala fide*, unnecessarily, the man who did it must answer for; it was outside the scope of his agency. But for any act done under our orders, Government must be responsible. We are the principal, he was merely our agent; such remedy as there may be, must be against the principal. There are many lawyers in this Council besides my Hon'ble friend Mr. Sinha, but I feel certain that even he must be well acquainted with the maxim, *Respondeat superior*. Let Government answer; it is we who have ordered these things to be done. If they were reasonable, in accordance with the necessities of the case, we must be responsible. We have not attempted by the Bill to preclude any possible action against Government. So far as validation goes, we are, as I said, validating nothing but existing sentences. One would also have thought that it might have been worth while for one or other of those who have spoken to-day to refer to the pledge that has been given that everybody, who is now in jail merely for a breach of a martial law regulation and nothing more, will be released. That is, it appears to me, a concession which answers a great deal of the most eloquent portion of the Hon'ble Pandit's speech.

"But my Hon'ble friend began with one of the most astounding arguments I have ever heard in any law court or even in this Council. He is much in love with the preambles of Acts, and he quoted from the preambles of the English Acts about acts that were necessary, and recitals that the putting in force of martial law was necessary; and he said that this is the only foundation for an indemnity. It is only justified if you can assume that martial law has been necessary. My Hon'ble friend went on to point out, somewhat disingenuously I thought, that we had, of course at his request, omitted the word 'necessary' from the preamble. Then came the astounding argument that because we had omitted the word 'necessary' from the preamble, therefore Government must give up the whole Bill. That is an argument which is solemnly addressed to a Council of some half a hundred reasonable men. Will it carry conviction to any man in this Council or outside it? I think the Hon'ble Pandit did not even refer to the reason why the recital of necessity which was in the English Act to which he referred was omitted here. Is it that he does not understand the reason for it, the reason why we have omitted the word 'necessary' from the preamble? Even the Hon'ble Mr. Sinha did not venture to suggest that Government does not believe martial law was necessary. I can only say that, speaking for myself as a responsible member of this Government, I have not the least doubt that it was necessary. But why did we leave out the recital of this at the request of the Hon'ble Pandit? Because it was said that there is a Commission coming out to examine that question and it would not be fair to prejudice it by putting this into the preamble..

(The Hon'ble Pandit Malaviya rose to make a remark).

The President:—"Order, order, the Hon'ble Member must sit down."

The Hon'ble Sir George Lowndes:—"That is the reason why the reference to necessity was omitted from the preamble, and not because we have had the least doubt that it was necessary. In the case of the English Act of 1889, to which the Hon'ble Pandit referred, there was no commission coming, and the conclusion of reasonable men was that it was necessary and therefore the recital of this appeared in the preamble of the Bill. But my Hon'ble friend's predilection, if I may so put it, for preamble was so great that he proceeded in the course of his argument to tell the Council that you do not find any recital of necessity in the South Africa Acts. I am glad that I am able to say that the Hon'ble Pandit in this respect is absolutely correct. The Council will perhaps be amused to know why it is correct—it is because no South Africa Act ever has a preamble. But in dealing with the South Africa Acts it was much more convenient for the Hon'ble Pandit to quote from the operative part of the Act, which he proceeded to do, without saying that he was doing so. In this case he quotes from the operative part of the Act because it suits him. When he is dealing with the English Act of 1789, as I pointed out on the previous occasion, he quoted only from the preamble and not from the operative part, because the operative part of this 1789 Act validated all acts done, whether they were necessary or not. Apparently, the—what shall I say—the necessities of elocution produce this unfortunate result, that when it pays the Hon'ble Pandit to quote one particular part of an Act, he quotes it; when it does not pay to quote that, he quotes the other part. I protest that is not a scheme, either of argument or logic, to which I have been brought up.

"Then my Hon'ble friend went on, with a magnanimity which I admire, to defend his absent friend—I hope I did not err again in that expression—his absent friend Raja Sir Rampal Singh. No one regrets more than I do, and I said it on a previous occasion, that the Hon'ble Raja Sir Rampal Singh has not been able to stay for this debate. But I am afraid I cannot recognise the fact that an Hon'ble

Member is not able to stay for the whole of the Council proceedings as disentitling me to reply to arguments he has used. The Hon'ble Pandit tells us that he has taken the trouble to send Raja Sir Rampal Singh a telegram asking him whether he had written that speech (of course it was a written one, we know that) and Raja Sir Rampal Singh has unblushingly admitted that he had. I accept the statement; I have no doubt that it is true, and I do not doubt that his was the hand that wrote it, but I am still inclined to think that though the hand was the hand of Esau, the voice was the voice of Jacob. But let me give that point up. But what does the Hon'ble Pandit's contradiction mean? It was not a statement of fact on my part. The Council will no doubt remember that all I said was that I thought the most charitable interpretation of Raja Sir Rampal Singh's speech was that it had been written for him by a friend. I always like to be charitable, but the Hon'ble Pandit now has told me that there is no room for charity and I must now take what the Hon'ble Raja said in all its baldness as a statement of fact by a gentleman from Oudh (who is not here to tell us anything more about it) as to the condition of the Punjab at a particular time. The Hon'ble Pandit went on to suggest that I was quite unjustified in referring to Mr. Chanda having come from Assam. Well I doubt if there was anything particularly unparliamentary in that reference, but the argument was a very simple one, and I will repeat it for the Hon'ble Pandit's benefit. I was not arguing that the Punjab wanted this Bill; that has been sufficiently explained by one of my Hon'ble friends opposite. All I was dealing with was the question, 'was there or was there not at the time we put martial law into force a state of affairs in the Punjab that the ordinary civil arm could not cope with?' And I said that it was a remarkable fact that with all these members here from the Punjab, men of weight, men of standing, men of honour, men of truth, that there was not one who could get up in this Council and say the situation was not one of that sort, and that it was only Hon'ble Members from Assam, from Oudh, and from Madras, who made that statement? We have plenty of members in this Council who come from the Province where those things were taking place and who knew—it was not the case of having an opinion—who knew for certain whether it was necessary to put martial law in force for the restoration of order or not, and I would still ask the Council to judge whether that is not an argument of some weight. You have them all here; do you believe they are untruthful, do you believe that they do not know what was going on in the Punjab? And yet I say there is not one who knows the facts who states that there was not a situation such as the civil arm could not deal with. And I repeat, it wanted a gentleman from Madras, a gentleman from Assam to say it—perhaps I must not say again the Special Commissioners from the United Provinces because that appeared to arouse some indignation on the part of my Hon'ble friend the Pandit. I really thought he was a self-constituted commissioner at that time, but he has told us he was a constituted commissioner by some body (I do not mean some person, but some body) of which he gave the name though I was unable to catch it. I am quite willing to assume that he was appointed a special commissioner by some body to inquire into the facts in the Punjab. But there again it does not affect the argument. The argument is that the Punjab people who know do not say this; the only people who say there was no rebellion there are people from outside who have only second-hand information. I apologise sincerely to the Hon'ble Pandit if I have over-stepped the bounds of courtesy by referring to him as a special commissioner for this purpose, and I am the more anxious to make the apology in that I understand from what he has told us to-day that a considerable portion of his duties was merely sanitary! The Hon'ble Pandit also referred to my having mentioned Mr. Sinha in this connection. There, I think, he is mistaken. I think he is confusing his two allies in this Council, Mr. Sinha and the Hon'ble Mr. Ayyangar. I do not doubt that he will offer suitable apologies afterwards. But I did not refer to Mr. Sinha in this connection. My Hon'ble friend Mr. Sinha had made no statement whatever on the subject of the situation in the Punjab; he very carefully abstained from doing this, and if I may say so, wisely. And here again, the larger part of the Hon'ble Pandit's speech on this point was a mere perversion of my argument. I was not dealing with the question whether this Bill was necessary I was dealing solely with the constitutional question whether, when martial law was proclaimed, a situation had arisen which necessitated its use, nothing else.

"With regard to the second portion of my Hon'ble friend's argument which dealt with certain questions of law, we know that under my Hon'ble friend's auspices a number of cases have gone to the ultimate court of appeal of the Empire, the Privy Council and are lying there for decision. I do not propose to answer my Hon'ble friend on these legal points. I will only say let them be urged in the Privy Council. As no doubt they will be; and let their Lordships attribute what weight to them they deserve. I am content at all events that they should judge upon them between him and me.

"The real point which the Council have got to consider—I venture to reiterate it once more, but for the last time I hope—is 'Do Hon'ble Members regard it as the first duty of Government to enforce law and order in this country and to protect the lives and property of its citizens? If they do recognise that that is the duty of Government, if Hon'ble Members wish that their lives and their property should be protected, and wish Government in cases of emergency to employ the ultimate force of the Army for that purpose, then they must, at the first possible opportunity, indemnify those who in carrying out the orders of Government have acted *bona fide* and in the belief that what they have done was reasonably necessary for the purpose. If Hon'ble Members think that it is not the duty of Government to protect their lives and property, if they do not wish that done, then let them refuse an Indemnity Act. But if they do that, they cannot expect protection when these great emergencies, these great crises, arise.

"Some reference was made by the Hon'ble Pandit to martial law in Bombay. Have Hon'ble Members forgotten the ghastly fate that overtook an Indian in connection with those disturbances? Have they forgotten how the mob seized one of their own community, a *mamlatadar*, soaked him in kerosene, set fire to him and burnt him alive? That is a fate which overlook, not a European bank manager, not a European lady missionary, but one of their own community. If they do not wish their lives and their property protected by Government, I venture to suggest that that is a fate that may overtake any one of them on the next occasion.

"Then the Hon'ble Pandit referred to the legal position of soldiers under martial law and he read us out quotations from law works on the point which, I am afraid, did not appeal to me very much, because the answer is so obvious. It is because soldiers may find themselves in this extraordinary position, of having on the one hand to fulfil the orders of their Commanding Officers on pain of being tried by court martial, and on the other of being tried by the civil courts, it may be for murder, if they do—it is because of this extraordinary position in which the soldier may find himself, that it is necessary to indemnify them. That is the reason and the object to a great extent of indemnifying them against actions, indemnifying them against suits and against criminal prosecutions. It is perfectly immaterial for the Hon'ble Pandit to read out long citations about the legal position of soldiers. I hardly cared to listen to them—the answer is so clear. It is because of that position that it is necessary to pass an Indemnity Act and has been so held in the other cases where martial law has been enforced throughout the Empire.

"There is much more to which I should have liked to reply in many passages of the Hon'ble Pandit's speech; but we are now on the second day of this debate nearly at eventide, and, I think, it would be kinder it I left the rest unanswered. I do not want the Council to think that it is because, there is no answer to the points that have been made by him, but only because it seems to me at this hour not to be worth attempting."

The Hon'ble Rao Bahadur B. N. Sarma:—"My Lord, we have listened with rapt attention to the powerful speeches which have been delivered by the Law Member in defence of the policy of the Government. All the points that have been raised have been threshed out for two days, and I do not propose to go into the facts at any length in order to justify the vote that I have to record on this motion. All that I ask is, that the Government Members should not be uncharitable in interpreting the attitude that some of us have had to take and have still to take with regard to this Bill on the facts which have been so far placed before us in this Council. I allude to that for the simple reason that, during the course of the debate, more than one reference has been made to the opposition of a few individuals in this Council to the introduction of this Bill and, later on, to their attempting to whittle down the measure, when they did not succeed in effecting their original object.

"My Lord, if there was opposition to the introduction of the Bill, there were ample grounds therefor; it is not necessary to repeat them. What we were entitled to do after the Bill was introduced was to make it, if possible, one which would be acceptable both to the Government as well as to the people. The primary object, we were told, of this Bill was to protect, not the Government, not the higher officials who initiated the policy, but the officers who executed, who carried out, the objects of the policy which was enunciated by the Government. I agree that the object is one to which no general exception can be taken. I said that these officers should not be allowed to be sued during the interval which may elapse before the Legislative Council is in a position to make up its mind as to the exact form the Bill should assume. Therefore it was that, both at the introductory stage, as well as when the Bill was brought up for consideration, I suggested the enactment of a provision that no suit should be entertained until the inquiry was over and a reasonable time elapsed, when the Government and the public would be in a position to sift the facts for themselves and arrive at fairly acurate conclusion. I felt, my Lord, that the object of the Government would be achieved without at the same time offending the susceptibilities, the reasonable susceptibilities of the people, and I made the suggestion in the hope that we should re-establish the Government in the confidence of the people.

"My Lord, the law need not he stated over again. In the absence of an Idemnity Bill it is acknowledged on all hands that the officers who may be put on their trial would have to show that there was a necessity for the particular measures that they took. Judicial Courts would be the proper tribunals to dispose of that question and also of the question as to whether martial law was necessary. That is a question of fact. But in all civilised countries these martial law proceedings have been followed by indemnity Acts making it unnecessary for judicial tribunals to consider the question as to whether martial law was necessary. Therefore, when we render it unnecessary for the judicial tribunal to go and ascertain as a question of fact whether martial law was necessary, it is necessary that we as the Legislative Council should come to some rational conclusion on that subject. It is all the more necessary in a Council of this description, where the Legislative Council is virtually the Executive Government. That is the reason why, my Lord, we, as the representatives of the people thought it was our bounden duty to defend the rights of the people to the utmost in so far as it was compatible with securing the necessary object the Government had in view, namely, the protection of its officers before the facts were thoroughly sifted. My Lord, that course was not allowed to us. Then, accepting the position that we should have to protect the officers and the soldiers, the question that we had to consider was as to whether on the facts that were placed by the Hon'ble Pandit Madan

Mohan Malaviya before the Council and cotroverted to a certain extent by the official members, on those facts as I say accepted for the time being as correct, was there any alternative for the Members of Council but to ask the Government to stay their hands and not to afford protection to all and sundry alike.

"The Hon'ble the Law Member says we do not want it, we only raise the presumption in all these cases but leave it open to the persons aggrieved to show that the presumpting is unreasonable. My Lord, I venture to say that no such presumption should be raised especially in the case of certain acts which have been the subject of discussion in this Council. If people grumble and are dissatisfied that undue presumptions have been made in favour of such actions, I do not think we can say that such grumbling or dissatisfaction is unreasonable. We felt it would be wrong to do so and that, my Lord, was the reason why we prayed, we begged, we implored that all actions prior to the proclamation of martial law should be excluded from the purview of this Bill.

"The Government wish to cover every act that cannot be justified in this Council to the satisfaction of us by raising this presumption. Therein lies the difficulty of some of us seeing eye to eye with the Government. The Government cannot believe that our object was merely to whittle down the measure so as to make the protection nominal, illusory and absolutely meaningless. Allusion has been made more than once to the circumstance (and the elucidation of the facts here is a sufficient answer) that people from other provinces should come forward and build up theories and enunciate principles, and advance facts which they can only know second-hand. Whatever justification there may have been for the charge before this debate, I venture to say that everyone, whether he comes from the Punjab or from outside, is now in a position to express his opinion. We now know what took place in the Punjab if we did not know before. I venture to reiterate what I said before, that members from outside the province of the Punjab should have been grossly remiss in the discharge of their duties if they had only looked upon this as a Punjab problem. It is rightly regarded as an all-India problem. It is true that we here who represent the people are at the present moment in a hopeless minority. Of the 13 non-official members elected by Provincial Legislative Councils we have only 4; of those who are elected by communal bodies there are 7, of those nominated only 2, of whom one was nominated by the Punjab Government after the disturbances. It is true that public opinion outside the Council Chamber is not adequately represented here had has never been. My Lord, there is one significant argument that has been used by the Law Member now and on a previous occasion by the Home Member, that some of the matters dealt with by the Hon'ble Pandit Malaviya would afford a good electioneering cry, but that they were hardly relevant to the subject under discussion. The significance of the admission is this, any member who does not defend the position as we defend it would have no chance with the constituency, and therefore that in advancing the arguments which have been used, we are really voicing public opinion. The Government seems to be therefore aware that what has been stated by us represents faithfully sentiments which rightly or wrongly are cherished by the people throughout the country. My Lord, there were certain passages-at-arms between the Hon'ble Pandit and the Hon'ble Mr. Thompson and the Hon'ble the Law Member. We have listened with some pain to the debate on these points. We have tried our level best to base our judgment on the material facts practically admitted by both sides. Nothing has been said either now or before this which really controverts the facts as stated by the Pandit. On relevant questions there has been no substantial contradiction. There may have been some trivial incidents, some matters not of essential importance which may have been inaccurate. Such being the state of things, we have tried, we have asked the Government to stay their hand in protecting all their officers until the public inquiry sets the matter at rest. The main line of the argument of the Hon'ble the Home Member, as well as the Law Member, was: 'Do you want the Government to uphold order or not? If you want the soldiers to protect your life and property, then you cannot expect them to do so unless you protect them.' We do not quarrel with the premises. The Hon'ble the Home Member, particulary appealed to the aristocracy. But even the professional classes have a stake in the country, and I do not therefore think that that was a very happy appeal, made as it was to a particular section of this legislative assembly. Everyone here has a stake in the country and is expected to look at the problem in a proper perspective and in just proportions. We know we should do nothing to weaken the hands of the Government especially in a country like India; but what we want is justice to all alike; we do not want any officer to be harassed by vexatious and unnecessary actions; but, my Lord, at the same time the golden mean has to be observed;

where certain facts have been divulged which necessitate an inquiry, all I say is the protecting cloak should not be cast on all alike equally. It is because vital constitutional principles are at stake, that we have taken so much trouble to weary the Government and the Legislative Council. We feel that this Council should not pass a final Act of Indemnity, unless it is satisfied that there was necessity for martial law in the Punjab. We think that this Legislative Council should not lend the weight of its authority to the proposition that the executive Government, whenever they feel that the civil arm is unable to cope with an emergency, should call in the aid of military and allow them to do what they like. We do not want an extension of the martial law doctrine to cases which occurred in peace and before the proclamations thereof. We do not want to accept here as a body the doctrine that martial law can be enforced or can be kept in force one minute longer, for the suppression of rebellion, whether armed or unarmed, the moment the rebellion is suppressed. Martial law cannot and ought not to be used for the mere purpose of maintaining order in the community. No Government is worth the name of Government if it cannot maintain order, by the civil power, once violent disturbances are suppressed; and it would be a dangerous doctrine to uphold that we may indemnify all the acts of Government the moment the Governor of a province says that he cannot maintain order, not merely without the aid of the military, but without the enforcement of martial law. That question, my Lord, is one of essential importance as to how long martial law can be kept in force, and here we have grave reasons for thinking that although the Government of India might have been justified, on the representations made by the Punjab Government—and when it was not in a position to ascertain the accurate position—and I am sorry that the Chief Justice has dragged himself in here, although it may be that the Government of India might have been justified in issuing its preliminary orders, there was no justification for keeping it in force for three months, and more, and most of the trials held in that period should not be upheld and ratified by this Council. We are thankful to the Hon'ble the Home Member for conceding to us that all those found guilty of infractions merely of Martial Law Ordinances would be released, provided they do not at the same time come under some provision of the Penal Code, special or local law....."

The Hon'ble Sir William Vincent:—"My Lord, the Hon'ble Member said Martial Law Ordinances, I think he means Martial Law Regulations."

The Hon'ble Rao Bahadur B.N. Sarma:—"I beg your pardon. I mean Martial Law Regulations. We are thankful for that concession, and it is a real concession and the other one is that the cases, of those who have not appealed to the Privy Council would also be governed by the principles and grounds of the Privy Council decision. It cannot but be acknowledged that that to a certain extent obviates some of the objections we had to the passing of the Bill. But, to my mind, the constitutional principles that are at stake, especially in a country like India, are of such vital importance that we as a legislative body would not be justified in passing a Bill of this description finally, pending the inquiry into the necessity for the enforcement of martial law, its duration, the measures adopted and as to the acts of individual officers who *prima facie* on the evidence before us here must be presumed to be guilty until the contrary is shown."

The Hon'ble Sir William Vincent:—"My Lord, before I address myself to the main motion, I should like to reply to two remarks of Mr. Sinha. I regret that he is not here, but it is not my fault that he is absent. The Hon'ble Member began by complimenting me, perhaps undeservedly, on the moderate tone I had adopted throughout the debate. He went on immediately afterwards, however, to cite with approval, with gusto, if I may say so, an extract from some paper, which condemned in no measured terms, the whole of the substance and language of my speech. This does not seem to me reasonable.

"I am content, however, to leave the matter to the decision of Council. I do not think that any Member here can say that I have been intemperate in my language in this debate.

"The Hon'ble Mr. Sinha then went on to suggest that, as I had quoted Mr. Gandhi in regard to the Indemnity Bill, I should remember also that Mr. Gandhi had repeatedly found fault with the convictions and sentences of various persons. My Lord, we are having these cases examined, but may I point out to the Council that, although Mr. Gandhi condemned these convictions, in spite of his feelings on that point, he has still supported this Bill? That is a fact which many Members of this Council might do well to remember. I did not quote him as an authority for whom I myself had any very great respect, but the Hon'ble Pandit Madan Mohan Malaviya having cited him frequently in this Council, as a man of the greatest weight and one almost inspired, I hoped that I might use the name of

Mr. Gandhi in appealing to him and to other Members of this Council to support the Bill.

"Turning to other speakers my Lord, may I say that in my opinion the whole debate on this motion to pass the Bill has resolved itself into an occasion for a discussion of totally irrelevant matters? All kinds of details have been brought up which really are not before the Council at this stage at all. Many Members have indeed taken the opportunity of the motion to answer criticisms that have been made of their speeches on previous occasions, and a part of the day at least was spent in recriminations. Statements of fact made on one side were almost inevitably answered by others, and the result has been, however, that the Council has been invited indirectly by some Members, like the Hon'ble Mr. Malaviya, and almost directly by others, such as the Hon'ble Mr. Thompson, to come to definite conclusions on inadequate information and *ex parte* statements, as to particular incidents during these risings. You have one member saying one thing : another saying something quite different; on many occasions neither of them speaking from first-hand knowledge; and on their statements this Council is asked to condemn or justify the conduct of individual officers. I use the word 'condemn' deliberately—I took down one statement used by the Hon'ble Mr. Madan Mohan Malaviya when he said that a particular officer was guilty of criminal dereliction of duty—I put it 'emphatically' to the Council that such a statement is neither fair nor reasonable. These are matters for the Committee. I will take one incident which has been repeatedly referred to, this unfortunate Jallianwala Bagh affair. My Lord, no one deplores the loss of life on that day more then the Government. It has been, and must be to all of us, a source of great distress, and it does not really make so very much difference from this point of view whether the number killed was 300 or 500. In either case, the loss of life is serious enough in all conscience, and greatly to be regretted. But we have no right in this Council either to justify or condemn that action. It is not part of our duty; it does not come within the scope of the Bill. General Hudson has, it is true, put before the Council certain considerations relating to this occurrence, but as I understood him—he was merely attempting to put the matter as it might have appeared to a military officer at the time and was not in any way putting his personal views before the Council. That is the way I understood his remarks. I mention this because his statements have been made the ground for attacks on him; and it was suggested he sought to justify what was done. I do not think that the Council, when they have considered the position, will for one moment accept that as a fair presentment of his intention. What I ask the Council to do now is, not to prejudge this matter in any way, neither to condemn nor to justify any action, neither to say a man is innocent nor to say he is guilty until the proper time for such a decision shall arrive. Does this question come within the scope of this debate? Is there anything in the Bill that justifies a man or condemns a man? I maintain there is nothing. All that the Bill enunciates is a principle. It does not say that a man is justified or blameworthy for his conduct on any particular occasion. It leaves that to the Court to decide from a legal point of view. In so far as administrative action is concerned, that is also a question outside the Bill altogether, which can be decided, as I have repeatedly explained to this Council, only after the Report of the Committee is received. What could be fairer? The question whether an officer acted *bona fide* or not is left to be decided from the legal point of view by the Courts save for this provision, that there is a presumption that he has acted *bona fide* and reasonably. Let me take the case again of Jallianwala Bagh. What is the position? If the action of any particular officer is found to be unjustifiable, if all the allegations made to-day are true, what will be the result? It will be a matter for the Court, either the Court will find it justifiable and reasonable or unjustifiable and unreasonable in which latter case the normal legal results, will follow. Similarly, so far as administrative action in concerned, if the action was unjustifiable, then undoubtedly the Committee will condemn it. But is it fair to any officer to condemn him behind his back, unheard and without his having an opportunity of making a statement and offering his explanation? Is it fair to him to come here and make statements which affect his character, his honour, his sense of justice, and his sense of humanity?

"My Lord, the Hon'ble Pandit Madan Mohan Malaviya made an admittedly powerful speech; many parts of it were very powerful, but I submit that it was as I have tried to point out to the Council, both irrelevant to the motion before us now and unjust to many who are not here. The Hon'ble Member in the course of the debate made more than one reference to the Almighty and to his conscience. I wish, my Lord, that it would induce him to be fair to others. I regard the whole of his speech, however, as a desperate attempt by creating prejudice to recover a position that was really lost. The whole principle of this Bill had been accepted by the Council on the understanding, as I say, that the question of *bona fides* or *mala fides* was to be decided by the Courts. When that principle has been accepted, the Hon'ble Member again attempts to prejudice the minds of the whole Council by citing specific incidents, the merits of which are really not before this Council at all.

"My Lord, the Bill has however been attacked as premature for more weighty reasons than these. It was said—at least if I understood the argument correctly—it was said 'you should pass no Indemnifying Bill because the Legislature has had no opportunity of satisfying itself as to the actions taken.' The answer to this argument seems to be very simple. We are not dealing with individual actions or specific actions at all. We are dealing with principles, that is, the principles upon which a man in such circumstances ought to be indemnified. If Council will not give a Government officer even this qualified indemnity, then he is liable in the courts for any action which is not legal or justifiable by the strict law though it may have been proper and necessary. Such an argument, namely, that you should not pass Act of Indemnity until you are satisfied as to the character of the act indemnified, would be of some weight and more could be said in favour of it, if we were here granting complete indemnity and completely validating all that has been done. My Lord, that is exactly what we are not doing, and the reason we are not doing more is because we do not think it would be right to ask for more complete indemnification at present. If Council will look at the older Acts, either the English Acts or the Indian Act of 1860, they will see that these Acts give complete indemnity to everybody for any acts done in suppressing disorders irrespective of any question of *bona fide*. The indemnity we propose to give is however definitely qualified, for reasons I have given, namely, because we cannot with the Committee coming on ask Council to pass a more comprehensive Act. By taking our present course, we leave it to the Courts to decide whether a particular action was *mala fide* or wrong from the legal point of view; and from the administrative point of view, we await the report of the Committee of Inquiry. My Lord, it is said that the words 'reasonable belief' mean nothing, to my mind the meaning is perfectly simple. The only legal definition of the term, I know, is in the Indian Penal Code, where reasonable belief is defined as belief for which there is sufficient cause. I will read the exact words 'A man is said to have reasonable belief if he has sufficient cause to believe it, but not otherwise.'

"Another objection taken to the passing of the Act now is, that the preamble has been altered since the Bill was introduced. This point has been dealt with so ably by my Hon'ble Colleague, that I really do not think I need dilate on it at any length. But I should like to put one aspect of it to the Council. First, we were told that by retaining the original words in the preamble we were making this Council admit that martial law was necessary. Well, we said 'All right; we will alter the preamble; we do not want to commit you to any such admission'; and we modified that portion of the preamble to which objection was taken. The next day two new objections are put forward, the first by the Hon'ble Mr. Malaviya who says 'You cannot pass the Bill because you have withdrawn that statement from the preamble,' though we did so to meet objections of non-official Members. The second was by the Hon'ble Mr. Sinha who said 'Oh, you have now admitted that martial law was not necessary.' Hon'ble Members have heard the whole of the discussion, and I leave it to them to decide whether they think that either of these arguments is of any weight.

"My Lord, it has been repeated more than once in this debate that martial law was not necessary. The facts are before the Council, and I do not want to reiterate anything which has been said already; but I have here a short statement of some of the leading outrages that occurred in the Punjab which, I think, will be interesting. There were 7 murders of Europeans, 15 serious assaults, some of them murderous, there were 44 cases of arson; there were 34 cases of serious tampering with railway lines, anyone of which might have caused a grave accident—I am quoting from information supplied to me—and there were 132 cases of cutting telegraph wires or destruction of telegraph posts and insulators. I think that with this additional information before it, this Council will conclude that there was some reason at least for supposing that this was not a case of ordinary disorder, for crimes of this kind are not committed in cases of local rioting.

"The Hon'ble Mr. Ayyangar (I wish I could make myself heard by him), indeed, went so far as to suggest that martial law was instituted merely because Sir Michael O'Dwyer wished to pay off old scores. I have read out to the Council the telegram that we received from the Punjab; the Council have heard from Mr. Hailey and from others well acquainted with the facts including my friend, the Hon'ble Major Umar Hayat Khan, what the actual position was. Is it generous, is it fair, is it honest, in these circumstances, for an Hon'ble Member of this Council to come forward and make or quote an allegation against Sir Micheal O'Dwyer of that character, to stab him in the back in this way? For myself I may say that I have heard many unfair things said in this Council—but I have never heard a more cowardly attack in the whole course of my experience.

"Then we had another allegation by the Hon'ble Pandit Malaviya to which I wish to make some reference. He made what was to my mind a very serious statement. An allegation that the telegram from the Punjab Government to the Government of India did not state the truth....."

The Hon'ble Pandit Madan Mohan Malaviya:—"The whole truth, I said."

The Hon'ble Sir William Vincent:—"The Hon'ble Member said 'truth' first though he subsequently corrected it. I took down the words....."

The Hon'ble Pandit Madan Mohan Malaviya:—"My Hon'ble friend did not take the words down accurately. I said 'the whole truth.'"

The Hon'ble Sir William Vincent:—"I maintain that what the Hon'ble Member first stated was 'truth'; he corrected it later. I submit in any case that there was no justification for such an allegation against the late Lieutenant-Governor of the Punjab. There is nothing whatever in the speech of the Hon'ble Member which can be held to be justification of such a serious accusation as that. Whatever were the exact words used—'the truth' or 'the whole truth'—the insinuation is that Sir Micheal O'Dwyer deliberately withheld facts from the Government of India, and I maintain that there is no information before Council to lead us to think that there is any basis at all for such a suggestion.

"Then it was said that the declaration of martial law was really due to unsympathetic treatment of the people by the Punjab Government. If that statement is correct, my Lord, what was the case in Bombay? Was Sir George Lloyd unsympathetic? We have heard nothing but praise of Sir George Lloyd's conduct throughout, yet we know that martial law was enforced in parts of Bombay for a short time, at any rate, and we do know that the most deplorable excesses were committed there. The Council has heard of this unfortunate Mamlatdar, who was burnt alive.

"The fact is, my Lord, that in many of these cases where martial law is declared, it is easy to criticize the action taken; and often the measures taken deprive the authors of evidence of the necessity for them. This is very well put in the Report of the Commission on the Jamaica Rising—in the following words: 'how much easier it is to decide such a question after' than before the event and sometimes the success of the measures adopted for the prevention of an evil deprives the authors of those measures of evidence they would otherwise have had of their necessity.' I maintain that this has been a great deal the position in the Punjab. The very success of the measures taken has deprived the authorities of evidence of their necessity.

"But, my Lord, we are not now deciding whether martial law was necessary or not, but whether in any case to protect our officers when they have acted *bona fide*? It was for this reason I deprecated the discussion of the necessity for martial law in this Council altogether. I asked the Council then to forbear from discussing that question, because it necessarily must come before this Committee of Inquiry. The position I have always taken up is, that we believe that martial law was necessary, but whether it was necessary or not we must protect our officers who have acted *bona fide*; and I have never yet heard any argument which has satisfied me that I was wrong on that point. We do not seek to indemnify our officers for specific acts; we are not doing so either administratively or in respect of legal liability; we are only laying down principles on which indemnity should be granted. I am told, however, that officers need no such protection, and they must depend on their protection under the common law. This point has also been dealt with by the Hon'ble the Law Member, and I will only say to Council that these references to legal dogmas leave me cold. The real question is a simple one, on which any man of sense can judge for himself. Each Member of this Council must judge, whether a soldier or any officer of Government who carried out the orders of his superior or did his duty in suppressing these disorders *bona fide* and honestly is or is not entitled to be indemnified against legal liability for his action. There is no good citing legal dogmas and constitutional theories in such circumstances. The question is 'are you going to afford the men reasonable protection or not?'

"Well, my Lord, I have placed all the facts relating to the Bill before the Council. I maintain now that it is a perfectly fair and reasonable measure, that it is entitled to receive the support of this Council, and I now leave the issue with all confidence in the hands of Hon'ble Members."

The motion that the Bill, as amended, be passed was put and agreed to.

APPENDIX VII
Miscellaneous

(1)—All-India Moderates' Conference

Sir Sivaswamy's Presidential Speech

The following is an extract from Sir P.S. Sivaswamy Iyer's Presidential speech at the All-India Moderates' Conference :—

I shall now pass on to a subject which has been engrossing the mind of the public even more than the subject of constitutional reforms. The disturbances in the Punjab in April last and the measures taken by the authorities to deal with them attracted the keenest and most widespread interest at the time. While the acts of lawlessness committed by the mobs were duly published at the time, the public were not kept equally informed of the doings of the authorities and the nature and extent of the measures adopted by them in the restoration of order. The movements of people to and from the Punjab were prohibited or restricted. Accused persons were deprived of the services of counsel from outside the province. A rigorous censorship was exercised over the press, and security was demanded from papers which had the temerity to publish accounts of the manner in which martial law was administered. Such information, however, as leaked out and was published sent a thrill of horror over the land. While all political organisations expressed their detestation of damage to life and property and communications and all the other outrages committed by the mobs and their approval of all measures reasonably necessary for the suppression of disorder, they felt it their duty to condemn the excesses of the authorities administering martial law and press for the prompt withdrawal of martial law. After a delay of several months, the promised Committee of Enquiry has been appointed and the inquiry has been going on for two months. It is to be deeply regretted that the Government should not have seen their way to suspend the sentences of the leading citizens, who were convicted in Lahore and Amritsar, and enable them to be present when evidence affecting them was being given at the inquiry and to give instructions to counsel for the cross-examination of the witnesses. It is also unfortunate that for this reason the Congress Committee, to whose patriotic labour we owe an ungrudging tribute of praise, should have decided to withhold their assistance from the Committee and let in no evidence on behalf of the people. Notwithstanding these disadvantages, the evidence tendered by the government, and especially the evidence of the European officers who were charged with the duty of restoring order, has thrown a flood of light upon the administration of the Punjab during those eventful months. The disclosures now made have confirmed the worst suspicions of the public as to the ruthless and inexcusable barbarity of the administration and have created a feeling of intense indignation throughout the country. In view of the fact that the inquiry is not yet concluded, a considerable measure of reserve is called for in expressing an opinion on the matters pending before them. It is neither possible, nor desirable at this stage to express any opinion as to the cause of the disturbances or as to the necessity for the employment of military force or for the introduction of martial law; but the evidence of the European officers which has been already taken has made it abundantly clear that martial law was continued long after the necessity for it, if any, had ceased, that the means adopted by the military authorities to put them down were far in excess of the requirements of the situation and that the proceedings of the officers concerned were not guided by any considerations of common sense, humanity or decency. Whether the disturbances in the various localities amounted only to riots or rebellion is a matter which may be left, for the present, to the decision of the Committee. It is well settled that necessity is the sole measure of the duration and extent of the force to be employed for putting down-an insurrection and restoring order; and that it is only when it is impossible for the ordinary courts of law to sit or enforce the execution of their judgments, that martial law can be indulged. There is nothing to show that except perhaps during the few days immediately following the disturbances the ordinary civil courts could not sit.

Apart from any question of the legality of the Ordinance providing for the trial of offences by special or martial law tribunals, there was no moral justification for the continuance of martial law or for the continuance of the special tribunals after the disturbances had been put down. The fact that trial by courts-martial is bound to be quicker or would serve as an example of terror to others and help to keep them in due awe and obedience is no justification whatever for the establishment or continuance of Martial Law. It is also clear that the

Martial Law officers had no right to treat contraventions of their own orders as offences, and proceed to try and punish people for infringement of their orders. Let us turn our eyes to some of the facts disclosed in the evidence of the principal European witnesses. The wholesale slaughter of hundreds of unarmed men at Jallianwala Bagh without giving the crowd an opportunity to disperse, the indifference of General Dyer to the condition of the hundreds who were wounded in the firing, the firing of machine guns into crowds who had dispersed and taken to their heels, the flogging of men in public, the order compelling thousands of students to walk 16 miles a day for roll-calls, the arrest and detention of 500 students and professors, the compelling of school children of 5 to 7 to attend on parade to salute the flag, the order imposing upon owners of property the responsibility for the safety of the Martial Law posters stuck on their properties, the flogging of marriage party, the censorship of mails, the closure of the Badshahi mosque for six weeks, the arrest and detention of people without any substantial reason and especially of people who had rendered services to the State in connection with the War Fund or ortherwise, the flogging of six of the biggest boys in the Islamiah school simply because they happened to be school boys and to be big boys, the construction of an open cage for the confinement of arrested persons, the invention of novel punishments like the crawling order, the skipping order and others unknown to any system of law, civil or military, the handcuffing and roping of persons and keeping them in open trucks for 15 hours, the use of aeroplanes and Lewis guns and the latest paraphernalia of scientific warfare against unarmed citizens, the taking of hostages and the confiscation and destruction of property for the purpose of securing the attendance of absentees, the handcuffing of Hindus and Muhammadans in pairs with the object of demonstrating the consequences of Hindu-Musalman unity, the cutting off of electric and water supplies from Indian houses, the removal of fans from Indian houses and giving them for use by Europeans, the commandeering of all vehicles owned by Indians and giving them to Europeans for use, the feverish disposal of cases with the object of forestalling the termination of martial law—are some of the many incidents of the administration of martial law, which created a reign of terror in the Punjab and have shocked the public.

It is a strange feature of the mental constitution of those military officers that they should have imagined that the steps they took were a remedy for the sullenness of the people and a means for promoting the popularity of the Government. We are naively told by General Sir William Beynon that instead of being unduly severe, the administration erred on the side of leniency, and that he and Sir Michael O'Dwyer approved of General Dyer's exploit. It is inconceivable that such things can ever happen under the name of martial law in England or even in Ireland. That they could have happened in India shows the ineptitude of the present system of government. It is obvious that the Government of India must have regarded the opposition to the Rowlatt Bill as a direct challenge of their authority and as a trial of strength between the people and the Government; and that having given the promise of support to the local authorities, they were prevented by panic and love of prestige from listening to the representations of Indian leaders, or making any attempt to see things for themselves. It is no wonder that the hearts of our people have been stirred by these doings to their inmost depths. The indecent haste with which the Indemnity Bill was rushed through the Imperial Council is now intelligible. It will also be clear how well-founded the objection of the people was to the provisions of the Rowlatt Bills which entrust the liberties of the subject to the mercy of the executive.

We do not know what the findings of the Enquiry Committee may be; but if we may be allowed to voice the wishes of the people we should ask, (1) for reparation for all serious hardship and suffering caused by unwarranted acts of severity, (2) for steps being taken to bring to justice any officials, high or low, civil or military, who may be found to have acted unreasonably and in excess of their powers or authorised such acts, (3) for the provision of safeguards against the recurrence of such things in the future and (4) for the abolition of flogging in the Indian Army. Let us see what reasonable safeguards it is possible to suggest. One remedy which may perhaps be thought of is that in dealing with internal outbreaks the civil authorities should only invoke the aid of military forces, but should not allow the introduction of martial law. This suggestion raises a very large issue and in view of the incidents of the martial law regime in Ireland, Egypt, India and Ceylon may deserve consideration; but it seems to me doubtful whether it is likely to be entertained as a practical proposition. No enactment of any declaration of rights, as suggested by our friends in the Congress, can avert the possibility of the introduction of martial law; for, by the very nature of the case martial law is a creature of necessity and transcends all law. Martial law is a state of no law, where the will of the General who commands the army prevails; but if, as is only too likely, the abolition of martial law for the purpose of suppressing internal outbreaks is put aside as an impracticable suggestion, we are entitled to ask that the constitutional limitations to which its exercise and duration are subject according to the opinion of eminent English jurists shall be authoritatively set forth either in a statute or in a memorandum of instructions to be issued to the Governor-General. It should be made clear that martial law should not be introduced, unless it is impossible for the civil courts to sit and exercise their functions. It is further necessary that the power of creating new offences for breach of regulations and providing penalties therefor should not be delegated to Military Officers; and that if courts-martial and civil courts are both sitting, any person not subject to the Naval Discipline Act or to Military Law, who is alleged to be guilty of the contravention of any regulation should be allowed to claim to be tried by a Civil Court instead of by a Court-Martial.

The happenings in the Punjab have emphasised the necessity for providing that the Indian element in the Executive Council of the Viceroy shall be at least equal to the European element. They point to the urgent need for the cheapening and quickening of cable communications with England. They have also demonstrated the evil effects of a prolonged exodus to the hills, and the consequent isolation of the Government from the world of humanity beneath.

(2)—The Indian National Congress

The Hon'ble Mr. Nehru's Address

The following are some extracts from the Hon'ble Pandit Motilal Nehru's Presidential Address at the Amritsar Congress :—

.......Fellow delegates, you have assembled here in deep mourning over the cruel murder of hundreds of your brothers and in electing your president you have assigned to him the position of chief mourner. That position I accept in all reverence and I sincerely thank you for it.......

.......In India the first fruits of the peace were the Rowlatt Bills and Martial Law. It was not for this that the War was fought, it was not for this that many hundreds of thousands laid down their lives. Is it any wonder that the peace has aroused no enthusiasm and that the vast majority of the people of India have refused to participate in the peace celebrations?

. . . .

We must also do reverence to the sacred memory of the dead who were killed in Amritsar and elsewhere in the Punjab, and to the living who were put to indignities worse even than death and suffered the most shameful barbarities. No monument in marble or bronze is needed to consecrate their memory. Our speeches here will be forgotten, the resolutions you pass may in the future have interest only for the historian, but India will never forget the sacrifice and the sufferings of these children of hers.

The Punjab

As I have already indicated, the Punjab has the right to claim the first attention of this Congress. But before I deal with the various problems which it presents for our consideration, I desire to congratulate you heartily, my fellow countrymen and women of the Punjab, and more specially those of Amritsar, for the courageous public spirit you have shown in holding the present session of your great National Assembly in this city. You resolved in happier times to invite the Congress to your Province, little dreaming of the dark days you were destined to go through before you were to realize your expectations. You lost no time in forming your Reception Committee and were cheerfully busying yourselves with your patriotic work when a great calamity suddenly descended upon you. You have borne this affliction, and at the same time have adhered to your resolve. Your spokesman at Delhi, who invited the Congress, lies in jail together with many of his colleagues. Yet you have not flinched or sought to cast aside the burden you had voluntarily undertaken. All honour to you for your devoted patriotism. All praise for your patient suffering.

India has suffered much at the hands of an alien and reactionary bureaucracy; but the Punjab has in that respect acquired a most unenviable notoriety. Competent observers have borne testimony to the spirit that has animated the Punjab administration ever since it came under British rule. Sir Henry Cotton and Mr. Bernard Houghton, both eminent members of the Indian Civil Service, have told us of the retrogressive and backward condition of the province and the militarist tendencies which hold sway there. Mr. Ramsay MacDonald in his book, "The Awakening of India" says:—

> "It is generally conceded in India that the most incompetent of the Governments is that of the Punjab. It takes its stand upon two foundation rocks. 'Prestige' and 'Sedition,' the meaning of the former being that it can do what it likes, and of the latter that if any Indian questions its doings his house will be raided and he will be deported.................. It has no notion of statesmanlike handling, no idea of political methods. The man in power simply uses his power whether it is in the form of a not too honest detective department or a not too discriminating executive or judiciary."

The proximity of the Punjab to the frontier has enabled its administrators time and again to enforce their will on successive Viceroys and Secretaries of State. The bogey of the frontier is exploited to the uttermost and the proposals made by the "man on the spot" seldom fail to secure acceptance at the hands of the higher authorities. With Delhi almost on the border and with Simla for its summer capital, the Government of the Punjab has the additional advantage of having the ear of the Viceroy; and it has thus come about that being the worst Government in India, it is the most favoured of all provincial administrations. Public life is not likely to thrive under these conditions and it is no wonder that for long there was no marked growth of political ideas in the Punjab.

In order to appreciate the causes which ultimately led to the catastrophe of April last and its sequel, it is desirable to consider briefly the forces which have been at work ever since the first pulsations of public life began to be noticed by the authorities. Before 1905 there was practically no public life in the Punjab, but the stupendous blunder of Lord Curzon in affecting the partition of Bengal in the face of a nation's resentment not only convulsed the affected province but sent a thrill of excitement and discontent throughout the country, which could not fail to arouse public activity in the Punjab. The introduction of the Colonization Bill in the local Legislative Council shortly after brought trouble to the very doors of the people. By this bill it was intended to curtail the valuable vested rights of the so-called colonists and to deprive them of the fruits of their labour which had converted the desolate wilds around Lyallpur into a smiling garden. A strong agitation followed and this was dealt with by the usual policy of repression. About this time, the editor and proprietor of the "Panjabee" newspaper were convicted. Shortly after the Colonization Bill was passed by the local Council. But these measures failed to put down the agitation which was continued with redoubled energy. The more excitable among the people came into conflict with the police, and there were riots in Lahore and Rawalpindi in April, 1907. Against the arrest and trial of the actual rioters no sensible person can have anything to say; but there was no justification for the arrest of Lala Hansraj Sawhney and some other leading public men, as was shown at their trial. Even less excusable was the deportation without trial of Lala Lajpat Rai and Ajit Singh. The policy of the Punjab Government in those days, and handed down as a legacy to succeeding Lieutenant-Governors, was to shut their eyes to their own reactionary administration and keep the Government of India and the Secretary of State in ignorance of the real causes of the disturbances by supplying them with coloured accounts and fixing responsibility for their own lapses on the poor "agitator." Be it said however to the credit of Lord Minto, that he refused to assent to the unjust law passed by the Punjab Council. But there was no lack of other weapons of repression in the already over-stocked armoury of the Punjab Government; and these continued to be freely used during the years 1907 to 1909. The methods adopted were the suppression of the press and the prosecution of individuals unacceptable to the Government. Needless to say, the young sapling could not weather the continuous storm it was subjected to and there was little manifestation of public life in the Punjab during the years 1910 to 1913.

But repression and terrorism have never yet killed the life of a nation; they but increase the disaffection and drive it underground to pursue an unhealthy course, breaking out occasionally into crimes of violence. And this brings further repression and so the vicious circle goes on. No one can but deplore violence and political crime. But let us not forget that this is the direct outcome of continued repression. It is due to the perversity of the executive which blinds itself to the causes of the discontent and, like a mad bull, goes about attacking all who dare to stand up against it.

Sir Denzil Ibbetson, the Lieutenant-Governor of the Punjab, during the troublous days of 1907, was not slow to perceive the "new air which was blowing through men's minds", but instead of adjusting his sails to this "new air" be chose to steer his course right against it. He, as well as his successor, followed the broad and easy path of piling repression on repression in accordance with the hallowed traditions of the Punjab Administration.

This was the state of the Punjab, when her destinies were placed in the hands of Sir Michael O'Dwyer. It was a splendid opportunity for a broadminded and generous-hearted statesman to strengthen the foundations of the Empire by doing the barest justice to the natural aspirations of a people, to whom the Empire owed so much. How Sir Michael acquitted himself of this high trust every Indian knows.

During the early days of Sir Michael O'Dwyer's rule occurred the *Komagata Maru* incident. The unfortunate men who had left their homes in a spirit of peaceful enterprise, many not wishing to return to India at all, found every door shut in their faces and were forced to return. The reception prepared for them by the Government of India, presumably at the instance of the Punjab Government, was the passing of the Ingress into India Ordinance, which empowered the Government to restrict the liberty of any person entering India. On landing in India they found themselves prisoners and, broken down as they were by the consistent ill-treatment they had received at home and abroad, they completely lost their heads and the unfortunate Budge-Budge riot was the result.

The *Komagata Maru* episode marked the recrudescence of unrest in the Punjab, and afforded a pretext to Sir Michael O'Dwyer to ask for more "effective power" from the unwilling Government of Lord Hardinge. During 1914 and the early part of 1915 insistent demands continued to be made for a *carte blanche* to deal with the situation; and a draft ordinance of a drastic character was submitted to the Government of India for approval and promulgation. At last Lord Hardinge, was compelled to yield and the Defence of India Act, which substantially embodied the provisions of this draft ordinance, was hurriedly passed through the Indian Council. How this "essentially war measure" has been used, not only in the Punjab but in the other provinces as well, to deal with matters wholly unconnected with the war, we all know. Sir Michael O'Dwyer was not slow to utilise it and soon after reported its "salutary effect" to the Government of India.

The years 1915 to 1917 were occupied with various conspiracy trials by special tribunals constituted under the Defence of India Act. The vernacular press was ruthlessly suppressed and hundreds of persons were interned under the Defence of India Act or the Ingress Ordinance. It was during this period that Lokamanya Tilak and Shrijut Bepin Chandra Pal were prohibited from entering the province lest they should introduce the virus of Home Rule here. . . . . .

War Activities

I now come to the war activities of the O'Dwyerian regime during which, in the name of patriotism and the Empire, methods were employed which were even worse than those I have so far noticed. These could only have been practised in the Punjab either by the direct sanction or connivance of Sir Michael O'Dwyer or by over-zealous subordinates in the hope of reward. The truth of the Persian saying—

به پنج بیضه که سلطان ستم روا دارد
زنند لشکریانش هزار مرغ به سیخ

(If a king tolerates one grain of oppression, his retinue will inflict a ton of misery)

was fully realised in the course of this strenuous period. For a short time after the beginning of the war, recruitment in the Punjab proceeded under normal conditions. But soon after, Sir Michael O'Dwyer made up his mind to acquire the distinction of being the foremost recruiting sergeant in India, and gentle pursuasion gave place to more vigorous methods. Then came the Prime Minister's appeal for increased war effort. Sir Michael O'Dwyer's energies now knew no limits. In his speech in the Punjab War Conference, he said:—

> "You know the Delhi programme. My application of it to the Punjab I can explain in a single sentence. Two hundred thousand men for the regular army, voluntaryism if possible,

conscription if necessary; twice the thousand men we have been asked for for the Indian portion of the Indian Defence Force; a war loan effort which will eclipse the last; the development to the utmost of our local resources; and by God's grace victory in the end."

These are noble words breathing a lofty patriotism for the Empire. But what regard was paid to the capacity of the province to fulfil the expectations of his ruler? At the Delhi Conference the total number of men to be supplied by India was determined to be 5,00,000. Of these Sir Michael O'Dwyer made up his mind to find no less than 40 per cent from his own province, the population of which including the Indian States is only 15 per cent. It was too big an undertaking even for the martial races of the Punjab, who had already contributed over 2,50,000 combatants and 70,000 non-combatants since the commencement of the war. Hence the broad hint conveyed in the words "voluntaryism if possible, conscription if necessary." The various officials engaged in recruiting lost no time in translating those words into action and the horrors committed in the guise of patriotic effort are still fresh in the memory of the victims. An ingenious "quota system" was devised under which a rough census of the male population of every village was taken and each village was called upon to furnish a certain number of recruits within a fixed time. If the required number was not forthcoming within the time given, various unlawful and oppressive methods were employed. Villages were punished collectively and individuals were subjected to great hardships and humiliation. I shall not here enter into any details as the Commissioners appointed by the Sub-Committee are enquiring into these cases of ill-treatment and will present to you their report in due course.

The Criminal law was openly abused and numerous proceedings were taken against innocent men under the provisions of Sections 107 and 110 of the Code of Criminal Procedure with the sole object of compelling the accused persons either to enlist or to supply recruits. There are judicial records in existence showing that those who did either the one or the other were acquitted, while those who did neither were convicted. In the report on the administration of Criminal Justice for 1917 it is stated :—

"District Magistrates have spent much time in recruiting work during the year. The large decrease in the number of persons called upon to give security under Section 110, Criminal Procedure Code, is in a great part due to the heavy recruiting for the army."

In the report for 1918 it is, again, stated :—

"Recruiting for the army continued to be one of the main factors in bad livelihood cases."

Nor was the abuse of law confined only to bad livelihood cases. The following passage occurs in the judgment of the Sessions Judge of Karnal setting aside the convictions of the appellants by the District Magistrate:—

> "The various orders passed by the District Magistrate from time to time clearly show that if these appellants had also supplied recruits from among their near relations or if they were fit for enlistment themselves they would have been let off, provided 20 recruits were made up from the village as was originally demanded from it."

Similar methods were employed to swell the provincial contributions to the war loan. It will be interesting to prepare statistics to show how many subscribers found it necessary to transfer their war bonds at heavy discount soon after their subscriptions were announced. One of the favourite methods to deal with those who did not satisfy the authorities with their war effort either in supplying recruits or contributing to the war loan was to enhance their income-tax. The following short extracts from the judgments of Collectors, rejecting objections to the enhancement, will be instructive:—

"He (the objector) has three sons and will not enlist one of them. He has not subscribed to any war fund or war loan although he could easily do so."

"Up to date he has not helped even by a single pice in any war fund or loan."

"He is a miser and has not helped with a single pie in any war fund or loan."

The inevitable result of the systematic oppression, the main features of which I have described, was to spread serious discontent throughout the province and it is not surprising that the pent-up feelings of the people occasionally found vent in the commission of serious offences. We have it on record that a Tehsildar in the Shahpur District was murdered and some of his companions sustained grievous hurt. In the same district, a mob offered resistance to the arrest of some men on a charge of dissuading people from enlistment with the result that it was fired upon and several casualties occurred.

In a recent speech made in Multan, Sir Michael O'Dwyer expressed the lament that "those who worked in organising recruiting for the division have had a most arduous task; they have had to contend against apathy, timidity, and even with open hostility which in some cases unfortunately culminated into riot, bloodshed, and defiance of authority in Multan and Muzaffargarh."

Mr. Montagu in his last speech on the Indian budget remarked:—

"Recruiting for the army has gone on in parts particularly affected by these disturbances with such zeal and enthusiasm that I think there is reason to believe that many a family was left without its bread-winner."

Did Mr. Montagu sufficiently realize the inwardness of the "zeal and enthusiasm" he referred to or the extent to which it was carried? The "unauthorised, objectionable and oppressive methods" employed by zaildars and lambardars under pressure of the authorities are described in the judgment of the Sessions Judge of Multan as "matters of common knowledge." It is evident that this "common knowledge" did not travel beyond the seas to England or we should have found some indication of it in Mr. Montagu's speech.

What I have so far said applies to all classes affected by recruiting and war loan activities, and concerns mainly "the man on the sod and the man behind the plough" for whom the late Lieutenant-Governor professed the warmest sympathy and solicitude. Let us now turn to another class of people for whom he never affected any feelings other than those of unqualified hatred and contempt—I mean the people known as the educated classes in general and the politically minded section of them in particular. I have already shown that public life was all but dead in the Punjab some years before Sir Michael O'Dwyer appeared on the scene. It showed some signs of revival on his assuming charge of the province, but was again put down by his masterful repression. There were, however, world forces at work which even the strongest man could not resist, and the people of the Punjab, whose "manliness, sanity, and practical commonsense" the then Lieutenant-Governor was never tired of extolling for his own purposes could not remain unaffected. The famous memorandum of the nineteen members of the Indian Council, the Congress-League Scheme of Constitutional Reforms, the historical announcement of the 20th August, 1917, the visit to India of Mr. Montagu himself and the publication of the Montagu-Chelmsford Report all came in quick succession to the utter bewilderment of Sir

Michael O'Dwyer. He saw Congress Committees spring up in important centres, and heard the whole province ring with the echoes of speeches made at public meetings and conferences, in the course of which his administration was freely criticised. Early in his career as Lieutenant-Governor, he had conceived an immense admiration for himself and his administration and so long as it was open to him, he suppressed all talk of the slightest change or improvement. When that was made impossible by the announcement of the 20th August and the developments which followed it, he made highly offensive and provocative speeches in his own and the Viceroy's Council which served the only purpose of adding to the bitterness of feeling on both sides. Up to the end of 1918, constitutional reforms were the all absorbing topic at almost all public meetings and he could not well interfere with them. But early in 1919 came a terrible visitation in the shape of the Rowlatt Legislation, which set a tremendous wave of agitation rolling in the country from one end to the other. It swept through the Punjab with the same volume and force as through other parts of India, and gave Sir Michael O'Dwyer the opportunity he sought. The people were no longer offering criticism which was invited by the Government, but had engaged themselves in a strong agitation against a set policy which the Government had made up its mind to carry out at all cost. This made all the difference with him; and with the convenient bogey of the frontier to trot out in case of need, he prepared himself to deal the last effective blow.

Satyagraha

The Rowlatt Bills, bad as they were, were made even worse and more unacceptable to us by the environment in which were they set. Mahatma Gandhi rightly pointed out that they were "the unmistakeable symptom of the deep seated disease in the governing body," a disease which soon after broke out in all its virulence and naked ugliness. To fight this disease Mahatma Gandhi started the great *Satyagraha* movement. A new force was introduced into our politics, a force with the most tremendous potentialities. India's masses were suddenly awakened and the message of *Satyagraha* entered the humblest home. Some of us did not entirely agree with the wording of the *Satyagraha* pledge, many were of opinion that the time had not come for civil disobedience. But few, I imagine, can disagree with the essentials of the doctrine. These as I conceive them, are truth, fearlessness and non-violence. And, as a corollary, I would add that it is the right of every man to refuse to obey any law which goes against his conscience and to which he cannot with due regard to truth submit, and to suffer the consequences for such disobedience. This is specially so where the laws are passed against the will of the people. I would here refer you to what an eminent American has said. Mr. Hadley, president of the Yale University, says:—"You can compel ignorant people to accept a statute, you can force bad men to obey it when they do not want to; but if a statute or a judicial decision passes the line of those duties which good and intelligent men as a body accept and impose upon themselves, it is at once nullified. The process of nullifying law has sometimes been called passive resistance."

The qualities I have mentioned above, whether you call them *Satyagraha* or by any other name, are essential if we are to take our rightful place amongst the nations of the world. We shall not be free or deserve freedom unless we have these qualities in an ample measure. Unless we adhere to truth and discard fear we cannot get rid of the slave psychology, the outcome of generations of repression, which has been our sad inheritance. And violence cannot avail us. That is the special weapon of the west and we cannot hope to win freedom by armed force. But even if we could do so, it would be a barren victory, a victory which would degrade and coarsen us and make us less fit to enjoy the freedom we had so won. We would develop the same vices against which we are contending now, and in our turn would start the game of repression.

The spirit of *Satyagraha* was nobly shown by the great and peaceful demonstrations of the 6th of April. That day must remain a red letter day for India. It was the greatest event of the year. Some persons, ignorant of history and Indian tradition, have likened the *hartal* to the general strike after the manner of the west, and have called it the forerunner of riot and bloodshed. But the *hartal* in India is a spiritual weapon, the old-time method of showing sorrow, of having grievances redressed by patient suffering. It has from time immemorial been resorted to to express grief at a national calamity, sorrow at the loss of a loved citizen. It is not used as a threat nor as a weapon against the forces of law and order. And this was fully shown on the *Satyagraha* Day, when the mighty demonstrations passed off peacefully without the slightest conflict with the police or military.

Some words of Mahatma Gandhi have been distorted to mean that the *Satyagraha* movement was the cause of the disturbances in

India. Fellow delegates, I say most emphatically that this was not so. Neither *Satyagraha* nor the *hartal* was the cause except in so far as they greatly displeased the authorities and made them provoke the people. There was no civil disobedience of laws in the Punjab. *Satyagraha* flourished more in other parts of the country and yet there was no disturbance there. The *hartals* of the 6th April did not cause any breach of the peace. It was only after two popular leaders of this city had been suddenly deported and Mahatma Gandhi, the most revered Indian of the day, had been arrested, that the passions of the populace broke loose in certain parts of the country. That would have been so even without *Satyagraha* or *hartal*. The disturbances were the result of the action of the authorities. They knew full well, in the Punjab at least, that the consequence of their provocative action would lead to trouble and they took measures accordingly.

Martial Law, and After

The events which followed must be fresh in your memory. Martial Law was enforced and for long the Punjab was almost cut off from the rest of the world. The truth was hidden from us and we had to rely on the one-sided accounts presented by Government for our benefit. Outsiders were not permitted to enter the charmed area, even Mr. Andrews being turned out of the province. Within a few days of the declaration of Martial Law, the All India Congress Committee demanded a full and impartial enquiry, and a little later appointed a Sub-Committee to conduct an enquiry. This Sub-Committee laboured for months and collected a great deal of evidence. It was hoped to present this evidence to the official committee which had been announced.

Lord Hunter's Committee

The appointment by the Government of India of Lord Hunter's Committee was most disappointing; but we waived our substantial objections to it and decided to co-operate, provided only full facilities were given to us to represent the people's case. At the earliest possible opportunity, we urged upon the Government that the presence of the Punjabee leaders, who were in jail, was necessary for a fair enquiry. For many days we were in frequent communication with the Punjab Government, and we were led to believe that our requests were being favourably considered by them. We refrained from going to the press, in order to avoid embarrassing the Government and waited patiently for their answer. That answer came on the eve of the Hunter Committee's arrival in Lahore. You must have seen the correspondence subsequent to this and our Sub-Committee's statement which have already appeared in the papers, and I can add but little. I would only point out to you that we tried to meet the Government as much as possible. We modified our original request for the release of all the leaders during the enquiry and agreed to the presence of only one or two of them at a time *in custody* before Lord Hunter's Committee, while evidence relating to them was being given. That was all we wanted and which the Government finally refused to give us. It was not an extravagant request. Even criminals have a right to be present in court during their trial. The Punjabee leaders are not being tried in the technical sense but their actions are being judged, they are being attacked by official witnesses and much of the blame and responsibility for the disturbances is being cast on them. Yet they were not allowed the privilege of the meanest criminal, although the officials of Government, who are as much on their trial and have at least as much to answer for, have had the fullest opportunities of appearing before the committee and conducting their case. Some of these officials have even been allowed the advantage of giving their evidence in camera. After the most anxious consideration the Sub-Committee came to the conclusion that "if it was to discharge the trust laid upon it, if it was to vindicate the national honour of the great Punjabee leaders, if it was to see truth and innocence established, it could not possibly engage in an enquiry, in which the people's party was so heavily handicapped." I feel confident that you will approve of and endorse the action your Sub-Committee took, and trust to its judgment in taking all necessary steps to obtain justice.

Meanwhile, Lord Hunter's Committee has pursued the even tenor of its way, roused occasionally by some particularly callous official admission. Their findings can but be *ex parte* decisions, based on the evidence of one party only. The other side of the shield will be presented to you by the Commissioners appointed by your Sub-Committee, who have strenuously laboured to collect and sift the evidence for the people. I do not overlook the fact that the proceedings of your Commissioners are in the legal sense as *ex parte* as those of Lord Hunter's Committee. There is, however, this to be said that your Commissioners have the additional advantage of considering the evidence given before the Hunter Committee. They have for good reasons deferred publishing their report and the evidence on which it will be based and this Congress will not have the advantage of having their considered opinion on the Punjab occurrences before it. This has also considerably handicapped me, as in the absence of your Commissioners' report, it is somewhat difficult for me to deal with some aspects of Martial Law.

But whatever findings the Commissioners appointed by the Congress Sub-Committee may arrive at the central facts of the recent tragic events have now become so crystallised as to enable us to form an adequate idea of the true nature of the horrors through which the Punjab has just passed. These central facts are now matters of common knowledge and emerge clearly above the few controversial points, which we may safely leave to our Commissioners. What we in this Congress are concerned with is not so much the fixing of individual responsibility for particular acts as the ascertainment of the spirit which runs through them all. I shall now, by your leave, touch on some of the main incidents and broad features of the occurrences which clearly indicate the spirit with which the people on the one side and the administration on the other were actuated.

Amritsar

I shall take the case of Amritsar, which stands out more prominently than any other, as affording in itself a complete illustration of the spirit on either side.

The people of Amritsar observed the 6th of April in the true *Satyagraha* spirit. So they did also the 9th April, the Ram Naumi day, and Muhammadans gladly and eagerly joined their Hindu brethren in celebrating the festival. There was no violence, no threats, and the processionists played the English National Anthem in honour of the Deputy Commissioner. That showed the psychology of the people of Amritsar on that Ram Naumi day—Hindus and Moslems observing the festivals together, and both joining to do honour to the King Emperor. The next few hours brought a strange transformation. The Bazaars were filled with mourning and the crowds that had rejoiced the night before, discarded their turbans and shoes in sorrow, for they heard that two of their loved leaders had been suddenly deported. And, after the old Indian fashion, they went unarmed and bare-headed towards the Deputy Commissioner's house to pray for the release of their leaders. They were fired at, some were killed and a number wounded. But I shall not here deal with the circumstances of or the necessity for this firing. Again, the temper of the crowd changed; and as is the way with crowds, it rapidly went to the other extreme. The passion for vengeance took possession of it and some parts of the mob committed those excesses for which we Indians cannot but hang our heads in shame. Whatever the treatment they had been subjected to, whatever the provocation offered, nothing can justify the murders which they committed, the shameful assault which they perpetrated on a defenceless woman, the arson and plunder of which they were guilty.

Yet again, the mood changed. After two or three hours of madness, the people, or rather such of them as had been guilty of the outrages, recovered control of themselves. They saw the folly of their doings and, without the intervention of the police or military, of themselves stopped the destruction.

Such was the behaviour of the people of this city on those fateful days. The psychology of a crowd is a difficult thing to fathom; but I cannot but think that the history of those days would have been differently written, if an attempt had been made to appreciate the view-point of the people.

Let us now consider some of the doings of the officials and the spirit which actuated them. They did not appreciate the inner significance of *Satyagraha* or the *hartal.* To them it was all a vast conspiracy, the forerunner of a second mutiny. They did not care to see what troubled the people, they did not search for the causes of this mighty movement. They looked upon the closing of shops and the meetings and the demonstrations as a personal insult to them. Even the fraternisation of Hindus and Moslems was anathema, an act in the great conspiracy. We all know what it is in this country for a body of men to walk bare-headed and bare-footed. It is the sign of deep grief, a token of a great calamity. But our rulers neither understand nor care to study the feelings and emotions of those whom they look upon as a subject race. In his evidence before Lord Hunter's Committee, Mr. Miles Irving, who was Deputy Commissioner of Amritsar at the time, was asked about the people who were proceeding to his house on the 10th. He stated:—

> "Yes, they were coming to my house, I understood. They were coming not to make any ordinary protest. When people come, they come properly clad, but these men had put off their *pugrees* and shoes and they intended violence.

Question:—It might have been the sign of mourning?

Answer:—If it was mourning, it was violent mourning."

So, Mr. Miles Irving, after a life-time spent in the Indian Civil Service, thinks that the taking off of turbans and shoes is a sign of coming violence. Ignorance of the habits of a people is never excusable in one whose duty it is to govern them. It becomes criminal when it leads to grave consequences.

The sudden deportation of Drs. Kitchlew and Satyapal was a typical act of our administrators. Having convinced themselves that there was revolution in the air, that conspiracies were being hatched, that the wonderful calm of the 6th and 9th of April hid strange currents underneath, they took the only step which appeals to the mind of a bureaucrat. They knew that this would greatly upset the people, they knew that there might be trouble, but what matter. Could they not crush them with the "ample resources" at their disposal? It did not strike them that the people could be reasoned with or could be conciliated. Nor did they think of having recourse to the ordinary law courts of the country. They do not believe in the intricacies or the delays of the law. They believe in making themselves the judges, and meeting out swift and stern justice to their opponents.

The Jallianwala Bagh

But saddest and most revealing of all was the great tragedy which occurred here on the Vaisakhi day. No Indian and no true Englishman can hear the story of the Khuni Bagh, as it is now aptly called, without a sickening feeling of horror. Our friend, Mr. C.F. Andrews, to whom this province and our country is so much indebted, has described it "as a cold and calculated massacre." He says, "I have gone into every single detail with all the care and thoroughness that a personal investigation could command and it remains to me an unspeakable disgrace, indefensible, unpardonable, inexcusable." Such is the verdict of an Englishman. What words, fellow delegates, can I use to express your feelings and mine whose kith and kin, were mercilessly shot down by the hundred in cold blood? Well may we grieve in the words of the Persian poet:—

گردید وطن غرقهٔ اندوه و محن وای۔ ایوای وطن وای

خیزید روید از پی تابوت و کفن وای۔ ایوای وطن وای

از خون جوانان که شده کشته در این راه، رنگین طبق ماه

خونین شده صحرا و گل و دشت و دمن وای۔ ایوای وطن وای

(Our country is flooded with sorrow and woe,
O, for our land woe!
Arise and for coffin and ceremonies go!
O, for our land woe!
With the blood of our men killed in this pursuit
The moon shines red:
Hill, plain, and garden blood-red glow:
O, for our land woe!)

The facts of this incident are before you, they have largely been admitted by the authorities. But I am not aware of any condemnation from the authorities, I do not know of any high official, who has protested against this grim occurrence. That is a revelation of official mentality which staggers me. General Dyer, the author of the deed, has almost boasted of his achievement. He has sought to justify it. To him it was a "merciful act" to fire without warning on an inoffensive crowd because it might have made fun of him if he had refrained from doing so. He admits that he could have dispersed it without firing, but that would have been derogatory to his dignity as a defender of law and order. And so, in order to maintain his self-respect, he thought it his duty to "fire and fire well" till his ammunition was exhausted and 2,000 persons lay dead and wounded. There ended his duty. It was none of his business, he tells us, to look after the dead and wounded. It was no one's business. The defenders of law and order had won a great victory, they had crushed the great rebellion. What more was needed?

This is the deed which received the benedictions of Sir Michael O'Dwyer. This is the deed, which has been defended by official after official before Lord Hunter's Committee. The plea of necessity is raised, the plea that the massacre produced a good effect on the surrounding districts. We have heard of these excuses before, when Louvain was razed to the ground, when atrocities were committed at Dinant and Termonde. For these crimes against humanity, the late Kaiser and his underlings are going to be tried. But General Dyer is secure. His late chief has blessed him and his colleagues in the civil and military administration of this country stand by him and applaud his deed.

Crawling

The shooting in the Jallianwala Bagh was not the only feat which General Dyer performed. His subsequent conduct was no less revealing of his perverted state of mind. He tells us that he "searched his brain" for a new punishment, a new terror for the people—something as General Hudson put it in the Imperial Council, to "strike the imagination". And the punishment that was devised did credit to General Dyer's ingenuity and ferocity. It was worthy of the days of the Inquisition. All Indians who happened to pass through a certain lane were forced to crawl on their bellies like worms. This was the punishment meted out to all innocent and peaceful men who went that way, because some hooligans had attacked Miss Sherwood in the lane some days before. No better method could have been devised to humble the people to the dust.

Of the other measures taken in Amritsar by General Dyer—the flogging in public places, the enforced salaaming, the cruel treatment of the best and most respected citizens—I shall not say much. They all tell the same tale of brutal terrorism, the attempt to crush the spirit of the people.

Lahore

General Dyer was not the only apostle of this cult. There were many others, who tried to rival his exploits in the other districts under Martial Law. Lt.-Col. Frank Johnson, the expert from Bechuanaland, pursued the policy of "thoroughness" in the Lahore area. A "false and malicious" rumour that the Government intended to interfere with the marriage customs of the people was contradicted by an official *communique* from Simla, and the contradiction was given due publicity. The rumour was set down as a base lie; and a Mohammadan marriage was arranged in a village not far from Lahore. It so happened that the whole marriage party, including the bridegroom, the priests and the guests, were flogged for having dared to assemble together during the Martial Law days. Col. Johnson has now been pleased to express his regret for this flogging and to tell us that it was due to the absence of tact in the official concerned. He himself exercised this "blessed virtue" by arresting 500 students and the professors of the Sanatam Dharma College and confining them in the fort, because a Martial Law notice was damaged by some unknown person. He welcomed the opportunity of doing so, he "was looking for it." He tells us that he was waiting for an opportunity to bring home to the people the power of Martial Law. To him a walk of 16 miles daily for the students for three weeks in the scorching Lahore sun of April and May was no hardship. It was "ordinary physical training of a mild form." But perhaps the most noticeable example of the tact and mentality of Col. Johnson was his order prohibiting more than two Indians from walking abreast. He tells us:—

"If more than two natives come and do not give way to a European, that is likely to lead to breach of the peace."

Question—Who would commit the breach of the peace, the European?

Answer—Undoubtedly.

Question—You think he would be justified in doing so?

Answer—Certainly.

And yet we are told of equal partnership in the Empire, and are asked to rejoice over the peace which has given this to us!

Gujranwala

In Gujranwala Col. O'Brien held sway, serene in the knowledge that he could do what he wished without let or hindrance prior to Martial Law, that his actions would be subsequently validated. This simple fact furnishes a more illuminating commentary on the new Indemnity Act, than all the learned arguments of Sir George Lowndes in the Imperial Council. We can now understand the whole-hearted support given to the measure by the Hon'ble the Chief Secretary to the Punjab Government and appreciate the wisdom of the provision in the Act, which throws on the complainant the burden of proving want of good faith in the accused official when he is armed with a certificate from a Secretary to the Government.

One of the steps taken by Col. O'Brien on the assurance of the Chief Secretary was to arrest Gauhar Singh, a lambardar, aged 60 years. Col. O'Brien states: "Gauhar Singh himself had committed no offience, but his two sons were wanted by the police and they were not forthcoming; and that was why their old father was arrested. He told us that he did not know where his sons had gone. An order was also passed confiscating his property. The order stated that until the arrest of Gauhar Singh's sons his property would be confiscated, that he be dismissed from the post of lambardar, and any one touching his property or cutting his crops would be shot." No comment from me is necessary.

In Gujranwala, as you are all aware, the gentle art of bombing from aeroplanes was practised, a bomb being actually dropped on a school boarding house full of boys. The manner in which bombs were dropped may be gathered from Lt. Dodkin's statement. He says: "I saw twenty or 30 people in a field talking to one another and dropped bombs on them. I did not know who they were, whether they had assembled for an unlawful purpose, but I bombed as my orders were to disperse crowds."

Another part of this district has come to be known as the Bosworth Smith area in memory of the horrors it underwent under the rule of a member of the Indian Civil Service, who for years past was in disgrace with the Punjab Government but was selected as specially qualified to administer Martial Law justice, and has since been rewarded by promotion.

Kasur

In Kasur Capt. Doveton evolved fancy and novel punishments for the people; and sought to teach them how to observe the ancient customs of India by touching the ground with their foreheads. He also had men stripped and flogged in the presence of prostitutes. His brother officer Lt. Col. Macrae meanwhile amused himself by having school boys flogged in public in order to set an example to all evildoers. The bigger boys were picked out at random perhaps because they could bear the whipping better. They were not gulity of any offence "it was their misfortune" Col. Macrae tells us; and I take it that the punishment he awarded was in good faith. All the male inhabitants, boys and men ten thousand in number, had to present themselves for the identification parade. The men arrested, 150 in number, were put in a cage placed on the station platform, and a public gallows was erected, entirely at the instance of the Punjab Government, before any one was tried or condemnad to death—so Col. Macrae informs us.

Hindu–Muslim Unity

Besides the attempt to terrorize the people the Punjab officials aimed a blow at the most valuable asset of our political life, the union between Hindus and Mohammadans. You are aware, fellow delegates, of the pathetic scenes of fraternization between Hindus and Muslims which took place during the recent disturbances at Delhi, Lahore and other places accompanied with shouts of *Hindu Musalman ki jai*. These expressions of fellowship in a common trouble were treated by the Punjab officials as heinous crimes amounting to open rebellion and waging war against the King, and a new offence was created which was defined as "fraternization of Hindus and

Mohammadans against the Government by law established." One of the most shameful acts of the Martial Law authorities was to ridicule the Hindu-Muslim entente publicly in various ways. The admission of Hindus to the Mohammadan mosques and of Mohammadans to the Hindu temples, the drinking of water or *sherbet* from out of the same glass by Hindus and Mohammadans were unmistakable signs of a far deeper union of the two than could be looked upon with equanimity by those who were interested in keeping them apart. And an attempt was made under official inspiration during the closing days of Martial Law to found separate political associations or *Sabhas* for Hindus, Mohammadans and Sikhs. I do not know what progress has been made in this direction, but I trust that my fellow countrymen of all communities will refrain from swallowing this fatal bait.

I have referred you, fellow delegates, to a very few of the admitted facts. It is not possible for me here to go into all the harrowing details of the numerous atrocities committed in the name of law and order. For these you will have to wait for the report of your Commissioners and the evidence they are collecting. Meanwhile I would beg of you to read carefully the evidence which has been tendered before Lord Hunter's Committee. I would request you to note the overbearing attitude of the official witnesses and their arrogance to the Indian members of the Committee. That will give you a greater insight into the official mind than any words of mine can convey. That will give you some idea of what our brethren in the Punjab have had to go through. And I would have you remember that these were the officers who presided over the Martial Law Summary Courts, who dispensed justice and inflicted heavy punishments and floggings.

Necessity for Martial Law

The question of the necessity or otherwise of the application of Martial Law to the situation which arose in April last is a question on which also we must await the considered opinion of our Commissioners on all the evidence taken by them and that tendered before Lord Hunter's Committee. The Government case has been put as high as it possibly could be before the latter, so far as the opinion of the authorities as to the real nature of the disturbances, and their apprehensions at the time as to what they might eventually lead to, are concerned. The point is whether their opinion and apprehensions were based on facts or were the result of panic. I shall abstain from embarrassing either our own Commissioners or Lord Hunter's Committee by offering at this stage any definite opinion of my own for your acceptance. But I think I am fully within my rights in pointing out that the question is not so much whether there was necessity for the application of Martial Law at any time as whether it was necessary when it was actually applied. It may be that Martial Law could be justified if it had been introduced at the time when the disturbances were actually going on, but it is an admitted fact that it was not so applied. What was done was to call on the military to help the civil administration, which is well within the discretion of every magistrate under our Criminal Law, but is very different from Martial Law. Whether or not it was necessary to hand over the entire civil administration to the military on the dates on which the Martial Law Ordinances and notifications relating to each district were issued is the next question before your Commissioners as well as Lord Hunter's Committee. I shall content myself with laying before you the official view. Mr Kitchin, the Commissioner of Lahore Division, has stated that Martial Law was not wanted for the purpose of recovering control but in order to prevent the spread of infection, and specially for the speedy trial of the numerous persons who had been arrested. Mr. Miles Irving tells us that the necessity for the continuance of Martial Law did not depend on anything that happened in his district. It depended on outside factors, on the situation on the frontier. General Dyer tells us that the city of Amritsar was a "model of law and order" after the 13th April.

Whatever the finding of your Commissioners and Lord Hunter's Committee as to the initial necessity for Martial Law may be, there is not the slightest doubt, on the admissions made by the official witnesses before Lord Hunter's Committee that there was absolutely no justification for keeping it in force for the unconscionable length of time during which its horrors continued to be perpetrated. Admittedly it was not required to maintain law and order and the only justification pleaded, besides the old story of the dangers arising from the proximity of the frontier, is that it enabled the offenders to be brought to speedy justice. But the Government had ample power under the statute law to constitute special tribunals for the trial of offenders and these would not have taken much longer to dispose of the cases than the Martial Commissions and Summary Courts did. The only difference would have been that people would have been saved the sufferings and indignities to which they were subjected under cover of Martial Law and that the accused would have had the advantage of defending themselves by counsel of their choice. The trend of the whole official evidence before Lord Hunter's Committee is that Martial Law was not required to meet the immediate necessities of the administration but merely for the purpose of striking terror into the hearts of the people, so as to avoid possible trouble in the future. I am, of course, not aware what secrets of state have been imparted to the Hunter Committee in camera by the Chief Secretary to the Punjab Government and General Hudson. But so far as the open proceedings before the Committee go, I can affirm with confidence that it was a gross abuse of Martial Law for which all concerned are liable to answer.

Martial law Cases

I do not intend discussing any of the hundreds of cases disposed of by the Martial Law Commissions and the Summary and Area Courts. They have caused the greatest misery to the people, the suffering which endures. Hundreds still lie in jail, many for having done what no honest man need be ashamed of. You will have some idea of the sentences inflicted, when I tell you that 108 persons were sentenced to death and the aggregate sentences of imprisonment amounted to the stupendous total of 7371 years and 5 months (allowing 20 years for a sentence of transportation for life). The figures for whippings, forfeitures, fines and impositions on villages and towns are not yet fully available. Those I have given for imprisonments have been compiled from the official statements presented to the Imperial Council. I am told that even these figures are incomplete and that the official statements do not contain many cases. Many of these sentences have been largely reduced by the present Lieutenant Governor. Clemency has been shown, where justice was needed. Injustice cannot be tempered with mercy. Sir Edward Maclagan is a kindly gentleman, who has tried to mitigate the rigours of his predecessor's regime; but he has not had the courage or the wisdom to break through the evil traditions he has inherited.

Sir Michael O'Dwyer's Responsibility

Such, in briefest outline, is the story of the Punjab. The responsibility of Sir Michael O'Dwyer for much that occurred here is admitted and established beyond doubt. I have endeavoured to show you the whole trend of his administration. It would appear that he was striving to make the Punjab a kind of Ulster in relation to the rest of India, a bulwark of reaction against all reform. "We now seem to be drifting into what is known as Birrellism in Ireland," he complained, "truckling to the extremists, encouraging the idea that we are going to hand over the administration to them." And even in his memorandum on the reforms he could not help lamenting that the Punjab politicians, "hitherto quiescent, were encouraged to assert themselves, and to come into line with other Provinces." To him there was little difference between a constitutional agitator and an anarchist. For both he had the same remedy—repression. But the remedy failed him and but increased the disease. And then he played his master card and brought in Martial Law to kill once for all the breed that agitates. He has failed again in his endeavour, but his policy has resulted in death for many and in utmost misery for thousands. For that he is fully responsible. He is responsible for the actions of General Dyer and his military colleagues in Amritsar; he is also responsible for the doings of his subordinates in the other districts under Martial Law.

Lord Chelmsford's Responsibility

But what shall we say of Lord Chelmsford? He must have known, or ought to have known, what was happening in the Punjab. The Congress Committee repeatedly drew his attention to it. Did he seek to interfere or cut short the agony? Has he received or considered any representation from this afflicted province presented to him from any sources which are not strictly official? Has he shown us any sympathy? Has he even been into the heart of the province to acquaint himself by personal enquiry on the spot concerning the tragedies which have taken place? We have not even heard that his "heart has bled for Amritsar." Lord Chelmsford occupies a very exalted position. He has received that position at the hands of his King and as a trust from the English people. How has he served his King and fulfilled this trust? Has he faithfully and adequately discharged his duty to his King and to his fellow countrymen by his persistent refusal to listen or to interfere, by his aloofness and by his absence from the scene of these happenings, when hundreds of His Majesty's subjects were done to death by the military and thousands put to shameful indignity?

Englishmen are, I believe, proud of the justice of British rule and zealous of their reputation. May I not ask them to consider whether Lord Chelmsford has shown himself an active guardian of their honour and worthy of the trust which they had reposed in him?

Indians seek for justice at the hands of the British Democracy. Will they tolerate this "frightfulness" in India and shield the authors of it? That is the acid test of British policy in India. On the answer to that depends the future goodwill of the Indian people.

The Lesson of the Punjab

Fellow delegates, I have ventured to trespass on your time to a considerable extent in dealing with the Punjab and the other matters which have acquired a special significance on account of the recent disturbances. Much has of late been said and written about the Punjab, much still remains. But the lessons which the crowded events of the year have to teach us and the English people are clear. To us they point to the path of steadfast endeavour, the path of sacrifice and patient ordeal. That is the only way to reach our goal. To Englishmen they teach the oft-repeated truth that tyranny degrades those who exercise it as much as those who suffer under it. And so it is that England, of old the champion of liberty, assumes a different guise in parts of her own dominions. England went to war to fight for the freedom of small nationalities, and yet a big nation under her sway continues to be unfree. In Belgium the German doings were condemned, but in India we still have the pure milk of Prussianism. And the man governed by the Prussian idea is much the same whether he is in the west or in the east. The logic of force is the only argument which appeals to him; military necessity justifies all severities. The object is always to strike terror and an act however "frightful" appears to him "merciful." Ordinary morality and humanity do not influence him and cruelty itself becomes laudable. It is for England to learn the lesson and put an end to conditions which permit these occurrences in her own dominions. If our lives and honour are to remain at the mercy of an irresponsible executive and military, if the ordinary rights of human beings are denied to us, then all talk of reform is a mockery. Constitutional reform without free citizenship is like rich attire on a dead body. Better to breathe God's free air in rags than be a corpse in the finest raiment.

The Declaration of Rights

The (Reforms) Act, as I have said, gives us some power, but it does not give us free citizenship or the power to check the misuse by the executive of the functions of law and order. It ignores the insistent demand of the country for a Declaration of Rights. This demand was clearly formulated by the Special Congress at Bombay and it was reiterated at Delhi last year. Subsequent events have but emphasised the necessity for it. No constitution can meet our needs, unless it is accompanied with a guarantee and a clear declaration of our elementary rights which have recently been so ruthlessly violated in the Punjab. No Indian can be blind to the fact that the protection of our fundamental civic liberties is a matter of the most urgent consequence. No statesman can shut his eyes to the supreme moral necessity of securing the faith of the Indian people in the inviolability of their rights of citizenship.

History teaches us that wherever the liberties of a people have been placed at the mercy of an executive possessing the power to enact all the laws it wanted, the advent of self-government has been preceded or accompanied by a statutory declaration of rights. This is what we find in most of the continental constitutions of Europe and in the American constitution. Even in respect of India, the British Parliament has in the past expressed a desire to protect the fundamental liberties of the people. As early as 1833, when Parliament first set itself to reconstitute the Indian legislature, it specifically limited the powers of this body by a historic clause, the full meaning of which has often been ignored by the Indian Government and the Indian courts. The Indian legislature, it declared, is to have no power "to make any law affecting the authority of Parliament or any part of the ancient laws of the constitution of the United Kingdom of Great Britain and Ireland whereon may depend in any degree the allegiance of any person to the Crown of the United Kingdom." But notwithstanding this, the steady tendency of the executive in India has been to ignore the implications of this limitation of the Indian legislature. The Congress has rightly therefore been on its guard against this danger which lay in the proposals for reform. In considering these proposals and in suggesting modifications to them, it has insisted upon one essential condition, that whatever the scheme of reforms may be, it should include as an indispensable part thereof a Declaration of Indian Rights. Judging from Indian conditions alone, it is imperative for this Congress to state, that without a repeal of the existing repressive law and a guarantee of the future inviolability of our civic rights, no reforms in the constitutional machinery of the country can be regarded as satisfying our immediate requirements. They will not lessen the risks or the rigours of any future reign of terror, that might at any time be inaugurated in the country by a panic-stricken executive.

It has been said that a demand for the declaration of Indian rights is unsupported by constitutional precedent within the Empire, and is inconsistent with a demand for full Home Rule. But we are still very far from full Home Rule, even under the new dispensation; and the bureaucratic agents of Parliament in India would still be in practically uncontrolled exercise of the power to suspend and suppress civic liberties. But even if India gets full Home Rule within the Empire, it is difficult to see why a Declaration of Indian Rights should necessarily be considered inconsistent with the demand for full legislative powers for the Indian assemblies. It is true that in many British constitutions conferring full responsible government, the need of specific guarantees has not been felt owing to the protection afforded by the great principles flowing from the rule of Common Law I have referred to above. But in cases where it was found that the tendency of the executive to encroach upon fundamental liberties was pronounced, the necessity of imposing limitations on the powers of even such responsible Legislatures has been recognised and acted upon. I shall here only cite the latest example of this kind, which occurred when the late Liberal Government passed the Irish Home Rule Act. Section 4 of this Act provides, among other things:

> "The powers of the Irish Legislature shall not extend to the making of any new law.. whereby any person may be deprived of life, liberty, or property, without due process of law, or may be denied the equal protection of the laws or whereby private property may be taken without just compensation.
>
> Any law made in contravention of this section shall be void."

It may be stated in this connection that the American Commonwealth has made a special feature of this Declaration of Rights, both in the Federal and in the State Constitutions. At the time when the Federal Constitution was originally framed, at the conclusion of the War of Independence, the proposal to embody a Declaration of Rights in the Constitution was discussed. This was given up owing to the delay involved in settling its terms in time for the Convention, but within a few years the necessity for doing so became apparent and the constitution was so amended as to include the Declaration of Rights. The terms of the declaration are far wider than those asked for by the Indian National Congress, which, in fact, has only adopted some of the important clauses of the section in the American Constitution.

The latest and the most instructive instance is that of the Philippines. The United States have not only conferred self government on them at the earliest possible opportunity but have granted to them, under the constitution established by the Jones Law, a Declaration of Rights similar to their own.

3—Sir Rabindranath Tagore's Protest

The following letter was sent by Sir Rabindranath Tagore to his Excellency the Viceroy.

"Your Excellency,

"The enormity of the measures taken by the Government in the Punjab for quelling some local disturbances has, with a rude shock, revealed to our minds the helplessness of our position as British subjects in India. The disproportionate severity of the punishment inflicted upon the unfortunate people and the methods of carrying them out, we are convinced, are without parallel in the history of civilised Governments, barring some conspicuous exceptions, recent and remote. Considering that such treatment has been meted out to a population disarmed and resourceless by a power which has the most terribly efficient organisation for destruction of human lives, we must strongly assert that it can claim no political expediency, far less moral justification. The accounts of insults and sufferings undergone by our brothers in the Punjab have trickled through the gagged silence, reaching every corner of India, and the universal agony of indignation roused in the hearts of our people has been ignored by our rulers—possibly congratulating themselves for imparting what they imagine as, salutary lessons. This callousness has been praised by most of the Anglo-Indian papers, which have in some cases gone to the brutal length of making fun of our sufferings, without receiving the least check from the same authority, relentlessly careful in smothering every cry of pain and expression of judgment from the organs representing the sufferers. Knowing that our appeals have been in vain and that the passion of vengeance is blinding the noble vision of statesmanship in our Government, which could so easily afford to be magnanimous as befitting its physical strength and moral tradition, the very least that I can do for my country is to take all consequences upon myself in giving voice to the protest of the millions of my countrymen, surprised into a dumb anguish of terror. The time has come when badges of honour make our shame glaring in their incongruous context of humiliation, and I for my part wish to stand shorn of all special distinctions, by the side of those of my countrymen who, for their so-called insignificance, are liable to suffer a degradation not fit for human beings. And these are the reasons which have painfully compelled me to ask Your Excellency, with due deference and regret, to released me of my title of knighthood which I had the honour to accept from His Majesty the King at the hands of your predecessor, for whose nobleness of heart I still entertain great admiration."

"Yours faithfully,
"RABINDRANATH TAGORE."

4—Mr. C. F. Andrews' Views

(a) Flogging in Public

The following letter by Mr. C. F. Andrews to the editor of the *Leader* was published in that paper on the 24th April, 1919:—

To the Editor of the Leader

"Sir,—I could scarcely credit the Associated Press telegram (though it must have been passed by the censor), which stated that there had been public whipping in the streets of Lahore. But now I have had a visit from an eye-witness, who has told me that he has actually seen it himself with his eyes and been sickened at the sight. I wish to write at once, as one Englishman among many, to express the shame and indignation which such news has brought to me. I do not think that the military authorities can understand the humilitation worse than death, which the people of this country feel at such a punishment, otherwise they surely would never have inflicted it. But they ought to know the truth and know it at once; for such things can never be forgiven or forgotten. Is it not possible for the Viceroy to assert his authority, as superior even to martial law, and to stop these acts before they are carried any further?

Yours faithfully,

Delhi C. F. ANDREWS

(b) Administration of Martial Law

In the course of a speech delivered at a meeting held at Lahore on Novemer 15, 1919, to bid him farewell on his departure to East Africa, Mr. C. F. Andrews said :—

"I hold as strongly as possible, that no provocation whatever can excuse the cowardly and brutal murders of the Englishmen by the mob which occurred at Amritsar and elsewhere, or burning of holy places of the Christian religion. Most cowardly and dastardly of all, I regard the murderous attack on Miss Sherwood, who was loved by every Indian who knew her and who was a true follower and disciple of the gentle Saviour Christ.

"But just as I condemn, without one single word of palliation or excuse, these acts, so all the more utterly and entirely do a condemn the cold and calculated massacre of the Jallianwala Bagh. The massacre of Glencoe in English history is no greater a blot on the fair name of my country, than the massacre at Amritsar. I am not speaking from idle rumour. I have gone into every single detail with all care and thoroughness that a personal investigation could command, and it remains to me an unspeakable, indefensible, unpardonable, and inexcusable disgrace.

"I am obliged to go on from that incident to what followed under martial law. I have seen with my own eyes very many who have endured the crawling order, the stripping of their persons naked in public under compulsion, men who had to grovel on their bellies in the dust, men who underwent public flogging, and a hundred other desecrations of man's image, which according to our Christian scriptures is made in the likeness of God.

"This ruthless and deliberate emasculation of manhood by the brute force of the military and police, appear to me no less an indelible stain on the fair honour of my country than the massacre at Jallianwala itself. These are the very few words which I have felt compelled as an Englishman to say, with regard to the culminating acts of disturbance.

"Every day that I have been working side by side with my Indian fellow-workers, the deep sense of the wrong done has come home to me, and each act has been in very truth an act of penance, of atonement. When in Lahore, I have gone out each morning to watch the sun rise over the great eucalyptus trees in the public gardens and I have walked there all alone trying to collect my thoughts for the day's work, and this morning there come to me out of the stormy time I have been passing through, these words from my own scriptures. 'He maketh his sun to rise upon the just and upon the unjust also. Be ye, therefore, perfect even as your father in Heaven is perfect.' These were the very words of Christ, my Master, when he taught his disciples that forgiveness was the final thing in life, not vengeance, love was the end not hate. That same word was uttered long before in India itself by Buddha, who came to save and help mankind. It was this alone which has given hope to me on this last day in Lahore, before my voyage out.

'He maketh his sun to rise upon the just and unjust.' 'Be ye therefore perfect even as your Father in Heaven is perfect.' We must probe down to the depth the wounds that have been made in order to draw out all the evil from them.

"I would urge you as you go forward, and face all the deeds of evil which have been done, not to dwell merely upon vengeance, but rather upon forgiveness; not to linger in the dark night of hate, but to come out into the glorious sunshine of God's love."

5—The Jallianwala Bagh Massacre

Colonel Wedgwood's Motion in the House of Commons

Colonel Wedgwood:—*(By Private Notice)* asked the Secretary of State for India whether pending the result of the Hunter Enquiry, Brigadier General Dyer has been relieved of his command; and, further, whether the Secretary of State has yet received a cabled report of General Dyer's evidence given before the Commission.

Mr. Montagu:—the answer to both parts of the question is in the negative. I may say I am in communication with the Viceroy on the whole matter.

Colonel Wedgwood:—Obviously this is too important a question to be dealt with in supplementary questions and, therefore, I give notice that I shall raise the subject on the adjournment to-day.

Colonel Wedgwood (*later*):—I rose because I wanted to raise a question which is different from the Irish question in locality, but very similar to it in general characteristics.

I want to raise the question of the Amritsar massacre, and the duty of this country towards India in that respect. The details of that massacre are unfortunately too well known to us. The English Press, with few exceptions, has taken the English view of the matter. The whole country has been horrified at what took place. Let me remind the House of what took place, and not from hearsay, but on the evidence given by the principal actor. Here enquiry will result in some trivial action. The thing must be put right. What happened? There was a religious festival and thousands of Punjabis had gone into Amritsar. The British officials were anxious, and the Deputy Commissioner on April 9 surrounded the notorious Drs. Satyapal and Kitchlew and carried them off. The news got about and their followers sent a mass deputation to the Deputy Commissioner demanding their release. The deputation was stopped, apparently by troops; it was only armed with sticks and as a result the troops fired and shot some of the demonstrators. Speeches were made over the bodies, and the mob turned and murdered three Englishmen and beat a lady. No one would excuse riots of that sort. On the evening of the 10th General Dyer arrived at Amritsar, and the Deputy-Commissioner handed over the civil power to him. He issued a proclamation by word of mouth that no meetings should be held.

Two days later, after there had been no sort of riot, nor murder, General Dyer heard that a meeting was to be held at the Jallianwala Bagh. He proceeded there with about 50 troops, half British, half Indian, and a certain number of Ghurkas, armed with their kukris. The Jallianwala Bagh is an open space half a mile square, which has one entry wide enough for three persons. The troops got in and lined up on a mound of debris. The walls, seven feet high, and the surrounding houses enclosed the people. There were, too, three alleys through which the people might have been able to pass. Within 30 seconds of the troops getting in, General Dyer gave orders to fire, and the crowd of people, estimated at anything from 5,000 to 20,000, who were sitting on the ground, peacefully listening to the mob oratory, were fired on. The result of the troops' fire into the mass of people we do not know. But we do know that Dyer's own estimate of the casualties resulting from ten minutes' continual individual firing was 400 to 500 killed and 1,500 wounded. What were the people to do? They could not escape. They were people who had not offered any violence and who had not been warned. These people were shot down. After ten minutes the ammunition was exhausted and the troops marched off, and they left 1,500 wounded there. There were men lying there for two days, dying of thirst, eating the ground, bleeding to death and nobody to look after them. Those relations who lived near came and carried away some of the wounded from among the heap of dead and dying, but the unfortunate country people died there miserably of their wounds. This is what is done in 1919 in British India. An English sportsman would take any amount of trouble or time to see that a wounded partridge was put out of its misery, but these wounded people were lying there for two days dying slowly. Think what this means. There has never been anything like it before in English history, and not in the whole of our relations with India has there ever been anything of this magnitude before. If you are to find anything so damning to the British reputation you have to go back centuries. In the ordinary English primer the only thing the ordinary person learns about British rule in India is about the Black Hole of Calcutta and the massacre of Cawnpore, where there was a well choked with corpses Centuries hence you will find Indian children brought up to this spot, just as they visit now the Cawnpore Well, and you can imagine the feelings of these Indians for generations over this terrible business (An Hon. Member: "What would you have done?") I should not have committed murder. Think what all this means! You will have a shrine erected there and every year there will be processions of Indians visiting the tombs of the martyrs, and Englishmen will go there and stand bareheaded before it. By this incident you have divided for all time races, races that might otherwise have loved one another. The right hon. gentleman has laid a foundation which might have led to a real co-operation with the British Empire but that has now been destroyed.

It has not only destroyed that; but it has destroyed our reputation throughout the world. You know what will happen. All the blackguards in America when they lynch niggers, will say "Oh, you did the same in India." When butcheries take place in Russia, whether it be by White or Red Guards, they will say "We never did anything like what you did in India"; and when we tell the Turks, "You massacred the Armenians," they will say, "Yes we wish we had the chance of getting 5,000 of them together and then of shooting straight." That is the sort of welcome that this will get, and all the decent people in the world will think that England really likes what happened at Amritsar, and that all this sort of thing is English. Really, we know that this sort of thing is the finest Prussianism that ever took place. The Germans never did anything worse in Belgium. This damns us for all time. Whenever we put forward the humanitarian view, we shall have this thrown into our teeth. What is it that differentiates this from all other horrors by Government in the past? If you have a mob distinctly out to kill and to loot, and the soldiers are called out to meet the mob they have got to stop it. Firing is justified in such cases. There may be hundreds killed in such a case, but, when soldiers are being stoned and hammered it is their duty, as well as their right, to resist.

The Secretary of State for India (Mr. Montagu):—The hon. and gallant Member knows that he is dealing with subjects which are *sub-judice* and he is forming his estimate of what happened on one column and a half report of the evidence of a single man who was in the witness-box for a whole day. He knows that no action of any sort or kind whatever can be taken affecting whoever it may be, to vindicate—if any action be necessary—the name of England for justice and fair play, until that report is received. I have never known a case where so many deductions have been drawn in this House from events which at the moment are being enquired into by an impartial tribunal.

Colonel Wedgwood:—I do not think that I have varied from the words used by General Dyer. He is accused out of his own voice. He himself said, "I did not take thirty seconds to decide whether to shoot." He himself said that the mob might have dispersed if he had asked them. He himself said that he fired on them because, if they had dispersed, they might have come back and laughed at him afterwards. He has made that clear, I wanted to point out, the difference between suppressing a mob doing violence and shooting down people who are not violent, because by that action terror might be inspired and prevent riots in the future. We have never justified the shooting down of people, not because they were endangering life, but because they might do so at some future time unless they were fired on.

(*It being eleven of the clock, the Motion for the Adjournment of the House lapsed, without Question put.*)

6—Commonsense of Coercion

To, The Editor, New Statesman

Sir,—'Let not a Prince,' declared Machiavelli, 'complain of the faults of a people under his rule, for they are due to his own negligence or his own example.' Perhaps, in modern conditions, we may substitute 'blunders' for 'example.' If a Government finds it necessary to shoot, the first question we should ask is, Why is the shooting necessary? Without cause men do not collect in mobs and loot. What is the cause of the riots? In particular, why have Indians, admittedly peaceful quietistic, and law-abiding to a fault, resorted to mob violence? The silly talk of Bolshevism, officially repudiated, merely shows the credulity of the Anglo-Indian mind. The only thing Bolshevistic in the Punjab events was the ferocity with which the Government repressed the riots. Their real cause is well-known. They were due to the Rowlatt Act coming as it did in the Punjab on a population irritated by a series of tyrannical war measures, the immediate cause being the arrest under *lettres de cachet* of Drs. Satyapal and Kitchlew, coupled with the forcible exclusion of Mr. Gandhi. Even in a most loyal people—and Sir Mr. O'Dwyer vouches for the loyalty of the Punjab in early years of the war—such a series of acts was bound to cause trouble, and the trouble came. None but a race of slaves, without courage or self-respect, would have meekly submitted. Have we forgotten our own history? Have we always been docile when our liberties were gravely threatened? There are limits beyond which no Government can go without risk of outbreaks, and the Simla and Punjab Governments easily overpassed those limits.

Bold and blind men are already busy white-washing the atrocities committed. They allege they were necessary to keep the peace and to prevent disorders. The case of Ahmedabad disproves that plea. But has not a Government which can keep the peace by such atrocities abrogated all claim to be considered a civilised Government? Has it not descended to the level of Enver Pasha and of Talaat Bey? If we can only preserve our rule by such means, the sooner we clear out of India, bag and baggage, the better. No purely Indian Government in this twentieth century would have provoked riots by a Rowlatt Act, nor repressed any riots by such means. Remember, the India of today is a transformed India, as all competent observers from Sir James Meston downwards agree. Nationalism, patriotism and an invincible will for self-government are everywhere enthroned. Old world racial and religious feuds are dying out quickly. If the bureaucratic Government of Simla cannot rise to the height of this brighter day, it has signed its own death warrant. It must be so placed under popular control as to render for ever impossible a repetition of the events in the Punjab. These events have, *teste* Mrs. Besant, for the first time produced amongst Indians a real hatred of the British people. That should give ground for thought. I will finish this letter as I began, with a quotation from Machiavelli:—'Better far than any number of fortresses is not to be hated by your people.'—Yours, etc.

BERNARD HOUGHTON
(*Late of the I. C. S.*)

SUPPLEMENT—1

Statement showing the Sentences passed by the Martial Law Commissions together with the orders of Government

No. and name of case	Serial No.	No. of accused according to schedule	Name of Accused with Father's Name	(1) Offence of which found guilty (2) Date of decision	Sentence passed by the Commissions	Sentence as determined by Government
1. **Badshahi Mosque** (Assault on Inspector Ali Gauhar of Criminal Investigation Department.)	1	1	Abdul Hai, son of Abdur Rahman.	(1) Section 121, 147, 332/149, Indian Penal Code. (2) 28th April 1919.	Transportation for life and forfeiture of property.	4 years' rigorous imprisonment.
	2	2	Bashir Ahmad, son of Nasir-ud-din.			2 years' do.
	3	3	Bhagat Ram, son of Kirpa Ram.			Do. do.
	4	4	Feroz Din, son of Nur Din ...			6 months' rigorous imprisonment. (Sentence to run concurrently with that in case No. 50.)
	5	5	Chanan Din, son of Shams-ud-din.			4 years' rigorous imprisonment.
	6	6	Labhu Ram, son of Tota Ram.			2 years, do.
	7	7	Tara Chand, son of Salig Ram.			Do. do.
	8	8	Har Narain, son of Ram Chand.			Do. do.
	9	9	Muni Lal, son of Jai Chand			Do. do.

SUPPLEMENT—1 *contd.*

No. and name of case	*Serial No.*	*No. of accused according to schedule*	*Name of Accused with Father's Name*	*(1) Offence of which found guilty (2) Date of decision*	*Sentence passed by the Commissions*	*Sentence as determined by Government*
2. **Crown** *Versus* **Balwant Singh** (*Ex*-sepoy who announced in Lahore that troops had mutinied and was carried in triumph to pulpit of Badshahi Mosque.)	10	1	Balwant Singh, son of Natha Singh	(1) Section 121, Indian Penal Code. (2) 28th April 1919.	Transportation for life and forfeiture of property.	5 years' rigorous imprisonment.
3. **Danda Fauj Case.** (Band of Club-men)	11	1	Chanan Din, son of Shamas Din.	(1) Sections 124-A, 143, Indian Penal Code	Transportation for life	4 years' rigorous imprisonment.
	12	2	Qamar Din, son of Din Muhammad.	(1) Sections 124-A/ 149, 143 Indian Penal Code	7 years' rigorous imprisonment	2 years' rigorous imprisonment
	13	3	Prem Narain Sircar, son of R. N. Sircar.		Do do	Do do
	14	4	Bashir, son of Chiragh Din		Rs. 250 fine or 6 months' rigorous imprisonment in default	No alteration
	15	5	Lal Din, son of Chiragh Din		2 years' rigorous imprisonment	6 months' rigorous imprisonment
	16	6	Lal Din, Son of Amir		3 year's rigorous imprisonment	Do do

	17	7	Sita Ram, son of Pheru Ram	(1) Sections 124-A/149, 143 143/109, Indian Penal Code (2) 29th April 1919.	6 months' rigorous imprisonment	No alteration
4. **Extortion Case**	18	1	Khuda Bakhsh, son of M Muhammad Ibrahim (Sub-Inspector of Police)	(1) Sections 161, 384/511, Indian Penal Code	3 years' rigorous imprisonment	No alteration
	19	2	Ahmad Din, son of Muhammad Kalu	(1) Sections 161/109, 384/109, Indian Penal Code (2) 30th April 1919	1½ years' rigorous imprisonment	
5. **Kasur Case** ... (Attack on train, murder of 2 British Soldiers), etc.	20	1	Chuni Lal, son of Nathu..		Death and forfeiture	4 years' rigorous imprisonment.
	21	2	Bir Singh, son of Hira Singh	(1) Section 121, Indian Penal Code (2) 30th April 1919	Do	No alteration
	22	3	Budha, son of Imam Din..		Do	
	23	4	Gaman, son of Kamene Beg		Do	
	24	5	Jawala, son of Bahadur...		Transportation for life and forfeiture	2 years' rigorous imprisonment
	25	6	Daulat Khan, son of Wahab Din		Death and forfeiture	No alteration
	26	7	Labhu, son of Chandu		Do	
	27	8	Charan Das, son of Harnam Das		Do	
	28	9	Sohna, son of Chuni Lal		Do	
	29	10	Balandu, son of Wazir		Do	

SUPPLEMENT—1 *contd.*

No. and name of case	*Serial No.*	*No. of accused according to schedule*	*Name of Accused with Father's Name*	*(1) Offence of which found guilty (2) Date of decision*	*Sentence passed by the Commissions*	*Sentence as determined by Government*
5. **Kasur Case** *Concld.*	30	11	Hira, son of Fatta	(1) Section 121, Indian Penal Code. (2) 30th April 1919.	Transportation for life and forfeiture	3 years' rigorous imprisonment.
	31	12	Kamal Din, son of Ghulam Mohi-ud-din		Death and forfeiture	4 years' do
	32	13	Jamal Din, son of Muhammad Khan		Do	2 years' do
	33	14	Bura, son of Nabi Bakhsh		Transportation for life and forfeiture	4 years' do
6. **Crown** *versus* **Ganesh Das**	—	—	—		Acquitted	
7. **Fazla Tongawala** (Seditious incitement)	34	1	Fazla, son of Umar Din	(1) Section 124-A, Indian Penal Code (2) 30th April 1919	Transportation for life	3 years' rigorous imprisonment
8. **Landa Bazar Riot** (Attack on Mr deGale, A.S.P.)	35	1	Beli Ram, son of Nihal Singh	(1) Sections 147/152 Indian Penal Code (2) 1st May 1919	3 years' rigorous imprisonment including 3 months' solitary confinement	2 years' do
	36	2	Ghulam Muhammad, son of Khairati			
	37	3	Nanak, son of Juman			

Amritsar National Bank Loot	38	1	Ramzan, son of Khaura	(1) Section 412, Indian Penal Code (2) 2nd May 1919.	7 years' rigorous imprisonment	2 years' rigorous imprisonment
	39	2	Ghafur, son of Amdu		5 years' do	1 years' do
	40	3	Muhammadu, son of Amdu		7 years' do	2 years' do
	41	4	Ahmad, son of Muhammad		5 years' do	1 years' do
10. **Do**	42	1	Ghafar Bat, son of Karim Bat	(1) Section 412, Indian Penal Code (2) 2nd May 1919	7 years' rigorous imprisonment	2 years' rigorous imprisonment
	43	2	Khaliq Wain, son of Rusal Wain			
	44	3	Aziz Mir, son of Rusal Mir			
	45	4	Rahman, son of Lassi			
11. **Do**	46	1	Manohar, son of Lassi	(1) Section 412, Indian Penal Code (2) 1st May 1919	7 years' rigorous imprisonment	2 years' rigorous imprisonment
	47	2	Khaliq, son of Jamal			
	48	3	Khalil Wain, son of Gafar Wain		5 years' do	6 months' do
	49	4	Anwar, son of Ghaffar			
	50	5	Munawwar, son of Jamal			
	51	6	Alia, son of Khizra			
	52	7	Rusla, son of Sattar		7 years' rigorous imprisonment	2 years' rigorous imprisonment
	53	8	Ahmdu, son of Khaura			
	54	9	Subhanju, son of Walli			
	55	10	Subhan, son of Ahmadu			

SUPPLEMENT—1 *contd.*

No. and name of case	Serial No.	No. of accused according to schedule	Name of Accused with Father's Name	(1) Offence of which found guilty (2) Date of decision	Sentence passed by the Commissions	Sentence as determined by Government
12. **Amritsar National Bank Loot**	56	1	Kaman, son of Ali Bakhsh.	(1) Section 412, Indian Penal Code. (2) Ist May 1919.	7 years' rigorous imprisonment.	2 years' rigorous imprisonment.
	57	2	Dina, son of Kadir Bakhsh.			
	58	3	Ghulam Rasul, son of Kishan Singh			
	59	4	Jhanda, son of Kahna ...			
	60	5	Muhammad Din, son of Pir Bakhsh.			
	61	6	Abdu, son of Baqir Khan.			
	62	7	Jan Muhammad, son of Nur Din.			
	63	8	Allah Ditta, son of Miran Bakhsh			
	64	9	Chiragh Din, son of Pira.			
	65	10	Nathu son of Ibrahim ...			
	66	11	Ghani, son of Sadiq ...			
	67	12	Bassa, son of Yar Muhammad			6 months' rigorous in imprisonment.
	68	13	Imam Din, son of Jamal Din			2 years' rigorous imprisonment.
	69	14	Muhammad Shah, son of Abdullah Shah.			
	70	15	Rahim Khan, son of Rusal Khan ...			Released.
	71	16	Jan Muhammad, son of Sadiq.			

13. **Do** ...	72	1	Muhammadu, son of Khizra...	(1) Section 412, Indian Penal Code (2) 3rd May 1919.	7 years' rigorous imprisonment	2 years' rigorous imprisonment
	73	2	Sadla, son of Nura ...			
	74	3	Fatta, son of Asad Joo ...			
14. **Do** ...	75	...	Mahaja, son of Fazal ...	(1) Section 412, Indian Penal Code (2) 3rd May 1919	7 years' rigorous imprisonment	2 years' rigorous imprisonment
15. **Do** ...	76	...	Fazal Din, *alias* Fajja, son of Muhammad.	(1) Section 412, Indian Penal Code (2) 3rd May 1919	7 years' rigorous imprisonment	2 years' rigorous imprisonment
16. **Do** ...	77	...	Allah Rakha, son of Umar Bakhsh	(1) Section 412, Indian Penal Code (2) 3rd May 1919	7 years' rigorous imprisonment	2 years' rigorous imprisonment
17. **Do** ...	78	...	Ruldu, son of Miru ...	(1) Section 412, Indian Penal Code (2) 5th May 1919	7 years' rigorous imprisonment	2 years' rigorous imprisonment
18. **Do** ...	79	...	Ghulam Muhammad, son of Miran Bakhsh	(1) Section 412, Indian Penal Code (2) 5th May 1919	7 years' rigorous imprisonment	2 years' rigorous imprisonment
19. Crown *versus* Moti Ram (Sedition and attempt to seduce police).	80	...	Moti Ram, son of Gur Das ...	(1) Rules 24/29 Defence of India Rules and section 124—A, Indian Penal Code. (2) 3rd May 1919.	Transportation for life.	2 years' rigorous imprisonment
20. **Amritsar National Bank Loot**	...	...	... ...	... ...	Acquitted.	
21. **Do** ...	81	...	Hari Ram, son of Bishan Das	(1) Section 412, Indian Penal Code (2) 5th May 1919	7 years' rigorous imprisonment	2 years' rigorous imprisonment

SUPPLEMENT—1 *contd.*

No. and name of case	*Serial No.*	*No. of accused according to schedule*	*Name of Accused with Father's Name*	*(1) Offence of which found guilty (2) Date of decision*	*Sentence passed by the Commissions*	*Sentence as determined by Government*
22. **Lahore Upper Mall Riot**	82	1	Ahmad Din, son of Barkhur Dar			
	83	2	Ata Muhammad, son of Jan Muhammad.	(1) Sections 121, 147, Indian Penal Code.		
	84	3	Basant Ram, son of Ram Lal		Transportation for life and forfeiture	2 years' rigorous imprisonment.
	85	4	Feroz Din, son of Nabi Bakhsh.	(2) 5th May 1919.		
23. **Gujrat case** ... (Riot, mischief and arson)	86	1	Ghulam Nabi, son of Dr. Allah Ditta.			6 months' rigorous imprisonment.
	87	2	Peshawari Lal, son of Ganesh Das.			Do.
	88	3	Abdul Shakur, son of Rahim Bakhsh.			Do.
	89	4	Najam Din, son of Allah Ditta.	(1) Sections 121, 147, 427, 435, 436 / 149 I.P.C.	Transportation for life and forfeiture	3 years' rigorous imprisonment.
	90	5	Ghulam Muhammad, son of Nabi Bakhsh.			2 years' rigorous imprisonment.
	91	6	Faqir Muhammad, son of Fazl Din.			1 years' rigorous imprisonment.
	92	8	Kidar Nath, son of Kahan Singh.			2 years' rigorous imprisonment.
	93	9	Arura, son of Kishen Chand.			3 years' rigorous imprisonment.

	94	11	Ranjha, son of Ilam Din	(1) Sections 121, 147, $\frac{427, 435, 436}{149}$ I. P. C.	Transportation for life and forfeiture.	3 years' rigorous imprisonment
	95	12	Kali Das, son of Hushnak Rai.			1 years' rigorous imprisonment
	96	13	Tufail, son of Karam ...			Do.
	97	15	Devi *alias* Budha, son of Bindra Ban.			2 years' rigorous imprisonment
	98	16	Fakira *alias* Muna, son of Jiwan.			1 years' rigorous imprisonment
	99	17	Raja Ram, son of Sawan Mal			2 years' rigorous imprisonment
	100	18	Amar Nath, son of Nihal Chand.			Do.
	101	19	Sadhu Singh, son of Narain Singh.	(1) Sections 121, 147, $\frac{427}{149}$, I. P. C.		1 years' rigorous imprisonment
	102	21	Ghulam Husain, son of Nur Bakhsh.	(1) Sections 121, 147, $\frac{427, 435, 436}{149}$ I. P. C. (2) 7th May 1919.		3 years' rigorous imprisonment
24. **Supplementary Gujrat Case.**	...	...	...	...	Acquitted.	
25. **Telegraph wire cutting.**	...	...	...	...	Withdrawn	
26. ...	...	...	...	...		
27. **Jalalpur Jattan** (Riot and mischief).	103	6	Abdul Aziz, son of Karm Ilahi.	(1) Section 124-A, Indian Penal Code.	Transportation for 10 years.	3 years' rigorous imprisonment
	104	7	Abdur Rashid, son of Ahmad Din.		Transportation for 14 years.	Do.

SUPPLEMENT—1 *contd.*

No. and name of case	Serial No.	No. of accused according to schedule	Name of Accused with Father's Name	(1) Offence of which found guilty (2) Date of decision	Sentence passed by the Commissions	Sentence as determined by Government
	105	8	Ahsan Ali, son of Bahadur Ali.	(1) Section $\frac{124\text{-A}}{149}$, Indian Penal Code. (2) 8th May 1919.	3 years' rigorous imprisonment	6 months' rigorous imprisonment.
	106	11	Mahma, son of Adha ...			
	107	12	Sardara, son of Jani ...			2 years' rigorous imprisonment
	108	17	Ghulam Muhammad, son of Ahdu.			
28. **Amritsar National Bank Loot**	109	...	Kesho Ram, son of Harbhagwan.	(1) Section 412, Indian Penal Code. (2) 8th May 1919	7 years' rigorous imprisonment	2 years' rigorous imprisonment
29. Do.	110	...	Mehr Din, son of Alia	(1) Section 412, Indian Penal Code. (2) 8th May 1919	2 years' rigorous imprisonment	6 months' rigorous imprisonment
30. Do.	111	...	Ali Muhammad, son of Rukh Din.	(1) Section 412, Indian Penal Code. (2) 8th May 1919	7 years' rigorous imprisonment	2 years' rigorous imprisonment
31. Do.	112	...	Khuda Bakhsh, son of Bahadur Khan	(1) Section 412, Indian Penal Code. (2) 8th May 1919	7 years' rigorous imprisonment	2 years' rigorous imprisonment

32. Do.	113	...	Nizam Din, son of Ghani.	(1) Section 412, Indian Penal Code (2) 8th May 1919.	7 years' rigorous imprisonment	2 years' rigorous imprisonment
33. Do.	...	...	...	...	Acquitted	
34. Do.	114	...	Feroz Din, son of Khair Din.	(1) Section 412, Indian Penal Code (2) 8th May 1919	7 years' rigorous imprisonment	2 years' rigorous imprisonment
35. **Aulakh case.** (Burning of Patwar-khana and records of six villages).	115	1	Ganda Singh, Lambardar	(1) Section 121, Indian Penal Code.	Death and forfeiture	7 years' rigorous imprisonment
	116	2	Makhan Singh ...		Death and forfeiture	7 years' rigorous imprisonment
	117	3	Singhara Singh ...		Do.	
	118	4	Ala Singh ...			
	119	5	Pala Singh ...	(1) Section 412, Indian Penal Code (2) 6th May 1919	Transportation for life and forfeiture.	3 years' rigorous imprisonment
	120	6	Sohan Singh ...			
	121	7	Gian Singh ...			
	122	8	Sucha Singh ...			

SUPPLEMENT—1 *contd.*

No. and name of case	Serial No.	No. of accused according to schedule	Name of Accused with Father's Name	(1) Offence of which found guilty (2) Date of decision	Sentence passed by the Commissions	Sentence as determined by Government
36. **Lohari Gate Riot**	123	1	Mahtab, son of Ghulam Dastgir	(1) Section 121, Indian Penal Code. (2) 9th May 1919.	Transportation for life and forfeiture	2 years' rigorous imprisonment
	124	2	Abdur Rahim, son of Buti.			
	125	3	Bishan Chand, son of Kishen Chand			
	126	4	Fazl Husain, son of Nur Husain			
	127	5	Jadu Mal, son of Mangha.			
	128	6	Ghulam Muhammad, son of Ramzan.			
37. ...	129	8	Shiv Das, son of Jhanda Mal			
38. ...	...	...	...		Acquitted	
39. **Gumanpura Railway Derailment Case.**	130	1	Lal Singh, son of Ishar Singh	(1) Sections 121, 124-A, 147/109, Indian Penal Code Section 126, Railway Act/ 109, I. P. C.	Death and forfeiture.	Transportation for life.

131	2	Ishar Singh, son of Bhagat Singh.		Transportation for life and forfeiture.	5 years' rigorous imprisonment
132	3	Inayat, son of Kaddu ...		Do ...	Do
133	5	Din, son of Kalu ...		10 years' rigorous imprisonment	3 years' rigorous imprisonment
134	6	Wasakhi, son of Kharak Singh		Transportation for life ...	5 years' do
135	7	Bishan Singh son of Phaggu		7 years' rigorous imprisonment	2 years' do
136	8	Lachhman, son of Guranditta	(1) Sections 126, Ry. Act, / 149, I. P. C. 147, I. P. C. (2) 10th May 1919	Transportation for life ...	5 years' do
137	9	Buta, son of Nandu ...		7 years' rigorous imprisonment	2 years' do
138	12	Buta Singh, son of Kharak Singh.		10 years' Do	3 years' do
139	13	Kishan Singh, son of Hakim Singh		7 years' Do	2 years' do
140	14	Jhanda, son of Hira ...		Transportation for life ...	5 years' do
141	15	Jhanda, son of Labhu ...		Do ...	Do

SUPPLEMENT—1 *contd.*

No. and name of case	Serial No.	No. of accused according to schedule	Name of Accused with Father's Name	(1) Offence of which found guilty (2) Date of decision	Sentence passed by the Commissions	Sentence as determined by Government
40. **(II) Gumanpura Railway Derailment Theft Case.**	142	1	Amrik Singh, son of Nihal Singh	(1) Sections 121, 147, 370/149 Indian Penal Code. (2) 12th May 1919.	2 years' rigorous imprisonment and Rs.100 fine or 6 months' rigorous imprisonment in default.	1 year's rigorous imprisonment, fine unchanged.
	143	2	Santu, son of Amrik Singh ...		30 stripes	No alteration.
	144	3	Kehr Singh, son of Nihal Singh.		3 years' rigorous imprisonment and Rs.100 fine or 6 months' rigorous imprisonment in default.	2 years' rigorous imprisonment, fine unchanged.
	145	4	Ram Singh, son of Mula Singh.		Do. do.	
	146	5	Kapur Singh, son of Anup Singh.		Do. do.	
	147	6	Bawa, son of Jai Kishen ...		Do. do.	
	148	7	Katha, son of Shaman ...		1 year's rigorous imprisonment.	No alteration.
	149	8	Mahandu, son of Chaughatta.		Do. do.	
	150	9	Teja Singh, son of Wir Singh.		3 years' rigorous imprisonment and Rs.500 fine or 6 months' rigorous imprisonment in default.	2 years' rigorous imprisonment, fine unchanged.

	151	10	Maghar Singh, son of Wir Singh		Do do	Do do	
	152	11	Ganda Singh son of Jawala Singh		6 months' rigorous imprisonment	No alteration.	
	153	12	Gulab, son of Shadi ...		30 stripes		
	154	13	Mehr Din, son of Kiman		Do		
41. —	—	—	—		Acquitted		
42. **Akalgarh Case** (Riot and mischief)	155	1	Badri Nath, son of Gulab Rai	(1) Section 506, Indian Penal Code	1 years' rigorous imprisonment and Rs.100 fine or in default 3 months' rigorous imprisonment.	6 months' rigorous imprisonment	Fine remitted.
	156	2	Bishan Das, son of Jiwan Mal	(1) Section 506 & 124-A, Indian Penal Code	1 year's rigorous imprisonment and Rs.100 fine or in default 3 months' rigorous imprisonment, under section 506; 1 years' rigorous imprisonment under section 124-A, to run consecutively.	1 years' rigorous imprisonment	
	157	3	Gokal Chand, son of Laiq Ram.	(1) Sections 506, Indian Penal Code	1 years' rigorous imprisonment and Rs.100 fine or in default 3 months' rigorous imprisonment.	6 months' rigorous imprisonment	
	158	4	Bishambar Das, son of Harbilas.				
	159	5	Sohan Singh son of Ram Mal	(1) Sections 506 & 124-A, Indian Penal Code	1 years' rigorous imprisonment and Rs.100 fine or default 3 months' rigorous imprisonment, under section 506; 1 years' rigorous imprisonment under section 124-A, to run consecutively.	1 years' rigorous imprisonment	

SUPPLEMENT—1 *contd.*

No. and name of case	Serial No.	No. of accused according to schedule	Name of Accused with Father's Name	(1) Offence of which found guilty (2) Date of decision	Sentence passed by the Commissions	Sentence as determined by Government
42. **Akalgarh Case** —concld.	160	6	Ishar Das, son of Gopal Das	(1) Section 506, Indian Penal Code.	1 year's rigorous imprisonment and Rs. 100 fine or in default 3 months' further rigorous imprisonment.	6 months' rigorous imprisonment Fine
	161	7	Utma, son of Amolak Ram ...	(1) Section 421, Indian Penal Code. (2) 14th May 1919.	Imprisonment till rising of Court	No alteration.
	162	10	Dulla Mal, son of Shankar Das			
43. **Barhoa Wire Cutting and Riot**	163	2	Rahmat Ullah, son of Daula	(1) Section 147, Indian Penal Code. (2) 10th May 1919.	3 years' rigorous imprisonment	No alteration.
	164	4	Nawab, son of Daula		2 years' rigorous imprisonment	
	165	5	Shahab Din, son of Daula ...		3 years' rigorous imprisonment	
	166	6	Ghulam, son of Daula ...		2 years' rigorous imprisonment	
	167	7	Ibrahim, son of Daula ...		Do. do.	
	168	9	Ahmad, son of Maulvi ...		Do. do.	
	169	10	Azim Bakhsh, son of Abdulla		3 years' rigorous imprisonment	

	170	11	Sharaf Din, son of Karam Ilahi		2 years' rigorous imprisonment	
	171	12	Ismail, son of Khuda Bakhsh		3 years' rigorous imprisonment	
	172	13	Azim Bakhsh, son of Umar Din		3 years' rigorous imprisonment	
	173	14	Ismail, son of Umar Din		Do do	
	174	15	Fatteh Muhammad, son of Umar Din		2 years' rigorous imprisonment	
	175	16	Muhammad Husain, son of Abdul Rahim			
	176	17	Abdul Rahman, son of Naman			
	177	20	Tek Chand, son of Ganga Ram			
	178	23	Din Muhammad, son of Chand	(1) Section 147, Indian Penal Code (2) 10th May 1919	2 years' rigorous imprisonment	No alteration.
	179	28	Muhammad Ali, son of Bagh			
	180	26	Nizam Din, son of Allah Ditta			
	181	30	Mehr Ali, son of Faqir Muhammad			
	182	31	Ilm Din, son of Nur Muhammad			
44. **Khem Karan Railway Station** (Looting Station, & c.)	183	1	Mauloo, son of Lali ...	(1) Sections 147, 395, $\frac{395, 426}{149}$, I.P.C. (2) 15th May 1919	Transportation for life	
	184	3	Jaggu, son of Chanda ...			3 years' rigorous imprisonment
	185	4	Gandu, son of Mamu ...		7 years' rigorous imprisonment	2 years' rigorous imprisonment
	186	6	Jammu, son of Ida ...		Do do	Do
					10 years' rigorous imprisonment	Do
	187	7	Arjan Singh, son of Diwan Singh		Transportation for life	3 years' rigorous imprisonment

SUPPLEMENT—1 *contd.*

No. and name of case	*Serial No.*	*No. of accused according to schedule*	*Name of Accused with Father's Name*	*(1) Offence of which found guilty (2) Date of decision*	*Sentence passed by the Commissions*	*Sentence as determined by Government*
45. **Kaira** (Lahore District) (False and exciting rumours)	188	1	Lehna Singh, son of Sohan Singh	(1) Sections 121, 124-A, 505, Indian Penal Code, and Rule 25 of Defence of India Act Consolidation Rules (2) 15th May 1919	Transportation for life and forfeiture	3 years' rigorous imprisonment
46. **Jalalpur Jattan Wire Cutting Case**	—	—	—	—	Acquitted	
47. **Amritsar National Bank Loot**	189	—	Hari Ram, son of Ganda Mal	(1) Section 412, Indian Penal Code (2) 15th May 1919	7 years' rigorous imprisonment	2 years' rigorous imprisonment
48. **Do**	190	—	Hans Raj, son of Hari Ram	(1) Section 412, Indian Penal Code (2) 15th May 1919	7 years' rigorous imprisonment	2 years' rigorous imprisonment
49. **Do**	191	—	Gyan Das, son of Ram Saran	(1) Section 412, I.P.C. (2) 15th May 1919	6 Months' rigorous imprisonment	No alteration.
Hira Mandi Riot (Lahore)	192	1	Faqir Chand, son of Ram Chand	(1) Section 121, I.P.C. (2) 15th May 1919	Transportation for life and forfeiture	2 years' rigorous imprisonment
	193	2	Nand Lal, son of Kanshi Ram			

	194	3	Siraj Din, son of Amir Bakhsh			
	195	4	Karam Chand, son of Brij Lal			
	196	5	Abdul Majid, son of Didar Bakhsh			
	197	6	Allah Rakha, son of Hira			
	198	7	Diwan Chand, son of Parma Nand			
	199	8	Anant Ram, son of Hari Chand			
	200	9	Jai Chand, son of Dharam Chand	(1) Section 121, I.P.C. (2) 15th May 1919	Transportation for life and forfeiture	2 years' rigorous imprisonment
	201	10	Imam Din, son of Mehr Din			
	202	11	Ramzan, son of Ghasita			
	203	12	Miran Bakhsh, son of Rahim Bakhsh			1 year's rigorous imprisonment concurrent with that given in case No. 18
	204	13	Bhagwan Das, son of Devi Ditta			
	205	15	Feroz Din, son of Nur Din			
	206	16	Jhanda Ram, son of Atma Ram			6 months' rigorous imprisonment
51. **Amritsar National Bank Loot**	207	—	Santa Singh, son of Ala Singh	(1) Sections 411/412, Indian Penal Code (2) 16th May 1919	5 years' rigorous imprisonment	1½ years' rigorous imprisonment
52. **Do**	208	—	Sardara, son of Dulo	(1) Sections 411/412, Indian Penal Code (2) 16th May 1919	5 years' rigorous imprisonment	1½ years' rigorous imprisonment

SUPPLEMENT—1 *contd.*

No. and name of case	Serial No.	No. of accused according to schedule	Name of Accused with Father's Name	(1) Offence of which found guilty (2) Date of decision	Sentence passed by the Commissions	Sentence as determined by Government
53. **Amritsar National Bank Loot**	209	—	Mehr Din, son of Fauju Khan	(1) Sections 411/412, Indian Penal Code (2) 16th May 1919	5 years' rigorous imprisonment	1½ years' rigorous imprisonment
54. **Do**	210	—	Jagat Ram, son of Tepla...	(1) Sections 411/412, Indian Penal Code (2) 16th May 1919	6 months' rigorous imprisonment	No alteration
55. **Do**	211	—	Kirpa, son of Parana ...	(1) Sections 411/412, Indian Penal Code (2) 16th May 1919	15 stripes ...	No alteration
56. **Do**	212	—	Kashmiri Lal, son of Ganda Ram	(1) Sections 411/412, Indian Penal Code (2) 16th May 1919	5 years' rigorous imprisonment	1½ years' rigorous imprisonment
57. **Do**	213	—	Maya Ram, son of Ganda Mal	(1) Sections 411/412, Indian Penal Code (2) 16th May 1919	2 years' rigorous imprisonment	6 months' rigorous imprisonment
58. **Do**	214	—	Mahama, son of Nur Din	(1) Sections 411/412, Indian Penal Code (2) 16th May 1919	15 stripes	No alteration.
59. **Khem Karan Supplementary**	215	1	Dyala, son of Bhagu	(1) Section 395, Indian Penal Code (2) 16th May 1919	7 years' rigorous imprisonment	2 years' rigorous imprisonment
	216	2	Panju, son of Haku		5 years' rigorous imprisonment	Do

60. **Hafizabad** (Sedition and attack on train and on British officer and child with him)	217	1	Mangal Sain, son of Nihal Chand	(1) Section 121, Indian Penal Code	Death and forfeiture	7 years' rigorous imprisonment
	218	2	Gujrati Mal, son of Thakur Das	(1) Do do	Do do	10 years' rigorous imprisonment
	219	3	Kesar Mal, son of Nanak Chand	(1) Do do	Do do	Do
	220	4	Diwan Singh, son of Prem Chand	(1) Section 122, Indian Penal Code	Transportation for life and forfeiture	6 months' rigorous imprisonment
	221	5	Dyal Singh, son of Beli Ram	(1) Section 121, Indian Penal Code	Do ...	3 years' rigorous imprisonment
	222	6	Jiwan Kishen, son of Gokal Chand	(1) Do do	Do ...	6 months' rigorous imprisonment
	223	7	Darya Mal, son of Daulat Ram	(1) Do do	Do ...	5 years' rigorous imprisonment
	224	8	Khushabi Mal, son of Kanshi Ram	(1) Do do	Do ...	3 years' rigorous imprisonment
	225	10	Gyan Singh, son of Mangal Singh	(1) Do do	Do ...	} 5 years' rigorous imprisonment
	226	11	Sundar Das, son of Atma Ram	(1) Do do	Do ...	}
	227	12	Harnam Singh, son of Nihal Singh	(1) Do do	Do ...	3 years' rigorous imprisonment
	228	15	Ismail, son of Fazl Din	(1) Do do	Do ...	Do
	229	16	Des Ram, son of Daulat Ram	(1) Do do	Do ...	1 year's rigorous imprisonment
	230	18	Mul Chand, son of Thakar Das	(1) Do do	Do ...	3 years' rigorous imprisonment
	231	19	Karam Chand, son of Ishar Das	(1) Do do (2) 19th May 1919	Death and forfeiture	1 years' rigorous imprisonment

SUPPLEMENT—1 *contd.*

No. and name of case	*Serial No.*	*No. of accused according to schedule*	*Name of Accused with Father's Name*	*(1) Offence of which found guilty (2) Date of decision*	*Sentence passed by the Commissions*	*Sentence as determined by Government*
61. **Nizamabad** (Riot, arson and dacoity)	232	1	Muhammad Hussain, son of Abdul Manan	(1) Section 121, Indian Penal Code	Death and forfeiture	10 years' rigorous imprisonment
	233	2	Basheshar Nath, son of Nihal Chand	(1) Do ...	Do ...	Do ...
	234	3	Din Muhamad, son of Muhammad Bakhsh	(1) Do ...	Do ...	Do ...
	235	4	Muhammd Azim, son of Nur Din	(1) Section 395, Indian Penal Code	20 stripes	No alteration
	236	5	Muhammad Hussain, son of Sharaf Din	(1) Section 121, Indian Penal Code	Transportation and forfeiture	7 years' rigorous imprisonment
	237	6	Abdur Rahman, son of Imam Din	(1) Do ...	Do ...	Do ...
	238	7	Abdullah, son of Nur Ahmad	(1) Do ...	Do ...	Do ...
	239	8	Muhammad Hussain, son of Ismail	(1) Do ...	Do ...	Do ...
	240	9	Rahmat, son of Muhammad Bakhsh	(1) Section 395, Indian Penal Code	20 stripes	No alteration

	241	10	Abdul Razzak, son of Ghulam Mohi-ud-Din	(1) Do ...	Do ...	Do ...
	242	11	Allah Ditta, son of Pir Bakhsh	(1) Section 121, Indian Penal Code	Transportation for life and forfeiture ...	7 years' rigorous imprisonment
	243	13	Allah Ditta, son of Muhammad Ditta	(1) Do ...	Do ...	Do ...
	244	14	Ahmad, son of Chirag	(1) Section 395, Indian Penal Code	20 stripes ...	No alteration.
	245	15	Abdul Karim, son of Chogatta	(1) Section 121, Indian Penal Code	Transportation for life and forfeiture.	7 years' rigorous imprisonment
	246	16	Amar Singh, son of Lachman Das	(1) Ditto ditto	Death and forfeiture ...	10 years' rigorous imprisonment
	247	17	Ata Ullah, son of Abdullah	(1) Section 436, Indian Penal Code	10 years' rigorous imprisonment	5 years' rigorous imprisonment
	248	19	Nizam-ud-Din, son of Ilm Din	(1) Section 121, Indian Penal Code	Transportation for life and forfeiture.	7 years' rigorous imprisonment
	249	22	Sardara, son of Maula Dad	(1) Section 412, Indian Penal Code	10 years' rigorous imprisonment	5 years' rigorous imprisonment
	250	23	Hazura, son of Lehna	(1) Ditto ditto	5 years' rigorous imprisonment	3 years' rigorous imprisonment
	251	24	Elahi Bakhsh, son of Umar Bakhsh	(1) Section 412, Indian Penal Code (2) 15th May 1919	7 years' rigorous imprisonment	Do ...
62. **National Bank Loot**	252	—	Ahmad, son of Nurani	(1) Section 412, Indian Penal Code (2) 15th May 1919	2 years' rigorous imprisonment	6 months' rigorous imprisonment

SUPPLEMENT—1 *contd.*

No. and name of case	Serial No.	No. of accused according to schedule	Name of Accused with Father's Name	(1) Offence of which found guilty (2) Date of decision	Sentence passed by the Commissions	Sentence as determined by Government
63. **Chuharkana** (Bridge burning and attack on train).	253	1	Jewan Singh, son of Ladha Singh	(1) Section 121, Indian Penal Code	Transportation for life and forfeiture	3 years' rigorous imprisonment
	254	2	Amolak Ram, son of Sohna Mal.		Ditto ditto ...	1 year's rigorous imprisonment
	255	3	Chuni Lal, son of Gobind Ram.		Ditto ditto ...	Released.
	256	4	Sultan, son of Sadulla ...		Ditto ditto ...	5 years' rigorous imprisonment
	257	5	Mehr Din, son of Arura ...		Death and forfeiture ...	10 years' rigorous imprisonment
Chuharkana (Riot, arson and dacoity) continued.	258	7	Wadhawa Singh, son of Dial Chand		Transportation for life and forfeiture	3 years' rigorous imprisonment
	259	9	Karam Chand, son of Harnarain.		Ditto ...	Ditto.
	260	10	Mahna Singh, son of Dhian Singh.		Death and forfeiture ...	10 years' rigorous imprisonment
	261	11	Kahan Singh, son of Lal Singh		Ditto ...	Ditto.
	262	13	Mandu, son of Jhanda ...			
	263	14	Rao, son of Bagh ...		Ditto ...	Ditto.
	264	15	Jahangir Singh, son of Mangal Singh.		Transportation for life and forfeiture	3 years' rigorous imprisonment
					Ditto ...	Ditto.

	265	17	Ladha Singh, son of Wir Singh.	(1) Section 121, Indian Penal Code (2) 23rd May 1919.	Ditto ...	Ditto
	266	18	Sundar Singh, son of Prem Singh.		Ditto ...	Ditto
	267	19	Ram Narain, son of Ishar Das.		Ditto ...	6 months' rigorous imprisonment
	268	20	Hans Raj, son of Duni Chand.		Transportation for life and forfeiture.	3 years' rigorous imprisonment
	269	21	Balbir Singh, son of Arjan Singh.		Do do ...	5 years' rigorous imprisonment
	270	22	Ishar Das, son of Billa Ram		Do do ...	4 years' rigorous imprisonment
	271	24	Teja Singh, son of Partab Singh.		Death and forfeiture ...	7 years' rigorous imprisonment
	272	25	Ujagar Singh, son of Sharm Singh.		Transportation for life and forfeiture.	5 years' rigorous imprisonment
	273	27	Kartar Singh, son of Tej Singh.		Death and forfeiture ...	7 years' rigorous imprisonment
	274	28	Bhagwan Singh, son of Bishan Singh.		Transportation for life and forfeiture.	2 years' rigorous imprisonment
	275	30	Allahdad Khan, son of Muhammad Arif Khan.		Do do ...	Do do ...
64. **Gujrat Riot Supplementary Case.**	276	1	Trilok Nath, son of Ishar Das.		Transportation for life and forfeiture.	2 years' rigorous imprisonment
	277	2	Narinjan Das, son of Lachman Das.	(1) Section 121, I. P. C. (2) 23rd May 1919.		
65. **Amritsar Rego Bridge (Murder of Sergeant Rowlands).**	278	1	Mahni, son of Amir Bakhsh.	(1) Sections 121 & 302, Indian Penal Code (2) 27th May 1919.	Death and forfeiture	No alteration.
	279	2	Muhammad Shafi, son of Muhammad Ju.			

SUPPLEMENT—1 *contd.*

No. and name of case	Serial No.	No. of accused according to schedule	Name of Accused with Father's Name	(1) Offence of which found guilty (2) Date of decision	Sentence passed by the Commissions	Sentence as determined by Government
66. **Attempt to murder Mr. Wale.**	280	...	Harnam Singh, son of Jiwan Singh.	(1) Section 307, I. P. C. (2) 26th May 1919.	Transportation for life...	Transportation for life. To run concurrently with the sentence in case No. 112.
67. **Bhagtanwala Case.** (Looting of Post Office and burning of Railway Station)	281	1	Nizam Din, son of Kamal	(1) Section 121, I. P. C.	Transportation for life and forfeiture	7 years' rigorous imprisonment
	282	2	Chaga, son of Muhammad Bakhsh.			Do do.
	283	3	Habib, son of Rahmat-ullah.			Do do.
	284	4	Shaman, son of Abdulla...			5 years' rigorous imprisonment
	285	5	Dhilli, son of Kadir ...			7 years' rigorous imprisonment
	286	6	Pira, son of Wariam ...			5 years' rigorous imprisonment (Enquiry made about age)
	287	7	Mani, son of Asdu ...			5 years' rigorous imprisonment
	288	8	Gurdit Singh, son of Kanhava.			Do do.
	289	9	Lal, son of Sawan ...			5 years' rigorous imprisonment (Enquiry made about age)

	290	10	Majha, son of Badar Din	(1) Section 121, I. P. C.	Transportation for life and forfeiture.	5 years' rigorous imprisonment
	291	11	Gaman, son of Kaka ...	(1) Section 412, I. P. C.	5 years' rigorous imprisonment	2 years' rigorous imprisonment
	292	13	Mana, son of Muhammad Bakhsh.	(1) Section 121, I. P. C.	Transportation for life and forfeiture.	2 years' rigorous imprisonment
	293	14	Dadu, son of Karam Din	(1) Do ...	Do ...	5 years' do.
68. **Gujranwala City Case No. 11** (Burning of Railway Bridges, Post Office, District Courts, Railway Station, Church, & c.)	294	1	Girdhari Lal, son of Wali Ram	(2) 29th May 1919.	Death and forfeiture ...	Transportation for life
	295	2	Abdulla, son of Fakiria ...		Transportation for life and forfeiture.	7 years' rigorous imprisonment
	296	3	Diwan Chand, son of Chandu Lal.		Do ...	Do
	297	4	Devi Dial, son of Diwan Chand.		Death and forfeiture.	10 years' rigorous imprisonment
	298	5	Dyal Singh, son of Gian Singh		Do ...	Ditto.
	299	8	Lachman, son of Ram Rattan	(1) Section 121, I. P. C.	Transportation for life and forfeiture.	7 years' rigorous imprisonment
	300	9	Lal Chand, son of Gokal Chand.		Do ...	Do.
	301	11	Muhammad Din, son of Shamas Din		Death and forfeiture.	10 years' rigorous imprisonment
	302	13	Mangal Singh, son of Gopal Singh.		Transportation for life and forfeiture.	7 years' rigorous imprisonment
	303	15	Ghulam Sap, son of Shamas Din.		Death and forfeiture.	10 years' rigorous imprisonment
	304	16	Kishen Chand, son of Devi Das.		Transportation for life and forfeiture.	7 years' rigorous imprisonment
	305	20	Sardari, son of Mula ...			
	306	21	Behari Lal, son of Harnam Das.	(1) Section 121, I. P. C. (2) 30th June 1919.	Transportation for life and forfeiture.	7 years' rigorous imprisonment
	307	22	Ganpat, son of Jowala Das.			

SUPPLEMENT—1 *contd.*

No. and name of case	*Serial No.*	*No. of accused according to schedule*	*Name of Accused with Father's Name*	*(1) Offence of which found guilty (2) Date of decision*	*Sentence passed by the Commissions*	*Sentence as determined by Government*
69. **Amritsar National Bank Loot.**	308	1	Ditta, son of Daula ...	(1) Sections 411 and 412, I. P. C. (2) 29th May 1919.	7 years' rigorous imprisonment	2 years' rigorous imprisonment
	309	2	Dindar, *alias* Amin Chand, son of Damodar.		3 years' rigorous imprisonment	1 year's rigorous imprisonment
	310	3	Mahanda, son of Miran Bakhsh.		7 years' rigorous imprisonment	2 years' rigorous imprisonment
	311	4	Waris, son of Shamira ...		Do. ...	Do.
	312	5	Mehr Din, son of Nihala		Do. ...	Do.
70. **Wrecking of Majith Mandi Post Office.**	313	1	Sharam Singh, son of Hakim Singh.	(1) Section 121, I. P. C. (2) 29th May 1919.	Transportation for life and forfeiture.	3 years' rigorous imprisonment
	314	2	Bhagwan Das, son of Guranditta.			2 years' rigorous imprisonment.
	315	3	Fazl Din, son of Hukam Din			Do.
71. *Tribune* **Case**	316	1	Kali Nath Roy, Editor, *Tribune*.	(1) Section 124-A, Indian Penal Code. (2) 28th May 1919.	2 years' rigorous imprisonment and Rs. 1,000 fine or in default 6 months' further rigorous imprisonment.	3 months' rigorous imprisonment. Fine maintained.
72. **Gujranwala City Case 1 (See No. 68)**	317	1	Amrik Rai, son of Parbat Rai		Death and forfeiture	10 years' rigorous imprisofiment.
	318	3	Dina, son of Labhu ...		Do ...	7 years' rigorous imprisonment.

	319	4	Jehana, son of Muhammad Bakhsh.	(1) Section 121, Indian Penal Code. (2) 26th May 1919.	Do....	Do.
	320	5	Beli, son of Harbhagwan		Transportation for life and forfeiture.	5 years' rigorous imprisonment
	321	6	Mukanda, son of Hira Lal ...		Do....	Do.
	322	7	Barkat, son of Mathra ...		Do....	2 years' rigorous imprisonment
	323	8	Bahadur Singh, son of Ram Singh.		Do....	5 years' rigorous imprisonment
	324	9	Nur Din, son of Buta ...		Do....	3 years' rigorous imprisonment
	325	10	Mehar Din, son of Muhammad Bakhsh.		Do....	Do.
73. **Amritsar** ... (Attempt to kill Miss Sherwood).	326	1	Sundar Singh, son of Kala Singh.	(1) Sections 121, 307, 147, 307/189, Indian Penal Code. (2) 31st May, 1919.	Death and forfeiture	Transportation for life.
	327	2	Wilayati, son of Dault Ram.		Do....	Do.
	328	3	Mangtu, son of Sant Ram		Do....	4 years' rigorous imprisonment
	329	4	Mela, son of Ganga Ram		Do....	7 years' rigorous imprisonment
	330	5	Mangtu *alias* Giddar, son of Maghi.		Do....	2 years' rigorous imprisonment
	331	6	Lal Chand, *alias* Lalu, son of Dyal Singh.		Do....	1 years' rigorous imprisonment
	332	7	Ahmad, son of Karim Bakhsh.		Do....	4 years' rigorous imprisonment
	333	8	Jila, son of Karim Bakhsh...		Transportation for life and forfeiture.	Released.
74. **Supplementary Nizamabad case** (See No. 61).	334	1	Bhagat Singh, S/o Surjan Singh.	(1) Section 121, Indian Penal Code. (2) 2nd June 1919.	Transportation for life and forfeiture.	5 years' rigorous imprisonment
	335	2	Muhammad Ali, son of Imam Din.			Do.

SUPPLEMENT—1 *contd.*

No. and name of case	Serial No.	No. of accused according to schedule	Name of Accused with Father's Name	(1) Offence of which found guilty (2) Date of decision	Sentence passed by the Commissions	Sentence as determined by Government
	336	3	Dittu, son of Ghamun ...			2 years' rigorous imprisonment
	337	6	Karim, son of Ahmad Din ...	(1) Section 121, I. P. C. (2) 2nd June 1919.	Transportation for life and forfeiture.	5 years' rigorous imprisonment
	338	7	Allah Ditta, son of Chanu ...			Do.
75. **Amritsar National Bank Murder** (Murder of 2 Europeans and looting of Several lakhs' worth of property)	339	1	Rattan Chand, son of Sita Ram			No alteration
	340	2	Bugha, son of Paira Mal ...			Do.
	341	3	Ghulam Hassan, son of Ida..			Do.
	342	4	Faqir, son of Pir Bakhsh ...			Do.
	343	5	Asadullah, son of Sultan Bakhsh.		Death and forfeiture	Transportation for life.
	344	6	Karm Chand, son of Faqir Chand			Do.
	345	7	Karim Bakhsh, son of Mehr Bakhsh.	(1) Section 121, Indian Penal Code.		7 years' rigorous imprisonment.
	346	8	Manohar Singh, son of Lehna Singh.			No alteration.
	347	9	Muhammadi, son of Aziz ...			Transportation for life.
	348	10	Jani, son of Muhammad Bakhsh.			10 years' rigorous imprisonment.

	349	11	Nizam, son of Rustam ...			Do.
	350	12	Feroz, son of Maula Bakhsh			Do.
	351	13	Chiragh, son of Sadarang			Do.
	352	14	Sadru, son of Makhan ...			Do.
	353	15	Ghulam Hassan, son of Makhan.	(1) Section 412, Indian Penal Code.	7 years' rigorous imprisonment	2 years' rigorous imprisonment
	354	16	Inayat, son of Pair Mal			10 years' rigorous imprisonment
	355	17	Ghulam Rasul, son of Ghulam Haidar.			Do
	356	18	Harnam Singh, son of Kala Singh	(1) Section 121, Indian Penal Code.	Death and forfeiture	Transportation for life
	357	19	Mehr Sain, son of Mandhoo	(2) 22nd June, 1919.		Do
	358	20	Sandhi, son of Husain Bakhsh			Do
	359	21	Roshan, son of Hyat Beg			10 years' rigorous imprisonment
76. **Amritsar Alliance Bank Murder** (Murder of European Manager).	360	1	Nizam Din, son of Kamal			Trasnportation for life
	361	2	Dina, son of Wazira ...			Do
	362	3	Umar, son of Kaim Bakhsh..	(1) Section 121, Indian Penal Code.		10 years' rigorous imprisonment
	363	4	Hussaina, son of Atar Din ...	(2) 12th June 1919.	Death and forfeiture	No alteration
	364	5	Aziz, son of Ahsan ...			Do.
	365	6	Ganda Singh, son of Bhangar			Transportation for life.

* Sentences stayed pending orders of Privy Council

SUPPLEMENT—1 *contd.*

No. and name of case	Serial No.	No. of accused according to schedule	Name of Accused with Father's Name	(1) Offence of which found guilty (2) Date of decision	Sentence passed by the Commissions	Sentence as determined by Government
	366	8	Husaina, son of Muhammad Shaikh			No alteration
	367	9	Sadiq, son of Ibrahim			Transportation for life
	368	10	Ram Chand, son of Phangan	(1) Section 121, Indian Penal Code (2) 12th June 1919.	Death and forfeiture	No alteration
	369	11	Kahna, son of Goman			Transportation for life
	370	12	Jalal Din, son of Sawan			Do
	371	14	Bishna, son of Labhu			No alteration
77. **Kasur Supplementary Case** (No. 5)	372	1	Nadar Ali Shah, son of Kaim Ali Shah		Death and forfeiture	Transportation for life
	373	2	Dhani Ram, son of Devi Ditta		Do do	No alteration
	374	4	Chiragh, son of Karim Bakhsh		Transportation for Life and forfeiture.	6 months' rigorous imprisonment.
	375	5	Allah Din, son of Dasondhi		Death and forfeiture	Transportation for life.
	376	6	Rehlu, son of Ahmad		Do do	3 years' rigorous imprisonment.
	377	7	Piran Ditta, son of Budha		Do do	Do
	378	8	Ram Saran Das, son of Gobind Ram		Transportation for life and forfeiture.	2 years' rigorous imprisonment.

379	9	Khushi Muhamad, son of Ilahi Bakhsh		Transportation for life and forfeiture	4 years' rigorous imprisonment
380	11	Nath Ram, son of Sunder Das		Death and forfeiture	No alteration
381	12	Diwan, son of Kishna		Transportation for life and forfeiture	10 years' rigorous imprisonment
382	14	Farzand, son of Ditta		Death and forfeiture	7 years' do
383	15	Khuda Dad, son of Nadir		Ditto	10 years' do
384	18	Panna Lal, son of Amir Chand		Transportation for life and forfeiture	7 years' do
385	22	Ganda Singh, son of Lehna Singh		Death and forfeiture	5 years' do
386	29	Bishan Singh, son of Hari Singh		Transportation for life and forfeiture	6 months' rigorous imprisonment
387	33	Jiwan Singh, son of Sham Singh		Do do	1 year's rigorous imprisonment
388	34	Khushal Singh, son of Hira Singh		Do do	Ditto
389	35	Tara Singh, son of Jawala Singh	(1) Section 121, Indian Penal Code.	Do do	3 years' rigorous imprisonment
390	36	Mahuga, son of Mahmun	(2) 28th May 1919	Do do	2 years' rigorous imprisonment
391	37	Santa Singh, son of Kundan Singh		Death and forfeiture	5 years' rigorous imprisonment
392	38	Pira, son of Buta		Transportation for life and forfeiture	3 years' rigorous imprisonment
393	39	Ali Muhamad, son of Imam Din		Do do	No alteration
394	41	Tirath Ram, son of Deoki Nath		Death and forfeiture	10 years' rigorous imprisonment
395	43	Bhura, son of Rupa		Transportation for life and forfeiture	7 years' rigorous imprisonment
396	47	Khetu Ram, son of Bakhshi Ram		Death and forfeiture	5 years' rigorous imprisonment
397	48	Allah Bakhsh, son of Shera		Ditto	No alteration

SUPPLEMENT—1 *contd.*

No. and name of case	Serial No.	No. of accused according to schedule	Name of Accused with Father's Name	(1) Offence of which found guilty (2) Date of decision	Sentence passed by the Commissions	Sentence as determined by Government
78. **Amritsar (Mrs Easdon's) case** (Attack on Municipal Zenana Hospital with a view to murder Mrs. Easdon, the Lady Doctor)	398	1	Mahesha, son of Amru	(1) Section 121, 147, 302/120-B, 426/149, Indian Penal Code	Death and forfeiture ...	5 years' rigorous imprisonment
	399	2	Harnama, son of Dasondha Singh			
	400	4	Karim Bakhsh, son of Shahiya			
	401	11	Muhamad Sadiq, son of Inayat Ullah			
	402	12	Gaman, son of Ghulam Nahi			
	403	15	Muhamad Akram, son of Muhamad Amin			
	404	16	Mussammat Mathri, wife of Mithan Lal	(1) Section 121, $\frac{147, 426}{109}$ 302/115, I.P.C. (2) 2nd June 1919	Transportation for life and forfeiture.	Released on 4th August 1919
79. **Supplementary Hafizabad Case** (Mischief and wire-cutting at station, removal of rails, and attack on Tahsil)	405	1	Tope Mal, son of Jhanda Mal	(1) Section 121, I.P.C. (2) 5th June 1919	Transportation for life and forfeiture.	5 years' rigorous imprisonment.
	406	2	Ishar Das, son of Kirpa Ram			Do do
	407	3	Mela Ram, son of Kirpa Ram			Do do
	408	4	Hari Singh, son of Ganda Singh			Released
	409	5	Mehtab Singh, son of Gopal Singh			3 years' rigorous imprisonment.
	410	12	Abdulla, son of Maula Bakhsh			Do do

	411	17	Kartar Singh, son of Aya Singh			Do.
	412	19	Murad, son of Fazal Din			Do.
	413	29	Sant Ram, son of Gurdas			Do.
80. **Amritsar Chartered Bank Case** (Mischief and arson)	414	1	Ibrahim, son of Ajmeri			4 years' rigorous imprisonment
	415	2	Gaman, son of Natha			Do.
	416	3	Nabi, son of Kalu	(1) Section 121, Indian Penal Code. (2) 5th June, 1919.	Transportation for life and forfeiture	Do.
	417	4	Ghauns, son of Alla Ditta			3 years' rigorous imprisonment
	418	7	Sadhu Singh, son of Sant Singh			7 years' do
81. **Toba Tek Singh Case** (Attempted derailment)	419	1	Jagat Singh, son of Hakim		3 years' rigorous imprisonment and Rs. 300 fine or 6 months in default.	No alteration
	420	2	Surain Singh, son of Khushal Singh		1½ years' rigorous imprisonment and Rs. 150 fine or 6 months in default	Do
	421	3	Wasawa Singh, son of Mehtab Singh	(1) Sections 25, Act, XIII of 1885/149, Indian Penal Code (2) 6th June 1919.	Do	Do
	422	4	Ujagar Singh, son of Santa Singh		Do	Do.
	423	5	Gurdit Singh, son of Wadhawa Singh		1 years' rigorous imprisonment and Rs. 100 fine or 6 months in default	Reduced to sentence already undergone & a fine of Rs. 50
	424	6	Pala Singh, son of Sunder Singh		Do	No alteration
	425	7	Thakar Singh, son of Narain Singh		1½ years' rigorous imprisonment and Rs. 100 fine or 6 months in default	Do.
	426	8	Wasakha Singh, son of Mangal Singh		Do do	Do.

SUPPLEMENT—1 *contd.*

No. and name of case	Serial No.	No. of accused according to schedule	Name of Accused with Father's Name	(1) Offence of which found guilty (2) Date of decision	Sentence passed by the Commissions	Sentence as determined by Government
81. **Toba Tek Singh Case**—*concld.*	427	9	Dhana Singh, son of Jhanda Singh	(1) Sections 25, Act XIII of 1885/149, I. P. C. (2) 6th June 1919	1½ years' rigorous imprisonment and Rs. 100 fine or 6 months in default	No alteration
	428	10	Thakar Singh, son of Chet Singh		1 year's rigorous imprisonment and Rs. 100 fine or 6 months in default	Do
	429	11	Lachman Singh, son of Arur Singh		Do do	Do
	430	12	Ladha Singh, son of Jamal Singh		Do do	Do
	431	13	Khan Muhamad, son of Bhana		1½ years' rigorous imprisonment and Rs. 150 fine or 6 months in default	Do
	432	14	Phagu, son of Bura		1½ years' rigorous imprisonment and Rs. 20 fine or 6 months in default	Do
	433	15	Gandu, son of Mangtu		Do do	Do
	434	16	Mian, son of Hira		Do do	Do
	435	17	Jiwan, son of Nanda		Do do	Do
	436	18	Sohni, son of Karam Ilahi		Do do	Do

82. ***"Partab"* Case**	437	1	Radha Kishen, son of Tara Chand—Editor, *"Partab"*	(1) Rule 25 of Defence of India Rules. (2) 7th June, 1919.	18 months' rigorous imprisonment and Rs. 500 fine or 6 months' more in default	2 months' rigorous imprisonment. Fine unchanged
83. **Guard Robinson's Murder case**	438	3	Kanhya, son of Ruldu Ram	(1) Sections 121/302, I.P.C. (2) 7th June, 1919.	Death and forfeiture	Transportation for life
	439	12	Jota Singh, son of Labh Singh	(1) Section 121, Indian Penal Code (2) 6th June, 1919.	Transportation for life and forfeiture	2 years' rigorous imprisonment
	440	6	Vir Singh, son of Thakur Singh			5 years' rigorous imprisonment
	441	10	Uttam Singh, son of Thakur Singh			Do
84. **Wagah** (Derailment of Armoured train)	442	1	Sulakhan Singh, son of Fauja Singh			10 years' rigorous imprisonment
	443	2	Asa Singh, son of Nehal Singh			5 years' rigorous imprisonment
85. **Wazirabad** (Rail wrecking)	444	1	Abdullah, son of Sultan Mahmud	(1) Section 121, Indian Penal Code.	Transportation for life and forfeiture	5 years' rigorous imprisonment
	445	2	Chiragh, son of Suba			Do
	446	3	Diwan Chand, son of Mul Raj			3 years' rigorous imprisonment
	447	5	Amar Nath, son of Badri Nath			Do
	448	6	Mula, son of Ghamun	Section 426, I.P.C.	15 Stripes ...	No alteration
	449	7	Girdhari, son of Karm Chand	(1) Section 121, I.P.C.	Transportation for life...	3 years' rigorous imprisonment
	450	8	Abdulla, son of Karim Bakhsh			
	451	9	Allah Rakh, son of Nizam Din			

SUPPLEMENT—1 *contd.*

No. and name of case	Serial No.	No. of accused according to schedule	Name of Accused with Father's Name	(1) Offence of which found guilty (2) Date of decision	Sentence passed by the Commissions	Sentence as determined by Government
85. **Wazirabad** (Rail wrecking)—*concld.*	452	10	Ditta, son of Karam Din			Released.
	453	11	Diwan. son of Jai Dial	(1) Section 121, I. P. C.	Transportation for life ...	6 months' rigorous imprisonment
	454	12	Imam Din, son of Shahna			3 years' rigorous imprisonment
	455	13	Muhamad Hussain, son of Muhamad Bakhsh			Do.
	456	14	Thakur, son of Prabh Dyal...			6 months' rigorous imprisonment
	457	15	Allah Ditta, son of Karim Bakhsh.			3 years' rigorous imprisonment
	458	17	Ramzan, son of Nizam ...	(1) Section 121, Indian Penal Code.	Transportation for life and forfeiture.	Do.
	459	18	Maddu, son of Umar Din ...			Do.
	460	20	Pala, son of Ram ...	(2) 31st May, 1919.		6 months' rigorous imprisonment
	461	21	Jawinda Mal, son of Duni Chand.			5 years' rigorous imprisonment
	462	22	Sardara, son of Budha ...			3 years' rigorous imprisonment
	463	23	Kirpa Ram, son of Kalyan Das.			5 years' rigorous imprisonment
	464	24	Inayat Ullah, son of Siraj Din.			Do.

86. **Jagdeo Khurd Dacoity.**	465	3	Ganga Singh, son of Pannu...	(1) All under Section 394/397, I. P. C. (2) 9th June 1919.	7 years' rigorous imprisonment	4 years' rigorous imprisonment
	466	4	Ram Singh, son of Isher...			
	467	8	Labhu, son of Mohla ...			
	468	9	Jaimal, son of Goga ...			
87. **Supplementary Gujranwala Case.** (See No. 68).	469	1	Muhamad Shafi, son of Umar Bakhsh.	(1) Section 121, Indian Penal Code. (2) 10th June, 1919.	Transportation for life and forfeiture.	4 years' rigorous imprisonment
	470	2	Sundar Singh, son of Sham Singh			Do
	471	3	Hayat, son of Budha ...			3 years' rigorous imprisonment
	472	4	Haria, son of Sukh Nand			4 years' rigorous imprisonment
	473	7	Amar, son of Faqiria ...			Do
	474	8	Shaukat, son of Guranditta..			Do
	475	9	Abdulla, son of Ladha ...			Do
	476	11	Babu, son of Ilahi Bakhsh...			Do
	477	14	Ismail, son of Ahmad Din			Do
	478	16	Muhamad Ju, son of Ghufar			3 years' rigorous imprisonment
	479	17	Anant Ram, son of Jawinda Mal			4 years' rigorous imprisonment
	480	18	Hira Singh, son of Kishen Singh.			Do
	481	19	Mohamda, son of Imam Din.			Do
88. ...	...	...	... ...	... ...	Acquitted. ...	... ...

SUPPLEMENT—1 *contd.*

No. and name of case	Serial No.	No. of accused according to schedule	Name of Accused with Father's Name	(1) Offence of which found guilty (2) Date of decision	Sentence passed by the Commissions	Sentence as determined by Government
89. **Amritsar National Bank Loot Case**	482	...	Nura, son of Ibrahim	(1) Section 412, Indian Penal Code. (2) 11th June, 1919.	1 years' rigorous imprisonment	6 months' rigorous imprisonment
90. **Do** ...	483	...	Lal Singh, son of Wadhawa Singh		Do	Do
91. **Do** ...	484	...	Allah Ditta, son of Kanda		7 years' rigorous imprisonment	2 years' rigorous imprisonment
92. **Do** ...	485	...	Rati Ram, son of Gurdas		Do	Do.
93. ...	...	...	...	...	Acquitted	...
94. **Do** ...	486	...	Basanta, son of Ralla	(1) In all cases under Section 412, I.P.C. (2) All decided on 11th June 1919, except *No. 95* which was decided on 16th June 1919	7 years' rigorous imprisonment	2 years' rigorous imprisonment
95. **Do** ...	487	...	Parma Nand, son of Sahiba		20 Stripes	No alteration
96. **Do** ...	488	...	Murad, son of Rahim Bakhsh		7 years' rigorous imprisonment	2 years' rigorous imprisonment
97. **Do** ...	489	...	Labhu, son of Allah Ditta		Do	Do.
98. **Do** ...	490	...	Rahim Bakhsh, son of Gulab		Do	Do.
99. **Dhaba Singh Railway Case** (Burning of bridge and removal of line)	491	1	Muhammad Din, son of Fazla		Transportation for life and forfeiture.	7 years' rigorous imprisonment
	492	2	Bahawla, son of Hakim		Do	Do
	493	3	Kharak Singh, son of Hira		Do	Do

	494	4	Amar Singh, son of Attar Singh.		Do.	Do.
	495	5	Waryam, son of Amir ...	(1) Section 121, I. P. C.	Do.	Do.
	496	6	Vir Singh, son of Mehr Singh	(2) 11th June 1919.	Do.	Do.
	497	7	Jagat Singh, son of Wadhawa Singh.		Do.	Do.
	498	8	Gian Singh, son of Diyal Singh.		Death and forfeiture ...	Transportation for life.
	499	9	Harnama, son of Hassa ...		Transportation for life and forfeiture.	
	500	10	Jhanda Singh, son of Hira Singh.		Do.	7 years' rigorous imprisonment
	501	11	Narain Singh, son of Kharak Singh.		Do.	Do.
						Do.
100. **Gujranwala Supplementary Case.** (See No. 68).	502	1	Gian Chand, son of Mela Ram.	(1) Section 121, I. P. C.	Transportation for life and forfeiture.	5 years' rigorous imprisonment
	503	2	Mukand, son of Lal Chand...	(2) 13th June 1919.		
	504	3	Budha, son of Ladha ...			
101. **Chheharta Case** (Train looting).	505	1	Banta Singh, son of Nihal Singh.		7 years' rigorous imprisonment	2 years' rigorous imprisonment
	506	2	Asa Singh, son of Man Singh		5 years' do. ...	18 months' rigorous imprisonment
	507	3	Natha Singh, son of Khushal Singh.		7 years' do. ...	2 years' rigorous imprisonment
	508	4	Banta Singh, son of Bagh Singh.	(1) Section 412, I. P. C. (2) 13th June 1919.	Do do. ...	Do.
	509	5	Maghar, son of Jani ...		5 years' do. ...	18 months' rigorous imprisonment
	510	6	Khazan Singh, son of Jhanda Singh.		7 years' do. ...	2 years' rigorous imprisonment
	511	7	Sundar Singh, son of Jhanda Singh.		Do do. ...	Do

SUPPLEMENT—1 *contd.*

No. and name of case	*Serial No.*	*No. of accused according to schedule*	*Name of Accused with Father's Name*	*(1) Offence of which found guilty (2) Date of decision*	*Sentence passed by the Commissions*	*Sentence as determined by Government*
101. **Chheharta Case** (Train looting)—*concld.*	512	8	Fauja Singh, son of Jindar Singh.	(1) Section 412, Indian Penal Code. (2) 13th June, 1919.	7 years' rigorous imprisonment	2 years' rigorous imprisonment
	513	9	Sharfu, son of Fajji ...		3 years' rigorous imprisonment	6 months' rigorous imprisonment
	514	10	Siraj, son of Hami ...		7 years' rigorous imprisonment	2 years' rigorous imprisonment
	515	11	Ujagar Singh, son of Jhanda Singh.		3 years' rigorous imprisonment	6 months' rigorous imprisonment
	516	12	Ujagar Singh, son of Talak Singh.		7 years' rigorous imprisonment	2 years' rigorous imprisonment
	517	13	Harnam Singh, son of Kesar Singh.		Do	Do
	518	14	Sohel Singh, son of Kharak Singh.		Do	Do
	519	16	Ishar, son of Vir Singh ...		Imprisonment till rising of Court.	No alteration
	520	17	Bhan Singh, son of Hira Singh.		7 years' rigorous imprisonment	2 years' rigorous imprisonment
	521	18	Teja Singh, S/o Jaimal Singh.		Do	Do
	522	19	Hazara Singh, son of Sulakhan.		3 years' rigorous imprisonment	6 months' rigorous imprisonment
	523	20	Harnam Singh, son of Kala Singh		7 years' rigorous imprisonment	2 years' rigorous imprisonment

102. **Gujranwala Leaders' Case**	524	1	Amar Nath, son of Bidhi Chand	(1) Section 121, I. P. C. (2) 17th June 1919.	Death and forfeiture	3 years' rigorous imprisonment
	525	2	Mangal Sen, son of D. Tulsi Das.		Transportation for life and forfeiture.	2 years' do.
	526	4	Labh Singh, son of Sundar Singh.		Do	6 months do.
	527	5	Mati Ullah, son of Habibullah		Do	1 year's do.
	528	6	Sarb Dial, son of Guran Ditta		Do	Do
	529	10	Jagan Nath, son of Brij Lal..		Do	Do
	530	11	Mohan Lal, son of Jawanda Mal.		Death and forfeiture	5 years' rigorous imprisonment
	531	13	Chuni lal, son of Bulaqi Ram.		Transportation for life and forfeiture.	4 years' rigorous imprisonment
	532	14	Behari Lal, son of Jawanda Mal.		Do	Do
	533	15	Haveli Ram, son of Mukand Lal.		Do	Do
103. **Amritsar, burning of Girls' Normal School.**	534	1	Imam Din, son of Ilahi. ...	(1) Section 121, I. P. C. (2) 16th June 1919.	Transportation for life and forfeiture.	4 years' rigorous imprisonment
	535	2	Fazal Din, son of Allah Ditta			5 years' do.
	536	4	Muhamad Sultan, son of Ilahi Bakhsh.			3 years' rigorous imprisonment
	537	5	Abdur Rahman, son of Abdur Razaq			Do
	538	7	Nanak Chand, son of Kahn Chand.		7 years' rigorous imprisonment	Do
	539	8	Ismail son of Phila ...			Do
104. **National Bank Loot**	540	...	Kake Shah, son of Karam Bakhsh.	(1) Section 412, I. P. C. (2) 17th June 1919.		2 years' rigorous imprisonment

SUPPLEMENT—1 *contd.*

No. and name of case	Serial No.	No. of accused according to schedule	Name of Accused with Father's Name	(1) Offence of which found guilty (2) Date of decision	Sentence passed by the Commissions	Sentence as determined by Government
105. **Malakwal No. I** (Sedition)	541	1	Bhoj Raj, son of Risal Singh.	(1) Both under Section 124-A, I. P. C. (2) 17th June, 1919.	Transportation for life and forfeiture.	2 years' rigorous imprisonment
	542	2	Ram Chandra, son of Fakir Chand...		Do ...	6 months' rigorous imprisonment
106. **Malakwal No. II**	...	...	... ...	... ...	Acquitted	... ...
107. **Malakwal No. III** (Wire-cutting)	543	1	Raja Ram, son of Ganga Ram	(1) Section 25, Act XIII of 1885 Section 149, I. P.C. (2) 17th June, 1919.	Sentenced to 6 months' rigorous imprisonment	No alteration
	544	2	Daulat Ram, son of Ganga Ram.			
	545	5	Karam Chand, son of Sham Das.			
	546	6	Alla Din, son of Mohkam Din			
	547	7	Abdur Rahman ...			
	548	8	Multani, son of Kishen Dial.			
	549	9	Muhamad Jafar, son of Ghulam Ali.			
	550	10	Ahmad Shah, son of Ghulam Mohi-ud Din.			
108. **Malakwal No. IV** (Derailment resulting in loss of 2 lives)	551	1	Raja Ram son of Ganga Ram.		Death and forfeiture	Transportation for life.
	552	2	Daulat Ram, son of Ganga Ram.	(1) Section 121, I. P. C. (2) 17th June, 1919.	Transportation for life and forfeiture.	2 years' rigorous imprisonment
	553	3	Karam Chand, son of Sham Das		Do	7 years' do.

	554	5	Sarwar, son of Muhamad Bakhsh.	(1) Section 121, Indian Penal Code. (2) 17th June 1919.	Death and forfeiture ...	Transportation for life.
	555	6	Fajju, son of Muhamad Bakhsh		Transportation for life and forfeiture.	7 year's rigorous imprisonment
	556	7	Nura, son of Mela.		Do do ...	Do
	557	8	Abdul Majid, son of Misalam		Do do ...	Do
	558	9	Multani, son of Kishen Dial		Do do ...	Do
109. **Supplementary Hafizabad Case** (See No. 60)	559	2	Hari Singh, son of Jawahir Singh.	(1) Section 121, Indian Penal Code. (2) 18th June 1919.	Transportation for life and forfeiture.	3 year's rigorous imprisonment
110. **Supplementary Amritsar National Bank Murder Case** (See No. 75)	560	...	Jairam Singh, son of Atma Singh	(1) Section 121, I. P. C. (2) 18th June 1919.	Death and forfeiture ...	Transportation for life.
111. **Supplementary Kasur Case** (See No.5)	561	1	Imam Din, son of Jhandu	(1) Section 121, I. P. C. (2) 17th June 1919.	Death and forfeiture ...	7 year's rigorous imprisonment
	562	2	Sharfu, son of Modi ...		Do ...	Do
	563	3	Kima, son of Budho ...		Transportation for life and forfeiture.	1 year's rigorous imprisonment
112. **Burning of Moman Railway Station**	564	1	Harnam Singh, son of Jiwan Singh.	(1) Section 121, I. P. C. (2) 17th June 1919.	Death and forfeiture ...	7 year's rigorous imprisonment to run concurrently with the sentence in Case No. 66.
	565	2	Banta Singh, son of Kala Singh.		Transportation for life and forfeiture.	5 year's rigorous imprisonment
	566	3	Mihan Singh, son of Chuhar Singh.		Do do ...	Do
113. **Amritsar Leaders' Case.**	567	1	Saif-ud-Din Kichlew ...	(1) Section 124-A, $\frac{124\text{-A}}{120\text{-B}}$ I. P. C.	Transportation for life.	2 year's rigorous imprisonment
	568	2	Satya Pal, son of Mani Ram.	(1) Section $\frac{124\text{-A}}{120\text{-B}}$ I. P. C.	Do do ...	Do

SUPPLEMENT—1 *contd.*

No. and name of case	Serial No.	No. of accused according to schedule	Name of Accused with Father's Name	(1) Offence of which found guilty (2) Date of decision	Sentence passed by the Commissions	Sentence as determined by Government
114. **Amritsar Leaders' Case** —*contd.*	569	4	Muhamad Bashir Din, son of Muhamad Hussain.	(1) Section 124-A, and 121, I. P. C.	Death and forfeiture ...	6 years' rigorous imprisonment
	570	5	Kotu Mal, son of Raghunandan Lal	(1) Accd, Nos. 5, 6 and 9 under Section $\frac{124\text{-A}}{120\text{-B}}$ I.P.C. only; Accd, Nos. 8, 10 and 12, also under Sec. 121, I.P.C.	3 years' rigorous imprisonment	6 months' rigorous imprisonment
	571	6	Narain Das Khanna, son of Tirath Ram.		Do ...	Do
	572	8	Anubhawan Nand, *Sunyasi*		Transportation for life and forfeiture.	2 years' rigorous imprisonment
	573	9	Dina Nath, son of Nanik Chand.		Do ...	Do
	574	10	Gurbakhsh Rai, son of Jai Gopal		Do ...	1 years' Do.
	575	12	Ghulam Muhamad, son of Seth Madho.		Do ...	2 years' Do.
	576	13	Abdul Aziz, son of Firoze Din.		Do ...	3 months' Do.
115. **Lahore Leaders' Case**	577	1	Harkishen Lal ...	(1) Sec. 121, I. P. C. (2) 5th July, 1919.		2 years' rigorous imprisonment
	578	2	Rambhai Datt ...	(1) Section 121 & 121-A, I. P. C. (2) 5th July, 1919.	Transportation for life and forfeiture.	3 years' Do.
	579	3	Duni Chand ...			Do
	580	10	Allah Din ...			1 year's rigorous imprisonment
	581	11	Mota Singh ...			Do